Are emerging markets another fad or one of the most important transformations in the world's political economy? Millions of lives in both rich and poor countries depend on the answer to this question. This handbook has all the analytical tools one needs to answer it and that is why it will become the indispensable reference on emerging markets.

Moisés Naím, author of the *The End of Power: From boardrooms to battlefields and churches to states, why being in charge isn't what it used to be.*

This Handbook is a welcome and overdue entry into the current economic development literature. While good separate texts have been on the market for most countries covered here, there has been no possibility of readers and researchers to be able make a ready inter-country comparison within one cover. The choice of the countries covered is excellent, and the selected authors are all well-known scholars in the their field. This is another jewel in the editor's and the publisher's literary crowns.

Jahangir Amuzegar, former Minister of Commerce and Minister of Finance, Iran, and a former executive director of the International Monetary Fund.

The BRIC economies are the first big story of the 21st century. Here Robert Looney has assembled the essential handbook, and a remarkable collection of authors, to tell their tale.

Barry Eichengreen, Professor of Economics and Political Science, University of California, Berkeley, and former senior policy adviser at the International Monetary Fund.

Everything you wanted to know about emerging market economies? The emerging market world is too big and moving too quickly for that. But I challenge you to find a more comprehensive review of what's happening – and likely to happen – in countries ranging from China to South Africa to Brazil to Russia. One-stop shopping for 'policy wonks' and international business professionals, not to mention the merely curious.

Peter Passell, former economics columnist for the *New York Times* and editor of the Milken Institute Review.

There are many studies of developing and emerging market economies, but the often quite different experiences of individual countries often get lost in the effort to generalize. Robert Looney's handbook fills this important gap with individual chapters on the most important and largest emerging economies, drawing on distinguished economists who know one or more of these economies well. It is a valuable contribution.

Dwight H. Perkins, Harold Hitchings Burbank Professor of Political Economy, Emeritus, Harvard University.

Handbook of Emerging Economies

The growth and increasing prominence of emerging economies is fundamentally changing the world economy. The continued expansion of emerging economies during and after the world financial crisis, in contrast with the much slower rates of growth in the debt-ridden developed world, has led influential observers to speculate that they will dominate the world economy by the middle of this century.

This Handbook, an invaluable tool for academics, economists, researchers and anyone with an interest in emerging economies, grew out of the need for a comprehensive examination and analysis of these dynamic emerging economies. To this end, the volume's major objective is to assess the circumstances under which the emerging economies will continue their rapid ascent. Its chapters capture the diversity and complexity of this important group of countries. Is the long-anticipated convergence between the developing and the advanced world finally under way on a broad scale? If so, which countries have the best chance of attaining developed country status in the foreseeable future? If not, what factors may prevent other countries from achieving that goal?

Part I: Introduction: an overview
Part II: The BRICS
Part III: Key lessons: the path to emerging status
Part IV: Diverse success stories
Part V: Likely success stories
Part VI: Possible candidates: the difficult road ahead
Part VII: Assessing the future

The Editor, Professor **Robert E. Looney**, is a Distinguished Professor at the Naval Postgraduate School, Monterey, California, who specializes in issues relating to economic development in the Middle East, East Asia, South Asia and Latin America. He has published 22 books and more than 250 articles in professional journals. As an international consultant, Dr Looney has provided advice and assistance to various governments and international organizations.

Handbook of Emerging Economies

Editor: Robert E. Looney

LONDON AND NEW YORK

First edition published 2014 by Routledge

2 Park Square, Milton Park, Abingdon, Oxfordshire OX14 4RN
52 Vanderbilt Avenue, New York, NY 10017

Routledge is an imprint of the Taylor & Francis Group, an informa business

First issued in paperback 2018

Copyright © 2014 Taylor & Francis

The right of the editor to be identified as the author of the editorial material, and of the authors for their individual chapters, has been asserted in accordance with sections 77 and 78 of the Copyright, Designs and Patents Act 1988.

All rights reserved. No part of this book may be reprinted or reproduced or utilised in any form or by any electronic, mechanical, or other means, now known or hereafter invented, including photocopying and recording, or in any information storage or retrieval system, without permission in writing from the publishers.

Notice:
Product or corporate names may be trademarks or registered trademarks, and are used only for identification and explanation without intent to infringe.

Library of Congress Cataloging in Publication Data
Handbook of emerging economies / edited by Robert E. Looney.
    pages cm. – (Routledge international handbooks)
  Summary: ""Analyses emerging and newly emerged economies. Covers the BRICS countries as well as possible other candidates for emerging economy status and offers an overview of current issues in development economics"–Provided by publisher"– Provided by publisher.
  Includes bibliographical references and index.
  1. Developing countries–Economic conditions. 2. Developing countries–Economic policy. I. Looney, Robert E., editor of compilation.
  HC59.7.H29676 2014
  330.9172'4–dc23
        2013040609

ISBN: 978-1-85743-670-9 (hbk)
ISBN: 978-1-857-43978-6 (pbk)

Typeset in Bembo
by Taylor & Francis Books

Europa Commissioning Editor: Cathy Hartley
Editorial Assistant: Amy Welmers

For Christopher
—thanks for some memorable chess games

Contents

List of illustrations	xii
List of contributors	xviii
Foreword – Deepak Lal	xxix
Preface	xxxix
List of abbreviations	xlii

PART I
Introduction: an overview — **1**

1 Introduction — 3
Robert E. Looney

2 Key trends in the world economy — 13
Uri Dadush

PART II
The BRICS — **31**

3 Brazil — 33
Albert Fishlow

4 Russia as an emerging economy — 46
Philip Hanson

5 The how and why of economic growth in India, 1950–2012 — 61
Surjit S. Bhalla

6 China after the international financial crisis: still emerging — 83
Pieter Bottelier

7 South Africa's difficult transition — 105
Robert E. Looney

Contents

PART III
Key lessons: the path to emerging status
135

8 Modern stage theories and their relevance for the emerging economies
Robert E. Looney
137

9 Beijing Consensus versus Washington Consensus
John Williamson
177

PART IV
Diverse success stories
185

10 The Israeli economy
Paul Rivlin
187

11 Singapore's success: after the miracle
Linda Y.C. Lim
203

12 The original sin in Chile's successful history of development
Patricio Navia
227

PART V
Likely success stories
243

13 Turkey
Fatih Özatay
245

14 Indonesia's ways to sustainable economic growth and development
Zamroni Salim
265

15 Mexico: emerging economy kept on a leash by mismatched monopolies
Francisco E. González
287

16 Middle-income trap of Malaysian economy: a political economy analysis
Vijayakumari Kanapathy and Herizal Hazri
306

PART VI
Possible candidates: the difficult road ahead
327

17 Argentina's present and its intriguing economic history
Domingo F. Cavallo
329

18 Viet Nam
Martin Rama
339

Contents

19 The Philippines: road to being an emerging economy   364
    Dante B. Canlas

20 Pakistan: an economy in extreme distress that could be revived   377
    Shahid Javed Burki

21 Egypt: too 'big' to succeed?   397
    Robert Springborg

22 Thailand: economic progress and the move to populism   416
    Peter Warr

23 Iran at a crossroads   440
    Reza Ghorashi and Hamid Zangeneh

24 Colombia: seeking prosperity through peace   458
    Nake M. Kamrany, Danielle N. Ramirez and Laura E. Armey

25 The Saudi Arabian model   475
    Robert E. Looney

PART VII
Assessing the future   501

26 The emerging powers and global governance: why the BRICS matter   503
    Leslie Elliott Armijo and Cynthia Roberts

27 Challenges of managing emerging economies   525
    Domingo F. Cavallo

28 Lessons of Korea for emerging economies: an unexpected journey from rags
    to riches, from crisis to recovery   531
    Bernhard J. Seliger

29 China and India, 2025: a macroeconomic assessment   539
    Charles Wolf, Jr and Alisher Akhmedjonov

    Index   555

List of illustrations

Figures

2.1	Average annual GDP growth in the G20 economies	14
2.2	Investment converging towards 15%–20% for mature economies	17
2.3	The United Kingdom has the greatest ability to catch the USA, Nigeria the least	19
4.1	Per capita GDP in 2011: Russia, Moscow and selected other countries	48
4.2	Between two crises: Russia's GDP growth and the Urals oil price, 1998–2009	49
4.3	How bad was 2009? The deterioration in GDP performance between 2008 and 2009 for the world, Russia and selected other countries	52
4.4	Contribution of different end uses of demand to the fall in GDP in 2009 year-on-year in the USA and Russia	53
4.5	Russian GDP and retail sales growth from the global crisis into 2013	54
4.6	Russia: projected working-age population, 2011–20	55
5.1	Five-year smoothed actual and potential GDP growth in India, 1951–2012	63
5.2	How well do interest rates (lagged) explain GDP growth in India, 1978–2012?	71
5.3	India and developing country median inflation: close correlation	74
5.4	Savings and investment (% share of GDP) and real interest rates	76
6.1	Food, producer and consumer price inflation (monthly, annualized percentage change, January 2006–December 2012)	84
6.2	China quarterly GDP growth, annualized, year-on-year and quarter-on-quarter seasonally adjusted, 2006Q1–2012Q4	85
6.3	Monthly bank lending (LHS) and three-month moving average growth	86
6.4	Shares in global GDP growth	90
6.5	China's household final consumption expenditure as % of GDP, 1998–2011	93
6.6	Household consumption annual growth rates for selected countries, 1998–2008	93
6.7	Demographic shifts in China	94
6.8	The rising share of services (tertiary) in China's GDP	95
6.9	Marginal return on aggregate investment (MPK) in China, 1950–2010	96
6.10	Marginal return on aggregate investment (MPK) in selected countries, 1965–2009	96
6.11	Investment/GDP ratios and capital stock per person for various countries in 2000 and 2011	97
7.1	South Africa, Malaysia, Korea and Singapore: patterns of per-capita income: 1960–2011	107

List of illustrations

7.2	South Africa, middle income countries: growth in per capita income: 1960–2011	109
7.3	South Africa, middle income countries: patterns of GDP per person employed: 1980–2011	109
7.4	South Africa: sector GDP shares, 1960–2011	110
7.5	South Africa: macro-aggregate shares of GDP, 1960–2011	111
7.6	South Africa, middle income countries, gross savings % GDP: 1960–2011	113
7.7	South Africa, Turkey, Indonesia, Malaysia, and Mexico: % of labor force unemployed, 1980–2011	115
7.8	South Africa, middle income countries, labor force participation rates: 1990–2011	115
7.9	South Africa, emerging economies, Boston Consulting Group sustainability patterns	117
7.10	South Africa, emerging economies: Boston Consulting Group, converting wealth into well-being	118
7.11	South Africa, emerging economies, patterns of voice and accountability: 1996–2011	119
7.12	South Africa, emerging economies, patterns of political stability/absence of violence: 1996–2011	120
7.13	South Africa, emerging economies, patterns of government effectiveness: 1996–2011	121
7.14	South Africa, emerging economies, patterns of regulatory quality: 1996–2011	122
7.15	South Africa, emerging economies, patterns of rule of law: 1996–2011	122
7.16	South Africa, emerging economies, patterns of control of corruption: 1996–2011	123
7.17	South Africa, emerging economies, Legatum Institute Economy/governance rankings	124
8.1	Contrasting emerging economy growth patterns	138
8.2	Per capita incomes relative to the United States, 1960 and 2008	139
8.3	Bremer/Kasarda Stage Theory	140
12.1	GDP per capita (constant 2000 US$), 1960–2010	228
12.2	Inflation and per capita GDP growth in Chile, 1960–2011	229
12.3	General government final consumption expenditure	231
12.4	Poverty rates and Gini coefficient, 1990–2011	239
13.1	Per-capita GDP of Turkey, BRIC countries and Korea relative to the US GDP in purchasing-power parity terms	246
13.2	Borrowing requirement, operational balance and interest payments of the public sector (general government): 1990–2011	248
13.3	Net international reserve position of Turkey and foreign debt of private sector: 1996–2011	254
13.4	Real GDP and net capital inflows (right axis): 1998Q1–2012Q3	255
13.5	Industrial production index (right axis) and current account balance: 1998Q1–2012Q3	256
13.6	GDP loss in the 2001 crisis and the global crisis	257
14.1	The components of economic growth in BRICS and Indonesia	270
14.2	Indonesia's exports shares by sector, 2000–11	275
14.3	Indonesia's import shares by sector, 2000–11	276
14.4	Indonesia's per capita GDP, economic growth and exchange rate	277

List of illustrations

15.1	Employment growth by sector occupational profile charge as a proxy of modernisation	288
15.2	Population growth and urbanization demographic explosion and urbanisation	289
15.3	Annual GDP and price changes the 1990s: another lost decade?	292
15.4	Annual GDP and price changes low growth, a big negative shock, and law inflation in the 2000s	293
15.5	Poverty headcount ratio in Mexico, 1992–2010	294
15.6	Domestic credit to private sector as % GDP at the tail end of credit expansion to unleash productive activity	297
15.7	Dependency ratio projections to 2040 (population 14 and under, 65 and over)	302
16.1	Relative growth performance	307
16.2	Key economic indicators	308
16.3	Ratio of public and private investment	309
16.4	Demand side sources of growth	310
16.5	Public sector deficit	311
16.6	Household debts as a % of GDP	317
16.7	Federal debts as a % of GDP	322
16.8	Avoiding the middle income trap	323
17.1	Domestic and foreign terms trade and the RER: 1945/1975	332
17.2	Public expenditure and fiscal deficit: 1945/1975	334
17.3	GDP and inflation: 1945/1975	334
17.4	GDP and inflation: 1975/1990	335
175	Domestic and foreign terms of trade and the RER: 1990/2012	336
17.6	GDP and inflation: 1990/2012	337
17.7	Public expenditure and fiscal deficit: 1913/2012	337
18.1	Rapid structural change	341
18.2	A globally integrated economy	342
18.3	From farmers to wage earners	343
18.4	Rapidly falling poverty	344
22.1	Thailand: real GDP per capita and its growth rate, 1951 to 2013	417
22.2	Real GDP in East Asia, 1986 to 1996	419
22.3	Real GDP in East Asia, 1996 to 2012	419
22.4	Composition of net annual investment, 1975 to 2005	421
22.5	Real and nominal interest rates, 1994 to 2006	424
22.6	Private investment and the stock exchange price index, 1977 to 2005	424
22.7	Investment shares of GDP in East Asia, 1993 to 2012	425
22.8	Sectoral shares of GDP, 1965 to 2012	426
22.9	East Asia: export dependence and the effects of the global financial crisis	428
22.10	Thailand, quarterly Real GDP per capita and its growth, 1995 to 2013	429
22.11	Poverty incidence and economic growth, 1962 to 2009	431
22.12	Population growth rate, 1960 to 2004	433
22.13	Infant mortality (deaths per 1,000 births), 1960 to 2012	433
23.1	Actual and hypothetical trend lines	449
24.1	Colombia: patterns of GDP and per capita GDP growth, 1991–2011	459
24.2	Colombia and US: projected GDP per capita growth paths, 2011–2040	460
24.3	Real GDP per capita ratio	461
25.1	Saudi Arabia and the "success stories" (1) (ppp, current international $s)	476
25.2	Saudi Arabia and the "success stories" (2) (ppp constant 2005 international $s)	477

List of illustrations

25.3	Government consumption	480
25.4	% Annual growth working age (15–64) population	481
25.5	Oil curse mapping	483
25.6	Voice and accountability (percentile)	485
25.7	Political stability/absence of violence	485
25.8	Government effectiveness	486
25.9	Regulatory quality (percentile)	487
25.10	Rule of law (percentile)	487
25.11	Control of corruption	488
25.12	Composite governance oil countries (percentile)	489
25.13	Total governance: "success stories"	490
25.14	Heritage House, economic freedom score: oil countries	491
25.15	Heritage House trade freedom score: oil countries	491
25.16	Heritage house, economic freedom score: "success countries"	491
25.17	Heritage house, trade freedom score: "success stories"	492
25.18	Break even oil prices	498
29.1	China-India macroeconomic comparisons: salient estimates, 2025	541
29.2	China-India GDP growth rate estimates by the three cluster, 2020–2025	547
29.3	Summary of the average, high and low estimates, for all 27 studies and by cluster	548
29.4	Fire GDP growth scenario, India and China, 2020–2025	550
29.5	Five scenarios: GDP's of China and India in 2025, Harker Exchange Rate	550
29.6	Five scenarios: GDP's of China and India in 2025, purchasing power party conversion rates	551
29.7	Meta-analysis process	552

Tables

2.1	Average annual GDP growth, % change	20
2.2	Percentage of population living in poverty	23
2.3	Size of the global middle and rich (GMR) class population	24
3.1	Aggregate economic data, 1900–39	36
3.2	Aggregate economic data, 1950–80	39
3.3	Aggregate economic data, 1985–2010	43
4.1	Russian hospitals without mains water supply and other facilities, 2010	48
4.2	GDP per employed person in Russia, Germany and the USA, 2009	51
5.1	GDP and related variables, different periods, 1951–2012	64
5.2	Sectoral growth rates, different periods, 1951–2012	66
5.3	Real interest rates and levels and changes in currency valuation, 1951–2012	67
5.4	Modelling the determinants of GDP growth in India, 1978–2012	67
5.5	Savings, investment, current account and fiscal deficits	72
5.6	Poor industrial growth in India	77
5.7	GDP growth, by factors	79
7.1	South Africa's sector growth patterns relative to middle-income countries	108
7.2	South Africa's changing productive structure relative to middle-income countries	110
7.3	South Africa's macroeconomic growth patterns relative to middle-income countries	111

List of illustrations

7.4	South Africa's changing macroeconomic structure relative to middle-income countries	112
8.1	Countries at various stages of development, 2010–11	143
8.2	Group means on governance dimensions, World Economic Forum development stages, 2010–11	144
8.3	Group means on economic freedom dimensions I, World Economic Forum development stages, 2010–11	145
8.4	Group means on economic freedom dimensions II, World Economic Forum development stages, 2010–11	146
8.5	Financial sector development	147
8.6	Factor analysis: growth potential/entrepreneurship linkages—total sample of countries	149
8.7	Factor analysis: growth potential/entrepreneurship linkages—country groups 1 and 2	152
8.8	Factor analysis: entrepreneurship linkages—country groups 2 and 3	154
8.9	Factor analysis: growth potential/entrepreneurship linkages—country groups 3 and 4	157
8.10	Factor analysis: growth potential/entrepreneurship linkages—country groups 4 and 5	159
8.11	Country group profiles	162
8.12	Determinants of entrepreneurial activity	164
8.13	Determinants of entrepreneurial activity, continued	165
8.14	Governance patterns by country grouping	166
8.15	Entrepreneurship and improved governance: WEF country groupings	167
8.16	Entrepreneurship and improved governance: WEF country groupings, continued	168
8.17	Entrepreneurship and improved governance: WEF country groupings, continued	168
8.18	Entrepreneurship and improved governance: discriminant analysis country groupings	169
8.19	Entrepreneurship and improved governance: discriminant analysis country groupings, continued	170
8.20	Entrepreneurship and improved governance: discriminant analysis country groupings, continued	170
8.21	Entrepreneurial activity by country grouping	171
8.22	Shadow economy and entrepreneurship	172
8.23	Determinants of the shadow economy	173
8.24	Determinants of the shadow economy, continued	174
10.1	Fiscal indicators, 1980–2010	190
10.2	Economic growth and financial stability, 1995–2011	193
10.3	Manufactured exports by technology intensity, 1990–2011	193
10.4	Labour market indicators, 2001–11	196
13.1	Main macroeconomic indicators	250
13.2	Gross national savings and total investment	253
13.3	Educational attainment and high-technology exports	260
14.1	Distribution of FDI in Indonesia by sector, 2004–10	273
14.2	High-technology exports	274
14.3	Agriculture value added and R&D	279

List of illustrations

16.1	Total factor productivity for Malaysia, 1991–2010	311
16.2	Key legislative reforms	319
17.1	Rates of growth of GDP per capita, 1870–2012	332
19.1	Real per capita income and average annual growth rate	365
19.2	Current account (CA), consolidated public sector account (CPSA) and savings-investment gap (S-I) as % of GDP	367
19.3	Tax effort (%) selected years	368
19.4	Share of foreign trade and internal taxes	368
19.5	Total factor productivity in the Philippines	372
19.6	Employment by educational attainment	373
22.1	Growth of GDP and its sectoral components in Thailand, 1951–2012	417
22.2	Aggregate growth accounting in Thailand, 1980–2002	420
22.3	Financing of aggregate investment in Thailand, 1973–2002	422
22.4	Thailand, Indonesia and Malaysia: contributions to expenditure on GDP, 1987–2006	423
22.5	Total factor productivity growth by sectors, 1980–2002	426
22.6	Percentage contributions to aggregate growth, 1980–2002	427
22.7	Poverty incidence and Gini coefficient, 1988–2009	430
23.1	Inflation rates	450
23.2	Inflation and purchasing power	452
25.1	Saudi Arabia: vulnerabilities	478
25.2	Saudi Arabia: volatility and correlation of oil revenue, spending and non-oil growth, 1980–2010	478
25.3	Saudi Arabia: output and employment by sector	479
25.4	Saudi Arabia: contributions to overall GDP growth, 2008–11	479
25.5	Saudi Arabia: Global Competitiveness Index rankings, 2012–13	493
25.6	Saudi Arabia competitiveness: strengths and weaknesses	494
25.7	Saudi Arabia key variables: forecast to 2030	498
26.1	Key global governance clubs, 2013	504
29.1	China-India macro-economic meta-analysis: summary of salient estimates, 2020–25	540
29.2	China-India GDP growth estimates by 2020–25, by academic authors	541
29.3	China-India GDP growth estimates by business organizations and authors, 2020–25	543
29.4	Business conditions in China and India, 2007	545
29.5	China-India GDP growth rate estimates by the three clusters, 2020–25	547
29.6	Some qualitative factors affecting China and India's performance	551

List of contributors

Robert E. Looney is a Distinguished Professor at the Naval Postgraduate School, Monterey, California. He received his PhD in Economics from the University of California, Davis. He specializes in issues relating to economic development in the Middle East, East Asia, South Asia and Latin America. He has published 22 books, including: *Economic Development in Saudi Arabia: Consequences of the Oil Price Decline*, with a foreword by Raymond Mikesell (Greenwich, CT: JAI Press, 1990); *The Economics of Third World Defense Expenditures*, with a foreword by Charles Wolf (Greenwich Conn.: JAI Press, 1995); *The Pakistani Economy: Economic Growth and Structural Reform* (Praeger Publishers, 1997); and *Iraq's Informal Economy: Reflections of War, Sanctions and Policy Failure* (Abu Dhabi: The Emirates Center for Strategic Studies and Research 2007); and is editor of two Routledge Handbooks: *Handbook of US–Middle East Relations* (2009), and *Handbook of Oil Politics* (2012). His current research involves assessing the economic causes and consequences of the Arab Spring.

Dr Looney is on the board of editors of *International Journal of World Peace* and *Journal of Third World Studies*. In addition, he has published over 250 articles in numerous professional journals including: *World Economics, Journal of Development Economics, Middle East Policy, Middle Eastern Studies, Orient, OPEC Review, Middle East Journal, Economic Development and Cultural Change, Journal of Energy and Development, Development Policy Review, American-Arab Affairs, Iranian Studies, Challenge, World Development, Pakistan Development Review, Modern African Studies, Asian Survey, International Organization, Mediterranean Quarterly, Mexican Studies, South Asia, Economia Internationale, Journal of Economic Development, Journal of South Asian and Middle Eastern Studies, The National Interest*, and *Contemporary South Asia*. As an international consultant, Dr Looney has provided advice and assistance to the governments of Iran, Saudi Arabia, Japan, Mexico, Panama and Jamaica, as well as to the World Bank, International Labor Office, Inter-American Development Bank, Stanford Research Institute, the RAND Corporation and the International Monetary Fund.

Alisher Akhmedjonov joined the Economics Department at Zirve University in Turkey in autumn 2010 as an Assistant Professor of Economics. He received his MA degree in Economics from the University of San Francisco and his PhD in Policy Analysis from the RAND Graduate School in 2010. His research interests are in the areas of economic development and applied microeconomics. He has been published widely, including in *Applied Economics, Economic Modelling* and *Economics Letters*.

Laura E. Armey is currently an Assistant Professor of Economics in the Defense Resources Management Institute at the Naval Postgraduate School. She received a BA in Anthropology and a BA and MA in Economics (2004), and a PhD in Political Economy and Public Policy

(2008) from the University of Southern California. Dr Armey previously worked as an analyst at the Cost Analysis and Program Evaluation division of the Office of the Secretary of Defense, where she provided economic analysis of defence policy. Her research focuses on the political and economic factors that affect civil wars and insurgencies. Most recently she has focused on the economics and politics of post-war reconstruction. This includes work that analyses the effectiveness of insurgents and counterinsurgents in Colombia. In addition, as a postdoctoral research fellow for the Institute for Communications Technology at the University of Southern California she began work analysing telecommunications markets and the impact of information technology in developing countries.

Leslie Elliott Armijo (PhD, University of California, Berkeley in Political Science/International Relations) studies the intersection of democratic politics and capitalist markets in emerging powers such as Brazil, India and other large Latin American and Asian countries. A long-time advocate of widening participation in global economic governance (see *Financial Globalization and Democracy in Emerging Markets*, 1999, and *Debating the Global Financial Architecture*, 2002), she argues that democratic consolidation in developing countries helps to mitigate the incidence and costs of economic crisis, as in 'Two Dimensions of Democracy and the Economy' (with C. Gervasoni, 2010). Armijo also has chronicled the rise of the BRICS countries and other emerging powers, as in 'The BRICs Countries (Brazil, Russia, India, and China) as Analytical Category: Insight or Mirage?' (2007); 'Brazil, the Democratic and Entrepreneurial BRIC' (with S. Burges, 2010); and 'The Systemic Financial Capabilities of Emerging Powers' (with L. Muehlich and D. Tirone, forthcoming). Other work considers how countries' positions in the global hierarchy of states influence their leaders' policies and preferences, including 'Absolute or Relative Gains? How Status Quo and Emerging Powers Conceptualize Global Finance' (with J. Echeverri-Gent, forthcoming). Armijo is a Visiting Scholar in the Hatfield School at Portland State University and a Non-Resident Faculty Fellow at the Center for Latin American and Latino Studies at American University. Her website is: www.lesliearmijo.org

Surjit S. Bhalla is Managing Director of Oxus Research and Investments, a New Delhi-based economic research, asset management and emerging-markets advisory firm. He taught at the Delhi School of Economics and worked at the RAND Corporation, the Brookings Institution, and at both the research and treasury departments of the World Bank. He has also worked at Goldman Sachs (1992–94) and Deutsche Bank (1994–96). He is author of *Devaluing to Prosperity: Misaligned Currencies and Their Growth Consequences* (2012) and *Imagine There's No Country: Poverty, Inequality, and Growth in the Era of Globalization* (2002). His research interests are fiscal policy (flat tax?), economic history (do institutions cause growth?), and macroeconomic policy (the role of exchange rates in economic development). He has been a member of several government of India committees on economic policy, most recently the committee on capital account convertibility. He is on the board of India's largest think tank and is an appointed member of the National Statistical Commission of India. He is also a regular contributor to newspapers and magazines on economics, politics and cricket. His first book, *Between the Wickets: The Who and Why of the Best in Cricket* (1987), developed a model for evaluating performance in sports.

Pieter Bottelier is an economist and China scholar. He has been Senior Adjunct Professor, Johns Hopkins University School of Advanced International Studies (SAIS) since 1999. His many positions include: Senior Advisor on China to the Conference Board, 2006–10, Non-resident Fellow at the Carnegie Endowment for International Peace, 2009–12, Adjunct

Lecturer at Harvard University KSG and at Georgetown University, 2001–03. He is the author of many articles and book chapters on China's economy. His World Bank career 1970–98 involved: senior adviser to the Vice-President for East Asia, 1997–98; chief of the Bank's resident mission in China, 1993–97; directorships for Latin America and North Africa, 1987–93; division chief for Mexico, 1983–87; resident chief economist in Jakarta, Indonesia, 1979–83; various assignments as desk economist for East and West African countries, 1970–79. Employment prior to the World Bank included: Lecturer at the University of Amsterdam, 1964–65; adviser to the Minister of Finance, Zambia, 1965–67; consultant to the United Nations Conference on Trade and Development (UNCTAD) on the global market for virgin and scrap non-ferrous metals, 1968; Chief Economist and Marketing Director of Zambia's state-owned copper company, 1968–70. His education includes: University of Amsterdam, 1954–62, Drs degree (MA equivalent), 1962. He was a Harkness Fellow of the Commonwealth Fund in New York for study in the USA, 1962–64; guest scholar at the Massachusetts Institute of Technology (MIT), 1962–63; research associate at the Brookings Institution, Washington, DC, 1963–64.

Shahid Javed Burki was educated at the University of Oxford as a Rhodes Scholar and at Harvard University as a Mason Fellow. He received advanced degrees in economics from both universities. He was at the World Bank for 25 years, from 1974 to 1999, where he held a number of senior positions including Director, China Department, and Vice-President, Latin America and the Caribbean. In 1996–97, on leave of absence from the World Bank, he served as Pakistan's finance minister. After retiring from the Bank, he served as CEO of EMP Financial Advisors, a Washington, DC-based private sector advisory agency. He is currently Chair of the Institute of Public Policy at the Beaconhouse National University, Lahore, Pakistan. He has written extensively on China, Latin America and Pakistan. He books include: *Transforming Socialist Economies: Lessons for Cuba and Beyond* (with Daniel Erikson), and *Changing Perceptions, Altered Reality: Pakistan's Economy under Musharraf, 1999–2007*. He is currently Visiting Senior Research Fellow at the Institute of South Asian Studies and a Senior Fellow at the Woodrow Wilson Center. His latest publications include the *Historical Dictionary of Pakistan* (fourth edition to be published in 2014). He is currently preparing a major work assessing the state of Afghanistan after 2014.

Dante B. Canlas is currently a Professor at the University of the Philippines School of Economics. He served as Socio-Economic Planning Secretary and concurrently Director-General of the National Economic and Development Authority from 2001 to 2002, under then President Gloria Macapagal-Arroyo. Dr Canlas was also the Executive Director of the Asian Development Bank (ADB) for Kazakhstan, Maldives, Marshall Islands, Mongolia, Pakistan and the Philippines from 2003 to 2004. He earned his BS in Mathematics, MA and PhD in Economics from the University of the Philippines. He was Visiting Professor at Northern Illinois University in De Kalb, Illinois, and Research Fellow at Princeton University in New Jersey.

Domingo F. Cavallo is currently a Partner at Global Source Partners LLC and the Chairman and CEO of DFC Associates LLC. He is also honorary President of Fundación Mediterránea, the research institute in applied economics he created in 1977 and presided between 1977 and 1987. He is also a member of the Group of Thirty. He was Minister of Economy (1991–96 and 2001) and Minister of Foreign Affairs (1989–91) of Argentina. He was twice elected National Congressman (1987–91 and 1997–2001). He also served as Chairman of the Central Bank of Argentina in 1982. He was Professor of Economics in the National University of Córdoba, Visiting Professor of Economics at the Stern Business School at NYU, Robert F. Kennedy

Visiting Professor of Latin American Studies at Harvard University and Senior Fellow in Global Affairs at the Jackson Institute on International Relations of Yale University.

Uri Dadush is Senior Associate at the Carnegie Endowment for International Peace. He analyses trends in the global economy and is especially interested in the effects of the rise of developing countries and the associated economic policy and governance questions. He is the co-author of four recent books and reports: *Inequality in America: Facts, Trends and International Perspective* (Brookings, 2012); *Juggernaut: How Emerging Markets are Reshaping Globalization* (Carnegie, 2011); *Currency Wars* (Carnegie, 2011); and *Paradigm Lost: The Euro in Crisis* (Carnegie, 2010). He has published over a dozen Carnegie papers and policy briefs as well as numerous journal articles. His opinion on current economic events appears frequently in the most prominent media. Before joining Carnegie, Dadush's experience was split evenly between the public and private sectors. In the private sector, where he led a number of business turn around situations, he was president and CEO of the Economist Intelligence Unit and Business International, part of the Economist Group (1986–92); group vice-president, international, for Data Resources, Inc. (1982–86), now Global Insight; and a consultant with McKinsey and Company in Europe. In the public sector, he served as the World Bank's director of international trade and director of economic policy. He also served concurrently as the director of the Bank's world economy group, leading the preparation of the World Bank's flagship reports on the international economy for over 11 years. During that period he was spokesperson for the Bank on global economic trends and on the ongoing international trade negotiations. Dadush holds a PhD in Business Economics from Harvard University and a BA and MA in Economics from the Hebrew University of Jerusalem.

Albert Fishlow is Professor Emeritus both at the University of California, Berkeley and Columbia University. He has also served as Professor of Economics at Yale and Paul Volcker Fellow at the Council on Foreign Relations. His published research has addressed issues in economic history, Brazilian and Latin American development strategy, as well as economic relations between industrialized and developing countries. His most recent book is *Starting Over: Brazil Since 1985* (Brookings, 2011).

Reza Ghorashi received his PhD in International Economics from Fordham University and is currently Professor of Economics and Coordinator of International Studies at Richard Stockton College of New Jersey. His research interests include compatibility of polity and economy with concentration on Iran. He has written on this subject both in English and Farsi. Among English publications are 'A Modern Society Facing a Pre-modern State', *Asian Affairs* 25 (2005); and 'Economic Globalization and Prospect for Democracy in Iran', *Iran Encountering Globalization*. A related area of his research deals with the impact of international trade on economic development. His English writings include 'Measuring Terms of Trade of LDCs', *American Economist* 22; and 'Marx on Free Trade', *Science & Society* 59(1).

Francisco E. González is the Riordan Roett Associate Professor of Latin American Studies at The Johns Hopkins University Paul H. Nitze School of Advanced International Studies (SAIS) in Washington, DC. He holds Master's (MPhil, 1997) and Doctoral (DPhil, 2002) degrees in Politics from the University of Oxford, and served as a British Academy Postdoctoral Fellow at Nuffield College, Oxford (2002–05). Before moving to Washington, DC, Professor González taught at the SAIS Bologna Center in Italy (2003–05), and previously was a Lecturer in Politics at St John's College, Oxford. Between 2000 and 2005 he was a junior faculty member at the University of Oxford's Department of Politics and International Relations. Professor González is the author of two books, both published by the Johns Hopkins University Press. First, *Dual Transitions from Authoritarian Rule: Institutionalized Regimes in Chile and Mexico, 1970–2000* was named 'Outstanding Academic Title of 2008' by *Choice*, the magazine for academic libraries. Second, in the spring of 2012 he published *Creative Destruction? Economic Crises and Democracy in Latin America*. He is a regular participant in commentary shows on CNN en Español, Voice of America, the Diane Rehm Show and Al Jazeera International. Professor González has received the 'Excellence in Teaching' award at SAIS (in 2006 and again in 2012), making him one of just a couple of SAIS faculty members to have received this honour twice.

Philip Hanson is an Associate Fellow of the Russia and Eurasia Programme at Chatham House, London and an Emeritus Professor of the Political Economy of Russia and Eastern Europe at the University of Birmingham. He has written among other things an economic history of the USSR from 1945–91 and a study of patterns of regional economic change in Russia. Past appointments have been at the Foreign & Commonwealth Office, UK, the UN Economic Commission for Europe, Radio Liberty, and Michigan, Harvard, Kyoto and Södertörns universities. He is currently working on contemporary Russian economic policy and business-state relations in Russia.

Herizal Hazri is the Deputy Country Representative in The Asia Foundation's Malaysia office. He is responsible for programme design and co-ordination for the Foundation's programmes in Malaysia. Prior to joining the Foundation, Herizal served as a consultant with several think tanks and public policy consulting firms internationally as well as in Malaysia. He is known particularly in the areas of economic development, politics, democracy and conflict resolution in the region. He has built good relationships with governments and multinational corporations, and has managed complex development programmes in a number of Asian countries such as Indonesia, Timor-Leste, Thailand, the Philippines, Cambodia, Myanmar, Pakistan, Afghanistan, Sri Lanka, Bangladesh, Taiwan, and his home country, Malaysia. Herizal has published works on political processes, Malaysia's economic development and is a constant contributor to the *In Asia* blog on development and democracy.

Nake M. Kamrany was born in Kabul, Afghanistan. He is currently a tenured Senior Professor of Economics and attorney at law teaching economic analysis of law, macroeconomics, the world economy and economic development. He is also Director of Program in Law and Economics at the University of Southern California. He received his BS at UCLA, MA and PhD at USC (1973), and JD at UWLA (1993). His previous professional appointments include MIT (1973–75), the World Bank (1969–73), UCLA, and Stanford Research Institute. He has served as adviser to the World Bank, UN Development Programme (UNDP), the governments of the USA, Ghana, Lebanon, the Philippines, Jamaica and the Sahel-Sudan countries of Africa, including Mali, Chad, Burkina Faso, Senegal and Niger, having published 12 volumes of research reports. He has 16 published books and over 100 professional papers in learned journals. He is the recipient of research grants from the Sloan Foundation, Advanced Research Project Agency, and Agency for International Development. Professor Kamrany's pioneering work includes: application of computerized system dynamic modelling approach in regional economic policy analysis of the Susquehanna River basin and the Grand River basin; rescheduling Ghana's and the Philippines' multi-million-dollar national debts; developing computerized programmable automation for application in the production of the discrete manufacturing sector; and the development of global income convergence models among nations in the 21st century.

Vijayakumari Kanapathy holds a PhD in Economics from the University of Malaya and is currently an independent consultant. Prior to that, she was attached to the Institute of Strategic and International Studies (ISIS) Malaysia, the Faculty of Economics at the University of Malaysia and the Socio-Economic Research Unit of the Prime Minister's Department. Her research interests include computable general equilibrium (CGE) modelling, international migration, and trade and industry policy studies. She has extensive work experience as a consultant to international agencies including the World Bank, International Labour Organization (ILO), UN Industrial Development Organization (UNIDO), World Intellectual Property Organization (WIPO) and UN Development Programme (UNDP), and the government of Malaysia.

Linda Yuen-Ching Lim is Professor of Strategy at the Stephen M. Ross School of Business at the University of Michigan, where she also served as Director of the Center for Southeast Asian Studies, 2004–09. A citizen of Singapore, Linda holds degrees in Economics from the universities of Cambridge (BA), Yale (MA) and Michigan (PhD), beginning her academic career as Assistant Professor of Economics at Swarthmore College, where she taught economic development. She has published numerous scholarly and popular media articles on Singapore's economy since 1976, including an early journal article on 'Singapore's Success: The Myth of the Free Market Miracle', *Asian Survey* (1983), and the book chapter 'Globalizing State, Disappearing Nation: Foreign Participation in Singapore's Economy' (with Lee Soo Ann, Institute of Southeast Asian Studies, 2010). Her work on Singapore and other South-East Asian countries has focused on international trade and investment, industrial policy, labour (including foreign and female labour), multinational and local business, including overseas Chinese business. Her current research is on Western and Asian business in Myanmar; foreign direct investment by Chinese companies in South-East Asia; and on local entrepreneurs in South-East Asia. Professor Lim has consulted and conducted executive education on Asian business, politics, economics and culture for multinational and Asian companies and associations, and government and international development agencies (e.g. Economic and Social Commission for Asia and the Pacific (ESCAP), International Labour Organization (ILO), UN Industrial Development Organization (UNIDO) and the Organisation for Economic Co-operation and Development (OECD)). A Trustee Emeritus of The Asia Society, a New York-based non-profit organization, she has served sequentially as an independent director of two publicly listed US tech manufacturing companies with extensive operations in China and Singapore.

Patricio Navia is a master teacher in Liberal Studies and Adjunct Assistant Professor at the Center for Latin American and Caribbean Studies at New York University. He is also a researcher and Professor of Political Science at the Facultad de Ciencias Sociales at Universidad Diego Portales in Chile. He holds a PhD in Politics from New York University, an MA in Political Science from the University of Chicago, and a BA in Political Sciences and Sociology from the University of Illinois at Chicago. He has been a Visiting Professor at Princeton, New School University, Universidad de Salamanca, Universidad de Chile and NYU Buenos Aires, and a Visiting Fellow at the University of Miami. He has published scholarly articles and book chapters on democratization, electoral rules and democratic institutions in Latin America. As founding director of Observatorio Electoral at Universidad Diego Portales, he edited *El sismo electoral de 2009. Cambio y continuidad en las preferencias políticas de los chilenos* (with Mauricio Morales, 2010), and *El genoma electoral chileno. Dibujando el mapa genético de las preferencias políticas en Chile* (with Mauricio Morales and Renato Briceño, 2009). His books *Diccionario de la política chilena* (with Alfredo Joignant and Francisco Javier Díaz), *El discolo. Conversaciones con Marco Enríquez-Ominami* (2009), *Que gane el más mejor: Mérito y Competencia en el Chile de hoy* (with Eduardo Engel, 2006), and *Las grandes alamedas: El Chile post Pinochet* (2004) have been bestsellers

List of contributors

in Chile. He is a columnist at *La Tercera* newspaper and *Buenos Aires Herald*, has previously penned columns at *Capital* and *Poder* magazines in Chile, and regularly writes for the *Infolatam* website. Since 2009 he has been a Fellow in the Americas Business Council and *Poder* magazine.

Fatih Özatay received his PhD in Economics from Ankara University in 1986. He worked in the research department of the Central Bank of Turkey from 1987 until 1995, when he joined the Faculty of Political Sciences of Ankara University. In May 2001 he was appointed Vice-Governor of the Central Bank of Turkey and also served as a member of the Monetary Policy Committee. He has been a Professor in the Department of Economics at TOBB University of Economics and Technology, and Director of the Finance Institute at the Economic Policy Research Foundation of Turkey (TEPAV) since April 2006. His main areas of interest are financial crises, monetary policy and the Turkish economy. His two recent books (in Turkish) are *Financial Crises and Turkey* (2009), and *Monetary Economics: Theory and Policy* (2011).

Martin Rama is the Chief Economist for the South Asia region of the World Bank, based in Delhi. His main priorities are to promote debate on difficult policy issues in the region, to lead the preparation of major reports on regional issues, and to oversee the overall quality of the Bank's analytical work in the region. To deliver on these tasks, he and his team actively engage with counterparts in government, academia, civil society and the business community. Until October 2012 Martin Rama was the Director of the 2013 *World Development Report, on Jobs*. The *WDR* is the main annual flagship of the World Bank, and the dean of such publications in the area of development economics. The Jobs report built on new research, in-depth case studies and extensive consultations. Over the previous eight years, until 2010, Martin Rama was the Lead Economist for Viet Nam, based in Hanoi. In this capacity, he oversaw the analytical programme of the World Bank in areas related to economic policy and poverty reduction. Prior to moving to operations, Martin Rama spent 10 years with the research department of the World Bank, mainly in Washington, DC, but providing cross-support to a large number of developing countries. Martin Rama gained his PhD in macroeconomics from the University of Paris in 1985. Back in his home country of Uruguay, he worked at CINVE, the country's largest think tank, and became one of its directors. In parallel with his World Bank duties, he was Visiting Professor in Development Economics at the University of Paris until 2005.

Danielle N. Ramirez's interest in Latin American political economy led her to pursue an academic career in Economics. Throughout her years at the University of Southern California Danielle focused her undergraduate and graduate research on the Cuban Embargo and the Colombian economy. It was then that she met Nake M. Kamrany PhD, JD, and with his guidance was able to delve even deeper into her research and overall interest in Colombia by co-authoring an article in the *Huffington Post* called 'Colombia's Economic Problems and Prospects'. Danielle graduated from USC with honours and as one of the founding members of the Global Income Convergence Group (GIC-G), a non-profit think tank concerned with the changing disparity of living standards among the world's countries. Danielle plans to pursue her passion for global economics through continued research and possibly a career with the United Nations.

Paul Rivlin is a senior fellow at the Moshe Dayan Center for Middle East and African Studies, Tel-Aviv University. He studied at Cambridge, London and Harvard universities and is the author of five books, *The Dynamics of Economic Policy Making in Egypt*, *The Israeli Economy*, *Economic Policy and Performance in the Arab World*, *Arab Economies in the Twenty-First Century*, and *The Israeli Economy from the Foundation of the State to the Twenty-First Century*, as well as publications on economic development in the Middle East, energy markets, defence and trade economics. Paul Rivlin is the Editor of *Iqtisadi*, the Middle East economics publication of the Dayan Center; he has lectured extensively overseas and has been a Visiting Professor of Economics at Emory University.

Cynthia Roberts (PhD, Columbia) is an Associate Professor of Political Science at Hunter College, CUNY; Adjunct Associate Professor and Senior Associate of the Saltzman Institute of War and Peace Studies, Columbia University. Professor Roberts is the author of a monograph, *Russia and the European Union: The Sources and Limits of 'Special Relationships'* (2007), and is completing a study on 'Russian Grand Strategy from Peter to Putin: Lessons for Emerging Great Powers'. Her articles on Russia, European and international security problems have appeared in such journals as *Comparative Politics, Survival, Europe-Asia Studies*, the *Washington Quarterly, Journal of Cold War Studies*, the *European Financial Review, Technology Review*, and in edited volumes. Professor Roberts is also a specialist on the BRICS and international power shifts, and served as editor and author of two articles of a special issue of *Polity* (January 2010) on 'Challengers or Stakeholders? BRICs and the Liberal World Order'.

Zamroni Salim is an economist at the Economic Research Center, the Indonesian Institute of Sciences. He graduated from the Graduate School of International Development (GSID), Nagoya University, Japan in 2009, with an undergraduate degree from Airlangga University, and a Master's degree from Massey University, Palmerston North, New Zealand (2003). His primary research interests include regionalism, economic integration and development, the Association of Southeast Asian Nations (ASEAN) and East Asian studies, and industrial economics. He has been a Lecturer at the School of International Relations, President University, Indonesia. His various positions also include the Habibie Center and the Ministry of Trade of the Republic of Indonesia—Research and Development on Trade Policies. He is an Editor of *Indonesian Economic and Business Studies* (RIEBS), *Buletin Ilmiah Litbang Perdagangan* (BILP, a scientific journal on trade-related issues under the Ministry of Trade), and the *Journal of Democracy and Human Rights* of the Habibie Center.

Bernhard J. Seliger is currently resident representative of the Hanns Seidel Foundation in the Republic of Korea (South Korea), based in Seoul, consulting with non-governmental organizations (NGOs), academic and public institutions in questions of unification. He has frequently travelled to the Democratic People's Republic of Korea (North Korea), where he implemented capacity-building projects, among others in economics, forestry and the introduction of the clean development mechanism. He serves as associate of *North Korean Review* as well as Founding Editor of the website www.asianintegration.org. In 2006 the honorary citizenship of Seoul was conferred on him by the future president of South Korea, the then-Mayor Lee Myung-Bak. Since 2007 Dr Seliger has been Senior Lecturer (Privatdozent Dr Habil) at the University of Witten/Herdecke, Germany. In 2004–06 Dr Seliger was Guest Professor at the Graduate School of Public Administration of Seoul National University and at the Graduate School of International Area Studies of Hankuk University of Foreign Studies. Previously, Dr Seliger was Assistant Professor at the Graduate School of International Area Studies of Hankuk University of Foreign Studies, 1998–2002; Assistant Researcher at the Institute for Economic Policy, Christian-Albrechts-University at Kiel, Germany, 1995–98, where he received a doctorate (DrScPol) in 1998. Dr Seliger holds a degree (Maîtrise en sciences économiques) from Université de Paris I (Panthéon-Sorbonne, France). Among Dr Seliger's research interests are institutional economics, economics of transformation and integration, and the economic development of Korea in North-East Asia. His latest book is *The Shrimp that Became a Tiger. Transformation Theory and Korea's Rise After the Asian Crisis* (Frankfurt: Peter Lang, 2013).

List of contributors

Robert Springborg is a Professor in the Department of National Security Affairs of the Naval Postgraduate School and Program Manager for the Middle East for the Center for Civil-Military Relations. Until August 2008 he held the MBI Al Jaber Chair in Middle East Studies at the School of Oriental and African Studies in London, where he also served as Director of the London Middle East Institute. Before taking up that Chair he was Director of the American Research Center in Egypt. From 1973 until 1999 he taught in Australia, where he was University Professor of Middle East Politics at Macquarie University. He has also taught at the University of California, Berkeley, the University of Pennsylvania, and elsewhere. His publications include *Mubarak's Egypt: Fragmentation of the Political Order; Family Power and Politics in Egypt; Legislative Politics in the Arab World* (with Abdo Baaklini and Guilain Denoeux); *Globalization and the Politics of Development in the Middle East* (with Clement M. Henry); *Oil and Democracy in Iraq; Development Models in Muslim Contexts: Chinese, 'Islamic' and Neo-Liberal Alternatives*; and several editions of *Politics in the Middle East* (with James A. Bill). He co-edited a volume on popular culture and political identity in the Gulf which appeared in 2008. He has published in the leading Middle East journals and was the founder and regular editorialist for *The Middle East in London*, a monthly journal that commenced publication in 2003. He has worked as a consultant on Middle East governance and politics for the United States Agency for International Development (USAID), the US State Department, the UNDP and various UK government departments, including the Foreign & Commonwealth Office, the Ministry of Defence and the Department for International Development. He is a member and past President (1991) of the Australasian Middle East Studies Association; member of the National Advisory Committee of the Middle East Policy Council, Washington, DC, 1997–; member of the Editorial Board of *The Middle East in London*, 2003–; member of the Editorial Board of the LMEI/SOAS Saqi Series on Contemporary Middle East Issues, 2005–; member of the Board of Trustees of the Committee for British Research in the Levant, 2005–; member of the Board of the British Society for Middle East Studies, 2004–; member of the Editorial Board of *Foreign Policy Bulletin*, 2005–; member of the Board of Trustees of the Arab-British Chamber of Commerce Foundation, 2007–; member of the Steering Committee of Il Vicino Oriente, September 2007–; member of the Editorial Board of the Routledge Series on the Political Economy of the Middle East, 2008–; and member of Phi Beta Kappa Epsilon of Minnesota, 2008–.

Peter Warr is Head of the Arndt-Corden Department of Economics, John Crawford Professor of Agricultural Economics and Executive Director of the National Thai Studies Centre, College of Asia and the Pacific, at the Australian National University. He studied agricultural economics at the University of Sydney and has a Master's degree in Economics from the London School of Economics and Political Science (LSE) and a PhD in Economics from Stanford University. His current research is on the relationship between economic policy, technological change and poverty incidence, especially in South-East Asia. Much of this work uses general equilibrium models, specially adapted to measure changes in poverty incidence. He has published extensively on the Thai economy and has been a Visiting Professor of Economics at Thammasat University and Chulalongkorn University in Bangkok, and at the University of Indonesia. He has also acted as a consultant to the World Bank, the Asian Development Bank, various United Nations agencies and AusAID. He has written or edited three books on the Thai economy, the most recent being *Thailand Beyond the Crisis* (Routledge, 2005).

John Williamson was born in 1937 and educated at LSE and Princeton University. He has taught at the Universities of York (1963–68) and Warwick (1970–77) in England, the Pontificia Universidade Católica do Rio de Janeiro (1978–81) in Brazil, as a Visiting Professor at MIT (1967 and 1980), LSE (1992), and Princeton (1996), and as an Honorary Professor at the University of Warwick (1985–2007). He was an economic consultant to the UK Treasury in 1968–70, where he worked on a range of international financial issues, and an adviser to the International Monetary Fund in 1972–74, where he worked mainly on questions of international monetary reform related to the work of the Committee of Twenty. He was a Senior Fellow at the Peterson Institute for International Economics in Washington, DC, from its founding in 1981 until his retirement in 2012. In 1996–99 he went on leave from the Institute to serve as Chief Economist for the South Asia Region of the World Bank. In 2001 he served as Project Director for the UN High-Level Panel on Financing for Development (the Zedillo Panel). He retains his British nationality. His publications have mainly concerned international monetary issues and include: *The Crawling Peg* (Princeton Essays in International Finance, 1965); *The Failure of World Monetary Reform, 1971–74* (Nelson, 1977); *IMF Conditionality* (1983); *The Exchange Rate System* (1985); *Political Economy and International Money* (Wheatsheaf, 1987); *Latin American Adjustment: How Much Has Happened?* (1990); *The Political Economy of Policy Reform* (1993); *Estimating Equilibrium Exchange Rates* (1994); *What Role for Currency Boards?* (1995); *The Crawling Band as an Exchange Rate Regime: Lessons from Chile, Colombia, and Israel* (1996); and *Exchange Rate Regimes for Emerging Markets: Reviving the Intermediate Option* (2000); 'What Should the World Bank Think about the Washington Consensus?' *World Bank Research Observer* (2000); *Curbing the Boom-Bust Cycle: Stabilizing Capital Flows to Emerging Markets* (2004); *Reference Rates and the International Monetary System* (2009); with Donald Lessard, *Financial Intermediation Beyond the Debt Crisis* (1985); with Marcus Miller, *Targets and Indicators: A Blueprint for the International Coordination of Economic Policy*; with Chris Milner, *The World Economy* (Harvester-Wheatsheaf, 1991); with Molly Mahar, *A Survey of Financial Liberalization* (Princeton Essays in International Finance, 1998); with Pedro Pablo Kuczysnki, *After the Washington Consensus: Restarting Growth and Reform in Latin America*; and co-edited with C. Fred Bergsten, *Dollar Adjustment: How Far? Against What?* From 2008 to 2012, he published with W.R. Cline a series of studies estimating countries' FEERs. (Except as noted, all are published by the Peterson Institute for International Economics.)

Charles Wolf, Jr is Senior Economic Adviser and Distinguished Corporate Chair in International Economics, RAND. He is a Professor of Policy Analysis in the Pardee RAND Graduate School, and received his BS and PhD degrees in Economics from Harvard. From 1967 until June 1981 he was head of RAND's Economics Department, and thereafter was director of RAND research in international economics. He was the founding Dean of the RAND Graduate School, and served in that capacity from 1970 to 1997. Dr Wolf is a Senior Research Fellow at the Hoover Institution, and was a director of Capital Income Builder Fund, Inc and Capital World Growth and Income Fund, Inc in 1986–2010. Dr Wolf has served with the Department of State, and has taught at Cornell, the University of California at Berkeley, UCLA and Nuffield College, Oxford. He is the author of more than 250 journal articles and the author or co-author of 24 books, including: *Foreign Aid: Theory and Practice in Southern Asia* (1960, Princeton Press); *Rebellion and Authority: An Analytic Essay on Insurgent Conflicts* (1970, Markham); *The Costs of the Soviet Empire* (1986, RAND); *Markets or Governments: Choosing Between Imperfect Alternatives* (1993, MIT Press); *The Economic Pivot in a Political Context* (1997); *Asian Economic Trends and Their Security Implications* (2000); *Straddling Economics and Politics: Cross-Cutting Issues in Asia, the United States, and the Global Economy* (2002); *Fault Lines in China's Economic Terrain* (2003); *Looking Backward and Forward: Policy Issues in the 21st Century* (2008); *Modernizing the North Korean System* (2008); *Enhancement by Enlargement: The Proliferation Security Initiative* (2008); *U.S. Combat Commands' Participation in the Proliferation Security Initiative* (2009); *A Smarter Approach to China's Currency* (2011, Policy Review); *China and India, 2025: A Comparative*

List of contributors

Assessment (2011); *China's Expanding Role in Global Mergers and Acquisitions Markets* (2011); and *China's Foreign Aid and Government-Sponsored Investment Activities: Scale, Content, Destinations and Implications* (forthcoming). He is a frequent contributor to the *Wall Street Journal*, the *Asian Wall Street Journal*, the *Wall Street Journal Europe*, the *Weekly Standard*, the *New York Times*, the *International Herald Tribune*, the *Los Angeles Times*, and the *International Economy*. Dr Wolf's main research and policy interests are the international economy, international security, and the relations between them.

Hamid Zangeneh is Professor of Economics at Widener University, Chester, Pennsylvania. His areas of specialization are macroeconomics, money and banking, and international economics. He has written on these subjects both in English and Persian. His publications have appeared in, among others, *Applied Economics, Public Budgeting and Financial Management, Middle East Policy Journal*, and *Iranian Economic Review*. He co-edited (with Cyrus Bina) *Modern Capitalism and Islamic Ideology* (St Martin's Press, New York, 1992), and edited *Islam, Iran, and World Stability* (St Martin's Press, New York, 1994). He has served as the treasurer and executive director of the Center for Iranian Research and Analysis (CIRA). He is a frequent guest on Voice of America Persian programmes, discussing Iranian economic and political issues. He is currently the editor of the *Journal of Iranian Research and Analysis*.

Foreword

Deepak Lal

I am very pleased to write this foreword for this Handbook, as it covers many countries on which I have worked over the past 50 years.[1] It is nice to see how they have got on over the years, and their prospects as 'emerging economies' as judged by an eminent roster of economists.

However, I must begin with a linguistic protest. It concerns the use of the term 'neo-liberal' in many of the chapters. As Polonius would have said, 'That's an ill phrase, a vile phrase'.[2] It is a meaningless term. As the Peruvian novelist, politician and Nobel laureate Mario Vargas Llosa has argued:

> A 'neo' is someone who pretends to be something, someone who is at the same time inside and outside something; it is an elusive hybrid, a straw man set up without ever identifying a specific value, idea, regime or doctrine … To say 'neoliberal' is the same as saying 'semi-liberal' or 'pseudo liberal'. It is pure nonsense. Either one is in favor of liberty or against it, but one cannot be semi-in favor or pseudo-in favor of liberty, just as one cannot be 'semi-pregnant', 'semi-living' or 'semi-dead'. The term has not been invented to express a conceptual reality, but as a corrosive weapon of derision, it has been designed to semantically devalue the doctrine of liberalism.
>
> *(Vargas Llosa 2000: 16)*

However, the correct term, 'economic liberalism', has, as Schumpeter (1954: 394) noted, 'acquired a different—in fact almost the opposite—meaning since about 1900 and especially since 1930; as a supreme if unintended compliment, the enemies of the system of private enterprise have thought it wise to appropriate its label'. *Faute de mieux*, the correct term to use for the set of classical policy prescriptions for an economy should be *classical liberalism*, to distinguish them from the quasi-socialist policies which currently go under the name of liberalism.

Classical liberal policies

There is an excellent account of this set of classical liberal policies in Domingo Cavallo's Chapter (27) in this volume, and I set out my outline as well as dealing with the objections made against them by contemporary 'liberals' in my *Reviving the Invisible Hand—The Case for Classical Liberalism in the Twenty-first Century* (Lal 2006). As Myint and I pointed out in our synthesis volume for the World Bank comparative study *The Political Economy of Poverty Equity and Growth—A Comparative Study* (Lal and Myint 1996: 326), 'our general argument for free-market policies is derived not from the formal properties of the perfect-competition model but on empirical grounds from experience and history'. The resulting classical liberal policy package can be summarized as consisting of free trade, Gladstonian finance, stable money and the maintenance of stable property rights to allow entrepreneurship to flourish with free entry by potential entrepreneurs and the exit of unviable firms. As many of the successful emerging economies of this volume have followed many, though not all, of these prescriptions, it can be taken as a vindication of the classical liberal policy package. Many have described this as the Washington Consensus. However, as John Williamson—the progenitor of this term—argues in his Chapter (9) in this volume, he would demur from this view, particularly regarding the support of many classical liberals for floating or fixed exchange rates as compared with Williamson's advocacy of managed rates.[3] However, he is right to question the desirability of the alternative Beijing Consensus, and its emphasis on industrial policy, on grounds similar to the ones for which I have argued in my own recent examination of these alternative policy packages (Lal 2012).[4]

Even the partial adoption of the classical liberal package, particularly that concerning freedom of trade and capital, provided the necessary environment for the 'catch-up' growth of the successful emerging markets, including the BRICS (Brazil, Russia, India, People's Republic of China and South Africa). Given their larger share of the global population, this has led to their growing weight in the global economy, but does this mean that these emerging markets, and in particular the BRICS, have now been uncoupled from the outcomes in the world economy, and provide an independent and more robust pole of growth? I think this is doubtful, as the recent downgrading of their contributions to proximate world growth, relative to the developed countries, by the International Monetary Fund (IMF) shows. This is in large part due to the failure of emerging markets to undertake the structural reforms (to complete their move to a full-fledged classical liberal economy) during the long global boom, induced by loose US monetary policy, from 2003 until the Great Recession of 2008. They were partially insulated from the global ripples of the Western banking crisis, as their banking systems were only partially integrated with the global system, and they had relatively strong fiscal balances, relatively flexible exchange rates and built up foreign exchange reserves as a lesson they had learnt from the 1990s debt crises.

The movement in emerging market dollar bond spreads over US Treasuries illustrates the recent rise and fall of the emerging market story. As James Mackintosh of the *Financial Times* noted, after the 1997 Asian crisis, emerging market (EM) bonds had by 2007 begun to behave in line with investment grade bonds. This lasted in the aftermath of the collapse of Lehman Brothers, but now EM bonds 'are back closer to junk than investment grade'. This is not because of any substantial downgrades by rating agencies, but because 'investors have begun to realize they made a mistake. While some emerging markets may be safe, taken together their politics, monetary policy and economic development remain immature—and thus very risky'.[5]

The BRICS

Given that emerging market growth did not suffer by much in the Great Recession, there was growing hubris, particularly in the BRICS. China and India undertook fiscal expansions to offset the possible economic contraction flowing from the global crisis. Both were flawed and have damaged their prospective growth rates. In both there was a statist turn in the 2000s. In China, through the continuation of financial repression, with the de facto deployment of its large household savings in unproductive infrastructural spending, leaving a large debt overhang.[6] In India, through an expansion of populist entitlements, predicated on the continuance of high growth rates, which have led to a fiscal and balance of payments crisis.

In both countries (and in Russia) their very success in liberalizing product markets, which generated high growth rates, has led to a surprising rise in rent seeking. This is to acquire the rents from land and natural resources, which have risen with the overall growth rate, but the rent seeking associated with the distribution of these rents has not in itself—unlike the rent seeking associated with the past monopoly rents arising from the controls on commodity markets—affected their growth rates. This is because the rent seeking associated with land and natural resources relates (in Marshallian terms) to pure 'economic' or 'quasi' rents, and is equivalent to levying lump sum taxes. The 'monopoly' rents associated with controls on product markets, by contrast, are equivalent to the levying of distortionary taxes-cum-subsidies, which in addition to their deadweight losses affect the marginal decisions of consumers and producers, thereby affecting economic performance. Though the appropriation of these pure 'economic' rents by the politically connected did not affect growth in the past, it has led to a political backlash in both countries which could (as it already has in India) damage their economic performance in the future (see Lal 2011).

Unlike China, India has also failed to end the 'monopoly' rents in the labour market arising from colonial labour laws (see Lal 2005: Ch. 9), for the small aristocracy of organized labour. By limiting the entry and exit of firms, and artificially raising the price of India's most abundant resource, they have damaged labour-intensive industrialization in India, so that the famed 'demographic dividend', on which so much faith has been placed for India's future growth prospects, could just as easily become a 'demographic bomb'. This failure to undertake structural reforms during the post-2000 boom, together with the wholly unjustified expansion of entitlements is, in my view, even more important than the tight monetary policy which Surjit Bhalla in his chapter (5) blames for the Indian economy's recent dismal growth performance being well below its potential. It is the populism associated with India's democracy that is responsible for the recent dimming of India's prospects, but as democracy does provide the avenues for course correction, perhaps Indian politicians will eventually in the face of a crisis[7] liberalize the labour market, and institute a legal framework to distribute the rents from land and natural resources.

China's prospects also remain uncertain, because although the path for continuing its past economic success has been clearly charted in the joint World Bank and Development Research Centre of China report entitled *China 2030*, and lucidly discussed in Pieter Bottelier's Chapter (6) in this volume, whether the current configuration of its polity will allow it to follow it remains in question. Francis Godemont (2012) of the European Council on Foreign Relations in an essay elegantly summarizes the current debate among the 'liberals' responsible for *China 2030* and the 'conservatives' who have been responsible for China's statist turn since the mid-2000s. He argues that the current deployment of China's massive household savings through financial repression is determined by the interests of the 'princelings' who increasingly control the Chinese Communist Party (CCP). Godemont notes that 'there are many indications that China's "princelings" (the children of past leaders) have formed a quasi-union', due to 'a 1992 decision inspired by Bo Yibo, a former close associate of Mao, that each leading "family" would be able to promote one child into top politics' (Godemont 2012: 4). As Carl E. Walter and Fraser J.T. Howie (2012) argue in an important book, this *nomenklatura* has benefited from the statist turn China has taken with the expansion of an opaque state financial and enterprise system, which has the trappings of a market system but not the substance. It has assumed the guise of Western corporations, while hiding their true nature, that they are a patronage system centred on the Party's *nomenklatura*. 'These companies are not autonomous corporations; they can hardly

Foreword

be said to be corporations at all. Their senior management and, indeed the fate of the corporation itself, are completely dependent on political patrons' (Walter and Howie 2012: 31). Whether the reformers will be able to win against this opposition of what *China 2030* describes as these 'vested interests', and reverse China's statist turn remains an open question.

Hence it is not surprising that as far as the two largest BRICS are concerned, the excellent Chapter (29) by Charles Wolf, Jr and Alisher Akhmedjonov shows the wide divergence in the estimates of academics, business economists and international agencies, of their future growth prospects. When judging how these two largest emerging economies will perform in the future, as politics as much as their economic fundamentals will determine the outcome, we are *faute de mieux* left 'looking through a glass darkly'.

Country studies in the LM framework

It may also be useful to view the various countries studied in this Handbook through the classificatory framework that was found useful in the Lal-Myint (LM) comparative study (Lal and Myint 1996: Ch. 2V and 6). We found it useful to categorize countries by a five-fold classification of polities and a three-fold classification of economies based on factor proportions. The latter were countries which, compared with the world endowment of capital, labour and land, were classified as 'labour abundant', 'land abundant' and 'intermediate'. This allows an application of the three-factor trade theoretic framework of Anne Krueger (1977), and formalized by Edward Leamer (1984, 1987), to yield a rich menu of alternative efficient development paths and the implied patterns of changes in the functional distribution of income (between the three factors of production: land, labour and capital), as with capital accumulation and population growth the factor endowments of the relevant countries change over time.

The polity

The five-fold classification of the polity distinguished between the objectives of the government and the constraints on its activities. On the latter, two basic types were distinguished: the autonomous and the factional state. In the former, the state subserves its own ends. In the latter, it serves the interests of the 'factions' that succeed in capturing the state.

Further subdivisions among these two broad groups based on differing objectives can be made. Among autonomous states, the first is the benevolent Platonic Guardian State of the 'public economics' textbooks, seeking to maximize some social welfare function, while the second is the predatory state, whose self-seeking can take either the form of the absolutist state seeking to maximize *net* revenue for the sovereign's use or the bureaucratic state maximizing public employment.[8]

A state is needed to provide the classical public goods of defence and justice. For their provision it needs a monopoly of coercive violence (including the power to tax) in its territory. It is therefore best viewed as a natural monopoly providing these public goods. Being as self-regarding as its citizens (except for the Platonic Guardian version), the autonomous state's public goods-cum-tax equilibrium—which yields the net rents it can obtain from its natural monopoly—will depend upon the extent to which its natural monopoly is contestable from internal and external rivals. The greater the barriers to entry, the greater the net revenue the state can garner for its own purposes. However, even if this contestability is very low, there will be a further constraint on the autonomous state's ability to levy confiscatory taxes. Particularly in developing countries, where a subsistence rural sector and a non-taxable 'informal' sector are common, as the net of tax income decreases, at some stage the 'prey' will exit the taxed sector and melt into the bush (as happened, for example, in Tanzania and Ghana in the 1960s and 1970s). While this puts an upper boundary on the tax rate even when the state's natural monopoly is not contestable, in practice, depending upon geography, military technology and the internal legitimacy of its rulers, the maximum tax rate will be much lower, and will depend on this degree of contestability.[9]

Of the three types of autonomous states, the Platonic Guardian provides the optimal level of public goods at least cost. The predatory state tax-cum-public goods equilibrium will be with a net revenue-maximizing tax rate (determined by the degree of contestability) and the provision of less than the ideal amount of public goods in the absolutist version, and an over-provision in the bureaucrat maximizing version.

The factional state, by contrast, has no objectives of its own. It serves those of whoever is successful in its capture. Two major types can be distinguished: the oligarchic state and a majoritarian democracy. The former limits the polity and hence the contestants to the state's capture, while the latter extends the polity to the adult population. As is well known from the median voter theorem, the 'predator' in a majoritarian democracy will be the median voter with their well-documented 'middle-class' capture of the unavoidable transfer states that result, in both developed and developing countries. Moreover, the tax rate will be the revenue maximizing one based on the so-called Ramsey tax rule,[10] as in the case of the autonomous predatory state, while the provision of public goods will be close to that of its bureaucrat maximizing version (with pure public goods being supplemented with 'merit good' provision).

Where do the countries in the chapters in this Handbook fit into this classification? First, the BRICS. Brazil, which was a predatory revenue maximizing state, moved into the factional state democratic category in the 1990s. India since its independence has and continues to be a majoritarian democratic factional state. Russia, when it was part of the USSR, was a predatory bureaucrat maximizing state, but has emerged into an oligarchic factional state ruled by various factions of the *silovoki*, but which in Vladimir Putin's latest turn seems to be turning into a Latin American-style absolutist revenue maximizing predatory state.[11] China, after its opening by Deng Tsiao Ping, was by and large an absolutist Platonic Guardian state, which since the 2000s has turned into a predatory revenue maximizing state with elements of an oligarchic state. South Africa, since the ending of apartheid, is a democratic factional state.

Of the success stories, Israel is clearly in the democratic category. Singapore has and continues to be a Platonic Guardian state. Chile moved from being a Platonic Guardian state under Augusto Pinochet, into the democratic category since his fall. Turkey, which was a Platonic Guardian state, has also moved firmly into the democratic category with the rise of Recep Erdoğan's Justice and Development Party (AKP). Indonesia, from being a predatory revenue maximizing state, has also moved into the democratic factional state category. Mexico, a predatory bureaucratic state during the long, uninterrupted rule by the Partido Revolucionario Institucional (PRI), has also become a democratic factional state, while Malaysia since its independence has been a democratic state.

Among the potential candidates for EM status, Argentina is a democratic state, as are the Philippines, Thailand and Colombia. Viet Nam and Saudi Arabia seem to be autonomous absolutist states of the Platonic variety. Iran and Pakistan are both predatory revenue maximizing states, while Egypt has been one since the fall of its monarchy, but its evolving form remains uncertain.

From the studies of the growth performance of these countries discussed in this volume there is evidently no clear relationship between the type of polity and economic performance, despite the divergent claims made by supporters of either democracy or authoritarianism. However, as in the Lal and Myint study, the relative resource endowment seems more important in explaining divergent policy regimes and outcomes than the polity.[12] Without going into a detailed discussion of each of these countries for which we would need the detailed factor proportions data that Leamer provided and which were used in the Lal and Myint study, the general pattern we observed till the early 1990s does also seem to apply to the countries in this Handbook.

Resource endowments

Thus, the *labour-abundant countries* (e.g. the Republic of Korea, Singapore, Israel and possibly Viet Nam), irrespective of their polities, have the easiest policymaking task. For them the standard economist's policy prescription (based on the two-factor Hechsher-Ohlin model) of initially developing labour-intensive industries and then moving up the ladder of comparative advantage is easy to follow.

First, this policy leads to politically desirable movements in the prices of factors of production (labour and capital). With wages rising as capital is accumulated, there is unlikely to be political resistance from the bulk of the population in factional states that realize the country's comparative advantage.[13] Meanwhile all types of autonomous state will also find that even their predatory ends are better served by undertaking the development of their only resource—the human—on which their revenues and prosperity depend. The major task of government is to provide an adequate infrastructure to reduce the transaction costs of the relatively small-scale organizational units that will predominate in the earlier stages of their development, and constantly to upgrade their human resources.

Second, if the country is small, the limited size of the domestic market makes reliance on foreign trade inevitable. Also, there is unlikely to be vertical import substitution when the ubiquitous *dirigiste* impulse leads to some departures from free trade. This means that when a switch to free trade is made, lobbies preventing competitive imports of intermediate inputs will not exist. The political cost of rectifying past mistakes are, therefore, likely to be lower than in the land-abundant or intermediate group of countries.

Third, their incremental comparative advantage is readily apparent to economic agents in both the private and public sectors. It is thus easier to pick 'industrial winners' and the consequences of picking losers or policies that stimulate them are more immediately apparent—as with Singapore's ill-judged attempt to jump a few rungs on the ladder of comparative advantage through an artificial raising of wages in the 1980s.

The comparative advantages of *land- and natural resource-abundant countries* are also likely to be clearer than for the intermediate group, but more difficult to realize than for the labour-abundant group of countries. This is for two reasons. First, with a higher supply price of labour than the labour-abundant countries, due to their more favourable land-to-labour ratios and abundant natural resources, their incremental comparative advantage is likely to lie on the relatively capital-intensive rungs of the ladder of comparative advantage. Public promotion may be required because of the ensuing lumpiness of investments, and the need to develop scarce skills and absorb complex imported technology. The dangers of 'bureaucratic failure' endemic to such promotion may then lead to a failure to realize their economic potential.

Second, if the rate of capital accumulation is not high enough, then with growing labour forces, their efficient development path could contain declining real wage segments. If the polity is subject to factional democratic pressures, this 'equilibrium' time path of real wages could lead to political pressure to resist the requisite real wage adjustments by turning inward. The polity could be at odds with the economy, with political cycles of economic repression (during factional 'populist' political phases), followed by liberalization (during autonomous political periods), as has been the case in most of Latin America.

Third, given the political imperative of avoiding the 'falling wage' segments of their development paths, such countries have attempted 'big push' development programmes, often

xxxiv

financed by foreign borrowing. This big push has often forced them into a fiscal and debt crisis and thence a growth crisis, as happened in Brazil in the 1980s.

Finally, given the rents available from natural resources, the inevitable politicization of their disbursement leads to 'transfer states', which inevitably bear harder on the revenue-generating sector when terms of trade decline, while raising entitlements when they improve. Thus natural resources may prove a 'precious bane', leading to polities that tend to kill the goose that laid the golden egg.

The stories of Brazil, Russia and South Africa among the BRICS, and Thailand, Mexico, Colombia, Iran and Saudi Arabia would fit these patterns in the political economy of natural resource- and land-abundant countries.[14] However, as the shining example of Chile with its rich copper deposits, and of Malaysia (discussed in this volume) show, natural resources are not always a 'precious bane'.

Finally, the *intermediate resource endowment* group have the most difficult task in terms of development policy. Their incremental comparative advantage is more opaque, so 'mistakes' are not so easily recognized or rectified, particularly by the public sector, which in the absence of any bankruptcy constraint resists the exit of inefficient firms. Second, this group is also more likely to face situations in which the polity is at times at odds with the pursuit of their comparative advantage. Two of the largest BRICS—India and China—fall into this category, as do Turkey, Indonesia, the Philippines and Egypt. All of these countries have initially sought to develop along a statist, inward-looking path against their comparative advantage, until a 'crisis' has forced them to change course and adopt a more appropriate open economy, market-friendly path. However, given the continuing hold of economic nationalism and *dirigisme* in the minds of their political elites, this change still remains insecure.

Modernity and tradition

In this context two other elements that my past research has emphasized may be relevant in assessing the future prospects of the countries discussed in this volume. The first concerns the common problem of reconciling tradition with modernity, which, with the rise and global expansion of the West, all the other Eurasian civilizations have faced. Given their ancient equilibrium between (what I termed in my Ohlin lectures) the 'material beliefs' (how to make a living) and 'cosmological beliefs' (how one should live) of their civilizations, which was shattered most often by superior Western arms, how could their wounded civilizations come to terms with the West without losing their souls?

There were three responses to this conflict between modernity and tradition. The first, adopted by Meiji Japan after its opening by Commodore Perry's 'black ships', was to modernize by adopting the West's material beliefs to provide military and economic strength, without changing its cosmological beliefs. It recognized that modernization did not entail Westernization. The second was to adopt the attitude of the clam for fear that modernization would undermine their ancient traditions. This route was advocated by many cultural nationalists, particularly in India by Mahatma Gandhi and his followers, including until recently the Hindu nationalist Bharatiya Janata Party (BJP). The third was to find a middle way between modernity and tradition, which usually took some socialist form.

Socialism is rooted in both the rationalism of the Enlightenment and the Romantic critique of modernization based on these rationalist ideas. Fabian socialism (unlike full-blooded communism embodying the manipulative Enlightenment's rationalism) had the most appeal in the Third World, as it combined the two faces: the utilitarian socialism of the Webbs (the Enlightenment strand), and the passionate critique of a dehumanizing capitalist society by the young Karl Marx,

R.H. Tawney and William Morris (the Romantic strand). It provided the formula for reconciling the two ambivalent rejections of the traditional and the modern, but its economic failure (and that of its cousin communism) led to the adoption by most countries of the first, the Japanese route, with the recognition that modernization did not entail Westernization.

The exception is most of the Islamic countries, which have tried all three routes. Apart from Erdoğan's Turkey, which has accepted modernity without giving up its Islamic cosmological beliefs, most of the others are still ensnared in this conflict between modernity and tradition, with the Islamists determined to follow the second route: that of the clam. The travails of Iran, Saudi Arabia and Pakistan outlined in this Handbook reflect this continuing conflict between modernity and tradition.

Mercantilism and economic nationalism

The second theme of relevance is the role of economic nationalism and the mercantilism it promotes. In his magisterial study *Mercantilism*, Eli Hecksher (1955) argued that the mercantilist system arose from the desire of the Renaissance princes of Europe to create nations out of the weak states with myriad disorderly groups they had inherited from the fall of the Roman Empire, by expanding the span of their economic control. A similar 'nation-building' motive underlay the system of mercantilist controls established in the Third World, but in both cases this attempt to create 'order' through *dirigisme* bred 'disorder' (through the growth of black markets, tax evasion, rent seeking and the growth of illegal activities in underground economies), with the state losing control over the economy. The most serious consequence for the state was the erosion of its fiscal base and the prospect of its un-Marxian withering away. In both cases economic liberalization was undertaken to restore the fiscal base, and thence government control over what had become ungovernable economies.

Though the new Age of Reform in the Third World has lasted, with its embrace, however imperfectly, of economic liberalization and globalization, there is the continuing danger that it could end, as the first age of European reform ended with the Great War and the dismantling of the 19th-century liberal international economic order. After the Second World War, a new 'classical' liberal international economic order was created under US aegis, which the Third World did not join until the 1980s–90s, but during these post-Second World War years, the pendulum between *dirigisme* and classical liberalism did not swing back completely in the West as in the first, 19th-century Age of Reform, with the gradual expansion of their welfare states and the resulting entitlement economies[15] that have emerged. The Great Crash and the following Great Recession were the denouement, when unsustainable entitlements led to explicit or implicit fiscal and debt crises in many developed countries (see Lal 2012a: ch. 10). Their backwash effects continue to affect the prospects of emerging economies. Their best hope remains that they and the developed world follow, as best as possible, the classical liberal economic package that ushered in the first great Age of Reform.

Notes

1 The comparative study of 21 developing countries till the late 1980s that Hla Myint and I undertook for the World Bank on *The Political Economy of Poverty Equity and Growth* (Lal and Myint 1996) contained detailed country studies of nine of the countries (Brazil, Singapore, Turkey, Indonesia, Mexico, Malaysia, Egypt, Thailand and Colombia), included in this Handbook. In addition, I have worked on and written about a number of the others (see Lal 1993, 2005, 2013).
2 *Hamlet*, Act 2, Scene 2, line 11.

3 This is a long standing disagreement I have had with John. See my discussion of managed (i.e. discretionary) as opposed to fixed or floating (automatic) exchange rate adjustments in Lal 2006: 97–100. The superiority of the automatic adjustment mechanisms is that they do not require the authorities to make guesses about an unknowable future.

4 See also Srinivasan (2000) on the relevance of the Washington Consensus for development policy.

5 James Mackintosh, 'The Short View', *Financial Times*, 13 September 2013, 21.

6 See my three recent columns, 'China's Statist Turn I, II, III', *Business Standard*, June, July, August, 2013. They can be accessed on my website: www.econ.ucla.edu/lal.

7 The role of crises in inducing reform was first outlined by Lal (1987) and deployed to explain the movement away from growth retarding policies in many of the countries covered in the Lal-Myint comparative study (see Lal and Myint 1996: Ch. 6.IV).

8 See Lal 1984 and Lal 1988: Ch. 13.2, for a model of the predatory state.

9 This model of the 'predatory state' was first developed in Lal 1984, and was extended and incorporated in my social and economic histories of India (Lal 1988), and the world (Lal 1998).

10 See Brennan and Buchanan 1980; Becker 1983, 1985; Lal 1990 (1994).

11 See my column, 'The Tsar in Winter', *Business Standard*, April 2012, www.econ.ucla.edu/lal.

12 The classification was based on a three-factor (land, labour and capital), multiple-good open economy model due to Krueger (1977), and its formalization in terms of a simple diagram by Leamer (1987).

13 However, as the rents from scarce land rise, there will be increasing pressure to find some way of providing 'social' housing, as in both Singapore and Hong Kong.

14 It should also be noted that Mexico's, Colombia's (and other Andean countries) and Pakistan's economies have also been inimically affected by the wholly unjustified and unwinnable US-led 'war on drugs' (see Lal 2012a: Ch. 7).

15 Entitlements are implicit or explicit subsidies which create politically determined income streams for various favoured groups. The implicit subsidies that investment banks derived from their access to the implicit subsidy provided by deposit insurance after the repeal of the Glass-Steagall Act in the USA were as much part of the entitlement economies created in the West as the more familiar entitlements of the welfare state.

Bibliography

Becker, G. (1983) 'A Theory of Competition Among Pressure Groups for Political Influence', *Quarterly Journal of Economics* 18(3): 371–40.

——(1985) 'Public Policies, Pressure Groups and Deadweight Costs', *Journal of Public Economics* 28(3): 329–48.

Brennan, G. and J.M. Buchanan (1980) *The Power to Tax: Analytical Foundations of a Fiscal Constitution*, Cambridge University Press, Cambridge.

Godemont, F. (2012) 'China at the Crossroads', *European Council on Foreign Affairs*, April, www.ecfr.eu.

Hecksher, E. (1955) *Mercantilism*, 2 vols, Allen & Unwin, London.

Krueger, A.O. (1977) *Growth, Distortions and Patterns of Trade among Many Countries*, Princeton Studies in International Finance No. 40, Princeton University, Princeton, NJ.

Lal, D. (1984) 'The Political Economy of the Predatory State', DED Discussion Paper No. 105, World Bank, Washington, DC.

——(1987) 'The Political Economy of Economic Liberalization', *World Bank Economic Review*, 1(2): 273–99 (reprinted in Lal 1993).

——(1988) *The Hindu Equilibrium*, vol. 1, Clarendon Press, Oxford.

——(1990) 'Fighting Fiscal Privilege: Towards a Fiscal Constitution', Social Market Foundation Paper No. 7; reprinted in D. Lal (1994) *Against Dirigisme*, ICS Press, San Francisco, CA.

——(1993) *The Repressed Economy: Causes, Consequences, Reform*, Economists of the Twentieth Century, Edward Elgar, Aldershot.

——(1998) *Unintended Consequences: The Impact of Factor Endowments, Culture and Politics on Long-run Economic Performance*, The Ohlin Lectures, MIT Press, Cambridge, MA.

——(2005) *The Hindu Equilibrium: India c.1500 B.C.–2000 A.D.*, abridged and revised edn, Oxford University Press, Oxford.

——(2006) *Reviving the Invisible Hand: The Case for Classical Liberalism in the Twenty-first Century*, Princeton University Press, Princeton, NJ.

——(2011) 'India's Post-Liberalisation Blues', *World Economics* 12(4): 1–12.

——(2012) 'Is the Washington Consensus Dead?' *Cato Journal* 32(3): 493–512.

——(2012a) *Lost Causes: The Retreat from Classical Liberalism*, Biteback Publishing, London.

——(2013) *Poverty and Progress: Realities and Myths about Global Poverty*, Cato Institute, Washington, DC.

Lal, D. and H. Myint (1996) *The Political Economy of Poverty, Equity and Growth: A Comparative Study*, Clarendon Press, Oxford.

Leamer, E. (1984) *Sources of International Comparative Advantage*, MIT Press, Cambridge, MA.

——(1987) 'Patterns of Development in the Three Factor, N-good General Equilibrium Model', *Journal of Political Economy* 95(5): 961–99.

Schumpeter, J.A. (1954) *History of Economic Analysis*, Oxford University Press, Oxford.

Srinivasan, T.N. (2000) 'The Washington Consensus a Decade Later: Ideology and the Art and Science of Policy Advice', *World Bank Research Observer* 15(2): 265–70.

Vargas Llosa, M. (2000) 'Liberalism in the New Millennium', in I. Vasquez (ed.), *Global Fortune*, Cato Institute, Washington, DC.

Walter, Carl E. and F.J.T. Howie (2012) *Red Capitalism*, Wiley, Singapore.

Preface

If one had to identify the major change in the world economy over the last 20 or so years, it would be the growth and increasing prominence of emerging economies. Many of these countries were already growing rapidly before the start of the 2008–09 global financial/economic crisis. Their continued rapid expansion in subsequent years, together with much slower rates of growth in the debt-ridden developed world, has led influential observers to speculate that they will dominate the world economy in another 20 or 30 years.

This book grew out of the need for comprehensive examination of these dynamic economies. To this end, the volume's major objective is to assess the circumstances under which the emerging economies will continue their rapid ascent. Its chapters capture the diversity and complexity of this important group of countries. Is the long-anticipated convergence between the developing and advanced world finally under way on a broad scale? If so, which countries have the best chance of attaining developed country status in the foreseeable future? If not, what factors may prevent other countries from achieving that goal?

The volume is divided into seven main sections. The first sets the stage by identifying the main trends in the world economy, then tracing the progress made and possible future growth paths of the emerging economies. Of particular interest is the manner in which the global economic/financial crisis of 2008–09 has affected the growth paths of the emerging and advanced economies.

The second section develops five country case studies, each devoted to a specific country of the BRICS (Brazil, Russia, India, People's Republic of China and South Africa). How did each manage to initiate growth and expansion? What factors appear critical to their success? What possible difficulties may they encounter in their attempt to close the gap with the advanced countries? Is there a common theme other than large size and strong growth that ties these countries together? What are the significant differences between these countries and can these factors account for their slightly divergent growth paths?

The third section comprises two chapters that develop a framework for assessing the growth prospects of the emerging economies. Views on emerging economies' prospects roughly fall into two broad groups. The first, an optimistic convergence-based model,[1] stresses the ability of emerging economies to adapt and implement technologies to close the gap quickly with more advanced economies. The second, less optimistic approach contends that convergence is not pre-ordained or automatic, but instead will depend on a sequence of internal economic and

xxxix

Preface

governance reforms. These reforms lay the necessary foundation to support more sophisticated productive structures. Failure to achieve significant progress in these areas is likely to condemn the emerging country to the so-called 'middle-income trap'[2] or simply to slow downs to the extent that they prevent the country from achieving advanced country status. With regard to reforms, the two competing approaches, the so-called Washington Consensus[3] and Beijing Consensus,[4] are contrasted.

The fourth section develops individual case studies of emerging economies (Israel, Singapore and Chile) that are often held up as examples of success stories. Here, the focus is on identifying those elements critical for each country's successful transition from low income status. What reforms appear to have aided the transformation of these economies? How have their governments recovered from possible policy errors? Are there possible lessons that can be applied to other countries?

The fifth section examines a further group of countries (Turkey, Indonesia, Mexico and Malaysia) that appear to be on the verge of high-sustained growth. Is there a common policy mix that has created this fortuitous situation? Or has each country charted its own particular foundation for future growth?

The sixth section looks at a group of countries comprising Argentina, Viet Nam, the Philippines, Pakistan, Egypt, Thailand, Iran, Colombia and Saudi Arabia. These countries have often had spurts of high growth intermixed with severe setbacks. While each has the potential for better performance and perhaps even advanced income status, their future success is far from assured. Are they the victims of an unfavourable external environment, or are policy short-comings, including the inability to undertake significant economic and governance reforms, the main factors impeding their growth?

The seventh and final section looks towards the future. What are the implications for global governance if the emerging economies continue to account for a larger and larger percentage of world trade and output? Many of the existing international organizations trace their origins back to the Bretton Woods[5] era, dominated by the advanced countries. In recent years global governance appears to have been in a severe drought.[6] What changes in global governance might be called for to give today's emerging economies more voice in and responsibility for the smooth functioning of the global system?

In addition to the country case studies in this volume, a large body of knowledge concerning economic policymaking in the emerging economies has been compiled over the years and analysed at length. What general lessons can we draw from country experiences? Are there some basic rules governing economic policy that all emerging countries should follow in their efforts to assure rapid and stable growth?

The Republic of Korea (South Korea) is a country that has arguably reached developed country status. The country's rise has been dramatic, casting doubts on the inevitability of the much discussed 'middle-income trap'. The country's success and occasional setbacks provide many lessons for other emerging countries about to transition into higher stages of development.

Finally, many observers feel that the state of the global economy over the next several decades will be largely determined by the growth patterns of China and India. A concluding chapter surveys current thinking about the prospects of these key countries.

In short, the proposed volume is integrated around a central theme: the rise of the emerging economies and transformation of the world economy brought on by their ascendency. The Handbook is more than a series of country studies. It is an original contribution to our understanding of a phenomenon that is reshaping the world and billions of lives.

Clearly, a book of this scope and sheer length could not have come to completion without the contributions of many individuals. In addition to the volume's many contributors, special

xl

thanks go to my colleagues at the Naval Postgraduate School, Bob Springborg, Robert McNab, Nazneen Barma, Jessica Piombo, Tom Bruneau, Maria Rasmussen and Harold Trinkunas, whose help and encouragement proved invaluable. Greta E. Marlatt of the Naval Postgraduate School Knox Library went far beyond the call of duty to keep me informed of the latest country and global developments throughout the course of the manuscript—a task only she could perform. Her 'Greta's Links' have been a life-saver on more than one occasion. Special thanks to Alison Phillips for her tireless efforts in ensuring the volume's readability and accuracy. Most of all, thanks go to Cathy Hartley, Europa Commissioning Editor, who conceived of the original study, provided ongoing guidance and most importantly provided good cheer and positive encouragement throughout.

Notes

1 Kemal Dervis, 'World Economy: Convergence, Interdependence, and Divergence', *Finance & Development*, September 2012, www.imf.org/external/pubs/ft/fandd/2012/09/pdf/dervis.pdf.

2 Cf. Barry Eichengreen, Donghyun Park and Kwanho Shin, 'Growth Slowdowns Redux: Avoiding the Middle-Income Trap', *VOX*, 11 January 2013, www.voxeu.org/article/growth-slowdowns-redux-avoiding-middle-income-trap.

3 Cf. John Williamson, 'What Should the World Bank Think About the Washington Consensus?' *World Bank Research Observer* 15(2), August 2000, 251–64.

4 Joshua Cooper Ramo, *The Beijing Consensus*, Foreign Policy Centre, London, 2004, fpc.org.uk/publications/TheBeijingConsensus.

5 'The Bretton Woods Conference, 1944', US Department of State, Office of the Historian, history.state.gov/milestones/1937-45/BrettonWoods.

6 Naazeen Barma, Ely Ratner and Steven Weber, 'The Mythical Liberal Order', *National Interest*, March–April 2013.

Abbreviations

ADB	Asian Development Bank
AEC	ASEAN Economic Community
AFD	direct fiscal funding
AFI	indirect fiscal funding
AFIO	Agricultural and Food Industries Organization
AFTA CEPT	ASEAN Free Trade Area-Comprehensive Effective Preferential Tariff
ANC	African National Congress
APEC	Asia-Pacific Economic Cooperation
ASEAN	Association of Southeast Asian Nations
ASGISA	Accelerated and Shared Growth Initiative for South Africa
AUC	Autodefensas Unidas de Colombia
BC	Beijing Consensus
Big Five+M	Brazil, Russia, India, China, Indonesia and Mexico
BIRD	Bi-national Industrial Research and Development
BIT	bilateral investment treaty
BJP	Bharatiya Janata Party
BN	Barisan Nasional
BNDES	Banco Nacional do Desenvolvimento Econômico e Social
BOP	balance of payments
BRICs	Brazil, Russia, India, China (People's Republic)
BRICS	Brazil, Russia, India, China (People's Republic), South Africa
BRIICS	Brazil, Russia, India, Indonesia, China (People's Republic), South Africa
BSP	Bangko Sentral ng Pilipinas
BTA	bilateral trade agreement
BTUs	British thermal units
C	Celsius
CAE	crédito con aval del estado
CAI	Capital Access Index
CBP	Central Bank of the Philippines
CCT	conditional cash transfer

CFT	centres for technical formation
CIA	Central Intelligence Agency
CIS	Commonwealth of Independent States
CIVETS	Colombia, Indonesia, Viet Nam, Egypt, Turkey and South Africa
CNA	National Accreditation Commission
CNAP	National Undergraduate Accreditation Commission
CNI	gross national income
Comecon	Council for Mutual Economic Assistance
COSATU	Congress of South African Trade Unions
CPF	Central Provident Fund
CPI	consumer price index
CPI	Corruption Perception Index
CTRP	Comprehensive Tax Reform Programme
DAP	Democratic Action Party
DBS	Development Bank of Singapore
ECLA	Economic Commission for Latin America
EDB	Economic Development Board
ELN	National Liberation Army
EM	emerging market
EMBI	Emerging Markets Bond Index
EO	executive order
EPU	Economic Planning Unit
ESF	Economic Stabilization Fund
ETP	Economic Transformation Programme
EU	European Union
FAO	Food and Agriculture Organization
FARC	Revolutionary Armed Forces of Colombia
FDI	foreign direct investment
FEG	Framework for Economic Growth
FIC	Foreign Investment Committee
FJP	Freedom and Justice Party
FRDLA	Fiscal Responsibility and Debt Limitation Act
FTA	free trade agreement
G20	Group of Twenty
G7	Group of Seven
GAFI	General Authority for Investments
GATT	General Agreement on Tariffs and Trade
GCC	Gulf Cooperation Council
GDP	gross domestic product
GEAR	Growth, Employment and Redistribution
GERAKAN	Malaysian People's Movement Party
GHG	greenhouse gas
GIC	Government of Singapore Investment Corporation
GLC	government-linked corporation/company
GMR	global middle and rich class
GNP	gross national product
GTP	Government Transformation Programme
HDB	Housing Development Board

Abbreviations

HEPR	Hunger Eradication and Poverty Reduction Programme
HIPC	Highly Indebted Poor Countries
IAI	Israel Aircraft Industries
IAPG	Inter-Agency Planning Group
IBRD	International Bank of Reconstruction and Development
ICC	International Criminal Court
ICT	information communications technology
IDB	Inter-American Development Bank
IDF	Israel Defence Forces
IFC	International Finance Corporation
IFI	international financial institution
IGO	international governmental organization
IMF	International Monetary Fund
IP	professional institutes
IRGC	Islamic Revolutionary Guard Corps
IRI	Islamic Republic of Iran
ISI	import substitution industrialization
IT	information technology
JIPSA	Joint Initiative on Priority Skills Acquisition
JMM	Jaringan Melayu Malaysia
KAMCO	Korean Asset Management Company
LGE	General Law of Education
Libor	London Interbank Offered Rate
LOCE	Organic Constitutional Law on Education
M-19	19 April Movement
MB	Monetary Board
MCA	Malaysian Chinese Association
MENA	Middle East and North Africa
MFN	most favoured nation principle
MIC	Malaysian Indian Congress
MIEGA	Masterplan of Indonesia's Economic Growth Acceleration
MinEkon	Ministry of Economic Development
MinFin	Ministry of Finance
MIST	Mexico, Indonesia, South Korea and Turkey
MIT	middle-income trap
MITI	Ministry of International Trade and Industry
MNC	multinational corporation
MOF	Ministry of Finance
MOU	Memorandum of Understanding
MP	Member of Parliament
MPI	Ministry of Planning and Investment
MQI	Minhajul Quran International
MQM	Muttahida Qaumi Movement
N-11	Next 11
NAB	National Accountability Bureau
NAB	New Arrangements to Borrow
NAFINSA	Nacional Financiera
NAFTA	North American Free Trade Agreement

xliv

NATO	North Atlantic Treaty Organization
NDAA	National Defence Authorization Act
NDP	National Development Plan
NDP	National Development Policy
NDPC	National Development Planning Committee
NEDA	National Economic and Development Authority
NEM	New Economic Model
NEP	New Economic Policy
NESDB	National Economic and Social Development Board
NFPE	non-financial public enterprise
NGP	New Growth Path
NIC	National Intelligence Council
NIOC	National Iranian Oil Company
NIRC	National Internal Revenue Code
NKEAs	National Key Economic Areas
NKRA	National Key Results Areas
NPL	non-performing loan
NTUC	National Trades Union Congress
ODA	overseas development assistance
OECD	Organisation for Economic Co-operation and Development
OFDI	outward foreign direct investment
OPEC	Organization of the Petroleum Exporting Countries
PAC	Programa de Aceleração do Crescimento
PAN	Partido Acción Nacional
PAP	People's Action Party
PAS	Pan-Malaysian Islamic Party
PC	Communist Party
PDC	Christian Democratic Party
PDS	Partido Democrático Social
PE	private equity
PEMANDU	Performance, Management and Delivery Unit
PEMEX	Petróleos Mexicanos
PGMs	platinum group metals
PKO	peace-keeping operation
PKR	People's Justice Party
PMDB	Partido do Movimento Democrático Brasileiro
PMET	Professional Management Executive and Technical
PMR	product market regulation
PPP	Pakistan People's Party
PPP	purchasing power parity
PR	permanent residence
PRD	Partido de la Revolución Democrática
PRI	Partido Revolucionario Institucional
PS	Socialist Party
PT	Partido dos Trabalhadores
QFII	qualified foreign institutional investor
R&D	research and development
R/P	reserves to production

Abbreviations

R2P	Responsibility to Protect
RA	Republic Act
RBI	Reserve Bank of India
RDP	Reconstruction and Development Programme
REIT	Real Estate Investment Trust
RM	Malaysian ringgit
RMB	renminbi
RQFII	renminbi qualified foreign institutional investor
RVAT	Reformed VAT
SCAF	Supreme Council of the Armed Forces
SCIC	State Capital Investment Corporation
SDRs	Special Drawing Rights
SES	Socio-Economic Survey
SET	stock exchange index of Thailand
SMEs	small and medium-sized enterprises
SNIT	simplified net income taxation
SNTE	Sindicato Nacional de Trabajadores de la Educación
SOCB	state-owned commercial bank
SOE	state-owned enterprise
SWIFT	Society for Worldwide Interbank Financial Telecommunication
TASE	Tel-Aviv Stock Exchange
TFP	total factor productivity
TI	Transparency International
TIMSS	Trends in International Mathematics and Science Study
TLCs	Temasek-linked companies
TPP	transpacific trade partnership
TPSEP	Transpacific Strategic Economic Partnership Agreement
UK	United Kingdom
UMNO	United Malay National Organization
UN	United Nations
UNCTAD	United Nations Conference on Trade and Development
UNSC	United Nations Security Council
US(A)	United States (of America)
USAID	US Agency for International Development
USSR	Union of Soviet Socialist Republics
VAT	value-added tax
VC	venture capital
WC	Washington Consensus
WEF	World Economic Forum
WEF GCI	World Economic Forum's Global Competitiveness Index
WMP	wealth management products
WPI	wholesale price index
WTO	World Trade Organization
ZAF	rand

Part I

Introduction: an overview

1

Introduction

Robert E. Looney

The emerging economies first caught the public's attention in 2001 when Jim O'Neill, then the chairman of Goldman Sachs' asset management division, coined the acronym BRIC depicting the four emerging economies, Brazil, Russia, India and the People's Republic of China.[1] At the time these countries appeared to have the best prospects in the developing world for high sustained rates of growth. The BRICs have three things in common: they each have a large population; cheap labour markets; and a vast amount of untapped potential. It was O'Neill's contention that while these countries might differ in other regards, these factors positioned the countries to take advantage of the growing opportunities afforded in a world of rapidly growing export markets and capital flows.

In the subsequent years it became apparent that the BRICs were simply an elite set of countries cut from a broader group of emerging markets. Through years of high rates of investment, economic reforms and prudent macroeconomic policy a broad group of developing countries were becoming well positioned to tap into the rapidly growing consumer markets in Europe and the USA.

With the global boom in 2003, emerging markets started to take off as a group. Their share of global gross domestic product (GDP) began a rapid climb, from 20% to the 34% that they represent today. Their share of the global stock market total rose from less than 4% to more than 10%.

Acronyms abound[2] with various groupings of emerging economies basking in the limelight. One group, coined the CIVETS (Colombia, Indonesia, Viet Nam, Egypt, Turkey and South Africa) by Robert Ward from the Economist Intelligence Unit, is attracting considerable attention and is judged by many to have even greater growth potential than the BRICs.

In 2005 the same Jim O'Neill identified another group of countries he thought had the greatest potential to be major economic leaders. He dubbed these countries N-11 or the Next 11. These are, in no particular order, Indonesia, the Republic of Korea (South Korea), Turkey, Mexico, Viet Nam, the Philippines, Iran, Bangladesh, Nigeria, Egypt and Turkey. O'Neill's latest group, MIST, includes Mexico, Indonesia, South Korea and Turkey—the four largest markets of the N-11 group. Other groupings have been proposed as a growing literature attempts to keep up with this rapidly expanding phenomenon.[3]

A problem with thinking in acronyms is that the focus tends to be on cleverness rather than economic fundamentals. The BRICS (which now include South Africa) themselves are quite a diverse group of countries. Russia has a declining population and is for all practical purposes a rentier state exporting raw materials and energy, India is a very poor country that has a sophisticated services sector, but little in the way of a manufacturing base capable of creating the large number of semi-skilled jobs one might usually expect for a country at its stage of development. China, a manufacturing giant, is larger than the others combined, while Brazil's recent growth can be attributed in large part to supplying China with food and raw materials.

Still, because of the widespread usage of the BRIC country grouping, the present volume retains that sub-set of countries. The remaining emerging economies are grouped on the basis of both their progress made to date as well as an initial rough assessment of their potential for further growth.

Uri Dadush (Chapter 2) introduces the burst of emerging economies into the global economy. In doing so, he provides an optimistic picture of the future: these economies are likely to continue with market-oriented policies that will assure their continued expansion. Specifically, he sees China overtaking the USA as the world's largest economic power, with India likely to join both as a global leader. Other emerging economies in Asia and Latin America will outpace Europe, driving a vast expansion of global trade and financial integration.

Dadush warns, however, that this optimistic picture will not occur automatically. For it to happen, the community of nations will need to work together to continue to build the international integration frameworks essential for trade, capital, people and technology to continue to flourish. They will jointly need to build stronger safeguards against massive financial crises. They will need to find a way to avert environmental catastrophe in the form of uncontrolled climate change. Above all, they will have to manage the historic power shift towards new actors from the developing world without resorting to war or protectionism.

The volume's assessment of the BRIC countries begins with Albert Fishlow's (Chapter 3) examination of the factors that have led to Brazil's spectacular rise in recent years. While Brazil's growth has been solid over the last several decades there is increasing concern about the future. As Professor Fishlow demonstrates, even to grow at an annual rate of 3% per capita, Brazil will need to raise its investment rate gradually from 19.5% (2010) to 25% of output. Stable growth must also be matched by corresponding increases in domestic savings. Brazil's massive public sector has to play a role by cutting expenditures while continuing its efforts to increase revenues. Most importantly, for higher growth to occur regularly, productivity gains will have to be generalized throughout the economy. Finally, Brazil's future development depends upon the successful integration of the agricultural, mineral, petroleum, manufacturing and services sectors.

In introducing Russia (Chapter 4), Philip Hanson reminds us that there is no such thing as a typical emerging economy, but Russia is more atypical than most. It is on the richer end of the scale of emerging economies with a per capita income that is more than twice China's level and more than four times India's. In addition, Russia has already industrialized once and has had a few decades as a superpower. It is an upper-middle-income country with many of the attributes of modernity but with deep-seated economic problems as well.

However, the country's strikingly deep recession in 2008–09 indicated a volatility that could not be accounted for simply by its being an oil exporter. A defective legal order and a lack of trust seem to lie at the root of its weak adaptation to the changed global environment after 2009. Unless these shortcomings can be met and resolved, the country's future growth will be well below both the ambitions of its leaders and the performance of which a country at its stage of development should be capable.

In introducing India (Chapter 5), Surjit Bhalla emphasizes the importance of economic reforms during 1991–93 in facilitating India's accelerating rate of growth. In subsequent years, growth has averaged 6.7% per annum; in the previous 40 years, growth had averaged only 4%

Introduction

per annum. India's growth post-1991 has the hallmarks of being exceptional; since 2003, an average of nearly 8% is akin to miracle growth.

By examining the various determinants of growth, and over different time periods, Dr Bhalla concludes that the pattern of long-term interest rates, and the level and change in currency valuation, are the strongest determinants of GDP growth. On the assumption that these elements will remain in the proper range, he concludes that the country's growth could recover from its slowdown over the last several years and return to the 7.0%–8.5% range.

No emerging economy is more important to the health of the global economy than that of China. As Pieter Bottelier observes (Chapter 6), the Chinese economy will be going through a major transition aimed at changing its growth model to make it more sustainable—less dependent on capital formation and external demand, and more so on domestic consumption. In doing so, the country will be facing formidable challenges, including rising labour and other production costs, rising public discontent due to many factors, including severe social inequality, disrespect by the government for some of its own laws, and increasingly serious and frequent environmental problems. A 'second transition' towards a less capital-intensive, more equitable and more sustainable growth pattern is likely, but will take a long time and require both economic and political change.

The final BRICS country, South Africa, is a recent addition to that group. Given the country's relatively small size and struggling economy, its BRIC membership has been controversial. Still, the country represents one of Africa's rare economic success stories. On the other hand the country has not been able to achieve rates of growth in the ranges necessary to pull large segments of the population out of poverty. As Robert Looney (Chapter 7) notes, with chronic unemployment around 25%, the current policy mix focusing almost exclusively on macroeconomic stability is unsustainable. For the longer term, much will continue to depend on the extent to which the government begins to commit itself seriously to major structural and policy reforms.

Part III of the volume provides several frameworks for guiding reforms and policymaking in the emerging economies. The experience of the BRICS suggests that even in fast-growing economies, growth often slows, transitions to more sophisticated productive structures are difficult and policymakers are often not prepared to meet the changing environment they face.

Building on these themes Robert Looney (Chapter 8) develops a stage framework for identifying the challenges to sustained growth many of the emerging economies are likely to encounter. The framework also serves as a rough guide in prioritizing the many governance and economic reforms countries must undertake to guarantee a fairly steady progression up the income ladder. A main finding of this analysis is the central role played in the growth process by entrepreneurship and the private sector. A clear pattern emerges whereby countries that encourage entrepreneurship and provide a suitable, conducive environment for private sector activity are better positioned to achieve high rates of sustainable growth.

The Washington Consensus, originating with the works of John Williamson, has traditionally been seen as the best policy set for encouraging private sector development and the efficiency that sector needs to play a dynamic force in the development process. However, perhaps as a result of China's rapid ascendency, the so-called Beijing Consensus, stressing a larger role for the state, has been increasingly finding adherents in the emerging world. John Williamson (Chapter 9) compares the two approaches and sees merit in each. Since no country could implement simultaneously all the features of either approach, the problem facing decision makers comes down to knowing the essential features in each that merit adoption.

Part IV focuses on three major success stories: Israel, Singapore and Chile. While each country has many unique characteristics, their experiences provide valuable lessons for countries

5

aspiring to developed country status. Their experience also suggests that rapid growth over a sustained time is not without costs that must be addressed at some point.

Through moving from state-led economic policymaking to economic liberalization, Israel has managed to achieve relatively fast economic growth, the remarkable development of high technology as well as financial stability. Despite these achievements, Paul Rivlin (Chapter 10) finds that the country still suffers from poverty, income inequality, inadequate public services and infrastructure. Also plaguing the country is a distinct lack of competition in key local markets. He is concerned that these problems may become endemic and threaten the future of the economy because they remove significant numbers of people from the labour market and result in poverty being passed down from one generation to the next. He concludes that Israel will have to find ways to combine elements of equity with economic growth if it wants to avoid increasing levels of domestic tension.

As Linda Lim (Chapter 11) rightly notes, Singapore has long been widely recognized as possibly the most successful case of development among emerging economies. She finds Singapore's economic success was the product not just of 'the right' policies, but also of favourable initial conditions (domestically and internationally), and 'the right' institutions, for the times. She contends that in addition Singapore's policies and institutions worked to deliver the results they did because they were integrated across economic, social and political arenas. Despite Singapore's success, she cautions that countries would be well advised to look more closely before trying to replicate the Singaporean model. Few countries are prepared to make the commitment to marshal and implement such a complex, interrelated set of public policies under the aegis of a strong centralized state. The authoritarian nature of Singapore's model may also have been effective in the 1960s, 1970s and into the 1980s, but would be less likely to produce the same result in the current competitive global environment.

She concludes that perhaps, then, the main quandary in Singapore's current economic policy conundrum is what to do about the role of the developmental state after the Miracle of Growth has been achieved. As other rich countries have found upon maturity, it is extremely difficult to 'stay on top', especially without a vibrant indigenous entrepreneurial class.

The Chilean success story has fascinated observers for years. As Patricio Navia (Chapter 12) documents, despite the origin of the country's economic model in the Pinochet dictatorship, Chile has been a success story of democratic consolidation and economic development. All economic indicators show significant progress. Democratic institutions are strong and getting stronger. Citizens are politically engaged and social movements are flourishing. As he shows, the pragmatic and gradual approach to economic and institutional reforms championed since democracy was restored explains why Chile has successfully avoided the pro-cyclical boom and bust trend that has characterized most other Latin American economies in the last two decades. Though the quality of life of all Chileans has improved, high levels of inequality remain a dark spot in the otherwise most successful story of economic development and democratic consolidation in Latin America in the past three decades.

Four countries—Turkey, Indonesia, Mexico and Malaysia—each in somewhat different settings, appear to be the top candidates to follow in the footsteps of Israel, Singapore and Chile. As Fatih Özatay (Chapter 13) shows, Turkish growth has been strong following the country's 2001 financial crisis thanks to strong macroeconomic policies put in place at the time. Still, the country's large balance of payments deficits make the economy vulnerable to external shock. Clearly, the government will have to address this and other long-standing issues before high and sustained growth can be safely assured. These include raising the country's notoriously low savings-to-GDP ratio, eliminating widespread informality and associated low productivity, and greatly improving secondary and tertiary education.

Indonesia has reached the point where the country's rich natural resources are no longer the main determinant of growth. Zamroni Salim (Chapter 14) feels that at this point the country's progress must be hinged more on the creation of a solid, competitive economy. He rightly concludes that in charting out a new course the country can benefit from the lessons learned by the BRICS countries. In particular, he sees the BRICS as a mirror for Indonesia to reflect on identifying gaps in its productive and policy environment. Areas of importance in this regard include government expenditure, investment, value-added technology exports, and sufficient attention to research and development (R&D) and innovation. If successfully implemented the result will be a new BRICS—or more exactly, the expansion of the BRICS to BRIICS.

Mexico's prospects have intrigued observers for years. The country has a vast potential for growth, but has underperformed over the last several decades. Francisco González (Chapter 15) attributes this sad state of affairs to, among other things, what he refers to as a landscape characterized by mismatched monopolies. Economically, the country is dominated by monopolies or concentrated oligopolistic structures in the main private and public production sectors. In this environment lack of competition has led to low productivity growth, underproduction, overpricing and strong blackmail power that tycoons in the private and public sphere have used against successive governments to avoid opening their sectors to competition. Rather than innovating, many of these firms devote most of their energy to preserving, and if at all possible augmenting, their dominance.

An absence of the rule of law is another area greatly impeding growth, foreign investment and innovative activity. Dr González concludes that the absence of the rule of law is the most important problem that Mexico confronts. Sadly, this is not a problem that can be simply decreed away or solved through silver bullet proposals. The confluence of the absence of the rule of law and the all-out armed response to the narcotics trade created a poisonous mix that has killed thousands, has tarnished Mexico's reputation, and increased the costs of doing business in the country.

Still, there is hope that the rejuvenated and reformed Partido Revolucionario Institucional (PRI), the country's long-dominant political party, will be able to make sufficient progress in the reform area so as to unleash a new economic resonance.

Vijayakumari Kanapathy and Herizal Hazri (Chapter 16) document Malaysia's remarkable transformation in the span of one generation from a poor, colonial plantation economy into a modern, upper-middle-income country. In this regard Malaysia represents one of the most extraordinary records of economic and human development in recent memory.

Still, the country's progress has not been without significant setbacks. Growth was interrupted following the 1997 Asian Financial Crisis. The country's economic progress has substantially mellowed since, resulting in Malaysia straying away from its goal of becoming a fully developed country by 2020. Today, while many Malaysians have recovered from the trauma of the 1997 financial crisis and are ready to move on to the next phase of development, another problem seems to have surfaced. Less than a decade from 2020, it is argued that Malaysia is finding itself caught in the so-called 'middle-income trap', where it has reached a relatively comfortable level of income, but cannot seem to take the next leap to developed nation status.

As the authors demonstrate, the solution to the country's middle-income trap is for a parallel socio-political transformation to match the significant progress made in the economic area. In this regard, there is a compelling need to improve the democratic process to ensure good governance and improved rule of law. They wisely conclude that there must be adequate checks and balances to maintain integrity of the key institutions of the government. Corruption must be checked, and there must be greater transparency and accountability so that the developmental outcomes are just.

Part VI assesses a fairly large group of countries, each facing major obstacles in its path up the income ladder. From time to time, each has shown bursts of growth and promise, but sustainable growth has not been possible. These countries are not nearly as favourably placed as Turkey, Indonesia, Mexico and Malaysia, yet one senses that with the right set of reforms and policy actions their prospects could change significantly and quickly.

In the 1990s Argentina seemed on the verge of significantly closing the gap between itself and the advanced countries of Europe. A major financial crisis in 2001 set the country back years. Yet growth returned and until very recently the country appeared positioned for another period of prosperity. As Domingo Cavallo, the chief architect of the country's 1990s boom, notes (Chapter 17), the country's Achilles heel of inflation and widespread relative price distortion is discouraging efficient investment and instead encouraging capital flight, land speculation and inefficient real estate investment. Whether the government will have the political will to tackle these problems remains to be seen. If it does, there is a chance the country might be able to resume the rules of the game that during the 1990s made Argentina the poster child of emerging economies.

Viet Nam is one of the world's most successful post-conflict economies and an example of what is possible under visionary leadership. As Martin Rama shows (Chapter 18), the country's economy is rather unique. The country is an agricultural powerhouse and a large exporter of garments and shoes; it is rapidly moving into the production of electronics. The speed of this transformation is remarkable: while in 2002 Viet Nam was still included in the list of Highly Indebted Poor Countries (HIPC), in 2010 it was already borrowing from the International Bank of Reconstruction and Development (IBRD), a sign of international creditworthiness.

At the same time, Viet Nam remains one of only five nominally communist countries in the world, together with China, Cuba, Laos and the Democratic People's Republic of Korea (North Korea). While more open in terms of public debate and internet access than the other countries in the group, it is a one-party system where dissent is not tolerated beyond what is seen as safe limits. While it is clearly a market economy, the authorities insist on its 'socialist orientation'. As Dr Rama asks, which of these two countries is the real Viet Nam? He concludes that the answer is both, and that this explains many of the specific traits of the country's performance since the beginning of its transition. The tension between these two apparently incompatible systems is also important to understand the prospects and challenges ahead.

The Philippines has been a latecomer. The country was not one of the original 'Asian Tigers' (South Korea, Taiwan, Hong Kong and Singapore) which experienced a growth rate in real per capita income of 5%–7% each year beginning in the late 1960s or early 1970s. However, as Dante Canlas demonstrates (Chapter 19), the country has, in more recent years, been laying a solid foundation to support higher rates of economic growth. His positive assessment is based largely on a series of reforms that have been pursued in succession by political administrations since 1986. These reforms may be broadly classified into, first, short-term macroeconomic policies designed for stable growth, and second, long-term structural policy reforms aimed at sustained and broad-based growth. Time will tell, but there is no denying that the Philippines finally may have positioned itself to be the next Asian Tiger.

The Pakistani economy is another case of bursts of rapid growth (1960s, 1980s), only to be followed with long periods (1970s, 1990s) of instability and below-par economic performance. Former Finance Minister Shahid Javed Burki (Chapter 20) is primarily concerned with the period from 2008 to 2013, when a new political system began to take shape and new relations with the world outside began to be developed.

While the country's poor economic performance in recent years has led many observers to conclude that the country's chances of becoming an emerging economy are slim, Burki is optimistic that the recent establishment of democratic institutions will begin paying high dividends. However, he cautions that the real economic issue at this point is the revival of confidence in the economy. For that to happen, the quality of governance must improve, and this is where policymakers need to focus.

As this volume was being prepared for publication the Egyptian economy, along with the rest of the country, was going through a period of great instability and uncertainty. As Robert Springborg observes (Chapter 21), the predominant theme of republican Egypt's economic history is that of rent seeking, external and internal. 'Cursed' by the resource endowment of a key geostrategic location, which is reinforced by being the largest, most powerful Arab state, possessing substantial hydrocarbon reserves, Egypt has substituted rents for reforms required for a productive, rapidly growing economy. Successive administrations have pursued national economic well-being primarily by attempting to garner public assistance from foreign suitors and by extracting oil and gas rents. As Professor Springborg concludes, if Egypt is to become a full-fledged emerging economy and join the hypothesized newly arriving second tier of BRICS, it must first overcome these curses. Sadly, in the summer of 2013, far from aspiring to BRICS status, the country was struggling simply to survive as a nation.

Thailand is unusual among middle-income developing countries in several respects. It was never colonized, a unique experience within South-East Asia. Perhaps partly because of that, Peter Warr (Chapter 22) feels that successive Thai governments have not been afraid to embark on deep trade and investment integration with the rest of the world. The country's trade and investment policies have been relatively open and its macroeconomic policies have generally been conservative and directed towards maintaining economic stability. The result has been satisfactory long-term growth, but also considerable exposure to global instability.

Professor Warr's assessment stresses the fact that Thailand's development model will have to shift if the country expects to keep moving up the income ladder. As things stand, inequality has increased at the same time as absolute poverty has declined. Education policy remains a serious problem. Public primary and secondary education remain archaic. Standards of rural education, in particular, remain low, and the poor quality of education received by most rural Thais dooms them to lives of economic disadvantage.

Despite a series of development plans under the Shah and Revolutionary government, Iran's vast economic potential remains largely untapped. As Reza Ghorashi and Hamid Zangeneh (Chapter 23) document, the country's failure to achieve significant progress in the socio-politico-economic progress areas can be attributed to a variety of factors. During the last three decades these include the Iran–Iraq War and the 1986 collapse of oil prices, both of which were beyond the government's control. On top of this the country was hit by a variety of economic sanctions while undertaking many self-inflicted and self-destructive policies.

Ironically, they see that many of the present impediments to progress easily might be overcome if Iran's ideological straightjacket were removed from the policymaking process. Over the years poor and inconsistent policymaking as well as little in the way of rule of law has created what veteran observer Homayoun Katouzian has often referred to as a 'short-term society'.[4] This environment creates an atmosphere of great insecurity for large segments of the population. Insecurity is further increased by numerous human rights violations. Laws and regulations are frequently revoked and modified. Lack of uniformity in the application of laws of the land, and uncertainty due to political instability, add to the sense of individual insecurity. Despite vast reserves of oil, in the absence of major governance and political reforms there is little hope for broad-based increased prosperity.

Colombia is beginning to attract widespread attention in the hope that many of the factors inhibiting past growth will be soon resolved. As Laura Armey, Nake Kamrany and Danielle

Ramirez (Chapter 24) note, growth has been constrained for over 40 years by a costly and ineffective drugs war policy. The illicit activity of drugs production and trafficking grosses approximately US$10–$20 billion a year that does not enter into official GDP estimates. In addition, FARC's (Revolutionary Armed Forces of Colombia) terrorism and intimidation has stifled Colombia's drive towards economic prosperity.

Colombia's inequality in the distribution of wealth, land and income, which is among the highest in the world, is at the forefront of ongoing conflict. One consequence of the country's internal conflict has been a partial abandonment of legitimate market activity, and an entrenchment of violence that threatens to undermine future growth. There is hope, but it requires that the government address corruption, income and land inequality—elements that to date have continued to empower FARC.

Saudi Arabia is not included in many of the lists of emerging economies. The country is included in this volume for the simple reason that the Kingdom is the single largest economy in the Middle East and North Africa, and because it possesses an estimated 16.1% of the world's proven oil reserves. As long as regional and domestic stability prevail, Saudi Arabia will remain a key player in the region and around the world.

Still, as Robert Looney suggests (Chapter 25), the country's future prosperity is far from assured. The Saudis face a rapidly closing window to transition to an economy that is less dependent on oil and more capable of self-sustained, job-creating growth. As he notes, the Saudi situation is a bit like global warming. Year-to-year developments don't produce enough change to elicit a dramatic shift in governmental policies or actions, yet the situation remains a ticking time bomb. The main danger may well be the Arab Spring forces that have forced the government to pursue a series of short-term measures—basically handouts to buy domestic tranquillity. Ultimately, these expenditures are likely to divert resources from the oil sector, resulting in lower oil exports, cutbacks in the country's long-term diversification programme and, ultimately, the financial inability of the government to meet the increasing demands of a rapidly growing and increasingly restive populace.

The final section of the volume, Part VII, looks at the future. Will global governance structures evolve to facilitate the continued expansion of the emerging economies? What are some of the keys to emerging country policymaking that will assure successful transitions to developed country status? What lessons can the Korean experience provide for those emerging economies about to transition into developed country states? What will the world economy, and most critically China and India, look like in 2025?

Leslie Armijo and Cynthia Roberts (Chapter 26) begin by examining how the rise of emerging powers might affect existing, Western-dominated, global governance regimes. Five main conclusions arise from their analysis. First, an underlying interstate shift in material capabilities is indeed underway, and at some point in the future there will be two dominant powers: the USA and China. Second, BRICS policymakers are eager to enhance their global influence by discovering common preferences that they can join forces to pursue. Third, it appears likely that the BRICS organization itself functions most readily as an 'outside option' for China to employ to exercise leverage within the major existing global governance institutions. Fourth, the BRICS' preferences, singly and jointly, for global governance turn on reform and evolution, not revolution. Fifth and finally, the BRICS may make a growing difference, but not always and not necessarily in ways that improve global governance or serve the collective good. As they note, none of this is entirely good news for a world that faces urgent global challenges that appear to be overwhelming the capacity of existing international institutions to produce meaningful co-operation.

As a policymaker himself, Domingo Cavallo fashioned some of the most innovative programmes of the day. With years of experience and reflection he has come to the conclusion that policymakers in emerging economies need to design new rules and institutions that depart from those inherited in ways that may become very disruptive of the traditional social order. Furthermore, in the course of applying economic policies quite different from those of the past, policymakers have to dampen the risk that, at time of crisis, the defenders of the old order will push to reverse the institutional changes already implemented. With these factors in mind, Dr Cavallo (Chapter 27) outlines 10 critical areas that policymakers need to heed if they are to sustain growth and provide better standards of living for their populations.

Many emerging economies about to transition to developed country status look to South Korea for guidance. As Bernhard Seliger expertly demonstrates (Chapter 28), the country has overcome a series of adversities to record remarkable rates of growth for over 30 years. As a result, the country has reached the status of a large and respected middle power on an equal footing with Japan. The country embraced institutional changes, it opened its markets further and overcame some of the old traumata haunting the former Japanese colony and divided nation, in particular the fear of losing its cultural identity by opening up.

South Korea became a confident middle power in world affairs, and a model for many countries searching for a recipe for development. However, as Dr Seliger warns, the South Korean developmental success cannot be emulated in a simplistic manner. The ingredients of its success were very specific and some of them may not work at all outside Korea. However, the Korean case certainly holds out hope for all countries searching for a way to develop their economies. The South Korean message is simple: poverty can be overcome, though the process usually will entail sacrifices of hard-working generations. Crises are often unavoidable, but can be used to get rid of institutional 'sclerosis' and free the economy to embark anew on a growth path.

In the final chapter (Chapter 29) Charles Wolf, Jr and Alisher Akhmedjonov attempt to close the circle started by Uri Dadush at the beginning: what will the world economy generally look like in 2025 and specifically how will China's and India's economies evolve up to that date? Not surprisingly, after reviewing 27 of the leading forecasts from governments, think tanks and academics, they conclude that there are too many degrees of freedom and uncertainties to arrive at a precise picture. Instead, one must think in terms of alternative scenarios generated under different sets of assumptions involving the key drivers of growth. It is interesting to note that several of these scenarios result in sharply contrasting future environments.

Will the boom times for the emerging economies return after a bit of a lull beginning in 2012? Or will it be some years before we have a better picture of the future? As *The Economist* observes:

> When a champion sprinter falls short of his best speeds it takes a while to determine whether he is temporarily on poor form or has permanently lost his edge. The same is true of emerging economies.[5]

Alas, the future retains its mystery. In any case, though, the evolution of the emerging economies will likely prove to be much more than just business as usual. It is hoped that readers of this volume will gain a deeper understanding of the forces likely to produce one of the greatest changes in the lives of billions of people.

Notes

1 Jim O'Neil, 'Building Better Global Economic BRICs', Global Economics Paper No. 66, Goldman Sachs & Company, New York, 30 November 2001.
2 Elaine Moore, 'CIVETS, BRICs and the Next 11', *Financial Times*, 8 June 2012.
3 See for example: Uri Dadush & William Shaw, *Juggernaut: How Emerging Markets are Reshaping Globalization*, Carnegie Endowment for International Peace, Washington, DC, 2011; Jim O'Neill, *The Growth Map: Economic Opportunity in the BRICs and Beyond*, Portfolio/Penguin, New York, 2011;

Ruchir Sharma, *Breakout Nations: In Pursuit of the Next Economic Miracles*, W.W. Norton, New York, 2012; Lawrence Edwards and Robert Z. Lawrence, *Rising Tide: Is Growth in Emerging Economies Good for the United States?* Peterson Institute for International Economics, Washington, DC, 2013; and Michael Spence, *The Next Convergence: The Future of Economic Growth in a Multispeed World*, Farrar, Straus and Giroux, New York, 2011.

4 Homayoun Katouzian, 'The Short-Term Society: A Study in the Long-Term Problems of Political and Economic Development in Iran', Lecture, UCLA International Institute, 16 June 2010, www.intern ational.ucla.edu/article.asp?parentid=115711.

5 'The Great Deceleration', *The Economist*, 27 July 2013, 10.

2

Key trends in the world economy

Uri Dadush

The world economy is undergoing an historic transformation, reflecting the rapid growth of developing countries and their integration into global markets. The resilience of developing countries during the Great Recession suggests that they will persist with market-oriented policies that underpin their growth and integration. The crisis—the epicentre of which was in the USA and Europe—has, if anything, accelerated their rising share of global economic activity.

Projections presented in this chapter suggest that the world's economic balance of power will shift dramatically.[1] The People's Republic of China will overtake the USA as the world's largest economic power, and India, its very recent dismal performance notwithstanding, is likely to join both as a global leader. Other emerging economies in Asia and Latin America will outpace Europe, driving a vast expansion of global trade and financial integration. Despite this, migration pressures from developing into advanced countries will intensify due to the marked differences in demographic patterns.

It is impossible to project over decades with any claim to precision. However, it is possible to portray likely long-term economic trends conditional on certain assumptions, and to sketch the broad contours of the world economy that would result from them. So the discussion that follows, even though it will contain hard numbers, should be interpreted as painting a plausible scenario, not as a point forecast.

Rather than show a large number of alternative futures, the chapter tries to identify this 'central tendency' or baseline—on the assumptions that market-oriented policies persist and that major political, economic and ecological disasters are avoided. It then briefly discusses the main risks. This approach has the defect of suggesting precision that is frankly illusive, but it helps to focus on the analysis of the baseline, economizes on the attention span, and gives the critical reader a clear target to shoot at and disagree with.

The chapter begins with a brief discussion of the long-term implications of the crisis. It next presents the main scenario: long-term growth projections for the world's major economies, the G20, from a model that uses a Cobb-Douglas production function as the base. It then briefly sketches some implications for the main channels of international integration: trade, financial flows, relative prices, migration and capital flows. The chapter also reviews risks to the forecast, including climate change, and concludes with some policy implications.

The crisis and its implications

In the run-up to the Great Recession, many developing countries, though not all, saw remarkable economic advances and a rise in living standards. Better policies, less debt and higher reserves helped them to weather the crisis.

Growth in the developing countries in the aggregate has exceeded that of the industrial countries by 2–3 percentage points a year since the turn of the century, 500 million people have been lifted out of poverty since 1990, and average life expectancy has risen to 70 years in many of them. Developing countries have integrated into the global markets for goods, capital and labour. Tariffs have been cut to one-third of their level in the early 1980s, trade has risen by 15 percentage points of gross domestic product (GDP) over the last 15 years, and foreign direct investment's (FDI) share of GDP has more than doubled. Remittances have surged. This rapid growth and integration has been associated with a cumulative and mutually reinforcing adaptation of various technologies imported from advanced countries. Growth has also been associated with better macroeconomic management: in the years prior to the crisis, developing countries saw a large decline in external debt to GDP, smaller fiscal balances and a large increase in foreign currency reserves.

The effects of the Great Recession were severe, but the developing countries were damaged less than industrial ones (see Figure 2.1).

Many developing countries saw relatively small decelerations in growth during the crisis, and some continued to grow quite rapidly, including three countries—China, India and Indonesia—that account for nearly half of the developing world's population, although India's very recent growth performance has been disappointing. Partial exceptions include several developing countries in Eastern Europe, some of which were hit worse than the industrial countries. The growth deceleration was pronounced in the USA and even more so in the large countries of Europe where a sovereign debt crisis related to the dysfunctional operation of the European single currency was triggered and continues to rage.

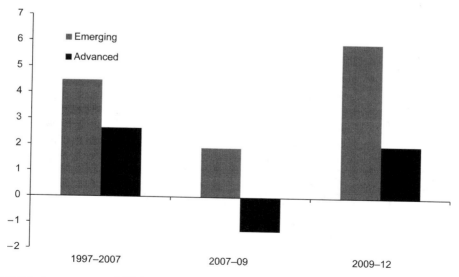

Figure 2.1 Average annual GDP growth in the G20 economies (% Change)
Source: IMF

While the trade and financial shocks initially affected every country in the world, the banking systems of most developing countries were relatively insulated. The prudent macro stance many of them adopted in recent years allowed them to adopt countercyclical policies and mitigate the crisis. Flexible exchange rates helped. Once the global panic subsided, confidence in emerging markets returned quickly, and capital flows were re-established, if well below those of the pre-crisis period.

However, even as a recovery takes shape in the USA, the legacy of the crisis is profound. In advanced countries, the post-crisis world is characterized by low growth as well as by greater volatility. Uncertainty persists as to the effect of the withdrawal of massive monetary stimulus and as large fiscal stimulus gives way to widespread austerity policies. The surge of public sector debt in advanced countries, now estimated by the International Monetary Fund (IMF) to be in excess of 100% of GDP in several, will constrain macroeconomic policies for years, and demand a structural adjustment in taxes and spending.

Contrary to the proclamations of some sceptics at the outset of the crisis, it appears unlikely that the episode will lead to a fundamental change in policies supporting free markets and global economic integration, partly because developing countries weathered the crisis well and because the largest advanced and developing countries have—albeit imperfectly—heeded the admonitions of the G20, the World Trade Organization (WTO), and others, not to repeat the self-defeating protectionism of the 1930s. Some of the institutional planks of the dominant policy paradigm, including the development banks and especially the IMF and the Financial Stability Board, emerged reinforced by the crisis. WTO disciplines, though porous, also proved their value, as did regional trade agreements. Central bankers, perhaps the most consistent proponents of the current policy paradigm, played an absolutely crucial role in fighting the crisis, also emerging stronger. They have become more active in financial regulation and surveillance.

Baseline scenario

Before the Great Recession the balance of economic power in the world was gradually shifting to the South and the East. Now, as industrial countries slowly resume growth along their pre-crisis long-term paths but do not recover the output lost during the crisis, developing countries—whose output losses were much lower—have already put the effects of the recession behind them. In the coming years the most successful of them, especially in Asia, look set to converge even more rapidly towards their advanced counterparts.

GDP projections to 2050 for the world's major economies—the 19 nations of the G20 (the European Union (EU) is excluded) and several large countries in Africa—are presented here. Based on a standard Cobb-Douglas output model, the projections build on a long history of studies, dating at least to the early 1970s. The concept of the 'Big Five' developing countries—China, India, Indonesia, Brazil and Russia—and the idea that their effects on the world economy would be profound was introduced in the World Bank's 1997 Global Economic Prospects.[2] Some years later Goldman Sachs unveiled the catchy BRIC acronym to denote these countries, minus Indonesia, which was then in deep crisis (but has since recovered and clearly belongs in the BRIC club). In the early 2000s Goldman Sachs[3] and PricewaterhouseCoopers[4] developed their own long-term projections of the world's largest economies.

Technological change, the single most important driver of economic growth, is usually incorporated in these precursor models exogenously; in other words, it is a given number generated outside the model. This is hardly satisfactory, especially as modern growth theory has attempted to identify the factors that drive technological change—such as the contestability of markets, openness and the skills of workers—and to incorporate them endogenously in models of economic growth models.

The model used in this book tries to incorporate this theory of technological change by making technological advances dependent on an underlying set of factors, which include the initial income gap relative to the most advanced countries, openness to foreign technology, the prevalence of competition, quality of the business climate, and levels of education.

Based on these assumptions, rapid growth in developing countries will result from a high, though slowing, population increase, as well as advances in total factor productivity (TFP) from technology absorption (conditional on the quality of education, governance, business climate and infrastructure, and declining over time as the gap with advanced countries closes). While investment rates in developing countries will also be higher than in industrial countries—a continuation of the trends observed over decades—technology will be more important than capital accumulation in driving growth in both groups.

The large shift in economic power that these projections imply will have far-reaching consequences for global economic governance and for relationships among countries and geographic regions. Kenichi Ohmae's 1980s concept of a triad—a world economy led by the USA, Europe and Japan—will be eclipsed by a new order, consisting of China, the USA and India. As foreshadowed by the Lisbon Treaty, Europe would have to operate increasingly under an EU banner in order to retain its historical influence, a hopeful assumption in light of the enormous strains caused by the euro crisis. International organizations such as the IMF and World Bank, whose governance structures still reflect the world as it was in 1945, must either adjust or be relegated to the margin.

How confident can one be that growth in developing countries will continue to outstrip that of advanced countries by a wide margin? The answer, based on an examination of the fundamentals driving growth, is 'very'.

Why drivers of growth favour developing countries

The main force propelling growth in developing countries is 'catch-up' of technology to that at the frontier as found in the USA and other advanced countries where total factor productivity is the highest in the world. However, it is not the only force: developing countries save and invest a higher proportion of their income (and have a relatively low capital stock at the outset); they also have relatively young populations and a surging labour force in contrast to the relatively stagnant and ageing labour force in advanced countries.

Young labour force

According to the Population Reference Bureau, the global population will rise from 7.1 billion in 2009 to 9.6 billion in 2050. According to the United Nations (UN), the global labour force will expand by 1.3 billion. Developing regions will see their workforces expand by close to 1.5 billion people, mostly in Africa and Asia, while the labour force in developed areas will shrink by more than 100 million workers. The working-age population in developed regions will fall from 62.8% of the population in 2009 to 52.0% in 2050. It will also decline in developing regions, but only from 61.1% to 59.5%.

Rising capital stock

Physical capital stocks will continue to accumulate as incomes rise and rates of savings will more than cover depreciation and allow for new investment, but as the capital stock rises relative to the labour force and to output, its return tends to decline as does the incentive to invest. Moreover, in industrial countries, savings as a share of GDP will likely decline as populations age rapidly and the dependency ratio rises. In developing countries, however, where capital-to-output ratios are much lower and the working population is rising rapidly, the incentive to invest (and the propensity to save) will remain high. China, which stands out as an exception among developing countries since its population is ageing rapidly, is nevertheless expected to see continued savings and investment rates, even though they decline from current extremely high levels.

Historically, developed countries have invested about 20% of GDP in fixed capital formation each year (see Figure 2.2). Developing countries have invested significantly more, with investment in China and some Asian countries averaging around 35%–40% or more.

Japan provides a useful case study, because the rapidity of its rise and then maturing over the post-war period allows us to trace its investment through very different stages of development. Japan's yearly investment rate peaked at 36% of GDP when its economy was growing rapidly and has moderated towards 20% in recent years. The Republic of Korea (South Korea) had a similar experience, with investment peaking at 40% of GDP in 1992 before declining to just below 30% since then.

Over the next 40 years China and India are expected to have the highest average investment rates, 33.8% and 33.5% per year, respectively. The United Kingdom and Germany are projected to invest at the lowest rates, 17.7% and 18.3%, respectively.

Technology catches up

Technological innovation will become a more important driver of growth as the means of production shift from traditional labour-intensive to industrial capital-intensive activities and to

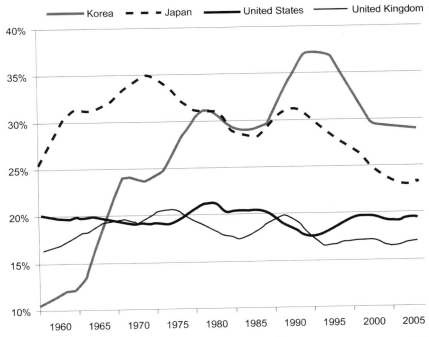

Figure 2.2 Investment converging towards 15%–20% for mature economies (% of GDP, five-year moving average)

Source: IMF

services sectors requiring specialized skills. Such a process is invariably accompanied by urbanization and large-scale emigration from the countryside.

As a comprehensive World Bank report on technology and development explains, 'Part of the strong projected performance for developing countries derives from stronger labor force growth, but much can be attributed to technological progress'.[5] The report shows that developing countries are continuing to absorb well-established technologies, such as electricity and sanitation. While the largest urban agglomerations and elite firms and individuals in developing countries typically have access to such technologies, rural areas and less favoured segments of society often do not. In developing countries, the main driver of technological innovation and productivity is the expanded use of well-established technologies to the less favoured regions and segments of society.

However, newer technologies, such as mobile phones and the internet, are also spreading rapidly to developing countries, partly because they are relatively inexpensive and require little government spending on infrastructure. Although advanced countries will remain the source of cutting-edge technological innovation, some developing countries will innovate by modifying technologies to suit local conditions.

The potential for technological catch-up is greater when TFP and per capita income are low. Thus, convergence of the poorest countries is potentially the fastest, but actual rates of catch-up will depend on each country's educational attainment, communication and transportation infrastructure, governance, and business and investment environment. These factors hold technological progress significantly below potential in low-income countries, but as educational attainment and openness to world trade rise, technologies spread faster. The availability of knowledge and information of all kinds at relatively low cost make the investment in communications infrastructure and access to the internet crucial. Such policies are central to the development process, and in this sense our model incorporates some features of endogenous growth theory.

An examination of the relevant indicators suggests that among major developing countries (those in the G20), Russia, China and Mexico are well prepared for faster adoption of foreign technologies, largely because of fairly high levels of educational attainment and supportive infrastructure. However, governance indicators in Russia and China are weak, suppressing technological convergence (adjusted for initial income), other things being equal.

Contrary to India's high-tech image, its spread of technology and speed of convergence (adjusted for initial income) are assumed to be among the lowest in the G20. It exhibits the lowest education indicators and worst business climate in the G20, while Indonesia has the G20's weakest communication infrastructure. Education, infrastructure and governance must improve before rapid technological advancement can occur in India and Indonesia. India's recent disappointing growth performance has been ascribed in part to such shortcomings.

In the model, the degree to which these factors will hold countries' technological growth below the potential is suggested by their estimated speed of convergence to the USA controlling for their income gap, with a score of 10 representing maximum ability to take advantage of technological catch-up (see Figure 2.3).

Projections: the 'rise of the rest'

As developing countries house a larger share of people, capital and technology, their share of global GDP will increase, dramatically shifting the economic balance of power. By the midpoint of this century the USA and Europe, long the traditional leaders of the global economy, will be joined in economic size by emerging markets in Asia and Latin America.

Key trends in the world economy

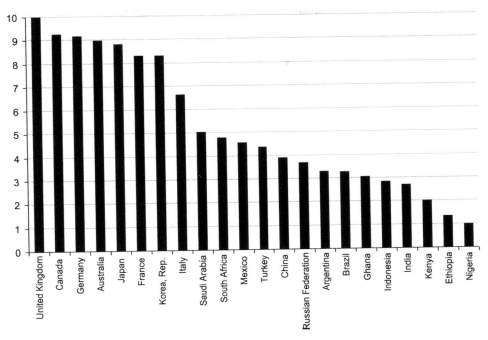

Figure 2.3 The United Kingdom has the greatest ability to catch the USA, Nigeria the least (index of technological catch-up conditions, 0 denotes slowest convergence to the USA, 10 denotes fastest)
Source: World Bank World Development Indicators (2009)

However, as these countries become the world's largest economies, as well as the most populous, they will not rise to be among the world's richest, breaking the decades-old correlation between economic size and per capita income. This notion of a low- or middle-income country becoming the world's largest economy—dating to at least 1993, when China was predicted to rise as a world power—now appears more likely.[6] The recent promotion of the G20 as the world's principal economic forum will likely mark the end of wealthy country dominance over the world economy and usher in a more integrated and complex economic era.

The baseline scenario assumes that markets stay open and macroeconomic policies remain sound; catastrophes—economic, natural, or geopolitical—are assumed not to occur. For these reasons the projections represent only an educated assessment of the present direction of the international economy.

To account for more immediate risks, such as a slow recovery and unfavourable debt dynamics in many advanced economies following the financial crisis, projections for the first five years are provided by the IMF's *World Economic Outlook*. For each of the 10 years that follow the model's predictions are an average of the model and the recorded growth rate during 1997–2007. By nudging the projections towards the trends of the pre-crisis decade—roughly the length of two complete business cycles—factors that affect growth in the medium term, such as political disruptions or natural resource windfalls, but are not incorporated in the long-term growth model, can be partly accounted for. Beyond that point the projections are entirely model-driven.

19

2050: a new economic order

The weight of global economic activity is already shifting substantially from the G7 countries towards emerging economies in Asia and Latin America. Over the next 40 years or so, this trend is expected to accelerate (see Table 2.1).

As labour productivity in the developing countries increases relative to that in the developed countries, wages will increase and the price of non-tradables relative to tradables will rise in developing countries, as predicted by the Balassa-Samuelson effect.[7] These changes, which imply an appreciation of real exchange rates in developing countries, will increase the importance of developing economies as export markets.

The total economy of the G20 is expected to grow at an average annual rate of 3.2%, rising from US$35 trillion in 2012 to $118 trillion in 2050 in real US dollars (constant 2000 prices). Over half of this $83 trillion expansion will come from six countries—Brazil, Russia, India, China, Indonesia and Mexico (the Big Five+M)—to eclipse the G7. US dollar GDP in these six economies will grow at an average of 5.2% a year; their share of G20 GDP will rise from 21% in 2012 to 43% in 2050. By contrast, GDP in the G7 will grow 2.2% a year, and their share of G20 GDP will decline from 71% to 48%.

In purchasing power parity (PPP), the shift is even more dramatic. Today, developing countries claim only 44% of the G20's GDP in PPP terms; by 2050 their share will rise to 61%. Again, the Big Five+M economies will be responsible for most of this growth, with their share rising from 38% to 54%.

Table 2.1 Average annual GDP growth, % change

	Pre-crisis trend 1997–2007	Crisis and recovery years 2007–12	Projections 2012–50	Real GDP (constant 2000 US$) 2012	2030	2050
Argentina	2.6	5.5	3.9	491	978	2,103
Australia	3.6	2.5	2.9	589	985	1,746
Brazil	2.8	3.1	3.9	981	1,954	4,200
Canada	3.3	1.2	2.6	918	1,456	2,433
China	9.6	9.3	5.6	3,747	9,990	29,707
France	2.4	0.0	1.7	1,532	2,075	2,907
Germany	1.6	0.7	1.4	2,172	2,789	3,683
India	7.0	6.8	5.7	1,106	3,001	9,093
Indonesia	2.7	5.9	5.0	307	739	1,961
Italy	1.5	−1.4	1.3	1,166	1,471	1,904
Japan	1.1	−0.1	1.3	5,125	6,466	8,372
South Korea	4.3	2.9	2.7	853	1,378	2,347
Mexico	3.3	1.6	4.3	753	1,606	3,729
Russia	5.7	1.8	3.3	448	803	1,538
Saudi Arabia	3.7	6.6	4.3	290	620	1,438
South Africa	4.0	2.2	4.4	202	439	1,038
Turkey	3.2	3.1	4.6	442	994	2,443
UK	2.9	−0.4	2.1	1,808	2,629	3,983
USA	3.0	0.6	2.7	12,061	19,483	33,195

Source: IMF; author's projections

The new triad

China, India and the USA will emerge as the world's three largest economies in 2050. Rapid annual growth of 5.6% and a strengthening currency—the renminbi's real exchange rate against the dollar is predicted to appreciate by more than 1% a year—will drive China's US dollar GDP up from $3.7 trillion in 2012 to $29.7 trillion in 2050, 90% as large as the USA in real dollar terms and 42% larger in PPP terms. Of all G20 countries India is predicted to post the fastest growth, of 5.7% a year, and its rapidly growing population, to become the world's most populous nation in 2030, will push its US dollar GDP to $9.1 trillion in 2050, nine times its current level. Its PPP GDP will be 61% that of the USA.

Despite these dramatic increases in total GDP, US per capita GDP will be more than three times that of China and almost 14 times that of India, complicating the US role in the global economy. US technological advantages will likely help it to maintain its position as a leader of the international community, but China's and India's much lower per capita incomes, combined with their large size, may reinforce their authority as their conditions will be perceived as more representative of the vast majority of the world population.

A more balanced world

The economic balance of power within the rest of the G20 will tilt towards emerging markets, as slowing growth in high-income countries—2.2% annually—is met with rapid expansion in the developing world—5.1% annually. However, excluding China and India, emerging markets will not supplant Europe and Japan as economic powers, but they will add new authoritative voices to the international dialogue.

Real GDP in India is expected to increase by 5.7% a year, surpassing the GDP of Japan, currently the world's third largest economy, in 2050; Brazil and Mexico are both expected to be larger than present-day China.

Japan's influence in Asia will likely recede with China's rise and Indonesia's rapid expansion. Japan will grow by a sluggish 1.3% a year, tied with Italy for slowest growth in the G20. Japan, Asia's most powerful nation in the 20th century, will be pressed to develop ever closer economic ties with China, an economy that will be twice as large as Japan's in US current dollar terms (market exchange rates) in 2050, and with India, which will be 1.7 times larger. Like Britain in past centuries, Japan will seek to promote a regional balance of power, implying continued close political and security ties with the USA.

The four largest countries in Europe are expected to grow by only 1.7% annually as their share of G20 GDP shrinks from 19% in 2012 to 11% in 2050. To retain their historical influence, European nations will likely need to collaborate and conduct their foreign policy increasingly under an EU banner. If the EU follows the 1.7% growth average of its four largest countries, real US dollar GDP will increase from $10.1 trillion to $19.1 trillion in 2050, placing it among the world's three largest economies.

Russia, historically a great power, may become a political outlier under this scenario. The world's largest country, and enormously rich in natural resources, its population in 2050 will be down to 109 million from 140 million today. With China, India and the USA, not only the world's three largest economies but also the world's three most populous, to its south and east, Russia may face mounting pressure to increase its economic and security ties with Europe if it is to maintain a voice in world affairs.

Can Africa break through?

The impressive advance in the G20 developing economies depicted by the baseline scenario conceals the plight of many of the poorest and less successful developing economies, which have been falling behind even as growth accelerated among a large part of the world's population. Owing to macroeconomic and political instability, barriers of distance and transport, environmental degradation, inadequate capacity, and explicit policy choices not to integrate in global markets, these countries remain outside the mainstream.

Among the outliers are Haiti, Myanmar (formerly Burma) and the Democratic People's Republic of Korea (North Korea), but most are in Africa. Can they do better? The answer—according to our model—is yes. Applying the projection methodology to the four large countries in sub-Saharan Africa—Ethiopia, Ghana, Kenya and Nigeria—suggests that in the absence of major conflicts, they could exhibit rapid growth over the next 40 years. Africa's rapidly increasing population will help drive growth in the near term, while large technological improvements can potentially sustain the expansion over coming decades, despite unfavourable (though improving) initial conditions in education, governance and infrastructure. These four African countries are projected to grow at an average of 5.5% a year to 2050. Relative to past decades of dismal performance, these growth rates represent a major acceleration, but they are not out of line with outcomes since the turn of the century.

Under this scenario the average per capita income in these countries will be less than half of India's and a fraction of China's, raising the possibility that African countries could become competitive with the Asian giants in labour-intensive manufactures, as well as destinations for outsourcing.

As incomes in China (and to some extent India) diverge from those in Africa, China and India could become major export destinations for Africa not only in raw materials but also in basic manufactures. There is, of course, nothing automatic about this outcome, as the ability to compete in the international market for manufactures will require a big improvement in the quality and predictability of the business climate and efficient investments in education, which may or may not be forthcoming.

The fall in extreme poverty and the rise of the global middle class

Not only will the economic landscape be dramatically changed by 2050, but the world will also be profoundly different in human terms. Over the next 40 years, millions, if not billions, of people around the world will be lifted out of the harshest forms of poverty (see Table 2.2). Accompanying this trend will be the emergence of a new global middle and rich class (GMR)—the segment of the global population that can demand advanced goods and services—in developing countries.[8]

In 2005 the World Bank estimated that more than 1.3 billion people—more than one-quarter of the world's population—lived in extreme poverty, consuming less than $1.25 a day in PPP terms. Nearly twice this number, or half of the world's population, lived on less than $2.00 a day. By 2050, according to projections in *Juggernaut*, a guide to the growing clout of emerging markets that was published by the Carnegie Endowment for International Peace in 2011, no country in the G20 will have more than 5% of its people in extreme poverty, though significant portions of society will still live on less than $2.00 a day.

Poverty rates are expected to come down significantly in Indonesia, Brazil, Mexico and Turkey, but growth in China and India—nations home to 48% of the world's population living on less than $1.25 a day in 2005—will be the driving force behind this shift. Over the past 25 years, more than 600 million people have emerged from poverty in China. (Excluding China, global poverty has actually increased since 1981.) From 2005 to 2050 China and India will lift 600 million more people from the most extreme forms of poverty.[9]

Key trends in the world economy

Table 2.2 Percentage of population living in poverty

Living on less than $1.25 a day					
	2005	2010	2020	2030	2050
China	15.9	7.9	3.1	2.0	1.2
India	41.6	34.5	10.4	4.1	2.5
Indonesia	27.4	18.1	7.4	4.1	2.3
Sub-Saharan Africa	45.8	39.7	26.2	16.1	8.4
Living on less than $2.00 a day					
	2005	2010	2020	2030	2050
China	36.3	19.5	5.1	3.2	2.0
India	75.6	64.1	40.5	19.6	4.0
Indonesia	55.9	47.4	29.8	13.0	3.7
Sub-Saharan Africa	69.6	62.5	49.0	35.8	16.9

Source: World Bank; *Juggernaut*

Economic growth will also bring relief to millions of poor in sub-Saharan Africa, but the region will remain the most impoverished. The benefits of the area's strong growth will be diffused across a rapidly expanding population, holding per capita incomes down in a region where more than half the population consumed less than $1.25 a day in 2005. Although the next 40 years will bring marked improvements, poverty will remain relatively high: in 2050, 8.4% of the population will still live on less than $1.25 a day, and 16.9% on less than $2.00 a day.

These trends certainly offer hope. They do not imply, however, that poverty will no longer be a serious economic and humanitarian concern. The higher poverty line—$2.00 a day—will satisfy basic human needs, but it will mean a miserable existence. Nor is absolute income the only measure of the human condition. Both within and across countries, enormous relative income disparities will severely limit the poorest segments' political voice, social integration, and access to economic markets and opportunities.

Many of those lifted from poverty will join the new GMR class. Estimates in *Juggernaut* show that the GMR population in the developing G20 economies is likely to grow from 739 million in 2009 to 1.9 billion in 2050 (see Table 2.3).[10] Today, 24% of the global GMR population resides in developing countries; by 2050, about 60% will do so.[11] However, the purchasing power of the GMR in advanced countries will be about 60% greater than that of the GMR in developing G20 countries.

Recent analysis suggests that these numbers may underestimate the size and growth rate of the global middle class. In July 2012, the Carnegie Endowment for International Peace published a paper, 'In Search of the Global Middle Class: A New Index', which used data on passenger cars in circulation and the size of the average household to approximate the size of this group. According to this direct measure of the affluent, the global middle class may be about 50% larger than commonly estimated using traditional household survey income-based measures, and may be growing between two and three times faster.

Trade and financial integration

Assuming that the world does not retreat into protectionism, the role of developing countries as exporters and importers will increase significantly over the next 40 years, reflecting their high growth rate and the rise of their middle classes. Their share of global exports will more than double. In addition, their dependence on developed country markets is projected to weaken as trade among developing countries overwhelms that among advanced economies. Patterns of

Table 2.3 Size of the global middle and rich (GMR) class population (million)

	2009	2020	2030	2050
Advanced economies	1,193	1,225	1,254	1,284
Developing G20 economies	368	740	1,295	1,958
China	118	375	779	1,092
Brazil	66	80	110	170
Russia	57	82	93	98
India	37	69	121	273
Mexico	37	51	72	111
Turkey	17	29	46	70
Indonesia	11	20	33	81
Argentina	17	21	28	40
South Africa	9	13	14	23
Large African economies				
Nigeria	4	6	10	22
Kenya	4	7	10	26
Ethiopia	3	6	11	34
Ghana	1	3	5	18

comparative advantage will shift as well, as incomes, wages, capital-labour ratios and education levels increase faster in successful developing countries than in industrial ones.

Financial integration will increase, and developing countries' share of capital flows will rise along with their participation in trade. Robust global growth, a favourable financing environment and domestic policy improvements led to a surge in private capital flows to developing countries before the financial crisis. Going forward, continuing policy improvements and rapidly expanding trade (which will attract FDI, as well as other flows thanks to improved creditworthiness) are likely to continue the upward trend in private capital flows. Even assuming that FDI grows in line with GDP, and not faster as in recent history, the share of developing countries in the world's net FDI inflows will jump from 25% in 2005–07 to 66% in 2050, according to *Juggernaut*. Many low-income countries will cross the ratings threshold to attract private portfolio flows and will see increased bank lending. Developing countries will also become larger investors, in both each other and industrial countries.

The greater financial integration of developing countries will present new opportunities. In Africa, for example, the prospects for aid flows have become even less certain with the advent of the crisis, but the potential for private capital inflows remains relatively untapped.

However, greater financial integration will also present new challenges for macroeconomic and regulatory policies. These policies need to ensure that capital is used effectively and does not simply respond to artificial distortions or market euphoria—and that safeguards are built against sudden stops and reversals in capital flows.

Prospects for relative prices

Commodity prices in the coming years will likely continue their gradual downward path relative to manufactured goods (the price surge in the mid-2000s notwithstanding). A broad array of empirical studies shows that primary commodity prices have declined historically relative to manufactured goods, with estimates of long-term decline ranging from −0.6% to −2.3% a year.[12] The reasons for the secular decline have also been widely explored, and include the low demand elasticity for primary commodities relative to manufactures and services, the growth of substitutes and the rapid technological advances that have reduced the cost of growing or extracting these materials.

In addition, the price of basic manufactured goods may be expected to continue to decline relative to knowledge-intensive goods and services. The declining price of manufactured goods relative to services is a well-documented feature of economic development. From 1950 to 2000 manufacturing productivity in the USA increased at an average annual rate of 2.8%, compared with 2.0% in non-farm business overall. From 1990 to 2002 manufacturing productivity's relative pace was even more impressive: 3.9% a year, compared with 2.3%. This strong productivity differential lowers the cost of producing manufactured goods, and thus their price, relative to services.

At first glance, the downward trend in primary commodity prices appears to be threatened by massive increases in demand from the acceleration of growth in large developing countries, including China and India, that are net importers of energy, materials and many agricultural commodities, but consider three offsetting effects. First, technological advances in both the production and use of commodities in a broad range of developing countries will increase supply and reduce demand. For example, the Food and Agriculture Organization (FAO) and the Organisation for Economic Co-operation and Development (OECD) argue that agricultural productivity is likely to increase in the medium term, and note that in Central and Eastern Europe as well as in sub-Saharan Africa it could rise significantly if existing technologies were implemented.

Second, investments in commodities also will rise. This is clearest in agriculture, where the potential for bringing more land under cultivation is huge. About 1.4 billion hectares are used for crops. FAO and OECD estimates show that an additional 1.6 billion hectares could be cultivated. Found in Africa and Latin America, the majority of this land is highly suitable for rain-fed crop production, though it requires large infrastructure investments and institutional improvements before it can be put to effective use. As new land is cultivated, it may take longer for yields there to catch up. Moreover, investment in the production of raw materials (including that financed directly by China and India) is also likely to rise, increasing supply.[13]

Third, global population growth is expected to slow, even as absolute numbers rise, which will directly translate into reduced demand growth for commodities. While a rise in per capita income will likely increase demand for other products, after a certain threshold income is reached, it should have no significant impact on demand for agricultural products.

Fundamentally, GDP growth has consistently outpaced the demand for commodities. While this downward trend in commodity intensity is not immutable, a major external change would be required to break it—nor is it clear what that change might be.[14] Some of the more disruptive technologies on the horizon, including biotechnology and miniaturization, could both reduce the demand for some commodities and greatly increase their supply. The drive to reduce carbon emissions could also begin to make a dent in energy use, but oil may be an important exception to the downward trend in commodity prices, as the exhaustion of easily accessible reserves places a floor on oil prices. Prospects for prices depend critically on the severity of the effects of climate change, which could cause shortages of food and land in some areas of the world.

Despite this long-term downward trend, commodity prices are likely to remain highly volatile, and price spikes such as the ones in the mid-2000s may recur, as they have today. The reasons for high volatility of commodity prices have also been widely explored. They include low short-term income and price elasticities of demand and supply, long lead times before investment and supply respond to changing demand conditions, weather factors in agricultural commodities, and policy-induced distortions that impede the orderly adjustment of markets. Newer sources of instability may include more variable weather due to climate change and increased use of commodities and commodity derivatives for speculation.

Increasing migration

Migration is already significant, with more than 200 million people residing outside their countries of birth today. Migration pressures have been reduced drastically by the Great Recession and its effects on labour demand, but pressures for increased migration are likely to intensify in the coming years. Demographic trends, wide and in some cases widening gaps in economic opportunity, spreading networks of migrants, more intensive communication, and greater ability to afford the cost and risk of migration will increase the mobility of workers. In the longer term, the effects of climate change are likely to increase greatly the need to migrate out of the worst-affected regions in developing countries

Risks

Even though the last 40 years have been relatively free of mega-shocks compared with the previous 40 (during which the Great Depression and the Second World War took place), they nevertheless included at least three major financial crises (the Debt Crisis of the 1980s, the Asian Financial Crisis, and the Great Recession of 2007–09), the fall of the Berlin Wall, and the emergence of China.

Although it is impossible to foretell where and how large shocks may originate, at least four classes of risk that could introduce major discontinuities that would undermine these projections can be identified.

Climate change

Climate change could severely reduce the prospects for global growth. While climate change is already occurring, the timing and extent of its most severe effects remain very difficult to pinpoint. It is assumed in the baseline that the positive growth factors discussed above will outshine any negative effects, but even a modest rise in temperatures of 2°C could sharply reduce welfare, particularly in developing countries. Without concerted efforts to control carbon emissions, much greater increases are likely, with particularly catastrophic implications for many developing regions.

Climate change may drive large migration flows from the most-affected regions (South Asia, East Asia and Africa) to the industrial countries, which are best able to cope with its effects and could even benefit from modest rises in temperatures.[15]

It could also exacerbate protectionist measures. Border adjustments to compensate firms for tighter emission standards have been incorporated in draft legislation in the US Congress, and are explicitly supported by at least one prominent European leader. They are perceived as profoundly inequitable by China, India and many other developing countries whose emissions are a fraction of those in industrial countries. The legitimacy of these border adjustments under WTO rules is questionable, and if enacted, they risk a large deterioration in international trade relations, with unpredictable consequences.

Geopolitical breakdown

The next 40 years may see one of the greatest shifts in economic and military power in history. China's influence will rise, compete with and perhaps overtake that of the USA, and major power shifts will occur within regions, with China and India relative to Japan, the great European powers continuing on a path of relative decline, and Brazil and possibly Mexico becoming more ascendant in Latin America.

Key trends in the world economy

History documents that these transitions have rarely been easy and that there is a high likelihood of hitting any number of flashpoints along the way. Even if major disputes over territory or regional influence are resolved peacefully, economic relations could be undermined by trade disputes, differences over dealing with climate change and many other issues related to the global commons, and major economic crises.

In short, globalization does not exist in a vacuum. Maintaining the cohesion of the international community is crucial to its continuation.

Financial crisis and depression

The world economy's near-demise at the turn of 2009 should remove any sense of complacency about the dangers lurking in international financial integration when adequate regulatory mechanisms and sound macroeconomic policies are lacking even in the world's most advanced economies.

Yet the ability of countries to turn the many lessons of the Great Recession into effective reforms remains unproven and even highly suspect. The reasons are multiple: they include the financial industry's resistance to reform, ideological differences about the appropriate role of regulation and market discipline, the difficulties of internationally co-ordinated action, the complexity of modern financial markets, and the weak capacities of both domestic and international regulators. Furthermore, the political challenges of dealing with macroeconomic imbalances of various kinds are formidable.

Arguably, the world economy emerges from the crisis a more, and not a less, dangerous place, reflecting large public debts, difficult-to-reverse financial sector support policies, large overhangs of liquidity, and greatly increased moral hazards, particularly in financial institutions deemed 'too big to fail'. These vulnerabilities will not soon disappear—indeed, they may become greater with the passage of time as the financial industry's appetite for risk returns once memories of the disaster begin to fade.

Protectionism

A relapse into protectionism presents perhaps the single most important risk to this forecast, since the growth projections are grounded in assumptions about technological catch-up and increased efficiency that depend on open international markets.

Given the densely interwoven fabric of today's global economy, and the vast set of rules under WTO and regional agreements, including international legal redress procedures, a large relapse into protectionism is likely only in the presence of the other risk factors discussed above. International markets could become closed in the event of a deterioration of great power relations to the point of open military or economic hostilities, an economic depression and rise in mass unemployment (as narrowly avoided in 2009), or profound divisions over climate change and the attempt to resort to trade sanctions as an enforcement mechanism. The risks to open trade would be compounded if more than one of these conditions occurred together: in general the risks of geopolitical breakdown, financial crisis and protectionism tend to rise in the presence of the others.

If any or all of the above risks materialize, growth may be significantly slower than estimated. For example, under a lower-growth scenario developed in *Juggernaut*, growth in industrial countries is expected to be 0.3–0.5 percentage points lower than in the base case, 1.0–1.3 points lower in China and India, 0.5–0.8 points lower in other emerging economies, and 1.5 point lower in non-G20 economies in sub-Saharan Africa. Under those assumptions, the G20 GDP will reach $109 trillion in 2050, 32% less than its baseline GDP. China and India will emerge as two of the three largest economies in the world, but both will remain smaller than the USA in dollar terms; however, China's PPP GDP will still surpass that of the USA to become the largest in the world. The relative weight of emerging markets in the global economy will still rise, with an average annual growth rate of 4.5% for the Big Five+M, compared with 1.6% growth in the G7.

Assuming no efforts to reduce emissions, carbon concentrations under this low-growth scenario would be less than that expected under the baseline growth rates, making the mitigation of climate change less daunting. However, slower growth could also reduce the space for necessary investments and make other trade-offs more difficult. Upholding the commitments put forth at Copenhagen would require a smaller reduction in emissions-to-GDP ratios, but the cost of these reductions (relative to GDP) could be even greater.

Conclusion

This chapter has argued that the world economy is undergoing a profound transformation, reflecting the acceleration of growth in developing countries, home to the vast majority of the world's population, and their increased integration into global markets. Although many countries have been left behind, large opportunities for greater efficiency have been exploited in recent years with the surges in international flows of trade, capital, labour and technology. However, the potential gains to come are much larger, with productivity and living standards in developing countries still a fraction of those in advanced countries, which are innovating at a rapid rate.

These opportunities could open new avenues for development in both the richest countries, which will find they can address vast new markets for their advanced products, and the poorest, which may find that the climb up the technological ladder through manufactures exports is possible as the giant economies of Asia migrate to more sophisticated products and present large new markets for both commodity and basic manufactures exports.

These favourable prospects are, however, far from a foregone conclusion, and no country can expect to capture the prize automatically. Sound domestic policies that favour integration into global markets—including macroeconomic stability, a sound business climate and appropriate investments in education—will be necessary for success. However, even more will be needed. The community of nations will need to work together to continue to build the international integration frameworks essential for trade, capital, people and technology to continue to flow. They will jointly need to build stronger safeguards against massive financial crises. They will need to find a way to avert environmental catastrophe in the form of uncontrolled climate change. Above all, they will have to manage the historic power shift towards new actors from the developing world without resorting to war or protectionism.

Notes

1 This chapter updates previous work, including the book *Juggernaut* (2011) by the author and William Shaw, and the paper 'The World Order in 2050' (2010) by the author Bennett Stancil. Excellent research assistance was provided by Zaahira Wyne.
2 World Bank 1997.
3 Wilson and Purushothaman 2003.
4 Hawksworth 2006.
5 World Bank 2008: 45.
6 Armington and Dadush 1993.
7 Balassa 1964; Samuelson 1964.
8 All individuals with a per capita income above US$4,000 in 2005 PPP terms are considered to be members of the global middle and rich class (GMR). This follows the World Bank definition, which

defines the middle class as those with per capita incomes between $4,000 and $17,000. Those with incomes above $17,000 are considered members of the rich class.

9 Poverty models are based on studies by Ravallion (2001), Ahluwalia *et al.* (1978), and Anand and Kanbur (1991). Poverty data are from World Bank (2009) and the United Nations University World Institute for Development Economics Research.

10 These include China, India, Russia, Brazil, Mexico, Argentina, Indonesia, Turkey and South Africa. Although Saudi Arabia is also a developing G20 economy, it was not included in these calculations because data were not available for its distribution of income.

11 This is the ratio of the GMR population in developing G20 countries to the total that includes the GMR in all advanced countries. It is assumed that more than 95% of the population in advanced countries is in the GMR class.

12 Grynberg and Newton 2007.

13 OECD/FAO 2009.

14 World Bank 2008.

15 The Intergovernmental Panel on Climate Change estimates that in Europe, Australia and New Zealand, growing seasons will lengthen, frost risk will fall, and new crops will become viable (Parry *et al.* 2007).

Bibliography

Ahluwalia, Montek S., Nicholas G. Carter and Hollis B. Chenery (1978) 'Growth and Poverty in Developing Countries', *Journal of Development Economics* 6: 299–341.

Anand, Sudhir and Ravi Kanbur (1991) 'International Poverty Projections', Policy Research Working Paper Series 617, World Bank, Washington, DC.

Armington, Paul and Uri Dadush (1993) 'The Fourth Pole', *International Economic Insights*, May/June: 2–4.

Balassa, Bela (1964) 'The Purchasing Power Parity Doctrine: A Reappraisal', *Journal of Political Economy* 72: 584–96, burbuja.udesa.edu.ar/materias/kawa/ecintmon/balassa64.pdf.

Dadush, Uri and William Shaw (2011) *Juggernaut*, Carnegie Endowment for International Peace, Washington, DC.

Dadush, Uri and Bennett Stancil (2010) 'The World Order in 2050', Carnegie Endowment for International Peace, April.

Grynberg, Roman and Samantha Newton (eds) (2007) *Commodity Prices and Development*, Oxford University Press, New York.

Hawksworth, John (2006) 'The World in 2050', PricewaterhouseCoopers, London.

Mankiw, N. Gregory (2003) 'The Manufacturing Sector', Remarks at the Exchequer Club, Washington, DC, 17 December.

OECD/FAO (Organisation for Economic Co-operation and Development/Food and Agriculture Organization) (2009) 'OECD-FAO Agricultural Outlook 2009–18', Paris.

Parry, Martin, Osvaldo Canziani, Jean Palutikof, Paul van der Linden and Clair Hanson (eds) (2007) *Climate Change 2007: Impacts, Adaptation and Vulnerability*, Cambridge University Press, Cambridge.

Ravallion, Martin (2001) 'Growth, Inequality, and Poverty: Looking Beyond Averages', Policy Research Working Paper Series 2558, World Bank, Washington, DC.

Samuelson, Paul (1964) 'Theoretical Notes on Trade Problems', *Review of Economics and Statistics* 46: 145–54, www.clarku.edu/faculty/mcallan/Econ308/Readings/samuelson.pdf.

United Nations University World Institute for Development Economics Research (UN-WIDER) (2008) World Income Inequality Database, Version 2.0c, May, www.wider.unu.edu/research/Database/en_GB/database/.

Wilson, Dominic and Roopa Purushothaman (2003) 'Dreaming with BRICs: The Path to 2050', Global Economics Paper 99, Goldman Sachs, New York.

World Bank (1997) *Global Economic Prospects and the Developing Countries*, Washington, DC.

——(2008) *Global Economic Prospects: Technology Diffusion in the Developing World*, Washington, DC, siteresources.worldbank.org/INTGEP2008/Resources/complete-report.pdf.

——(2009) *2009 World Development Indicators*, Washington, DC.

Part II
The BRICS

3

Brazil

Albert Fishlow

Introduction

Brazil is now one of the world's principal economies. Gross national product (GNP) in 2012 ranked sixth or seventh, and population fifth. In per capita terms, adjusted by purchasing power parity, results were less illustrious. Brazil stood closer to 80th. Size alone did not translate into national productivity.

That was especially true during much of the 19th century, before income growth began to accelerate after the 1870s. During the 20th century Brazil achieved one of the highest rates of expansion among developing countries until the lost decade of the 1980s, when improvement was essentially nil. That last experience coincided with a return to civil governance and a series of failed attempts to terminate mounting inflation in two elected administrations. None the less, that period was short, and lessons were learned.

With the Plano Real of 1994, growth and price stability finally took hold. Happily, that course has continued up to the present. Along with expanding income, poverty declined and the very unequal income distribution began to improve. The Bolsa Família, a conditional cash transfer programme, contributed to this result, as did a greater than average rise in the minimum wage. Attention turned to other social programmes, like health, education and social security, bringing improvements to all. In 2010, in rapid recovery from the Great Recession, economic expansion mounted to new heights of 7.5%. Expectations resurged: Brazil was not condemned to Sisyphean failure to achieve an advance to first world status.

With Dilma Rousseff's presidency beginning in 2011, lower growth and higher inflation have returned. Seeking to cope with that recurrence has become a central issue as Brazil girds itself for the presidential campaign in 2014. In the last section of this chapter I return to present policy choices and their future implications, but beforehand, some brief discussion of the past will help in appreciating the challenges that lie ahead.

Looking back much longer[1]

Portuguese colonial possession of Brazil, originating with Pedro Álvarez Cabral's discovery in 1500, extended until 1822. Remissions to Portugal were financed by the export of precious metals, diamonds, tobacco, cotton and sugar produced under slavery. As other Latin American countries struggled for freedom through military revolt in the post-Napoleonic era, Brazil's independence emerged more peacefully. The Prince Regent, Dom Pedro I, already in Brazil as a result of prior French invasion of Portugal in 1807, simply accepted dominion as Emperor Dom Pedro I. That substitution came with a transfer of previous Portuguese debt, a dominant position of England as a source of manufactured products, and a continuation of slave importation for almost another 30 years.

Brazil succeeded in only slow expansion until the great international flow of trade and capital beginning in the 1870s. That much seems to be agreed upon. Despite the increase in coffee production, which by the 1830s accounted for more than 40% of aggregate exports, the domestic economy did not take off. Gains occurred before 1870 principally as a consequence of special circumstances: a rise in coffee prices, a late surge in sugar exports, and favourable, but temporary, effects of the US Civil War on cotton exports. Terms of trade rose by 50%, principally as a result of cheaper prices of imports between 1830 and 1850, with little change thereafter. The long war of the Triple Alliance with Paraguay in the 1860s did change the distribution of government expenditures and their magnitude, creating large deficits and inflation, as well as increasing the foreign debt. Like the US Civil War, there seem to have been only limited consequences for economic activity as a whole. According to Abreu and Lago, per capita income grew by approximately 0.2% annually between 1822 and 1870, and the population by around 1.5%.

From 1870 to 1913 Brazil entered more vigorously into the world economy. Immigration occurred from Italy to southern Brazil along with domestic movement from the north-east. Railways expanded, with large foreign investment in response to governmental guaranteed rates of return. Coffee exports multiplied, as did later expansion of rubber sales abroad. Domestic production of textiles began to expand, in the aftermath of the Encilhamento's rapid burst of inflation and devaluation in the first years of the new republic after 1889. Despite a brief relapse thereafter, and a need to renegotiate its external debt in 1898, Brazil benefited once more from improved terms of trade in the decade before the First World War. Indeed, for the first time, Brazil adhered to the gold standard. During this period, the population expanded by 2.2% annually, and national per capita income by at least 2.5%, but much higher productivity growth was to be found in the thriving southern part of the country, possibly to the extent of allowing expansion of 1.5% per capita.[2]

Per capita income remained one-fifth that of neighbouring Argentina, and had declined from perhaps one-half of the US level in 1820 to about one-10th in 1913. Brazil, despite its great size and its greater advance after 1870, lagged considerably behind other Latin American countries. Integration into an expanding international economy had come late and in a diluted form. Regional differences between the north-east and the south would continue to widen in the 20th century as more active protective policies of state engagement to enhance industrial production evolved. Concern about coffee producers stockpiling excess supply in order to regularize price came earlier. Brazil managed better than most other Latin American countries to reconcile the divergent interests of its nascent import-substituting manufacturing sector and its still dominant agricultural class. A larger state and tolerance for inflation were two significant reasons.

The Great Depression: a saviour[3]

Despite early efforts at import substitution in the 1890s and subsequent rapid growth of manufactures between 1906 and 1912, Brazil on the eve of the First World War had only a primitive industrial structure. Textiles continued to be imported; external sources accounted for more than one-third of consumption. Although considerable advances in the production of processed foodstuffs had occurred, agricultural imports remained large, rivalling those of iron and steel. The domestic capital goods sector was essentially non-existent. No more than 3% of the labour force was engaged in manufactures.

The war interrupted this development process based upon the continuing expansion of exports and the beginning of import substitution. Trade was curtailed, especially imports, and population inflows were much lower. There was irregular and slower industrial growth, a reduced rate of capital formation imposed by limited access to imports, and evidence of rising urban profits inspired by higher inflation.

International conflict was therefore not a great stimulus for industrialization, but neither was it an unequivocal check. Absence of imports reversed an earlier rise that was gathering force owing to abundant foreign exchange generated by the Amazon rubber boom. These windfall gains found their way into a considerable post-war expansion of industrial capacity. None the less, Brazilian industrialization was still fragile. As late as 1919 imports of manufactures constituted almost as large a contribution to industrial supply as domestic value added. External competition remained, despite protection afforded by high tariffs.

That threat became apparent during the 1920s. Conservative domestic monetary policy had as its objective appreciation of the milreis. Industrial growth slowed under tight credit and cheaper imports. Between 1922 and 1926 it virtually stagnated, recovering thereafter. Had the influx of imports not occurred—financed in part by rapid expansion of foreign loans—industrial growth in those years perhaps would have been close to 8%. As a consequence, the decade ended with excess capacity and uncertain direction.

The Great Depression definitively resolved both. Brazil was among the countries initially hardest hit, not least because new investments in coffee undertaken in the 1920s began to yield output only in the early 1930s. Coffee prices fell by 60% between 1929 and 1931, and continued at low levels thereafter. Consequently, Brazilian capacity to import never went beyond two-thirds of its earlier magnitude.

Yet, Brazil succeeded in sustaining an industrial growth rate of more than 10% annually between 1932 and 1939; that of gross domestic product (GDP) attained almost 6%. In the first instance, government policy stimulated demand by protecting, at least partially, the internal income of coffee producers, through the purchase and destruction of coffee stocks, as well as by a speedy real devaluation. Coffee sector receipts modestly recovered between 1932 and 1936. Second, federal government deficits, some not initially intended and generated by the uprising in the state of São Paulo, also helped. Third, there was an expansive monetary policy.

The role of coffee policy alone should not be exaggerated. Not much more than 10% of total income was generated by the sector, and receipts were not fully sustained. In the absence of compensatory action there, however, results clearly would have been less positive. Brazil proceeded as autonomously as it did because the economy was not so open: the ratio of exports to GDP was not much more than 15%. That independence granted scope for national action.

Supply responded initially on the basis of the excess capacity accumulated in the 1920s. Competitive imports fell rapidly as limited foreign exchange was diverted to debt service. Labour intensity of production increased during the decade as extra shifts were employed fully to utilize scarce capital. New investment was undertaken during the period, but in amounts limited by access to imported machines and concentrated in the newer sectors.

Rapid growth in manufactures during the decade was underwritten by a massive substitution of imports. In aggregate, about half of the observed increase in industrial sector value added can be explained by reduced import supply. Most rapidly growing industries were found in the intermediate and capital goods sectors, reflecting earlier domestic production of consumer goods: textiles, shoes, clothing and foodstuffs. Industry became increasingly concentrated in São Paulo, which even before the depression was more oriented to these technologically advanced sectors.

By 1939 Brazil's manufacturing sector employed some 9.5% of the labour force. Some diversification had occurred. Industry remained, however, relatively backward. Import substitution driven by necessity, while impressive, imposed a capital-scarce industrialization less capable of international competition. That was despite constant real wages—a possibility sustainable only for short periods under special economic and political circumstances. Industrialization under the impulse of adverse shocks is not without some limitations.

Table 3.1 provides a summary of income, inflation, trade and fiscal data from 1900 to 1939. Up until 1913 data were scarce. As Luis Catão has recently shown, research can produce a better measure of price movements from 1870 to 1913.[4] A smaller gain occurred as economic globalization proceeded between 1900 and 1913, with much more rapid advance after the early 1930s. In the first instance, outward orientation and British foreign investment predominated. In the second, it was closure and domestic demand alone that drove the economy at a much greater rate in the midst of the Great Depression.

Import substitution unfurled[5]

Post-Second World War industrialization evolved as a deliberate policy of state intervention. That differentiates it from earlier advances. Three elements characterize the disequilibrium model that emerged.

One was reliance upon commercial policy to implement a large transfer of resources between agriculture and industry. Early on, an overvalued exchange rate taxed agriculture while subsidizing industry through providing low-cost imports. Later, however, this advantage to industry via more favourable exchange rates had to give way to direct fiscal support as primary export prices fell soon after the Korean War.

That imposed a new characteristic of rapid industrial growth previously absent: accelerating inflation. Rising government expenditures to support subsidies, essential infrastructure and urbanization were not matched by increased taxes. The fiscal deficit accordingly grew, and was financed by accommodating monetary expansion and forced domestic savings as inflation progressively rose.

The third characteristic was reliance upon foreign capital. Direct investment within the dynamic industrial sector matched the entrepreneurial and technological requirements of more

Table 3.1 Aggregate economic data, 1900–39

	1900	1913	1929	1939
GDP (bill)[a]	12,332	21,734	44,941	67,712
Product per capita[a]	680	919	1,366	1,681
annual rate of growth	2.3%	2.5%	2.1%	(4.2%)[b]
Inflation rate	−8.96%	−4.10%	−3.57%	2.01%
Investment/product	4.21%[c]	20.33%[d]	10.98%	13.06%
Exports/product	18.6%	14.8%	11.9%	11.2%
Government expenditure/product	15.0%	18.1%[d]	13.7%	16.0%
Fiscal balance/product	−3.1%	−2.8%	−0.6%	−2.5%
Current account/product	3.5%	–	–	1.1%

Source: ipeadata, *Estatísticas Históricas do Brasil*; Raymond W. Goldsmith, *Brasil 1850–1984: Desenvolvimento Financeiro sob um Século de Inflação*, São Paulo, 1986
Notes: [a] These data are in 2012 US$; per capita data utilize population estimates as corrected by Mortara, not those in ipeadata; [b] 1932–39; [c] Value is for 1901; [d] Values for 1913 are high owing to large public investment that year.

sophisticated and diversified manufactures. Consumer durable and intermediate sectors then favoured by the government could not have expanded domestic auspices. Foreign investment was especially needed to finance imports of capital goods as export receipts stagnated and terms of trade fell after 1953.

All three elements so central to the Brazilian import substitution model were subject to reversal. Exchange overvaluation eventually took its toll on any diversified supply of exports. That began to inhibit access to imports. The necessary taxes went beyond the temporary of bonanza coffee profits. Forced savings relied upon a continuing rise in the rate of inflation, and such an acceleration provoked additional distortions. Not least of these was the cyclical effect upon real wages of urban workers. Apparent wage gains would fall short of any real increase when price increases were greater than they had been. As inflation mounted to 40% by the end of the decade, union resistance mounted.

Foreign investment supplemented by private short-term capital inflows attracted by very favourable returns were not stable and dependable sources of finance. Investment was bunched as large projects were undertaken to the point of completion, as in the automobile sector. This was not a smooth process even for an economy as large as Brazil's. Time was then needed to allow the growth in supply to catch up with demand.

Efforts to resolve these contradictions in time proved inadequate. Exports responded only slowly to more favourable policies, and confronted a competitive world market where prices of primary products were falling. Fiscal and monetary policy operated irregularly and inadequately. Foreign capital flows dried up, provoking continuing balance of payments crises in the early 1960s and partial and unsuccessful short-term liberalization under the guise of the International Monetary Fund (IMF).

It later became fashionable to criticize this flawed import substitution industrialization from the perspective of the successful Asian development strategies of the late 1960s and early 1970s that relied upon industrial exports. Three observations on the Brazilian experience place the policies that were pursued in a more favourable light.

First, the contribution of import substitution during the 1950s was not a significant component of the domestic demand for manufactures. The ratio of imports to domestic production was already quite low by 1949 and its subsequent decline during the decade accounts for less than one-fifth of the observed growth of manufactures. This is in sharp contrast to the Great Depression experience. Even a constant import–income ratio would have permitted significant growth of manufactures.

In the second instance, Brazilian industrialization was not as inefficient as the inflated tariff structure made it appear. Impossibly high rates of effective protection are the result of temporary measures to deal with the balance of payments, and do not measure real cost differentials. The economic miracle of the late 1960s had its basis in the diversified industrial structure and excess capacity derived from the past rather than divine mystery. Brazil's subsequent positive export performance in manufactures benefited from subsidies, but not entirely. That capital-intensive industrial development was accompanied by a 2.4% annual rate of productivity growth that far exceeded previous experience.

Third, exchange rate devaluation to encourage exports would have been inadequate. Primary product specialization in the later 1950s did not represent a feasible solution. Brazil faced international competition from other producers, even in coffee. Policies and priorities logically favoured industry under such circumstances, and were not as prejudiced against external market opportunities as some retrospective views suggest.

In any event, Brazilian import substitution led to increasing domestic inflation and balance of payments disequilibrium in the early 1960s. The IMF intervention was too little and too late to help. Political circumstances—the resignation of President Jânio Quadros and the apparent radicalization of his successor, President João Goulart—rapidly deteriorated. US aid contributions from the Alliance for Progress were caught up in fears of foreign influence. By the end of March 1964, the military intervened and imposed a quite different economic solution.

The Brazilian miracle

That new model was characterized by greater integration into international markets; by a larger and more centralized fiscal capacity; by a structure of subsidies and incentives favouring profits rather than wages; by enactment of monetary correction to diminish inflation induced distortion; by institutional reforms modernizing and altering the rules of the social security system, internal financial markets, tax laws, etc.; and by technocratic economic management as a counterpart to authoritarian political control.

For all its frank commitment to capitalism, this strategy never corresponded to a free enterprise prototype. Brazilian economic strategy has been more pragmatic and rooted in an interventionist tradition. Government participation in the economy, an object of rightist criticism in 1963, actually increased after military intervention. Public investment, whether direct in infrastructure or through state enterprises, rose as a percentage of capital formation. Regulation of economic activity did not wither away. Subsidies and incentives proliferated and so did price controls; they were accepted and welcomed so long as private profits also grew. Public control over resources expanded via taxes as well as forced savings accumulated through the social security system.

Nor did the prior emphasis upon industrialization alter. Agricultural exports did not receive anything like the same subsidies as manufactures, and indeed continued to be implicitly taxed by protection against foreign industrial imports. Agricultural production for domestic consumption received comparatively little attention, not surprisingly since the principal foodstuffs were primarily produced by small and medium-sized units. Foreign investment and modern capital-intensive technology were again welcomed.

This model has been praised for the extraordinary growth it fostered between 1968 and 1973: a rate of aggregate expansion in excess of 10% a year is no mean achievement. Yet it was also criticized for its failure to distribute income more equitably and expand access to public services to the poor. Both reactions have a basis. Indeed, this same combination of concerns about production and distribution continues to this day.

Here I wish to stress the special character and importance of Brazilian integration into world capital markets as a component of the model. Despite rapid and unprecedented export volume growth (about 10% since the mid-1960s) and favourable price trends of the same magnitude, Brazilian recovery involved even more rapid import expansion. The current account balance moved from a surplus in 1965 and 1966 to a deficit of 2.3% of GDP in 1971–73; by the end of 1973, before the rise in oil prices had its full consequence, the external debt registered 17% of GDP compared to about 10% in 1967.

That acceleration of product growth represents debt-led, rather than export-led growth. External resources, predominantly on commercial terms as Brazil for the first time became a factor in the Euro-dollar market, guaranteed availability of foreign exchange for voracious import requirements. Those resources also permitted a surge in investment that did not have to be financed domestically at the expense of consumption. They rendered unnecessary any internal capital market reforms to achieve equivalent finance.

External indebtedness continued to expand after 1973 at even more rapid rates. The quadrupling of oil prices caught Brazil just when internal bottlenecks and cyclical excesses were creating internal economic adjustment problems and inflation was resurgent. Especially vulnerable to the rise in oil prices because 80% of its oil consumption needs were satisfied by imports, Brazil opted to postpone its adjustment to external imbalance by relying even more heavily on debt. By the end of 1978 the external debt had mounted to more than US$40 billion, representing 25% of GDP.

Such debt-financed adjustment produced less positive economic returns than the earlier phase of debt-led growth. Aggregate expansion during the 1970s proceeded at rates almost half of the earlier period, and with a stop-go alternation reflecting the absence of a strategy to deal both with the external crisis and internal imbalances in agriculture, not to mention accumulating social disparities. Debt management has been weak, permitting massive acquisition of reserves and domestic monetary expansion. Limitation of imports—held virtually constant in nominal terms between 1974 and 1978 through stricter controls—created difficulties. Inflation, at high levels since 1974, accelerated to rates approaching 100%. Oil prices went up again in June 1979.

Despite this deteriorating scenario of the 1970s, the extent of Brazil's advance between 1950 and 1980 is quite impressive. Table 3.2 provides some quantitative data. Continued domestic protection allowed industrial production to flourish and urbanization to advance. Brazil was the leader not only within Latin America, but even challenged the Republic of Korea (South Korea) and Taiwan as they rapidly expanded. Within a world where developing countries for the first time began to keep pace with the industrialized countries, and even exceeded them, Brazil stood out.

That was not to last. In December 1979 the government recognized the crisis confronting Brazil. A new liberalization package and a new strategy were proclaimed. This was a second coming of Finance Minister Antônio Delfim Netto. It was less beneficial than his first. The heterodoxy advanced in 1979 soon gave way to orthodox austerity in November 1980. No longer were external banks willing to offer much needed finance. Debt-led recession finally came, and stayed.

Proliferating deterioration of the international economy in the wake of US attempts to reduce its double-digit inflation rate did not help. Not until 1984 would Brazil again achieve rising per capita incomes. Before then, in 1982, after an election that was favourable to the opposition, Brazil went once more to the IMF, as it had 20 years before. A series of altered agreements ensued, at every regular evaluation, but high inflation did not yield. That breakthrough was only to occur later.

In those deteriorating circumstances, the original intent of the military to appoint one final general in the indirect presidential election of 1985 gave way. A civilian would be chosen

Table 3.2 Aggregate economic data, 1950–80

	1950	1973	1980
GDP (bill)[a]	120	632	1,022
Product per capita[a]	2,310	6,290	8,590
annual rate of growth		4.50%	4.60%
Inflation rate	9.0%	29.6%	92.1%
Investment/product	12.8%	20.4%	23.6%
Exports/product	9.2%	7.8%	9.0%
Government expenditure/product	19.8%	22.2%	24.0%
Fiscal deficit/product[b]	2.23%	−2.59%	0.60%
Current account/product	0.8%	−3.3%	8.6%[c]

Source: ipeadata, IMF, World Bank
Notes: [a] These data are in US$ of 2012; [b] excludes deficits of state enterprises; [c] overvaluation biases direct calculation; I have tried to compensate.

instead. As it turned out, a fusion of the minority political opposition, the Partido do Movimento Democrático Brasileiro (PMDB), and part of the Partido Democrático Social (PDS), the majority party, occurred. Tancredo Neves would win as president-elect, and José Sarney as his vice-president-elect.

An unfortunate illness interceded, and Tancredo never served. Instead, Sarney assumed leadership of the new republic in its first years. Ever since, a new constitution, much amended to be sure, has prevailed, and direct elections have been held regularly. Inflation was definitively tamed by the Real Plan in 1994. Social programmes received increased attention and expenditure. Civil society has flourished, to the extent of presidential impeachment, and in 2012 judicial conviction of many in the Partido dos Trabalhadores (PT—Worker's Party) leadership for participation in the *mensalão* scandal of 1995. Brazil truly started over in 1985.

Starting over[6]

In 1985, the Sarney government simultaneously confronted two immediate tasks: restructuring the political system inherited from prior military rule and ending a continuing inflation of more than 200% annually that had defied the efforts of the IMF.

The 1988 Constitution accomplished the first objective, after considerable debate and differences that regularly led on to creation of new political parties peopled by those exiting older ones. Frequently, individual ambitions seem to dominate any substantive divergence. At the last count, there were more than 70 amendments in place, and more than 25 parties represented in Congress.

The heterodox 1986 Cruzado Plan, intended to implant price stability, had less success. After an initial rapid decline to single-digit price increases, by the end of the year, after an election where the PMDB won a congressional majority (the only time a single party was to do so), price and wage controls had to be scrapped. They were no longer working. Not long after, the finance minister had to go. Despite following ministers and plans, any relief was temporary. Indeed, Brazil became unable to meet the required payments of interest and principal to private creditors. Inflation accelerated to a level of 80% per month by March 1990, prior to the inauguration of President Fernando Collor.

The awaited Collor Plan had its roots in the Erhard Plan of post-Second World War Germany. There a sharp reduction in the quantity of money in circulation achieved success. In Brazil, despite achieving a large primary surplus on the fiscal side, the Collor Plan did not. Shock treatment did not work owing to erratic monetary policy, a fluctuating exchange rate and a labour market in disequilibrium. There was no anchor to guarantee price stability. Both heterodox and orthodox approaches need to persuade the public of likely success. Otherwise, initial confidence fades and inflation rapidly returns as governments have no alternative but to increase the quantity of money.

In October 1982 Vice-President Itamar Franco assumed the presidency following the successful vote in the Câmara on Collor's trial for impeachment. Immediate return to higher growth was the goal. Inflation persisted, although the finance ministers appointed did not. There could be no coherent economic policy when the average ministerial stay was less than two months.

That all changed when Fernando Henrique Cardoso took office in 1993, assembling a group of economists that had been vital to the formulation—but not the application—of the earlier Cruzado Plan. This time, the arrangement would be done correctly, allowing market adjustments for prices and wages rather than holding them fixed. Administered public sector prices were able to adjust as well. This time there was no automatic inflation trigger built in, and indexing was abolished for assets of less than a year. A primary fiscal surplus and a restrictive monetary policy checked demand, while abundant international reserves, capital inflow, favourable terms of trade and lower tariffs allowed income growth to exceed product expansion. There was a genuine anchor provided by a stable exchange rate.

An initially hesitant public gradually came to believe in the stability of the real. They did so in time to elect Cardoso as president and he took office on 1 January 1995.

During his two terms, important changes occurred. Privatization, already on the agenda during previous administrations, accelerated. There was no movement back, despite the election of PT successors. Financial reform took place. While costly, and internal debt rose as a consequence, failure of domestic banks after the Real Plan was managed successfully. So was consolidation of state and municipal indebtedness. Trade liberalization, already underway since the Collor years, was maintained. Social security, health and education were revamped through constitutional amendment.

When financial crisis threatened in early 1999, following the earlier Asian and Russian downturns, forcing large devaluation and recession, the government responded by assuring regular primary fiscal surpluses and raising federal revenues. Brazil received pledges of more external assistance from the IMF and other international agencies than had any other country previously. Social policy, the intended objective of the second term, had to yield. The Law of Fiscal Responsibility was passed in May 2000 and transformed the budgetary process. An altered economic structure took shape. Fiscal discipline became a requirement, and has remained an obligation—with mounting flexibility during recent years. Exchange rate variability was introduced. Inflation targeting became the practice of the Central Bank.

These accomplishments were more appreciated internationally than domestically. Cardoso's presidency ended with his declining popularity, and a rash of additional problems. Lack of rainfall in 2001 created an energy shortage; then came the US downturn, and the terrorist attacks of 11 September 2001. In December there was the Argentine exit of President Fernando de la Rua. Foreign inflows virtually ceased in 2002 as a clear break with recent advances threatened, amid still another agreement with the IMF for greater assistance.

Continuity first, but changes later

Luiz Inácio Lula da Silva, a labour leader and organizer of the PT, rose to president of Brazil on 1 January 2003. His inauguration afforded great joy to the left, not only in Brazil, but in the rest of Latin America. Lula promised profound forthcoming change in his inaugural address, rejecting the free market policies of his predecessor and emphasizing a campaign to eliminate hunger and want among the poor.

Immediate economic challenges, however, took priority. The exchange rate had devalued as his victory became likely, and the Central Bank interest rate, SELIC, had risen to more than 25%, yielding much the highest real rate in the entire world. His choice of Henrique Meirelles as head of the Central Bank (who remained in that position until the end of 2010) and of Antônio Palocci as minister of finance went a long way towards easing the anxiety of the international financial community. Together, the two managed to restrain internal demand by enlarging the fiscal primary surplus, and only slowly reducing interest rates. Recession in this first year could, and would, be blamed upon the inadequate policies of the Cardoso administration.

No Plan B, the hope of many fervent PT adherents, was ever to substitute that initial conservative stance. Those supporters sought full reversal of prior privatization and a Brazil that was receptive to globalization and foreign direct investment (FDI). Instead, to their chagrin, came an early proposal by the government for a constitutional amendment designed to limit the deficit accruing in state pensions, this time by imposing constraints for the first time upon employees in the public sector.

The economy responded with high average rates of growth in the years after recovery began to take hold in 2004. There was no miracle, but steady gains appeared not only in domestic performance, but also in the export growth of commodities, favoured by improving terms of trade. That led to a continuously large positive commercial surplus and, much more briefly, a surplus on the current account. Brazil was able to pay off its debt to the IMF, and as exchange rates regularly strengthened, to attract FDI and financial inflows. Reserves began to increase, and interest rates moved down—too slowly, as far as the industrial sector was concerned.

Upon re-election in the autumn of 2006, Lula launched the Programa de Aceleração do Crescimento (PAC), a set of public, and associated private, investments designed to accelerate the rate of growth to 5% per year. The largest components of the PAC, and its successor PAC II, were directed towards infrastructure and Petrobrás, but this effort was slow to get fully underway and could not manage to achieve its goals. Brazil experienced accelerating growth in 2007 and 2008, but investment managed to attain only 17% of GDP, too low to guarantee sustainable expansion.

At the end of 2008, subsequent to the failure of Lehman Brothers within the USA in September, Brazil got caught up in the Great Recession spreading to all parts of the world. There was no exemption for developing countries as the proponents of Third World decoupling had hoped. Two negative quarters of performance rapidly cooled the excess expansion of domestic demand. The Banco Nacional do Desenvolvimento Econômico e Social (BNDES) was given increased resources to lend, and reductions in taxes on consumer durables were put in place, as policy offsets to the decline.

Recovery rapidly occurred. The final tabulation for 2009 came out barely negative—a far cry from more pessimistic predictions—and in the final year of Lula's mandate there was growth of 7.5%, bringing memories of the miracle years at the end of the 1960s and 1970s. SELIC rates, after falling to their lowest real levels in many years, around 5%, again moved upwards as the Central Bank sought to curb inflationary pressures. With continuing inflows of external money, the exchange rate appreciated and new taxes upon entry of foreign capital were imposed. Terms of trade again turned favourable, augmenting domestic income.

Adding to Brazilian optimism are substantial oil deposits off the coast. These sub-salt holdings promise to place the country among principal world petroleum producers over the next decade. They will require substantial investment for their development. Brazil passed legislation elevating the role, and profit share, of Petrobrás vis-à-vis private companies. Henceforth, the latter can bid for drilling rights only through production-sharing agreements, rather than by operating independently. In September 2010 Petrobrás transferred a sizeable amount of capital to the government in return for the proven Tupi field. This was the first stage of what many, especially political leaders, see as a bonanza of future riches available for expanded social programmes.

The period from 2003 to 2010 saw expansion of income at a rate of 4%. According to the PT, if one excludes 2003, the rate increases to 4.4%, a much better result than that experienced during the previous eight-year Cardoso period. Inflation came down, the real interest rate declined, poverty fell and income distribution improved as the Bolsa Família, incorporating more than 20% of the population, was launched. Minimum wages, too, grew well beyond the rise in income. Added to all of this were palpable improvements in education, health and greater provision of pensions for old age. A new lower-middle class, encompassing some 35 million persons, especially benefited as income distribution continued to improve.

Lula, as a consequence, was widely lauded for these accomplishments. He travelled abroad even more than his predecessor, and was honoured everywhere. Foreign policy became a central theme. Brazil reached out to Africa, the Middle East and Asia. A quest for a permanent position on the UN Security Council moved upward on the agenda. Brazil asserted leadership of the developing countries in the still unfulfilled Doha Round. Regular meetings with the other BRICs (Brazil, Russia, India and the People's Republic of China) were established. Brazil became an active member of the G20, an international grouping of the world's leading economies. At the same time, Brazil terminated the ongoing negotiations for a Free Trade Area of the Americas, preferring instead to emphasize its association with other countries, particularly Mercosul (the Southern Common Market), in South America.

Close to the end of the Lula term, Brazil even reached out to play a role as a mediator in the Middle East, jointly with Turkey. That came to nought. The Security Council soon rejected the apparent accord. However, Brazil's stature as an international player was enhanced, at least for a time.

It was little wonder that Dilma Rousseff won the subsequent election handily, despite no prior electoral experience. The PT, despite the publicized mensalão crisis, whereby allied members of Congress received regular payments, managed to emerge with new gains, notably in the poorer north-east, the birthplace of Lula. President Dilma started with a larger majority, constructed of many political parties, than Lula had achieved in either of his electoral victories.

Table 3.3 provides a statistical summary of renewed expansion from 1980 to 2010. Despite the positive results of recent years, all did not sit well for the new administration. Investment remained too low to achieve the growth of 5% that was the immediate objective. The exchange rate was overvalued, hampering exports, particularly of manufactured products. Educational quality continued to be a major issue, and one not entirely resolved by spending more money. Indeed, the cumulative social expenditures of Brazil were well above the Organisation for Economic Co-operation and Development (OECD) average, without evidence that they were having the desired outcome. Political reform continued to lag, too: constitutional change altering the multitude of candidacies for the Congressional House seemed unlikely ever to happen.

Looking forward

In the first two years of Rousseff's presidency, aggregate economic performance went from bad to worse. In 2011 growth was 2.7%; in 2012 it was a mere 0.9%. All of this happened despite Central Bank reduction of interest rates to a nominal SELIC rate of 7.25% by the end of 2012. Along with it came additional Treasury credits to BNDES for expanded lending to the industrial sector. Public banks put pressure on the private sector by lowering their interest rates as

Table 3.3 Aggregate economic data, 1985–2010

	1985	1994	2002	2010
GDP (bill)[a]	1084	1288	1571	2146
Product per capita[a]	8170	8450	8990	11250
annual rate of growth		0.4%	0.7%	2.8%
Inflation rate	248.5%	2252.0%	10.60%	8.2%
Investment/product	18.0%	20.8%	16.4%	19.5%
Exports/product	13.0%	9.5%	14.1%	10.9%
Government expenditure/product	23.8%	29.2%	39.5%	38.1%
Fiscal deficit/product	−4.7%	1.1%	−1.2%	−1.7%
Current account/product	−0.1%	−0.3%	−1.5%	−2.2%

Source: ipeadata, IMF, World Bank
Notes: [a] These data are in US$ of 2012.

well. There was greater control over fiscal policy (partially eroded by postponing federal payments until the new year and similar delay mechanisms) to compensate. A better mix of fiscal and monetary decisions happened, but renewed growth did not.

Admittedly, the world economy did not help, but the principal blame was unresponsive domestic supply. Investment declined as a percentage of output, while real wages went up, and unemployment continued at record lower levels. What dynamism there was stemmed from consumption, assisted by lower taxes and greater credit, but domestic industry as a whole failed to advance sharply despite a considerable devaluation of the real.

Rousseff's strong initial commitment was to industrial policy and a domestic sector increasing its share of product and utilizing more sophisticated technology. That undoubtedly remains, but in 2013, with low growth persisting, inflation still high, and Central Bank interest rates again on the rise, a new direction has been signalled. BNDES has turned its attention to looming infrastructure requirements: ports, roads, railroads, airports, electricity generation and transmission, housing and others. That is reinforced by preparations for the upcoming World Cup in 2014 and Olympic Games in 2016, and, of course, there is the reality of an upcoming presidential election in which Rousseff, with impressive public support, is favoured.

There remain two sharply different domestic perceptions of the Brazilian economic future. One, emanating from the PT, seeks a partial return to protection, import substitution and public sector expenditure as key. A large and expanding state is fundamental. The other emphasizes a need to take advantage of a globalizing world affording opportunities for greater Brazilian trade participation, with the North as well as the South. This is hardly a free enterprise alternative, but one in search of efficient intervention. The state will hardly disappear, nor shrink in importance. In particular, education will be a prime area of importance.

To a considerable extent, *Brasil em 2022*, produced at the very end of the Lula administration, conveys the former. That document specifies an annual growth rate of 7%, along with impressive social gains and much greater income equality. Those hundreds of objectives— although some are mutually inconsistent—have hardly been forgotten. In April 2013, at an event announcing expanded public works, Rousseff reiterated that doubling income per capita by 2022 remained the goal.[7]

That is a miracle of historic Chinese proportions, but one achieved with considerably less drastic means. Brazil accomplished its miracle with an investment rate that was less than half China's, a labour force already urban, much greater government less reliance on social objectives, and international trade. Social security obligations will rise in future years, gradually eliminating the primary surplus, and increasing the financial deficit, even with lower real interest rates. Potential profits from the sub-salt oil reserves run the risk of lower international petroleum prices stemming from expanded use of 'fracking' technology in the USA and elsewhere.

Even to grow at an annual rate of 3% per capita, half that proposed above, Brazil will need to raise its investment rate gradually to 25% of output, as other Latin American countries have been doing, matched by gains in domestic savings. The public sector has to play a role by cutting expenditure while continuing its revenue stream. Ending annual escalation of pensions by the rate of increase of minimum wages is a place to start. So is a real sovereign wealth fund to prevent export price booms from stimulating more domestic consumption.

Indeed, for higher growth to occur regularly, productivity gains will have to be generalized throughout the economy. Brazil's future development depends upon integration of the agricultural, mineral, petroleum, manufacturing and services sectors. Present-day commodity exporters differ greatly from those in the past that relied on goods such as sugar and coffee. Their competiveness stems from efficiency. Few countries benefit from such a diversified base. Perhaps God is truly Brazilian.

Perhaps the most important task of all political persuasion. Brazilian citizens, including those who have moved recently in to the lower-middle class, must learn the virtue of postponing immediate gratification for the greater good. This is a different message from that emphasized in the past. The ability to move forward to a higher, and sustainable, level of annual growth depends upon lower domestic consumption. Otherwise, the future will become more clouded. Another recent projection can be found, from the largest private Brazilian bank, Itaú, for 2020.[8] Its base scenario suggests an annual increase of only of 3%, declining to 2.8%. Brazil can, and should, do better.

Notes

1 I have benefited from the recent paper by Marcelo de Paiva Abreu and Luiz Aranha Correa do Lago, 'A Economia brasileira no Império, 1822–89', *PUC Texto para Discussão No. 584*, 2010, as well as Marcelo de Paiva Abreu (ed.), *A Ordem do Progresso*, Editora Campus, Rio de Janeiro, 1990, in this and later sections. My own 'Origins and Consequences of Import Substitution in Brazil', in L.E. di Marco (ed.), *International Economics and Development*, Academic Press, New York, 1972, is also relevant.

2 Raymond W. Goldsmith, *Brasil 1850–1984: Desenvolvimento Financeiro sob um Século de Inflação*, São Paulo, 1986, is often invoked for estimates going back to the 19th century, but with little basis. He uses real imports and exports, money stock and a small selection of salary rates with the latter two deflated by incomplete price indexes. The subject of 19th-century growth—which seems to have been too slow by most accounts—is complicated by the circumstance of slavery, with sharp differences in income levels.

3 See my 'Brazilian Development in Long-Term Perspective', *American Economic Review*, May 1980, 102–8, and additional references cited there for more detail. Marcelo de Paiva Abreu and Afonso S. Bevilaqua, 'Brasil Como una Economía Exportadora', in Enrique Cárdenas, José Antonio Ocampo y Rosemary Thorp (eds), *La Era de las Exportaciones Latinoamericanas*, Mexico City, 2003, provides further and more recent contributions to the literature on this period.

4 Luis A.V. Catão, 'A New Wholesale Price Index for Brazil During the Period 1870–1913', *Revista Brasileira de Economia* 46(4), out./dez. 1992: 519–33.

5 I dealt with this period (and the next) in much more detail in two essays: 'Some Reflections on the Post-1964 Brazilian Economic Policy', in Alfred Stepan (ed.), *Authoritarian Brazil*, New Haven, CT, 1973; and 'A Tale of Two Presidents', in Alfred Stepan (ed.), *Democratizing Brazil*, New Haven, CT, 1989. Once again, for additional recent references, see Abreu, Bevilaqua and D.M. Pinho, 'Sustitución de Importaciones y Crecimiento en Brasil (1890–1970), in Enrique Cárdenas, José Antonio Ocampo y Rosemary Thorp (eds), *Industrialización y Estado en la América Latina*, Mexico City, 2003.

6 My book, *Starting Over*, Brookings, 2011, covers the period from 1985 to 2010 and affords many relevant additional references.

7 *Brasil em 2022* and the underlying submissions of goals from ministries and agencies can be found on the website of the Secretaria de Assuntos Estratégicos. In the Plan's Preparatory Papers from the ministries, also available, many key objectives have a lesser level than is later cited in the final document. For example, the rate of growth proposed is 6%, not 7%; investment as a proportion of income is set at 23%, not 25%; fertilizer production is not to attain 100%, but for potassium, 70%; high school education is to become universal, but 80%; social security coverage is to reach 80%, not 100%; and so on. Influenced by the exceptional growth in 2010, the final report winds up bolder than initially proposed. Dilma's statement regarding the increase in income per capita can be found on the *Mercopress* site, 13 April 2013.

8 This report from Banco Itaú is entitled *Brasil 2020*, and was published on 12 April 2013.

4

Russia as an emerging economy

Philip Hanson

There is no such thing as a typical emerging economy, but Russia is more atypical than most. It is on the richer end of the scale of emerging economies: the International Monetary Fund (IMF) puts its 2011 per capita gross domestic product (GDP) in international dollars at $16,736 (at purchasing power parity—PPP).[1] That is more than twice the level of the People's Republic of China and more than four times that of India. In addition, Russia has already industrialized once and has had a few decades as a superpower. To say it is 'emerging' begs a great many questions. It is an upper-middle-income country with many of the attributes of modernity but with deep-seated economic problems, as well.

In this chapter we shall begin with some background; next, take a look at the uneven nature of Russian development levels; then we review recent growth patterns, the economy's sensitivity to the oil price and the macroeconomic policies that have been deployed to handle that sensitivity. We go on to consider the effects of the 2008–09 global crisis; the implications for Russia of the changed global environment, and controversies over policies to minimize present and future risks. That leads, finally, to a review of fundamental features of the Russian business environment, and whether they are an obstacle to any return to stronger growth.

Background: three circumstances affecting Russia's contemporary development

Three of the circumstances surrounding Russia's current development deserve to be singled out: it is a major oil exporter; it is emerging not from underdevelopment but from distorted development; and it is the main successor state of what was once a superpower, ruled by a communist party.

The first of these characterizations needs no elaboration at this stage. Its importance will be considered in a later section. The other two are worth a few words by way of introduction.

Industrialization and urbanization began in Tsarist Russia at the end of the 1860s, but greatly accelerated under Soviet rule from the end of the 1920s. Soviet industrial development included two major injections of foreign technology, in the early 1930s and through US Lend-Lease in the Second World War, but was otherwise conducted in semi-isolation. It was successful above all in military production, enabling the USSR to defeat Germany on the Eastern Front and later to match the USA in nuclear weapons, including inter-continental ballistic missiles. Industrialization

46

therefore happened much earlier than in China, India or other large emerging economies with which Russia is now grouped. It was accompanied by a rapid build-up of scientific and technical education, and research and development (R&D). Russia inherited the lion's share of the R&D and production capability of the USSR.

That inheritance distinguishes Russia from other present-day emerging economies. Probably the most helpful part of it is the mature and fairly strong educational system that remains to this day. The damaging part of the inheritance is a production structure that had been put in place by central planning. This structure reflected prices and a product mix that bore little or no relation to relative costs and scarcities; it had been completely sealed off from international competition. In 1992 Russian policymakers made a decisive move to an open and, in principle, free market economy. The country proved to be full of enterprises that could not pay their way.

Some combination of drastic restructuring of old enterprises and their replacement by new firms was needed to produce a healthy economy. Russia today can be seen as an economy in which that necessary redevelopment has made some headway but still falls short of what is needed. The restructuring of a defective, mis-developed economy is not a problem faced by other large emerging economies: China, adding a new, market economy onto a continuing state-planned economy and not dismantling the old system, faces somewhat different problems.

At the same time, past development, albeit distorted, has contributed to Russia's moderately advanced level of provision of services such as education and health care. In the 2012 ranking of 187 countries in the United Nations (UN) Human Development Index, Russia comes 55th, well above Brazil (85th), Turkey (90th) or China (101st).[2]

The consequences of having been a communist-run superpower are less tangible than those of inheriting a distorted economy. Russians are still subject to authoritarian rule, albeit of a rather soft nature, but without the enforced unifying influence of an official ideology or an all-powerful ruling party. There remains from superpower days a widespread assumption that Russia should still be something more than a regional power. This political legacy carries implications for economic policy. For example, joining the European Union (EU) was never a remotely plausible objective and policy anchor for Russia, in the way it was for the Baltic states or Poland. Many, probably most, Russians believe that Russia has to develop in its own, uniquely Russian way.

The varied development levels of Russia

Considered as a single whole, Russia is, as has already been noted, an upper-middle-income country. That means that its per capita GDP in PPP terms is of the order of $16,000 in current international dollars, placing it significantly above another large Eurasian emerging economy, Turkey. Like Turkey, however, and indeed like all emerging economies, its development level is highly uneven within the nation's borders.

For example, Moscow, if taken in isolation, would appear to have the development level of some of the most advanced economies in the world. Figure 4.1 illustrates this.

Figure 4.1 also illustrates the considerable gap in development level, at the national level, between Russia and the other BRIC or BRICS countries (Brazil, Russia, India, China and South Africa). The numbers suggest that Turkey, on this indicator, is relatively close.

The obverse of Moscow's advanced state of development is that there are other parts of the country that are poorly developed to a degree that the casual visitor to Moscow would think unlikely. Table 4.1 illustrates this with information on the backward state of a fringe of public facilities—in this case, hospitals.

Philip Hanson

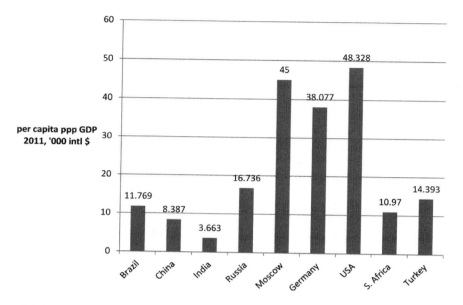

Figure 4.1 Per capita GDP in 2011: Russia, Moscow and selected other countries (PPP in international dollars, '000s)
Source: IMF World Economic Outlook database of October 2012, except for Moscow, for which the estimate is derived from Rosstat regional data and the IMF figure for Russia as a whole

Table 4.1 Russian hospitals without mains water supply and other facilities, 2010 (%)

Without main water supply	6.0
Without central heating	9.5
Without sewerage	8.3
Without a telephone landline	5.8

Source: Rosstat, www.gks.ru/bgd/regl/b11_34/IssWWW.exe/Stg/d01/02-11.htm

These are no doubt remote and relatively small facilities. The proportion of the population obliged to use them is very likely below the percentages in the table. Even so, they serve as a reminder of the extreme unevenness of Russian development.

Recent patterns of growth, up to the global financial crisis

We begin with a brief overview of the early years of the post-Soviet economy and then look more closely at the inter-crisis years, 1998–2008, and then at more recent developments.

The USSR collapsed as a state at the end of 1991. The economy, both of Russia and of the rest of the USSR, had already begun to decline. Recorded output fell from 1989. By then, the Soviet economy was, in the words of George Soros, 'a centrally planned economy with the center knocked out'.[3]

Attempts at market reform began, most clearly, with the decontrol of prices on 2 January 1992. This and other measures can be seen as attempts to create a market economy in conditions where many of the institutions of such an economy did not exist. The situation has been called one of 'systemic vacuum'. In addition, there was massive resistance, both elite and popular, to the changes. It was not surprising that the reform process was chaotic. Production declined until 1997, briefly turned upwards in that year and then fell again in the financial crisis of summer 1998. The officially estimated decline in output between 1989 and 1998 was about 40%.

Russia's subsequent recovery and, indeed, its period of boom had their roots in the latter months of 1998 and early 1999. The enforced depreciation of the rouble from around six to the US dollar to somewhat over 20 kick-started the recovery. It meant that a so-called 'nominal anchor' for macroeconomic policy, in the form of an exchange rate 'corridor', was abandoned. This unintended change of policy proved to be a blessing. Domestic producers of consumer goods and equipment were suddenly able to compete with imports, pay their workers, pay their suppliers and generally unblock the flow of rouble settlements.

The exchange rate boost was soon followed by an upturn in the oil price. The boom that then lasted until mid-2008 was essentially propelled by oil exports at mostly rising prices. The importance of oil in the Russian story can hardly be exaggerated. Crude oil, natural gas and oil products between them have in recent years accounted for three-fifths to two-thirds of Russia's merchandise exports, equivalent to about 18% of GDP. Extraction tax plus export duties on hydrocarbons have been providing about half of federal budget revenue.[4]

The effect of rising oil prices over most of the 1998–2008 period was to strengthen Russia's terms of trade. That allowed gross domestic income, in real terms, to rise faster than GDP. That process was sustainable so long as the oil price kept rising. It allowed final spending to rise faster than production, so that household consumption, real wages and retail sales tended to rise appreciably faster than GDP—which itself was increasing at around 7% a year.

It has been shown that a number of Russian economic indicators in this period moved in lock-step with the international oil price, the Russian stock market (RTS) index and the dollar value of non-oil and -gas company sales, to cite just two.[5] The broad picture is illustrated in Figure 4.2, with the Urals oil price tracked against the right-hand vertical axis and year-on-year percentage changes in GDP measured on the left. The correspondence between steep rises in

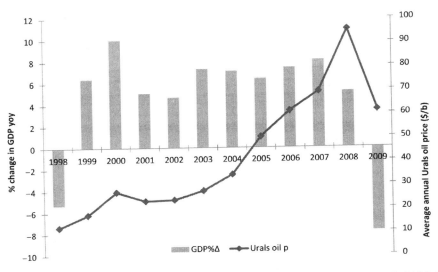

Figure 4.2 Between two crises: Russia's GDP growth and the Urals oil price, 1998–2009 (annual % change and $ per barrel)
Source: Rosstat and Central Bank of Russia

the oil price (measured between annual averages) and particularly strong growth in GDP in the same year is not perfect, but the synchronized collapse of both in 2009 is striking.

Russia's growth in this period can be described as consumption led and oil fuelled. Buoyant consumer demand was the main driver of growth among final end uses of demand. Growing hydrocarbon revenues drove the incomes of the state, of companies and of households, fuelling that demand.

Oil and gas revenues drove growth despite the fact that part of those revenues was taxed away and 'sterilized' by channelling it into the stabilization fund from 2004.[6] Despite a high marginal rate of taxation of oil revenues, enough of the hydrocarbon rents still entered the flow of state, company and household income to push up demand.

It would be misleading to treat Russia, at this boom period or later, as a petro-state. Its economy is large and diverse. The metals sector is a major net exporter and foreign investor, and the array of manufacturing and services capabilities, though containing only a handful of internationally competitive businesses, is extensive. None the less, Russia's role as a major exporter of oil and gas presented problems for policymakers during the boom, and continues to do so.

At the root of these problems are the large rents available from hydrocarbons exports. Rent has been traditionally defined as earnings above supply price. In the case of oil and gas that means revenue obtainable in excess of the cost of extraction and necessary transportation. The rent can be used in a variety of ways, from subsidizing energy prices to domestic users, to subsidizing other lines of business, to building up a sovereign wealth fund to benefit the population at some later date.

It is not necessarily used efficiently. The notion of an 'oil curse' or a natural resource curse more broadly is controversial. What can be agreed is that there are risks attendant on being a major natural resource exporter. In times of boom the rising values of commodity exports may raise the exporting nation's exchange rate, reducing the competitiveness of other industries. The ready flow of oil money in good times can tempt politicians into wasteful expenditure, leaving the state with debts it may be unable to meet when oil prices fall. More speculatively, the availability of hydrocarbons or other natural resource rents may blunt pressures to innovate and develop new lines of business.

Oil-cursed or not, the Russian economy flourished during its inter-crisis period, 1998–2008. It is one thing to say that the growth was consumption driven and oil fuelled. That conveys an important truth about the demand side of the process, but how was the additional production generated? In other words, what were the sources of growth on the supply side?

One way of answering this question is to use the growth accounting approach, in which the growth of output is broken down into the part that can be accounted for by increased inputs of labour, the part accounted for by increased inputs of capital, and the residual not attributable to either of these, usually labelled total factor productivity (TFP) growth

$$g(Y) = \alpha g(K) + (1-\alpha)g(L) + g(TFP)$$

where g denotes annual rate of growth, Y = GDP, K = capital stock, L = labour force and α is the elasticity of output with respect to a change in K.[7]

Masaaki Kuboniwa has estimated from quarterly data the apparent sources of Russian growth in the boom period from the first quarter of 1999 through the second quarter of 2008.[8] Average annual growth of GDP over this period was 7.5%, and Kuboniwa estimates that capital stock grew at an estimated 3.2% per year and employment at 0.8% per year. He concludes that TFP was probably the dominant source of growth, contributing 4.6 of the 7.5 percentage points of GDP growth.

The implication is that in Russia during the boom period the productivity of labour and capital combined (TFP) was rising rapidly. In view of the usual array of criticisms of the Russian economy, including poor business climate and weak competitive processes, this may at first sight look implausible. However, a few moments' reflection suggests that it is not necessarily far-fetched. Parts of the old, inefficient Soviet economy remained in place, it is true, but there were large shifts of labour and capital from less to more productive—previously neglected—activities. A scientist who moves from being grossly under-employed in an undistinguished research lab to a busy life as a taxi driver is very likely increasing GDP by his or her move.

Whole new industries have come into being that either did not exist or barely existed in Soviet times: recruitment agencies, travel agencies, applications software. Empty or half-empty heavy engineering works or industrial research institutes have lost people, by and large, to better-paying employment; that employment often, if not always, will also be more productive than the working life they have left behind.

In addition, fixed investment in equipment has consisted predominantly of imported machinery. This is likely to embody levels of technology and productivity higher than those embodied in domestically built machinery. It will tend to raise productivity levels in the direction of the levels obtaining on that equipment in its country of origin.

There was still a long way to go, in that direction. At the end of the boom period aggregate Russian labour productivity still lagged far behind that of the most advanced countries. Table 4.2 illustrates this.

There is another way of looking at the pattern of growth during the boom period. Whatever the precise scale and origins of TFP growth, this was a time when the growth of capital inputs into the Russian economy was not particularly rapid. For an emerging economy, a growth rate of capital stock of around 3% a year is not particularly impressive. This reflects the modest and fairly stable share of fixed investment in Russian GDP: slightly above 20% and notoriously far below the figure for China in recent years, where it has been in the high 40s.

The growth of employment during this period was of course a helpful influence. It was the product of mostly falling unemployment, together with some continued growth in the working-age population (including some net immigration, mostly from other Commonwealth of Independent States (CIS) countries). The population as a whole was falling during this period, but not the population of working age. The significance of labour force numbers for Russia now is that in contrast to the boom period, they are beginning to fall. The significance of this will be considered in the next section.

Growth during the boom was accompanied by gradually falling inflation, budget surpluses, balance of payments current account surpluses and a strong growth in reserves of gold and foreign exchange. The primary reason for this happy state of affairs was the rising oil price, but prudent fiscal management also played a part.

Consumer price inflation (December-to-December) was 84.4% in the crisis year of 1998, when a massive devaluation of the rouble forced import prices up dramatically.[9] Thereafter

Table 4.2 GDP per employed person in Russia, Germany and the USA, 2009 ('000 US$ at purchasing power parity)

Russia	30.5
Germany	69.9
USA	100.9

Source: IMF, *World Economic Outlook* database of October 2010, except Russian employment numbers from Rosstat, www.gks.ru/bgd/regl.b10_01/1ssWWW.exe/Stg/d12/3-2.htm

consumer inflation fell steadily to 2006, when it finally attained single figures: 9.0%. The federal budget was in surplus from 2000 to 2008. The current account balance was positive throughout, even in 1998 and 2009.

In 2007, apparently under the pressure of parliamentary and (in 2008) presidential elections, the fiscal stance was relaxed somewhat. This contributed to consumer inflation moving back into double figures in 2008. We shall return in a later section to the subject of macroeconomic policies.

Growth patterns: the 2008–09 crisis and after

The global financial crisis hit Russia during 2008, most conspicuously through a steep fall in the oil price. The monthly average price per barrel of Urals oil reached $129.30 in July 2008 and by December had plummeted to $38. By July 2009 it had edged back up to $64.30.[10] The annual average figures shown in Figure 4.2 capture only a little of this volatility.

We have already noted the sensitivity of the Russian economy to the Urals oil price—that is to say, the export price of Russian oil. In the crisis of 2008–09 that sensitivity seems to have been severe.

The deterioration of Russian GDP performance between 2008 and 2009 was extreme. Figure 4.3 illustrates this. The bars represent the change in performance between the two years (the percentage change in year 2008 minus the percentage change in 2009) for the world, Russia and selected comparator countries.[11]

There were some small countries in which economic activity fell more sharply than in Russia—Lithuania, for example—but among larger economies, Russia's deterioration was unusually sharp. The 2009 decline in Russian GDP was the greatest in any G20 nation. It was also unusual among oil exporters, except for Kuwait. The Saudi economy, for instance, slowed to a crawl but just about continued to grow. It does not seem likely that the severity of the Russian recession can be blamed simply on the fall in the oil price.

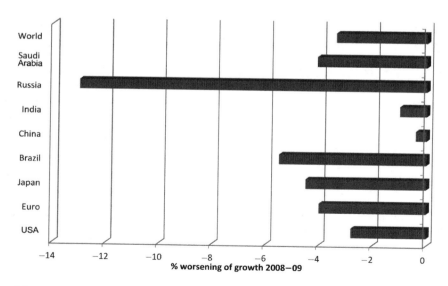

Figure 4.3 How bad was 2009? The deterioration in GDP performance between 2008 and 2009 for the world, Russia and selected other countries.
Source: IMF World Economic Outlook database, October 2012.

Arithmetically, an exceptionally large part of the fall in Russia's economic activity in 2009 can be ascribed to an unlikely source: a very large reduction in inventories (stocks of goods). Year-on-year changes in inventories are in most economies predominantly only a tiny component of the change in GDP. In Russia in 2009 they were the largest single contributor to the fall. Figure 4.4 illustrates this, comparing the sources of GDP decline in that year in the USA and in Russia.

This unusual feature of the Russian recession was spotted by observers[12] but for the most part treated as an oddity explicable perhaps by the lack of experience on the part of Russian business in managing inventories through a downturn. An alternative explanation by Nikita Krichevskii,[13] however, deserves attention. Krichevskii[14] showed how a number of leading Russian companies had moved very large amounts of funds out of the country in late 2008. He showed that in at least some cases this process had been carried so far that working capital was cut substantially, and steep falls in inventories followed.

We cannot be sure that this is the key to the unusual drop in Russian economic activity, but it is a plausible hypothesis. It may help us to understand some more recent developments. The implication is that a sudden, steep fall in the oil price creates uncertainty bordering on panic in Russia—or at least that it did so on this occasion—notwithstanding the presence of the stabilization fund, of low public debt and of large foreign exchange reserves. This somewhat hectic response would characterize a business community that is deeply wary about the behaviour of the state at the best of times, and liable to become especially worried at a time of global crisis. Behind such behaviour, if our surmise is correct, lies the general lack of protection of property rights by a rule of law. That is a subject to which we shall return when we consider the renewed slowdown of late 2012–early 2013.

At all events, the Russian recession was a steep one. It was also relatively short-lived, enduring for four quarters. The well-stocked stabilization fund helped the authorities to put in place a fiscal stimulus package, net of automatic stabilizer effects, of about 2.8% of GDP.[15] The money was not necessarily wisely spent, but that was not an outcome confined to Russia. It helped recovery.

Russia has not returned to its pre-2008 trend rate of growth. In this it is not very different from most other countries. The particular influences on Russia's longer-term slowdown, however, are in part distinctive.

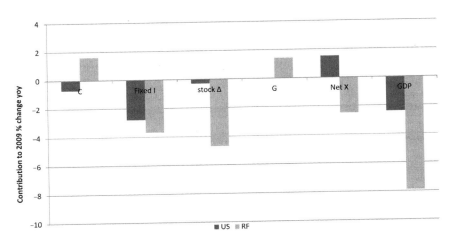

Figure 4.4 Contribution of different end uses of demand to the fall in GDP in 2009 year-on-year in the USA and Russia (percentage points)
Source: US Department of Commerce Bureau of Economic Analysis; Rosstat

GDP growth in 2010 and 2011 was somewhat over 4%, followed by a further slowdown from mid-2012. Figure 4.5 illustrates the course of events.

In Figure 4.5 the time intervals are irregular, going from annual to quarterly to monthly as one moves to the right. This gives an emphasis to what are at the time of writing the most recent developments.

Two different processes seem to be involved in this slowdown. The first is the medium-term effect of changed circumstances in comparison with the inter-crisis boom period. The second may be a more short-term impediment to growth.

The main medium-term changes in Russia's circumstances since the 1998–2008 period are the following:

- The world as a whole is growing more slowly, and Europe, which takes over one-half of Russia's merchandise exports, fluctuates between stagnation and decline.
- The world financial system, adjusting to a 'balance sheet recession', is making less credit available than before. Russian banks and corporations, which had been able to borrow rather freely in the earlier period, are among the losers.
- Uncertainty about future global demand for hydrocarbons and therefore about future volumes and prices of oil and gas sales has increased. This concern is enhanced by developments in the supply of shale oil and shale gas from sources outside Russia.
- For demographic reasons the available Russian workforce has plateaued and is expected to decline. During the pre-crisis boom, employment was still growing (see above).
- The main demographic change is a plummeting number of new young entrants to the labour force. This is likely to reduce labour mobility and the rate at which skills are upgraded.

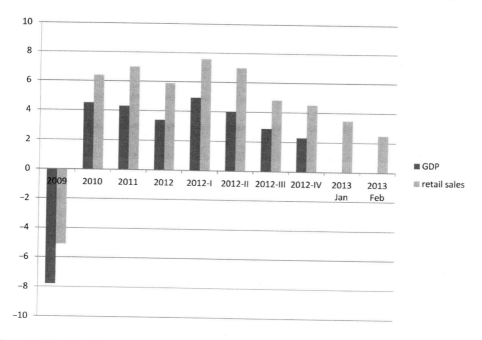

Figure 4.5 Russian GDP and retail sales growth from the global crisis into 2013 (% change year-on-year)
Source: Rosstat

- There may also be some increase, whether justified or not, in concern about corruption and possible political instability.

The net outflow of private capital from Russia is often cited as a symptom of recent loss of business confidence.[16] This may be a misinterpretation. A net outflow of private capital has been recorded from Russia in every post-Soviet year except 2006 and 2007 (there was also a near-balance between inflows and outflows in 2005). One might take the view that confidence was beginning to grow in 2005–07, and has subsequently been lost, but that can only be a matter of speculation.

The demographic impediment to growth is illustrated in Figure 4.6.

Figure 4.6 shows the middle of three variant projections by the Russian Statistical Service (Rosstat) of the future working-age population (15–65 years), allowing for projected net immigration. If Kuboniwa's[17] estimate of the sensitivity of Russian output to changes in labour inputs (see the previous section) is correct, the damage to growth directly resulting from this demographic change would be modest. The working-age population is projected to fall by about 1% per annum to 2020. Any raising of the pension age (currently 60 for men and 55 for women) seems to be politically taboo, but some increase in the already considerable number of pensioners in employment is possible, perhaps stimulated by increased years-of-service requirements needed to qualify for full state pension.[18] If those in work or actively seeking work diminished in number in 2013–20 by, say, 0.7% per annum, the change from employment growth in the boom period would be -1.5% per annum, with a Kuboniwa-style effect on output of approximately -0.5% a year.

To this would be added some reduction of TFP growth because of the reduction in the rate of reallocation of labour and the slower growth of human capital posited above—due to the falling number of young labour force entrants.

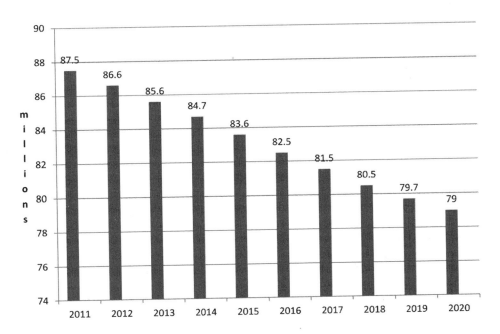

Figure 4.6 Russia: projected working-age population, 2011–20 (millions)
Source: Rosstat

Labour shortages are already present. The effects extend beyond those just described. Part of the extreme unevenness in Russian development is a sharp differentiation of regional labour markets. Large, dynamic regions, of which Moscow city is the extreme case, have had over-full employment for some time, while the numbers of unemployed remain quite high in places like Dagestan or Tyva. Further tightening of aggregate labour supply will severely constrain output in Moscow, St Petersburg, Moscow region, Tatarstan and other more active areas, slowing overall growth and increasing inflationary pressure.

If all the changes in Russia's circumstances, demographic and international, are taken together, growth at the '5%–6%' demanded by President Vladimir Putin looks unattainable in the medium term unless either the growth rate of the capital stock or the growth of total factor productivity, or both, are substantially increased. As things stand, the IMF, for example, projects Russian GDP growth to 2017 at just below 4% per annum.[19] This is a healthier prospect than the developed world faces but is no higher than IMF projections for the world as a whole. One might suppose that almost by definition, the trend rate of growth in an emerging economy should be clearly above that for the entire global economy. How else would an emerging economy emerge?

The second process that may be at work is an additional, shorter-term deceleration in late 2012 and early 2013 (see Figure 4.5). It might prove to be only a brief dip in performance superimposed on the medium-term slowdown. At the time of writing it is impossible to say whether this is the case or whether something more substantial is happening.

Leading indicators are not encouraging. Sales of cars and light commercial vehicles were up in 2012 as a whole, compared with 2011, but the December figure was at about the same level as December 2011. Rail freight loadings (in tons) were up by a modest 2.4% in 2012 as a whole, but down by 3.7% year-on-year in December. In January the slide in rail freight continued: down 7.3% in 'turnover' (ton-kilometres). Sales of new cars and light goods vehicles were only 2% up year-on-year in February 2013. With industrial sector growth slipping (year-on-year) from 4.0% in the first quarter to 1.7% in the fourth and then turning negative in January of 2013, the deterioration in freight transport indicators does not appear to be anomalous. Rosstat estimates that industrial production, which includes extractive industry, was 1.5% down year-on-year in January–February 2013.[20]

The background to this unexpected additional slowdown seems to be a loss of confidence on the part of Russian business. This is provoked in part by growing uncertainties about the global, and especially the European, economy, but that is not the only worry. Retail sales growth has slowed as banks have restricted the growth of consumer lending.[21]

Critics of the Putin regime point to profound social concerns: a growing dissatisfaction with prevailing corruption and the lack of a rule of law. The fundamental issue of reform will be taken up in the penultimate section of this chapter; here it must suffice to note this claim while also noting that it is not clear that the business environment is getting worse.

In March 2013 the collapse of the two leading banks in Cyprus, Laiki and Bank of Cyprus, dealt an additional blow to Russian business confidence. Cyprus had become a major offshore financial centre for Russian companies. Many Russian-owned private companies are controlled by their owners through holding companies on the island, and many transactions are routed through Cyprus. This includes 'round-tripping' by corporate capital. In 2011 a third of all Russian outward foreign direct investment (FDI) went to Cyprus and about a quarter of all inward FDI came from Cyprus.[22] In other words, a large amount of funding was recycled through the island's holding companies and banks. Some of the funds flowing through Cyprus are illicit money that is being laundered, but much of the flow is legal, and is responding to low tax rates in Cyprus and the desire to put assets beyond the reach of a predatory Russian state.

The Cyprus bail-out by the 'troika' of the European Central Bank, European Commission and IMF imposes substantial losses on holders of deposits above €100,000 in the two banks, puts capital controls in place for an uncertain period, and has probably ended Cyprus' functioning as an offshore financial centre. The direct and immediate loss to Russian depositors in the two banks might be of the order of 0.2% of Russian GDP.[23] The damage to business confidence, coming at an already difficult time, may in the medium term be more costly.

Policy and reform: policy issues

Russia could, by common consent, be doing better. President Putin wants to see GDP growth averaging at least 5%–6% per year over a decade. Most independent projections for the next few years, at least, are in the range 3%–4%. The leading Russian private bank, Alfa Bank, projects GDP growth for 2013 at only 2.8%.[24] Given a starting point of labour productivity about three-sevenths' the level of Germany's (see Table 4.2), there should be scope for the Russian economy to grow faster than 3%–4% on average in the longer run.

There are two modes in which policymakers can address this issue: through policy changes and through reform. Policies could operate through government spending and taxation, perhaps favouring particular activities by means of tax breaks, or might be restricted to fiscal and monetary discipline aimed at minimizing inflation. Reforms would be institutional changes such as altering employment law or, for example, altering the status and functioning of law courts and law enforcement.

There is a lively debate in Russia on both policies and reforms. Participants in that debate are in many cases advocating both policy changes and reforms, and the two modes of influencing the economy are not mutually exclusive. For ease of discussion, however, we treat them separately: policies in this section and institutional reform in the next.

The policies most actively discussed in Russia recently have been to do with macro management and industrial policy, with some active, related debates over privatization and pensions. The discussions will be reviewed here only in brief outline.

On fiscal policy, there is a long-running intra-governmental difference of approach between the Ministry of Finance (MinFin) and the Ministry of Economic Development (MinEkon). The MinFin approach was advocated with great professionalism and a fair degree of success by Aleksei Kudrin[25] when he was Minister of Finance from 2000 to 2011. The line has been stalwartly defended by his successor, Anton Siluanov. It is to give priority to balancing the budget (strictly speaking, the federal budget, but the combined federal and sub-national budgetary balance is always close to the federal balance), restricting the non-oil and -gas budget deficit and building up fiscal reserves in the form of the Reserve Fund and the Fund of National Prosperity.

The MinEkon approach is to give a higher priority than MinFin would do to state spending aimed at improving the economy's capacity to innovate and diversify, even if that might entail a small and temporary budget deficit. With central government debt at only about 10% of GDP, this might seem a modest ambition.

Kudrin,[26] however, has consistently stressed two things: the need to be able to cope with a large and abrupt fall in the oil price (for which he had prepared Russia well in 2008) and the highly ineffective nature of Russian public spending. He deplored the rise over time in the 'break-even oil price' of the federal budget: the average annual price per barrel of Urals oil at which the federal budget would be just in balance. This had been $57.5 in 2007 and was set, he contended, to be $117.2 in the budget planned for 2012.[27] Kudrin made this observation after he had resigned from MinFin. It reflects the retreat into which he had been forced by the spending lobbies.

The recommendations that emerged from a review of Russia's official state 2020 strategy[28] favoured a modest version of the MinEkon line, incorporating a short period of small federal budget deficits. So far, in practice, the oil price has been such that both MinFin and MinEkon could be said to have had some success. However, the highly ambitious spending targets for military re-equipment threaten to breach the MinFin line.

Behind this central policy debate there is a more general division between conservatives *à la Russe* (standing for a strong state and top-down economic policies) and small-government, free market liberals. The former have been happy to delay further privatization and to 'reform' the state pension system so as to reduce almost to nothing its funded pillar. That self-financing component of the state pension system might have helped to create a core of institutional investors in the shape of pension funds, and thus assist the deepening of what are at present very shallow financial markets.

Here the disagreements over policy begin to shade into more fundamental matters: the core interests of different groups of people and the basic institutional question of the rule of law.

Fundamental reform issues

The business environment in Russia is routinely described as poor. Various international ratings and ranking support this view. In the World Bank's 2013 Ease of Doing Business rankings, Russia was 112th out of 185 countries and 40th out of 49 upper-middle-income countries. The Organisation for Economic Co-operation and Development's (OECD) product market regulation score for Russia in 2008 (higher indicating less competition and more state interference) was 3.094, against an OECD average of 1.340 and a rating for Greece of 2.374. In the World Bank's governance scoring for 'rule of law', which can lie between a worst score of -2.5 and a best score of +2.5, Russia is marked at -0.78, compared with Turkey at +0.08.[29]

These scores and rankings have, needless to say, their limitations. Despite them, post-Soviet Russia has spawned some internationally competitive companies, such as Yandex (search engines) and Kaspersky Lab (anti-virus software), and retained some effective older capabilities. It is also the case that a number of foreign firms that have set up business in Russia have prospered. We are not talking about a black hole.

At the same time, there is a problem with law and law enforcement, and therefore with property rights, and therefore with incentives to invest and innovate. One of the recommendations of the expert group revising the 2020 national strategy was that there should be independent courts and that there should cease to be privileged and unprivileged economic actors. This last was an allusion to firms that have political protection and those that do not, and to the widespread practice of enlisting corrupt officials in blocking competition from potential rivals.

There is indeed a common practice that goes well beyond blocking competition: *reiderstvo*, literally 'raiding'. This includes using the police and courts to have a competitor arrested on trumped-up charges and their business assets seized. Occasionally, something of this sort impinges on a foreign-owned company and attracts attention in the media outside Russia. This happened, notoriously, in the case of Bill Browder's Hermitage Capital Management, issuing eventually in the Magnitsky affair.[30] *Reiderstvo*, including the arrest of Russian businesspeople, is, however, a common event. Reportedly, some 50,000 people a year are arrested for alleged 'economic crimes'.[31] Examples can be found on the website www.nocorruption.biz associated with the business association Delovaya Rossiya, which has been trying to combat this practice.

In one view, this vulnerability of businesspeople to persecution and exploitation by officials and their business cronies is part of a deeply engrained system ('*sistema*') of informal governance that is part of the way in which Russia has long operated.[32] At all events, the establishment of a

Russia as an emerging economy

rule of law cannot simply be achieved by a simple policy decision, though legislation might be a necessary part of a much more basic set of changes.

It is not certain that Russia's long-term economic performance would be greatly improved by the introduction of something more closely resembling the rule of law, but it is plausible. Insecurity of property rights deters investment, including investment in research, development and innovation. It may well be at least part of the reason for the comparatively limited development of small business in Russia.[33]

Why should radical change be so difficult? The chief problem is that those currently in positions of power have made their way in the system of informal governance in which cronyism and corruption dominate. An individual high official or tycoon may personally disapprove of the state of affairs and yet find it immensely difficult to change.[34]

Conclusions

Russia is a comparatively high-income emerging economy. Its development is geographically very uneven. The structure of the economy has been distorted by past investment decisions made under central planning. In the boom years of 1998–2008 Russia grew strongly and could be said, at any rate in terms of per capita income, to be catching up with the advanced world. However, the country's strikingly deep recession in 2008–09 indicated a volatility that could not be accounted for simply by its being an oil exporter.

A defective legal order and a lack of trust are not unique to Russia by any means but they seem to lie at the root of its weak adaptation, compared to some other emerging economies, to the changed global environment after 2009. In early 2013 Russia seemed to face a prospect of comparatively sluggish growth: stronger than was expected in Europe but well below both the ambitions of its leaders and the performance of which a country at its stage of development should be capable.

Notes

1 IMF World Economic Outlook database of October 2012.
2 The UN HDI is based on such measures as life expectancy at birth and years of education, as well as on per capita gross national income (GNI) per head. For the 2012 data (2013 report), see hdr.undp.org/hdr4press/press/report/summaries/HDR2013_EN_Summary.pdf.
3 *Wall Street Journal*, 7 December 1989.
4 Hydrocarbons export data from the Central Bank of Russia (www.cbr.ru); dollar GDP from Bank of Finland BOFIT Russia Statistics; federal budget revenue by origin from the Russian government's Economic Expert Group (www.eeg.ru).
5 Clifford Gaddy and Barry W. Ickes, 'Russia after the Global Financial Crisis', *Eurasian Geography and Economics* 51(3), 2010: 281–311.
6 The stabilization fund was split in 2008 into a Reserve Fund and a Fund of National Prosperity. The former is, as the name suggests, a reserve fund to prop up state spending in the event of falling oil prices while the latter was intended to be a long-term investment fund akin to a sovereign wealth fund.
7 This growth accounting equation is based on the assumption that the production function—the relationship between inputs and outputs—is a Cobb–Douglas function with (in aggregate) constant returns to scale, so that the labour and capital coefficients add to one.
8 Masaaki Kuboniwa, 'Russian Growth Path in Light of Production Function Estimation Using Quarterly Data', in Iikka Korhonen and Laura Solanko (eds), *From Soviet Plans to Russian Reality*, Helsinki: WSOYpro.OY, 2011, 39–53.
9 This and other macroeconomic figures quoted in the remainder of this section are taken from the macro data appendix of Alfa Bank's *Russian Economic Monitor*, 3 December 2012—a handy compilation of Russian official data.

59

10 Central Bank of Russia, cbr.ru/statistics/print.aspx?file=macro/macro_08.htm&pid=macro&sid=oep, 2008, and cbr.ru/statistics/print.aspx?file=macro/macro_09.htm&pid=macro&sid=oep, 2009.

11 In Russia's case this is a drop from +5.2 to −7.8, or 13%. For several others, e.g. China and Saudi Arabia, it is a slowdown, i.e. a fall from one positive number to another, smaller positive number.

12 Ol'ga Kuvshinova, 'Spad pro zapas' [A Fall because of Stocks], *Vedomosti*, 2 October 2009.

13 Nikita Krichevskii, 'Postpikalevskaya Rossiya: novaya politiko-ekonomicheskaya real'nost'' [Post-Pikalevo Russia: The New Politico-economic Reality], 2009, www.krichevsky.ru (accessed 27 March 2013).

14 Ibid.

15 Philip Hanson, 'Russia: Crisis, Exit and ... Reform?' *Journal of Communist Studies and Transition Politics* 27(3–4), 2011: 456–76.

16 The estimated net private capital outflows in 2012 were US$56.8 billion (cbr.ru/statistics/print.aspx?file=credit_statistics/capital_new.htm&pid=svs&sid=itm_18710), equivalent to 2.8% of GDP.

17 Kuboniwa, 'Russian Growth Path in Light of Production Function Estimation Using Quarterly Data'.

18 In late 2012 and early 2013 there was considerable controversy about reforms to the state pension system. At the time of writing these have not been finalized, but a simple rise in the pension age is strongly resisted.

19 IMF World Economic Outlook database of October 2012. Several projections by other bodies, made since those data, are a shade lower.

20 www.gks.ru/bgd/free/B04_03/IssWWW.exe/Stg/d01/51.htm for industrial output in January–February 2013. Earlier data from www.rzd.ru (railways) and *Vedomosti*, 11 March 2013.

21 In February 2013 the Central Bank of Russia expected bank credit to increase during the year by not more than 15%–20%. That may seem quite high, but it is only about half the rate of expansion of consumer credit in 2012. See Tat'yana Voronova, 'Banki snizhayut stavki po depozitam naseleniya' [Banks Lower Rates on Deposits of the Population], *Vedomosti*, 4 February 2013.

22 Central Bank of Russia data, www.cbr.ru. At the time of writing data for 2012 were incomplete, but the picture in January–September 2012 was similar to that in 2011, in broad terms.

23 Author's very rough estimate. For background see Bank of America Merrill Lynch, *Russia Macro Watch*, 25 March 2013; Yurii Barsukov, 'Poteri kiprskikh vkladchikov rastut na glazakh' [Losses of Cyprus Depositors Grow before their Eyes], *Kommersant*, 27 March 2013; Philip Hanson, 'Russian Caution Over Cyprus Comes Despite Damaging Economic Effect', *City A.M.*, 26 March 2013.

24 Alfa Bank, *Russia Economic Monitor*, 4 March 2013.

25 Aleksei Kudrin, 'Bortom k volne' [Riding the Wave], *Kommersant*, 15 October 2011.

26 Ibid.

27 In the event the 2012 federal budget was minimally in deficit (-0.1% of GDP) at an average oil price of $110.4 per barrel: Economic Expert Group, www.eeg.ru/pages/22 (accessed 28 March 2013).

28 *Promezhutochniy doklad o rezul'tatakh ekspertnoi raboty po aktual'nym problemam sotsial'no-ekonomicheskoi strategii Rossii na period do 2020 goda* [Interim Report of the Results of Expert Work on Current Issues in Russia's 2020 Strategy], *Kommersant* website (accessed 19 August 2011).

29 www.doingbusiness.org; www.oecd.org/economy/pmr; www.govindicators.org.

30 For an account of the original scam, see 'Testimony of William Browder, CEO, Hermitage Capital Management', US Commission on Security and Cooperation in Europe, 23 June 2009.

31 Yulia Yakovleva, '"Delovaya Rossiya" predlagayet perepisat' stat'yu o moshenichestve' ['Delovaya Rossiya' Proposes a Revision of the Article on Swindling], *RBK Daily*, 11 March 2012.

32 Alena Ledeneva, *Can Russia Modernise? Sistema, Power Networks and Informal Governance*, Cambridge University Press, Cambridge, 2012.

33 OECD, *OECD Reviews of Innovation Policy: Russian Federation*, Paris, 2011, provides estimates of employment in firms with fewer than 100 employees, plus numbers of unincorporated sole traders in 2009; the total is only 21% of total employment.

34 For a full statement of this argument see Philip Hanson and Elizabeth Teague, 'Liberal Insiders and Economic Reform in Russia', Chatham House REP 2013/01, www.chathamhouse.org/publications/papers/view/188985.

5

The how and why of economic growth in India, 1950–2012

Surjit S. Bhalla[1]

Introduction

The changing growth pattern in India over the last 60–odd years, and the determinants thereof, is the major focus of this chapter. Particular emphasis is given to the developments since 1991, an economic crisis and major economic reforms year. Since that year, growth has averaged 6.7% per annum; in the previous 40 years, growth had averaged only 4% per annum. India's growth post-1991 has the hallmarks of being exceptional; since 2003, an average of nearly 8% is akin to miracle growth. However, the last two years have witnessed a negative miracle, with gross domestic product (GDP) growth collapsing to 5% in 2012, from a near 10% level just two years earlier.

Economic growth is a well-researched subject. The challenge is to explain the puzzles in the pattern of growth. For example, despite major economic reforms in 1991, there was no acceleration in India's growth rate in the 1990s over the 1980s growth rate of around 5.5% per annum. Yet another conundrum: Indian growth suddenly accelerated to above 8% growth in the early 2000s and did so for eight long years, and just as suddenly dropped to 5.5% in the last two years. Thus, there are four questions that need to be answered about Indian growth. First, what caused India's growth to *accelerate* in the 1980s? Second, what *prevented* India's growth from accelerating in the 1990s, as would have been forecast by the magnitude of the 1991 economic reforms? Third, what caused the growth rate to accelerate sharply in 2003/04 *without* the benefit of any new reforms, major or minor? Fourth, what caused the recent sharp deceleration in India's growth? This chapter attempts to find an explanation for these different aspects of economic growth in India.

The plan of the chapter is as follows. The next section is devoted to an understanding of the stages, and determinants, of economic growth. One insight that this review provides is the estimate that due to factor reallocation alone—movement of labour from low-productivity agriculture to somewhat higher-productivity non-agriculture—GDP growth was expected to be around 5% in the 1980s. The following section documents the growth process for the pre-reform years 1950–90. These early decades were dominated by the 'old' policies of import substitution, currency overvaluation and heavily repressed capital markets. Then detailed tests are provided of the determinants of economic growth in India, most likely very similar to the determinants in other developing countries as well. Perhaps surprisingly for India (and its policymakers), the most important variable explaining GDP fluctuations in India is the pattern of real long-term interest rates. Some other determinants of growth are also examined, e.g. fiscal deficits, and found wanting. The next section is concerned with explaining growth (and the puzzles) post-1991 and has three parts—one each for the periods 1992–96, 1997–2002, and 2003–12. After that the odd reality of the low share in GDP of industrial output is discussed, followed by the future path of growth.

Determinants of economic growth

In his classic study, Nobel laureate Arthur Lewis (1955) outlined the four principles of growth: factor accumulation, human capital, institutions and policy. While there are four principles, the *proximate* causes of growth, again according to Lewis, are three: 'effort to economize (efficiency); increase of knowledge and its application; and increasing the amount of capital or other resources per head' (Lewis 1955: 11).

There are some additional factors. One, in particular, deserves prominent mention and that is 'catch-up'. Work by Barro and Sala-i-Martin now allows us to put a value to this catch-all term. Catch-up means the ability of poorer countries to grow faster than rich countries and do so for two reasons: first, income growth for poorer countries can be enhanced by simple technology transfer rather than be based on the research and production of new technology, an inherently slow process; and second, poorer countries have cheaper labour, and a labour force whose wages are lower in international productivity adjusted terms. The net result—poor countries can grow at about 0.5% to 1.5% per annum faster than their rich country peers, *ceteris paribus*. In other words, in identifying determinants of growth, it is important to recognize that the poor countries have a natural (comparative?) advantage to grow faster.

An important addition to the list of determinants is the role of institutions. Another Nobel laureate, Douglas North, has talked extensively about the importance of institutions, and other authors, especially the joint work of Acemoglu and Robinson, have provided empirical support for this 'factor'. Indeed, one of the four parts in Lewis's book is on the importance of institutions. However, Bhalla (2012) subjects the institutions hypothesis to some stringent tests, and especially tests that conduct a 'horse race' between institutions and the importance of a competitive exchange rate. In less than a quarter of more than 4,000 models was the institutions variable significant; in striking contrast, measures of currency valuation were a significant factor in over 70% of the models.

Tests of institutions versus competitive exchange rates confirm that Western institutions equals faster growth may not be a realistic equation. Chang (2005) is also critical of the institutions hypothesis and speculates that the correlation between levels of income (and/or faster growth) and institutions is reflective of the fact that higher incomes lead to the demand for better institutions—a result that finds considerable support in Bhalla's (2007) study of the middle class.

Further support for the notion that institutions may be an overrated determinant of growth is revealed by the nature and magnitude of exceptional Chinese growth during the last 30 years. Their growth was particularly high by any standards and the presence of Western-style institutions particularly low. That this exceptional growth does not fit known paradigms of growth has been argued by Justin Lin (2012), among other (especially Chinese) scholars. Lin argues that it was the nature of state intervention, state selection and state guidance that propelled the People's Republic of China to hitherto unknown possibilities of growth. According to Lin, none of the factors associated with faster growth—openness, competitive exchange rates, institutions—were really present in China. Interestingly, Lin's book does not contain a single mention of currency undervaluation.[2]

Thus, although there are several factors that contribute to economic growth, the debate about the important determinants is wide open. Some insight can be obtained by breaking up economic growth into the sum of its three components: factor accumulation (labour and capital) and productivity growth. If determinants of the individual components are identified, one can reach a consensus about the causative factors associated with growth. Note that among factors, only capital can be increased at a fast, even forced pace. The oldest policy to accelerate growth is therefore to apply more capital and grow faster. Russia did it under Stalin and, according to some, so did East Asia. The simple point is that higher inputs can mean higher output, but several developing countries, especially India and China, along with Russia and others, e.g. the Economic Commission for Latin America (ECLA) found that in the relatively closed economy days prior to the 1980s that investment without openness (or competitive exchange rates), or investment without competition, was a sure recipe for some growth today but only at the expense of slower long-term growth.

That capital accumulation was not enough was also argued by Young (1995) and Krugman (1994) in the mid-1990s. However, the conclusion that East Asian countries grew primarily due to high investment rates is incorrect; there was more capital input in these economies, and more productivity growth (owing to openness and competitive exchange rates). Between 1960 and 1995 East Asian economies, excluding China, grew at a rate above 6% per annum and an average total factor productivity growth above 2% per annum. So besides capital accumulation, one needs to examine the competitive environment in which the investment takes place: a closed or open economy, an overvalued or undervalued exchange rate, high or competitive real interest rates.

The varied Indian experience over the last six or more decades is examined via the prism of the determinants of investment and productivity growth. There are six broad stages of Indian growth post independence (see Figure 5.1). In stage I, the five-year average growth was

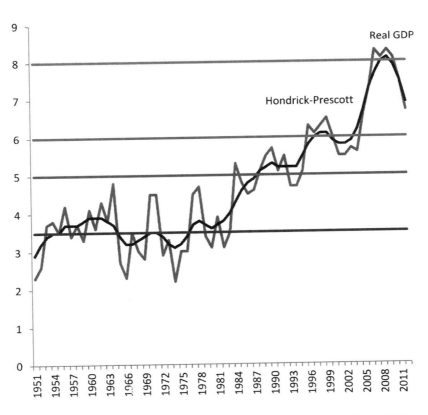

Figure 5.1 Five-year smoothed actual and potential GDP growth in India, 1951–2012

consistently below 5% in the period 1950 to 1980, but what is noteworthy is that about once every decade average GDP growth did poke above the 5% barrier.[3] In Stage II, starting in the early 1980s, there was a marked acceleration in GDP growth to above 5.5% per annum. Stage III is the growth acceleration for the three-year period starting in 1994—an acceleration of 5.9% per annum in the 1980s having reached 8% in 1996. Stage IV (1997 to 2002) is the surprising slowdown; note the near-vertical decline in the figure, and the fact that this was just a few years after the 1991 reforms. During these years, GDP growth averaged only 5.4% per annum, making the average post-reform growth equal to the pre-reform growth of the 1980s. Just as miraculously (though there is a consistent explanation provided below), the average GDP growth rate accelerated to 8.4% per annum in 2003–10. This is Stage V. Just as miraculously, the growth rate collapsed in the last two years, registering only 5% in 2012—a figure considerably below recent trend growth. This is Stage VI.

Some of the findings are presented here: the 5.4% GDP growth rate of the 1980s did *not* represent a significant departure from the growth rate that should have been expected. One reason this conclusion might have been missed by most analysts is that there was a global slowdown in the 1970s, a period when Indian growth declined to an average of only 2.8% per annum (see Table 5.1). Hence, the acceleration or break with trend in the 1980s seemed to be large, when in reality there was only a gradual, and minor, acceleration to above-trend growth. Second, the 1991 reforms did lead to a sharp acceleration to above 7% GDP growth for a few years, but this 'new' level was not sustained due to an overly hawkish and inappropriate monetary policy. Real long-term interest rates[4] rose to near double-digit levels in the late 1990s

Table 5.1 GDP and related variables, different periods, 1951–2012

Period	GDP and related variables (in %)				
	Population	Per capita real GDP	Real GDP	Hondrick Prescott potential growth (HP)	Total factor productivity growth rates
Decades					
1951–59	1.8	1.7	3.5	3.6	—
1960–69	2.2	1.7	3.8	3.5	−1.0
1970–79	2.1	0.7	2.8	3.4	−0.8
1980–89	2.1	3.3	5.4	4.8	1.9
1990–99	2.0	3.7	5.6	5.6	2.5
2000–09	1.5	5.4	7.0	7.2	2.0
2010–12	1.4	4.9	6.3	6.3	1.4
Periods					
1951–69	2.0	1.7	3.7	3.6	−1.0
1951–89	2.1	1.8	3.9	3.9	0.1
1992–02	1.7	5.0	6.7	6.6	2.5
1993–96	2.0	4.6	6.6	5.9	3.3
1997–02	1.8	3.4	5.2	5.8	1.9
2003–10	1.5	6.6	8.0	7.7	2.5
2003–12	1.4	6.1	7.5	7.3	2.1
Average	1.9	2.9	4.8	4.8	1.0

Source: RBI, *Handbook of Statistics on the Indian Economy*; World Bank Indicators; Bhalla 2012; authors' computation
Note: All variables are average annual rates of growth.

The how and why of economic growth in India

and not surprisingly, growth collapsed. This fact alone helps answer two of the above questions: the non-acceleration in GDP growth in the 1990s post-reforms *and* the 'miracle' high growth in 2003–10.[5] With the change of government in 1996, new policymakers adjudged that administered savings deposit rates were too high; in a space of four years, 1999–2003, these rates were reduced by 450 basis points. Inflation stayed the same, and hence real lending rates declined by a record amount. This 'reform' set the stage for the investment and growth boom starting in 2003. However, many commentators and analysts believe that the recent high growth was a consequence of overheating, and *not* because of a structural shift in the economy; this debate is taken up in some detail later in this chapter.

In an eerie replay of the mid-1990s, there has been a sharp increase in real rates during the last two years, especially in 2012. Again, the cause is very likely the overly hawkish monetary policy.[6] While other factors are no doubt responsible, analysis suggests that at least half of the 5 percentage point decline in GDP growth was due to an inappropriate level of short-term policy rates. Thus, an important part of the explanation of Indian growth rates post-1991 is the operation of monetary policy; in this regard, not unlike many emerging economies, but unlike many developing economies in the pre-globalization era before the 1980s, monetary policy has now taken centre stage.

The first low growth planning stage, 1950–90

The economic environment at independence: planning is equal to development

At the time of India's independence, the world was emerging from the double whammy of the Depression and the Second World War, but in the first post-war decade, a lot changed. In the West, government-planned reconstruction achieved wonders—the European economies enjoyed unprecedented economic growth. Economic depression had become a distant memory, and it seemed that *some* planning was extremely productive. Some European countries, and particularly those with a strong left-wing tradition like England, extended enormously the role of the government. For the state to intervene was for the state to do good.

With India's colonial master choosing a strong(er) role for the state, planning became the norm in the 1950s, and bigger planning meant a better future. The original purpose of increased government intervention—avoidance of severe economic macroeconomic contraction—was lost in the assumed superiority of government in handling *all* economic activities. Western economists also purported to show the duality/equality between a market, individual system and a government/central planning system. This theoretical equivalence ignored all of the political dangers pointed out by some, especially Hayek.

Friedman's important study *Capitalism and Freedom* in the early 1960s was to be the last warning before truly mega-planning in most of the developing, and several of the developed economies. (The USA escaped the worst excesses.) So isolated were the forces of liberalism—Hayek, Friedman and Bauer—that what they taught, and advocated, did not make even the reading lists of important US universities. So universal was the hold of democratic socialism and/or planning that the phrase 'economic freedom' and/or 'economic liberties' is not to be found in most (or any) economic literature published between 1962 and 1988. The lack of *any* discussion of economic freedom by economists, and the considerable political science and economic literature on political freedom (see Bhalla 1997, 2007 for a sample) only emphasizes the stranglehold of prevailing 'liberal' economic opinion. Discussion of political freedom was politically correct; discussion of economic freedom was politically incorrect. Economics and public policy departments at liberal Eastern universities did not even mention Hayek, let alone study his prescient analysis

65

of economic freedom and growth; and Friedman was mentioned only for his views on monetarism and for his 'battle' with fiscalism.

In terms of patterns, there are three noteworthy factors about India in those early years (around 1951). First, the share of agriculture in GDP was high, around 50%. The share of industry was only 15%, which by 1962 had reached 20%. Some 50 years later, in 2012, the share of industry in GDP had not increased that much, at only 26%. Table 5.2 shows the sectoral growth rates since 1951.

India had a deeply overvalued exchange rate of around 180% at the time of independence: this was nearly identical to the real exchange rate in the late 19th century (Bhalla 2012). If the currencies were overvalued 100 years earlier, they were far more so in 1950, after almost 80 years of faster growth in the USA than at home.

Whether it was false nationalist pride, or ignorance, India persisted with a large, more than 100% overvaluation until the early 1980s, and it was not until 1998 that the exchange rate was fairly valued (Table 5.3 reports period averages; currency valuation in India was −1.6% in 1998; see Bhalla 2012 for details).

This overvaluation led to a distorted pattern of development. Agriculture was ignored, industry emphasized; import substitution was the rule, imports were favoured and exports were taxed. It was a familiar tale in those days. The fact that we have the opposite problem today indicates how much the development models, and the world, have changed. Industrialization in a hurry meant a neglect of agriculture, and an overvaluation of the currency—an average overvaluation level of 124% with the beginning decade level at 154% and the end decade (1980s) average level at 93%. Given that the average coefficient of currency valuation is −0.015 for a large sample of countries (Bhalla 2012) and for India (see Table 5.4), this meant that close to 2% of annual GDP growth was lost to the biases engineered by the 'import substitution' policy of industrialization.

Table 5.2 Sectoral growth rates, different periods, 1951–2012

| Period | Sectoral output growth | | | |
	Agriculture	Industry	Services	GDP
Decades				
1951–59	2.6	5.7	—	3.5
1960–69	2.3	6.0	4.2	3.8
1970–79	1.0	3.4	4.3	2.8
1980–89	4.2	5.8	6.1	5.4
1990–99	3.1	5.5	7.1	5.6
2000–09	2.4	7.4	8.3	7.0
2010–12	4.8	5.1	8.7	6.3
Periods				
1951–69	2.4	5.9	4.2	3.7
1951–89	2.5	5.2	4.9	3.9
1992–02	3.1	6.8	8.1	6.7
1993–96	4.2	7.8	7.4	6.6
1997–02	0.9	4.9	7.5	5.2
2003–10	3.9	8.2	9.2	8.0
2003–12	3.8	7.7	9.1	7.5
Averages	2.6	5.6	6.2	4.8

Source: RBI, *Handbook of Statistics on the Indian Economy*

The how and why of economic growth in India

Table 5.3 Real interest rates and levels and changes in currency valuation, 1951–2012

Period	Currency undervaluation	Change in currency undervalue	IMF Def	Productivity adjusted change	Real interest rates
Decade					
1951–59	153.8	−3.1	−0.9	−2.2	—
1960–69	137.8	−3.4	−1.0	−2.4	4.5
1970–79	122.5	1.8	0.4	1.4	3.8
1980–89	93.0	−7.0	−3.2	−3.8	7.8
1990–99	21.2	−6.9	−3.6	−3.3	6.8
2000–09	−26.6	−2.7	1.5	−4.2	6.2
2010–12	−28.3	2.7	1.9	0.8	5.3
Period					
1951–69	145.4	−3.3	−1.0	−2.3	4.5
1951–89	126.1	−2.9	−1.2	−1.7	5.8
1992–02	−9.6	−3.7	0.5	−4.1	6.4
1993–96	19.3	−5.7	−1.2	−4.5	6.2
1997–02	−9.7	−6.0	−2.5	−3.5	7.8
2003–10	−29.4	−0.4	4.4	−4.8	5.3
2003–12	−29.3	−0.4	2.8	−3.2	5.4
Average	77.1	−3.3	−1.0	−2.3	6.1

Source: RBI, *Handbook of Statistics on the Indian Economy*; Bhalla 2012; authors' computations

Table 5.4 Modelling the determinants of GDP growth in India, 1978–2012

	Interest rate lagged (%)	Currency valuation (%)		Fiscal deficit (%)	R-square	No. of obs
		Level	Change			
1978–2012						
Model 1	-0.764**				0.407	35
Model 2		−0.020**			0.255	35
Model 3			−0.412*		0.314	35
Model 4				−0.051	0.077	35
Model 5	−0.628***	−0.012*	−0.325**	−0.101	0.650	35
1993–2012						
Model 6	−0.675***				0.386	20
Model 7		−0.022			0.090	20
Model 8			−0.213*		0.176	20
Model 9				0.299	0.123	20
Model 10	−0.883***	−0.008	−0.364***	−0.138	0.782	20

Notes: Statistical significance: * $p<0.1$; ** $p<0.05$; *** $p<0.01$; both the real interest rate and currency valuation levels are entered with one period lag.

Some of the reasons for the initial gap, i.e. the sorry state of India's industrialization in the Nehru era, 1950 to the late 1960s, is explored intensively by Bhagwati and Desai (1970). Their book, *India: Planning for Industrialization—Industrialization and Trade Policies since 1951*, was the first wake-up call to Nehruvian socialism and is a must-read for anyone wanting to understand how, why and where Indian industrial development went wrong—*especially given the rich industrial and entrepreneurial heritage*, a point the authors emphasize.

67

GDP growth accelerates, 1980–90

GDP growth shows a clear acceleration from an average of 2.8% in the 1970s to a level of nearly double that in the 1980s: 5.4% per annum. It is this acceleration that several authors have noticed (e.g. DeLong 2001; Panagariya 2004; Rodrik and Subramanian 2004a; Virmani 2004a; Kohli 2006) and commented upon.

That the acceleration in the 1980s was not due to economic reforms of any magnitude is a conclusion supported by two facts. First, the conclusion about a large acceleration or breakout in GDP growth is based on a comparison of the 1980s vs the 1970s. For most countries, the 1970s are a bad 'benchmark', as they were a turbulent period for the world economy, with food, commodity and oil prices sky-rocketing and bringing in their wake stagflation. Further, the 1960s growth is understated because of the presence of back-to-back drought years of 1965/66 and 1966/67. Average GDP growth increases from 3.8% to 4.3% per annum during 1951–69 if these drought years are excluded, and what little acceleration is present (from 4.4% to 5.4% per annum) is easily explained by the reallocation of labour from agriculture to industry (see below). The 1980s were a lot better in terms of lower oil prices and lower world inflation. India was not immune to these events. Second, there was only a marginal increase in the investment rate for the two decades, from 19% in 1970–79 to 21% in 1980–89.

Not much increase in factor inputs and no reforms, and yet some consistent acceleration in GDP growth. A detailed perusal of the data on India suggests the following alternative interpretation.

Reallocation of labour from agriculture to industry

India was a predominantly rural economy at the time of independence in 1947, with agriculture accounting for approximately 75% of the workforce and 55% of GDP. The development literature, whether of the unlimited supplies of labour à la Lewis, or the structural change school of Chenery, recognizes that in the early stages of development, the *extra* growth that an economy receives is due to the reallocation of labour from the low-productivity agricultural sector to the higher-productivity non-agricultural (industrial) sector. Only later do factor accumulation and technological change matter as contributors to higher growth. This factor reallocation has been estimated by Robinson (1971) to average around 16% to 18% of the early growth in developing countries.

Reallocation is a long-term process and a simple accounting exercise indicates that if the economy was growing at 4% in the 1950s, and India had an agricultural share of 55%, and that agricultural and industrial growth was roughly 2.6% and 6.0%, respectively, then 30 years later the average GDP growth rate, on factor reallocation alone, would be expected to be 5% per annum. Actual GDP growth in the 1980s amounted to 5.4% per annum! In other words, there was no acceleration in GDP growth in the 1980s due to a better investment climate (which would show up in a higher investment rate, which did not happen), or any economic reforms.

Modelling Indian growth

A key question in growth empirics is to establish the determinants of human and capital factor accumulation. The determinants of human capital accumulation are well known. Policies to increase enrolment and school quality have been well discussed, and accepted. Somewhat controversial are the presumed determinants of investment. It is widely acknowledged that just as the demand for labour is on a downward slope, so is the demand for investment.

There was one reform in the 1980s: the exchange rate began to be less overvalued and, as noted above, devaluations and economic reforms post-1991 meant that the exchange rate became fairly valued in the late 1990s. This meant that the price of an investment good (in international prices) became cheaper as the exchange rate became less overvalued. The price of an investment good is the price for capital, and the price of capital incorporates both the real exchange rate and the real interest rate.

One of the interesting features of the Indian economy, and policy, is the relative scarcity of experts who think that interest rates matter at all in determining investment. This feature has especially come to the forefront in the last few years when the GDP growth has steadily collapsed to only 5%. Policymakers at the Indian central bank (Reserve Bank of India, or RBI) have been emphasizing that it is not. Various causes have been mentioned as determinants of the growth slowdown, especially 'policy paralysis' in the form of non-clearance of government-aided projects, political uncertainty, etc. Unduly tight monetary policy is rarely mentioned as a factor. Is it true that interest rates do not much affect investment in India? This subject is examined below.

Currency valuation matters

In addition to interest rates, another important determinant of investment is the competitive nature of the exchange rate. This is explored in detail in Bhalla (2012), where it is shown that the profitability of investments is affected by the real exchange rate: the more the exchange rate is undervalued, the higher the profitability, and the higher the rate of investment, *ceteris paribus*. How, though, does one define the real exchange rate? Balassa (1964) and Samuelson (1964) argued that the equilibrium real exchange rate was affected by productivity growth—the higher such growth relative to the benchmark, e.g. the USA, the greater the tendency for the real exchange rate to appreciate. This definition is extensively discussed and successfully tested in Bhalla (2012), from where the estimate of the real exchange rate and currency valuation (log percentage difference between the two) is used in this chapter.

If the level of currency valuation is available for any given year, the logarithm (log) *change* in such valuation can easily be computed as the sum of two (log) change components: change due to a conventional International Monetary Fund (IMF) component that adjusts currency and inflation rate differentials with respect to a base currency or economy (e.g. the USA), and change due to 'standing still'. The latter generally occurs when a country manages its currency to *prevent* the nominal appreciation being engineered by 'markets' via strong capital flows, etc. Real devaluation from strength leads to reserve accumulation and makes your currency more competitive—a win-win situation for the individual country. By contrast, the IMF component is often the result of devaluation from weakness, i.e. when the fundamentals of the economy collapse due to high inflation and/or slower growth.

Both components add up to the change in currency valuation. An increase in inflation, *ceteris paribus*, leads to an appreciation of the exchange rate. When this appreciation is corrected via a nominal exchange rate depreciation, it can be termed as devaluation from weakness. However, when the exchange rate is *prevented* from appreciation due to either lower inflation, or other fundamentals, then the resulting real exchange rate change is depreciation from strength.

An undervalued currency directly leads to greater profitability of investments (both domestic and foreign direct investment—FDI), a higher investment rate, and therefore higher growth. Indirectly, higher FDI can lead to greater efficiency of investments and therefore higher growth. A detailed cross-country analysis for the period 1960 to 2011, yields the following result (Bhalla 2012): no matter what the time period (before or after 1980), or specification, the impact of currency undervaluation on the investment rate is large: each 10% increase in currency under-valuation leads to almost a 1% increase in the investment rate. In a reduced form *growth* model, the same significant relationship holds; each 10% increase in undervaluation leads to a 0.1–0.2 percentage point increase in GDP growth.

In testing for the impact of change in currency valuation on growth, it matters whether a real devaluation is of the strong variety or of the weak type. In growth regressions of the type reported in Table 5.4, real depreciation due to weak fundamentals has no impact on growth; by contrast, real depreciation due to standing still has a strong impact on growth. Each 10% depreciation adds about 1–2 percentage points to GDP growth. This is particularly true for the long time period 1978 to 2012, but the coefficient is not significant for the more recent period 1993–2012.

The level of currency undervaluation is also significant, but only in the longer period 1978–2012 regressions. The coefficient is similar to that found in Bhalla (2012) for a cross-section of countries, around −0.02, i.e. each 10 percentage point increase in currency undervaluation[7] leads to a 0.2 percentage point increase in GDP growth. This magnitude may appear small but is not actually the case: the Indian currency was overvalued by close to 60% in 1990, so the elimination of this overvaluation in the decade 1991–2001 meant that the economy was able to grow at almost 1.2 percentage points faster than in the pre-1991 reform years.

The importance of interest rates

It is one of the most basic laws of economics: the price of a good affects its demand, e.g. the price of capital (the real interest rate) affects the demand for investment and hence GDP growth. In developing countries like India, imperfect capital markets may mean that there is a lot of noise in measures of interest rates and inflation and hence the effect of the price of capital on investment is inadequately captured. Nevertheless, the hypothesis remains that real interest rates matter for investments and growth.

Strangely, and this is one of the strong and near-unique characteristics about the Indian growth experience, discussions about interest rate policy have been conspicuous through their absence. Except for five short years, 1998–2003, it is fair to state that the importance of interest rates has been neglected in India. Reflecting this (misguided) lack of policy emphasis, most writing on Indian growth has also ignored this important dimension. Panagariya (2008) makes little mention of interest rate policy as a determinant of Indian growth. Ditto for most other contributors in the debate on Indian growth, e.g. Acharya, Rodrik and Subramanian, DeLong and Kohli. Virmani does discuss the role of interest rates but empirically finds a zero effect, most likely because he (erroneously) uses the WPI deflator as a measure of inflation.[8]

Table 5.4 documents the results of several models of economic growth for India with three determinants: the real interest rate lagged one period, currency valuation, also lagged one period, and the consolidated fiscal deficit. Two start years are chosen, 1978 and 1993, the latter year chosen two years after the start of the reforms in 1991. In that year, growth was only 1.4%, and a dummy variable for that year is included in regressions for the 1978–2012 period. The real interest rate is defined as the nominal lending rate of the State Bank of India, India's largest bank, minus the inflation rate as measured by the GDP deflator.[9] Currency undervaluation levels are taken from Bhalla (2012), and the consolidated centre plus state fiscal deficit estimates are taken from official documents.

The major result emerging from the several growth regressions reported in Table 5.4 is that not only do interest rates matter, but they are the strongest determinant of growth. Note both the strong significance and near constancy of the coefficient for the real interest rate at around −0.6 to −0.9—i.e. for each 1 percentage point increase in the real interest rate, real GDP growth is −0.8 percentage points lower. The explanatory power of the model is also very large: for the 20

The how and why of economic growth in India

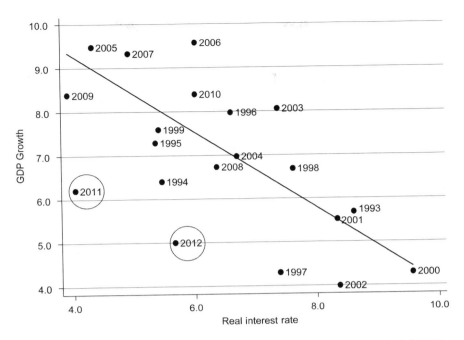

Figure 5.2 How well do interest rates (lagged) explain GDP growth in India, 1978–2012?

post-reform years 1993–2012, the R-squared is 0.39 with just one variable (real interest rates lagged); the R-squared is about the same for the longer 35-year period 1978–2012.

Figure 5.2 documents a simple scatter plot of (one period lagged) real interest rates and GDP growth. The exceptionally slow growth years of 2011 and 2012 are major negative outliers, with the post-crisis stimulus year a major positive outlier. Note that estimates for both 2004 (the first boom year) and 2008 (crisis year) have low prediction errors, along with 1991 and 1992, and the high growth year 2010 is on the line.

There is an extremely close correspondence between the two variables, including a matching of the turning points (the correlation coefficient is above 0.77). Real interest rates increased by over 400 basis points from 5.4% in 1994 to 9.6% in 1999. The growth rate declined from 8.0% in 1996 to 4.3% in 2000. The acceleration in GDP growth (8.1% vs. 4.0% the previous year) started in 2003/04, ostensibly because of good weather; agricultural growth topped 9% in that year. In the background is the real clue of real interest rates, as they fell to a low of 4.3% in 2004/05, the lowest since 1979. Only the great financial crisis brought the real rates lower in 2008, but by 2012 such rates had climbed to 6.7%, the highest in the new era of growth, 2003/04 onwards.

Fiscal deficits and growth

In addition to real interest rates and currency valuation, there is a third, often talked about determinant of growth—the magnitude of fiscal deficits. The share of fiscal deficits in GDP, along with other related shares (savings, investment and current account deficit) are reported in Table 5.5. How fiscal deficits affect the economy is controversial. The direction of causality is often not clear: is it high fiscal deficits that cause low growth, or is it that low growth leads to

Surjit S. Bhalla

Table 5.5 Savings, investment, current account and fiscal deficits (% GDP)

Period	Savings	Investments	Current account deficit	Fiscal deficit
Decades				
1951–59	11.1	11.7	–0.6	—
1960–69	14.6	15.0	–0.4	—
1970–79	18.6	18.0	0.0	–4.0
1980–89	20.8	22.6	–1.8	–7.3
1990–99	23.7	24.9	–1.2	–6.7
2000–09	30.1	30.6	–0.5	–8.6
2010–12	31.1	35.0	–3.9	–8.5
Periods				
1951–69	12.9	13.4	–0.5	—
1951–89	16.4	16.9	–0.7	–5.6
1992–02	27.6	28.4	–0.9	–7.8
1993–96	24.1	25.2	–1.1	–5.6
1997–02	24.0	24.4	–0.4	–9.6
2003–10	32.6	33.8	–1.2	–7.9
2003–12	32.3	34.0	–1.8	–8.0
Average	20.5	21.3	–0.9	–6.8

high fiscal deficits? In India, the debate is compounded by the fact that for most of the post-1970s period, fiscal deficits were the result of abnormally high administered interest rates on savings deposits. For most of the last 15 years or so, interest payments have accounted for over 80% of the entire fiscal deficit in the economy. Administered interest rates, in the form of interest rates on 'small savings' offered by different state governments, were kept at a nominal level of 12.5% or higher until 1999. In none of the models explored in Table 5.4 is the fiscal deficit variable at all significant in explaining GDP growth.

This result is not surprising since fiscal deficits are more in the nature of an outcome rather than an input. Some of their effect is already captured by the presence of the variable of real interest rates. However, it is surprising that in none of the models, and even when entered by itself, is the fiscal deficit variable statistically significant.

In Bhalla (2000) a direct connection between administered interest rates and the fiscal deficit was outlined. It was argued that if repressive interest rates were to be reduced, the fiscal deficit would be lower, real interests would be lower, growth would be higher—a virtuous cycle. The prospects for such an eventuality were outlined in detail in Bhalla (2000):

> the consolidated (State plus Center) fiscal deficit has stayed constant around 9–10% of GDP for the last twenty years. Abnormally high interest rates (no arbitrage with world rates possible because of a closed capital account) have resulted in higher cost of borrowings ... interest payments have increased from 3% of GDP in the early eighties to almost 8% of GDP today; as a proportion of the fiscal deficit, the percentage is 35% in the early eighties, and more than 75 per cent today. High interest rates are a major *cause* for the high fiscal deficits in India.
>
> (*Bhalla 2000: 2*)

Starting in February 1999 small savings rates began to be reduced, and over the next four years were reduced by a total of 450 basis points. In the years 1999 to 2003 the government had

The how and why of economic growth in India

proceeded to cut administered interest rates on deposits from 12.5% to 8.0%. It is this reduction in interest rates (note, not monetary policy RBI action but fiscal policy Ministry of Finance action) that sowed the seeds of the boom in investment and growth that India experienced from 2003 onwards. This decline in interest rates also allowed the fiscal deficit to decline both from the higher growth effect and, as noted above, also from the effect of significantly lower interest payments.

Growth begins, 1992–96

The most significant economic story of India in the post-independence era is the story of economic reforms in 1991. That year India faced its most serious economic crisis. After a decade of 'high' growth in the 1980s, the economy stuttered into 1991 as foreign reserves collapsed to near zero and GDP growth to only 1.4%. Elections were held; the new government, under the leadership of Prime Minister Narasimha Rao and Finance Minister Manmohan Singh, was different in style and structure than any previous government. Given that Finance Minister Singh's Oxford PhD thesis was on the necessity of export growth for successful development, perhaps it was not a coincidence that foreign trade initiatives defined the economic reforms.

These reforms were major. In a short period of time, they achieved the following: devaluation of the rupee by 20%, reduction in the peak tariff rate of 300% to 110%, elimination of the Monopolies and Restrictive Trade Practices Act, and a structural adjustment loan from the IMF. In 1995 the Indian economy felt the full impact of these reforms as growth accelerated to above 7% for two consecutive years, 1995/96 and 1996/97. Agricultural growth fluctuations had caused GDP growth often to grow above 7% (e.g. in 1964, 1967, 1975, 1988, etc.), but this was the first time such growth had occurred without a snap back from a preceding drought year. However, soon the economy slowed and registered an average growth rate of only 5.4% for the period 1997–2002.

Growth should have been in the 7%+ range throughout the 1990s—an acceleration of 1.5% per year was consistent with the magnitude of the economic reforms and the gradual elimination of currency overvaluation. The two-year (1995–96) acceleration to potential had some unintended consequences. In the mindset of many Indian politicians and policymakers the 'large' acceleration over the Hindu rate of growth of 3.5% was suggestive of overheating, and overheating meant the onset of high, and higher, inflation. So when the growth acceleration occurred, the RBI reacted and as a first recourse, put on the monetary brakes.

The central bank's actions, the monetary tightening, clearly imply an assumed trade-off between growth and inflation. While there might have been a trade-off between the two during the closed era pre-1990,[10] there was considerably less chance of such a trade-off following the opening-up of the economy in 1991. India became a considerably more open economy with economic reforms. Outside influences on growth and inflation were bound to be greater with an open economy than a closed economy. One outside influence, singularly under-appreciated by Indian policymakers, is the relationship between domestic inflation and world inflation, the latter as measured by the median inflation rate in the developing world in that particular year. Figure 5.3 documents the surprisingly close relationship between median developing country inflation[11] and Indian inflation, at least since 1980. The correlation between the two series (1980 to 2012) is a high 0.72 and almost all the turning points are near simultaneous. It appears that monetary policy was tightened in India at almost exactly the same time as inflation began to fall world-wide in the mid-1990s.

73

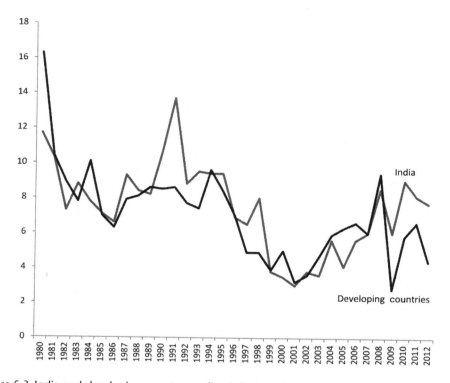

Figure 5.3 India and developing country median inflation: close correlation
Note: Inflation is measured by the GDP deflator, while developing countries' inflation is the median value for each year.

Growth falters, 1997–2002

In the mindset of the Indian politicians, and most policymakers, it was inconceivable that the Indian economy could grow at East Asian growth rates; hence the doubling of the rate of growth above Hindu rates of 3.5% was considered impossible. Such growth was viewed as overheating and deserving of a strong policy response. Possibly it was the crisis of 1991 that prevented the monetary policymakers from realizing that an expansion from 5.5% to 7.5% growth was the mildest of accelerations. Even though there was a large and rapid decline in world-wide, and domestic, inflation in the mid- to late 1990s, the monetary authorities did not respond by easing.

And by keeping savings deposit rates at high double-digit levels (12.5%), and inflation collapsing, real rates reached double-digit levels in the late 1990s. This caused GDP growth to revert back to around 5.0% to 5.5%.

In 1999, when inflation reached a low of 2.9%, the government took the first major step towards interest rate reforms. It was not the Central Bank that changed its policy; it was the Ministry of Finance which began the necessary process of aligning savings deposit rates with inflation (and market) realities. Within a space of four years, savings deposit rates were brought down from 12.5% to 8%, and government bond yields were at 5.7% in 2003, down from 12% levels that prevailed in the late 1990s.

In 'normal' economies, such a reduction in long-term real interest rates would ordinarily be headline news for several years. Analysts would relate industrial growth, GDP growth, stock prices to this mega event. After all, in Western economies a mere 25 basis point change in interest rates is a momentous occasion. So it is in several developing economies, including China. However, as noted earlier, a defining feature of India's political economy and policy-making is that the level of interest rates is not considered that important in either determining investment or growth.

Growth accelerates, 2003–10, and slows down 2011–12

The new Congress government came to power in May 2004, after an agriculture-induced robust growth of 8.1% in 2003/04. During the preceding five years, GDP growth averaged only 5.6% per annum, about equal to the long-term average of the 1980s and 1990s. However, with no growth-friendly policy inputs post-2002, and several anti-growth initiatives, the economy averaged close to 9% growth for eight years, a record by any yardstick.

No economic reforms and growth acceleration: what happened? Many, including several economists, senior government officials, *The Economist* and the IMF claimed that the acceleration was proof of overheating and growth much in excess of potential GDP growth of around 6%–7%. Others, e.g. Bhalla (2006, 2010), claimed that there was a structural break in the Indian growth rate starting in 2003, and that the potential GDP growth of India, without any additional economic reforms, was close to 8%+—a finding supported by statistical exercises like the Hodrick–Prescott filter (see Figure 5.1).

The increase in growth in 2003–10 was the sharpest, and longest, in Indian history: a large 4 percentage point acceleration to around 9% per annum. However, in an eerie replay of the mid-1990s, this growth acceleration was also met with scepticism. As with the mid-1990s, most analysts, economists and especially the monetary authorities doubted the sustainability of this acceleration and felt that the economy was in a substantial overheating phase. The base case belief remained that any growth rate above 6% to 7% per annum was not sustainable.

This scepticism suggests that India may be *sui generis*. No policymaker, and very few analysts, pointed to the earlier decline in real interest rates as an important cause, let alone *the* cause, for India's belated entry onto the high-growth stage. Models of GDP growth reported above indicate that a 400 basis point decline in long-term interest rates would lead to an approximately 3 percentage point increase in GDP growth. This is exactly what happened.

However, subsequently growth collapsed to the long-term 5.5% range and this has led many observers to question the 8%+ time path of Indian growth. The reasoning is as follows. The period 2002 to 2007 coincided with global liquidity and global expansion, with the result that many countries were observed to be overheating and growing above long-term trends. This was a rising tide that lifted all boats, including India. Subsequent to the Great Recession, growth rates in many developing countries are significantly below their 2003–07 averages, as is the case with India.

However, the collapse of GDP growth in 2011 and 2012 to levels last seen in the 1980s and 1990s has led many commentators, and government officials, to speculate that what happened in India during 2003–10 was the exception and not the rule. It is argued that global liquidity and associated expansion led the Indian economy to accelerate—indeed, to overheat—and that the reduction to 5% to 6% levels is just reversion to the 'normal' mean. The rising tide lifted all boats. The tide withdrew, and so did India.

While the global tide theory is compelling, it misses out on one very important development vis-à-vis India. It is that both savings and investment rates increased sharply post-2002. Savings rates had hovered in a narrow range around 24% in the previous decade (1993 to 2002) and investment rates had averaged the same. In just five years since 2002, savings and investment rates increased by 12 and 13 percentage points, respectively.

As shown in Table 5.5 and Figure 5.4, investment rates increased from an average 23% level 1980–2002 to 11 percentage points higher in 2003–12. No other country has shown this increase in investment rates; indeed, most countries (including China) have shown a decline in the investment rate, especially post-2007. The explanation for the decline in Indian growth rates has to go outside of the conventional wisdom of a rising tide; as discussed above, it had substantially to do with an inappropriate monetary policy.

The Indian interest rate story helps to complete the circle and explain Indian growth puzzles. Unwarranted tight monetary policy, and much higher than warranted real interest rates, brought the Indian economy crashing down from a potential GDP growth rate of 7.5% to less than 5%. Reversal of this policy brought the economy back to 7.5%; further decline in the level of undervaluation (from 13% overvaluation in 1996 to 30% undervaluation in 2006) has added another percentage point to GDP growth: hence, a potential GDP growth in India of at least 8.5% per annum.

Low industrial growth

One of the striking features of the Indian economy is the very low share of industrial output in GDP *and* the relatively low growth of industrial output. One of the most accepted theorems of development is that the labour that is released from agriculture is absorbed by industry. In India, this has not been the case, despite the fact that the share of industry was already small to begin with. Compared with China, in the year just before the Great Recession, industry's share of GDP in India was only 26%; in China it was 22 percentage points higher at 48%, i.e. almost twice the size.

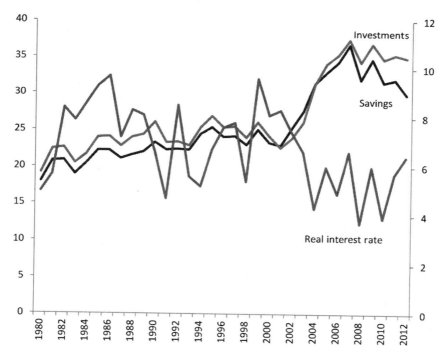

Figure 5.4 Savings and investment (% share of GDP) and real interest rates

What explains this radically differential pattern? One important factor is initial conditions. In 1965 and 1980 the industrial share in China was 35% and 49%, respectively; the corresponding figures for India were 19% and 22%. So the share of industry in India has always been behind, way behind, that of China. Since the attitudes towards economic freedom were much the same in India and China prior to 1980, this large difference is hard to explain. One possible explanation is that since industry was part of the state sector in China, and originally was part of the private sector in India, it did not come under the 'exploitative' filter in China. In India, especially during the period 1947–91, profits and money-making were not something in which an upper-caste Brahmin was supposed to indulge in. Add to that Fabian socialism and old-fashioned communism, and one had a heady recipe for disaster. Marginal tax rates on individual income peaked at 97.5% under the socialist Indira Gandhi; her dynasty rules India even today.

Industrialists have been under constant suspicion, and taxation, in India. Until recently, and compared to most of its Asian competitors, Indian industry has paid a higher cost of capital, and paid higher taxes. The one advantage it ostensibly had, cheap labour, was reduced to zero (if not lower) by both an overvalued exchange rate and restrictions on employers for hiring and firing. All of these policies have contributed to India's pitifully lower share of industry, compared to an economy at its level of development and size.

The bias against industry also shows up in the results. Table 5.6 reports the highest 10-year moving average growth in industrial value added achieved in different countries. Data are till 2011 and are revealing. The maximum 10-year average achieved in China was 12.9%; the maximum ever achieved in India was 7.6%, a figure almost half that of China. Out of 150-odd developing countries,[12] India's rank is 77. There are several countries that have achieved a 10-year

Table 5.6 Poor industrial growth in India

| | Industrial growth | | |
Country	Average	Max 10 years	Rank max 10 years
Algeria	4.5	16.6	6
Côte d'Ivoire	5.9	14.2	12
Indonesia	6.6	13.3	18
China (People's Repub.)	9.1	12.9	20
Thailand	7.9	12.1	28
Korea (Repub.)	8.4	12.0	29
Egypt	5.4	10.7	41
Malaysia	6.4	10.4	44
Pakistan	6.6	10.3	46
Brazil	4.1	10.0	49
Bangladesh	5.5	10.0	50
Singapore	6.7	8.9	62
Turkey	5.3	7.7	75
Philippines	4.0	7.7	76
India	5.6	7.6	77
Mexico	3.7	7.1	86
Chile	3.3	6.7	92
Sri Lanka	5.3	6.5	95
South Africa	2.5	6.3	100
Argentina	2.3	5.8	108

industrial growth rate higher than that of India: Egypt has done it, Brazil has achieved it, and Pakistan and the Philippines have surpassed India's growth.

What the future holds

The big concern, and debate, in India today is its potential rate of growth, and how quickly it is likely to achieve it. There are statistical methods (like the Hondrick–Prescott filter) to arrive at an estimate of potential GDP growth. The results of this method (reported in Figure 5.1 and Table 5.1) suggest that potential GDP growth was above 8% but if the last two years' growth is a 'valid' observation, then potential GDP growth is down to 6%.

Alternative estimates of potential growth can also be derived from economic 'fundamentals'. There are at least three different methods for arriving at the forecast of growth rates. The first method relies on a sectoral approach, i.e. growth in the three different sectors (agriculture, industry and services) are forecast, based on past patterns, to arrive at an assessment of the future. The second method is a production function approach, with most importantly the estimate of growth in investment or capital inputs. The third method relies on the catch–up and policy (mostly currency undervaluation and interest rates) models discussed earlier.

Method 1: forecast based on sectoral growth rates

The sector-based estimate of potential GDP growth of 7.8% per annum is arrived at as follows. Services presently account for close to 56% of Indian GDP, industry for 27% and agriculture 18%. Industry has never averaged more than 7% growth on a sustained basis to date but there is reason to believe that history will not repeat itself. Between 2003 and 2010, industrial growth averaged 8.2% per annum (see Table 5.2). This was over eight continuous years and only the unusual nature of the economy during the last two years (policy paralysis and high interest rates) has brought the decadal average to 7.7%. It is 'reasonable' to expect industrial growth averaging 8% per annum with economic reforms in India. If this happens, then the historical relationship between services and industrial growth (arbitraged through the labour market) suggests that services will grow by 9%. If agriculture grows at 3.5%, the combined GDP growth rate will be 7.8%.[13]

Method 2: production function approach

Factor accumulation: cross–country data suggest that it is rare for an economy to jump to an investment level of around 35% of GDP and not stay at those levels for a considerable length of time. As Table 5.5 shows, in India during 2003–12 just such a jump in investment shares was observed. An investment-to-GDP ratio of 35% implies that the growth of capital stock is close to 9% per annum. This 'episode' of increasing investment rates, and then stabilization around 40%+ levels, is likely to occur over the next several years. Labour force and employment growth has been slowing to around 1.8% per annum. Assuming a capital share in output of 55%,[14] expected GDP growth, with zero productivity growth, is 5.8% per annum. Total factor productivity growth in 2003–10 averaged 2.5% per annum; hence, a production function approach yields 8.3% as India's potential GDP growth (see Table 5.7).

Method 3: currency undervaluation and real interest rates

The level of currency undervaluation in India has stayed in the 25% to 30% range for the last several years. The variation has been present in the two components of the change in currency

The how and why of economic growth in India

Table 5.7 GDP growth, by factors

Period	Capital	Labour force	Total factor productivity	GDP
Decades				
1951–59	4.3	—	—	3.5
1960–69	5.7	3.8	−1.0	3.8
1970–79	4.4	2.8	−0.8	2.8
1980–89	4.7	2.3	1.9	5.4
1990–99	4.1	2.0	2.5	5.6
2000–09	7.2	1.9	2.0	7.0
2010–12	8.2	1.6	1.4	6.3
Periods				
1951–69	5.0	3.8	−1.0	3.7
1951–89	4.8	2.9	0.1	3.9
1992–02	6.0	1.9	2.5	6.7
1993–96	4.1	2.0	3.3	6.6
1997–02	4.4	1.8	1.9	5.2
2003–10	8.4	1.9	2.5	8.0
2003–12	8.4	1.8	2.1	7.5
Average	5.2	2.5	1.0	4.8

valuation. The statistically relevant 'standing still' depreciation was at a healthy −4.8% per annum between 2003 and 2010. Given that a conservative estimate of the impact coefficient of this variable is around 0.2, it was observed that around 1% GDP growth was contributed by this real depreciation. Over the last two years, the depreciation has turned into an appreciation at the rate of 0.8% per annum (implying productivity growth less than the numeraire country, the USA).

If Indian growth were to re-emerge (and the two growth forecast models above suggest that this is likely), then 'standing still' depreciation is also likely to occur, and this could add around 1% to GDP growth. An inflation decline, followed by Reserve Bank action, could also mean a decline in real interest rates of 100 to 200 basis points. Taking 150 as an average estimate, and a coefficient of around 0.7, one obtains extra GDP growth of 1%. Adding these two 'extras' to the average of the last two years of 5.7%, one obtains an estimated GDP growth of (5.7 + 0.8 + 1) 7.5%.

Combining the four different estimates of future growth, one obtains the following range for potential GDP growth in India: 7.5% to 8.5%. Only the future will tell whether India can emerge out of its self-imposed darkness to be one, if not the fastest growing economy in the world.

Conclusions

This chapter has examined the sources, and determinants, of GDP growth in India for the last 60-odd years. Empirical evidence was provided for the important and substantive role played by interest rates, and currency valuation, in determining investments, productivity and GDP growth. The sharp rise in real interest rates, induced by very tight monetary policy at a time of *falling* inflation rates in the mid- to late 1990s resulted in industrial (and GDP) growth being killed before it reached its potential. The reversal of this interest rate hike, and reduction to realistic and competitive levels during 1999–2002, is a major reason for the miraculous growth acceleration observed starting in 2003.

Aiding and abetting this process of an economy moving towards a new and higher potential GDP growth of around 8.5% was the maintenance of an increasingly competitive exchange rate since 1993/94. The chapter also offered a 'new' explanation for the much discussed, and much hyped, growth acceleration observed in the 1980s. Reallocation from agriculture to industry resulted in the potential growth rate being as high as 5%, almost equal to the 'high' growth observed in the 1980s.

By examining the various determinants of growth, and over different time periods, this study reaches the strong conclusion that the pattern of long-term interest rates, and the level and change in currency valuation, are the strongest determinants of GDP growth. Examination of the different episodes of growth shows that invariably, post-1980, the behaviour of real interest rates is the best predictor of the magnitude and direction of GDP growth

It appears that a structural break in India's growth occurred in 2003, just over a full decade after the economic reforms of 1991–93. Those reforms were incomplete, and particularly so in the financial, fiscal and monetary sectors of the economy. The gradual relaxation of controls, along with a movement towards market-determined interest rates starting in 1999, meant that post-2003 (when administered interest rate reform was complete) a structural break was possible. As part of this structural break, investment and savings rates have both jumped in India to the mid-30s+ levels.

The final conclusion about Indian growth pertains to forecasts of future growth. A variety of methods suggest that such growth, *ceteris paribus*, is likely to be in the 7.0% to 8.5% range.

Notes

1 I would like to thank Manoj Agrawal and Josh Bali for excellent research assistance.
2 Recall that China was branded a 'currency manipulator' by the USA as long ago as 1994.
3 This does not show in Figure 5.1 because the figure shows five-year averages of GDP and potential growth.
4 Throughout, real long-term interest rates refer to private bank lending rates (as per the largest public sector bank in India, the State Bank of India) minus inflation as measured by the GDP deflator.
5 The Indian fiscal year runs from April to March, so reference to the year 2003 is actually to the fiscal year 2003/04.
6 In a Taylor rule evaluation of 27 central banks, Bhalla *et al.* (2011) found the Indian central bank to be the most unwarrantedly hawkish in its operation of monetary policy.
7 Note that currency overvaluation is a positive number and undervaluation a negative number.
8 For reasons unknown, both the major economic departments in the government of India, the Ministry of Finance and the RBI, have used, and continue to use, the wholesale price index (WPI) inflation measure as a 'correct' indicator of inflation. It is well known, both in the case of India and elsewhere, that the WPI is a misleading indicator of inflation and should not be preferred for policy direction.
9 Use of the consumer price index as an inflation gauge in India is problematical for several reasons: first, prior to 2010, there were two separate indices—one each for urban and rural areas; second, post-2010, the CPI has an abnormally high share of food in its basket—around 50%. In reality, the agricultural share in India's GDP is less than 18%. The GDP deflator has the disadvantage of a three-month time lag. Nevertheless, it is preferred especially for historical analysis for which precise dating is *not* a factor.
10 However, there is close to zero empirical evidence to support the existence of a trade-off pre-1980.
11 Throughout, unless otherwise specified, inflation is as measured by the GDP deflator.
12 Oil-dependent countries and countries with a population less than one million are excluded.
13 All forecasts are contingent upon a 'neutral' world economy; short-term cycles, linking India to events and economies abroad, are to be expected.
14 A panel growth model for developing countries for the period 1960–2010 yields a capital share estimate of 55%.

Bibliography

Acemoglu, Daron, Simon Johnson and James A. Robinson (2005) 'Institutions as the Fundamental Cause of Long-Run Growth', *Handbook of Economic Growth*, North Holland, December.

Acharya, Shankar (2006) *Essays on Macroeconomic Policy and Growth in India*, Oxford University Press, Oxford.

Balassa, B. (1964) 'The Purchasing Power Parity Doctrine: A Reappraisal', *Journal of Political Economy* 72: 584–96.

Bardhan, Pranab (2005) 'Institutions Matter, but Which Ones?' *Economics of Transition* 13(3): 499–532.

Barro, Robert J. and Xavier Sala-I-Martin (1992) 'Convergence', *Journal of Political Economy* 100(2), April: 223–51.

Barry, Norman P. (1979) *Hayek's Social and Economic Philosophy*, The Macmillan Press, London.

Bhagwati, Jagdish and Padmini Desai (1970) *India: Planning for Industrialization*, Oxford University Press, London.

Bhalla, Surjit S. (1997) 'Freedom and Economic Growth: A Virtuous Cycle?' in Axel Hadenius (ed.), *Democracy's Victory and Crisis: Nobel Symposium 1994*, Cambridge University Press, Cambridge.

——(1999) 'Chinese Mercantilism: Currency Wars and How the East was Lost', ICRIER Discussion Paper, March.

——(2000) 'Financial Sector Policies in India—*Apne Pair pe Apni Kulhadi*', Chapter 2 in Surjit S. Bhalla (ed.), *New Economic Policies for New India*, Proceedings of an ICSSR Conference, Hari Haran Press, New Delhi, February.

——(2002) *Imagine there's No Country: Poverty, Inequality and Growth in the Era of Globalization*, Institute of International Economics, Washington, DC.

——(2006) *Mid-Year Review of the Indian Economy 2006–2007: India at a Structural Break*, India International Centre.

——(2007) *Second Among Equals: The Middle Class Kingdoms of India and China*, draft, Peterson Institute of International Economics, Washington, DC, May, www.oxusinvestments.com.

——(2010) 'Indian Economic Growth, 1950–2008: Facts & Beliefs, Puzzles and Policies', in Acharya Shankar and Rakesh Mohan (eds), *India's Economy: Performance and Challenges, Essays in Honor of Montek Ahluwalia*, Oxford University Press, New Delhi.

——(2012) *Devaluing to Prosperity: Misaligned Currencies and Their Growth Consequences*, Peterson Institute for International Economics, Washington, DC.

Bhalla, Surjit S., Ankur Choudhary and Nikhil Mohan (2011) *Central Banks: The Good, The Bad and The Ugly*, Oxus Investments, July, www.oxusinvestments.com.

Bloom, David E. and David Canning (2004) 'Global Demographic Change: Dimensions and Economic Significance', NBER Working Paper 10817, September.

Bosworth, Barry P. and Susan M. Collins (1996) 'Economic Growth in East Asia: Accumulation Versus Assimilation', *Brookings Papers on Economic Activity*, Fall.

——(2003) 'The Empirics of Growth: An Update', *Brookings Papers on Economic Activity*, 2, 113–206.

Chang, Ha-Joon (2005) 'Understanding the Relationship between Institutions and Economic Development: Some Key Theoretical Issues', WIDER Jubilee Conference, *Change* 40(3): 523–44.

DeLong, J. Bradford (2001) 'India Since Independence: An Analytic Growth Narrative', in Dani Rodrik (ed.), *Modern Economic Growth: Analytical Country Studies*, July.

Easterly, William, Michael Kremer, Lant Pritchett and Lawrence Summers (1993) 'Good Policy or Good Luck? Country Growth Performance and Temporary Shocks', *Journal of Monetary Economics* 32, December: 459–83.

Freidman, Milton (1965) *Capitalism & Freedom*, University of Chicago Press, Chicago, IL.

——(1966) *Essays in Positive Economics*, University of Chicago Press, Chicago, IL.

Hayek, F.A. (1976) *The Road to Serfdom*, University of Chicago Press, Chicago, IL.

Joshi, Vijay and I.M.D. Little (1994) *India Macroeconomics and Political Economy 1964–1991*, The World Bank, Washington, DC.

Kapur, Devesh and Pratap Bhanu Mehta (eds) (2006) *Public Institutions in India, Performance and Design*, Oxford University Press, Oxford.

Kochhar, Kalpana, Utsav Kumar, Raghuram Rajan, Arvind Subramanian and Ioannis Tokatlidis (2005) 'India's Pattern of Development: What Happened, What Follows', IMF Working Paper, December.

Kohli, Atul (2004) *State-Directed Development. Political Power and Industrialization in the Global Periphery*, Cambridge University Press, Cambridge.

——(2006) 'Politics of Economic Growth in India, 1980–2005', *Economic and Political Weekly*, 1 April, 8 April.

Krugman, Paul (1994) 'The Myth of Asia's Miracle', *Foreign Affairs* 73(6): 62–78.

Lewis, Arthur W. (1955) *The Theory of Economic Growth*, George Allen & Unwin, London.

Lin, Justin Yifu (2012) *The Quest for Prosperity: How Developing Economies Can Take Off*, Princeton University Press, Princeton, NJ.

Little, I.M.D, Richard N. Cooper, W. Max Corden and Sarath Rajapatiarana (1993) *Booms, Crises, and Adjustment, the Macroeconomic Experience of Developing Countries*, Oxford University Press, Oxford.

Mooley, D.A., B. Parthasarathy, K. Rupa Kumar, N.A. Sontakke, A.A. Munot and D.R. Kothawale (2003) 'IITM Indian Regional/Subdivisional Monthly Rainfall Data Set (IITM-IMR)', India Meteorological Department, www.tropmet.res.in/pub/data/rain/iitm-imr-readme.txt.

Nehru, V. and A. Dhareshwar (1993) 'A New Database on Physical Capital Stock: Sources, Methodology and Results', *Revista de Analisis Economiico* 8: 3–59.

North, Douglass C. (2005) *Institutions, Institutional Change and Economic Performance*, Cambridge University Press, Cambridge.

Panagariya, Arvind (2004) 'India in the 1980s and 1990s: A Triumph of Reforms', IMF Working Paper WP/04/43, March.

——(2007) Why India Lags Behind China and How it Can Bridge the Gap, *World Economy* 30(2), February: 229–48.

——(2008) *India: The Emerging Giant*, Oxford University Press, New York.

Pritchett, Lant (2001b) 'Where Has All the Education Gone?' *World Bank Economic Review* 15(3): 367–91.

Robinson, Sherman (1971) 'Sources of Growth in Less-Developed Countries: A Cross-Section Study', *Quarterly Journal of Economics* 85: 391–408.

Rodrik, Dani (ed.) (2003) *In Search of Prosperity: Analytic Narratives on Economic Growth*, Princeton University Press, Princeton, NJ.

Rodrik, Dani and Arvind Subramanian (2004a) 'From "Hindu Growth" to Productivity Surge: The Mystery of the Indian Growth Transition', Draft.

——(2004b) 'Why India Can Grow at 7 Per Cent a Year or More: Projections and Reflections', *Economic and Political Weekly* XXXIX(16), 17 April: 1591–96.

Samuelson, Paul A. (1964) 'Theoretical Notes on Trade Problems', *Review of Economics and Statistics* 46: 145–54.

Shenoy, B.R. (1968) *Indian Economic Crises: A Programme of Reform*, Economics Research Centre, Berkeley, CA.

Singh, Manmohan (1962) *India's Exports*, Oxford University Press, Oxford.

Virmani, Arvind (2004a) 'India's Economic Growth: From Socialist Rate of Growth to Bhartiya Rate of Growth', ICRIER Working Paper No. 122, February.

——(2004b) 'Sources of India's Economic Growth: Trends in Total Factor Productivity', Working Paper No. 131, ICRIER, May.

——(2006) *Propelling India from Socialist Stagnation to Global Power: Vol. 2: Policy Reforms*, Academic Foundation.

Young, Alwyn (1995) 'The Tyranny of Numbers: Confronting the Statistical Realities of the East Asian Growth Experience', *Quarterly Journal of Economics* 110: 641–80.

6

China after the international financial crisis

Still emerging

Pieter Bottelier

Recent economic developments 2007–12: main points

The last five years have been tumultuous for the People's Republic of China's economy, reflecting both domestic and international turmoil. The problems did not start with the global financial crisis (triggered by the collapse of Lehman Brothers in the USA in September 2008), but with the high domestic consumer price index (CPI) and house price inflation in 2007 that followed years of double-digit growth and the accumulation of very large external surpluses. China's current account surplus reached a record high of 10.1% of gross domestic product (GDP) in 2007. On top of that there were substantial 'hot money' inflows from abroad, attracted by a property boom in major cities and the expectation of renminbi (RMB) appreciation. To slow the pace of appreciation, the central bank intervened heavily in the foreign exchange market and sterilized excess liquidity in the banking system resulting from external surpluses by raising reserve requirements and/or selling central bank bills. In retrospect the sterilization effort may not have been aggressive enough, as both CPI (especially the food price component) and property price inflation became serious in 2007 (see Figure 6.1).

Beijing responded to the inflation problem of 2007 with relatively aggressive monetary tightening. This action was probably more effective than had been expected; food price inflation declined quickly, while house prices began to fall in the fourth quarter of 2007, triggering a slump in the construction business. Developers began to lay off construction workers, mostly migrants, in large numbers.[1] Many in government began to worry that GDP growth was slowing too quickly. At that time a new problem developed: export orders began to fall as a result of the financial crisis that had been brewing in the USA since 2006. Mounting subprime mortgage defaults and related bankruptcies created occasional credit crunches and fears of worse to come. Many Chinese exporters had to scale back production and lay off workers. By July 2008 the government became so concerned about the growing unemployment problem (affecting mostly migrants) that it re-froze the RMB/US$ exchange rate[2] to provide at least some protection to exporters. Financial sector problems in the USA intensified, especially after the collapse of Bear Stearns in March 2008. While China's exports were still growing, new

83

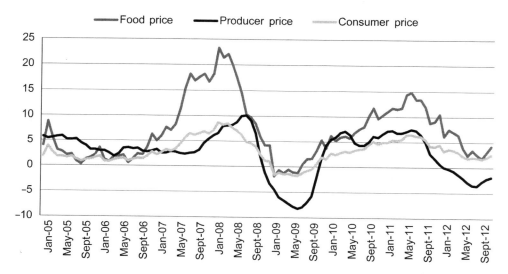

Figure 6.1 Food, producer and consumer price inflation (monthly, annualized percentage change, January 2006–December 2012)
Source: NBS, Bloomberg

export orders dropped fast. As is well known, the global financial system went into a stupor following the collapse of Lehman Brothers (15 September 2008), causing a sharp contraction of global trade, including exports from China, which by the end of 2008 had laid off an estimated 20 million workers in export industries. Total migrant unemployment at that time was probably some 30–40 million.[3] Quarter-on-quarter GDP growth fell to near zero in the final quarter of 2008.

It was under those dire circumstances that China launched an aggressive stimulus programme. It was the first major economy to do so after the international financial system froze and exports collapsed. A RMB 4 trillion ($586 billion) programme was announced in Beijing on Sunday 9 November, only eight weeks after the collapse of Lehman Brothers. The bulk of the stimulus money was to come in the form of bank loans. The fiscal component—mostly in the form of budget subsidies for consumption and various social programmes such as 'affordable housing' and job re-training—probably accounted for less than 20% of total stimulus spending from late 2008 to mid-2010. There is no reliable *ex post* accounting of China's stimulus programme, but it is almost certain that total incremental (stimulus) spending from late 2008 to mid-2010, most of which was credit-financed, exceeded the original RMB 4 trillion by a wide margin. Credit expansion alone during the period of most intensive stimulus spending—December 2008 to April 2010—exceeded the pre-crisis 'normal' by at least RMB 7 trillion. Additional (stimulus-related) fiscal outlays during that period were probably of the order of RMB 1.4 trillion.

With the benefit of hindsight, it is clear that China's stimulus programme, in particular its credit component, was too large and created serious 'hangover' problems (including housing bubbles in several major cities) which might have been avoided if more time had been taken to prepare the programme more carefully. None the less, it is also clear that the programme was extremely effective in quickly restoring growth and full employment. Well before the end of 2009 the economy was booming again and fears of recession had been replaced by fears of economic overheating. GDP growth for 2009 as a whole, in spite of the facts that the contribution of net exports was significantly negative and that the year started with near zero growth, was an astonishing 9.2%. The quick resumption of growth in 2009 was largely due to the massive, mostly credit-financed, investment programme, in infrastructure. China's investment/GDP ratio, already very high in preceding years, reached an unprecedented 47.2% in 2009, temporarily relegating to the back burner the rebalancing objective of the 11th Five-Year Development Plan (2005–10) to reduce the investment ratio.[4]

In early 2010, when inflation was once again rising rapidly, Prime Minister Wen Jiabao made the control of inflation, including the control of asset price inflation, a top priority. The government was especially concerned about sharp price increases for residential properties in major eastern cities, which frustrated the aspiration of China's emerging middle class to own an apartment, and were feared to become a serious social problem.

The main reasons why China's stimulus programme was so effective in quickly restoring growth (see Figure 6.2) and full employment are:

- Unlike the USA, China was not overleveraged when the crisis hit and its fiscal condition was strong. Consequently, stimulus spending quickly translated into incremental aggregate demand. The various US stimulus programmes (which in the aggregate, relative to GDP, remained much smaller than China's) only partially compensated for private sector deleveraging; aggregate demand in 2009 fell and growth became negative in the USA and many other advanced economies.
- China had gained considerable experience with stimulus programmes in the years following the Asian Financial Crisis of 1997/98 and had effective planning capability at different levels of government. China's political and administrative system is well organized to design, prepare and implement big projects, especially infrastructure. Implementation tends to be quick and relatively efficient, especially when the interests of central and local government are aligned, as was the case when China's stimulus programme was launched. Later, when many local governments had gained a fiscal incentive to promote property price increases to boost local revenues, while Beijing wanted to cool the property sector (to protect national financial stability), the stimulus programme ran into trouble as will be discussed later. It was

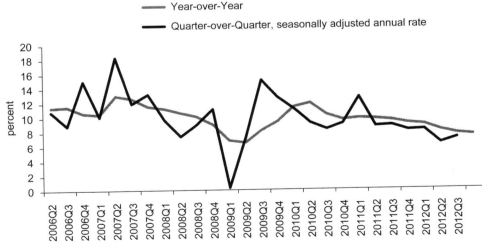

Figure 6.2 China quarterly GDP growth, annualized, year-on-year and quarter-on-quarter seasonally adjusted, 2006Q1–2012Q4
Source: NBS and author's calculations

effectively discontinued around mid-2010 when the programme's main objectives had been already been achieved.

- As a result of aggressive reforms since the late 1990s, China's banks—among the world's weakest a decade earlier—were in relatively good shape when the crisis hit. They were able to respond quickly to the government's call for additional lending and had ample liquidity to finance it. As all of China's large banks remain state controlled, Beijing can influence bank lending in ways that Washington cannot.

The housing bubble: a key part of the narrative

The biggest negative side effect of China's otherwise effective stimulus programme and a potential threat to financial stability was the sharp increase in land and residential property prices in major eastern cities. This was mainly due to the extremely large expansion of credit in 2009 and (to a lesser extent) in 2010 (see Figure 6.3).[5]

Beijing knew well the risks associated with uncontrolled asset bubbles and in early 2010 decided to make bubble control a top priority.[6] It had carefully studied the experience of other countries, including Japan's real estate and stock exchange bubbles of the late 1980s and the US housing bubble prior to the start of its collapse in 2007. Mindful of the negative effects on the construction sector of relatively aggressive monetary tightening in 2007, Beijing decided to be more cautious this time and to rely heavily on a range of administrative measures aimed at reducing speculative house buying.[7] In addition, as part of its stimulus programme, Beijing launched a large, nation-wide, subsidized 'affordable housing' scheme for migrants and other low-income groups. Given that the programme depends mainly on the allocation by local governments of land and financial resources, implementation is very uneven across China, but it is seen by Beijing as a key instrument to influence urban house prices from the supply side of the market, and pursue social objectives at the same time.

A factor that reinforced Beijing's decision to rely more on administrative measures for bubble control than on conventional monetary policy was the fact that the housing bubble was concentrated in a limited number of big cities; in 2009 and 2010 it was not national in scope, as it was in the USA during the years leading up to the financial crisis. Residential property prices

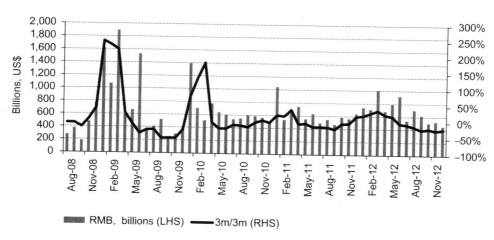

Figure 6.3 Monthly bank lending (LHS) and three-month moving average growth (RHS)
Source: Bloomberg

rose steeply in Beijing, Shanghai, Shenzhen, Guangzhou and a few other major eastern cities, but remained relatively stable in most tier 2 and tier 3 cities. The housing affordability problem, therefore, was a local, not (yet) a national problem. A policy of increasingly restrictive administrative house-buying controls (supported by mild monetary tightening) was started in April 2010. However, fueled by excess liquidity in China and 'hot money' inflows from abroad, the speculative property fever was so high that it took more than a year for markets to cool noticeably. It was a nail-biting period for the government in Beijing. Some officials and academics argued for early monetary relaxation to counteract slowing growth and growing pessimism in the business community, but the top leadership remained determined to control the property bubble as a top priority. Part of the demand for residential properties in big eastern cities came from abroad, especially overseas Chinese wanting to possess a 'pied-à-terre' in China for themselves or their children, or as an investment. Expectations of continuing RMB appreciation strengthened demand from abroad, at least through the first half of 2012. Another factor that made bubble control so difficult was collusion between large state-owned enterprises (SOEs) with excess cash, local governments and property developers. The initial alignment of interests between the central and local governments broke down as a result and poorly regulated financial intermediation outside the normal channels took off.

SOEs with extra cash were reluctant to deposit the money in state banks at artificially low interest rates, preferring instead to make some extra profit by lending it directly to borrowers willing to pay a higher rate of interest than charged by state banks, a form of shadow banking.[8] Other forms of shadow banking also blossomed, as will be discussed later. Meanwhile, incentives facing municipal governments became increasingly misaligned with those of the central government. Many local governments had become dependent for local revenues on land leases and were for that reason reluctant to co-operate in efforts aimed at cooling property markets. Finally, after more than a year of such efforts by Beijing, towards the end of 2011, property markets— turnover and prices—finally began to stabilize, permitting a mild relaxation of monetary policy. However, residential housing prices did not decline suddenly and sharply, as happened in the USA in 2006/07 and in Japan in 1990/91. A banking crisis was thus avoided in China, although there were plenty of developers, construction companies and speculators, including foreign hedge funds that ran into financial problems, sometimes because they had 'shorted' China.

Beijing's determination to control the housing bubble, while passively accepting the economic slowdown that resulted, paid off. Other factors, including slower export growth, contributed to the overall economic slowdown (from the second quarter of 2010 to mid-2013), but it was reduced investment in new commercial real estate that accounted for most of it. This is explained by the fact that because of its high urbanization rate, the contribution of urban housing construction to China's GDP growth is unusually high, about 17% in 2009.[9] Therefore, a reduction in new housing construction quickly generates powerful negative ripple effects elsewhere in China's economy. Owing to the size of the economy and its import dependency for many commodities, there are also important international spillover effects, especially in commodity markets.

When, contrary to prevailing international pessimism about China's economic prospects during most of 2012, the economy began to stabilize in the third quarter[10] (while the housing bubble seemed finally under control), Beijing took heart. Monetary policy was relaxed a little more, while the National Development and Reform Commission approved an additional RMB 1 trillion of infrastructure projects to promote growth further. This relatively modest stimulus programme contributed to China's improving economic performance in the fourth quarter of 2012 and the expectation that relatively robust growth (around 7.5%) would be achieved in 2013. Private investment also picked up in the second half of 2012, which lends additional weight to this relatively optimistic expectation.

It thus appears that Beijing has been largely successful in controlling a potentially dangerous housing bubble, at least so far. This should be recognized as a remarkable achievement, but there is no guarantee, of course, that speculative buying and excess liquidity will not return to the housing market in the future, generating new bubbles. It is worth noting that China reacted to the threat of a housing bubble very differently from the USA and other advanced economies, and did so with determination and skill, using a combination of administrative and monetary policy instruments. It is doubtful that China could have controlled the bubble through conventional monetary policy alone. It would have risked recession and another round of massive lay-offs. Owing to its unique political system, Beijing was able to employ administrative (rationing) tools—such as buying restrictions and minimum down-payment for mortgage loans—that are not in the tool kit of advanced market economies. The same factors that enabled China to launch a huge and effective stimulus programme quickly in November 2008 enabled the government to deal with the various 'hangover' problems that resulted from excessive credit expansion, at least so far.

Speculative fever in China's property sector is probably not a thing of the past. The government has to ensure that urbanization proceeds in an orderly fashion and that future credit expansion will not be excessive. This has become an even greater challenge since the emergence of an extensive shadow banking system over which the government has incomplete control. The most effective way to avoid property bubbles in China is probably financial sector liberalization, including interest rate deregulation and further capital account opening. Similarly, the most effective way to reduce incentives for undesirable forms of shadow banking is probably deregulation of interest rates.

The speculative property fever in China may have its origins in the way urban housing was privatized from the late 1990s. Prior to 1998 most urban housing in China was owned by the state. SOEs and other agents of the state were responsible for providing housing to their employees. There was no commercial housing market to speak of and mortgage financing was generally unavailable. Rents were heavily subsidized. Then came the Asian Financial Crisis, which changed everything. In 1998 the newly appointed State Council under Prime Minister Zhu Rongji decided to privatize almost all urban housing as quickly as possible and to shift other remaining social burdens on SOEs (mainly health care and education) to agencies of the government. The main objectives of housing privatization were:

- to relieve SOEs of the financial burden of providing (and maintaining) subsidized housing, so that they could become more competitive and survive after China entered the World Trade Organization as a full member (which finally took place in 2001);
- to increase productivity through the increased labour mobility that came with the development of a commercial housing market;
- to create a major new source of domestic demand (for home improvement and appliances), so as to reduce the expected negative effects of slowing or falling external demand.

As a mortgage industry had not yet developed, China had little choice but to transfer house ownership rights, mostly to current occupants, at prices far below potential market levels. In this way, most urban housing was privatized by 2003. China's private homeownership ratio is now higher than in most advanced economies, including the USA. The domestic economic consequences of this unprecedentedly large privatization, combined with the unprecedentedly large associated wealth transfer from the state to individual households (resulting from below-market transfer prices) are extremely important, but not well understood. In some ways the urban housing privatization of 1998–2003 dominated economic developments in China during the first decade of this century, like the de-collectivization of agriculture from the late 1970s had influenced development in the 1980s. Supported by a rapidly emerging mortgage loan industry, private developers and construction companies quickly filled the void in the supply of new and the maintenance of old housing. The private housing market, for rental or ownership, greatly enhanced labour mobility and accelerated urban growth. As urban households began to spend a growing portion of their disposable income on real estate, the share of consumption in GDP declined.

Another unintended consequence of China's massive housing privatization of 1998–2003 was the birth of speculative property fever. Since house ownership was typically transferred at prices well below market, the state imposed sell restrictions on the new owners for the first three-to-five years. Anyone wishing to sell during this period had to give the original owner, i.e. the state or a work unit (*danwei*) of the state, the right of first refusal at the original transfer price. When that period was over, which in most cases was around 2003, free market rules kicked in and many of the new private owners used the opportunity to convert the implicit equity transfer they had received, into cash used to buy a bigger, better house, or additional property.

Thus apartments in major cities such as Beijing, Shanghai and Shenzhen became attractive investment objects and an alternative to deposit accounts or state bonds at artificially low interest rates. Additional demand from overseas Chinese and foreign investors reinforced the upward pressure on property prices resulting from domestic financial repression. The price trend was further strengthened by the expectation of RMB appreciation against the dollar. Much of the 'hot money' inflow into China since the early 2000s, especially since July 2005 when the fixed RMB/US$ exchange rate policy was discontinued, was fueled by the expectation that property prices and the exchange rate would appreciate.

When the economy slowed, from mid-2010 through the first half of 2012, and Beijing's efforts to cool the housing market began to have some effect (from late 2011), speculative property fever dissipated and many Chinese decided to take their money out of the country, thus generating net 'hot money' outflows from China in 2012. Other factors, including tax evasion and fear that political reform might stagnate or take a wrong turn, contributed to the outflow. The same factors underlie reports about record numbers of wealthy Chinese seeking foreign citizenship or residence permits. Ironically, much of the current outflow of private money from China is used for speculative real estate purchases in the USA, Canada, Europe and Australia.[11]

China's growing share in the global economy and dominant share in global growth

China's role in the world economy continues to expand rapidly. According to the International Monetary Fund (IMF), its share in global GDP (measured at purchasing power parity (PPP) exchange rates) increased from 11.4% in 2008 to 14.3% in 2011 (the same as the eurozone and almost three times that of India), while the USA's share fell from 20.7% to 19.1%.[12] China's contribution to global growth in 2009 and 2010 was about 50% (see Figure 6.4). Its share for the period 2013–18 is projected to be about one-third, falling to a little under 30% thereafter, until 2025. In recent years China became the world's largest merchandise exporter/manufacturer (in terms of gross output value), producer of energy, and second largest user/investor in renewable energy, producer and market for automobiles, steel, cement, many other construction materials and, unfortunately, also largest emitter of greenhouse gases. It is currently the world's second largest importer after the USA and will probably become number one soon. China's output and foreign trade would be much smaller, had it not been for the large presence of foreign-invested enterprises in its economy. For example, well over half its exports and most industrial innovation is accounted for by foreign-invested enterprises. A large part of income earned in

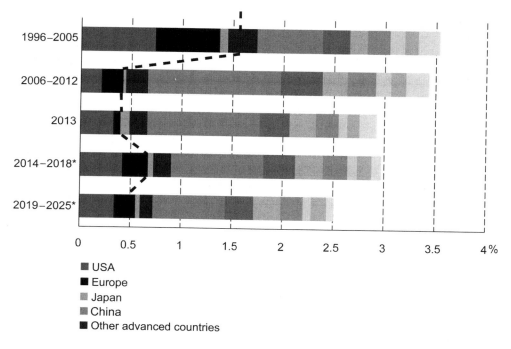

Figure 6.4 Shares in global GDP growth (measured at PPP exchange rates)
Source: The Conference Board, *Global Economic Outlook for 2012*

manufacturing accrues to foreign business partners. China's current role as 'workshop for the world' is unique. This role is likely to diminish in relative importance as China's production costs are rising relative to those of most other countries, which reduces its international competiveness.

Owing to its large current account surpluses during most of the past decade and net 'hot money' inflows, China's foreign reserves grew significantly and accounted for about one-third of the world's total at the end of 2012. On the basis of current growth trends and exchange rate expectations, it is reasonable to expect that China's GDP (measured at market exchange rates) will equal that of the USA by about 2022—sooner if GDP is measured at PPP exchange rates. China's influence on many commodity markets is already dominant, owing to the country's rapid growth and high import dependency for raw materials, accounting for about 45% of merchandise imports in 2011. Since China first severed the link between its currency and the dollar (July 2005), until the end of 2012, the nominal RMB/US$ exchange rate has appreciated by about one third. In real terms it appreciated by 42%–52% depending on the use of inflation index, CPI or GDP deflator.[13]

China's rapidly growing import demand and outward investment are having significant spillover effects on other economies, especially in developing Asia, Africa, Latin America, Australia, the former USSR and Europe. In 2006 the USA was still the world's dominant trader; it was the largest trading partner for 127 countries, versus 70 for China. In 2011 a major shift had occurred: China was the largest trading partner for 124 countries and the USA for 76.

Another factor underlying China's increasingly important role in the global economy is the rapid growth of China's outward foreign direct investment (OFDI). During the period 1990–2007 China accounted for about 1% of global OFDI, but after the financial crisis, while many Western countries curtailed their OFDI, China's share in the total increased to about 5% in

China after the international financial crisis

2010.[14] It is expected to grow further, as China diversifies its foreign exchange reserves while at the same time facilitating foreign investment by private Chinese enterprises.

USA–China trade

Bilateral USA-China merchandise trade has expanded more than four-fold between 2001 and 2011, from US$121.5 billion to $503.5 billion. During the decade US exports to China grew faster than US imports from China, 18.4% versus 14.6% per annum. None the less, owing to the base number effect, the bilateral trade imbalance continued to widen, from $83 billion in 2001 (accounting for 19.4% of America's overall merchandise trade deficit) to $315.1 billion in 2012 (when China's share had increased to almost 60% of the total). As a result of the economic recession in Europe, the USA replaced the European Union (EU) as China's largest trading partner in 2011. China is now the third largest destination for US exports (after Canada and Mexico), but still accounted for only 7% of the total. The USA also accounted for 7% of China's imports in 2011, but ranked number five as a source of imports into China. During the past 10 years, US exports to China have been growing about seven times faster than US exports to the rest of the world.

China's imports of services are growing faster than its merchandise imports and China's services trade balance is becoming increasingly negative. This is the main reason why China's current account surplus has fallen faster than its merchandise trade surplus, since both peaked in 2007. The USA has a growing bilateral surplus in services and in agricultural trade with China.[15] The most rapidly growing category of service imports by China is tourism. The number of Chinese travelling abroad for vacation or business purposes has grown enormously. The World Tourism Organization estimates that the number will rise to 100 million by 2020 (from 70 million in 2011). The most popular destinations for Chinese tourism abroad are Hong Kong, Taiwan (recently opened to mainland tour groups), and neighbouring countries in Asia and Europe. Chinese tourism to the USA has remained modest so far, partly because of cumbersome and costly visa regulations.

In spite of substantial RMB/US$ appreciation since 2005 and the fact that China's current account surplus has come down dramatically from 10.1% of GDP in 2007 to 2.3% in 2012,[16] many in the US government continue to blame the country's large trade deficit and associated job losses on China's exchange rate policy, an explanation that is even less credible today than it was six to eight years ago.[17] China, on the other hand, continues to complain about US export restrictions on certain high- and dual use technical equipment and services. Trade spats and conflicts over specific investment proposals have intensified. China was initially very unhappy about Washington's push for a broad, 'high-standards' transpacific trade partnership (TPP),[18] entry conditions for which seemed designed to exclude China, but may yet decide to join, as Japan did in early 2013. Since China's share in Pacific trade is by far the largest, a TPP without China would potentially be very troublesome. China meanwhile, in line with the growing recognition on both sides that US-Chinese economic relations are extremely important, and in spite of mutual strategic distrust, agreed to start negotiations for a bilateral investment treaty (BIT). If China decides to stay out of the TPP, a bilateral China-USA free trade agreement should be considered.

Many economies have benefited from China's rise; Africa seems to be a special case. Decades of stagnation were followed by sustained high growth (about 5% on average) since about 2000, almost everywhere on the continent. Many factors are responsible for this remarkable turnaround. China is probably one of them. Bilateral Africa-China trade has been growing at an astonishing rate of 27% per annum since 2000, topping $100 billion in 2011. OFDI from China to Africa is growing rapidly, and although the accumulated total—about $15 billion by the end of 2011—is still small compared to that from traditional Western sources, annual flows are rapidly increasing.[19] Private Chinese investment in Africa, which is rapidly growing in both absolute and relative importance, is mainly concentrated in small-scale manufacturing and service industries. Some private manufacturing enterprises in China, hit by falling margins due to rising wages[20] and other production cost increases, are reported to be relocating to Africa. In addition, numerous Chinese are emigrating to Africa to start small businesses there. While Chinese SOEs are mainly involved in large-scale mining and construction projects (oil and other minerals, infrastructure, housing), the presence of small- and medium-scale manufacturing and service companies owned by private Chinese companies and individuals has become ubiquitous in many African countries.

Economic rebalancing: consumption and investment

Finding the right balance between consumption and investment is not a new challenge for China. There has been a tendency to favour capital formation over consumption ever since the establishment of the People's Republic in 1949. Mao Zedong followed Stalin's development strategy, which emphasized heavy industry and state ownership. The fact that so many of the country's leaders were trained as engineers, often in the USSR, may help to explain a continued policy bias in favour of building factories and infrastructure. However, when Deng Xiaoping pushed for market reforms in the late 1970s, one of his first actions was to scuttle Hua Guo Feng's 10-year Soviet-style development plan and replace it with a two-year Interim Plan that gave priority to consumption, agriculture and light manufacturing over heavy industry. Something similar occurred in the early 1960s, when the magnitude of the disaster of Mao's 'Great Leap Forward' and the need to promote consumption growth were recognized. A high priority of China's current Five-Year Plan (2011–15) is to change China's growth model from investment and export-led growth to greater emphasis on domestic consumption.

Many authors have pointed to the decline in China's household consumption/GDP ratio (from 46.5% in 2000 to 34% in 2009) as evidence of a serious economic imbalance requiring corrective action. In some ways they are right. China's household consumption/GDP ratio (although rising modestly in 2010 and 2011, but not in 2012; see Figure 6.5) remains the lowest in the world for any major economy. Greater reliance on domestic consumption growth may indeed help to make growth more sustainable. However, the popular notion that China is *under-consuming* is highly questionable. China's consumption growth rate is in fact very high by international standards—the highest in the world for any major economy since 2000 (see Figure 6.6)

The two main reasons why China's consumption/GDP ratio fell so low are that, first, investment and GDP grew even faster, *not* because consumption growth was low; and second, the proportion of household income spent on housing has vastly increased since the privatization of urban housing in China (mainly during the period 1998–2003), mentioned before. Such expenditures are typically not included in household consumption statistics, but, as Jonathan Anderson points out, if they were, China's household consumption/GDP ratio would have remained about level since 2000.[21]

In short, China's consumption 'problem' is not what it seems to be. China is the most rapidly growing consumer market already, and per capita consumption growth has been the highest in the world for many years. The feasibility and wisdom of pushing China's household consumption growth beyond the average of recent years is questionable. In light of the expectation of slower GDP growth in the years ahead, it will in fact be difficult to keep consumption growth at current levels. Should consumption growth be fueled by increased credit card use, there is a risk that China will run into the same household leverage problems as the Republic of Korea (South Korea) did a few years ago. Economic rebalancing has to be achieved mainly by reducing

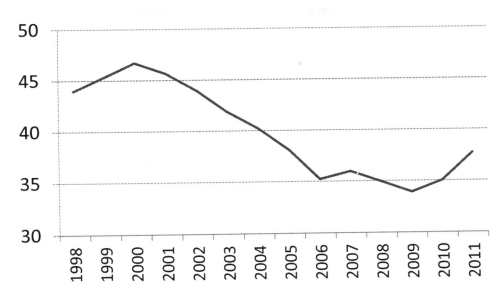

Figure 6.5 China's household final consumption expenditure as % of GDP, 2005–12, seems to have bottomed out in 2009
Source: World Bank DataBank

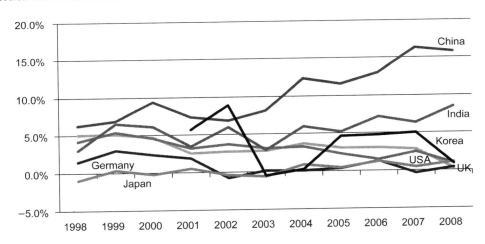

Figure 6.6 Household consumption annual growth rates for selected countries, 1998–2008
Source: World Bank DataBank

investment *growth* and by improving the quality of investment. The political leadership has to be willing to accept lower overall GDP growth. This is precisely what appears to be happening.

The best ways to promote economic rebalancing in China at the practical level are:

- Abolishing the household registration (*hukuo*) system. As this implies giving equal access to urban services to all, fiscal implications for many local governments will be serious. Therefore, abolishing the system will require fiscal reform and can only be done gradually.

- Strengthening rural property rights (mainly land and housing) to make them tradable and usable as collateral for bank loans. Paying fair compensation for land needed for public purposes is, of course, also very important.
- Improving the efficiency of domestic capital markets, e.g. by eliminating administrative quotas and price controls such as ceilings on deposit rates (which would increase household disposable incomes). China should also license more private banks and create an explicit deposit insurance system. Market-determined deposit rates would make it more difficult and more costly for the government to subsidize favoured industries. Such discriminatory practices remain a source of economic distortion and friction between China and its trading partners.
- Reducing the need for precautionary savings by perfecting and extending social security and social safety nets for all as quickly as possible. As this will entail additional budget expenditures, broader fiscal reforms, including the sharing of revenues and expenditure responsibilities between different levels of government, will be needed. A possible source of additional revenues to finance additional social spending by the government is higher SOE dividend payments. This could contribute to slower SOE investment growth and economic rebalancing.

Since these policies are consistent with the objectives of China's current Five-Year Plan, it is reasonable to expect that they will be actively pursued. Other reasons why economic rebalancing is likely to progress in the future are:

- Driven, in part, by rapid demographic changes (see Figure 6.7), real wage increases may well continue to grow faster than GDP.[22] As a consequence, the share of household income in GDP would rise, which, assuming no change in saving behaviour, means that household consumption would rise relative to GDP.
- As the share of services in GDP continues to increase (see Figure 6.8), it should become easier to maintain full employment at a lower investment growth rate (owing to the lower

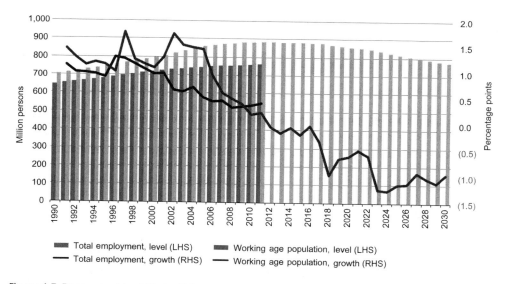

Figure 6.7 Demographic shifts in China
Source: US Census Bureau, NBS, The Conference Board

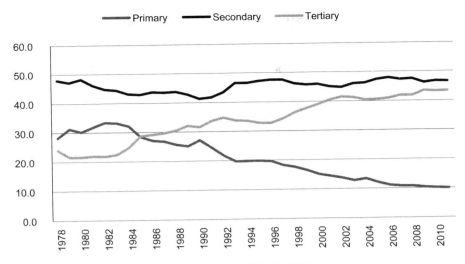

Figure 6.8 The rising share of services (tertiary) in China's GDP
Source: NBS

average capital intensity of services), while real wage growth may accelerate (owing to higher average skill requirements in service industries).
- Government 'consumption' in the form of budget outlays for social services (health, education, social safety nets, etc.) is rising in absolute terms and as a percentage of total government spending.

Many analysts have argued that China's investment/GDP ratio is too high and that the country is wasting resources, because the return on capital has become too low. China's gross investment/GDP ratio is indeed exceptionally high (see Figure 6.9), but that does not necessarily mean that the economy would benefit from a reduction in the investment/GDP ratio. Although it becomes harder to allocate and use capital efficiently when the investment ratio reaches very high levels, as is the case in China, the real issue is the efficiency of investment. The decline in China's marginal productivity of capital (MPK) is neither a new nor a unique phenomenon (see Figure 6.10 and Figure 6.11), but it has rightly become a serious concern in recent years. There is no objective standard to determine an optimal level for a country's investment/GDP ratio. Reducing the ratio per se should not be a rebalancing objective; it will not automatically increase the efficiency of capital, which should be the central focus. Besides, it should be recognized that China's saving ratio is very high—more than adequate to finance all investment at the aggregate level—and that its capital stock per capita is still very low. Catching up in development usually requires high investment to create potential for future productivity growth.

The economic efficiency of some investment in China, especially in residential housing and government buildings in some cities or counties, is indeed highly questionable, but there is also evidence of good quality capital formation. A prominent Beijing economics research firm recently concluded that investment in industry (which accounts for about 43% of gross investment) tends to be relatively efficient.[23] In general, China's unusually high investment rate is not a matter of international concern, because China can afford it; national savings are in fact more than sufficient to finance even the exceptionally high investment of recent years. China remained a net capital exporter through 2012.

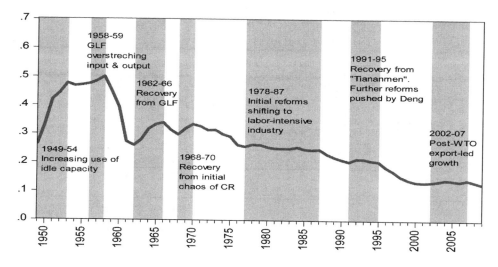

Figure 6.9 Marginal return on capital investment (MPK) in China, 1950–2010
Source: World Bank DataBank

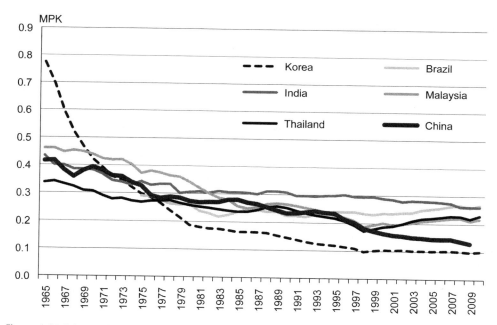

Figure 6.10 Marginal return on investment (MPK) in selected countries, 1965–2009
Source: Harry X. Wu, 'China's Growth and Productivity Performance Revisited', The Conference Board China Centre, 2013

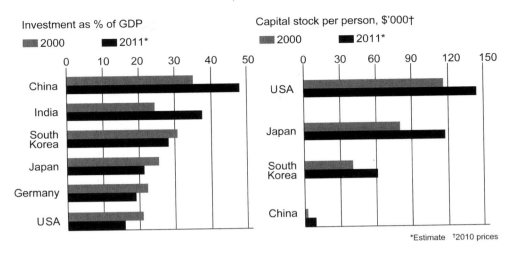

Figure 6.11 Investment/GPD ratios and capital stock per person for various countries in 2000 and 2011
Source: *IMF, HSBC, The Economist*

China has invested heavily in industry and infrastructure. Its physical infrastructure—roads, rail, ports, bridges, power and transmission, telecommunications, etc.—is superior in quality and quantity to that of other developing countries at a comparable level of income. Lack of infrastructure is generally not a constraint on development in China, as it is in many other developing countries. It is true that some of China's physical infrastructure is underutilized at present, but if the economy keeps growing rapidly, as expected, that is only a temporary problem. Generally, it has been China's practice to build infrastructure ahead of demand; it is perhaps the only large developing country that has been able to afford this practice so far.

Yet, now that transition to a more sustainable growth model has become a national priority, it is reasonable to allow for (but not necessarily aim at) lower investment growth. As mentioned, the policy focus should be on improving the efficiency of capital. Several factors will more or less automatically lead to slower investment growth in coming years:

- It is becoming more commonly accepted in China that environmental protection has to be given priority over raw GDP growth.
- Slower growth in external demand (exports) will probably lead to slower growth in manufacturing and related investment: China's share in global trade cannot continue to grow indefinitely.
- A gradual adjustment of bank deposit rates to market levels, an announced government objective, will tend to increase the cost of capital for investors.
- A rise in the share of services in GDP (see Figure 6.8) will tend to reduce the amount of capital needed per additional job.
- As fiscal constraints are likely to increase, government budget outlays for the financing of infrastructure will probably grow more slowly than in the past, or shrink.

While recognizing that the emphasis in economic rebalancing has to be on improving the efficiency of capital allocation and use, the recent joint World Bank-Development Research Centre *China 2030* report (see next section), estimates that it will take 15–20 years to reduce

China's investment/GDP ratio from an average of 46.2% for the period 1995–2010, to a more sustainable level of 34%.

Another major rebalancing challenge will be to reform the fiscal system such that it remains healthy and able to support social development in a lower growth environment. It will be necessary to ensure that incentives facing local governments are aligned with national priorities. This was not the case in recent years when Beijing wished to control real estate bubbles while many local governments, because of their dependence on land leases for local revenues, had an interest in rising property prices.

In rebalancing the economy, a big challenge will be to change the incentive framework facing government and party officials. It remains skewed in favour of investment and output growth, especially at the local government level. 'Downward accountability'[24] of officials at all levels has to be strengthened to ensure more efficient use of capital, more effective social policies and better environmental protection.

China 2030

The World Bank continues to be an important player in China. Its most recent contribution to the thinking about economic development and reform is *China 2030*, a 500-page report produced jointly with the Development Research Centre, the in-house think tank of the State Council (China's Cabinet). This was the first time a major economic report was produced collaboratively between the World Bank and the government. The three previous long-perspective, comprehensive World Bank economic reports on China,[25] along with many hundreds of more narrowly focused economic and sector reports produced since 1980, were all the exclusive responsibility of the World Bank. Like its predecessors, *China 2030* analyses in detail what had been achieved, what went wrong, while identifying the main challenges ahead. Much of the report is focused on the question of how China can avoid the 'middle-income trap'.[26] The report recommends adopting six key directions for a new development strategy, which can be summarized as follows:[27]

1 Strengthen the foundation for a market-based economy: by redefining the role of government, developing the private sector, promoting competition in output markets, and deepening reforms in the land, labour and financial markets. While providing relatively fewer 'tangible' public goods and services directly, the government should provide more 'intangible' public goods and services like systems, rules and policies that increase production efficiency, promote competition, facilitate specialization, enhance the efficiency of resource allocation, protect the environment, and reduce risks and uncertainties.

2 Accelerate the pace of innovation: by creating an open innovation system in which competitive pressures encourage Chinese firms to engage in product and process innovation not only through their own research and development (R&D), but also by participating in global research and development networks. Much needs to be done to ensure that China's already relatively high level of investment in R&D yields commercially viable innovations that will help firms move up the value chain and compete internationally. To this end China should improve the technical and cognitive skills of university graduates and build a few world-class research universities with strong links to industry. It should foster 'innovative cities' that bring together high-quality talent, knowledge networks, dynamic firms and learning institutions, and allow them to interact without restriction. The availability of and access to patient risk capital for private start-up firms needs to be increased.

3 'Go green': greener development and increasing efficiency of resource use will not only improve the level of well-being, but could potentially drive rapid, sustained growth as well. China should not replicate the experience of advanced countries that got rich first and cleaned up later. Instead, China should boost environmental protection and technological advancement as part of the development process. This will require a combination of incentives, regulations, standards and public investments that will promote low pollution and high efficiency in energy and resource use.

4 Expand opportunities for all: to access decent jobs, finance, social services and portable social security to reverse inequality, help households manage employment- and age-related risks, and further enhance labour mobility. To achieve this will require more and better-quality public services to underserved rural and migrant populations, improving the efficiency and quality of core health and education services, and enhance equality of opportunity to benefit from social services and social security. Such reforms will need to be facilitated by phased reforms of the *hukuo* system to reduce disparities in social entitlement for migrants.

5 Strengthen the fiscal system: by increasing the efficiency of the tax structure, improving government financial management, and ensuring that local governments have adequate financing to meet heavy and rising expenditure responsibilities. A key element of future fiscal strategy should be to reorient public expenditure composition towards social and environmental challenges.

6 Develop and protect mutually beneficial relations with the world: by becoming a proactive stakeholder in the global economy, actively using multilateral frameworks and shaping the global governance agenda of international trade, global financial stability, climate change, food security and the international aid architecture, among others.

Financial sector reform and risks

In China's gradual transition from plan to market, the financial sector did not become a reform priority until the late 1990s when the Asian Financial Crisis hit. Until that time the closed financial system, with some exceptions, remained essentially an instrument of the state to mobilize and allocate financial resources in accordance with plan priorities and support market reforms in the real economy. State banks were essentially fiscal agents of the state, while the non-banking part of the financial system remained relatively small and underdeveloped. Between 1998 and 2005 all major state banks (with one exception)[28] were reorganized, relieved of costly social obligations (such as education, health care, housing and social security for their workers and retirees) and most of their non-performing loan portfolio, audited according to international standards, recapitalized and listed on the Hong Kong and Shanghai stock exchanges. The reform of the banking system was more aggressive and more successful than the reform of non-bank financial institutions, including the two stock exchanges (Shanghai and Shenzhen). However, even the bank reforms were limited in scope. The banks, though listed, and with minority foreign strategic partners represented on their boards, remain majority state-owned and subject to both interest rate controls and credit guidelines.

From around 2007 the development of financial intermediation by non-bank financial institutions (bond markets, venture capital (VC) and private equity (PE) funds, trust loans, bill discounting and other forms of 'shadow banking') has picked up considerably. The pace of reform intensified as a result of various bottom-up and top-down pressures generated by the international financial crisis that broke in 2008. In addition, from 2009 China made serious efforts to promote the international use of its currency (the RMB) for trade settlement and investment financing. In 2012 the pace of financial sector reform, including capital account opening, further accelerated. The following announcement and measures taken in 2012, illustrate the direction financial reform is taking:

- In February China's central bank announced on its website that 'preconditions for China to liberalize its capital account have become mature'. The statement was based on an internal study, which concluded that the benefits of an open capital account for China's economy outweigh the costs and that the time is ripe to pursue the necessary reforms more aggressively. In the first phase of the reform plan (3–5 years), the government plans to further loosen controls on foreign direct investment outflows, while encouraging foreign investment by Chinese enterprises, using either foreign exchange or RMB funds, depending on the circumstances. The second phase (5–10 years) would focus on broadening and deepening domestic capital markets and on opening financial markets to foreign capital. Quantitative controls on cross-border capital flows are to be gradually replaced by market-oriented price controls. Actual developments since February 2012 confirm the seriousness of this plan.
- The qualified foreign institutional investor (QFII) ceiling on foreign portfolio investment in China was raised from $30 billion to $80 billion.
- The daily RMB trading band in the interbank foreign exchange market was doubled (to 2%).
- Informal money markets in the city of Wenzhou, in Zhejiang Province, known as a bastion of private enterprise and a model for private-sector development by other cities, were legalized, while restrictions were relaxed on investment abroad by Wenzhou residents. RMB bank credit is already being made available for this purpose.
- Controls on almost all lending rates were removed, while controls on deposit rates were somewhat relaxed.
- Tax reductions for services sector enterprises were introduced to support these financial reforms.
- RMB internationalization was further promoted by the development of offshore markets and/or special currency arrangements with London, Singapore, Taiwan and by additional currency swap agreements with other central banks.
- To promote further Hong Kong as China's premier offshore RMB market, a special scheme for the re-entry into China of RMB funds (RQFII) was introduced.
- The virtual explosion of 'shadow banking' in recent years was not responded to by outright suppression, as might have been the government's reaction in earlier decades, but by efforts better to regulate and supervise those markets.
- Small, medium-sized, very small and micro enterprises now have much better access to bank credit and other sources of finance than in earlier years.[29]
- Illiquid B-share listings in Shanghai and Shenzhen were permitted to migrate to the much more liquid and higher-priced Hong Kong H-share market.
- Owing to the sharp reduction in China's trade and current account surpluses as well as capital flight from China in 2012, intervention by the People's Bank of China (the central bank) in the foreign exchange market to prevent RMB appreciation virtually ceased that year. There have even been reports that at least on one occasion the central bank intervened in the opposite direction, to prevent RMB depreciation.
- The emphasis on monetary policy has begun to shift from direct quantitative controls to more conventional open market operations, influencing interest rates and bank liquidity indirectly, as is the practice in advanced economies.
- Although their effectiveness remains to be demonstrated, special measures were taken to guard against over-borrowing by local governments through front companies.

- Limited-scale experiments with new financial instruments and market techniques such as shorting, index futures trading, securitization and credit default swaps, were continued.

None of these developments by themselves represents a fundamental breakthrough in financial sector reform, but they are important steps and, in the aggregate, add up to a quantum leap in financial reform. Additional reforms, including the licensing of more private banks, interest rate liberalization, the creation of an explicit deposit insurance scheme, removal of restrictions on the opening of foreign bank branches and steps to open the capital account further, are needed and expected. One of the consequences of recent financial sector reforms is that the relative importance of *financial repression*[30] is rapidly diminishing. Generally, though, system risks have increased (see the next section, on shadow banking), and China's financial system is changing in the right direction. Illustrations of improvement are:

According to official sources:

- The share of small and medium-sized enterprises (almost entirely privately owned) in total enterprise credit extended in 2012 increased significantly (to more than half of new credit and over 35% of bank credit outstanding). Conversely, the share of large enterprises (mostly SOEs) declined. The share of credit extended to household businesses (including consumer credit) increased to almost 20%.
- The share of bank loans priced above the government's benchmark (minimum) lending rate increased from 40% in 2008 to 63% in 2012. This means that banks are increasingly risk-pricing their loans and diversifying assets on their balance sheet.
- Mainly as a result of rapidly growing shadow banking, the non-bank share of new credit increased from 8% in 2002 to almost half in 2012. Evidently, China's traditional bank-dominated financial system is changing. Many new financial institutions and instruments have entered the market in recent years.

Although financial sector reform in China was long delayed (while attention was focused on reforms in the real economy), it is fair to say that the pace of reform has increased significantly since the financial crisis of 2008. However, the system of financial repression, though gradually becoming less important, remains intact for the benefit of large state banks and other enterprises (mostly SOEs) favoured by the government. Though the road to complete currency convertibility is still long, there is, for the first time, a 5–10-year plan to open the capital account and to make the RMB usable as an international reserve currency.

The process of financial sector liberalization, which accelerated in recent years, is reminiscent of China's 'dual-track' approach to market reform, as applied to agricultural and other markets in the 1980s and 1990s. Could it be that policymakers and technical experts in Beijing responsible for managing and reforming China's financial system are deliberately permitting a large, relatively lightly regulated shadow banking system based on market pricing to develop in parallel with traditional financial intermediation by state banks, with the intention of merging the two segments of the market at some point? If this is indeed the government's unspoken strategy and if it turns out to be successful, we may be witnessing over the next 5–10 years the final chapter in the transformation of China's financial sector.

Shadow banking[31]

The biggest risk facing China's financial system in the next few years is that the lightly regulated shadow banking system becomes too big, permitting over-leveraging and creating pockets of instability that, in a worst-case scenario, could undermine the entire system. Fortunately, the government appears to be well aware of potential dangers and determined to avoid losing control. In most countries the bulk of shadow banking takes place outside the banking system; it is the business of non-bank financial institutions such as hedge funds, money market funds, PE and VC funds, as well as smaller players such as pawn shops and kerb markets. China has known those kinds of shadow banking for many years, but they accounted for a small part of financial intermediation and did not present a risk to stability. Things began to change in the wake of the massive stimulus programme launched by China in response to the international financial crisis of 2008. To avoid financial system risks from becoming unmanageable, the government must indeed get a firm handle on shadow banking as soon as possible.

The amount of additional credit pumped into the economy in 2009 and 2010, mainly as a result of the government's stimulus programme, was so large that leverage ratios (for many local governments and corporations) have become a matter of concern. Some corporations began to function as banks by lending their surplus cash (outside the banking system) directly to others. The most important form of shadow banking that developed in recent years, however, is the introduction by banks and other financial intermediaries, of largely unregulated wealth management products (WMP) and 'trust' loans, to avoid controls on bank deposit rates. Since much of this business is kept off balance sheets, statistics on shadow banking are incomplete.

The total amount of shadow banking credit outstanding in China at the end of 2012 was estimated at about RMB 27 trillion, about 55% of GDP and 43% of total bank credit outstanding. Since the global average ratio of shadow bank credit to regular bank credit is over 100%, shadow banking in China is still relatively modest in size. The problem is that the rate of increase of shadow banking in China, especially off-balance sheet WMP and trust loans, has been very high in recent years—much higher than GDP growth or bank credit expansion—especially in 2012.

What will Beijing do if/when some banks cannot make good on WMP they sold? It has already happened a few times, but the amount of money involved was too small and the cases too isolated to trigger a wider bank run. Although no detailed information has been made available, it is believed that Beijing did not intervene in those recent cases on behalf of the WMP holders, so as to avoid moral hazard. The potential of more serious problems arising, however, has to be taken seriously.

On the one hand, Beijing does not want to suppress free market financial intermediation; on the other, it is responsible for maintaining financial stability. If indeed it is Beijing's strategy to allow a gradual liberalization of financial markets on the basis of a 'dual-track' transition approach, difficult dilemmas cannot be avoided. Success in shadow banking is critical in the transition to a market-based financial system. It will help to improve efficiency in the allocation and use of capital, a critical factor in making China's growth more sustainable. In the meantime, China will have to live with greater risks and greater volatility in financial markets. There is no fail-safe short cut to financial sector liberalization.

The risks to financial stability arising from poorly regulated shadow banking and over-leveraging by some categories of borrowers, underline the need to strengthen government oversight of the financial system, to broaden and deepen domestic capital markets, further to relax controls on interest rates and to continue shifting the emphasis in monetary management from direct to indirect controls. As the financial system liberalizes, efficiency of the allocation and use of financial resources will improve, while the scope for hidden subsidies to favoured borrowers will shrink. Since the creation of level playing fields for all economic agents will require a re-thinking of the role of the state in the economy, financial sector liberalization will also be a factor driving political reform.

Notes

1 In China's statistical system migrant worker lay-offs are not included in official unemployment data. The full extent of the unemployment problem caused by the slowdown in urban housing construction in 2007/08 is therefore not known, but it probably amounted to 10–20 million by the third quarter of 2008. In times of economic difficulty, migrant workers are usually the first to be laid off in China.

2 As no official announcements was made, the precise date of the refreezing is not known.

3 To put this number in perspective, China's total migrant population at that time was estimated at 220 million. Hence, the (unrecorded) unemployment rate among this group of urban workers (unprotected by social safety nets) was of the order of 14%–18% by the end of 2008.

4 Different measurements of gross investment yield different results for the calculation of China's investment/GDP ratio. If inventory changes are included, the ratio increases to a little over 48% in 2010 and 2011; if inventories are excluded the ratio falls to a little over 44% in 2011, which is still extraordinarily high by international comparison.

5 With the benefit of hindsight, it can be safely said that bank credit expansion in 2009 and 2010 was excessive and became the source of new problems, such as asset price inflation. It should also be noted that the credit expansion depicted in Figure 6.3 is limited to regular bank loans. Since 2009, China has seen a veritable explosion in shadow banking, including a variety of credit instruments offered by non-bank financial institutions and banks alike. For additional comments on shadow banking, see the final section of this chapter.

6 Beijing's policy response to its developing housing bubble was markedly different from Washington's in the years leading up to the financial crisis of 2007/08. The US Federal Reserve believed that bubbles could not be clearly identified or effectively controlled. The prevailing opinion was that it was easier to clean up after a bubble had burst.

7 Such measures included restrictions on the purchase of property by citizens and foreigners who already owned one or more apartments, higher down payments and higher mortgage interest rates for the purchase of additional properties. Implementation details were left to local authorities.

8 The term shadow banking usually refers to financial intermediation by non-bank financial institutions such as hedge funds, money market funds, PE and VC funds, but it may also include financial intermediation by non-financial institutions and corporations, and off-balance sheet intermediation by banks, as has become popular in China in recent years. (See section on shadow banking.)

9 A comparable rate for the USA in a normal year would be 3%–4%.

10 Third quarter growth in 2012 (7.4%) was lower than second quarter growth (7.6%) measured year-on-year. However, if measured quarter-on-quarter, seasonally adjusted, it was higher. Hence the observation that China's economy began to stabilize in the third quarter of 2012.

11 There is no direct, precise way to measure 'hot money' inflows or outflows. Estimates are usually based on the difference between changes in foreign exchange reserves at the end of a period and what can be explained on the basis of officially recorded current account and capital account transactions during that period, i.e. 'errors and omissions' in the balance of payments. In China's case 'hot money' outflows may have been as high as US$40–$60 billion from January 2012–June 2013, but this was not a threat to financial stability.

12 'World Economic Outlook', April 2009 and April 2011.

13 The RMB also appreciated significantly against a representative basket of currencies, but less than against the dollar: about 27% in nominal terms and 34%–45% in real terms, depending on the choice of inflation index, CPI or GDP deflator.

14 'China's Emerging Role as a Global Source of FDI', USITC Executive Briefing on Trade, January 2012.

15 US agricultural exports to China account for about one-third of the total and consist mainly of soybeans, cotton and corn.

16 In spite of this sharp decline, the IMF considers China's current account surplus for 2012 to remain well above the level consistent with fundamentals and desirable policies, and expects it to rise to close to 3% of GDP by 2014. At a G20 meeting in Seoul in 2010 US Treasury Secretary Timothy Geithner proposed that as a rule, current account surpluses or deficits should not be allowed to exceed 4% of GDP.

17 A country's current account surplus or deficit is necessarily equal to its domestic saving/investment gap. The USA has for decades had a serious national saving deficit. The fact that a large part of the USA's trade deficit with the rest of the world is accounted for by China reflects, first, the fact that many Japanese, Korean and Taiwanese suppliers have shifted all or part of their production to China

for cost reasons, and second, that China is a very efficient supplier of imports into the USA. China's exchange rate has very little to do with the USA's overall trade deficit. Besides, it is important to remember that in our globalized world with multi-country production chains, the bilateral US–Chinese trade imbalance says little or nothing about the distribution of gains from that trade. Various studies have concluded that the balance of domestic value added in the bilateral trade is very different from the gross trade balance and that the USA may well gain as much or even more than China does.

18 President Obama proposed in 2009 to broaden and deepen significantly the original Transpacific Strategic Economic Partnership Agreement of 2005 (TPSEP) between New Zealand, Brunei, Singapore and Chile. The proposal was accepted in principle at the APEC summit of 2010. Apart from the four original members, the following countries are currently participating in the negotiations: USA, Australia, Peru, Viet Nam, Malaysia, Mexico, Canada and Japan.

19 China's Ministry of Commerce, 'Statistical Bulletin on China's Outward Foreign Direct Investment', 2010.

20 Manufacturing wages in China's eastern provinces have been rising 8%–12% on average per annum in real terms since the early years of this century.

21 Private communication. Jonathan Anderson is president of Emerging Advisors Group in Beijing.

22 For example, the minimum wage in Dongguan, a major export processing centre in Guangdong Province has risen by almost 200% in dollar terms since 2004, almost 10% in real terms per annum.

23 Warwick Simons, 'China's Surprisingly Efficient Allocation of Capital', GKDragonomics, 10 January 2013. In the manufacturing sector, there are some notable exceptions to this. For example, China's solar panel, steel, shipbuilding and automobile industries significantly over-expanded in recent years. There are no reliable statistics on capacity utilization in China's manufacturing sector, but the overcapacity problem is recognized as serious in some other industries as well.

24 What is needed is an incentive framework rewarding efficiency, social development and environmental protection, both at the national and local levels. The current system still tends to reward capital formation and raw GDP growth, often regardless of efficiency and sustainability.

25 *China Socialist Economic Development* (1981); *China Long-Term Development Issues and Options* (1983); and *China 2020* (1997).

26 Defined as the observed inability of many middle-income developing countries to continue rapid growth after they have exhausted the advantages of low-cost labour and easy technology adoption.

27 Based on Chapter 2 in *China 2030. Building a Modern, Harmonious, and Creative High-Income Society*, conference version. This version of the report (which is available at www-wds.worldbank.org/external/defa ... WPOP127500China020300complete.pdf, accessed 10 January 2012) was extensively discussed at public meetings in China in 2012.

28 The last of the four largest state commercial banks, Agricultural Bank of China, went public in 2010. It had a larger load of non-performing loans than other state banks and had to perform social functions for the state for a longer period.

29 ChiNext, a NASDAQ-type exchange for high-tech start-ups was opened as a special board in Shenzhen in 2009.

30 Financial repression may be defined as a quasi-fiscal system of artificially repressed deposit and lending rates, designed to favour state investments and state banks at the expense of depositors. The system enabled China to maintain state-sponsored investment far above the level that would otherwise have been possible. As the formal fiscal system and domestic capital markets are maturing, the need for financial repression diminishes. The end of financial repression in China is in sight.

31 The quantitative information in this section is based on various central bank reports and on research by Citibank, made available in the form of a bulletin to subscribers dated 11 January 2012.

7

South Africa's difficult transition

Robert E. Looney

Introduction

South Africa projects many contrasting images. On the one hand, the country represents one of Africa's rare economic success stories. The country has one of the largest, most diversified and developed economies of sub-Saharan Africa. The economy's growth and development has been steady, if not spectacular, and its progress has been favourable enough to enable the country to join the elite emerging economy group, the BRICS (Brazil, Russia, India, People's Republic of China, South Africa), as Africa's only member. Considerable progress has also been made in the establishment of democratic institutions anchored in one of the world's most progressive constitutions.

The country possesses well-developed financial, communications, energy and transport sectors. Its stock exchange is the largest on the continent and the world's 18th largest, while the country's currency, the rand (ZAF), is among the most actively traded emerging market currencies. The country's strong financial services infrastructure, political stability and solid regulatory environment, have made the country an attractive destination for foreign direct investment (FDI), as well as an entry point and base for many multinational corporations' African operations.

While South Africa has long had the potential to become one of the world's most dynamic economies, the country has not been able to achieve rates of growth in the ranges necessary to pull large segments of the population out of poverty.[1] The South African Reserve Bank's latest estimate of annual long-run potential output growth is 3.5%, a rate considerably below the 5%–6% expansion needed to make a significant dent in the country's massive pool of unemployed. In recent years even the 3.5% rate has often been unattainable. At present, the country is more highly integrated with the global economy and more exposed than most of its neighbours to the volatility of European demand and financing.

The poor state of the economy has led the normally overly cautious World Bank to conclude that the country may be trapped in a vicious circle of slow growth, low investment and limited job-creating capacity.[2] Other observers have drawn similar conclusions: 'South Africa remains a country of imbalances, disparities, distortions and a number of paradoxes.'[3] The most prominent of these negative attributes are the persistence of large-scale poverty, high levels of inequality, high crime rates, and a dualistic economic and social structure.[4]

The sections that follow trace South Africa's economic progress over the last several decades in an attempt to identify those factors that appear to be constraining growth, creating conditions of high chronic unemployment (25% in 2013), preventing the elimination of poverty, limiting improvements in well-being and impeding the development of a more equitable society.

Demographic patterns

South Africa's demographic patterns have shifted considerably over time, with implications for the country's longer-term growth. South Africa has a population of approximately 50.59 million (2011), growing at a rate of around 1% per annum with 62% classified as urban and 38% rural. Life expectancy is around 52 years.

According to the 2010 census 80% of South Africans are of black African ancestry, divided among various ethnic groups and spoken languages. The constitution recognizes 11 languages, including Zulu, spoken by 23.8% of the population, Xhosa (17.6%), Afrikaans (13.3%), Sepedi (9.4%), English (8.2%), Setswana (8.2%), Sesotho (7.9%) and Xitsonga (4.4%).[5]

Immigration patterns have shifted dramatically over the years, with arrivals from Europe exceeding 20,000 people per year during the late 1960s and early 1970s. However, in the late 1970s and 1980s the number of whites leaving South Africa tended to exceed the new arrivals. In the early 21st century, another dramatic shift occurred with a sizeable influx of immigrants and refugees from other African countries fleeing political persecution or seeking greater economic prospects, especially from neighbouring Zimbabwe.[6]

The population is relatively young. Some 72% of black South Africans are under 35. In many developing countries, especially those in East Asia, falling birth rates helped to create a 'demographic dividend'[7] which has helped to accelerate economic growth by reducing the proportion of dependent children and elderly in the population relative to the proportion of working-age adults. Similar demographic patterns exist in South Africa, with fertility falling steadily over the past half century, from 6.4 births per woman in 1950–60 to 2.4 births in 2005–10.

Everything else being equal, per capita income has grown more rapidly during this time as resources are freed up from child rearing and directed towards productive investment. However, this is predicated on the country's relatively large working-age population finding productive roles in the economy. Unfortunately, in South Africa's case this has not happened, and the country may have missed its window for tapping this mechanism for accelerated economic growth. Of the 4.4 million unemployed, almost three-quarters (72%) are younger than 34. For those aged 15–19, the unemployment rate is 65%, for those aged 20–24 it is 49%, and for those aged 25–29 it is 34%.

While there is little chance of a dramatic increase in growth stemming from the country's population dynamics, the situation is not unfavourable for the next several decades, with a shrinking child population compensating for an elderly population that is beginning to expand. In 2010 each worker was supporting an average of 1.8 individuals outside of the working-age population. This was down from a peak of 2.1 in the 1960s.

Relative progress

At least three distinct phases characterize the country's economic progress since 1960: the period of apartheid expansion 1960–80, a briefer period of the demise of apartheid (1981–93), and finally the period of post-apartheid growth and recovery 1994–present.

Patterns of growth

In the 1960s South Africa's per capita income was similar to that of the future 'tiger' economies of South-East Asia (see Figure 7.1). However, South Africa's average growth on a per capita basis was only 2.3% in 1960–80[8] (versus 3.4% for the upper middle-income countries and 2.2% for the lower-middle-income countries). The most dramatic shift in relative incomes occurred during the 1981–93 period when South Africa's per capita income contracted at an average annual rate of 1.7% for an overall decline of 18.5%. During this period per capita incomes in both the upper- and lower-middle-income countries averaged 1.4% (see Table 7.1).

Since 1993 (1994–2011) South Africa's per capita income has averaged 1.6% per annum. This rate was considerably below that of 4.5% achieved by the upper-middle-income countries and 3.6% for the lower-middle-income group. As a result of these growth patterns, South Africa's large lead in per capita incomes over that of the upper-middle-income countries has shrunk considerably (see Figure 7.2), with the latter converging quickly with South Africa. However, comparing countries on the basis of GDP per person employed suggests that the upper middle-income countries as a group closed the gap and passed South Africa in around 2006 (see Figure 7.3).

Associated with these overall patterns of income growth has been a fairly dramatic shift in the composition of South Africa's economy (Figure 7.4). Agriculture's share of gross domestic product (GDP) averaged 7.8% during the 1965–80 period, only to average 3.4% in 1994–2011 (see Table 7.2). Correspondingly, manufacturing's share of output declined from 22% in the 1965–80 period to 18.8% in 1994–2011, while services expanded from 51.9% in the earlier period to 64.5% during 1994–2011.

South Africa also experienced some significant shifts in productive sector composition relative to that in other middle-income countries. For example, industry's share of South African GDP averaged 40.3% during 1965–80, while that of countries in the upper-middle-income group averaged 37.5%. By 1994–2011 South Africa's share had declined to 32.1% while that of the upper-middle-income group had increased to 36.9%.

South Africa's major macroeconomic aggregates have also undergone major changes since 1960. Generally, these aggregates follow a pattern similar to that of the productive sectors—relatively rapid growth during 1960–80, followed by a sharp decline over the 1981–93 period, with a slower expansion (relative to the first period and other upper-middle-income countries) after 1993 (see Table 7.3). Of the leading aggregates, capital formation has experienced the

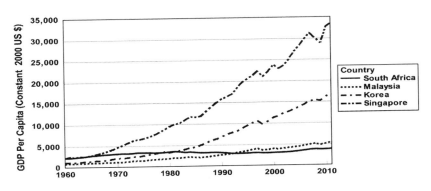

Figure 7.1 South Africa, Malaysia, Korea and Singapore: patterns per-capita income 1960–2011
Source: World Bank, World Development Indicators, April 2013.

Robert E. Looney

Table 7.1 South Africa's sector growth patterns relative to middle-income countries (average annual rates of real growth)

	South Africa	Upper-middle-income countries	Lower-middle-income countries
GDP per capita			
1960–80	2.3	3.4	2.2
1981–93	−1.7	1.4	1.4
1994–2011	1.6	4.5	3.6
GDP			
1960–80	4.7	5.4	4.6
1981–93	0.6	2.9	3.7
1994–2011	3.3	5.4	5.3
Agriculture			
1960–80	2.9	n.a.	0.2
1981–93	0.6	2.1	2.6
1994–2011	1.4	2.8	3.0
Industry			
1960–80	4.4	5.8	6.2
1981–93	−0.3	3.2	3.9
1994–2011	2.1	6.3	3.3
Manufacturing			
1960–80	6.8	5.9	5.7
1981–93	−0.4	5.0	4.3
1994–2011	2.7	6.6	5.6
Services			
1960–80	4.7	6.4	5.2
1981–93	1.1	3.1	4.9
1994–2011	4.0	5.3	6.4

Source: Computed from World Bank, *World Development Indicators*, April 2013

greatest period-to-period change, growing at an average rate of 6.1% (1960–80), declining at an average rate of 4.6% (1981–93), and then recovering to expand at an average annual rate of 5.6% (1994–2011). Corresponding figures for capital formation in the upper-middle-income countries were 6.9%, 2.4% and 6.9%.

While not contracting during the 1981–93 period, exports of goods and services have grown considerably slower than have most other middle-income countries. In particular, South Africa's exports have averaged growth of only 3.2% since 1994, compared with 9.3% for the upper-middle-income countries and 8.1% for the lower-middle-income countries.

The South African government's consumption has been relatively stable, averaging 6.4% (1960–80), 3.2% (1981–93) and 3.1% during the most recent period. On the other hand, household consumption has been considerably more volatile at 4.5% (1960–80), 0.3% (1981–83), and 3.65 (1983–2011).

South Africa's macroeconomic trends have produced some sharp shifts in the composition of aggregate demand (see Figure 7.5). The general pattern is one of increasing relative share of consumption and falling shares of savings and investment. In terms of future growth, there is increasing concern about the decline in the country's rates of capital formation and savings. South Africa's gross capital formation (see Table 7.4) declined from averaging approximately

108

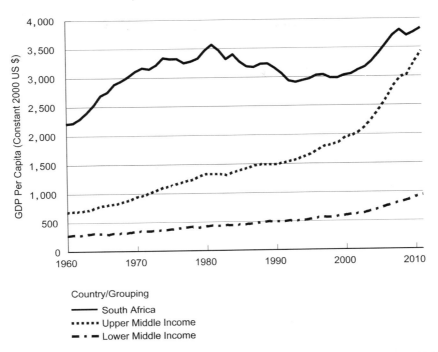

Figure 7.2 South Africa, Middle income countries: growth in per capita income: 1960–2011
Source: World Bank, World Development Indicators, April 2013

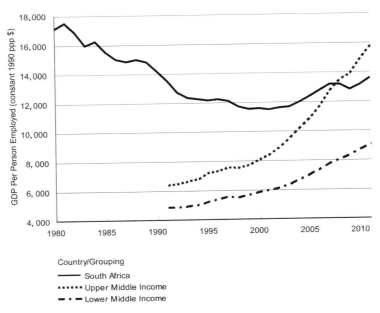

Figure 7.3 South Africa, middle income countries: patterns of GDP per person employed 1980–2011
Source: World Bank, World Development Indicators, April 2013

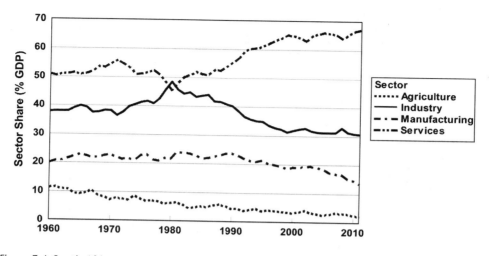

Figure 7.4 South Africa: sector GDP shares, 1960–2011
Source: World Bank, World Development Indicators, April 2013

Table 7.2 South Africa's changing productive structure relative to middle-income countries (% GDP)

	South Africa	Upper-middle-income countries	Lower-middle-income countries
Agriculture			
1965–1980	7.8	21.3	36.3
1981–1993	5.0	15.9	27.0
1994–2011	3.4	9.0	19.7
Industry			
1965–1980	40.3	37.5	24.1
1981–1993	41.0	39.5	29.1
1994–2011	32.1	36.9	31.8
Manufacturing			
1965–1980	22.0	26.8	15.9
1981–1993	22.8	26.9	16.9
1994–2011	18.8	22.5	17.5
Services			
1965–1980	51.9	41.2	39.5
1981–1993	53.4	44.6	43.8
1994–2011	64.5	54.0	48.4

one-quarter of GDP in 1960–80, to an average of 20.7% (1981–93), only to decline further to an average of 18.0% in the period since 1993. By contrast, both the upper-middle-income countries (23.3%, 26.5% and 27.0%) and the lower-middle-income countries (17.7%, 23.1% and 25.5%) saw a fairly dramatic rise in their share of GDP allocated to capital formation while controlling consumption.

Correspondingly, South Africa has suffered a fairly dramatic fall in the country's gross savings rate (Figure 7.6). Gross savings as a share of GDP declined from an average of 24.6% in 1960–80 to 21.5% (1981–93), only to fall further to 15.6% in the period since 1993. Comparable figures for

Table 7.3 South Africa's macroeconomic growth patterns relative to middle-income countries (average annual rates of real growth)

	South Africa	Upper-middle-income countries	Lower-middle-income countries
Gross capital formation			
1960–1980	6.1	10.2	6.9
1981–1993	−4.6	3.6	2.4
1994–2011	5.6	12.1	6.9
General government consumption			
1960–1980	6.4	6.2	6.3
1981–1993	3.2	3.9	4.0
1994–2011	3.1	4.8	5.3
Household consumption			
1960–1980	4.5	n.a.	3.8
1981–1993	0.3	2.9	3.6
1994–2011	3.6	4.4	5.3
Imports of goods and services			
1960–1980	4.1	n.a.	6.4
1981–1993	−0.4	0.8	1.3
1994–2011	5.6	8.9	7.9
Exports of goods and services			
1960–1980	2.6	n.a.	6.0
1981–1993	2.7	3.9	3.7
1994–2011	3.2	9.3	8.1

Source: Computed from World Bank, *World Development Indicators*, April 2013

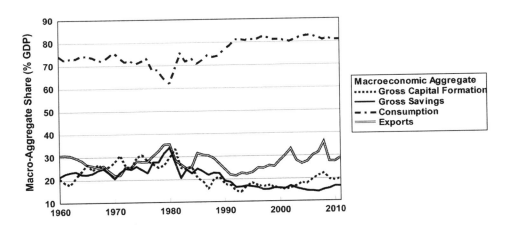

Figure 7.5 South Africa: macro-aggregate shares of GDP, 1960–2011
Source: World Bank, World Development Indicators, April 2013

Table 7.4 South Africa's changing macroeconomic structure relative to middle-income countries (% GDP)

	South Africa	Upper-middle-income countries	Lower-middle-income countries
Gross capital formation			
1960–80	25.6	23.3	17.7
1981–93	20.7	26.5	23.1
1994–2011	18.0	27.0	25.5
Private sector capital formation			
1960–80	24.8	n.a.	n.a.
1981–93	16.0	n.a.	11.4
1994–2011	12.5	15.0	16.9
Gross savings			
1960–80	24.6	n.a.	n.a.
1981–93	21.5	25.3	21.1
1994–2011	15.6	28.0	25.1
General government consumption			
1960–80	12.7	10.3	11.0
1981–93	18.4	13.0	11.9
1994–2011	19.4	14.9	11.5
Household consumption			
1960–80	58.9	63.7	73.6
1981–93	56.3	59.8	68.6
1994–2011	62.0	55.9	66.5
Imports of goods and services			
1960–80	25.2	12.4	14.7
1981–93	21.7	17.2	19.7
1994–2011	27.0	25.8	29.1
Exports of goods and services			
1960–80	28.0	11.7	12.4
1981–93	26.4	17.7	16.1
1994–2011	27.7	28.0	26.0
Trade			
1960–80	53.2	24.1	27.1
1981–93	48.1	34.8	35.9
1994–2011	54.7	53.9	55.1

Source: Computed from World Bank, *World Development Indicators*, April 2013

the upper-middle-income countries (28.0%) and lower-middle-income countries (25.1%) in this latter period suggest that South Africa's funding gap of the difference between capital formation and domestic savings is increasing dramatic, relative to countries of similar income.

A low domestic savings rate means that South Africa runs structural deficits on the current account of the balance of payments (-6.4% of GDP in the second quarter of 2012). As FDI inflows are relatively small, the economy relies heavily on foreign purchases of bonds and equities to fund its current account deficits. Cumulative foreign purchases of equities since 1994 amount to ZAF 420 billion (about US$48 billion). A substantial proportion of these shares bought by foreigners are in mining companies.

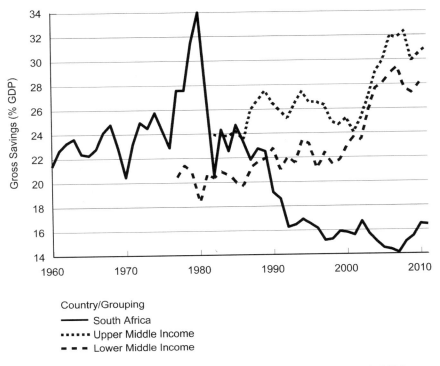

Figure 7.6 South Africa, middle Income countries, gross savings % GDP: 1960–2011
Source: World Bank, World Development Indicators, April 2013

In fact, minerals and mining have played, relative to other middle-income countries, a much more significant role in South Africa's economy. While the country exhibits few of the natural resource curse symptoms (inflation, deindustrialization) often found in other mineral/oil economies, the sector tends to be very capital intensive and has not contributed significantly to job creation over the last several decades.

Despite its limited role in job creation the mining sector has been a key element in South Africa's economy ever since the discovery of diamonds and gold in the mid-to-late 1800s. The country's early industrialization was heavily based on mineral wealth and on supplying inputs to the mining industry. With the depletion of many of the sector's initial deposits and the growth of other sectors, mining's share of GDP had declined to only 7.5% by 1971.

Volatility has characterized the sector's growth in recent decades. Rising gold prices in the 1970s produced a resurgence in the sector's importance, and by 1980 its share of GDP had expanded to 20.6%. A sharp decline in the gold price after 1980, falling ore grades, rising costs and generally weaker global commodity prices resulted in mining's share of GDP falling to a low of 6.5% in 1997. Initially a weaker rand—and later, dramatically higher global commodity prices and rising non-gold mining production—saw mining's share of GDP rise to 9.8% in 2011.

Falling annual gold production from 1,000 tons in 1980 to 187 tons in 2011 resulted in gold's share of exports declining from 50% in 1980 to 10% in 2011. Rising prices and output of platinum group metals (PGMs) mean that these now surpass gold's contributions to exports. Despite the dramatic fall in gold production, mining exports still make up the bulk of South Africa's exports: in 2010 primary and processed mineral exports amounted to 46.6% of all exports.

Other mining-related exports such as steel and processed diamonds contributed a further 16.3%; total mining-related exports amounted to 63.0% of total exports that year (64.0% in 2011).

Human development

The Human Development Index (HDI) paints another picture of South Africa. The index represents a broader definition of well-being and provides a composite measure of three basic dimensions of human development: health, education and income. Between 1980 and 2012 South Africa's HDI score increased at a rate of 0.9% annually—from 0.570 to 0.629. While South Africa ranks only 121 out of 187 countries, the country remains well above the sub-Saharan regional average (0.475).[9] However, while South Africa had a relatively large lead in the mid-1990s over the average for medium human development countries, this was lost in 2007. Since 2007 South Africa has continued to fall further behind the medium human development countries.

Income inequalities and unemployment

Growth has also been highly uneven in its distribution, perpetuating inequality and exclusion. With an income Gini of around 0.70 in 2008 and consumption Gini of 0.63 in 2009, South Africa stands as one of the most unequal countries in the world. The Gini coefficient is a measure of inequality with values from 0 (complete equality) to 1.0 (complete inequality). The top decile of the population accounts for 58% of the country's income, while the bottom decile accounts for 0.5%, and the bottom half less than 8%.[10] In large part, this is an enduring legacy of the apartheid system, which denied the non-whites (especially Africans) the chance to accumulate capital in any form—land, finance, skills, education, or social networks.

Another factor contributing to increased income disparities has been a dramatic shift in the shares of income received by labour and capital. In 1995 wages and salaries made up 50% and profits 27% of gross national income. By 2002 wages and salaries had declined to 45% with profits increasing to 30%.[11] Clearly, most of the gains of growth during this period were captured by capital.

This dramatic shift in income shares can be explained in part by the economy's inability to create jobs commensurate with high population growth rates and the overall expansion of the economy. Unemployment in South Africa has increased from around 8% in 1980 to over 25% (early 2013)—a figure considerably above that found in other major emerging economies (see Figure 7.7). The discouraging effect of chronic unemployment no doubt accounts in part for the country's relatively low labour participation rate (see Figure 7.8). Despite an almost 30% increase in per capita GDP since the late 1990s, the country's chronic unemployment and low labour participation rates have resulted in reductions in poverty being considerably less than might have been anticipated. While the factors underlying the country's serious inability to create jobs are complex, there is little doubt that higher rates of growth will be needed if significant reductions are to occur.

Unfortunately, despite nearly 20 years since the end of apartheid, poverty still exists largely along racial lines. Between 1995 and 2008 white mean per capita income grew by over 80%, while African income grew by less than 40%. Poverty remains overwhelmingly black: in the poorest quintile of households, 95% are Africans. At the other end of the scale, almost half of the wealthiest 20% of households are white, even though whites make up less than 10% of the total population.[12]

Pending a sudden acceleration in the rate of economic growth, the government has relied increasingly on social assistance grants. As documented by the World Bank, non-contributory and means-tested (except for foster care) financial transfers from the budget account for more than 70% of the income of the bottom quintile (up from 15% in 1993 and 29% in 2000). As the Bank notes:

South Africa's difficult transition

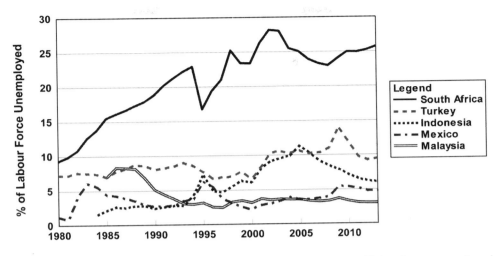

Figure 7.7 South Africa, Turkey, Indonesia, Malaysia and Mexico: % of labor force unemployed, 1980–2011
Source: IMF World Economic Outlook Database, April 2013

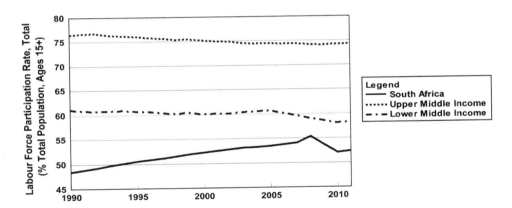

Figure 7.8 South Africa, middle income countries, labor force participation rates: 1990–2011
Source: World Bank, World Development Indicators, April 2013

With the social grants, the entire spectrum of population ranked by income percentiles saw income growth between 1995 and 2005. But without the grants as part of income, those below the 40th percentile saw a significant decline in their income. In other words, without the grants, two-fifths of the population would have seen its income decline in the first decade after apartheid.[13]

Clearly, the country's serious disparities of income and high levels of poverty will take years to rectify and will require major shifts in government policy from short-term redistributive programmes with a longer-term horizon to longer-term programmes capable of supporting self-sustained expansions in income. An examination of the country's sources of growth provide a macro perspective on what might be possible.

Robert E. Looney

Sources of growth

Estimates of the sources of South Africa's growth suggest that several sharp changes have occurred over the years. Faulkner and Loewald's[14] examination of these patterns breaks down the post-1971 period into several relevant sub-periods, as follows: 1971–84 apartheid growth; 1985–94 final decade of apartheid; 1995–2000 first phase of post-apartheid; and 2001–07 second phase of post-apartheid.

Their results suggest a structural shift in the relative strength of the components that contribute to South Africa's economic growth. In particular, factor inputs (capital and labour) have diminished in importance, while technological progress has increased. This pattern is consistent with the high levels of investment in the 1980s, together with the increased competition and technological inflows as South Africa became more integrated into the global economy after 1994.

While comparable figures for the period after 2007 are unavailable, Faulkner and Loewald anticipated that with increased macroeconomic stability:

> Lower rates of inflation and interest should support: a rise in the contribution of private sector capital, further encouraging the crowding in effects of public infrastructure investment. The contribution to growth from labor as a factor of production will rise with better employment growth, the adjustment of firms to the democratic labor law framework, lower inflation, and a better balance between real wage growth and labor productivity.[15]

Assessing South African growth dynamics

While South Africa's past trends relative to other middle-income countries are clear, identifying the causal mechanisms responsible for the country's somewhat unique pattern of growth, especially as it pertains to underperformance, poverty, income distribution and unemployment, is far from straightforward.

Factors affecting well-being

One promising approach developed by the Boston Consulting Group[16] assesses the country's general welfare by measuring the well-being of the population. In this approach an overall well-being score is derived by examining 10 key dimensions: income, economic stability, employment, income equality, civil society, governance, education, health, environment and infrastructure. The Boston approach not only examines a country's current level of well-being, but also its recent progress—that is, how well-being has changed over the last five years.

Both the current level of well-being and recent progress are measured on a scale of 0 to 100, with 100 representing the highest level among the 150 countries included in the original Boston sample. In addition, the Boston approach analyses the long-term sustainability through identifying the enablers that help each of the 10 dimensions of socio-economic development to continue. This long-term sustainability score provides an indication of a country's ability to sustain improvements over the next generation.

A comparison of South Africa, the BRICs (Brazil, Russia, India and China), and this volume's likely success stories, Turkey, Mexico and Malaysia, produced several interesting patterns. A plot of each country's current level score with that of its long-term sustainability score shows the two fairly closely related (see Figure 7.9). That is, there is a fairly steady progression of higher long-term sustainability scores associated with current level scores. The line in Figure 7.9 represents an exponential trend with countries lying above the line having relatively brighter

South Africa's difficult transition

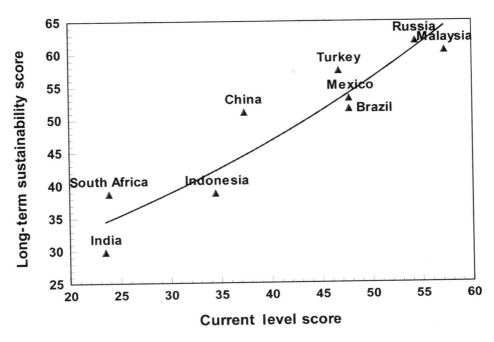

Figure 7.9 South Africa, emerging economies, Boston Consulting Group sustainability patterns
Source: Boston Consulting Group, *From Wealth to Wellbeing*, Appendix, 2012

future prospects given their current situation, and countries below the line facing relatively less advantageous prospects.

South Africa and India share both the lowest current level and long-term sustainability scores. As South Africa lies above the exponential trend, its future looks a bit brighter than India's. Still, by the Boston measures of progress, South Africa has a significant gap to close before its economy can be considered on the same level as many of the other successful emerging economies. In addition, the government's attempts at providing increased levels of well-being may, under current conditions, be extremely difficult. An examination of wealth to well-being—a metric that adjusts current levels of well-being by GDP per capita—finds (see Figure 7.9) that South Africa comes out (with the notable exception of India) well below that of the BRIC countries and our sample of successful emerging economies.

Similarly, South Africa has had great difficulty in translating its recent growth into improved well-being. A plot of South Africa's progress in well-being (see Figure 7.10) against the country's recent growth (2006–11) shows South Africa well below the country regression line linking the two variables. The contrast with Brazil is particularly striking: for a similar range of growth, Brazil had an improved well-being score nearly twice that of South Africa.

No doubt much of South Africa's difficulty in attaining higher levels of well-being can be linked to the legacy of apartheid. As noted earlier, although per capita GDP growth has improved from a period of contraction in the 1980s, annual rates of growth have remained relatively low, averaging 1.6% from 1994 to 2011.

A number of empirical studies confirm South Africa's difficulties in converting growth into well-being. Odhiambo[17] examined the so-called 'trickle-down effect' in attempting to answer one critical question: does economic growth in South Africa trickle down to the poor through

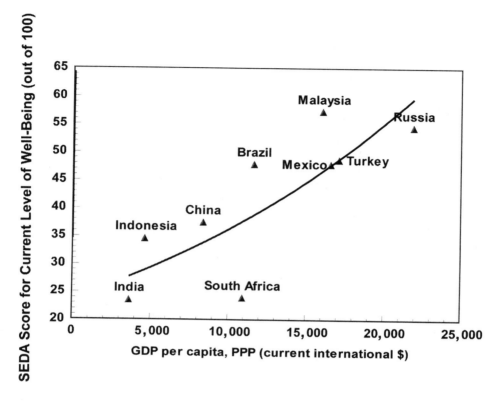

Figure 7.10 South Africa, emerging economies: Boston Consulting Group, converting wealth into well being
Source: Boston Consulting Groups, *From Wealth to Well Being*, Appendix, 2012

job creation? In this study two proxies were used to measure the incidence of poverty in South Africa: household consumption per capita and infant mortality. His empirical findings fail to support the trickle-down effect between economic growth and poverty reduction in South Africa. Moreover, the results show that there is no causal relationship between economic growth and poverty reduction in either direction. The results apply irrespective of whether the poverty level is measured by real per capita consumption or by the infant mortality rate.

The role of governance

Limited progress in improving some aspects of governance may have played a role in affecting South Africa's below-par economic performance in recent years. Numerous empirical studies[18] have found significant links between such governance dimensions as democracy, corruption, rule of law, government effectiveness and overall economic performance.

While rating countries on the basis of their relative progress in improving governance is inherently subjective, with different sources often providing conflicting results, the World Bank's Governance Indicators data set[19] regularly provides a set of rankings incorporating the full extent of our knowledge about this critical aspect of development. The World Bank data set estimates six dimensions of governance for 213 economies over the period 1996–2011.

South Africa's difficult transition

These dimensions are: voice and accountability; political stability and absence of violence; government effectiveness; regulatory quality; rule of law; and control of corruption. To assess South Africa's progress, comparisons are made with our group of likely success stories, Indonesia, Malaysia, Mexico and Turkey.

Voice and accountability 'reflects perceptions of the extent to which a country's citizens are able to participate in selecting their government, as well as freedom of expression, freedom of association and a free media'. On this dimension South Africa scores well above the sample group. Since 1996 (see Figure 7.11), South Africa's scores have ranged in the low 70th percentile to the mid-60th percentile. Only Malaysia comes close to matching South Africa's progress in this dimension. However, Malaysia has yet to score in the 60th percentile.

The World Bank data suggest a slight downward trend in voice and accountability since 2004 when the country reached the 73.56th percentile. Following this peak, the country's score declined fairly steadily, winding up at the 65.73 percentile in 2011.

However, other sources looking at the components of this governance measure paint a slightly different picture. Through a series of public attitude surveys, the prestigious Afrobarometer's latest survey of public opinion found that personal satisfaction with South Africa's democracy has gone up from 49% in 2008 to 60% in 2011.[20] In sum, it is safe to say democratization has been one of South Africa's major accomplishments. However, the country is still classified as a 'flawed democracy' in the Economist Intelligence Unit's Democracy Index.[21]

Political stability/absence of violence reflects perceptions of the likelihood that the government will be destabilized or overthrown by unconstitutional or violent means, including politically motivated violence and terrorism. South Africa does not have the lead over the other sample countries that it did with voice and accountability. Still, the country started out (1996) at only the 31st percentile (see Figure 7.12) and experienced steady improvement until 2007, when the country had risen to the 52nd percentile. At that time South Africa had the highest score of our sample countries. Since 2007 South Africa fell to the 46th percentile (2009), only to improve

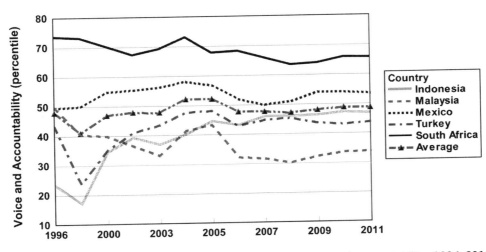

Figure 7.11 South Africa emerging economies, patterns of voice and accountability: 1996–2011
Source: World Bank, Worldwide Governance Indicators, 1996–2010
Reflects perceptions of the extent to which a country's citizens are able to participate in selecting their government, as well as freedom of expression, freedom of association, and a free media.

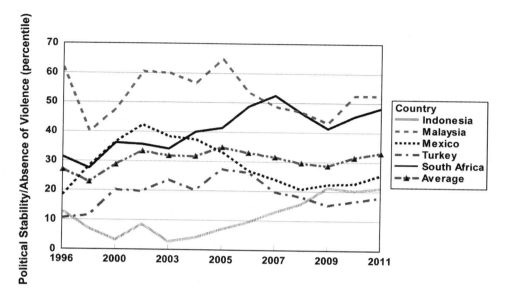

Figure 7.12 South Africa, emerging economics, patterns of political stability/absence of violence 1996–2011
Source: World Bank, Worldwide Governance Indicators, 1996–2011.
Reflect perceptions of the likelihood that the government will be destabilized and overthrown by unconstitutional and violent protest, including politically motivated violence and terrorism.

again to the 48th by 2011. Currently, South Africa ranks slightly behind Malaysia in attainment of this important governance dimension.

These patterns seem to be at odds with the common perception of the increasing number of violent protests in South Africa. As Lavery documents, from the 'rolling mass action' of the 1980s[22] to the service delivery demonstrations of the 1990s and 2000s, South African citizens have regularly participated in mass protests to impact public option and influence policymakers on political economic or social matters.[23] Carl Death[24] goes further, to contend that political protests have visibly increased in frequency and intensity in South Africa in recent years.

However, detailed interviews conducted by Afrobarometer over the period 2000 to 2011 do not support the increasing frequency of protest position. In fact, these surveys suggest that South Africans have become more likely to say they would never protest. Over the same period there was a decline in the percentage of South Africans who reported that they have attended a protest in the past year.

In sum, it is fairly safe to say that the country has achieved steady if not spectacular gains in political stability/absence of violence. These gains may be fragile, with evidence that poverty appears to be one of the major predictors of active protest.[25]

Government effectiveness reflects perceptions of the quality of public service, the quality of the civil service and the degree of its independence from political pressure, the quality of policy formulation and implementation, and the credibility of the government's commitment to such policies. Here the picture painted by the World Bank is not as favourable. In 1996 South Africa had the highest score among the sample countries, the 79th percentile. However, there has been a continuous, albeit gradual, deterioration in this key dimension of governance (see Figure 7.13). By 2011 the country's score had declined to 65%, the average for the group as

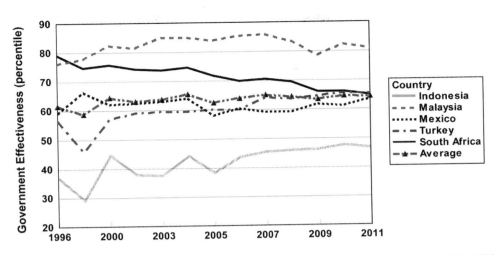

Figure 7.13 South Africa, emerging economies, patterns of government effectiveness 1996–2011
Source: World Bank, Worldwide Governance Indicators, 1996–2010
Reflect perceptions of the purity of public services, the quality of policy boundaries and implementation, and the credibility of the government's commitment to such policies.

a whole and approximately the same as that of Mexico and Turkey. At this time South Africa's ranking was considerably behind that of Malaysia.

The Fitch credit rating agency has expressed concern over the declining effectiveness of the government, and in January 2013 downgraded South Africa, warning that 'social and political tensions have increased as subdued growth, coupled with rising corruption and worsening government effectiveness, has constrained the government's ability to ... redress historical inequalities'.[26]

Regulatory quality reflects perceptions of the ability of the government to formulate and implement sound policies and regulations that permit and promote private sector development. South Africa scores fairly well on this government dimension (see Figure 7.14), but as in the case of government effectiveness, has not been able to sustain marked improvements since the early 2000s. South Africa ranked in the 63rd percentile in 1996, slightly above Mexico, but considerably below Malaysia (73rd). Considerable improvement took place up to 2003 when the country reached the 74th percentile and was the highest ranked of our sample countries. However, since 2003, there has been a steady decline in regulatory quality with South Africa levelling off at the 66th percentile in 2011. This was approximately the same ranking as Turkey, but below Malaysia at the 74th percentile.

Lack of better progress in this area has no doubt taken a toll on the economy, especially with regard to the country's overall growth rate and, in particular, that of the private sector. Focusing on product market regulation (PMR)—a measure of the extent to which the regulatory framework is supportive of competition in markets for goods and services, the Organisation for Economic Co-operation and Development (OECD) has found some significant statistical relationships linking PMR with income gaps with countries in the upper half of the OECD income distribution.[27] Regressing restrictiveness of product market regulation on gaps in GDP per capita, the OECD finds a correlation coefficient of −0.79 that is significant at the 1% level.

Plotting South Africa and our sample countries produced a roughly similar pattern (see Figure 7.15) in both the OECD analysis and the one presented here. South Africa lies to the

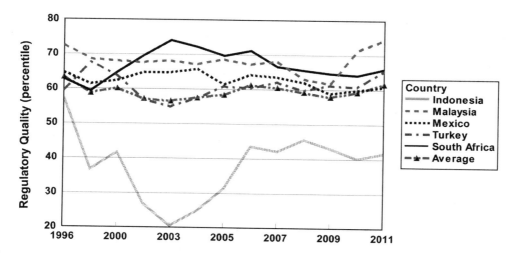

Figure 7.14 South Africa, emerging economies, patterns of regulatory quality to 1996–2011
Source: World Bank, Worldwide Governance Indicators, 1996–2011
Reflect perceptions of the dailery of the government to formulate and implement sound policies and regulations that permit and pollute minor seeker development

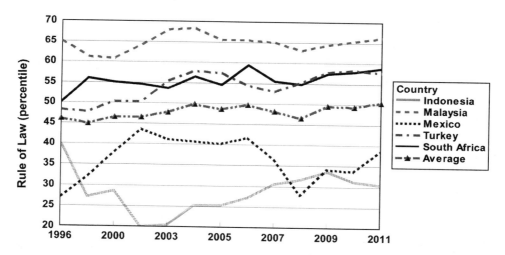

Figure 7.15 South Africa, emerging economies, patterns of rule of law 1996–2011
Source: World Bank, Worldwide Governance Indicators, 1996–2011.
Reflects perceptions of the extent to which peers have confidence in and divide by the rules of society and in particularly the purity of coutiser empowerment, property rights, the police, and the courts, as well as the likelihood of crime and violence.

right of the regression line, suggesting that its income gap, while large (–75) is not as large as might be anticipated given the restrictiveness in its product markets.

As the OECD notes, there are a number of mechanisms that might account for this pattern. For one thing, promoting competition by lowering (domestic and border) barriers to entry and levelling the playing field for different firm types can encourage the movement of capital from low- to high-productivity firms and sectors, thereby improving resource allocation.

South Africa's difficult transition

There is also evidence that that lower PMR speeds the international diffusion of new technologies and production techniques. Greater competition can also stimulate job creation and increase employment levels in the long run. Finally, there is some evidence that stronger competition may have particularly beneficial effects for the purchasing power of lower-income groups.

Rule of law reflects perceptions of the extent to which agents have confidence in and abide by the rules of society, and in particular the quality of contract enforcement, property rights, the police, the courts, as well as the likelihood of crime and violence. The country has made fairly steady progress in this area. Starting in the 50th percentile in 1996, the country's rule of law score increased to the 56th percentile in 1998 and finally the 59th by 2011 (see Figure 7.16). At the present time the country still lags Malaysia (66th percentile), but is considerably above the average for our sample countries (50th percentile).

Still there are some major concerns over limited progress in several rule of law sub-components. In its latest report on competitiveness, the World Economic Forum (WEF) highlights the poor security situation as an important obstacle to doing business in South Africa: 'The high business costs of crime and violence (134th) and the sense that the police are unable to provide sufficient protection from crime (90th) do not contribute to an environment that fosters competitiveness.'[28]

Lack of employment opportunities has contributed to poverty and crime, raising the spectre of a vicious circle in which increasing social insecurity reduces business confidence and investment, leading to slower economic growth and lower job creation.[29] Recent business surveys have identified crime as the leading constraint on investment, followed by the cost of capital, labour regulations and skills shortages.[30]

Research at the World Bank[31] suggests that drivers of crime are varied and complex, but the models of behaviour to which young people are exposed and the levels of care and support that they receive play a key role. The research shows that violence is for many young people a part of life; it is a feature of their homes, schools and communities, and has become an accepted component of young people's social interactions. Many poor children are also growing up in home environments

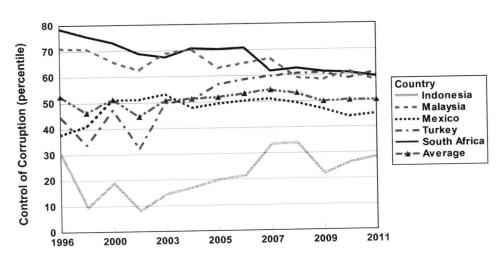

Figure 7.16 South Africa emerging economies, patterns of control of corruption: 1996–2011
Source: World Bank, Worldwide Governance Indicators, 1996–2010
Reflect perceptions of the extent to which public power is exercised for future gain, including both party and found forms of corruptions, as well as "capture" of the able by elites and private interests.

where they lack the developmental investment needed to become healthy, well-adjusted adults. 'These drivers are compounded by shortfalls in childcare, afterschool care and recreation, which could help to steer children toward more pro-social modes of behavior; parenting practices that promote violence; and young people's limited opportunities for personal growth.'

Control of corruption reflects perceptions of the extent to which public power is exercised for private gain, including both petty and grand forms of corruption, as well as 'capture' of the state by elites and private interests. Initially (1996), South Africa had the highest country ranking (79th percentile) in our country sample. Unfortunately, since 1996 progress has been limited (see Figure 7.17) and the country has seen a rather continual fall in this important governance dimension. From 2004 to 2006 the country's ranking fell to the 70th percentile, only to decline further to the 60th percentile by 2011. At this time South Africa's ranking was similar to that of Malaysia and Turkey, but still above the sample average of the 50th percentile.

Deteriorating progress in combating corruption has been noted by a number of concerned organizations. According to Corruption Watch, corruption is on the rise in South Africa. The latest Transparency International Corruption Perceptions Index ranks South Africa 69th out of 176 countries. The findings also reveal that South Africa is sliding in the rankings from year to year. The WEF's *Global Competitiveness Report* further showed that corruption was one of the most-cited hindrances to doing business in South Africa.

There is little doubt that widespread corruption in South Africa has taken a serious toll on the country's growth. Nepotism, patronage and corruption have also played a significant role in bleeding the state of scarce resources. This is most acute at the level of local government, but more recently, the central government has had to send special task teams to take over the administration of selected provincial government departments where incompetence and corruption rendered them totally incapable of delivering on their constitutional mandate.[32]

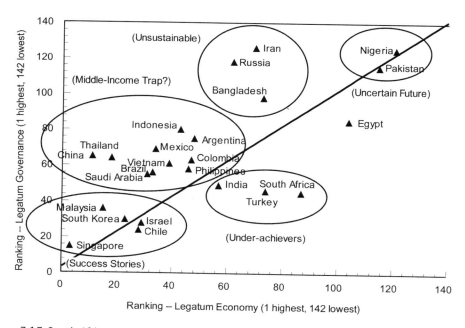

Figure 7.17 South Africa, emerging economies, Legatum Institute Economy/Governance Ranking

Corruption is increasingly becoming a matter of concern to citizens in all walks of life. While the South African government has verbally committed itself in unequivocal terms to the eradication of corruption, high-profile cases and grassroots experience are fuelling public perceptions of a government squandering public funds. It has been estimated that as much as 30% of all public spending is creamed off in various scams.[33]

In sum, South Africa's progress in the area of governance has been mixed. While the country has relatively high levels of governance in each of the key dimensions, there has been limited improvement in most categories since 1996. In addition, the areas that might have a significant effect on economic growth, government effectiveness and control of corruption have shown signs of secular deterioration.

Given the importance attached to governance in facilitating and supporting economic growth in the emerging economies one might expect a rough one-to-one relationship between these two variables. The Legatum Prosperity Index provides a useful framework for testing this proposition. The overall Index incorporates eight key elements: economy; entrepreneurship and opportunity; governance; education; health; safety and security; personal freedom; and social capital.

Values for the economy dimension are computed on the basis of a five-year growth rate (2010); confidence in financial institutions (% positive, 2011); and satisfaction with living standards (% positive, 2011). The Legatum governance dimension comprises: confidence in the government (% positive, 2011); confidence in the judiciary; and the World Bank's government effectiveness measure.

A plot of the Legatum country governance ranking against its economic ranking for this volume's emerging economies (BRICS, diverse success stories, likely success stories and possible candidates) produced an interesting pattern of five groups and one outlier (Egypt). The first group, uncertain future, comprises Bangladesh and Pakistan. This group fits the prediction of a roughly one-to-one link between economic performance and governance attainment. Unfortunately, in their cases the countries score very low in both areas.

A second group, unsustainable, includes Iran, Russia and Bangladesh. These countries have fared fairly well economically, but on the basis of limited governance. No doubt in Russia's and Iran's cases, very favourable oil markets in recent years have been translated into higher rates of economic growth.

The third group of countries, middle-income trap? is by far the largest and includes Indonesia, Argentina, Mexico, Thailand, Colombia, the Philippines, Brazil, Viet Nam, China and Saudi Arabia. The commonality here is very good economic performance that is not directly matched by progress in governance. Each country has achieved proportionally better economic rankings than in the area of governance. Indonesia and Argentina are the extreme cases, with the Philippines, Colombia, Viet Nam and Saudi Arabia much closer to the one-to-one balance.

This group of countries may be approaching the controversial 'middle-income' trap—countries that will stagnate at per capita incomes in the $12,000 to $15,000 range unless they undertake major reforms in governance, if they are to continue their progression to higher levels of government. As is often the case, vested interests, bureaucratic inertia and a tendency to deal with short-run stabilization problems over longer-term growth issues prevents or limits the creation of a sound governance structure capable of improving competitiveness and allowing transition to more sophisticated industries and services.

The fourth group of countries, success stories, consisting of Malaysia, the Republic of Korea (South Korea), Israel, Chile and Singapore, correspond roughly to this volume's group of success stories: countries that have had sustained rates of economic growth enabling them to support high and rising standards of living. These countries also follow the expected one-to-one pattern of governance/economy.

South Africa is in a fifth group of countries, underachievers, along with India and Turkey. These countries have made good progress in improved governance, but have not been able to leverage these gains into better economic performance. Their economies are operating at a sub-optimal level, not capable to taking advantage of a relatively solid governance foundation. Of the three countries, South Africa has by far the largest gap between its actual and expected economic ranking.

There may be several explanations for South Africa's economic underperformance. First, the measure of governance used by the Legatum Institute focuses largely on government effectiveness, confidence in the government and confidence in the judiciary. As noted above, South Africa's government effectiveness, while relatively high, has been on a marked downward trend, suggesting an increasing inability on the part of the government to cope with an increasingly complex domestic and external environment—changes in governance may be more important that the average level in affecting economic performance. Second, since corruption is not directly factored into the Legatum governance dimension, the corrosive effects of this dimension have reduced the country's factor productivity (labour, capital and total factor productivity) and hence are a drag on the economy. Third, there are other areas in which reforms have lagged to such an extent that they cannot be compensated for by improved governance as measured by the Legatum method. No doubt other explanations exist for South Africa's disappointing economic performance in recent years, but the three noted here are good starting points

One explanation has been suggested by empirical research[34] undertaken by the International Monetary Fund (IMF). In this study South Africa's pattern of growth is compared directly to a panel of 10 countries with rapid rates of per capita income growth: China, Viet Nam, India, Russia, Poland, Ukraine, South Korea, Bangladesh, Iran and Romania.

As with the analysis above, the comparative approach provides a useful perspective on South Africa's progress: good performance relative to the period of apartheid may still come up short when viewed from the perspective of other successful countries. The IMF identified (mainly for the period 1996–2007) the main constraints on South African growth as, first, a low investment rate, second, insufficient labour productivity gains, and third, lower openness to trade and slower technical progress relative to faster-growing countries.

Underinvestment was singled out as the major factor underlying South Africa's relatively slow rate of growth. Despite a pick-up in recent years, the investment rate is low compared to faster-growing countries. Boosting investment is therefore critical for accelerating growth.

In turn, the country's relatively low rate of investment was largely attributed to the country's relatively low savings rate. From a policy perspective, the country's savings could be increased with greater savings efforts by the private and public sectors. However, the IMF held out little scope for a dramatic increase in private savings, noting that:

> the low level of private saving in South Africa mainly results from structural factors like shifts in demographics, urbanization, and financial sector deepening that are not easily affected by public policies. The two factors that most explain the difference in the private saving rate between South Africa and the panel of comparators (apart from the persistence term) are both demographic: the young dependency ratio and the urbanization rate.[35]

On the other hand, restraining government consumption was seen as an effective way of increasing public savings and thus the overall savings rate.

Competitiveness

On the surface, competitiveness would not appear to be a major cause of South Africa's economic underperformance. The country has made significant progress in many of the key areas affecting competitiveness, ranking 52nd (up from 54th in 2010–11, but down from 50th in

2011–12) out of 144 countries in the WEF's 2012–13 *Competitiveness Report.*[36] According to the WEF's measure, South Africa has the highest overall level of competitiveness in sub-Saharan Africa and is third placed among the BRICS economies.

A somewhat different picture emerges, however, when looking at the main components of the WEF competitiveness measure. The WEF's overall competitiveness measure is a composite of 12 pillars: (1) institutions, (2) infrastructure, (3) macroeconomic environment, and (4) health and primary education. These are grouped as a Basic Requirements sub-index. Pillars (5) higher education and training, (6) goods market efficiency, (7) labour market efficiency, (8) financial market development, (9) technological readiness, and (10) market size, form the Efficiency Enhancers sub-index. Finally, pillars (11) business sophistication, and (12) innovation form the Innovation and Sophistication Factors sub-index. The WEF classifies South Africa as being in Stage 2, or efficiency driven. Countries in this group have a GDP per capita in the range of $3,000 to $8,999. For this group of countries, the three sub-indexes' weights of importance in affecting overall competitiveness are 40% for Basic Requirements, 50% for Efficiency Enhancers and 10% for Innovation and Sophistication factors.

South Africa's ranking on the various pillars shows that the country has an inherent advantage, particularly in terms of other sub-Saharan countries, due to its economic size, ranking 25th. South Africa also has made good progress as reflected by the quality of its institutions (43rd), business sophistication (38th), innovation (42nd), and its goods market efficiency (32rd). The country's greatest strides have been in financial market development (3rd). According to the WEF, this ranking indicates 'high confidence in South Africa's financial markets at a time when trust is returning only slowly in many other parts of the world'.[37] These combined attributes make South Africa the most competitive economy in the region.

Unfortunately, this progress may be more than offset by glaring deficiencies in several key areas. South Africa ranks 113th in labour market efficiency (representing a decline of 18 places in 2011–12). The country is plagued by little co-operation in labour-employer relations (144th or last), flexibility of wage determination (140th), hiring and firing practices (143), and pay and productivity (134th).

Education is another area where the country has serious deficiencies, ranking very low in several key areas: quality of primary education (132nd); primary education enrolment (115th); quality of higher education and training (140th); quality of maths and science education (143rd); and internet access in schools (111th).

The country also lags in providing for the population's basic health with: business impact of malaria (100th); business impact of tuberculosis (132nd); business impact of HIV/AIDS (132); and life expectancy (132nd).

The poor security situation remains another important obstacle to doing business in South Africa. The high business costs of crime and violence (134th) and the sense that the police are unable to provide sufficient protection from crime (90th) do not contribute to an environment that fosters competitiveness.

Although the country has relatively good institutions by regional standards, there are several areas that may be having a serious impact on business: trust in politicians (88th); business costs of crime and violence (134th); reliability of police services (90th); burden of government regulation (123rd); and organized crime (111th).

Restrictive labour regulations, inefficient government bureaucracy, inadequate supply of infrastructure and corruption are the main factors often noted as being the most difficult obstacles to doing business in South Africa.

Policy approaches to create self-sustained equitable growth

The previous sections have identified a number of areas in which improvement is needed if the country is to achieve high sustained rates of growth with broad-based equity and the alleviation of poverty.

No doubt some of the skills shortages can be attributed to the deliberate exclusion[38] of black people from the education system and from skilled occupations under apartheid. During apartheid, education was strictly segregated; spending on white students was 10 times higher than for black students. However, the vestiges of the apartheid system remain de facto as the families of poorer black families are not able to afford the tuition fees charged by the better schools. Furthermore, the quality of education freely available to the poorer segments of South African society is regularly ranked as one of the worst[39] in the world by organizations, as noted above, such as the WEF and the Legatum Institute.[40] The result is increased polarization with rising incomes for the educated, formal sector workers. The undereducated, burdened by stagnant wages and low productivity, are forced to take refuge in the informal[41] economy.

However, there's another equally persuasive explanation for the country's dual economy—one that has become increasingly topical since the onset of labour strife. That is South Africa's industrial relations[42] structure, another (albeit indirect) remnant of the apartheid era. While many developing countries have a nascent union movement, South Africa's unions under apartheid developed along more advanced industrial country lines. Their strong adherence to and enforcement of minimum wages laws in the post-1994 era has stifled[43] the development of many low-cost, labour-intensive industries that would normally employ large numbers of semi-skilled and unskilled workers.

Union power together with the government's attempts to respond to the demands of its 'working poor' constituencies have resulted in a pattern of wage increases that are above the rate of inflation and unrelated to productivity. With labour costs rising faster[44] than productivity, many smaller labour-intensive firms, facing competition from low-cost imports, have either had to go out of business or risk the chance of prosecution for non-compliance. Many have been forcibly shut down.

With productivity's role diminished in the determination of wages, factors such as labour market imperfections (price and wage rigidities, entry restrictions, employment protection legislation) have combined with the collective bargaining framework to reduce labour mobility and thus job creation.

Rather than focus on labour market reforms[45] better to link wages with productivity and reduce job entry impediments, however, the government has approached the problem through broad, sweeping plans that are strong on vision but weak on details and means of implementation. Unfortunately, while raising expectations at the time of their announcement, the results have generally fallen short of their lofty goals.

Over the years the government has developed many plans and strategies in its attempt to achieve better economic performance and the creation of an equitable growth path.

The Reconstruction and Development Programme (RDP)

The RDP served as the African National Congress's (ANC) 1994 election manifesto. By placing most of its emphasis on the reduction of poverty, the programme was seen by many as overly leftist-oriented, yet had broad popular support. As might be expected for a first attempt at planning, the RDP was over-ambitious, given the limited state capacity of the first post-apartheid administration. The programme was abandoned after two years with little success in meetings its goals.[46]

Growth, Employment and Redistribution (GEAR)

The RDP was replaced by a programme called Growth, Employment and Redistribution (GEAR). GEAR was championed by then-Deputy President Thabo Mbeki, who announced at the time: 'Just call me a Thatcherite.'[47] In that spirit, GEAR incorporated much of the neo-liberal, Washington Consensus[48] in vogue at the time. It built on the principles of trade liberalization, market deregulation, privatization of state-owned enterprises, and macroeconomic stabilization through 'responsible' fiscal and monetary policies. Clearly, GEAR was conceived on the notion that fairly orthodox economic policy must be the foundation on which to build the growth required to defeat poverty and unemployment.

GEAR's strong commitment to a stable, conservative macroeconomic framework set in motion an approach to South African policymaking that has largely endured to the present day. However, there are notable exceptions: instead of liberalization, labour market regulation increased while privatization was only partially implemented. The programme ended in 2000, having failed to meet its growth and employment goals. The growth rate, while improving during the last decade of apartheid, was barely sufficient to keep pace with the growth of the population. More tellingly, the dual problems of poverty and income inequality were worsening, apparently confirming the programme's critics' position that it was in direct conflict with some of the country's more immediate problems: the reduction of poverty and a more equal division of wealth.[49]

Over the years GEAR's critics have stressed the inappropriateness of the neo-liberal approach to solving South Africa's economic problems. In particular, many regard GEAR's cautious fiscal and monetary policies (aimed at meeting an inflation target) as insufficiently expansionary. Resentment of GEAR remains, with the Congress of South African Trade Unions (COSATU) referring to it as the '1996 class project'.[50]

Accelerated and Shared Growth Initiative for South Africa (ASGISA)

It was not until 2006 that a successor to GEAR was launched: the Accelerated and Shared Growth Initiative for South Africa (ASGISA), which aimed at halving both unemployment and poverty by 2014, through increased average economic growth rates of at least 4.5% per year in 2005–09 and at least 6.0% in 2010–14.

This programme, which enjoyed the support of all key social stakeholders, has focused its attention on questions of infrastructure development, skills enhancement, the promotion of small and medium-sized enterprises (SMEs), and the capacity of the organs of state to promote social development.

Central to its purpose ASGISA identified a list of binding constraints. In contrast to many developing world plans, the list was made short enough and focused sufficiently to enable the implementation of a coherent and consistent set of policies. Simultaneously, the government asked the Harvard Group to apply its diagnostics approach to identify the constraints they felt were impeding the economy's progress.

While the lists of constraints identified by ASGISA and Harvard share some similarities, there are some significant differences. Specifically, the Harvard Group placed more emphasis on raising exports and toward this end recommended a more active management of the rand (exchange rate) to assure South Africa's products were competitively priced.

Both the government and the Harvard Group identified skills shortages as important constraints. However, the two differ in their approach to the problem. The Harvard Group emphasizes the need to facilitate legal immigration. Outside of a few efforts to attract South African expatriates, the government's preferred approach is to address shortages through education and training—the Joint Initiative on Priority Skills Acquisition (JIPSA).

With regard to industrial policy the Harvard Group argues that downstream beneficiation (the transformation of a mineral, or a combination of minerals, to a higher-value product) should not be part of state-led industrial policy. By contrast, some influential groups within the government have lobbied for a more active public sector involvement in targeted industries, including measures to stimulate beneficiation of mineral resources.

Harvard and ASGISA also differed over the effectiveness of state intervention, with the Harvard Group sceptical that state intervention would be effective in eliminating the country's more serious bottlenecks, while many in the government felt that the government should move to transforming the public sector into a development state, in a manner along the lines of many of the East Asian emerging economies.

As it turned out, although some progress was made in areas such as infrastructure development, issues such as insufficient skills development and capacity within state departments limited the effectiveness of ASGISA in meeting its goals. Despite a substantial—albeit unsustainable—post-2005 growth spurt, joblessness still affected one in four of the workforce, even on a narrow definition of unemployment, and over half of all young blacks.

By various measures, inequality and poverty were still rising. Especially in the wake of the 2009 recession—caused by a combination of external and domestic factors—the prospects of future growth rising even close to the 6%+ target were negligible.

New Growth Path

In 2010 the New Growth Path[51] (NGP) was introduced with the 2020 target of reducing the unemployment rate from 25% to 15%, via the creation of five million new 'decent' jobs. Though most of the jobs will be in the private sector, that sector has been highly sceptical of the plan, claiming that it lacks credibility.[52] Specifically, to create five million jobs by 2020, South Africa would need a growth rate[53] of at least 5% per year just to make a dent in current levels of unemployment, and considerably more to meet the planned job creation targets. The likelihood of that being achieved is pretty low. According to the IMF, South Africa's GDP is projected[54] to stay well under 4% until 2018.

One hears little today of the NGP. Instead, the government has moved on to a new plan, the National Development Plan[55] (NDP), with similar grandiose promises of full employment, this time by 2030. This effort would require 11 million extra jobs, again hardly a feasible goal.

Why the diversion of attention from proven labour market reforms to questionable massive state intervention to solve the country's economic problems? One possible explanation harks back to mindsets formed during the apartheid days. South Africa under apartheid fancied itself as a developmental state—that is the use of government planning and focused public policy to accelerate economic growth along the lines successfully implemented at the time in many East Asian countries.

Many of apartheid's key development state agencies are still in place, including the Industrial Development Corporation, the Land Bank and the Southern African Development Bank. Many in the government think that by using these agencies, a new developmental state that is democratic and non-racial could be successful where the apartheid variant failed.

Unfortunately, going down the development state road is likely to end in stagnation, as in the apartheid era. The reasons are different, however. The apartheid developmental state[56] was unsustainable because it was premised on excluding the black majority, leaving the apartheid state virtually bankrupt by the late 1980s. The developmental states of East Asia achieved their rapid industrialization during the post-war pre-oil crisis era of the Bretton Woods international economic order, which for a generation delivered unprecedented sustained non-inflationary growth in the world economy, accompanied by a tolerance of tariff and non-tariff barriers. The contemporary world economy of highly competitive export markets and lower overall world economic growth calls for open, liberalized markets. By moving in the opposite direction in this new and rapidly changing setting, the developmental state is not a suitable or indeed a feasible path for South Africa to take at this time.

Will the post-apartheid dream of freedom, equity, tolerance, multi-racial harmony and a more prosperous South African existence come to an end, undermined by a failed economy unable to eliminate the vestiges of apartheid? Or will the government muster the courage to confront effectively the many problems it faces? One hopes it will, but to date the authorities are providing little cause for optimism.[57] As one wise observer put it, in the spirit of Nelson Mandela:

> As a country, what we are called upon to do is to think and act collectively ... and most important of all, change our national political behavior in ways that are properly aligned to our national strategic goals.[58]

How wonderful it would be if the country could return to Mandela's dream.

Economic outlook

South Africa's economic prospects over the next several years are not particularly bright and it will be nearly impossible for the government to effect growth rates in the 5% range necessary to make a significant reduction in unemployment.

The sources threatening growth are both external and internal. Interest rates remain at historic lows, inflationary pressures linger, and ratings agencies are now watching the government's fiscal discipline more closely: neither monetary nor fiscal policy currently offers much scope for counter-measures. Even worse, on 16 April 2013 the Reserve Bank governor warned of the risk of 'stagflation'.[59]

While the economy's deceleration to 0.9%[60] growth in the first quarter of 2013 was a shock to many, it is unlikely, barring a major eurozone crisis, or a marked slow down in the world economy, that the economy will dip into a recession. Instead, the most likely prospect is of continued sideways drift, with the government embattled with labour disputes and falling investor confidence. Longer-term, much will continue to depend on the extent to which the government begins to commit itself seriously to major structural and policy reforms.

Notes

1 BartelsmannStiftung, *BTI 2012: South Africa Country Report*, 2012, 4, www.bti-project.de/fileadmin/Inhalte/reports/2012/pdf/BTI%202012%20South%20Africa.pdf.
2 *South Africa: Economic Update: Focus on Savings, Investment and Inclusive Growth*, World Bank, July 2011, siteresources.worldbank.org/INTSOUTHAFRICA/Resources/SAEU-July_2011_Full_Report.pdf.
3 BartelsmannStiftung, *BTI 2012: South Africa Country Report*.
4 BartelsmannStiftung, *BTI 2012: South Africa Country Report*, 6.
5 South Africa's Population, www.southafrica.info/about/people/population.htm#.UdBa3Zy0RY8.
6 Anne Hammerstad, *Linking South Africa's Immigration Policy and Zimbabwe Diplomacy*, South African Foreign Policy and African Drivers Programme, Policy Briefing 42, December 2011.
7 *Youth Population in South Africa: Prospects for the Demographic Dividend*, Human Science Research Council, 2009, www.foresightfordevelopment.org/sobipro/55/582-youth-population-in-south-africa-prospects-for-the-demographic-dividend.

8 Unless indicated otherwise all data are from the World Bank, *World Development Indicators*, April 2013, data.worldbank.org/data-catalog/world-development-indicators.

9 United Nations, *Human Development Report 2013, The Rise of the South: Human Progress in a Diverse World*, UNDP, New York, 2013.

10 World Bank, *South Africa: Economic Update: Focus on Inequality of Opportunity*, July 2012, viii.

11 Elke Zuern, 'Why Protests Are Growing in South Africa', *Current History*, May 2013, 175.

12 Ibid., 175.

13 World Bank, *South Africa: Economic Update: Focus on Inequality of Opportunity*, July 2012, viii.

14 David Faulkner and Christopher Loewald, *Policy Change and Economic Growth: A Case Study of South Africa*, Working Paper No. 41, Commission on Growth and Development, Washington, DC, 2008.

15 Ibid., 20.

16 *The New Prosperity: Strategies for Improving Well-Being in Sub-Saharan Africa*, The Boston Consulting Group, Boston, MA, May 2013.

17 Nicholas M. Odhiambo, 'Growth, Employment and Poverty in South Africa: In Search of a Trickle-Down Effect', *Journal of Income Distribution* 20(1), March 2011.

18 Dani Rodrik and Mark Rosenzweig, 'Development Policy and Development Economics: An Introduction', in Dani Rodrik and Mark Rosenzweig (eds), *Handbook of Development Economics*, Vol. 5, North Holland, Amsterdam, 2009.

19 info.worldbank.org/governance/wgi/sc_country.asp.

20 Institute for Democracy in South Africa, 'South Africa: Results of the Afrobarometer Round 5', 15 March 2012, allafrica.com/stories/201203150769.html.

21 *Democracy Index 2012: Democracy at a Standstill*, Economist Intelligence Unit, London, 2013.

22 Doreen Atkinson, 'Taking to the Streets: Has Developmental Local Government Failed in South Africa?', in Sakhela Buhlungu, John Daniel, Roger Southall and Jessica Lutchman (eds), *State of the Nation: South Africa 2007*, HSRC Press, Cape Town, South Africa, 2007, 53–77.

23 Jerry Lavery, 'Protest and Political Participation in South Africa: Time Trends and Characteristics of Protestors', *Afrobarometer Briefing Paper* No. 102, May 2012.

24 Carl Death, 'Troubles at the Top: South African Protests and the 2003 Johannesburg Summit', *African Affairs* 109(437), 2010.

25 Lavery, 'Protest and Political Participation in South Africa', 6.

26 Quoted in William Wallis and Andrew England, 'South Africa: A Faded Rainbow', *Financial Times*, 17 February 2013.

27 *Economic Policy Reforms: Going for Growth*, OECD, Paris, 2010.

28 *The Global Competitiveness Report 2012–2013*, World Economic Forum, Geneva, 2013, 41.

29 John Page, *Africa's Growth Turnaround: From Fewer Mistakes to Sustained Growth*, Working Paper No. 54, Commission on Growth and Development, Washington, DC, 2009, 21.

30 *Post Apartheid South Africa: The First Ten Years*, International Monetary Fund, Washington, DC, 2005, 74.

31 *Country Assessment on Youth Violence, Policy and Programs in South Africa*, World Bank, Washington, DC, June 2012, 1.

32 BartelsmannStiftung, *BTI 2012: South Africa Country Report*, 30.

33 R.W. Johnson, 'Zuma's First Year', *Current History*, May 2010.

34 Luc Eyraud, 'Why Isn't South Africa Growing Faster? A Comparative Approach', Working Paper, WP/09/25, International Monetary Fund, Washington, DC, February 2009.

35 Ibid., 17.

36 *The Global Competitiveness Report 2012–2013*, World Economic Forum, Geneva, 2013.

37 Ibid., 37.

38 Bernard Makhosezwe Magubane, *Reflections on the Challenges Confronting Post-Apartheid South Africa*, Discussion Paper Series No. 7, UNESCO, Management of Social Transformations, Paris, 1995, www.unesco.org/most/magu.htm.

39 'Education in South Africa: Still Dysfunctional', *The Economist*, 21 January 2012, www.economist.com/node/21543214.

40 *The 2012 Legatum Prosperity Index*, Legatum Institute, London, 2012, webapi.prosperity.com/download/pdf/SOUTH%20AFRICA_710.pdf.

41 'The Scope of the South African Informal Economy, and Some Private Attempts to Empower this Sector', Young Business Leaders, 10 October 2012, www.ybl.co.za/south-african-informal-economy-formal/.

42 'The Sins of Wages', *The Economist*, 24 May 2013, www.economist.com/blogs/baobab/2013/05/south-africa-s-economy.

43 Nicoli Nattrass and Jeremy Seekings, 'Job Destruction in the South African Clothing Industry: How an Unholy Alliance of Organised Labour, the State and Some Firms is Undermining Labour-intensive Growth', Working Paper 323, University of Cape Town, Centre for Social Science Research CSSR, Cape Town, South Africa, 2013, www.cssr.uct.ac.za/pub/wp/323.

44 'Productivity Drops to 50-Year Low in SA', *Mail & Guardian*, 11 March 2013, mg.co.za/article/2013-03-11-job-index-the-same-but-huge-dip-in-labour-productivty.

45 Abebe Aemro Selassie, 'What Ails South Africa?' *Finance & Development* 48(4), December 2011, www.imf.org/external/pubs/ft/fandd/2011/12/selassie.htm.

46 Mats Lundahl and Lennart Petersson, *Post-Apartheid South Africa: An Economic Success Story?* UNU-WIDER, Helsinki, 2009.

47 Sipho Kings, 'South Africa Shaped by Thatcherism', *Mail & Guardian*, 12 April 2013.

48 See Chapter 9 of this volume for John Williamson's summary of the approach.

49 'Is South Africa's New Growth Path Capable of Creating Jobs?' *Political Analysis South Africa*, 28 September 2012.

50 Charles Simkins, 'Poverty, Inequality and Democracy, South African Disparities', *Journal of Democracy* 22(3), July 2011: 105–19.

51 *The New Growth Path*, South African Government Information, 23 November 2010, www.info.gov.za/view/DownloadFileAction?id=135748.

52 'Is South Africa's New Growth Path Capable of Creating Jobs?' *Political Analysis South Africa*, 28 September 2012, www.politicalanalysis.co.za/2012/09/28/is-south-africas-new-growth-path-capable-of-creating-jobs/.

53 'South Africa Needs 5 Percent Growth to Create Jobs', *The Economic Times*, 19 July 2010, articles.economictimes.indiatimes.com/2010-07-19/news/27621633_1_south-africa-climate-change-dent.

54 International Monetary Fund, *World Economic Outlook Database*, April 2013 edition, www.imf.org/external/pubs/ft/weo/2013/01/weodata/index.aspx.

55 *The National Development Plan 2030*, South African Government Information, 15 August 2012, www.info.gov.za/issues/national-development-plan/.

56 William Gumede, *Delivering the Democratic Developmental State in South Africa*, Development Bank of South Africa, Development Planning Division Working Paper Series No. 9, 2009, www.dbsa.org/Research/DPD%20Working%20papers%20documents/DPD%20No%209.pdf?AspxAutoDetectCookieSupport=1.

57 Claire Bisseker, 'Economy on the Edge', *Financial Mail*, 6 June 2013, www.fm.co.za/fm/CoverStory/2013/06/06/economy-on-the-edge.

58 Aubrey Matshiqi, 'Perfect Storm of Economic, Political Developments is Avoidable', *Creamer Media's Engineering News*, 12 June 2013, www.engineeringnews.co.za/article/perfect-storm-of-economic-political-developments-is-avoidable-2013-06-12/page:366.

59 Linda Ensor and Ntsakisi Maswanganyi, 'Stagflation Danger for SA Growth Warns Marcus', *Business Day Live*, 17 April 2013, www.bdlive.co.za/economy/2013/04/17/stagflation-danger-for-sa-growth-warns-marcus.

60 Franz Wild and Mike Cohen, 'South Africa's GDP Grows at Slowest Pace Since Recession', *Bloomberg*, 28 May 2013, www.bloomberg.com/news/2013-05-28/south-africa-s-economic-growth-slows-in-first-quarter.html.

Part III

Key lessons
The path to emerging status

8

Modern stage theories and their relevance for the emerging economies

Robert E. Looney

Introduction

Global growth has benefited greatly over the last 20 years from the increased expansion of world trade and related surge in growth in the emerging economies. Whether growth in the emerging world will continue at its recent pace has become a critical question for the global economy and the millions of citizens who live in these countries.

All economies evolve and develop over time, and there have been many theories constructed over the years that have attempted to give both descriptive and predictive explanations for their growth. These fall into two broad categories: (1) growth as a continuum, and (2) growth as a progression through a sequence of stages.

The continuum approach, with its origins in neo-classical economic theory,[1] assumes that markets function to provide signals of impending bottlenecks and that there is sufficient flexibility in the economy to respond and alleviate these constraints to growth before serious diminishing returns set in. In this model, bottlenecks usually take shape as factor inputs traded in markets. As they become relatively scarce, their rising prices signal the necessity to firms of substituting cheaper inputs into the productive process as a means of remaining competitive. While there are always external shocks causing ups and down in growth, the long-term pattern is clear: drawing on a common pool of technology, a smooth convergence takes place between high- and low-income countries.[2]

Experience suggests, however, that many fast-growing economies experience periods of slow growth or even stagnation[3] well before converging with advanced countries. Stage theories, often drawing on their Marxian origins,[4] implicitly assume that markets do not always provide the correct signals as to increased scarcity and/or that many of the potentially binding factors are not traded in markets so that their constraining effects cannot easily be gauged and preventive action taken.

Modern stage theories, beginning with the work of Michael Porter[5] at the Harvard Business School, built on the initial framework developed by W.W. Rostow,[6] usually view the growth process as one entailing a series of transformations that economies go through as countries move from extreme poverty to wealth.[7] At the initial stages of development, Porter sees a factor-driven economy gaining its competitive advantage from natural resources, favourable conditions for growing crops, and low-cost labour sources. This initial stage sets the foundation for an investment-driven economy drawing on the willingness of firms and individuals to invest in modern plant, equipment and technologies. Finally, an innovation-driven economy evolves based on firms creating novel processes, products and business models. However, smooth growth cannot be assumed. There is always the danger that through mis-steps, bad luck or poor policy decisions, economies may be become trapped at the first or second stage of development.

The emerging economies have thus experienced both patterns of growth noted above: continuum and stage. For years (see Figure 8.1) growth in the Republic of Korea (South Korea) and Singapore was rather rapid and steady, propelling both to high-income stages. By contrast, South Africa, Thailand, Malaysia and Brazil have exhibited more of a stage period pattern of growth with stops and starts.

Most typically in the post-war era, many countries have managed to reach middle-income status (roughly Porter's investment driven stage), but few have gone on to become high-income (innovation stage) economies. Rather, after an initial period of rapid ascent, many countries have experienced a sharp slowdown in growth and productivity at a particular stage of development, or what has been popularly dubbed the 'middle-income trap'. Research at the World Bank[8] suggests that of 101 middle-income economies in 1960, only 13 (see Figure 8.2) reached high-income status by 2008: Equatorial Guinea, Greece, Hong Kong SAR (China), Ireland, Israel, Japan, Mauritius, Portugal, Puerto Rico, South Korea, Singapore, Spain and Taiwan (China).

The standard variant of the middle-income trap develops along the following lines:[9]

1 As economies move from low- to middle-income status, they can compete internationally by moving from agricultural to labour-intensive, low-cost manufactured products.
2 Using imported technologies, late-developing economies can reap productivity gains as workers shift from the agricultural sector to the manufacturing sector.
3 Eventually, the pool of transferrable unskilled labour is exhausted, or the expansion of labour-absorbing activities peaks.

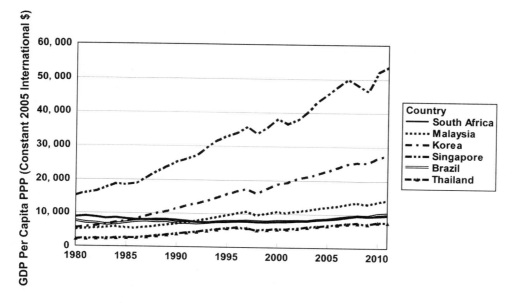

Figure 8.1 Contrasting emerging economy growth patterns
Source: World Bank, World Development Indicators, April 2013.

Modern stage theories and emerging economies

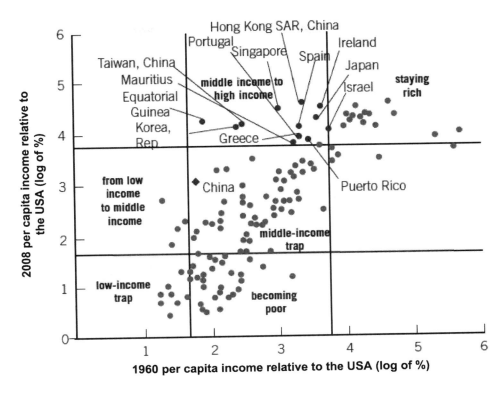

Figure 8.2 Per capita incomes relative to the United States, 1960 and 2008
Source: *Online 2030: Building a Modern, Harmonious, and Creative High – Income society* (Washington, DC: World Bank, 2012).

4 As countries reach middle-income levels, real wages in urban manufacturing rise or market share is lost, and gains from importing foreign technology diminish. Productivity growth from sectoral reallocation and technology catch-up are eventually exhausted, international competitiveness is eroded, output and growth slow, and economies become trapped, unable to transcend to high-income status.

While certainly plausible, this explanation does not provide an explanation as to why countries fail to recognize what is unfolding and begin to take action to neutralize or offset the process before it sets in to the extent that growth is impaired.

An alternative characterization of a middle-income trap has been developed in a recent World Bank paper.[10] Although this analysis fundamentally agrees that productivity slowdowns are a major cause of middle-income traps, it differs from the existing literature in terms of the reasons why productivity growth may weaken and what type of public policies can help avoid such a slow-growth equilibrium.

In particular, several factors may affect productivity growth, including individual decisions to acquire skills, access to different types of public infrastructure, and knowledge network externalities—which are defined as the possibility that a higher share of workers with advanced levels of education has a positive impact on performance, that is, the ability to benefit from existing knowledge, of all workers engaged in innovation activities.

Another variant—failure to sequence governance and economic reforms correctly—may be found in a new stage theory developed by Jennifer Bremer and John Kasarda.[11] Bremer and

Kasarda view transition as occurring in three phases (see Figure 8.3). The first phase typically begins when a low-income country begins to industrialize rapidly, launching an agrarian-industrial transition and the complex transformations in urbanization, income growth and economic diversification that accompany it. A process that is similar but not identical to Rostow's[12] take-off occurs.

If growth is sustained for a decade or more, the country may reach the second transition phase, in which industrial production per capita can increase as much as three-fold, growth in low value-added manufacturing is rapid and sustained, and rising incomes lead to the emergence of a middle class. Assuming this middle phase is successful, the country will likely reach the advanced phase in 10–20 years. Countries that are currently in the advanced phase include Brazil, Poland, Russia and Turkey.[13]

While the process can be smooth and continuous, countries can become trapped in either of the first two stages. Failure to adopt choice-based systems encompassing both market-based economic reforms and democratic political institutions and organizations make it very difficult to escape the first stage. The resulting inefficiencies and a lack of incentives for entrepreneurship inhibit more dynamic growth patterns.

Without the adoption and proper sequencing of such reforms, countries cannot progress up the ladder to more sophisticated production structures and, as a result, will face rising popular discontent and instability.[14]

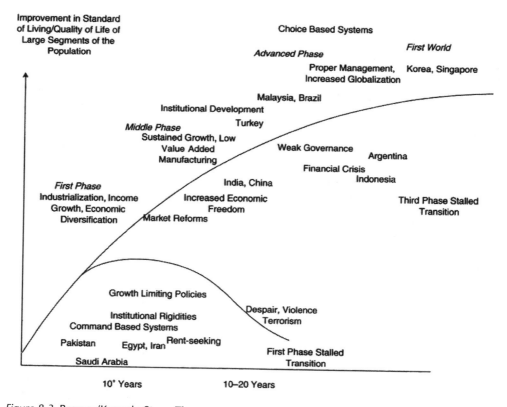

Figure 8.3 Bremer/Kasarda Stage Theory
Constructed from: Jennifer Bremer and John D. Kasarda, "The origins of Terror" Implications for US Foreign policy, talken Institute Review, Quarter, 2002.

Similarly, failure to enact proper governance reforms in the second phase can result in a failed transition to the third stage. Or, the country's economy may become very prone, like Argentina in the late 1990s, to financial crisis through lacking the right regulatory structures. In either case growth is halted and the country falls further and further behind better-prepared countries. The message: deficient governance structures and/or inadequate economic reforms can result in growth-stopping diminishing returns to factor inputs.

Why do the two patterns—continuum and stage—continue to exist simultaneously? One answer might be that the successful continuum countries are simply better (or luckier) at anticipating problems and overcoming them.

As *The Economist* magazine noted:

> Development is a long and arduous process, during which economies continuously evolve in scope as well as size. Potential traps lurk at every level of income. There is no reason to single out the middle levels. In a recent paper Mr Kharas and a co-author likened the middle-income trap to the bunkers that lie in wait for golfers. Not every player falls into them, but every golfer should worry about them.[15]

The purpose of this chapter is to develop an empirical framework for identifying the likely constraints impeding growth of various emerging economies at each stage of their development. A cursory survey of the literature suggests myriad inhibiting factors. Those most frequently identified as key development constraints include: (1) lack of competitiveness due to limitations in factors ranging from infrastructure to education to technological capacity; (2) limited governance in areas such as rule of law and anticorruption; and (3) insufficient economic reforms that hinder open markets and trade.

Each of these broad categories is made up of a number of individual variables, which are explored in-depth below. The examination of the variables is instructive, both in illuminating the wide range of constraints emerging economies face and in illustrating the diversity of opinion as to the paramount factor or factors that inhibit their growth.

Potential competitiveness constraints

The World Economic Forum's Global Competitiveness Index (WEF GCI) provides an excellent starting point for examining the changing environments emerging economies face in their progress towards developed country status. Drawing on the work of Harvard's Michael Porter,[16] the index provides a benchmark for identifying impediments to a country's competitiveness.[17] The GCI takes into account macroeconomic as well as the core microeconomic foundations of national competitiveness, which it defines as 'the set of institutions, policies, and factors that determine the level of productivity and thus income of a country'.[18]

The WEF's approach depicts global competitiveness as a weighted average of many different components, each of which affects some aspect of competitiveness. These components fall into 12 main groups, or '12 pillars of competitiveness'.[19] These pillars are: institutions; infrastructure; the macroeconomic environment; health and primary education; higher education and training; goods market efficiency; labour market efficiency; financial market development; technological readiness; market size; business sophistication; and innovation.

Following Porter's[20] earlier work, the WEF further assumes that countries progress through three distinct stages: (1) factor driven, (2) investment driven, and (3) innovation driven. Using regression analysis, the forum has found that certain pillars are more important at one stage than at others. Institutions, infrastructure, macroeconomic stability, and health and primary education are key in the factor-driven stage. Higher education and training, goods market efficiency, labour market efficiency, financial market sophistication, technological readiness, and market size predominate during the efficiency-driven stage. Business sophistication and innovation play a critical role in the innovation-driven stage.

Drawing on this framework, the WEF is able to classify individual countries into one of these three stages. Each country is assigned to a development stage based on: (1) its level of gross domestic product (GDP) per capita measured at market exchange rates—a proxy for wages (used by the WEF because internationally comparable data on wages and purchasing power parity are not available for all countries covered); and (2) the extent to which countries are factor driven, as proxied by the share of exports of primary goods in total exports.

The forum deems countries falling between two stages as 'in transition'. As these countries develop, increasingly more weight is given to the pillars that will assure their competitiveness when they move on to the next development stage. In this way, the GCI rewards countries that do what is needed to ensure a smooth transition and penalizes those that fail to prepare for the next stage. Table 8.1 provides a summary of the World Economic Forum stage classifications as of 2010. For the purposes of this chapter and its empirical model, the WEF stages have been relabelled as Groups 1 to 5, as indicated in parentheses under the main headings on Table 8.1.

In addition to global competitiveness per se, development may be affected by deeper determinants of growth, including governance variables such as corruption, political stability and the rule of law.[21] Another body of literature observes that the various dimensions of economic freedom (or the lack thereof) have had a profound effect on the progress of many emerging economies.[22]

Limited institutional development: governance

While rating countries on the basis of their relative progress in improving governance is inherently subjective, the World Bank[23] regularly provides a set of rankings incorporating the full extent of our knowledge about this phenomenon. The World Bank data set estimates six dimensions of governance for 213 economies over the period 1996–2009. These dimensions are: voice and accountability; political stability and absence of violence; government effectiveness; regulatory quality; rule of law; and control of corruption. The values for each of the governance figures range from a low of −2.5 to a high of +2.5, with a mean of zero for each country's sample.

The means for the five-group sample for 2009 (see Table 8.2) show a fairly steady progression on each governance dimension, from low for Group 1 to high for Group 5. The one notable exception to the pattern is a drop in the voice and accountability dimension as countries move from Group 1 to Group 2.

Limited progress in economic freedom

No indices exist of the prevalence of choice-based systems central to the Bremer/Kasarda model. However, the Fraser Institute's Economic Freedom of the World[24] and the Heritage Foundation and *The Wall Street Journal*'s Index of Economic Freedom[25] are good proxies in that they measure the relative progress of countries in moving towards a deregulated, limited government, free market environment. The Heritage Foundation data set was chosen for this study because it contains a larger sample of countries.

Table 8.1 Countries at various stages of development, 2010–11

Stage 1	Transition From 1 to 2	Stage 2	Transition From 2 to 3	Stage 3
(Group 1)	(Group 2)	(Group 3)	(Group 4)	(Group 5)
Bangladesh	Algeria	Albania	Bahrain	Australia
Benin	Angola	Argentina	Barbados	Austria
Bolivia	Armenia	Bosnia	Chile	Belgium
Burkina Faso	Azerbaijan	Brazil	Croatia	Canada
Burundi	Botswana	Bulgaria	Estonia	Cyprus
Cambodia	Brunei	Cape Verde	Hungary	Czech Republic
Cameroon	Egypt	China	Latvia	Denmark
Chad	Georgia	Colombia	Lithuania	Finland
Côte d'Ivoire	Guatemala	Costa Rica	Oman	France
Ethiopia	Guyana	Dominican Republic	Poland	Germany
The Gambia	Indonesia	Ecuador	Puerto Rico	Greece
Ghana	Iran	El Salvador	Slovakia	Hong Kong (SAR)
Honduras	Jamaica	Jordan	Taiwan (China)	Iceland
India	Kazakhstan	Lebanon	Trinidad and Tobago	Ireland
Kenya	Kuwait	Macedonia	Uruguay	Israel
Kyrgyzstan	Libya	Malaysia		Italy
Lesotho	Morocco	Mauritius		Japan
Madagascar	Paraguay	Mexico		Korea, Repub.
Malawi	Qatar	Montenegro		Luxembourg
Mali	Saudi Arabia	Namibia		Malta
Mauritania	Sri Lanka	Panama		Netherlands
Moldova	Swaziland	Peru		New Zealand
Mongolia	Syria	Romania		Norway
Mozambique	Ukraine	Russian Federation		Portugal
Nepal	Venezuela	Serbia		Singapore
Nicaragua		South Africa		Slovenia
Nigeria		Thailand		Spain
Pakistan		Tunisia		Switzerland
Philippines		Turkey		United Arab Emirates
Rwanda				United Kingdom
Senegal				USA
Tajikistan				
Tanzania				
Timor-Leste				
Uganda				
Viet Nam				
Zambia				
Zimbabwe				

Source: Xavier Sala-i-Martin *et al.*, 'The Global Competitiveness Index 2010–2011: Looking Beyond the Economic Crisis', in Klaus Schwab (ed.), *The Global Competitiveness Report: 2010–2011*, World Economic Forum, Geneva, 2010, 11

Robert E. Looney

Table 8.2 Group means on governance dimensions, World Economic Forum development stages, 2010–11

World Economic Forum stages		Voice	Political stability	Government effectiveness	Regulatory quality	Rule of law	Control of corruption
1	Mean	−0.547	−0.685	−0.714	−0.562	−0.761	−0.731
	No. of countries	38	38	38	37	30	38
	Std deviation	0.557	0.813	0.389	0.443	0.461	0.388
	Pakistan	−0.997	−2.756	−0.933	−0.499	−0.925	−1.097
2	Mean	−0.739	−0.300	−0.267	−0.278	−0.415	−0.402
	No. of countries	25	25	25	25	22	25
	Std deviation	0.649	0.787	0.582	0.710	0.552	0.723
3	Mean	0.015	−0.175	0.061	0.137	−0.223	−0.165
	No. of countries	29	29	29	29	23	29
	Std deviation	0.620	0.666	0.412	0.453	0.545	0.442
4	Mean	0.657	0.598	0.802	0.902	0.720	0.572
	No. of countries	15	15	15	15	13	15
	Std deviation	0.680	0.320	0.303	0.331	0.378	0.456
5	Mean	1.127	0.761	1.462	1.358	1.443	1.488
	No. of countries	32	32	32	32	28	32
	Std deviation	0.547	0.558	0.430	0.350	0.454	0.661
Total	Mean	0.051	−0.038	0.183	0.240	0.109	0.097
	No. of countries	139	139	139	138	116	139
	Std deviation	0.932	0.882	0.932	0.886	0.989	1.006

Source: World Economic Forum, *The Global Competitiveness Report, 2010–2011*, World Economic Forum, Geneva, 2010

To measure economic freedom, the Heritage Index takes 10 different factors into account: (1) trade policy, (2) fiscal burden of government, (3) government intervention in the economy, (4) monetary policy, (5) banking and finance, (6) capital flows and foreign investment, (7) wage and prices, (8) property rights, (9) regulation, and (10) the informal market. These factors are designed to measure the openness of countries to competition, the degree of state intervention in the economy, and the ability of the courts to enforce rules and property rights. The Heritage Foundation emphasizes that countries must score well in all 10 factors in order to improve their economic efficiency and, consequently, the living standards of their people.[26]

An examination of the group means by World Economic Forum groupings (see Table 8.3 and Table 8.4) shows a pattern similar to that found in the governance dimensions: countries show steady progress in economic reforms as they move from Group 1 to Group 5. The one major exemption is in the fiscal area, where lower levels of government spending and taxes are considered freer. Given the expansion of government spending in the advanced countries, Groups 4 and 5 score low on this dimension.

Deficiencies in entrepreneurial access to capital

The Milken Institute's Capital Access Index (CAI) provides an additional perspective on for example Pakistan's progress in supporting entrepreneurship and a modern economy. This index scores the ability of entrepreneurs to gain access to financial capital in countries around the

Modern stage theories and emerging economies

Table 8.3 Group means on economic freedom dimensions I, World Economic Forum development stages, 2010–11

World Economic Forum stages		Overall freedom score	Business freedom	Trade freedom	Fiscal freedom	Government spending	Monetary freedom
1	Mean	54.300	55.460	69.537	77.051	75.168	69.886
	No. of countries	38	38	38	37	37	37
	Std deviation	5.867	11.605	7.503	9.418	15.816	5.591
	Pakistan	55.2	71.7	67.0	80.5	88.8	69.4
2	Mean	57.260	65.150	74.792	82.204	71.667	66.329
	No. of countries	24	24	24	24	24	24
	Std deviation	9.639	16.136	10.320	11.229	15.905	7.024
3	Mean	61.890	67.110	78.090	80.517	71.893	71.928
	No. of countries	29	29	29	29	29	29
	Std deviation	6.263	9.410	7.970	7.884	16.450	4.942
4	Mean	68.910	72.550	84.136	80.693	63.229	72.879
	No. of countries	14	14	14	14	14	14
	Std deviation	4.936	9.822	7.166	9.408	17.512	4.184
5	Mean	73.190	85.470	86.391	64.234	49.128	78.613
	No. of countries	32	32	32	32	32	32
	Std deviation	6.899	10.272	3.562	14.439	19.451	3.810
Total	Mean	62.330	68.380	77.696	76.059	66.496	72.055
	No. of countries	137	137	137	138	136	138
	Std deviation	10.057	15.860	9.818	12.693	19.661	6.649

Source: Heritage Foundation, Index of Economic Freedom database, 2010

world. The CAI measures not only the breadth, depth and vitality of capital markets, but also openness in providing access without discrimination, a measure of global progress in the democratization of capital.

The seven components of the CAI are:

1 Macroeconomic environment: the favourableness of conditions for running and financing a business, based on such variables as inflation, interest rates, tax rates and financial sophistication relative to international norms.
2 Institutional environment: the extent to which institutions support and enhance business financing activities, based on variables that include the enforceability of property rights, the impartiality of the judicial system, the efficiency of bankruptcy procedures and the levels of corruption.
3 Financial and banking institutions: the involvement of deposit-taking institutions in financing businesses, based on such variables as the extension of credit to the private sector, the soundness of financial institutions, the ease of access to bank loans and the efficiency of the banking system.
4 Equity market development: the importance of equity financing of business operations, based on such variables as stock market capitalization relative to GDP, stock market liquidity and changes in the number of listings.
5 Bond market development: the importance of bond financing for businesses, based on variables such as the value of private and public bonds relative to GDP and securitized asset issuance relative to GDP.

Robert E. Looney

Table 8.4 Group means on economic freedom dimensions II, World Economic Forum development stages, 2010–11

World Economic Forum Stages		Investment freedom	Financial freedom	Property rights	Freedom from corruption	Labour freedom
1	Mean	41.180	43.290	30.210	27.010	57.600
	No. of countries	38	38	38	37	37
	Std deviation	14.861	12.318	8.918	6.482	14.868
	Pakistan	30	40	30	25	49.8
2	Mean	45.430	43.750	35.220	31.000	60.429
	No. of countries	23	24	23	24	24
	Std deviation	22.508	16.101	14.498	11.425	19.769
3	Mean	54.310	53.450	40.170	38.140	63.403
	No. of countries	29	29	29	29	29
	Std deviation	16.568	12.328	13.462	8.855	12.870
4	Mean	68.570	63.570	62.500	54.500	66.621
	No. of countries	14	14	14	14	14
	Std deviation	11.673	13.927	13.552	10.559	15.062
5	Mean	75.310	70.630	80.940	74.530	66.678
	No. of countries	32	32	32	32	32
	Std deviation	12.885	12.165	12.472	14.213	18.589
Total	Mean	55.550	53.980	48.440	43.970	62.366
	No. of countries	136	137	136	137	137
	Std deviation	20.911	17.141	23.577	21.328	16.561

Source: Heritage Foundation, Index of Economic Freedom database, 2010

6 Alternative sources of capital: the level of usage of diverse financing sources, such as venture capital, credit cards, and non-public stock offerings or other private placements.

7 International funding: the availability of foreign capital to businesses in a particular country, based on such variables as the volatility of exchange rates, international reserve holdings, portfolio and foreign direct investment, capital inflows and outflows, and sovereign ratings.

As the example of South Asia attests (see Table 8.5), development of sophisticated capital markets capable of providing adequate funding to the private sector has lagged significantly in many parts of the world. However, because of the many dimensions of this factor, generalizations are difficult. For many countries progress has been slow in some areas, while significant gains have been made in others.

Constraints on growth and entrepreneurship

It is unrealistic to expect that many countries would be able to address all the potential constraints identified in the previous section. Hausmann, Rodrik and Velasco suggest that a better approach is to identify and address the one or two most binding present constraints. To this end, they propose that each country use a decision tree methodology to identify binding constraints and policy options. Their framework focuses on the short term, identifying constraints as they emerge rather than attempting to anticipate future impediments to growth.[27]

While the Hausmann approach provides a good starting point, a more dynamic approach that includes factors such as entrepreneurship may be more appropriate for longer-term analysis that

146

Table 8.5 Financial sector development

	Rank	Score
Capital Access Index: summary		
Pakistan	74	3.93
India	44	5.51
Sri Lanka	72	3.96
Bangladesh	85	3.48
Macroeconomic environment		
Pakistan	110	3.75
India	63	5.83
Sri Lanka	113	3.50
Bangladesh	99	4.17
Institutional environment		
Pakistan	70	4.82
India	71	4.76
Sri Lanka	56	5.35
Bangladesh	110	3.24
Financial and banking institutions		
Pakistan	72	3.90
India	46	5.10
Sri Lanka	62	4.40
Bangladesh	69	4.00
Equity market development		
Pakistan	40	5.17
India	14	6.50
Sri Lanka	40	5.17
Bangladesh	33	5.50
Bond market development		
Pakistan	45	4.25
India	33	5.25
Sri Lanka	76	2.50
Bangladesh	62	3.50
Alternative sources of capital		
Pakistan	74	1.75
India	18	6.25
Sri Lanka	72	2.00
Bangladesh	86	0.75
International funding		
Pakistan	93	2.75
India	25	5.50
Sri Lanka	76	3.42
Bangladesh	97	2.50

Source: Compiled from James R. Barth, Tong Li, Wenling Lu and Glen Yago, *Capital Access Index 2009: Best Markets for Business Access to Capital*, Milken Institute, Santa Monica, CA, April 2010

is focused on how countries move through the five stages in the WEF framework. Despite increased state activity in many of the emerging economies, entrepreneurship will still play a key role in driving investment, introducing new technologies and upgrading production sophistication to levels sufficient to transition to higher stages of development.

It is also unlikely that entrepreneurship and growth face the same constraints simultaneously as countries progress to higher levels of development. Given an increasing number of countries experiencing stalled growth and failed take-offs it is also critical to get a sense of sequencing of reforms and their dynamics at work. Does increased entrepreneurial activity place sufficient pressure on governments to advance a reform agenda? Or do government-led reforms usher in a new wave of entrepreneurship? Identification of the normal sequencing may be critical in assuring growth as an ongoing process.

As a first step in the analysis, the World Economic Forum Competitiveness Indicators (WEF), the World Bank Governance Indicators (WB), and the Heritage Foundation Index of Economic Freedom (EF) were merged into a single database.[28] Added to this were the World Bank's database on entrepreneurial activity[29] and the size of the shadow economy (percentage of GDP) in individual countries.[30] The shadow economy is relatively large in many of the key emerging economies.[31] It is included in part to track the country's movement towards an efficient competitive economy, since the literature on entrepreneurship and growth stresses the necessity of transforming informal/shadow activities into formal entities with higher productivity and taxpaying potential.[32]

Key dimensions of growth potential and entrepreneurship

The first step in the analysis was to assess the main trends in the data, as well as examine the development situation of a sample country, Pakistan. The key questions examined were:

1 Of the 28 potential constraints on growth contained in the merged database, how many distinct phenomena are represented?
2 Do the same elements impact increased entrepreneurship and growth potential, or is each linked to a separate set of conditions?

To answer these questions, a factor analysis was undertaken for the total sample of country groupings (Groups 1–5), as well as for sequential subsets of country groupings through the five stages of development.[33]

The rotated factor matrix (see Table 8.6) identified five main trends or dimensions in the combined data set for the total sample of countries. Factor 1 variables were loaded on a dimension associated with economic freedom; Factor 2 variables on fiscal freedom and state of governance; Factor 3 variables on health/education/trade; Factor 4 variables on labour efficiency/freedom and institutions; and Factor 5 variables on a competitiveness dimension.

In the total sample of countries, growth potential is most highly associated with several components of Factor 5, the competitiveness dimension, namely, the WEF's (a) market size, (b) macroeconomic environment, (c) business sophistication, and (d) infrastructure. However, a sharp picture does not emerge, as growth potential is also associated to a lesser extent with Factors 1–4.

Entrepreneurship does not seem to be highly associated with any of the main trends in the data. Instead, this key variable is fairly equally associated with Factor 1 (economic freedom), Factor 3 (health/education), and Factor 4 (labour market freedom and efficiency). Although causation cannot be firmly established at this point, a safe assumption is that entrepreneurship is

Table 8.6 Factor analysis: growth potential/entrepreneurship linkages—total sample of countries (loadings on principal dimensions)

Key indicators	Main dimensions				
	Factor 1 Economic freedom	Factor 2 Fiscal/governance	Factor 3 Health/education	Factor 4 Labour market efficiency	Factor 5 Growth/competitiveness
EF investment freedom	0.803	0.198	0.362	0.131	0.013
EF financial freedom	0.761	0.162	0.317	0.166	0.145
EF monetary freedom	0.725	0.240	0.026	0.067	0.301
EF overall economic freedom score	0.710	0.100	0.352	0.524	0.213
WB regulatory quality	0.662	0.382	0.438	0.313	0.284
WEF financial market development	0.481	0.246	−0.024	0.443	0.473
EF business freedom	0.428	0.247	0.363	0.389	0.203
EF fiscal freedom	−0.211	−0.807	−0.017	0.118	−0.328
EF government spending	−0.075	−0.748	−0.382	0.118	0.082
WEF innovation	0.223	0.613	0.176	0.387	0.545
WB rule of law	0.482	0.574	0.412	0.352	0.294
WB voice and accountability	0.537	0.570	0.448	−0.008	0.147
EF property rights	0.532	0.566	0.292	0.378	0.307
WB control of corruption	0.506	0.555	0.373	0.402	0.278
EF freedom from corruption	0.507	0.546	0.362	0.399	0.307
WEF technological readiness	0.440	0.512	0.471	0.295	0.403
WB government effectiveness	0.493	0.503	0.426	0.374	0.375
WEF health and primary education	0.161	0.304	0.747	0.181	0.367
EF trade freedom	0.492	0.087	0.715	0.088	0.072
WER higher education and training	0.219	0.485	0.624	0.267	0.442
WB political stability	0.382	0.355	0.596	0.273	0.098
WEF labour market efficiency	0.202	0.109	0.210	0.818	0.093
EF labour freedom	0.007	−0.195	0.043	0.759	−0.056
WEF institutions	0.354	0.505	0.172	0.618	0.310
WEF goods market efficiency	0.495	0.356	0.183	0.580	0.416
Entrepreneurship	0.395	0.136	0.423	0.455	−0.074
WEF market size	−0.021	0.191	0.033	−0.160	0.812

(continued on next page)

Table 8.6 (continued)

Key indicators	Main dimensions				
	Factor 1 Economic freedom	Factor 2 Fiscal/ governance	Factor 3 Health/ education	Factor 4 Labour market efficiency	Factor 5 Growth/ competitiveness
WEF macroeconomic environment	0.353	−0.101	0.298	0.116	0.647
Growth potential	0.304	0.414	0.388	0.402	0.639
WEF business sophistication	0.329	0.529	0.186	0.303	0.636
WEF infrastructure	0.341	0.416	0.490	0.279	0.542
Country factor scores					
Pakistan	−0.323	−0.036	−2.532	−0.648	0.183
Difference: Pakistan–Group 1	0.122	0.060	−1.244	−0.580	0.948
Mean factor scores					
Group 1 countries	−0.445	−0.096	−1.288	−0.068	−0.765
Group 2 countries	−0.741	−0.616	−0.022	−0.133	−0.013
Group 3 countries	−0.148	−0.613	0.078	−0.234	0.132
Group 4 countries	0.346	−0.254	0.882	−0.158	−0.256
Group 5 countries	0.567	0.878	0.425	0.334	0.444

Notes: Extraction method: IBM SPSS 19.0 Principle Component Analysis. Rotation Method Variamax with Kaiser Normalization. Rotation converged in nine iterations. WEF = World Economic Forum data set; EF = Heritage Economic Freedom data set; WB = World Bank Governance data set. Entrepreneurship: World Bank, Enterprise Snapshots (WBGES) 2010.

positively affected by improved economic freedom, better health/education, and progress in freeing labour markets, a key area in facilitating the establishment of new firms. The mean factor scores by WEF country groupings suggest development through the various stages is associated with steady improvements in governance (Factor 2), and to a lesser extent economic freedom (Factor 1), with a sizeable jump in governance occurring when countries transition from Group 4 to Group 5.

In terms of creating an environment for the growth of entrepreneurship, Pakistan, for example, scores slightly above Group 1 countries on economic freedom but has one of the lowest attainments on health/education and is below the group average in labour market development. The country appears to be well above the Group 1 mean for potential growth (Factor 5), a finding that may be due simply to the dominance of market size in contributing to this dimension.

It is likely that many of the key linkages between growth potential and entrepreneurship are blurred due to the great diversity of country environments. To sharpen the focus, a more detailed analysis was undertaken of the various country subgroupings. For our purposes, a key issue is that of facilitating Pakistan's movement up the development ladder. Do the factors impacting growth and entrepreneurial activity in these individual groupings differ from those for the total sample of countries, and if so, which are critical?

The biggest difference between the patterns for Group 1 and Group 2 countries and those of the total country sample is a sharpening in the area of growth potential. When the factor analysis is confined to Group 1 and Group 2 countries (see Table 8.7), the growth potential term (Factor 1) is narrowly associated with health and primary education, followed by higher education and training and then infrastructure. In terms of economic freedom, openness to trade is also an important element contributing to a country's growth potential at this stage of development. Several elements of competitiveness reflected by Factor 3—business sophistication, financial market development, and innovation—are important to a lesser extent.

In Factor 1, the elements that contribute to expanded growth potential, Pakistan is considerably below the Group 1 norm. While it surpasses even Group 2 countries on the competitiveness elements of Factor 3, this advantage may be due to the country size component of this factor. The significant difference in the means of Group 1 and Group 2 for Factor 1 suggests that forces in addition to increased per capita income[34] are instrumental in allowing countries to make this transition.

As in the case of the total country sample, the factors determining entrepreneurship for Groups 1 and 2 are more diffuse and less focused. Factor 1, education/health, was a main contributor to the expansion of new firms, just as it was to growth potential. Also important were Factor 4, economic freedom, and Factor 5, improved labour market efficiencies and freedom.

While for the countries in Group 1 immediate focus must be on accomplishing the transition to Group 2, they should also anticipate the challenges involved in transitioning to the higher groups. To this end, a factor analysis of WEF country groups 2 and 3 was undertaken which produced several interesting pattern shifts (Table 8.8).

Replacing Group 1 countries with Group 3 countries in the sample shows that country growth potential is increasingly influenced by several components of governance and economic freedom. Growth potential loads heavily on Factor 1, institutions and competitiveness. While competitiveness elements such as business sophistication and financial market development play an important role, so also do the World Bank's government effectiveness, rule of law and control of corruption. Similarly, the Heritage Foundation measures of property rights and freedom from corruption now figure importantly in contributing to improved growth potential.

The factors associated with entrepreneurship also shift. For the Group 2 and 3 countries, entrepreneurship loads heaviest on Factor 3, democracy/political stability, with trade freedom

Table 8.7 Factor analysis: growth potential/entrepreneurship linkages—country groups 1 and 2 (loadings on principal dimensions)

Key indicators	Main dimensions							
	Factor 1 Growth education	*Factor 2 Governance*	*Factor 3 Competitiveness*	*Factor 4 Economic freedom*	*Factor 5 Labour freedom efficiency*	*Factor 6 Democracy*	*Factor 7 Macroeconomic stability*	*Factor 8 Political stability*
WEF health and primary education	0.899	0.065	−0.041	0.000	−0.124	0.171	−0.122	0.093
WEF higher education and training	0.896	−0.131	0.167	−0.058	0.025	−0.269	−0.019	0.022
WEF infrastructure	0.879	0.222	0.221	0.097	−0.046	0.008	0.019	−0.105
Growth potential	0.796	0.195	0.454	−0.105	0.032	0.163	0.210	0.083
WEF technological readiness	0.651	0.115	0.497	0.163	0.126	−0.171	0.261	−0.103
EF trade freedom	0.594	−0.311	−0.357	0.300	0.096	−0.138	0.151	0.214
WB control of corruption	0.019	0.920	−0.006	0.147	−0.081	−0.019	0.004	0.040
WB rule of law	0.132	0.819	0.216	0.154	−0.015	−0.124	−0.006	0.114
EF freedom from corruption	−0.069	0.808	−0.074	0.203	−0.209	−0.255	0.136	−0.196
WB government effectiveness	0.391	0.700	0.190	0.377	0.050	0.013	−0.026	0.073
WEF institutions	−0.025	0.681	0.251	−0.185	0.389	0.338	−0.132	0.201
EF property rights	−0.092	0.660	0.336	0.272	−0.084	−0.274	−0.164	0.019
WEF business sophistication	0.349	0.051	0.879	−0.060	−0.154	0.038	0.052	−0.084
WEF financial market development	0.044	0.055	0.875	0.231	0.065	−0.099	−0.120	0.012
WEF innovation	0.065	0.284	0.767	−0.345	−0.049	0.034	0.138	0.111
WEF goods market efficiency	0.103	0.393	0.724	0.178	0.218	0.187	−0.041	−0.031
WEF market size	0.296	−0.117	0.561	−0.243	−0.318	−0.068	0.194	−0.270
EF fiscal freedom	0.076	−0.448	−0.480	0.286	0.088	0.193	−0.354	0.117
EF financial freedom	0.035	0.082	−0.101	0.890	−0.045	−0.105	−0.007	0.162
EF overall freedom score	0.044	0.172	−0.106	0.870	0.310	0.222	0.052	−0.132
EF investment freedom	−0.082	0.184	0.002	0.853	0.093	0.052	0.003	0.042
WB regulatory quality	0.229	0.312	0.238	0.802	0.140	−0.142	−0.005	0.018
EF labour freedom	−0.006	−0.097	0.010	0.150	0.849	0.018	−0.110	−0.156

Table 8.7 (continued)

Key indicators	Main dimensions							
	Factor 1 Growth education	*Factor 2 Governance*	*Factor 3 Competitiveness*	*Factor 4 Economic freedom*	*Factor 5 Labour freedom efficiency*	*Factor 6 Democracy*	*Factor 7 Macroeconomic stability*	*Factor 8 Political stability*
WEF labour market efficiency	−0.089	−0.072	0.007	0.105	0.834	0.0130	−0.034	0.393
Entrepreneurship	0.474	−0.067	−0.273	0.445	0.522	−0.179	0.173	−0.116
EF government spending	−0.075	−0.216	0.216	0.232	−0.186	0.779	0.196	−0.057
WB voice and accountability	0.049	0.242	0.305	0.269	−0.283	−0.705	−0.045	0.147
WEF macroeconomic environment	0.309	−0.102	0.046	−0.077	−0.060	0.267	0.828	0.148
EF monetary freedom	−0.412	0.086	0.074	0.467	−0.171	−0.035	0.628	−0.089
WB political freedom	0.249	0.300	−0.273	0.252	0.199	−0.155	0.160	0.690
EF business freedom	0.258	0.270	−0.374	0.362	0.349	0.295	0.015	−0.482
Factor scores								
Pakistan	−0.912	−0.863	0.658	−0.301	−0.916	0.675	−0.780	−2.520
Difference: Pakistan–Group 1	−0.307	−0.740	0.717	−0.159	−0.850	0.748	−0.655	−2.627
Mean factor scores								
Group 1 countries	−0.605	−0.123	−0.059	−0.142	−0.066	−0.073	−0.125	0.107
Group 2 countries	0.907	0.185	0.089	0.212	0.099	0.109	0.187	−0.160
Difference: Group 2–Group 1	1.512	0.308	0.148	0.354	0.165	0.182	0.312	−0.267

Notes: Extraction Method: IBM SPSS 19.0 Principle Component Analysis. Rotation Method Variamax with Kaiser Normalization. Rotation converged in 15 iterations. WEF = World Economic Forum data set; EF = Heritage Economic Freedom data set; WB = World Bank Governance data set. Entrepreneurship: World Bank Enterprise Snapshots (WBGES) 2010.

Table 8.8 Factor analysis: entrepreneurship linkages—country groups 2 and 3 (loadings on principal dimensions)

Key indicators	Main dimensions						
	Factor 1 Institutions/ competitiveness	*Factor 2 Economic freedom/governance*	*Factor 3 Democracy/ political stability*	*Factor 4 Labour efficiency/ freedom*	*Factor 5 Health/ education*	*Factor 6 Macroeconomic stability*	*Factor 7 Government spending*
WB government effectiveness	0.864	0.250	0.136	0.069	0.088	0.009	−0.044
EF property rights	0.837	0.239	0.105	−0.115	0.002	−0.189	0.100
WEF institutions	0.807	0.133	−0.225	0.117	0.248	0.192	−0.125
Growth potential	0.804	−0.356	−0.069	0.131	0.054	0.384	0.147
WEF goods market efficiency	0.802	0.231	0.005	0.221	0.072	0.187	0.225
WEF business sophistication	0.801	−0.273	0.080	−0.155	−0.171	0.162	0.252
WB rule of law	0.787	0.163	0.187	−0.008	0.351	−0.049	−0.250
WEF financial markets development	0.764	0.123	0.174	0.103	−0.410	0.179	0.066
EF freedom from corruption	0.762	0.347	0.268	−0.200	0.204	−0.091	−0.078
WEF infrastructure	0.718	−0.238	−0.175	0.096	−0.114	0.022	0.154
WEF innovation	0.702	−0.613	−0.041	0.018	0.017	0.194	−0.082
WB control of corruption	0.693	0.370	0.360	−0.251	0.268	−0.123	−0.173
WEF technological readiness	0.566	−0.119	0.449	0.053	−0.048	0.378	−0.247
EF investment freedom	−0.034	0.837	0.316	−0.117	0.003	−0.028	−0.028
EF overall economic freedom	0.390	0.827	0.166	0.203	0.083	0.022	0.233
EF financial freedom	0.206	0.746	0.250	0.153	−0.225	−0.045	0.168
EF business freedom	0.295	0.666	−0.337	0.182	−0.065	0.086	−0.142
WEF market size	0.081	−0.610	−0.023	−0.349	−0.232	−0.039	0.289
WEF higher education and training	0.424	−0.61	0.161	0.243	0.284	0.092	−0.334
WB regulatory quality	0.544	0.609	0.425	0.194	−0.047	−0.051	0.040
EF monetary freedom	0.142	0.562	0.077	−0.256	0.055	0.435	0.030
WB voice and accountability	0.130	0.166	0.840	−0.072	−0.148	−0.101	−0.150
Entrepreneurship	0.187	0.140	0.602	0.202	0.470	0.029	−0.070
EF trade freedom	−0.228	0.421	0.598	0.289	0.143	−0.027	0.349

Table 8.8 (continued)

Key indicators	Main dimensions						
	Factor 1 Institutions/ competitiveness	*Factor 2 Economic freedom/governance*	*Factor 3 Democracy/ political stability*	*Factor 4 Labour efficiency/ freedom*	*Factor 5 Health/ education*	*Factor 6 Macroeconomic stability*	*Factor 7 Government spending*
WB political stability	0.143	0.069	0.509	0.160	0.239	0.426	−0.304
WEF labour market efficiency	0.059	−0.014	0.182	0.889	0.079	0.126	0.059
EF labour freedom	0.071	0.169	−0.065	0.836	0.164	−0.147	−0.182
WEF health and primary education	0.224	−0.291	−0.013	0.152	0.718	0.022	−0.103
EF fiscal freedom	−0.206	0.426	0.156	0.401	0.582	0.025	0.204
WEF macroeconomic environment	0.095	0.006	−0.068	0.002	−0.024	0.864	0.189
EF government spending	0.261	0.135	−0.208	−0.101	−0.057	0.240	0.736
Mean factor scores							
Group 2 countries	−0.453	−0.089	−0.666	0.150	−0.079	−0.303	0.243
Group 3 countries	0.226	0.044	0.333	−0.075	0.040	0.151	−0.121
Difference: Group 3–Group 2	0.679	0.133	0.999	−0.225	0.119	0.454	−0.364

Notes: Extraction Method: IBM SPSS 19.0 Principle Component Analysis. Rotation Method Variamax with Kaiser Normalization. Rotation converged in 18 iterations. WEF = World Economic Forum data set; EF = Heritage Economic Freedom data set; WB = World Bank Governance data; Entrepreneurship: World Bank Enterprise Shapshots (WBGES) 2010.

also sharing a strong association with increased entrepreneurial activity. While health and education (Factor 5) remain important, they become secondary to institutional development as countries move up the development ladder.

For Groups 1 and 2, the seven factors (see Table 8.7) show the largest differences in Factors 1 and 3, which are associated with growth and entrepreneurship. This result implies that countries face a number of significant barriers in making the transition from Group 2 to Group 3.

The observed patterns of growth potential and entrepreneurship carry over to the analysis of country groups 3 and 4. Growth potential is most strongly associated (see Table 8.9) with variables reflecting governance—especially government effectiveness, rule of law, political stability, freedom from corruption, and property rights—together with elements of competitiveness, such as the WEF's measure of institutions.

Entrepreneurship in Group 3 and 4 countries has its greatest loadings on Factor 2, economic freedom/democracy, and Factor 5, health and education. Key elements in Factor 2 include investment freedom, voice and accountability, trade freedom regulatory quality and overall economic freedom. This pattern demonstrates a subtle shift from fairly loose associations between these factors and entrepreneurship for Groups 1 and 2, to a strengthening of governance factors for Groups 2 and 3, to a greater balance between governance and economic freedom for Groups 3 and 4.

Also striking is the apparent weakening of the relationship between entrepreneurship and the factors surrounding growth competitiveness, which is fairly strong for Groups 1 and 2 but declines significantly as countries move to Groups 2–3 and 3–4.

For Groups 4 and 5 (see Table 8.10), growth potential is defined by a balance of competitiveness, governance and economic freedom. In contrast, entrepreneurship has little or no connection with these variables, loading weakly on the final factor, which largely comprises measures of monetary freedom.

The factor analysis by country groupings demonstrates the shifts that occur in the linkages associated with growth potential and entrepreneurship as the development process proceeds. In terms of growth potential, this pattern begins with a limited number of basic elements such as infrastructure and education/health, proceeds next to institutions associated with improved governance, then to governance and more economic freedom, and culminates in a final balance among all three elements: competitiveness, governance and economic freedom.

In terms of entrepreneurship, the pattern moves from weak association with these three groups of variables in early stages of development, to stronger links with democracy and political stability, to economic freedom, and finally to a state in which there are few links to competitiveness/governance and economic freedom. These patterns suggest a tentative working hypothesis comprising three parts: (1) if entrepreneurship affects national growth potential, it does so indirectly through its influence on the institutional environment; (2) once under way, entrepreneurship appears to spur a process of governance reform and further economic liberalization; and (3) this process is largely complete once countries reach stages 4 and 5, in which factors outside the variables examined here may play a more significant role.

Discriminant analysis: key constraints on group advancement

A pattern noted above was that the differences in means between groups were most significant on those factors loading heavily on growth potential and entrepreneurship (with the exception of entrepreneurship and Factor 5, growth competitiveness, for the Group 1 and 2 countries). This pattern suggests that a relatively small number of variables associated with growth potential and entrepreneurship may control movement from one stage to another.

Table 8.9 Factor analysis: growth potential/entrepreneurship linkages—country groups 3 and 4 (loadings on principal dimensions)

Key indicators	Main dimensions							
	Factor 1 Growth institutions competitiveness	Factor 2 Economic freedom/ democracy	Factor 3 Fiscal freedom	Factor 4 Business/ financial freedom	Factor 5 Health/ education	Factor 6 Labour market freedom	Factor 7 Government spending	Factor 8 Monetary freedom
WEF institutions	0.888	−0.047	0.348	0.068	0.052	0.055	0.038	0.050
Growth potential	0.849	−0.163	−0.140	0.299	0.181	0.256	0.081	0.041
WB government effectiveness	0.828	0.372	−0.096	0.241	0.193	0.035	−0.055	−0.033
EF freedom from corruption	0.822	0.483	0.137	−0.035	0.050	−0.074	0.012	−0.063
EF property rights	0.789	0.446	−0.053	0.035	0.100	0.000	0.168	0.040
WB rule of law	0.784	0.447	0.079	0.077	0.246	0.096	−0.200	−0.080
WEF innovation	0.768	−0.281	−0.300	0.037	0.303	0.223	−0.060	−0.069
WB control of corruption	0.759	0.567	0.132	−0.122	0.085	−0.026	−0.038	−0.060
WEF goods market efficiency	0.758	0.096	0.298	0.305	−0.062	0.262	0.199	0.222
WEF business sophistication	0.729	−0.097	−0.299	0.153	−0.025	0.150	0.341	0.164
WEF infrastructure	0.704	−0.080	−0.120	0.465	0.181	−0.051	−0.022	−0.201
WEF financial market development	0.701	0.032	−0.048	0.223	−0.290	0.199	0.040	0.404
WB political stability	0.496	0.370	0.213	−0.096	0.251	0.000	−0.420	−0.021
EF investment freedom	0.053	0.881	0.282	0.066	0.092	−0.193	0.071	0.087
WB voice and accountability	0.075	0.832	−0.204	−0.161	0.154	0.002	−0.129	0.041
EF trade freedom	−0.007	0.811	0.201	0.157	−0.066	0.125	−0.172	0.071
WB regulatory quality	0.511	0.703	0.006	0.322	0.080	0.213	−0.073	0.146
EF overall economic freedom score	0.472	0.637	0.330	0.271	−0.049	0.115	0.340	0.163
Entrepreneurship	0.080	0.509	0.091	−0.090	0.400	0.505	0.031	−0.207
EF fiscal freedom	−0.111	0.056	0.841	0.170	−0.027	0.230	0.088	−0.044
WEF market size	−0.004	−0.292	−0.791	−0.022	−0.189	0.055	0.093	−0.089
WEF macroeconomic environment	0.355	−0.144	0.140	0.747	−0.145	0.095	−0.074	−0.075
EF business freedom	0.165	0.228	0.086	0.632	0.168	0.005	0.284	0.114
EF financial freedom	0.033	0.561	−0.001	0.622	−0.141	0.229	−0.003	0.214
WEF health and primary education	0.118	0.037	0.160	−0.038	0.889	0.057	−0.071	0.050

(continued on next page)

Table 8.9 (continued)

Key indicators	Main dimensions							
	Factor 1 Growth institutions competitiveness	*Factor 2 Economic freedom/ democracy*	*Factor 3 Fiscal freedom*	*Factor 4 Business/ financial freedom*	*Factor 5 Health/ education*	*Factor 6 Labour market freedom*	*Factor 7 Government spending*	*Factor 8 Monetary freedom*
WEF higher education and training	0.547	0.092	−0.201	−0.010	0.646	0.127	−0.263	−0.135
WEF technological readiness	0.482	0.378	−0.148	0.341	0.541	0.026	−0.265	0.078
WEF labour market efficiency	0.251	0.113	0.149	0.295	0.175	0.803	−0.053	0.059
EF labour freedom	0.233	−0.168	0.529	−0.138	−0.223	0.530	−0.091	0.001
EF government spending	0.141	−0.097	0.005	0.056	−0.158	−0.062	0.895	0.009
EF monetary freedom	0.026	0.163	0.039	0.040	0.027	−0.016	0.024	0.945
Mean factor scores								
Group 3 countries	−0.296	−0.313	0.023	−0.107	−0.120	0.062	0.280	0.084
Group 4 countries	0.710	0.752	−0.055	0.257	0.288	−0.148	−0.671	−0.203
Difference: Group 4–Group 3	1.006	1.066	−0.078	0.365	0.408	−0.210	−0.951	−0.287

Notes: Extraction Method: IBM SPSS 19.0 Principle Component Analysis. Rotation Method Variamax with Kaiser Normalization. Rotation converged in 15 iterations. WEF = World Economic Forum data set; EF = Heritage Economic Freedom data set; WB = World Bank Governance data. Entrepreneurship: World Bank Enterprise Shapshots (WBGES) 2010.

Table 8.10 Factor analysis: growth potential/entrepreneurship linkages—country groups 4 and 5 (loadings on principal dimensions)

Key indicators	Main dimensions					
	Factor 1 Competitiveness governance/, economic freedom	Factor 2 Fiscal freedom	Factor 3 Financial/ investment freedom	Factor 4 Macroeconomic environment	Factor 5 Market size	Factor 6 Entrepreneurship/ monetary freedom
EF freedom from corruption	0.916	0.033	0.192	0.141	−0.127	0.118
WB control of corruption	0.904	0.005	0.188	0.176	−0.170	0.141
WB government effectiveness	0.887	−0.008	0.199	0.274	−0.084	0.201
WB rule of law	0.881	−0.100	0.239	0.183	−0.156	0.155
WEF higher education and training	0.879	−0.154	0.059	−0.058	0.063	0.053
Growth potential	0.873	0.046	0.140	0.351	0.266	−0.046
EF property rights	0.850	−0.015	0.255	0.120	−0.088	0.249
WEF innovation	0.843	−0.106	0.045	0.159	0.319	−0.086
WEF institutions	0.838	0.123	0.120	0.365	−0.175	0.054
WEF business sophistication	0.826	−0.174	0.074	0.250	0.342	−0.060
WEF technological readiness	0.806	−0.137	0.318	0.080	0.015	0.096
WEF goods market efficiency	0.790	0.249	0.198	0.397	−0.018	0.172
EF business freedom	0.757	0.066	0.192	−0.144	0.162	0.270
WEF health and primary education	0.745	−0.211	0.003	−0.168	0.085	0.467
WEF infrastructure	0.738	0.073	0.131	0.131	0.368	0.043
WEF labour market efficiency	0.683	0.487	0.277	0.166	−0.057	0.048
WB regulatory quality	0.651	0.048	0.529	0.372	−0.049	0.256
EF total economic freedom score	0.631	0.551	0.426	0.142	−0.039	0.238
EF government spending	−0.040	0.828	0.023	0.031	−0.054	0.063
EF fiscal freedom	−0.337	0.824	−0.123	−0.075	−0.207	−0.047
WB voice and accountability	0.395	−0.663	0.293	−0.172	−0.117	0.251
EF labour freedom	0.276	0.625	0.085	0.143	0.053	0.111
EF investment freedom	0.263	0.017	0.838	0.025	−0.052	0.015
EF financial freedom	0.231	−0.051	0.740	0.261	0.164	0.197
WEF macroeconomic environment	0.169	0.109	0.193	0.836	0.077	−0.120

(continued on next page)

Table 8.10 (continued)

Key indicators	Main dimensions					
	Factor 1 Competitiveness governance/ economic freedom	Factor 2 Fiscal freedom	Factor 3 Financial/ investment freedom	Factor 4 Macroeconomic environment	Factor 5 Market size	Factor 6 Entrepreneurship/ monetary freedom
WEF financial market development	0.427	0.165	0.123	0.760	−0.032	0.278
WEF market size	0.252	−0.108	0.000	0.141	0.821	−0.115
WB political stability	0.510	0.022	−0.209	0.192	−0.530	0.005
EF trade freedom	0.154	−0.043	0.445	0.129	−0.479	−0.158
Entrepreneurship	0.177	0.311	0.251	−0.041	−0.303	0.719
EF monetary freedom	0.348	−0.174	−0.045	0.288	0.407	0.626
Mean factor scores						
Group 4 countries	−1.033	0.458	−0.722	−0.018	−0.534	−0.624
Group 5 countries	0.344	−0.153	0.024	0.006	0.178	0.208
Difference: Group 5–Group 4	1.377	−0.611	0.746	0.024	0.712	0.832

Notes: Extraction Method: IBM SPSS 19.0 Principle Component Analysis. Rotation Method Variamax with Kaiser Normalization. Rotation converged in 8 iterations. WEF = World Economic Forum data set; EF = Heritage Economic Freedom data set; WB = World Bank Governance data; Entrepreneurship: World Bank Enterprise Snapshots (WBGES) 2010.

The WEF uses two criteria for allocating countries into five stages of development. The first is the level of GDP per capita at market exchange rates as a proxy for wages, since comparable data on wages are not available for all countries. The second is the extent to which countries are factor driven, as proxied by the share of minerals in total exports. For example, countries in which minerals make up 70% or more of average total exports over a five-year period are deemed to be factor driven.[35]

The inability of many countries to sustain steady growth raises the more interesting question of whether there are specific impediments that might cause a country to get 'stuck' in one of these groups. Rather than per capita income and primary product exports, are there specific governance/competitiveness/economic freedom variables associated with each pair of country groupings that constrain or delay the development process until threshold levels are reached? While not conclusive proof of causation, if the hypothesis derived from the factor analysis is correct, we should expect to find that entrepreneurship is a leading force in affecting—either directly or indirectly—these key transition variables.

To test this theory, a discriminant analysis[36] was undertaken to determine which variables were statistically significant in correctly classifying countries in each of the five WEF stages of development. The discriminant results start with Groups 1 and 2, with group membership gradually expanded to see which variables come into play when more developed countries are added to the sample.

Of the 28 possible profiling elements (see Table 8.11), only two were statistically significant in separating Group 1 and 2 countries into distinct groupings based on competitiveness/ governance and economic freedom. In order of importance, these were the WEF's innovation variable and the WEF's infrastructure variable, which together correctly classified 82.5% of countries into their original WEF groupings. In the case of both variables, Group 2 countries had a significantly higher level of attainment, especially with regard to infrastructure.

Broadening the discriminant analysis to include Group 3 countries produced another distinct profiling pattern. Four variables were statistically significant in profiling the combined group of countries into their three original WEF groupings with 75.0% accuracy. In declining order of statistical importance, these variables were: the WEF's measure of technological readiness; the WEF's innovation; the WEF's infrastructure; and finally, the World Bank's measure of governance, voice and accountability.

In contrast to the other key transition variables which show steady progress as countries move to higher groupings, the mean group scores for voice and accountability decline for Group 2 countries before increasing dramatically for Group 3. This finding suggests that authoritarian regimes may be more adept at initiating a growth process. On the other hand, reliance on the military has not always resulted in sustained growth. Clearly, for most countries democratic institutions and government accountability must be immediately strengthened to sustain its progress from Group 1 to Group 2, with governance reforms continuing to facilitate the transition to Group 3.

When the discriminant sample is further expanded to include countries in Group 4, the WEF's overall growth potential variable contributes to group delineation. Some 72.9% of the countries are correctly classified in their respective WEF groupings. The growth potential term increases steadily from the lower to the higher country groupings, suggesting that a balanced attainment of many of the competitiveness measures is critical for continued advancement.

Finally, when the discriminant analysis included all five groups, six key variables were identified that create a distinct competitiveness/governance/economic freedom environment. In addition to innovation, infrastructure and growth potential, the WEF's higher education and training, the World Bank's rule of law, and the Heritage Foundation's monetary freedom variables are statistically significant in correctly classifying 75% of the countries in their original WEF groupings.

Table 8.11 Country group profiles

Groups 1 and 2 (82.5% placement as WEF)	Pakistan 90.4% in WEF Group 1					
	Mean values discriminant groups					
Discriminating variables in order of importance	*Group 1*	*Group 2*				*Pakistan*
WEF innovation	2.79	2.96				3.03
WEF infrastructure	2.53	3.72				2.75

Groups 1, 2 and 3 (75.0% placement as WEF)	Pakistan 89.4% in WEF Group 1					
	Mean values discriminant groups					
Discriminating variables in order of importance	*Group 1*	*Group 2*	*Group 3*			*Pakistan*
WEF technological readiness	2.77	3.27	3.67			2.94
WEF innovation	2.80	2.95	3.05			3.03
WEF infrastructure	2.52	3.66	3.80			2.75
WB voice and accountability	−0.49	−0.95	0.16			−1.00

Groups 1, 2, 3 and 4 (72.9% placement as WEF)	Pakistan 94.1% in WEF Group 1					
	Mean values discriminant groups					
Discriminating variables in order of importance	*Group 1*	*Group 2*	*Group 3*	*Group 4*		*Pakistan*
WEF technological readiness	2.78	3.29	3.67	4.38		2.94
WEF innovation	2.79	2.95	3.13	3.36		3.03
WEF infrastructure	2.50	3.71	3.80	4.64		2.75
WEF growth potential	3.47	4.07	4.19	4.36		3.48
WB voice and accountability	−0.53	−0.93	0.22	0.72		−1.00

Groups 1, 2, 3, 4 and 5 (75.0% placement as WEF)	Pakistan 97.0% in WEF Group 1					
	Mean values discriminant groups					
Discriminating variables in order of importance	*Group1*	*Group 2*	*Group 3*	*Group 4*	*Group 5*	*Pakistan*
WEF innovation	2.77	2.99	3.05	3.31	4.68	3.03
WEF higher education and training	2.85	3.81	4.11	4.7	5.41	2.91
WEF infrastructure	2.46	3.62	3.77	4.63	5.61	2.75
EF monetary freedom	70.67	65.03	72.66	73.67	79.14	69.4
WEF growth potential	3.44	4.06	4.12	4.36	5.09	3.48
WB rule of law	−0.77	−0.46	−0.21	0.72	1.53	−0.93

Notes: SPSS 19.0 Stepwise Multiple Discriminant Analysis; WEF = World Economic Forum Competitiveness data; EF = Heritage House Economic Freedom data set; WB = World Bank governance data set.

Regression analysis: key linkages surrounding entrepreneurship

The factor and discriminant analyses were both suggestive of the potentially key role that entrepreneurship could play in many emerging economies' transition to higher levels of development. However, while identifying key relationships, neither method is capable of definitively establishing causal relationships between entrepreneurship and other key competitiveness/governance/economic freedom variables. To fill this gap, a regression analysis was performed on the country sample to determine the specific factors that contribute to entrepreneurship.

Factors contributing to increased entrepreneurship

Neo-liberal thought purports that economic liberalization and increased efforts in many of the WEF's categories of competitiveness can produce an environment conducive to the creation of new small and medium-sized enterprises (SMEs).[37] This assumption underlay the neo-liberal approach to economic reform in Chile after the fall of Allende and later became the rationale for many of the dramatic market reforms in post-communist Eastern and Central Europe.[38] To test this proposition, the World Bank's entrepreneurship (density) was regressed on the WEF's competitiveness data set and the Heritage Foundation economic freedom variables. As with the discriminant analysis, the analysis began with Groups 1 and 2 and gradually expanded to the more developed country groupings.[39]

Of the competitiveness and economic freedom variables, entrepreneurship in Group 1 and 2 countries responded most strongly to improved trade freedom, followed by business freedom (see Table 8.12). These two variables alone accounted for more than 50% of the fluctuation in entrepreneurship for this sample of countries.

When the sample was expanded to include Group 3, competitiveness factors, especially technological readiness and labour market efficiency, took on an added role in facilitating increased entrepreneurial activity. Increased freedom from corruption was also a critical factor at this juncture.

With the addition of Group 4, economic freedom factors were replaced by variables reflecting increased competitiveness, namely, technological readiness and labour market efficiency (see Table 8.13). The fact that the economic liberalization reforms impact primarily the early stages of development was confirmed through regressions omitting Group 1 countries. For Groups 2, 3 and 4, and for 3 and 4 separately, only competitiveness variables—technological readiness and labour market efficiency—were statistically significant in affecting entrepreneurship.

With market liberalization, especially trade freedom and business freedom reforms, opportunities for increased entrepreneurial activity open up for Group 1 countries. Further increases in market reforms do not appear as critical in influencing movement through the higher stages of development, although a key market reform may still make a significant contribution to the growth of new firms.

However, while market reform can produce increased entrepreneurial activity, it is most likely (based on the experiences of several of the former European communist countries) not sufficient in and of itself to create a virtuous circle of continued growth and reform.

Entrepreneurship and governance

The literature suggests that the impact of entrepreneurship on governance may play a major role in determining whether initial growth will be devolve into a vicious, or evolve into a virtuous, circle of development.[40] According to Havrylyshyn and Wolf,[41] a vicious circle is precipitated when the first set of entrepreneurs and other vested interests, content merely to live off their

Robert E. Looney

Table 8.12 Determinants of entrepreneurial activity (stepwise regression)

	Standardized coefficient	t	Sig	df	R	R square	Adjusted R square
WEF Group 1							
Model 1							
EF trade freedom	0.584	3.447	0.002	23	0.584	0.341	0.312
Model 2							
EF trade freedom	0.565	4.114	0.000				
EF business freedom	0.495	3.598	0.002	22	0.765	0.585	0.547
WEF Groups 1 and 2							
Model 1							
WEF technological readiness	0.503	3.775	0.000	42	0.503	0.253	0.236
Model 2							
WEF technological readiness	0.547	4.330	0.000				
EF fiscal freedom	0.326	2.583	0.013	41	0.598	0.358	0.327
Model 3							
WEF technological readiness	0.540	4.451	0.000				
EF fiscal freedom	0.266	2.131	0.039				
WEF labour market efficiency	0.260	2.101	0.042	40	0.649	0.422	0.378
Model 4							
WEF technological readiness	0.381	2.762	0.009				
EF fiscal freedom	0.254	2.119	0.041				
WEF labour market efficiency	0.273	2.301	0.027				
EF freedom from corruption	0.292	2.132	0.039	39	0.734	0.482	0.429

Notes: Stepwise Regression Model: IBM SPSS 19.0; country groupings are those from the World Economic Forum Competitiveness 2010–11 data set. Data Set: WEF = World Economic Forum Competitiveness data set; EF = Heritage Economic Freedom data set; entrepreneurship data: World Bank Enterprise Snapshots (WBGES) 2010; regression analysis was entrepreneurship on the combined WEF and EF data sets; additional variables: SHADOW = Size of the Shadow Economy (% GDP), WEFGROUP, group prediction dummy.

rents, derail the development process by blocking further governance (and possibly economic) reforms. In contrast, the creation of a virtuous circle requires entrepreneurs to take a longer-term view and push for continuing reforms to spur additional growth and increase profits.[42]

The analysis thus far appears to support this theory. The components of governance, with the exception of voice and accountability, show steady improvement as countries move to higher and higher groupings. The level of improvement for both the WEF groups and the discriminant groupings used in this model appears to peak as countries move from Group 3 to Group 4 (see Table 8.14). Control of corruption also improves markedly at this level, but reaches its maximum rate of improvement during the transition from Group 4 to Group 5.

Are these patterns, in fact, associated with pressure from entrepreneurial groups for further reforms, especially in the area of governance? After controlling what appears to be a normal improvement in governance as countries develop, does increased governance contribute an additional amount to the upgrading of national governance dimensions? If a pattern exists, it may do so with a lag due to the time it takes to realize major changes in areas like rule of law or control of corruption. Thus, we would expect major gains in governance to follow somewhat behind flurries of increased entrepreneurial activity.

Regression analysis was used to identify possible linkages between improved levels of governance and entrepreneurship. As there appears to be a normal progression of regression

Table 8.13 Determinants of entrepreneurial activity, continued (stepwise regression)

	Standardized coefficient	t	Sig	df	R	R square	Adjusted R square
WEF Groups 1, 2, 3 and 4							
Model 1							
WEF technological readiness	0.616	5.585	0.000	51	0.616	0.380	0.367
Model 2							
WEF technological readiness	0.563	5.260	0.000				
WEF labour market efficiency	0.269	2.508	0.015	50	0.670	0.449	0.427
WEF Groups 2, 3 and 4							
Model 1							
WEF technological readiness	0.529	3.373	0.001	36	0.529	0.280	0.260
Model 2							
WEF technological readiness	0.383	2.703	0.011				
WEF labour market efficiency	0.378	2.663	0.012	35	0.633	0.401	0.367
WEF Groups 3 and 4							
Model 1							
WEF labour market efficiency	0.536	3.237	0.003	26	0.536	0.287	0.260

Notes: Stepwise regression model: IBM SPSS 19.0; country groupings are those from the World Economic Forum Competitiveness 2010–11 data set; data set: WEF = World Economic Forum competitiveness data set; EF = Heritage Economic Freedom data set; entrepreneurship data: World Bank Enterprise Snapshots (WBGES) 2010; regression analysis was entrepreneurship on the combined WEF and EF data sets; additional variables: SHADOW = Size of the Shadow Economy (% GDP), WEFGROUP, group prediction dummy.

improvement by group (again with voice and accountability the exception), a control stage dummy variable was included as an independent variable—assuming values of 1, 2, 3, 4 and 5 to reflect the various country groupings. For the regressions involving the WEF stages, these values replicate the country groupings. In a similar fashion, for the analysis of the progression of governance improvement through the discriminant stages, the dummy assumed the value of each of the assigned groupings.

For the WEF Groups 1 and 2 (see Table 8.15), there are very weak linkages between entrepreneurship and increased levels of governance, with slight improvements occurring in the areas of political stability and regulatory quality. For the other measures of governance, no statistically significant linkages were found.

The picture improves somewhat for countries in Groups 2 and 3. For these countries, expanded entrepreneurship results in improved governance, with the exception of government effectiveness. However, as indicated by the adjusted r2 term, these linkages are not particularly strong.

Entrepreneurial linkages improve dramatically for countries in WEF Groups 3 and 4 (see Table 8.16). Again, entrepreneurship is statistically significant for all categories of governance, with the exception of government effectiveness. More importantly, in contrast to the previous groupings, the adjusted r2 values move into the 40% and 50% range, with the exception of voice and accountability. That is, entrepreneurship accounts for nearly half the observed fluctuations in governance after controlling for the normal patterns of improvement.

Finally, countries in Groups 4 and 5 (see Table 8.17) show few linkages between improved levels of governance and increased entrepreneurial activity. Entrepreneurship is statistically significant only in the case of regulatory quality, and even here it is a secondary factor after taking into account the progression of stages.

Robert E. Looney

Table 8.14 Governance patterns by country grouping (group means)

WEF country group	Voice and accountability	Political stability	Government effectiveness	Regulatory quality	Rule of law	Control of corruption
Group 1	−0.547	−0.685	−0.714	−0.562	−0.760	−0.732
Group 2	−0.739	−0.300	−0.267	−0.278	−0.394	−0.403
Difference: Group 2–Group 1	−0.192	0.385	0.447	0.284	0.366	0.329
Group 3	0.015	−0.176	0.016	0.137	−0.178	−0.165
Difference: Group 3–Group 2	0.754	0.124	0.283	0.415	0.216	0.238
Group 4	0.657	0.598	0.802	0.902	0.715	0.572
Difference: Group 4–Group 3	0.642	0.774	0.786	0.765	0.893	0.737
Group 5	1.127	0.761	1.462	1.358	1.436	1.488
Difference: Group 5–Group 4	0.470	0.163	0.660	0.456	0.721	0.916
Discriminant country group						
Group 1	−0.535	−0.694	−0.751	−0.569	−0.774	−0.737
Group 2	−0.638	−0.279	−0.340	−0.374	−0.455	−0.481
Difference: Group 2–Group 1	−0.103	0.415	0.411	0.195	0.319	0.256
Group 3	−0.083	−0.299	0.008	0.165	−0.215	−0.201
Difference: Group 3–Group 2	0.555	−0.020	0.348	0.539	0.240	0.280
Group 4	0.650	0.577	0.789	0.889	0.719	0.557
Difference: Group 4–Group 3	0.733	0.876	0.781	0.724	0.934	0.758
Group 5	1.200	0.769	1.561	1.419	1.530	1.629
Difference: Group 5–Group 4	0.550	0.192	0.772	0.530	0.811	1.072

Source: Data from World Bank Governance Indicators data set for 2009

A slightly different pattern emerges when countries are examined in the discriminant analysis framework. Again, there are few linkages for Groups 1 and 2 (see Table 8.18), outside political stability and regulatory quality, between expanded entrepreneurship and higher levels of governance. The linkages that do occur are extremely weak and barely significant.

Linkages are strengthened somewhat, especially in the area of voice and accountability, once countries reach Groups 2 and 3. Here, entrepreneurship, along with the stage progression term, accounts for more than 60% of the variance across countries in voice and accountability. More importantly, for countries in these groups, entrepreneurship has a statistically significant link to all governance measures.

In sharp contrast to the findings reported above for the WEF stages, countries in discriminant Groups 3 and 4 show no statistically significant linkages with entrepreneurship (see Table 8.19). In all cases, the discriminant stage dummy has high levels of statistical significance for all measures other than voice and accountability.

Another sharp contrast occurs between the two country grouping systems for Groups 4 and 5. As noted, there was only a weak linkage between entrepreneurship and regulatory quality for

Modern stage theories and emerging economies

Table 8.15 Entrepreneurship and improved governance: WEF country groupings

Governance measures	Standardized coefficient	t	Sig	R square adjusted
WEF country groups 1 and 2				
Voice and accountability		No variables statistically significant		
Political stability				
Entrepreneurship	0.376	2.184	0.031	0.141
Government effectiveness				
WEF stage group dummy	0.418	2.475	0.019	0.146
Regulatory quality				
Entrepreneurship	0.444	2.619	0.014	0.168
Rule of law		No variables statistically significant		
Control of corruption		No variables statistically significant		
WEF country groups 2 and 3				
Voice and accountability				
WEF stage group dummy	0.376	2.504	0.017	
Entrepreneurship	0.331	2.208	0.034	0.288
Political stability				
Entrepreneurship	0.500	3.368	0.002	0.228
Government effectiveness				
WEF stage group dummy	0.408	2.608	0.013	0.142
Regulatory quality				
Entrepreneurship	0.478	3.171	0.003	0.205
Rule of law				
Entrepreneurship	0.476	3.160	0.003	0.204
Control of corruption				
Entrepreneurship	0.402	2.855	0.007	
WEF stage group dummy	0.387	2.746	0.100	0.373

Note: Stepwise regression: dependent variables listed in order of entry; data: governance measures, World Bank Governance Indicators; entrepreneurship: World Bank, Enterprise Snapshots (WBGES), 2020; all data are for 2009.

countries in WEF Groups 4 and 5. In the discriminant country scheme (see Table 8.20), entrepreneurship forms a highly significant link to four areas of governance: government effectiveness, regulatory quality, rule of law and control of corruption.

What might account for these differences between country grouping schemes? As with governance (see Table 8.14), entrepreneurial activity increases as countries move through the sequence of groupings (see Table 8.21). However, increases in entrepreneurship between stages vary somewhat by grouping scheme. For the WEF classification framework, the highest percentage increase in entrepreneurship occurs between Groups 2 and 3, with a marked fall-off in entrepreneurial activity between Groups 3 and 4. In the case of the discriminant country scheme, a big jump in entrepreneurial activity occurs between Groups 1 and 2. In contrast with the WEF scheme, there is also a relatively large increase in entrepreneurship between Groups 3 and 4.

If we assume some delay between surges in entrepreneurship and improvements in governance, these different patterns of entrepreneurial expansion are roughly in line with the observed contrasts in governance between the two classifications.

In the case of the WEF countries, the pattern is fairly straightforward: the big gains in governance observed in Groups 3 and 4 follow the maximum rate of growth in entrepreneurship that occurs between Groups 2 and 3. Owing to the big drop-off in entrepreneurial expansion

167

Table 8.16 Entrepreneurship and improved governance: WEF country groupings, continued

Governance measures	Standardized coefficient	t	Sig	R square adjusted
WEF country groups 3 and 4				
Voice and accountability				
WEF stage group dummy	0.398	2.690	0.011	
Entrepreneurship	0.363	2.450	0.020	0.306
Political stability				
WEF stage group dummy	0.563	4.179	0.000	
Entrepreneurship	0.282	2.096	0.440	0.425
Government effectiveness				
WEF stage group dummy	0.702	5.580	0.000	0.477
Regulatory quality				
WEF stage group dummy	0.616	5.186	0.000	
Entrepreneurship	0.341	2.870	0.007	0.553
Rule of law				
WEF stage group dummy	0.654	5.694	0.000	
Entrepreneurship	0.312	2.716	−0.011	0.582
Control of corruption				
WEF stage group dummy	0.593	4.592	0.000	
Entrepreneurship	0.290	2.246	0.032	0.472

Note: Stepwise regression: dependent variables listed in order of entry; data: governance measures, World Bank Governance Indicators; entrepreneurship: World Bank, Enterprise Snapshots (WBGES), 2020; all data are for 2009.

Table 8.17 Entrepreneurship and improved governance: WEF country groupings, continued

Governance measures	Standardized coefficient	t	Sig	R square adjusted
WEF country groups 4 and 5				
Voice and accountability				
WEF stage group dummy	0.395	2.652	0.012	0.156
Political stability		No variables statistically significant		
Government effectiveness				
WEF stage group dummy	0.610	4.743	0.000	0.355
Regulatory quality				
WEF stage group dummy	0.418	2.998	0.005	0.284
Entrepreneurship	0.296	2.124	0.040	
Rule of law				
WEF stage group dummy	0.621	4.882	0.000	0.369
Control of corruption				
WEF stage group dummy	0.545	4.008	0.000	0.279

Note: Stepwise regression: dependent variables listed in order of entry; data: governance measures, World Bank Governance Indicators; entrepreneurship: World Bank, Enterprise Snapshots (WBGES), 2020; all data are for 2009.

Modern stage theories and emerging economies

Table 8.18 Entrepreneurship and improved governance: discriminant analysis country groupings

Governance measures	Standardized coefficient	t	Sig	R square adjusted
Discriminant analysis country groups 1 and 2				
Voice and accountability		No variables statistically significant		
Political stability				
Entrepreneurship	0.376	2.184	0.037	0.141
Government effectiveness		No variables statistically significant		
Regulatory quality				
Entrepreneurship	0.444	2.619	0.014	0.168
Rule of law		No variables statistically significant		
Control of corruption		No variables statistically significant		
Discriminant analysis country groups 2 and 3				
Voice and accountability				
Discriminant stage group dummy	0.679	6.326	0.000	
Entrepreneurship	0.294	2.741	0.010	0.617
Political stability				
Entrepreneurship	0.500	3.368	0.002	0.228
Government effectiveness				
Entrepreneurship	0.361	2.256	0.031	0.105
Regulatory quality				
Entrepreneurship	0.407	2.761	0.009	
Discriminant stage group dummy	0.313	2.128	0.041	0.280
Rule of law				
Entrepreneurship	0.476	3.160	0.003	0.204
Control of corruption				
Entrepreneurship	0.456	3.178	0.003	
Discriminant stage group dummy	0.293	2.043	0.049	0.316

Note: Stepwise regression—dependent variables listed in order of entry; data: governance measures, World Bank Governance Indicators; entrepreneurship: World Bank, Enterprise Snapshots (WBGES), 2020; all data are for 2009.

when countries reach Groups 3 and 4, entrepreneurship ceases to play a significant role in governance change in Group 4 and 5 countries.

The same general lagged pattern occurs for the discriminant country groupings, albeit not quite as sharply. For these countries, the largest rate of increase in entrepreneurship occurs between Groups 1 and 2. These increases are followed by improved governance in Groups 2 and 3, especially in voice and accountability, where entrepreneurship and the group dummy accounted for more than 60% of the observed variance across countries.

While there is a slight drop-off in the rate of growth of entrepreneurial activity from Group 2 to 3 and Group 3 to 4, it is not nearly as dramatic as the decline from Group 3 to Group 4 in the WEF scheme. As a result, entrepreneurship continues to play a significant role in improving governance for countries in Groups 3 and 4. With a 15% higher increase in entrepreneurship between Groups 3 and 4 than that observed with the WEF countries, entrepreneurship continues to play a significant role in the upgrading of governance for countries reaching Groups 4 and 5.

From these results, one can tentatively conclude that successful movement through higher stages of development has been associated with entrepreneurial gains resulting in subsequent improvements in governance, as seen in the virtuous circle pattern of successful reform-led growth.

Table 8.19 Entrepreneurship and improved governance: discriminant analysis country groupings, continued

Governance measures	Standardized coefficient	t	Sig	R square adjusted
Discriminant Country Groups 3 and 4				
Voice and accountability				
Discriminant stage group dummy	0.560	3.823	0.001	0.292
Political stability				
Discriminant stage group dummy	0.689	5.378	0.000	0.458
Government effectiveness				
Discriminant stage group dummy	0.877	10.337	0.000	0.762
Regulatory quality				
Discriminant stage group dummy	0.796	7.435	0.000	0.622
Rule of law				
Discriminant stage group dummy	0.893	11.222	0.000	0.791
Control of corruption				
Discriminant stage group dummy	0.812	7.868	0.000	0.649

Note: Stepwise regression: dependent variables listed in order of entry; data: governance measures, World Bank Governance Indicators; entrepreneurship: World Bank, Enterprise Snapshots (WBGES), 2020; all data are for 2009.

Table 8.20 Entrepreneurship and improved governance: discriminant analysis country groupings, continued

Governance measures	Standardized coefficient	t	Sig	R square adjusted
Discriminant Country Groups 4 and 5				
Voice and accountability				
Discriminant stage group dummy	0.497	3.531	0.001	0.227
Political stability				
Discriminant stage group dummy	0.346	2.273	0.029	0.097
Government effectiveness				
Discriminant stage group dummy	0.770	8.628	0.000	
Entrepreneurship	0.256	2.872	0.007	0.695
Regulatory quality				
Discriminant stage group dummy	0.613	5.364	0.000	
Entrepreneurship	0.312	2.733	0.010	0.499
Rule of law				
Discriminant stage group dummy	0.752	7.795	0.000	
Entrepreneurship	0.224	2.319	0.026	0.643
Control of corruption				
Discriminant stage group dummy	0.722	7.069	0.000	
Entrepreneurship	0.233	2.282	0.028	0.600

Note: Stepwise regression: dependent variables listed in order of entry; data: governance measures, World Bank Governance Indicators; entrepreneurship: World Bank, Enterprise Snapshots (WBGES), 2020; all data are for 2009.

Modern stage theories and emerging economies

Table 8.21 Entrepreneurial activity by country grouping

Country grouping	Entrepreneurship	
	Discriminant country grouping	WEF country grouping
Group 1	0.404	0.472
Group 2	0.993	0.990
(% difference)	59.32	52.32
Group 3	2.036	2.374
(% difference)	51.23	58.30
Group 4	3.736	3.417
(% difference)	45.50	30.52
Group5	6.267	5.948
(% difference)	40.39	42.55

Notes: World Bank: The 2020 World Bank Group Entrepreneurship Snapshots (WBGES); World Bank Entrepreneurship data set: number of newly registered limited liablility firms per 1,000 working-age population (those aged 15–64) for the year 2009.

Entrepreneurship, governance and the shadow economy

One of the main impediments to competitiveness and sustained growth is the development of a large shadow, or informal, economy. Numerous studies have documented that while the shadow economy may provide a temporary haven for the unemployed, its low level of productivity and tax potential ultimately causes a drag on sustained rates of economic growth.[43] Furthermore, the development of a large shadow economy is usually one of the symptoms of the vicious circle noted above. Often, with the development of a large shadow economy, insurgent and criminal groups are able to establish secure sources of financing for their operations, further contributing to ongoing instability and economic decline.[44]

As might be expected, the size of the shadow economy declines as countries pass through the various stages of development, although this reduction appears to stall at around 35% of GDP at the Group 3 level before declining rapidly to 15.25% as countries reach Group 4. While the shadow economy contracts as entrepreneurial activity increases, it does so at a differential rate (see Table 8.22).

To test whether the reduction in the shadow economy is a direct result of increased entrepreneurship or the result of a more indirect process stemming from the improved governance associated with increased entrepreneurial activity, regressions were undertaken beginning with Group 1 and gradually expanding the group sample size. For these countries (see Table 8.23), improved goods market efficiency was the strongest factor reducing the size of the shadow economy, followed by innovation (a key element affecting the expansion of entrepreneurship for this group of countries) and fiscal freedom. The last term is logical since higher tax rates at early stages of development have been known to force many firms into informal (tax-avoidance) activities. These three variables account for more than 80% of the variance in the size of the shadow economies across this group of countries. Beyond these variables, entrepreneurship was not statistically significant in contributing to the regression equation.

Expanding the sample to include Group 2 countries produced a shift in factors affecting the size of the shadow economy. Now, innovation becomes the most important variable, followed by investment freedom. Regulatory quality is a marginally significant variable in increasing the size of the shadow economy. Improved regulatory quality at this stage of development may force firms that are unable to comply into the shadow economy. Finally, expanding the sample to include Group 4 and 5 countries (see Table 8.24) resulted in the rule of law playing the dominant role in the shadow economy's reduction.

Table 8.22 Shadow economy and entrepreneurship

Country grouping	WEF country grouping	
	Shadow economy	Entrepreneurship
Group 1	40.56	0.472
Group 2	35.54	0.990
(% difference)	−14.12	52.32
Group 3	35.1	2.374
(% difference)	−1.25	58.30
Group 4	27.86	3.417
(% difference)	−25.99	30.52
Group5	15.25	5.948
(% difference)	−82.69	42.55

Notes: Entrepreneurship: The 2020 World Bank Group Entrepreneurship Snapshots (WBGES) data set—newly registered limited liability firms per 1,000 working age population; shadow economy (% GDP) from Andreas Buehn and Friedrich Schneider, 'Shadow Economies and Corruption All Over the World: Revised Estimates for 120 Countries', *Economics: The Open-Access, Open-Assessment E-Journal*, 27 October 2009.

The results for the shadow economy are roughly consistent with the entrepreneur-led virtuous circle described above and, in that sense, close the circle. For Group 1 countries, economic reforms, especially in the areas of trade and improved business freedom, jump-start entrepreneurial activity (seeTable 8.12). As entrepreneurial activity takes hold, this class begins to generate more resources for growth and supportive government services. With growth, political stability becomes easier to maintain (see Table 8.15). For successful countries that are able to continue moving up the development scale, further growth and expansion in entrepreneurial activities result in the broad improvements in governance required for sustained growth. These patterns occur in WEF Groups 3 and 4, with subsequent dramatic declines in the size of the shadow economy in Groups 4 and 5.

Assessment

Whether expanding numbers of entrepreneurs will play this positive role depends on which of Mancur Olson's[45] coalitions dominate over time. Olson distinguished between distributional coalitions, which are seen as leading to outcomes inimical to economic growth, and encompassing coalitions, which are seen as potentially aiding economic growth in a society. For Olson, the equilibrium-upsetting crisis of losing a war explained post-war growth in Japan and Germany. By making possible reforms that neutralized entrenched vested interests, the crisis produced a fresh environment in which the benefits of public institutions and policies could be distributed more widely.

The Olsonian framework enables a deeper insight into stalled development. The answer to many emerging economies' stalled-out progress, or the middle-income trap can, in large part, be traced to Olson's distributional coalitions that are capable of blocking reforms.

Summarizing our main empirical findings as they pertain to emerging country growth: first, entrepreneurial activity is a key element in driving the growth process through progressive stages of economic development. Successful countries whose development relies on increased entrepreneurial activity appear to sustain growth through a series of ongoing reforms initiated by this growing stakeholder group. As a result, they are able to establish virtuous circles of increased economic liberalization, extended entrepreneurship, expanded growth and improved governance, which lead in turn to further growth and development. Second, increased trade

Table 8.23 Determinants of the shadow economy (stepwise regression)

	Standardized coefficient	t	Sig	df	R	R square	Adjusted R square
WEF Group 1							
Model 1							
WEF goods market efficiency	−0.816	−5.099	0.000	13	0.816	0.667	0.641
Model 2							
WEF goods market efficiency	−0.553	−3.637	0.003				
WEF innovation	−0.464	−3.054	0.010	12	0.901	0.812	0.781
Model 3							
WEF goods market efficiency	−0.547	−4.151	0.002				
WEF innovation	−0.673	−4.155	0.002				
EF fiscal freedom	−0.317	−2.222	0.048	11	0.933	0.871	0.835
Pakistan	Actual = 37.1% Predicted = 37.5%						
WEF Groups 1 and 2							
Model 1							
WEF innovation	−0.638	−3.970	0.001	23	0.638	0.407	0.381
Model 2							
WEF innovation	−0.679	−4.494	0.000				
EF monetary freedom	−0.318	−2.105	0.047	22	0.711	0.506	0.461
Pakistan	Actual = 37.1% Predicted = 39.6%						
WEF Groups 1 2 and 3							
Model 1							
WEF innovation	−0.449	−3.255	0.002	42	0.449	0.201	0.182
Model 2							
WEF innovation	−0.521	−3.802	0.000				
EF investment freedom	−0.287	−2.099	0.042	41	0.528	0.279	0.244
Model 3							
WEF innovation	−0.671	−4.478	0.000				
EF investment freedom	−0.623	−3.009	0.005				
WB regulatory quality	0.426	2.099	0.042	40	0.592	0.350	0.302
Pakistan	Actual = 37.1% Predicted = 42.7%						

Notes: Stepwise regression model: IBM SPSS 19.0; country groupings are those formed from a discriminant analysis of the combined data set; data set: WEF = World Economic Forum competitiveness data set; EF = Heritage Economic Freedom data set; WB = World Bank Governance Indicators data set; entrepreneurship data: World Bank Enterprise Snapshots (WBGES) 2010; regression analysis was the size of the shadow economy (% GDP) on the combined WEF, WB and EF data sets; additional variable: WEFGROUP, WEF Grouping from the WEF 2010–11 Competitiveness Report.

Robert E. Looney

Table 8.24 Determinants of the shadow economy, continued (stepwise regression)

	Standardized coefficient	t	Sig	df	R	R square	Adjusted R square
WEF Groups 1, 2, 3 and 4							
Model 1							
WB rule of law	−0.517	−4.315	0.000	51	0.517	0.267	0.253
Model 2							
WB rule of law	−0.505	−4.363	0.000				
WEF market size	−0.254	−2.195	0.333	50	0.576	0.332	0.305
Pakistan	Actual = 37.1%	Predicted = 42.0%					
WEF Groups 2, 3 and 4							
Model 1							
WB rule of law	−0.503	−3.429	0.001	36	0.503	0.253	0.232
WEF Groups 3, 4 and 5							
Model 1							
WB rule of law	−0.804	−9.835	0.000	53	0.804	0.646	0.639
Model 2							
WB rule of law	−0.793	−10.041	0.000				
WEF market size	−0.176	−2.231	0.298	54	0.823	0.677	0.665

Notes: Stepwise regression model: IBM SPSS 19.0; country groupings are those formed from a discriminant analysis of the combined data set; data set: WEF = World Economic Forum competitiveness data set; EF = Heritage Economic Freedom data set; WB = World Bank Governance Indicators data set; entrepreneurship data: World Bank Enterprise Snapshots (WBGES) 2010; regression analysis was the size of the shadow economy (% GDP) on the combined WEF, WB and EF data sets; additional variable: WEFGROUP, WEF Grouping from the WEF 2010–11 Competitiveness Report.

liberalization and improvements in the business climate are the most important factors for stimulating entrepreneurial expansion at early stages of development. Finally, the first and second points suggest that entrepreneurial efforts could be expanded in the short term without major improvements in governance.

Notes

1 Robert M. Solo, 'The Last 50 Years in Growth Theory and the Next 10', *Oxford Review of Economic Policy* 23(1), Spring 2007: 3–14.
2 Arvind Subramanian, 'This is a Golden Age of Global Growth (Yes, You Read That Right)', *Financial Times*, 7 April 2013.
3 Robert Looney, 'Failed Economic Take-offs and Terrorism in Pakistan: Conceptualizing a Proper Role for U.S. Assistance', *Asian Survey* XLIV(6), November/December 2004: 771–93.
4 Cf. Benjamin Higgins, 'The Marxist Model: Growth and Collapse', in *Economic Development*, revised edn, Norton, New York, 1968, 76–105.
5 Michael E. Porter, *The Competitive Advantage of Nations*, Free Press, New York, 1990.
6 Walt W. Rostow, *The Stages of Economic Growth: A Non-Communist Manifesto*, Cambridge University Press, London, 1960.
7 The Porter framework has been refined and expanded over the years in the World Economic Forum, *Global Competitiveness* reports.
8 Pierre-Richard Agenor, Otaviano Canuto and Michael Jelenic, 'Avoiding Middle-Income Traps', *Economic Premise*, World Bank, 8 November 2012.
9 Ibid.
10 Ibid.
11 Jennifer Bremer and John Kasarda, 'The Origins of Terror: Implications for U.S. Foreign Policy', *Milken Institute Review*, Fourth Quarter, 2002.

12 Rostow, *The Stages of Economic Growth*.

13 Bremer and Kasarda, 'The Origins of Terror'.

14 Ibid.

15 'Middle-Income Claptrap', *The Economist*, 16 February 2013.

16 See, for example, Michael Porter, 'Enhancing the Microeconomic Foundations of Prosperity: The Current Competitiveness Index', in Klaus Schwab (ed.), *The Global Competitiveness Report 2001–2002*, World Economic Forum, Geneva, 2001; and Michael Porter, 'The Microeconomic Foundations of Prosperity: Findings from the Business Competitiveness Index', in Klaus Schwab (ed.), *The Global Competitiveness Report 2007–2008*, World Economic Forum, Geneva, 2007.

17 X. Sala-i-Martin, J. Blanke, M. Drzeniek Hanouz, T. Geiger, I. Mia and F. Paua, 'The Global Competitiveness Index: Measuring the Productive Potential of Nations', in Klaus Schwab (ed.), *The Global Competitiveness Report, 2007–2008*, World Economic Forum, Geneva, 2007, 3.

18 Klaus Schwab, preface to *The Global Competitiveness Report 2010–2011*, ed. K. Schwab, World Economic Forum, Geneva, 2010, 4.

19 Ibid.

20 Porter, 'Enhancing the Microeconomic Foundations of Prosperity'.

21 Dani Rodrik and Mark Rosenzweig, 'Development Policy and Development Economics: An Introduction', in Dani Rodrik and Mark Rosenzweig (eds), *Handbook of Development Economics, Vol. 5*, North Holland, Amsterdam, 2009.

22 See, for example, J. Gwartney, J. Hall and R. Lawson, *Economic Freedom of the World 2000 Annual Report*, Fraser Institute, Vancouver, 2000.

23 World Bank, *Worldwide Governance Indicators*, info.worldbank.org/governance/wgi/sc_country.asp.

24 James Gwartney and Robert Lawson *et al.*, *Economic Freedom of the World 2010 Annual Report*, Fraser Institute, Vancouver, 2010.

25 *The 2011 Index of Economic Freedom*, The Heritage Foundation, Washington, DC, 2011.

26 Ibid.

27 Ricardo Hausmann, Dani Rodrik and Andrés Velasco, 'Getting the Diagnosis Right: A New Approach to Economic Reform', *Finance & Development*, March 2006.

28 Preliminary analysis suggested that while the Milken Institute Capital Access data set provided some interesting insights to the Pakistani situation, because of its relatively narrow focus it did not contribute a significant amount of information over and above that provided by the other three data sets.

29 World Bank, Enterprise Snapshots (WBGES), 2010 which comprises the number of newly registered limited liability companies per 1,000 working-age people (ages 15–64).

30 Data compiled in Friedrich Schneider and Andreas Buehn, 'Shadow Economics and Corruption All Over the World: Revised Estimates for 120 Countries', *Economics: the Open Access, Open-Assessment E-Journal*, 27 October 2009.

31 Ibid.

32 Friedrich Schneider with Dominik Enste, *Hiding in the Shadows: The Growth of the Underground Economy*, International Monetary Fund, Washington, DC, 2002.

33 See the classic work by Irma Adelman and Cynthia Taft Morris, 'A Factor Analysis of the Interrelationship Between Social and Political Variables and Per Capita Gross National Product', *Quarterly Journal of Economics*, November 1965, for a discussion of the method and interpretation of results. See also their 'Factor Analysis and Development', *Journal of Development Economics*, August 1982.

34 As noted below, the WEF basis of classifying industries into its five groups is heavily dependent on per capita incomes in defined ranges.

35 World Economic Forum, *The Global Competitiveness Report 2010–2011*, 10.

36 Irma Adelman and Cynthia Taft Morris, 'Performance Criteria for Evaluating Economic Development Potential: An Operational Approach', *Quarterly Journal of Economics*, May 1968. See also Randal Jones, 'A Model for Predicting Expropriation in Latin America Applied to Jamaica', *Colombia Journal of World Business*, Spring 1980, for an early example of the use of factor and discriminant analysis in classifying countries and assessing the requirements for progression from one group to another.

37 Robert Looney, 'Neo-liberalism', in Vol. 2 of R.J. Barry Jones (ed.), *Routledge Encyclopedia of International Political Economy*, Routledge, London, 2001, 1106–10.

38 Ibid.

39 The results presented here are for countries classified in groups derived from the discriminant analysis. However, a separate analysis of the WEF groupings produced a similar set of findings.

40 From somewhat different perspectives, this theme is touched upon in William Baumol, Robert Litan and Carl Schramm, *Good Capitalism, Bad Capitalism and the Economics of Growth and Prosperity*, Yale University Press, New Haven, CT, 2007, and Raghuram Rajan, *Saving Capitalism from the Capitalists*, Crown Business, New York, 2003.

41 Oleh Havrylyshyn and Thomas Wolf, 'Determinants of Growth in Transition Countries', *Finance & Development* 36(2), June 1999.

42 Ibid.

43 See, for example, Robert Looney, 'The Economic Consequences of Conflict: The Rise of Iraq's Informal Economy', *Journal of Economic Issues*, December 2006; and Robert Looney, 'Iraq's Shadow Economy', *Revista Internazionale di Scienze Economiche e Commercialli*, December 2005.

44 Robert Looney, 'The Business of Insurgency: The Expansion of Iraq's Shadow Economy', *The National Interest*, Fall 2005.

45 Mancur Olson, *The Rise and Decline of Nations: Economic Growth, Stagflation and Social Rigidities*, Yale University Press, New Haven, CT, 1982. See also Mancur Olson, 'The South Will Fall Again: The South as Leader and Laggard in Economic Growth', *Southern Economic Journal*, 1983.

9

Beijing Consensus versus Washington Consensus[1]

John Williamson

Ever since I suggested that there was a useful measure of consensus at the end of the 1980s about the policies that Latin American countries needed to adopt in order to end the debt crisis and start building a brighter future, a vast number of consensuses have been proclaimed. Apart from my own Washington Consensus, there is the augmented Washington Consensus (with parts from which I differ profoundly), the Barcelona Agenda (which was almost called a Consensus), the Beijing Consensus, the Beijing-Seoul-Tokyo Consensus (the 'BeST Consensus'), the Buenos Aires Consensus, the Copenhagen Consensus (though this dealt with different issues and was not aimed at replacing the Washington Consensus), the London Consensus, the post-Washington Consensus, the Santiago Consensus, the Seoul Consensus and the Singapore Consensus. Doubtless other cities have had consensuses named after them.

Let me state at the outset that I do not believe that listing desirable policies solves all of the profound problems of economic development. I agree with Dani Rodrik[2] in believing that there are also issues of priority and implementation that agreement on the objectives does not address. I nevertheless do believe that a clear view of the proximate objectives is valuable. I also believe that there are major differences between alternative statements of what commands a consensus. Accordingly, I take the view that I have a topic worth discussing.

Since I do not propose to inflict on the reader a summary of a dozen or so different policy agendas that have been claimed to be relevant, I have a first problem of deciding which of the several candidate consensuses I wish to discuss. In view of the widespread interest in the subject, it is natural to include the Beijing Consensus. In view of the widespread use of the term, plus its pioneering role in initiating the debate, it is also natural to include the Washington Consensus. However, the latter confronts a major problem: the term has been used in at least two major senses, and the present author has no sympathy for the one that has reached the most widespread status. To describe the Washington Consensus as embodying neo-liberal, minimalist state views (as the popular view of the Washington Consensus does) implies that these doctrines command, or commanded, a consensus in Washington, which is not factually correct. In my view this version of the Washington Consensus was invented only to be a whipping boy. Accordingly, I shall use the term in my original sense, which bears little relationship to the popular, or populist, version, although I make occasional references to major differences. (Among the consensuses listed above, the one that comes closest to my original sense, though it is expressed less clearly, is the Seoul Consensus.)

177

John Williamson

The Beijing Consensus

An immediate problem in discussing the Beijing Consensus is to know what it means. The term was introduced by Joshua Cooper Ramo,[3] but he offered no list of the recommended policies.[4] I concluded in a prior discussion that the Beijing Consensus should be defined as the policies pursued by the People's Republic of China.[5] This has the virtue of being what most of the enthusiasts appear to mean by their use of the term, and it is also the sense in which Stefan Halper[6] uses the term in his book with that title.

Hence in this paper we shall contrast the policies pursued by China with those called for by the Washington Consensus.

My version (as opposed to the popular version mentioned above) of the Washington Consensus may be summarized as follows:[7]

1 Fiscal discipline. Governments should aim to restrict budget deficits to a level that can be financed in a non-inflationary manner. (I should have added that if interpreted as a medium-run objective this can be a corollary to, rather than competitive with, fiscal policy being conducted in a counter-cyclical manner.) *No view was taken, or is implied, about the right combination of expenditure restraint and tax policy to achieve fiscal discipline.*
2 Public spending. Governments should redirect public expenditure from low-priority expenditures like general subsidies to education, health and infrastructure.
3 In redesigning tax policy, governments should aim to raise revenue using a broad tax base combined with moderate marginal tax rates.
4 Governments should aim for domestic financial liberalization. (I initially focused only on interest rate liberalization, which is too narrow a focus; I failed to acknowledge the importance of accompanying liberalization with the establishment of effective financial supervision; and I did not make it clear that I regarded the liberalization of capital flows as a low-priority objective.)
5 The exchange rate should be unified and set at a level that is competitive. (I define a competitive rate as one that is not overvalued, i.e. is either correctly valued or undervalued.)
6 Governments should liberalize trade, initially by tariffying import restrictions and subsequently by reducing tariffs. It was admitted that views differ about both the speed with which tariffs should ideally be reduced and the expediency of allowing the process to be interrupted by adverse economic developments.
7 Inward foreign direct investment (FDI) should be allowed without restriction.
8 State enterprises should be privatized. (The statement is somewhat bald, but was intended to imply that every Latin American country had state enterprises that would be better off privatized rather than that there is never a justification for state enterprise.)
9 Entry and exit to industries should be deregulated.
10 Secure property rights should be extended to the informal sector.

Having thus specified the competing frameworks, our remaining task is to ask which of them provides a better guide to successful development.

Gradualism versus shock treatment

Many adherents of the Beijing Consensus (henceforth BC) explicitly favoured gradualism (based on Deng Xiaoping's calling for feeling the stones when crossing a river), whereas the subject is not broached by the Washington Consensus (henceforth WC), because I did not perceive it to be a major issue facing Latin America in 1989. When I have been forced to face the issue subsequently, I have argued that gradualism has merits when there is a society that has not already fallen apart and a leader who is confident of remaining long enough to effect his/her reforms. However, often those conditions are unrealistic: the economies in question have already broken down, or else a leader feels that s/he has to act quickly before s/he loses office. I certainly do not believe that many of the former communist societies had the opportunity to effect gradual and effective reform in 1989–91.

Encouraging innovation

This has again been explicitly favoured by many adherents of the BC, while the WC is silent on the topic. One could make a case similar to that offered above for not including this topic in the WC, but in this case there is an argument for regarding the omission more seriously. A popular recent development has been the tendency to assert the existence of a 'middle-income trap'[8] and one antidote suggested is to change the mix of industries in which a country specializes to more technology-intensive, or innovation-intensive, ones. I am concerned that the notion of a middle-income trap has never been properly demonstrated and that it may well be an illusion (Williamson 2012b), but I did not claim to prove the converse, and the possibility should be taken seriously. The Beijing Consensus, unlike the WC, mentions a possible antidote.

There is also a possible downside. The key to catch-up growth is imitation, not innovation, and it is possible to waste resources reinventing the wheel (as Brazil used to do in the days when it prohibited the importation of computers).

Macroeconomic stability

This was a major theme in the WC (items 1–3, though monetary policy was not mentioned, betraying the historic origins of the WC). Beijing has maintained something close to price stability ever since 1949, even during the Great Leap Forward and associated famine, when there was a massive increase in food prices. When necessary, notably during the world recession starting in 2008, it has employed Keynesian policies of demand stimulation in order to keep the economy near full capacity operation. In giving a high priority to maintaining macroeconomic balance, China has proved typically Asian. This part of the WC has never been problematic in Asia.

Other countries have now followed the Asian and WC lead: rapid inflation has been essentially eliminated from Africa and Latin America. Item 1 of the WC is not controversial. There have of course been innumerable fights (not least in Washington) about the mix of expenditure cuts and tax rises used to achieve fiscal discipline, but the goal is no longer seriously contested. As I emphasized in the preceding presentation of the WC, the mix that should be used was not a part of my version of the WC, although the populist version of the WC called for this to be achieved through expenditure reduction.

An open economy

Points 5, 6 and 7 of the WC deal with this topic, calling for a competitive exchange rate, trade liberalization and opening towards inward FDI. (My version of the WC, unlike the popular version, specifically did *not* call for countries to engage in general capital account opening.) Beijing liberalized inflows of FDI very early in the reform era and beginning in the mid-1990s reduced protection substantially as a condition for joining the World Trade Organization (WTO), so there is no contradiction on points 6 and 7. Exchange rate policy is less clear. By a 'competitive' exchange rate I understand one that is not overvalued, so that technically Beijing (which has in practice used an undervalued exchange rate as the main tool for achieving its occasionally large and certainly consistent current account surpluses) satisfied this one too. Moreover, if one measures the openness of the economy in the traditional way, by the ratio of exports to GDP, then the Chinese economy is the most open large economy in the world.

I none the less feel some qualms about declaring China guiltless in terms of its external relations. This is primarily because it remains opposed to any attempt to impose an international discipline on exchange rates,[9] and certainly has not abandoned the practice of running an undervalued exchange rate and the resulting current account surplus.

The contradiction between Beijing and Washington centres on the question of currency valuation. There are two separate issues in contention: one is the method of determining the exchange rate, the other concerns the level of the exchange rate. The two are often confused. China long fixed its exchange rate in terms of the US dollar, and then after announcing that it was going to start floating it, in fact moved to a crawling appreciation against the dollar. Holding its exchange rate at an undervalued level involved large intervention, and many US economists objected to the intervention per se (and argued that the renminbi (RMB) should instead float), rather than to the level at which the intervention occurred. My own objection is centred unambiguously on the level, and I have no objection to the fact of intervention: in fact, I favour a managed exchange rate, which implies a need for regular intervention. (Those who demand that China floats seem to have great faith that the RMB would be better behaved than many other floating rates have proved, and float to a level at which the current account and/or the basic balance would be in equilibrium, so that the two demands would have similar results.)

I do not think the central issue on which Beijing and Washington differ is well caught by the WC (primarily because this was written for Latin America at a time when there was a prospect of the region developing current account surpluses). The fundamental issue is whether surplus countries have a duty as members of the international community to take action to curb their surpluses. Even though I believe the demands coming from Washington have confused this message by expressing it as a demand for floating, the basic demand seems to me entirely reasonable, and I would like to see it codified as an International Monetary Fund (IMF) duty to avoid large surpluses. The fact that Beijing resists the notion of placing a limit on the surpluses that countries should pursue is a disservice to far more than the USA: it also makes life far more difficult for most other developing countries, as well as the cause of building a robust international system, and to the immediate prospects of restoring prosperity in the advanced world.

Market liberalization

The demand for market liberalization is expressed in points 4, 6, 8, 9 and perhaps 10 of the WC. This is surely the most basic difference between Beijing and the WC: the fact that even stripped of the absurdities of demands for a minimal state and a belief in the ubiquity of perfect competition (characteristics of the popular version of the WC but emphatically not my version), the WC is basically pro-market while Beijing allows a far larger role for the state. Indeed, since macro-stabilization and opening up to international trade (globalization) are nowadays uncontroversial in most of the developing world, one infers that it was this aspect of the WC that provoked the strong reactions to it.

On the general topic of market liberalization, I would offer two reactions. The first is that Beijing has in fact undertaken a fair measure of market liberalization, and that it is this that prompted the impressive growth of the Chinese economy, rather than the continuing existence of state-owned enterprises (SOEs). By the end of the 1990s China had already liberalized most commodity (though not factor) prices. In 1978 three-quarters of manufactures in China were produced by SOEs, while this figure had fallen to under one-quarter by 2010. (This decline is not an artefact of changing definitions: SOEs include those that have listed on national or foreign stock exchanges but still have major government participation.) Desire to proclaim a BC is more a characteristic of Western than of Chinese economists.

The second is that there are different forms of market economy, and it is far from obvious that the only way, let alone the right way, to define a market economy is by the absence of the state. This is shown most clearly by the fact that many countries have developed an anti-monopoly (anti-trust) policy. If the maintenance of vigorous competition is dependent upon state action, and one regards a market economy as characterized by competition, than a market economy depends on state action. Of course, it is state action of a particular kind, and does not suggest that all state actions (such as nationalization or the institution of an industrial policy) are to be welcomed. The point is that one cannot judge a market-oriented policy by the test that was often used in the aftermath of the crisis, the minimization of the role of the state.

Four, maybe five, forms of market liberalization were included in my statement of the WC. The first is financial liberalization. In the light of subsequent history, it is quite clear that a liberalization of the financial system needs to be accompanied by adequate prudential supervision. Without this, there is a serious danger of the financial system being abused as a conduit for transferring wealth to the particular individuals who control the financial institutions. Provided this is done, the logic of financial liberalization is that investment decisions are best made on a decentralized basis by individual credit managers considering whether the prospective risk/return characteristics of particular investment projects appear sufficiently attractive to merit support. Presumably there are those who do not accept this logic and envision countervailing advantages in investment decisions being made centrally by 'the planners', which would justify opposition to this element of the WC.

The second element of market liberalization included in the WC is trade liberalization. Opponents of liberalization have often pointed out that most presently developed countries went through a phase of protecting their infant industries when they were developing, and therefore accuse of hypocrisy those who argue that presently developing countries should liberalize trade. There are several answers to this critique. First, past levels of protection were modest compared to the barriers that many hopefully developing countries erected in the post-war period. Second, it may be that protection was a bow to sectional interests that impeded overall development in the now-developed countries, rather than the boon to development that is portrayed. It is certainly not true that every presently developed country embraced protection at some stage: Hong Kong provides the most vivid counter-example. Third, while it is difficult to refute the argument that some protection of infant industries may help to establish new industries, it is easy to point to examples of industries that have failed to grow up and continued to need protection for many years.

One should also note that the WC is to be judged as a whole rather than by its independent parts. It is absurd to blame Argentina's trade liberalization for its economic collapse and ignore Argentina's failure to maintain a competitive exchange rate; trade liberalization only makes sense if there are thriving export industries into which the resources displaced from import-competing industries can flow.

The third policy favoured by the WC that furthers market liberalization is privatization. China showed no hurry to privatize, and many of the remaining state industries proved useful in one capacity that had largely been overlooked during the long period of world prosperity that preceded the world crisis. Specifically, they provided a direct means of rapidly injecting additional demand into the economy at the start of the recession, which enabled China to recover from the world recession far more quickly than other countries. Small companies and private individuals also benefited from the rapid credit expansion by the state-owned banks, but the majority of the additional spending was done by SOEs.

It is, however, wrong to regard this as the only factor at stake in choosing the size of the state sector. Most analyses, including comparisons of the performance of various sectors in China, favour privately owned over state-owned companies. For example, the study by the World Bank and the Development Research Centre of China's State Council[10] calculated the return on equity in state and private companies over the years 1998–2009 and showed that the return was always greater in private enterprises, approaching being double by 2009. Similarly, the National Bureau of Statistics has found the return on equity was always greater in the private sector, and was most recently over 14% (versus under 6% for the state sector). Despite this, privatization probably heads the list of the unpopular elements of the WC. One reason for this is without much doubt the manner in which privatization has often been undertaken: corruptly, so as to channel rents to cronies. Clearly privatization needs to be handled transparently and in a manner that can be expected to have no first order effects on income distribution, and this should have been added to the WC to have any hope of producing a statement of consensus views.

The fourth element of the WC that was intended to promote a market economy was deregulation. I was careful to specify that by this I meant the abolition of restrictions on entry and exit; I did not make the mistake of calling for the wholesale abolition of regulations intended to promote such causes as consumer safety, financial probity, worker welfare and environmental sustainability. The model was the spate of deregulation in the USA of things like airlines and trucking that had been started by the Carter Administration. Most countries, both developed and developing, maintain quite unnecessarily many restrictions on entry to certain industries, including the liberal professions.

The final element of the WC that has often been taken to be pro-market was the furthering of property rights, with the emphasis on extending these to the informal sector reflecting specifically (though not exclusively) Latin America. Secure property rights are usually reckoned to be of fundamental importance to growth in a market economy, since no one has an incentive to take care of the future unless they expect to be the major beneficiary. Dani Rodrik has often remarked on the paradox of China's fast growth rate in view of its dubious property rights.

I never claimed that the WC contained all the elements needed for fast growth. If one asks what the East Asian countries that enjoyed fast growth had in common, the answer is a demographic transition; competitive exchange rates; good education; high savings; and macroeconomic stability. If one excludes Hong Kong, one can add an active state role, typically taking the form of an industrial policy. Demographic factors are exogenous. A competitive exchange rate was applauded (explicitly) in the WC. Education made it only parenthetically, in point 2, but there would seem no contradiction. High savings were not mentioned at all, because this was not perceived as an obstacle to Latin American countries escaping from the debt crisis in 1989, but it is difficult to envisage a coherent objection. Macro stability was certainly emphasized by the WC. In any event, the element on which opponents of the WC have seized (notwithstanding the embarrassment of Hong Kong, which was simply declared a city-state and therefore irrelevant) is industrial policy.

A lot seems to hang on exactly what is understood by 'industrial policy'. If one interprets it in the traditional sense of 'picking winners', there is little reason to think that the state is particularly good at it, and the serious counter-objection that investment projects should be decided by those who stand to win or lose, depending on the outcome. However, if it is interpreted in the sense that Dani Rodrik[11] does, of government recognizing that it has a responsibility for compensating firms for the main external effects to which they are subject (i.e. for internalizing externalities), then only a rabid believer in the popular version of the WC would be likely to object.

Authoritarianism

A conspicuous feature of Chinese policy is the hostility evident to any sort of democratic ideal. Despite the recent revelations about the wealth accumulated by some of the leaders, it is not clear that the Chinese leadership wants to hang on to power for the sake of material advantages, in which case one is faced by the conundrum of explaining just why they oppose democracy. One possible motivation is the fear that populists would win a democratic election, which has been known to happen in the West. Another possible explanation is a genuine belief that democracy is a Western rather than a universal value, coupled with a belief that it is their mission to oppose all things Western. Whatever the explanation, it is a fact that they act in an authoritarian way.

Not only do they refuse to countenance democracy at home, but they always oppose efforts to use the international organizations to spread any sort of democratic (or, for that matter, human rights) notions. This is done in the name of national sovereignty, which means that it is often popular with the public of the affected state as well as (naturally) with their rulers.

The WC contained no reference to democracy either, essentially taking the view that recovery from the debt crisis was possible whatever the political system (both in a newly restored democracy like Brazil and in a country like Mexico, which was still an autocracy in 1989). I am firmly convinced that this is right for reasons that I explain[12] based on Doucouliagos and Ulubaşoğlu:[13] that there is no relation (or only a very weak relation) from the form of government to the rapidity of growth. Admittedly, there are some economists who argue that growth is dependent up: on having 'inclusive' institutions.[14] Now inclusive institutions are not quite the same as democratic institutions, and it is possible that China has developed an inclusive form of non-democracy. It would be interesting to know what this is. (This argument, which seems essential to their thesis, is nowhere made in Acemoglu and Robinson.[15])

Concluding remarks

There are two reasons why following the WC might not induce rapid growth, quite apart from the possibility embraced by the critics that the policies are basically wrong. The first is that it was not constructed for that purpose, and therefore it omits certain policies that are essential. The second is that it was designed to be an expression of consensus views, and if some essential policies were espoused only by a minority then they would not appear. In practice I would judge the first factor to be the overwhelmingly important one. The examination of the individual policies recommended by the WC did not reveal any to be inappropriate, let alone harmful.[16]

If growth is essentially replicable, i.e. if following the same policies achieves similar results (because growth is not heavily dependent on natural features of the economy), then one knows that adopting the BC will result in fast growth. The problem (since in practice one cannot exactly adopt all the policies) is in knowing which are the essential features of Beijing's policies that merit adoption. For example, I would doubt whether China's resistance to democracy or its friendship with dubious regimes has speeded growth, though it is possible (some would argue that democracy complicates the problem of acquiring the resources needed for investment projects). As regards the essential features responsible for China's fast growth, I would personally plump for the list offered earlier of the five or six commonalities between East Asian fast growers: demographic transition; competitive exchange rate; good education; high savings; macro stability; and perhaps a government that actively aims to internalize externalities. As argued earlier, there is some, but not much, overlap between these policies and those in the WC. This does not make the policies listed in the WC silly or inappropriate or harmful, it simply means that they need supplementing to have a list of the objectives that should be pursued by a country interested in achieving rapid growth. Then, as admitted at the beginning, there are also issues of priority and implementation that have to be addressed.

Notes

1 The author is indebted to Nicholas Lardy for helpful comments, but he is absolved of all responsibility for views expressed.
2 Dani Rodrik, *One Economics, Many Recipes*, Princeton University Press, Princeton, NJ, 2007.
3 Joshua Cooper Ramo, *The Beijing Consensus*, The Foreign Policy Centre, London, 2004.
4 He tells us that the Beijing Consensus consists of three theorems, but these are not sufficiently well defined to identify the Beijing Consensus.
5 John Williamson, 'Is the Beijing Consensus Now Dominant?' *Asia Policy*, 13 January 2012: 1–16.
6 Stefan Halper, *The Beijing Consensus: How China's Authoritarian Model Will Dominate the Twenty-first Century*, Basic Books, New York, 2010.
7 John Williamson, *Latin American Adjustment: How Much Has Happened?* Institute for International Economics, Washington, DC, 1990.
8 See, for example, World Bank and Development Research Center of China's State Council, *China 2030, Building a Modern Harmonious and Creative High-Income Society*, World Bank, Washington, DC, 2012.
9 It has argued that setting an exchange rate is an inherent feature of national sovereignty. Since an exchange rate is by definition the ratio permitting one currency to be converted into another, this is not true. In international monetary economics this is known as the 'n-1 problem', which was resolved by the passivity of the USA in the Bretton Woods system. China appears to have taken this passivity as an inherent fact of life rather than a policy choice.
10 World Bank and Development Research Center of China's State Council, *China 2030*, 212.
11 Dani Rodrik, *Normalizing Industrial Policy*, Working Paper No. 3, Commission on Growth and Development, Washington, DC, 2008.
12 John Williamson, 'Some Basic Disagreements on Development', paper presented at a Panel at the High-Level Knowledge Forum for Rethinking Development Policy held by KDI and the World Bank, Seoul, 2012.
13 Hristos Doucouliagos and Mehmet Ali Ulubaşoğlu, 'Democracy and Economic Growth: A Meta-Analysis', *American Journal of Political Science* 52(1), 2008: 61–83.
14 Daron Acemoglu and James Robinson, *Why Nations Fail: The Origins of Power, Prosperity, and Poverty*, Crown Business, New York, 2012.
15 Ibid.
16 I reached a similar conclusion when I was invited by the World Bank to consider the appropriateness of the Washington Consensus as a formula for development (see Williamson 2005).

Bibliography

Acemoglu, Daron and James Robinson (2012) *Why Nations Fail the Origins of Power, Prosperity, and Poverty*, Crown Business, New York.

Doucouliagos, Hristos and Mehmet Ali Ulubaşoğlu (2008) 'Democracy and Economic Growth: A Meta-Analysis', *American Journal of Political Science* 52(1), January: 61–83.

Halper, Stefan (2010) *The Beijing Consensus: How China's Authoritarian Model Will Dominate the Twenty-first Century*, Basic Books, New York.

Ramo, Joshua Cooper (2004) *The Beijing Consensus*, The Foreign Policy Centre, London.

Rodrik, Dani (2007) *One Economics, Many Recipes*, Princeton University Press, Princeton, NJ.

——(2008) *Normalizing Industrial Policy*, Commission on Growth and Development Working Paper No. 3.

Williamson, John (1990) *Latin American Adjustment: How Much Has Happened?* Institute for International Economics, Washington, DC.

——(2005) 'The Washington Consensus as Policy Prescription for Development', in T. Besley and N.R. Zagha (eds), *Development Challenges in the 1990s: Leading Policymakers Speak from Experience*, World Bank, Washington, DC.

——(2012a) 'Is the Beijing Consensus Now Dominant?' *Asia Policy* 13, January: 1–16.

——(2012b) 'Some Basic Disagreements on Development', paper presented at a Panel at the High-Level Knowledge Forum for Rethinking Development Policy held by KDI and the World Bank in Seoul.

World Bank and the Development Research Center of China's State Council (2012) *China 2030: Building a Modern, Harmonious, and Creative High-Income Society*, World Bank, Washington, DC.

Part IV

Diverse success stories

10

The Israeli economy

Paul Rivlin

Introduction

This chapter analyses current problems facing the Israeli economy and its historical development. In recent years Israel has experienced relatively fast economic growth, the remarkable development of high technology as well as financial stability. Despite these achievements the country suffers from poverty, income inequality, inadequate public services and infrastructure, as well as a lack of competition on local markets.

The development of the economy since independence

The achievements of the Israeli economy over the last 64 years have been immense. The population has grown from 600,000 Jews and 150,000 Arabs at independence in 1948 to an estimated six million Jews and 1.6 million Arabs at the end of 2012. In addition, about 400,000 people were classified as neither Jews nor Arabs. The gross domestic product (GDP) rose from just over US$6 billion in 1950 to an estimated $240 billion in 2012 (in 2012 prices and exchange rates). As a result, GDP per head increased from $4,560 to $30,000 during that period, a more than six-fold rise in real terms.[1]

Between 1948 and 2012 Israel absorbed over three million immigrants, one million of whom arrived in the 1990s. These developments took place despite the background of conflict that has existed since the state was created. The Middle East conflict has resulted in numerous wars, the isolation of Israel from its neighbours and economic boycotts against it, and the civilian population has suffered thousands of casualties as a result of terrorist attacks. Furthermore, Israel had few natural resources until the recent discoveries of gas reserves in its territorial waters in the East Mediterranean.

When Israel was founded, it had both an egalitarian social ethos and relatively equal distribution of income. The political life of the state was dominated by the Labour Party and its mainly left-wing allies. Labour Zionists came to Palestine from Europe in the pre-state period in order to create a new type of Jewish society and a new type of Jew. They aspired to return to manual labour, particularly on the land, and to change both the Jewish psyche and society by building a socialist economy in which people would be self-reliant and value manual work, in contrast to the experience of the diaspora. In this sense their mission was revolutionary. Unlike agriculture and industry, the services sector was considered parasitic and intellectuals were viewed suspiciously by Labour leaders. The Socialist Zionists initially sought fraternal relations with Arab workers and peasants and wanted to include them in the labour union federation, called the Histadrut, but opposed their employment by Jewish capitalists at lower wages than Jews would take. In the 1920s, as conflict between Jews and Arabs increased, the Labour movement created the Hagana, a defence force that became the basis of the Israeli army in 1948.

The effects of the Holocaust in Europe and the cost of the War of Independence (in which 1% of the Jewish population was killed), were the background to a major effort of national renewal. The effects of war and mass immigration stretched resources to the hilt and the government implemented policies of austerity, centralized control including rationing. While most of the population had a low standard of living, there was, for many, a sense of mission. Following independence, the most significant changes were the welding of military groups into the Israel Defence Forces, the introduction of state education systems, and the government's increased responsibility for social welfare, employment and attempts to absorb immigrants.

After independence, events gradually weakened the ideology of the ruling Labour movement. In the 1950s many unskilled Jews from North Africa and the Middle East immigrated, and they were largely employed in low-status positions. They were often sent to development towns on the periphery of the country, where basic industries were set up to employ them within the policy framework of import substitution. These industries were not always established on an economic basis, and the immigrant workers were employed on low wages. With the education of the younger generation, productivity and real wages rose, but immigrants from the Middle East and North Africa largely failed to take leading positions in the Labour-run economy and the Histadrut.

Attempts to minimize Arab employment in the Jewish economy continued until the early 1950s. The aim was to maintain employment and wages for the large number of largely unskilled Jewish immigrants. Gradually this broke down, and Israeli Arabs started to work in Jewish agriculture and in particular in construction. These patterns were reinforced after 1967, when Israel gained control of the West Bank and Gaza, with its Palestinian population that numbered one million. Within a few years, Arabs from these areas began to supplant Israeli Arabs and Jews of Middle Eastern and North African origin in low-status occupations such as construction work. The latter thus moved up the ladder in terms of their work status, gaining jobs in the services and public sectors.

Since the 1960s there has been a reversal of the Jewish work ethic as enunciated by the Socialist Zionists. The services sector grew; Israeli Arabs, Palestinians and then other foreign workers were employed in the manual jobs that Jews did not want. The idea that manual labour would contribute to the redemption of the Jewish people also came into conflict with the desire, and the need, for higher education. In a country lacking raw materials and fuel deposits, it was realized that the labour force was virtually the only economic resource. Increasing skill levels would therefore make an important contribution to economic development. Investment in education and training increased, which reduced the prestige of agriculture, construction and other sectors reliant on manual labour. Government, with its large bureaucracy, became a growing source of employment in the services sector, while inflation led to the growth of financial services, especially banking. These factors reinforced the movement away from manual and industrial employment.

The waves of immigration that followed independence were not self-financing and the costs of absorbing them were huge. Although Israel achieved independence and survived the invasion by neighbouring Arab states in 1948, the conflict imposed major losses of life and other costs.

The government's main task was to obtain sources of capital to finance investment so that the economy could grow and provide employment. This was not an easy task given Israel's isolation and perilous strategic position in the Middle East. However, it was achieved with the aid of the international Jewish community, German reparations and some assistance from the US government. These sources of finance were used to develop local industry that provided employment for immigrants and supplied the basic needs of the population. Economic policy was very pragmatic: Labour governments relied on the private sector and even on foreign entrepreneurs to develop industries based on import substitution. These policies were very successful in achieving growth: between 1950 and 1965 Israel's national income rose by more than five-fold in real terms, and national income per head rose 2.5 times. By the 1960s, when industries began to experience saturated local markets, a free trade agreement was negotiated with the European Economic Community that gradually changed Israel into an export-led economy. This agreement can be seen as a turning point, moving the economy towards a liberal international trade system that took 30 years to implement.

The balance of payments remained precarious for the first 50 years of Israel's history and whenever the current deficit reached a level that was hard to finance, the government was forced to squeeze the economy and devalue the currency, thus slowing the rate of growth and reducing imports. In the first decade of the 21st century this constraint ended and Israel began to experience surpluses on the current account of the balance of payments, net inflows of capital and an appreciating exchange rate together with economic growth. This was a huge transformation that has enabled the economy to survive the recent international recession better than much of developed world. Structural change, most notably the development of high technology resulted in large increases of both exports and foreign investment in Israel. The development of this sector was closely related to Israel's efforts to increase self-reliance in military technology and the success of economic stabilization and liberalization policies followed since the mid-1980s.

Given Israel's isolation from the rest of the Middle East and the costs of defence and immigrant absorption, what made rapid economic growth possible? The short answer is that Israel began its independent history with a highly educated and motivated population.[2] Hundreds of thousands of immigrants began to arrive in the country as soon as independence was declared and immigration continued throughout the war that lasted until armistice agreements were signed with neighbouring Arab states in 1949. This was achieved at considerable cost but once the war ended Israel began to concentrate on economic development. Economic policy was highly pragmatic and capital was obtained from abroad enabling vital investments in industry and the infrastructure to be made. In addition, investment in education was maintained, thus increasing the level of human capital.

The 1960s also saw a strengthening of industrial policy as a result of the French arms embargo. Israel had relied on French armaments from the 1950s until the Six-Day War of 1967 when President Charles de Gaulle banned further sales. This provided a strong impetus to the development of the arms industry in Israel, which had its origins in the pre-state period. Decisions to make Israel's army one of 'quality' to match Arab numerical superiority were to have profound consequences for industrial development and economic growth. The USA recognized Israel as a regional power and extended military and economic assistance. Military assistance meant that Israel obtained US technology and this was absorbed 'hands on' with Israeli experts visiting the plants manufacturing the equipment they were buying, testing and even modifying it. This provided crucial opportunities for learning-by-doing and a web of connections between Israeli and US companies. Gradually, this spilled into civilian sectors, thus helping to stimulate the high-technology sector.

The dramatic victory in the Six-Day War gave the economy a huge boost that lasted until the Yom Kippur War of 1973. The latter was, however, followed by much slower growth compounded by large budget deficits, accelerating inflation—which reached an annual rate of nearly 500% in the first half of 1985—balance of payments and foreign debt problems. Following mismanagement on a grand scale, hyperinflation was only brought under control with a radical stabilization programme introduced in July 1985, by which time the economy had suffered what became known as a decade of lost growth. The stabilization of 1985 was accompanied by the gradual liberalization of many sectors of the economy. This provided the basis for fast economic growth when the massive immigration from the USSR began in late 1989. Economic relations with the USA developed as a result of the free trade agreement signed between the two countries in 1985 covering industry, agriculture and services. In the 1990s one million immigrants arrived, largely from the former USSR. They helped to transform the economy by expanding the local market and thus creating economies of scale. The availability of US loan guarantees encouraged an inflow of capital to balance that of labour and thus provide the basis for economic growth. The more liberal economic order encouraged foreign investment, especially in high technology.

The relationship between stabilization and liberalization is an important issue. The stabilization programme reduced the role of the state and introduced a new, more liberalized economic order. The transformation of the fiscal position that resulted from the 1985 programme is shown in Table 10.1. Between 1980 and 2010 the reduction in public sector spending was equivalent to 32% of GDP. Spending on domestic interest payments, subsidies and domestic defence (i.e. defence spending within Israel) fell by just over 15%. Other spending, mainly on civilian services and public sector investment fell by 17%. The results of this transformation included a decline in the budget deficit, the internal debt and a long-term squeeze on social and infrastructure spending. The first two effects were, of course, beneficial and were accompanied by the deceleration of inflation and improvements in the external accounts (see below). The latter had negative effects on the social economy and contributed to widening income gaps and inadequate public services for the population as a whole.

In the early 1990s foreign trade and capital markets were liberalized. During the years 1996–2003 economic growth decelerated to an annual average rate of only 2.7%, which, when allowing for population growth, meant that GDP per head was the same in 2003 as it had been in 1997. This therefore has been called the 'second lost decade'. The main reason for the lack of growth was the negative impact of monetary and fiscal policies designed to reduce inflation still further, the collapse of the high-tech boom in 2001 and the second *Intifada*, or Palestinian revolt. In 2004 the tax on income from investments at home and abroad was equalized. This encouraged Israelis to find higher returns abroad and contributed to a rise in investment income. The boom—centred on the high-technology sector—encouraged a huge increase in foreign

Table 10.1 Fiscal indicators, 1980–2010 (% of GDP)

	Total public spending	Domestic interest payments	Subsidies	Domestic defence spending	Total public revenues
1980	74.0	7.5	8.4	13.5	62.0
1990	57.7	6.6	2.8	10.1	52.9
2000	52.6	4.4	0.8	6.7	49.9
2010	42.0	2.9	0.7	5.1	40.7

Source: Bank of Israel, Annual Reports 2001 and 2011

investment and was largely export-based. This pushed the balance of payments current account into surplus and as a result the foreign debt became negative, meaning that Israel accumulated net foreign assets. The stream of income on these assets helped to strengthen the current account of the balance of payments. By 2004 economic growth had recovered and continued at a rapid rate until 2008. In 2005 the Bank of Israel abolished the 'exchange rate path' that it used to prevent excessive changes, but from 2009 it bought billions of dollars to limit the rise in the shekel against the dollar and other foreign currencies. In 2010 Israel joined the Organisation for Economic Co-operation and Development (OECD).

The Israeli economy in the 21st century is characterized by several outstanding features. The first is the high level of defence spending. The second is financial strength demonstrated in and since the international financial crisis of 2008–09. This was manifested in the balance of payments, the government budget and the banking system, and reflects the cautious way that the economy has been managed since 1985. Behind this financial strength has been the rapid development of high-technology exports and associated foreign direct investment in Israel. There are serious problems in the labour market due to the low participation rates of Arab women and Jewish ultra-orthodox men. Finally, Israel suffers from poverty and serious problems of inequality.

Defence

One of the most important elements of Israel's economy is the very high level of defence expenditure. Israel spends a greater share of its national resources on defence than most Western countries and has done so for more than 20 years. In 2010 defence expenditure equalled 6.3% of GDP in Israel, 4% in the USA and 2.6% in the UK.[3] These costs were not always so high: the era of high volumes of defence spending in Israel began in the 1960s.

In 1950 Israel spent about $475 million on defence, equal to about 8.5% of GDP. In 1975 this had increased 35-fold in real terms to reach a peak of about $16.6 billion or 30% of GDP. By 2012 it had fallen to about $14 billion, about 8% of GDP (these figures are all in 2012 prices). Allocations for defence as a share of GDP fell afterwards but they remain very large in absolute terms. In recent years defence spending has risen in real terms. In 2011 the defence budget amounted to nearly $13 billion, which accounted for 14.3% of government spending. This included about $3 billion of US aid, but does not include extra-budgetary allocations.

For Israel defence is both a burden and a service. If a country is threatened and decides to defend itself then defence is a service that it chooses to acquire, like education or health. It ensures that life can continue and in this respect defence is like other publicly provided services. If defence is viewed as an expenditure that results from the pressures of the military-industrial complex or because of mistaken political policies, then it may be regarded as a burden. The funds spent on defence could go to improving civilian services or reducing taxation. The allocation of resources to defence reduces the costs of insecurity but at the same time it reduces the volume of resources available to the civilian economy. Most Israelis agree that defence spending is necessary; however, most would also prefer the volume of this defence spending to be lower.

The Six-Day War of 1967 pushed up defence costs, as did the War of Attrition along the Suez Canal that followed it until 1970. Each war brought a rise in absolute levels of defence spending, and following the Yom Kippur War spending did not return to previous levels. The growing cost of military equipment and the need to increase the size of the armed forces to match those of the Arab countries led to an increase in defence spending. The peak in budgeted defence expenditure was reached between 1973 and 1975, when defence consumption reached crippling levels. In 1990 defence expenditure funded by domestic sources (excluding US military aid) was 58% higher in real terms than in 1970. During this period, national income had increased by 52%. Between 1970, a year of fighting along the Suez Canal, and 1990, a year in which the country experienced quiet along its borders, the burden had therefore increased.

From the mid-1980s purchases of equipment from Israeli companies were also partly funded by the USA, mainly for the development of the Lavi fighter by Israel Aircraft Industries (IAI). Funds received by the Israeli government were exchanged for local currency, which was then used to pay domestic companies for work on the Lavi. The dollars were sold by the government to other sectors in the economy, thus reducing its need to raise revenue by other means. In 1987 the Lavi project was cancelled as a result of US and domestic political and financial pressure. Hundreds of engineers were released from IAI and they became part of the backbone of the civilian high-technology sector.

Despite the decline since the 1970s, the defence budget still accounts for a larger share of GDP than in most countries, even after removing US military assistance from the budget. Not all defence costs are covered by the budget. Compulsory military service for men remains three years and for women two years, and the absence from the labour force of these tens of thousands of potential workers results in a significant loss of production. Conscripts are paid a nominal wage and therefore carry the costs of their service through their loss of earnings. The economy also loses their potential output in the civilian sector and this cost, which has been estimated at about 1.7% of GDP, has to be added to the budget in order to assess the full cost of defence. Other extra-budgetary costs include the construction and maintenance of shelters, storing fuel, guarding many civilian premises in the public and private sector, and even maintaining larger foreign exchange reserves than a country at peace would require.

On the beneficial side, the military has trained thousands of young people in high technology and has stimulated production in that sector. The government also released technology developed in the military for civilian use.

Financial strength

During the period 2008–12 the economy grew by an average annual rate of 3.3% compared with a global average of 2.9%. Government debt as a share of GDP declined from 78.4% to 74.0%.[4]

Israeli banks were in relatively good shape when the international financial crisis developed in 2008 and so the government did not have to engage in expensive rescue operations that have increased public sector debt in the USA and some major European countries. The very cautious financial policies implemented since 1985, the gradual liberalization of capital markets together with the rapid growth of high-tech industries have been the main factors behind this stability. Israeli financial institutions had very limited exposure to the financial instruments that collapsed on international markets. Israeli banks had very limited reliance on domestic and international financial markets as sources of funds. Banking supervision was strong: the Basel II framework was being implemented and banks raised their risk-weighted capital ratios. The most complex financial instruments such as those involving securitization were absent in Israel. Finally, foreign banks had very limited presence in domestic financial intermediation. On the other hand the increased integration of the economy in the international financial system, economic growth resulting in increased savings and business demand for capital and structural changes in the financial system all increased the effects of the international financial crisis on the Israel economy.[5]

Table 10.2 shows how the current account of the balance of payments and the foreign debt position were transformed in the late 1990s and early 2000s.

The Israeli economy

Table 10.2 Economic growth and financial stability, 1995–2011 (US$ billion, unless otherwise stated)

	GDP growth, annual average, %	Budget deficit/ GDP, %	Internal public debt/ GDP	Current account balance	Foreign direct investment in Israel	Net foreign assets, annual average
1995–2002	3.9	3.6	96.0	−2.7	2.7	−27.7
2003–11	4.2	3.0	84.5	4.2	7.5	3.1

Source: Central Bureau of Statistics, *Statistical Abstract of Israel*, 2012; Bank of Israel, *Annual Report*, 2011

High technology

The development of high technology has been Israel's success story: it has been the main source of economic growth in the last 20 years and there is much optimism about its future. One of the definitions of high technology used in Israel is the level of technological intensity, illustrated in Table 10.3. This classifies industries by the amount of capital equipment per worker and the age of the capital stock. The table shows that as a result of a near 10-fold increase in high-technology exports, their share in total industrial exports rose from 30% in 1990 to 47% in 2011.

High technology includes office and computing equipment, electronic components, aircraft and electronic communication equipment, equipment for control and supervision, and pharmaceuticals. Medium high-technology industries are chemicals and petroleum refining, machinery and equipment, electronic equipment and electrical motors, transport equipment. Medium low-technology industries are mining and quarrying, rubber and plastics, non-metallic mineral products, basic metals, ships and boats, jewellery and silversmith articles. Low-technology industries are food products, beverages and tobacco, textiles, wearing apparel and leather, paper, printing and wood products.

As the high-technology sector developed in the 1990s, especially in telecommunications and computers, Israel's output and exports of these and related products expanded rapidly. Although the share of manufacturing industries in GDP declined, there was rapid structural change within that sector. Between 2000 and 2011 total industrial production rose by 31% while that of high-technology industries increased by 75%.

Some of the high-technology companies that were sold to large US corporations had relatively few employees and, as was customary, payments to employees included options to buy shares. As a result of the sale of these companies, a number of employees, some of whom had been in employment for only a few years or less, received millions of dollars in shares or cash.

Table 10.3 Manufactured exports by technology intensity, 1990–2011 (US$ million)

	Low technology	Medium-low technology	Medium-high technology	High technology	Total
1990	1,492	1,537	2,390	2,278	7,697
1995	1,823	2,542	3,388	4,549	12,302
2000	1,812	3,171	4,833	11,188	21,005
2005	2,087	4,751	6,962	11,767	25,566
2011	2,272	7,780	14,183	21,517	45,752

Source: Central Bureau of Statistics, *Statistical Abstract of Israel*, 2011

The owners or founders of these companies did even better. This had effects on the distribution of wealth and income and thus on consumption patterns.

Employment as well as wages rose much faster in high technology than elsewhere in the economy. As the high technology labour force was more skilled than those in other sectors, it was better paid, partly because the labour market for highly skilled workers is international. In periods of fast growth, there were shortages of skilled labour and high-technology firms bid workers away from each other by increasing wages. This further increased average pay in the sector and pushed it above levels paid elsewhere in the economy.

There are several explanations for Israel's technological success. The first is that it was a response to adversity. The country has experienced wars and boycotts since its foundation and has had to develop technology in order to survive. The defence relationship with the USA has given Israel access to technology from the most sophisticated economy in the world and close business links have developed as a result. Israel has a very informal culture—the Zionist socialists rebelled against the formality of life in Europe—and some say that its management culture in both the civilian and military sectors are influenced by this.[6] The second is that emphasis has been put on education, including scientific and technological training at the higher level.

The high-technology sector is more globalized than any other in the economy, had its origins in import substitution applied to the defence sector and to government involvement more generally. It was closely connected to developments in Israeli defence policy and in government investments made in academic research and other research. In 1948 Israel Defence Forces (IDF) established the Science Corps, charged with developing their weapons and equipment. In the 1950s military industry developed to provide for the country's needs for armaments and technologies that it could not obtain from abroad. Israel had the best institutions of education and scientific research in the Middle East: two technological universities: the Technion, the Israel Institute of Technology in Haifa (founded in 1924); and the post-graduate Weizmann Institute of Science in Rehovot (founded in 1933). In addition, Israel now has five universities and numerous degree-awarding colleges. In the early 1960s Israel set up two nuclear research plants.

By the 1960s most research and development (R&D) was carried out in the public sector. Since then, the private sector has played an increasing role. Output was concentrated first in information and communications technology (ICT) hardware and then in ICT software. The aim of R&D was to create new products and the government saw the private sector as the main agent for carrying out these activities. It confined itself to providing funds, encouraging the diffusion of know-how from the military and the universities to the private sector.

One of the most important factors in enabling Israel to develop high technology was the willingness to experiment. In a country that has always been at war and has experienced many years of shortages, the need to devise ad hoc solutions has become second nature. This was particularly true in the IDF and the military industries and has permeated all sectors of the economy. The 'hands-on' approach is the essence of learning by doing, ultimately a significant source of economic growth.[7] Israel imported military and civilian equipment but seldom bought 'turnkey' projects. The aim was always to learn how to operate equipment, to train Israeli personnel and often to improve what was acquired abroad, to adapt it to local conditions and needs.

Israel has achieved a comparative advantage in R&D based on development in defence and academic institutions. The government's focus on the enhancement of technological cutting-edge capabilities enabled firms to develop new products. This made it possible for Israeli IT companies to supply the rest of the world initially in hardware and then in software. The government encouraged public–private sector co-operation and links with foreign firms when appropriate. All this was made possible by investments in education, the encouragement of R&D in the defence sector and policies that gave high priority to science and technology. This was partly facilitated by the informal but close links that existed between key political leaders and the scientific and technological elite. Another important step taken by the government was the creation in 1968 of the Office of the Chief Scientist of the Ministry of Trade and Industry, which was given a budget to invest in R& d in the public and private sectors.

Until the late 1960s support was confined to national R&D laboratories, academic R&D, defence-related R&D and agricultural research. Between 1969 and 1987, as a result of the new impetus, industrial R&D expenditure grew at 14% per year. The next major development was the passing in 1985 of the Law for the Encouragement of Industrial Research and Development. This has been the main piece of legislation that has defined government policy towards industrial R&D ever since. The aims of the law were to develop science-based, export-oriented industries, which would promote employment and improve the balance of payments. In order to do this, the legislation was designed to provide the financial means to expand and exploit the country's technological and scientific infrastructure, including its high-skilled human resources. In recent years government funding has declined from a peak of $520 million in 2001 to $400 million in 2011.[8]

In 1976 the Israeli and US governments set up Bi-national Industrial Research and Development (BIRD), with an endowment of $110 million that reached $205 million in 2007. Its aim was to encourage co-operation between Israeli and US companies jointly to develop and market new products.[9] Over time it brought many Israeli and US firms together: by 2011 it had approved 845 projects, provided $295 million in grants and its investments had yielded $4.5 billion in sales.[10] Since the 1990s an increasing volume of funds has been raised from venture capitalists in the USA and Israel. This was made possible by the maturity of the high-technology industry, the stability of the economy, the globalization of international capital markets, and government programmes directed towards the venture capital sector.

The labour market

While the economy has demonstrated financial strength, social gaps have widened. The development of high technology has increased the returns to education. This has resulted in the creation of a well-paid sector of skilled workers. The fact that there was international demand for their skills (many Israelis are employed in the USA) meant that wages in Israeli high technology were pushed up. In contrast, those with low skill levels were subject to competitive pressures working in the opposite direction. Until the 1990s they faced competition from Palestinian workers and then from workers brought in from the Far East. These labour market pressures are, of course, not unique to Israel, but when combined with other factors prevailing in the labour market, their effect has been severe.

Table 10.4 shows some of the main trends in the labour market between 2001 and 2011. The number of employees rose by 30% but the number employed in the public sector increased by 60%, compared to 34% in the business sector. The large increase in public-sector employment was one indicator suggesting that the liberalization of the economy was limited. About 10% of the labour force was foreign (Palestinian and from other countries) but this is an underestimation as there are many thousands of unregistered, illegal workers in Israel. One official estimate is that in 2012 there were 95,000 people who had overstayed their tourist visa plus 55,000 illegal migrants and asylum seekers. These were the known ones; many believe that the number is much higher.[11]

Labour force participation rates rose even among the two groups with very low averages, Arab women and Jewish ultra-orthodox men. Despite that, their rates remained very low.

Table 10.4 Labour market indicators, 2001–11 (million)

	2001	2011
Working-age population	4.605	5.585
Employees	2.532	3.313
of whom: Israelis	2.270	3.025
Palestinians	0.014	0.066
Other foreign workers	0.248	0.222
Public sector	0.574	0.920
Business sector	1.769	2.387
Unemployed	0.193	0.181
Total rate of labour force participation (%)	66.6	71.9
Participation rate of Arab women (%)	19.6	26.8
Participation rate of Jewish ultra-orthodox men	38.9	45.6

Source: Bank of Israel, *Annual Report*, 2001, 2011

The labour market is also characterized by low participation rates among two large minority groups. In 2011 the total participation rate was 57.5%, that among men 62.4% and among women 52.7%. That among Arab women was 26.1% and among ultra-orthodox men 45.6%. Although the participation rates of these two groups have increased in the last decade (from 19.6% and 38.9%, respectively, in 2001), they remain very low. The results include a loss of output in the economy and low earnings among families in the Arab and ultra-orthodox communities. These are also major causes of income inequality and poverty.[12]

Participation rates are lower than in the OECD and there is a link between education levels and participation rates: the lower the level of education, the lower the participation rate. The male employment rate has remained very low, at 60.7% in 2001 and 62.3% in 2011, while the female rate increased from 48.2% to 50.6% during the same period. Not only were participation rates correlated with education, but so were wage rates.[13] As many in the Arab and Jewish ultra-orthodox communities did not gain school leaving certificates (or attained them at a low level), so low earnings were concentrated among those who went to work.

Income distribution and poverty

Between 2002 and 2011 the Gini coefficient of income distribution before taxes and transfers fell by 0.4% to 0.4973. The Gini coefficient is defined as a ratio with a range from 0 and 1 (or 0% to 100%). A low Gini coefficient indicates more equal income or wealth distribution, with zero corresponding to perfect equality while higher Gini coefficients indicate more unequal distribution, with 1 corresponding to perfect inequality. These figures suggest that the factors causing inequality have weakened in recent years. The index for income after taxes and transfers increased from 0.3675 to 0.3794. In 2002 government measures, in the form of taxes and benefits, to redistribute income reduced the gap between net and gross income by 31.5%, while in 2011 they reduced the gap by 23.7%.[14]

In Israel the poor are officially defined using a relative poverty measure, as those having an income below 50% of the median income. In the OECD the rate is 60%, although figures for 50% and 70% are also reported. The standard of living of a household depends not only on its income but also on its needs determined by its size. The additional income needed by each additional person in a family declines as family size increases because there are economies of scale. To measure poverty an equivalence scale is constructed to calculate what each member of

The Israeli economy

a family needs. The economies of scale assumed abroad are much greater than those in Israel, which is one reason that more people are recorded as poor in the latter.

In 2011 1.84 million people, or 24.8% of the population, lived in poverty after allowing for direct taxation and subsidies. In 2002 the share was 21%. This includes Arabs living in East Jerusalem, many of whom have Israeli resident status and are thus registered with the Israeli National Insurance Institute. The rate of poverty is one of the highest in the OECD and there are several reasons for this. The first is low earnings: many Israelis in full-time employment earn less than the official minimum wage and there are even public sector employees who are entitled to income supplements because they earn less than the official minimum. The low-skilled labour force grew with the import of Palestinian and then other foreign workers. This helped to moderate wage rises for the lower paid. Furthermore, the availability of low-paid jobs in the manufacturing sector has been reduced by the effects of globalization. The resulting unemployment of Israelis (unemployed Palestinians and other foreigners leave the Israeli labour market when demand for labour falls) also puts downward pressure on wages. The second is a set of factors special to Israel, associated with two minority groups: the Arabs and the Jewish ultra-orthodox communities. The Arab community, which accounts for about 20% of the population, suffers very high levels of poverty largely because of low earnings and the low participation of women in the labour force. Low earnings reflect both lower skill levels than the average for the population and also discrimination. Arabs are not welcome in the higher-paying high-technology sector even when they have the requisite skills, although this is gradually changing. Arab women tended to work in the home for traditional reasons but those who want to enter the labour market face discrimination. Large family size lowers income per capita and reduces the resources that can be invested in each child. In 2011 56.6% of Arabs were classified as living in poverty.

In the ultra-orthodox, or Haredi community, which accounts for about 8% of the population, the reluctance or even refusal of many parents to provide their children with basic studies in English, maths, science and citizenship means that they cannot obtain a school leaving certificate. This severely limits their future earning ability and helps to confine them and their families to poverty which is also worsened by very large average family size. The preference of many ultra-orthodox men for state-subsidized religious study further limits income and places a large burden on the state budget. As a result, this section of the population, which is growing faster than any other, produces less and relies on the rest of society for subsidies. In 2011 55% of the ultra-orthodox population was poor. One of the most worrying factors about this is that the younger generation inherits poverty as a result of the inadequate ultra-orthodox education system that concentrates on religious studies and does not provide the adequate basic education that is the pro-condition for participation in the labour market at anything other than a very low skill level. Both the Arab and ultra-orthodox communities have larger-than-average families and as a result poverty among children increased from almost 27% in 2002 to 35.5% in 2011.[15]

Economic concentration

The Israeli economy suffers from a lack of competition in key internal markets including food, cement, banking, ports, water, automobiles, public transport, pension provision and fuels. In all these markets there are few producers or suppliers and in some of them there are severe restrictions on imports. The food industry benefits from high taxes and other restrictions on imports and from an exemption to laws limiting monopoly practices. These are in turn designed to maintain agricultural production and processing.[16] This is in contrast to other sectors of the economy, such as textiles, that were subject to competition from cheap sources of imports from the early 1990s. High food costs have serious welfare and distributional consequences.

The most blatant private sector monopoly is that of cement: there is only one producer in Israel and that company accounts for 85% of the market. Imports account for 15% and there is only one licensed importer. A government report noted that there are monopolies in port and transport facilities for imported cement and that reform would require more producers as well as changes in the ports and transport system.[17] In addition to monopolies and cartels in many markets the ownership of much of the economy is very concentrated, with owners in one sector having significant holdings in other sectors of the economy. One of the most important studies of concentration in the Israeli economy found that between 1995 and 2006, of the 650 public companies traded on the Tel-Aviv Stock Exchange (TASE), 20 major business groups controlled about 160 listed companies and close to half of total stock market capitalization. The 10 largest groups controlled 30% of market capitalization, among the largest shares in the Western world. These groups were family-controlled and highly diversified across different industries, and about 80% of all group-affiliated companies belong to business pyramids. Business groups were dominant especially in the financial sector, where half of banks and insurance companies were group-affiliated.[18]

More recent research by an official commission found that concentration had increased in recent years. In 2011 24 business groups controlled some 136 companies of the 569 listed on TASE. This 23% of companies accounted for 68% of capitalization (with the exception of one large company, Teva, that is not associated with any other business group and which accounted for 24% of capitalization). The 10 largest business groups account for 41% of total capitalization with assets. The five largest business groups have assets equal to almost 63% of GDP, and the largest business group has assets equal to19.4% of GDP.[19]

One example of this diversified ownership structure was the Discount Investment Corporation which controls 48% of a supermarket chain (which has 21% of the market), 44% of the shares in a mobile phone company (which has 35% of the market), 75% of the cement monopoly, 65% of a national newspaper, 59% of the country's main paper manufacturer and 55% of a leading insurance company.[20]

Concentration does not encourage efficiency and the extent of concentration, therefore, has a negative impact on the economy.[21] Much is in the form of pyramid ownership in which minority but controlling shareholdings are acquired in one company and through it in others.

Concentration also exists in the public sector. The government in effect owns or controls over 90% of the land in Israel; there is one generator and distributor of electricity and most international flights use one airport. The sea ports are state owned and competition between them is very limited. The railways are a natural monopoly but bus services remain dominated by two co-operatives, despite liberalization. Workers' committees (labour unions) often opposed reforms that would introduce or increase competition and threaten the level of employment and wages of their members.[22] As a result of the political and economic strength of these workers' committees, reforms have often been delayed.[23] The strength of these workers' committees is demonstrated by the fact that management in the ports cannot deal with rampant nepotism, which affects the recruitment of new workers.[24]

The cost of West Bank settlements

The Israeli economy has been severely burdened by costs of construction, maintenance and guarding of settlements in the West Bank. What were the costs? If the settlements that now accommodate hundreds of thousands of people had not been built, then alternatives inside the

The Israeli economy

1967 border would have had to be constructed. They would either have been new settlements or expansions to existing ones, or both. In either case, they could have reinforced the development of existing peripheral areas such as the Galilee or, even more so, the Negev, which is under-populated and underdeveloped, helping to achieve economies of scale. These are the first costs of the West Bank settlements that should be calculated, but they have never been carried out as they involve asking very complex, hypothetical questions. The Ministry of Finance has noted that the economy of the Negev will benefit from the current construction of a group of new military bases and a town for military personnel and their families. This could have been replicated many times over if resources allocated to settlement building had gone there or to the Galilee instead.[25]

The second set of costs is related to security. The location of the settlements in the Palestinian areas, sometimes near or even in populated areas, gave rise to high security costs that would not have arisen if they had been built inside the green line. This is not to deny that the latter would require some security.

The third cost is that of dismantling settlements. Israel abandoned the settlements it built in the Sinai when the area was returned to Egypt in the early 1980s, including the small town of Yamit that had been built on the North Sinai coast. In 2006 Israel left the Gaza Strip and closed four settlements in the northern part of the West Bank. Thousands of settlers were rehoused and compensated. The total cost of the evacuation of Israeli settlements in Gaza has been estimated at about $2.5 billion, over 1% of GDP, spread over a two- to three-year period.[26] This figure is a transfer cost imposed by the government on taxpayers and is not necessarily equal to the loss to the economy. The economic loss is measured by the effect of higher taxation (or deficit financing) that the government imposes. If it creates disincentives to work then it will result in a loss of output; if it does not, it may lead to a loss of welfare for taxpayers but not necessarily to a commensurate loss for the economy. Although the government budget has nearly been balanced in recent years, this has not been a costless process: many painful cuts have been made in public spending and the internal debt remains high. Offsetting the costs of relocation by increasing taxation helps to maintain the budget in balance but indirect, negative effects on growth mean that national income is smaller than it otherwise would be and so the budget deficit/GDP ratio will also be higher. No estimates have been made of these effects in Israel. A peace treaty with the Palestinians will require abandoning large numbers, if not all, of the settlements, with thousands of homes and other facilities in which billions of shekels have been invested.

Between 1967 and 2003 Israel spent over $15 billion on the settlements, or $480 million a year, excluding security costs (in 2012 prices). Security costs have been calculated at between 1.6 billion and 2.7 billion shekels a year, depending on the level of violence. If an average of $450 million a year is used, then the annual cost, including security, averaged $960 million, or nearly 0.4% of GDP in 2012. A rough calculation based on these figures suggests that between 1967 and 2012 Israel spent about $43 billion on West Bank settlements and security.[27]

There have been other negative effects of Israeli settlement building. First, they have had direct effects on Israel's foreign economic relations. The most obvious example was the unwillingness of President George Bush, Sr, to extend loan guarantees to Israel in 1991 owing to settlement building. With the election of a Labour-led government under Yitzhak Rabin in June 1992 and the announcement of a change in priorities away from spending on settlements, the USA agreed to provide loan guarantees. As the Israeli government continued to spend money on settlements, $1.4 billion was deducted from the volume of loan guarantees that were made available.

How far did Israel's settlement activity directly contribute to the conflict and how much did that cost? These are very controversial issues and one Israeli organization has tried to provide answers. It suggests that most of Israel's woes can be accounted for by the occupation of

199

the West Bank (and Gaza), together with the construction of settlements.[28] The implication that an Israeli withdrawal from the territories occupied in 1967 would bring peace is questionable, but this does not invalidate the view that occupation and settlement have exacted high costs.

The *additional* cost of the settlements—above what they would have cost if they had been built in Israel—has been estimated at $8 billion for the period 1979–2008, or about 0.3% of annual national income.[29] This does not allow for the fact that had the settlements been built in Israel (either as separate villages and towns or as extensions of existing ones) then economic development inside the green line, Israel's 1967 border, would have been enhanced.

Gas

Israel has an estimated 800 billion cubic metres of natural gas reserves in its territorial waters, part of the Levantine Basin of the East Mediterranean. In 2012 these reserves had an estimated current value of $240 billion. They are expected to play a major role in the economy in the near future by raising output and tax revenues, creating new business in infrastructure, processing and manufacturing, improving the country's energy balance, which has always heavily relied on imports, strengthening the balance of payments and possibly improving Israel's geopolitical position if it becomes a gas exporter.[30]

In 2013 gas production was expected to add 1% to the growth rate of national income, which is forecast at 3.8%. It is also forecast to reduce imports by 3%, or $2.5 billion. The effect will increase in the coming years as more gas is brought on stream.[31] The Israeli find is part of what the USA has estimated could be 3.4 trillion cubic metres of technically recoverable gas in the Levant basin.[32]

Conclusions

The strengthening of the economy while society has become weaker is a reversal or perceived reversal: for many years Israelis felt that their society was strong but their economy weak. That seems paradoxical given that between 1948 and 2012 Israel attracted just over three million immigrants, a very large number for a country whose population at the end of 2012 was eight million. In 1948 two-thirds of the population was born abroad; in 2012 one-third of the population comprised immigrants. The effects of immigration are central to Israel's economic history. Economic policy has been dominated by the search for capital that would permit the growth of employment and output, given the increase in the supply of labour made possible by immigration. During the last decade this has increasingly come from foreign investment, something that has transformed Israel's economy, especially the country's balance of payments.

Israel has also experienced a profound change from a state-led economy to a much more liberalized and globalized one. It has developed a consumer society based on the Western model in which the satisfaction of individual wants rather than collective needs is paramount. Public spending on social programmes has been reduced and the distribution of wealth has become more unequal.

Israel's very fast GDP and GDP/capita growth rates in the 1950s suggest that government intervention in the early stages of economic development can be beneficial. Since then it has moved broadly in the manner advocated by economists and has benefited in terms of economic growth and rising living standards. In the last 20 years wide gaps have opened in the distribution of income, wealth and educational achievement. Poverty has become chronic and deep. There is a risk that these problems may become endemic and threaten the future of the economy because they remove significant numbers of people from the labour market and result in poverty being passed down from one generation to the next. Israel will have to find ways to combine elements of equity with economic growth if it wants to avoid major domestic tension. Given the precariousness of its position in the Middle East, the need for internal cohesion is great, but as yet not fully recognized.

Notes

1 Central Bureau of Statistics, *Statistical Abstract of Israel*, Jerusalem, 2012, cbs.gov.il/reader/shnaton/templ_shnaton.html?num_tab=st02_02&CYear=2012; Central Bureau of Statistics, Press Release, Preliminary National Account Estimates for 2012, No. 360/2012, 31 December 2012, cbs.gov.il/reader/newhodaot/hodaa_template.html?hodaa=201208360; Central Bureau of Statistics, *Monthly Bulletin of Statistics*, December 2012, cbs.gov.il/www/yarhon/b1_h.htm.

2 Richard A. Easterlin, 'Israel's Development: Past Accomplishments and Future Problems', *The Quarterly Journal of Economics* 75(1), February 1961.

3 *The State Budget 2011–12* (Hebrew), mof.gov.il/BudgetSite/StateBudget/Budget2011_2012/Lists/20112012/Attachments/1/Budget2011_2012.pdf; Stockholm International Peace Research Institute (SIPRI), *Military Expenditure Database*, milexdata.sipri.org.

4 Bank of Israel Press Release, 'Research Department Staff Forecast for 2012–13', June 2012, www.bankisrael.gov.il/press/eng/120625/120625ghj.pdf; IMF, *World Economic Outlook*, October 2012, www.imf.org/external/pubs/ft/weo/2012/02/index.htm; Remarks by the Governor of the Bank of Israel at the Bank of Israel Research Departments annual seminar, 27 December 2012, www.boi.org.il/en/NewsAndPublications/LecturesSpeechesAndPresentations/Pages/neum261212-a.aspx.

5 Bank of Israel, *Annual Report 2008*, 13–14, www.boi.org.il/en/NewsAndPublications/RegularPublications/Pages/eng_doch08e.aspx.

6 Dan Senor and Saul Singer, *Start Up Nation: The Story of Israel's Economic Miracle*, The Hachette Book Group, New York, 2010, 67–83.

7 Kenneth J. Arrow, 'The Implications of Learning by Doing', *The Review of Economic Studies* 29(3), 1962: 155–73.

8 Office of the Chief Scientist, Ministry of Industry, Trade and Employment, *Program to Support Research and Development, 2011–12*, Hebrew, www.moit.gov.il/NR/rdonlyres/0BA7755A-4F76-4520-9A67-A4216C30E071/0/mopspreads.pdf.

9 Gil Avnimlech and Morris Teubal, *Israel's Venture Capital (VC) Industry: Emergence, Operation and Impact*, 2002, economics.huji.ac.il/facultye/teubal/VCPaper1%20-%20Dilek%20Book.pdf.

10 Israel-US Bilateral Industrial Research and Development Foundation, *Annual Report*, 2011, www.birdf.com/_Uploads/dbsAttachedFiles/AnnualReport_2011.pdf.

11 Gilad Nathan, *The OECD Expert Group on Migration (Sopemi) Report: Immigration in Israel 2011–12. Research and Information*, The Knesset, Jerusalem, 2012, www.knesset.gov.il/mmm/data/pdf/me03131.pdf.

12 Bank of Israel, *Annual Report*, 2011, Chapter 5, www.boi.org.il/en/NewsAndPublications/RegularPublications/Documents/Doch2011/pe_5.pdf.

13 Ayal Kimhi, *Labor Market Trends: Employment Rate and Wage Disparities*, Taub Center Policy Paper no. 2112.07, taubcenter.org.il/tauborgilwp/wp-content/uploads/E2012.07-Kimhi.pdf.

14 National Insurance Institute, *Annual Report 2011*, Poverty and Social Gaps, National Insurance Institute, Jerusalem, 2012, Hebrew, www.btl.gov.il/Publications/oni_report/Documents/oni2011.pdf.

15 Bank of Israel, *Annual Report 2011*, www.boi.org.il/en/NewsAndPublications/RegularPublications/Pages/eng_doch11e.aspx.

16 The Trajtenberg Report, *The Cost of Living and Competitiveness*, hidavrut.gov.il/sites/default/files/%20%D7%A1%D7%95%D7%A4%D7%99.pdf.

17 The Committee to examine Structural Change and Increased Competition in the Cement Sector, Ministry of Finance, November 2012, www.mof.gov.il/Lists/List26/Attachments/439/%D7%AA%D7%99%D7%A7%D7%95%D7%9F%202.pdf.

18 Konstantin Kosenko, *Evolution of Business Groups in Israel: Their Impact at the Level of the Firm and the Economy*, Bank of Israel, www.boi.org.il/deptdata/mehkar/papers/dp0802h.pdf.

19 Lucian Bebchuk, *Corporate Pyramids in the Israeli Economy: Problems and Policies*, 2012, 4, mof.gov.il/Lists/CompetitivenessCommittee_4/Attachments/3/Opinion_2.pdf; and Yuval Tzuk, *The Market Value of Traded Companies*, Tel Aviv Stock Exchange, Tel-Aviv, 2012, www.tase.co.il/TASE/Statistics/ResearchReviews/2012/Research_2012_02_173708.htm.

20 Discount Investment Corporation, *Stock Info IBD Company*, www.dic.co.il; Dun's 100, Israel's Largest Enterprises, duns100.dundb.co.il/comp_eng_600064463/IDB%20Group.

21 Stanislav Sokolinski, *Business Groups in Israel*, Koret Milken Institute, 2012, 3–4, www.milkeninstitute.org/publications/publications.taf?function=detail&id=38801359&cat=ResRep.

22 Reuben Gronau, 'Structural Changes in the Israeli Public Utilities: The Reform That Never Was', in Avi Ben Bassat (ed.), *The Israeli Economy, 1985–1998*, The MIT Press, Cambridge, MA and London, 2002, 309–48.

23 *Haaretz*, www.haaretz.com/business/israel-electric-seeking-to-delay-reform-for-10th-time.premium-1.481997.

24 *The Marker*, 16 January 2013, www.themarker.com/dynamo/1.1908144.

25 Ministry of Finance, *Main Points of the Budget 2009*, 91, govx.mof.gov.il/BudgetSite/StateBudget/Budget2009/Lists/2009/Attachments/1/ikarey2010.pdf.

26 Imri Tov, 'The Disengagement Price Tag', *Strategic Assessment* 8(3), November 2005, www.inss.org.il/publications.php?cat=21&incat=&read=194.

27 Paul Rivlin, *The Israeli Economy from the Foundation of the State through the 21st Century*, Cambridge University Press, New York, 2011, 143–65.

28 Shlomo Swirski, *The Cost of Occupation, The Burden of the Israeli-Palestinian Conflict*, The Adva Center, Tel-Aviv, 2008, www.adva.org/uploaded/costofoccupation2008fullenglish%281%29.pdf.

29 Ephraim Kleiman, 'Not all the Result of the Occupation: The Influence of 40 Years of Israeli Rule of the Palestinian Territories on the State of Israel', in Ephraim Lavie (ed.), *40 Years of Occupation: The Effects on Israeli Society*, The Tami Steinitz Center for Peace, Tel-Aviv University, 2009, 183–94 (Hebrew), 191.

30 *The Report of the Inter-ministerial Committee to Examine the Government's Policy Regarding Natural Gas in Israel*, The Ministry of Energy and Water Resources, Jerusalem, 2012, energy.gov.il/Subjects/NG/Documents/NGReportSep12.pdf; APCO Forum, *Israel's Natural Gas Sector*, www.apcoworldwide.com/content/PDFs/telaviv_israels_natural_gas_sector.pdf.

31 Bank of Israel, *Quarterly Research Staff Forecast*, December 2012, www.boi.org.il/en/NewsAndPublications/PressReleases/Documents/Meeting%20with%20Forecasters.pdf.

32 *The Economist*, 'Drill or Quarrel Gas in the Eastern Mediterranean', 12 January 2013, www.economist.com/news/business/21569452-politics-could-choke-supplies-big-new-offshore-gasfields-drill-or-quarrel.

11

Singapore's success

After the miracle

Linda Y.C. Lim[1]

Singapore has long been widely recognized as possibly the most successful case of development among emerging economies in the 20th century. This has resulted in a large literature—both academic and popular—on the country's economic development, quite out of proportion to its small size and unique circumstances.[2] This chapter will not repeat or synthesize this literature, since it is well known. Instead, I shall, first, provide a brief retrospective summary of the country's economic policy and performance in the 20th century since independence in 1965, considering the extent to which these are replicable (or not) in other countries; and second, discuss the many developmental challenges the now-rich country faces in the 21st century, reflecting on whether they cast doubt on the wisdom and sustainability of some of its past and current policies, and the prospective implications for other developed as well as emerging economies that may seek to emulate Singapore as a 'model'.[3]

Given this focus, the chapter draws heavily on current public policy debates in Singapore and recent research by Singapore-based economists and other social scientists. A collective conclusion is that industrial policy, population policy, immigration policy, housing, health, social security, monetary and fiscal policy are all heavily interconnected and interdependent in a 'complex system', such that operating one policy lever has consequences (including unintended and undesirable consequences) for other policy arenas and the system as a whole. This reality limits both the replicability of the Singapore model in other economies, whether emerging or developed, and the policy options for Singapore as it struggles to emerge from its current development dilemmas.

The 'miracle' economy: from independence to maturity in the 20th century

Singapore's transformation from colonial port-city to newly industrialized economy in the 20th century shared much with the experience of the other 'Asian Tigers' of the Republic of Korea (South Korea), Taiwan and Hong Kong, as noted in the voluminous scholarly literature of the time, the World Bank's 1993 study of *The East Asian Miracle*,[4] and continued policy reflections since, focused on lessons for other emerging economies.[5]

From a market perspective, these economies in the 1960s and 1970s developed through free trade by specializing in the export of labour-intensive manufactures based on comparative advantage (relative resource endowments). From a 'developmental state' perspective, they relied heavily on state-interventionist policies which used industrial policy of selective protection and subsidies to direct capital investment to particular sectors, and provided public investment in infrastructure and education to increase productivity. Industrialization was further facilitated by conducive macroeconomic policy (including fixed and undervalued exchange rates, and high domestic savings[6]) and authoritarian political regimes which ensured labour peace and 'affordability', and efficient, centralized policymaking with effective implementation.

Singapore resembled Hong Kong, but differed from South Korea and Taiwan, in continuing with the free trade and capital flows of the British colonial era, including openness to foreign direct investment (FDI, whereas both trade and FDI were only selectively 'free' in South Korea and Taiwan). It resembled South Korea and Taiwan, but differed from Hong Kong, in practising industrial policy.[7] Significantly, it also differed from all three other 'Tigers' in relying much more heavily on multinationals than local enterprises, and on imports of foreign labour and talent, in addition to tight state control of land and the domestic labour market.[8]

Political democratization in Taiwan in 1987 and South Korea in 1988 accelerated the shift in resource-based comparative advantage that both economies experienced, as now-permitted labour activism raised wages, currencies were allowed to float upward (but remained 'managed'), the influence of state industrial policy and enterprises moderated (but did not disappear), and local private enterprises rapidly expanded and globalized their operations. There were no similar political changes in Hong Kong and Singapore, but China's opening around 1980 facilitated the relocation of Hong Kong's labour-intensive manufacturing there, to be replaced by finance and other services.

In Singapore, manufacturing competitiveness was maintained through the 1980s and 1990s by state industrial policy that encouraged the substitution of capital for labour, and technological upgrading, even as foreign labour imports preserved some labour-intensive parts of the manufacturing value chain. Exchange rate management also helped, with Singapore running globally unprecedented current account surpluses of around 25% of gross domestic product (GDP) every year for over 30 years in a row. This has maintained manufacturing at over 20% of GDP[9]—again unprecedented among high-income countries—largely by attracting huge amounts of FDI into particular targeted sectors ranging from petrochemicals in the 1960s to pharmaceuticals in the 2000s, with electronics in between. It has also maintained and even expanded the economic role of the state, with a proliferation of government-linked companies or GLCs (resulting from the partial privatization of state agencies and enterprises) and two of the world's leading sovereign wealth funds, GIC (Government of Singapore Investment Corporation) and Temasek.[10]

This state-driven development model succeeded in delivering high rates of GDP growth over nearly four decades, such that Singapore now ranks as one of the world's richest countries by per capita income.[11] It also ranks high globally in many private sector comparative indices, such as for 'competitiveness',[12] 'economic freedom',[13] 'business environment',[14] 'science and mathematics education',[15] among others. However, the model is of limited relevance to other countries today, given recent changes in the dynamics of the world economy (and political economy), and peculiarities of the Singapore case itself.

When Singapore and the other Asian Tigers embarked on their export manufacturing development strategy, they were individually and collectively small players in a world market where there were few other open economy competitors with the same market comparative advantage (relative labour intensity) and policies to develop sector-specific competitive advantage (investment incentives, industrial targeting, export promotion). Today, there are many more large emerging economies with similar market advantages (most notably the People's Republic of China), while the evolution of World Trade Organization (WTO) trade rules has limited international tolerance for 'export subsidies', 'trade-related investment measures', 'currency manipulation' and other 'beggar-my-neighbour' policies. Singapore gets away with continuing many of these policies because it is both relatively small, and very open in trade and capital flows; given that its policies benefit multinationals, their home countries are unlikely to protest 'unfair competition'.

From the 1960s to the 1980s Singapore and the other Asian Tigers also found ready access for their exports in the robustly growing and open USA, other developed Western and Japanese markets, at a time when those countries' companies were rapidly internationalizing their production networks amid global trade liberalization. Today, most rich countries face stagnant or slow-growing economies burdened with ageing populations and unsustainable fiscal burdens, making them less tolerant of imports from countries perceived as not observing 'a level playing field'. Following the global financial crisis of 2008–09, tightening financial regulations and reduced tolerance for 'tax havens' may also reduce the scope of offshore financial services and industrial investment incentives that countries like Singapore can offer international capital.[16] With political liberalization accompanying market economic reforms around the world since the 1990s, many emerging economies today also have limited tolerance for the type of state-heavy policies that propelled authoritarian Singapore's economic development.

Behind the 'miracle' in the 20th century

Singapore's economic development benefited from many favourable 'initial conditions', including an excellent geographical position and deep-water port at the crossroads of intra-Asian and international maritime trade, good infrastructure and commercial institutions developed by the British colonial authorities, free trade and capital flows which facilitated its role as a regional entrepôt within South-East Asia, and an entrepreneurial, largely immigrant population engaged in trading networks with their neighbouring countries of origin.[17] Despite this, GDP growth was slow and unemployment high at independence in the mid-1960s, when the city of 1.5 million was already middle-income (with the second highest income in Asia after Japan). The beginnings of offshore sourcing in labour-intensive manufacturing by Western and Japanese corporations, and the experiences of Puerto Rico, Mexican border *maquiladoras*, and South Korean and Taiwanese export-processing zones, provided a model for industrialization and employment creation that was also adopted in the 1970s by some of Singapore's South-East Asian neighbours, especially Malaysia and the Philippines in the electronics industry.

As in these other economies, government policies and institutions in Singapore played an important role in attracting FDI in labour-intensive export manufacturing. The role in investment promotion of Singapore's lead development agency, the Economic Development Board (EDB), is well-known,[18] but perhaps less attention has been paid to the complementary roles of other government agencies and policies in facilitating rapid industrialization. The efficiency-enhancing role of infrastructure agencies—the Port of Singapore Authority, Changi Airport, Jurong Town Corporation (industrial estates), Public Utilities Board, Urban Redevelopment Authority, etc.—is obvious, but social policy has also played a less obvious role in increasing productivity and creating the conditions for successful growth.

Most notably, Singapore's Housing Development Board (HDB) has housed some 85% of the population since the 1980s, building and maintaining 'public' housing units which most residents own. The provision of affordable housing helped keep wages low, while the integration of industrial premises into residential housing estates provided an easily accessible supply of factory labour.[19] Investments in public health and education increased labour productivity and skills, while a vigorous family planning campaign encouraged low fertility and greatly increased female labour force participation. Social security was provided through a Central Provident Fund (CPF) or 'forced savings' scheme under which employers and employees contributed mandated proportions (ranging from 20% to 50%) of employees' salaries to individual accounts managed by the CPF. Although meant to be savings for retirement, employees could and did use these funds to purchase housing—and later, also for medical and (limited) educational expenses, and equity investments in certain 'blue chip' GLCs.[20]

Such institutional innovations enabled the Singapore government to provide high-quality public and social goods and services without running public sector deficits. It frequently articulated its abhorrence of 'subsidies' and a 'welfare state' even while extending the long arm of the state, directly and indirectly, into more and more sectors of the economy.[21] Most public sector agencies earned surpluses through user charges, and the government budget itself was almost always in surplus, with revenues exceeding expenditures nearly every year. 'Singapore Inc.' became a frequently invoked moniker in the international business press, even before the privatizations of the 1990s and 2000s turned monopolistic state agencies into publicly listed corporations (e.g. Singapore Airlines, Neptune Orient Lines, Singapore Telecoms, Singapore Mass Rapid Transit, etc.), dominating the market capitalization of the Singapore Stock Exchange. State agencies and GLCs (in which the government holds controlling minority shares) essentially prosper by providing goods and services at profit-making prices to the private sector.[22]

The government also influences wages and salaries in a number of ways. First, it controls the supply of labour through visa and immigration policies. Second, it influences the demand for labour through its investment promotion activities. Third, it is a major employer through the public sector and GLCs (influencing both demand and the supply price of labour). Fourth, it is the dominant participant in the tripartite (government, unions, employers) National Wages Council which comes up with annual wage increase guidelines for the private sector. Fifth, it controls the labour movement[23] and exerts considerable influence on the private business sector.[24]

The state's early ability to organize itself efficiently enabled it to 'get the basics right' with lightning speed and limited political backlash as it embarked on an 'extreme makeover' of the city. Being able quickly to deliver good infrastructure, low inflation, fiscal balance, political stability,[25] policy predictability and low corruption enabled it to outcompete cheaper neighbours to become the preferred regional headquarters of multinationals. This, then, developed agglomeration and other first-comer advantages that became part of its competitive advantage in later years.

The fact that Singapore has been politically a 'one-party state' for three generations has much to do with the social and institutional underpinnings of its economic success in the 20th century. Unchallenged political authority enabled the ruling People's Action Party (PAP) to undertake many developmental policies that in more pluralistic democracies might have encountered opposition, including from vested interests, and threatened a loss of power. Potentially contentious policies included labour controls, compulsory land acquisition and allocation, and the 'crowding out' of the local private sector in both product and factor markets by multinationals and the state sector (which has not happened in the other Asian Tiger economies). The country also ranks far below its per capita income rank in comparative rankings, which include variables such as 'political freedom', 'human development' and 'well-being'.[26]

After the 'miracle': developmental challenges of the 21st century

Singapore's development model of the 20th century might not be replicable in other emerging economies because they do not face the same favourable initial conditions that Singapore and other Asian Tigers enjoyed then, and/or they do not possess the political will or institutional capacity necessary to enact and implement the comprehensive social as well as economic policies that Singapore could undertake in the 20th century. Another reason why countries might not follow the Singapore model is that 21st-century internal and international developments have revealed the model's own shortcomings in continuing to deliver positive results for its population.

The most critical shortcoming of Singapore's growth model is its sustainability—or lack thereof. Almost from the beginning, studies have shown that GDP growth in most periods was achieved mainly through increasing the quantum of inputs—of capital, labour, even land[27]—rather than their productivity.[28] This strategy may have been efficient in developing a middle-income economy with underutilized resources (e.g. the high unemployment of the 1960s), and the ability to 'borrow' internationally (e.g. by participating in multinational networks) to 'catch up' to the global technological frontier. It becomes much more difficult in a high-income (and thus high-cost) economy with fully employed resources now at the global technological frontier, but lacking the domestic market size, production scale and indigenous entrepreneurs to innovate for global markets.

The logic of international economics is that resource-based comparative advantage shifts, sometimes rapidly, such that activities that are competitive in one location at one period of time eventually become uncompetitive as domestic and international factor markets change. Given its small size and extreme openness to and dependence on world markets (with exports, including re-exports, accounting for over 200% of GDP), Singapore would be particularly vulnerable to shifts in comparative advantage. Indeed, barely half a dozen years after the launch of its labour-intensive export manufacturing strategy in the late 1960s, the country reached full employment and began importing foreign labour (initially from Malaysia) as a means of delaying the loss of comparative advantage in labour-intensive manufacturing. A few years later (1979–82), the government switched course, launching what it called a 'second industrial revolution' with a 'high-wage policy' aimed at increasing labour productivity and upgrading technology through capital-labour substitution. Ever since, variable labour importation has been an important policy tool in creating competitiveness and in counter-cyclical management (with 'tightening' taking place in times of weak GDP growth and slack labour market demand, to limit domestic unemployment, and 'easing' taking place when demand was strong, to reduce inflationary pressures). This has arguably delayed the 'economic restructuring' to higher productivity levels that the government itself has called for more than once a decade since the 1970s.[29]

In seeking to manage and facilitate inevitable shifts in comparative advantage, the modus operandi of Singapore state development agencies, led by the EDB, has been to pick particular 'new' sectors they think are promising, then attract foreign companies in these sectors to Singapore by showering them with investment incentives (tax breaks, R&D and training subsidies, employment subsidies, cheap land, special buildings). Since these are capital- and skill-intensive industries, offering capital subsidies and the freedom to hire specialized employees from around the world are effective inducements. Singapore has also worked on constantly improving its competitive advantages of location, infrastructure, logistics, legal, regulatory and tax regimes, and the general business environment—all of which contribute to its popularity as a global financial centre and regional headquarters for multinationals. However, these efforts have not been entirely successful,[30] given the high capital cost and risks of picking new industries at the uncertain technological frontier, Singapore's chronic lack of the scale required to develop robust, long-lived clusters, and the rising local costs inevitably associated with the simultaneous development of many different sectors competing for scarce land, labour and talent resources, and with the privatization (and hence profit-seeking higher prices) of some previously publicly provided goods and services.

The turn of the 21st century saw Singapore's economy suffer in quick succession from several external shocks: the late 1990s Asian Financial Crisis which hurt financial services, the early 2000s crash of the dotcom bubble which hurt high-tech and IT, and the SARS near-epidemic which temporarily devastated tourism and hospitality. An Economic Review Committee in 2003[31] affirmed the continued importance of manufacturing, particularly the 'four key clusters' of electronics, chemicals, biomedical sciences and engineering, as well as the development of educational, medical, financial and tourist services, and 'creative industries', for a growing Asian middle class. Following the global financial crisis of 2008–09, an Economic Strategies Committee in 2010[32] expanded these activities to include 'green urban solutions' and developing Singapore as a global 'hub' and 'node' for financial and business services, R&D, consumer research, 'commercialization and innovation', and 'complex manufacturing and manufacturing-related services', on top of established industries like trading, logistics and ICT, though the most visible addition to the economy was the opening of two major casinos (called 'integrated resorts').

Despite (or perhaps because of) this proliferation of diversified new sectors, GDP growth declined, volatility increased (particularly in the highly capital-intensive and 'lumpy' pharmaceuticals sector), and productivity growth slowed as GDP growth was achieved largely by input-intensive means (increasing capital and labour). While the government was mainly concerned with maintaining GDP growth, economists (and even some ruling party 'backbencher' MPs) were already questioning the quality of growth and distribution of its benefits, noting: (1) increased volatility (and its negative impact on domestic investment, employment and growth);[33] (2) the very low ratio of wages and of domestic consumption (about 35% each) in GDP and concomitantly high savings (45%) occurring disproportionately in the highly profitable multinational and state corporate sectors;[34] (3) stagnation in median incomes and decline in incomes of the bottom decile; (4) worsening income inequality with one of the highest Gini coefficients among rich countries (0.478 before and 0.459 after government taxes and transfers)[35] and declining social mobility;[36] (5) persistent consumer price and asset inflation, particularly of land and housing;[37] (6) Singapore's relatively poor performance in newly popular measurements of 'well-being' that include non-income metrics such as working hours, consumption, inequality and life expectancy;[38] and (7) environmentalists added concerns over high energy consumption, the loss of green and wild spaces, and the intensifying negative externalities of congestion, pollution and loss of cultural heritage sites in what was already the most densely populated country in the world (7,253 people per sq km in 2010).[39]

Several factors appear to have contributed to the real or perceived decline in Singaporeans' well-being, even as the country climbed the charts of the richest nations in the world, ranking first in the proportion of households with over US$1 million in assets under management (15.5%).[40] First, pushing growth in many different new high-tech, high-skill sectors divided Singapore's already limited talent pool, preventing the development of critical mass in any given industry, while requiring heavy dependence on specialized foreign talent, given the desire to 'develop new capabilities in emerging technologies such as micro-electromechanical systems, nanotechnology and photonics'.[41] Second, the vast expansion in numbers of foreign workers admitted in a very short space of time[42] led to inevitable national clustering in workplaces and residences, alleged discriminatory hiring practices, a perceived 'glass ceiling' for Singaporean professionals, and extreme congestion in transportation and housing scarcity as the government's physical planning fell behind the numbers it admitted. Third, a massive influx of low-skilled foreign workers (in construction, domestic service, cleaning and other services), and of white-collar clerical and retail workers, depressed wage growth among low- to middle-income Singaporeans, while a similar influx of highly skilled 'global talent' attracted with above-world-market salaries, and ultra-wealthy tax haven-seeking capital owners/investors[43] contributed to visibly widening income and wealth disparities in the already densely packed island city-state.[44]

Fourth, at the same time, the ruling party stuck to its long-standing aversion to social (but not corporate) subsidies, raising a consumption tax while maintaining low income tax rates, and privatizing what were previously public goods like health care, housing, transportation and utilities. With only a few large, now profit-seeking, players in what might be considered 'natural monopoly' sectors, the predictable result was rising user charges and oligopolistic rents.[45] The impact on social welfare was particularly noticeable in health care.[46] In housing, a change around 2000 in the goal of public housing policy from 'affordability' to 'asset enhancement' penalized new buyers, resulting in large and long mortgage burdens for young couples whose starting professional salaries have increased only fractionally relative to the cost of public as well as private housing over the past decade. 'The government itself has acknowledged that the emerging homelessness problem is due in part to some who gambled on asset appreciation and lost.'[47] Not surprisingly, Singaporeans complain that they are 'paying more and more for less and less' (including residential housing space in HDB flats), while living costs (pushed up in part by foreign demand) escalate much more rapidly than average wages (held down by foreign supply, and the related low productivity gains), resulting in a sense of 'downward mobility'[48] in what residents are constantly reminded is one of the world's richest countries.

That the situation had become politically and socially, if not economically and environmentally, unsustainable, was revealed by two elections in 2011. In the May general election, the PAP which had ruled since the 1960s with only one or two token opposition parliamentarians, saw its share of the popular vote drop to 60% (the lowest since independence), while its share of parliamentary seats dropped from 98% to 93%.[49] In the four-way contest for the elected presidency in August, the government's candidate won with 35% of the vote, or a 0.3% margin. These unprecedented results were seen by the ruling party as a loss of popularity; the prime minister apologized to the population, the cabinet was reshuffled with some of the most unpopular ministers replaced, and many new policies were hurriedly announced, particularly to increase the availability of public housing and transportation. Also politically significant was the decision to reduce cabinet ministers' salaries—then and still today the highest in the world.[50] Since then, two by-elections were also won by the main opposition Workers' Party, most recently in January 2013 with a 55% majority against the PAP candidate.

Right after this last by-election loss, the government released a White Paper on Population Policy,[51] which met with overwhelming public opposition, including some from ruling party backbenchers (reflecting the views of their electoral constituents).[52] It laid out plans for what Singapore might be in 2030, with a 6.9 million population (vs 5.3 million currently), of whom 45% would be immigrants or temporary foreign workers (with 15,000 to 25,000 new permanent residents a year, down from 79,000 in 2008[53] and on top of a current stock of 500,000 permanent residents), required because native Singaporeans' abnormally low total fertility rate of 1.2 children per woman and rapidly ageing population would make it otherwise impossible to achieve 3%–5% GDP growth (high for a developed economy). The government later acknowledged that a lower GDP growth rate was likely, given the maturity of the economy, that it would focus on increasing productivity and reducing (but not eliminating) reliance on foreign labour, and that the 6.9 million figure was not a target, but a 'planning parameter' for infrastructure purposes, and even 'a worst-case scenario'. It also enacted yet more pro-natalist policies to encourage Singaporeans to have more children, including shorter waits for HDB housing for young couples, and cash bonuses for each baby, though such policies have been around for 30 years without having much impact (though one could argue that without them, the birth rate might be even lower).[54]

Many of Singapore's problems today are shared by other high-income developed economies, especially by their dense urban areas. These include low birth rates, rising income and wealth inequality, reduced social mobility, traffic congestion, expensive housing and reliance on an immigrant labour force. The difference in Singapore is mainly one of degree—its birth rates are lower, income and wealth inequality greater, housing more expensive,[55] and reliance on foreign labour most extreme. As its economy is also more state driven (e.g. with the government housing 85% of the population, admitting the large numbers of foreign workers and actively pursuing industrial policy), public policy must explain some of the differential, though the ultimate constraint may simply be the country's extreme land shortage.

The government's growth and investment promotion policies, and their requirement for large inputs of foreign labour and talent, probably have the greatest impact on the economy, since they distort the allocation of resources by influencing relative prices. In terms of sectoral targeting, the White Paper mentioned the government's intention to grow the following 'new industries': biomedical, digital media, petrochemicals, advanced electronics, green energy, in addition to existing sectors of logistics, fashion, food, marine and environmental engineering. Not mentioned were the already large established sectors of trade, finance and tourism/hospitality, other sectors identified (above) by the Economic Review Committee (2003) and Economic Strategies Committee (2010), or the new sectors of 'space industries' and 'Big Data' analytics and storage, announced after the release of the White Paper (2013). All these sectors require investment incentives or corporate subsidies (because they would not be market competitive otherwise); all would compete with each other for scarce local resources including land and skills, pushing those costs up; all would require heavy recruitment of foreigners (with the resultant negative externalities of congestion, asset inflation and social unease); while simultaneous development of multiple sectors would undermine the likelihood that each would be able to reach the critical size and scale required for global market competitiveness. Since these sectors are selected for being capital- and skill-intensive, their returns would accrue disproportionately to high-income owners of capital and skills (mostly foreigners), thus worsening income inequality. Large inflows of capital would either cause currency appreciation that would reduce the competitiveness of more labour-intensive export sectors (such as tourism) or aggravate (already rising) domestic inflation (if the currency were not allowed to appreciate). Some sectors would add to Singapore's already high energy consumption and consume scarce land, with negative consequences for environmental sustainability and 'spatial justice'.

The impact of these industrial and labour policies on birth rates probably works through the housing market. Young dual-income couples needing both to work longer and save more to purchase housing[56] delays the age of marriage, while the need to service housing loans, the high costs of childcare, limited living space (especially for those who take in tenants to help pay for their mortgages), and expensive and inconvenient transportation, discourage childbearing. This is true also in other cities around the world. To the extent that children are an 'inferior good' (for whom demand falls as income rises) in a materialist consumerist society and among the highly educated, this trend should continue in Singapore as the proportion of university-educated Singaporeans rises from the current 27% to the targeted 40% of the age cohort, and population density increases. Some scholars also argue that corporate career pressures, long working hours and a highly stressful school system are responsible for young Singaporeans' low marriage and fertility rates.[57] High housing prices, the use of CPF retirement savings to pay for them, and the erosion of CPF savings given the low interest rate they earn relative to inflation, also causes many Singaporeans to fear that they will be unable to support themselves in retirement, with a recent survey revealing that 56% of 2,000 respondents would like to emigrate.[58] Complicating the situation, several GLCs are now dominant players in private property development of high-end commercial and residential properties, with their REITs (Real Estate Investment Trusts) profiting handsomely from soaring prices and rentals.[59]

In their criticisms of the White Paper and its vision of Singapore in 2030, Singaporeans have generally called for slower GDP growth with better distribution, including a higher share of the proceeds of growth for Singaporeans (vs foreign workers and employers) and those on low incomes; a recent poll by the government's 'feedback unit' found that nearly nine in ten Singaporeans support measures to tighten the inflow of foreign workers.[60] The government itself proposes higher productivity growth as a means to assuring higher incomes, but it appears to assume continued dependence on low-skilled foreign workers and labour-intensive methods in sectors such as construction, food and beverages, and domestic service, even though this itself discourages investments in productivity improvements, technological and institutional innovations,[61] and sociological transformations that are commonplace in other rich countries, and discourages Singaporeans from entering these occupations because they remain low-wage, low-status and populated by low-skilled foreigners. Instead, the government's approach, as revealed in its 2013 Budget, for example, is a two-pronged one: lifting more Singaporeans into what are called PMET (Professional Management Executive and Technical) jobs that pay higher wages (rather than allowing wages for non-PMET jobs to rise), and providing more social subsidies to low-income households (rather than enabling them to earn higher wages through the market), in direct contradiction of its long-standing opposition to income transfers because they make people 'lazy'. In short, its plan appears to be to continue with resource allocation distortions and then to compensate those who lose by such distortions (such as the wage repressing effects of low-wage foreign labour imports) through fiscal handouts (known locally as 'giveaways').[62]

Apart from local objections, and the questionable wisdom of 'growing new sectors' which mainly provide jobs for foreigners and can only survive by hiring them, there is concern that foreign workers may not be available in the medium to long term. As the gap between employment and living standards in Singapore and migrant source countries like China, India, Malaysia and the Philippines narrows, and as the multinationals that employ these workers increasingly move to their home locations because they have larger labour and talent pools, as well as lower costs and larger, more rapidly growing markets, it may become harder for Singapore to attract such workers, while those who do come may not stay permanently since they have family in their home countries and eventually better economic opportunities there for themselves and their children. It is possible, even likely, that 'new industries' heavily subsidized by the Singapore state may eventually move to the larger origin countries of their migrant employees. Thus the strategy of attracting investment by providing capital subsidies and ease of hiring foreign labour and talent is probably not sustainable. Already multinationals say that inflation, rising costs and expensive property prices, as well as shortages of staff, are making Singapore a less attractive location for investment.[63] Local businesses, which tend to be more labour intensive, are also challenged by rising costs and labour shortages;[64] the government has instituted a variety of assistance schemes to help them to upgrade, and will cover wage increases for most of their workers over the next three years.[65] Like multinationals, some will have to relocate as businesses have always done with shifting comparative advantage.[66]

These 21st-century developments suggest that the past success of Singapore's economic model is not sustainable. Even the government argues in support of its policies that the country has 'no choice' but to import large numbers of foreigners, and does not have a strategy for what it can and should do after 2030, since then there will be even more rapidly diminishing returns to the policy of adding yet more capital and labour to the already overcrowded island.[67] Singapore's accumulation of excess foreign reserves and its early establishment of sovereign wealth funds to manage government surpluses and invest them abroad was originally designed to provide the country with a financial cushion against external shocks and domestic downturns. It appears now that foreign reserves will be further increased 'to strengthen our social safety nets, and to cope with volatility and uncertainty',[68] since the government continues to be averse to raising revenues through taxes (which range from 12% to 17% of GDP, compared with the 34% Organisation for Economic Co-operation and Development (OECD) average).[69]

Lessons for emerging economies

Many lessons have been, and continue to be, drawn from Singapore's economic development experience for other emerging economies; they range from the general[70] to the specific.[71] There is certainly much to admire and emulate from public policy in Singapore. Two recent books by former Singaporean civil servants engaged in policymaking are particularly recommended. *Dynamics of the Singapore Success Story: Insights by Ngiam Tong Dow* outlines the political and institutional, educational and social, financial and banking 'pillars' of Singapore's building of a knowledge-based economy, and also considers the implications of its experience for China.[72] The chapters in *Behavioural Economics and Policy Design: Examples from Singapore* show how behavioural economics informs policies such as traffic management, environmental management, electricity retail, discretionary transfers, health and retirement policy, and provide useful lessons for developed countries as well.[73]

In terms of the broader themes of this volume, another book, by a long-time International Monetary Fund economist on South-East Asia, *Singapore's Success: Engineering Economic Growth*, perhaps best captures international development agencies' enthusiasm for Singapore's development as a model for developing countries.[74] It concludes with these words:

> Key themes emerged from Singapore's success story. These include: the role of saving in allowing the buildup of first-rate infrastructure; the growth potential of increased labor force participation and immigration; the central importance of economic development among national goals; sharing opportunities for growth widely to make people more productive through better health and education; the macroeconomic resilience and employment-creating potential provided by flexible wage policy; competent civil service and integrity of governance; fiscal discipline and setting aside surpluses during boom years; win-win relations with MNCs [multinational corporations] and labor; maintaining racial harmony; learning from others pragmatically; the rule of law; and well-designed policies …
>
> Singapore followed an integrated approach to development. Outcomes, policies, institutions, social and cultural values, and the political dynamics of implementation all reinforced each other. The government pursued this comprehensive strategy across a range of areas such as fiscal, monetary policy, education, health, transportation, housing, finance, wage policy, legal system and law enforcement, labor markets, and political stability and legitimacy.[75]

From this expert practitioner perspective, then, Singapore's economic development was a success because it was comprehensive and integrated across all dimensions of public policy, and social and cultural institutions. This alone can be a daunting and difficult path for other emerging economies to follow, which is presumably the reason for Paul Romer's suggestion of establishing a separate city-state.[76] Ghesquiere and other foreign admirers of the Singapore model skirt around the one institution which has arguably been essential to the 'growth-enhancing institutions' and 'political economy of implementation' that enabled its economic success—and that is the political institution of the one-party authoritarian state. A very different view is projected by some other Western writers focused on the country's non-economic institutions, where they find governance a problem due to its concentration in a small interrelated elite.[77] It is beyond this author's expertise and this chapter's scope to consider governance issues, except to note that in other emerging economies such a concentration of political and economic power is typically considered antithetical to, rather than supportive of, successful economic development.[78]

More interesting, in my view, is how and why the Singapore model—so admirable in so many respects and for so long—has stumbled in the 21st century, in terms of maintaining high living standards, economic opportunity and social satisfaction for its citizen population, requiring a return to the input-intensive growth that is typically associated with less-developed economies that have fewer strategic choices. After four decades of rapid GDP and income growth, Singapore's economy today is even more dependent on increasing inputs of foreign labour and talent, foreign capital and technology, and even increasing land area by artificial means, at the cost of increased inequality, reduced social mobility, rising inflation, greater risk and volatility, and declining quality of public and social goods and services (all of which the government, to its credit, acknowledges). It has failed to develop a model of sustainable growth despite achieving a highly educated population (human capital) and accumulating huge amounts of financial capital through the world's highest savings rate and foreign exchange reserves (which indicate that wages and consumption continue to fall behind top-line GDP growth, or that Singaporeans are much less well-off than their nominal or even real GDP per capita suggests). Seen in this light, the ruling party's declining political popularity is unsurprising.[79]

Theories about domestic causes of these public policy shortcomings relate mainly to failures of governance arising from the single-party system and its concentration/overlap of political and economic power, leading to lack of diversity of thought and competition of ideas ('groupthink'), the persistence of cognitive ideological biases long after they have ceased to be valid, and the self-interest of an academically selected elite of lifetime civil servants heavily networked with state and quasi-state agencies and GLC senior management, all of them highly compensated for their responsibilities over the allocation of public resources.[80] However, for the purposes of this volume, it is more useful to consider if any general lessons may be derived from the Singapore experience for economies that are still 'emerging'.

A first possible lesson is the limitations of globalization as a development strategy. There is no question that Singapore and other emerging economies would not have succeeded as they did in industrializing, raising incomes and moving towards post-industrial status, without participating in globalization, particularly liberalizing trade and foreign direct investment, and exporting to global markets. However, the 21st century has also revealed some of the downsides of globalization especially for small, open economies like Singapore. These include extreme volatility arising from external GDP shocks; vulnerability to destabilizing global capital flows resulting from other countries' monetary and currency policies; and the unreliability of multinational investors as long-term members of a national private sector, since their own corporate fortunes and strategies change with globalization and the accompanying shifts in comparative and competitive advantage, such that 'piggy-backing' on specific multinationals is no longer an assured path to growth given heightened technological dynamism, business cycle volatility and general uncertainty in the world economy.[81]

Singapore's attempt to deal with export volatility through industrial diversification has had limited success, while its accumulation of foreign reserves managed by sovereign wealth funds has been variously criticized for: (1) maintaining currency undervaluation; (2) depriving the economy of funds that might be better used for domestic consumption, investment and a more robust social safety net; (3) resulting in financial losses from bad investments overseas; and (4) undermining the sovereignty of other nations.[82] Singapore's extreme openness to capital inflows puts upward pressure on its currency (undermining export competitiveness), contributes to domestic inflation (including politically sensitive house price inflation)[83] and income and wealth inequality, and has exposed it to criticisms at home and abroad of being a tax haven and money-laundering centre.[84]

The heavy and prolonged reliance on multinationals is what most differentiates Singapore from other successful Asian emerging economies—Taiwan, South Korea, Hong Kong, even Malaysia,

Thailand and China—all of which have developed large local private enterprises with the capacity for competitive survival at home and successful globalization abroad as national comparative and competitive advantages have shifted. Singapore, in contrast, has remained heavily dependent on foreign multinationals, not simply by being open to FDI, but actually attracting specific state-chosen investments with extensive subsidies of capital expenditures and of labour (through liberal labour importation policies, training and education).[85] The subsidies required to attract and retain such foreign investment tend to increase with capital and skill intensity and technological specificity, yet are no assurance that the companies will remain, since from a corporate perspective subsidies are only one variable in location and investment decisions.[86] Providing subsidies to any company or industry also diverts scarce resources (land, labour, talent, capital) from other companies and industries. While multinationals do provide supply chain opportunities for local companies, they also 'crowd out' or compete with them for scarce resources, given limited land and full employment. This is one reason why many local Singapore companies are 'much bigger abroad than at home', given larger markets and more resources in neighbouring countries, and competition at home from MNCs and GLCs. Concerns have also been expressed that the heavy dependence on foreigners may distort economic development and hamper the continued evolution of participatory democracy.[87]

A second possible lesson for emerging economies is the limitations of state industrial policy as a country moves up the technology and income ladder, and it becomes more costly, risky and difficult to pick sectors in which to 'strategically invest' (or subsidize). Some sectors may not survive when subsidies are withdrawn, and the resources, e.g. labour and skills, they leave behind might be too specific (geared to fill niches in MNCs' global value chains) to be transferable to other sectors. There are also other risks associated with industrial policy, such as vested business interests (lobbying for subsidies), bureaucratic entrenchment (of state agents responsible for industrial policy), and the 'crowding out' of private business by state agencies and GLCs as well as MNCs. The main problem is that after decades of resource allocation distortions, downsizing the state and 'unwinding' to market forces is difficult, and there may be few local entrepreneurs available to drive the growth of a market economy.[88] However, public policy in a market economy is supposed to focus on the well-being of (domestic) consumers, not (foreign) producers. A national economy should begin with its domestic resource base, paying attention to both comparative advantage and strategic differentiation in the sectors it chooses to develop. In a developed economy, this resource allocation decision should be made by private enterprise actors risking their own money in response to (local and global) market forces, not by state actors. The transition from a state-driven to a market-driven economy which comes with development is a difficult one, at which Singapore has not yet shown itself successful. Fortunately, the government's new focus on 'inclusive growth' shows that it recognizes that it is important that growth benefits everyone; unfortunately (in my view), it seems to want to achieve this by continuing with its problematic growth model to date (subsidize foreign skills and capital) and then compensating locals who do not benefit, out of the public purse.

A third possible lesson, somewhat counter to the previous one, is that privatization is not always the answer, certainly where public goods and social services are concerned. Since the 1990s the Singapore state has progressively privatized what used to be social goods, even as it continued with and even ratcheted up its subsidies of the multinational (and local) corporate sector. The housing, transportation, health and education sectors have been liberalized or corporatized to allow prices to be set by international market forces, including foreign demand, prioritizing returns to foreign as well as local shareholders, with social goods being 'commoditized' as export products. This has contributed to rising costs of living for Singaporeans, whose wages did not

Lessons for and from developed countries

Singapore has become something of an icon for many 'policy wonks' in developed countries. In the West, conservative politicians and economists like it for its low taxes, lack of welfare spending, big budget surpluses,[89] free trade and capital flows, corporate subsidies, labour controls, pro-business policies and pro-market rhetoric; liberals like it for its activist state and industrial policies, what they think are social subsidies, good education and anti-market fundamentalism; everyone likes the absence of corruption and regrets the lack of political freedoms. What, besides an impressively successful state public relations apparatus, explains the dissonance between the foreign plaudits and the local dissatisfactions highlighted in this chapter?

A recent *New York Times* blog post by Nobel prizewinning economist and Columbia University Professor Joseph Stiglitz,[90] widely reprinted in Singapore and elsewhere, illustrates some of the reasons. First, foreign commentators are often inadequately if not wrongly informed about Singapore. For example, Professor Stiglitz asserts that a quarter of the Singapore labour force was unemployed at independence in 1963—it was half that (at 12%); he praises Singapore for having a progressive tax system when it is less progressive than that in the USA and Western Europe, with a top corporate tax rate of 17% and top personal income tax rate of 20%; his claim that the government's intervention in wage bargaining between workers and firms 'tilts the balance towards groups with less economic power' is unsubstantiated, certainly given the stagnation and decline of median and especially low-decile wages since 2000; he totally disregards the hundreds of thousands of low-wage foreign workers with no bargaining rights; his claim that the education system ensures that it is 'not just the children of the rich' who have a chance at upward mobility is contradicted by the government's own efforts to counter demonstrated low social mobility, which it considers troubling.

Second, information about Singapore is selectively and uncritically presented, primarily to serve the foreign commentator's own policy agenda in his home country. Thus Professor Stiglitz lauds the fact that 90% of Singaporeans own their own homes, paid for by their CPF savings, which he praises for inculcating 'individual responsibility' for personal welfare. He does not note that the conflation of savings for retirement and home payments has become a serious social issue given housing price inflation and population ageing, with 47% of Singaporeans over the age of 60 having insufficient CPF savings to support themselves in retirement; he fails to note that this 'individualized' solution to social welfare needs disadvantages those—particularly women—who are unable to have continuous, lifelong, full employment, and being tied to earnings, translates wage differentials into unequal access to health care (also provided out of CPF forced savings) and retirement income. He also disregards the disadvantages that lower-income parents and children suffer in the education system, which has given rise to large private investments in expensive out-of-school tuition and enrichment classes that they are less able to afford.[91]

Third, there is a tendency by Western commentators especially to judge Singapore by different (and lower) standards than they uphold for themselves and other Western societies. For example, Stiglitz says of Singapore that:

> It's true that Singapore, a highly centralized state, has been ruled for decades by Mr. Lee's People's Action Party. Critics say it has authoritarian aspects: limitations on civil liberties; harsh criminal penalties; insufficient multiparty competition; and a judiciary that is not fully

independent. But it's also true that Singapore is routinely rated one of the world's least corrupt and most transparent governments, and that its leaders have taken steps toward expanding democratic participation.

while he says of the Nordic countries that:

I believe the economic achievements of the Nordic countries are in large measure a result of the strongly democratic nature of these societies. There is a positive nexus not just between growth and equality, but between these two and democracy.[92]

Professor Stiglitz is not alone among liberals in his infatuation with Singapore. *Washington Post* and NPR (National Public Radio) commentator Matt Miller is a self-described 'gushing fan of Singapore's public policy achievements', recently praising its high ministerial salaries, low expenditure on health care (just 4% of GDP), home ownership policies, transport facilities, 'fiscal stewardship' based on a 'culture of self-reliance' and 'no redistributions', and 'low-tax, business-friendly environment'.[93] For former Democratic Governor of the state of Michigan Jennifer Granholm, it is Singapore's practice of industrial policy to attract foreign investment that is attractive, recounting that a panel of multinational CEOs she interviewed all agreed that Singapore 'has the best formula for attracting their investment'.[94]

This, then, is the reason for the dissonance. As US liberals have long argued, what is good for the corporation—minimal regulation, offshore tax havens, outsourcing—is not necessarily good for the country. Singapore ranks high on indices that measure the business environment for multinational investors—low taxes, no corruption, lots of state subsidies, freedom to take capital in and out and hire people from anywhere in the world.[95] However, this is not the same as the well-being of native Singaporeans, as measured by income, inequality, working hours, access to affordable housing, health care, social security, education and social mobility—without even considering negative externalities like congestion, environmental degradation, loss of cultural heritage and even 'nationhood'.

Interestingly, many Singaporean social scientists find themselves attracted to the 'Scandinavian model' of small, open economies with modest growth, low income inequality, strong social safety nets and high measurements of well-being, even 'happiness'. However, in a speech to economists and parliamentarians in June 2012, Prime Minister Lee Hsien Loong said that this would not work because 'higher taxes would likely be unpopular among Singaporeans and make the economy less competitive'. Some of his audience (including ruling party MPs) argued that a 'middle ground' is possible, since Singapore can increase public spending over the current 17% of GDP (perhaps to the over 20% ratio that prevailed up to the late 1990s), and that tax rates alone are not the only source of Singapore's competitiveness.[96]

Conclusion

In this chapter I have reviewed one of the most successful cases of economic development in modern times: one that, unusually, has been held up as a model for both emerging and developed economies, and has won plaudits from all sides of the political spectrum. I argue, in line with other development researchers and practitioners, that Singapore's economic success in the 20th century was the product not just of 'the right' policies, but also of favourable initial conditions (domestically and internationally), and 'the right' institutions, for the times. I further argue, as some others have, that Singapore's policies and institutions worked to deliver the results they did because they were *integrated* across economic, social and political arenas. Thus the relevance for other countries is limited, since few, if any, can (or want to) marshal and implement such a complex, interrelated set of public policies under the aegis of a strong centralized state whose political power has been unchanged for over half a century.

I deviate from the international development establishment consensus, but concur with local Singaporean scholars and analysts, in noting that the results of Singapore's public policy complex have been less positive for average Singaporeans than they have been for international business and for global and local elites, in the 21st century; that this view is widely shared in Singapore and is reflected in recent electoral results and a much more open public discourse.[97] I further argue that the past Singapore growth model is unsustainable, because of changes in the international environment, and domestic resource and social constraints.[98] In particular, I note the limits of globalization, state industrial policy and privatization of social services as contributors to growth and welfare, especially for a high-income country; and like other Singaporeans, I question the efficiency and equity of growth based on continuous large imports of foreign capital and labour induced by ever-expanding corporate subsidies.

The Singapore government is nothing if not responsive to the developmental and political challenges it faces, and is finally embarking on policies (long recommended by local economists) to limit foreign labour dependence, increase productivity and increase social subsidies for Singaporeans, even if it means slower GDP growth and 'painful restructuring'. It has accepted that manufacturing's share of the economy will continue to decline. The low productivity of the services sector (measured by value added per employee and as compared with other high-income countries) offers many opportunities for increased efficiency, growth and higher incomes,[99] as does the continued growth and rising incomes of Singapore's 600 million South-East Asian neighbours, for whom it will continue to serve as a regional financial, commercial, trade, transport, information and recreational 'hub'.

The public policy dilemma the government now faces arises from the very interdependence of economic and social policies and institutions which led to the country's past success; it turns out that they cannot be easily disentangled and restructured. Take, for example, housing policy which once contributed to economic growth but is now a drag on it due to asset inflation. Turning housing from an affordable social good into a financial asset interacts negatively with demographics—both on fertility rates of the young, and on consumption of retirees who have 'nowhere else to go'. Allowing the free inflow of foreign capital and labour also contributes to housing price inflation,[100] reducing cost competitiveness while undermining social stability, all of which discourage investment, growth, entrepreneurship and innovation.[101] CPF 'locks up' individuals' forced savings, channelling them disproportionately into housing (and state assets), leaving inadequate amounts for health care and retirement subsistence, and inhibiting the development of a healthy domestic (as opposed to global) financial services sector that could channel savings into local value-creating enterprises. HDB and GLCs in the property development business employ large numbers of low-wage foreign construction workers and earn their profits (and senior management bonuses) off the increased costs of households and businesses, creating potential conflicts of interest. This results in Singaporeans, as they get richer and older, saving more and more—now, nearly half their income—for basic subsistence (housing, health care), which limits the growth of the domestic consumer sector and the entrepreneurship it could generate. The government is now taking steps to reduce housing speculation and inflation (by increasing supply, increasing transaction and mortgage costs for those with more than one private property, and limiting the increased demand from more foreign workers), but this risks diminishing the asset values (and retirement savings) of property-owning households, as well as the profits and equity values of property GLCs in which citizen savings and offshore capital are invested. Encouraging and rewarding state agencies (and their management) for earning surpluses (a source of pride for 'Singapore Inc.') also transfers income from households and the private sector to the state, which then invests the surpluses offshore in sometimes risky private investments in foreign countries rather than in public or social goods at home. Meanwhile a well-compensated state and quasi-state bureaucracy and GLC management have little incentive to restructure themselves out of their high-earning jobs to relinquish scarce resources and market space for private sector investment.

From a governance perspective, the expansion of the state and the proliferation of individual ministries and agencies and their activities has resulted in duplication, competition and a weakening of the central co-ordination function of the state.[102] The recent launch of the Population White Paper from the National Population and Talent Division in the Prime Minister's Office revealed a lack of co-ordination and consultation among different government departments, most notably exemplified by the controversial (and hastily withdrawn) identification of nurses (a short-supplied profession into which the Ministry of Health has long been trying to attract more students and workers) as 'low skilled'. Multinational employers have also mentioned their frustration with conflicting messages they get from different ministries: for example, the Ministry of Trade and Industry's EDB promises them they can hire skilled foreigners freely, while the Ministry of Manpower rejects their applications for employment visas.[103] Equally important, a now larger but less centralized state is less able to impose its own, perhaps more divided, political will on an increasingly politically restive and active citizenry.

Perhaps, then, the main quandary in Singapore's current economic policy conundrum is what to do about the role of the developmental state *after* the miracle of growth has been achieved. As other rich countries have found upon maturity, it is extremely difficult to 'stay on top', especially without a vibrant indigenous entrepreneurial class. How should and can the state reduce and reshape its role at a stage and era when innovation, and not imitation or superior execution, is the source of sustainable competitiveness? How does it deal with the limits to changing comparative and competitive advantage through state action (e.g. immigration policy, capital flows, technology and infrastructure development, and tax and regulatory regimes)? How does the state balance its political obligation for the social welfare of its citizenry with its economic goal to be 'Number 1' in servicing international capital? How does it manage the challenges that both bureaucratic division and democratic pluralism pose to economic growth? What is the proper nature of a state, or a nation, in a globalized era which some argue is increasingly defined by competing state—or even national private—capitalisms? It may be that Singapore's development conundrum is a general one after all, not just for economies that are still 'emerging', but also for all high-income, open economies. However, there is a special poignancy to the Singapore case, given the apparent belief of its long-time political leaders that here subordination of the hitherto carefully nurtured nation is necessary for economic survival. The resulting tension is perhaps best summed up by this recent foreign comment on a local heritage-conservation controversy:

> This is what Singapore's government has always done: look around corners on behalf of its people and plan ahead, confident enough in the infallibility of its policymaking and in the inevitability of its re-election to ignore pressure groups and to scorn pandering to populism. Even its critics contend it has been successful. But times have changed. Social media have turned silent, isolated dissent into more concerted, vocal protest. The political opposition— with less than 10% of the seats in parliament—seems a long way from power. But with 40% of the popular vote in 2011, it can no longer be dismissed as irrelevant. For its part, the government makes much these days of its willingness to 'listen'.
>
> In this context, the struggle over Bukit Brown takes on a wider meaning. The improbable coalition of birdwatchers, conservationists and heritage buffs trying to stop the

road are testing the government's promises of a new responsiveness, or, put another way, the strength of its conviction that it still knows best. The argument over the fate of the graveyard may look like a tussle over Singapore's past. But it is really about its future.[104]

Notes

1 Thanks are due to Tilak Abeysinghe, Manu Bhaskaran, Richard Doner, Gunter Dufey, Donald Low, Irene Ng, Pang Eng Fong, Kanwaljit Soin and others for their very helpful comments on earlier versions of this paper. Any remaining errors of fact or interpretation are mine alone.

2 My own early contributions to this literature include Pang Eng Fong and Linda Lim, 'Rapid Growth and Relative Price Stability in a Small Open Economy: The Experience of Singapore', in Vittorio Corbo, Anne O. Kreuger and Fernando Ossa (eds), *Export-Oriented Development Strategies: The Success of Five Newly Industrializing Countries*, Westview Press, Boulder, CO, 1985, 79–110; Linda Lim, Pang Eng Fong and Ronald Findlay, 'Singapore', in Ronald Findlay and Stanley Wellisz (eds), *Five Small Open Economies*, Oxford University Press for the World Bank, New York, 1993, 93–137.

3 The Singapore 'model' has been praised and singled out for emulation (often for different reasons) by a wide range of noted economists, including Michael Porter, Robert Reich, Paul Romer, Joseph Stiglitz, Lester Thurow and many media columnists; some of these will be considered later in this chapter.

4 World Bank, *The East Asian Miracle: Economic Growth and Public Policy*, Oxford University Press, Oxford, 1993.

5 See, for example, Dani Rodrik, 'Normalizing Industrial Policy', Commission on Growth and Development, Working Paper No. 3, The World Bank, Washington, DC, 2008.

6 For a summary explanation of high East Asian savings, see, for example, Linda Y.C. Lim, 'Rebalancing in East Asia', in Stijn Claessens, Simon Evenett and Bernard Hoekman (eds), *Rebalancing the Global Economy, A Primer for Policymaking*, Center for Economic Policy-Making, London, 2010, 32–35.

7 See, for example, Robert E. Wade, *Governing the Market: Economic Theory and the Role of Government in East Asian Industrialization*, Princeton University Press, Princeton, NJ, 1990; Jung-en Woo, *Race to the Swift: State and Finance in Korean Industrialization*, Columbia University Press, New York, 1991; Linda Y. C. Lim, 'Foreign Investment, the State and Industrial Policy in Singapore', in Howard Stein (ed.), *Asian Industrialization and Africa: Case Studies and Policy Alternatives to Structural Adjustment*, St Martin's Press, London and New York, 1995, 205–38.

8 Linda Y.C. Lim, 'Singapore's Success: The Myth of the Free Market Economy', *Asian Survey* 26, 1983: 756–64, summarises the role of the state in Singapore's early economic development.

9 Manufacturing was over 25% of GDP until the downturn following the 2008–09 global financial crisis.

10 GIC's funds come from government surpluses, which include foreign exchange reserves accumulated from balance of payments surpluses, and other government cash surpluses. Temasek developed from a holding company for entities such as DBS (Development Bank of Singapore), Singapore Airlines and other GLCs, often referred to as TLCs (Temasek-linked companies).

11 In 2010 Singapore had a per capita income of US$40,070 in nominal terms, and $55,790 in purchasing power terms, which ranked seventh in the world, according to the World Bank's *World Development Indicators* 2012, Table 1.1, www.worldbank.org.

12 Singapore perennially ranks second (to Switzerland) in the annual *Global Competitiveness Report* rankings of the World Economic Forum, most recently in 2012–13, www.weforum.org.

13 Singapore perennially ranks second (to Hong Kong) in the Heritage Foundation's annual *Index of Economic Freedom*, most recently in 2013, www.heritage.org.

14 Singapore ranked first in the World Bank and International Financial Corporation's *Doing Business 2013* report, www.doingbusiness.org.

15 Singapore typically ranks among the top 10 countries in the OECD's Programme for International Student Assessment, including in 2012, www.oecd.org/pisa.

16 In the short term, regulatory tightening benefited Singapore's financial centre as tax-avoiding global capital fled there from Switzerland and other Western countries. The bulk of Singapore's private wealth management services are accounted for by Asian investors, so its 'strict bank-secrecy laws and a poor record on exchanging information' (*The Economist* 'Special Report on Offshore Finance', 16

February 2013, 14) may continue without detriment to this sector. A potentially more serious concern is the international effort to require that taxes on MNCs be assessed in the geographical location where particular activities occur, such that transfer pricing to shift income (e.g. attributable to intellectual property) to low-tax jurisdictions like Singapore is limited.

17 Singapore also had unfavourable initial conditions, such as lack of natural resources and domestic market, labour unrest and the withdrawal of British military services accounting for one-third of GDP, which conditioned its choice of development strategy. See, for example, Richard F. Doner, Bryan Ritchie and Dan Slater, 'Systemic Vulnerability and the Origins of Developmental States: Northeast and Southeast Asia in Comparative Perspective', *International Organization* 59, 2005: 327–61.

18 www.edb.gov.sg.

19 HDB was particularly successful in rebuilding communities dislocated by extensive urban redevelopment. Its public housing estates included community centres, residents' committees, childcare and recreational facilities, all of which helped to form new communities and promote peaceful social relations in a multiracial and multireligious society (though an alternative interpretation was that these social goods and the 'grass-roots' organizations that managed them were designed to consolidate the ruling party's popularity and power).

20 Linda Y.C. Lim, 'Social Welfare in Singapore', in Kernial Singh Sandhu and Paul Wheatley (eds), *Singapore: The Management of Success*, Oxford University Press, Oxford, 1989, 171–97, describes the rationales (including ideological rationales) for Singapore's housing, education, health and social security policies from the 1960s to the 1980s.

21 One example is the National Trades Union Congress (NTUC), nominally an autonomous labour movement co-operative, but controlled by the ruling party for decades, headed by PAP cabinet ministers or members of parliament and widely seen as an extension of the government. NTUC runs many enterprises including the island's largest supermarket chain, insurance, taxis and resorts.

22 See, for example, Linda Low, *The Political Economy of a City-State: Government-Made Singapore*, Oxford University Press, 1998.

23 See Note 21. Strikes are also illegal throughout the economy; in 2012, the 'first strike in 25 years' resulted in striking bus drivers from the People's Republic of China being arrested, prosecuted, jailed and deported; one subsequently complained of 'lack of freedom' and workers' rights in Singapore, and the unfriendliness of Singaporeans, and claimed that some Bangladeshi workers were paid so little that they went without food, sg.news.yahoo.com/former-smrt-bus-driver-why-we-went-on-strike-part-ii-083616951.html. However, earlier, control of the labour movement facilitated adjustments such as redundancies, as argued in Yuen Chi Ching and Lim Ghee Soon, 'Globalization, Labour Market Deregulation and Trade Unions in Singapore', in Chris Rowley and John Benson (eds), *Globalization and Labour in the Asia-Pacific*, Frank Cass, London, 2000, 154–73.

24 For example, membership of the Singapore Business Federation is compulsory for all businesses in Singapore, and it is often headed by former civil servants (including currently).

25 This was achieved in part through vigorous suppression of a left-wing labour movement and political opposition.

26 For example, Canada's Fraser Institute ranks Singapore as 'partly free' (4 out of 7, where 1 is most free) in terms of political and civil liberties, www.fraserinstitute.org; the United Nations Human Development Index ranks it far lower in HDI than in per capita income (though granting a major jump since 2011 based on political liberalization), www.hdr.undp.org. Charles I. Jones and Peter J. Klenow, 'Beyond GDP? Welfare Across Countries and Time', National Bureau of Economic Research (NBER) Working Paper No. 16352, September 2010, find that Singapore has the greatest (negative) gap between per capita GDP and well-being of any of the 134 countries studied, with a welfare score of less than half that of Hong Kong despite a slightly higher per capita GDP.

27 Singapore has thus far reclaimed about 20% of its land from the sea, a process that is slowing due to the technical difficulties of reclaiming land from deeper waters, and the difficulty of obtaining reclamation materials (sand, rocks, earth) from neighbouring countries, most of which have now banned the export of such materials.

28 See, for example, Lee Tsao Yuan, 'Growth without Productivity: Singapore Manufacturing in the 1970s', *Journal of Development Economics* 19, 1985: 25–38; Alwyn Young, 'A Tale of Two Cities: Factor Accumulation and Technical Change in Hong Kong and Singapore', in O.J. Blanchard and S. Fischer (eds), *NBER Macroeconomics Annual 1992*, MIT Press, Cambridge, MA, 1992, 13–54; Alwyn Young, 'The Tyranny of Numbers: Confronting the Statistical Realities of the East Asian Growth Experience', *Quarterly Journal of Economics* 110, 1995: 641–80; Paul Krugman, 'The Myth of Asia's Miracle', *Foreign*

Affairs 73/6, 1994: 62–79; Koji Nomura and Tomomichi Amano, 'Labor Productivity and Quality Change in Singapore: Achievements in 1974–2011 and Prospects for the Next Two Decades', KEO Discussion Paper No. 129, September 2012, Keio Economic Observatory, Keio University.

29 See, for example, Pang Eng Fong and Linda Lim, 'Singapore's Foreign Workers: Are They Worth the Costs?' *Asian Wall Street Journal*, 4 August 1981; Pang Eng Fong and Linda Lim, 'Foreign Labour and Economic Development in Singapore', *International Migration Review* 16, 1982: 548–76; Pang Eng Fong and Linda Lim, 'Wage Policy in Singapore', in *Government Wage Policy Formulation in Less-Developed Countries: Seven Country Studies*, International Labour Office, Geneva, 1989, 75–101. For a more recent study, see Hui Weng Tat and Aamir Rafique Hasmi, 'Foreign Labour and Economic Growth: Policy Options for Singapore', *Singapore Economic Review* 52, 2007: 53–72. For a gender perspective, see Linda Y.C. Lim, 'Beyond Gender: The Impact of Age, Ethnicity, Nationality and Economic Growth on Women in the Singapore Economy', unpublished manuscript presented at the 25th anniversary of the Association for Women in Action and Research (AWARE) at the National University of Singapore, 5 March 2011, revised 13 July 2011.

30 The Singapore government claims that it is quick to stop supporting sectors that fail to perform, for example, scaling back on support for life sciences (biomedical) research when this cluster was (predictably) slow to deliver on commercial results, and when some of the 'international research stars' recruited from abroad to lead the effort left the country. However such a trial-and-error method of choosing sectors to subsidize has a high opportunity cost. In my field research in Singapore in 2012 and 2013 I came across partially or completely empty new buildings in dedicated technology research parks, and what other tenants told me were 'white elephant' operations soon to leave the premises that were occupied. Both local and foreign technology start-ups I visited, as well as larger multinationals with hundreds of employees, said that as many as 85% of their employees were foreigners, including recent Asian scholarship graduates from Singapore universities, who could obtain permanent residence (PR) status 'in one month', before foreign labour visa rules were tightened beginning in 2011.

31 www.mti.gov.sg/ResearchRoom/Documents/app.mti.gov.sg/data/pages/507/doc/1%20ERC_Main_Committee.

32 www.mti.gov.sg/ResearchRoom/Documents/app.mti.gov.sg/data/pages/885/doc/ESC%20Full%20Report.pdf.

33 Choy Keen Meng, 'Singapore's Changing Economic Model', in Terence Cheong (ed.), *Management of Success: Singapore Revisited*, Institute of Southeast Asian Studies, Singapore, 2010, 123–38. See also various essays in Choy Keen Meng, *Studies on the Singapore Economy*, World Scientific Publishing, Singapore, 2012.

34 Tilak Abeysinghe and Choy Keen Meng, 'The Aggregate Consumption Puzzle in Singapore', *Journal of Asian Economics* 15, 2004: 563–78; Linda Y.C. Lim and Lee Soo Ann, 'Globalizing State, Disappearing Nation: The Impact of Foreign Participation in the Singapore Economy', in Terence Chong (ed.), *Management of Success: Singapore Revisited*, Institute for Southeast Asian Studies, Singapore, 2010, 139–58; Hoon Hian Teck (Singapore Management University, Economics), 'The Future of Wages in Singapore', *The Straits Times*, 5 February 2013.

35 Department of Statistics, Singapore, cited in Goh Chin Lian, 'Gap Widens but Workfare Helps', *The Straits Times*, 21 February 2013; and Fiona Chan, 'Reducing Inequality', *The Straits Times*, 9 March 2013; this represented a worsening since 2000 (0.430) and 2010 (0.452), during which time the ratio of the average income of the top quintile of employed households to that of the bottom quintile also increased, from 10.1 to 12.9. For discussions of the causes of high and rising inequality, see Donald Low, 'The Four Myths of Inequality in Singapore', 26 April 2011, sites.google.com/site/reflection singapore/Downhome/Topic1/thefourmythsofinequalityinsingapore; Manu Bhaskaran, Ho Seng Chee, Donald Low, Tan Kim Song, Sudhir Vadaketh and Yeoh Lam Keong, 'Inequality and the Need for a New Social Compact', in Kang Soon Hock and Leong Chan-Hoong (eds), *Singapore Perspectives 2012 Singapore Inclusive: Bridging Divides*, World Scientific Publishing, Singapore, 2013, 125–78, and other chapters in this volume from the Institute of Policy Studies, Lee Kuan Yew School of Public Policy, National University of Singapore; Hui Weng Tat, 'Economic Growth and Inequality in Singapore: The Case for a Minimum Wage', *International Labour Review* 152, 2013: 107–23; Linda Y.C. Lim, 'Beyond Gender'. For an early analysis, see Pang Eng Fong, 'Growth, Inequality and Race in Singapore', *International Labour Review* 25, 1975: 508–23.

36 Irene Y.H. Ng, 'The Political Economy of Intergenerational Income Mobility in Singapore', *International Journal of Social Welfare* 22, 2013: 207–18; Irene Y.H. Ng, 'Education and Intergenerational Mobility in Singapore', *Educational Review* (Early online view Doi:10.1080/00131911.2013.780008).

37 Tilak Abeysinghe and Gu Jiaying, 'Lifetime Income and Housing Affordability in Singapore', *Urban Studies* 48, 2011: 1875–91.

38 Jones and Klenow, 'Beyond GDP?' 'In 2010 full-time resident male workers worked 50.7 hours a week … sales and service workers worked 52.5 hours (54.2 hours for those aged 50–59) and plant and machine operators 52.1 hours (54.7 hours for those aged 50–59)', Singapore labour force data cited in Linda Y.C. Lim, 'Beyond Gender'.

39 For one of many examples, see Geh Min, 'Singapore: Home or Hotel?' *The Straits Times*, 4 March 2013, and an earlier commentary by Linda Lim and Geh Min, 'When Less Is More', *The Straits Times*, 30 June 2008. See also www.bukitbrown.org, www.bukitbrown.com and other sites on the government's plan to demolish part of Singapore's oldest cemetery, a green area, to make way for roads, mass rapid transit, and new housing for an expanded population, similar to the planned demolition of an historic downtown school complex for condominium development, www.facebook.com/saveoldschool.

40 Boston Consulting Group, 2010, reported in *Bloomberg News*, 4 April 2012 with this caveat: 'Singapore is ending a program that allowed wealthy foreigners to "fast track" their permanent residency if they kept at least S$10 million in assets in the country for five years. The moves are aimed at slowing the rapid surge in property prices, which have been driven in part by wealthy investors and which have rankled Singaporeans.'

41 Economic Review Committee, 2003. For example, the expansion of financial services diverted local university students from engineering to business and finance, resulting in university engineering departments recruiting students from China and other countries, who then fulfilled their scholarship bonds by working for the required number of years in Singapore's semiconductor, petrochemical and other industries. Many of these subsequently left Singapore for China or other countries (such as the USA, Canada and Australia).

42 About two-thirds of jobs created in Singapore between 2006 and 2011 went to foreigners, or well over 100,000 per year; together with their dependents, it is likely that the foreign population grew by nearly one million (or 25% of Singapore's total population) in just six years. The increase slowed to 32,200 in 2012 (excluding construction and domestic service workers), Amelia Tan, 'Inflow of Foreign Workers Slows Down', *The Straits Times*, 16 March 2013. In 2010 the foreign-born accounted for 45% of the population and 38% of the total labour force.

43 The government and media have been particularly proud that Brazilian Facebook co-founder Eduardo Saverin and US investor Jim Rogers both left the USA to take up residence (instantly granted) in Singapore.

44 A slew of recent articles in the international press have highlighted Singapore's attractiveness to ultra-wealthy global elites. See, for example, Shibani Mahtani, 'Singapore Takes a Gamble on Glitz', *Wall Street Journal*, 3 October 2012, and 'Singapore: Wealth over the Edge', *WSJ Money*, Spring 2013. A recent report ranks Singapore third (behind London and New York) among cities 'important to high net-worth individuals', predicting that it will outrank New York in 10 years with property continuing 'to feature strongly in the investment portfolios of the rich', Cheryl Ong, 'Singapore "Set to be No. 2 Wealth Centre in the World"', *The Straits Times*, 12 March 2013.

45 At one time minimum rentals were set for hawker stalls in food centres, benefiting landlords at the expense of small entrepreneurs and relatively low-income consumers. However, telecoms charges did fall with privatization and increased competition.

46 Singapore lacks a comprehensive health insurance programme, such that a high proportion of citizens' medical costs are borne out of pocket. Public health services have been squeezed by the deliberate expansion of the high-earning private medical sector, an 'exportable service' catering disproportionately to wealthy foreigners, and overwhelmed by the sudden large increase in population, such that waiting times as well as service quality are perceived to have declined, even before population ageing has increased demand.

47 Irene Y.H. Ng, 'Can we Fix Inequality?' 23 September 2010, www.salt.org.sg. It is not known how many of the growing numbers of homeless and poor are the victims of 'problem gambling' following the opening of the casinos, which have delivered high profits to their foreign owners (Las Vegas Sands of the USA and Genting of Malaysia) and large tax revenues to the government, including from the entrance fee imposed on Singaporeans (but not on foreigners) in an effort to discourage their visits.

48 Tan Ern Ser (National University of Singapore, Sociology), quoted in Joyce Hooi, 'Singapore's Emigration Conundrum', *Business Times*, 6 October 2012.

49 Decades of gerrymandering explain the large discrepancy between the popular vote and parliamentary representation. Besides some genuine appreciation for the government's achievements, tight

media control, pre-election distributions (popularly known as 'goodies'), a limited nine-day election campaign, and lingering fears from the past persecution of opposition politicians, explain what in other countries would be considered a respectable popular vote share for the government.

50 No. 1-ranked Singapore Prime Minister Lee Hsien Loong's annual salary of US$2.85 million in 2011 was five times that of No. 2-ranked Donald Tsang of Hong Kong, seven times that of No. 5-ranked President Barack Obama of the USA, and 40 times that of average per capita GDP in Singapore (as calculated by *The Economist*, 5 July 2010). As part of the post-2011 salary revision, political leaders' and senior civil servants' annual bonuses are now linked to unemployment and median and bottom quintile wage increases, as well as to GDP growth which previously was the sole metric.

51 *A Sustainable Population for a Dynamic Singapore*, www.population.sg.

52 See, for example, Donald Low, Yeoh Lam Keong, Tan Kim Song and Manu Bhaskaran, 'Economic Myths in the Great Population Debate', www.ipscommons.sg; Linda Lim, 'How Land and People Fit in Singapore's Economy', 21 February 2013, www.sg.news.yahoo.com; and numerous traditional media articles and blog posts from January to March 2013. On 17 February 2013 a protest rally against the White Paper attracted 4,000 people at Hong Lim Green; the gathering was the 'largest in 40 years', given strict limitations on freedom of assembly.

53 For comparison, note that the much larger USA grants only 65,000 H1-B visas a year for highly skilled foreigners, though this number has been as high as 180,000 in the past and is expected to be raised in the near future.

54 For more on this subject, see Youyenn Teo, *Neoliberal Morality in Singapore: How Family Policies make State and Society*, Routledge, London, 2011, and the White Paper on Population Policy (Note 51).

55 See, for example, www.economist.com/houseprices for international comparisons by various metrics.

56 Tilak Abeysinghe (National University of Singapore, Economics), research reported in 'Move Beyond Economics to Boost Fertility', *The Straits Times*, 25 January 2013.

57 See, for example, reports on The Population Conundrum Roundtable on Singapore's Demographic Challenges, Institute of Policy Studies, Singapore, 3 May 2012, www.spp.nus.edu.sg, especially remarks by Pauline Straughan (National University of Singapore, Sociology).

58 Mindshare survey reported in Joyce Hooi, 'Singapore's Emigration Conundrum', *Business Times*, 6 October 2012. Some 65% of respondents did not believe that they would be able to retire comfortably in Singapore, 73% thought that public housing prices are 'getting out of hand', 75% agreed that 'I should not be spending my entire working life paying off my housing loan', 72% said they 'could not afford to get sick due to high medical costs', and 69% said that 'there are too many foreign workers taking up job opportunities in our society today'. According to the World Bank, there are 300,000 Singaporeans living and working abroad (about 9% of the total native population, although government figures put the number at 200,000 or 6%, one-third of whom left in the last 10 years), with Malaysia the top destination, followed by Australia, the UK and USA (all with lower per capita incomes than Singapore).

59 GLCs in the property development and REIT business include Capital Land, Mapletree, Keppel (core business: shipbuilding and marine services), and Singapore Press Holdings (core business: media).

60 Tessa Wong, '"Most Support Curbs" on Foreigner Inflow', *The Straits Times*, 19 March 2013.

61 'Has the Ideas Machine Broken Down?' *The Economist*, 12 January 2013, reviews work by Paul Romer and others that suggests that the availability of abundant cheap labour not only discourages investment in productivity but also reduces innovation and increases income inequality.

62 The recent appearance of credit and training programmes for small-scale entrepreneurs like hawkers is a potentially hopeful sign of a different philosophy emerging.

63 Survey by *The Economist* Corporate Network, reported by Yasmine Yahya in 'S'pore Losing Shine Among MNCs: Poll', *Business Times*, 8 January 2013. In February eight international chambers of commerce signed a letter to the government expressing their concerns with the tightening of employment visas for foreigners.

64 Aaron Low, 'Bosses Fear Further Curbs on Foreign Manpower', *The Straits Times*, 31 January 2013.

65 Note that local SMEs, like MNCs, have long received a variety of government subsidies, mostly for upgrading and retraining; however, because they are less capital-intensive than MNCs and less likely to be in the targeted high-tech and 'new industries' which receive the bulk of 'incentives', they receive fewer subsidies each.

66 Besides productivity growth, moderating property prices, rents and inflation from a slower-growing population, and slower appreciation of the Singapore dollar with lower inward FDI, could partly compensate for rising labour costs. Linda Lim, 'Can Slower Growth Lead to a Stronger Nation?' *The Straits Times*, 22 February 2013.

67 In addition to replacing 20-storey buildings with 50-storey ones, the government is also promoting joint development of the Iskandar project in the neighbouring Malaysian state of Johor, and exploring more ways for Singaporeans to live and work underground.

68 Prime Minister Lee Hsien Loong at the first Singapore Summit, quoted in Teh Shi Ning, 'S'pore to Build up its Foreign Reserves Shield', *Business Times*, 22 September 2012.

69 Chia Ngee Choon (National University of Singapore, Economics), 'How Progressive is the New Tax Structure?' *The Straits Times*, 28 February 2013, also notes that overall social spending is 'just above a third of the OECD average'; the 2013 Budget raises various levies on luxury car and investment housing purchases, mainly to reduce traffic congestion and housing price inflation, but they also have a progressive distributional impact.

70 For example, Mac Margolis, 'The Next Singapore: Honduras Ponders an Extreme Economic Makeover', *Newsweek*, 8 October 2012, reports on an effort to create a 'semi-autonomous, free-market charter city' like Hong Kong or Singapore 'to tap investment, migrant workers and innovation from around the world', an idea inspired by Paul Romer (New York University, Economics), www.chartercities.org.

71 Ravi Velloor, 'S'pore Held up as Model in Reducing Trade Barriers', *The Straits Times*, 24 January 2012, notes the World Bank's and Bain & Co.'s praise for Singapore's 'strategic initiatives to cut trade barriers', which facilitate the globalization of multinational supply chains.

72 Zhang Zhibin (ed.), *Dynamics of the Singapore Success Story: Insights by Ngiam Tong Dow*, Singapore: Cengage Asia Learning, 2011. Note that in the past several years, Mr Ngiam, once Singapore's top civil servant in charge of economic development, has been publicly critical of the government's more recent 21st-century policies, including the emphases on property and finance as sources of employment and income.

73 Donald Low (ed.), *Behavioural Economics and Policy Design: Examples from Singapore*, Singapore: World Scientific Publishing, 2012, for the Civil Service College.

74 Henri Ghesquiere, *Singapore's Success: Engineering Economic Growth*, Singapore: Thomson Learning, 2007. Dr Ghesquiere served on the staff of the IMF in 1978–2005, and was director of the IMF's Singapore Regional Training Institute in 2004–05.

75 Ibid., 167–68.

76 However, see also Jonathan Watts, 'Plans for Honduras Start-up City Hit by Transparency Concerns: Blow to Plan's Credibility as NYU Professor Paul Romer Says He Has Been Unable to Act as Its Guarantor and Watchdog', *The Guardian*, 7 September 2012.

77 See, for example, Ross Worthington, *Governance in Singapore*, RoutledgeCurzon, London and New York, 2003; Michael D. Barr and Zlatko Skrbis, *Constructing Singapore: Elitism, Ethnicity and the Nation-Building Project*, Copenhagen, Denmark: Nordic Institute of Asian Studies (NIAS Press) Democracy in Asia No. 11, 2008. One of the well-known facts about governance that these authors note is that Singapore has had only three prime ministers since 1959, with the third, current Prime Minister Lee Hsien Loong, being the son of the founding Prime Minister Lee Kuan Yew, while his wife Ho Ching is the long-time head of the sovereign wealth fund Temasek.

78 As Ghesquiere also notes, 'Good institutions can take a variety of forms. Each country must fashion the specifics of its policies and institutions tailored to its own local geographical and historical conditions' (Ghesquiere, *Singapore's Success*, 168). Singapore's model differs from those of South Korea and Taiwan, but all had the political will and determination to impose their chosen models on their populations in the early stages of industrial development.

79 With rising affluence, education, and the spread of the internet and social media, especially among youth and post-Arab Spring, it is tempting to suggest that this unpopularity is due to a desire for greater political freedoms. However, the public discourse and popular rhetoric including online is heavily weighted toward so-called 'bread-and-butter' issues of stagnating incomes and worsening distribution, housing and health care costs, etc. for which government policy allowing the massive influx of foreigners is held partly to blame. Singaporeans did not seem to mind high salaries for political leaders and senior public officials, when their own economic situation was good, and the public sector appeared to be performing well; their ire was raised only when several repeated failures in public services (escape of a terrorist suspect from jail, mass transit overcrowding and breakdowns, frequent severe flooding, high cost and reduced availability of housing and health care, etc.) called into question the competence of highly compensated civil servants whom 'we pay well to do the job'. As many of the commentators cited here note, the past 'social compact' in which Singaporeans supposedly accepted curbs on their political freedoms in exchange for economic and social advancement has broken down because of the state's failure to deliver the latter, even as political freedoms have gradually improved.

80 For thoughtful reflections on post-2011 governance challenges in Singapore, see the following essays by former civil servant Donald Low: 'What Went Wrong for the PAP in 2011?' www.facebook.com/notes/donald-lows-fc/what-went-wrong-for-the-pap-in-2011/209993849034597; 'Sustaining Good Governance in an Era of Rapid and Disruptive Change', speech at the IPS Singapore Perspective Conference, February 2013; 'Reframing the National Conversation', IPS Commons, www.ipscommons.sg/index.php/categories/politics/86-reframing-the-national-conversation; 'Governing in the New Normal', *The Straits Times*, 10 September 2011. Singapore justifiably ranks as the least corrupt country in Asia, No. 5 globally in 2012, www.transparency.org, though recent years have seen a rise in high-profile cases of corruption related to government procurement contracts.

81 See, for example 'Here, There and Everywhere', *The Economist* Special Report on Outsourcing and Offshoring, 19 January 2013.

82 For example, during the financial crisis Singapore's sovereign wealth funds incurred large losses from their investments in Western financial institutions such as Citigroup, Merrill Lynch and UBS; their telecommunications investments in Indonesia, Thailand and Australia caused political controversy and also resulted in losses.

83 Emerging economies suffering from the same problems have in recent years imposed a variety of capital controls that are increasingly sanctioned by the IMF; see, for example, Dani Rodrik, 'Global Capital Rules', www.project-syndicate.org, 7 April 2013. This is not possible for Singapore, given the reliance of its financial services sector on open capital flows, but in 2012 the Monetary Authority of Singapore added macro-prudential measures to what had previously been only exchange rate management in its monetary policy.

84 For example, in 2013 Singapore was found to be the centre of a global soccer-fixing syndicate, presumably facilitated by the ease of money transfers.

85 At the extreme, the Singapore EDB has paid for the salaries of engineers and other skilled employees of multinationals such as Microsoft and Hewlett-Packard; such jobs tend to disappear when subsidies are withdrawn, since by definition they do not make market sense for the employing multinationals. There have also been media reports of young Singaporeans graduating with previously encouraged 'life sciences' degrees being unable to find suitable employment (e.g. the celebrated case of a Stanford PhD 'new citizen' from China found driving a taxi).

86 During my 2013 research visit to Singapore, more than half of the taxi drivers I engaged were in the business (which, unusually, is limited to Singapore citizens only), after being laid off (after 8–20 years as production managers, logistics and procurement officers, warehouse supervisors, sales and marketing managers, even an engineer) from MNCs, mostly in electronics (e.g. disk drives), but also in consumer goods; many blamed age discrimination for the loss of their previous jobs.

87 'Foreigners beholden to the state for its beneficence and their own presence are unlikely to challenge its authority, in the way that an independent, globally competitive and non-state-dependent domestic entrepreneurial class—still weak and largely absent in Singapore—might', Linda Y.C. Lim and Lee Soo Ann, 'Globalizing State, Disappearing Nation', 155. Some Singaporeans (particularly active online) go further in subscribing to the 'conspiracy theory' that the goal of the government's immigration policy is to 'dilute' native Singaporean votes with those of 'new citizens' who are much more likely to support the ruling PAP.

88 Linda Lim, 'Why Local Entrepreneurs are Vital', *The Straits Times*, 12 May 2009, makes the case for local entrepreneurs as agents of economic growth going forward.

89 Conservatives do not seem to realize that public sector surpluses are derived from private sector deficits, since they mean that the state collects more in revenues from the population than it delivers in expenditures.

90 Joseph E. Stiglitz, 'Singapore's Lessons for an Unequal America', *The New York Times*, 18 March 2013, opinionator.blogs.nytimes.com/2013/03/18/singapores-lessons-for-an-unequal-america/. Professor Stiglitz has been a frequent visitor to Singapore over many years.

91 These arguments were cogently made by Teo You Yenn (Nanyang Technological University, Sociology), 'How Stiglitz Weakens Change in S'pore', www.todayonline.com/print/98231, one of many critical comments on the Stiglitz article.

92 Stiglitz, 'Singapore's Lessons for an Unequal America'.

93 Matt Miller, 'What Singapore can Teach Us', *Washington Post*, 2 May 2012.

94 Cited in Sharon Chen, 'Can the Singapore Model Solve US Unemployment Crisis?' www.asiancorrespondent.com, 21 October 2011.

95 For example, as noted by Hoon Hian Teck, 'The Future of Wages in Singapore': 'The ready access to the supply of foreign workers kept labour costs low while the increase in value added per worker

boosted the profitability of manufacturing firms. This boost to profits very likely benefited both multi-national corporations (MNCs) as well as small and medium-sized enterprises (SMEs).'

96 Robin Chan and Aaron Low, 'Find Middle Ground: Economists, MPs', *The Straits Times*, 11 June 2012. See also Donald Low, 'Squaring the Circle the Scandinavian Way', www.facebook.com/notes/donald-lows-fc/squaring-the-circle-the-scandinavian-way/389281347772512.

97 Contrary to Professor Stiglitz's attributing Singapore's recent political liberalization to its 'leaders' having 'taken steps to expand political participation', this is more the result of the spread of the internet and social media, and the emergence of a 'new generation', as acknowledged by Prime Minister Lee Hsien Loong in a recent *Washington Post* interview, reported by Andrea Ong, 'Govt Will Need to be More Open, Says PM', *The Straits Times*, 17 March 2013. There has been a notable increase in well-educated young professionals participating in the political opposition, motivated in large part by the perception of declining living standards and economic opportunities for themselves and their fellow citizens in 21st-century Singapore.

98 For details, see Linda Lim, 'Singapore's Economic Growth Model: Too Much or Too Little?' *Ethos* 6, May 2009: 32–38.

99 See, for example, Choy Keen Meng, 'Rethinking Singapore's Growth Model', *Today*, 7 November 2009.

100 For example, residential property (and REITs) are major investment asset classes for foreigners attracted to Singapore as a 'safe haven' for international and offshore capital (private banking and wealth management are promoted as part of the financial services sector), while permanent residents compete with citizens for scarce public housing, and foreign workers crowd and push up rents in both the public and private housing sectors.

101 An example of resulting resource misallocation was the discovery that government-subsidized industrial space was being illegally converted into dormitories to be rented out to foreign workers (also with 'nowhere else to go') for a much higher return than manufacturing could yield.

102 For example, nearly every ministry has its own research and training units which both conduct in-house activities and outsource them to private sector (often foreign) consultancies, professional service providers and commercial market research firms (e.g. McKinsey, KPMG, Gallup, Nielsen, etc.). Anecdotally it appears that Singapore government agencies and GLCs may account for as much as one-third of the business in the professional services private sector; their custom (like their capital) is also a reason for other companies to set up in Singapore, e.g. US start-ups with which I have had contact, in the medical technology, IT and telecoms sectors.

103 Meanwhile, the Ministry of Home Affairs grants permanent residence (permission to immigrate and settle permanently, not just to work temporarily) on other criteria, including education and race, given the government's long-standing belief that the racial proportions of the population existing at independence should be preserved.

104 Banyan, 'Grave Concerns', *The Economist*, 6 April 2013. See also Linda Lim, 'Singapore: Place or Nation?' *The Straits Times*, 16 June 2006; Linda Lim, 'Can Money Ease Loss of Memories?' *The Straits Times*, 21 June 2007; Geh Min, 'Singapore: Home or Hotel?' (2013).

12

The original sin in Chile's successful history of development

Patricio Navia

Since the end of the Pinochet dictatorship in 1990, Chile has been a success story of democratic consolidation and economic development. All economic indicators show significant progress. Democratic institutions are strong and getting stronger. Citizens are politically engaged and social movements are flourishing. The origin of the so-called Chilean miracle can be traced back to the neo-liberal economic model adopted under the Pinochet dictatorship, but the pragmatic and gradual approach to economic and institutional reforms championed since democracy was restored explains why Chile has successfully avoided the pro-cyclical boom and bust trend that has characterized most other Latin American economies in the last two decades. Though the quality of life of all Chileans has improved, high levels of inequality remain a dark spot in the otherwise most successful story of economic development and democratic consolidation in Latin America in the past three decades.

The origin of the Chilean miracle

Although it is an inconvenient fact for advocates of market-friendly policies, the Chilean economic model dates back to the brutal Augusto Pinochet dictatorship (1973–90). The original sin of the so-called Chilean miracle raises results from its illegitimacy of origin and the authoritarian conditions under which the reforms were first implemented. Moreover, it transforms Pinochet into the father of today's Chile. As in the epic *Star Wars* film series, Chile can be described as a Luke Skywalker having to deal with the trauma of being the son of the villain Darth Vader. Building the strength to move past the traumatic origin—without forgetting the atrocities of human rights violations—has been a difficult task for Chile. While on the one hand the economic model has allowed it to lift millions out of poverty and has converted Chile into one of the most developed countries in Latin America, the legacies of human rights violations perpetrated by the military dictatorship still haunt Chileans and will always be an indelible mark on the nation's history.

As Figure 12.1 shows, compared to Latin America and the rest of the world, the Chilean economy was an underperformer in the 1960s. In the 1970s and early 1980s the country experienced two severe economic crises. Since 1983—10 years into the authoritarian period— the Chilean economy entered into a stable growth pattern that has lasted for more than three

Figure 12.1 GDP per capita (constant 2000 US$), 1960–2010
Source: author with data from World Development Indicators, World Bank

decades. In the early 1990s, after democracy was restored, the Chilean economy surpassed the Latin American average in per capita terms. More recently, during the first decade of the new century, the Chilean economy has grown to a per capita higher than the world economy average. As the growth trajectory of the economy began under military rule, the origins of the three-decade period of economic expansion cannot be disassociated from the controversial legacy of the Pinochet dictatorship. However, since Chile only surpassed the Latin American average after democracy was restored—and because the period of economic growth has survived the authoritarian regime by more than two decades—the credit for the successful performance of the Chilean economy must also go to the democratic governments that implemented reforms, in their own words, to transform the neo-liberal economic model into a socially oriented neo-liberal model, or as neo-liberalism with a human face.[1]

Figure 12.1 shows that while in the 1960s the Chilean economy barely grew and in the 1970s it followed a boom and bust trajectory, since the mid-1980s Chile has experienced gradual and sustained economic growth. More than impressive growth—which Chile has none the less enjoyed occasionally—the big story behind Chile's success is its gradual and incremental growth path and the ability to avoid prolonged stagnation or recessionary setbacks. While the rest of Latin America continues to go through periods of rapid growth followed by stagnation or recession, Chile has moved forward as it has maintained a pattern of moderate growth and has successfully avoided declines.

Since the 1930s Chilean governments have championed import substitution industrialization (ISI) policies with mixed results.[2] Protectionist policies fostered the emergence of an industrialized and manufacturing sector, but negatively impacted competitiveness. Protectionist policies favoured the organized labour sector to the detriment of the large majority of the population

Chile's successful history of development

that remained in the informal sector or in rural areas. The state strengthened its control over the formal sector with regulations and labour legislation that protected workers, but the limited dynamism of the private sector and the falling competitiveness of the Chilean economy prevented economic development and condemned a majority of Chileans to a life of poverty and destitution.

As Figure 12.2 shows, the Chilean economy presented a common pro-cyclical pattern in the 1960s, with boom and bust periods. After reformist Christian Democratic Party (PDC) Eduardo Frei was elected (1964–70), his government further deepened ISI policies, with the partial nationalization of the copper industry, and launched an ambitious agrarian reform initiative aimed at empowering the rural unorganized labour sector and reducing wealth inequality.[3] Though Frei's reforms brought inflation down, the economy continued to grow at a slow rate. Rapid population growth—triggered by massive migration to urban areas where living conditions and access to health and education were much better—further limited the effect of economic development. By 1970 the Frei 'revolution in liberty' reformist economic model was greatly discredited and most Chileans wanted change. In the 1970 election, the country was almost equally split three ways. Former conservative President Jorge Alessandri (1958–64) campaigned on a fiscally conservative and business-friendly platform. PDC candidate Radomiro Tomic campaigned on further defending Frei's reformist policies and left-wing candidate Salvador Allende, the leader of a coalition comprising the Communist Party (PC), Socialist Party (PS) and other left-wing parties, campaigned on a revolutionary platform that would put the state at the centre of economic activity. Allende won with 36.6% of the vote, just above Alessandri (35.3%). Tomic ended in third place (28.1%). Though turn-out was high (56.2%), it was

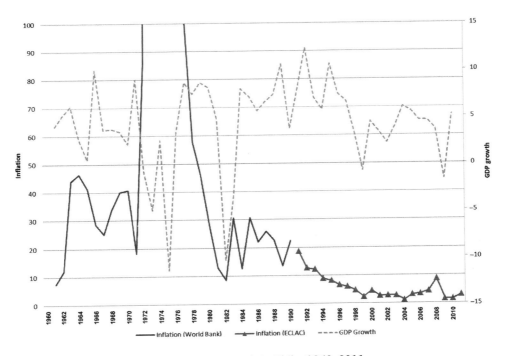

Figure 12.2 Inflation and per capita GDP growth in Chile, 1960–2011
Source: author with data from World Development Indicators, World Bank Inflation in 1971–1977 was 414%, 665%, 335%, 251% and 106%

229

lower than in 1964 (61.6%). Almost half of voting-age Chileans were still excluded from the political process.[4]

As no candidate received an absolute majority, the constitution mandated Congress to name the president from among the two candidates with the most votes. Following a complex negotiations with socialists and communists, the PDC voted for Allende, thus making him the first Marxist to be democratically elected in the world. The PDC required Allende's commitment to limit the scope of his nationalization plans. As president, Allende moved swiftly to fully nationalize copper—partially nationalized under his predecessor. The Socialist president also pushed for significant wage increases and implemented aggressive expansionary policies that quickly overheated the economy and triggered hyperinflation. Allende faced the militant opposition of the business sector and the USA, which feared the effect of Allende's democratic victory would combine with the influence of the 1959 Cuban revolution to make Latin America a fertile ground for revolutions and for the expansion of its Cold War enemy, the USSR.

Less than three years into his six-year term, in a bloody military coup on 11 September 1973, Salvador Allende's Popular Unity government was overthrown by the military. The reasons for the democratic breakdown have been discussed extensively elsewhere.[5] The role of the USA in destabilizing Allende[6] and the political polarization that took place in those years[7] have been cited as reasons for the military coup, but the impact of the failed economic policies implemented by the Popular Unity government cannot be ignored.[8] As Figure 12.2 shows, the economy was in an undeniable state of crisis when Allende was deposed.

Claiming that the Allende government had violated the constitution and citing the growing economic crisis—with high inflation, price control, black markets and growing nationalization of the productive sector—the military took power. The military junta, led by the head of the army, General Augusto Pinochet, had a much clearer goal of what it stood against than a plan of what to do to put the economy back on its feet.

At the same time that it committed atrocious human rights violations against political opponents, the military government began to implement policies that sought to stabilize the economy. As Figure 12.2 shows, it took a few years to bring inflation down from its record levels of 1973. Although it first simply focused on reversing the nationalization initiatives implemented by Allende, the military government soon went further beyond and began to implement market-friendly policies that ended up becoming Pinochet's biggest legacy.[9]

After the economy was stabilized, from the late 1970s until it ceded power to a democratically elected government in 1990, the Pinochet dictatorship implemented sweeping neo-liberal economic reforms.[10] Promoted by a group of young economists trained in the 1960s at the University of Chicago (the Chicago Boys), the neo-liberal policies sought to reduce the role of the state in the economy. Thus, state enterprises were privatized, legislation that gave the government oversight powers was repealed and new legislation that promoted private and foreign investment was adopted. As Figure 12.3 shows, the size of the state began to decline rapidly after the country emerged from its 1973–75 recession.

The military was able to implement all the reforms under authoritarian rules, repressing the opposition and labour unions that were adversely affected by the market-friendly policies. The implementation of the reforms is intrinsically associated with the massive human rights violations that characterized the Pinochet regime: the overwhelming discretionary power the military had allowed General Pinochet to build a new institutional set-up. The 1980 constitution, custom-made for Pinochet, established a protected-democracy framework[11] and also established the foundations for the market-friendly economic model.[12] However, the constitution also became a trap for the military dictatorship. As even custom-made shoes bind, the 1980 constitution became the

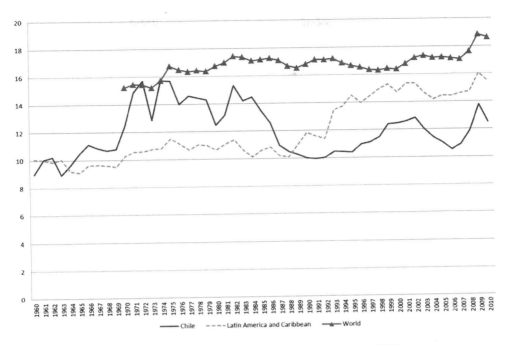

Figure 12.3 General government final consumption expenditure (% of GDP)
Source: author with data from World Development Indicators, World Bank.

roadmap for the restoration of democracy in Chile.[13] In fact, though most of the authoritarian components of the 1980 constitution have been amended and modified since democracy was restored in 1990,[14] the institutions and constitutional prerogatives on which the market-friendly economic model is based remain intact. In that sense, Pinochet remains the father of the neo-liberal economic model in Chile. The democratic governments that have ruled the country since 1990 have further deepened the model and have also legitimized it, by introducing reforms to reduce poverty, increase social spending and strengthen the regulatory role of the state.

The main tenant of the neo-liberal reforms implemented under Pinochet was that the state was an obstacle for economic development. Thus, by reducing the size of the state and limiting its functions, the *creative destruction* power of capitalism would be unleashed and economic growth would bring about development. As Figure 12.3 shows, after increasing in the 1960s, central government consumption expenditure substantially decreased under the authoritarian regime and remained low until democracy was restored. Since then, there has been a gradual upward trend, but it remains relatively weak compared to the rest of Latin America and to the world in general. As Chile's growth has been driven primarily by the private sector and as the state has a limited role in affecting economic output, the Chilean model can be properly characterized as neo-liberal. The market-friendly focus on institutions and government policies is intrinsically associated with the growth experienced in the past three decades. However, as critics repeatedly argue, the limited role of the state on the economy has also allowed for income and social inequality to remain high. The cost of the economic expansion experienced by Chile has been high levels of inequality. That remains Chile's largest social unmet challenge. If it is not addressed properly, it can also constitute a threat to Chile's long-term stability and to the country's chances of becoming the first Latin American country to enter the elite of industrialized nations.

The economic plan of the military focused on promoting market-based mechanisms and limiting the role of the state in economic activities and social interactions. As a result, the Chilean state today has a limited—and sometimes non-existent—role in areas where the state is the leading economic actor elsewhere, like elementary and secondary education or pensions. In Chile, the role of the state is mostly limited to a regulatory oversight power. Though some key public sector companies were not privatized under the military dictatorship (most notably the copper-producing CODELCO), the sweeping economic reforms implemented by the Chicago Boys substantially reduced the size of the public sector and limited the role of the state as an economic engine.

Today, the role of the state in Chile is limited. A Chilean child can be born in a private clinic paid for by her parents' private health insurance. The child will attend private day care and spend her entire elementary and secondary school years in a private school partially funded by a public voucher programme. She will attend a private university. When she starts working, her monthly mandated retirement deduction will go directly to a private pension of her choice. She will drive an automobile on privatized highways and will pay her utility bills to private companies that bring electricity, gas and telecommunications to Chilean homes. When she dies, she will be buried in a private cemetery. She can go her entire life with minimal interaction with the state. To be sure, the state does have regulatory power over most sectors, but its regulatory muscle and its enforcement power are limited.

This neo-liberal paradise is built on an intricate set of institutional features put in place in the 1980 constitution. The constitution explicitly bans the state from participating in productive economic activity and establishes broad protections of private property. Though a number of key reforms were introduced by the military in the 1970s, the most important reforms were adopted after the 1980 constitution was approved and General Pinochet began an eight-year presidential term in March 1981.

The most important early reform in the 1970s was the Foreign Direct Investment Statute (Decree Law 600 of 1974), designed to attract foreign capital and to reverse the negative effect of the nationalization effort championed by Presidents Frei and Allende. By building an institutional set-up that protected foreign investment, the military government sent a clear signal of commitment to market-friendly policies. The reversal of several nationalizations enacted under Allende and the privatization of other public sector companies was also intended to attract foreign investors as the country was in dire need of capital. Low domestic savings and high government expenditures had stalled economic development. The stabilization phase in the mid-1970s set the foundations for more innovative and controversial reforms adopted later.

Among the important reforms implemented by the dictatorship in the 1980s were the educational overhaul that transferred schools from the national to municipal governments, the privatization of the pension system, the partial privatization of health care and the nationalization of public sector companies. Deregulation of several economic sectors also fostered the growth of private enterprises and restricted government's ability to block private initiatives, though it also limited the regulatory power of the state to protect and enforce consumers' rights.

A case study: educational reform

One of the most controversial reforms after the passage of the 1980 constitution involved education. In discussing it in detail, I explain the ideological tenants of all the reforms adopted under the military. The goal of the reforms was to reduce the discretionary power of the state, to introduce market mechanisms that would foster competition and establish incentives to reduce information asymmetries and level the playing field to reward meritocracy and productivity.

Prior to the dictatorship, the state had almost complete control of the educational system. Those with access to public education, especially tertiary education, received a good education, but access was limited. In fact, in 1960, while 80% of the population had received an elementary education (six years), 14% had completed a secondary education, and only 4% of those aged between 20 and 24 years were enrolled in tertiary education. By 1970 elementary education coverage reached 93% of children, secondary education 50%, and 9% of those aged between 20 and 24 years were enrolled in tertiary education.[15] In 1980 95% had received an elementary education, 65% a secondary education and only 11% of those in the 20–24 age group were enrolled in tertiary education.[16]

In 1973 the military government took control of eight universities (two public and six private). As universities had been a centre of political activism in the 1960s, the authoritarian government seized control of tertiary education and limited its political influence. Under military control, enrolment was frozen and funding was cut. In 1980 university funding was divided into two types, direct and indirect fiscal funding (AFD and AFI, respectively). AFD was complemented by AFI, a direct subsidy to universities associated with the 20,000 students with the best scores in entrance exams. By associating AFI funding with entrance exam scores, the government introduced incentives for universities to compete for the best students. The two public national universities were divided into smaller regional universities. Decree Law 3541 also allowed for the creation of non-profit private universities, for-profit private professional institutes (IP) and for-profit centres for technical formation (CFT), thus allowing for-profit tertiary education. Before 1980 there were six non-profit private universities, which were run by educational foundations (including some by the Catholic Church). The number of public and government-funded non-profit private universities increased from eight before 1980 to 20 by 1990 and government-funded IPs fluctuated from seven in 1984 down to two in 1990.[17] A number of private universities, IPs and CFTs not funded by the government were also created after 1980. When democracy was restored in 1990, there were 40 private universities, 80 IPs and 168 CFTs.[18]

In 1981 the government also introduced elementary and secondary education reforms.[19] Public schools were transferred to municipal governments. A voucher system was established to fund elementary and secondary education. Private for-profit schools were allowed. A subsidy for each child was to be paid directly to the municipality or the private school owners. Competition was introduced between private and municipal schools. Since parents could choose which schools to send their children to, there would be market incentives for schools to offer quality education.

Public school elementary and secondary enrolment decreased from 80% to 60% between 1980 and 1990, while voucher school enrolment increased to 30% by 1990. The other 10% of children attended fully private schools.[20] In 1990 elementary education coverage reached 95% of children and secondary education 78%.[21] Since 2003, there was constitutionally mandated universal elementary and secondary school coverage. Voucher school enrolment continued to increase progressively under democratic rule. By 2008 it had reached 45%, the same share of children attending municipal schools.

One day before it left office in 1990, the military dictatorship passed a comprehensive education bill that incorporated all the changes made under Pinochet. The bill secured deregulation, guaranteeing the presence of private for-profit education at the elementary and secondary levels and ensuring the municipalization of education. As the bill required a supermajority vote for future changes (an organic constitutional bill that required a 4/7 majority of seating members of both chambers), it became especially difficult for the incoming democratic government to alter the educational system that had been designed and implemented under the dictatorship.

The expansion of tertiary education began after democracy was restored. In 1990, 249,482 college-aged Chileans were enrolled in tertiary education, 13% of the 18–24 age group. Of them, 131,702 were enrolled in universities. Some 20 years later, in 2009, the number was 876,243 (30.8% of the respective age group). Five-fold growth brought the number of university students to 576,600 in 2009. Most of the increase came from growth in private university enrolment. In 1990 one in every six university students was enrolled in a private institution. In 2009 the number of students enrolled in private institutions (258,960) was almost identical to those enrolled in public institutions (276,683).[22]

Though first implemented under military rule, the market-friendly educational reforms were consolidated after democracy was restored in 1990. After Pinochet was defeated in a plebiscite in 1988, a coalition of centre-left political parties, the Concertación, led a successful transition to democracy. The Concertación won four consecutive presidential elections between 1989 and 2005. Concertación governments developed aggressive earmarked social spending policies to alleviate poverty. Since limited social spending was prioritized to help the poor, old policies that granted universal access to social services were replaced with new policies that focused spending on the lowest two quintiles of the population. The implementation of targeted social policies was considered too moderate or insufficiently universal by some critics.[23] The Concertación defended them because of their more immediate and stronger effect on reducing poverty.[24] Independent observers and right-wing think tanks agreed.[25]

The four Concertación governments (1990–2010) applied the same logic to education. They put the focus of social spending on promoting universal access to elementary and secondary education. Under President Patricio Aylwin (1990–94), educational policies 'targeted individual schools directly with additional resources and disregarded (and at times interfered with) market mechanisms'.[26] The focus of educational policies shifted from 'access and quality in the 1980s to "quality and equity", although equity was not a particularly important component in education policies instituted during the Aylwin administration'.[27] The most important reforms were a teacher labour statute that protected employment and established a single pay structure for teachers in municipal schools, and a reform that targeted the worst performing primary schools. The shared financing mechanism top-up co-pay—which allowed parents to complement the government voucher in private but not in municipal schools—was also implemented under Aylwin.

Under President Eduardo Frei (1994–2000), educational reform focused on increasing teachers' pay, transparency of school level test scores and the adoption of the extended school day for municipal and voucher schools. The reform required massive government investment in infrastructure for municipal and private schools. Formerly controlled by militants of Concertación parties, the Colegio de Profesores fell under the control of the Communist Party, a left-wing opposition party, in 1995.

Under President Ricardo Lagos (2000–06), a constitutional reform in 2003 made secondary education mandatory. In addition, the Lagos administration focused on promoting access to voucher schools to vulnerable students. Schools that received government subsidies had to accept a minimum of 15% of vulnerable students—defined as those from families so classified by the government's social programmes scheme. Though there were plenty of mechanisms available to schools not to comply with that requirement, this reform sought to use the government subsidy to foster school integration. The government aimed to reverse the growing segregation by parents' income in Chilean schools that resulted in lower-income families sending their children to municipal schools and middle-class families choosing voucher schools. The Lagos administration also introduced a teacher evaluation scheme. Though the government had tried since the early 1990s to introduce a mechanism to assess the quality of teachers, an effective opposition by the Colegio de Profesores derailed those efforts. Criticized as insufficient and only applied to municipal schools, the 2004 teacher evaluation reform constituted a major change in educational accountability. The government also introduced a more transparent mechanism to select

Chile's successful history of development

municipal school principals, a move that undermined the power of unionized teachers but was cleverly passed using the argument that it would allow the removal of principals who had been appointed during the military dictatorship.

Shortly after Michelle Bachelet (2006–10) became the first woman president in Chile, student protests rocked the country, in May 2006. The movement started at public secondary schools and soon spread to other municipal and voucher schools. Soon after, the movement spread to public universities and other higher education institutions. As the government was slow to react, the movement soon dominated the political agenda and forced Bachelet to shuffle her cabinet on 14 July, replacing the ministers of the interior (her chief of cabinet), education and economics. Bachelet also appointed an ad hoc 81-member presidential advisory council on education, charged with drafting a proposal to reform the educational system at all levels. The committee eventually produced two reports, reflecting the lack of consensus on the role of the private sector in the provision of educational services, funding for private and public education, and the regulatory role of the state over private institutions.

In April 2007 Bachelet sent a legislative bill to Congress to replace the existing Organic Constitutional Law on Education (LOCE) with a new General Law of Education (LGE). In August 2009 the new LGE was promulgated (Law # 20.370). Although the legislation itself did not immediately change the institutional set-up, it did constitute a departure from the strict neo-liberal framework under which the educational system had evolved during the dictatorship and which had prevailed once democracy was restored. The LGE explicitly stated a number of values and principles that were put on the agenda by the student protests, such as equality, universal access to quality education, inclusion and participation. Yet, it did not include three key student demands, the end of for-profit education, the transfer of public schools from municipal governments to the national government, and the banning of student selection mechanisms by voucher schools. The LGE banned student selection up to the sixth grade, but in a way that made it unenforceable. Since it provided a new framework for education, a series of other reforms were triggered by the adoption of the LGE. Some of those reforms were introduced as bills during the Bachelet administration, but they were only approved under President Sebastián Piñera. Some of those bills are still making their way in the legislative process.

In January 2010 the candidate of the centre-right Alianza, Sebastián Piñera, won the presidential election, putting an end to the 20-year period of four consecutive Concertación governments. During Piñera's (2010–14) first year in office, the government altered the legislative agenda to reflect its own priorities and ideology. As the distribution of seats in Congress also changed, giving the Alianza and its allies a slim majority in the House and keeping a Concertación majority in the Senate, the government's need to bargain with Congress also affected the educational legislative agenda. A devastating earthquake a few days before Piñera's inauguration also influenced government priorities. In education, reconstructing schools destroyed by the earthquake overtook educational reform as the first government priority in 2010. Student mobilizations—and in general other social expressions of discontent—decreased dramatically in 2010, in part due to the presidential honeymoon and also because of the earthquake that relegated other priorities.

In 2011 the student movement returned with renewed strength. Unlike 2006 the movement focused this time on tertiary education. Since 1990 tertiary education had evolved in the same direction of insufficient regulation and a mix of public and private providers that competed to attract students. Tertiary education enrolment increased rapidly from the early 1990s, from fewer than 200,000 to more than one million in 2011. The bulk of tertiary education growth came from professional institutes, technical centres and private universities. During the 1990s growth in private education was constrained by costs and regulations. Private institutions charged higher tuition than public and traditional universities, and regulations required them to

235

be under government supervision for several years before they could obtain 'autonomy', a classification that allowed them to open new sites and offer new degrees at their discretion.

The growth in private education put pressure on the government to expand the subsidized loan system (*crédito fiscal*) to private universities. However, the opposition of traditional and public universities forced the Lagos administration to implement an alternative funding scheme. A different government subsidized loan (*crédito con aval del estado*—CAE) was introduced for private universities in 2006. Unlike the *crédito fiscal*, the CAE was obtained from a private bank, not from the university itself. In addition, while the *crédito fiscal* has a fixed rate of 2% (in inflation-indexed *unidad de fomento*, or unit of account), the CAE had a 5.8% interest rate. Conditions for repaying the *crédito fiscal* were also more lenient than for the CAE.

In order to introduce an accountability mechanism, the new CAE legislation required universities to be accredited by the recently created National Accreditation Commission (CNA), an autonomous institution that replaced the old National Undergraduate Accreditation Commission (CNAP). To be eligible to receive the CAE, students had to belong to low-income families and attend accredited universities. There were five areas of accreditation: educational administration, undergraduate education, graduate education, research and community linkages, but only the first two were mandatory and required for CAE eligibility. Universities could receive accreditation from one to seven years. IPs and CFTs were not eligible for CAE loans.

Not surprisingly, universities rushed to obtain accreditation to be eligible for government-subsidized CAE loans. As a result of this new funding opportunity, enrolment in private universities increased dramatically after 2006. By 2011, when the student protests erupted under Piñera, thousands of students had already attended private universities and had pending loans with private banks accumulating interest. Since loans had to be repaid even if a student dropped out of school, for many low-income students their CAE loans became a burden rather than an upward mobility opportunity. As drop-out rates were high in private universities and higher among first-generation university students, access to CAE loans generated perverse incentives. Even among those who graduated, the cost of their degree at some private universities of low quality far exceeded their income potential. Thus, the expectation that a university degree would provide an opportunity for upward mobility did not materialize. In fact, recent research has shown that for those with some university education and for many with a university degree from a non-elite university, the returns of educational spending can be negative.[28]

Universities expanded their degree offerings to attract more students. Getting accreditation became a must for universities to grow. Though they are not legally allowed to profit, many universities engaged in profit making by expanding their programme offerings, attracting low-income students and getting them to apply for CAE loans. Even if those students dropped out after a few semesters, the university would still have collected their CAE-financed tuition. Repaying the loans would be the student's obligation while universities kept their profit. Though all private universities must be non-profit foundations, several institutions have a parallel for-profit company that owns the buildings and rents them to the university to extract profit, or they extract profits by offering other services at above-market rates to the non-profit university owned by the same company.

Since CNA accreditation is a requirement for CAE eligibility, for-profit universities actively sought to obtain accreditation. Lax regulatory mechanisms and outright corruption in the CAN allowed many underperforming and low-quality schools to get accreditation. In addition, since students were allowed to get CAE loans to attend universities that were in the process of accreditation, a low-quality school could still extract rents from the state through student loans and offer below-par education to mostly low-income and underperforming students who were not admitted to higher-quality institutions. As the cost of higher education is not correlated with the quality of education, many students ended up attending expensive schools that provided them with low-quality education.

The protests of 2011 were led by public university student federations. Thousands of students marched to protest against the educational system in place. Student leaders concentrated their criticisms on different components of the for-profit (*lucro*) educational model. Private for-profit universities that were benefiting from CAE became the symbol of what was wrong with the higher educational system. Student protest demands included a combination of calls for expanding public education, improving the quality of education across all types of institutions, phasing out private for-profit schools and moving towards universal and free access to higher education. Though it agreed with the focus on improving quality and expanding access to low-income Chileans, the Piñera administration staunchly opposed expanding public higher education and defended the focalized nature of government-subsidized loans for higher education. Because some of the governments' officials—including the education minister—had been involved in private universities suspected of hiding a for-profit scheme, and because President Piñera argued that education was a consumption good—enraging students who argued in favour of education as an inalienable right—there was little room for dialogue and negotiation. Protests continued throughout 2011, twice forcing Piñera to sack his minister of education.

The evolution of educational reform in Chile highlights the way in which the market-based reforms introduced by the military have been both modified but also legitimized after the restoration of democracy. By putting a focus on expanding access and earmarking public spending to benefit the lowest two income quintiles, the Chilean government has sought to correct market imperfections. However, by mending the reforms rather than undoing them, democratic governments have also further consolidated the market-based fundamentals of the Chilean economic model.

Market-friendly institutional constraints

Market-based reforms were also introduced by the military in the pension system, health, housing, transportation and in public works.[29] After democracy was restored, a sophisticated build-operate-and-transfer scheme was designed to promote private investments in public works.[30] That allowed public spending in public works to focus on socially relevant sectors that were not attractive to private investors.

The privatization of the pension system in 1982 and the adoption of an individual pension savings account sought to prevent the impending crisis of the existing generous but not widespread pay-as-you-go system. The new pension system represented a heavy cost for the public sector as the state continued to fulfil its commitment to those in the old system but stopped receiving contributions from those in the workforce whose pensions were not being saved in private for-profit pension fund companies. Information asymmetries unfavourable to workers and insufficient competition between the pension funds have generated widespread criticism of the system. As many of the workers who are now retiring had big gaps in their contributions, their accumulated pension funds are not sufficient to guarantee them a decent pension. In 2008 a pension fund reform that guaranteed a state-provided minimum pension was introduced. That created an additional burden for the state, although a sovereign wealth fund was also established, using excess revenues from copper exports.

A health reform in 2005 that introduced a state-guaranteed treatment for a basket of common illnesses also modified the existing strict market-based mixed private-public health provision scheme. In the past 20 years, several smaller reforms in housing policies and poverty alleviation policies also intended to correct market-based imperfections and to introduce universally guaranteed minimum state-provided services for functions that were partially or fully privatized under military rule.

When democracy was restored in 1990, the incoming Concertación government was critical of the market-based mechanisms introduced by the dictatorship. However, the rapid economic growth the country was experiencing at the time and the institutional constraints left in place by the dictatorship in the constitution limited what the Concertación could do.

The conditions under which the transition took place were admittedly difficult. The military retained oversight power on several democratic institutions and General Pinochet stepped down from the presidency but remained as head of the army. Those limitations further restricted the range of action of the new government. As governments have to choose among different priorities, and because the Concertación wanted to avoid testing the strengths of democratic institutions, the Aylwin administration chose to focus on reducing poverty rather than on changing the foundations of the economic model. Thus, rather than pushing for reforms that would move the country away from the neo-liberal model, the Aylwin administration focused its efforts on social spending. Aylwin wanted to transform the economic model into what came to be known as the neo-liberal model with a human face. The Concertación governments embraced the social market economic model as its own. If Pinochet is the father of the economic model, under Aylwin the Concertación became a deserving stepfather.

The institutions left in place by the military were intended to block an electoral majority from introducing changes that could unilaterally change the economic model. Thus a number of counter-majoritarian provisions were put in place in the constitution. Although the constitution established a strong presidential system, Congress has an effective power to block the executive. A bicameral Congress is elected through an unusual electoral system. Each district elects two legislators and seats are assigned by proportional representation, but because only two seats are distributed in each district, the winning party must obtain twice as many votes as its competitors to gain both seats. Otherwise, one seat goes to the winning party and the other goes to the losing party. The electoral system can be described as an insurance against defeat. The winning party will find it difficult to transform its electoral majority into a seat majority. The losing party benefits as it retains half of the seats with only one-third of the votes. This counter-majoritarian feature was implemented by the outgoing dictatorship to prevent the Concertación from transforming its electoral majority into an overwhelming seat majority in Congress when democracy was restored. In addition, the constitution also provided for non-elected senators, who comprised 19% of the Senate. As those non-elected senators were appointed by the outgoing regime, the Concertación had a minority in the Senate despite having won a majority of the elected seats.

A number of other institutional features were put in place in the constitution to force the winning coalition to bargain with the losing coalition to implement reforms. Strong enforcement mechanisms were also put in place to facilitate compromise. The institutional set-up also fostered the emergence and consolidation of strong parties that had long-term horizons. As a result, political parties ended up negotiating with ideological opposites to change the status quo. From 1990 to 2005 a number of constitutional reforms were adopted that gradually eliminated authoritarian enclaves from the constitution and eliminated non-democratic features (including the non-elected senators). Those reforms further strengthened democratic institutions but also helped to legitimize the institutional set-up initially imposed by the authoritarian government.

To be sure, the Aylwin administration and subsequent Concertación administrations introduced corrective changes to focus social spending on the neediest. Earmarked spending was the Concertación's response to the limited size of the public sector that the Pinochet government had enshrined in the constitution. Since public resources were scarce, the government sought to

Chile's successful history of development

spend almost exclusively on the lowest two quintiles of the population. The earmarked social spending policies produced impressive results in poverty reduction in the years following democratic restoration. As Figure 12.4 shows, poverty declined from 38.4% in 1990 to 20.5% in 2000. Since then, poverty has declined more slowly to reach 14.4% in 2011.

Reductions in inequality have been more difficult to come by. Figure 12.4 also shows that the Gini coefficient has barely moved since 1990. As the economy has grown steadily, the small decrease in inequality can be seen as good news. Inequality tends to increase during periods of economic growth. Despite a solid economic expansion, Chile did not see its inequality levels increase. The government's effort to focus social spending on the lowest two quintiles helped to keep inequality at bay while the economy expanded and millions were lifted out of poverty.

However, the fact that inequality remains high poses a long-term threat to the success and stability of the Chilean economy and its democratic system. Since democracy is built on the premise of majority rule, high levels of inequality constitute an unstable equilibrium. If the majority of the people earn salaries below the mean, they will probably end up voting for candidates who promise redistribution. If social mobility is limited, the push for redistribution will be even stronger. The threat of confiscation for those whose salaries are well above the national mean will also feed instability.

The tax structure in place in Chile also limits the effect of social spending on reducing inequality. The most important tax in place in Chile is a value-added tax (VAT) that charges an across-the-board 19% tax on most goods and services. Although there is also a progressive income tax structure, the large majority of Chileans are exempt. Higher-income Chileans have access to a number of legal and semi-legal tax breaks and loopholes that reduce their effective marginal tax. Companies pay a 20% tax rate on their earnings, but they can also delay their payment if they reinvent their earnings.

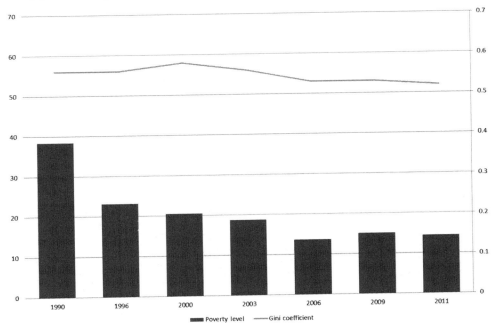

Figure 12.4 Poverty rates and Gini Coefficient, 1990–2011
Source: CASEN dara, www.minidenodesdrellosocial.job.cl

As a result, the taxes people pay as a proportion of their income can actually be higher for those in the middle-income quintiles than for those in the top quintile. Those in the middle who consume all of their earnings end up paying a higher tax rate (19% VAT tax on all they consume) than those in the top income brackets. Those at the bottom also pay 19%, but they benefit from earmarked social spending. Thus, the lowest two quintiles pay 19% of their income in taxes, but they received a bulk of government social spending. Those in the middle two quintiles also end up paying 19% of their income, but they receive little by way of government subsidies. Those in the top income bracket take advantage of tax breaks for savings and investments and might end up paying a lower marginal tax than those in the middle. To be sure, they do not receive government subsidies either, but their contributions are lower than those in the middle-income brackets.

The 2011 student protests can also be understood as the revolt of the middle class. Those in middle-income groups took to the streets to protest against the economic model. Since the role of the state is limited to a weak regulatory function and to subsidizing those at the lowest end of the income ladder, those in the middle believe that they get the short end of the stick. They contribute at the highest tax rate and receive very little in return. As they took to the streets to demand stronger public sector presence in education—and polls also show support for a stronger public sector role in health, pensions, housing, labour rights protection and utilities—the Chilean middle class began to show its muscle. In a well-functioning democracy, interest groups and public opinion play an important role in influencing public policy and government spending. In Chile, the student protests of 2011 can be seen as a signal that the market-friendly economic model imposed by the authoritarian regime is in trouble. However, one can also interpret the social movements as an indication of the opposite. Precisely because the market-friendly model promotes competition and protects the rights of consumers, the Chilean citizenry—and especially those in the middle-income quintiles—has embraced the basic tenets of the model and has begun to push for their interests, wants and needs. The ability of the elites and policymakers to adjust the economic model to make it fairer to those in the middle who pay the highest tax rates and get little in return will determine if Chile can successfully move beyond its present level of development to become the first Latin American country to join the select club of industrialized nations.

Notes

1 Patricio Navia, 'Chile: Democracy to the Extent Possible', *Latin American Research Review* 45, 2010: 298–328.
2 Paul Drake, Paul, 'Chile: 1930–58', in L. Bethell (ed.), *Chile Since Independence*, Cambridge University Press, New York, 1993; Ricardo Ffrench-Davis, *Políticas económicas en Chile. 1952–1970*, Ediciones Nueva Universidad, Santiago, 1973; Patricio Meller, *Un Siglo de Economía Política Chilena*, Editorial Andrés Bello, Santiago, 1998.
3 Robert R. Kaufman, *The Politics of Land Reform in Chile. 1950–1970. Public Policy Institutions and Social Change*, Harvard University Press, Cambridge, MA, 1972; Timothy R. Scully, *Rethinking the Center. Party Politics in Nineteenth- and Twentieth-Century Chile*, Stanford University Press, Stanford, CA, 1992.
4 Patricio Navia, 'Participación electoral en Chile 1988–2001', *Revista de Ciencia Política* 24, 2004: 81–103.
5 Stefan de Vylder, *Allende's Chile. The Political Economy of the Rise and Fall of the Unidad Popular*, Cambridge University Press, Cambridge, 1976; Ian Roxborough, Philip O'Brien and Jackie Roddick, *Chile, The State and Revolution*, Macmillan, London, 1977; Paul Sweezy and Harry Magdoff, *Revolution and Counter Revolution in Chile*, Monthly Review Press, New York, 1974; Arturo Valenzuela, *The Breakdown of Democratic Regimes: Chile*, Johns Hopkins University Press, Baltimore, MD, 1978.
6 J. Faundez, 'Chilean Constitutionalism before Allende: Legality without Courts', *Bulletin of Latin American Research* 29, 2009: 34–50; Peter A. Goldberg, 'The Politics of the Allende Overthrow in

Chile', *Political Science Quarterly* 90, 1975: 93–116; James Petras and Morris Morley, *The United States and Chile. Imperialism and the Overthrow of the Allende Government*, Monthly Review Press, New York, 1975; Robinson Rojas Sandford, *The Murder of Allende and the End of the Chilean Way to Socialism*, Harper and Row Publishers, New York, 1975; P.E. Sigmund, 'The "Invisible Blockade" and the Overthrow of Allende', *Foreign Affairs* 1974: 322–40.

7 Genaro Arriagada, *De la vía chilena a la vía insurreccional*, Editorial del Pacífico, Santiago, 1974; James W. Prothro and Patricio E. Chaparro, 'Public Opinion and the Movement of Chilean Government to the Left, 1952–72', *The Journal of Politics* 36, 1974: 2–43; Arturo Valenzuela, *The Breakdown of Democratic Regimes: Chile*, Johns Hopkins University Press, Baltimore, MD, 1978.

8 Sergio Bitar, *Chile 1970–1973. Asumir la historia para construir el futuro*, Pehuén, Santiago, 1995; Stefan de Vylder, *Allende's Chile. The Political Economy of the Rise and Fall of the Unidad Popular*, Cambridge University Press, Cambridge, 1976; Francisco S. Zapata, 'The Chilean Labor Movement Under Salvador Allende', *Latin American Perspectives* 9, 1976: 85–97.

9 Ascanio Cavallo, Manuel Salazar and Oscar Sepúlveda, *La historia oculta del régimen militar*, Grijalbo, Santiago, 1997; Arturo Fontaine Aldunate, *Los economistas y el presidente Pinochet*, Zig-Zag, Santiago, 1988; Juan Gabriel Valdés, *Pinochet's Economists: The Chicago School of Economics in Chile*, Cambridge University Press, New York, 1995.

10 Barry P. Bosworth, Rudiger Dornbusch and Raul Labán, *The Chilean Economy. Policy Lessons and Challenges*, Brookings Institution, Washington, DC, 1994; Ricardo Ffrench-Davis, *Economic Reforms in Chile. From Dictatorship to Democracy*, University of Michigan Press, Ann Arbor, MI, 2002; Felipe Larraín and Rodrigo Vergara, *La transformación económica de Chile*, Centro de Estudios Públicos, Santiago, 2000.

11 B. Loveman, 'Military Dictatorship and Political Opposition in Chile, 1973–86', *Journal of Interamerican Studies and World Affairs* 28, 1986: 1–38; Brian Loveman, 'Protected Democracies and Military Guardianship: Political Transitions in Latin America, 1978–1993', *Journal of Inter American Studies and World Affairs* 36, 1994: 105–89.

12 Renato Cristi, *El pensamiento político de Jaime Guzmán. Autoridad y libertad*, LOM, Santiago, 2000; Renato Cristi and Pablo Ruiz-Tagle, *La república en Chile. Teoría y práctica del Constitucionalismo Republicano*, LOM, Santiago, 2006.

13 Robert Barros, *Constitutionalism and Dictatorship: Pinochet, the Junta, and the 1980 Constitution*, Cambridge University Press, New York, 2002.

14 Claudio Fuentes, *El pacto. Poder, constitución y prácticas políticas en Chile (1990–2010)*, Ediciones Universidad Diego Portales, Santiago, 2013; Claudio Heiss and Patricio Navia, 'You Win Some, You Lose Some: Constitutional Reforms in Chile's Transition to Democracy', *Latin American Politics and Society* 49(3), 2007: 163–90.

15 José Pablo Arellano, 'La reforma educacional chilena', *Revista de la Cepal* 73, 2001: 83–94.

16 Ibid.

17 José Joaquín Brunner, *Educación superior en Chile. Instituciones, mercados y políticas gubernamentales (1967–2007)*, Ediciones Universidad Diego Portales, Santiago, 2009.

18 Ibid.

19 A. Mizala, 'La economía política de la reforma educacional en Chile', *Serie de Estudios Socio Económicos CIEPLAN* 36, 2007; D. Salinas and P. Fraser, 'Educational Opportunity and Contentious Politics: The 2011 Chilean Student Movement', *Berkeley Review of Education* 3, 2012.

20 G. Elacqua, D. Contreras, F. Salazar and H. Santos, 'The Effectiveness of Private School Franchises in Chile's National Voucher Program', *School Effectiveness and School Improvement* 22, 2011: 237–63.

21 José Pablo Arellano, 'La reforma educacional chilena', *Revista de la Cepal* 73, 2001: 83–94.

22 Rodrigo Rolando, Juan Salamanca and Marcelo Aliaga, *Evolución Matrícula Educación Superior de Chile*, Sistema Nacional de Información de la Educación Superior, Ministerio de Educación, Santiago, 2010.

23 Silvia Borzutzky, *Vital Connections. Politics, Social Security and Inequality in Chile*, University of Notre Dame Press, Notre Dame, IN, 2002; Silvia Borzutzky, 'Social Security Privatisation: The Lessons from the Chilean Experience for Other Latin American Countries and the USA', *International Journal of Social Welfare* 12, 2003: 86–96; Joseph Collins and John Lear, *Chile's Free Market Miracle: A Second Look*, The Institute of Food and Development Policy, Oakland, 1995; Marcus J. Kurtz, *Free Market Democracy and the Chilean and Mexican Countryside*, Cambridge University Press, New York, 2004; Peter Winn, 'Victims of the Chilean Miracle. Workers and Neoliberalism in the Pinochet Era, 1973–2002', Duke University Press, Durham, NC, 2004.

24 Edgardo Boeninger, *Democracia en Chile. Lecciones para la gobernabilidad*, Editorial Andrés Bello, Santiago, 1997; Comité Interministerial de Modernización de la Gestión Pública, *El Estado al servicio de la gente. Balance 1994–2000*, Ministerio Secretaría General de la Presidencia, Santiago, 2000; Dante Contreras, 'Poverty and Inequality in a Rapid Growth Economy: Chile 1990–96', *The Journal of Development Studies* 39, 2003: 181–200; Javier Martínez and Alvaro Díaz, *Chile. The Great Transformation*, Brookings Institution, Washington, DC, 1996.

25 Felipe Larraín and Rodrigo Vergara, 'La transformación económica de Chile', Centro de Estudios Públicos, Santiago, 2000.

26 Gregory Elacqua and Pablo Gonzalez, 'Education under the Concertación: Freedom of Enterprise or Freedom of Choice?' in K. Sehnbruch and P. Siavelis (eds), *Democratic Chile: The Politics and Policies of an Historic Coalition, 1990–2010*, Lynne Rienner Press, Boulder, CO, 2013.

27 Ibid.

28 Sergio Urzúa, 'La rentabilidad de la educación superior en Chile. ¿Educación superior para todos?' *Documento de Trabajo Centro de Estudios Públicos* 386, 2012.

29 Rossana Castiglioni, *The Politics of Social Policy Change in Chile and Uruguay*, Routledge, New York, 2005; Rossana Castiglioni, 'Social Policy Reform and Continuity under the Bachelet Administration', in J. Diez and S. Franceschet (eds), *Comparative Public Policy in Latin America*, University of Toronto Press, Toronto, 2012; Rossana Castiglioni, 'The Politics of Retrenchment: The Quandaries of Social Protection under Military Rule in Chile, 1973–90', *Latin American Politics and Society* 43, 2001: 37–66; Silvia Borzutzky, *Vital Connections. Politics, Social Security and Inequality in Chile*, University of Notre Dame Press, Notre Dame, IN, 2002; Silvia Borzutzky, 'Social Security Privatisation: The Lessons from the Chilean Experience for Other Latin American Countries and the USA', *International Journal of Social Welfare* 12, 2003: 86–96; Silvia Borzutzky, 'From Chicago to Santiago: Neoliberalism and Social Security Privatization in Chile', *Governance: An International Journal of Policy and Administration* 18, 2005: 655–74.

30 Eduardo Engel, Ronald Fischer and Alexander Galetovic, 'The Chilean Infrastructure Concessions Program: Evaluation, Lessons and Prospects for the Future', in F. Larraín and R. Vergara (eds), *La transformación económica de Chile*, CEP, Santiago, 2000.

Part V

Likely success stories

13

Turkey

Fatih Özatay[1]

Introduction

Following the turbulent 1990s, Turkey faced a severe financial crisis in 2001. From then up to the onset of the global crisis, important steps towards achieving macroeconomic stability were taken. Fiscal policy has been remarkably disciplined, public debt has been reduced sharply, the financial sector has been deepened, strengthened and well regulated, and inflation and risk perception have significantly declined. Following the relative deterioration in fiscal indicators due to sharp output loss during the global crisis, the improvement trend observed between 2002 and 2007 continued after 2008. The first natural question that follows is whether Turkey's goal to achieve macroeconomic stability has been accomplished, and if not, what problems remain.

Figure 13.1 shows the evolution of per capita gross domestic product (GDP) in Turkey, expressed in purchasing power parity dollars as a percentage of US GDP.[2] Despite favourable developments in the Turkish economy during the last decade, there has been only a mild increase in this ratio. Moreover, the per capita GDP gap between Turkey and the USA is still considerable: Turkey's per capita GDP was 25.4% relative to the US level in 2010. Figure 13.1 compares and contrasts Turkey's per capita GDP with respect to the BRIC countries (Brazil, Russia, India and the People's Republic of China) and the Republic of Korea (South Korea), all as percentages of US GDP as well. The rise in per capita GDP growth relative to the USA is much more pronounced in China, South Korea and Russia, compared with Turkey, in the last decade. While the per capita GDP of Turkey as a percentage of US income increased by 6 percentage points between 2001 and 2010, the percentage point increases were 15.6 for South Korea, 13.5 for Russia, 9.5 for China, 3.4 for India and 2.9 for Brazil. Instead of 2001 and 2010, when the 1990–2001 and 2002–10 averages are compared, a similar picture emerges— however, this time China's performance is better than that of Russia. The differences as percentage points between these two periods are as follows: Brazil −2.8, Turkey 1.7, India 1.9, Russia 4.6, China 7.5, South Korea 20. The second question that we will pose is about the main reasons behind the mediocre growth performance of Turkey.

We will discuss the positive radical change in the macroeconomic policy environment in the aftermath of the 2001 crisis in the second section. Notwithstanding these improvements, developments during and after the global financial crisis showed that shocks that emanate from

245

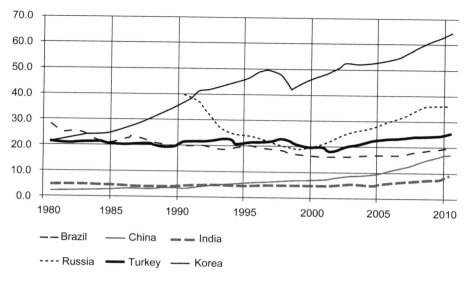

Figure 13.1 Per capita GDP of Turkey, BRIC countries and Korea relative to the US GDP in purchasing power parity terms (US dollars of 2005%)
Source: Author's calculations based on Penn World Tables version 7.1 (Heston Summers and Bettina 2012).

instability elsewhere can affect Turkey. Foreign demand for Turkish exports was significantly reduced, whereas increased risk averseness caused net capital outflow from Turkey during the global crisis. In this environment, business and consumer confidence declined and the domestic credit stock contracted. Output loss was in the order of that observed during the 2001 crisis. However, this time, something happened which would have been unthinkable during the preceding crises: Turkish policymakers took counter-cyclical policies as a response to GDP contraction. This was certainly a positive achievement of the economic policies implemented in the post-2001 crisis period. However, it also became clear that Turkey was still vulnerable to changes in global financial conditions. One of the main underlying reasons for the sharp output loss was net capital outflows. The second serious warning about how the Turkish economy is sensitive to sudden reversals in the international risk appetite was signalled by extremely low interest rate-cum-quantitative easing policies by developed countries in the aftermath of the global crisis. This time capital inflows surged and led the Turkish lira to appreciate, domestic credit to expand, and the current account deficit to widen. The main culprit for the vulnerability of the Turkish economy to fluctuations in global financial conditions is a low and declining domestic savings rate. Since there is still a high degree of liability dollarization, changes in the direction of capital flows have important repercussions on the economic activity and create a number of problems for policymakers. The third section discusses limits to economic policymaking under these conditions.

Establishing macroeconomic stability is a necessary condition for sustainable growth. However, it is not a guarantee for catching up with the developed world. As emphasized at the outset, the per capita GDP gap between Turkey and the developed world is still considerable. In the fourth section, we turn to this most important challenge for Turkey and discuss various underlying issues. While a rather long list of growth constraints can be made especially for emerging economies, we focus on what we think are the most binding. We point to low savings-to-GDP ratios, widespread informality and associated low productivity, and an unsatisfactory level of human capital as the main culprits. The final section concludes the chapter.

Towards macroeconomic stability, 1980–2012

The last two decades of the 20th century witnessed weak financial sectors, huge public deficits, a rise in public debts, monetization attempts, balance of payments problems, high and in some cases hyperinflation, and volatile as well as low growth in a number of developing countries. Such macroeconomic imbalances frequently ended with crises leading to sharp increases in unemployment and significant recessions. Accumulated fiscal problems did not allow most of these countries to implement counter-cyclical polices to reorient their economies to a normal growth path. On the contrary, pro-cyclical policies became the hallmark of the developing world at least until the beginning of the new millennium. One of the main challenges for developing countries facing these problems was to put their houses in order without jeopardizing growth and employment, as well as to 'graduate' from the pro-cyclicality camp. None the less, this was not an easy task and most of the time a rise of opposition led economic policymakers to halt such programmes, leaving their countries prone to new crises.

Turkey was not an outlier: having faced a number of crises and with the exception of the last 'home-made' crisis of 2001, Turkey could not sustain any adjustment programme put in place as a response to a crisis and hence made itself vulnerable to a new crisis. However, the aftermath of 2001 was different.

The 1980s: liberalization[3]

Turkey implemented an inward-oriented growth policy until the end of the 1970s. The inability of the existing system to give a proper response to the severe balance of payments crisis in the second half of the 1970s led policymakers to search for a better policy framework and institutional structure. Consequently, Turkey launched a structural adjustment programme in 1980. Initially, the main emphasis was on the deregulation of the financial system. One of the results of this deregulation was the mushrooming of 'bankers' who promised rather high real returns in order to collect deposits. Such Ponzi schemes led to the financial crisis of 1982.

Taking lessons from this premature liberalization, and starting from 1983, reforms were more evenly distributed between deregulation and the establishment of institutional foundations for the smooth functioning of the financial system. The regulatory power of the monetary authorities was strengthened. The Banking Act of 1985 introduced provisions regarding the capital structure of banks, their obligatory audit, and the protection of deposits. The structural reform efforts seemed to be weakened as of 1988, alongside the first signs of a deterioration in the fiscal position.

The 1990s: macroeconomic imbalances and 'home-made' crises[4]

The 1990–93 period witnessed high budget deficits, increasing public debt-to-GDP ratios, high real interest rates and high inflation. When the public sector borrowing requirement reached almost 6.6% of GDP, which was known by the public as 8.6% of GDP,[5] by the end of 1993, policymakers tried to change the financing mechanism of the deficit and relied heavily on central bank resources. This attempt at 'financial engineering'—despite the lack of effort to reduce the budget deficit, trying to decrease the debt burden by tapping the central bank—led the Turkish economy into a serious financial crisis at the beginning of 1994. The Turkish lira depreciated by almost 70%, overnight the interest rate jumped to 700% from a stable pre-crisis level of around 70%, and the economy contracted by 5.3%.

Following a short-lived decline in the aftermath of the 1994 crisis, the public-sector borrowing requirement-to-GDP ratio followed almost an uninterrupted upward trend and finally reached 9.8% in 1999 (or in other words 13%).[6] After the 1994 crisis, the interest payment burden of the public sector was also rather high. The part of the interest burden stemming from the real interest rate was significant; that is, the operational budget was in deficit (see Figure 13.2). Monetary policy was mainly accommodative; as a result, the average consumer inflation rate between 1994 and 1999 jumped to 86% from 66% of the 1990–93 period average. The average treasury borrowing rates during these periods were much higher: the 1994–99 period average was 127.5%, whereas the 1990–93 average was 76.6%.

As a result of these developments, the public debt-to-GDP ratio increased to 39.8% at the end of 1999 from 25.3% in 1990. Despite the fact that a public debt stock of 39.8% of GDP seems rather innocuous, especially compared to what has been observed in most of the developed countries since 2008, this would be a misinterpretation for two reasons. First, taking into account the publicly known GDP figures of that time, the debt-to-GDP ratio was 53%. Second, given imperfect financial markets, an important part of this debt had to be rolled over in domestic financial markets. However, the financial sector was rather shallow in the 1990s and even this 'innocuous' level of debt was putting an upward pressure on borrowing rates. Indeed, the public debt-to-M2 ratio was 102.6% at the end of 1999.[7] Note that in the same year the average borrowing rate of the treasury was 109.6% whereas the average consumer inflation rate was 64.8%.

There were other indicators pointing to lax fiscal policy as well. From 1992 growing government debt instruments that were still outstanding and the increasing financing needs of the Treasury led the government to financing some activities through loans taken from state-owned banks. Instead of repaying the principal and the interest accrued, the Treasury allowed these non-performing loans to be treated as performing loans by state-owned banks. In fact, this was a hidden budget deficit which was termed duty losses of the state-owned banks'. It was not known to the public and thus the public sector borrowing requirement and the operational

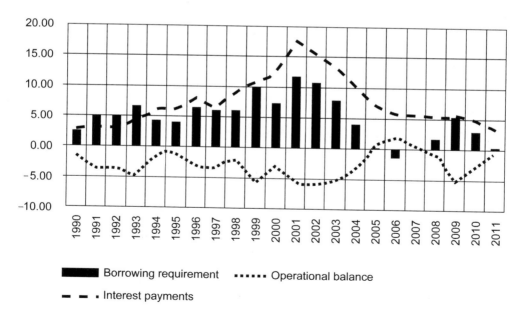

Figure 13.2 Borrowing requirement, operational balance and interest payments of the public sector (general government) 1990–2011 (% of GDP)
Source: Ministry of Development. Operational balance is author's calculation

deficit in Figure 13.2 do not reflect this hidden deficit.[8] When this practice began in 1993, the hidden budget deficit was 0.4% of GDP. The following year it increased to 1.1%. As of the end of 1999, the cumulated stock was almost 10.2% of GDP. Put differently, between 1993 and 1999 the average annual hidden deficit was in the order of 1.5% of GDP.

The poor fiscal policy was reflected on the balance sheet of the financial sector as well. This led to an increase in government debt instruments, especially on the balance sheets of private banks. Some of the private banks were funding government debt instruments through rather short-term liabilities, which caused them to default when hit by a sharp rise in interest rates when the 2001 crisis erupted. As discussed above, it also caused a significant deterioration in state-owned banks by accumulating duty losses. The ratio of non-performing loans to total loans was alarming. There was a significant open foreign exchange position as well as an important maturity mismatch.[9]

Turkey attempted to change this picture and signed a standby agreement with the International Monetary Fund (IMF). The new programme started to be implemented at the beginning of 2000. In addition to orthodox elements, the programme relied on a pre-announced crawling peg system as well. The primary surplus-to-GDP ratio increased to 5.4% in 2000 from a mere 1.0% in the previous year. Year-end inflation sharply declined to 39%. A parallel reduction was observed in the Treasury borrowing rate. GDP growth increased to 6.8% (see Table 13.1).

However, the positive reversal was short lived. In the second half of November 2000 the first signs of a severe crisis were observed. At the end of December average interest rates were almost four times higher than the levels at the beginning of November and more than five times higher than the pre-announced year-end depreciation rate of the Turkish lira. This unsustainable situation came to an end on 19 February 2001, when the prime minister announced that there was a severe political crisis resulting in a rush on foreign currency, which caused sharp capital outflows. On that date, overnight rates jumped to 6,200%. Three days later the exchange rate system collapsed. The Turkish economy contracted in 2001 by 5.7% and the unemployment rate increased by 1.9 percentage points (see Table 13.1).

The aftermath of the 2001 crisis: towards macroeconomic stability

The fragile banking system and the triggering factors closely related to the banking sector were the main reasons behind the 2001 crisis (Özatay and Sak 2002). The sky-high overnight rates and the collapse of the fixed exchange rate system brought a significant number of banks—including systemically important state banks—to the verge of default. In the aftermath of the collapse of the peg, the Turkish lira entered into free fall. This created great inflationary pressures on the one hand, and further enormous problems for the banking and corporate sectors on the other. The risk perception for Turkey reached unprecedented levels: the Emerging Markets Bond Index (EMBI)[10] spread jumped to 1,061 basis points in mid-April 2001 from 400 basis points at the beginning of January 2000. Consequently, business and consumer confidence collapsed.

To bring an end to this unsustainable situation, Turkey signed a new stand-by agreement with the IMF. The new programme that was put into force in mid-May 2001 had three main pillars: banking sector reform, macroeconomic discipline with a significant fiscal consolidation, and an ambitious structural reform agenda aiming to change radically the existing structure of economic institutions. The floating exchange rate regime was centre stage of the programme which was supported by IMF and World Bank credits. Özatay states what was expected from the programme:

i) reduce default risk, ii) decrease real interest rates, iii) prevent further depreciation pressures on the exchange rate which at that time was obviously overshot and then bring the

249

Table 13.1 Main macroeconomic indicators (% of GDP)

	2000	2001	2002	2003	2004	2005	2006	2007	2008	2009	2010	2011
Nominal GDP (US$ billion)	266.3	195.1	232.1	304.1	392.2	482.8	528.6	646.8	733.4	614.1	730.2	773.2
GDP per capita (US$ PPP)[a]	7,983	7,594	8,085	8,577	9,725	10,899	11,884	12,650	12,854	12,177	13,294	14,393
GDP growth rate (%)	6.8	−5.7	6.2	5.3	9.4	8.4	6.9	4.7	0.7	−4.8	9.2	8.5
Unemployment rate (average, %)[b]	6.5	8.4	10.3	10.5	10.8	10.6	10.2	10.3	11.0	14.0	11.9	9.8
Inflation rate (consumer, year end, %)	39.0	68.5	29.7	18.4	9.3	7.7	9.7	8.4	10.1	6.5	6.4	10.4
Inflation rate (consumer, average, %)	55.0	54.2	45.1	25.3	8.6	8.2	9.6	8.8	10.4	6.3	8.6	6.5
Total domestic savings	17.0	17.0	17.3	15.1	15.7	15.4	16.0	15.1	16.1	12.8	13.1	13.9
Gross fixed investments	20.8	15.1	17.6	17.6	19.4	20.0	22.1	21.1	21.8	14.9	19.5	23.8
Fiscal policy indicators												
General government balance	−7.3	−11.8	−10.8	−7.9	−4.1	−0.1	1.3	−0.2	−1.7	−5.5	−3.0	−0.4
General government primary balance	5.4	5.8	4.5	5.4	6.3	7.1	7.5	5.7	3.8	0.3	1.5	3.0
Central government												
Balance	−7.9	−11.9	−11.5	−8.8	−5.2	−1.1	−0.6	−1.6	−1.8	−5.5	−3.6	−1.4
Primary balance	4.4	5.2	3.3	4.0	4.9	6.0	5.4	4.2	3.5	0.0	0.7	1.9
Revenues	22.9	24.3	22.7	22.2	22.0	23.5	22.9	22.6	22.1	22.6	23.1	22.9
(Tax revenues)	17.7	18.2	17.2	18.1	18.0	18.4	18.1	18.1	17.7	18.1	19.2	19.6
Non-interest expenditures	18.6	19.1	19.4	18.2	17.1	17.6	17.4	18.4	18.6	22.6	22.4	21.0
Interest expenditures	12.3	17.1	14.8	12.9	10.1	7.0	6.1	5.8	5.3	5.6	4.4	3.3
Gross debt stock	38.2	74.1	69.2	62.2	56.6	51.1	45.5	39.6	40.0	46.4	43.1	39.9
Banking sector (year-end values)												
Capital adequacy ratio (%)		20.8	25.1	30.9	28.8	23.7	21.9	18.9	18.0	20.6	18.9	16.5
Non-performing credit/total credit (%)	12.4	41.4	21.2	11.5	6.0	4.7	3.7	3.5	3.7	5.3	3.7	2.7
Total credit volume	19.1	14.0	14.0	14.6	17.8	24.1	28.9	33.9	38.7	41.2	47.9	52.6
Total credit/asset (%)	30.5	19.9	23.0	26.5	32.4	38.4	43.8	49.1	50.2	47.1	52.2	56.1
Balance of payments												
Exports	10.4	16.1	15.5	15.5	16.1	15.2	16.2	16.6	18.0	16.6	15.6	17.4
Imports	20.5	21.2	22.2	22.8	24.9	24.2	26.4	26.3	27.5	22.9	25.4	31.1

Table 13.1 (continued)

	2000	2001	2002	2003	2004	2005	2006	2007	2008	2009	2010	2011
Current account balance	−3.7	1.9	−0.3	−2.5	−3.7	−4.6	−6.1	−5.9	−5.7	−2.2	−6.4	−10.0
Net capital inflow	4.7	−0.8	0.6	1.0	3.4	4.0	6.1	5.8	5.1	1.5	6.0	8.5
Foreign direct investment	0.0	1.5	0.4	0.4	0.5	1.9	3.6	3.1	2.3	1.1	1.0	1.8
Gross external debt	47.9	68.6	60.8	44.2	38.6	35.2	38.6	34.5	45.2	42.2	41.0	44.7
(Gross external debt of private sector)	22.0	25.4	20.2	15.0	15.3	17.4	22.4	22.2	30.3	27.0	26.8	29.6
Central bank foreign exchange reserves (average)[c]	9.2	10.6	10.4	10.1	9.0	8.7	11.2	10.8	10.5	11.6	10.7	12.0
Real exchange rate index (average)[d]	102.4	84.4	94.0	100.0	103.9	114.3	113.0	122.2	123.2	114.6	127.0	112.3
Confidence indicators												
Secondary market treasury rate (%, average)	39.8	91.4	64.9	46.1	24.5	16.3	17.8	18.3	19.4	11.7	8.5	8.8
Average maturity of borrowing (months)	14.2	4.9	9.4	11.9	14.6	28.0	28.0	34.2	31.1	32.6	43.1	38.2
EMBI Turkey spread (average, index)	488	889	761	628	354	273	226	214	383	364	220	261
EMBI Turkey–EMBI global	−264	51	−14	66	−83	−43	26	24	−2	−92	−59	−48
Business confidence index (average)[e]	101.0	76.8	102.0	104.1	106.8	102.8	102.4	111.5	90.1	87.3	110.3	110.5

Notes: [a] IMF World Economic Outlook database, October 2012. 2011 value is the estimate of the IMF. [b] Values above 100 denote confidence is increasing. [c] Including gold. [d] An increase denotes real appreciation. [e] Due to the methodology change as of the beginning of 2007, 2001-2006 and the rest are not comparable. Source: Treasury (Public Debt Management Statistics and Turkish Economy both available at the website), Banking Regulation and Supervision Agency, Central Bank of Turkey, Turkish Statistics Institute.

exchange rate to more reasonable levels through market forces, iv) improve balance sheets of the corporate and banking sectors whose liabilities denominated in foreign currency far exceeded their assets in foreign exchange, v) increase credit supply to the private sector by re-capitalizing the banking sector, decreasing the risk perception of the banking sector, and reducing the amount tapped by the public sector from the sources of the banking sector, and vi) boost private demand through the combined impact of these factors.

(2012: 2)

On the eve of the new programme, the central bank law was changed. Extending credit to the public sector was prohibited, price stability became the main objective of the central bank which was empowered to use monetary policy tools freely to achieve this aim, and together with a number of other changes it has had instrument independence since then. Simultaneously with the central bank reform, the rehabilitation of the banking sector started. The programme first aimed to solve the problem of the accumulated debt of the Treasury at the state banks. The number of branches and employees were reduced sharply. Private banks were strengthened, and their capital adequacy ratios were increased. Vulnerability to foreign exchange mismatch was minimized. The autonomy of the regulatory and supervisory authority was secured. Its technical capacity was increased. International standards in banking legislation were adopted.

Following these initial steps, the agricultural support system was redesigned. Steps were taken to enhance transparency, budget discipline and accountability in the public sector. Redundant positions were eliminated. Various laws were enacted to improve the investment environment. Independent regulatory and supervisory agencies were established. Two of the last major moves were the currency reform at the beginning of 2005—six zeros were dropped from the currency—and the start of formal inflation targeting at the beginning of 2006.

Mainly as a result of the bank restructuring efforts, the public debt-to-GDP ratio jumped to 74% at the end of 2001 from the previous year-end level of 38%. Despite challenges raised by this unprecedented level of debt ratio, policymakers stuck to fiscal discipline.[11] Consequently, just before the beginning of the global financial crisis, the financial sector was sound and fiscal policy was in order. As of the end of 2007, the general government budget was almost in balance and public debt was reduced to 40% of GDP. Thanks to both the successful implementation of the programme and favourable external conditions—notably, low global interest rates up to 2004—most of the macroeconomic indicators, with the exception of the current account deficit and persistent unemployment rate, improved and the risk perception for Turkey decreased considerably. Inflation came down to 9.7%. Almost all of the indicators point to a strong banking sector: the non-performing loans-to-total loan stock ratio was at considerably low levels, the capital adequacy ratio was rather high and the credit-to-asset ratio had increased significantly. The increase in credit volume helped the fiscal consolidation process not to undermine growth performance. The 2002–07 average GDP growth rate was 6.8%, a rather remarkable level compared to the long-term 4.6% average growth rate of Turkey (see Table 13.1).

Low savings rate, liability dollarization and vulnerability to global financial shocks

Notwithstanding the radical positive change in the macroeconomic policy environment in the aftermath of the 2001 crisis, there are two important pending problems that have the potential to undermine macroeconomic stability. First, the domestic savings rate is low and moreover has been declining in the last couple of years, rendering Turkey vulnerable to changes in global financial conditions. Second, there is still a high degree of liability

Table 13.2 Gross national savings and total investment (% of GDP)

	1980–89	1990–99	2000–09	2010–12
Savings				
Brazil	18.5	17.1	16.8	18.2
China	39.1	40.7	46.4	51.8
India	20.8	23.7	30.1	31.6
Russia	—	27.3	30.0	27.0
Turkey	21.5	21.6	15.8	13.5
South Korea	31.7	35.9	31.8	31.7
Investment				
Brazil	18.9	18.0	17.5	20.4
China	39.9	39.1	41.3	48.4
India	22.6	24.9	30.6	34.9
Russia	—	26.8	20.8	21.9
Turkey	22.7	22.4	19.0	21.7
South Korea	31.5	35.2	29.5	29.3

dollarization. These two problems mean that fluctuations of capital flows have important repercussions on economic activity.

Low domestic savings

As shown in Table 13.1, the domestic savings-to-GDP ratio is low and moreover has been declining in recent years. The low savings rate restricts investment growth as well, and leaves it 'at the mercy' of changes in international financial conditions. An investment rate higher than that implied by the domestic savings rate causes the current account balance to deteriorate. Table 13.2 compares domestic savings and investments of Turkey with those observed in the BRIC countries and South Korea. Among this group, Brazil and Turkey are the two countries with the lowest savings rates. Moreover, in 2010 and 2011 Turkey's average savings rate was even significantly below Brazil's level, which itself has a considerably low savings rate compared to the other of the BRIC countries and South Korea. The investment-to-GDP ratio is well below the investment ratios of China, India and South Korea, but in the order of investment ratios in Brazil and Russia.

Liability dollarization

The net international reserve position of Turkey as a ratio to GDP showed an improvement after the 2001 crisis up to 2005. Since then it has deteriorated, though with some fluctuations. The 2011 value was US$321 billion (41.5% of GDP). A similar movement has been observed in the foreign debt of the private sector (see Figure 13.3). Note that not only has the foreign indebtedness of the private sector increased, but also its net foreign exchange position has deteriorated. The net foreign exchange position of the non-financial firms in Turkey was −16.8% of GDP in the second quarter of 2012, indicating a worsening trend since the end of 2003 when it was 6% of GDP.

Impact on economic activity

The low savings rate and the accompanying need for net capital inflows on the one hand and liability dollarization on the other cause fluctuations in capital flows with important

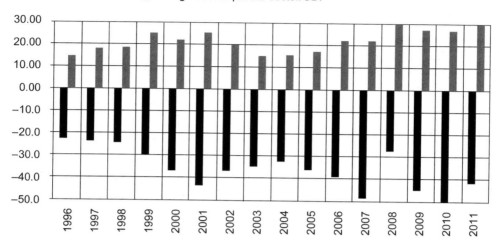

Figure 13.3 Net international reserve position of Turkey and foreign debt of private sector: 1996–2011 (% of GDP)
Source: Central Bank of Turkey

repercussions on economic activity. A number of channels are at work behind the link between capital flows and economic activity. First, with a surge in capital inflows, both financial and non-financial firms can more easily access foreign finance. Furthermore, financial firms can boost the liability of the non-financial sector by converting external funds they obtained from abroad to domestic credit.[12] Consumer credit and trade credit also pick up under these conditions. As a result, economic activity accelerates with a surge in net capital inflows. For the same reasons, net capital outflow periods generally witness a slowdown in economic activity.

The second channel is the sensitivity of the balance sheets of financial and non-financial firms to fluctuations in asset prices caused by capital flows. There is a wealth of literature showing the close connection between capital flows and sovereign spreads. Global liquidity conditions, global risk appetite and releases macroeconomic news in financial centres, in addition to domestic fundamentals, affect the sovereign spreads of emerging economies.[13] Other things being the same, an increase in global liquidity and an associated decrease in risk aversion increase demand for financial assets of emerging economies, whereas a surge in risk aversion decreases demand for these assets. Consequently, one generally observes a significant co-movement between spreads, domestic interest rates and exchange rates. For example, for the period January 2002–October 2012 the coefficient of correlation between monthly rates of change in Turkish EMBI spreads and monthly rates of change in the exchange rate is 0.65, whereas the coefficient of correlation between monthly rates of change in Turkish EMBI spreads and monthly changes in the benchmark Treasury rate is 0.53.[14] Moreover, in periods with sharp changes in risk aversion, such correlations increase.[15]

Under these conditions, capital inflows have a tendency to improve balance sheets. First, an increase in risk appetite for Turkish financial assets fuels net capital inflows and leads to an appreciation pressure on the lira. Given significant foreign exchange exposure of corporate sector, the appreciation of the currency improves the balance sheets of the corporate sector.

Second, as a result of capital inflows, asset prices rise and cause a parallel increase in net worth of the corporate sector. Obviously, capital outflows lead to the opposite effect.

Kesriyeli *et al.* (2013) provide evidence of expansionary effects of real appreciation through increases in investments and profitability for firms with high liability dollarization in Turkey. The results of Kara *et al.* (2007) reinforce these findings, which show that real exchange rate lead to an expansion in Turkish economic activity. Note that such effects highly depend on the level of dollarization. For example, Levy-Yeyati and Sturzenegger (2009) show that in the absence of dollarization, real exchange rate appreciations are associated with slow growth or contraction, whereas financial dollarization may reverse this effect. In the same vein, Frankel (2005) points to the contractionary effects of devaluation in highly dollarized economies. Note also that improvements in the balance sheets of non-financial firms ease credit constraints that they face. Both demand for and supply of credit tend to rise due to improvements in the balance sheet, leading to a parallel increase in domestic credit expansion. A rise in capital inflows increases direct borrowing of both financial and non-financial firms from the rest of the world as well. Consequently, loan growth boosts economic activity. Clearly, balance sheet deterioration leads to the opposite effect.[16]

Figure 13.4 shows the quarterly seasonally adjusted evolution of the levels of real GDP and net capital inflows in Turkey. The significant positive correlation between real GDP and net capital inflows is striking. The significant negative correlation between the current account deficit and industrial production index (both seasonally adjusted) is even more visible in Figure 13.5. These facts, which are closely related to inadequate domestic savings rates in Turkey, have rendered the Turkish economy highly vulnerable to changes in capital flows.[17] Consequently, the risk appetite of financial investors has been an important determinant of the economic activity in Turkey at least since the liberalization of the capital account in 1990.

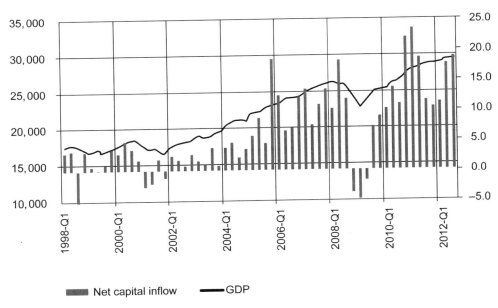

Figure 13.4 Real GDP and net capital inflow (right axis) 1998Q1–2012Q3 (All series are seasonally adjusted, net capital in flow is in billion US dollars and seasonally adjusted by the author).
Source: Central Bank of Turkey and Turkish Statistic Institute

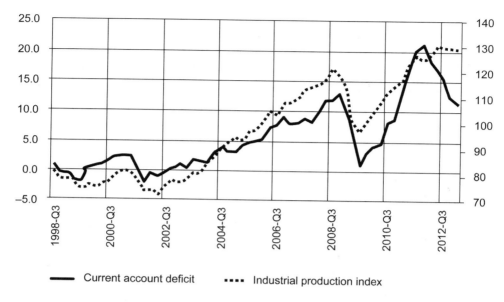

Figure 13.5 Industrial production index (right axis) and current account balance: 1981Q1–2012Q3 (all series are seasonally adjusted, current account deficit is in billion US dollars and sasonally adjusted by the author).
Source: Central Bank of Turkey and Turkish Statistics Institute

Global shocks and economic policymaking

Globalization has considerably increased financial and trade linkages between countries, rendering emerging economies vulnerable to global shocks even though their macroeconomic fundamentals are sound, subject because they are to punishment on the one hand international financial markets and on the other to domestic imbalances. In this section, we discuss the economic policy response to three episodes of significant change in capital flows.

The first two are the net capital outflow episodes in 2001 and during the 2008–09 period. The third is the surge in net capital inflows during 2010 and the first half of 2011. Table 13.1 gives annual net capital inflows to GDP ratios. Annual figures may mask higher-frequency sharp U-turns in capital flows. Figure 13.4 shows the evaluation of seasonally adjusted quarterly net capital inflows measured in millions of US dollars and indicates the above-mentioned three periods. One may as well look at unadjusted quarterly net capital inflows as a percentage of annualized GDP values to gain a clearer picture. The first episode: 2001 Q1 −0.6, Q2 −1.1, Q4 −1.0. The second episode: 2008 Q4 −0.8; 2009 Q1 −0.7. The third episode: 2010 Q1 1.5, Q2 2.6, Q3 1.4, Q4 2.7; 2011 Q1 3.0, Q2 3.0. Note also that the first two capital outflow episodes were preceded by significant inflows, rendering the following outflows more damaging.

It should be noted that the underlying reasons for net capital outflows during the first two episodes were entirely different. The first one was a response to the weak fundamentals of that period and triggered the 2001 crisis. Hence, it belonged to the 'punishment' category. The second was caused by the global financial crisis. Below, we analyse fiscal policy in these two periods. The output losses in both of these periods are shown in Figure 13.6. We argue that while a counter-cyclical policy response was possible during the global crisis, policymakers at the time of the 2001 crisis did not have the same 'luxury' at their disposal. We then turn to the

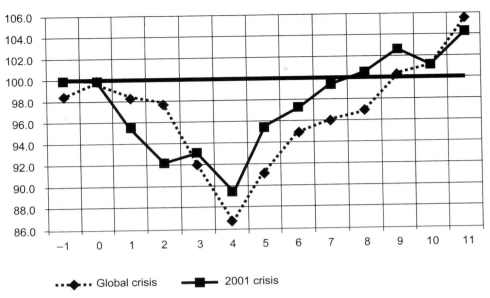

Figure 13.6 GDP loss in the 2001 crisis and global crisis (Quarterly index values. The maximum seasonally adjusted GDP value observed at the start of the downturn (T=0) is set to 100 in each of the crises. For the 2001 crises T=0 is the fourth quarter of 2000, whereas for the global crisis T=0 is the first quarter of 2008).

Source: Author's calculations based on Turkish Institute of Statistics data.

surge in net capital inflows during 2010 and the first half of 2011. We concentrate on constraints on monetary policy during this episode.

Fiscal policy during the 2001 crisis

As discussed above, immediately after the 2001 crisis the banking restructuring process began. Prospective deficits hidden in the balance sheets of state banks were cleared through an injection of Treasury debt instruments. Additionally, the restructuring and recapitalization of the financial sector—especially state banks—caused the public debt-to-GDP ratio to increase twofold.[18] Similarly, the general government deficit-to-GDP ratio increased from 7.3% in 2000 to 11.8% at the end of 2001 (see Table 13.1).

Despite the fact that the economy was in a sharp downturn and eventually showed an obvious tendency to contract, it was counterproductive to loosen fiscal policy to increase domestic demand. The main reason was that there had already been a considerable rise in debt sustainability concerns stemming from this rather poor fiscal position. Various confidence indicators given in the last section of Table 13.1 imply that throughout 2001 and to a certain extent 2002 confidence in the Turkish economy was rather fragile. Under these conditions, a loosening of fiscal policy would further boost public debt and the associated risk premium. Moreover, such concerns were self-fulfilling, increasing real interest rates and putting significant real depreciation pressure on the lira, which further increased public debt and intensified sustainability concerns.

Indeed, during the first years of the programme, financial markets were rather reactive to signals they perceived as possible deviations from the implemented programme. Emir *et al.*

(2007) report on the impact of such reactions on domestic interest rates. Using daily data for 16 May 2001 (the starting date of the programme) to 31 December 2002 for the Turkish economy, they show that almost all of the sharp rises in the secondary market benchmark rates were associated with good or bad political news releases. These news releases were generally related to the necessary action that should be taken by the Turkish government, as promised in the stand-by agreement signed with the IMF.

A further increase in risk perception for Turkey which was already at record high levels certainly would have caused further capital outflows, decreased confidence, depressed private sector consumer and investment expenditures, and undermined efforts to recover economic growth. Based on these considerations, economic policymakers of the time opted for fiscal austerity-cum-structural rehabilitation measures.

Fiscal policy during the global crisis

The global financial crisis hit Turkey through four channels. First, the financial and non-financial firms, after enjoying large amounts of capital inflow on the eve of the global crisis, became net debt payers to the rest of the world. Second, the decline in foreign demand caused a sharp contraction in exports. Third, the domestic banking sector cut its credit lines to the non-banking corporate sector and households. Fourth, business confidence declined considerably. In this environment, output contracted significantly (see Figure 13.6). The first set of fiscal stimulus measures was announced in late March 2009. The special consumption tax rates on a limited number of sectors were temporarily reduced. The second set of measures was related to the labour market. The third set of measures targeted the credit market. In mid-June 2009 budget support to credit guarantee mechanisms was announced.[19]

The IMF (2009) attempted to measure the magnitude of fiscal stimulus measures taken by the G20 countries. According to the IMF estimates, among these countries, the lowest fiscal stimulus was given by Turkey, at 1.1% of GDP, closely followed by Brazil and India (both 1.2% of GDP).[20] Note that the corresponding average values for the developed countries and the remaining countries in the G20 are 3.5% and 3.8%, respectively (IMF 2009). However, what is important is that rather than a pro-cyclical policy, a counter-cyclical policy was implemented, and moreover it was not punished by the markets: there was not an extra increase in risk perception for Turkey due to these measures, and the EMBI spread of Turkey was below the EMBI global level (see Table 13.1).

Surge in capital inflows and monetary policy, 2010–11

The global crisis severely hit most of the developed economies. The response of these countries to the crisis led to record low levels of interest rates and an unprecedented amount of global liquidity. Capital inflows increased sharply during 2010 and the first half of 2011 in most of the emerging economies and Turkey as well. Starting in 2010, this new wave of influx led to rapid domestic credit expansion. For example, in its April 2011 *World Economic Outlook*, the IMF reported a significant pick-up in real credit growth in Brazil, Colombia, India and Indonesia in real per capita terms in the range of 10%–20%, and in Turkey exceeding 20% (IMF 2011: 20–21).[21] The surge in capital inflows caused the lira to appreciate in real terms as well. The real effective exchange rate was 116.8 at the end of 2009. It rose to 127.6 in June 2010, and to 131.3 in October 2010.[22]

As a response, the central bank started to use a new monetary policy framework in November 2010, and as time evolved, the framework was revised in line with new developments.[23] Özatay (2013) documents various shortcomings of the new policy. The central bank increased the required reserve ratios in several steps to curb rapid credit expansion, starting from October 2010 to April 2011. However, as an inflation targeting central bank, since it was fixing its policy rate, it had to accommodate money demand. Towards the end of 2010 the economy was growing well above the potential growth rate, and consequently demand for credit was increasing. The banking sector was more than eager to meet this demand. Given that short-term borrowing through open market operations from the central bank was a close substitute for the deposits lost to the central bank as a result of required reserve ratios, the banking sector increased its borrowing from the central bank. Consequently, required reserves held at the central bank and the short-term borrowing from the central bank moved upwards in tandem.[24] Despite significant required reserve ratio increases, rapid credit growth continued in the first three quarters of 2011, indicating limits of monetary policy in an open emerging economy with low savings rates and liability dollarization.

The same period witnessed another example of this limit. As a reaction to appreciation pressures, the central bank sought to depreciate the lira by widening the interest rate corridor (the gap between its lending and borrowing rates) and significantly reducing the overnight borrowing rate as well. Consequently, it deliberately let overnight market interest rates diverge from its policy rate, jeopardizing the importance of its policy rate.[25] Starting in August 2011, global risk appetite followed a downward trend due to worsening economic conditions in Europe, putting pressure on the lira which had already been depreciating due to the policy of the central bank. As a response to a sharp rise in risk aversion, this time the central bank both increased its lending rate and let the market rate fluctuate upwards and diverge from its policy rate in an upward direction. First as a result of the central bank's new policy and then due to a decline in the global risk appetite, the lira depreciated considerably. The value of an equally weighted euro and dollar currency basket increased with respect to the lira by 25% in the October 2010–December 2011 period. Consequently, both headline and core consumer inflation increased significantly and remained well above the inflation rates of its peers.[26]

The most important challenge: convergence

As discussed in the introduction, and shown in Figure 13.1, despite a mild increase in growth in recent years, the story of Turkey is not one of catching up. This is the most important challenge that the Turkish authorities face. Understanding the reasons underlying convergence and non-convergence has been keeping development and growth economists busy for decades. Discussing plausible factors behind the Turkish non-convergence and providing solid results are extremely important tasks, but obviously beyond the scope of this chapter.[27] We will instead compare some salient features of the Turkish economy with the BRIC countries and South Korea, and then try to achieve some results regarding the binding growth constraints.

The first and the most important issue in the short-to-medium term is the low savings rate in Turkey. In the second section, we compared savings and investment rates of Turkey with those of the BRIC countries and South Korea. During the 2010–11 period the Turkish savings-to-GDP ratio was in the range of 26% to 50% of the savings rates of these countries (excluding Brazil), and 74% of Brazil's. Low savings rates restrict investment growth and in Turkey they are well below the investment ratios of China, India and South Korea.[28]

Dani Rodrik, using the framework of Hausmann *et al.* (2008), discusses binding growth constraints faced by the Turkish economy. He states that 'regardless of the nature of the binding constraint, raising growth in the future will necessitate a significant increase in domestic saving effort' (Rodrik 2009: 20). One should also note that breaking the link between capital inflows and growth by raising domestic savings would also reduce liability dollarization. This would be an important step towards establishing a 'normal' relationship between real exchange rate developments and growth, instead of what is generally observed, i.e. real appreciation causing growth through favourable balance sheet effects but putting a ceiling on the deepening of the tradable sector.

The natural question that follows is how one can accomplish this task. Rodrik (2009) points to a need for increasing structural surplus of the public sector. A recent World Bank study first analyses determinants of savings rates in Turkey and then makes some projections for Turkey's savings rate by using the estimates of Loayza et al. (2000).[29] One of the findings of the report is that increasing public savings can increase domestic savings, provided that measures taken rely on the formalization of the economy. The tax base in Turkey has been rather narrow—an obvious reflection of a relatively large informal economy—with two important consequences.[30] First, Turkey is one of the Organisation for Economic Co-operation and Development (OECD) countries that has very low tax revenue relative to its GDP. The OECD average for tax revenues-to-GDP ratio was 33.8% in 2010, whereas it was 25.7% in Turkey. Second, the composition of tax revenues has been shifted significantly towards indirect taxation in the last decade. In 2010 the proportion of indirect taxes in total taxes was 48.4% in Turkey (32.5% OECD average).[31]

Firms in the informal sector are unproductive and create an obstacle for firms operating in the formal sector to grow and become more competitive in foreign markets. Based on Taymaz (2009), the World Bank (2010: Chapter 4) provides some estimates for productivity differences between formal and informal firms in Turkey. For manufacturing firms the productivity gap is estimated at 150% and for the services sector it is 140%. Controlled for some factors, the difference drops to 19% for the manufacturing sector and to 62% for the services sector, but they are still considerably high.

No doubt formalization is not a growth panacea, but these estimates still indicate that there can be considerable per capita GDP gains through a formalization reform. Furthermore, some extra tax revenue created by such a reform could be used for programmes aimed at increasing the human capital level of employees working in the informal sector to find better jobs. Such a move would certainly increase the political feasibility of the whole reform process by decreasing resistance to it.

By increasing domestic savings, a high growth episode can be obtained. However, there is no guarantee that it will be sustainable, as documented by Hausmann et al. (2005). Eichengreen et al. (2013) show that continued growth episodes are generally related to two important factors. First, as the level of secondary and tertiary education rises, and second as the share of high-technology products in manufacturing exports increases, slowdowns become less likely. Table 13.3 compares Turkey with the BRIC countries and South Korea from this perspective. Regarding the high-technology

Table 13.3 Educational attainment and high-technology exports

	Brazil	China	India	Russia	Turkey	South Korea
Average years of schooling for population aged 15 and over, 2010						
Total	7.54	8.17	5.13	11.52	7.02	11.85
Secondary	2.12	2.88	1.64	4.82	2.32	4.95
Tertiary	0.24	0.29	0.18	1.59	0.29	1.13
Percentage ratio of high-technology exports to manufactured exports						
1990–99 average	6.6	11.3	5.3	10.8	1.8	23.6
2000–09 average	14.0	26.2	6.6	12.0	2.3	31.3
2010	11.2	27.5	7.2	8.8	1.9	28.7

export ratio, Turkey's performance is the worst among these countries. Educational attainment is not satisfactory either. It is noteworthy that a recent study on binding growth constraints for Turkey pinpoints these two factors as the most important (Atiyas and Bakış 2011).

The low domestic savings rate on the one hand and the last two indicators on the other point to the fact that the continuation of even the modest growth performance of Turkey in the last decade is in jeopardy. To increase its growth and make it sustainable, Turkey has to change this scenario. One positive development in this regard is that a new voluntary private pension scheme supported by public funds was put into force as of the beginning of 2013 to raise the domestic savings rate. However, it is too early to judge the effectiveness of this scheme.

Since, as mentioned above, we aimed to focus on binding constraints, let us refrain from enlarging our list but instead emphasize one more point. The female labour force participation rate in Turkey is extremely low: 28.8% in 2011. In other words, Turkey cannot make use of this potential. However, if female participation rate were to increase, there is no guarantee that this potential would be used. Obviously, in order for this addition to the labour force to be productive, women should be employed in the first place. That is, on the one hand there should be demand for this extra labour force and on the other these people should satisfy the human capital requirements of employers. Put differently, the low female participation rate problem, once alleviated, would immediately become an education and low savings problem, which are two of our three binding constraints.

Conclusion

The turbulent 1990s led Turkey to face a severe financial crisis at the beginning of 2001. In the aftermath of the 2001 crisis, Turkey put its house in order with considerable success. Fiscal discipline was established, the financial sector was strengthened considerably and a number of important institutional reforms were implemented. As a result, inflation fell to single digits, the average growth rate increased and risk perception for Turkey declined significantly. Despite these positive developments, the global financial crisis caused considerable loss of output. Similar economic contractions were observed in 1994, 1998–99 and 2001. However, this time, thanks to much stronger macroeconomic fundamentals as a result of the economic programme put in place after the 2001 crisis, policymakers had room to manoeuvre.

Two important challenges remain. First, the Turkish economy is still vulnerable to fluctuations in capital flows. Both a surge in capital flows and sudden reversals cause problems for economic policymakers. The main underlying reason is the low savings rate and still important level of liability dollarization in Turkey. Second, the per capita GDP gap between the developed economies and Turkey is substantial. Moreover, despite some signs of narrowing in recent years, the width of the gap persists. While reasons behind the second challenge are more deep-rooted, both are related. There are other significant growth bottlenecks as well. However, to list them all clearly would have turned this chapter into a 'laundry list', from which we refrained. Instead, we have focused on what we regard as the most important problems, i.e. the low savings-to-GDP ratio, widespread informality and associated low productivity, and an unsatisfactory level of secondary- and tertiary-level schooling.

Notes

1 I'm grateful to Ufuk Demiroğlu, Hasan Ersel and Cihan Yalçın for their helpful comments.
2 Per capita GDP values are in purchasing power parity (2005 US dollars) and taken from the Penn World Tables version 7.1 (Heston *et al.* 2012).

3 This section and the following are drawn from Özatay 2000, Özatay and Sak 2002, and Ersel and Özatay 2011.

4 The sources of data of this section are as follows: fiscal indicators are from the Treasury and the Ministry of Development; GDP and inflation figures are taken from The Turkish Institute of Statistics.

5 Public sector refers to the general government, i.e. excluding state economic enterprises. Throughout this chapter we use a newer GDP series which was released as of the beginning of 2007 and on average is 30% higher than the old GDP readings. Note that from a risk perception perspective, what is relevant is the GDP of that time. That is, the public sector borrowing requirement was 8.6% of GDP for economic agents at that time.

6 See the previous note.

7 M2 includes foreign exchange deposits.

8 See Özatay and Sak 2002 for details, especially Tables 4 and 7.

9 See Özatay and Sak 2002.

10 The EMBI spread is the yield on an emerging country sovereign bond and bond issued by a government of the developed world with identical currency denomination and maturity.

11 We discuss these challenges in the third section.

12 Özmen et al.(2012) show that appreciation reduces the savings rate of the non-financial corporate sector.

13 Among others, see, for example, Gonzales-Rozada and Levy-Yeyati 2006; and Özatay et al. (2009). For a sample of 18 emerging economies and for the period from 31 December 1997 to 29 December 2006, Özatay et al. (2009) show that the long-term evolution of EMBI spreads of these countries depends on global liquidity conditions, risk appetite, crises contagion and US macroeconomic news, as well as domestic macroeconomic fundamentals. The sample covers Argentina, Brazil, Bulgaria, Colombia, Ecuador, Egypt, Mexico, Malaysia, Morocco, Panama, Peru, the Philippines, Poland, Russia, South Africa, Turkey, Ukraine and Venezuela.

14 The highest cross-correlation coefficients are on variables with zero lag. The exchange rate is the domestic currency defined as a unit of a basket of equally weighted US dollars and euros.

15 For example, in the spring of 2004, financial market perceptions regarding the timing of FED rate hikes changed. Expecting an early upward cycle in FED rates, risk aversion increased. Consequently, during the 2 January–30 June 2004 period the correlation coefficient between the benchmark Treasury rate and exchange rate jumped to 0.93. There are several other similar periods as well. In the first half of 2006, again due to a change in expected FED policy, risk aversion increased. Consequently, the correlation coefficient between the two series increased to 0.93.

16 Using quarterly Turkish data for the period 1994–2006, Özatay (2008) shows that once fluctuations in disposable income were controlled, there was a significant influence of consumer credit growth on consumption growth. Moreover, along with business confidence and real income, the real volume of credit extended to the corporate sector was an important determinant of private investment expenditures.

17 During the 1998 Q1–2012 Q3 period the maximum cross-correlations are at lag zero and as follows: 0.78 between real GDP and net capital inflows, −0.91 between real GDP and current account balance, 0.80 between industrial production and net capital inflows, −0.93 between industrial production and net capital inflows.

18 The publicly known debt-to-GDP ratio for 2001 was 104% compared to 54% in 2000. See Note 5 for an upward GDP revision in 2007.

19 See Özatay (2010) for a more detailed evaluation.

20 The estimate for Turkey does not include the measures taken in June 2009.

21 In Turkey, in nominal terms, the annual rates of credit growth in the last two quarters of 2010 and in the first quarter of 2011 were as follows: 34.9%, 32.2% and 30.1% for domestic currency denominated loans; 34.5%, 34.0% and 34.3% for consumer loans.

22 The Central Bank's real effective exchange rate index. An increase denotes real appreciation.

23 The Central Bank of Turkey (2011) states this new policy as follows: 'In the period from the adoption of the new policy framework in November 2010 to intensifying uncertainties in the European economy in August 2011, the Central Bank aimed at limiting short-term capital flows and preventing excessive appreciation of the Turkish lira on the one hand, and ensuring more controlled growth in domestic credit and domestic demand on the other. Due to the strong risk appetite and the surge in short term capital flows in this period, the Central Bank widened the interest rate corridor by reducing the overnight borrowing rate. Thus, interest rates in overnight markets were let to be lower

Turkey

than policy rates, which gave rise to an increase in the downward volatility of overnight market rates and a decline in very short-term capital flows. Meanwhile required reserve ratios were raised significantly in the same period to avert excessive credit growth and contain domestic demand.'

24 The average maturity of deposits was 45 days at that time, whereas banks borrowed from the CBT in the short-term money market with a one-week maturity.

25 See Note 15 for this policy.

26 With the start of the new policy, in various reports the Central Bank had frequently compared the value of the lira against the US dollar and euro with a group of countries in order to evaluate effectiveness of its new policy framework. At the end of 2011 the consumer inflation rate in these countries and Turkey (in ascending order) and percentages were as follows: Czech Republic 2.4; Colombia 3.7; Indonesia 3.8; Mexico 3.8; Hungary 4.1; South Korea 4.2; Chile 4.4; Poland 4.6; South Africa 6.1; Brazil 6.5; Turkey 10.4 (IMF 2012).

27 There is a wealth of research on this topic: see for example, Acemoğlu (2009, especially Chapters 1 and 4), Acemoğlu and Robinson (2012), Rodrik (2007), and for a survey Benassy-Quere et al. (2010: Chapter 6), among others.

28 Ganioğlu and Yalçın (2013) stress the importance of investment-savings difference as an important determinant of growth. Looking from this perspective, low savings rate constraints together with dependence on risk appetite of foreign investors to overcome this constraint are among the most important determinants of Turkey's growth performance.

29 World Bank (2012b).

30 World Bank (2010: Chapter 2) shows that informality in Turkey is widespread, but not excessively high with respect to its peers.

31 Values are taken from the OECD tax database.

Bibliography

Acemoğlu, D. (2009) *Introduction to Modern Economic Growth*, Princeton University Press, Princeton, NJ.

Acemoğlu, D. and J.A. Robinson (2012) *Why Nations Fail*, Crown Business, New York.

Atiyas, İ. and O. Bakış (2011) *Türkiye'de Büyümenin Kısıtları (Growth Constraints in Turkey)*, İstanbul, Tüsiad Report No: 2011/11/519 (in Turkish).

Barro, R.J. and J.W. Lee (2010) 'A New Dataset of Educational Attainment in the World, 1950–2010', NBER Working Paper No. 15902, April.

Benassy-Quere, A., B. Coeure, P. Jacquet and J. Pisani-Ferry (2010) *Economic Policy: Theory and Practice*, Oxford University Press, Oxford.

Central Bank of Turkey (2011) 'Monetary and Exchange Rate Policy for 2012', Central Bank of Turkey, www.tcmb.gov.tr.

Eichengreen, B., D. Park and K. Shin (2013) 'Growth Slowdowns Redux: New Evidence on the Middle-income Trap', NBER Working Paper No. 18673.

Emir, O.Y, F. Özatay and G. Şahinbeyoğlu (2007) 'Effects of US Interest Rates and News on the Daily Interest Rates of a Highly Indebted Emerging Economy: Evidence from Turkey', *Applied Economics* 39 (1–3), January–February.

Ersel, H. and F. Özatay (2011) 'Monetary Policy in Turkey: The Reasons for Introducing IT and the Outcome', in M. Boughzala and D. Cobham (eds), *Inflation Targeting in MENA Countries*, Palgrave Macmillan, New York.

Frankel, J.A. (2005) 'Mundell-Fleming Lecture: Contractionary Currency Crashes in Developing Countries', IMF Staff Papers 52(2).

Ganioğlu, A. and C. Yalçın (2013) 'Domestic Savings and Growth: Are Foreign and Domestic Savings Perfect Substitutes in Financing Domestic Capital? A Cross-Country Study', forthcoming as CBT Working Paper.

Gonzales-Rozado, M. and E. Levy-Yeyati (2006) 'Global Factors and Emerging Market Spreads', Inter-American Development Bank Working Paper, No. 552.

Hausmann, R., L. Pritchett and D. Rodrik (2005) 'Growth Accelerations', *Journal of Economic Growth* 10: 303–29.

Hausmann, R., D. Rodrik and A. Velasco (2008) 'Growth Diagnostics', in J. Stiglitz and N. Serra (eds), *The Washington Consensus Reconsidered: Towards a New Global Governance*, Oxford University Press, New York.

Heston, A., R. Summers and A. Bettina (2012) 'Penn World Tables 7.1', Center for International Comparisons of Production, Income and Prices at the University of Pennsylvania, July.

Ilzetski, E., E.G. Mendoza and C.A. Vegh (2012) 'How Big (Small?) are Fiscal Multipliers', mimeo, University of Maryland.

IMF (2009) 'The State of Public Finances: A Cross-country Fiscal Measure', IMF Staff Position Note, SPN/09/21.

——(2010) 'Recovery, Risk, and Rebalancing', *World Economic Outlook*, October.

——(2011) 'Tensions from the Two-speed Recovery: Unemployment, Commodities, and Capital Flows', *World Economic Outlook*, April.

——(2012) World Economic Outlook Database, October.

Kara, H., F. Öğünç, Ü. Özlale and Ç. Sarıkaya (2007) 'Estimating the Output Gap in a Changing Economy', *Southern Economic Journal* 74: 269–89.

Kesriyeli, M., E. Özmen and S. Yiğit (2013) 'Corporate Sector Liability Dollarization and Exchange Rate Balance Sheet Effects in Turkey', *Applied Economics*, forthcoming.

Levy-Yeyati, E. and F. Sturzenegger (2009) 'Fear of Appreciation: Exchange Rate Policy as a Development Strategy', in G. Hammond, R. Kapur and E. Prassad (eds), *Monetary Policy Frameworks for Emerging Markets*, Edward Elgar Publishing, Cheltenham.

Loayza, N., K. Schmidt-Hebbel and L. Servén (2000) 'What Drives Private Saving Across the World?' *The Review of Economics and Statistics* LXXXII(2).

Özatay, F. (2000) 'The 1994 Currency Crisis in Turkey', *The Journal of Policy Reform* 3(4).

——(2008) 'Expansionary Fiscal Consolidations: New Evidence from Turkey', Economic Research Forum Working Paper No. 406.

——(2010) 'Europe: Counter-Cyclical Policies in Light of the Global Financial Crisis: The Case of Turkey', *Journal of Globalization and Development* 1(1), Article 18.

——(2013) 'A Note on the New Monetary Policy of the Central Bank of Turkey', in A. Arı (ed.), *The European Debt Crisis: Causes, Consequences, Measures and Remedies*, Cambridge Scholar Publisher, Cambridge.

Özatay, F., E. Özmen and G. Şahinbeyoğlu (2009) 'Emerging Market Sovereign Spreads, Global Financial Conditions and US Macroeconomic News', *Economic Modelling* 26: 526–31.

Özatay, F. and G. Sak (2002) 'Banking Sector Fragility and Turkey's 2000–2001 Financial Crisis', in S.M. Collins and D. Rodrik (eds), *Brookings Trade Forum 2002*, The Brookings Institute, Washington, DC.

Özmen, E., S. Şahinöz and C. Yalçın (2012) 'Profitability, Savings and Investment of Non-Financial Firms in Turkey', CBT Working Paper No. 12/14.

Penn World Tables (2012) 'Penn World Tables 7.1', Center for International Comparisons of Production, Income and Prices, University of Philadelphia, Philadelphia, PA, July.

Rodrik, D. (2007) *One Economics—Many Recipes*, Princeton University Press, Princeton, NJ.

——(2009) 'The Turkish Economy after the Crisis', Turkish Economic Association Discussion Paper No. 2009/9.

Taymaz, E. (2009) *Informality and Productivity: Productivity Differentials between Formal and Informal Firms in Turkey*, METU Economic Research Center Working Paper No: 09/01, Ankara background paper of Country Economic Memorandum Report No: 48523-TR.

World Bank (2010) *Informality: Causes, Consequences, Policies*, Turkey Country Economic Memorandum, Report No: 48523-TR.

——(2012a) 'World Development Indicators', data.worldbank.org/data-catalog/world-development-indicators.

——(2012b) *Sustaining High Growth: The Role of Domestic Savings*, Turkey Country Economic Memorandum, Report No: 66301-TR.

14

Indonesia's ways to sustainable economic growth and development

Zamroni Salim

Introduction: road to the giant emerging economy

With globalization and the increasing tension from open competition, the developing countries have tried to overcome their handicaps to economic growth. Developing countries have had to face their own specific problems but, in general, there might be common problems, such as low rates of human development, high dependence on natural resources, poor infrastructure, and sometimes getting caught in the economic trap of being part of the developing world without making any effort to prepare for a developmental leap.

Brazil, Russia, India, the People's Republic of China and South Africa, the BRICS economies, stand out from the other economies of the developing world. The BRICS countries restructured their economies fundamentally by using their abundant resources as an engine of growth. It has been predicted that China's economy will be 35% larger than that of the USA by 2050. Similarly, India's economy has been predicted to be 83% of the size of the US economy (in gross domestic product (GDP) value) by that time. In 2040 the BRICS countries are projected to have a larger combined GDP than six developed countries: France, Germany, Italy, Japan, the UK and the USA; by 2050, the BRICS economies will contribute 50% of global GDP.[1] Meanwhile, Indonesia is also predicted to become a giant economy, though it will not be as big as the economies of China and India. Indonesia will be 14% of the US economy by 2050 compared with just 4% in 2009.[2]

How do these economies compare at present? According to the World Bank's[3] classification of countries by income groups, Indonesia was a lower-middle-income country; BRICS countries, such as Brazil, Russia, China and South Africa, were at a higher level, as upper-middle-income countries. India was in the same class as Indonesia at the lower-middle-income level. There is still a wide gap in terms of gross national income (GNI) per capita between lower- and upper- middle-income values, US$1,006 to $3,975 and $3,976 to $12,275, respectively. With these figures in mind, Indonesia needs, at least, to follow with its own adjustments bearing in mind the specific characteristics of its economic and non-economic resources.

This chapter discusses current economic conditions and the possibility that Indonesia as an emerging economy will be one of the BRICS economies.[4] An overview of the concepts of economic growth, development and sustainability sets the scene for this chapter. The next parts deal with Indonesia's economy and development in comparison to BRICS economies, and entry points to achieve the economic success of BRICS economies by discussing the engines of growth and how to get sustainable development. The concluding remarks discuss how Indonesia might develop to be one of the new BRIICS economies.

Economic growth, development and sustainability

This section discusses briefly the concept of economic growth and the interchangeability of economic development with economic growth. Discussion of economic growth, or in other terminology, economic development, is an area of specialized economics that has attracted many scholars, but the area of economic growth overall is quite large and home to many unknowns and challenges.[5] In this chapter, economic growth, especially that of Indonesia, is discussed through the concept of endogenous growth with some determining factors, including technological advances and innovation, with the possibility of sustainable growth.

The predominant effort in the study of economic growth was by Robert Solow,[6] using neo-classical growth theory with its assumption of diminishing returns in the economy. Since then, much has changed and knowledge has expanded; advances in technology and human capital development have emerged to help solve problems in the economy. Endogenous growth theory opened a new window to investigate economic growth and economic development in broader terms.[7] Since the introduction of endogenous economic growth, the study of the contribution of technology inclusion, knowledge and innovation to economic growth has become more interesting and challenging. Technological change in the endogenous growth theory compensates for the economic problem of diminishing returns as postulated by the classical and neo-classical economists.

The main reasons for different rates of economic growth between rich and poor countries were to do with productivity, and differences in productivity were attributed to the technology advantages that could be exploited by industries and firms. The factors differentiating the economies of poor and rich countries are the presence or lack of capital, technology, education and division of labour in the production process, and these factors are the basic indicators of high and low economic growth. The factors behind the success of economic development, as argued by Wydick,[8] basically need a condition of well-developed institutions to co-ordinate the overall resources to achieve greater development with better outcomes. At a certain point in time, the accumulated effect of these factors influencing growth is reflected in the level of domestic development. Investment is one of the channels that leads to the adoption and development of technology and innovation in any country. The adoption of new technology by the BRICS countries was gradual rather than immediate through the new investment flows into their economies.[9]

Sustainable growth refers to endogenous structural change with the improvement of technology and environmental sustainability. Indeed, sustainable economic growth requires the conservation of resources over time. The lack of a neo-classical optimization criterion model could not account for sustainability without the formulation of strong hypotheses about technological changes or time preference in the model.[10] Under endogenous structural change, a country may grow at a constant rate with no effect on the level of resource endowment.[11] It means that the endogenous growth has been supported by more productive resources and exaggerated by technology and innovation. At the micro level, in order to increase its productivity and competitiveness and to enjoy profits, the firm has to innovate.

The BRICS countries should rely not only on traditional factors of production such as labour and capital, but also on the technological development as reflected in total factor productivity

(TFP). Through additional technological advances, the BRICS countries could effectively utilize their potential resources.[12] The ability of an economy to achieve sustainable annual growth of GDP in order to benefit its people should be maintained and improved. It has to sustain improvements in welfare, in its many aspects, over time. The sustainability of economic growth with the endogenous factors of technology and innovation is a critical condition to get more productive, competitive and sustainable economic growth; and, further, it will direct an economy to follow similar pathways to the BRICS countries.

The BRICS and Indonesia: a comparison

By searching the globalized world, we can find several groups of countries that have been trying to exist alongside, contribute to and to some extent influence the rest of the world.[13] At the top level of these groupings we have the G7 and Organisation for Economic Co-operation and Development (OECD) countries with their strong, influential positions in the world, not only in economic affairs but also in other ways, such as their social and political systems. There is also the G20 group, of which Indonesia is a member. In more general terms, we find emerging economies over the past two decades have been standing above the common herd of developing countries. We may also recognize that the rest of groupings are less influential to the world economy.

The major emerging economies in the BRICS group have increasing influence not only in economic but also in political and social areas. The BRICS group has taken political initiatives to reform global governance. Emerging economies have been gaining a larger share of global GDP compared to the rest of the world (including the developed countries) and this increasing share is predicted to be sustained over the next decades. As a group the emerging countries were reported to have a higher resilience in dealing with the effects of the global crisis of 2007–09. China and India and a number of emerging Asian economies have been in the lead to recover faster than most developed countries. The more resilient economies owe their success to their stronger policy frameworks and to their smaller financial, external and fiscal vulnerabilities. With these environmental policies, the emerging economies are in a better place to apply countercyclical monetary and fiscal policies.[14] In the global world, their size and growth rate will be shaping the dynamic movement of oil prices, emerging market stock prices and exchange rates.[15] The power to change world prices is growing owing to the increasing size of domestic markets (large populations with greater purchasing power) and greater diversification of products supplied around the world.

The BRICS economies graduated from the emerging economies with some additional features. Besides their increasing contribution to global economic growth and outputs, they come with features such as large human capital, competitive labour, access to natural resources and an ability to maintain the momentum of increasing internal demand.[16] With those endowments, the BRICS countries are the new engines of growth in the global constellation.[17]

The BRICS countries experienced higher TFP growth rates, as did Indonesia, compared to other developed countries, but still their contribution ratios to economic growth were much lower than those in industrialized countries such as Japan and the USA. Higher TFP contributions ratios to GDP growth in developed countries show the substantial technology advances in the economy. In 2004 the average TFP contribution to GDP in the BRICS was 46%, while the rest, contributors of traditional labour and capital input, hold the remaining 54%. However, their TFP growth was related to the force of rapid economic growth, not to substantial innovation and technological advance.[18]

Technologically driven endogenous growth is the key means by which the BRICS countries will achieve sustained growth. The BRICS countries, especially China, have driven their economies to be more productive and endogenously employ technology advances. Technological progress has now been an important factor generating China's economic growth to be sustainable. In this respect, productivity growth emerged as the main contributor to economic growth through improvement in efficiency (catch-up or convergence), or technological progress or innovation.[19]

The higher growth rate of TFP in the BRICS countries does not synchronize with their technological advance that enables them to utilize effectively their potential resources to catch up with the developed countries. Related to technological advances that could speed up the convergence,[20] the convergence speed of Indonesia is relatively lower (at 0.5%) than other South-East Asian countries such as Thailand and the Philippines. Meanwhile, the BRICS economies presented a higher convergence speed of 1.5% for India and Brazil and 2.0% for Russia and China. Other more advanced countries like Japan, Taiwan and the Republic of Korea (South Korea) are the highest at 4.0%.[21] The possibility of convergence in economic development and growth may not be realized in the case of emerging economies unless they can handle risk and establish better financial institutions to accelerate trade, foreign direct investment (FDI), short-term capital flows, knowledge and movement of labour.[22] Unexpectedly, they might come to a divergence in catching up with the developed world.

From an historical perspective, Indonesia experienced quite good TFP to GDP growth. Van der Eng calculated the contribution of TFP growth, by accounting for the growth of non-residential capital stock and education-adjusted employment, which was, on average, 7%–13% took place during the period 1880–2008.[23] The growth of capital stock played a larger part than the growth of education-adjusted employment. The largest contribution of TFP growth during the period 1967–1998, when its contribution was around 56%–61%. The higher growth rate of Indonesia's economy during that period was perhaps based on 'perspiration', rather than 'inspiration', which supported the miraculous growth of Asian countries.[24] In other words, the higher economic growth during these periods was not the consequence of technological development, but of the larger capital inflow through FDI, mostly in extractive industries. The Indonesian government should pay greater attention to the development of a more productive economy. As such, Indonesia's high economic growth was much more investment-driven and accompanied by low TFP growth and the small contribution of TFP to economic growth.[25]

Emerging economies are characterized by a set of factors such as their higher and faster economic growth, and they operate their economies under various business, cultural, economic, financial, institutional, legal, political and social environments.[26] Despite the current global position and other supporting factors, there are still some deterrents to economic growth in the BRICS countries, some of which are related to the weakness of institutions and to foreign debt. Institutional weaknesses affect economic growth and are still a common problem in the BRICS countries. The institutional problems are related to enterprise management, the availability of education and training for employees, reliability of professional management, and consumer satisfaction.[27]

The absence of, or weakness within, economic institutions could generate weak economic growth or to some extent create counterproductive effects with some determinants such as a country's rate of saving, trade dependence and FDI.[28] Institutional governance has a significant control on aggregate country risk and on the rate of technological progress and innovation. Traditions and bureaucratic behaviour contribute to economic growth and development. Owing to the inflexibility of traditions and bureaucratic behaviour, they might sometimes act as barriers to innovation. In fact, such inflexible traditions and bureaucratic behaviour may inhibit new innovation. This is because, sometimes, the defenders argue that innovation in governance and development could reduce their existence and power (in terms of social, economic and political power). By paying attention to the other problems in the BRICS and other emerging economies, including Indonesia, institutional problems are not as simple to resolve as the lags in technological advance. Institutional development is sometimes more complicated and takes longer to effect.

Foreign debt or foreign currency liabilities are quite a common feature and are seen as financial weakness in emerging economies. The foreign currency debt in the circumstances of the global financial crisis could reduce economic growth and total output, even though its effect is temporary or permanent depending on the debt and the ability to pay.[29] Unpaid foreign debt could possibly destroy the economy and push it to the next stage of crisis.

Back to the 1997–98 crisis: the emerging economies had the very important experience of having remarkable development and economic growth, followed by a crisis. The large foreign debt and huge government deficits had been a nightmare. They started to fight the crisis with a critical policy of privatization to reduce public debt, arranging better access to capital and improving incentives and efficiency in the economy.[30] Privatization could induce the strengthening of institutional frameworks, reducing political and legal uncertainty.[31] The economic crisis in Indonesia put pressure on the government to promulgate competition law as part of economic stabilization and reform programmes. The international development and lending agencies, including the World Bank, urged the Indonesian government to adopt laws that would encourage competition.[32] With those reforms, better institutional conditions prevailed.

Indonesia substantially developed institutional reforms after the economic crisis. Almost all sectors were reformed, especially political and economic institutions. The reforms influenced the current development of economic growth under more stable macroeconomic conditions and a stable political environment.

The entry points to the BRICS level

The BRICS economies have become more influential as their contribution to the global economy has increased. Brazil, Russia, India, China and South Africa have established their shares of world economic power in terms of GDP, flow of trade and investments, and in promising sustainable economic growth. How will Indonesia, which claims to be as rich in resources, be included as a fully fledged member of this economic group?

The engines of sustainable growth

Indonesia experienced remarkable growth especially before the crisis of 1997–98. The growth was mainly owing to sound macroeconomic policies, and the reorientation of the economy to a free and open market.[33] From the macroeconomic model, GDP is constructed from consumption, investment, government expenditure and net trade (exports minus imports). The engines of growth for the comparable BRICS countries and for Indonesia are elaborated from this standpoint (see Figure 14.1).

The economies of the BRICS and Indonesia have been more dependent on domestic consumption, which has played a significant role in their economic growth. The consumption levels of the BRICS countries and Indonesia are presented in Figure 14.1, which includes other components of GDP. The average level of steady consumption in these countries was 60%–70%. From this standpoint, Indonesia has also made significant contributions from time to time. A stable consumption level in Indonesia's economy has helped the country to emerge in good shape from the crisis in 2008 and even from the recent crisis in the eurozone.

For developing Asian countries, the structure of growth with a larger consumption share has had the positive effect of showing their economies to be more resilient during the crisis, in which they had only two quarters of negative growth. Public consumption worked well, especially in circumstances when the net exports of the respective countries largely resulted from a decrease in imports, not an increase in exports, during that period.[34] Most developing

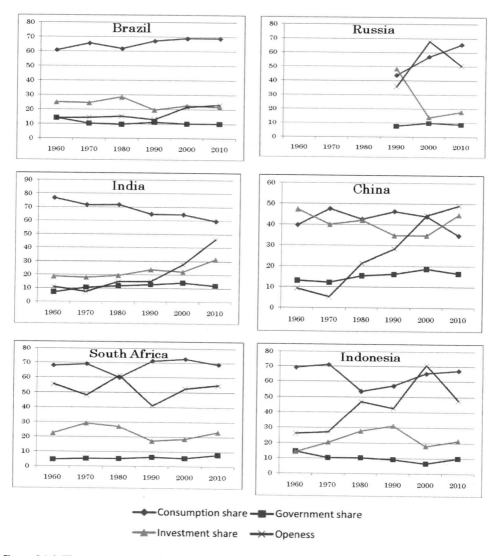

Figure 14.1 The components of economic growth in the BRICS and Indonesia

Asian countries, including Indonesia, experienced public consumption as the engine of economic growth even during the economic crisis of 2008–09. The correction to less global demand was compensated by the increase in domestic consumption.

The government share of the structure of GDP was around 10% for the BRICS and Indonesia during the period 1960–2010. A different approach was used in China, where budgetary expenditures increased to nearly 20% in 2000 and slightly decreased thereafter. The fiscal stimulus also had a positive effect on the endurance of the economy. Indonesia and other developing countries, such as Malaysia, the Philippines, Singapore and Thailand, had growth improvements of 0.5%–1.5%, but China had a 0.7%–2.3% improvement. The greater efforts by the government of China through higher government expenditure created a more enduring, as well as a more productive, economy during the most recent crisis.

Fiscal policy has been seen as a main tool other than monetary policies to counter economic recession. The effects of the increase in government expenditure have been much more profound than have the increases in interest and other monetary policy tools. In spite of the dominant strategy of fiscal policy, in general, macroeconomic policies were essential to counter the negative effects of the 2008–09 global crisis in most developing Asian countries.

Investment: foreign direct investment

Investment is one of the engines of economic growth for developing countries. Different from the two previous determinants, consumption and government expenditure, investment is not fully controlled by domestic or national factors. Instead, some investment decisions are determined by global factors that are beyond the control of the national authority. A national government may issue an attractive investment policy, but the decision to invest is made by outsiders.

Investors have their own reasons for placing their funds in specific countries and sectors, but there are some FDI determinants controlling their decisions: market attractiveness (size, spending power and growth of the market); low-cost labour and skills (labour cost); and natural resources and infrastructure.[35] In addition, Pravin studied the economic, institutional and political factors controlling the inflow of FDI in the BRICS countries.[36] It has been found that the economic determinants in BRICS countries are more significant in controlling the flow of FDI than institutional and political factors. For efficient production, being close to the raw materials, such as abundant natural resources, makes for cost efficiency, but this is not the case for the BRICS countries, where the ready availability of natural resources has, conversely, negative effects on total FDI inflow. In other words, natural resources were not the dominant factor in attracting FDI, but instead more emphasis was put on secondary and even tertiary industries.

The United Nations Conference on Trade and Development (UNCTAD)[37] argued that there are some countries whose performance in attracting FDI was below their potential. These countries might have potential for economic determinants but a policy climate that is not attractive to investors. Some developing countries with emerging market status and potential investment growth recently experienced FDI flows below expectations. These countries include the Philippines, South Africa, India, Mexico and Indonesia. UNCTAD suggested that for these countries to achieve their potential FDI inflows, they must pay attention to policy options (that are friendly to investors) and innovations, instead of focusing only on economic determinants.

The expanding economies of Asian countries have been shaped significantly by capital accumulation. Even though their labour input, education and total factor productivity were positive, their effect was not so significant at inducing economic growth. Lee and Hong argued that past performance of economic growth would not be mirrored in the next few decades because of the lowering marginal productivity of capital.[38] The possible decreasing performance of economic growth could be avoided as long as the countries have the capability to ensure an increasing productivity rate. It has been argued, and empirically proven, that FDI increases productivity. Increased productivity could come from better working environments, training and technology upgrades. In addition, new companies entering an industry or area increase competition and induce other companies (local or foreign) to improve working conditions.

Why, though, does investment not come easily to developing countries? With respect to the existing conditions controlling FDI, the developing economies have worked hard to encourage more investors to their countries, but a large gap remains and is increasing the difference between advanced and emerging or developing countries. By using the FDI Index, Groh and Wich explained why the shares of FDI were still very different between advanced and emerging or developing economies.[39] The developed countries attracted more than 75% of FDI owing to the appropriate legal and political systems as well as sufficient and developed infrastructures.

For Indonesia, FDI inflow has not been so remarkable because of disincentives such as limited infrastructure, and relatively complicated and time-consuming investment procedures, which remain unsolved. The competition emerged not only between the developing countries (including Association of Southeast Asian Nations (ASEAN) members) but also with developed countries that are more advanced in technology, infrastructure and developed institutions. In general, several specific conditions have made Indonesia an attractive investment destination: abundant and cheap natural resources, especially minerals and quarrying products; increasingly large markets for final products; and cheap labour. Of those three factors, cheap labour is increasingly endangered because of the dynamic conditions in the labour market and reforms to labour law pending in the national legislative programme.

The global FDI flow rebounded in 2010 after the deep slump following the global financial crisis that erupted in 2008. In 2010 FDI inflows amounted to more than $3,000,000 million.[40] This amount was much lower than before the financial crisis of 2007, when it was around $9,000,000 million. Investment in Indonesia has been falling steeply, from $9,318 million in 2008 to $4,877 million in 2009. The 2009 figure was still lower than the average FDI inflow after the recovery from the 1997–98 crisis.

Globally, in 2011 the FDI inflow to developed countries increased significantly compared to 2010, but it was still below the pre-crisis figure for 2008. The positive sentiment of global inflows helped Indonesia to regain FDI. The FDI inflow to developing countries increased by about 12%, to around $770,000 million, mainly driven by the increase in Asia of around 10%; however, Latin America and the Caribbean increased by 16%. The larger increases, at 25%, took place in the transition economies. UNCTAD's *World Investment Prospects Survey (WIPS)* 2012–14 declared that Indonesia was one of the top five FDI destinations, which meant, with respect to the obstacles to investment, that Indonesia was still a promising destination for FDI for investors (transnational corporations). According to the *WIPS* report, China offers the best prospects for investment, India is ranked third, Brazil fifth, Russia eighth and South Africa 14th. Those figures confirm that the emerging economies of the BRICS countries and Indonesia still have good prospects for attracting FDI.

Where has the FDI flowed to in Indonesia's economy? The manufacturing sectors received the most FDI in Indonesia in 2004–10, as shown in Table 14.1. This sector absorbed the largest portion of FDI, in which the annual average was 38.29%. Second to the manufacturing sector was mining and quarrying, with a share of 20.86%. The second position of mining and quarrying does not support the statement by Pravin about the insignificance of natural resources in attracting FDI to BRICS countries.[41] In Indonesia, a larger share of FDI to the extractive industries shows that this sector is still very profitable. This sector is interesting for foreign investors because it preserves the high benefits for operating companies in Indonesia as well as their companies overseas in one group (for multinational companies). The benefits are lower prices and the continuity of input supply. Other attractive sectors for FDI were transport, storage and communication, financial intermediation, and the wholesale and retail trades. The large domestic market and consumption level gave impetus to the fast growth of these latter sectors.

Trade: exports and imports

Apart from the pros and cons of the global effects of the current crises in European countries and in the USA, international trade is in fact the channel for the emerging economies to improve their growth performance and a way to recover from the crisis. During the 2008–09

Indonesia's economic growth and development

Table 14.1 Distribution of FDI in Indonesia by sector, 2004–10

	2004	2005	2006	2007	2008	2009	2010	2004–10
Agriculture, hunting and forestry	6.69	0.04	4.58	4.13	2.11	−1.07	2.15	2.18
Fishing	0.00	0.11	0.08	0.27	−0.27	0.21	0.39	0.14
Mining and quarrying	5.94	14.70	6.55	27.48	38.74	26.70	14.25	20.86
Manufacturing	39.30	63.13	34.41	34.82	24.92	32.26	37.37	38.29
Electricity, gas and water supply	0.00	1.94	−0.02	−0.88	−0.60	1.09	1.53	0.60
Construction	−0.85	1.56	1.73	2.81	0.26	0.14	−0.37	0.75
Wholesale and retail trade	−10.08	0.72	7.62	3.10	12.44	1.50	18.51	8.29
Hotel and restaurant	0.00	0.00	0.14	−0.14	0.17	0.00	0.01	0.03
Transport, storage and communication	10.74	4.61	12.06	13.27	1.44	36.89	17.96	12.94
Financial intermediation	20.55	9.35	20.91	19.64	20.68	3.06	3.07	12.23
Real estate, renting and business activities	−0.85	0.20	−0.29	−0.06	−2.16	−0.51	0.20	−0.44
Others	28.56	3.61	12.19	0.53	2.28	−0.23	4.92	4.81
Total	100.00	100.00	100.00	100.00	100.00	100.00	100.00	100.00

Source: Produced from Bank Indonesia, 2012, *Statistics of Indonesia's Economic and Finance (SEKI)*

crisis, the total volume of global trade decreased owing to falling demand from main trading players, such as the European Union and the USA. The countries that had higher dependency on specific markets tended to have a significant contraction in their trade. Then the contraction in trade depressed their economic growth. Trade direction and market diversification are crucial to compensate for the decreasing demand from the importing countries.[42]

The export structures of Brazil and Russia were mainly dependent on exports of commodities (which account for 51.8% and 79.5% of their total exports, respectively), while China and India mainly depend on exports of manufactured products (93.4% and 64.0% of their total exports, respectively).[43] During the 2007–09 global financial crisis, the financial dependency of Brazil and Russia on the US economy was much greater than that of China and India. India and China have established more trade networks with the rest of the world.

Indonesia is rich in natural resources. Raw materials, particularly minerals and mineral products, are predominant in Indonesian exports but plastics, rubber and other articles, and base metals have also been increasing their share (see Figure 14.2). From the manufacturing sectors there has been a tendency to decrease volumes of exports, in particular of machinery and mechanical appliances, electrical equipment, and textiles and textile articles. The textile industry was dominant in contributing to labour absorption and share in GDP, especially in the 1980s–90s. On the import side, imported products were mainly capital goods such as machinery and mechanical appliances, electrical equipment, base metals and articles of base metal, vehicles, aircraft, marine vessels and associated transport equipment (see Figure 14.3).

The trade patterns of the countries have also had an effect on economic growth. Indeed, the pattern of trade specialization induces long-term economic growth. Countries that are more dependent on the export of natural resource-based products might fail to grow sustainably (or grow at a lower rate) if they cannot diversify their export structure.[44] The inability of the producers or exporters of primary commodities to develop more dynamic patterns of trade specialization in the economy could reduce long-term economic growth. The initial step to achieve long-term economic growth is restructuring resource-based industries to natural resource-processing industries. The next step is to create industries with more added value in the economy. The ability of one country to export more value-added and differentiated products (up to the final

Zamroni Salim

Table 14.2 High-technology exports (% of manufactured exports and current US$)

	Brazil	Russia	India	China	South Africa	Indonesia
High-technology exports (% of manufactured exports)						
1990	6.46	—	3.94	—	—	1.59
2000	18.73	16.07	6.26	18.98	7.00	16.37
2005	12.84	8.44	5.80	30.84	6.66	16.55
2006	12.08	7.78	6.07	30.51	6.46	13.47
2007	11.87	6.88	6.40	26.66	5.58	11.00
2008	11.65	6.47	6.78	25.57	5.12	10.90
2009	13.20	9.23	9.09	27.53	5.35	12.87
2010	11.21	8.85	7.18	27.51	4.28	11.36
High-technology exports (US$ million)						
1990	1,053.13	—	497.83	—	—	144.31
2000	5,990.41	3,907.96	2,062.49	41,735.54	990.53	5,774.42
2005	8,031.34	3,820.37	4,139.24	215,928.41	1,759.56	6,671.06
2006	8,418.10	3,866.05	4,876.30	273,131.52	1,790.06	6,034.49
2007	9,076.35	4,108.63	5,997.79	302,773.30	1,832.87	5,356.42
2008	10,285.56	5,071.30	7,738.41	340,117.84	1,974.04	5,762.69
2009	7,896.04	4,527.43	10,728.45	309,600.89	1,364.42	6,038.55
2010	8,121.87	5,193.36	10,086.63	406,089.69	1,420.05	6,673.36

Source: Food and Agriculture Organization (FAO), 'FAOSTAT', 2012
Note: High-technology exports cover products with high R&D intensity, such as aerospace, computers, pharmaceuticals, scientific instruments, and electrical machinery.

goods) may not be sustained in the long run without employing technology, innovation and educated/skilled human resources. Export-driven policies have significantly increased the real per capita income of the countries.

Trade patterns are related also to the ability of industrial sectors to create production networks. Networking is a key component to win the global competition. Regional production networks in emerging economies are closely related to the progress of economic crises. The companies tried to create the networks either in resources, production, distribution and marketing just after the crisis hit the economies. As a comparison, at the country level, in the case of ASEAN countries, the group named ASEAN Plus emerged after the Asian crisis in 1997–98. The companies in emerging markets needed to maintain their strategic focus after the crisis, to survive and expand their operations. Problems of regional expansion sometimes emerge because of the over-emphasis on the magnitude of domestic markets and the treating of export markets as additional business. Companies tend to postpone their expansion overseas because they want to be more competitive in their domestic markets.[45] They have to be established first in domestic markets before expanding their business globally. Economic liberalization in periods of economic crisis has had positive and negative effects on industrial structure. Successful companies benefited from the liberalization, shown by increases in the quality of products, price competitiveness, variety of products or product differentiation, and the power of distribution channels.

How could the (additional increase) in productivity, some of which follows from the investment channel, and more dynamic patterns of trade specialization, control longer and even sustainable economic growth for the country? There is a bilateral causal relation between productivity and exports and, hence, in tandem, they induce economic growth. The productivity gain could be obtained by productive and competitive firms entering foreign markets.

Indonesia's economic growth and development

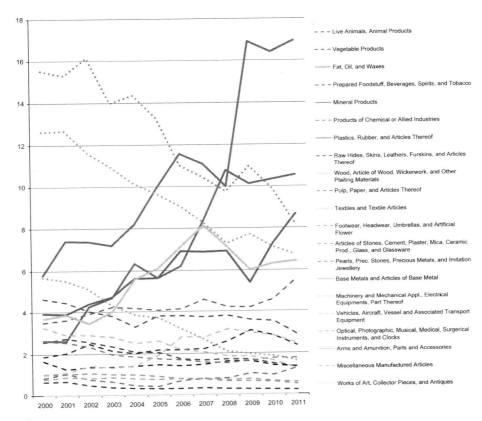

Figure 14.2 Indonesia's exports shares by sector, 2000–11

Controllable factors of exchange rates and inflation

The engines of growth, discussed earlier, may not generate higher real incomes if the respective country cannot handle what we call 'lubricants' for the economy.[46] The lubricants we shall discuss are inflation and the exchange rate. Rocha and Moreira studied policies that can potentially reduce the economic vulnerability of the emerging market economies around the globe.[47] The policies relate to financial liberalization, public debt management, consistent economic growth, development of domestic financial markets and improvements in governance indicators (the rule of law and the quality of regulation), and are important in restoring those economies from their slower growth.

Looking back at the longer periods of economic growth of Indonesia, it can be seen that exchange rate and inflation policies made a significant contribution to steering the economy back onto the right track (see Figure 14.4). The higher economic growth has not had a real effect on increasing social welfare because the nominal GDP has been eroded by higher inflation and an uncontrolled exchange rate. History shows how Indonesia's economy collapsed during the Asian crisis even after a period of higher economic growth, which led, in the 1990s, to it being described as one of the Asian Tigers.

Until recently, these two macroeconomic instruments have been managed properly in Indonesia. The inflation rate has been kept under two digits (being firm between 4% and 6% since 2000). In addition, the exchange rate has also been controlled by the central bank with prudent market interventions to ensure stability in its market rate.

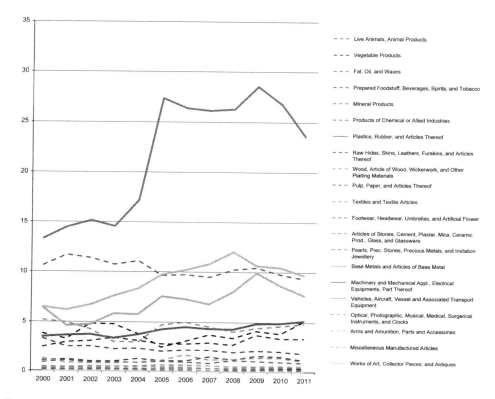

Figure 14.3 Indonesia's Imports shares by sector, 2000–11

Indonesia is becoming a net oil importer and fluctuations in the oil price will put pressure on the current account especially, and on the national budget and development planning generally. Adjustment to the national budget and related policies are necessary to anticipate the possibility of an unexpected depreciation. The depreciation of the currency of net importing countries in the long run emerges because of the adverse terms of trade effect and, in the short run, because of the expectation of future depreciation will also take place.[48]

Indonesia has dramatically changed its currency regime, a result of the 1997–98 economic crisis, from managed floating to free floating. Under certain conditions (if the market rate of the rupiah is not in accord with a specified range of medium-term inflation), the central bank intervenes to ensure that the rupiah gets back on track. Inflation targeting has become a prime choice of the central bank to guide the economy and to ensure stability of the rupiah.[49] Indonesia devalued the rupiah in 1986 to achieve export competitiveness and maintain purchasing power parity (PPP).[50] Following the Asian Financial Crisis, Indonesia applied a floating exchange rate regime to accommodate fluctuations of the rupiah with some intervention by the central bank.

Factors that ensure sustainable development

With globalization, where the domestic economy seems to be always open to international competition, sustainable growth depends very much on external factors. The remaining question of the sustainability of economic resilience to global shocks still exists. External shocks can

Indonesia's economic growth and development

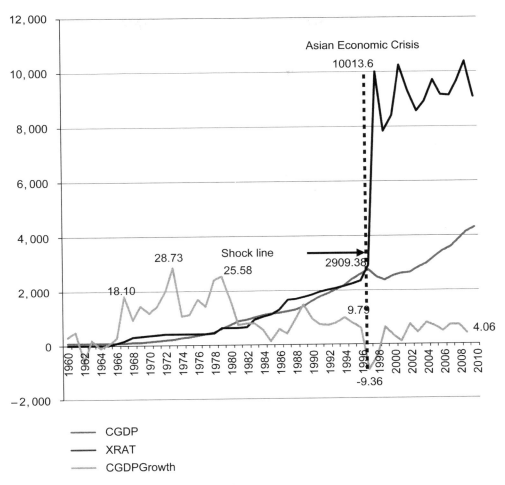

Figure 14.4 Indonesia's per capita GDP, economic growth and exchange rate
Note: CGDP refers to per capita GDP, XRAT refers to exchange rate of Indonesia's Rupiah against the US$ and CGDPGrowth refers to economic growth based on per Capita GDP

hamper or quite easily destroy the domestic economy. As a response, the domestic economy has to be stable and resilient when up against global shocks.

Auty records the necessary conditions for sustainable, equitable and rapid economic development.[51] The conditions include relatively equitable access to land and primary education; effective markets and public accountability; open trade policies and a diversified, competitive economy (diversification in competitive manufacturing). Those conditions are essential to ensure that an economy is resilient to (global) shocks and also to preserve sustainable economic growth. Those conditions are not sufficient without the fifth factor of political state development with the following characteristics: sufficient autonomy for logical and consistent economic policy, and sufficient political will to achieve long-term social welfare.

'Accelerated industrialization' is a programme, initiated in 2012, to develop industrial sectors in Indonesia to accelerate and expand development and economic growth. There are several policies to encourage industrial development, such as the domestic industry security policy, infrastructure development, improving the quality of service by the bureaucracy, improving and harmonizing regulations, fiscal policy, and human resource development for industry.[52]

The staple trap relates also to increasing income inequality. While an inefficient labour market continues to provide jobs for the surplus rural labour, it tends to result in holding down the remuneration of those at the bottom of the labour scale. At the same time the labour unions effectively represent only those in the protected capital-intensive manufacturing sector.[53]

Research and development

Indonesia needs to have industrial restructuring policies that emphasize the development of manufacturing industries under the base line of a developed agricultural sector. This would benefit the economy by creating more collected domestic value added in overall sectors. Restructuring in industries must be implemented and aimed first at the more competitive industries, such as the extractive agro-based industries, to enable them to produce not only exported raw material but also intermediate goods.[54] Such restructuring also helps to develop industries that produce final goods for consumers. As part of the effort to increase industrial competitiveness and sustainable economic growth, top priority must be given to increasing the skills and education of the labour force, to improving technology and to ensuring there is adequate research and development (R&D). One of the big differences between developed and developing countries is the mobility of industrial labour. Inefficient workers are a prominent characteristic of the labour force in developing countries, mainly because of their lack of competency and capability. This immobility has to be minimized, so the workers are easily able to move and adjust to new industries or other competitive sectors.

China and India were the leaders in spending on agricultural R&D, together with Brazil and Russia. There was increasing expenditure by the middle-income countries from 39% in 2000 to 46% of total agricultural R&D spending in 2008. The budget allocation for agricultural R&D in Indonesia was very low, though there was significant growth in R&D generally during the same period.[55]

Of the BRICS economies and other developing countries, China and India lead in R&D spending. China's share was 12.0% in 2010 and this increased to 14.2% in 2012; meanwhile India followed with 2.6% in 2010 and 2.9% in 2012 of total spending on R&D (see Table 14.3). What of Indonesia's R&D spending? Even though the R&D funding in Indonesia has not progressively increased, it has been directed to better purpose. Indonesia's R&D-to-GDP ratio was 0.05 and 0.07 for the years 2004 and 2005, respectively.[56] Indonesia spent 0.10% in 2010 and 0.20% in 2012—that is, it increased by 100% within two years (see Table 14.3). The increased spending was encouraging even though the amount in nominal US dollars was lower than other emerging countries.

The projection of Indonesia's economy

Indonesia's President Soesilo Bambang Yodhoyono was optimistic that Indonesia would be on the shortlist of the 10 big economies in the world within the next two decades.[57] The president based his hopes on the continuing good economic performance of the country over the past five years under firm, conducive and prudent macroeconomic policies, and appropriate fiscal policy. Similarly, the vice-president was optimistic about Indonesia's economic growth over in the next two decades. Vice-President Boediono mentioned three conditions necessary to achieve economic parity with developed countries: entrepreneurship, innovation and the eradication of hindrances to creativity.[58] The synergy of science and technology is important to support and improve national economic development and its competitiveness.

Table 14.3 Agriculture value added and R&D

	Brazil	Russia	India	China	South Africa	Indonesia
Agriculture, value added (% of GDP)						
1980	11.01	—	35.39	30.17	6.20	23.97
1990	8.10	16.61	29.02	27.12	4.63	19.41
2000	5.60	6.43	23.12	15.06	3.27	15.60
2005	5.71	4.97	18.81	12.12	2.67	13.13
2006	5.48	4.52	18.29	11.11	2.88	12.97
2007	5.56	4.41	18.26	10.77	3.37	13.72
2008	5.91	4.40	17.78	10.73	3.22	14.48
2009	5.63	4.69	17.72	10.33	3.04	15.29
2010	5.30	4.00	17.74	10.10	2.48	15.31
Agriculture value added per worker (constant 2000 US$)[1]						
1980	1,090.13	—	307.84	179.38	1,913.73	449.81
1990	1,624.68	—	365.19	257.54	2,287.22	492.79
2000	2,348.05	1,953.16	420.16	357.58	2,669.08	531.54
2005	3,090.89	2,478.43	449.58	432.90	3,173.83	611.39
2006	3,305.94	2,620.11	461.77	455.27	3,080.87	639.71
2007	3,544.76	2,666.19	484.58	472.15	3,239.49	652.16
2008	3,859.69	2,893.12	479.49	498.50	3,683.31	682.89
2009	3,833.86	2,992.04	479.01	520.71	3,661.71	709.69
2010	4,182.45	2,730.84	507.01	544.96	3,950.87	730.01
Agricultural machinery, tractors per 100 sq km of arable land[2]						
1980	121.16	—	23.50	77.14	138.85	1.17
1990	143.80	—	60.70	66.63	107.89	2.23
2000	138.21	60.06	128.51	81.77	49.01	1.96
2005	129.45	39.44	—	—	—	—
2006	129.19	36.16	—	—	—	—
2007	—	33.37	—	—	—	—
2008	—	29.95	—	—	—	—
2009	—	27.10	—	—	—	—
R&D expenditure (% of GDP)[3]						
2000	1.02	1.05	0.77	0.90	—	0.07
2005	0.97	1.07	0.78	1.32	0.90	—
2006	1.00	1.07	0.77	1.39	0.93	—
2007	1.07	1.12	0.76	1.40	0.92	—
2008	1.08	1.04	–	1.47	0.93	—
2009	—	1.25	—	—	—	0.08
2010	1.10	1.03	0.80	1.48	0.93	0.10
2012	1.25	1.08	0.85	1.60	0.95	0.20
GDP, US$ billion, PPP						
2012	2,402	2,492.00	4,859.00	12,434.00	579.00	1,203.00

Source: FAO, 'FAOSTAT', 2012; Advantage Business Media, *2012 Global R&D Funding Forecast*, 2011
Notes: [1] Agriculture value added per worker is to measure the agricultural productivity. It covers forestry, hunting, and fishing, cultivation of crops and livestock production. [2] Agricultural machinery is calculated from the number of wheel and crawler tractors (excluding garden tractors) used in agriculture. Arable land is land under temporary crops, temporary meadows, land under market or kitchen gardens, and land temporarily fallow (FAO, 2012). [3] Expenditures for R&D are current and capital expenditures (both public and private) used to increase knowledge (knowledge of humanity, culture, and society), and the use of knowledge for new experiments and applications. R&D includes basic research, applied research, and experimental development.

Through its Master Plan (MP3EI), the Indonesian government has declared its intention to accelerate and expand economic growth based on Law 17 of 2007 (Long-term National Development Planning 2005–25). According to MP3EI, Indonesia is projected to have a per capita GDP of $14,250 to $15,500 and a GDP of $4,000,000 million – $4,500,000 million in 2025.[59] Those targets of per capita GDP and GDP could be achieved if Indonesia's real economy were to grow by 6.4% to 7.5% in the period 2011 to 2014, and followed by 8.0% to 9.0% in the following decade. The long-term target could be achieved if the inflation rates during the periods were kept to the modest rate of 3%.

The projection of Indonesia's economy was supported in a report by Hawksworth and Tiwari, which predicts the GDP growth rate to be around 5.8% with a per capita GDP growth rate of 4.1%. Indonesia will be ranked eighth with a GDP of $6,205 (PPP terms), but the current BRICS countries, except South Africa, will be in higher positions.[60]

To reach the position by 2025 of per capita GDP of almost $14,900, Indonesia needs extra incentives; it cannot be left doing business as usual. So, there should be additional extraordinary measures to lift the economy to the position predicted by Hawksworth and Tiwari, and hoped for by the Indonesian people.

How can Indonesia realize its dream by 2025? There are three channels that Indonesia should follow: increasing value added in the economy by integrating production chains of natural resources, and increasing the value added by human resources in or between the economic growth poles; increasing production and marketing efficiencies to increase national competitiveness and endurance; and empowering a national innovation system to create an innovation-driven economy. The technological and innovation leaps are necessary conditions to attain the targeted GDP figures. The most efficient developed infrastructure and logistic sectors have to be built as soon as possible to catch up with the economies of the BRICS and the developed countries.[61]

Innovation was a very expensive option in the economy, at least until the 1990s when the Indonesian government started to recognize the importance of R&D for long-term growth.[62] The utilization and the development of science and technology, and the formulation of industrial technology coincided with the enactment of consistent patent, trademark and copyright laws in 1997, which were an initial step towards generating endogenous growth. In addition, public research institutions and universities in Indonesia have been empowered through increasing budgets, which accounted for about two-thirds of total R&D expenditure, while the rest was from the private sector.

The main goal of the initiative to develop innovation is the achievement of sustainable growth. In terms of concept, Indonesia is on track to achieve economic growth by incorporating science and technology to boost growth and social welfare. In order to increase innovation as part of increasing technology advances and research development, the Indonesian government has plans to develop the innovation system by applying the concept of Innovation 1-747.[63] It refers to:

- 1% of GDP per year to support R&D.
- Seven innovative ecosystem improvements (regulations to support innovation, research centres and small and medium-scale enterprise development), and infrastructure revitalization for R&D.
- Four modes to accelerate economic growth (industrial development for basic needs, creative, science and technology, and strategic industries).
- Seven targets of innovation in 2025 (increasing the number of patents, assuring intellectual property rights, higher international-standard qualifications for science, technology and R&D, and the achievement of sustainable economic growth).

The challenges for sustainable growth

Logistics and infrastructure

In spite of the abundant natural resources and large population (both consumers or labour), Indonesia still has difficulties and, to some extent, impediments in its path to sustainable growth. Indonesia may not achieve its vast potential as a BRIC country because of key shortages that keep the costs of production elevated. The most persistent impediment, among others, to economic growth, is poor, or what can be classified as less developed, infrastructure.

In general, Indonesia has logistical problems. This sector is vital to the distribution of materials and goods from the point of origin (extraction) to the production process, and then to consumers (final destination). In principle, Indonesia and other ASEAN member countries have agreed to liberalize their logistics sector in 2013 as part of the common goal of achieving the ASEAN Economic Community (AEC) in 2015. With this strong commitment, Indonesia should prepare more to develop its logistics sector and, in particular, its infrastructure.

The Logistics Performance Index for Indonesia, on average, has been in the mid-range among the ASEAN countries—that is, it was slightly higher than that of new members of ASEAN, such as Laos, Cambodia and Myanmar (formerly Burma), but much lower than that of already established members such as Thailand, Malaysia and Singapore. The big disparity in customs and import clearance procedures could undermine efforts to build efficient supply chains not only in Indonesia but also for ASEAN as a whole. Just-in-time production management is vital if Indonesia is to increase its international competitiveness.

The World Economic Forum recorded the infrastructure quality in Indonesia in 2010 and compared it with the other ASEAN countries. The infrastructure quality in Indonesia was relatively poor. On the quality of roads, Indonesia was 94th (of the 133 countries being surveyed). Its position was far below India, China, Thailand and Malaysia. Other components of infrastructure that were found to be poor were the condition of railways, sea ports, air transport, the electricity supply and telephone lines.

Indonesia has been working hard to build a better infrastructure by introducing a scheme of public-private partnerships, as stipulated in the ministerial regulation no. 4 of 2010. In spite of well-documented regulation, its implementation is still far from complete. The public-private partnership scheme is basically part of the bigger infrastructure developmental concept of the Masterplan of Indonesia's Economic Growth Acceleration (MIEGA), which is in line with a broader ASEAN Connectivity. MIEGA comprises three pillars: the development of the potency of the economy; national connectivity and human resources; and science and technology development.

Indonesia, especially its capital, Jakarta, the centre of business in Indonesia, recently suffered large floods. Why is it that Indonesia has suffered from inadequate infrastructure for such a long time? The recent extensive flooding is just another example. The uneven development of infrastructure in Jakarta has meant that shopping malls, business districts and office centres have been built but there has been a lack of will and ability to build a mass rapid transport system, engineer drainage, clear slum areas and ensure security.

The responsibility for building a better Jakarta is not just that of the Jakarta Municipality Mayor but also of the central government of Indonesia. The shortages of funds, of holistic development planning and the isolation of infrastructure issues by political interests are some of the reasons why Jakarta, and other metropolitan cities, are underdeveloped and far from being cities friendly to growth, development and their inhabitants.

Economic curse and people's behaviour

Under the concept of the 'Paradox of Plenty', countries endowed with rich natural resources often do not build prosperity and economic power from those resources but instead stagnate.[64] The resource curse condition could create 'who cares' societies.[65] For the bureaucrats, it means over-exploitation of national resources (including budgets). For consumers, the resource curse phenomenon tends to influence their excessive consumption of specific resource-abundant products, such as subsidized fuel in Indonesia. The over-consumption of energy in Indonesia can be shown by the much larger energy intensity of 470 toe per million of GDP than that of OECD countries at around 200.[66]

Energy subsidies in industrial and developing countries cause economic efficiency losses. Removing subsidies could give significant environmental benefits (the reduction of carbon dioxide emissions) as well as real GDP gains.[67] In Indonesia, the fuel subsidy is to help poor people to enjoy a lower price for products in general (increasing economic welfare), but in the real world the benefit to poor families is reduced because of their limited income and consumption of fuel. The larger share of the subsidy, indeed, goes to the richer people in the economy. It needs a wise and firm policy of removing the complex structure of energy subsidies.[68] The incentive of a money transfer would not be a good policy because it tends to be used for unproductive activities and increased consumption. Indonesia should think about a compensation policy that could increase the skills and productivity of new job seekers, through, for example, vocational training that would have lasting benefits.

The statement that there is no positive correlation between natural wealth and other kinds of economic wealth in resource-abundant countries may be applicable to Indonesia.[69] The country has not experienced strong export-led growth and sustained rapid economic growth, but has tended to have a high-price economy. The resource curse is a warning sign for societies that have suffered from high levels of corruption and have sluggish checks and balances on political decision making.[70] The curse of economic development being highly dependent on natural resources comes about through deterioration in the quality of the institutions of government in the country, which are then not able to reduce or prevent corruption, waste and mismanagement.

The above statements should be seen as a warning sign for the country to avoid resource curse traps that might cause it to deviate from the goal of sustainable economic growth. The exit strategy from the resource curse is through institutional reform to strengthen governance, and to install political checks and balances so that economic reality can be a guide to the economic, social and political aspects of the energy subsidy.

The Indonesian government has an energy mix policy with the two main goals of securing the energy supply for maintaining and improving industrial growth, and increasing the share of renewable energy to be on the path to green growth. The energy mix policy is to encourage the exploration of potential alternative energy, and energy in consumption. As part of this policy, renewable energy use is to go from zero in 2005 to 17% in 2025. The use of fossil fuel energy is to be cut from 55% in 2005 to 20% in 2025. This policy also stipulates the increasing use of natural gas from 22% in 2005 to 30% in 2025. The policy is also directed to cause the economy to be more sustainable or, in other words, it is recognized as green growth.

This green growth has been related to the green economy for sustainable development and poverty reduction. It means that the process of economic development with all kinds of resources should preserve their use for the next generation and work for the future. Different from China, India and overall developed countries, the source of greenhouse gas (GHG) emissions came mainly from peat fires and deforestation, not from industrial economic activities. The contribution of the Indonesian GHG emissions to its GDP is around 0.6%, which was quite small compared to Indonesia's contribution of 4.97% of global GHG emissions.[71] These figures send the message that Indonesia should restructure its sectoral economic activity from being based on raw materials and low value-added products to more finished goods with larger added values. In addition, the second message is that preservation of natural resources for future generations must be started right now before they are gone forever. Technology innovation may help to enable efficient industries with larger added values.

Sustainable economic growth must assure the people in the country that they are to enjoy equal welfare (shown as a lower income inequality). The economic development policies issued by the government must, inclusively, encourage people to be more productive.

Concluding remarks

The BRICS countries are a relatively new paradigm in international development. It could induce other developing or emerging countries to be more active in contributing globally. This paradigm may give encouragement and inspire other developing countries to use their resources to achieve sustainable growth and development. Indonesia should take this positive BRICS sentiment to employ its resources at the potential level.

The richness in natural resources is no longer a main determinant for Indonesia to reach the current economic growth and development. Development must be planned and settled outside the 'resource curse' box and directed to be a more competitive economy.

The features and figures of the BRICS can be used as a mirror for Indonesia to see the existing gaps of factors controlling sustainable growth, including government expenditure, investment, value-added technology exports, and sufficient attention to R&D and innovation. Industrial restructuring policy can be used to increase more value-added products in industry once the developed infrastructure (logistics in general) and developed agricultural sector are preserved in the economy. Technological advance and innovation, by inviting investment and R&D, would bridge the gap of the current development stages between Indonesia and the BRICS countries.

The increasing endowment of human capital, technological advance and innovation under developed infrastructure could preserve Indonesia with strong sustainable economic growth and development. The new giant economy, as the next member of the BRIICS, is feasible and reasonable for the currently developing country of Indonesia.

Notes

1 M. Papa and N.W. Gleason, 'Major Emerging Powers in Sustainable Development Diplomacy: Assessing Their Leadership Potential', *Global Environmental Change* 22(4), October 2012: 915–24; S.A. Basher, A.A. Haug and P. Sadorsky, 'Oil Prices, Exchange Rates and Emerging Stock Markets', *Energy Economics* 34, 2012: 227–40.

2 J. Hawksworth and A. Tiwari, *The World in 2050—The Accelerating Shift of Global Economic Power: Challenges and Opportunities*, PricewaterhouseCoopers, London, 2011.

3 World Bank/International Bank for Reconstruction and Development, *World Development Report 2012: Gender Equality and Development*, World Bank, Washington, DC, 2012.

4 Once Indonesia joins this group, BRICS will change to BRIICS.

5 D. Acemoglu, 'Introduction to Economic Growth', *Journal of Economic Theory* 147, 2012: 545–50. C. Kenny and D. Williams, 'What Do We Know About Economic Growth? Or, Why Don't We Know Very Much?' *World Development* 29(1), 2001: 1–22.

6 Robert M. Solow, 'A Contribution to the Theory of Economic Growth', *Quarterly Journal of Economics* 70, 1956, 65–94.

7 As conceptually structured by R.E. Lucas, 'On the Mechanics of Economic Development', *Journal of Monetary Economics* 22(3), 1988: 42; P. Romer, 'Increasing Returns and Long-Run Growth', *Journal of Political Economy* 94, 1986: 1002–37.

8 B. Wydick, *Games in Economic Development*, Cambridge University Press, Cambridge, 2008.

9 Acemoglu, 'Introduction to Economic Growth'.

10 V. Martinet and G. Rotillon, 'Invariance in Growth Theory and Sustainable Development', *Journal of Economic Dynamics & Control* 31, 2007: 2827–46.

11 R.E. Lopez, G. Anriquez and S. Gulati, 'Structural Change and Sustainable Development', *Journal of Environmental Economics and Management* 53, 2007: 307–22.

12 X. Yao, C. Watanabe and Y. Li, 'Institutional Structure of Sustainable Development in BRICs: Focusing on ICT Utilization', *Technology in Society* 31, 2009: 9–28.

13 These groups are not directly or intentionally related to a group of countries under regional trading arrangements or many kinds of free trade agreement.

14 K. Rocha and A. Moreira, 'The Role of Domestic Fundamentals on the Economic Vulnerability of Emerging Markets', *Emerging Markets Review* 11, 2010: 173–82.

15 Basher *et al.*, 'Oil Prices, Exchange Rates and Emerging Stock Markets'.

16 R. Aloui, M.S.B. Aïssa and D.K. Nguyen, 'Global Financial Crisis, Extreme Interdependences, and Contagion Effects: The Role of Economic Structure?' *Journal of Banking & Finance* 35, 2011: 130–41.

17 M. Papa and N.W. Gleason, 'Major Emerging Powers in Sustainable Development Diplomacy: Assessing Their Leadership Potential', *Global Environmental Change* 22(4), 2012: 915–24.

18 Yao *et al.*, 'Institutional Structure of Sustainable Development in BRICs'.

19 Y. Wu, 'Is China's Economic Growth Sustainable? A Productivity Analysis', *China Economic Review* 11, 2000: 278–96.

20 The ability of developing countries to catch up with the development level of developed countries is measured by the convergence speed. The convergence speed is measured through the average value of infrastructure and total expenditure on R&D as representative of potential technological strength of the countries. The infrastructures (for health and environment, science and technology, and education) showed the basic condition and environment required to catch up with technological advancements, while total expenditure on R&D is a representation of the input in technology development (Yao *et al.*, 'Institutional Structure of Sustainable Development in BRICs').

21 Yao *et al.*, 'Institutional Structure of Sustainable Development in BRICs'.

22 J.E. Stiglitz, 'Globalization and Growth in Emerging Markets', *Journal of Policy Modeling* 26, 2004: 465–84.

23 P. van der Eng, 'The Sources of Long-term Economic Growth in Indonesia, 1880–2008', *Explorations in Economic History* 47, 2010: 294–309.

24 P. Krugman, 'The Myth of Asia's Miracle', *Foreign Affairs* 73(6), 1994: 62–78.

25 J.M. Page, 'The East Asian Miracle: An Introduction', *World Development* 22, 1994: 615–25.

26 C. Kearney, 'Emerging Markets Research: Trends, Issues and Future Directions', *Emerging Markets Review* 13, 2012: 159–83.

27 Yao *et al.*, 'Institutional Structure of Sustainable Development in BRICs'.

28 P. LeBel, 'The Role of Creative Innovation in Economic Growth: Some International Comparisons', *Journal of Asian Economics* 19, 2008: 334–47.

29 M.D. Bordo, C.M. Meissner and D. Stuckler, 'Foreign Currency Debt, Financial Crises and Economic Growth: A Long-Run View', *Journal of International Money and Finance* 29, 2010: 642–65.

30 Z. Salim, 'Indonesia in the G20: Benefits and Challenges Amidst National Interests and Priorities', in W. Hofmeister (eds), *Perceptions and Perspectives for Global Governance*, Konrad-Adanauer Stiftung, Singapore, 2011a.

31 E.C. Perotti and P. Oijen, 'Privatization, Political Risk and Stock Market Development in Emerging Economies', *Journal of International Money and Finance* 20, 2001.

32 World Bank and the International Bank for Reconstruction and Development, *World Development Report 2002: Building Institutions for Markets*, 2002.

33 J.H. Cassing, 'Economic Policy and Political Culture in Indonesia', *European Journal of Political Economy* 16, 2000: 159–71.

34 K. Hong and H.C. Tang, 'Crises in Asia: Recovery and Policy Responses', *Journal of Asian Economics* 2010, doi:10.1016/j.asieco.2012.07.002.

35 United Nations Conference on Trade and Development (UNCTAD), *World Investment Report 2012: Towards a New Generation of Investment Policies*, 2012.

36 The factors includes market size, trade openness, natural resources as economic determinants and macroeconomic stability (inflation rate), political stability, little risk of violence, government effectiveness, good regulatory quality, control of corruption and accountability, rule of law as potential institutional and political determinants. Jadhav Pravin, 'Determinants of Foreign Direct Investment in

BRICS Economies: Analysis of Economic, Institutional and Political Factor', *Procedia—Social and Behavioral Sciences* 37, 2012, 5–14.

37 UNCTAD, *World Investment Report 2012*.

38 J.W. Lee and K. Hong, 'Economic Growth in Asia: Determinants and Prospects', *Japan and the World Economy* 24, 2012: 101–13.

39 The differences may be detected by using the FDI Index. This index is a composite index measuring the attractiveness of one country for FDI based on the key drivers of economic activity, the legal and political system, the business environment, and infrastructure. Alexander Peter Groh and Matthias Wich, 'Emerging Economies' Attraction of Foreign Direct Investment', *Emerging Markets Review* 13, 2012, 210–29.

40 ASEAN Secretariat, *ASEAN Investment Report 2011: Sustaining FDI Flows in a Post-crisis World*, ASEAN Secretariat, Jakarta, November 2011.

41 Pravin, 'Determinants of Foreign Direct Investment in BRICS Economies'.

42 C.G. Tsangarides, 'Crisis and Recovery: Role of the Exchange Rate Regime in Emerging Market Economies', *Journal of Macroeconomics* 34, 2012: 470–88.

43 Tsangarides, 'Crisis and Recovery'.

44 S.M. Mursheda and L.A. Serino, 'The Pattern of Specialization and Economic Growth: The Resource Curse Hypothesis Revisited', *Structural Change and Economic Dynamics* 22, 2011: 151–61.

45 J. Anand *et al.*, 'Strategic Responses to Economic Liberalization in Emerging Economies: Lessons from Experience', *Journal of Business Research* 59, 2006: 365–71.

46 The term 'lubricant' is the variable controlling the temperature of the economy. Overheating may reduce the real value of the output or income of the people in the country.

47 Rocha and Moreira, 'The Role of Domestic Fundamentals on the Economic Vulnerability of Emerging Markets'.

48 Basher *et al.*, 'Oil Prices, Exchange Rates and Emerging Stock Markets'.

49 E. Tanuwidjaja and K.M. Choy, 'Central Bank Credibility and Monetary Policy in Indonesia', *Journal of Policy Modeling* 28, 2006: 1011–22.

50 Y. Hadiwibowo and M. Komatsu, 'Trilemma and Macroeconomic Policies Under Different Financial Structures in Indonesia', *Journal of Asian Economics* 22, 2011: 302–10.

51 R.M. Auty, 'The Political Economy of Resource-Driven Growth', *European Economic Review* 45, 2001: 839–46.

52 Ministry of Industry Republic of Indonesia, *Industry Facts and Figures 2012*, Ministry of Industry Republic of Indonesia, Jakarta, 2012.

53 Auty, 'The Political Economy of Resource-Driven Growth'.

54 Z. Salim, 'Structural Change in Indonesian Economy: Natural Resource-Based Industries', *World Bank Discussion*, Jakarta, 28 June 2011b.

55 N. Beintema *et al.* 'ASTI Global Assessment of Agricultural R&D Spending Developing Countries Accelerate Investment', *International Food Policy Report*, 2012.

56 C.H. Yang and Y.H. Chen, 'R&d, Productivity, and Exports: Plant-Level Evidence from Indonesia', *Economic Modelling* 29, 2012: 208–16.

57 This optimism of the president was aired during his visit to Berlin, Germany, on 5 March 2013. Detik Finance, *Laporan dari Berlin: Promosi Investasi di Jerman, SBY Sebut RI akan Jadi Negara 10 Besar Ekonomi Dunia* [The Report from Berlin: Investment Promotion in Germany, SBY Stated that Indonesia will be one of the World's Top Ten Economies], finance.detik.com/read/2013/03/05/130839/2186070/4/promosi-investasi-di-jerman-sby-sebut-ri-akan-jadi-negara-10-besar-ekonomi-dunia?f990101mainnews (accessed 5 March 2013).

58 Kompas, 'Boediono: Tiga Syarat Indonesia Jadi Negara Maju' [Boediono: Three Conditions for Indonesia to be Developed Countries], accessed 17 January 2013.

59 Indonesia Coordinating Minister for Economy, *The Master Plan of Indonesia's Economic Acceleration and Enlargement for Economic Development*, 2011.

60 J. Hawksworth and A. Tiwari, *The World in 2050—The Accelerating Shift of Global Economic Power: Challenges and Opportunities*, PricewaterhouseCoopers, London, 2011.

61 Indonesia Coordinating Minister for Economy, *The Master Plan*.

62 C.H. Yang and Y.H. Chen, 'R&D, Productivity, and Exports: Plant-Level Evidence from Indonesia', *Economic Modelling* 29, 2012: 208–16.

63 Indonesia Coordinating Minister for Economy, *The Master Plan*.

64 M. Sandbu, 'Natural Wealth Accounts: A Proposal for Alleviating the Natural Resource Curse', *World Development* 34(7), 2006: 1153–70.

65 'Who cares' society is a term used to show the condition of society, where their activity is used just for their own (family) purposes and see the use of resources (natural resources) for short period of time. They never look at future uses and future generation. In addition, others do not care about what happens as long as their own belongings are not affected or deducted.

66 'toe' refers to ton of oil equivalent. Another figure of energy use in Indonesia is the larger elasticity of energy use. The elasticity in Indonesia was around 1.84 compared to developed countries of less than 1 (1998–2003). Larger energy intensity indicates a higher price or cost of energy conversion to GDP. Ministry of Energy and Mineral Resources, *Blue Print of National Energy Management 2006–2025*, Ministry of Energy and Mineral Resources of Republic of Indonesia, Jakarta, 2006.

67 World Bank and the International Bank for Reconstruction and Development, *World Development Report 2003: Sustainable Development in a Dynamic World Transforming Institutions, Growth, and Quality of Life*, 2003.

68 Indonesia still uses the national poverty line which is equal to US$0.92 a day in 2012, which is far from any category that the World Bank used of $1.25 and $2.00 a day. (Badan Pusat Statistik, *Kemiskinan: Jumlah dan Persentase Penduduk Miskin* [Poverty: The Number and Percentage of Poor People], BPS, Jakarta, 2012.) The differences of the poverty line had significant effects on the recorded poverty incidence in the country. According to the survey data in 2009, those living below the poverty line were just around 14.2%; meanwhile, by applying the World Bank poverty line of $1.25 and $2.00 recorded 18.7% and 50.7%, respectively. The lower number of people below the poverty line tends to drive the national policy away from the right target of how to increase the Human Development Index and social economic welfare.

69 J.D. Sachs and A.M. Warner, 'Natural Resources and Economic Development: The Curse of Natural Resources', *European Economic Review* 45, 2001: 827–38.

70 M. Brückner, 'Natural Resource Dependence, Non-Tradables, and Economic Growth', *Journal of Comparative Economics* 38, 2010: 461–71.

71 J. Jupestaa *et al.* 'Managing the Transition to Sustainability in an Emerging Economy: Evaluating Green Growth Policies in Indonesia', *Environmental Innovation and Societal Transitions* 1, 2011: 187–91.

15

Mexico

Emerging economy kept on a leash by mismatched monopolies

Francisco E. González[1]

Bottom-line diagnosis: downside pressures given 'mismatched monopolies' but strong potential for growth and development

In a nutshell, Mexico's political economy will continue to be dominated by what I identify as a landscape characterized by mismatched monopolies. Economically, the country is dominated by monopolies or oligopolistic competition in the main private and public production sectors. Such concentration has led to low productivity growth, under-production, over-pricing, and strong blackmail power that tycoons in the private and public sphere have used against successive governments to avoid opening their sectors to competition, and to preserve and if possible to augment their dominance. In turn, the political sphere, concentrated and effective in terms of vertical command and control between the 1940s and the mid-1990s, gave way to the decentralization of authority, the fragmentation of the exercise of power, and particularly the strengthening of private groups that usurped the state's prerogative as the only source of the use of public force in its territory.

In spite of the economic and political forces that have created a stable, sub-optimal equilibrium that concentrates power, resources and influence in few individuals and groups, Mexico is one of the few 'trillion–dollar club'[2] emerging economies with close to 120 million inhabitants, which gives it the scale and scope for domestic-led growth. It shares a 2,000–mile border and has a free trade agreement with the USA, the richest, most powerful country in the world and one of the largest consumer markets, which gives Mexico the capacity for export-led growth too.

In the sphere of geopolitics, Mexico was identified since the turn of the 21st century as one of nine 'pivotal states' in the developing world with which US foreign policy had to keep special engagement because of their regional weight.[3] In the world of international financial flows, Mexico's profile has also gained prominence recently. Living in the shadows of the so-called BRICs (Brazil, Russia, India and the People's Republic of China) in the 2000s, Goldman Sachs identified a 'Next 11' (N–11) group of emerging economies in 2011, whose four largest markets it dubbed MIST, and include Mexico, Indonesia, South Korea (Republic of Korea) and Turkey.[4] Productive use of significant foreign inflows could act as a catalyser that enables

287

sustained, high domestic as well as export-oriented growth in Mexico. The current government under President Enrique Peña Nieto (2012–18) has moved decidedly against some of the main public and private monopolies and while there is no silver bullet that can transform in the short term the concentrated economic landscape, major changes are under way for the first time in more than one and a half decades. The dice are rolling.

Birth and growing pains of an emerging economy

The Mexican miracle, 1940–70

Mexico, a federal republic made up of 31 states plus the capital city, was ruled uninterruptedly by an authoritarian, civilian regime under the Partido Revolucionario Institucional (PRI) between 1929 and 2000. Politically, the system was highly centralized under the authority of the president-in-turn, elected every six years. The golden rule of the system was and remains no re-election to public office, not only for the president but also for governors, federal and state legislators. Economically, positive external shocks like the Second World War and the Korean War helped growth, given the high demand for raw commodities and Mexican migrant labour in the USA. Successive PRI governments managed the country's economy quite conservatively—high real interest rates, low foreign borrowing, and low fiscal deficits—particularly between the early 1950s and the start of the 1970s.

The 1940–70 period, known as the 'Mexican miracle' delivered average annual gross domestic product (GDP) growth of 6%–7% and low inflation rates of 2%–4%.[5] Governments invested in rural but much more so in urban infrastructure as they embraced in the 1940s the strategy of import-substitution industrialization (ISI). Significant public investment in education, health care and housing fed the growth of the manufacturing and services sectors and a concomitant fall in subsistence agriculture (see Figure 15.1). A process of fast modernization characterized by growth in literacy, life expectancy and the middle classes helped to move the country from a poor to a middle-income country in less than four decades. Mexico's population more than

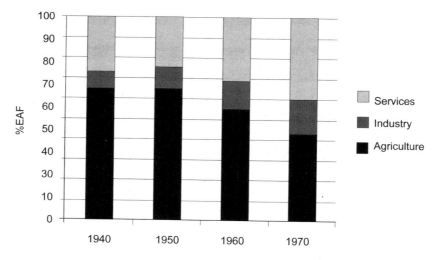

Figure 15.1 Employment growth by sector occupational profile charge as a proxy of modernisation
Source: Data elaborated by the author from the *Oxford Latin America History Economic Database*, 2007

doubled during this period—from under 30 million to more than 80 million—and the growth rate of the urban population outpaced significantly that of rural dwellers (see Figure 15.2). The label 'miracle' has to be qualified because, among other things, a majority of rural dwellers, still a majority of the population, was left behind, and poverty rates, particularly extreme poverty, grew during this period.

Economic populism and recurrent booms and busts, 1970–82

The image of a sucking, overbearing, disorderly state that crowded out private initiative through nationalization (84 firms in 1970 to 1,155 in 1982), overspending, and unsustainably expansive economic policies mostly applies to the 12 years of economic populism that include the presidencies of Luis Echeverría (1970–76) and José López Portillo (1976–82). Economic and social modernization had created a revolution in expectations among urban dwellers who protested in favour of pluralism, and which put increased pressure on the straightjacket of authoritarian, vertical command-and-control PRI rule. The regime suffered an existential crisis following the repugnant student massacres it carried out in 1968 and 1971.

Echeverría and López Portillo's governments tried to defuse political protest through economic largesse. The former declared in 1973 that the economy would be run from the executive's office (Los Pinos), and this led to a damaging personalization of economic policy characterized by exploding foreign indebtedness (US$3.2 billion in 1970 to $16 billion in 1976), fiscal deficits (2.5% to 9.3% of GDP in 1971 and 1975, respectively), and inflation (5% in 1970 to 17% in 1976). These trends culminated in 1976, the last year in office of Echeverría, with a balance-of-payments crisis and the first disorderly macro-devaluation of the Mexican peso since

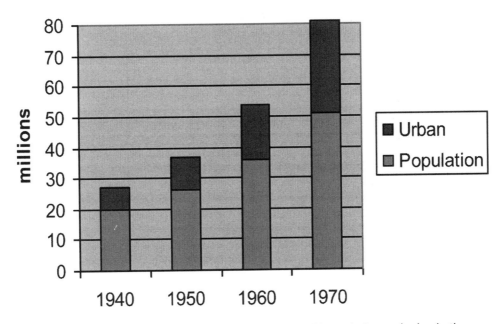

Figure 15.2 Population growth and urbanization demographic explosion and urbanisation
Source: Data elaborated by the author from the *Oxford Latin American History Economy Database*, 2007

Francisco E. González

1954. The government had to request a line of credit from the International Monetary Fund (IMF) in exchange for austerity policies.

In spite of this constraining inheritance, López Portillo shook off in 1978 the internationally mandated austerity plan in the wake of apparent shining prospects. The large-scale development of Mexico's oil infrastructure and cheap international credit resulting from the recycling of so-called 'petro-dollars' in the wake of the 1973–74 and 1979–81 global oil shocks gave López Portillo a temporary window of opportunity to re-enact the personalized, state-led, expansionary economic policymaking style of his predecessor. The experiment, likewise, ended in tears during the president's last year in office, 1982. Acceleration of foreign indebtedness ($20 billion in 1972 to $80 billion in 1982), growing fiscal deficits (11% to 18% of GDP in 1975 and 1982, respectively), accelerating inflation (17% in 1976 to 57% in 1982) and a twin process of rising international interest rates and lowering oil prices created a perfect storm, in large part manufactured by López Portillo's imprudent, hubristic one-sided policies. The government and the private business class fell out dramatically, as the president nationalized the banking industry as revenge for the massive capital flight that growing macroeconomic imbalances precipitated, and which the regime considered unpatriotic. This time the magnitude of the crisis was such that it led to the so-called 'lost decade' of growth and development not only in Mexico but throughout Latin America.

Change of course: painful adjustment, adoption of neo-liberalism and continuation of busts, 1982–2000

Aside from the IMF, the other official international financial institutions (IFIs) based in Washington, DC, i.e. the World Bank and the Inter-American Development Bank (IDB) became heavily involved in giving short-term financial help conditional on strict orthodox management—through austerity-induced policies and regular payment of interest and principal on foreign debts. The team that took over Mexico's government led by President Miguel de la Madrid (1982–88) had a cohesive core of young US-trained technocrats who embraced such orthodox external debt management. They set the roots of the return to orthodox macroeconomic policies that have dominated ever since. This group of young economists, public administrators and public policy experts established a credible, solid presence both at home and abroad. Of particular relevance was their trusted operators' presence in the main multilateral agencies in Washington, DC, as well as in the capitals of private financial markets, New York and London.

Following the austerity-based approach sanctioned by the USA and the multilateral institutions was not a foregone conclusion despite its embrace by the young technocrats. In 1984–85 negotiations among the largest external debtors in Latin America, i.e. Brazil, Mexico and Argentina, might have led to the formation of a debtors' club to co-ordinate actions and force softening creditors' conditions. Some members of de la Madrid's cabinet supported this strategy, but the technocrats, led by future President Carlos Salinas (1988–94), convinced the chief executive to stay the course, keep paying the country's debt obligations, and seek a unilateral rapprochement with the government of the USA to try to craft better paying conditions and fresh credit lines. Among other things, Mexico gave up its long-term opposition to free trade by joining the General Agreement on Tariffs and Trade (GATT) round in 1986.

The triumph of this approach did not translate automatically into a return of growth and less stringent living conditions for a majority of Mexicans. Between the end of 1982 and the end of 1988, when de la Madrid stepped down, total GDP growth was 0.2%, average annual inflation was 87%, and real wages suffered a massive contraction of 40%. Like his two predecessors, de la

Madrid's last year in office also experienced a crisis of confidence, related in part to the big New York stock market collapse of October 1987, and uncertainty about future economic management once he stepped down.

However, the commitment to stick to what by then had come to be known as the neo-liberal approach (i.e. stabilize and adjust via stringent fiscal and monetary policies, and implement structural reforms to re-orient economies in free market directions) and the objective to forge a closer economic relationship with the USA meant that Carlos Salinas's presidency was widely welcomed and supported, if not at home, given significant opposition by left-wing movements and parties that came together as the Partido de la Revolución Democrática (PRD), then certainly by the conservative, social, Catholic Partido Acción Nacional (PAN), the US government, banks and other businesses, and the multilateral lending community.

The overall financial flows' dynamic changed for the first time as Mexico, having been a net capital exporter since the early 1980s, became a big recipient of fresh foreign capital ($3.5 billion in 1989 to $33 billion in 1993) in search of high yields. In the early 1990s Mexico's share of capital inflows in Latin America was around 40%. The confidence Salinas's economic team inspired helped the country to become the first nation to undergo successful sovereign debt restructuring via the Brady bond scheme, whereby past, high-interest debt was sold at discounted prices and indebted countries were able to draw fresh resources from their creditors under advantageous conditions. Domestic and international elites also praised Salinas's policies of whole-scale privatization, particularly returning banks to private ownership; deregulation, capital account liberalization, and pursuing trade liberalization by signing the North American Free Trade Agreement (NAFTA) with the USA and Canada; granting central bank autonomy (although he still interfered in the bank's decision making); and rejoining into a single ministry the public revenue-raising and spending functions, which López Portillo had split.

A key short-term goal of the Salinas presidency was to combat inflation to restore confidence in the economy, and more specifically to force price change convergence between Mexico and the USA. He enacted an incomes policy and pegged the Mexican peso to the US dollar, and both anchors were quite successful, although the latter one, combined with trade liberalization since the mid-1980s plus the enactment of free capital movements in 1989, sowed the seeds of currency appreciation, growing current account deficits and eventually, like his three predecessors, a disorderly macro-devaluation and financial crisis, in his case (having refused to enact it) after he left office.

Salinas's successor, Ernesto Zedillo (1994–2000), also a US-trained technocrat who had been at the forefront of Mexico's external debt management, did not possess the political networks and support inside the PRI that his predecessor exploited successfully to promote economic reforms. Moreover, having promised 'well-being for your family' as his campaign slogan, less than one month after coming into office he faced a dramatic collapse in growth and a spike in inflation as a consequence of the sovereign and private debt crisis that ensued and came to be known as the 'tequila effect' in the world of emerging economies. Big US banks, pension funds and hedge funds were perilously exposed to Mexico's so-called 'Tesobonos', i.e. dollar-indexed bonds, and having been refused help by the US Congress, President Bill Clinton and his Secretary of the Treasury Robert Rubin engineered a Mexican bail-out. Using $20 billion from the Economic Stabilization Fund (ESF), they got the IFIs to cough up another $30 billion. The $50 billion bail-out helped to put a floor on the continuation of speculation and further economic decline in Mexico.

Like the previous decade, the 1990s ended up eroding living standards and well-being for a majority of Mexicans. Per capita income in real terms continued to decline as inflation outpaced growth throughout the decade (see Figure 15.3). For a party whose main source of legitimacy

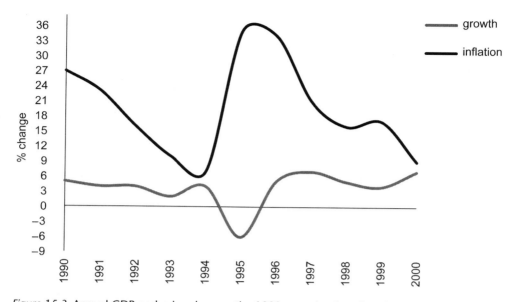

Figure 15.3 Annual GDP and price changes the 1990s: another lost decade?
Source: Data elaborated by the author from the World Bank, *World Economic Indicators* http://data.worldbank.org/country/mexico, accessed Feb. 13, 2013.

had been gradual economic improvement, relative social peace and political stability, the last in the four successive end-of-presidency crises (1976, 1982, 1987–88, 1994–95) was the straw that broke the camel's back. The long period of strong, centralized authority and vertical command-and-control exercise of power had come to an end. To garner broad support for renewed austerity policies imposed by the IFIs, Zedillo offered a political reform in 1996 that severed the control of elections from the minister of the interior, traditionally a sturdy *priísta*. The effects of this move were not long in coming as voters punished the PRI in the mid-term elections of 1997—the party lost the simple majority in the lower chamber—and later voted against the 71-year continuation of its rule by giving the presidential electoral victory to Vicente Fox (2000–06) of the PAN.

The PAN governments: macroeconomic orthodoxy and growth underperformance, 2000–12

The PAN inherited monetary and fiscal policies with a strong non-expansionary bias. On the monetary side, during the Zedillo years the Banco de México (central bank) adopted a policy of inflation targeting (3%+ or −0.5% annual price change), which helped to bring down the price increase spiral created by the 1994–95 macro-devaluation, but at the cost of keeping credit scarce and expensive, which left without financing possibilities a majority of small and medium-sized enterprises (SMEs) as well as most households. On the fiscal side, the IMF-mandated austerity after that crisis slashed spending once again. In addition, the Fox government pushed for the adoption of a fiscal rule in 2006 which established a zero target for the public sector balance, given five-year projections that, among other factors, take into account fluctuations of the international price for oil, a key contributor to the annual federal budget (see below, on energy and the fiscal conundrum). Still, according to fiscal policy experts the Mexican fiscal rule has kept government spending in a pro-cyclical direction, which has led to limited savings that in turn weakened the government's capacity to respond counter-cyclically during the 2008–09 global financial meltdown.[6]

Mexico's macroeconomic performance in the 2000s was mixed but on the whole perceived by international and domestic observers as mediocre. The average annual growth rate was 2.17%, significantly lower than other large, emerging markets like the BRICs and, crucially, very sluggish regarding the creation of formal employment. Better news came from the inflation figures, which were kept in single-digit numbers and under 7% every year-on-year. The end results (see Figure 15.4) might have been disappointing, but at least this was the first decade in which growth rates outpaced inflation rates for several years; macroeconomic fundamentals remained solid; and the country's production structure and links, particularly with the USA, started bearing fruit in the form of high, sustained growth of manufacturing exports that were not limited to low value-added, cheap goods, as between the 1960s and 1990s, but included growing proportions of sophisticated high value-added goods, given increased local sourcing in the auto and auto parts industry, electronics and microprocessors, and aeronautics.

Aside from the orthodox macroeconomic management inheritance, the PAN governments also inherited a targeted social policy inaugurated under Zedillo, known originally as *Progresa* and renamed *Oportunidades*. This so-called conditional cash transfer (CCT) programme became a blueprint for the adoption of similar programmes around the world as multilateral financial institutions identified such social policy as a new paradigm to further poverty reduction and development.[7] While successful at helping to cut the percentage of the population living below the national poverty line from around 69% in 1996 to 43% in 2006, the 2008–09 global financial crisis led to an increase above 50% by 2010 and, moreover, close to two-thirds of the country's rural population remained below the national poverty line (see Figure 15.5).

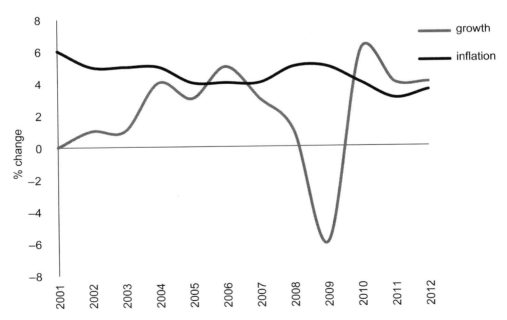

Figure 15.4 Annual GDP and price changes low growth, a big negative shock, and law inflation in the 2000s

Source: data elaborated by the author from the World Bank, *World Economic Indicators*, http://data.worldbank.org/country/mexico, accessed 13, 2013

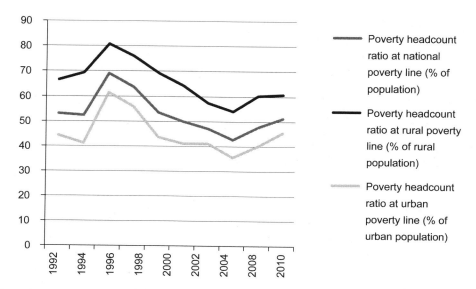

Figure 15.5 Poverty headcount ratio in Mexico, 1992–2010
Source: data elaborated by the author from the World Bank, *World Economic Indicators*, http://data.worldbank.org/country/mexico, accessed 14 January 2013.

Central political authority and the exercise of power by the executive continued to weaken during the PAN years in government, in spite of the attempt by President Felipe Calderón (2006–12) to reverse it. Economically, his government continued with the inherited orthodoxy but suffered several adverse shocks, some exogenous and others self-inflicted. It had to deal with the 2008–09 global financial crisis, which given its epicentre in the USA and Mexico's deep economic integration and dependence on this country meant a very significant decline. The rate at which growth declined in 2009 was even higher than after Mexico's own currency and banking crisis in 1994–95. The 2009 decline was compounded by the outbreak of the H1N1 flu pandemic, which devastated the country's tourism industry, a significant contributor to GDP (8%–10%).

Moreover, and more controversially, Calderón launched a 'war on drugs' shortly after coming into office in December 2006. The large-scale operations that ensued (more than 50,000 military and police on the ground), intended to rein in drug cartel violence that had increased significantly since 2003–04, produced the opposite effect as leadership decapitation of some organized criminal groups led to splintering, fragmentation and proliferation of gruesome, indiscriminate violence in many cities and significant swathes of the country's territory. By the time Calderón stepped down towards the end of 2012, more than 60,000 individuals had been killed and thousands disappeared as a consequence of the 'war'. Although impossible to quantify, the economic costs of insecurity and violence (see below), Mexico's international as well as its self-image suffered significant reputational damage. So much so that the US Joint Forces Command grossly overestimated the impacts of the conflict and declared Mexico a potential 'failed state' in a 2009 report,[8] which US government officials later were forced to downplay.

Return of the PRI: opportunities, challenges and limitations ahead

After two successive PAN governments, and given a generalized sense of fear and concern around the country, the Mexican population returned the PRI to power in the 2012 elections.

Enrique Peña Nieto (2012–18), a representative of a younger generation of *priístas*, took the helm of a $1.2 trillion economy, close to 120 million inhabitants, low growth/low inflation, the continuation of whole-scale organized criminal violence, and a wave of intense citizen expectations about the need and possibility to turn things around—a tall order.

Still, perceptions about Mexico's potential in the global economy started changing for the better even before the 2012 PRI presidential victory. Around the end of 2010 and early 2011 official publications (IMF, World Bank, Organisation for Economic Co-operation and Development—OECD) and financial/economics commentary in high-circulation outlets like *The Economist* and the *Financial Times* noted the strong recuperation Mexico's economy experienced after the 2008–09 global fallout, manufacturing exports' dynamism, a fall in Mexicans northbound in search of work in the USA, and the continued foreign investment in the country in spite of the insecurity and violence on the ground. The finance media started talking about Mexico as a potential 'Aztec tiger'.

Mexico started being compared favourably with Brazil—a source of great pride, given that the latter country monopolized the limelight in the 2000s. Loss of market share given an explosive growth in Chinese exports to the USA since the former joined the World Trade Organization (WTO) in 2001 started reversing, particularly in sophisticated, bulkier, high value-added goods. A 20-year opportunity to raise growth rates was identified, given a so-called 'demographic bonus' whereby the country's dependency ratio[9] will be lower until the 2030s. Praise continued to be bestowed by IFIs and the USA on the solid fundamentals that more than a decade of orthodox macroeconomic policy allowed Mexico to gain credibility and stature in the highly competitive world of foreign investment. Finally, social policy, spearheaded by *Oportunidades*, was extolled as a blueprint to combat poverty and create lower levels of socio-economic exclusion and wasted opportunity.

These positive developments co-exist with major challenges, from putting a floor on insecurity and violence, revamping the criminal justice system and counting with professional, non-corrupt law enforcement services to large-scale infrastructure investing, particularly in the energy, transport, industrial and construction sectors, as well as significant redistribution of resources and opportunities to close high levels of inequality and improved but still high and persistent poverty. Injecting competition into Mexico's highly concentrated economic sectors, both in the private and public spheres, as well as reconstructing the state's capacity to exercise its authority effectively across the country's territory are essential if the so-called 'Aztec tiger' appellation is to be realized. The rest of this chapter examines the main opportunities, challenges and limitations that Mexico's emerging economy will confront in the foreseeable future, given the mix of factors identified above.

Energy and fiscal conundrum

Mexico has been a top-10 global crude oil producer since the early 1980s. Until now, the constitution (Article 27) prohibits private participation in the exploration and production of oil, leaving concentrated risk of these activities on the shoulders of the state-owned oil monopoly firm Petróleos Mexicanos (PEMEX). Nationalized in 1938, the industry has remained a source of nationalist pride and self-determination among the country's population. However, decades of under-investment, corruption and very generous entitlements for the firm's 140,000 employees (PEMEX has very low productivity levels compared not only to private but also most other state-owned energy companies in the world) have ended up endangering Mexico's energy security. PEMEX reached peak production of close to 3.5 million barrels per day in 2004, and since then has experienced a significant fall in production (around 2.5 million barrels per day in 2011 and 2012), which if not reversed could lead to the country becoming a net crude importer in the 2020s. Allowing this to happen would be sheer madness because the country sits 'on estimated 115 billion barrels of oil equivalent, comparable to Kuwait'.[10]

The politicization of PEMEX highlighted above has been compounded by Mexico's federal government use of the company's earnings for budgetary purposes. Between 25% and 40% of annual budgets are made up of PEMEX proceeds, starving the firm of investment to keep high reserves to production (R/P) ratios. The situation is so absurd that PEMEX pays higher taxes than its gross annual earnings, forcing the company to borrow in international capital markets to pay its fiscal obligation and keep current operations. Mexico has weak fiscal capacity and is one of the medium-income countries with the lowest take of revenue to GDP (15% to 19% in contrast to the average for OECD countries of around 35%). This situation, identified by public finance experts as 'fiscal precariousness', has been a function, among others, of high dollar liquidity given oil exports.[11] The last major fiscal overhaul in Mexico took place in 1977–78, when value-added tax (VAT) was introduced. The fiscal system is characterized by too many special regimes that have granted tax exemption to a majority of large firms operating in most sectors. Property taxation, the backbone of local revenue capacity in many advanced and developing countries, is weak given precarious revenue-raising capacity by Mexican municipal and state governments. Income taxes, while at competitive rates, could be more progressive. Charging VAT on food and medicines, the proceeds of which could be redistributed to low-income families via social programmes like *Oportunidades*, would create a paper trail that would allow the government to know who generates what, where and when, which would increase its revenue-generating capacity.

A mild reform of PEMEX in 2008 has liberated some resources ($4 billion–$5 billion annually) for exploration and production, and significant finds were made in the deep waters of the Gulf of Mexico in 2012. Major international oil companies invest around $15 billion in exploration annually so PEMEX remains at a great disadvantage. Moreover, the company has been left far behind in technological development, and therefore requires foreign expertise if it is to bring online production of newly found reserves in the next decade.

The Peña Nieto government promised to tackle fiscal and energy problems in tandem, which makes sense given their deep inter-dependence. While the government has said time and again that it will not reform article 27 of the constitution to allow the privatization of PEMEX, it could still attract significant interest from leading private as well as state-owned companies with the cash and know-how that are needed to turn current circumstances around. Neither a wholesale move towards 'risk contracts' (seen as the legal instrument of privatized hydrocarbon exploration or production), nor the status quo of 'service contracts' (seen as the legal instrument of state control and private participation in revenue only via fees) have to be the outcome of an effective energy reform. A constitutional reform that allowed 'production-sharing contracts' would be a halfway move that would allow private investors to book newly found reserves as part of their assets while the state would retain control of projects, would also be able to book reserves, and would be able to experiment with different types of public-private partnerships to maximize the effectiveness and security of oil exploitation.

The financial system and credit scarcity

Chronic fiscal precariousness has resulted in low levels of public investment. The investment component of GDP and its growth has remained under-par because private investment has also been low. The key to low investment lies in the financial system, whose concentration in the private sector and weakness in the public has tied down productive activity because of credit scarcity. Mexico has one of the lowest ratios of credit to the private sector as a proportion of

GDP (see Figure 15.6). Very high ratios between 2007 and 2011 were not a panacea, as the cases of countries that went into financial overdrive, like Ireland, Spain, the USA and Great Britain, at 200% or more show in the figure. Still, high-growth emerging economies like India, Brazil, Chile and South Korea found themselves in the 50% to 100% range, whereas Mexico was significantly lower in the mid-20% range.

The problem with Mexico's private banking sector is its oligopolistic structure. After the 1994–95 financial collapse, the government sold a great majority of national private banks' shares to foreign banks. As a result, close to 90% of banks' equity is owned by large global banks. Two firms (BBVA-Bancomer and Citibank-Banamex) account for close to 50% of deposit accounts. The four largest banks account for 85%–90% of credit and debit card transactions (the two above plus Santander and HSBC). The only large bank owned by a majority of Mexican shareholders is Banorte. Most banking profits come from high fees that the main players charge for their services rather than the extension of credit for productive activity and the interest that should result from such lending. For example, fees for standard services like ATM use have been found to be 10 times higher in Mexico than in the foreign banks' home countries.[12]

The banking oligopoly operates like a classic rent-seeker rather than as an allocator of capital to productive investment opportunities. SMEs are particularly affected because credit is scarce and expensive. Mexico's largest firms, with access to foreign capital markets at competitive interest rates, have been spared the pain of inadequate financing, thus contributing to their not joining what could be a powerful coalition of borrowers, from industry titans to SMEs, as well as households, to force policy changes that inject competition and lending to the economy.

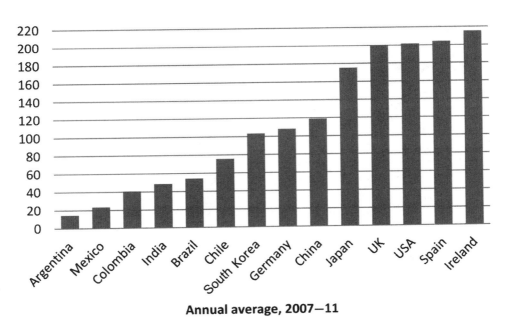

Figure 15.6 Domestic credit to private sector as % GDP at the tail end of credit expansion to unleash productive activity
Source: Data elaborated by the author from the World Bank, *World Economic Indicators*, http://data.worldbank.org/indicators/FS.AST.PRVT.GD.7S, accessed 14 November 2012

Francisco E. González

In turn, state-owned development banks played a central role in financing large-scale as well as medium-sized and small businesses in Mexico between the 1940s and the external debt crisis of 1982. Banks like Nacional Financiera (NAFINSA), Banrural, Banobras and Bancomext were vital to keep open access for credit. The so-called 'lost decade' (1980s) and later on the 1994–95 financial crisis and its consequences ('the tequila effect') led to a dramatic retrenchment of state-led credit extension. In great contrast to Brazil, where the state-owned Banco Nacional do Desenvolvimento Econômico e Social (BNDES) is a successful, leading provider of credit and whose portfolio is larger than all credit provided by the World Bank and the IDB in Latin America, Mexico's state development banks almost stopped making a contribution to productive activity.

More recently, since the 2008–09 global financial collapse, there has been a slight revival of state development banks' financing, with around $67 billion disbursed as part of the counter-cyclical effort to turn around declining economic activity given the international bust.[13] An adequate financing landscape that permits Mexico's economy to grow at 5% to 7% in a sustained way has as a necessary though insufficient condition a careful but continued expansion of state bank development credit, but also and more fundamentally, injection of competition through policy changes that enact significant carrots and sticks for the oligopolistic foreign-dominated private banks in order that they act as channels of productive investment rather than lazy, fat rentiers.

The other most visible concentrated sectors: telecommunications and the media

The rise of other highly visible and influential monopoly sectors in Mexico's economy was also a consequence of the privatization process under President Carlos Salinas. In the case of telecommunications, an explicit aim of the privatization was to keep Teléfonos de México (Telmex) as a monopoly rather than breaking it up to generate competition and low profits for suppliers. Carlos Slim's investment group Carso, with the help of loans from NAFINSA, won the bid and since then has dominated the system (around 80% of landlines and 70% of cellular telephony and broadband in 2012). The telecoms monopoly, now named América Móvil, helped to catapult a businessman from a middle-income country where around half the population lives below the poverty line, to become the richest man in the world for several years now, according to *Forbes'* annual rich list. The OECD has estimated the welfare loss (loss of consumer surplus from overcharging and low level of coverage) between 2005 and 2009 at $129.2 billion or 1.8% of GDP per year.[14]

In the mass media sector, the Salinas reforms brought about one of the dominant actors in television with the privatization of the state's channel and the creation of TV Azteca, owned by Ricardo Salinas Pliego (around 25% of the market in free channel television). The heavyweight in this sector, however, was not a recent creation but rather a third-generation family-dominated business, Televisa (around 70% of the market), headed by Emilio Azcárraga Jean. This duopoly controls 95% of the free-to-air TV market. Their deep penetration and omni-presence throughout the Mexican territory have given them incredible power to help set the public agenda, shape the reputations of public personalities (from politicians and businessmen to artists and sports stars), and filter news coverage and content.

Laws and regulation exist to manage in theory these sectors. However, federal regulators until now have remained relatively toothless and in spite of many legal actions against their dominance, they have remained relatively untouched. The federal government passed new anti-competition laws in 2011 to try to raise the costs for the continuation of single or two-player dominance in key sectors of the economy, but it is too early to assess how effective such efforts will be. To date, rather than an effective challenge being mounted by the state, the challenge to these dominant players has come from one another. Amounting to a clash of titans, Slim's, Azcárraga's and Salinas Pliego's empires have been challenged by their attempt to move into each other's turf.[15] Azcárraga joined Salinas Pliego in the cellular telephony business by buying into the latter-controlled Iusacell, to challenge the dominance of Slim's Telcel. In turn, Slim has been trying to get into the television business. His América Móvil is a dominant player throughout Latin America in so-called 'triple-play services' (i.e. calls, internet and television), but in Mexico he remains barred from the latter.[16]

Now the clash of the titans is being stirred by the Peña Nieto government. With apparent support from the main opposition parties, PAN and PRD, the administration wants to 'strengthen government regulators, auction two new national television networks, and lift restrictions on foreign investment for fixed-line telephony, among other steps'.[17] While still uncertain about the outcome of such reform attempts, and even if they are successful, the size, penetration and resources of dominant players will give them significant advantages to keep their large sector share; however, what for many years appeared to be a monolithic landscape is being disturbed.

The Chinese challenge: reversal of an onslaught?

Not content with a precarious fiscal-energy situation as well as a concentrated, fee-driven, low-lending banking sector, a monopoly in telecommunications, and a duopoly in visual media, Mexico faced a formidable external challenge in the 2000s. After China became a member of the WTO in 2001, it started eating away at Mexico's market share of the US consumer market. By 2003 China had replaced Mexico as the second largest source of US imports, and by 2006 it displaced it as the second largest US commercial partner after Canada.[18] Substantially lower Chinese average hourly wages ($0.62 compared to $5.06 in Mexico in 2003) led to an exodus of final assembly (*maquiladora*) plants, the Mexican production of which contracted by 30% between 2000 and 2012.[19] Analysts highlighted that Mexico as well as Central American and Caribbean countries' specialization in assembling US inputs for re-exporting to the USA as finished goods in areas such as apparel, textiles and electronics, are vulnerable because of China's 'combination of endowments, scale, fast productivity growth, and an omnipresent state'.[20]

What many in Mexico perceived as a Chinese onslaught has been mitigated by a variety of factors, and estimates by domestic and international private businesses as well as governments suggest a reversal of the trend. On the one hand, China's own economic growth success has eroded some of the earlier comparative advantages it enjoyed. Most notably this has occurred in the wage compensation gap. Flexitronics, a Singapore-based electronics maker with 100,000 workers in China and 40,000 workers in Mexico, reports that the average hourly wage has climbed to $2.50 per hour in the former, while it is $3.50 including benefits in the latter, and expectations are that wages in China will top Mexican wages in the future.[21] The reduction in the wage gap is consistent with what other businesses report. HSBC says Mexico's wages were almost 400% higher than Chinese wages a decade ago, but that difference has eroded to only 29%. This dramatic change is partly explained by the demographic crunch in the working-age population that China is suffering, whereas more than half of the Mexican population is under the age of 29, and therefore the country can take advantage of a demographic bonus.[22]

Another important change that has helped to water down Chinese comparative advantages is distance. With the trebling of oil prices since the shocks of the early 2000s, fuel and other associated transportation costs have grown significantly, making Mexico's proximity to the USA a cost-effective choice that has translated into 'near-shoring' or 're-shoring' of production that had relocated to Asia in the 2000s. In particular, heavier, bulkier goods can be produced in

Francisco E. González

Mexico and shipped to the final market in the USA, but also increasingly to other Latin American countries, at a fraction of the cost, once transportation is factored in, than in China. A very visible example of this trend has been the rise of an aerospace industry that was close to non-existent one and half decades ago. Boeing of the USA and Bombardier of Canada have built plants in Mexico to take advantage both of proximity and similar time zones to remain competitive. The end result has been an industry with around $17 billion in investment and growing.[23] Also, products that depend on the customization of orders, where short-term fashion and fast inventory turnover are dominant, or where short supply chains help production by enabling innovation, correction and improvement on the go, are especially suited for near-shoring. It takes between 20 days and two months for goods to be shipped from China to the USA, while it takes two days to one week from Mexico.[24]

Another advantage that can be a double-edged sword but seems to be working in Mexico's favour is its trade openness, which I analyse in the next section.

A trading powerhouse: strengths and weaknesses

Until the mid-1980s Mexico's official position had remained a staunch defence of national sovereignty and self-determination. Economically, this had meant a committed pursuit of ISI and its concomitant policies—among them, trade protection. It was not until the external debt crisis of the 1980s touched bottom in 1985–86 that Mexican authorities were forced to embrace IFI's prescribed liberalization reforms and Mexico joined the GATT. The conventional wisdom is that Mexico became an open economy as a consequence of the signing of NAFTA, which started operating in 1994. By the time NAFTA started being implemented Mexico had already had eight years of domestic exposure to foreign goods markets. The result has been mixed but there is no question that Mexico in the 2010s is a crossroads of global trade.

With 12 free trade treaties that grant it preferential access to 44 countries' markets and more manufactured exports than the rest of Latin American countries combined by 2012, the 1980s debt crisis forced Mexico's economic path away from raw commodities exports, particularly oil, and forced it to diversify. Without minimizing the problem of oil due first and foremost to public finance dependence on the sale of crude for the annual federal budget, the country avoided the fate of petro-states such as Venezuela and Ecuador. Oil accounted for around 80% of Mexico's exports in the early 1980s, but today it represents less than one-quarter. By 2010 the country's trade openness coefficient at 58.6% was higher than China's at 47.9%, and a world away from Brazil's at 18.5%.[25]

Although attractive as a destination where many intermediate goods can be shipped from many parts of the world free of charge so that they can be put together and then be taken to the USA as a final consumer destination market, a high trade openness coefficient is a double-edged sword. If Mexican exports have been growing at high rates at least since the signing of NAFTA, why has GDP growth not followed? Some economists have identified Mexico's low foreign trade multiplier as a key that explains this conundrum. Betting on being an assembly platform that re-exports finished goods has meant that the country's marginal propensity to import is much higher than that of less open economies like Brazil (0.329 vs 0.055). This means that for each dollar Mexico exports it gains $1.7, whereas for each dollar Brazil exports it gains $2.3.[26] In short, trade openness helped Mexico to diversify away from oil exports and into manufactures. It has made it an attractive country for foreign direct investment (FDI) looking for a cheap, reliable entry into the great US consumer market. As a consequence, the country has become 'the world's biggest exporter of flat-screen televisions, BlackBerrys and fridge-freezers, and is climbing up the rankings in cars, aerospace, and more'.[27] However, this model has also meant that Mexico relies on too many imports of expensive-input to re-export finished goods, and this continues to keep overall GDP growth low and the current account under pressure.

Human capital: a significant bottleneck, but improvements

One of the main unrealized gains given Mexico's high openness coefficient has come from its relative scarcity of skilled labour. Relative abundance in this factor of production could contribute to raise the local-content inputs of finished export goods, which in turn would lower the country's high marginal propensity to import that the current export structure requires. The human capital bottleneck has at its core an inefficient, low-quality education system. According to the World Economic Forum's *Global Competitiveness Report 2010*, Mexico was near the bottom in measures of quality of education (120th out of 139 countries). In spite of near universal primary school attendance, there are high rates of year repetition and, crucially, a high dropout rate at the high school level with half of students enrolled per year failing to graduate.[28]

Many factors have been highlighted as contributing to this structural problem. In spite of public spending in education at comparable levels with average OECD countries—Mexico is a member and usually an outlier regarding quality of public spending—outcomes in international standardized tests for literacy and basic maths and reasoning like the Programme for International Student Assessment (PISA) show very poor outcomes. Of the factors highlighted, the most important is probably the long-term capture of the education system by the Sindicato Nacional de Trabajadores de la Educación (SNTE) and its lifer leader Elba Esther Gordillo. The official national trade union has had veto power over contracts, hiring, incentives, sanctions and teachers' placement (i.e. teaching positions can be bought or sold or passed on to relatives). The current PRI government under President Peña Nieto has dealt a blow to this repugnant state of affairs by signing after Congress the most sweeping reform in this sector for decades. For starters, the government ordered the arrest and jailing of Gordillo on a variety of charges, from the embezzlement of hundreds of millions of dollars to organized crime. In turn, the government will carry out the first census of the country's education system. The reform will create uniform standards for the teaching profession, taking away control from the union to hire and fire or to pay for the thousands of 'phantom' teachers who receive an official wage slip twice a month without showing up at schools, let alone teaching.[29] Even though significant improvements can be expected, there is no silver bullet that can turn around such a deeply ingrained low-productivity, patronage-driven, highly corrupt system. This was, none the less, a key blow to one of the most pernicious monopolies plaguing Mexico's emerging economy.

Tertiary education enrolment, although still behind the Latin American average, improved from 18% to 30% between 1999 and 2008.[30] Of particular importance has been the growth in numbers of manufacturing-related graduates in areas such as engineers, rising from 0.4 in 1,000 individuals in 1999 to 0.8 in 2012, whereas the USA's numbers have been more or less flat in the same period at around 0.6. Such skilled labour availability is behind firms' growing allocation of high value-added operations such as parts design of cars, computers and mobile phones to their Mexican subsidiaries.[31]

Human capital improvement has also been a function of better public health. Up until the early 2000s, only individuals in formal employment and their immediate family were covered by public health insurance. This system left out the 50%+ of the working population who labour in the informal sector, who were left to fend for themselves, a minority being able to afford private health insurance and the majority without any coverage. The introduction of the *Seguro Popular* in 2004 has meant that in spite of significant variation in quality of health care provided, Mexico has moved decidedly in the direction of universal coverage.[32] A key achievement from the perspective of human capital and its contribution to economic growth is that universal coverage has reduced the incidence of 'catastrophic health expenditure and impoverishing health expenditure', whereby upwardly mobile poor or lower middle-class families lose their assets to pay for very expensive treatment for one or more of their kin.[33]

A final factor that bodes well for human capital and its contribution to economic growth is the demographic bonus from which Mexico can gain, given a falling dependency ratio until the 2030s (see Figure 15.7). To put this in context, whereas back in 1980 there were slightly more than seven dependents for every 10 workers, that proportion had dropped to around five dependents, and projections suggest it will continue to drop to around 4.5 in 2020–30, after which time the number of dependents will start to grow as a proportion but at much lower rates than those experienced by southern European countries, Japan, China, and even the USA, for example. A demographic bonus does not translate automatically into higher growth rates. Taking advantage of this trend requires significant public and private investment into productivity-growth activity, of which human capital investment remains the best positioned to yield medium- and long-term benefits.

The mother of all ills: absence of the rule of law, insecurity and violence

At root, Mexico's mismatched monopolies problem is a function of the absence of the rule of law. Economic, political and social activity are prey to the arbitrariness of power, money and influence rather than equality of individuals before the law irrespective of such attributes. In this, Mexico is part of a large herd rather than an exception. The concert of nation-states has many more members where the rule of law is seriously defective than those where it is quite effective.

In modern Mexico, a particularly defective criminal justice system developed in tandem with the hegemony of the PRI. Rather than serving as a deterrent of anti-social and criminal

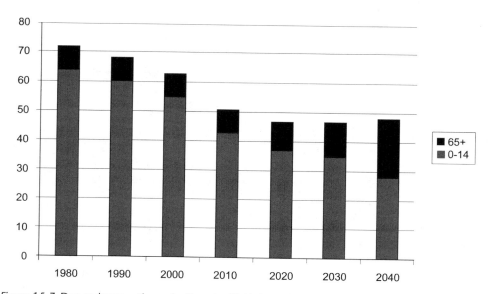

Figure 15.7 Dependency ratio projections to 2040 (population 14 and under, 65 and over)
Source: Elaborated by author with data from Mexico's Consejo Nacional de la Población, accessed 26 February 2012, http://www.conapo.gob.mx/es/CONAPO/Proyecciones

Mexico

behaviour, a function that the hegemonic party fulfilled, the criminal justice system was headed by attorneys-general and their sprawling subordinate networks, whose function was:

> more one of social containment, focusing on threats from subversive groups, than the control of crime ... the Supreme Court and the circuit courts steered clear of any kind of control of arbitrary police work and of the technical quality of criminal investigations ... confession, the defendant's first statement delivered in the office of the public prosecutor, was the declaration with the most probative value, because of its spontaneity ... The criminal investigation, if it can be called that, was primarily based on coercion, intimidation and physical abuse of a detainee by the judicial police and the public prosecutor, with the purpose of extracting confessions.[34]

This characterization remains by and large standard practice in Mexico in spite of a significant criminal justice system reform passed by President Calderón's government in 2008. The constitutional reform aims to transform the criminal justice system from a Roman law, written one into an adversarial one, similar to the Anglo-American tradition, based on public trial by peers rather than behind-closed-doors pen pushing. The system is slowly being implemented but great variation exists because each of the country's 32 states has leeway in terms of accepting the system and then implementing in a standardized way. As long as justice in Mexico is the purview of power, money and influence, the physical integrity, validity of contracts, security of property and the individual right to enjoy freedom from arbitrary coercion remain seriously threatened, as they are throughout the territory on a daily basis.

The so-called war on drugs or war against organized crime did not help either. Unleashing more than 50,000 state agents—military and police—to combat drugs traffickers at the end of 2006 created a situation whereby countless innocent civilians ended up in the crossfire. Organized criminals did not respect any law except that of survival of the cruellest, while state authorities did not have a framework of rule of law that kept them from carrying out myriad human rights abuses in the name of the war against drugs.

The narcotics trade is an integral part of the Mexican economy which, according to some estimates, directly employs 450,000 individuals while the livelihoods of some 3.2 million depend on this trade (and this excludes the people and money used to counter it).[35] In turn, a cost-benefit analysis of the net impact of insecurity and violence on economic activity in Mexico concludes that total annual income from the drugs trade fluctuates between $3 billion and $8 billion, compared with $15.5 billion spent on security. Insecurity creates direct and indirect costs for individuals, firms and governments, and 'crime and homicide rates are correlated with income inequality, unemployment, and lack of progress in social development'.[36]

The absence of the rule of law is beyond any doubt the most important problem that Mexico confronts. Sadly, it is not a problem that can be decreed away or solved through silver bullet proposals. The confluence of the absence of the rule of law and the all-out armed response to the narcotics trade created a poisonous mix that has killed thousands, has tarnished Mexico's reputation, and increased the costs of doing business in the country. International bureaucracies and the US government, not only the Mexican authorities, have been responsible for fanning the flames of barbaric violence leading growing numbers of Mexicans to believe that 'their people get killed whereas the United States, with its soft gun laws, arms the traffickers, launders their money and consumes their product'.[37]

The overlap of economic concentration and political fragmentation, undergirded by an absence of the rule of law and domestic and international forces that have strengthened the arbitrariness and lawlessness on the ground through an all-out use of coercion in the recent past, is the most fundamental challenge that Mexico's present and future authorities face. This challenge does not only stand in the way of the country being able to realize its potential as a high-growth, prosperous emerging economy, but also even more fundamentally as a nation-state in which political stability, social peace and a majority shared sense of gradual advancement prevails. Without the latter attributes, the former will remain unstable and elusive, and Mexico's emerging economy will continue to underperform, disappoint, and the dice will be loaded in favour of downside risks and headwinds.

Notes

1 The author is grateful to Julia Fox and Shanna Edberg for their superb research assistance. This analysis would not have been possible without their motivation, dedication and commitment.

2 Aside from the BRIC economies, South Korea and Mexico were identified in 2009 as the six 'trillion-dollar club' emerging economies. See Peterson Institute for International Economics, 'The Trillion Dollar Club: Spring 2009', www.iie.com/events/event_detail.cfm?EventID=105.

3 Robert S. Chase, Emily B. Hill and Paul Kennedy (eds), *The Pivotal States: A New Framework for U.S. Policy in the Developing World*, W.W. Norton, New York, 1999.

4 Eric Martin, 'Goldman Sachs's MIST Topping BRICs as Smaller Markets Outperform', *Bloomberg News*, 7 August 2012, www.bloomberg.com/news/2012-08-07/goldman-sachs-s-mist-topping-brics-as-smaller-markets-outperform.html.

5 All figures, unless otherwise referenced, can be found in Francisco E. González, *Dual Transitions from Authoritarian Rule: Institutionalized Regimes in Chile and Mexico*, Johns Hopkins University Press, Baltimore, MD, 2008, Chapters 2, 4 and 6.

6 Juan Carlos Berganza, 'Fiscal Rules in Latin America: A Survey', Banco de España, Documentos Ocasionales n. 1208, 2012, 26–27, www.bde.es/f/webbde/SES/Secciones/Publicaciones/PublicacionesSeriadas/DocumentosOcasionales/12/Fich/do1208e.pdf.

7 See Ariel Fiszbein and Norbert Schady et al., *Cash Transfers: Present and Future Poverty*, World Bank, Washington, DC, 2009, siteresources.worldbank.org/INTCCT/Resources/5757608-1234228266004/PRR-CCT_web_noembargo.pdf.

8 Bernd Debusmann, 'Among Top U.S. Fears: A Failed State Mexican State', *The New York Times*, 9 January 2009, www.nytimes.com/2009/01/09/world/americas/09iht-letter.1.19217792.html?_r=0.

9 The concept is defined as the proportion of non-working (infants, the young in schooling, and the older non-working) to working inhabitants in a given country.

10 John Paul Rathbone, 'Oil Reform Poised to Spark Rush for Mexico', *Financial Times*, 28 February 2012, www.ft.com/intl/cms/s/0/3ee499c4-80d8-11e2-9c5b-00144feabdc0.html?ftcamp=published_links%2Frss%2Fglobal-economy%2Ffeed%2F%2Fproduct#axzz2MCoqjQNJ.

11 Jesús Reyes Heroles, 'Mexico's Fiscal and Energy Conundrum', speech delivered at the Johns Hopkins University School of Advanced International Studies (SAIS), Washington, DC, 5 April 2012.

12 Heiner Schulz, 'Foreign Banks in Mexico: New Conquistadors or Agents of Change?' Wharton Financial Institutions Center Working Paper #06-11, 10 January 2007.

13 Greg Brosnan, 'Mexico Development Banks Leapfrog Private Banks', *Emerging Markets*, 22 March 2010, www.emergingmarkets.org/Article/2449744/Mexico-development-lenders-leapfrog-private-banks.html.

14 Organisation for Economic Co-operation and Development, *OECD Review of Telecommunication Policy and Regulation in Mexico*, OECD Publishing, 2012, 9, www.oecd.org/fr/mexique/oecdreviewoftelecommunicationpolicyandregulationinmexico.htm.

15 Adam Thomson, 'Televisa Key to Changing Mexican Ecosystem', *Financial Times*, 13 February 2012, 17.

16 John Paul Rathbone and Adam Thomson, 'Slim Sticks to his Principles Despite Recent Setbacks', *Financial Times*, 26 February 2013, 17.

17 David Luhnow and Juan Montes, 'Mexico Tackles Powerful Telecoms Interests', *Wall Street Journal*, 28 February 2013, online.wsj.com/article/SB10001424127887323978104578332520592448046.html.

18 Edgardo Arturo Ayala and Mario Villarreal, 'The Dragon Menace: Is China Displacing Mexico's Trade with the United States?' *Análisis Económico* 24(55), 2009: 327–46, 328.

19 Christopher E. Wilson, 'Working Together: Economic Ties between the United States and Mexico', Woodrow Wilson International Center for Scholars Mexico Institute, Washington, DC, November 2011, 35.

20 Mauricio Mesquita Moreira, 'Fear of China: Is There a Future for Manufacturing in Latin America?' *World Development* 35(3), 2007: 355–76, 372.

21 David Luhnow and Bob Davis, 'For Mexico, an Edge on China', *Wall Street Journal*, 16 September 2012, online.wsj.com/article/SB10000872396390444318104577587191288101170.html.

22 Adam Thomson, 'Mexico: China's Unlikely Challenger', *Financial Times*, 19 September 2012, www.ft.com/cms/s/0/9f789abe-023a-11e2-b41f-00144feabdc0.html#axzz2Ll5dVjjI.

23 Ibid.

24 Ibid.

25 Ibid.

26 Jaime Serra Puche, 'Openness and Growth in Mexico', Keynote Address, El Colegio de México and Center for Inter-American Policy and Research, Tulane University, 'Mexico at the Crossroads: Learning from History, Facing the Future', conference, 18 November 2011, cipr.tulane.edu/articles/detail/904/Conference-Nov.17-18-2011-Mexico-at-the-Crossroads-Learning-from-History-Facing-the-Future.

27 *The Economist*, 'The Rise of Mexico', 24 November 2012, www.economist.com/news/leaders/21567081-america-needs-look-again-its-increasingly-important-neighbour-rise-mexico.

28 J. Puryear, L. Santibáñez and A. Solano, 'Education in Mexico. Emerging Markets' Forum', Inter-American Dialogue, Washington, DC, 2012, www.thedialogue.org/PublicationFiles/Educationin Mexico0322.pdf.

29 Eduardo Castillo, 'Mexican President Signs Education Reform', Associated Press, 26 February 2013, abcnews.go.com/International/wireStory/mexican-president-signs-education-reform-18592352.

30 Puryear *et al.*, 'Education in Mexico'.

31 Thomson, 'Mexico'.

32 Elisabeth Malkin, 'Mexico's Universal Health Care is Work in Progress', *New York Times*, 29 January 2011, www.nytimes.com/2011/01/30/world/americas/30mexico.html?pagewanted=all&_r=0.

33 F.M. Knaul *et al.*, 'The Quest for Universal Health Coverage: Achieving Social Protection for All in Mexico', *The Lancet*, 16 August 2012, www.thelancet.com/journals/lancet/article/PIIS0140-6736(12)61068-X/abstract.

34 Ana Laura Magaloni, 'Arbitrariness and Inefficiency in the Mexican Criminal Justice System', in Paul Kenney and Mónica Serrano (eds), *Mexico's Security Failure: Collapse into Criminal Violence*, Routledge, New York and London, 2012, 94–5.

35 Stephen D. Morris, 'Drugs, Violence and Life in Mexico', literature review in *Latin American Research Review* 47(2), 2012: 216–23.

36 Eleanor Sohnen, 'Paying for Crime: A Review of the Relationship between Insecurity and Development in Mexico and Central America', Migration Policy Institute and Woodrow Wilson Center for International Scholars, Washington, DC, December 2012, 17.

37 *The Economist*, 'Illegal Drugs: The Great Experiment', 23 February–1 March 2013, 14.

16

Middle-income trap of Malaysian economy

A political economy analysis[1]

Vijayakumari Kanapathy and Herizal Hazri

Introduction

Malaysia has been remarkably successful over the past few decades in achieving rapid growth and transformative development. State institutions are well developed and social indicators and quality of life have shown striking improvement. At roughly US$14,215 gross domestic product (GDP) purchasing power parity (PPP) per capita, and a nominal GDP per capita of US$8,100, Malaysia has transformed from a poor, colonial plantation economy into a modern, upper-middle-income country in the span of one generation. This represents one of the most extraordinary records of economic and human development in recent memory.

In spite of this impressive development, Malaysia's robust growth for more than three decades was interrupted following the 1997 Asian Financial Crisis. Through a series of tough measures taken by the then Prime Minister Mahathir Mohamed, Malaysia was one of the first countries in South-East Asia to recover from the crisis. However, its economic progress has substantially mellowed since, resulting in Malaysia straying away from its goal of becoming a fully developed country by 2020. Today, while many Malaysians have recovered from the trauma of the 1997 financial crisis and are ready to move on to the next phase of development, another problem seems to have surfaced. Less than a decade from 2020, it is argued that Malaysia is finding itself caught in the so-called 'middle-income trap' (MIT), where it has reached a relatively comfortable level of income, but cannot seem to take the next leap to developed nation status.

Malaysia's development has been helped and hindered by aggressive state-led strategies for economic and social restructuring. The New Economic Policy (NEP) was introduced in 1970, to eradicate poverty and restructure society to remove the identification of race or ethnicity with economic status and/or function. While the NEP was meant to benefit the poor irrespective of their racial background, it has unfortunately institutionalized an affirmative action-type system which favoured bumiputera-owned enterprises in public procurement and trade policy. While the overall wealth of the country grew and poverty declined during the 20 years of the NEP, Malaysia emerged in the 1990s with strained ethnic relations, and growing patronage and corruption. Race-based economics went hand in hand with race-based politics. Political parties and coalitions have evolved since independence along strong ethnic and racial lines. The very policies that put Malaysia on its path to success 50 years ago may be holding it back today.

Acknowledging the problem, the Malaysian government has put in place brave reform initiatives under its New Economic Model (NEM) in just four years of the premiership of Najib Razak. These initiatives, dubbed by many the most extensive government socio-economic strategy ever tabled in Malaysia, is testimony to Malaysia not having a shortage of ideas about development strategy. Despite relatively good results recorded to date, there is a sense of uneasiness among reform-minded Malaysians that Najib's plans are not sustainable and will not succeed unless the current political conditions in Malaysia change. It is widely argued that to find Malaysia's way out of the MIT must include economic, and more importantly, political reform strategies. In this context, this chapter takes a political economy approach in analysing the MIT of the Malaysian economy.

The chapter first reviews Malaysia's economy and identifies the features or symptoms that characterize Malaysia as an MIT economy, and critically examines the underlying socio-economic challenges that confront the economy. Following that, we explain how and why the fundamental socio-economic challenges are inextricably linked to the political economy dynamics of the country. A macro or country-level framework of analysis will be used to examine the political economy environment and circumstances that frustrate or facilitate policy reforms. The following section explores an improved socio-political framework to advance into the next stage of development.

Malaysia in the middle-income trap?

Macroeconomic challenges

Figure 16.1 illustrates Malaysia's relative growth performance vis-à-vis selected Asian economies that shared similar growth trends in the initial years but have taken on divergent growth trends. Japan, the Republic of Korea (South Korea), Singapore and Malaysia all registered somewhat similar GDP per capita trends in the 1970s, but these trends have assumed different paths. In

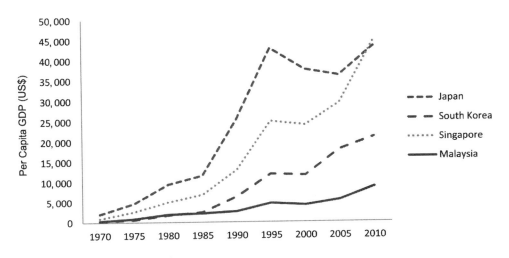

Figure 16.1 Relative growth performance
Source: United Nation Statistics Division

contrast to all of these economies which have gone on to become high-income economies, Malaysia risks falling into an MIT. The Malaysian economy grew briskly from 1970 onwards to attain upper-middle-income status by 1992, but since 1997 growth has remained relatively subdued and volatile. Malaysia's per capita GDP is now less than half of that of South Korea and about a quarter of that of Japan or Singapore.

The economy grew at an annual average of 5.1% from 2000 to 2009, or just half of that from 1987 to 1997 (10.4% in 1987–97). The growth path has also been relatively volatile, ranging from a recession (-1.7%) in 2000 to a high of 7.2% in 2010 (see Figure 16.2).

None the less, unemployment and inflation have been relatively low and stable. Low unemployment is due in large measure to the presence of contract migrant workers, who bear the brunt of unemployment during the slowdowns. Low-skilled foreign labour accounts for about 20%–25% of total employment in the country and they are the first to be fired in the event of a slowdown and retrenchment, giving rise to a stable employment rate in the country.[2] Excess capacity, increased liberalization of the economy, subsidies for essential goods and cheaper imports from low-cost producers such as China and India explain the relatively low inflation rates.

Corporate and financial restructuring and liberalization since 1998 have also contributed to growing reserves and a healthier financial scenario. Despite the macroeconomic stability Malaysia's lacklustre economic performance had raised serious concerns, especially with respect to declining private investment and its implications for sustainable growth.

An analysis of the sources of growth from the demand side indicates that the traditional drivers of growth have lost their momentum. The most significant change is the drastic fall in gross fixed capital formation or total investment. Total investment as a share of GDP declined steadily at about 3.4% per annum from 1997 to 2011, or by almost half from 43.0% in 1997 to about 22.0% in 2011 (see Figure 16.3). This is largely due to the sharp decline in private investment which fell sharply from around 74.0% of total investment in 1997 to about 34.0% in 2003, but

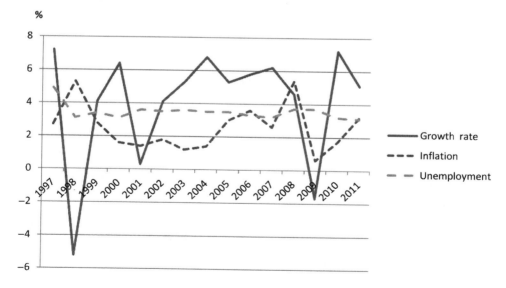

Figure 16.2 Key economic indicators
Source: Ministry of Finance, *Economic Report*, various issues

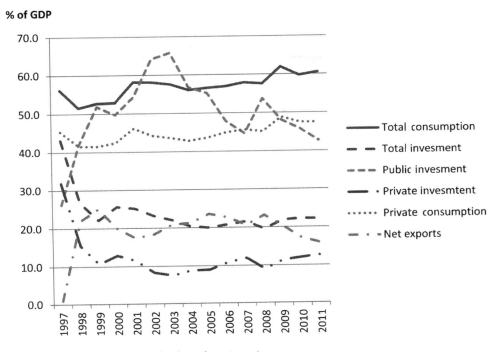

Figure 16.3 Ratio of public and private investment
Source: Ministry of Finance, *Economic Report*, various issues

recovered somewhat to around 57.0% in 2011 (see Figure 16.4). As a result, its contribution to growth declined sharply from about 32.0% in 1997 to about 13.0% in 2011.

The slack in private activity was offset by public expenditure, in particular public investment. Public investment grew at an annual average of 5.4% during this period, increasing its contribution to growth from only 26.0% in 1997 to a peak of about 66.0% in 2003 (see Figure 16.3). It has since declined to about 43.0% in 2011. This has raised an important policy issue as to whether public investment is crowding out private investment. In this respect, the dominant role of relatively large government-linked corporations (GLCs) and the government investment firm Khazanah Nasional Berhad, which are governed by both social and economic objectives are of particular concern. A recent study suggests that a large share of GLC firms in a particular industry has a deterrent effect on non-GLC firms' investment in that industry.[3]

Private consumption has remained more or less stable, varying between 42.0% and 48.0% during this period. This trend is reflective of stagnant or weak growth in wages in recent years.

Though net exports have remained positive since 1999, its contribution to growth has declined sharply from about 22.0% in 1998 to about 16.0% in 2011. This is primarily due to the drastic decline in export expansion. Total exports grew at an annual average of 6.0% from 2000 to 2011, compared to about 14.0% from 1987 to 1997. Despite slower export growth, net export was able to contribute about 16.0% to GDP as import growth experienced a sharper decline from about 18.0% per annum to about 6.0% during the same period. This is due to high import content of Malaysian exports.

The Malaysian economy was propelled by all four drivers of growth in the 1990s, but now two of them—private investment and net exports—are providing far less traction. To offset

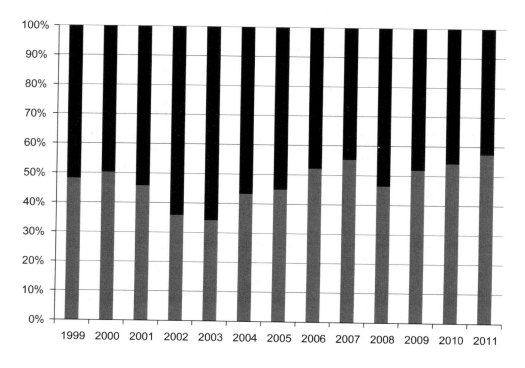

Figure 16.4 Demand side sources of growth
Source: Ministry of Finance, *Economic Repair*, various issues

these trends, public investment has risen significantly. Such a growth scenario is unsustainable in the longer run, however, especially with a rising public sector deficit. The public sector deficit has risen from 3.3% of GDP in 2006 to 4.8% in 2008, and is expected to rise further to a whopping 6.7% in 2009 (Figure 16.5). It is targeted to decline to 4.5% in 2012 and to 3.0% by 2015.

Based on the Global Competitiveness Index, Malaysia is becoming less attractive as an investment destination. Its global position has dropped to 24 in 2010 from 21 in 2009. Yusuf and Nabeshima[4] attribute the underlying factors behind the decline in private investment to the adjustment to over-investment in the 1990s, primarily in real estate and to declining profitability of selected segments of production as export prices have plummeted and terms of trade have deteriorated. The weakening of investment is also a reflection of the limited capacity of Malaysian firms to diversify through innovation into areas that bring higher returns. Domestic firms have a weak track record on innovation as reflected in the relatively low level of R&D expenditure and the low number of researchers in contrast to its nearest competitors. This phenomenon is amplified by the relatively low and declining total factor productivity (TFP) for Malaysia (see Table 16.1). The TFP growth rate declined from 2.5% in 1991–95 to 1.1% and 1.3%, respectively, under the seventh and eighth Malaysia Plans.

It is clear that the above-mentioned macroeconomic trends do not reflect a transitory phenomenon associated with global business cycles but the beginning of a more permanent shift to a slower growth phase. These developments also raise questions about the longer-term

Middle-income trap of Malaysian economy

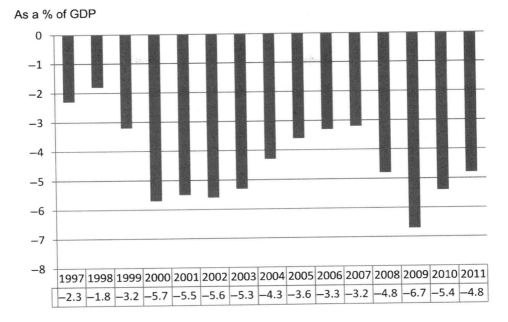

Figure 16.5 Public sector deficit
Source: Ministry of Finance, *Economic Report* various issues
Note: figures for 2003 to 2011 are preliminary figures.

Table 16.1 Total factor productivity for Malaysia, 1991–2010

Five-year plans	TFP (%)
6th Malaysia Plan (1991–95)	2.5
7th Malaysia Plan Period (1996–2000)	1.1
8th Malaysia Plan Period (2001–05)	1.3
1987–97*	1.7
1998–2007*	1.6

Source: Five-Year Plans, various issues
Note: * Figures taken from Chart 3-1 of the 10th Malaysia Plan.

economic and social prospects of the Malaysian economy which threaten to undo past achievements. Cracks in Malaysia's resilience to withstand internal and external shocks emerge in the form of rising inequities in the economy vis-à-vis the weakening position of labour and the falling standard of living, especially of the lower- and middle-income groups, sustained decline in investment as noted above, and rising emigration of much-needed high-skilled labour and large-scale immigration of low-skilled labour to sustain the viability of existing industries.

Though absolute poverty has fallen drastically, relative poverty in the country remains high. The overall incidence of poverty has declined from 10.0% in 1995, to 5.5% in 2004, and 3.8% in 2008, but income inequality is relatively high. The Malaysian inequality index, as measured by the Gini coefficient, was near 0.44 in 2008,[5] comparable to countries such as Indonesia and Viet Nam.[6] Wages are also relatively low. A 2009 study of 1.3 million Malaysian workers by the Ministry of Human Resources showed that almost 34.0% earned less than 700 Malaysian ringgit (RM) a month. Undoubtedly, the large presence of low-skilled migrants has moderated wage growth in the country.

Malaysia has a long history of out-migration, but recent trends indicate a rise in the number of highly educated and skilled Malaysians emigrating in search of better employment and living standards. According to a World Bank study, the number of Malaysian migrants rose more than 100-fold in a 45-year period, from 9,576 Malaysians in 1960 to 1,489,168 Malaysians in 2005.[7] More recent figures released by the deputy foreign minister show that 304,358 Malaysians migrated from March 2008 to August 2009, compared with 139,696 Malaysians in 2007. On the contrary, Malaysia imports large-scale low-skilled labour to ensure the profitability and viability of low-wage industries. Malaysia currently hosts about 1.8 million documented migrant workers and an estimated two million undocumented migrants. These migration trends do not bode well for a nation that seeks to move up the value chain.

The underlying weaknesses in the economy were officially recognized as early as the mid-1990s and various policies and initiatives to address the structural problems have been implemented, as detailed in successive Five-Year Development Plans beginning with the Seventh Malaysia Plan (1996–2000), as well as in the Third Outline Perspective Plan (2001–10). Despite the wide array of policies and heavy investment in programmes over the last two decades to 'shift from input-driven to productivity-driven growth' and to a 'knowledge-based economy for sustained growth and competiveness', structural weaknesses continue to plague the economy, preventing it from operating at a more optimal level. To recognize why the extensive economic solutions have produced less-than-desired outcomes and slowed the pace of transition to high-income status, it is imperative to examine the underlying socio-political dynamics. The following explores the larger overarching problem of relatively weak socio-political institutions that have compromised the implementation of sound economic policies.

Political economy analysis of the Malaysian economy

Structure and institutions

Malaysia is a multi-ethnic society with Malays accounting for the dominant share at about 60.3%, followed by the Chinese (22.9%), the Indians (7.1%) and other indigenous communities such as the Kadazans and Bajaus in Sabah and the Dayaks in Sarawak. In its formative years, much of Malaysia's political movement was dominated by race-based organizations. This was mainly due to the restrictive inter-ethnic relationship policy that the colonial British government had imposed in Malaya. These race-based political organizations later formed a coalition that succeeded in negotiating for independence in 1957. While it was a perfect political formulation to unite a nation highly divided—a legacy of the maxims of *divide et impera* practised within the British colonies it had, inevitably resulted in a political process heavily influenced by ethnic considerations.

The formation of the Alliance Party in 1957 marked the beginning of race-based political partnership that would determine almost all aspects of nation-building initiatives in Malaysia afterwards. Policy decisions with respect to growth and development, for instance, had to address concerns of inter-ethnic equity. However, with the decline in growth and the increase in intra-ethnic inequity in recent years, class concerns have emerged to confound ethnic considerations.

Malaysia is a resource-rich nation with a diverse population, rich biodiversity and natural resources such as high-quality timber, oil and gas, and large tracts of fertile land. It is also located in one of the most dynamic regions in the world.

Malaysia is a constitutional monarchy where the Yang di-Pertuan Agong, or king, is the head of state, whose role is largely ceremonial. The constitution provides for the establishment of three main branches of the government, i.e. the parliament or the bicameral legislative branch, which consists of the House of Representatives (Dewan Rakyat) and the Senate (Dewan Negara); the executive branch led by the prime minister and his or her cabinet ministers; and the judiciary branch headed by the Federal Court. The following will analyse how the separation of powers between the three bodies was progressively undermined, with the executive branch exerting greater control over decisions with respect to the use, production and distribution of resources in the country.

The present ruling regime, the Barisan Nasional (BN, or Coalition Front),[8] which has ruled the country since independence in 1957, is a coalition of ethnically based parties. The leader of the United Malay National Organization (UMNO), the dominant party within the coalition, is also the prime minister of the country. Thus the apex of power is vested in the leadership of the UMNO and it controls the process of inter-ethnic bargaining. The prime minister balances his role as arbiter between the rival claims of ethnically based coalition partners and retains support from within the UMNO and the rank and file of Malay voters. Thus 'inter-elite bargaining and accommodation' between the three main ethnic groups was the main approach to building consensus in a fractious society divided by race, religion and culture.[9] Sensitive and contentious issues were resolved within the governing councils by representatives of the three communal parties. However, the original power-sharing system of 'inter-elite bargaining and accommodation' broke down following the worst-ever inter-ethnic conflict in 1969, and a new political framework for governance emerged.

The 1969 racial riots were a turning point in the country's political, economic and social development. Politically, a new coalition framework emerged when the alliance was expanded to include members of the opposition parties, thus further diluting the checks and balances to power. A national ideology, the Rukunegara (National Principles),[10] was introduced and the 'racial bargain' agreed upon earlier became non-negotiable through amendments to the constitution.[11] These included amendments to sensitive ethnic issues such as Malay special rights, status and power of the Malay rulers, the position of Islam and Malay as the sole national language, and the rights of the non-Malays with respect to religion and language.

The new political framework with the UMNO-led Barisan National enhanced the power of UMNO leadership and contributed to a sharp rise in patronage. The prime minister 'became less accessible and could deal with the other coalition leaders on a one-to-one basis, playing off one against the other'. The role and power of the governing coalition council was reduced to 'an institution of ritualized confirmation for political agreements worked out by the Prime Minister'.[12] Debate and discussion on policy proposals within the cabinet was much more muted. It was now more concerned with issues of administrative jurisdiction and inter-agency co-ordination. However, when occasional organized public protest against policy initiatives rose, the cabinet became a venue for making partial adjustments and corrections to policy to placate protesters. Thus elite bargaining in the cabinet was minimized and no longer preceded the formulation of fundamental policy objectives. When there was inter-elite bargaining, it revolved around the role of the prime minister, who dispensed favours, patronage and the occasional policy concessions in a web of bilateral arrangements and agreements.[13]

Under the new political framework, the NEP, launched in July 1971, was a tool to promote national unity by eradicating poverty irrespective of race and eliminating race identification with economic function. The restructuring of society was to be based on an increasing economic pie so that no community would feel a sense of deprivation from the process. The NEP set targets with respect to poverty eradication and ownership of wealth and employment.[14] The

NEP was originally scheduled for a period of 20 years from 1971 to 2000, but it was continued under a new name—the National Development Policy (NDP). Despite the weakness in its implementation and calls for a review from several quarters, consensus from the various communities was forged by focusing the extended policy on growth, ideology and vision.

Policymaking process

The laws of the nation are passed by parliament, but the cabinet remains the highest decision-making body in the country with policies originating from a variety of sources, though primarily from the federal government. The three central government agencies, i.e. the Economic Planning Unit (EPU) within the Prime Minister's Department, the central bank, or Bank Negara, and the Ministry of Finance (MOF) initiate and lead discussion on economic policies. The central bank is responsible for monetary and exchange rate policies, while the fiscal policy is under the purview of the MOF. The EPU is in charge of overall development planning, including the formulation of the five-year development plans and their respective mid-term reviews, as well as plans with respect to specific areas, such as the Privatization Master Plan, the Human Resource Plan, etc. Policies may also originate from agencies or ministries responsible for the various sectors, but are often led by the three central agencies. Policy co-ordination is carried out through the Inter-Agency Planning Group (IAPG), whose members include the three central agencies and selected ministries and departments. The IAPG is activated for the preparation of the five-year development plans and for policy matters that arise in between the planning cycles. The EPU is the secretariat, while technical working groups provide the technical support.

A parallel policy initiative by the federal government is through the National Development Planning Committee (NDPC), which is responsible for policy inputs for the five-year development plans from senior officials and technocrats. The EPU is the secretariat, while the chief secretary to the government is the chairman of the NDPC. Policy papers for consideration by the NDPC are either prepared by EPU or submitted from outside through the EPU. The MOF and central bank have their own committees and secretariats to handle their respective policy interests. The central bank submits its policy matters and provides briefings to the minister of finance and other senior officials. Other important state sources of policy initiatives include the non-financial public enterprises (NFPEs) and the GLCs.[15]

The policies originating from the various state-centred sources are tabled in the cabinet by the respective ministers. The cabinet is, however, the final arbiter of policies. At the cabinet level, there are also various councils, committees and task forces that initiate and discuss policies on priority areas.

The non-government sources of policy initiatives include the private sector, trade associations, trade unions, universities, think tanks and selected non-governmental organizations (NGOs). Policy inputs from these diverse sources are solicited through public-private dialogue, the most popular being the Annual Budget Dialogue with MOF and the Ministry of International Trade and Industry (MITI) dialogue on industrial policy. Apart from these regular events, there is a long list of committees, working groups and task forces that are led by government agencies as and when necessary. At this forum, non-government bodies representing diverse interest groups and expertise are invited to provide policy inputs and to review and reassess old and new policies.

Apart from these domestic sources, international agencies of which Malaysia is a member such as the World Bank, International Monetary Fund (IMF) and the Asian Development Bank (ADB) have also been significant sources of policy advice. Though Malaysia is not heavily reliant on them for funds, they do provide valuable policy inputs through their country reports. For instance, the recent country reports termed the *Malaysian Economic Monitor* by the World Bank

Middle-income trap of Malaysian economy

have addressed critical areas of concern for reinvigorating growth to avoid the MIT. Likewise, the IMF produces an annual country report in line with its Annual Article IV Consultations.

Though major policies have to be debated and passed by parliament, the cabinet was the de facto arbiter on policies as the Barisan Nasional government has had an overwhelming majority in parliament until the 2008 election. Once decisions are made, support for them is solicited through nation-wide dissemination of information on the rationale and objectives, as well as on programmes and target recipients. Policy information is traditionally channelled by politicians and technocrats via the government-controlled media through interviews, conferences and seminars. A new supplementary approach is to post detailed information on policies and programmes online via the respective state agency websites. Political support is also solicited by the component parties of the ruling coalition at their respective national assembly. This is an important avenue for party delegates to voice their opinions openly and for political leaders to give swift response, with the help of invited technocrats. Elected leaders also garner grass-roots support by visiting their respective parliamentary constituencies to explain and obtain feedback on policies and programmes. Dissent on policies were considered and resolved at the cabinet level.[16]

Strengths and weaknesses of the political system

The well-established institutional framework for policymaking has contributed to swift and speedy decisions to tackle major economic challenges, especially during periods of boom and bust. Malaysia also inherited a strong and well-functioning machinery from British rule for effective administration of policies. In the aftermath of the 1969 ethnic clashes amid high unemployment, the state was able to transform the economy from predominantly agricultural activities to a more broad-based industrialized economy driven by foreign direct investment. Again in the early 1980s, when Malaysia succumbed to the slump in commodity prices that coincided with a downturn in electronics and textiles, two leading export sectors, it launched a second round of the import substitution policy based on heavy industries and trimmed the size of the public sector through a privatization scheme. In the 1990s, when it faced mounting competition for investment and markets from emerging large economies, it introduced various policies to address structural weaknesses, and further liberalized the economy.

How the political system and decision-making process works in reality depends largely on leadership. The political leadership has ensured political stability in the country through a fine balance between safeguarding the interests of the country's bumiputera majority and the interests of the non-bumiputeras.

However, insufficient checks and balances led to increasing concentration of power within the executive, especially under the leadership of Dr Mahathir, the fourth prime minister. During his 22-year period in office, from 1981 to 2003, he was able to consolidate his power and enhance his role in decision making. This is exemplified through a number of power contestations in which he succeeded. In 1983, he introduced constitutional amendments to reduce the power of the king to delay assent to a bill that had been enacted in parliament. He also removed royal immunity from the rule of law in 1992. He further compromised the independence of the judiciary when in 1998 he removed the sitting lord president of the Supreme Court of Malaysia, suspended five Supreme Court judges and dismissed two others. He also consolidated his power within UMNO when he was challenged by two senior UMNO members in the 1987 UMNO General Assembly.[17] Following his victory, he amended the UMNO constitution to enhance further the power of the president.[18]

Apart from increased concentration of power within the executive, any strong opposition to the government was neutralized through the use of draconian laws such as the Sedition Act,

Internal Security Act, the Official Secrets Act and other state institutions such as the police and the courts. The media[19] were tightly controlled and laws governing free speech, free assembly and free association were unjustly applied. All of these meant that there was lack of transparency and accountability, which has led to gross abuse of power.

It is now officially acknowledged that the 'NEP has addressed inter-ethnic imbalances' but 'its implementation has also increasingly and inadvertently raised the cost of doing business due to rent-seeking, patronage and often opaque government procurement. This has engendered pervasive corruption, which needs to be addressed earnestly'.[20]

The way in which the NEP and its successor the NDP (1991–2000) was implemented also led to the weakening of the very foundations of the society that ensures sustainable growth in an increasingly competitive global arena. From its original intentions of equalization of opportunities, the NEP morphed into focusing on equalization of outcomes. The unintended consequences have been the weakening of public education at all levels, a decline in the public health delivery system and in the efficiency of the bureaucracy. Corporate restructuring, mandated through the divestment of 30% of the stake to bumiputeras, led to abuse and nurtured a patronage system and a crutch mentality. Government contracts were not openly tendered but given to bumiputera companies, many of which did not have the capability or capacity to carry them out. This led to what is popularly known as the 'Ali Baba'[21] system, in which layers of sub-contracting escalated costs and produced poor-quality work.

The Privatization Scheme spearheaded by Dr Mahathir became an important vehicle for transferring government assets into private hands at prices far below their market value. Corruption and patronage via privatization led to leakages of government resources to a select group of favoured businessmen, both Malay and non-Malay, through negotiated tenders, outright granting of licences and permits, as well as questionable land transfers and conversions.

Apart from the ethnic-based political system, religion also plays a role in the nation's political process, particularly since the 1970s. The Parti Islam SeMalaysia (PAS, or Pan-Malaysian Islamic Party), a party founded upon religion, is the only Islamic-based party in the country and it aims to transform Malaysia into an Islamic state, one that would adhere to *Shari'a* law and the Islamic penal code. It currently governs the state of Kelantan. Though PAS has to some extent influenced UMNO to move to the right to appease UMNO's more conservative elements, its role in introducing its own ideology into the national political process has to some degree been blunted by its membership in the opposition coalition. However, it has occasionally tried to influence people's public lifestyles in the states it governed[22] and also use its religious credentials to oppose the ruling regime's stand on corruption.

Socio-political challenges

The weak macroeconomic trends highlighted above, i.e. the sharp decline in investment, slow productivity increase, sluggish and volatile growth with rising inequity, were paralleled by a weakening socio-political environment that began to impinge on the quality of life of the average Malaysian. The standard and quality of living further weakened with the rise in the cost living and the increase in crime rates. The price of essential food items escalated following world-wide food shortages and rising demand from emerging economies, while house prices skyrocketed, making house ownership a pipe dream for the middle- and lower-income households. The rise in the incidence of neighbourhood crime has compelled urban dwellers to hire private neighbourhood security guards.

The weakening position of the middle-income class is further reflected in the steady rise in household debt from 44.6% of GDP in 2000 to 74.2% in 2011, prompting the central bank to tighten credit card facilities (see Figure 16.6). According to the IMF country report, households in Malaysia have amassed consumer debt in excess of RM 600 billion.[23]

The changing political economy landscape

Popular dissatisfaction with the management of the economy was further aggravated by the exposure of a slew of high-profile corporate scandals, corruption and abuse of power in the country. The simmering popular discontent with the state of affairs in the country surfaced during the March 2008 general elections, when traditional supporters severely punished the ruling coalition government. As a result, the opposition parties clinched unprecedented gains that changed the political landscape of the country. For the first time in 52 years, the ruling Barisan Nasional lost its two-thirds' parliamentary majority which it had held since 1973, and ceded control of five states including Selangor and Penang, two of the more developed states.[24] By capturing these states and the metropolitan areas in the Federal Territory, the opposition controlled close to half of the economy in terms of GDP.

The Barisan Nasional controlled 140, or 64%, of the 222 parliamentary seats. Moreover, Barisan Nasional's margin of victory in the successful constituencies fell. Its popular vote count dwindled to around 50% from 63% in the 2004 election. All component parties with the Barisan coalition fared badly. The Malays withdraw their support for UMNO and it won only 66 parliamentary seats in the Peninsular, while the Malaysian Chinese Association (MCA) won 15, the Malaysian Indian Congress (MIC) three, and the Malaysian People's Movement Party (GERAKAN) two. On the contrary, the opposition garnered 47.2% of the popular vote, with the largest number of seats won by the Party Keadilan Rakyat (PKR, or People's Justice Party), followed by the Democratic Action Party (DAP) and the PAS. It was obvious that ethnic factors played a much smaller role than in previous elections. Voting crossed ethnic lines, with more Indians and Chinese voting for PKR.

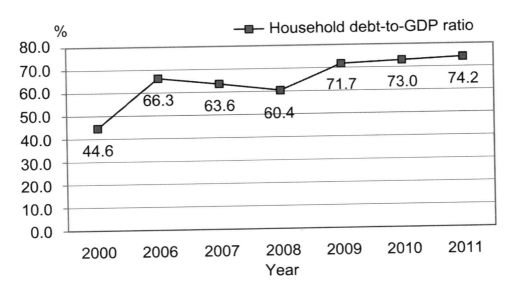

Figure 16.6 Household debts as a % of GDP
Source: Bank Negates Malaysia, as cited in IMF (2013), p. 31

Since the 2008 election, the opposition has ruled the four states with varying degrees of success. It has also made significant progress in establishing consensus and forming a rare coalition (Pakatan Rakyat, or People's Pact) to voice the concerns of the younger generation, who are more educated and politically savvy.

Activists from civil society have also been credited for the strong performance of the opposition in the 2008 elections. They have contributed to strategizing opposition collaboration, standing as candidates, informing debates and expanding media options.[25] Of particular significance was the Hindraf-led (Hindu Rights Action Front) campaign of late 2007 that culminated in the historic march of 25 November that year. That march was crucial to the withdrawal of Indian electoral support for BN in the 12th general election. Since then, the scale and role of activists from both sides of the political divide have expanded. Their voices with respect to a wide range of issues such as electoral reform,[26] judicial independence, corruption, freedom of assembly, media freedom, human rights and women's rights, and environmental protection have grown louder.

Undoubtedly, one of the key drivers of change has been the internet. In an environment of overwhelming control and domination of the print media and broadcast news by the state, the internet has brought about drastic political and cultural changes in contemporary Malaysia. Malaysia's internet penetration is currently around 62% and there is active participation on social media via Twitter, Facebook, YouTube and on political blogs.

The Barisan Nasional government had to face a new political reality which demanded greater transparency and accountability. Of particular significance is the expanding middle-income Malay society that has become so diverse socially, culturally and politically. This dominant political force spawned by the NEP views the notion of Malay political unity that has been traditionally used by UMNO to galvanize Malay support with less enthusiasm. Cracks in Malay political unity became more visible with the rise of the Reformasi Movement in the aftermath of the sacking of the former deputy prime minister in September 1998, who was then charged with sodomy (a crime in Malaysia) and corruption.[27] This movement has since grown and transformed into a viable opposition party and a coalescing force within the opposition coalition.

The 2008 election debacle led to a change in the leadership of UMNO, the dominant party in the ruling coalition. Under the new leadership a national stock-taking exercise was carried out to help revive support for the ruling coalition and to revisit the national goal to transform the nation into a high-income economy by adopting a more sustainable and inclusive policy. A far-reaching and comprehensive national transformation process was announced under four key pillars to achieve the developed nation status by 2020 and to address the people's concerns. These include: (1) Malaysia: People First, Performance Now; (2) Government Transformation Programme (GTP); (3) Economic Transformation Programme (ETP); and (4) the Tenth Malaysia Plan (2011–15).

The reform process

Under the new leadership, a set of liberalization measures were introduced in 2009 to revive investment. Of significance were the changes made with respect to bumiputera equity rules. The Foreign Investment Committee (FIC) that regulated the 30% bumiputera equity quota was suspended. Instead, a new mechanism, the Ekuiti Nasional Berhad (Ekuinas), was created to achieve the 30% equity target of the NEP.[28] In addition, full foreign equity ownership for 27 services sub-sectors was now allowed.

The New Economic Model: Part 1 launched in March 2010 was an honest and critical assessment of the dilemma facing the country.[29] For the first time, the state openly acknowledged the risks and challenges facing the economy and identified the main problems contributing to sluggish growth as follows: (1) declining private investments; (2) difficulties in doing business;

(3) low value-added industries; (4) low-skilled jobs and low wages; (5) stagnating productivity growth; (6) insufficient innovation and creativity; and (7) lack of appropriately skilled human capital.[30] The NEM also critically addressed the underlying problems and challenges and the painful policy changes needed to put the country back on the right track. Both the NEM and Tenth Malaysia Plan (2011–15) recognized that 'excessive focus on ethnicity-based distribution of resources has contributed to growing separateness and dissension'.[31] Instead, it focused on leveraging Malaysia's diversity and ensuring equal opportunities. It advocated inclusive growth by targeting assistance to the bottom 40% of households, ensuring equitable and fair opportunities through transparent processes, allowing access to resources on the basis of needs and merit, and having a sound institutional framework for better monitoring and effective implementation.[32] The New Economic Model: Concluding Part mapped the industrial upgrading and restructuring policies and strategies that will enable the aspiration of attaining a high income and developed-nation status by 2020.[33]

The GTP[34] aimed to improve public-sector delivery in key areas of public concern while the ETP[35] was designed to get Malaysia out of the MIT and propel the country to developed-nation status by 2020. A new agency called Performance, Management and Delivery Unit (PEMANDU), was formally established in 2009 under the Prime Minister's Department, responsible for monitoring and assessing the initiatives under both programmes.

The government also introduced the long-awaited National Minimum Wage Legislation.[36] Despite the backing from trade unions and other worker representatives, the state had to backtrack on the implementation of the policy and allow a one-year deferment for smaller firms, following strong opposition from the business community. Further, foreign workers who also benefit from the minimum wage ruling will have to pay their levy, which was previously borne by employers. The trade union movement in Malaysia is relatively weak and it currently represents only about 10% of the workforce.

Apart from economic transformation, there was a raft of legislative reforms to improve civil liberty (see Table 16.2). These legislative reforms include the repeal of some legislation that was deemed highly controversial and the introduction of new legislation more in line with international norms and the constitutional right to freedom of speech, assembly and association.

Table 16.2 Key legislative reforms

1	The Banishment Act 1959, The Restricted Residence Act 1933, The Proclamations of Emergency 1966, 1969 and 1977	Revoked after more than 40 years. All ordinances under them ended June 2012
2	Malaysia Volunteer Corps (Rela) Act 2011	Rela's enforcement powers removed, will not be allowed to carry firearms
3	Peaceful Assembly Act 2011	To replace Section 27 of the Police Act. Police permits no longer required for public assemblies
4	Security Offences (Special Measures) Act 2012	Internal Security Act (ISA) 1960 repealed and replaced with this new Act. Detention without trial scrapped, maximum 28-day detention for investigation
5	Printing Presses and Publication Act (PPPA) 1981	Publishing licences annual renewal and home minister's absolute discretion removed
6	Elections Offences Act 1954	Provisions on polling centre and printed materials amended
7	Universities and University Colleges Act 1971	Amended to allow students participation in politics

However, much of the new legislation has been criticized for incorporating new and stricter restrictions and penalties.

The Internal Security Act 1960 (ISA), the most controversial piece of legislation, which permitted long-term detention without trial and other rights-restricting legislation have been replaced. The Banishment Act 1959 and the Restricted Residences Act 1933 were the first to be rescinded, followed by three emergency declarations and the emergency-related laws they made possible. The Security Offences (Special Measures) 2012 Act (SOSMA) replaced the ISA on July 31 2012. SOSMA reduced initial detention without charge from 60 to 28 days, and required that a suspect be charged in court or released thereafter. One of the rescinded laws, the Emergency (Public Order and Crime Prevention) Ordinance 1969, had been regularly used to hold criminal suspects indefinitely without charge or trial.

Legislation affecting freedom of assembly was also introduced. Section 27 of the Police Act 1967 which criminalized the gathering of three or more people in a public place without a licence was repealed by the Police (Amendment) Act 2012. It was replaced by the Peaceful Assembly Act 2012 as the principal piece of legislation dealing with public gatherings. However, the new law introduced new restrictions, including a broad ban on 'moving assemblies' of any kind. Static protests are also prohibited closer than 50 metres from many prohibited sites, making it difficult to hold an assembly in an urban setting. Other restrictions include empowering the police to set assembly conditions such as time, place and date, after taking into consideration other groups' objections or 'any inherent environmental factor'. Police were also given the power to use all 'reasonable force' to break up a protest.

The University and University Colleges Act 1971 was amended to lift the ban on student participation in politics. Electoral reforms such as the use of indelible ink to avoid multiple voting and expanded overseas postal balloting were also introduced.

Corruption is one of the priority areas under the National Key Results Areas (NKRA) programme. Steps taken thus far include the Whistleblower Protection Act 2010 the setting up of 14 special corruption courts; the naming and shaming website; open tenders; and the introduction of integrity pledges or pacts. Despite these measures, Malaysia's ranking in the Corruption Perception Index (CPI) by Transparency International (TI) fell to 54 in 2012 from 23 in the first TI CPI in 1995. According to the financial watchdog Global Financial Integrity, illicit capital flight from Malaysia was estimated at $285 billion (about RM 880 billion) in 2001–10. Further, about 50% of businesses surveyed said they lost deals because they refused to pay bribes. It appears that corruption in the country has been so institutionalized that measures at the national level have failed to make much of a dent. Corruption weakens Malaysia's competitiveness and attractiveness as a destination for investments.

Underlying these reform measures is a new socio-political reality that threatens the interests of the conservative elements within UMNO. Though the president of UMNO wields strong power, traditionally the youth and women's wings within UMNO function as formidable pressure groups. UMNO Youth, in particular, holds a strong position on ethnic matters and against any compromise and concession to non-Malays that might weaken Malays' rights or advantage. Following the 2008 debacle, even more extremist groups with similar objectives have emerged outside UMNO, such as the Pertubuhan Pribumi Perkasa Malaysia (PERKASA) and Jaringan Melayu Malaysia (JMM). The reform efforts as advocated following the 2008 elections often fell short as they were constrained by these pressure groups.

2013 general elections

In the 2013 general elections, held on 5 May, the Barisan Nasional government was returned to power, but with a further reduction in the margin of victory. Its popular vote dropped to 47% from

50%, while it only managed to garner 133 of the 222 parliamentary seats, down by seven from 2008. It also lost 230 state seats out of 505, making it its worst electoral showing in history. The three major components parties within Barisan also witnessed a further deterioration of their support. MCA won only seven parliamentary seats, MIC four seats and GERAKAN one seat.

On the contrary, the opposition won 89 parliamentary seats and garnered a majority of 51% of the popular vote. The voting pattern reflected a clear divide both along ethnic lines and between urban and rural areas. DAP emerged the strongest with 38 seats, while PKR and PAS won 30 and 21 seats, respectively. All three parties, however, increased their popular vote and their representation throughout the nation. They won about 46% of the state seats and made significant inroads in the states of Terengganu, Perak and even Johor, which traditionally has been the heartland of UMNO.[37] However, the ruling government was able to recapture Kedah, which had been governed by PAS since 2008.

However, the 2013 election has been marred by strong allegations of irregularities. Gerrymandered constituencies meant that with only 47% of the popular vote, the ruling party was able to win 60% of the 222 parliamentary seats. Rallies protesting against the election results have been held throughout the nation, while the opposition has filed 39 petitions contesting the results of the elections.

Despite the alleged irregularities, the general election has permanently altered the political landscape of the country. The era of a two-thirds' majority for the ruling coalition has dissipated and a stronger and more formidable opposition coalition has emerged. The opposition has clinched representation in all the states, though its support is mainly urban. Moreover, it has a more multi-ethnic representation than the ruling coalition. The 2013 elections also saw a political reawakening, with the highest voter turnout at around 80%. Whether this trend will be sustained remains to be seen.

Towards a revised socio-political framework

The state reform measures may not have produced the desired political impact for the ruling government as seen in the 2013 elections, but it did have some positive economic impact. Malaysia has bucked global trends to record higher growth driven by strong domestic demand. Public and private investment was driven by large-scale projects under the economic transformation programme, while consumption was boosted by high employment, pre-election government transfers and easy credit. However, growth is still behind the average 6.0%[38] targeted under the Tenth Malaysia Plan (2011–15) to attain high-income status by 2020.

The discretionary fiscal stimulus, the national transformation programmes and the recent extensive government transfer/assistance programme targeting lower-income households and the youth[39] have inevitably contributed to a sharp rise in government debt. The debt has more than doubled from RM 216.6 billion in 2004 to RM 501.6 billion in 2012, or from 45.7% of GDP to 53.5% during this period (see Figure 16.7). Malaysia's statutory debt ceiling was set at 40.0% of GDP in 2003, but has since been gradually adjusted upwards to 45% in 2008 and 55% in 2009. Although about 97% of the debt is denominated in the RM, this trend has serious implications for policy autonomy as well as increasing the risks of capital flight. Of particular concern is the sharp rise in contingent liabilities of the government following the increase in government statutory guarantees which increased to 15% of GDP.[40] The high budget deficit and ballooning government and household debts pose fiscal and financial risks, given the uncertain global economic outlook.

The political economy review shows that recent reform measures by and large continue to focus on the symptoms rather than the deep-rooted causes for the MIT. It is apparent that

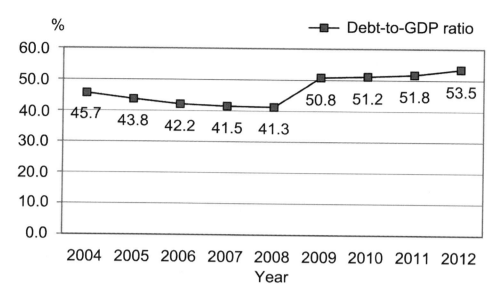

Figure 16.7 Federal debts as a % of GDP
Source: Bank Nepara Malaysia, *Monthly Statistical Bulletin*, various issues

attempts at implementing the requisite reforms from within the existing socio-political structure have been less than adequate. The state reform efforts have been contested vigorously by strong pressure groups that benefit from business as usual. As a result, changes to long-standing rules and regulations that broaden and deepen the democratic space have at best been modest. The following explores areas of policy support to sustain the momentum of socio-political reforms to improve overall governance in the country.

The 2008 and 2013 election outcomes are clear indications that Malaysian society has changed drastically and the old political framework of governance is beginning to lose its legitimacy. The elections also exposed the weaknesses of the ruling coalition arrangements. It was no longer able to represent the diverse interests of the new generation of Malaysians. The catalytic changes have given traction for an improved framework of political governance to meet changing realities, both at home and abroad. Internally, the socio-political dynamics have transformed significantly, with the growing educated urban middle-income class, while externally the nation faces an increasingly competitive global environment.

Malaysia needs a revised political economy framework: one that is no longer focused on ethnicity. The vast majority of those in the lower income categories are Malays. Thus a shift from an ethnic-based to needs-based approach to uplift the poor income households would benefit the vast majority of Malays. Affirmative action programmes must also be geared towards equalization of opportunities, rather than equalization of outcomes.

There is also a need further to deepen and broaden the democratic processes in the country. The central pillar of a truly democratic nation is its legitimacy through free and fair elections. Equally important are sufficient checks and balances to ensure the integrity of key institutions of the political process, as shown in Figure 16.8. Finally, the rights and liberty of all Malaysians, irrespective of race or creed, should be fully guaranteed and protected. As noted above, the impetus to change in all respects has heightened since 2008 and the ruling regime has responded with significant reforms unimagined in the nation's 56-year history. It is important to leverage

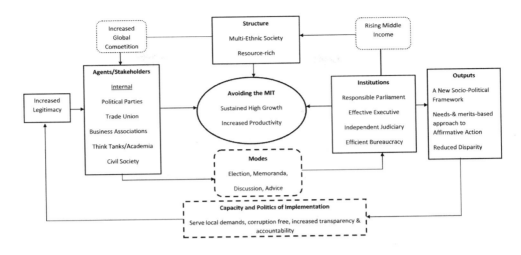

Figure 16.8 Avoiding the middle income trap
Source: Adapted from Diagram 2, p. 21 Leftwich (2008) "From Drivers of change to the Politicast of Development: Redefining the Analytical Framework to Understand The Politics of the Places where we work, Part 3: Final Report", Department of politics, University of York, July

the evolving environment to institute further reforms to improve Malaysia's competitiveness and to keep up with Malaysia's enhanced role in the international arena.

To ensure that the government in power is legitimate, the electoral process must be free, fair and transparent. As noted earlier, some nominal reforms have been introduced following strong pressure from advocacy groups, but fundamental reforms for a truly free and fair election have yet to be implemented. The Election Commission does not inspire the confidence of the electorate, as about 92% of Malaysians recently surveyed wanted the electoral rolls cleaned up before the 2013 elections. Though Malaysians are able to vote freely, the electoral system remains skewed in favour of the incumbent government. The electoral process must be refined further to ensure a more level playing field. The structural bias in favour of the ruling regime through gerrymandering needs to be resolved. The present structure is such that key constituencies belonging to the coalition government are in sparsely populated rural areas, while opposition strongholds are predominantly in heavily populated urban areas, giving excessive weight to the coalition government vote. The independence of the Election Commission and the integrity of the electoral process must be upheld. There must be transparency in the administration of voter lists, supervision of the voting and counting procedures, and unbiased enforcement of the Elections Offence Act.

There is also a need to decentralize power. As the economy grows and becomes more complex, it will become increasingly difficult to deal with local situations. Policymakers require large amounts of information and a feel for on-the-ground sentiments. They also need to address local issues of opportunity and distribution. The beneficiaries at the local level have the right to choose their local council. Local councils deal with matters that affect the lives of residents much more directly than, say, the state or federal government. Therefore, reinstating local government elections or the 'third vote' is a step in the right direction. The Penang state government move to reinstate local council elections has been thwarted by the federal government.[41]

The rising political activism in the country is encouraging and central to strengthening the democratic institutions. To increase transparency and the flow of information further, the contentious Official Secrets Act must be replaced with a Freedom of Information Act, which has already been passed as law in Selangor and Penang.

The separation of powers as enshrined in the constitution must be restored. This would entail the supremacy of parliament, an independent judiciary, an efficient civil service and an effective executive. This in turn would require a free press and an impartial and professional police and military that safeguards the security of the nation.

Concluding remarks

Malaysia attained middle-income status by 1992 but its transition to high-income status has been interrupted by relatively slow growth since the Asian Financial Crisis of 1997, raising concerns of being trapped in the middle-income category. The moderate and volatile growth has been underpinned by sluggish productivity growth, lack of innovation and skills, and a low level of investment in technology, all of which are symptoms of an MIT.

The state has recognized the underlying structural weaknesses in the economy and since the mid-1990s it has introduced a wide spectrum of policies and programmes to shift from an 'input-driven to productivity-driven growth', and to a 'knowledge-based economy for sustained growth and competiveness'. However, the vast array of economic solutions has produced less-than-desired outcomes. A political economy approach is adopted to identify and evaluate the underlying socio-political dynamics that undermine and weaken the implementation of sound economic policies.

Malaysia's rapid progress in the past has been driven by a strong and stable government. Timely and sound economic policies have ensured macroeconomic stability and a business-friendly environment. However, Malaysia's socio-political system has failed to evolve to meet the enormous economic challenges brought on by increased globalization and competition for investment and markets.

The ongoing economic and government transformation programmes may have spiked growth in the short term, but sustainable, broad-based growth to escape the MIT requires parallel socio-political transformation that addresses the overarching problem of weak socio-political institutions. There is a compelling need to shift from an ethnic-based to a needs-based policy, to address imbalances in society as well as improve the democratic process to ensure that good governance and the rule of law prevail. There must be adequate checks and balances to maintain the integrity of the key institutions of the government. Corruption must be checked and there must be greater transparency and accountability so that the developmental outcomes are just. Moving forward, Malaysia will have to improve efforts to address political reform as well as to combat entrenched institutional problems like corruption. These issues will not be easily solved. But if the history of Malaysia over the past 50 years is any indication, it can, with careful policies and political will, make progress and achieve its aspirations of "a nation that is fully developed along all the dimensions: economically, politically, socially, spiritually, psychologically and culturally"[42]

Notes

1 This research was made possible through a grant from The Asia Foundation. The opinions expressed here are solely of the authors and do not necessarily reflect those of The Asia Foundation.
2 V. Kanapathy, 'High-Skilled versus Low-Skilled Labor Migration: Managing a Complex Agenda in Malaysia', paper presented at the International Conference on East Asian Labor Migration, organized by East Asian Development Network and Philippines Institute of Development Studies, Manila, 9 March 2007.

3 J. Menon and H.N. Thiam, *Are Government-Linked Corporations Crowding Private Investment in Malaysia*, ADB Economic Working Paper Series, No. 347, April 2013, www.adb.org/sites/default/files/pub/2013/ewp-345.pdf.

4 S. Yusuf and K. Nabeshima, '*Tiger Economies Under Threat: A Comparative Analysis of Malaysia's Industrial Prospects and Policy Options*', The World Bank, Washington, DC, 2009.

5 A Gini coefficient of 0 indicates perfect equality and 1 perfect inequality.

6 World Bank, *Malaysia Economic Monitor—Inclusive Growth*, The World Bank, Washington, DC, April 2010, www.worldbank.org/my.

7 World Bank, *Malaysia Economic Monitor—Brain Drain*, The World Bank, Washington, DC, April 2011, www.worldbank.org/my.

8 The Alliance was formed in 1952 through an alliance between the United Malay National Organization (UMNO) and the Malaysian Chinese Association (MCA), and later with the Malaysian Indian Congress (MIC) in 1954. In 1974, it co-opted several other smaller parties and was renamed Barisan Nasional.

9 Gordon P. Means, *Malaysian Politics: The Second Generation*, Oxford University Press, 1991.

10 The Rukunegara or national ideology was introduced on 31 August 1970 and included five basic principles of belief in God, loyalty to king and country, upholding the constitution, rule of law, and good behaviour and morality.

11 Zainal Aznam Yusof and Deepak Bhattasali, 'Economic Growth and Development in Malaysia: Policy Making and Leadership', Working Paper No. 27, Commission on Growth and Development, 2008, 26.

12 Means, *Malaysian Politics*, 286; R.S. Milne and Diane K. Mauzy, *Malaysian Politics Under Mahathir*, Routledge, London, 1999.

13 Means, *Malaysian Politics*.

14 Constitutional amendments gave powers to the king to reserve academic places in institutions of higher learning, for Malays in areas where they were disproportionately represented.

15 These are agencies that operate as private entities, but the government has a high equity stake in them.

16 Yusof and Bhattasali, 'Economic Growth and Development in Malaysia', 35.

17 The 1987 UMNO crisis led to a split in UMNO and the formation of a new political party called UMNO Baru (New UMNO).

18 Yusof and Bhattasali, 'Economic Growth and Development in Malaysia', 28.

19 Mainstream media are tightly controlled through printing licences that must be renewed annually. The Publications and Printing Presses Act (PPPA) gives the minister the absolute discretion to grant or to revoke such licences.

20 National Economic Advisory Council, *New Economic Model for Malaysia Part 1*, NEAC, Putrajaya, Malaysia, 2010a, 7.

21 'Ali Baba' refers to a system whereby the contracts are obtained by Malay companies while the work is actually done by others.

22 It also governed the state of Kedah from 2008 until it lost its mandate in the 2013 elections.

23 International Monetary Fund, 'Malaysia 2012, Article IV Consultation', IMF Country Report, No.13/51, Washington, DC, February 2013.

24 Within a year, Barisan Nasional regained control of the state of Perak following a court battle when three state assemblymen (two from PKR and one from DAP) quit their respective parties.

25 L. Meredith Weiss, 'Edging Toward a New Politics in Malaysia: Civil Society at the Gate?' *Asian Survey* XLIX(5), September/October 2009.

26 Bersih (Coalition for Clean and Fair Elections), together with other electoral advocacy groups, such as Mafrel (Malaysians for Free and Fair Elections) and Pusat Komas, has spearheaded the demands for electoral reforms. They have successfully organized three protests by tens of thousands of people demanding electoral reforms beginning from 2011.

27 He spent the next six years in prison, and in 2004 was acquitted on the charge of sodomy and released.

28 The abolishment of the FIC lifted the 30% bumiputera equity requirement for listed companies. To increase bumiputera equity in the economy, Ekuinas was established as a government-linked private equity funding to invest in high potential growth potential companies.

29 National Economic Advisory Council, *New Economic Model for Malaysia Part 1*.

30 Ibid. 44.

31 National Economic Advisory Council, *New Economic Model for Malaysia Concluding Part*, NEAC, Putrajaya, Malaysia, 2010b, 10.

32 Ibid., 10.

33 National Economic Advisory Council. *New Economic Model for Malaysia, The Concluding Part*, NEAC, Putrajaya, Malaysia, 2010b.

34 Seven National Key Result Areas (NKRAs) were identified to spearhead the government's transformation: (1) reducing crime; (2) fighting corruption; (3) improving student outcomes; (4) raising living standards of low-income households; (5) improving rural basic infrastructure; (6) improving urban public transport; and (7) addressing the cost of living.

35 The 12 areas of focus under the ETP known as National Key Economic Areas (NKEAs) include 11 industries and one geographic area as follows: oil, gas and energy; palm oil; financial services; tourism; business services; electronics and electrical; wholesale and retail; education; health care; communications, content and infrastructure; agriculture; Greater KL.

36 The mandatory monthly minimum wage was set at RM 900 for the Peninsular and RM 800 for Sabah and Sarawak, effective 1 January 2013.

37 Sarawak held its elections much earlier. Including Sarawak, there are a total of 576 state seats, of which about 42% is currently held by the opposition.

38 The growth rate was 5.1% in 2011 and 5.6% in 2012.

39 With the impending elections, the state has offered cash payouts to low-income households, smartphone rebates to young people, and stepped up an affordable housing scheme aimed at college graduates and young adults, who represent a large portion of the new voters.

40 International Monetary Fund, 'Malaysia 2012, Article IV Consultation', IMF Country Report, No. 13/51, Washington, DC, February 2013.

41 In May 2012 the Penang State Legislative Assembly passed the Local Government Elections (Penang Island and Province Wellesley) Enactment 2012, which provides for the Election Commission to conduct local government elections in Penang. However, it was declared *null and void* by the court.

42 The definition of developed Malaysia as presented by then Malaysian Prime Minister Tun Dr Mahathir Mohamad by the year 2020 to the Malaysian Business Council, 28 February 1991

VI

Possible candidates
The difficult road ahead

17

Argentina's present and its intriguing economic history

Domingo F. Cavallo[1]

Present and prospects

At the beginning of 2013 the Argentine economy showed clear signs of stagnation with 25% annual inflation; the country risk was more than twice that of Spain and Italy, countries that are suffering crises not very different to the crisis Argentina suffered in 2001; and there was a black market premium in the foreign exchange market of around 50%. This happened in spite of the fact that the country has been reducing its foreign debt since 2002.

While most economies of Latin America suffer from excessive capital inflows, in Argentina capital has been flying out at a rapid pace. The accumulated capital flight since 2007 has reached more than US$80 billion, which represents almost 20% of gross domestic product (GDP). This happened because during the last decade, Argentina's economic policies have defied basic principles of good economic management.

Those basic principles include a countercyclical fiscal policy that tries to generate fiscal surpluses (or at least fiscal balance) when the external conditions feed an economic boom and confine fiscal deficits to recessionary scenarios; a monetary policy that targets inflation; trade and exchange rate policies that promote international trade; efforts to improve the investment climate; and reliance on the markets and private initiative to allocate scarce resources to investment and production.

The Argentine economy since 2002

Instead, during the last decade, fiscal policy has been pursuing an ever-increasing level of government expenditure to keep effective demand expanding, even when the economy was clearly overheated. To finance this increasing level of government expenditure the government has introduced and maintained very distortive taxes on exports, financial transactions, and the wage bill. If tax revenues fell short of expenditures, then financing did not come from debt but from monetary expansion.

Price stability has been abandoned as a target of monetary policy. Instead, the central bank tries to perform the role of a development bank, unconcerned with price stability. To prevent inflation from spiralling, the government has relied upon a public utility rates freeze, taxes and quantitative restrictions on exports of agricultural and energy products, price controls on basic consumer goods and, lately, upon exchange controls to prevent the rapid devaluation of the peso that would be the natural outcome of these policies.

The encouragement for private investment came from increased demand of import substitution goods that benefited from increased tariff protection and of those domestic goods that were not subjected to price controls. Private investment in real estate, as a hedge against inflation, was also encouraged by negative real interest rates on bank deposits. However, private domestic and foreign investment in key sectors of the economy, like energy, transportation and agriculture was discouraged by price controls, distortionary taxes, trade restrictions and exchange controls which lately have prevented dividend distribution and capital repatriation.

Companies that had been privatized during the 1990s were expropriated with the intention of improving management and investment, but this had the opposite effect. The end result has been increased fiscal deficit and inefficient investment.

How and why did it happen?

During the 1990s Argentina had defeated hyperinflation and inaugurated a period of stability and the growth of a market economy, well integrated into the global trade and capital flows, with a very strict monetary rule. At the time of a sharp deterioration in terms of trade, between 1999 and 2001, this strategy did not help to prevent recession turning into deflation and fed a debt problem.

Unfortunately, instead of fixing the debt problem in an orderly way and changing the monetary rule to allow for more flexible inflation targeting, the new authorities that emerged from the political crisis of December 2001 opted for a disorderly debt default and a change in the monetary regime. The new monetary regime started with the destruction of the contractual base of the economy by forcing the conversion into pesos of all the contracts that had been written in US dollars.

The default and forced conversion of contracts provoked an extreme devaluation of the peso and opened the door to a very damaging freeze of public utility rates, price controls, distortionary taxes and all manner of administrative interventions thought as substitutes for an inflation-targeting monetary rule.

An expansionary fiscal policy was, at the beginning, very useful to reactivate the economy and renew growth, even without significant investment in key sectors of the economy that had been very well capitalized during the previous decade. However, with the significant improvement in terms of trade since 2003, the government found in the distortionary taxes introduced during the emergency period, particularly in export taxes, a politically very useful instrument to finance populist policies and accumulate political power. The external bonanza allowed the government to finance policies that are in sharp contrast with the basic principle of good economic management. There is no doubt that in the long run these policies will be non-sustainable, but what is not at all clear is how long they will last.

How far is Argentina's return to good economic management?

Most independent observers think that Argentina is at least three years away from a return to good economic management, for two reasons: (1) because the chances that the current government changes its approach to economic policymaking are negligible and a new government can only be elected by the end of 2015; and (2) because the current crisis may continue until 2015 without becoming so extreme as to force the current government to enact a drastic turn in economic policies.

It is very unlikely that the current government will decide on a turn because it lacks the human resources necessary to move towards good economic management. The ministers, vice-ministers and advisers either lack the professional training and experience to come out with rational economic reform proposals or interpret reality through a melange of Marxist-Keynesian ideological glasses that are completely inappropriate to detect solutions for an economy that is trapped in autarky and stagflation. Furthermore, the president doesn't want to listen to anybody who praises price stability, integration to the world economy and allocation of resources through private initiative and market mechanisms because she considers those to be neo-liberal concepts that have been developed by the US government and Washington-based institutions to exploit under-developed economies. A new government, with different views, may only come to power by the end of 2015, after the general elections that will take place in October of that year.

The probability that an aggravation of the crisis may force the current government to turn towards rational economic policymaking, as happened after the 'Rodrigazo'[2] in 1975 or after 'hyperinflation' in 1989–90, is low because the very favourable terms of trade that Argentina has enjoyed since 2003 are expected to persist at least over the next two to three years. Therefore, the fiscal crisis may not become as acute as it became in 1975 and in 1989–90. Taxes on exports, thanks to the very favourable terms of trade, have provided, and will very likely continue to provide, extraordinary financing in order to make it possible to prevent in the short term the current fiscal-monetary situation to become completely unsustainable and explosive.

Therefore, the prediction of most independent observers is that in the next three years the Argentine economy will evolve with higher, but still non-explosive, inflation, some ups and downs in the level of economic activity that will not change the current picture of stagnation, and increasing distortive state interventions in the economy that will only widen the gap between black market and official prices, particularly in the market for foreign exchange.

Unfortunately for Argentines, the country has such high productivity in agriculture, was so efficiently capitalized during the 1990s and has benefited from such extraordinarily favourable terms of trade since 2003, that the government can hide the negative effects of its policies and postpone the time of reckoning until after the next presidential election.

It will be the responsibility of opposition leaders and influential stakeholders to help the people realize that the policies on course will eventually produce a disaster, and to put an end to the nonsense economic policies of the last decade. If they do not succeed in this endeavour, the prospects for Argentina after 2015 will be very dark.

On the other side, the abundance of natural and human resources ready to be put into action with good economic policies as soon as a new government tells the people the truth about the economic situation, offers opportunities that not many countries around the world actually have.

Resource abundance may therefore be a blessing or a curse depending on the ability and honesty of the new leadership that will very likely emerge from the electoral process of 2015.

History usually provides some insights on how the dice are loaded. So, let's turn to the intriguing history of the last 100 years.

A century of economic frustrations

During the first wave of globalization that came to an end with the eruption of the First World War, Argentina was one of the most successful emerging economies of the time. The political system worked according to the rules of the National Constitution enacted in 1853 and accepted by the Province of Buenos Aires in 1860. Between 1870 and 1913 the Argentine economy grew faster than that of the USA, Canada, Australia, New Zealand and Brazil, five countries that, like Argentina, are well endowed with natural resources and attracted large inflows of capital and immigrants from Europe. This period is known as the 'golden age' of the Argentine economy. However, the history of the 100 years that have elapsed since 1914 is very different.

The traumatic inter-war period, 1913–45

In common with most of the countries that were actively engaged in international trade and finance, Argentina suffered from the numerous shocks that emerged after the First World War, the European hyperinflation of the 1920s, the Great Depression of the 1930s and the Second World War.

Exports increased during the wars thanks to the neutrality of the country, but difficulties with importing intermediate inputs and capital goods affected growth from the supply side. The Great Depression reduced demand for exports and deteriorated the terms of trade.

Economic adversity fuelled corporate defensive attitudes of increasingly organized interest groups. Democratic institutions were weakened and corporations, including the armed forces, captured increasing political power.

Table 17.1 Rates of growth of GDP per capita, 1870–2012

Period	The golden age, 1870–1913	The traumatic inter-war period, 1913–45	From the first to the third presidency of Perón, 1945–75	Stagflation and hyperinflation, 1975–90	Stability and growth, deflation and counter-reform, 1990–2012
Argentina	2.5	0.4	2.1	−1.5	2.7
Australia	1.1	0.9	2.2	1.8	2.0
Brazil	0.3	1.7	3.7	1.1	1.5
Canada	2.3	1.5	2.3	1.9	1.3
New Zealand	1.2	0.9	2.0	0.6	1.4
USA	1.8	2.5	1.1	2.4	1.4
World	1.3	0.9	2.3	1.5	1.9

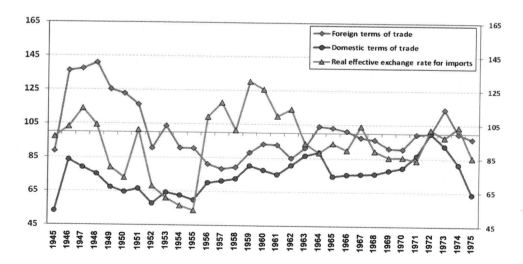

Figure 17.1 Domestic and foreign terms of trade and the RER: 1945/1975

Argentina's present and economic history

In 1930 Argentina suffered the country's first military coup and during the rest of the period the governments were either military or civilians elected in rigged elections. In 1943 a second military coup took place.

From the first to the third presidency of Juan Domingo Perón, 1945–75

After being a prominent member of the military government that seized power in 1943, Perón was democratically elected as president in 1946, defeating a broad coalition of political parties that was organized around the Radical Party and included the conservatives, socialists and communists.

From the very beginning of his ascent to power, Perón saw the encouragement of labour-intensive manufacturing, construction and domestic services as a way to shift the functional distribution of income away from capital/land-intensive agriculture in favour of urban workers. The instruments to implement this strategy were multiple exchange rates, high import duties and quantitative restrictions to imports that could potentially be locally produced, and implicit or explicit taxes on exports of agricultural goods.

In practice it was the continuity of the import substitution growth strategy that during the Second World War was an ad hoc consequence of the short external supply of manufactured goods, but after the end of the war and even when world markets for most products started to normalize and very soon the high demand for agricultural exports would reverse, Perón decided to deepen this import substitution strategy as an income redistribution policy.

The trade and exchange rate policies pursued produced a significant gap between the domestic and foreign terms of trade: producers' prices for exported agricultural goods were lowered in relation to the price received by producers of import-competing manufactured goods.

The desired effects on urban real wages were brief because the policies produced the stagnation of agriculture, a drastic reduction in exports, and difficulties in financing the importation of intermediate and capital goods required for the efficient production of manufactured goods and domestic services.

As a result, expansion of industry was interrupted by supply constraints and low productivity during the early 1950s and, even when industrial expansion resumed, particularly after the commencement of foreign direct investment during the years of President Arturo Frondizi, overall growth was lower than during the golden age, lower than in Australia and Canada in the same period, and also significantly lower than in neighbouring Brazil.

In addition to the import substitution growth and redistribution strategy, Peróns government brought about a very large increase in government expenditure and fiscal deficits. In the beginning the fiscal deficits were financed by levies on wealth and past savings, but eventually they had to be financed increasingly by monetary expansion. Inflation became a persistent phenomenon, but with the exception of 1958, a year of a drastic removal of repressed inflation, inflation hovered at around 30% per year. The worst inflationary experience was still to come.

Even though both the price distortions and the high government expenditures and very large fiscal deficits of the late 1940s started to be reversed during the second presidency of Perón and even more after his removal from power, a third presidency of Perón in 1973 reinstated them.

In 1973 Perón commenced his third period as president at a time of very favourable external terms of trade, not very different from those that existed during the beginning of his first presidency. In just three years similar policies to those applied since 1945 were fully implemented:

333

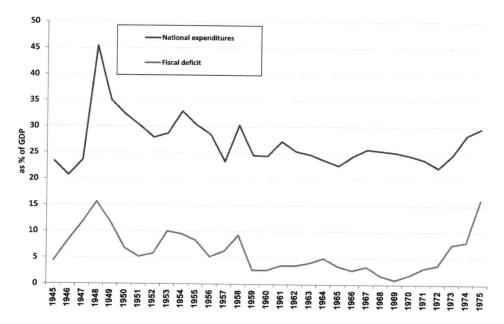

Figure 17.2 Public expenditure and fiscal deficit 1945/1975

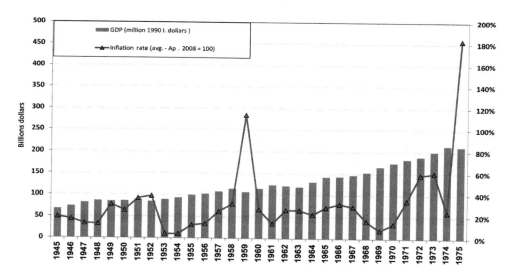

Figure 17.3 GDP and inflation 1945/1975
Source: own elaboration based on INDEC and Maddison's data

agricultural prices were heavily taxed; manufacturing, construction and domestic services were actively encouraged; public spending increased sharply and large fiscal deficits were financed by massive monetary expansion.

This time terms of trade reversed much more rapidly than in the late 1940s, and the political power of the government was much curtailed by the death of Perón and the intensification of the war between the military and the guerrillas. In that context, an attempt by María Estela

Argentina's present and economic history

('Isabelita') Martínez de Perón to reverse the policies as Perón himself had done after 1949, generated very large social conflict and ended in an inflationary explosion in June 1975.

Stagflation and hyperinflation, 1975–90

The 15 years that followed the inflationary explosion of 1975 were characterized by inflation above 100% per year and frustrated attempts to introduce partial economic reforms that failed to reverse the climate of stagnation and high inflation.

The growth performance during this period was very poor. Per capita income declined at a rate of 1.5% per annum while the world expanded at a rate of 1.5% per year. By the end of this period the Argentine economy ran into hyperinflation. Between March 1989 and March 1990 the rate of inflation reached 11,000%.

Stability and growth, deflation and counter-reform, 1990–2012

The traumatic experience of 1975–90 created the political conditions for a complete reorganization of the economy: an ambitious economic reform that pursued a full integration of Argentina into the global economy framed by a monetary system very similar to that of the initial decades of the 20th century.

During the first quarter of 1991 the Argentine government passed the Convertibility Law, which created a new monetary system based on the peso, convertible one-to-one to the dollar, fully backed by foreign reserves.

At the same time taxes on agricultural exports were eliminated, import duties reduced and quantitative restrictions on imports removed. State-owned companies were privatized after competition was reinstated in the markets, whenever possible, or otherwise clear regulatory frameworks

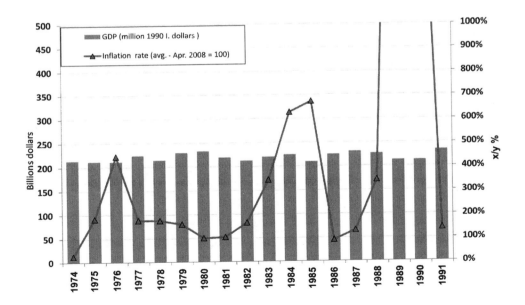

Figure 17.4 GDP and inflation 1975/1990

were set up for markets that operated under conditions of natural monopoly. Government expenditures were reduced, the tax system simplified and the fiscal deficit eliminated.

The rate of inflation was down to 3% per annum in 1994. The country enjoyed four consecutive years of rapid growth.

In 1995 a sudden stop of capital inflows derived from the crisis in Mexico generated a recession, but the International Monetary Fund (IMF) and other financial institutions, including international private banks, provided lending of last resort and the country recovered in one year without any alteration in the rules of the game. Argentina renewed rapid growth in 1996 until 1998.

As a consequence of several external shocks, particularly the devaluation of the real in February 1999, the depreciation of the euro during 1999 until mid-2002, and the recession of 2001 in the USA, the economy entered into recession in the late 1990s. With a sharp deterioration in the terms of trade and the impossibility of devaluing the currency, the recession was accompanied by deflation and created a climate of virtual depression.

From 1999 government expenditure increased as a proportion of GDP as a consequence of the recession and the increase of interest costs on the public debt, particularly that of the provinces with the local banking system. For the same reasons, revenues started to decline and the fiscal deficit began to increase. This fiscal deterioration fed another sudden stop in capital inflows.

From the last quarter of 2000 foreign capital started to leave the country and in 2001 there was a new sudden stop of capital inflows that produced illiquidity in the banking system. As the banks had lent to the provinces and these had difficulty in continuing to service their debts, several banks became insolvent and neither the central bank nor the government had the resources to help them.

The IMF, which provided some funding for a few months in 2001, decided in November to withdraw its support when the government announced an orderly restructuring of the public debt. A run on the banks forced the government to decree restriction in cashing out of bank deposits which created riots and brought about the fall of the government.

In the midst of political chaos, a new provisional government decided to abandon convertibility, transformed all financial obligations, including bank deposits, from dollars into

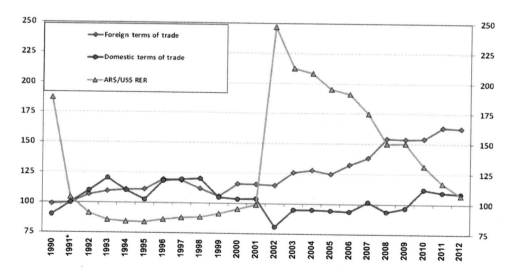

Figure 17.5 Domestic and foreign terms of trade and the RER 1990/2012

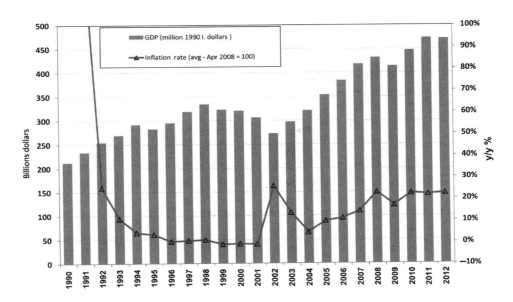

Figure 17.6 GDP and inflation 1990/2012

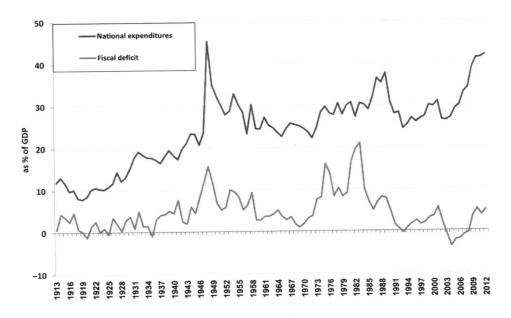

Figure 17.7 Public expenditure and fiscal deficit 1913/2012

inconvertible pesos, and the currency suffered a very large devaluation. The price of the dollar jumped from 1 peso to 4 pesos between January and September 2002. Inflation was reintroduced into the economy. In 2002 the consumer price index (CPI) increased by 42%.

Initially, the government froze wages, pensions and public utility rates, and introduced taxes on agricultural exports and price controls on beef and other items in the consumer basket.

In 2003, as foreign terms of trade started to recover and the US dollar started to weaken, the Argentine economy, which between 1998 and 2002 had suffered a 25% decline in GDP, began to recover very rapidly and the peso began to appreciate. The peso price of the dollar went down from 4 to slightly below 3, and inflation declined to 3% in 2003.

The new government, led by Néstor Kirchner, allowed wages to increase gradually in 2003 and more rapidly from 2005. Government expenditure also started to increase rapidly and in 2006 already represented the same proportion of GDP as in 2001, in spite of a sharp reduction in the interest cost of the public debt achieved after the compulsory debt restructuring of 2005.

As monetary policy targeted growth rather than inflation, the central bank intervened to stop the appreciation of the peso. From 2005, as wages started to recover, government expenditure increased at a rapid pace and, as monetary expansion was committed to preventing the appreciation of the peso, inflation started to increase again.

Inflation accelerated to 6% in 2004, 12% in 2005 and 10% in 2006, when price controls produced a temporary reduction, but it jumped to 18% in 2007 and to 24% in 2008. The government, instead of using monetary policy as an anti-inflationary tool, decided to cheat with the official measurement of inflation, which from 2007 was fixed (by data manipulation) at around 8% per annum.

The economy continued to grow quickly, except during 2009, when the global recession and a conflict with the farmers produced a recession interval. The growth was pushed by very favourable external terms of trade and large fiscal and monetary stimulus for domestic demand.

The intervention of the government in the markets, the restrictions to foreign trade, the freezing of public utility rates, the renationalization of public utility companies and the large increase in government expenditure and tax pressure constituted in practice a counter-reform of the economy in comparison with the reform of the 1990s.

Even so, the period 1990–2012 displayed a rate of growth of per capita GDP even higher than that of the golden age. The Achilles heel of the Argentine economy is not only inflation, which again has become a persistent phenomenon, but also the many relative price distortions that are discouraging efficient investment and instead encouraging capital flight, land speculation and inefficient real estate investment.

By 2012 stagflation had become the new reality and, as described in the first part of this chapter, the prospects are that stagflation may last for several years before new political conditions permit the resumption of the rules of the game that during the 1990s made Argentina the poster child of emerging economies.

Notes

1 With the collaboration of Mariano Giachetti.
2 A drastic change in the price level provoked by a simultaneous increase in public utility rates, the price of foreign exchange and nominal wages that inaugurated a period of much higher inflation.

18

Viet Nam

Martin Rama[1]

An extraordinary journey

At the end of the American war Viet Nam was a country with a dilapidated infrastructure and two dysfunctional and disconnected economies. In the north, decades of central planning had led to very low productivity and generalized shortages. In the south, collectivization had brought to a standstill the once dynamic but chaotic market economy supported by the US war machinery. A decade later, at the beginning of the renovation process (*Doi Moi*), Viet Nam was one of the poorest countries in the world, often on the edge of famine. Four years after the transition to a market economy had started income per capita was below US$100 in current terms, and total exports of goods and services barely reached $1 billion in current terms. Precise estimates are not available, but close to 90% of the population might have lived on less than $1 a day in purchasing power parity (PPP) terms back then.

Today, Viet Nam is a middle-income country. It may not be growing as quickly as it did during the first two decades after *Doi Moi*, but its income per capita has reached $1,600 in current terms. Based on recent trends, less than 10% of the population lives on less than $1 a day in PPP terms, and social indicators are comparable to those of high middle-income countries. Infant mortality, for instance, dropped from 40 per 1,000 children under the age of one in 1986, to 14 by 2010. The country has become a magnet for foreign direct investment (FDI), receiving inflows accounting for 8% of its gross domestic product (GDP) on average over the last six years. Exports of goods and services reached $127 billion in current terms in 2012. Viet Nam is an agricultural powerhouse and a large exporter of garments and shoes; it is rapidly moving into the production of electronics. The speed of this transformation is remarkable: while in 2002 Viet Nam was still included in the list of highly indebted poor countries (HIPC), in 2010 it was already borrowing from the International Bank of Reconstruction and Development (IBRD), a sign of international creditworthiness.

At the same time, Viet Nam remains one of only five nominally communist countries in the world, together with the People's Republic of China, Cuba, Laos and the Democratic People's Republic of Korea (North Korea). While more open in terms of public debate and internet access than the other countries in the group, it is a one-party system where dissent is not tolerated beyond what is seen as safe limits, and crackdowns on bloggers, journalists and certain religious groups remain common. While it is clearly a market economy, the authorities insist on its 'socialist orientation'. Government spending accounts for almost one-third of GDP, more than in most developing countries. The number of state-owned enterprises (SOEs) has declined steadily, and most of them operate on a commercial basis, but increasingly powerful 'economic groups' inspired by the *chaebol* (conglomerates) of the Republic of Korea (South Korea) are state owned and controlled. Although private publishing houses are gradually developing, there are no privately-owned media in TV and broadcasting.

Which of these two countries is the real Viet Nam? The answer is: both. This explains many of the specific traits of the country's performance since the beginning of its transition. The tension between these two apparently incompatible systems is also important to understand the prospects and the challenges ahead. The country's 'socialist orientation' is often dismissed as irrelevant lip service to an old ideology, but that would be a mistake as this orientation shapes its governance and influences important aspects of its economic policies. Viet Nam is also described as China with a 10-year lag, but that is not correct either, as the same nominally communist structures function in different ways in the two countries. Viet Nam's development experience is more unique than it may seem at a first glance, and that also makes its prospects different from those of other emerging economies.

The path to prosperity

The economic transformation experienced by Viet Nam over these three decades has much in common with that observed in other successful East Asian countries. Growth accelerated as smallholder agriculture became more productive, supporting the development of off-farm rural employment and the gradual migration of household members to towns and cities. In line with the 'flying geese' pattern initiated by Japan, light manufacturing activities previously performed by other countries in the region migrated to lower-cost Viet Nam. In the process, cities developed and the services sector expanded. At first, much of the urban economic activity was associated with either SOEs or household businesses, but gradually the private sector developed and wage employment, formal or informal, became much more prevalent.

Structural change

Reasonably reliable national account figures for Viet Nam are only available since the late 1980s. Back then, agricultural output represented 46% of GDP; by now, it only accounts for 21% (see Figure 18.1). For some time, productivity gains in farming were so large that the output share of the sector barely declined, in spite of urban-rural migration. As in other countries, the flip side of the decline of the agricultural share of GDP was a steady growth in the share of services. However, what distinguishes Viet Nam from other developing countries is the rapid growth of manufacturing output, from 12% of GDP in 1990 to 21% in 2005 and currently still 19%. While the services sector keeps growing, the share of manufacturing in Viet Nam's GDP is high by international standards.

The transformation of agriculture was nothing short of miraculous. In the 1980s the country was at the edge of famine, with rice—the country's basic staple—being a desperately scarce commodity. Since the 1990s Viet Nam has been alternating with India as the second world exporter of rice, measured in tons, and it could overtake Thailand as the top exporter in 2013. Coffee production had been disrupted by the American war and was negligible after reunification, but one decade after *Doi Moi* Viet Nam displaced Indonesia to become the second world exporter, and it overtook Brazil as the top exporter in 2012. Success in food production happened across the board. Today, Viet Nam is the largest exporter of black pepper and cashew

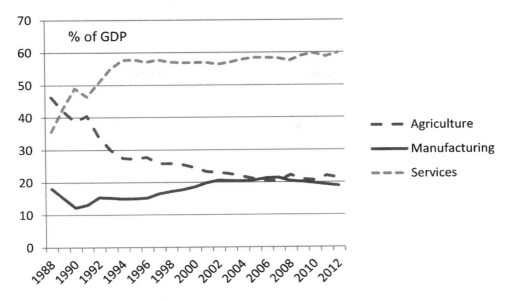

Figure 18.1 Rapid structural change
Source: World Bank (2013)

nuts, both relatively unimportant products at the beginning of the economic transition. The story is similar with aquaculture, with Viet Nam now occupying fourth place in the global rankings among exporters of fish and fishery products.

In manufacturing, the initial phases of development were concentrated in garments and footwear, with thousands of firms—mainly a combination of East Asian foreign investors and Vietnamese SOEs—serving orders from the likes of Target and Macy's in the USA. At some point, several of the major producers of sports footwear, such as Adidas and Nike, were indirectly employing more than 60,000 Vietnamese workers each. However, the transition to higher value-added products did not take long. In 2010, when Viet Nam's per capita GDP was barely $1,200 in current terms, Intel opened its biggest chip-making plant world-wide in Ho Chi Minh City. Canon and Panasonic are producing a large share of their global supply of printers in Hanoi's outskirts. As of 2012 hi-tech products accounted for 17% of total exports, up from 5% in 2007. This trend is bound to continue, as shown by Samsung's case, which had first set its eyes on Viet Nam to produce low-end mobile phones, but is now shifting to the production of tablets. By 2017 its annual exports are expected to exceed $30 billion.

The dramatic growth of agricultural and manufacturing exports has transformed Viet Nam into one of the most globally integrated economies. In 1988 foreign trade represented less than 20% of GDP. As of 2012 it had attained 180% (see Figure 18.2). This figure puts Viet Nam in the same league as countries such as Malaysia or the Netherlands, except that their population is much smaller. No other country with a population of a comparable size is as open as Viet Nam.

The transformation of the services sector was less dramatic, but not less real. At the beginning of the transition, there were five state-owned commercial banks (SOCBs) in Viet Nam, and they were all more or less crippled by non-performing loans (NPLs) to SOEs. At present, there are 27 commercial banks, of which five are fully foreign-owned. Three of the SOCBs have been partially privatized, all of them with a strategic foreign partner. The share of state capital in the banking system declined from 87% in 2005 to 34% in 2010. Banking credit reached 136%

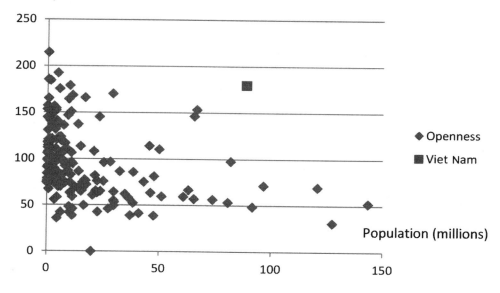

Figure 18.2 A globally integrated economy
Source: World Bank (2013)

of GDP in 2010, compared to 35% a decade earlier. Stock market capitalization, a meagre 1% of GDP in 2005, hovers now at around 23%. More striking perhaps is the growth of the information technology (IT) sector. Led by FPT a genuine start-up, Hanoi alone exported $2.3 billion in software in 2012.

More jobs, new jobs

This transformation did not happen by accident. With a vast majority of the population living in rural areas, and with the traditional power base of the Communist Party being in the villages, focusing on agricultural productivity was a necessity when the reform process started, despite the Party's industrializing amibitions. However, ever since decision makers in Viet Nam have had an almost obsessive focus on job creation. This was not only due to a socialist ideology attaching a high importance to productive work. Labour force participation rates in Viet Nam are among the highest in the world; at 77%, they are remarkably high in the case of women. This makes the creation of gainful employment opportunities critical to meet the expectations of the population—even more so in a country facing a massive youth bulge, where the median age of the population is 27 years.

As a result of substantial gains in education and health, and also due to the two-child policy applying to civil servants and SOE workers, the fertility rate of Viet Nam plummeted, from five children per woman in 1984 to two in 1996. The country was thus confronted with one of the fastest demographic transitions ever. Down the road, this transition raises the spectre of a rapidly ageing society, but for the last three decades it has resulted in the entrance of roughly 1.7 million young people into the workforce every year. Smallholder farming had the virtue of being labour-intensive, but soon after massive numbers of additional jobs needed to be created in cities. While the services sector is labour-intensive too, it is characterized by self-employment and family work in activities with low productivity. Labour-intensive manufacturing, on the other hand, opened a faster way to the development of wage employment.

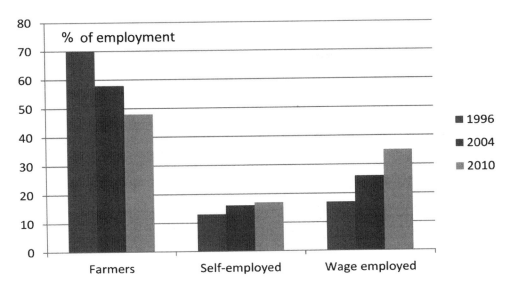

Figure 18.3 From farmers to wage earners
Source: World Bank (2013)

In the mid-1990s 61% of the people at work were farmers. Today, the proportion has fallen to less than half. With economic reforms, self-employment and work in household businesses became more prevalent. Their growth was especially fast in the initial phases of economic transition. However, wage employment in the private sector soon picked up, accounting at present for roughly one-quarter of total employment.

This change in the composition of employment was facilitated by a high degree of labour market flexibility. Barriers to geographical mobility are lower than in China. Rural-urban migrants do not carry with them all the entitlements to services they had in their villages, but access to basic health and education is granted to their children in urban areas, and more advanced education and health services are often not available in the villages anyway. Labour regulations are relatively rigid on paper, and compliance with labour standards is higher than in other countries specialized in exporting products from light manufacturing, such as Bangladesh or Cambodia. However, there is quite a lot of flexibility in practice, especially through the use of contract labour by firms, and the extensive reliance on overtime work as an important part of labour earnings. The global financial crisis revealed that flexibility (Cling *et al.* 2011). With its strong export orientation, Viet Nam was a natural candidate for massive job losses in manufacturing. Instead, workers accepted large wage cuts. The urban unemployment rate only climbed from 4.3% of the labour force in 2007 to 6.5% in 2009, and declined rapidly afterwards.

The change in the composition of employment has been accompanied by a rapid change in the skills mix of the workforce. In the decades after *Doi Moi* Viet Nam moved rapidly in the direction of attaining full primary education coverage and expanding the coverage of secondary education. By 2011 gross enrolment rates in secondary education had reached 77%. Over the last few years, the emphasis has shifted to the expansion of pre-school coverage to four-year-olds and tertiary education reform. Universities used to be public and struggled with governance issues similar to those faced by SOEs. The reform aims at setting standards for all universities, public or private, and at supporting the emergence of four model universities from industrial countries. Progress in addressing the governance issues faced by public universities has been more limited. Nevertheless, in 2011 the gross enrolment rate in tertiary education had reached 24%.

The combination of the change in the composition of employment and the change in the skills mix of the workforce resulted in a rapid growth of labour earnings. Strict comparisons over time are difficult, because the individual earnings of farmers, the self-employed and workers in household business cannot be measured precisely. Based on data from household surveys, the average growth in individual labour earnings, in real terms, was close to 10% per year. Wages remain low by international standards, as a worker in a light manufacturing industry typically earns less than $150 per month, and that is with heavy overtime.

The emergence of a middle class

Riding on high labour force participation rates, low unemployment rates and rapidly growing labour earnings, Viet Nam experienced one of the fastest poverty reductions ever documented (Glewwe et al. 2004). Using an internationally comparable poverty line, set at $1.25 per day PPP, the poverty rate fell from an estimated 63.7% of the population in 1993 to 16.7% by 2008 (see Figure 18.4). This is a decline of 3.13 percentage points per year, which compares favourably with the 2.82 percentage-point decline experienced by China between 1981 and 2005 (Ravallion 2011). Poverty is increasingly concentrated among ethnic minority populations, especially in the central highlands and the south-central coast, where it touches more than three-quarters of the population. Urban poverty, on the other hand, has fallen to 6%. While this figure may be an underestimate, due to the difficulty of household expenditure surveys adequately covering rural-urban migrants, extreme poverty is clearly on the way to being eradicated in cities and in the two deltas where most of the population lives.

The case of ethnic minorities, and especially of those living in the central highlands, is different (Baulch et al. 2010). The 54 officially recognized ethnic groups of Viet Nam represent

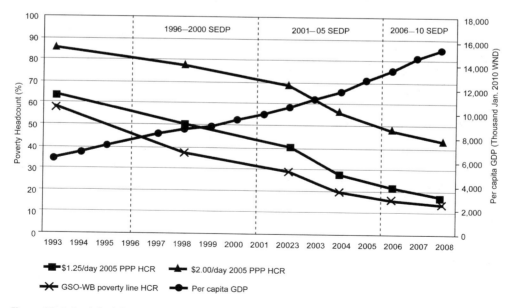

Figure 18.4 Rapidly falling poverty
Source: World Bank (2012)

14.3% of the population, but account by now for nearly half of the poor and more than two-thirds of the extreme poor. This is not for lack of government attention to their fate. Gradually the education levels and access to services by minorities are catching up with those of the *Kinh* and *Hoa* (Chinese) majority, and some minority households in the lowlands (such as the *Dao*) are increasingly indistinguishable, from a consumption point of view, from majority households. Even in the northern mountains, from where the Party led the independence struggle against the French colonial regime, minorities have experienced strong gains in living standards. However, those in the central highlands face a greater level of social exclusion, perhaps a legacy of their support for the southern regime during the American war. The spectacular development of coffee production and other crops was associated with the conversion of the forest land to agricultural land. This conversion was accomplished through a massive state-led relocation of *Kinh* people and northern minority groups to the area, depriving locals of the commons on which they used to live (Bayrak *et al.* 2013). Cultural and language barriers also make the integration of these groups more difficult (Nguyen *et al.* 2012).

By now, about two thirds of the population lives on more than $2 a day PPP. The social progress accomplished since *Doi Moi* extends beyond gains in private consumption, as it is also reflected in strong improvements in human development indicators. The literacy rate among the adult population was 93% in 2010. Life expectancy at birth has reached 73 years for men and 77 for women, comparable to industrial countries. Gains in life expectancy are associated with better health outcomes, as the country successfully navigated its epidemiological transition. By 2010 three-quarters of all deaths were due to non-communicable causes such as cardiovascular diseases and traffic accidents, a pattern observed in more affluent societies. With a lag, the progress in access to education and health services is similar in the case of ethnic minorities (Swinkels and Turk 2006).

Motorbikes may be the most visible indicator of this social transformation. Confronted with dramatic infrastructure shortages, the government encouraged the local production of motorbikes as the easiest way to connect people to markets. By 2007 more than two million new units were being sold every year, and there was one registered motorbike for every five inhabitants. Models are becoming increasingly fancy and expensive, and a growing share of the population is now shifting to cars—an unambiguous sign of prosperity. While earnings may still be low by international standards, a large fraction of the population has the traits associated with middle classes elsewhere. Many in this group are urban wage earners, a growing number of them have access to financial instruments such as bank accounts and credit cards, and they are increasingly covered by formal social protection systems such as health insurance and old-age pension programmes.

This group also belongs to the modern world in other ways. Viet Nam experienced one of the fastest penetrations of telecommunications in the world, and its government put emphasis on internet access as a priority. As of 2012, there were more than 36 million internet users, representing roughly 40% of the population (International Telecommunications Union 2013). This share is three times higher than in India, which has a similar income per capita and is a global powerhouse in information technology. It is close to that of China, whose income per capita is three times higher than Viet Nam's. Given the relatively limited censorship of internet content, the Vietnamese middle class is more exposed to global views and debates than that of many developing countries.

Leadership and vision

It is easy to be disappointed by Viet Nam's recent growth slowdown, or by its government's reluctance to reform the state sector thoroughly, or by the crackdowns on dissidents and journalists (Hayton 2008), but it would be short-sighted to ignore the country's remarkable accomplishments. The period of adherence to central planning principles was brief compared to other countries in the then communist bloc: *Doi Moi* happened less than a decade after reunification, and a full five years before the collapse of the USSR. The economic transformation that followed was almost as rapid as China's, but it was considerably more inclusive from a social point of view. Over the years after *Doi Moi*, Viet Nam avoided the collapse in economic activity suffered by countries in the former USSR and the increase in inequality experienced by China. The obvious question is: how did it happen?

From war to Doi Moi

At the time of reunification there was a clear consensus among the country's senior leaders that the planned economy model was superior, as had been made evident by Viet Nam's military defeat of much stronger 'capitalist' powers. The possibility of keeping the economic model of the south, even on a temporary basis, was not seriously entertained. Central planning carried respect as the tool that had taken Russia's backward agrarian economy all the way to space conquest in barely four decades. In Viet Nam, its deficiencies had been masked by the massive assistance from the USSR during the American war. All this resulted in an almost unconditional consensus on the need for state or collective ownership, administrative prices and Party leadership.

With such an assertive state of mind, the period that followed reunification was in many ways brutal. This was the time when the name of the Party was changed from Labour to Communist, and the name of the country from Democratic to Socialist Republic. While building on the experience of other countries in the Soviet bloc, a Vietnamese version of the planned economy model was adopted. This version was an attempt to industrialize agriculture rapidly, through collectivization, infrastructure investment and machinery. The operation of this model, in turn, required a minimum scale, which districts alone were supposed to provide. This version of the planned economy came to be known as 'the district as a fortress'.

Less than a decade later, the country was on the brink of economic collapse. Production grew more slowly than the population, leading to a decline in living standards even compared to the harsh war period. Tension with China led Viet Nam to join the Council for Mutual Economic Assistance (Comecon) bloc in 1978, a decision it had hesitated to make for two decades. This resulted in much higher prices for imports than before, when domestic prices from the USSR applied to goods shipped to Viet Nam. The inadequacy of the planned economy model became more evident in the south, where reunification was associated with a dramatic change in the organization of the economy. Food shortages emerged, pushing Viet Nam close to famine. In the late 1970s massive numbers of people fled the country, at risk of their lives. By then material and spiritual conditions had become unbearable.

Confronted with this economic reality and the ensuing population discontent, a set of local leaders took on changing the course of events. They initially did so through initiatives known as 'fence-breaking' experiments. What these initiatives had in common was their reliance on market mechanisms. The local leaders behind them were desperately seeking approaches that would work, and to understand why they worked. The process required experimentation beyond what was allowed by the rules; sometimes dangerously so. However, these local leaders were politically 'bullet proof', given their track record during the independence struggle and the American war. Most of the fence-breaking experiments took place in the south, which is not surprising given that market mechanisms were a fresh memory there and the entrepreneurial spirit was still alive. However, fence breaking had precedent in the north, going back to 1966. What had been treated by the Party as a dangerous deviation back then, started to be seen as innovative 'unbundling' one decade later.

At the time, the Politburo had 10 members, but most of the decision-making power was concentrated in four of them. Having an open discussion on the fence-breaking experiments with the Politburo would have been self-defeating for these local leaders, as even the reform-minded members would not have dared to support them. Instead, the local leaders identified the mechanisms at work in each of the experiments and targeted the key Politburo members who would be more interested in learning about them. Those members were approached on an individual basis, and invited to see first-hand the experiment selected for demonstration purposes. By the time the support of the four key Politburo members had been secured, larger-scale economic reform was in hand, without having to resort to wasteful fights, purges or internal coups. The local leaders responsible for the fence-breaking experiments were invited to take on bigger responsibilities, and led the *Doi Moi* process (Rama 2008).

The China factor

A commonly held view has Viet Nam's reform process as an imitation of China's, with a 10-year lag. The reality is more complex. Chinese advisers to Viet Nam had played an important role after independence from France, when Maoism was highly regarded by Vietnamese leaders. However, the implementation of land reform along Chinese lines in north Viet Nam resulted in many unnecessary deaths, shocking the population and pushing President Ho Chi Minh to take distance from it. From 1956 onwards Chinese orientations such as the Great Leap Forward, people's communes or the Cultural Revolution started to be watched with concern. The Cultural Revolution, in particular, was interpreted as an attempt to suppress debate in the face of economic decline. From then onwards, the influence of the USSR on Viet Nam increased.

China's influence diminished further in the years following reunification. Deng Xiao Ping came to power in 1978 and initiated the reform process in 1979. However, this was also the year when China invaded the northern border of Viet Nam, further fuelling tension between the two countries. At that time, Vietnamese leaders regarded China's economic reforms and its modernization drive with suspicion, as the initiative of a betrayer of socialism. There was more receptiveness to the changes happening in Russia after 1985, under Mikhail Gorbachev. However, Vietnamese leaders were also sceptical about Russia's political reforms, which were seen as a source of turbulence, undermining the Party's authority and interfering with the smooth implementation of more urgent economic reforms.

If China was an important driver of economic reform in Viet Nam, it was mainly for fear that the gap in economic power between the two countries would become dangerously wide. China had occupied north Viet Nam for several centuries, followed by 1,000 years of intermittent wars. Compared to that, the struggle for independence from France and the American war were relatively brief periods. The most recent military episode in that 1,000-year conflict was the short but bloody border war of 1979, prompted by Viet Nam's military invasion of Cambodia. Closer to today, tension between the two countries remains high on the status of the Spratly Islands.

Throughout this period one constant has been that China is always the larger power and Viet Nam the smaller. Indeed, with a population of 88 million, Viet Nam ranks with a medium-sized Chinese province. While China has rarely been able to dominate Viet Nam in recent times, this asymmetry creates systemic differences in interests and perspectives between the two sides, making the smaller partner much more sensitive to the relationship than the bigger one (Womack 2006; Thayer 2010). It is telling that the most elegant streets in Hanoi's French Quarter still bear the names of heroes in the wars against China, not against France or the USA.

In spite of the fears of Chinese expansionism, Vietnamese senior leaders chose to give precedence to the benefits from economic co-operation. Their determination to 'become friends with all countries', at the time of *Doi Moi*, can be seen in this light. Before, a distinction was made between three groups of countries. Those in the socialist group, embracing 'proletarian internationalism', were siblings. Countries in the Third World group, which had in common their efforts to free themselves from colonialism, were friends. The remaining countries, capitalist and imperialist, represented the enemy; China also fell into this last group. Treating the USA and China as partners, rather than enemies, represented a major step away from confrontation, but it also became a strategic way to counterbalance these two major powers.

There was also a strong emphasis on cultivating economic relationships with Taiwan (China) and Chinese communities overseas to support the domestic reform effort. A milestone in this respect was the deal struck between the Communist Party of Ho Chi Minh City and the Kuomintang, in the early years of reform, about Saigon South. This is an area near the centre of the city that had remained under-developed before reunification because the Viet Cong was well implanted in it, which made it very dangerous. The deal granted the Kuomintang land-use rights for an unlimited period of time—something still uncommon in Viet Nam—in exchange for investment in infrastructure and productive capacity. Since then the Kuomintang today has divested its enterprises and most of the Saigon South investors are fully private, but this remains one of the most modern and wealthy areas of the country—one that is becoming the hub of modern services, from medicine to education to software.

While there is much admiration among Viet Nam's senior leaders for China's remarkable accomplishments, to this day they do not represent their main reference model. China's reforms, from the distribution of collective land to the financing of urban infrastructure, are always carefully studied and often adapted to the Vietnamese context, but they are seldom copied uncritically. Singapore and South Korea are arguably higher in Viet Nam's reference list. Lee Kwan Yew was a direct mentor of Vietnamese senior leaders, often travelling to Viet Nam after *Doi Moi* to provide guidance. Singapore's combination of market principles with a considerable degree of political control makes it particularly attractive to Vietnamese leaders. South Korea has become more of a model in recent years, as the government has tried to support the emergence of national champions in the spirit of the *chaebol*. Viet Nam has also had a strong policy engagement with the World Bank (Nguyen and Turk 2011), while China has preferred to rely on it for investment projects and analytical work.

Selection and promotion of cadres

As the experience of *Doi Moi* shows, the reform process of Viet Nam is basically a co-operative way of processing change, in which key participants go to lengths to avoid 'defeating' others, even if that entails costly compromises and slow decision making. Seeking consensus seems to be a long-rooted tradition in Viet Nam—one that some historians trace back to army chief Hung Dao, who in the 13th century urged his generals to avoid divisions in order to stand a chance of winning against the much more powerful China. Regardless of its origins, it can be argued that this tradition has also permeated the Vietnamese Communist Party. Over its history, it is difficult to pinpoint a major political purge or an episode where one Party group physically suppressed another. 'You live-I die' contests were not the rule. Vietnamese institutions encourage the construction of broader policymaking coalitions, have more competitive selection processes, and place more constraints on executive decision making than exists by way of institutions in China (Malesky *et al.* 2011).

A commonly held view interprets Viet Nam's reform process as the victory of 'reformers' over 'conservatives', but that is misleading. In such an interpretation, key decision makers stand on one or the other side of some invisible line, whereas circumstances gradually shift the balance of power in favour of the reformist camp (Gainsborough 2010). In practice it is difficult to tell who is on each side of that line. Many of Viet Nam's senior leaders were conservatives at some points in their lives and reformers at some other points. *Doi Moi* was the story of a reformist mindset gradually winning over: the conservatives were not displaced, they were convinced. Some of the same leaders who embraced the planned economy model at the time of reunification were leading the reform process by the time of *Doi Moi*.

It would also be misleading to interpret reforms at the defeat of an old northern guard by a younger business-oriented and more Western-inclined group of southerners. The key steps in the reform process were handled by local leaders without any formal Western training and with limited exposure to the outside world. The most obvious example is Vo Van Kiet, the head of the Communist Party in the south during the American war and the main champion of reform in Viet Nam. Not only did he lack any formal Western training, but as he was actively advocating further reform in recent years, he could not be considered young, even by the lenient standards of East Asian societies. A similar pattern can be found at lower levels in the hierarchy (Rama 2008).

While a centralization of power took place in the Party during the American war, the *Doi Moi* process reinstated the primacy of consensus building. After the death of Party Secretary Le Duan, centralized decision making was replaced by strong leadership without individual leaders. There was a move towards balancing the weight of different regions (north, centre and south) in the overall distribution of senior positions. Accumulation of multiple positions by the same person was not allowed. Retirement rules were strictly enforced, even if this could result in losing highly qualified individuals. From then on, in lieu of an individual, there was a team whose members were waiting for each other. In the absence of a leader whose prestige would be comparable to that of President Ho Chi Minh, the collective became the decision-making body.

With the end of the independence wars, and the failure of central planning, economic performance emerged as the single most important source of legitimacy for the Party. There is an overlap between state and Party, and the frontier between politics and administration remains muddied, but Party functions are increasingly focused on setting the vision and handling human resource management at the senior level. The primary ladder of success for cadres is a mix of educational standards, tests and performance outcomes. Promotion within the Party structure often involves testing the ability of a high-potential member to operate and deliver in a province he or she was not originally from. Implementation is the key, because officials are expected to act according to local situations rather than strictly to apply general laws and regulations. Hence much policy innovation begins as local experiments prove to be successful and are generalized (Womack 2011).

Socialism and new ideas

Consensus building was associated with a determination to avoid creating losers in the political arena. At the time of *Doi Moi*, shifting from a centrally planned economy to one relying on market mechanisms was not presented as the rejection of the 'sacred principles' of socialism, but rather as a tool for their implementation. Even today, a statue of Vladimir Lenin stands in one of Hanoi's most central squares. Agreement was reached that markets were not a capitalist invention, as they existed in previous phases of economic development.

To distinguish economic reform from the renunciation of core principles, the expression 'market economy with a socialist orientation' was coined. This may sound like a vague concept, one that can be easily dismissed as cynical lip service to old ideologies without any practical implication, but the expression may be more meaningful than it seems at first glance. The socialist orientation is generally meant to imply a stronger emphasis on equality and a bigger role for the state, compared to a 'capitalist' market economy. Arguably, this is still too general, and may fail to provide guidance on how markets should be organized in practice, yet this very vagueness might have helped to avoid potentially difficult discussions and give reassurance to those concerned about abandoning Viet Nam's political system.

In practice, the vagueness of the notion means that there is considerable openness to entertain new ideas. The question is: what makes a new idea economically interesting and politically acceptable? At the risk of simplifying, there are three main sources of innovative ideas in Viet Nam: international experience, local think tanks and experimentation on the ground. The relative importance of these sources varies depending on the circumstances, but the impact of new ideas is amplified when an effective communication channel exists with senior leaders. Such communication often involves 'bullet-proof' mediators, who can convince the highest instances of the Party without running the risk of being labelled as revisionists. For important reforms, technical soundness or attractive packaging are not enough. Senior leaders must be convinced that recommendations are based on the reality of the country, would serve its best interests and would be compatible with political stability.

In an almost paradoxical manner for a country ruled by a Communist Party, this cautious attitude and the emphasis on relevance have led to a deep sense of mistrust of anything that may look ideological, regardless of whether it is inspired by the 'sacred principles' of socialism or in economic 'first principles'. Inductive reasoning tends to be favoured over deductive approaches. Piloting new ideas and extensively discussing the outcomes is a common practice—one that represents a defensible approximation to policy evaluation. There is no scaling-up of the pilot programmes until consensus has been reached on their merits. Admittedly, this process takes time and often leads to frustration, but the Vietnamese approach to processing and accepting new ideas also reduces the risk of major policy blunders and costly policy reversals.

The key transformations

Land and agriculture

In less than one lifetime, Viet Nam radically reformed its rural economy twice, first collectivizing agriculture then de-collectivizing it. The 1988 Land Law mandated the break-up of the agricultural collectives, scheduling more than four-fifths of the country's agricultural land area for effective privatization over a relatively short period. Initially, the collectives and local cadres still set production quotas and allocated land across households for fixed periods. Farmers with a surplus were free to sell their output at market prices. What is surprising is how egalitarian this process was. The central government had little choice but to leave the allocation of land to households in the hands of local officers it could not easily control. The risk of capture by local cadres and their friends and families was thus considerable. Yet, Viet Nam's agrarian reform was done in a relatively equitable way, giving everyone within the commune roughly the same irrigated-land equivalent (Ravallion and van de Walle 2008).

While this reform was similar to China's 'household-responsibility system', introduced there in the late 1970s, Viet Nam soon went further. In 1989, a number of years before China, it allowed a private market in agricultural output. However, the most radical step came with the 1993 Land Law, which introduced official land titles and permitted land transactions for the first time since communist rule began. Land remained the property of the state, but usage rights could be legally transferred, exchanged, mortgaged and inherited. A further resolution in 1998 removed restrictions on the size of landholdings and on the hiring of agricultural labour. Economic efficiency was clearly the primary objective of these reforms.

The productivity gains and reductions in poverty associated with these reforms are undeniable. A negative relationship exists between land productivity and farm size in Viet Nam, and it is robust to differences in village-related factors such as soil quality, irrigation facilities and prices (Vu *et al.* 2012). Labour productivity is of course lower on smaller plots, and over time land concentration should increase economic efficiency, but initially the reallocation of land to households on an equitable basis substantially increased yields. Across countries, growth originating in agriculture induces income growth among the poorest segments of the population to a much larger extent than growth originating in the rest of the economy, a pattern that is confirmed in Viet Nam's case (de Janvry and Sadoulet 2010). While it is not possible mechanically to attribute poverty reduction to agricultural reforms, it is telling that Viet Nam's poverty rate plummeted in the following years (Benjamin and Brandt 2004). A connection can also be established between these reforms and the subsequent decline in child labour (Edmonds and Turk 2002).

One concern was whether freeing-up land markets, in a context in which other markets were still heavily distorted, could lead to distressed land sales, growing landlessness and the emergence of a group of poor rural labourers. Nowadays there are rising signs of rural land-lessness, especially in the Mekong Delta, where de-collectivization often involved returning the land to previous owners rather than distributing it evenly across households. The question is whether the introduction of a land market results from distress sales, or rather from farmers selling their land to pursue more rewarding activities. The evidence so far seems to support the second hypothesis, implying that the process of land concentration is a positive force towards greater efficiency, but the process entails both gainers and losers, including among the poor (Ravallion and van de Walle 2008).

Global integration

Becoming friends with all countries, one of the mottos of *Doi Moi*, also had economic impli-cations. In 1990, four years into the reform political process, a resolution was passed to seek integration in the global economy. This resolution led to the renewal of relationships with the World Bank and the International Monetary Fund (IMF) on an unofficial basis in 1993, and to joining these two organizations and the Association of Southeast Asian Nations (ASEAN) in 1995. Importantly, it led to steps to bring the US embargo to an end and to open-up trade ties with other nations, but the most important milestones in the process were the bilateral trade agree-ment (BTA) with the USA and the accession to the World Trade Organization (WTO). Talks towards the BTA opened in 1995 and were completed in 2000. The application to the WTO was made in 1994, but Viet Nam only became serious about it in 2003; from that point onwards accession only took four additional years. While Viet Nam entered the WTO under a 'non-market economy' status, its accession in 2007 basically completed its global integration process.

Getting there was challenging. Vietnamese senior leaders knew little about the global econ-omy, and for quite some time were approaching negotiations from a 'concessions approach', but the BTA, the most demanding agreement of that sort signed by the USA up to that point, provided an enormous learning opportunity. The BTA covered three-quarters of what was required for WTO accession, and it was from it that senior leaders learned about key principles such as most favoured nation, non-discrimination, technical barriers, anti-dumping and the like (Katz 2012). In 2003 the strategic decision was made by the Party to switch from a 'concessions approach' to a 'development approach', in which international agreements would be used to lock-in domestic reforms. The BTA and the WTO were followed by implementation plans including the promulgation of an effective enterprise law, of major improvements in contract law, of new laws on financial instruments and capital markets, on revisions to tax and land laws, and an array of regulations on regulatory transparency, e-transactions, competition, bankruptcy and the like.

Global integration was unambiguously beneficial to Viet Nam. Provinces that were more exposed to tariff cuts in the USA as a result of the BTA experienced faster decreases in poverty; they also experienced faster wage growth for workers with low levels of education (McCaig 2011). Following the BTA, Viet Nam also experienced a large decline in employment in small household businesses, as workers reallocated towards larger firms. The probability of working in household businesses declined most in industries that faced the largest US tariff cuts (McCaig and Pavcnik 2011). When export markets were closed using the easy anti-dumping procedures allowed by Viet Nam's 'non-market economy status', as in the case of basa fish exports, poverty increased (Brambilla *et al.* 2012). FDI also had positive effects on the Vietnamese economy. Vertical productivity spillovers, making suppliers to foreign companies more efficient, were significant (Le and Pomfret 2011), and there were also horizontal spillovers, resulting in higher exports from domestic firms (Nguyen and Sun 2012).

Public finance

The economic reforms of Viet Nam involved a greater reliance in market mechanisms, but they also entailed a profound transformation of the way public resources were allocated and their use monitored. The most important milestone in this respect is the Law on the State Budget, passed in 2002 (World Bank 2004, 2005).

Together with other measures, this law consolidated three big shifts in power within the Vietnamese state (World Bank 2009). In the control and command economy, the key decisions were made by the Ministry of Planning and Investment (MPI), whose authority spanned not only decisions related to infrastructure, but also the allocation of public monies to SOEs. By now, the MPI retains a leading role on public investment, but the preparation and execution of the state budget is firmly in the hands of the Ministry of Finance (MOF). Just a glance at the MOF headquarters in Hanoi is enough to realize who is in command now. The second major shift in power concerns the enhanced oversight role of elected bodies, including the National Assembly and People's Councils at lower levels of government. The 2002 State Budget Law conferred the authority on the National Assembly to call ministers, and even the prime minister, to account. A sensitive vote of confidence in senior leaders, including the prime minister and the president, took place for the first time ever in 2013, and its outcome could not be taken for granted. The third shift concerns the growing role of the State Audit of Viet Nam, a technically independent and increasingly assertive agency that reports directly to the National Assembly.

In parallel, a considerable dose of power was devolved to the provinces. Nation-wide programmes and mandates were established, but their implementation was left in the hands of local authorities, which could also mobilize additional resources in their support. Taxation and decisions related to public debt were left in the hands of the central government, but clear formulas were introduced to allocate resources to provinces across sectors and programmes. They resulted in a massive transfer from rich to poor provinces: cities such as Hanoi and Ho Chi Minh City retain only one-quarter of their tax revenue, whereas poor provinces such as Phan Thiet fund up to three-quarters of their budget from central funds (World Bank 2004). This arrangement is arguably one of the main reasons why broad indexes of inequality, such as the Gini coefficient, have remained constant despite very rapid economic growth.

Competition between provinces to boost economic activity and attract FDI ended up being one of the major drivers of reforms over the last decade (Tran *et al.* 2009). Allowing provinces to find their own way forward was central to Viet Nam's economic development. Ever since the run up to *Doi Moi* experimentation at the provincial level has allowed dramatic turn-arounds, but the approach was institutionalized by the State Budget Law of 2002. This is how Danang could use its privileged coastal resources and the availability of land from the former US air base to undertake a complete urban renewal, focused on a green image. One-third of the population had to change housing over a period of eight years to allow the retrofitting of social services and modern urban infrastructure, including by now fibre optic cabling. The city has become a magnet for high-end tourism and modern services, and has the third highest income per capita in the country.

Danang may be one of Viet Nam's most successful provinces, but it is not an exception. Across all of Viet Nam, measures strengthening the investment climate at the provincial level are correlated with performance indicators at the firm level (Malesky and Taussig 2009; Tran *et al.* 2009). There is also evidence to suggest that in those provinces that are making most progress in economic reform the private sector played an important role. Not against government but with government. There was no formal public-private coalition but the dynamic was one of proactive government seeking input from the private sector, and the latter lobbying for and contributing to responsive and effective government (Schmitz *et al.* 2012).

If anything, it can be argued that decentralization has gone too far in Viet Nam. The median province size is too small to make it the optimal constituency to decide about major infra-structure projects or skills policies. Too many coastal provinces end up wanting to develop their own deep-sea ports, whereas regional universities have become fragmented as participating provinces have chosen to retake their part. Local elected bodies also lack the technical capacity to conduct their oversight role in an effective way. Viet Nam has started a recentralization process, by piloting a removal of elected People's Councils in 93 districts throughout the country, stratifying the selection by region, type of province and urban versus rural settings. So far recentralization has significantly improved public service delivery, from quality of roads to health care to agricultural extension. More surprisingly, perhaps, it has improved the quality of governance as measured by the amount of corruption experienced by Vietnamese citizens (Malesky *et al.* 2012).

Private sector development

Letting the private sector grow on the sides of the dominant state sector was another key ingredient of the reform process. Lump-sum separation packages provided in the early 1990s to 1.1 million redundant SOE workers allowed many of them to start their own household businesses. Back then a high degree of informality was compatible with the burgeoning of private initiative. Subsequently, the Enterprise Law of 1999 made it possible for hundreds of thousands of micro- and small enterprises to formally register. Vietnam may not be a star in Doing Business ratings, but a policy environment that was conducive to the growth of a vibrant private sector was put in place.

An aspect of the reform process which is often criticized is the limited privatization of state assets. To some extent, this criticism is unjustified, as the land reform process of the 1990s was one of the largest-scale privatizations ever. However, it is true that divestiture has been much less radical in the case of SOEs. The implications of this choice are less significant than in other formally planned economies, as Viet Nam never managed to go too far in the direction of capital-intensive, state-led industrialization, as did the former USSR and China. However, SOEs still control large shares of total capital, prime urban land, employment and finance, and the private sector could arguably use those resources more efficiently. Greater separation between business and policymaking could also result in lower corruption.

The Vietnamese leadership was reluctant to reform state ownership, because it was seen as the symbol of socialism, an instrument of power, and a tool to make strategic choices. This view was comforted by the experiences of China and the former USSR. While the former retained its overstaffed state sector more or less intact during the early stages of its transition to a market economy, the latter went for a shock therapy which included the mass-privatization of SOEs. In the eyes of senior Vietnamese leaders, this rushed-through process was responsible for the collapse in economic activity that followed, a collapse China successfully avoided by letting the private sector grow on the sides first. Senior leaders were also concerned about the transfer of ownership to private investors at a time when no reliable price discovery mechanism existed for state assets. In their eyes, the potential cost from corruption in the privatization of SOEs was greater than that associated with their production inefficiency (Rama 2008).

The Vietnamese approach to SOE reform favoured strengthened incentives over changes in ownership. SOEs were gradually allowed to make their own production and investment decisions, instead of following plan instructions (Fforde and de Vylder 1996). The rules governing employment and pay were progressively disconnected from those applying to civil servants. Directed credit from financial institutions was abolished, which resulted in a harder budget constraint. A generous separation package was introduced to facilitate employment restructuring (Rama 2002). Partnering up with foreign investors also brought in more advanced managerial practices. Indeed, in the earlier phases of economic transition, when many of the institutions of a market economy were still incipient, green field FDI projects were rare. Having an SOE as a partner, on the other hand, ensured some protection against the unknowns of one of the frontier outposts of economic development. This is how Vinatex, an umbrella corporation for SOEs in the textile sector, became a major exporter of garments (Rup and Rodie 2012).

A similar approach was applied in the services sector. For instance, in 2005 the decision was made to bring in strategic investors to all SOCBs, a transformation that is still under way. However, the most remarkable illustration of this approach concerns telecommunications. The liberalization of this sector started in 1993, when Mobiphone was established as an SOE, out of what was until then a government administration. By 1995 Vinaphone, a second SOE, had been established as a competitor to Mobiphone. Gradually, the number of players was expanded, and private participation in the capital of the SOEs was allowed. While the sector remains overwhelmingly state owned, fierce competition between these multiple players resulted in the fastest rate of penetration of telecommunications in the world.

While the focus has been on strengthening incentives, rather than reducing ownership, the relative size of the state sector has fallen steadily over the years. There were roughly 12,000 SOEs when the reform started. About half of them were closed, in the early 1990s, when the collapse of the USSR resulted in a major economic crisis in Viet Nam. Since then, their number has continued declining, as shares were given to the workers first, then auctioned, then made available through initial public offerings. Today there are about 1,300 enterprises that are 100% state owned, and a similar number where the state has a controlling share of the capital (World Bank 2011). SOEs contribute about 27% of GDP, and absorb 18% of banking credit (compared to 44% in 2000).

Urbanization

Based on the share of the population living in cities, Viet Nam remains an agrarian country. However, the statistics are somewhat misleading, as there is a continuum between urban and rural areas, and a substantial part of this fringe is officially classified as rural, even if its economy is very much connected to that of nearby cities. The urban population of Viet Nam is actually growing rapidly, perhaps by 3.4% per year. Urbanization has been in many ways successful.

Major cities, including Ho Chi Minh City, Hanoi and Danang, are poles of economic dynamism (World Bank 2012a). Ho Chi Minh City and its region host 45% of overall manufacturing production. Heavy and hi-tech manufacturing activity is more intense in the Hanoi region (55% and 39%, respectively), but there appears to be a strong convergence of welfare, and life has improved in smaller cities too. Claiming that Viet Nam has seen urbanization without slums would be an exaggeration, but not a very big one.

High population density contributes to successful urbanization, and indeed density in the Red River delta and the Mekong delta, where Hanoi and Ho Chi Minh City are located, is among the highest is the world. Explicit policy choices have also enhanced the agglomeration effects associated with successful cities. The infrastructure shortfall at the beginning of the transition pushed the authorities to support actively the development of the motorcycle industry, in the expectation that two-wheelers would help connect people to jobs and markets across the country. Today, Viet Nam produces two million motorcycles per year, and is home to almost 7% of the motorcycles in the world. All have four-stroke engines, to limit pollution, and cheap models sell for just a few hundred dollars apiece. The decision to engulf traditional villages in the cities' expansion, instead of razing them for urban development projects, also ensured the proximity of people and jobs. In an economy where many economic units are household-based, the lack of segregation between residential, commercial and industrial areas has allowed the informal sector to benefit from the dynamism of the modern part of the economy.

Granting land-use titles to urban dwellers has been a slow and complex process, especially in areas where overcrowding makes it difficult to determine who the 'legitimate' occupants of each dwelling are. However, informal ownership did not deter the private sector from investing heavily in housing. Creative models involving buyer financing and post-development ownership transfer were developed to support investment before a secure land title would be available, and they worked despite the shortcomings of laws, contracts and courts (Kim 2008). However, the conversion of agricultural land to urban land remains an issue. Government-set prices for reclaimed land are been gradually aligned with market prices, but the huge gap between market prices before and after urban development is at the centre of disputes on the fairness of compensation.

Heavy investment in urban infrastructure has also contributed to the dynamism of Vietnamese cities. Data from 65 utility companies show that only 12% of households in their catchment area had access to the water network in 2002, but 70% were connected by 2007. Some 67% of urban households already had a toilet in 2009, and about 96% of Vietnamese households, including almost all urban households, today have access to electricity. Congestion and limited competition in the trucking industry still result in high freight transport costs in Ho Chi Minh City, but the rapidly expanding container-handling capacity in the nearby deep-water port is creating an installed capacity that will be larger than Singapore's entire current throughput by 2015. For the first time in the country's history, this port is connecting Viet Nam with Western Europe and North America via direct ocean services (World Bank 2012a).

Social protection

During the quarter of a century since the beginning of the reforms the social policies of Viet Nam went through a radical transformation. It is perhaps in this area where the tension between the socialist ideal and market orientation turned out to be more difficult to handle. Before *Doi Moi*, the government had done a reasonably good job of providing basic health and education to everybody, even in remote villages. However, civil servants and workers in SOEs were entitled to social protection mechanisms, such as maternity leave and an old-age pension, which were not available to the rural masses. The story of reforms in the social sectors since then has turned around two main challenges. The first one is how to preserve access by the poor to health and education services as the latter are reorganized on a commercial basis (deliberately or not) and increasingly require out-of-pocket payments. The second challenge is how to build universal social protection systems in an economy that is still to a large extent rural, and where the formalization of private sector activities in urban areas is still incipient.

While most service providers in education and health remain public in Viet Nam, they increasingly started to charge user fees of different sorts (Lieberman and Wagstaff 2009). This might have been to a degree the result of a deliberate policy to strengthen incentives, as had been done in the case of SOEs. However, to a large extent the change resulted from the combination of insufficient public budgets and a more affluent population, ready to pay in order to get better services. Except that not everybody was equally affluent. To try to redress the inequalities, provinces started putting together programmes to support access by the poor to health and education services (Dang *et al.* 2007). Many of these programmes were designed in haste and their success varied, but as usual in Viet Nam, provincial experimentation provided a fertile ground to learn and scale up. Progressively, the myriad provincial programmes were consolidated under two major nation-wide umbrellas: the Hunger Eradication and Poverty Reduction Programme (HEPR) and the so-called Programme 135 for ethnic minorities and the poorest villages.

HEPR had households as its beneficiaries, while Programme 135 had villages. In both cases there was a relatively sound targeting mechanism to determine who should receive support. In the case of HEPR, local authorities 'knew' their households, and often held village assemblies to agree on who was poorest. There was unevenness across villages on the implicit poverty threshold, but within-village rankings were remarkably accurate, beating what more sophisticated proxy means-testing methods could accomplish (Nguyen and Rama 2007). Both programmes were also characterized by a limited emphasis on cash transfers to households, seen in Viet Nam as creating dependency and undermining incentives to work. HEPR allowed households classified as poor to be exempt from out-of-pocket payments in health and education (although this exemption did not apply to 'unofficial' payments). Programme 135 made resources available to local communities for investments in basic infrastructure, out of a pre-determined list including access roads, schools, health care centres, market halls and the like.

A potentially more fundamental transformation was the introduction of universal social protection systems. Key milestones in this process were the passing of a Social Insurance Law in 2006 and a Health Insurance Law in 2009. The most original feature of these two laws is their attempt to design programmes that are the same for the poor and the non-poor, or for formal and informal sector workers, but have different financing modalities. In health insurance, the premium is automatically paid for by the budget in the case of the poor, and heavily subsidized for the near-poor if they choose to enrol. Participation is mandatory for formal sector workers, on a contributory basis, and a calendar was established to extend coverage to various groups, in a compulsory way, so as to make the programme universal. In social insurance, the benefit formulas for old-age pensions are the same for formal and informal workers. Participation by the latter is still on a voluntary basis, and is unlikely to pick up without the kind of subsidization offered for health insurance, but portability is ensured by design (Castel 2008).

The challenges ahead

Stop-and-go macroeconomics

Until 2007 Viet Nam had faced few episodes of macroeconomic instability, and as a result the conduit of macroeconomic policy was seldom a matter of debate. With economic transition and the subsequent collapse of the Soviet bloc (the main market for Vietnamese exports) there was a short period of turbulence in the late 1980s and early 1990s. Consumer prices increased by more than 400% in 1986, but a dose of stability was quickly reinstated by the authorities. Also, in the aftermath of the East Asian crisis there was an economic slowdown, bringing the annual GDP growth rate down for two consecutive years. Other than that, however, stability was the rule. The budget deficit and the growth rate of domestic credit fluctuated around 5% of GDP and 30% per year, respectively. The inflation rate oscillated between 2% and 10% per year. There were no balance of payments crises and no banking crises. The authorities seemed to have the tools needed to steer the economy in the short term and much of the debate was on how to advance the reforms that would bring long-term economic growth.

Things changed when Viet Nam was in the final stages of WTO accession. By then there was a clear overheating, reflected in a construction boom, a stock price bubble and a ballooning current account deficit (Pincus *et al.* 2008). The authorities reacted with a set of tightening measures, only to be hit by the global crisis one year later. In 2008, much like China, they adopted a massive stimulus package, including a budget deficit in excess of 8% of GDP. SOEs were also encouraged to scale up their investments. The package was successful at containing the decline in economic activity, which could have been dramatic given Viet Nam's strong outward orientation, but by 2009 the balance of payments was again under stress, and international reserves had fallen below two months of imports. A tight macroeconomic policy stance, including credit growth rates close to zero at some points, followed for the next two years. As exports kept growing steadily, the level of international reserves recovered, but economic activity languished. NPLs reached dangerous levels among banks exposed to the construction sector and to small and medium-sized enterprises producing for the domestic market. In 2013 concern about slow growth and banking sector stress prompted a new phase of expansionary policies, in what seems to be a never-ending cycle of stop-and-go measures. By now, macroeconomics policies are at the centre of the debate and less attention is paid to reforms.

The prevalent explanation for this unhappy state of affairs attributes macroeconomic instability to the large size and unreformed nature of Viet Nam's state sector. In this explanation, SOEs in an investment overdrive mode generate excess demand and fuel the construction frenzy. The government emphasis on infrastructure projects only amplifies the pressure, but low investment efficiency by the public sector means that GDP growth is not commensurate with the volume of resources spent, reinforcing excess demand.

This explanation is attractive in its combination of structural forces and macroeconomic outcomes, but on closer examination it is not totally convincing. The relative size of Viet Nam's state sector was greater before WTO accession that after it. While it is true that SOEs were heavily involved in the construction sector at the end of 2006, they were basically responding to market incentives, and their overall investment was about $500 million, compared to $17 billion in capital inflows from abroad (World Bank 2008). Besides, government control over SOEs made the response to the global crisis more effective than in other countries, because it could rely on moral suasion (in addition to budget deficits) to adjust the level of aggregate demand.

A more plausible explanation for stop-and-go macroeconomics has to do with the uneven development of Viet Nam's asset markets. Domestic agents can fluidly arbitrate between dong, dollars and gold. WTO accession and the growing size and sophistication of financial intermediaries have made these transactions easier. On the other hand, only a small fraction of assets are actually traded. While the number of listed companies increased from 22 to 311 between 2003 and 2012, and stock market capitalization increased from less than 1% of GDP to 23% during the same period, the float portion remains small. Most shares are in the hands of government, former SOE employees and private business owners, not traded on the market.

Similarly with real estate: most Vietnamese households own their homes, but relatively few properties in the most valuable urban areas have the full papers needed to support commercial investments. The small float implies that portfolio adjustments have a large impact on asset prices, but changes in asset prices generate wealth effects even when the assets are not traded, and this in turn amplifies portfolio adjustments. In this context, standard macroeconomic measures may end up having disproportionately large effects on economic activity.

A country like Viet Nam may also need to accept a higher level of inflation than standard macroeconomic analysis would recommend. At the beginning of the economic transition domestic prices were extremely low in dollar terms, as reflected in a PPP factor of more than 7 in the 1990s. Two decades later, the PPP factor was roughly 3. A doubling of prices measured in dollar terms over two decades is equivalent to them increasing by around 3.5% per year. Because FDI requires a predictable economic environment, especially for firms that import large amounts of intermediate inputs to export finished products a few months later, Viet Nam is likely to continue intervening in the foreign exchange market with the goal of stabilizing the exchange rate. This means that inflation in Viet Nam should be roughly 3.5 percentage points higher than international inflation, and the gap could widen as local products move up the quality ladder. With Viet Nam being a very open economy, the impact of macroeconomic policy on the inflation rate is bound to be limited as long as the dong remains (unofficially) pegged to the dollar.

In sum, contractionary or expansionary policies may not have a large impact on the prices of goods and services, but they could greatly influence asset prices, and become a source of instability if not appropriately fine tuned. The development of asset markets should gradually reduce aggregate volatility, as it did in China over a decade ago, but in the meantime Vietnamese authorities could do better if they adapted their short-term policies to the characteristics of the economy in the aftermath of its WTO accession. Insufficient attention to the impact of macroeconomic policies on asset prices, could result in an unwarranted volatility of economic activity and exacerbate banking sector risks.

Too big to fail (and to succeed?)

The reform of the state sector remains an important policy priority on its own, regardless of the macroeconomic situation. However, the traditional discourse on the inefficiency of SOEs and their privileged access to key markets, while valid in general, may distract attention from one of the most serious challenges facing Viet Nam nowadays.

The share of resources absorbed by SOEs has declined steadily over time, as their number shrank and the private sector expanded. SOEs do remain much more capital-intensive than both domestic private firms and FDI companies, but this is mainly because of the sectors in which they operate, which include utilities. A vast majority of Viet Nam's remaining SOEs operate in competitive product markets. The share of the state sector as a whole may still be large in sectors such as textiles, chemicals or machinery, but the number of affiliates under the major SOEs in each of these sectors is large, and they tend to operate independently from each other. Meanwhile, the number of private firms and FDI companies in these sectors has grown substantially. Even in telecommunications, where the number of operators is limited, competition is fierce. Because the incentives SOEs face by now are similar to those of private enterprises, and in addition their managers are criminally liable if they incur losses, performance is acceptable. Across all the SOEs for which data are available, the average ratio of pre-tax profits to turnover increased from 5.5% to 9.5% between 2006 and 2010 and the average debt-to-equity ratio declined from 4.0 to 3.3 over the same period. As of 2012, SOEs were contributing 22% of total government revenue through tax payments, or a staggering 38% if PetroVietnam was counted as well.

Larger SOEs are more leveraged and have lower profitability, but for now it would be difficult to claim that they are basket cases. EVN is one of the best power utilities in the developing world, having extended electricity coverage from roughly half of households in the 1990s to 96% at present, and having brought commercial losses below 8%. Viettel was named the best telecoms service provider in emerging markets in 2012; today it is one of the main operators in neighbouring South-East Asian countries and it is venturing into Latin America. PetroVietnam is running exploration projects and operating oil fields in two dozen countries. The obvious bad performer, Vinashin, is so almost by design. Given its prospects to gain global market share the government allowed it to increase its leverage substantially, raising debt overseas on its behalf, but the global crisis, which resulted in several large contracts falling through, pushed Vinashin to the brink of insolvency. Since then, however, it has slashed its workforce by half and is in the process of restructuring its debts.

The really serious challenge faced by Viet Nam is not as much the drag on resources or the lack of efficiency of SOEs in general as it is the moral hazard potential created by *chaebol*, like economic groups. The performance of these very large SOEs may not be terribly bad nowadays, even when considering the Vinashin episode, but the combination of their sheer size and weak governance raises two major threats. The first is the standard 'too big to fail' problem. The public and publicly guaranteed debt of economic groups may be moderate relative to GDP, but their total debt is large and it is unlikely that the government would let them go bankrupt in the event of adverse shocks, bad investments, or a combination of the two. The drain on public resources could then be really large.

The second threat comes from the fact that economic groups are too large not only in economic terms but also in political terms. Smaller SOEs can be regulated by the relevant line ministries and government agencies as are private firms and FDI companies. Their financial reports can be overseen by the Ministry of Finance (MOF) and the exercise of state ownership rights can be allocated to a for-profit agency to avoid a conflict of interests with regulators and strengthen incentives for good performance. However, economic groups often have higher technical expertise than the ministries and agencies supposed to regulate them, and their scale and number of affiliated enterprises makes it difficult even for the MOF to grasp fully their real financial situation. Economic groups are thus a power within the state.

Current SOE reform efforts go in the direction of preventing them from investing out of their core business areas, strengthening their monitoring and assessing the appropriateness of their investment projects. Reform efforts also go in the direction of privatizing more than half of the remaining 1,300 SOEs. These are welcome moves but they will not address the moral hazard problem in the case of the larger SOEs. Upgrading the regulatory capacity of line ministries and relevant agencies, transferring the exercise of state ownership rights out of the regulators, and strengthening oversight by the MOF are key priorities at this point.

The legitimacy of wealth

Shared prosperity is perceived by the Party as one of the main foundations of its legitimacy, and a guarantee against social discontent. Shared prosperity depends on access to quality services, gainful employment opportunities and protection against adverse shocks. So far, Viet Nam has done well on all three fronts, as shown by the emergence of a solid middle class. As could be expected with the integration to the global economy, returns to skills have increased substantially, favouring those with more education, and the effects have been amplified by the ensuing changes in the composition of employment (Oostendorp and Doan 2010). Nevertheless, inequality has remained stable at relatively low levels. Not surprisingly, the Vietnamese were among the four most optimistic people in the world according to the 2010 Gallup World Poll, and among the top two in the 2012 Happy Planet Index, but there are two disturbing spots in this encouraging picture, and they are at the two ends of income distribution.

At the low end, the persistent poverty of some ethnic minority groups, and especially of those in the central highlands, is a reminder that not everybody is benefiting from growth to the same extent. Ethnic minorities are doing better than in the past, and probably much better than minorities in other countries at a similar development level. However, they do not seem to be catching up. Their hardship may not raise questions about the extent to which prosperity is really shared, though. The dominant view among the *Kinh* and *Hoa* majority is that poverty among ethnic minorities is not due to lack of opportunity but rather to their 'backward' behaviour, including not sending their children to school, not relying on modern medicine, or not working hard enough. Thus, disturbing as the situation at the low end may be, it is unlikely to alienate Viet Nam's growing middle class.

It is different with the situation at the high end. In just a few years since Viet Nam started approaching WTO accession, a small population group with staggering wealth has emerged. It includes a few billionaires (in dollar terms), and its consumption is conspicuous to an extent that is at odds with traditional Vietnamese values. The wealth of some of the members in this group comes from genuine entrepreneurship, but many simply made extraordinary gains through the up-and-down swings of asset prices, and especially of land. As prime land with full papers is scarce, and reliable information on listed firms is limited, the general perception is that only those with very good connections can have access to the best deals. As with the 'princelings' in China, this disproportionately fortunate top end is becoming a source of disenchantment among Viet Nam's growing middle class.

The standard response to a development of this sort is to scale up the fight against corruption. Many of today's industrial countries went through a period of 'robber barons' as their cities expanded and fortunes were made on land and urban infrastructure. Greater transparency in urban planning and in public procurement, stronger legal systems, citizen feedback mechanisms and a whistleblowing media can all help to contain and then reduce corruption, but the experience of today's industrial countries shows that it may take decades to get there. In the meantime, ensuring a greater stability of asset prices and taxing capital gains on land bear a greater promise to restrain the growth of extravagant wealth that is not associated with genuine entrepreneurship.

A democratic transition?

An important question is whether the need for stronger democratic accountability will become an acceptable idea, as the need for efficient market mechanisms did at the time of *Doi Moi*. The transformation process unleashed then has resulted in dramatic changes in the Vietnamese economy and society. Linkages between sectors, across borders and through finance make policy-making considerably more complex. The relationship between state and society has changed as well with the explosion in the number and diversity of stakeholders. Collecting relevant feedback and responding to it is much more difficult in light of this growing economic complexity and social diversity.

Caricaturing only slightly, when *Doi Moi* was launched, Viet Nam was a country made of rural households engaged in small-scale agriculture and urban households linked in one way or another to the public sector. Therefore, the diversity of issues and concerns faced by the Vietnamese people was limited too. Back then, the Party could not go wrong by favouring the average farmer in the deltas, or the average public sector worker in the cities, even if this approach did not work so well for ethnic minority households in the highlands. A quarter of a century later a sizeable middle class has emerged, with expectations to match. In addition to small-scale agricultural units and the public sector, there is a thriving private sector. Hundreds of thousands of enterprises have been created, whereas a sizeable minority of Vietnamese households runs a small business of one sort or another. The diversity of production and exports has also increased remarkably, with new dynamic sectors emerging one after another. Understanding the issues faced by all these groups, and addressing them properly, amounts to an enormous information-processing task, and it is not certain that Viet Nam currently has the means to do so in an effective manner.

The challenge is clearly understood by senior leaders. While there is now consensus on the need to rely on market mechanisms wherever possible, the internal debate has gradually started shifting towards the need for 'democratization', and its appropriate pace and modalities.

If the experience of *Doi Moi* is of any guidance, change is unlikely to come from external pressure or to be processed outside the Party. Back then, local developments and experimentation on the fringe of the system were critical to stimulate change, but it was the Party that transformed those local developments into larger-scale reforms. Fences were broken locally but they were dismantled centrally. The local leaders who launched this dynamic were highly placed in the Party structure, and this is one of the reasons why they were 'bullet proof'. These were mostly people who had fought in the war, had been tested for their political beliefs and were trusted by the Politburo. What these local leaders did was not subvert the order, but rather convey to higher levels in the structure the solutions they had come up with, out of their own ingenuity and that of the local population. This is why their new ideas received attention.

For Viet Nam to engage in a more determined democratic transition it will be important to find pathways giving reassurance to senior leaders that greater accountability will not come at the cost of higher instability. That may involve enhancing citizens' rights and participation while not necessarily embracing a Western multi-party political system (Womack 2011). Substantive steps have been taken in that direction already, including the shifting of increasingly large responsibilities to the National Assembly and People's Councils, as well as the emphasis on 'grassroots democracy' at the commune level. Additional initiatives could include shifting law-drafting initiative to the National Assembly, enhancing the oversight functions of People's Councils at local levels, upgrading legal aid services, allowing the direct election of city mayors, and supporting referendum initiatives at local levels.

Note

1 Chief Economist for South Asia, the World Bank. This article builds on my experience as the World Bank's Lead Economist for Viet Nam, from 2002 to 2010. It draws extensively upon the annual *Viet Nam Development Report*, the preparation of which I led from 2002 to 2009. It also builds on one year of conversations with the late Vo Van Kiet, in 2009–10, conversations that served as the basis for a paper for the Growth and Development Commission. The article also reflects rich exchanges over time with Viet Tuan Dinh, Quang Hong Doan, Duc Minh Pham, Dang Phong and Vivek Suri on economic reforms; with James Anderson, Soren Davidsen, Minh Van Nguyen and Huong Thi Lan Tran on public finance and governance; with Dang Hung Vo on urbanization; and with Nisha Agrawal, Sarah Bales, Paulette Castel, Nga Nguyet Nguyen, Thang Nguyen, Rob Swinkels and Carolyn Turk on poverty reduction and social protection. I am grateful to Yue Li for her input on the relationship between Viet Nam and China, to Paulette Castel, Quang Hong Doan and Deepak Mishra for insightful comments on a previous draft, and to Claudia Berg for her effective research assistance. While I am indebted to all of those cited above, the responsibility for the article is entirely mine. The views in it are personal, and should not be attributed to the World Bank.

Bibliography

Baulch, Bob, Hoa Thi Minh Nguyen, Phuong Thi Thu Phuong and Hung Thai Pham (2010) 'Ethnic Minority Poverty in Vietnam', *CPRC Discussion Draft*, Chronic Poverty Research Centre, London.

Bayrak, Mucahid Mustafa, Tran Nam Tu and Paul Burgers (2013) 'Restructuring Space in the Name of Development: The Socio-cultural Impact of the Forest Land Allocation Program on the Indigenous Co Tu People in Central Vietnam', *Journal of Political Ecology* 20: 37–52.

Benjamin, Dwayne and Loren Brandt (2004) 'Agriculture and Income Distribution in Rural Vietnam under Economic Reforms: A Tale of Two Regions', in Paul Glewwe, Nisha Agarwal and David Dollar (eds), *Economic Growth, Poverty and Household Welfare in Vietnam*, The World Bank, Washington, DC, 133–85.

Brambilla, Irene, Guido Porto and Alessandro Tarozzi (2012) 'Adjusting to Trade Policy: Evidence from US Antidumping Duties on Vietnamese Catfish', *Review of Economics and Statistics* 94(1): 304–19.

Castel, Paulette (2008) 'Voluntary Defined Benefit Pension System Willingness to Participate the Case of Vietnam', unpublished manuscript, available at SSRN 1379607, Hanoi.

Cling, Jean-Pierre, Mireille Razafindrakoto and Francois Roubaud (2011) 'Assessing the Potential Impact of the Global Crisis on the Labour Market and the Informal Sector in Vietnam', unpublished manuscript.

Dang, Huong Boi, Phuong Khanh Nguyen, Sarah Bales, Chen Jiaying, Henry Lucas and Malcolm Segall (2007) 'Rural Health Care in Vietnam and China: Conflict Between Market Reforms and Social Need', *International Journal of Health Services* 37(3): 555–72.

de Janvry, Alain and Elisabeth Sadoulet (2010) 'Agricultural Growth and Poverty Reduction: Additional Evidence', *World Bank Research Observer* 25(1), February: 1–20.

Edmonds, Eric V. and Carrie Turk (2002) 'Child Labor in Transition in Vietnam', Unpublished manuscript, The World Bank, Hanoi.

Fforde, Adam and Stefan de Vylder (1996) *From Plan to Market: The Economic Transition in Vietnam*, Westview Press, Boulder, CO.

Gainsborough, Martin (2010) *Vietnam: Rethinking the State*, Zed Books, London

Glewwe, Paul, Nisha Agarwal and David Dollar (eds) (2004) *Economic Growth, Poverty and Household Welfare in Vietnam*, The World Bank, Washington, DC.

Hayton, Bill (2008) *Vietnam: Rising Dragon*, Yale University Press, New Haven, CT.

International Telecommunications Union (2013) *Percentage of Individuals using the Internet 2000–2012*, Geneva.

Katz, Sherman (2012) 'Best Practices of Vietnam WTO Accession: A Case of Political Leadership', CSPC Working Paper, Center for the Study of the Presidency and Congress, Washington, DC.

Le, Hoi Quoc and Richard Pomfret (2011) 'Technology Spillovers from Foreign Direct Investment in Vietnam: Horizontal or Vertical Spillovers?' *Journal of the Asia Pacific Economy* 16(2), May: 183–201.

Lieberman, Samuel S. and Adam Wagstaff (2009) *Health Financing and Delivery in Vietnam: Looking Forward*, The World Bank, Washington, DC.

Kim, Annette Miae (2008) *Learning to be Capitalists*, Oxford University Press.

Malesky, Edmund J., Cuong Viet Nguyen and Anh Tran (2012) 'The Economic Impact of Recentralization: A Quasi-Experiment on Abolishing Elected Councils in Vietnam', unpublished manuscript, Australian National University, Canberra.

Malesky, Edmund and Markus Taussig (2009) 'Out of The Gray: The Impact of Provincial Institutions on Business Formalization in Vietnam', *Journal of East Asian Studies* 9(2): 249–90.

Malesky, Edmund, Regina Abrami and Yu Zheng (2011) 'Institutions and Inequality in Single-Party Regimes: A Comparative Analysis of Vietnam and China', *Comparative Politics* 43(4): 409–27.

McCaig, Brian (2011) 'Exporting Out of Poverty: Provincial Poverty in Vietnam and U.S. Market Access', *Journal of International Economics* 85(1), September: 102–13.

McCaig, Brian and Nina Pavcnik (2011) 'Export Markets, Household Businesses, and Formal Jobs: Evidence from the U.S.-Vietnam Bilateral Trade Agreement', unpublished manuscript, Hanoi, July.

Nguyen, Dao Thi Hong and Sizhong Sun (2012) 'FDI and Domestic Firms' Export Behaviour: Evidence from Vietnam', *Economic Papers* 31(3), September: 380–90.

Nguyen, Hoa Thi Minh, Tom Kompas, Trevor Breusch and Michael B. Ward (2012) 'Language, Mixed Communes and Infrastructure: Sources of Inequality and Ethnic Minorities in Vietnam', Working Paper 1207, Crawford School of Public Policy, Australian National University.

Nguyen, Nga Nguyet and Martin Rama (2007) 'A Comparison of Quantitative and Qualitative Poverty Targeting Methods in Vietnam', Q-Squared Working Paper No. 32.

Nguyen, Thang and Carolyn Turk (2011) 'Soft Rain Penetrates the Earth Better than a Storm: A Brief History of Government-World Bank Partnerships on Poverty Reduction in Vietnam', unpublished manuscript, Hanoi.

Oostendorp, Remco H. and Quang Hong Doan (2010) 'The Impact of Trade Liberalization on the Return to Education in Vietnam: Wage Versus Employment Effect', *Tinbergen Institute Discussion Paper*, September.

Pincus, Jonathan, Vũ Thành Tự Anh and T. Le Thuy (2008) 'Vietnam: A Tiger in Turmoil', *Far Eastern Economic Review* 171(4): 28.

Rama, Martin (2002) 'The Gender Implications of Public Sector Downsizing: The Reform Program of Vietnam', *The World Bank Research Observer* 17(2): 167–89.

——(2008) 'Making Difficult Choices: Vietnam in Transition', Growth and Development Commission Working Paper 40, The World Bank, Washington, DC.

Ravallion, Martin (2011) 'A Comparative Perspective on Poverty Reduction in Brazil, China, and India', *World Bank Research Observer* 26(1): 71–104.

Ravallion, Martin and Dominique van de Walle (2008) *Land in Transition: Reform and Poverty in Rural Vietnam*, Palgrave Macmillan and the World Bank, New York.

Rup, Jürg and Janet Bealer Rodie (2012) 'Vietnam: A Small Tiger is Growing Up', *Textile World* 162(5), September–October: 24–26.

Schmitz, Hubert, Dau Anh Tuan, Pham Thi Thu Hang and Neil McCulloch (2012) 'Who Drives Economic Reform in Vietnam's Provinces?' *IDS Research Reports* 76.

Swinkels, Rob and Carrie Turk (2006) 'Explaining Ethnic Minority Poverty in Vietnam: A Summary of Recent Trends and Current Challenges', unpublished manuscript, The World Bank, Hanoi.

Thayer, Carlyle A. (2010) 'Vietnam and Rising China: The Structural Dynamics of Mature Asymmetry', *Southeast Asian Affairs* 392–409.

Tran, Thi Bich, Quentin R. Grafton and Tom Kompas (2009) 'Institutions Matter: The Case of Vietnam', *Journal of Socio-Economics* 38(1), January: 1–12.

Vu, Thi Hoa, Tung Phung Duc and Hermann Waibel (2012) 'Farm Size and Productivity: Empirical Evidence from Rural Vietnam', unpublished manuscript, Universität Göttingen and University of Kassel-Witzenhausen, Göttingen.

Womack, Brantly (2006) *China and Vietnam: The Politics of Asymmetry*, Cambridge University Press, New York.

——(2011) 'Modernization and the Sino-Vietnamese Model', *International Journal of China Studies* 2(2), August–September: 157–75.

World Bank (2004) 'Governance', *Vietnam Development Report*, The World Bank, Hanoi.

——(2005) 'Managing Public Expenditure for Poverty Reduction and Growth. Public Expenditure Review and Integrated Fiduciary Assessment', The World Bank, Hanoi.

——(2007) 'Social Protection', *Vietnam Development Report*, The World Bank, Hanoi.

——(2008) 'Capital Matters', *Vietnam Development Report*, The World Bank, Hanoi.

——(2009) 'Modern Institutions', *Vietnam Development Report*, The World Bank, Hanoi.

——(2011) 'Market Economy for a Middle-Income Vietnam', *Vietnam Development Report*, The World Bank, Hanoi.

——(2012a) 'Vietnam Urbanization Review. Technical Assistance Report'. *Report No. 66916-VN*, The World Bank, Hanoi.

——(2012b) 'Well Begun, Not Yet Done: Vietnam's Remarkable Progress on Poverty Reduction and the Emerging Challenges', *Report No. 70798-VN*, The World Bank, Hanoi.

——(2013) *World Development Indicators*, The World Bank, Hanoi.

19

The Philippines

Road to being an emerging economy

Dante B. Canlas

Robert E. Lucas, Jr, in his *Econometrica* article entitled 'Making a Miracle',[1] used the Philippines as an example of a country that had failed to transform itself into an economic miracle. Lucas used the phrase to describe a process of productivity growth and industrial transformation associated with profound improvements in living standards of the country's population. He had in mind the transformation that at the time had been occurring in the Republic of Korea (South Korea), Taiwan, Hong Kong and Singapore in East and South-East Asia, economies that in about three decades from 1960 had witnessed a growth rate in real per capita income of 5% to 7% each year. I will refer to a country showing signs of undergoing such a transformation as an emerging economy.

About two decades later, Ruchir Sharma, in his book, *Breakout Nations: In Pursuit of the Next Economic Miracles*,[2] included the Philippines in his list of developing countries likely to become an economic miracle in the second decade of the 21st century. The main basis for inclusion in the list hinges on 'growth that surpasses expectations'. This brings to mind the so-called BRIC countries (namely, Brazil, Russia, India and the People's Republic of China), which some observers had tagged earlier as breakout nations. What did the Philippines do to merit significantly improved prospects? Is the country's real per capita income showing a tendency towards convergence—i.e. catching up with the established economic miracles?

A quick look at the recent growth performance of the Philippine economy over the past three decades, juxtaposed with two other middle-income South-East Asian economies, namely Thailand and Indonesia, may provide some insights into the positive assessment that is now evolving regarding the Philippine economy. Table 19.1 shows data taken from the World Bank's *World Development Indicators*.[3] In the 1980s the average real per capita income each year of the Philippines declined by 0.8%, compared to growth rates of 6.0% and 4.5% in Thailand and Indonesia, respectively. The Philippines recovered in the 1990s with an average annual growth rate of 0.58%. The recovery gained strength in 2001–10, growing by 2.52% each year.

In 1983 the Philippines experienced a balance of payments crisis that forced the government to declare a moratorium on foreign debt servicing. To overcome its liquidity problems, the government arranged a standby loan agreement with the International Monetary Fund (IMF). The latter's preferred financial programming techniques and conditionality lending practices anchored on tight fiscal and monetary policies resulted in a deep recession in 1984–85. Real gross domestic product (GDP) growth declined by 11% during the two-year period. The

364

The Philippines

Table 19.1 Real per capita income and average annual growth rate

Country	1980 real per capita income, y, in 2000 US$	Growth rate of y 1981–90 in %	Growth rate of y 1991–2000 in %	Growth rate of y in % 2001–10	2010 real per capita y in 2000 US$
Philippines	1,088	(0.80)	0.58	2.53	1,375
Thailand	772	6.0	3.64	3.26	2,774
Indonesia	356	4.46	3.15	3.52	1,034

Source: World Bank, *World Development Indicators*

economy recovered in 1986, and gathered strength up to 1989. However, in view of the deep recession in 1984–85, the 1980s proved to be a lost decade for the country.

Political shocks in 1990, including attempted *coups d'état* against the president of the republic and natural disasters, caused economic activities to decline in 1991. A new president was elected in 1992, but an electric power shortage in 1992–93 kept the economy weak and it did not gain strength until 1994. The growth was sustained up to 1997, despite the emergence that year of the Asian Financial Crisis that was triggered by the devaluation of Thailand's baht. The growth rate of real GDP slowed down, ending flat in 1998. A new president was elected in 1998, but lack of fiscal discipline under the new administration caused the budget deficits of the national government to balloon, which caused interest rates to rise and growth to slow down. Still, given the strength of the recovery in 1994–97, a moderate growth rate in per capita income was posted in the 1990s.

Entering the first decade of the 21st century, the economy was again battered by several shocks, economic and non-economic. In 2000 allegations of the president's involvement in an illegal numbers game led to the Philippine Senate impeaching the president, resulting in his eventual unseating in 2001. None the less, the economy posted a positive growth rate in real GDP that year. Then came the US terrorist attacks of 11 September 2001 (9/11), events that led the US government to declare a war against terrorism. That war had repercussions on the Philippine economy in view of the country's problems with Muslim rebels in its southern part. In any event, the economy proved sufficiently resilient by posting an annual average growth rate in real per capita GDP of 2.53% during the period 2001–10.

The economic growth in 2001 ushered in the longest recovery in the past few decades. Policymakers responsible for the economy have in succession managed to temper the volatility of output, keeping business fluctuations moderate. The economy dodged a recession in 2009, with real GDP managing to grow by 0.1%, in spite of the 2008 global financial crisis that was triggered by the collapse of the subprime housing loan market in the USA.

In 2010 real GDP grew by a strong 7.6%. This moderated to 3.6% in 2011. In 2012 real GDP grew by 6.6%, the highest among South-East Asian economies. Clearly, the country's growth performance has improved considerably since the 1980s. The remarkable growth performance of the economy in the past few years is one reason for the improved assessments of the country's macroeconomic performance in the future.

For a developing economy to converge or catch up with more developed ones, its real per capita income must exhibit growth on a sustained basis. To provide a quantitative tone, in a country where real per capita GDP grows by 6.9% each year, a doubling of real per capita GDP every 10 years can be expected. Several factors, both economic and non-economic, matter for growth of real per capita income in the long run.[4] Among the economic factors, it is important in the short run to avoid unwanted business fluctuations by using appropriate macroeconomic policies.[5] In the long run, it is vital for the economy to overcome the usual tendency towards diminishing marginal productivity in both factors of production: labour and capital. As the new

365

endogenous growth theory emphasizes, such growth is rooted in capital accumulation, whereby capital is defined broadly to include not only physical, but also human, technological and social overhead capital.[6]

For the Philippines, having experienced recurrent boom-and-bust cycles that forced the government to tap standby lending facilities of the IMF on a recurrent basis, it is useful to revisit the macroeconomic policy reforms that have contributed to an economic recovery and laid the foundation for that recovery to gather strength. Meanwhile, among the long-term factors, it is widely recognized that human capital investment, especially education, is vital to economic growth. Acting in combination with other forms of capital, human capital can lead to increasing returns.[7] Moreover, since education is a core value of the Philippine people, enshrined in the constitution, an investigation of the role of education in the growth process is warranted.

To begin with, this chapter examines the various short-term macroeconomic policy reforms that the Philippines has pursued to minimize unwanted business fluctuations. Then, in relation to growth over the long term, the chapter assesses the role that human capital accumulation, focused on education, has played.

Moreover, since economic policy reforms since 1986 have sought to integrate the Philippine economy with the rest of the world's, it is useful to examine the growth effects of foreign trade policy reforms. For instance, the governments since 1986 have in succession pursued trade and investment liberalization, a measure that can be relied on to trigger growth over the long term.

The chapter then discusses the macroeconomic policy reforms designed to minimize unwanted business fluctuations, and looks at key aspects of capital accumulation that have long-term growth effects, starting with human capital.

Macroeconomic policy reforms

Both fiscal and monetary policies have long been recognized as constraints to sustained growth in the Philippines, a point that was stressed in Canlas et al.[8] and reiterated by the National Economic and Development Authority (NEDA).[9] Fiscal policy is often singled out as the most binding constraint to the country's sustained growth, particularly the relatively low tax effort, or tax revenues as a proportion of GDP. Fiscal and monetary policies, however, are closely related, and are commonly viewed in tandem.

Fiscal policy is often viewed as encompassing measures that affect the size of the public debt, including taxation and government spending, while monetary policy spans policies affecting the composition of that debt between money and non–interest-bearing liabilities of the government. When the monetary authority or central bank accommodates by lending to the government to finance its deficit, money supply rises, which constitutes the non–interest-bearing liabilities of the government. However, when the monetary authority does not accommodate, then the government through the National Treasury issues interest-bearing debt claims.

In the short run, the choice of financing a deficit may entail differential impacts on output and the general price level.

Fiscal policy

Any deficit in the national government budget has to be financed; when the government borrows to finance the deficit, the public debt rises, resulting in heavier debt servicing. The fiscal history of the Philippines indicates persistent deficits in the budget of the national government. In the 1970s, for instance, the Philippine government pursued an expansionary fiscal policy in an attempt to ward off the recessionary effects of the two oil price shocks in 1974 and in 1979.

The Philippines entered the 1980s with a large public debt, largely foreign. When interest rates rose on a global basis in the early 1980s as a result of disinflation moves by the US Federal Board, the government found debt servicing quite burdensome, eventually forcing it to default on its foreign held component.

Following the debt moratorium and tapping of a standby loan from the IMF, the government resorted to fiscal and monetary tightening. That ushered in the recession of 1984–85, the longest in the post-war economic history of the Philippines, in which real GDP declined by 11% during the two-year period.

The fiscal position of the government has long been at the core of the liquidity crisis repeatedly faced by the Philippines. In a small, open economy like the Philippines, the current account deficit is identical to the budget deficit of the public sector and the savings–investment gap of the private sector. Table 19.2 shows such a decomposition of the current account deficit three years before the government declared a debt moratorium. It is shown that the budget deficit of the government as a percentage of GDP, after a near-balance in 1980, rose to 4.8% in 1981, which then ballooned to 5.3% in 1982. It moderated to 3.3% following the declaration of a debt moratorium in 1983.

The problem posed by the budget deficit of the national government returned in 1990, when the budget deficit reached 4.8% of GDP. Fiscal policy was subsequently tightened, forcing the consolidated public sector account to moderate to 2.1% of GDP in 1991. Real GDP growth slowed down to 0.5% that year.

A large government budget deficit as a percentage of GDP may also be an offshoot of weak economic growth. The tax system has automatic stabilizers that lose their vitality in an economy that is slowing down. The stabilizers include revenues from personal income and corporate income taxes. This was evident in 2009, when the budget deficit of the national government swelled again to 3.9% of GDP as a result mainly of the economic slowdown that emerged in the aftermath of the 2008 global financial crisis. So, in 2010 the fiscal position of the government was still deemed as the most binding constraint to growth in the Philippines, triggering earnest calls even in government for fiscal reform.[10]

It is well recognized that government spending at all levels has to be reined in, while protecting core values in education, health and infrastructure, but more importantly, it is widely agreed that insofar as raising the tax effort is concerned, there is still plenty of room for improvement. Table 19.3 shows figures on the tax effort (total tax revenue divided by GDP for the given year) for selected years. In the years prior to the 1983 foreign debt crisis, the tax effort was declining and averaging only about 10% each year. In 1986 a series of measures aimed at improving tax collection and tax administration started. From about 10.6% in 1985, the tax effort improved, peaking at 17% in 1997 before it weakened again.

Table 19.2 Current account (CA), consolidated public sector account (CPSA) and savings-investment gap (S-I) as % of GDP

Year	CA	CPSA	S-I
1980	(5.9)	0.46	(6.4)
1981	(6.2)	(4.8)	(1.4)
1982	(9.0)	(5.3)	(3.7)
1983	(8.3)	(3.3)	(5.0)

Source: Basic data: *Bangko Sentral ng Pilipinas* for CA; Departments of Finance, and of Budget and Management for CPSA; S-I is calculated as a residual

Table 19.3 Tax effort (%), selected years

Year	1980	1981	1982	1985	1990	1995	1997
Tax effort	11.4	10.3	9.9	10.6	14.1	16.3	17.0

Source: Basic data from National Statistical Coordination Board, *Philippine Statistical Yearbook*
Note: Tax effort is defined as total tax collection divided by GDP.

In 1986, following the restoration of democratic political institutions, the administration under the leadership of President Corazon Aquino started a tax reform package. One major motivation for these reforms stemmed from the recurrent liquidity crises of the past that were rooted in the recurrent budget deficits of the government. In addition, the introduction of foreign trade policy reforms gave rise likewise to the need to strengthen the internal tax system.[11] The Aquino administration started an import liberalization and tariff reduction programme. As border or customs tariffs and trade taxes declined, strengthening the internal tax system became an imperative, particularly personal and corporate income and indirect taxes. Since reliance on foreign trade taxes was being reduced, internal tax collection had to be beefed up to compensate for the foregone border taxes. Table 19.4 shows the long-term shares of customs tariffs to total taxes declining and those of internal taxes increasing.

In 1987, President Aquino issued an executive order (EO) that introduced a 10% value-added tax (VAT) on all sales transactions not explicitly excluded from this first EO on VAT. In addition, a Republic Act (RA) was enacted that amended the National Internal Revenue Code (NIRC). The latter introduced a 'simplified net income taxation', or SNIT, for the self-employed and professionals in an attempt to widen the tax base, accompanied by a reduction in marginal tax rates.

The Fidel Ramos administration, which succeeded that of Aquino's in 1992, resumed the tax reform programme. It expanded the coverage of the VAT law. In 1998, the end of the Ramos term, an RA called the Comprehensive Tax Reform Programme (CTRP) was enacted, which further sought to expand the tax base while reducing marginal tax rates. One outcome of the reform measures covering tax policy and administration during the Ramos administration was a significant increase in the tax effort. In 1997 the tax effort peaked at 17%, enabling the national government to post a budget surplus for the first time since the late 1970s.

In 1998 the Joseph 'Erap' Estrada administration took over the reins of government. The budget deficit of the national government expanded as spending rose without any accompanying tax measure. Estrada was unseated in 2001, but the need to raise tax revenues again became urgent.

The Gloria Macapagal Arroyo administration assumed power in 2001. The tax effort weakened during this administration, down from 16.9% prior to the 1997 Asian Financial Crisis, to 12.4% in 2004. Therefore, pressure mounted to enhance tax collections. In response, the

Table 19.4 Share of foreign trade and internal taxes (%)

Tax type	1980	1985	1990	1995	1997
Internal	56.9	69.4	68.5	67.7	76.4
Customs	38.0	27.8	30.2	31.4	23.0
Others	5.1	2.8	1.3	0.9	0.6
Total	100.0	100.0	100.0	100.0	100.0

Source: National Statistical Coordination Board, *Philippine Statistical Yearbook*

administration caused the enactment of an RA called the Reformed VAT (RVAT), which expanded coverage and raised the rate to 12% from 10% in 2007.

In 2010 the tax effort remained a major challenge to the new Aquino administration, which during 2012 shepherded in the enactment of a law that restructured taxes on cigarettes and alcoholic beverages, and indexed them to inflation. Accompanied by disciplined government spending, the budget deficit of the national government declined to about 2% of GDP in 2012.

The tax reform programme, going forward, will continue to rely a great deal on internal rather than border taxes. For direct taxation, this strategy calls for strengthening collection and administration of personal income and of corporate income taxes. A noticeable trend is the growing share of indirect taxes to total tax revenue, mainly on account of improvements in VAT collection.

With the share of indirect taxes increasing, questions emerge about tax incidence, particularly the regressivity of indirect taxes. Indirect taxes are considered regressive since the burden on low-income taxpayers is disproportionately large. As a proportion of earned income, people with low income pay a larger amount in taxes. There's little that can be done to reduce such a burden, except to make government spending progressive—that is, low-income taxpayers should benefit more from any additional unit of government spending. In line with making government spending progressive, the Aquino administration has prioritized some spending programmes in the national government budget for low-income households, such as the 'conditional cash transfer' programme for the poor.

Monetary policy

At this point, there is wide agreement among economists that monetary policy should be based on rules rather than discretion.[12] The main reason for this is to minimize the uncertainty and guessing game, an economic volatility that emanates from discretionary monetary policy. In doing so, monetary policy serves to provide a stable and predictable environment for the private sector. This is supportive of growth to the extent that market agents are able to implement their production and consumption plans with minimum risk and uncertainty.

Monetary policy rules in the Philippines have been evolving and undergoing refinement over time.[13] In the early 1970s, following the decision to allow the world's major currencies to go on a generalized float against one another, the monetary authority, i.e. the Central Bank of the Philippines (CBP), followed suit by adopting a flexible exchange rate system. However, the CBP reserved the right to intervene in foreign exchange markets to keep the exchange value of the Philippine peso against the US dollar within a targeted band. The CBP essentially observed exchange rate targeting as a monetary policy rule.

Under such targeting in which the CBP tried to keep the nominal exchange rate within a narrow band, the system in place resembled a fixed exchange rate system.[14] When the CBP embarked on an expansionary monetary policy, the country's inflation rate exceeded that of the USA, thereby making imports from the latter attractive. As the demand for imports increased, the demand for US dollars likewise rose. When the CBP accommodated, official foreign reserve assets held by the CBP declined. The erosion continued amid non-stop inflationary policy on the part of the CBP. The situation generally triggered a speculative attack against the Philippine peso, thereby accelerating the erosion of official foreign reserves. When the latter fell to a critically low level, a liquidity crisis ensued, resulting in a balance of payments (BOP) crisis and an abandonment of narrow exchange rate targeting.

The CBP then allowed the exchange rate to move within a wider band. At the same time, the CBP embraced monetary aggregate targeting as the dominant monetary policy rule. One factor that influenced the adoption of such a monetary policy rule stemmed from the fact that in the 1990s the Philippines was still tied to an IMF programme. In this context, the conduct of fiscal and monetary policies was based on financial programming techniques that the IMF imposed on its client countries with BOP problems.

From the standpoint of the IMF, a BOP problem means an excess of aggregate demand over aggregate supply. Demand management techniques are thus deemed essential. Inflationary monetary policy is to be curtailed. Money demand and supply need to balance. Disinflationary monetary policy means money supply growth has to decline. In the short term, however, disinflation results in adverse output effects.

Disinflation and recession occurred in the early 1980s, after the Philippine government declared a moratorium on foreign debt servicing and it tapped a standby loan from the IMF for the necessary liquidity. Tightened monetary (and fiscal) policy led to the recession of 1984–85.

Monetary aggregate targeting had its downside. Demand for money could be unstable at times, rendering such targeting unfeasible. In 2002 the CBP adopted inflation targeting.[15] Under this monetary policy rule, the central bank or monetary authority announces a target inflation rate, and uses its array of monetary policy tools to achieve the inflation target. When, for instance, the actual inflation rate exceeds the target, the monetary authority may cause interest rates to rise to tighten money supply and curb inflation. It is important for the monetary authority to maintain constant communication with the public so that its intentions are properly communicated, its messages shorn to the extent possible of uncertainty.

Inflation targeting requires that the monetary authority has both policy and instrument independence. Policy independence means that the fiscal authority does not influence policy-making of the monetary authority. Through instrument independence, the monetary authority wields enough tools of its own to achieve its inflation target. In line with this independence, an institutional reform in 1993 created an independent Bangko Sentral ng Pilipinas (BSP). One of the important provisions of the law called for a Monetary Board (MB), the majority of members of which were appointed by the president of the Philippines from the private sector. Prior to this reform, members of the president's cabinet who sat in an ex officio capacity dominated the MB.

A prior issue is this: is inflation a monetary phenomenon? Friedman had said that 'inflation is always and everywhere a monetary phenomenon'.[16] With a quantity theory of money in mind, if the central bank increases the money supply from a position of balance, then the real money stock exceeds the demand for it. To restore balance, the general price level must rise, which means that the inflation rate, defined as the percentage change in the general price level, must also rise.

Canlas[17] has tested a quantity theoretic model of inflation in the Philippines. The theoretical model implies a one-for-one impact of money growth on the inflation rate. Some econometric techniques, including first-order differencing for stationarity, finding the optimal lag length, and Granger causality tests are put to work. Time-series data are used. For the period 1973–90, the regression results show that money growth has a contemporaneous positive effect on the inflation rate, but less than one-for-one. The optimal lag length of the effect of money growth on inflation using Hsiao's[18] test is shown to be one year; in subsequent regressions, however, the effect of money growth lagged one year is insignificant. Overall, there is empirical support for an inflation model based on the quantity theory of money.

Since the adoption of inflation targeting in 2002 as a monetary policy rule, the general price performance of the Philippine economy has improved tremendously. During the period 2005–12 the inflation rate averaged only 5% each year, except in 2009, when relative-price shocks emanating from food and energy products intervened and caused the inflation rate to increase to 8% that year. Since then the inflation rate has again moderated to an average of about 4% each year.

Monetary policy can be trusted to promote growth insofar as it dampens inflationary expectations. As the latter is dissipated, interest rates decline with salutary effects on investment. An increase in investment is expected to support growth. However, an increase in physical capital is subject to diminishing marginal productivity, which in the long run dampens growth. The challenge, therefore, is to overcome this tendency towards diminishing marginal productivity, while producing growth over the long term.

Towards long-term growth

Investing in human capital

A major force that propels growth in the long run emanates from the accumulation of human capital, which is commonly associated with the knowledge and skills or efficiency units that people bring to the workplace. Given diminishing marginal productivity of physical capital, accumulation of the latter alone is not sufficient to yield positive growth in the long run. The model of Solow[19] emphasized the importance of investment or capital accumulation for growth.[20] It is insightful in terms of accounting for growth in a given country, but is not designed to account for growth convergence in a large cross-section of heterogeneous countries. Modern economic growth theory, or what is often referred to as endogenous growth, has thus extended the Solow growth model in trying to account for long-term growth in a number of developed countries and to account for convergence (or lack of it) in a large sample of countries.[21]

Human capital accumulates in various ways, including investments in education, training, health and nutrition. Health investments enable people to develop their physical skills, such as manual dexterity and visual acuity.[22] However, it is education and training that are popularly linked to human capital investment. Various levels of education, for instance, are credited with helping to raise literacy and cognitive skills and equip people with knowledge and scientific skills. Moreover, human capital investment is associated with other aspects of household behaviour, including desired family size and labour force participation.[23] Many countries, especially those that have succeeded in achieving growth in real GDP over a long-term period, have made it a point to invest in quality education at all levels, from basic to tertiary education.

In empirical studies that seek to determine the sources of growth, much of the growth stems from total factor productivity (TFP). This refers to the efficiency in use of all factors of production, e.g. labour and capital. The role of education in enhancing TFP is well understood and widely accepted in the economics profession. It seems clear that education and training equip people with efficiency units that are useful in the workplace.[24] On the job, people accumulate more skills, which further raises their human capital, as Mincer,[25] for instance, emphasized.

At the same time, however, family members' uses of time include non-market activities, such as attending to the education, health and nutritional needs of children, which leads to accumulation of human capital that eventually gets transmitted within the household across generations.[26] In countries that are able to produce across time highly trained and educated workers and who can master production techniques that continuously emerge in a modernizing economy, aggregate production efficiency is increased in the long run, with positive effects on TFP.

Following Solow,[27] Denison,[28] and Jorgenson and Griliches,[29] the growth rate of output is decomposed into the sum of the growth of labour and capital plus TFP, which is taken as a residual. Early empirical studies tended to show that much of the growth rate of output stems from growth of TFP. The latter is widely regarded as technological progress, which emanates from a variety of factors, including research and development (R&D) or knowledge production, and realization of scale economies. The latter follows as a matter of course from knowledge production, which is human capital-intensive and has dimensions of a public good.[30] That is, knowledge generated by one firm may spill over to all firms in the industry. So, as TFP improves, the tendency towards diminishing marginal productivity is overcome, resulting in positive growth rates of output over a long period of time.

Attempts to decompose the sources of output growth in the Philippines shows that in the 1980s and the 1990s, much of the growth of output was due to increases in labour and capital, while TFP contributed only a small proportion (see Table 19.5). In the 1980s TFP was −1.62%. This turned +0.25% in the 1990s, accounting for 9.9% of the growth rate of real GDP. During the period 2001–06 TFP gained strength and increased to 2.4%, which is about 50% of the real GDP growth rate.

To account for the improvements in TFP, it is insightful to note trends in educational attainment in the Philippines, and its impacts on the skill composition of the labour force. A rising share of skilled workers can be counted on to contribute to TFP improvements.

Investing in education

Recognizing the significance of education in the process of economic growth and development, the Philippine Constitution of 1987 provides for allocating the biggest proportion of the expenditure programme of the government budget to education. The national government has long been the major provider of education in the Philippines, particularly in basic education, which consists of elementary and secondary education levels. The latter are provided without out-of-pocket costs to parents who enrol their children in public schools.

At the tertiary education level, the national government runs a network of state colleges and universities, wherein tuition fees are charged, but at subsidized rates. The rest of the demand for tertiary education is met through private colleges and universities.

Moreover, the government supports skills training through a system of post-secondary schools offering technical and vocational education and training. Here, private institutions co-exist with government-run institutes.

Table 19.6 shows the distribution of workers by educational attainment. It is seen that the proportion of unskilled workers (those with only elementary schooling) has been declining over the past two decades. Meanwhile, the share of semi-skilled to skilled workers (those with secondary and tertiary schooling) has been rising.

Investments in education and training lead to growth through another transmission mechanism. By narrowing the differentials between earnings and non-work income, income

Table 19.5 Total factor productivity in the Philippines

Period	Growth of capital	Growth of labour	TFP
1981–1990	2.05	1.37	(1.62)
1991–2000	1.77	0.87	0.25
2001–06	1.12	1.24	2.41

Source: Dante Canlas, Rowena Cham and Juzhong Zhuang, 'Development Performance and Policy', in D. Canlas, M.E. Khan and J. Zhuang (eds), *Diagnosing the Philippine Economy: Toward Inclusive Growth*, Asian Development Bank and Anthem Press, 2008, Table 2.9

The Philippines

Table 19.6 Employment by educational attainment (%)

Education	1991	2001	2006
Elementary graduate	24.2	19.2	16.8
High school graduate	18.1	23.2	24.9
Tertiary and above	10.9	13.2	14.4

Source: Basic data: National Statistics Office, *Philippine Labor Force Survey*, various issues

inequality is reduced. Persistent income inequality tends to be deleterious to growth in so far as such inequality raises political pressure to implement redistributive programmes that are financed by raising taxes. Rising taxes on personal and business income tend to erode marginal productivity of labour capital that can be privately captured, with dampening effects on capital accumulation, both human and physical, and growth. However, by reducing the proportion of poor individuals and households, political pressure for redistribution may be eased.

Technological progress, trade policy and growth

It is widely known that growth comes not just by producing increasing quantities of the same good, but also by producing new products of ever-increasing quality.[31] Growth of Apple, Inc., for instance, comes not from producing the same MacBook or iPad, but from newer and more powerful versions of these products. Moreover, further growth is obtained not by selling in the same market but by accessing new markets for an expanding array of new products. Trading countries differ in their endowments of knowledge capital. The developed countries with large endowments of knowledge capital do a good deal of R&D and are thus able to produce and trade a wide range of new products.[32] Over time, developing countries that adopt open trade regimes may acquire production knowledge about some of these new products through imitation, with salutary effects on output growth. Clearly, technological progress and trade policies do matter.

Trade in intermediate products is one of the fastest growing segments of international trade. These intermediate products are normally result from investment in R&D. They lie at the core of an increasing number of new products of higher quality. In the crop sector of agriculture, for example, the discovery of high-yielding seed varieties has significantly raised the yields per hectare of rice and corn. In information technology, the microchip revolution has permitted the manufacture of supercomputers with huge memories and storage capacity, allowing various industries in the service trades, such as banking and finance, and retail and wholesale trade, to increase productivity.

The rise of intermediate products emerging from R&D is taking place in a system involving separable and multi-stage production processes. This has given rise to outsourcing. Firms in developed countries subcontract the labour-intensive stages of production to firms in less-developed countries, for instance, but this can also be done under a vertical integration arrangement if the firm from the developed country finds it more efficient to do so.

Considering that R&D yields knowledge that spills over to entities beyond the R&D proponents themselves, there is a public policy concern that it may be under-produced. Third parties may capture the returns from R&D but the original R&D proponents may not be fully compensated. People tend to invest only up to the marginal rate of return that they can appropriate. Since the private returns fall short of the social rate, then there is room for some form of subsidy to avoid under-investment in knowledge production.

Dante B. Canlas

Philippine trade policy reforms

In 1986 the Philippine government ushered in some trade policy reforms aimed at integrating its economy with that of the rest of the world and making local firms internationally competitive. To kick-start this reform process, the government liberalized imports and embarked on a tariff reduction programme. Later on, it also liberalized entry of foreign direct investment (FDI).

In the 1950s trade policy was based on import substitution. The government encouraged domestic firms to manufacture goods that at the time were being imported in large amounts, ostensibly to save on scarce foreign exchange, and to 'learn by doing'. The local firms were protected from competing imports through high import tariffs and quantitative restrictions, using infant industry arguments. The firms, however, relied on imported capital equipment and intermediate products. Since they were selling their products solely in the domestic market, the goal of saving on foreign exchange was not achieved. Moreover, since the Philippines was starting with a low human capital base, new products that could be exported did not emerge. The foreign exchange earnings of the country were derived largely from exports of agricultural and mineral products. Since these foreign exchange earnings were not adequate to finance the import needs of the import-substituting industries, the country experienced recurrent liquidity problems accompanied by the collapse of a fixed peso-US dollar exchange rate. Eventually, reliance on import substitution declined. Import liberalization and tariff reduction combined to shrink the size of import-substituting industries.

In 1994 the Philippines acceded to the World Trade Organization (WTO), which was anchored on a 'most favoured nation principle' or MFN. Under MFN, tariffs and other commercial policies extended to one member country of the WTO cannot be withheld from other member countries. In addition, the Philippines has actively participated in regional preferential trading arrangements. One of these is the Association of Southeast Asian Nations (ASEAN) Free Trade Area-Comprehensive Effective Preferential Tariff (AFTA-CEPT), which envisions non-tariff barriers among member countries, starting with manufactured products, and later on extending to trade in agricultural goods and in services.

Today, the Philippines is a small, open economy that is integrated with the rest of the world through trade in commodities, securities and national currencies. It adopts a flexible exchange rate system and allows international mobility of capital. It has significantly reduced its public debt as a proportion of GDP, and it is touted as ready for investment grade status.

Concluding remarks

Several development observers regard the Philippines at this point as an emerging economy or break-out nation, poised to join the South-East and East Asian economies that are now considered to be newly industrializing. This positive assessment derives largely from the structural reform programme that has been pursued in succession by political administrations since 1986, all of which have contributed to the sustained growth of real GDP since 2001. The policy reforms may be broadly classified into, first, short-term macroeconomic policies designed for stable growth, and second, long-term structural policy reforms aimed at sustained and broad-based growth.

The importance of short-term stabilization may be appreciated by taking an historical perspective. For nearly four decades from the 1950s, growth in the Philippines was hampered by inappropriate macroeconomic policies that resulted in unwanted volatility and business fluctuations. Political administrations since 1986 have in succession tried to address these concerns. Beginning in 1986, following the dismantling of martial law rule and restoration of democratic political institutions, the administration exerted efforts to strengthen the fiscal position of the national government by instituting a responsible deficit reduction programme. Monetary policy was rendered independent with the enactment of monetary authority independent of the fiscal authority. These measures helped to usher in economic recoveries from BOP crises and GDP declines, while putting a lid on inflation.

Moreover, attention was paid to growth-enhancing reforms, such as increased investment in capital broadly defined to include human and knowledge capital, in an effort to achieve long-term growth. In addition, the government pursued trade liberalization policies, anchored on import liberalization and tariff reduction. The government also liberalized FDI, which allowed ownership in several industry areas; restriction or limits on foreign ownership were announced in the so-called negative lists that are being shortened through time. Privatization of several industries that monopolized some sectors previously was pursued, such as those in oil and petroleum, commercial banking and telecommunications.

The economy has responded positively to these policy reforms. In 2001 the economy recovered from a political shock and posted GDP growth that has been sustained in spite of the intervention of shocks like 9/11, the global financial crisis of 2008, and the eurozone debt crisis of 2012. The economy has achieved sufficient resilience as it has become integrated with the global economy through trade in commodities, securities and national monies.

Entering the second decade of the 21st century, the economy is expected to achieve a sufficiently high growth rate in real GDP, with stable prices amid continuing challenges like the weak recovery in the USA, the debt problems of some eurozone countries and the growth slowdown in China.

The current administration is restoring credible political leadership and this is serving the economy well. Not only is the current leadership committed to market-friendly policies, but it is likewise aggressive in addressing concerns about good governance, including fighting corruption and strengthening the legal and judicial system. The latter, for instance, is vital to the success of the infrastructure programme of the government at both national and local levels. Since the programme is anchored on public-private partnership, contractual performance and sound adjudication in case of contractual disputes are critical. All this investors find quite appealing, a necessary condition to becoming an economic miracle.

Notes

1 Robert Lucas, Jr, 'Making a Miracle', *Econometrica* 61, 1993: 251–71.
2 Ruchir Sharma, *Breakout Nations: In Pursuit of the Next Economic Miracles*, W.W. Norton and Co, New York, 2012.
3 World Bank, *World Development Indicators*, data.worldbank.org/data-catalog/world-development-indicators (accessed 4 August 2011).
4 See, for example, Robert Barro, *Economic Growth and Convergence*, Occasional Papers no. 46, CS Press for International Center for Economic Growth, San Francisco, CA, 1994.
5 See Stanley Fischer, 'Does Macroeconomic Policy Matter? Evidence from Developing Countries', Occasional Papers no. 27, CS Press for International Center for Economic Growth, San Francisco, 1993.
6 Paul Romer, 'Increasing Returns and Long-Run Growth', *Journal of Political Economy* 94, 1986: 1002–37; Paul Romer, 'Human Capital and Growth: Theory and Evidence', *Carnegie-Rochester Conference Series on Public Policy* 32, 1990: 251–86; Robert Lucas, Jr, 'On the Mechanics of Economic Development', *Journal of Monetary Economics* 22, 1988: 3–42.
7 Romer, 'Increasing Returns and Long-Run Growth'; Robert Barro and Xavier Sala-i-Martin, *Economic Growth*, McGraw-Hill, Inc. New York, 1990.
8 Dante Canlas, Rowena Cham and Juzhong Zhuang, 'Development Performance and Policy', in D. Canlas, M.E. Khan and J. Zhuang (eds), *Diagnosing the Philippine Economy: Toward Inclusive Growth*, Asian Development Bank and Anthem Press, Manila and London, 2008.

9 NEDA, *A Strategic Framework and Action Plan for Inclusive Growth*, Monograph, Metro Manila, National Economic and Development Authority, 2010.

10 NEDA, *A Strategic Framework*.

11 Dante Canlas, 'Tax Reforms in the Philippines', in *Asian Tax Reforms: Issues and Results*, Proceedings of an International Symposium, Hitotsubashi University, Tokyo, 1998.

12 Finn Kydland and Edward Prescott, 'Rules Rather than Discretion: The Inconsistency of Optimal Plans', *Journal of Political Economy*, 1977: 473–91.

13 Dante Canlas, 'Business Fluctuations and Monetary Policy Rules in the Philippines: With Lessons from the 1984–85 Contraction', delivered as the *Bangko Sentral ng Pilipinas* Sterling Chair in Monetary and Banking Economics, 2012.

14 Dante Canlas, 'Monetary Policy and Exchange Rate in the Philippines', in Augustine H.H. Tan (ed.), *Monetary and Financial Management in Asia in the 21st Century*, World Scientific, Hackensack, NJ, 2002.

15 For an exposition on the intellectual development of inflation targeting, see Svensson, Lars, 'Inflation Targeting as a Monetary Policy Rule', *Journal of Monetary Economics*, 1999a: 607–54; and 'Inflation Targeting: Some Extensions', *Scandinavian Journal of Economics*, 1999b: 337–61.

16 Milton Friedman, *The Counter-Revolution in Monetary Theory*, first Wincott Memorial Lecture, delivered at the Senate House, University of London, 16 September 1970, 24.

17 Dante Canlas, 'Inflation in a Low-Income Country: Tests Based on the Quantity Theory of Money', Discussion Paper 9209, School of Economics, University of the Philippines, 1992.

18 C. Hsiao, 'Autoregressive Modeling and Money-Income Causality', *Journal of Monetary Economics*, 1981: 85–106.

19 Robert Solow, 'A Contribution to the Theory of Economic Growth', *Quarterly Journal of Economics* 70, 1957: 65–94.

20 See Dante Canlas, 'Economic Growth in the Philippines: Theory and Evidence', *Journal of Asian Economics* 14, 2003: 759–69, for tests of the Solow model in the Philippine context.

21 For an exposition on the origins and key doctrines of endogenous growth, see Paul Romer, 'The Origins of Endogenous Growth', *Journal of Economic Perspectives* 8, 2000: 3–22.

22 For empirical tests supportive of the positive growth effects of education on output growth using an endogenous growth model, see Jess Benhabib and Mark Spiegel, 'The Role of Human Capital in Economic Development: Evidence from Aggregate Cross-Country Data', *Journal of Monetary Economics* 34, 1994: 143–73.

23 Gary Becker, Kevin Murphy and Robert Tamura, 'Human Capital, Fertility, and Economic Growth', *Journal of Political Economy* 98, 1990: S12–S37; Robert Tamura, 'Human Capital and Economic Development', *Journal of Development Economics* 79, 2006: 26–72.

24 Gary Becker, *Human Capital: A Theoretical and Empirical Analysis*, Columbia University Press for the National Bureau of Economic Research, New York, 1964.

25 Jacob Mincer, 'On-the-Job Training: Costs, Returns, and Some Implications', *Journal of Political Economy* 70, 1962: 50–77.

26 Gary Becker, 'A Theory of the Allocation of Time', *Economic Journal* 75, September 1965: 493–517.

27 Solow, 'A Contribution to the Theory of Economic Growth'.

28 Edward Denison, 'Sources of Growth in the United States and the Alternatives Before Us', Supplement Paper no. 13, Committee for Economic Development, New York, 1962.

29 Dale Jorgenson and Zvi Griliches, 'The Explanation of Productivity Change', *Review of Economic Studies* 34, 1967: 249–80.

30 Gene Grossman and Elhanan Helpman, 'Product Development and International Trade', *Journal of Political Economy* 97, 1989: 1261–83.

31 Nancy Stokey, 'R&D and Economic Growth', *Review of Economic Studies* 62, 1995: 469–89.

32 Grossman and Helpman, 'Product Development and International Trade'.

20

Pakistan

An economy in extreme distress that could be revived

Shahid Javed Burki

Pakistan's future has never seemed more uncertain than it appeared at the start of 2013, the time of writing. The country faced difficulties on many fronts. The economy was weakening; it appeared highly unlikely that the governing coalition in Islamabad would be able to take the steps to bring growth back to the level needed to absorb the two million additional workers who join the workforce every year. The International Monetary Fund (IMF), in its Article IV consultations with Islamabad conducted in the spring of 2012, estimated that the economy needed to expand by 7% a year to keep unemployment from increasing. It forecast a rate of increase of at 3.4% in 2012–13[1] although, as discussed below, Hafeez Sheikh, the finance minister, expected a higher rate of growth. The country's external situation was weakening as it prepared to service the large amount of accumulated debt, in particular the amount owed to the IMF. There was no doubt that Pakistan needed external support, particularly from the USA, but relations with the USA remained patchy.

This chapter examines how Pakistan has fared in the five-year period from 2008 to 2013 when a new political system began to take shape in the country and new relations with the world outside began to be developed. Both are important for determining which direction— more accurately directions—the economy will take in the next few years. I will begin by referring to a debate in December 2012 between Dr Hafeez Sheikh, Pakistan's finance minister during most of this period, and some Washington-based economists who keep a close watch on the state of the Pakistani economy. Two interpretations emerged about the economic situation from these two assessments—one from the government and the other from some of its critics. There were elements of exaggeration in both.

In an interview given by the finance minister before he left for his autumn 2012 visit to Washington, DC, an impression was given that the economy was on the mend. 'The country's economic fundamentals are stable enough to absorb global and domestic challenges, meet international obligations and provide room for the revival of private investment', he told Khaleeq Kiani of *Dawn*, Pakistan's largest-selling English-language newspaper. He said that the country's gross domestic product (GDP) was likely to grow at a rate of 4.3% in 2012–13, with the output of agriculture increasing by 4.4%, that of manufacturing by 4.1%, and that of services by 4.6%.

377

Investment, while still low from the perspective of the developing world, was expected to increase to 13.1% of GDP. Contributions to total national investment by both the public and the private sectors will increase significantly. The rate of inflation was set to decline to 7.7% compared to 11.0% in 2011–12. There was also considerable fiscal consolidation, with higher amounts of tax returns while the government's spending was kept under control.[2]

Some commentators, including Mohammad Yaqub, former governor of the State Bank of Pakistan, and Meekal Ahmad, formerly an adviser in the office of the executive director at the IMF responsible for a number of Muslim countries including Pakistan, rejected the finance minister's optimistic interpretation of the situation. In their comments published in the Pakistani newspapers, they interpret the situation very differently. They were of the view that the country was sitting on a number of fault lines. The fiscal deficit was very high and was being met by excessive borrowings from commercial banks which had crowded out the private sector. While the current account deficit at less than 3% seemed manageable, large payments had to be made to the IMF to service the loan the institution had provided to cover the 2008–12 period. These would drain the foreign exchange reserves maintained by the State Bank. This had put the rupee, the domestic currency, under great stress. By spring 2013, the rupee had breached the psychological barrier of 100 to the US dollar.

Two months after the finance minister had spoken so optimistically about the state of the economy, his own ministry put out two statements that painted a very different picture. According to these the country's financial health was precarious. The 'Fiscal Policy Statement' and the 'Debt Policy Statement, 2012–13', both released on 4 February, suggested that the goals laid down in the Fiscal Responsibility and Debt Limitation Act of 2005 (FRDLA) had not been met. The first goal was to reduce the revenue deficit to zero no later than June 2008, or three years after the administration headed by General Pervez Musharraf piloted the legislation through the national assembly. That did not happen. The revenue deficit stood at 3.2% of GDP in 2008, declined to 1.2% in 2009, increased to 1.7% in 2010, jumped to 3.3% in 2011 and stood at 2.5% at the end of fiscal year 2012. One natural consequence of this was the increase in the amount of public debt. FRDLA required the government to bring down public debt to 60% of GDP by 2008 and then maintain it at that level. Instead, the ratio increased to 61.3% in 2011–12 from 60% in 2008–09. The third goal was related to expenditure by the government on social sectors and for poverty alleviation. That goal was also not achieved. The share in GDP of education expenditure increased marginally from the 1.8% average in 2008–11 to 2.1% in 2011–12, still very low for a developing country with a very young population. Health expenditure remained between 0.6% and 0.8% of GDP. The total expenditure on social sectors and poverty-related programmes declined from 9.3% to 8.2% in 2012. There was now greater dependence on domestic rather than foreign debt, and within domestic debt on short-term debt. This would further increase the total burden carried by the state.[3]

The minister's critics saw Pakistan faced with one of its most serious economic crises which could bring it sooner rather than later to the IMF for an emergency loan. The Fund, for its part, would no doubt insist on, in the language it uses about the countries in Pakistan's situation, several 'prior actions'. These could include increases in tariffs for electricity and natural gas and significant reductions in subsidies. The Fund would also demand a noticeable increase in the abysmally low tax-to-GDP ratio. All three actions were needed to stabilize the government's finance at a sustainable level. However, the problem with the programme was its political practicality as the country approached another general election in the first half of 2013.

There was also plenty of negative commentary in the Western press about Pakistan and the situation in the country as it prepared for the elections. One of the many comments made in the columns that appeared in the US newspapers provides a flavour of the way that the country was viewed from the outside. A long article contributed to the op-ed page of the *Baltimore Sun* by Pakistan-watcher, Joe Brinkley, suggested that 'distracted by the deadly violence in Mali and Algeria, no one seems to be paying much attention to the tragicomedy underway in Pakistan. This matters because recent events demonstrate without equivocation that Pakistan is an utterly failed state—but one that possesses nuclear weapons. The country is tumbling down the abyss'.[4] The world, he concluded, needed to take notice of this situation and prepare itself to act to prevent the country from slipping into total political and economic chaos.

Viewed from these different perspectives, the situation in Pakistan on the eve of the 2013 elections was precarious. There was a consensus both inside and outside Pakistan that most systems in the country were now dysfunctional. The most worrying development of recent years was the emergence of extremism, a movement joined by those who were working towards a radical change in the system of governance. For them, the liberal democracy that the rest of the world had decided was the best way to govern was anathema for a Muslim state. These groups and people who gave them their support had to be reintegrated into society. Through their anti-state activities, they had cost the economy dearly and ruined the country's reputation in the international community.

Some questions needing answers

Which way is Pakistan headed? The question, as is to be expected, has many answers, but the question itself can be divided into several components. When we talk about Pakistan's future are we referring to the shape its politics will take as it keeps moving through this period of transition? The move towards the establishment of a new political order was slow. There were many hiccups on the way. Although the country began to move towards the development of a new political system following the elections held in February 2008, there was some apprehension that the process might be interrupted. There was some fear that the military may intervene once again in the country's political life. However, the men in uniform chose to stay in their barracks. In the spring of 2013 the administration led by the Pakistan People's Party (PPP) in Islamabad completed its five-year term, a first in Pakistan's history. Does this mean that democracy as the system of governance had taken hold in the country?

Given the country's history could we be certain that the military establishment would not be tempted to take over once again, as it did four times in the past? In this context we should ask the question whether the politicians and the political system will be able to tackle the problem created by the rise of Islamic extremism. Therefore, in discussing the future, do we have to keep in mind the likely outcome of the struggle between several different ideologies that are engaged in many battles being fought in the country? For instance, will Pakistan succumb to the forces of extremism as many both inside and outside the country fear? Or will the large and growing middle class prevail and choose the path of liberalism and modernization? Staying in the political arena, will the country be able to put together a political order that will succeed in accommodating diversity? Prominent among the many forces that were pulling and pushing the country in several different directions were not only Islamic extremists. There were also elements in the country who did not accept its integrity. Will the separatist forces have their way and break up the country into several smaller parts?

Turning to economics, will the country find a way to reverse the declining trend in the rate of growth that began almost 50 years ago and has sped up in the last five years? The exceptionally poor performance of the economy since 2008 leads to another important question. Is democracy bad for the Pakistani economy? Will the policymakers find a way to build on the strength the country still has and come up with a strategy that would take the economy on to a higher plane? If policymaking fails to take advantage of the country's potential, how far will it fall behind the rest of South Asia? At the time of writing Pakistan was South Asia's sick man. Will it be able to recover and what would it take for the economy to regain health?

At least over the short term (defined as the next three years) Pakistan will remain dependent on external assistance to move the country out of the economic slump of 2008–12. Will there be support from the quarters that have helped the country in the past? How will the USA's changing strategic interests—in particular following the pullout from Afghanistan—affect its relations with Pakistan? Could Pakistan fall back on the People's Republic of China once again, as it did in the late 1990s when it faced bankruptcy? Will the IMF come to the country's assistance once again? The Fund is the institution of last resort for countries facing economic stress, but Pakistan has had difficult relations with it for decades. Given that history, will the Fund be less inclined to provide help this time around, or if it does, will it come up with a set of conditions that will be politically difficult to solve?

What about Pakistani society and social and political development? There is no doubt that like many Muslim countries, Pakistani society has become more conservative in terms of the religious faith of the majority of the population. This has had consequences for the status of women in Pakistani society. Will this trend continue and push the country back or will the reaction to some of the acts committed by extremist forces produce a reaction? What will the impact on the country be of the attempted assassination of the 14-year-old Malala Yousafzai, an education activist from the district of Swat, adjacent to the tribal belt? The international attention received by the young woman—she was selected as runner-up for *Time* magazine's 'person of the year' award, coming after President Barack Obama—should have positive consequences. The international focus on her and her work has highlighted both the problem Pakistan faces and the opportunities that could unfold from the activism she and her associates were promoting. As Aryn Baker of *Time* magazine wrote, in 'trying to kill Malala, the Taliban appear to have made a serious mistake. They wanted to silence her. Instead they amplified her voice … If Malala decides to continue her crusade, hers will be a platform backed with financial means and wired with well-connected allies'.[5] Would her prominence help finally to convince the moderate elements in society to assert themselves? Liberating women from the shackles into which extremists would like to put them would be of enormous benefit to the economy's future. Will the large number of well-trained and educated women now graduating from institutions of higher learning be allowed to enter the country's economic life and help to shape the country's future?

This may be the right moment to attempt some answers to these questions. However, as Nate Silver reminds us in his book, *The Signal and the Noise*, many predictions fail even when the questions being asked are relatively simple ones.[6] The questions I have raised above are not simple; to predict where Pakistan will be in the next few years is at best an exceedingly difficult task. The questions cannot be answered alone; they have to be taken together. One of the running themes of this chapter is that each aspect of Pakistan's current situation—political, economic, social and historical—affects the other, but I would argue that political development must take precedence over other desired changes. Therefore, whichever way the political order evolves will have enormous consequences for the development of the economy and shaping of the social structure.

How should we look at Pakistan's future? With despair as many do? Or with some hope as I tend to? Let me begin by quoting from an article by Thomas Freidman of the *New York Times*. The US journalist knows the Middle East well and has in recent years written several in-depth pieces about the countries in the region. According to him, pluralism does not work in the Arab world.

Muslims are killing Muslims across the Middle East and Central Asia today: Sunnis versus Shias, Pashtuns versus Pashtuns, and Kurds versus Turks. Christians are not doing well there either. The absence of pluralism and the prevalence of 'rule or die politics'—either my sect or party is in power or I'm dead—is the dominant political trend in the Arab-Muslim region today. Nobody trusts anybody, but it is impossible to build a modern innovation economy without trust.[7]

As already discussed, these types of conflicts are also occurring in Pakistan. The Sunnis are killing Shi'as; the muhajirs are attacking the Pashtuns and the Pashtuns are hitting back; the Baluchis are expelling the Punjabis from their province; and the extremists are assassinating or attempting to kill the leaders who are espousing a more moderate version of Islam. Could, at some stage, trust among these communities develop for those who are not of them? Might this happen also in Pakistan if a new inclusive political order took shape? My main argument in this work is that Pakistan has begun to move forward in this area. The process has begun with palpable political progress.

Establishment of a durable political order

Academics have also begun to devote time to studying nation-building failures. This was the subject of a book by Daron Acemoglu and James Robinson that appeared in 2012 with the telling title of *Why Nations Fail*.[8] According to them, nations fail when their institutional structures are designed to give the elite the capacity to extract resources from those who do not have access to political power. Extractive political institutions lead to the creation of similar institutions on the economic side, with each reinforcing the other.

The process of the development of durable and representative political orders has in recent years become the subject of intense academic inquiry. Those who have studied the phenomenon have reached the same conclusions. Francis Fukuyama has concluded in *The Origins of Political Order* that it takes a long time before a broadly structured order gets to be built. He worries that the movement is not always in one direction; it can be interrupted. Instead of political development, political decay can be the result.[9] Using a multidisciplinary approach, Acemoglu and Robinson, distinguish between two different types of societies. There are those in which extractive systems dominate, and there are those in which inclusive systems have taken root. For those that are caught in the first type, progress towards the second is difficult. It often takes revolutions to dispense with extractive systems in favour of those that are inclusive.

Using this academic research as the background, what should be concluded about the situation in Pakistan? Some progress was made in the period since 2008 in establishing a political order that would ultimately fully represent most segments of the population. Continuing progress, however, will need to overcome a number of challenges. The military that so often disrupted political progress in the past must be persuaded to stay out of politics. That is likely to happen partly because of the rise in power of civil society. Looking at the Arab Spring, those who are in command of the armed forces seem to have concluded that another intervention would be strongly resisted by the various institutions now active in politics. The judiciary is one of them, but 'people power' is an even more important deterrent. This means that the executive, the legislature, the judiciary and civil society each will have to respect the political space in which they operate. That has begun to happen but still to a limited extent. It will remain a work in progress for some time to come. Another area requiring progress is to build robust and workable relationship between the governments operating at different levels. This is perhaps the greatest challenge to be met to establish a political order that delivers services people want from the state. It is to the credit of the PPP-led government that it supported the writing and passage by the legislature of the 18th amendment to the constitution. The changes in relations between the federal and provincial governments envisaged by the amendment were still in the process of implementation at the time of writing. The federal authorities were still attempting to figure out how to finance the additional authority transferred to the provinces while keeping for itself the resources it needs for the execution of a number of vital functions. However, the need for the devolution of power to the governments one level below that of the provinces is proving to be problematic. The provinces rejected the local government development plan put in place in 2001 by the administration headed by President Pervez Musharraf. As was the case with the groups that dominated the central government, those who wield authority in the provincial capitals were also reluctant to transfer some of their power to the local governments. The provinces allowed the Musharraf system to lapse. The Sindh legislature passed a new local government law on 1 October 2012, but it ran into a different kind of political issue. With considerable authority transferred to urban municipalities where the Muttahida Qaumi Movement (MQM) wield political power, it was resented by the rural interests represented in the PPP.

It was only in the last five-year period following the establishment of democratic institutions that people representing different points of view have begun to work together within the still-evolving parliamentary system. The federal government, dominated by one particular party—the Pakistan People's Party—flexed its muscles to block the smooth working of the provincial administrations in which other parties led. However, Islamabad pulled back before the breaking point was reached. We should recall that in the early 1970s, the government headed by Zulfikar Ali Bhutto in Islamabad removed the administrations in Khyber-Pakhtunkhawa and Baluchistan since they were under the control of parties other than the governing PPP. The federal government asserted its authority by using strong-arm tactics. The constitution, authored by Bhutto himself, was not strictly followed. The requirement that relations between governments at different levels must be conducted strictly within the constitutional framework was tested by the events in Baluchistan in the opening days of January 2003. The dismissal of the Baluchistan government by President Asif Ali Zardari in January followed growing demands by the province's Shi'a community for its removal. The community was attacked by Lashkar-i-Jhangvi, an extremist Sunni group. They were of the view that the attack on them was because of the weakness of the provincial government to protect the entire citizenry. Having removed the provincial chief minister and his cabinet, the president took the decision to go to the national assembly to seek approval for his action. This was a constitutional requirement.

Although considerable progress was made in developing a new political order, there were serious tensions among the elements that comprised it. Relations between the executive branch headed by President Zardari and the judiciary under the command of the tough-minded Iftikhar Mohammad Chaudhry, chief justice of the Supreme Court, continued to race up and down on a roller-coaster. The court continued to pursue cases of alleged corruption by the senior members of the administration including the president. It also forced Yousaf Raza Gilani out of the premiership and began to move against his successor, Raja Pervaiz Ashraf. However, the new prime minister promised to write a letter to the Swiss authorities to revive the corruption case against the president. He showed the judges the language the government wished to use in the latter and accepted the changes suggested by the judges. However, it wasn't just the Supreme Court that was being difficult. Other courts also jumped into the fray. The Lahore High Court told President Zardari that he had to choose between the two jobs he concurrently held: the presidency and the co-chairmanship of the PPP. According to the traditions established since 1973, the year in which the constitution was adopted, the president was required to give up his party membership. The courts also continued to pursue several cases of alleged corruption against senior office holders and their families. Zardari, instead, had played a highly partisan role using the chairmanship of the PPP to exert a tight grip over the executive branch. This was traditional as well, but it was exercised during the time when military men served as presidents.

In January 2013 the court ordered the arrest of Prime Minister Ashraf in what was generally referred to as the 'power rental case'. This was related to the contracts given to a number of private entrepreneurs to establish power generation plants to overcome the severe power shortages that were taking a heavy toll on the economy. An investigation carried out by the Asian Development Bank came to the conclusion that a very high price was paid by the government to the people who set up the rental units. The owners also received large down-payments from which, it was alleged, hefty payments were made to Minister Ashraf, who then held the portfolio of water and power. Several of his senior colleagues were also alleged to be involved in the 'scam'. The Supreme Court took note of the bank's report and ordered an inquiry into the conduct of the minister in charge of the power portfolio along with 16 other officials of the organization. The court ordered the National Accountability Bureau (NAB) to hold an inquiry into the case. When the NAB stalled in its lukewarm efforts, the court ordered the arrest of the serving prime minister and the other senior officials alleged to have been involved. The case took a bizarre turn when a young officer engaged in investigating the case was found dead in his Islamabad hotel room. The government said that he had committed suicide. The man's parents said that he was murdered.

A country in turmoil

In these difficult circumstances the question most often asked by those who watched the country from within as well as outside was: where was Pakistan headed and could it avoid failure? 'The point is that the prospect of disaster, no matter how obvious, is no guarantee that nations will do what it takes to avoid that disaster', wrote Paul Krugman, the Nobel Laureate, in a column published in July 2012 in the *New York Times*.[10] His reference was not to Pakistan but to Europe, where a dithering leadership was letting the continent slide towards an economic abyss. However, the possibility of disasters on several fronts did not seem to focus the minds of the policymakers in Pakistan either. Nation failure—the opposite of nation building—became a popular topic in policy and academic discourse in 2012 as a number of countries in the Islamic world were convulsed by social upheaval. While the Arab Spring was watched, studied and analysed with great interest, there were even greater concerns about the nearly dysfunctional states of Afghanistan and Pakistan. Their future was also of equal interest for the security establishments in the West, in particular in the USA.

Engineers have known for as long as they have been engineering that it was the fear of failure that drove the field forward. Could the same be said about nation building, a field that had been practised as well as studied but in which there were more failures than successes? Engineers always hoped that their designs would succeed but as Henry Petroski, an expert who taught engineering failure at Duke University, wrote in his book, 'no matter what the technology is, our best estimates of its success tend to be overly optimistic'.[11] Statesmen who have delved in nation building—their own or that of other countries whose development they could and would like to influence—also knew failure. President Barack Obama's experience with nation building in the Islamic world provided a good example of failures, perceived or otherwise, leading to policy adjustments. David Sanger, who wrote a book on the US president's on-the-job education in the area of nation building, described how an almost total about-turn occurred in his thinking. In October 2009, a few months after assuming the presidency, Obama announced a plan for Afghanistan that would not only advance US security but also provide 'opportunity and justice—and not just in Kabul, but from the bottom up in the provinces'. He thought in terms of a 'civilian surge' made up of agricultural specialists and educators, engineers and lawyers, to fashion a new Afghan economy—in fact a new Afghan society. As Robert W. Merry, an historian who has studied US presidents,[12] wrote in his reaction to the Sanger account, Obama's 'goal was a level of societal coherence, and governmental functionality never before seen in that mountain redoubt of a country'.[13] That goal, of course, was not reached, and within two years Obama had reversed his course. At the end of 2011 the president convened a committee and put it in charge of narrowing his Afghan mission to its bare essence. Its task was to find a quick way to reach for the exit, but reaching the exit without incurring too heavy a cost meant working with Pakistan and re-establishing a relationship that was not rocked by suspicion and ill-feeling on both sides. That was not on the cards. However, not unlike Afghanistan, Pakistan also seemed to many to be headed towards failure.

What gives Pakistan-watchers pause about the country's future is the rise of Islamic extremism. Those who belong to these groups have been able to force their point of view by using violence. Often they have resorted to the use of lethal force to press their views on society at large. This was evident in the case of Malala Yousafzai. However, we should not lose sight of the fact that the extremists represent a very small segment of society. They were able to make their presence felt for two reasons: the state's weakness and the use of religion as the driving force. The reaction to the attempted murder of the 14-year-old girl may have finally persuaded the silent majority to raise its voice. That said, there are some who are troubled by the fact that the expression of disgust at the incident did not bring about palpable change. The *New York Times* headlined one of its stories on its extensive coverage of the attempt on the teenager's life by saying that 'the Malala moment may have passed'. I believe that this is not the case. Change comes slowly, especially when religion is involved to press a particular point of view.

While what Friedman says in the above-noted article about Muslim societies in the Middle East is certainly true, it is not the case with Pakistan. This is for two reasons. The mayhem on which the pessimists focus is being perpetrated by extremists of many different persuasions, but they are small in number. Society will have to develop ways to deal with them. How well has one part of the Muslim community in South Asia done in achieving the purpose for which it was given a home of its own? Many would answer this question by saying 'not very well', but that would not be the right response, on several scores. When compared with other Muslim societies not too distant from Pakistan's borders, the country's citizens have not done too badly and that realization should inform their approach towards the future. Turkey is the only country whose recent performance has been better than that of Pakistan, and we should remember that it took the Turks a long time to find their feet. Like Pakistan, they too experimented with a number of ways to govern themselves before adopting a form of governance that has worked well for them. The same model could work for Pakistan.

Pakistan is much more diverse than any of the Muslim countries in the Middle East and Central and West Asia. Diversity in Pakistan has led to a fair amount of violence. Shi'as have been targeted by several Sunni groups in Karachi as well as in Baluchistan and the northern areas. Under pressure the Shi'as have sometimes hit back. There is continuing violence between the Muhajir community in Karachi and other ethnic groups in the city. Baluchistan's native population has turned on other ethnic groups—in particular the settlers from the province of Punjab—to cleanse their territory of the people who are considered to be foreign. Christians and Hindus, the two main religious minorities, have been harassed in many different ways. Christians in particular have been subjected to the diktat of the blasphemy laws—the Hudood Ordinance. All this does not suggest a society that is tolerant of people who are not in the mainstream. That notwithstanding, Pakistan seems to be slowly moving towards a situation in which institutions and laws will begin to yield workable pluralism. As discussed above, a constitutional solution was found to deal with the rise of sectarianism in places such as Baluchistan where the people from different sects of the same religion have found it difficult to co-exist. The relative harmony that existed before the ill-fated attempt to Islamicize society was shattered by the rise of sectarian violence. Even within Sunni Islam, people holding different points also resorted to violence. Wahhabis have taken to burning Sufi shrines; the small Ahmadiya community continues to be discriminated against to the extent that many are seeking asylum in Europe, Canada and the USA; and the extremists are targeting the few members of the faiths other than Islam that remain in the country.

It was to use politics to address these growing intra-faith quarrels that a Sufi cleric arrived in Pakistan from Canada in December 2012 and shook the political world. Dr Tahirul Qadri, the head of Minhajul Quran International (MQI), first held a large public meeting in a Lahore public square on 23 December and then followed it with a march on Islamabad accompanied by tens of thousands of his followers. He had correctly concluded that poor governance was at the heart of Pakistan's many problems. After being promised that fair elections would be held in the spring of 2013 supervised by a caretaker administration to supervise them, he allowed his congregation to disperse from Islamabad.

There are of course strong links between economics, governance and politics. These links are in several different directions. It is almost always politics that determines the direction in which the economy develops, but there are also important links pointing in the opposite direction. As discussed at length before and as will be discussed later in the chapter, Pakistan's economy is under great stress. To have it recover from this pressure that has reduced the rate of GDP growth to a very low level, Pakistan will have to have good working relations with the USA. The USA has remained an important source of finance for the country.

Relations with the USA

Good relations with the USA matter a great deal for Pakistan since Islamabad's resource situation, always poor, deteriorated sharply on the eve of the 2013 elections. It will have to rely on external finance for years to come—for as long as it does not reform the structure of the economy, which would make it possible to rely more on domestically generated resources for development. Washington was and will continue to remain for several years to come the most important source of funds for Pakistan. It could provide a significant amount of capital from its own budget—a promise made by Washington in a bill signed into law by President Obama in the autumn of 2009. The Kerry-Lugar-Berman bill promised Pakistan US$4.5 billion of economic assistance in the form of grants over the five-year period from 2009 to 2014. Washington also told Islamabad that it would be prepared to provide the same level of support beyond 2014. This pledge was to assure Pakistan that US support would be available even after the USA pulled out of Afghanistan. However, this promised programme of support ran into serious political and operational problems.

The year 2011 proved to be one of the more difficult in the USA's often rocky relations with Pakistan.[14] In January a Central Intelligence Agency (CIA) operative killed two young men in broad daylight on a busy Lahore street. He was taken into custody but released after a lot of pressure was exerted on Islamabad by the Obama Administration, and also after the payment of 'blood money' allowed under Islamic law. In May Osama bin Laden, who had been hiding in a large house in Abbottabad, deep inside Pakistan, was killed during an operation carried out by US Navy Seals. The city housed the Pakistan Military Academy. Islamabad was informed of the attack only after the Seals had flown out of the country, carrying with them the body of the al-Qa'ida leader. Islamabad was not pleased that its sovereignty had not been respected and that the Americans had penetrated so deep into its territory. In late November a US attack on a Pakistani post near the border with Afghanistan killed 24 soldiers. This proved to be the last straw on the already burdened Pakistani back. Under pressure from the military, Islamabad stopped the flow of material to the US troops operating in Afghanistan. The USA retaliated by stopping the flow of all funds to Pakistan, putting the latter under considerable economic strain.

There were also operational problems with US assistance to Pakistan. Even when the funds were available, the US Agency for International Development (USAID) was able to develop a viable strategy for its support. As pointed out by a study group organized by the Washington-based Woodrow Wilson Center, the US-funded programme remained poorly defined and poorly implemented.[15]

Following strenuous efforts by both sides, relations began to improve. On 3 July 2012 a statement made by the US Secretary of State Hillary Clinton apologizing for the unintentional attack by US forces in November, marginally cleared the air. It was followed by the signing of a memorandum of understanding (MOU) in Rawalpindi by the two governments three weeks later. The MOU included an agreement with the USA for reopening the supply route to Afghanistan. It was expected to bring some financial rewards. The Obama Administration indicated that it would request from Congress $1.1 billion in aid for Pakistan. This money was owed to Islamabad for the services that had already been provided. Pakistan, however, estimated the amount at $3 billion. There was, however, no mention of the flow of funds from the Kerry-Lugar-Bermen bill, which was supposed to put Pakistan-US relations on a firmer ground. Even if the US Congress acted with dispatch—uncertain, given Pakistan's very low reputation in that body—it might ease the financial situation for a while. This happened in the week of 20 July, when the USA deposited $1.1 billion with the State Bank of Pakistan. However, the basic arithmetic will not change. Pakistan spent much more than it collected in taxes; its imports cost more than it was able to earn from exports. The State Bank of Pakistan had begun to lose reserves and the rupee came under pressure.

There were other US decisions that will have consequences for Pakistan. The USA's decision to pull out of Afghanistan and complete the process by the end of 2014 left Pakistan guessing about its impact. 'Washington seems to be settling for a degree of managed instability in Afghanistan dealt with by the Afghan National Army and American social forces', wrote Tanvir Ahmad Khan who was once the top diplomat in Pakistan and knowledgeable about the Afghan situation.

> Such a scenario will hurt the interests of most regional powers. For Pakistan it will be a nightmare. The situation in Afghanistan is, to say the least, dynamic and may gravitate towards greater crisis, including civil war or many mini civil wars … Washington is redefining its objectives in Afghanistan within the larger context of the strategic reconfiguration of Asia that it seeks. Much also would depend on the modalities of disbursing the assistance of $16 billion pledged at the Tokyo conference [held in July].[16]

By the end of 2012 Islamabad did an about-turn in its traditional position with respect to the activities of the Taliban.[17] Having helped to create the group in 1996 for the purpose of bringing peace to Afghanistan, Islamabad had shown considerable reluctance to convince the group to come to a political understanding with the government in Kabul headed by President Hamid Karzai. For years Pakistan's intelligence agencies had taken the position that it would be to their advantage if the void left in Afghanistan once US forces fully withdrew were to be filled by the Taliban groups that operated from the bases and sanctuaries located on their side of the border.

In its 'Banyan' column, *The Economist* examined in detail the change in Pakistan's policy stance concerning Afghanistan. 'Pervez Musharraf, Pakistan's former president did little to disguise the loathing he felt for his Afghan counterpart', wrote the magazine in its issue of 9 February 2012.

> By contrast, Mr Musharraf's successor Asif Ali Zardari, seems to have found in Mr Karzai a new best friend. In Britain this week, sharing a podium with their host, David Cameron, the two men beamed, clasped hands and pledged what Mr Cameron called 'an unprecedented level of co-operation'. They even agreed to work towards a peace agreement with the Taliban with in the next six months. This reflects a change in Pakistan's strategy far more profound than can be explained by Mr Zardari's more emollient character.[18]

Pakistan made a number of gestures before the meeting in London. In November Islamabad received Afghanistan's High Peace Council and then freed 20 Afghan Taliban prisoners. A peace roadmap was developed in which Pakistan was to have a central role. It was agreed to set up an office in Doha, the capital of Qatar, where the various sides to the dispute would hold consultations.

Pakistan's changed position was largely the result of its improved and improving relations with India, a country with which it had quarrelled ever since the two won independence in 1947. Starting in 2011, the two countries embarked on a course that should lead to improved relations, particularly in the area of trade.

Change is inevitable

Will Pakistan stay on its present course and eventually plunge into a deep and dark abyss, or will it pull back and alter course? Change, whether intended or unintended, will happen in Pakistan. Whether the government steps in to bring about long-delayed structural adjustments, some developments in a country such as Pakistan are inevitable. Both the population and the economy will grow; more people will move into the urban areas, even into the crowded cities, such as Karachi, Lahore and Faisalabad; and the technologies behind many production processes will improve. The structure of the economy will be reshaped with more output originating from what economists loosely describe as the service sector. Goods and commodities will flow between the country's different parts in increasing amounts. What public policy could do is to slow some of the expected negative changes (such as the rate of growth in the population), or hasten some of those that are positive (such as the rate of growth in the gross national product).

I will begin with population growth. According to the government, since 2010 the population has increased at the rate of 2% per year. With about 185 million people living in the country in 2013, it is more than six times its size when what is called Pakistan today became an independent state. An increase from 30 million in 1947 to 185 million in 2013 implies a rate of growth of 2.8% a year over this period. This did not remain unchanged all this time. At the time of its birth, Pakistan's population was increasing at the rate of less than 2% a year. The pace picked up in the 1950s and 1960s, as it did in most of the developing world. The government—sometimes with the help of developing agencies such as the World Bank—was able to provide better health services. As a result infant, child and maternal mortality rates declined and life expectancy increased. In the early 2010s, the infant mortality rate was 71 per 1,000 live births—still high, but considerably lower than a decade or two ago—and the maternal mortality rate was 276 per 100,000 births while life expectancy was 67 years.[19] This meant that over time the population became younger. In 2013 the median age of the population was only 22 years, one of the lowest in the world. This means that of the 185 million people who possibly live in the country (this number, at best, is an informed guess, since mostly for political reasons the country has not conducted a population census since 1998), 92.5 million are below that age.

If working age is defined as between 15 and 65 years, in Pakistan about 120 million people fall in this category. This group supports another 65 million non-working people (the very young, the very old and the infirm), which means that every non-working person has two people providing support. Pakistan, in other words, has a very low dependency ratio. Economists call this the 'demographic window of opportunity', which opens when there are more people working (or able to work) than those they need to support. In Pakistan's case this window opened a decade or so ago and will be shut in about three decades. Most countries that grew rapidly in the past few decades, such as those in East Asia, made use of this opportunity. This is where public policy enters the picture. With good policies and with good governance a rate of GDP growth of 6% to 8% per year is not beyond Pakistan's reach.

Without appropriate policies the economy will continue to grow at about half that rate. The growth rate is seldom less than the rate of increase in the population. It is usually a bit more depending upon how much capital is being accumulated and how much technical change is occurring. Even in a stagnant economy—which is what official numbers suggest Pakistan has today—capital continues to be added to the process of production and technological improvements continue to take place. The recent penetration of mobile telephony is one example of this, while another is the rapid replacement of bicycles with motorcycles in most parts of the country. This is speeding up the pace at which transactions and social interactions take place. Even with poor economic management the rate of growth will be a percentage point or two above the rate of increase in population. In the current situation, in other words, the economy will inevitably increase at a rate of 3% to 4% per year, which is what it has done since the arrival of democracy in the country.

Some Pakistan-based economists believe that these low numbers don't tell the real story of Pakistan's recent development. There is no doubt that the state of the economy and its performance over time should by analysed on the basis of data, but for Pakistan statistics on many aspects of economic change are either not available or are seriously out of date. As the newspaper columnist David Brooks wrote in a February 2013 article, 'if you ask me to describe the philosophy of the day, I'd say it is data-ism. We now have the ability to gather huge amounts of data. This ability seems to carry with it certain assumptions that everything that can be measured should be measured; that data is a transparent and filters out emotionalism and ideology; that data will help us to do remarkable things like tell the future'.[20] Unfortunately, that is not the case for Pakistan. Policymakers in the country have not shown much interest in basing economic policymaking on data and solid information. This resulted in the adoption of policies that could not reach their specified goals. Poor demographic data, including information about the rate of urbanization, is one of the several reasons why policy was made without much knowledge of what was really happening.

The pace of urbanization has picked up in most of the developing world and Pakistan is not an exception. In fact, the rate of increase in Pakistan's urban population was more rapid than the rest of the developing world. This was because of migration not just from rural to urban areas but from beyond Pakistan's borders. Three international migrations—two into the country and the third from the country to the world outside—have enormously affected the country's economic, political and social development. In 1947 when Pakistan was created and for a couple of years after that, the country received eight million Muslim refugees from various parts of India. A large number came from the Urdu-speaking provinces. Some six million Hindus and Sikhs left Pakistan for India, leaving the country with an additional two million people in a population of 30 million. The absorption of this horde was one of the great public policy successes in Pakistan's history. The other large migration into Pakistan was from Afghanistan during that country's two wars, starting with the USSR's occupation in 1979, followed by the 2001 invasion of the country by the USA. The number of displaced Afghans who took refuge in Pakistan has fluctuated between two and four million, depending upon the conditions in their homeland. While there are no accurate estimates of the number of Afghans who have settled permanently in Pakistan, two million would be a good working guess. Accommodating such a large number of people in various parts of the country is another story of Pakistan's overlooked success.

These two inward movements of people changed the ethnic and religious orientation of Pakistani society. Pakistan in 2013 is more Muslim than it was in 1947. Then one-third of the total population was non-Muslim; now the proportion is less than 5%. The 'Muslimization' of the country led to its progressive Islamization. It also became less tolerant of religious diversity. Pakistan is also more 'muhajir'. A significant proportion of the people in Karachi and some other cities in the country's south trace their origins to those who took refuge after the partition of British India in 1947. These two changes have proven to be of enormous consequence for the development of the country. The most telling result is the country's rapid urbanization and the extraordinary growth of what Steve Inskeep has called the instant city of Karachi. In 1947 Pakistan had about four million people living in urban areas when it became an independent state. In 2013, 66 years later, it had 80 million urban people, 20 times as many as in 1947. All the major cities in the world have grown rapidly during the past half century. Los Angeles has tripled in size; Houston has expanded six-fold; Istanbul is about 10 times its former size; Urumqi is about 23 times more populous than the estimate for 1950. 'And then there is Karachi', writes Inskeep. 'Conservative estimates suggest that it is at least thirty times larger than in 1995—meaning that there are at least thirty residents today for everyone at the war's end'.[21]

Karachi grew not only as a result of international migration. It also received millions of people from its own hinterland and from the country's north and east. It is by far the most cosmopolitan city in Pakistan and also the one with the most pronounced mix of ethnic and linguistic groups. The fact that the city's diverse population has learned to live in reasonable social and economic harmony is a measure of its success. The fact that the city often sees eruptions of extreme violence is an indication of its failure to govern itself. Karachi has seen more violence than other cities of Pakistan because of its diversity and also because of the inability to put in place institutions for political management. It still does not have the institutional structure that can help it to satisfy the different aspirations of its diverse population while also helping to resolve their differences. Karachi has been both a success and a failure as a megacity.

Large-scale rural-to-urban migration experienced by Pakistan inevitably changed the structure of the country's economy. Urbanization in a relatively poor country means the movement of people from an economy of subsistence to that of dependence. In the countryside most people produce most of what they need to consume. Relocated in the urban world, they have to depend upon the supply of goods and services in the formal and informal markets. In economies where most demand for products and services is domestic, the services sector tends to grow more rapidly than the rest of the economy. This is the case in Pakistan where well over half of the officially calculated value added in the economy comes from the services sector. This would not have been the case had the vast majority of the population remained rural. Also, had Pakistan focused greater attention on developing external markets for its agricultural and industrial products, GDP would have expanded at a faster rate. The manufacturing sector in East Asia expanded at an extraordinarily high rate owing to the external demand for its products. This did not happen automatically; it was a consequence of the vigorous encouragement provided by the state to manufacturing enterprises.[22] This could have happened in Pakistan as well, if the state had been more mindful of the opportunities that were available in international markets. Not adopting export-orientation as the driving force for the economy has meant a stagnation in its share in the international marketplace. Over the last couple of decades, Pakistan's share has improved only marginally from 0.12% in 1980 to 0.16% in 2010, 30 years later. At the same time, some of its competitors have increased their shares by significant amounts. China increased its share from 0.8% to 14.8% in the same 30-year period, India went from 0.46% to 1.40%, Turkey from 0.07% to 0.89%.[23]

Another 'what if … ?' in Pakistan's economic history concerns its relations with India. At the time of the partition of the Indian sub-continent the areas that now make up the state of Pakistan were the major suppliers of food grains to the food-deficit areas in the north-east of the British colony. However, in 1949 India imposed a trade embargo on its neighbour, which forced Pakistan to industrialize rapidly, dependent as it was on India for most manufactured goods that its citizens needed. Had relations with India not deteriorated, agriculture would have remained a more important sector of the economy. Now that relations have begun to improve, it will have a profound impact on Pakistan's rate of economic growth as well as on the structure of its economy. With openness to India, some of the sectors that can produce goods and commodities competitively for the large and rapidly expanding Indian markets will no doubt develop rapidly. In a book published in 2011, I estimated that Pakistan could add as much as 2.4% a year to its GDP by the year 2025.[24]

These, then, are some of the developments that have occurred and are occurring. They could have happened differently had the policymakers and public policy addressed some of the underlying aspects of the economy. Had appropriate policies been adopted at the right time, the economy would have been much larger than its present size and the rate of population growth would have been much lower. The two taken together would have meant a much higher income per head of the population; lower personal and regional income disparities; less violent cities; more tolerant society; and a pluralistic political culture. Could the directions in which changes are occurring at this time be altered by the adoption of the right sets of policies? The answer is obviously yes and that brings me to the next section in which I spell out some of the policies that could aid Pakistan's future development.

Shaping the future

It would take a multi-pronged approach to bring Pakistan out of the deep crisis it faced as the democratic government reached the concluding months of its fifth year in office. In the area of economics, public policy will have to address the issue of poor governance. It will need to deal with the failure of the state to raise sufficient resources for delivering public goods to an increasingly frustrated and disgruntled citizenry. There was the need to overcome serious shortages of goods and services critical for industrial output as well as household consumption. There was work to be done to reduce interpersonal and inter-regional income inequalities. Physical infrastructure needed to be improved and what had already been built needed to be maintained. It had not fully dawned on the policymakers that global warming was likely to prove disastrous for Pakistan, making the already stressed water situation even more problematic. The list of 'dos' was a long one. Pakistan had dealt with many crises in the past. What was different this time around was that a number of problems surfaced at the same time. Their coming together produced a perfect storm which required a great deal of thinking on economic policies that would be appropriate for Pakistan at this time.

What should be the development agenda for the policymakers at this delicate moment in the country's economic history? There were at least five areas that needed the policymakers' urgent attention: revival of growth; increasing domestic resource mobilization; reconnecting the country with the world; reducing income disparities; and investing in the development of the large human resource. Each of these areas required a series of government actions. What needs to be done in one area will impact on the remaining four. In other words, a comprehensive approach that dealt with the short term is the need at this precarious hour. Long-term thinking could wait while the short term was being fixed.

There were three possible public policy approaches to placing the Pakistani economy on the trajectory of higher GDP growth. This could be done by the adoption of policies that tend to go under the title of the 'Washington Consensus'. Or the country could follow the approach developed and published in 2011 by the Planning Commission in Islamabad. Or Islamabad could follow a two-step strategy that I have advocated in earlier writings. I will take up each of these three in turn, albeit briefly.

As already indicated, the IMF in its 'Article Four' consultations with Islamabad had correctly underscored the need to bring growth back to the economy. It believed that a rate of growth of 7% per year was needed in order to accommodate two million new entrants to the workforce. In fact, there was recognition among some, but not all, economists that getting the economy to grow again was a two-step process: first ensuring the survival of the economy and then working to revive it. The economy's fast descent into a state of near-chaos needed to be arrested and that required a different set of measures from those that would get the economy to grow again. However, it was not only the finance minister who believed that the economy was on the mend and that the worst was over. This was also the view of some of the Pakistan-based economists such as S. Akbar Zaidi, the author of a highly respected textbook on Pakistan. He and several others believed that excessive pessimism about the state of the economy was largely based on the thinking of a group of professionals who had left the country decades ago to work in institutions such as the World Bank and the IMF, or in New York- or London-based commercial banks. They had dealt with a number of countries around the world but had only a vague notion about the reality of the Pakistani situation. In an article in *Dawn* Zaidi labelled the group 'suitcase economists', since some of them had returned to occupy senior positions in the government, but only for short periods of time.[25] They had subscribed to the thinking embedded in what came to be called the Washington Consensus. The policies advocated by this approach looked at broad economic indicators such as the rate of GDP growth, the rates of national savings and investments, and the fiscal and balance of payments deficits. If these measures of economic performance were not in line with what was expected of a healthy economy, there was an urgent need to bring about structural changes. Most of these should be made in the context of 'openness'—opening the economy to trade and foreign capital flows, and also to domestic entrepreneurship. Once these measures were adopted, the state needed to step back and leave a great deal of space for the private sector. The government should neither control economic assets nor attempt to dispatch the economy in any particular direction. That should ideally be left to Adam Smith's proverbial 'invisible hand'. This style of economic management was imported into the country by the members of the 'suitcase economists' group.

This economic philosophy was put to use in several countries that faced extreme economic stress, first in the 1980s and then in the 1990s. The first set of problems arose as a result of the excessive borrowing by a group of middle-income oil-importing countries that saw sharp increases in their import bills because of the jump in the price of oil. The Arab embargo of 1973 was the first reason for the oil price increase. Another increase took place after the 1979 Islamic Revolution in Iran. Rather than cut oil consumption, the affected middle-income countries borrowed heavily from both the US and European banks in order to maintain oil consumption at the same level. Once faced with default, the countries turned to the international finance (IMF) and development (the World Bank and the Inter-American Development Bank) institutions for help. This was provided, but on the condition that the countries adopted Washington Consensus-type structural adjustments. The result was what economic historians call the 'lost decade of growth': the 1980s.

The second crisis came in the 1990s and was a consequence of strict adherence to the Washington Consensus on the part of several 'open' economies of East Asia. In the Republic of Korea (South Korea), Thailand, Indonesia and Malaysia private consumption and investment were fuelled by the easy availability of finance from the financial institutions in the West. These flows came in at adjustable rates, and when those went up because of the some belt-tightening in the West, the East Asians found themselves heading towards bankruptcy. The irony of this situation was that it was the very openness of the economies that produced the 1996–97 East Asian Financial Crisis. Among those who made this connection was the Nobel Laureate Joseph Stieglitz, who at that time was the chief economist at the World Bank.

The point of making this slight digression into economic theory, policy and practice is to provide the background against which some well-respected Pakistani economists are thinking unconventionally about the situation in the country in 2013, as well as what needs to be done to secure a better future. Given the above-mentioned statement by Finance Minister Sheikh, these non-conventional voices are having an impact on the making of public policy.

This group of economists believes that the state of the economy should be interpreted not just in terms of official macroeconomic numbers, but also by what is happening in the part of the economy that is loosely referred to as the 'underground'. As the name implies, this is the part of the economy that does not come to the surface. The reasons for hiding under the ground are mixed: to avoid paying taxes, to evade regulation by the many agencies of the state, to employ millions of workers who have arrived in cities such as Karachi as illegal migrants, and to deal in the products that are banned for consumption (drugs and alcohol). Little analytical work has been done to estimate the total value added by the underground economy. There is plenty of anecdotal evidence and some secondary information to suggest that the economy's real size may be considerably larger than suggested by official data. Working from official data, it appears that consumption was increasing at a rate that was a multiple of the rate of increase in the national product. There were sharp increases in the sales of such consumer durables as bicycles and motorcycles. The numbers begin to make some sense if the overall size of the economy was considerably larger than that suggested by official statistics. If this conclusion is correct, then no drastic reorientation of public policy is required. What is needed is fine-tuning to improve some aspects of the economy and not an application of the Washington Consensus.

Whether a fundamental structural change of the economy is needed or not, the fact remains that Pakistan is not raising as much in terms of government revenues as required to fulfil a number of unmet or poorly met needs. The tax-to-GDP ratio touched the lowest level in decades in 2010, falling below 9%. If the size of the economy is twice as large as some economists maintain, then the ratio is even lower. This does not augur well for the economy's future. The state does not have the means to invest in a number of areas which are necessary for the economy to move forward. In spite of a number of efforts made by the government in Islamabad to get the tax system to produce higher yields, government revenue remains low. The reason for this is largely politics. Even before the return of democracy, the government's efforts to mobilize more resources from the tax system floundered. During the early part of the Musharraf administration (1999–2008) the government tried to intimidate shop owners into paying taxes.

Islamabad used military personnel to accompany tax officials as they made their rounds of the shopping areas. This did not work.

There were, however, many things wrong with official thinking about the state of the Pakistani economy. Much of this was being done at the Planning Commission, some at the Ministry of Finance, some more at the Ministry of Commerce, and some was also coming out of the provincial capitals. There were some useful materials produced particularly at the Planning Commission. What the Planning Commission called the Framework for Economic Growth paper, or FEG, had some innovative material. It was right to focus on what it labelled the 'soft side' of the development equation. The commission claimed that for Pakistan to increase the rate of economic growth it needed to invest in the softer aspects of development and not continue to commit large sums of money on bricks and mortar development schemes that have dominated the Public Sector Development Plan.[26]

The 'soft side' advocated by the Planning Commission included institution building, human resource development, increasing the capacity of the private sector to innovate, reducing the regulatory burden carried by private enterprise, and changing and modernizing urban regulation so that cities became the most dynamic part of the economy. What really irked the Planning Commission were the zoning regulations in many cities that prevented vertical development. This inhibited the economic role of the city centre. The Commission was also concerned about the declining efficiency and effectiveness of the various civil services. It called for a fundamental restructuring and reform of the civil administration. All these were worthwhile goals and they needed to be included in an approach aimed at long-term growth. However, they didn't constitute a strategy that could pull Pakistan out of the deep economic hole it had by then dug for itself.

The FEG was an approach that will deliver rewards over the long term. It will do very little to solve Pakistan's current economic problems. There were several of these, but unfortunately not many among them found their way into official thinking. The following are some of the many problems crying out for policymaking attention, listed in no particular order: Pakistan's longest-lasting recession, with no end in sight; continuing violence, some of it directed at the state; increasing isolation from the world; continued dependence on external capital flows for financing low levels of public-sector investment; the loss of confidence on the part of the investment community, both inside and outside the country, in Pakistan's economic future; low rates of domestic savings and low tax-to-GDP ratio; very little public sector investment in improving the quality of the large human resource; a declining share in international trade; poor relations between the federal government and provincial administrations; and the increasing incidence of public sector corruption.

The list is even longer than this but there was no systematic official response to most of these problems. A soft power-focused strategy of growth would work well in realizing the economy's large but neglected potential. However, the impact of this focus will be felt only after a long time. Pakistan was now regarded as a fragile state by development institutions such as the World Bank. In one of its recent *World Development Reports* the Bank also picked up some of the soft factors in the growth function.[27] These, it suggested, were essential ingredients of long-term sustainable development, but it emphasized—correctly, I believe—that it will take a generation or two before fragile economies such as Pakistan could begin to use these factors effectively in the development equation.

If neither the Washington Consensus-type of approach nor the approach advocated by the Planning Commission's growth framework were appropriate for Pakistan's situation in early 2013, is there a third way? I will attempt an answer to this question by focusing on four points. First, the year 2012/13 was a bit better than the year before, but it did not mean that the economy was finally out of the woods. Second, Pakistan was not different from most other countries. Difficult economic situations are almost always the result of public policy. In 2008–13 Pakistan was engaged in making a transition from a controlled to a reasonably open political system. Policymakers were necessarily confronted with difficult choices to prevent the transition to the new political order from being compromised. The positive side to this development was that a durable and representative political system was coming into being in which people would have a voice. Third, one of the more important reasons for the economy's indifferent performance was the poor quality of governance that was on offer. There are ways of improving governance and some of these were being factored into the active discourse on corruption as the country approached another set of elections. Fourth, there were a number of positive features in the Pakistani economy. They could become part of the growth framework being developed by the Planning Commission. I can point to seven positives even while the country is faced with a dismal economic and security situation. This jump in the rate of growth will require some bold policy steps by the government operating out of Islamabad. The positives are agriculture with a high growth potential; small and medium-sized enterprises that have the skill base to become parts of international supply chains; the opening-up of the economy to India; an enviable geographic space at the crossroads of what could become important lines of international commerce; rapidly growing cities that could become the engines of economic growth; the entry of one million well-trained and skilled women into the economy every year; and large diasporas willing to play important roles in the development of the homeland. These factors, were they to be incorporated in the growth equation, could pull the country back from economic stagnation and set it on a plane of high and sustainable GDP growth. Pakistan, properly managed, could achieve a rate of growth of between 7% and 8% in the next three to five years.

The third way, therefore, suggests tackling the problem of economic stagnation by first increasing investor confidence in the economy. This should be attempted by whichever government takes office following the 2013 elections. Two decisions should be adopted within six months to one year following the assumption of office of the new administration. Two different public policy announcements should be the focus of immediate attention. The first should be aimed at the reform of the existing accountability system. The NAB should be headed by an individual who has the confidence of the citizenry. His or her appointment should result from the same kind of process that was put in place by the recent amendments to the constitution for selecting the senior members of the judiciary as well as the person to lead the Election Commission. The NAB's investigation agencies as well as its courts should be fully autonomous, reporting only to the institution's head and once a year to the national legislature. A programme for reforming the civil service should be the second area of focus. A well-researched and comprehensive reform document was produced in 2008 by a commission headed by Ishrat Husain, former governor of the State Bank of Pakistan. This report could become the basis of the reforms to be undertaken.

The third area of action should be the preparation of a three-year development plan that goes well beyond the FEG announced by the Planning Commission in 2011. It should be built on the seven positives identified above, with the roles to be played by both the public and private sectors clearly set out. The three-year development strategy should also incorporate the provincial plans covering the same period, say 2014 to 2017. This plan should be developed by the Planning Commission, which should also be tasked to oversee the plan's implementation. The reason why I have called this a two-step approach is that the first series of actions will be taken within the first 6–12 months after the induction into office of a new government. The more detailed growth plan should be prepared for implementation over the period ending in the financial year 2016–17.

Conclusion

No matter how one looks at the economy—in conventional or unconventional terms—that it is under stress is suggested by the vast army of unemployed or underemployed youth. If these people cannot be given reasonably productive jobs in the economy, many of them will opt out and start looking for other ways of meeting their needs. When the state is weak there is great temptation to work outside its space—a well-known reaction by the deprived, which has received academic attention from political scientists such as Samuel P. Huntington and political economists such as Albert O. Hirschman.[28] There is no doubt that many recruits to the organizations that pursue extremism as a way of achieving their objectives are attracted to them for economic reasons. Extremism in the country is not increasing only for ideological reasons; it has become good business for those who organize it and those who become its foot soldiers.[29] The Benazir Income Support Fund was one way of dealing with this situation and what was known about it seemed to suggest that it was working reasonably well. On top of this the government—in particular the provincial administrations—should give serious thought to the launching of public works programmes in both rural and urban areas. A great deal could be done by such programmes to improve the quality of life for those who are seeing its deterioration with every passing day. However, the real economic issue at this moment is the revival of confidence in the economy. For that to happen, the quality of governance needs to improve. It is on this that the policymakers need to focus.

Experiences from other parts of the world show that appropriate sets of economic policies and good-quality leadership can quickly turn a situation around. This happened in Latin America in the 1990s.[30] It is happening now in some parts of the African continent. However, these changes always occur when those who lead are committed to improving general welfare and not just their own economic situation and that of their families and close associates. It requires political will to take difficult decisions especially when they are not favoured by some powerful segments of society. Most of these conditions do not exist in Pakistan as the country moves towards another election, but they may appear as a consequence of the cleaning of the political house resulting from the next poll. One can only hope that the wait will not be a long one. Anatole Lieven, the author of an acclaimed book on Pakistan, observed that there are plenty of signs that the country is a troubled rather than a failed state.[31]

Notes

1 International Monetary Fund, 'IMF Executive Board Concludes 2011 Article IV Consultation and Proposal for Post-Program Monitoring with Pakistan', Public Information Notice No. 12/10, 6 February 2012, Washington, DC.

2 Khaliq Kiani, 'Fears are Baseless', *Dawn*, 2 December 2012, 11.

3 Khaliq Kiani, 'Govt Admits Breaching Debt Limits', *Dawn*, 5 February 2013, 9.

4 Joe Brinkley, 'Pakistan Coming Apart at the Seams', *The Baltimore Sun*, 28 January 2013, 13.

5 Aryn Baker, 'The Fighter Malala Yousafzai', *Time*, 31 December 2012, 98.

6 Nate Silver, *The Signal and the Noise: Why So Many Predictions Fail but Some Don't*, The Penguin Press, New York, 2012.

7 Thomas L. Friedman, 'Our Secret Sauce', *The New York Times*, 24 October 2012, A23.

8 Daron Acemoglu and James A. Robinson, *Why Nations Fail: The Origins of Power, Prosperity, and Poverty*, Crown Business, New York, 2012.

9 Francis Fukuyama, *The Origins of Political Order: From Pre-human Times to French Revolution*, Farrar, Giroux and Strauss, New York, 2011.

10 Paul Krugman, 'Europe's Great Illusion', *The New York Times*, 1 July 2012, 21.

11 Henry Petroski, *To Forgive Design: Understanding Failure*, The Belknap Press of Harvard University, Cambridge, MA, 2012.

12 David E. Sanger, *Confront and Conceal: Obama's Secret Wars and Surprising Use of American Power*, Crown Publishers, 2012; Robert W. Merry, *Where They Stand: The American Presidents in the Eyes of the Voters and Historians*, Simon & Schuster, New York, 2012.

13 Robert W. Merry, 'The Obama Doctrine', the *New York Times Book Reviews*, 15 July 2012, 19.

14 See Denis Kux for the history of US-Pakistan relations, *The United States and Pakistan, 1947–2000*, Johns Hopkins Press, London, 2001.

15 Woodrow Wilson Institute of International Scholars, *Aiding without Abetting: Making Civilian Assistance Work for Both Sides*, Washington, DC, July 2011.

16 Tanvir Ahmad Khan, 'Our Afghan Policy', *Dawn*, 17 July 2012, 7.

17 One of the good sources for understanding the rise of the Taliban is Ahmed Rashid, *Taliban: Islam, Oil and the New Great Game*, I.B. Tauris, London, 2000.

18 Banyan, 'A Decent Interval', *The Economist*, 9 February 2012, 43.

19 The data are from The World Bank, *World Development Indicators, 2011*, Washington, DC, Tables 2.16 to 2.22, 94–120.

20 David Brooks, 'The Philosophy of Data', the *New York Times*, 2 February 2012, 19.

21 Steve Inskeep, *Instant City: Life and Death in Karachi*, Penguin Press, New York, 2011, 3.

22 The development of the countries with miracle economies was examined by the World Bank in *The East Asian Miracle: Economic Growth and Public Policy*, Oxford University Press, New York, 1993.

23 Institute of Public Policy, *Fifth Annual Report 2012: The State of the Economy: The Punjab Story*, Lahore, 2012, Table 2.9, 28.

24 Shahid Javed Burki, *South Asia in the New World Order: The Role of Regional Cooperation*, Routledge, 2011, 180.

25 S. Akbar Zaidi, 'Suitcase Economists', *Dawn*, 31 December 2012, 7.

26 Planning Commission, *Pakistan: Framework for Economic Growth*, Government of Pakistan, Islamabad, 2011.

27 The World Bank, *World Development Report, 2011: Conflict, Security, and Development*, Oxford University Press, New York, 2011.

28 See Samuel P. Huntington, *Political Order in Changing Societies*, Yale University Press, New Haven, CT, 1968; and Albert O. Hirschman, *Exit, Voice and Loyalty: Response to Decline in Firms, Organizations and States*, Harvard University Press, Cambridge, MA., 2004.

29 The factors that motivate people—in particular young people—to sacrifice their lives in pursuit of various causes is examined in Riaz Hasan, *Life as a Weapon: The Global Rise of Suicide Bombings*, Routledge, London, 2011. Chapter five, 101–21, examines the situation in Pakistan.

30 The author, as vice-president for Latin America and the Caribbean at the World Bank, had personal experience of the fast and positive response of a number of countries in the region that changed both the leaders as well as public sector policies in order to handle difficult situations. Under his direction, the World Bank was deeply engaged in helping the countries in the region out of the deep economic and social crises they faced in the second half of the 1990s.

31 Quoted in Rahul Jacob, 'Zardari Court Battles Masks Pakistan Gains', *Financial Times*, 28 July 2012, 13.

21

Egypt

Too 'big' to succeed?

Robert Springborg

The predominant theme of republican Egypt's economic history is that of rent seeking, external and internal. 'Cursed' by the resource endowment of a key geostrategic location, which is reinforced by being the largest, most powerful Arab state, possessing substantial hydrocarbon reserves, Egypt has substituted rents for reforms required for a productive, rapidly growing economy. Successive administrations have pursued national economic well-being primarily by attempting to garner public assistance from foreign suitors and by extracting oil and gas rents. They have, moreover, surrendered steadily more of the economy to the military and security services that prop up executive power.

During the Cold War, for example, Gamal Abd al-Nasir (Nasser) sought with initial success to induce the USA and the USSR to compete for Egypt's favours, only ultimately to overplay his hand and fall firmly into the latter's orbit. Egypt's economy under Nasser thus traced a more or less steady decline. Initially buoyed by confiscation of assets from foreigners and wealthy Egyptians, especially non-Muslims, as well as by assistance from the West, which was terminated in 1965, the Egyptian economy slid downhill as it was locked ever more tightly into the Soviet embrace.

Rent seeking in the communist world was not very remunerative, as Nasser's successor, Anwar Sadat, appreciated. Replacing the Soviets with the Americans as geopolitical patrons and as inspirations for the domestic economic model, Sadat reaped immediate and substantial dividends. Fearful of the negative political repercussions for their new client-president of the legacy of crumbling infrastructure he had inherited from Nasser's Arab socialism, the Americans and their Western allies moved quickly to assist the upgrading and expansion of virtually the entire physical infrastructure, including power generation and distribution, roads and public transport, sewer and water delivery systems, schools, ports, and so on. Geostrategic rental income was augmented by a dramatic increase in hydrocarbon rents resulting from the quadrupling of oil prices in 1973–74, which benefited Egypt directly as its limited but long-established oil production was simultaneously expanding toward its historic maximum of almost one million barrels per day, and indirectly through subventions from newly enriched Saudi Arabia and other Gulf states. So while Egypt's rental income soared under Sadat, especially if remittances are included in that category, industry and agriculture languished as Egyptians sought opportunities in the Gulf, Libya and elsewhere, or in the newly expanding tourism and construction industries at home. The rapid rise in Egypt's per capita gross domestic product (GDP) during the Sadat era was due

397

not to expansion of the sectors producing tradable goods, whether agricultural or industrial, which were in fact negatively impacted by a predictable bout of Dutch disease, but to the surge of geostrategic and direct and indirect hydrocarbon rents. Sadat was fortunate in his final two years in office that the downturn in subventions from the Arab Gulf states resultant from his 1979 peace with Israel was offset by the surge in oil revenues as a result of the price run-up associated with that year's Iranian revolution.

While Sadat largely escaped the vagaries inherent in dependence upon rents, his successor, Muhammad Hosni Mubarak, who served as president almost three times longer than he did, had to cope with many substantial fluctuations. However, even the dramatic see-sawing of the national economy after 1981, accompanied by stagnating national savings, an infrastructure deteriorating yet again because of inadequate investment, and an increase in poverty, especially in politically volatile Upper Egypt, did not induce Mubarak to divert from the rent-seeking path trodden by his predecessors.[1] In free fall as a result of the collapse of oil prices in the mid-1980s, the economy, and possibly Mubarak himself, were saved by the West's US$30 billion debt forgiveness as a reward for Egypt's militarily negligible but politically vital participation in Operation Desert Storm, launched in 1991 to throw Iraqi forces out of Kuwait. The respite was relatively brief, however, for oil prices plunged again in 1996–97, imposing another round of economic hardship on Egypt. The structural adjustment programme that had been agreed in 1991 as a condition for the debt write-down, but which had been only partially implemented, was reinvigorated. Initially, this was in the form of devaluation and tariff reduction and then, after the formation of the Ahmad Nazif cabinet in July 2004, with what seemed to be more thoroughgoing reforms, including new taxation legislation, overhaul of foreign investment procedures and acceleration of privatization, including of one of the big four state-owned banks. By 2008 Egypt was listed by the World Bank as a 'top reformer' on its Ease of Doing Business Index, while prior to the global economic downturn of 2007–08 its annual GDP growth rate had doubled to over 7% and foreign direct investment (FDI) had accelerated from less than 1% of GDP to 8.9% in 2007.[2] By the 'coup-volution' of January–February 2011, the government and even some independent analysts were asserting that neo-liberal reforms had finally placed the Egyptian economy firmly on the path to sustained growth and emerging market status.[3]

In reality, GDP growth after 2002 was due primarily to the simultaneous dramatic rise yet again in hydrocarbon rents, this time from expanding gas production and its export as well as utilization for energy-intensive processing, such as in the cement, fertilizer and steel industries. The Nazif reforms ultimately proved to be marginal, with the currency remaining essentially pegged to the dollar, hence progressively more overvalued; selective but important sectors retaining tariff and non-tariff protection; privatization resulting primarily in transfer of assets to regime cronies and the military and ultimately not affecting the remaining three state-owned banks, whose tentacles continued to extend throughout the financial services sector; and government spending as a percentage of GDP remaining in excess of one third as the civil service continued to expand and food and energy subsidies consumed ever more of the budget, thus reducing capital expenditure to negligible proportions.[4] By contrast, external and internal hydrocarbon rents expanded dramatically. The run-up in the global oil price to the maximum of just under $150 per barrel reached in 2008 resulted in a flood of petrodollars into Egypt from the Gulf producers, whose investments, concentrated in real estate and tourism, accounted for at least half of FDI and whose tourists in Egypt contributed about half of gross revenues in that vital sector, accounting as it does for 12% of total employment. Of the remaining amount of FDI, the greatest proportion was in Egypt's own rapidly expanding gas industry, exports from which took off after 2002. By 2007 gas accounted for almost all of the 52% of the country's total exports derived from fuels. The contribution of tradable goods to export earnings steadily declined.[5]

These indirect Gulf oil- and direct domestic gas-fired booms both ended suddenly in 2008, with predictably immediate, negative consequences for economic activity. Indeed, rising unemployment and poverty were major causal factors of the uprising of early 2011. The end of the Mubarak era was thus presaged and probably caused by the dramatic downturn in hydrocarbon rents, the impact of which was further magnified by the proportionately steady reduction in public foreign assistance. US civilian aid, for example, was placed on a glide path in 1998 that took it from almost $815 million annually to $411 million in 2008, and then to $250 million thereafter. Since 1948 the USA has provided Egypt with almost $72 billion in aid.[6] Some three decades after Mubarak had taken power, Egypt's political economy remained heavily based on rent seeking, with predictably negative consequences for sustained growth. Its $148 GDP per capita in 1960, for example, almost equalled the Republic of Korea's (South Korea) $155, whereas by 2010 South Korea's had risen to $20,700 while Egypt's $2,698 was about one-10th as much.[7] For the period 1987 to 2006 Egypt's average per capita GDP annual growth was 2.2%, compared to a lower-middle-income country average of 5%.[8] Its exports of manufactured goods were more or less the same as Turkey's when Mubarak assumed power in 1981, whereas 30 years later Turkey's were almost 15 times greater.[9] Manufacturing as a percentage of value added annually averaged 17.8% in Egypt from 1987 to 2006, dropping by several percentage points after that time. By comparison, the lower-middle-income country average for the same 20-year period was 25%, more than 40% higher than Egypt's. Manufactures' share of merchandise exports declined steadily from an average of 38.5% in 1997–2001 to 18.6% in 2007.[10]

Whether considered a sub-type of rent seeking, or a distinctive structural impediment to economic growth, the military economy established by Nasser, then expanded by Sadat before being dramatically upgraded into a sprawling economy within the economy by Mubarak, is the second key factor causing Egypt's comparative economic failure. Unaccountable to civilian authority, opaque in its dealings, and having expanded far beyond its origins in the production of ammunition and small arms into a conglomerate producing a vast array of civilian goods and services, the military economy is further paralleled by an 'officer economy' and an 'officer republic'.[11] The former consists of private firms founded by serving or retired military and security service officers who trade on their connections within the state to obtain contracts, licences and access to subsidized commodities (especially energy and hydrocarbons), as well as to secure agency agreements to represent foreign entities in domestic markets.[12] Together, during the Mubarak era the military economy ('Military Inc.') and the officer economy slowly strangled the country's private sector, leaving the only surviving successful, large-scale enterprises being those controlled by presidential cronies, many of whom are now languishing in prison or in exile with their firms in legal limbo.[13] Indeed, it was largely the resentment of allocation of rents to these cronies of the Mubarak family that caused the military to turn on the president in February 2011. The 'officer republic', a term coined by Yezid Sayigh to refer to the penetration and control of the state administration by active duty and retired officers, which dramatically increased under Mubarak, facilitates the further growth of 'Military Inc.' and the officer economy, while simultaneously degrading the state's administrative capacities and rendering them still less accountable, transparent and efficient.[14]

The Egyptian economy has thus been doubly cursed: by the resource of rents from its geostrategic and hydrocarbon assets, and by the subordination of the state and the economy to the military. If Egypt is to become a full-fledged emerging economy and join the hypothesized newly arriving second tier of BRICs (Brazil, Russia, India and the People's Republic of China), it must overcome these twin curses. With limited potential for agricultural growth and being the world's largest wheat-importing nation, while suffering directly from declining gas prices and its own gas supply problems, and indirectly from sagging global oil prices, Egypt has no choice other than to produce industrial goods for export. For this to happen it must deal with its twin curses and then proceed to address some of the policy and structural constraints that have heretofore impeded industrialization. The key question, then, and the one to which the remainder of this chapter is devoted, is whether or not the political system that has emerged in the wake of the 2011 'coup-volution' can escape the trap of rent seeking, rationalize and render accountable the military economy, and overcome structural obstacles to growth.

Hopeful early prognoses and signs

The euphoria that greeted the fall of the Mubarak regime extended to assessments of economic prospects, which were generally seen as favourable. Despite some destruction to government buildings and public infrastructure, interruptions to production, pervasive insecurity of person and property, and a rapid drawdown of the country's foreign exchange holdings, coupled with downgrades by leading rating agencies of Egypt's sovereign debt, the general view was that these were temporary problems, unavoidable costs of overthrowing a corrupt dictatorship.

Underpinning this positive assessment was a widely shared belief that Egypt possesses untapped economic resources and that the failure to draw upon them was due to the ineptitude and corruption of the *ancien régime*. Now liberated from that oppressive regime and its parasitic crony capitalists, accused of spiriting hundreds of millions of dollars out of the country, a new leadership would be able to capitalize on the country's substantial assets, to say nothing of retrieving the country's stolen wealth.[15] The standard list of such assets typically included the burgeoning, young population of some 83 million with a median age of 24, hence the largest domestic market and labour force in the Arab world; the strategic location as the hinge between Asia and Africa, in close proximity to a Europe easily accessed through the Suez Canal; respectable energy reserves and production and the potential to serve as an inter-regional energy gateway; and finally, 'good will', by which is implied the country's attractiveness to foreign investment, but for most the distinction between Egypt as investment opportunity and Egypt as geostrategic ally, hence worthy of strategic rents, was not clearly drawn.

Turkish-Egyptian bilateral relations illustrate the ambiguity between Egypt viewed as investment prospect as opposed to geopolitical ally or client. For some the growth of Turkish investment in Egypt prior to 2011 and its promised surge thereafter was seen as a sign that the so-called 'flying geese' intra-regional model of development had finally descended into the Middle East. Japan's role as lead 'goose' in providing capital and technology to its Asian neighbours would now be emulated by Turkey, with Egypt serving as its China, or at least its South Korea or Taiwan. This optimistic appraisal was reinforced by a rapid, dramatic improvement in broader bilateral relations, accompanied by promises of further Turkish investment and formation of various joint associations and Egyptian business organizations modelled on Turkish prototypes.[16] For others, however, Turkey's reinvigorated economic and political courtship of Egypt reflected the geopolitical ambitions of its Islamist leadership and their alleged neo-Ottomanism, rather than any intent or capacity for it to serve as a Japanese-style 'goose' leading the way for trailing Egypt. Despite the ambiguity over Egypt's 'good will' as an economic or political asset, hence confusion over its transformative potential for the economy, the very concern with the subject suggested that most Egyptian observers at least valued the country's external connections as positive forces for its development, rather than as threats to which a return to an inward-looking development strategy of the Nasserist type would be appropriate.

Supporting the generally positive outlook of the country's asset base and its appeal to external actors, whatever that appeal might be, were some encouraging economic signs, at least for the initial year following the coup-volution. Despite the continuing global economic recession, worker remittances of almost $8 billion, the 10th largest amount among developing countries, constituting almost 4% of Egypt's gross national product (GNP), declined only slightly from their peak of $8.7 billion in 2008.[17] Foreign reserves plummeted from $36 billion to some $12 billion during the 15 months after February 2011, but then seemed to stabilize. Despite that drop, the Egyptian pound, informally pegged to the dollar, lost less than 5% of its value against that currency in the first year and a half following the uprising. Inflation, which had reached 18% in 2008, declined from 12.8% to 10.2% between 2010 and 2011.[18] Suez Canal revenues remained steady at just over $5 billion.

Initial optimism, however, began to fade as the political transition bogged down and the country's economic problems intensified.[19] Political turmoil extracted a greater economic price than had first been imagined, as reflected by growing macroeconomic imbalances. Moreover, global recession rendered economic recovery yet more challenging, while domestic structural constraints to growth, far from disappearing almost overnight as the most optimistic had hoped back in February 2011, seemed to intensify. None of the alleged billions of illegally gained and expatriated dollars were recovered. Finally, the new political leadership was unable to convince the public that it had a coherent development plan and the capacity to implement it. Political disaffection mounted in tandem with economic stagnation, raising the question as to whether the early optimism following the coup-volution was misplaced. The possibility of Egypt becoming a failed state was seen as having grown substantially by *Foreign Policy*, which ranked the country only 49th most likely in the world to fail in 2010, then 45th in 2011, but a much worse 31st in 2012.[20] A question that will now be addressed by examining immediate and longer-term constraints is whether Egypt's economic and even broader future could be as bleak or perhaps bleaker than its past?

Macroeconomic imbalances and uncertainties

The coup-volution intensified underlying macroeconomic imbalances. Budget deficits which had averaged around 7% of GDP even during the gas-fired 'golden years' of neo-liberal reforms in the first decade of the 21st century, blew out in 2011 to 10% and then in 2012 to over 12%. The chronic current account deficit nosedived in the first nine months of 2012 to $6.4 billion, almost 50% more than for the same period in 2011. By the end of the fiscal year the deficit had further widened to almost $8 billion, the largest in current dollars in Egypt's history.[21] Egypt's exports declined by one-fifth from 2010 to 2011.[22] Foreign reserves plummeted by two-thirds to some $12 billion, but the creative accounting habitually used in official calculations overstated the balance by at least one-quarter. Not included in the creative accounting was the non-payment of fees owed to foreign oil and natural gas companies, which amounted to some $7 billion by October 2012.[23] FDI, which had dropped from a high of $11 billion in the 'golden years' to less than $1 billion in the wake of the global economic crisis of 2007–08, went into reverse, with $16 billion of capital taking flight between February 2011 and October 2012.[24] With little business activity and uncertain prospects, the financial sector began to contract. French banks BNP Paribas and Crédit Agricole pulled out in the autumn of 2012.[25] Egypt's leading investment bank, EFG-Hermes, having taken a huge hit to its capital base and with its leadership under threat of prosecution for alleged Mubarak-era indiscretions, was taken over by Qatari interests.[26] Moody's, Fitch, and Standard and Poor's steadily downgraded Egypt's sovereign debt after spring 2011, more or less in tandem with rising interest rates on new bond and treasury bill issues, which climbed to over 15% before the end of 2011.[27]

These accelerating imbalances resulted from the government's inadequate, indeed counter-productive reactions to socio-political and -economic forces unleashed by the coup-volution.

Competition between the key political actors, including the military led by the Supreme Council of the Armed Forces (SCAF), Islamists, including both Muslim Brotherhood and Salafis, and secularists ranging from Nasserists to liberals, delayed promulgation of a constitution, prevented reform of the vital security sector, and subordinated economic decision making to political calculations, most apparent of which was populist outbidding. As a result, normal government functioning was impaired, the most obvious manifestation of which was pervasive insecurity of life and property, while successive decisions, whether initially by the SCAF or subsequently by the Muslim Brotherhood government installed in June–July 2012, essentially amounted to throwing what public money was available at proliferating problems.

Mubarak had sought to bolster his regime in its final days by pledging to hire an additional 250,000 civil servants, a commitment that he was soon in no position to honour, but which was subsequently reaffirmed by the SCAF and then implemented by the Brotherhood government. Stimulated by chronically low wages and encouraged by the ambiguous new legal and political contexts, as well as by the absence of the once pervasive security services, and organized by a host of newly formed unions, employees of virtually all types, ranging from doctors to professors to train and taxi drivers, commenced collective industrial action, including strikes and sit-ins.[28] The vital Ain al-Sukhna port was closed intermittently in the last quarter of 2012 as a result of industrial action. According to one prominent businessman, more than 400,000 jobs had been lost in 2011 due to unrest.[29] The SCAF and the Brotherhood governments vacillated in response, but in general gave ground on wages, salaries and conditions for civil servants and employees in state-owned enterprises, thereby further inflating the already prodigious government wage bill. Just after his election, for example, President Muhammad Mursi announced a 15% pay rise for civil servants and pensioners, and increased a projected rise of 10% in military pensions to 15%.[30] In an attempt to deter rural unrest, agricultural subsidies, most notably for cotton, were increased to the point that the government's guaranteed purchase price rose above international levels.[31] In order to protect globally inefficient industries, ranging from steel to textiles, threatened by imports even before the rounds of wage rises, the government reimposed tariff and non-tariff barriers that had been lowered or dropped altogether by the Nazif cabinet.[32] Instead of recommencing the stalled privatization, the government moved in the opposite direction in the telecommunications industry, announcing that the fourth mobile phone network would be government owned.[33] Despite various declarations of intent to reduce energy subsidies, at 20% among the world's highest as a share of the government's budget, the only concrete step that had been taken by the end of 2012 was a price increase on the highest of the three octane grades of gasoline. Fuel subsidies cost the government more than $17 billion in 2011, about 7% of GDP.[34] The yet more sensitive issue of food subsidies remained politically too challenging for any of the transitional governments to touch.

Unable for political reasons to put a cap on runaway spending, the government of President Mursi turned, as had its predecessors dating back to the Nasser period, to foreigners to foot the bills. The Muslim Brotherhood and its offshoot Freedom and Justice Party (FJP), had in 2011 condemned the SCAF for seeking a standby agreement of some $2.3 billion with the International Monetary Fund (IMF), claiming that it violated Egypt's sovereignty and Islamic principles. Once in power a year later, however, Mursi's FJP government commenced negotiations with the IMF for a $4.8 billion loan. Immediately following his election in June 2012, President Mursi began globetrotting in search of assistance from various governments, including those of China, Turkey, Qatar, Saudi Arabia and others. In the event he obtained commitments of $1 billion from the Turks and the Qataris, $200 million from the Chinese, as well as the payment of $500 million that constituted the outstanding balance of the $1 billion earlier promised by the Saudis to the SCAF. The consensus figure estimated in late 2012 for Egypt's immediate needs from foreign sources for 2013 was \$12–\$15 billion, suggesting that Mursi's efforts had been inadequate. Many Egyptian commentators, including a former ambassador in Washington, in fact criticized him for appearing as not just hypocritical in seeking IMF support, but as an international beggar, thereby marring post-authoritarian Egypt's image while failing to articulate a coherent foreign policy appropriate for the country's new status.[35]

Mursi's excessive rhetoric and exaggerated claims before domestic audiences stimulated not just criticism, but ridicule. The 'Mursimeter' of indicators by which he invited the Egyptian public to judge his performance after 100 days included several that would clearly take years for any government to implement, as many observers noted.[36] His counter to widespread criticism of the failure to combat inflation was to observe that the price of mangoes had fallen, giving rise to derisory comments along the lines of 'let them eat mangoes!'[37] His claim that along with a brain trust within the FJP he had drawn up a 'renaissance plan' to guide Egypt's economic salvation was dismissed as rhetoric by none other than a putative member of that inner group, his own mentor Khairat al-Shater.[38] Mursi's enthusiasm for strengthening relations with Turkey extended to claims that a new joint venture aircraft industry would be established, an unlikely prospect given the capital and technology required.[39]

The ever deepening economic crisis and the president's pie-in-the-sky approach to resolving it undermined confidence in the government as well as the economy. Particularly troubling for those hopeful of a democratic transition was the Brotherhood's obvious intent to gain as much control over the state administration as possible, while presiding over the promulgation of a constitution that facilitated such control and legitimated it at least partially with reference to Islamic principles. The reversion to time-tested authoritarian methods of rent seeking from foreign sources, combined with allocation of entitlements to domestic constituencies, reinforced the interpretation of the Brotherhood's primary ambitions as being the authoritarian Islamicization of Egypt, even if gradual in its application. While at the end of 2012 it was premature to pass judgement on intent, to say nothing of outcome, was is not too early to assess both the SCAF's and the Brotherhood's efforts to govern Egypt as having resulted in few political or economic gains. Consequently, the country's political and economic futures remain wide open. It is not beyond the realms of possibility that military officers disenchanted with this state of affairs will once again intervene in politics. Nor is it impossible that the political tug-of-war now underway between Islamists and secularists of various outlooks and loyalties will finally result in the mutual realization that a 'pacted' democratic transition would best serve their interests. So, the possible range of political outcomes extends from democracy to authoritarianism, the latter presumably of either an Islamist or direct military nature.

Such political uncertainty has profoundly negative economic consequences. So long as it persists the economy will remain precarious at best. Moreover, the chronic afflictions of rent seeking and a bloated military economy have yet to be addressed. Both may in fact have been reinforced as a result of the Brotherhood and the military having essentially partitioned the political economy to their mutual advantage. However, even if the slide back into authoritarianism is averted and a more effective, democratic government less in need of rents and more able and willing to subject the military to control by civilian institutions is established, a range of structural problems will confront that government's efforts to stimulate economic growth.

Structural constraints

Governments in republican Egypt have underinvested in physical and human infrastructure, choosing to rely heavily on public foreign assistance to 'top-up' domestic spending on education, health care, transportation, power generation, water and sewer services, and so on. The inevitable results of inadequate spending on public goods are weaknesses in the labour force and physical infrastructure. The comparative advantage of Egypt's large population thus lies more in market size than in skilled and semi-skilled manpower. Crumbling infrastructure deters foreign investment while increasing costs to domestic producers. Although governance is not strictly speaking a structural constraint to economic growth, as it is not a factor of production, its underperformance in Egypt is so long-standing and systemic and its improvement requiring such profound and difficult changes, that it amounts to a structural impediment.

Measures of both broad human resource capacities and characteristics of the labour force specifically reveal why the 83 million Egyptians have not constituted more of a magnet for investors seeking relatively inexpensive labour for production processes, as they have in many comparator countries, such as Bangladesh, Thailand, Turkey and Malaysia, all of which have outperformed Egypt on most measures of development. Thailand, whose population is similar to that of Egypt, for example, had a GDP about half Egypt's in 1970, but by 2010 it was almost three times higher.[40] On the United Nations Development Programme's overall Human Development Index, Egypt scores 20 places below its ranking on GDP per capita, while on the narrower Education Index it is 35 places below the level it should achieve according to its GDP per capita.[41] Only about two-thirds of adult Egyptians are literate, a ratio somewhat below that for the Arab world as a whole (71%) and far behind that of Turkey at 89% or Thailand at 94%.[42] More than two in five of Egyptian women are illiterate.[43] About one-quarter of Egyptians live below the poverty line of income less than $2 per day, a ratio only more negative in the Arab world in Morocco, Sudan and Yemen. Fewer than one in 10 Turks live in poverty so defined.[44] Poverty in Egypt increased between 2010 and 2012, rising from 21.6% to 25.2% overall, while going from 43.7% in Upper Egypt in 2009 to 51.4% in 2012. In 2000 the overall poverty rate had been 16.7%.[45] Poverty is closely associated with inequality. Within North Africa salary inequality is only higher in Morocco than it is in Egypt, with both being substantially more unequal than Algeria, Tunisia and Libya.[46]

As for the education system, it emphasizes quantity over quality and largely fails to address the needs of the poor. Combined gross enrolment in education of those in the relevant age cohorts is 76%, which exceeds the Arab country average of 66% and even that of Turkey, which is 71%.[47] Yet, the quality of that education, as indicated not only by comparatively high illiteracy rates, but by international test results, is relatively low. Egyptian pupils' performance on the Trends in International Mathematics and Science Study (TIMSS) tests administered in 2003 were well below international averages in mathematics and science and fell yet further when retested four years later.[48] In analysing the results the World Bank noted the comparatively high proportion of Egyptian students who failed to reach the low benchmark of 400%–40%, compared to 32% and 23% for Lebanese and Iranian students, respectively.[49] The Bank's explanation of Egypt's lopsided result is that the two lowest income quintiles perform extremely poorly, the gap between rich and poor students being greater in Egypt than any other Middle East and North Africa (MENA) country.[50] Net enrolments of children in the poorest one-fifth of the population are below half at 15 years of age.[51]

While inequality is one explanation of educational underperformance, inadequate government expenditure is another. Relative to GDP per capita, Egyptian teachers are the lowest paid in the MENA region, their average salary being only one-and-a-half times per capita GDP.[52] As comparatively low as Egypt's spending on education is, it is money not well invested. Male high school graduates earn only 6% more over their lifetimes than those who had no schooling whatsoever. Returns to educational expenditure in Egypt are lower than in all regional comparators, including Morocco and Tunisia.[53] The 8% return achieved in 2000 compared to more than double that rate achieved by Argentina, Chile and Uruguay.[54] One careful study of the impact of public expenditures in Egypt concluded that 'as a whole (education spending) has a negative effect on growth'.[55] The World Economic Forum ranked Egypt's higher education 126th out of 134 countries and 128th on the degree to which it satisfied the needs of the country's labour market.[56] Some 10% of graduates from tertiary educational institutions are in science and engineering, about half the average share in the MENA region as a whole. In Turkey and China the comparative percentages are 24% and 30%, respectively.[57]

Given that the overall recruitment pool from which the labour force is drawn is comparatively poor as well as poorly and even miseducated, it is not surprising that the labour force is relatively non-competitive. The overall labour force participation rate of 49% compares to Bangladesh's 71% and Thailand's 72%.[58] Female labour force participation at 24% is half the total of males and females combined. In Bangladesh and Thailand the female rate is 57% and 64%, respectively.[59] Egypt ranks 108th on the 'Third Billion Index' of 128 countries on the economic empowerment of women.[60] Booz and Company estimates that the increase in Egypt's GDP by 2020 would be about one-third if the female matched the male employment rate, the highest increase that could be achieved in this manner of the counties studied, outpacing even India's potential gain despite the fact that India ranks lower on the female empowerment index.[61] The Egyptian labour force is widely perceived as being poorly trained, a standard lament of potential investors. In response to various complaints of this sort at the annual Euromoney conference on Egypt in October 2012, for example, a spokesman for the FJP conceded the issue, noting that 85% of the labour force was unskilled.[62] One cause of the poor training of the labour force is the lack of investment by businesses in their workers. A World Bank survey in 2007 of the frequency of companies offering training to their employees revealed that only companies in Guinea-Bissau were less likely to do so than those in Egypt.[63] The inadequate production of graduates competent in science, mathematics and engineering poses a direct obstacle to exporting firms stimulating and being supported by backward linkages into the economy. On the measure of local availability of specialized research and training services, the World Economic Forum places Egypt in the 46th percentile, compared, for example, to Turkey in the 61st, Tunisia in the 68th and India in the 76th.[64] Not surprisingly, unemployment is a chronic problem that has been further aggravated by the coup-volution, rising from less than 10% to almost 13% in official figures, with the youth jobless figure reported at one-quarter of job seekers. Both figures are widely assumed to understate the problem by a significant magnitude.[65]

Even during the period of comparatively rapid economic growth after 2000, Egypt's labour force continued to reflect and contribute to the structural deficiencies of the economy. The share of informal employment rose from 57% in 1998 to 61% in 2006, with fully three-quarters of new entrants to the labour force during this period entering informal employment. Employment in manufacturing industry grew at half the rate of overall employment growth. Small, undercapitalized firms absorbed an ever greater share of the labour force, with some two-thirds of those working in the private sector by 2006 employed in firms of fewer than 10 workers.[66] Of these workers, about one-third earned less than $1 per day and another third less than $2 per day.[67] A recent study of informality in the MENA region concludes that it 'has been found to be one of the main causes of the productivity gap between developed and developing countries. In addition, there is a strong negative correlation between a firm's formal/informal status and its productivity in developing countries'.[68] In Egypt formal firms are 3.6 times more productive than informal ones, and micro- and small enterprises are almost six times more likely to be informal in Egypt than in Turkey.[69] Instead of being upgraded, integrated into global manufacturing production chains and increasingly well paid, Egypt's labour force is relying ever more heavily on marginal, poorly paid employment in the black economy which provides little opportunity for skills enhancement.

Various indicators also suggest deficiencies in Egyptian management of the factors of production, the summation measure being the country's overall total factor productivity (TFP) rating. A recent German study revealed it as being 25% and 40% lower than China's and Brazil's, respectively.[70] A 2011 World Bank study noted that if Egypt does not improve its TFP, vital to which is public management and firm-level technological innovation, 'a high rate of economic growth is not feasible at current rates of national saving and would require a saving effort that is highly unrealistic'. It concludes that if TFP were to grow at 2% annually it would lead to a 4% annual growth rate of GDP at a national savings rate of some 20%–25%, compared with the 80% savings rate required if TFP is not improved.[71] The comparatively poor state of Egypt's human resources, as reflected in inadequate public and private sector management, to say nothing of the broader labour force, thus poses a sizeable obstacle to growth and one not easily overcome even if far greater amounts of capital were available.

Egypt's physical infrastructure is similarly non-competitive. As the World Bank study just cited notes, 'since the mid-1990s infrastructure investment has suffered a substantial decline—mostly due to lower public investment'.[72] Comparative rates of gross capital and gross fixed capital formation reflect the decline. For the period 1987 to 1991 the former as a percentage of GDP was 28.6% and the latter 28.3%, whereas for the period 1997–2001 they were 19.7% and 19.3%, respectively, before declining yet further during the first few years of the 21st century.[73] By comparison, lower-middle-income country averages for the two measures from 1987 to 1991 were 31.9% and 26.4%, roughly the same as Egypt's, but they then accelerated in the 1997–2001 period to 29.9% and 28.1%, respectively, a full 10% of GDP more than Egypt's. Public spending on the agricultural sector has declined faster than in any other Arab country, at more than 3.8% per annum over the last decade, a decline which largely explains stagnation in this sector. By contrast, Turkey and Iran have increased such expenditure and their agricultural sectors have grown rapidly, at over 17% annually in the latter's case.[74] Among the Arab countries only Yemen and Sudan are more food insecure than Egypt.[75] Egypt's infrastructure, including power generation, sewer and water treatment, railways and roads, and so on, progressively denied investment from both foreign assistance and indigenous funding sources, steadily deteriorated during the last two decades of the Mubarak era.[76] Accompanying and in many cases caused by this deterioration were growing environmental problems, including poor air and water quality, resulting in turn in increased incidence of health problems such as bronchial and intestinal diseases. Particulate matter concentration in the air in Egypt's cities with populations above 100,000, for example, is only worse in some six other countries, a result primarily of congested roads and inadequate alternative modes of transport.[77] Movement of goods into, out of and within the country is time consuming and expensive, thereby posing a major deterrent to the country's participation in globalized production chains. So, too, do increasingly frequency power outages and interruptions to water delivery deter investment. The Aon Hewitt 2012 People Risk Index measures the risks that organizations face in the areas of demographics, education government support, talent development and employment practices when deploying staff globally to 131 cities. On that measure Cairo ranks 112th.[78]

That Egypt's poor governance can even be thought of as a structural obstacle, implying extended time and substantial effort for its reduction or removal, suggests how profoundly weak that governance is. Egypt's scores are consistent on the various governance measures recorded by the public international organizations such as the World Bank and the IMF, their subordinate organizations such as the International Finance Corporation (IFC), and private organizations such as the Heritage Foundation, *The Economist*, or the Bertelsmann Foundation. In virtually all rankings Egypt is below the MENA average, a sub-region that in the aggregate ranks at or near the bottom on most globally comparative governance measures. Moreover,

Egypt's performance, with the notable exception of its standing on the IFC Ease of Doing Business Index, has been declining. The World Bank's governance indicators, for example, first issued in 1996, were the progenitors of all such measures that followed. On five of those six indicators, Egypt performed better in 1996 than it did in 2010 or 2011, and on five of the six its performance deteriorated over those last two years.

The outlier is Egypt's ranking on the IFC Ease of Doing Business Index. Egypt was the world's 'top reformer' in 2008, jumping 26 places out of 178 countries. This was due primarily to it having established the General Authority for Investments (GAFI)—a 'one-stop shop' for business start-ups.[79] GAFI's director subsequently resigned because the agency was unable to fend off interference from other bureaucratic actors. Egypt has since slid back to 109th place out of 185 countries.[80] If Egypt still did not rank 26th on the indicator 'starting a business', which is due to the legal changes involved in creating GAFI rather than to its actual performance, its score would be well back below the starting point of its ascent during the Nazif prime ministry. Presently, it ranks 165th, for example, on 'dealing with construction permits', 145th on 'paying taxes' and 152nd on 'enforcing contracts'.[81] It takes on average 1,010 days to enforce a contract in Egypt, far and away the longest period in the MENA region, with only Syria coming close at 872 days.[82] So, in reality Egypt is not such an easy place in which to do business, the IFC's index notwithstanding.

The Economic Freedom Index compiled by the Heritage Foundation and *The Economist* rated Egypt a low 57.9 in 2012, 1.2 points lower than 2011 and 100th in the world, well below the global and even regional averages. The 2012 report noted that 'deeper institutional reforms are critically needed to sustain long-term growth and stable economic development'.[83] It is worsted in the MENA region only by Yemen, Syria, Algeria, Iran, Iraq and Libya. Possibly the best summary measure of governance is the broad indicator, 'extent of bureaucratic red tape', reported by the World Economic Forum. Egypt is almost at the bottom of global rankings on this measure, being in the 7th percentile, compared to Algeria in the 49th, Morocco in the 38th, Tunisia in the 72nd, and even notoriously bureaucratic and corrupt India being in the 50th percentile.[84] The extremely high rate of informality of business firms in Egypt, which in turn comprises a huge drag on the country's overall level of productivity, is due to 'the burden of regulations and paperwork ... and inadequate access to financing'.[85] Not surprisingly, Egypt ranks in the 20th percentile on the measure of 'access to credit' on the World Bank's global competitive measures. In the MENA region only Morocco and Algeria are ranked lower, while Bangladesh, Turkey and Pakistan are in the 56th, 89th and 94th percentiles, respectively.[86] Lack of access to credit, especially for small and medium-sized enterprises, results from the disproportionate share of bank capital that goes to purchase sovereign debt and to cover the losses of state-owned enterprises, as well as to regime cronies in loans lacking adequate collateral backing.[87] It is also a consequence of the high risk of lending in the absence of a responsive legal-judicial system. Indeed, credit risk analysis remains rudimentary in Egyptian banks, presumably part of the magnitude of that challenge. Small wonder that Egypt has for many years been in the bottom 10% of countries on the World Bank's measure of non-performing loans, with only Algeria in the MENA region having a higher ratio of bad loans.[88] The World Economic Forum's comparative study of the risk to businesses of regulatory capture by the government ranks Egypt the highest in the MENA region.[89]

Whether viewed narrowly as administrative effectiveness or more broadly to include measures of particular concern to business, such as regulatory capacities, rule of law and freedom from corruption, governance in Egypt has been profoundly inadequate since well before the World Bank commenced its quantification in 1996. The optimism that greeted the coup-volution was based primarily on the hope that increased voice and accountability would lead to improvements in other aspects of governance. In the event, Egypt's score on the Bank's voice and accountability indicator did go up slightly in 2011, but it was clear in 2012 that any further increase would depend on a transition to democracy that at this stage appears to have stalled. In any case, improved voice and accountability would not lead immediately and directly to enhanced government effectiveness, greater rule of law and so on. Political will is a necessary, but not sufficient, condition. Institutional capacities would have to be built for governance to be substantially improved. That inherently is a long-term project, one that Egypt's rulers have avoided for a good half-century, making its prospects appear now to be less than promising.

Prospects

Underlying the structural constraints of poor human and physical infrastructure and chronically bad governance to rapid economic growth, is a political economy forged by rent seeking in turn underpinned by a politically powerful, economically parasitical military. What are the prospects that rent seeking will give way to a focus on reconfiguring the state to provide competent macroeconomic management and protection of rights of property and person while building what Amr Adly has labelled 'state escorting institutions', by which he means those capable of guiding and assisting the private sector to become globally competitive?[90]

Possibly those prospects are better now than previously, for both positive and negative reasons. Although the coup-volution's birthing of a new leadership has been uneven and protracted, that process will ultimately be completed. The outcome, whether semi-authoritarian Islamist, inclusive democratic, or even a Pakistani-style cohabitation between the military and Islamic-leaning civilian politicians, might well be a substantial improvement. In any case the new leadership, whatever its predilections and capacities, will confront the negative challenge of declining rents, which paradoxically could have positive effects in the long run. Rent dependency is not viable below a certain ratio of rents to recipients, a ratio that Egypt probably exceeded during the Mubarak era. As its population continued to grow, especially in the vital 15–24-year-old job-seeking cohort, hydrocarbon rents began to decline proportionately, then to plummet after the fall in gas prices in 2008. There is little to no likelihood that direct or indirect hydrocarbon rents will catch up with the needs of the ever expanding population. What amounts to a global over-supply of gas resulting from new extraction technologies has brought the price down from as much as $12 per one million British thermal units (BTUs) at the height of the 2002–08 boom, to as low as $2 now. Egypt also faces a chronic gas supply problem and is already unable to provide sufficient quantities for its existing liquefaction facilities to operate at full capacity. Growing domestic demand is outpacing increases in supply, so the prospects for expanding gas exports are dim.[91]

As for the indirect rents and income provided by subventions, remittances, investments and tourism originating in the oil-rich states, all are under threat. With the exception of Qatar, ruling families in all the other Gulf Cooperation Council (GCC) states remain suspicious, even hostile to Egypt's Muslim Brotherhood, as reflected in the comparatively paltry funds they have provided the country since the coup-volution.[92] However, even if those relations were warm, the GCC states will be increasingly hard pressed to provide subventions. They are consuming ever larger shares of their hydrocarbon rents with allocations to their own expanding and politically restless populations. Although remittances have remained substantial at around $8 billion annually, of which far and away the largest share is generated in GCC countries, with the 1.5 million Egyptian workers in Saudi Arabia contributing the most, those remittances do not accrue directly to the Egyptian government. Moreover, remittances as a share of GDP are on a downward trajectory which will steepen as Egypt's population and GDP increase and opportunities for labour in the oil-exporting countries decline, in which in any case they have been stagnant for years. The primary investments in Egypt originating in GCC countries were in real estate and tourism, sectors that have been hardest hit by the global recession and political unrest in the region. It is not only that demand has diminished, but on the supply side the key Gulf-based real estate companies and connected financial institutions are themselves in financial trouble from which they are unlikely to emerge for many years. Finally, tourism is a fickle industry, with tourists easily deterred and attracted by alternative destinations. Sour state-to-state relations between Egypt and the GCC countries, if they continue, will exert further downward pressure on an industry already struggling.

Other potential external sources of rent are equally unpromising. Neither the USA nor the European Union (EU) has rushed to Egypt's assistance in the wake of the coup-volution. The international financial organizations have followed their lead. The IMF has yet to conclude the standby agreement on which it commenced negotiations in the spring of 2011. The World Bank has approved some additional project finance, but in the tens of millions only. This drip-feed of international public assistance to Egypt is unlikely to turn into a torrent. Global economic recession combined with aid fatigue renders Western donors reluctant to commit large sums, especially in conditions of political uncertainty. Indeed, opposition in the US Congress which held up through November 2012 a tranche of $450 million of the $1 billion in debt relief the Administration promised Cairo in May 2011 from what are essentially funds left over from the overall US aid budget, results from suspicion of Islamism in general and the Muslim Brotherhood in particular.[93] These suspicions, whether in the USA or Europe, are unlikely to vanish. Depending on events, particularly in relation to Israel and to domestic human rights, they could easily intensify. In the almost two years following the coup-volution the EU managed to scrape together only $652 million in total budgetary support for Egypt.[94] China is not an alternative, with President Mursi having managed to pry out of Beijing's grasp a paltry $200 million on his visit there. Nothing more was said to be in the pipeline. In sum then, both hydrocarbon and public foreign assistance rents are on downward trajectories that are unlikely to be reversed.

As for the military and officer economies, they will remain intact so long as the military continues to assert substantial political power. Presently, the Muslim Brotherhood has struck a deal with it, essentially partitioning the state so that the military is given a free hand in its traditional domains of national security policy, internal operations of the military and control over the sprawling military economy, including privileged access for officers into the civilian economy. This condominium over the political economy is unlikely to last, if only because the competition between the Brotherhood and officers for economic spoils will intensify as those spoils, linked as most are to direct and indirect hydrocarbon rents, diminish.

Three alternative outcomes seem possible. One is that the Brotherhood instrumentalizes the military, subordinating it to its will. A second is that the military strikes back, removing the Brotherhood at least temporarily and establishing its pre-eminence for the foreseeable future. A third is that democratic civilian political institutions become sufficiently robust and empowered to subordinate the military to their oversight and control. It is only the third outcome that would result unequivocally in the military economy being made transparent, accountable and dramatically smaller. If the military stages a coup it is not going to divest itself of its economic assets. If the Brotherhood succeeds in instrumentalizing the military, it might choose to transfer the military business empire into its own hands. That would be a lateral move, not forward progress on the path to accountability, transparency and downsizing. So, it is essentially only the democratization scenario that holds out real hope for eliminating the economic drag effect of the military's meddling in the economy, for which in turn a precondition is shrinking the half-million-strong military and its budget. Unfortunately, democratization coupled with demilitarization is the least likely of the apparent scenarios and, in any case, would take an extended period to play out. So, it appears that the struggle over the military economy might well intensify as rents decline, adding another element of potential political destabilization.

Finally, the political drama in Egypt is being played out at a time that could hardly be less propitious for an economically favourable ending. The rise of the BRICs occurred during the period of rapid global economic expansion and accompanying resource boom that commenced in the new millennium but which now seems to have run its course. Even the BRICs are experiencing declining growth rates amid speculation that their respective models will not be equal to the challenges of sustaining growth over the long haul.[95] As for the BRIC wannabes, the pressures are yet greater because they are smaller and have thinner resources and other reserves upon which to draw. The new normal seems to be for substantially slower global economic growth in the coming years. In such conditions the prospects for a country such as Egypt to reverse dramatically a long-standing downward slide of exports of tradable goods seems improbable. Global conditions do not support a repeat of the East Asian economic miracle along the southern shores of the Mediterranean. Furthermore, the states located there, including Egypt, do not have human and physical resources as well as governance capacities in any way equivalent to those of the lead goose Japan and the following geese of South Korea, Taiwan, Singapore, and so on. Turkey on the northern Mediterranean does not have sufficient economic lift to pull Egypt or other southern Mediterranean Arab states along in its wake. So, Egypt is going to be left to wrestle with its own political and economic challenges to a degree it has not previously experienced. The decline in its rental income will place yet more pressure on its decision makers. Indeed, it is already doing so. According to *The Economist*, Egypt scored lower in 2012 on its 'wiggle-room index', which measures the scope to ease fiscal and monetary policy, than any other country.[96] It is hoped that the negative incentives will propel decision makers in the direction of undertaking the long-delayed reforms essential to addressing the structural obstacles to more rapid growth. Having for half a century or so been too big to succeed, Egypt may soon become small enough to be forced to try to do so.

Postscript

Completed in late 2012, this chapter noted interlocking political and economic trends that headed downward from the time of President Mubarak's ouster. The rate of descent further steepened in the first half of 2013 as President Mursi and the Muslim Brotherhood exploited their influence over economic and national security policies in a vain attempt to tighten further their grip on power. The resultant economic and political crises came to a head in June–July, with the largest demonstrations in Egypt's modern history legitimating the military's intervention to remove Mursi and the Brotherhood from power. Not wanting to exercise power in its own right and seeking to legitimate the new order with both domestic and international audiences, the military immediately proposed a 'roadmap' for democratic transition that included the appointment of an acting civilian president and the formation of a civilian cabinet. Although some of the former civilian opposition elements were uneasy about the military's role and decisions, their distrust and dislike of the Brotherhood was sufficient to sustain the tactical alliance with the military, at least at the outset. The Muslim Brotherhood was offered by the military and their new civilian political allies the choice of carrot or stick. The former was in the form of an invitation to participate in the cabinet and forthcoming parliamentary and presidential elections. The latter was for the organization to face a purge of its leadership and a possible all-out effort by the military and security services to crush it. Egypt thus continued to face profound political uncertainty, with possible scenarios ranging from the three main political actors agreeing on a transition to democracy, to virtual civil war. As a result, the rate of devaluation of the Egyptian pound accelerated, the national debt was further downgraded by rating agencies, now reaching junk status for all, and revelations of less than three months of import cover and less than two months' supply of wheat stimulated talk in the region and the West of an international effort to save the country from collapse. Far from aspiring to BRIC status, Egypt in the summer of 2013 was struggling to survive as a nation.

Notes

1 On savings and infrastructure see Constantino Hevia and Norman Loayza, *Saving and Growth in Egypt*, World Bank, Policy Research Working Paper 5529, January 2011, www-wds.worldbank.org/servlet/WDSContentServer/WDSP/IB/2011/01/13/000158349_20110113095021/Rendered/PDF/WPS5529.pdf.

2 Data reported in Clement Moore Henry and Robert Springborg, *Globalization and the Politics of Development in the Middle East*, Cambridge University Press, Cambridge, 2010, 173.

3 The term 'coup-volution' was coined by Nathan W. Toronto, 'Egypt's Coup-volution', *Middle East Insight* 6, 16 February 2011, blog.nus.edu.sg/middleeastinstitute/2011/02/16/egypts-coup-volution/.

4 On government expenditure see www.heritage.org/index/pdf/countries/Egypt/pdf.

5 For an assessment of Egypt's gas-fired boom, see Robert Springborg, 'Gas and Oil in Egypt's Development', in Robert Looney, *Handbook of Oil Politics*, Routledge, New York, 2011, 295–311.

6 Jeremy Sharp, 'Egypt: Background and US Relations', Congressional Research Service Report for Congress, 13 September 2012, www.fas.org/sgp/crs/mideast/RL33003.pdf.

7 *index mundi*, www.indexmundi.com/facts/egypt/gdp-per-capita and www.indexmundi.com/facts/korea/gdp-per-capita. Contributing to the growing GDP gap was the differential rate of population growth. In 1960 both had populations around 25 million, whereas by 2005 Egypt's was some 73 million while South Korea's was 48 million. Paul Rivlin, *Arab Economies in the Twenty-First Century*, Cambridge University Press, Cambridge, 2009, 119–20.

8 Henry and Springborg, *Globalization and the Politics of Development in the Middle East*, 173.

9 Amr Adly, *The Political Economy of Trade Liberalization: Turkey and Egypt in the Post-Liberalization Era*, unpublished PhD thesis, Department of Political and Social Sciences, European University Institute, September 2010, 11.

10 Henry and Springborg, *Globalization and the Politics of Development in the Middle East*, 176.

11 On the military economies see Shana Marshall and Joshua Stacher, 'Egypt's Generals and Transnational Capital', *Middle East Report* 262, Spring 2012: 12–18; Shana Marshall, 'Egypt's Other Revolution: Modernizing the Military-Industrial Complex', *Jadaliyaa*, 10 February 2012; Zeinab Abul-Magd, 'The Generals' Secret: Egypt's Ambivalent Market', *Sada*, Carnegie Endowment, Washington, DC, February 2012; and Zeinab Abul-Magd, 'The Army and the Economy in Egypt', *Jadaliyya*, 23 December 2011.

12 On the two types of military economies, see Robert Springborg, 'Economic Involvements of Militaries', *The International Journal of Middle East Studies* 43(3), August 2011: 397–99.

13 The term coined by Ayesha Siddiqa in reference to Pakistan is very applicable to Egypt. See Ayesha Siddiqa, *Military, Inc.: Inside Pakistan's Military Economy*, Oxford University Press, Oxford, 2007.

14 Yezid Sayigh, 'Above the State: The Officers' Republic in Egypt', *The Carnegie Papers*, Middle East, August 2012.

15 Gamal Essam el-Din, 'Catching the Big Fish', *al Ahram Weekly*, 18–24 October 2012, weekly.ahram.org.eg/2012/1119/eg4.htm; Gamal Essam el-Din, 'Stepping up the Money Hunt', *al Ahram Weekly*, 6–12 September 2012, weekly.ahram.org.eg/2012/1113/eg11.htm.

16 On the most central of these organizations see 'The Turkish Ambassador Meets with EBDA Board of Directors', EBDA, www.ebda-egypt.com/index.php?option=com_k2&view=item&id=28:the-turkish-ambassador-meeting-with-ebda-board-of-directors&Itemid=309; Nadine Maroushi, 'Senior Brotherhood Member Launches Egyptian Business Association', *Egypt Independent*, 26 March 2012.

17 The World Bank, *Immigration and Remittances Handbook*, 201, siteresources.worldbank.org/INTLAC/Resources/Factbook2011-Ebook.pdf.

18 *Index mundi*, www.indexmundi.com/g/g.aspx?c=eg&v=71.

19 The change of heart is reflected in the views of Mustapha Nabli, one of the leading Arab experts in the World Bank and who briefly served as head of Tunisia's central bank following the overthrow of Ben Ali. Like many of his former World Bank colleagues, including Ahmad Galal, presently head of the Cairo-based Economic Research Forum, Nabli was initially optimistic about the prospects for economic reform, but by the autumn of 2012 he was clearly pessimistic. He commented caustically then that Egypt and Tunisia 'are in for a rough ride' because of unsustainable spending and inability to attract foreign investment. Ahmed Feteha, 'Arab Spring Economies Will Get Worse before Rebound: Tunisia's Former Top Banker', *Ahram Online*, english.ahram.org.eg/NewsContentPrient/3/0/56715/Business/0/Arab-Spring-econo.

20 Doaa el-Bey, 'Relative Failings', *al Ahram Weekly*, 19– 26 September 2012, sites.google,com/site/weeklyahramorgegissue1115/home-1/relative-failings.

21 Ahmad Namatallah and Alaa Shahine, 'Egypt Current Account Deficit Widens', Bloomberg, 10 June 2012, www.bloomberg.com/news/2012-06-10/egypt-current-account-deficit-widens-as-tourism-fdi-fall-1-.html and www.businessweek.com/news/2012-09-10/egypt-current-account-gap-widens-capital-outflows-increase. Between 1982 and 1988 the current deficit averaged US$3.6 billion, or about 9% of GDP. During the Nazif governments the deficit shrank and in fact the current account was in positive balance in 2007, before then beginning its unbroken descent with $1.4 billion and $3.4 billion deficits in 2008 and 2009, respectively. The trade account remained in chronic deficit throughout the Nazif era, as discussed in Rivlin, *Arab Economies*, 116.

22 'A Guide to Egypt's Challenges: The Economy', *Ahram Online*, 16 August 2012, english.ahram.org.eg/NewsContentPrint/1/0/49601/Egypt/0A-G.

23 Reem Leila, 'Towards a Politics of Consensus', *al Ahram* Weekly, 16–23 October 2012, weekly.ahram.org.eg/2012/1118/eg7.htm.

24 'Minister: US$16 bn Worth of Investments Left the Country After the Revolution', *al masry al youm*, 10 October 2012, www.egyptindependent.com/node/1164251.

25 Niveen Wahish, 'French Banks Go Home', *al Ahram Weekly*, 27 September–3 October 2012, weekly.ahram.org.eg/2012/1116/ec5.htm.

26 Stanley Reed and Sara Hamdan, 'Egypt's Disarray Puts a Leading Regional Investment Bank in Play', *The New York Times*, 15 June 2012, B1; Sherine Abdel-Razek, 'Breaking News at EFT', *al Ahram Weekly*, 7–13 June 2012, weekly.ahram.org.eg/2012/1101/ec2.htm; Heba Saleh and Simeon Kerr, 'EFG-Hermes Faces its own Arab Spring', *Financial Times*, 7 June 2012, 16.

27 'Fitch Downgrades Egypt Currency Rating over Political Uncertainties', 16 June 2012, www.egyptindependent.com/print/920216.

28 Joel Beinin, 'The Rise of Egypt's Workers', *The Carnegie Papers*, June 2012.

29 The port's operations were also interrupted by a dispute over new regulations imposed on Dubai Ports, the licensee managing the port, by the Mursi government. See Sherine Abdel-Razek, 'Conditional Commitment', *al Ahram Weekly*, 4–10 October 2012, weekly.ahram.org.eg/2012/1117/ec2.htm. On the job losses claimed by Ahmed el-Sweidy, see Ahmed Kotb, 'Finding the Way Out', *al Ahram Weekly*, 14–20 June 2012, weekly.ahram.org.eg/print/2012/1102/ec2.htm.

30 'Pensions Up', *al Ahram Weekly*, 5–11 July 2012, weekly.ahram.org.eg/2012/1105/ec4.htm.

31 Mona al-Fiqi, 'Supporting Cotton', *al Ahram Weekly*, 4–10 October 2012, weekly.ahram.org.eg/2012/1117/ec1.htm.

32 Ahmed Kotb, 'Protect Egypt's Steel', *al Ahram Weekly*, 4–10 October 2012, weekly.ahram.org.eg/2012/1117/ec3.htm; and 'Import Controls in the Balance', *al Ahram Weekly*, 2–8 February 2012, weekly.ahram.org.eg/2012/1083/ec1.htm.

33 'Mobinil Executive: State Attempting to Monopolize Market', *al Masry al Youm*, 15 August 2012, www.egyptindependent.com/node/1051471.

34 Heba Saleh, 'Poor Braced for Hardship as Egypt Seeks Path to Ending Fuel Subsidies', *Financial Times*, 18 October 2012, 2.

35 Nabil Fahmy, 'Egypt's Mursi gets Marks for Speed, not for Style in Foreign Policy', *al Monitor*, 15 October 2012.

36 Dina Ezzat, 'Morsi's Promises for his First 100 Days in Office', *al Ahram Weekly*, 11–17 October 2012, weekly.ahram.org.eg/2012/1118/eg111.htm.

37 Dina Ezzat, 'First Interview Fails to Impress', *al Ahram Weekly*, 27 September–3 October 2012, weekly.ahram.org.eg/2012/1116/eg2.htm.

38 Mursi in fact dispatched him to Doha, Qatar, in October 2012 in an attempt to secure the funds that the emir of that country had previously promised. That al-Shater saw fit to bring with him former

businessman Rashid Muhammad Rashid, a leading light in the Nazif cabinets to whom the SCAF had offered the prime ministry but then indicted him for corruption when he rejected the offer, suggested that the emir had some doubts about Mursi and his government's ability to manage donated funds and the economic crisis more generally. Rashid's presence was obviously intended to assuage the emir's doubts. Dina Ezzat, 'Brotherhood Shater, former Mubarak-era Minister Secure Qatari Loan to Egypt', *Ahram Online*, 21 October 2012, english.ahram.org/eg/NewsContentPrint/3/0/55939/Business/0/Brotherhood-Shater. On Shater's denial of the existence of the 'Renaissance Plan', see Emad Gad, 'The Awareness Factor', *al Ahram Weekly*, 27 September–3 October 2012, weekly.ahram.org.eg/2012/1116/op173.htm.

39 Sayed Abdel-Maguid, 'Turkish Delight', *al Ahram Weekly*, 4–10 October 2012, weekly.ahram.org.eg/2012/1117/eg1.htm.

40 Rodney Wilson, *Economic Development in the Middle East*, second edn, Routledge, London, 2012, 29.

41 Henry and Springborg, *Globalization and the Politics of Development in the Middle East*, 27.

42 Ibid., 27.

43 Leila, 'Towards a Politics of Consensus'.

44 Henry and Springborg, *Globalization and the Politics of Development in the Middle East*, 28.

45 'Government Report: The Poor Represent a Quarter of Egypt's Population', *al Masry al Youm*, 16 October 2012, www.eguyptindependent.com/node/1180436; and Sherine Abdel-Rezek, 'Living in Poverty', *al Ahram Weekly*, 9–15 February 2011, weekly.ahram.org.eg/2012/1084/ec1.htm.

46 Henry and Springborg, *Globalization and the Politics of Development in the Middle East*, 31.

47 Ibid., 27.

48 World Bank, *Arab Republic of Egypt Improving Quality, Equality, and Efficiency in the Education Sector: Fostering a Competent Generation of Youth*, Human Development Department Middle East and North Africa Region, 29 June 2007, 9; National Center for Educational Statistics, 'Trends in International Mathematics and Science Study 2007', nces.ed.gov/timss/table07_3.asp.

49 World Bank, *Arab Republic of Egypt*, 11.

50 Ibid., 1.

51 Abdeljalil Akkari, 'Education in the Middle East and North Africa: The Current Situation and Future Challenges', *International Education Journal* 5(2), 2004: 149.

52 World Bank, *Arab Republic of Egypt*, 29.

53 Ibid., 26.

54 Yasmine Fahim and Noha Sami, 'Adequacy, Efficiency and Equity of Higher Education Financing: The Case of Egypt', *Prospects* 41, 2011: 52.

55 Clemens Breisinger, Olivier Ecker, Perrihan al-Riffai and Bingxin Yu, 'Beyond the Arab Awakening: Policies and Investments for Poverty Reduction and Food Security', Food Policy Report, International Food Policy Research Institute, February 2012, 27.

56 Cited in Fahim and Sami, 'Adequacy, Efficiency and Equity of Higher Education Financing', 58.

57 Marcus Noland and Howard Pack, *The Arab Economies in a Changing World*, The Peterson Institute, Washington, DC, 2011, 36.

58 data.worldbank.org/indicator/SL.TLF.CACT.ZS/countries.

59 data.worldbank.org/indicator/SL.TLF.CACT.FE.ZS/countries.

60 'Economic Contribution of Women', *The Economist*, 20 October 2012, 85.

61 Ibid., 85.

62 Sherine Abdel-Razek, 'A Good Story to Tell', *al Ahram Weekly*, 11–17 October 2012, weekly.ahram.org.eg/2012/1118/ec1.htm.

63 Cited in Henry and Springborg, *Globalization and the Politics of Development in the Middle East*, 188.

64 Ibid., 104.

65 Mohamed el-Erian, 'The Arabian Horse', *Foreign Policy*, 30 July 2012, www.foreignpolicy.com/articles/2012/07/31/the_arabian_horse. Labour demand was reported as falling by 20% over the year ending May 2012. 'Egypt Labour Demands Falls 20 pct in May: State Figures', *Ahram Online*, 9 July 2012, english.ahram.org.eg?News/47252.aspx.

66 Ragui Assaad, 'Labor Supply, Employment, and Unemployment in the Egyptian Economy, 1988–2006', in Ragui Assaad (ed.), *The Egyptian Labor Market Revisited*, American University in Cairo Press, Cairo, 2009, 1–52.

67 Alia el Mahdi and Ali Rashed, 'The Changing Economic Environment and the Development of Micro- and Small Enterprises in Egypt, 2006', in Ragui Assaad (ed.), *The Egyptian Labor Market Revisited*, American University in Cairo Press, Cairo, 2009, 83–116.

68 Rana Hendy and Chahir Zaki, 'On Informality and Productivity of Micro and Small Enterprises: Evidence from MENA Countries', Working Paper 719, Economic Research Forum, Cairo, October 2012, 3.

69 Ibid., 5.

70 Tilman Brück, Christine Binzel and Lars Handrich, 'Evaluating Economic Reforms in Syria', DIW Berlin, Politikberatung Kompakt, for GTZ, cited in Henry and Springborg, *Globalization and the Politics of Development in the Middle East*, 147.

71 Constantino Hevia and Norman Loayza, 'Saving and Growth in Egypt', Policy Research Working Paper 5529, The World Bank, Development Research Group, January 2011, i.

72 Ibid., 24.

73 Henry and Springborg, *Globalization and the Politics of Development in the Middle East*, 173.

74 Breisinger *et al.*, 'Beyond the Arab Awakening', 22.

75 Ibid., 34.

76 As a consequence Egypt has been facing increasingly frequent power and water shortages of ever greater duration. See, for example, 'Sherine Abdel-Razek, 'Power Deficits to Continue', *al Ahram Weekly*, 16–22 August 2012, weekly.ahram.org.eg/2012/1111/ec1.htm; Reem Leila, 'Power to the People?' *al Ahram Weekly*, 25–30 July 2012, weekly.ahram.org.eg/2012/1108/eg5.htm; and 'Market Thirsty for Bottled Water', *al Ahram Weekly*, 9–15 August 2012, weekly.ahram.org.eg/2012/1110/ec3.htm.

77 World Bank, *World Development Indicators*, data.worldbank.org/indicator/EN.ATM.PM10.MC.M3.

78 Aon Hewitt People Risk Update, aonpeoplerisk.com/2012-Update; and 'Risky Cairo', *al Ahram Weekly*, 14–20 June 2012, weekly.ahram.org.eg/2012/1102/ec4.htm.

79 *Doing Business in Egypt, 2008*, The World Bank and the International Finance Corporation, Washington, DC, 2007, www.wbginvestmentclimate.org/uploads/DB08_Subnational_Report_Egypt.pdf.

80 For an assessment of how Egypt 'gamed' the Ease of Doing Business Index and the role of GAFI in that, see Robert Springborg, 'Governance in Egypt', in Abbas Khadim, *Handbook of Governance in the Middle East*, Routledge, London, 2012.

81 Ease of Doing Business in the Arab Republic of Egypt, IFC Doing Business, World Bank Group, www.doingbusiness.org/data/exploreeconomies/egypt.

82 Rodney Wilson, *Economic Development in the Middle East*, second edition, Routledge, London, 2013, 170.

83 The Heritage Foundation, Economic Freedom Index, www.heritage.org/index/ranking.

84 Noland and Pack, *The Arab Economies in a Changing World*, 154.

85 Hendy and Zaki, 'On Informality and Productivity of Micro and Small Enterprises', 8.

86 Noland and Pack, *The Arab Economies in a Changing World*, 125.

87 Robert Springborg, 'The Hound that Did not Bark: Solving the Mystery of Business Without Voice in Egypt', in Steffen Hertog, Giacomo Luciani and Marc Valeri (eds), *Business Politics in the Middle East*, Routledge, London, 2012.

88 Henry and Springborg, *Globalization and the Politics of Development in the Middle East*, 107.

89 Magdi Amin, Ragui Assaad, Nazar al-Baharna, Kemal Dervis, Raj M. Desai, Navtej S. Dhillon, Ahmed Galal, Hafez Ghanem, Carol Graham and Daniel Kaufmann, *After the Arab Spring: Economic Transitions in the Arab World*, Oxford University Press, Oxford, 2012, 48.

90 Amr Adly, *State Reform and Development in the Middle East: Turkey and Egypt in the Post-Liberalization Era*, Routledge, London, 2012.

91 Robert Springborg, 'Gas and Oil in Egypt's Development', in Robert Looney (ed.), *Handbook of Oil Politics*, Routledge, London, 2012, 295–311. In an ominous sign of likely intensifying gas supply problems, in November 2012 Orascom Construction Industries had to close three fertilizer plants when EGAS, the state-owned gas supplier, abruptly stopped the flow of gas, ostensibly for maintenance procedures. Earlier in the year it had cut off gas to several plants in the Delta. Simultaneously the government announced it had opened negotiations with Qatar and Algeria to import gas. 'Update: OCI Halts Fertilizer Plants after Gas Supply Cut', *Egypt Independent*, 6 November 2012, www.egyptindependent.com/news/update-oci-halts-fertilizer-plants-after-gas-supply-cut.

92 Alain Gresh, 'Gulf Cools Toward Muslim Brothers', *Le Monde Diplomatique*, November 2012, mondediplo.com/2012/11/.

93 Thalia Beaty, 'The Purpose of U.S. Aid to Egypt Needs Re-Examining', *The Daily Star*, 29 October 2012, www.dailystar.com.lb/Opinion/Commentary/2012/Oct-29/193012-the-purpose-of-us-aid-to-egypt-needs-re-examining.ashx#axzz2BZFuY64o. Steven Lee Meyers, 'Emergency Aid to Egypt Encounters an Objection', *New York Times*, 29 September 2012, A11.

94 Reem Leila, 'Seeking EU Aid', *al Ahram Weekly*, 20–26 September 2012, sites.google.com/site/weeklyahramorgegissue1115/home-1/seeking-eu-aid.

95 See for example Ruchir Sharma, 'Broken BRICS', *Foreign Affairs* 91(6), November/December 2012: 2–7; and Robert J. Samuelson, 'The BRIC Rescue that Wasn't', *The Washington Post*, 15 October 2012, www.washingtonpost.com/robert-j-samuelson/2011/02/24/ABSZV8O_page.html. The MSCI emerging market index was flat in 2012 and remained at about one-third below its 2007 peak. 'Dream On?' *The Economist*, 21 July 2012, 59.

96 'Free Exchange: Shake it all About', *The Economist*, 28 January 2012, 75.

22

Thailand

Economic progress and the move to populism[1]

Peter Warr

Introduction

Thailand is unusual among middle-income developing countries in several respects. It was never colonized, a unique experience within South-East Asia. Perhaps partly because of that, successive Thai governments have not been afraid to embark on deep trade and investment integration with the rest of the world. Its trade and investment policies have been relatively open and its macro-economic policies have generally been conservative and directed towards maintaining economic stability.

Long-term economic growth has been good. The lead-up to the Asian Financial Crisis of 1997–98 was a notable exception to the record of both conservative economic policies and sustained growth. Events originating within the country triggered a serious financial crisis affecting about half of East Asia. The crisis operated through Thailand's overextended financial system and produced a serious economic contraction. The 2008–09 global financial crisis again interrupted long-term growth, though this time the impact did not operate through Thailand's financial system but through sharply reduced demand for Thailand's exports, caused by recession among the major importing countries. Since the global financial crisis the rate of growth has remained below the long-term trend.

This chapter first reviews economic developments, with a focus on the growth of the Thai economy. It then looks at the implications of these events for social progress, including poverty reduction and health. The following section summarizes recent political developments, especially the rise of populism, and asks whether Thailand is now subject to a 'middle-income trap'. The final section concludes.

Economic growth: impressive performance despite turbulence

Aggregate economic performance

At the end of the Second World War Thailand was one of the world's poorest countries, having been stagnant for at least a century (Manorungsan 1989) and suffering significant damage during the war itself. Most economic observers of the time rated its prospects poorly (Ingram 1971). Half a century later, in the mid-1990s, these negative assessments had been replaced by euphoric descriptions of Thailand as a 'Fifth Tiger', following in the footsteps of the Republic of Korea (South Korea), Taiwan, Hong Kong and Singapore, having achieved a combination of rapid growth, macroeconomic stability and steadily declining poverty incidence, extending over several decades.

This growth performance is summarized in Figure 22.1, showing the level of real gross domestic product (GDP) per capita in each year (vertical bars) and its growth rate (solid line) for the period 1951 to 2013. The figure identifies six periods of Thailand's recent economic history: I pre-boom (until 1986); II boom (1987–96); III Asian Financial Crisis (1997–99); IV recovery from the Asian Financial Crisis (2000–07); V global financial crisis (2008–09); and VI recovery from the global financial crisis (2010–12). Table 22.1 provides a summary of average growth rates during each of these periods.

During the period 1968 to 1986 the average annual growth rate of Thailand's real gross national product (GNP) was 6.7% (almost 5% per person), compared with an average of 2.4%

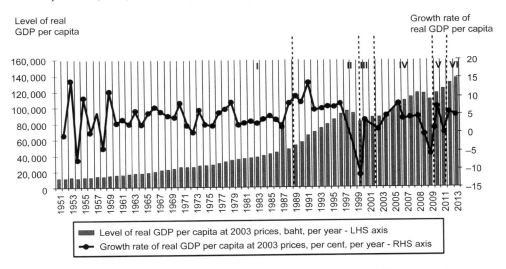

Figure 22.1 Thailand real GDP per capita and its growth rate, 1951 to 2013
Source: Author's calculations, using data from National Economic and Social Development Board (NESDB), Bangkok
Note: The data for 2013 are projections from NESDB, Bangkok.

Table 22.1 Growth of GDP and its sectoral components in Thailand, 1951–2012 (% per annum)

Period	Pre-boom 1968–86 I	Boom 1987–96 II	Asian financial crisis 1997–99 III	Recovery 2000–07 IV	Global financial crisis 2008–09 V	Recovery 2010–12 VI	Whole period 1968–2012
Total GDP	6.7	9.5	−2.5	5.1	0.1	4.8	6.0
Agriculture	4.5	2.6	0.1	3.2	2.8	2.8	3.4
Industry	8.5	12.8	−1.7	6.1	−0.9	4.2	7.6
Services	6.8	9.0	−3.6	4.5	0.6	5.9	5.9

Source: Bank of Thailand, data for 1951–86; National Economic and Social Development Board, data for 1987–2011; World Bank, *World Development Indicators*, data for 2012
Note: Roman numerals refer to the regions identified in Figure 22.1.

for low- and middle-income countries, according to World Bank data. Then, during the decade 1987 to 1996 the Thai economy boomed and throughout this period it was the fastest growing in the world. As we shall see below, Thailand's boom was driven by very high levels of investment, both domestic and foreign, in physical capital. Even more remarkable than the rate of growth over this long period was the stability of the growth. Not a single year of negative growth of real output per head of population was experienced during the four decades from 1958 to 1996, a unique achievement among oil-importing developing countries. Thailand's performance was often described as an example others might emulate. Its principal economic institutions, including its central bank, the Bank of Thailand, were often cited as examples of competent and stable management.

The crisis of 1997–98 changed that story dramatically. The domestic economy was in disarray, with output and investment contracting; poverty incidence was rising; the exchange rate had collapsed, following the decision to float the currency in July 1997; the government had been compelled to accept a humiliating International Monetary Fund (IMF) bail-out package; the financial system was largely bankrupt; and confidence in the country's economic institutions, including the Bank of Thailand, was shattered. Internationally, Thailand was now characterized as the initiator of a 'contagion effect' in Asian financial markets, undermining economic and political stability and bringing economic hardship to millions of people.

The economic damage done by the crisis of 1997–99 and the hardship that resulted were both substantial. The crisis eroded some of the gains from the economic growth that had been achieved during the long period of economic expansion, but it did not erase them. At the low point of the crisis, in 1998, the level of GDP per capita was almost 14% lower than it had been only two years earlier, in 1996. Nevertheless, owing to the sustained growth that had preceded the crisis, this reduced level of 1998 was still higher than it had been only five years earlier, in 1993, and was seven times its level in 1951.

Following the crisis, Thailand's rate of economic recovery was moderate. The rate of growth of real GDP was somewhat below its long-term trend rate and it was not until 2003 that the level of real GDP per capita recovered to its pre-crisis level of 1996. Foreign direct investment (FDI) declined dramatically from 1998 onwards and private domestic investment remained sluggish. Despite the slower than expected recovery, in 2007 the level of real economic output per person was 20% above its 1996 pre-crisis level and almost 10 times its level of 1951. The average annual rate of growth of real GDP per person during this entire period of five and a half decades from 1951 to 2008 was 4.2%.

The global financial crisis of 2008 affected Thailand primarily through trade in goods—a contraction in demand for its manufactured exports—rather than through financial markets. The effect was smaller than the Asian Financial Crisis of a decade before, but still significant, and it had political consequences. Unemployment among unskilled and semi-skilled industrial workers, many from the north-east and north regions of the country, contributed to the political instability of the 2008 to 2011 period, though it was not the only cause, culminating in July 2011 with the election of the populist Pheu Thai ('for Thais') government, led *in absentia* by the exiled former Prime Minister Thaksin Shinawatra.

Figures 22.2 and 22.3 place the experience of the last two and a half decades in comparative perspective. Data on real GDP are presented for eight East Asian economies, including Thailand. The pre-crisis period of 1986 to 1996 is covered in Figure 22.2, with each country's 1986 level of real GDP indexed to 100. The crisis and post-crisis periods of 1996 to 2012 are shown in Figure 22.3, with 1996 real GDP this time indexed to 100. Figure 22.2 shows that Thailand's boom was the largest of the countries shown, but only marginally so. Singapore, Malaysia, Indonesia, South Korea and Taiwan were not far behind.

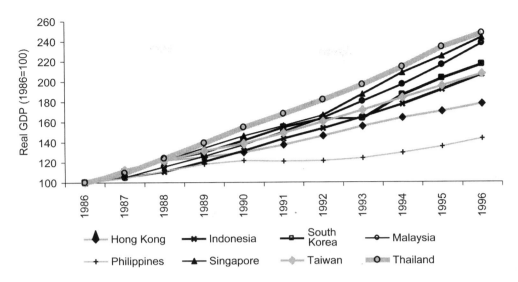

Figure 22.2 Real GDP in East Asia, 1986 to 1996
Source: Author's calculations, using data from Asian Development Bank, *Key Indicators for Asia and the Pacific* (various issues)

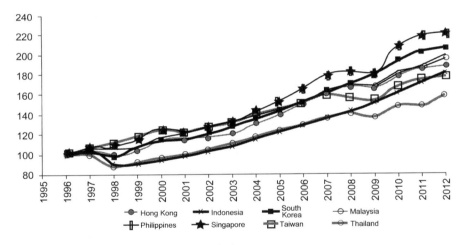

Figure 22.3 Real GDP in East Asia, 1996 to 2012
Source: Author's calculations, using data from Asian Development Bank, *Key Indicators for Asia and The Pacific* (various issues)

Figure 22.3 shows that in 1998 serious contractions occurred in South Korea, Malaysia and Indonesia, but that relative to 1996, Thailand's initial contraction was the most severe. Along with Indonesia, its contraction has also been the most long-lasting. Thailand's contraction was initially larger than Indonesia's, but Indonesia did not experience a recovery as large as Thailand's in 1999. It is commonly said that Indonesia's economic crisis was more severe than Thailand's, but these data reveal a somewhat different story. Using the pre-crisis year of 1996 as a base, their time paths of real GDP, relative to the 1996 base, were remarkably similar. The main difference is that since 2008 Indonesia was less affected by the global financial crisis, mainly because the share of manufactured exports in GDP is significantly lower in Indonesia.

Sources of aggregate growth

Where did Thailand's economic growth come from? Explaining long-term growth involves distinguishing between growth of the quantities of factors of production employed and growth in their productivity.[2] We now discuss a growth-accounting exercise for Thailand, covering the years 1980 to 2002. The present section presents this analysis at an aggregate, economy-wide level and the following section disaggregates the analysis by sectors.

The assumption being made in this kind of analysis is that output was primarily supply constrained—aggregate demand was not the binding constraint on output. This assumption seems reasonable for the period prior to the Asian crisis of 1997–99, but the crisis and recovery periods from 1997 onwards were characterized by a deficiency of aggregate demand. A growth accounting framework, which focuses on the determinants of aggregate supply, is therefore of limited relevance for such periods. The data relating to that period are included here mainly for completeness.

Data on labour inputs are adjusted for changes in the quality of the workforce by disaggregating the workforce by the educational characteristics of workers and weighting these components of the workforce using time series wage data for the educational categories concerned. Data on land inputs are similarly adjusted for the changing quality of land inputs by disaggregating by irrigated and non-irrigated land and then re-aggregating these components using data on land prices. In Table 22.2 the resulting estimates of factor growth rates are contained in the first column. The second column provides average factor cost shares over time, compiled from factor price data. These factor cost shares add to unity, imposing the assumption of constant returns to scale. The factor cost shares used in the calculations vary over time. The summary data shown in the table are the averages of these shares.

The third column on factor contributions to growth weights the growth rates of factors by their cost shares, producing an estimate of the degree to which the growth of output (6.01%) is attributable to growth of each component. These data are then used to calculate total factor productivity (TFP) as a residual. The final column shows the estimated percentage contribution of each component to the overall growth rate.

Table 22.2 Aggregate growth accounting in Thailand, 1980–2002

	Annual growth rate (% per year)	Average cost share (%)	Contribution to total growth (% per year)	Contribution to total growth (%)
Output	6.01	n.a.	n.a.	100.0
All factors	5.41	100.0	5.41	90.0
Raw labour	2.19	40.2	0.88	14.7
Human capital	2.49	11.2	0.28	4.6
Physical capital	9.05	46.9	4.24	70.6
Agricultural land	1.12	1.8	0.02	3.3
Aggregate TFP growth	n.a.	n.a.	0.60	10.0

Source: Author's calculations, using data from the National Economic and Social Development Board
Note: n.a. means not applicable.

The outstanding point is the rapid growth of the physical capital stock. The capital stock grew more rapidly than output in both the pre-boom and boom periods. This growth of the capital stock accounted for 70% of the growth of output.[3] Growth of the size of the labour force contributed about 15% of the growth of output, but improvements in the quality of the labour force made only a modest contribution, explaining less than 5% of overall growth. Indeed, the performance of Thailand's educational sector has been among the weakest in East Asia. Secondary school participation rates were low and did not improve greatly during the pre-boom and boom periods (Sirilaksana 1993). Similarly, since the 1960s the expansion of the cultivated land area has been small. Growth of the stock of land was not the source either. TFP growth was only moderately important, accounting for 10% of output growth.

It is perhaps unsurprising that the explanation for Thailand's impressive growth lies primarily in the growth of the physical capital stock. Both domestic and foreign investment grew rapidly, but the growth *rate* of foreign investment was larger from about 1987 (Warr 1993). Foreign investment plays an important role in introducing new technology and in the development of export markets. Nevertheless, the quantitative importance of foreign investment in Thailand's capital stock accumulation is easily exaggerated. Figure 22.4 makes this point by decomposing Thailand's total annual level of investment into three components: domestic private, public, and foreign direct investment. It does this for each of four years: 1975, 1985, 1995 and 2005. Of these three components, domestic private investment is by far the largest and FDI by far the smallest. In 2005 their contributions to the overall level of investment were: private domestic investment 69.5%, public investment 26.8%, and FDI 3.7%. Private investment by Thais themselves was the dominant contributor to overall capital accumulation.

How was the investment financed? Did the funds come from domestic savings or from borrowings from abroad? Table 22.3 presents an accounting of this issue based on the identities

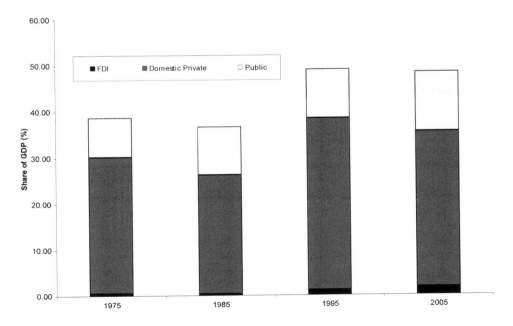

Figure 22.4 Composition of net annual investment, 1975 to 2005
Source: Author's calculation using data from National Economic and Social Development Board, Bangkok

Table 22.3 Financing of aggregate investment in Thailand, 1973–2002

| | | | Average share of each component (%) | | | | |
| | | | | Foreign savings | | | |
	Private savings	Government savings	Total	Long-term capital inflow	Short-term capital inflow	Decline in reserves	Total savings = total investment
Pre-boom (1973–86)	112.9	−16.7	3.8	5.1	2.1	−3.4	100
Boom (1987–96)	93.1	−11.4	18.2	4.1	22.8	−8.7	100
Crisis (1997–98)	160.9	−23.2	−37.7	17.3	−70.4	15.4	100
Post–crisis (1999–2002)	142.3	−6.4	−36.2	11.3	−35.4	−12.1	100
Whole period (1973–2002)	115.9	−19.0	3.1	5.3	1.1	−3.4	100

Source: Author's calculations, using data from Bank of Thailand and the National Economic and Social Development Board

that: (1) total investment = household savings + government savings + foreign savings; and (2) foreign savings = long-term capital inflow + short-term capital inflow − change in international reserves of the central bank. By far the most important source of finance was the private savings of the Thais themselves.

Contrary to the common perception that Thailand's boom (1987 to 1996) was financed largely by foreign capital, this source, consisting of private FDI plus foreign government investment by overseas development assistance (ODA), accounted for an average of only 5% of total investment. During the pre-boom period, FDI accounted for about 61% of the inflow of long-term foreign capital and ODA accounted for the other 39%. During the boom period, these proportions were 73% and 27%, respectively. Short-term capital inflows, consisting of borrowing from abroad plus portfolio inflows plus domestic bank accounts held by foreigners were a more important source, accounting for 23% of total investment. During the boom, government dissavings (budget deficits) reduced the funds available for investment by 11% and increases in the international reserves of the Bank of Thailand reduced it by a further 9%.

It is instructive to compare the boom period (1987 to 1996) with the pre-boom period (1973 to 1986). The major difference was in the proportion of total investment that was financed by short-term capital inflows. This proportion increased from 2% before the boom to 23% during the boom. It financed investment, but it also sowed the seeds of the crisis of 1997–99. The accumulated stock of mobile foreign-owned capital grew to levels far exceeding the stock of the Bank of Thailand's foreign exchange reserves. If the owners of these funds chose to withdraw them from Thailand, the Bank of Thailand would be unable to defend its fixed exchange rate. This is what happened in July 1997 (Warr 1999, 2005).

In summary, growth of the physical capital stock was the most important contributor to Thailand's aggregate growth, accounting for 70% of all growth over the period 1981 to 2002. Most of this investment was financed from Thai domestic private savings. The notion that Thailand's accumulation of physical capital was financed by FDI and/or foreign aid is a myth. Total foreign capital inflows, FDI plus ODA accounted for only about 5% of total investment. ODA was less than one-third of this foreign capital inflow. That is, the quantity of ODA explains only 1.5% of total investment over this period, and thus under 1% of total growth.

Before leaving the subject of Thailand's aggregate economic performance, one further topic requires attention. Why has Thailand's recovery been so slow? As noted above, the crisis was a

Thailand

Table 22.4 Thailand, Indonesia and Malaysia: contributions to expenditure on GDP, 1987–2006

Country/period	Consumption	Investment	Government	Net exports	Total
Thailand					
Pre-crisis (1987–96)	54.8	38.9	9.9	–5.0	100
Crisis (1997–99)	54.0	27.0	10.5	8.5	100
Post-crisis (2000–06)	57.6	26.0	11.3	5.3	100
Indonesia					
Pre-crisis (1987–96)	55.0	27.8	9.1	0.4	100
Crisis (1997–99)	65.0	24.5	6.5	5.0	100
Post-crisis (2000–06)	62.1	23.7	7.7	6.6	100
Malaysia					
Pre-crisis (1987–96)	48.8	37.2	12.8	1.2	100
Crisis (1997–99)	43.5	35.0	10.5	11.5	100
Post-crisis (2000–06)	46.1	23.0	12.6	18.3	100

Source: Author's calculations, using data from World Bank, *World Development Indicators*, various issues

contraction in aggregate demand, rather than a contraction in productive capacity. Labour and capital were underutilized because there was insufficient demand for Thai output. Where did this contraction in demand come from? Table 22.4 addresses this point. The upper section of the table shows contributions to the composition of expenditure on GDP in Thailand during the pre-crisis boom (1987–96), the crisis (1997–99), and the post-crisis recovery period (2000–05). During the crisis the share of investment in GDP collapsed by 13 percentage points. Investor confidence was severely damaged by the events surrounding the crisis, and during the post-crisis recovery period this share did not recover sufficiently to restore Thailand's long-term rate of growth.

Why has this occurred? High interest rates are not the answer. Figure 22.5 shows that although Thailand's interest rates increased during the crisis, they have been at historically low levels since 2000. A clue is provided by Figure 22.6, which shows the relationship between the stock exchange index of Thailand (SET) and the level of private investment. Investment follows the SET, but with a lag. The stock exchange index may be viewed as an indicator of investor confidence. Investors have lost confidence in the capacity of the Thai economy to generate a satisfactory return on their investments.

This problem is not unique to Thailand. Table 22.4 shows similar calculations for two other crisis-affected economies, Indonesia and Malaysia. The pattern is very similar. Finally, Figure 22.7 shows annual data on the share of investment in GDP in five crisis-affected East Asian economies: Thailand, Indonesia, Malaysia, the Philippines and South Korea. Although the contraction of private investment in Thailand is at least as large as any other (Malaysia is similar), the figure shows that the problem of sluggish recovery of investment is shared by several East Asian economies. It would not seem appropriate to look for country-specific causes. The decline of investor confidence is region-wide, at least among the countries seriously affected by the crisis. The crisis showed the possibility that investors could be bankrupted by macroeconomic events over which they have no control and where they have little or no forewarning.

Sectoral economic performance and productivity growth

How do the major sectors of the Thai economy compare in terms of productivity growth? Table 22.1 summarizes the sectoral composition of Thailand's growth performance since 1968. The growth of industry, especially export-oriented manufacturing, has far outstripped

423

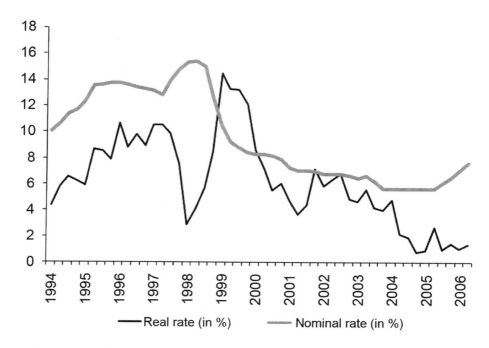

Figure 22.5 Real and nominal interest rate, 1994 to 2006
Source: Author's calculations, using data from Bank of Thailand, Bangkok

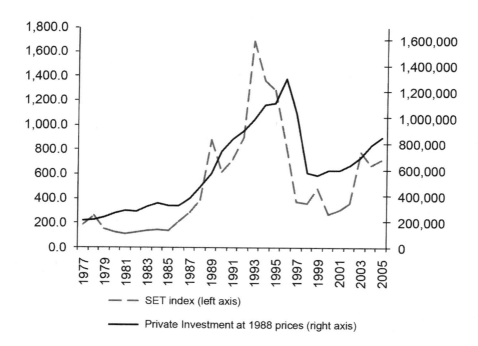

Figure 22.6 Private investment and the stock exchange price index, 1977 to 2005
Source: Author's calculations, using data from National Economic and Social Development Board, Bangkok and Stock Exchange of Thailand, Bangkok

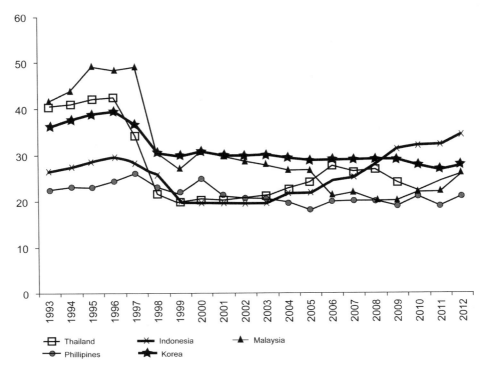

Figure 22.7 Investment shares of GDP in Asia, 1993 to 2012 (per cent)
Source: Author's calculations, using data from World Bank, *World Development Indicators* (various issues)

agriculture, implying that agriculture's share of GDP has declined significantly. This point is confirmed by Figure 22.8, which shows the rapidly changing composition of output in Thailand.

Observations of this kind are typical for rapidly growing economies. As aggregate output per person expands, agriculture tends to contract as a share of total output, while the share of industry expands. However, a common misinterpretation of this phenomenon is that the agricultural sector is 'stagnant' while industry is 'dynamic'. The misinterpretation lies in confusing the fact that the *level* of factor productivity in agriculture tends to be lower than in industry (and in services) with differences in the *rate of growth* of productivity. The data for Thailand indicate that although the level of factor productivity is indeed lower in agriculture, the growth of productivity is much more rapid there than in other sectors. The key point is that Thai agriculture has been expanding its output, albeit more slowly than the rest of the economy, with *declining* shares of the nation's resources.

The evidence for this conclusion, together with a set of calculations for agriculture, industry and services, is summarized in Table 22.5. This sectoral analysis mirrors the aggregate analysis reported in Table 22.2.[4] The data used in this analysis again cover the years 1980 to 2002 and include:

- employment of labour by educational category by sector;
- physical capital used by each sector;
- use of land in agriculture, adjusted by the extent of irrigation coverage; and
- cost shares for each of the above factors of production by sector.

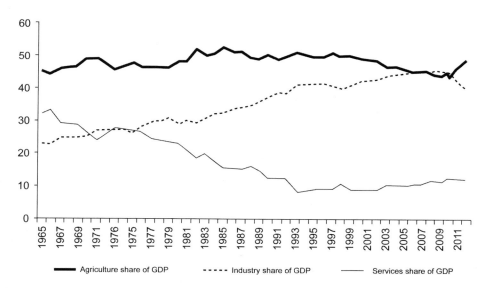

Figure 22.8 Sectoral shares of GDP, 1965 to 2012 (per cent)
Source: Author's calculations, using data from World Bank, *World Development Indicators* (various issues)

Table 22.5 Total factor productivity growth by sectors, 1980–2002

Average growth rates (% per annum)	Aggregate	Agriculture	Industry	Services
Output	6.01	2.64	8.09	5.53
Raw labour	2.19	1.50	5.25	3.47
Human capital	2.49	9.43	11.35	6.90
Physical capital	9.05	8.50	13.84	18.47
Agricultural land	1.12	1.12	0.00	0.00
Average cost shares (%)				
Raw labour	40.2	59.0	30.4	31.0
Human capital	11.2	3.9	12.0	9.2
Physical capital	46.9	13.0	57.6	59.8
Agricultural land	1.8	24.1	0.0	0.0
Decomposition of output growth (% per annum)				
Output growth	6.01	2.64	8.09	5.53
Factor growth	5.41	0.47	9.20	7.04
TFP growth	0.60	2.17	−1.11	−1.51
Decomposition of aggregate TFP growth (% per annum)				
Aggregate sectoral TFP growth	−0.85			
Reallocation effect	1.45			

Source: Author's calculations, using data from the National Economic and Social Development Board

For convenience, the first column of Table 22.5 repeats the findings at the aggregate level, discussed above. The sectoral findings may be summarized as follows. First, although output (value added) grew more slowly in agriculture (2.64%) than in either industry (8.09%) or services (5.53%), it was the only major sector to record positive TFP growth. This TFP growth in agriculture contributed one-20th of the overall growth of GDP. In agriculture, the growth of output of 2.64% per year was achieved by factor input growth of 0.47% and TFP growth of 2.17%. TFP growth therefore accounted for 82% of the growth of value added in agriculture.

Second, the analysis decomposes the aggregate productivity growth component just described into one component due to growth in productivity in individual sectors, each weighted by its share of GDP, and a second component due to the reallocation of resources among sectors of differing TFP. This analysis indicates that the *level* of factor productivity in agriculture remained significantly lower than elsewhere in the economy, despite its higher TFP growth over this period. The movement of factors of production out of agriculture thus further contributed to economic growth by raising the productivity of these factors. Indeed, this reallocation effect contributed 24% of the growth of aggregate output that actually occurred. It was almost five times as important for overall growth as the growth in the productivity of the factors that remained within agriculture.

The results of the analysis indicate that agriculture's contribution to economic growth in Thailand included impressive rates of TFP growth, but its main contribution occurred through releasing resources that could be used more productively elsewhere, while still maintaining output, rather than through expansion of agricultural output. It is seriously wrong to characterize Thai agriculture as 'stagnant', based merely on the fact that output growth is slower in agriculture than in other sectors. If agriculture had really been stagnant, economic growth would have been substantially lower because it would not have been possible to raise productivity significantly within agriculture or to release resources massively while still maintaining moderate growth of output.

Table 22.6 summarizes the results of this analysis by showing in the first column, the contributions to overall growth of aggregate factor growth (90% of total growth) and aggregate measures TFP (10%). It then decomposes this aggregate TFP growth into its sectoral components and the part that is due to the reallocation of resources from low productivity sectors (mainly agriculture) to higher productivity sectors (mainly industry). This distinction was apparently first identified empirically by Jorgenson (1988) in the context of US productivity growth. Although agriculture generated positive TFP growth, the aggregate of sector-level TFP growth was negative. All of the 10% of GDP growth accounted for by aggregate TFP, and

Table 22.6 Percentage contributions to aggregate growth, 1980–2002 (%)

	Whole period 1980–2002	*Pre-crisis period 1980–96*
Aggregate factor growth	90.0	80.3
Aggregate TFP growth	10.0	19.7
Agriculture TFP growth	5.0	2.9
Industry TFP growth	−7.1	−1.1
Services TFP growth	−12.0	0.7
Reallocation effect	24.1	17.3
Total	100.0	100.0

Source: Author's calculations, using data from the National Economic and Social Development Board

more besides, is accounted for by the reallocation of resources. The second column shows that these qualitative conclusions are not reversed if the analysis is confined only to the resource-constrained, pre-crisis period.

Recent economic developments: sluggish recovery

The global financial crisis of 2008–09 affected Thailand, along with most of East Asia, mainly through reduced export demand, rather than through financial channels. This point is illustrated in Figure 22.9, which is based on data for 12 Asia-Pacific countries, indicating the relationship between the size of the economic contraction that occurred with the global financial crisis and the country's export share in GDP. Those countries most dependent on exports, like Thailand, suffered the largest contractions. Those less dependent on exports, like India, the People's Republic of China and Indonesia, were less affected.

Continued slow growth in Europe, Japan and the USA constrains Thailand's capacity to use exports as the vehicle for recovery from the global financial crisis. Domestic political turmoil within Thailand from 2006 to 2011 added to these difficulties. Figure 22.10 summarizes real economic growth by quarter from 1995 to the second quarter of 2013. The vertical grey bars indicate the level of real GDP (total, not per capita) and the black line represents the year-on-year growth rate of this variable. Despite a sluggish global environment, the Thai economy is performing moderately well. Devastating flooding reduced growth in 2011 to 3.7%. In 2012 real growth was reported at 6.5% and growth in 2013 was projected at 4.3%. Inflation remains moderate at around 3%. A serious threat to public finances is posed by the government's disastrous rice 'pledging' programme, which is really a subsidized rice-purchasing scheme designed to bid-up the domestic price of rice, thereby benefiting at least part of the current government's rural support base.

Social progress: improved living standards amid high inequality

Is economic growth really so important? If all the benefit from growth went to those who were already rich, its social value would surely be questionable. Do the poor benefit? What happens

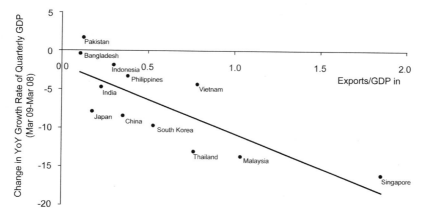

Figure 22.9 East Asia: export dependence and the effects of the global financial crisis
Source: Author's calculations, using data from World Bank, *World Development Indicators* (various issues)

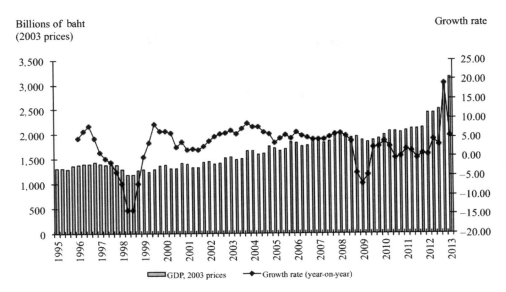

Figure 22.10 Thailand, quaterly Real GDP per capita and its growth, 1995 to 2013
Source: Author's calculations, using data from National Economic and Social Development Bank, Bangkok

to other dimensions of well-being such as health? Within Thailand, as elsewhere, there is considerable debate about these issues. We shall review the evidence in this section.

Poverty incidence and inequality

Despite much dispute about measurement and conceptual issues, all major studies of poverty incidence and inequality in Thailand agree on some basic points:

- Poverty is concentrated in rural areas, especially in the north-eastern and northern regions of the country.
- Absolute poverty has declined dramatically over the last four decades, but inequality has increased.
- The long-term decline in poverty incidence was not confined to the capital, Bangkok, or its immediate environs, or to urban areas in general, but occurred in rural areas as well. Since 1988, the largest absolute decline in poverty incidence occurred in the poorest region of the country, the north-east.
- Large families are more likely to be poor than smaller families.
- Farming families operating small areas of land are more likely to be poor than those operating larger areas.
- Households headed by persons with low levels of education are more likely to be poor than others.

The following discussion draws upon the official poverty estimates produced by the Thai government's National Economic and Social Development Board (NESDB), which, like all other available poverty estimates, are based upon the household incomes collected in the National Statistical Office's Socio-Economic Survey (SES) household survey data. Despite their imperfections, these are the only data available covering a long time period, having been collected since 1962. The early data were based on small samples, but their reliability has improved steadily, and since

Peter Warr

1988 the raw data have been available in electronic form. Table 22.7 summarizes the available official data for the two decades from 1988 to 2009.

Declining poverty incidence, rising inequality

Table 22.7 focuses on the familiar headcount measure of poverty incidence: the percentage of a particular population whose household incomes per person fall below the poverty line. The table confirms that most of Thailand's poor people reside in rural areas. Until recently, the SES data were classified according to residential location in the categories municipal areas, sanitary districts and villages. These correspond to inner urban (historical urban boundaries), outer urban (newly established urban areas) and rural areas, respectively. Poverty incidence is highest in the rural areas, followed by outer urban, and lowest in the inner urban areas. In 2004 rural areas accounted for 64% of the total population but a stunning 93% of all people below the poverty line.

The final column of Table 22.7 shows the Gini coefficient of inequality. This index potentially takes values between 0 and 1, with higher values indicating greater inequality. The index for Thailand rose significantly over the 20 years shown. Combined with the reduction in absolute poverty which occurred at the same time, this means that the real incomes of the poor increased with economic growth, but the incomes of the rich increased even faster.

The data reveal a massive decline in poverty incidence up to 1996, a moderate increase to 1998 and a further increase over the following two years. During the eight years from 1988 to 1996 measured poverty incidence declined by an enormous 21.4% of the population, an average rate of decline in poverty incidence of 2.7 percentage points per year. That is, each year, on average 2.7% of the population moved from incomes below the poverty line to incomes above it. Over the ensuing two years ending in 1998 poverty incidence increased by 1.5% of the population.

Table 22.7 Poverty incidence and Gini coefficient, 1988–2009

	Poverty incidence (headcount measure, % of population)			Inequality (Gini coefficient)
	Aggregate	*Rural*	*Urban*	*Aggregate*
1988	44.9	52.9	25.2	0.487
1990	38.2	45.2	21.4	0.515
1992	32.5	40.3	14.1	0.536
1994	25.0	30.7	11.7	0.520
1996	17.0	21.3	7.3	0.513
1998	18.8	23.7	7.5	0.507
2000	21.3	27.0	8.7	0.522
2002	15.5	19.7	6.7	0.507
2004	11.3	14.3	4.9	0.493
2006	9.5	12.0	3.6	0.503
2007	8.5	10.7	3.3	0.509
2009	8.1	10.4	3.0	0.489

Source: Data for 1988–2006 from National Economic and Social Development Board, www.nesdb.go.th/Default.aspx?tabid=322 (accessed 15 September 2012); data for 2007–08 from Thailand Development Research Institute, Bangkok, calculated from Socio-Economic Survey raw data
Note: Both poverty incidence and inequality are based on incomes rather than expenditures in these data. Higher values of the Gini coefficient indicate greater inequality. Data are available on a two-yearly basis from 1988 to 2006, after which annual data are available, except for 2008.

Alternatively, over the eight years ending in 1996 the absolute number of persons in poverty declined by 11.1 million (from 17.9 million to 6.8 million); over the following two years the number increased by one million (from 6.8 to 7.9 million). Thus, according to the official data, measured in terms of absolute numbers of people in poverty, the crisis reversed 9% of the poverty reduction that had occurred during the eight-year period of economic boom immediately preceding the crisis.

Recently released data show a strong relationship between poverty incidence and education. According to the NESDB data, of the total number of poor people in 2002, 94.7% had received primary or less education. A further 2.8% had lower secondary education, 1.7% upper secondary education, 0.48% had vocational qualifications and 0.31% had graduated from universities. Thailand's poor are overwhelmingly uneducated, rural and living in large families. However, they are not necessarily landless.

Poverty reduction and economic growth

What caused the long-term decline in poverty incidence? It is obvious that over the long term, sustained economic growth is a necessary condition for large-scale poverty alleviation. No amount of redistribution could turn a very poor country into a rich one. Long-term improvements in education have undoubtedly been important, but despite the limitations of the underlying SES data, a reasonably clear statistical picture also emerges on the short-term relationship between poverty reductions and the rate of economic growth. The data are summarized in Figure 22.11, which plots the relationship between changes in poverty incidence, calculated from Table 22.7, and the real rate of growth of GDP over the corresponding periods.

Although the number of data points is small, the implications seem clear. Periods of more rapid economic growth were associated with more rapid reductions in the level of absolute

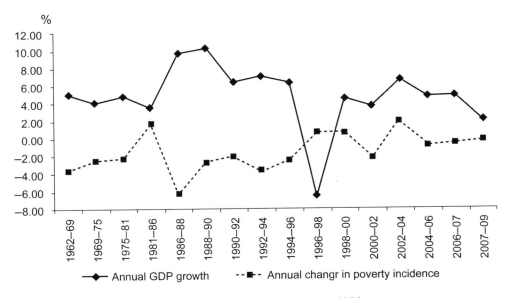

Figure 22.11 Poverty incidence and economic growth, 1962 to 2009
Source: Author's calculations using poverty data as in Table 22.7 and GDP data at constant prices from National Economic and Social Development Board, Bangkok

poverty incidence. Moderately rapid growth from 1962 to 1981 coincided with steadily declining poverty incidence. Reduced growth in Thailand caused by the world recession in the early to mid-1980s coincided with worsening poverty incidence in the years 1981–86. Then Thailand's economic boom of the late 1980s and early 1990s coincided with dramatically reduced poverty incidence. Finally, the contraction following the crisis of 1997–98 led to increased poverty incidence. The recovery since the crisis has been associated with significant poverty reductions, although the strong correlation between the rate of poverty reduction and the rate of growth seems to have weakened in the most recent periods.

On the other hand, no such simple short-term relationship can be found between the change in inequality over time and the rate of growth. The rate of growth does not seem to be a significant determinant of short-term changes in the level of inequality. Other social factors are undoubtedly playing a role, but research on this issue remains inconclusive.

Non-economic social change

The economic transformation that Thailand has experienced was achieved with substantial environmental and other costs. Pollution of air and water sources has been well documented and the expansion of the agricultural land area has been partly at the expense of deforestation, with negative effects on land erosion and the siltation of rivers and dams. Economic change has coincided with massive social change as well. Thai and foreign commentators agree that not all of this social change was necessarily beneficial. For example, the decline of village institutions and traditional values are widely lamented. Drugs trafficking has included both illegal export of drugs such as marijuana and heroin and domestic use of drugs such as meta-amphetamines. It has had a corrupting influence. Other social evils such as trafficking in women and child prostitution reportedly persist. In addition, rising wages in Thailand have attracted illegal migrants from neighbouring countries such as Myanmar (Burma), Cambodia and Laos, with occasional social conflict resulting. Not surprisingly, it is difficult to assemble solid evidence on the extent of these problems.

Despite these genuine problems, evidence can be advanced for substantial social progress accompanying Thailand's economic growth. The discussion will focus on three components of social change: population growth, and infant and maternal mortality.

Population growth

In the 1960s Thailand's population growth rate was around 3.5% per annum. Population growth at these rates puts enormous strain on a country's education and health systems. A programme of family planning was instituted in the 1960s and these efforts have been an outstanding success. Four decades later, population growth was well under 0.8% per annum and still falling (see Figure 22.12). Thailand's population will peak in around 2025. The nation's capacity to provide improved education and health services for its youth is greatly enhanced by these demographic changes, but declining population growth rates brings adjustment problems as well. Rural depopulation is an inevitable consequence of declining overall growth rates and rural-to-urban migration. Thailand's population is rapidly urbanizing and this requires adjustment to the provision of government services and infrastructure facilities.

Infant and maternal mortality

Improvement in the quality of life has been accompanied by startling improvements in standard health indicators. Important examples are shown in Figures 22.13 and 22.14. In 1960 infant

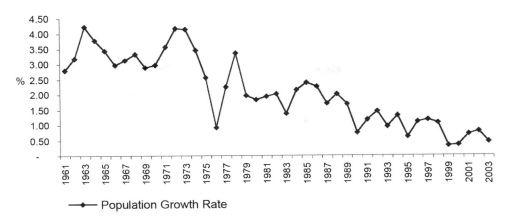

Figure 22.12 Population growth rate, 1960 to 2004 (% per year)
Source: Author's calculations using data from National Statistical Office, Bangkok

mortality rates were around 50 deaths per 1,000 births at the national level. In 2002 the corresponding morality rate was 6.5 (see Figure 22.12). This dramatic decline occurred in all major regions of the kingdom. In 1960 no region had an infant mortality rate below 40 per 1,000 births; by 2002 no region was above 7.5 deaths per 1,000 births.

Maternal mortality rates have declined even more rapidly. The data are summarized in Figure 22.13. In 1960 the average rate of maternal mortality was 420 deaths per 100,000 live births, at the national level. By 2002 this same national rate was 15 deaths per 100,000 live births. These achievements in public health were widespread throughout the kingdom. In 2002 no major region had a maternal mortality rate above 30 deaths per 100,000 live births. Economic growth is far from

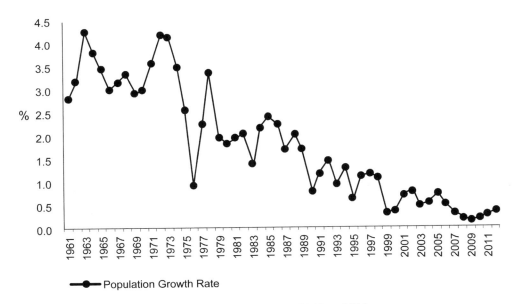

Figure 22.13 Infant mortality (deaths per 1,000 births), 1960 to 2012
Source: Author's calculations using data from Division of Vital Statistics, Ministry of Public Health

Recent political developments: populism and the middle-income trap

In July 2011 Thailand elected a new government, with a majority of seats won by the Pheu Thai Party. The new government is led by Yingluck Shinawatra, younger sister of the fugitive former Prime Minister Thaksin Shinawatra. It is commonly said that the Pheu Thai Party is 'populist', while the former government, led by Abhisit Vejjajiva of the Democrat Party, is more representative of the urban, monarchist Thai establishment. Thaksin is now based in Dubai, having been convicted while abroad of conflict of interest during his 2001–06 period in office. He was sentenced to two years' imprisonment but has refused to return to serve the sentence. Although Yingluck is now prime minister *in situ*, her older brother is widely considered the leader *in absentia*. Less than two months after Thaksin declared her as his choice for party leader, Yingluck found herself prime minister. Despite a lack of prior political experience she has a pleasant manner and an admirably explicit policy agenda, announced by her brother from Dubai. This programme was widely described as 'populism', but what does this label mean and what does it imply for Thailand's future?

Populism

Wikipedia describes 'populism' as an ideology of socio-political thought that emphasizes the difference between 'the people' and 'the elite', and comments that in practice populist discourse typically buttresses an authoritarian, top-down process of political mobilization in which a charismatic leader addresses the masses directly, rather than through political parties or other institutions. The *Cambridge Dictionary* adds that populism is in opposition to 'statism', which holds that a small group of professional politicians know better than the people and should therefore make decisions on their behalf. In their book *Populism in Asia*, Kosuke and Phongpaichit (2009) note that populist rhetoric is typically complemented by 'anti-intellectualism, anti-elitism, and often anti-foreign sentiments'.

More recently, in his book on populism in Latin America, *Left Behind: Latin America and the False Promise of Populism*, the UCLA economist Sebastian Edwards (2012) describes economic populism as an emphasis on public expenditures that win political support through poorly evaluated large public projects and short-term redistributions towards targeted groups, as opposed to public investments that raise long-term productivity, all combined with large-scale corruption and a disregard of the fiscal consequences of these policies.

Do these descriptions really apply to Pheu Thai and its putative leader Thaksin? On 23 April 2011 Thaksin announced his party's economic policies for the anticipated election, speaking to a meeting of the Pheu Thai faithful by video transmission from Dubai. Thaksin outlined a detailed set of economic initiatives with two components: capital-intensive mega-projects and redistributive initiatives designed to attract new sources of political support.

Thaksin's agenda

The proposed mega-construction projects include:

- a 30–60 km wall to protect Bangkok from flooding;
- a water diversion project to bring water to 25 Thai river basins, diverted from Myanmar (Burma), Laos and Cambodia;

- a high-speed train linking Bangkok with major cities;
- a 'land bridge' (not a canal) linking the Gulf of Thailand with the Andaman Sea; and
- 10 new electric train lines in Bangkok.

Each of these mega-projects is popular with a significant segment of the population, and like all construction projects in Thailand they offer the prospect of huge kickbacks for politicians and others. There is every possibility that at least some of these mega-projects, or some variant of them, would make economic sense once they were properly evaluated, but Thaksin shows no interest in waiting for that to be done. The projects are described as approved already.

The redistributive initiatives include:

- a three- to five-year debt moratorium for people owing 500,000–1 million baht;
- a 10-million-baht minimum revenue guarantee for local administrative organizations;
- a farmers' credit card project, presumably backed by the government;
- a 15,000-baht per month minimum salary guarantee for bachelor's degree graduates;
- a 1-billion-baht education fund for state and private universities;
- a tax cut for first-home buyers;
- a tax cut for first-car buyers;
- free wi-fi in public areas;
- a guaranteed price of 15,000 baht per ton for unmilled rice; and
- an increase in the minimum wage to 300 baht per day.

The increase in the minimum wage was one initiative on which the Democrats agreed, but their proposed increase was smaller (250 baht per day). Many of the initiatives outlined above are reminiscent of Thaksin's policies during his period in office of 2001–06, ended by a military coup. In addition, Thaksin recycled two promises from the 2001 election, in which he won an unprecedented parliamentary majority:

- eliminate the drugs problem within 12 months; and
- eliminate poverty within four years.

Following the 2001 election, 'eliminate the drugs problem' proved to mean giving the police permission to kill anyone suspected of being a drugs dealer. The police themselves are widely said to be the most important drugs dealers, so the policy was interpreted by many as a licence for the police to remove their business competitors. More than 2,000 extra-judicial murders occurred, none were properly investigated and of course no one was ever charged. Although the policy was reportedly popular with Thaksin's supporters, the drugs problem was not eliminated. Neither was poverty.

A feature of Thaksin's proposed policy measures is that unlike the Democrats, they do not ignore rural people. Despite decades of rural–urban migration and the growth of Bangkok in particular, two thirds of the Thai people still reside in rural areas, including almost all of the country's poorest people. In *Populism in Asia*, the chapter 'Thaksin's Populism', by Pasuk Phongpaichit and Chris Baker points out that prior to 2000, Thaksin had shown no interest in agricultural policy and his speeches had not used the term 'the people'. Thaksin is a businessman. He knows how to sell things. His political insight was to recognize that populist rhetoric offered him the chance to win the support of Thailand's huge, relatively impoverished and disaffected rural population. He has done so with unprecedented success.

Thaksin similarly did not succeed in eliminating poverty during his earlier period in office. I have shown elsewhere that the annual rate at which poverty declined under Thaksin's government was lower than the historical average over the preceding three decades, even though global economic conditions were relatively favourable during Thakskin's period in office (Warr 2009a). In my view, there was one principal reason. Thaksin's redistributive expenditures were implemented at the expense of productive investments, especially in agriculture, the economic base of most of Thailand's poor.

In a recent paper, a Thai colleague and I demonstrated that during Thaksin's period of government expenditure on agricultural research and extension declined as a proportion of agricultural output by 77% and 60%, respectively (Suphannachart and Warr 2011). Numerous studies, including our own, demonstrate that agricultural research is a powerful driver of productivity growth in agriculture and hence a driver of sustained poverty reduction (Sussankarn and Tinakorn 1998). Redistributions toward the poor can reduce poverty, but their once-only effect lasts only as long as the redistributions continue. There is no sustained effect on the productivity of the recipients.

Thailand's middle-income trap

The 'middle-income trap' is an empirical generalization based mainly on East and South-East Asian experience: once a country reaches middle-income levels the growth rate often declines and graduation from middle-income to higher-income levels stalls. I will describe what this means, how it come about, how it really does apply to Thailand, how current policies are making it worse, and what needs to be done to escape this situation.

During the decade of economic boom ending in 1997 Thailand's average annual growth rate of real GDP per person was a remarkable 8.4%. Like most booms, this one ended badly. It collapsed with the Asian Financial Crisis of 1997–99. Since 2000 the corresponding growth rate has been 4.1%. The immediate culprit was a contraction of private investment, which declined as a proportion of GDP from an average of 30% to 18% over the same two periods. The effect of lower investment was two-fold: it reduced aggregate demand, lowering income in the short run, and it reduced the rate of capital formation, lowering long-run growth prospects (Warr 2005, 2009b).

As we have seen above, a decline in this investment ratio occurred in all of the crisis-affected Asian economies, including Indonesia, Malaysia, the Philippines and South Korea. The decline in Thailand was one of the largest. The contraction of investment occurred primarily among Thai-owned, rather than foreign-owned, firms. Put simply, after the crisis Thai firms became less confident about their prospects and hence less inclined to invest. An expectation of this kind is self-fulfilling. It reduces investment, which does indeed ensure that growth will be lower.

Beneath these short-term macroeconomic events lies a deeper and longer-term phenomenon. Between the 1960s and 1990s Thailand achieved the transition from a poor, heavily rural backwater to a middle-income, semi-industrialized and globalized economy (Manorungsan 1989; Ingram 1971). The transition was primarily market-driven and the central policy imperative was to avoid those policies that impeded absorption of low-cost labour into export-oriented, labour-intensive manufacturing and services. This transition required some elementary market-supporting policy reforms: promoting a stable business environment (not necessarily meaning stable politics); open policies with respect to international trade and foreign investment; and public provision of basic physical infrastructure, including roads, ports, reliable electricity supplies, telecommunications and policing sufficient to protect the physical assets created by business investment.

This transition has now occurred in most of East and South-East Asia and the pattern was similar in all countries that undertook the basic policy reforms listed above. During this transition average real incomes rose significantly, the share of the workforce employed in agriculture contracted and the incidence of absolute poverty fell. The core of this growth process is expansion of the physical capital stock, resting overwhelmingly on private investment (Krugman 1994; Vines and Warr 2003). The private financial system facilitates the link between private savings and business investment, but the process is self-limiting. As labour moves from low-productivity agriculture to more rewarding alternatives elsewhere, wages are eventually driven up. As wages rise, the profitability of labour-intensive development declines. As the return to investment in physical capital falls, the rate of private investment slackens and growth slows. The frontier for further expansion of labour-intensive, export-oriented development soon moves to other, lower-wage countries. The result is the dreaded 'middle-income trap'. This describes Thailand and Malaysia today and China in the very near future.

Progress from middle-income to higher-income levels requires a different kind of policy reform, addressing a market failure that the private financial system cannot resolve: the undersupply of human capital. Human capital is a crucial input, created primarily by investment in education, broadly defined, but it differs from physical capital in that it does not provide the collateral that can ensure repayment of loans. Unlike physical assets, human beings can walk away. The private financial system is therefore unable to support investment in human capital. Individual families can and do invest heavily in the education of their own children, but because their resources are limited and because the recipient of the educational investment reaps only part of the returns it generates, this is insufficient to resolve the overall underinvestment in human capital.

Increasing the supply of human capital is central to overcoming the middle-income trap. It raises labour productivity directly and raises the return to physical capital, encouraging greater investment in physical capital as well. In Thailand, as in many other middle-income countries, the problem lies in the quality of education and not just the bare numbers of total school enrolments. The problem is primarily not at the tertiary level but at the primary and secondary levels. Massive public investment and reform of the education curriculum is needed to redress these problems, requiring the raising of sufficient tax revenue to finance it, and combating the backward and self-serving practices of the Ministry of Education and the teachers' unions. These are formidable obstacles.

During Thailand's boom almost everyone gained, including the poor, though not all at the same rate. Economic expectations rose, even among groups like lower-income rural people, who previously benefited only marginally from economic growth. However, when the boom collapsed in July 1997, the new opportunities vanished and the newly expanded expectations were crushed. A sense of economic and political injustice, latent for decades, then became more acute. For a large number of people redistributive politics then became more appealing as a focus for their anger and as a vehicle for collective economic advancement. Opportunities then arose for political entrepreneurs who could mobilize the frustration and use it to capture power.

Enter Thaksin Shinawatra. He had made a fortune by exploiting government-granted concessions in the telecommunications industry and been a deputy prime minister under two conservative governments in the 1990s, but in around 2000 Thaksin saw the political opportunity created by the frustrated expectations of many low- and middle-income people, especially those in the predominantly rural north and north-east regions. He articulated the discontent felt by these people and offered hope. According to his new rhetoric, Thailand's problem was not a flawed macroeconomic strategy that had strangled growth, but injustice inflicted on 'the people' by their fellow Thais, 'the elite'. Thaksin would look after them. This was standard Latin American-style populism and it worked. Thaksin's new party won an unprecedented election victory in 2001 and repeated the achievement in 2005.

What is wrong with that? At one level, nothing. It is simply democracy in action. However, a problem remains, in that Thaksin's short-term populism fails to address the underlying long-term sources of the middle-income trap and distracts attention from them. The policy platform successfully taken to the 2011 elections illustrates this point. Aside from the problem of paying for its spending initiatives, the important point is what the policy did *not* contain: anything about reforming Thailand's antiquated systems of primary and secondary education, the single greatest impediment to long-term economic progress in the country (Sirilaksana 1993); anything else about raising the long-term productivity of Thailand's masses of unskilled and semi-skilled workers; anything about reforming the country's regressive and inadequate tax system; or anything about reducing corruption.

Conclusions

Thailand's economic experience over the last six decades confirms the value of an open economic system in promoting long-term growth, but it also confirms that greater openness means greater exposure to global instability. The economic hardship within Thailand caused by the Asian Financial Crisis of 1997–99 and the global financial crisis of 2008–09, and their subsequent political ramifications within the country, illustrate this point. Despite this qualification, it is hard to deny the overall economic benefits that six decades of openness have delivered for the majority of the Thai people.

Not all aspects of the Thai development strategy have been successful. Inequality has increased at the same time as absolute poverty has declined. Education policy remains a serious problem. Public primary and secondary education remain archaic. Standards of rural education in particular remain low, and the poor quality of education received by most rural Thais dooms them to lives of economic disadvantage even if they migrate to the urban centres. The long-term neglect of environmental degradation is a further failure of Thai policy. This applies to pollution control, inland deforestation, contributing to increased flooding, the denudation of coastal mangrove forests and the wasteful management of the country's water resources.

Notes

1 The excellent research assistance of Ramesh Paudel is gratefully acknowledged.
2 The seminal paper in this area is Solow 1957. See also Young 1994; and Krugman 1994, for a discussion of these issues in a wider Asian context.
3 The macroeconomic significance of investment in Thailand is analysed in more depth in Vines and Warr 2003.
4 See also Sussankarn and Tinakorn 1998, for an earlier discussion of these issues.

Bibliography

Asian Development Bank (various years) *Key Indicators for Asia and the Pacific*, Asian Development Bank, Manila.
Bank of Thailand (2012) www.bot.or.th/english/Pages/BOTDefault.aspx (accessed 15 September).
Edwards, Sebastian (2012) *Left Behind: Latin America and the False Promise of Populism*, University of Chicago Press, Chicago, IL.
Ingram, James C. (1971) Economic Change in Thailand: 1850–1970, Stanford University Press, Stanford, CA.
Jorgenson, Dale W. (1988) 'Productivity and Postwar U.S. Economic Growth', *Journal of Economic Perspectives* 2: 23–42.
Kosuke, Mizuno and Pasuk Phongpaichit (2009) *Populism in Asia*, Singapore University Press, Singapore.
Krugman, Paul (1994) 'The Myth of Asia's Miracle', *Foreign Affairs* 73: 62–78.

Manorungsan, Sompop (1989) 'Economic Development of Thailand, 1850–1950', *Institute of Asian Studies Monograph* 42, Chulalongkorn University, Bangkok.

Ministry of Public Health (n.d.) eng.moph.go.th (accessed 15 September 2012).

National Economic and Social Development Board (n.d.) www.nesdb.go.th (accessed 15 September 2012).

Sirilaksana, Khoman (1993) 'Education Policy', in Peter Warr (ed.), *The Thai Economy in Transition*, Cambridge University Press, Cambridge.

Solow, Robert M. (1957) 'Technical Change and the Aggregate Production Function', *Review of Economics and Statistics* 39(3): 312–20.

Suphannachart, Waleerat and Peter Warr (2011) 'Research and Productivity in Thai Agriculture', *Australian Journal of Agricultural and Resource Economics* 55(1): 35–52.

Sussankarn, Chalongphob and Pranee Tinakorn (1998) *Productivity Growth in Thailand, 1980 to 1995*, Thailand Development Research Institute, Bangkok.

Vines, David and Peter Warr (2003) 'Thailand's Investment-driven Boom and Crisis', *Oxford Economic Papers* 55: 440–64.

Warr, Peter (1993) 'The Thai Economy', in Peter Warr (ed.), *The Thai Economy in Transition*, Cambridge University Press, Cambridge.

——(1999) 'What Happened to Thailand?' *The World Economy* 22, July: 631–50.

——(2005) 'Boom, Bust and Beyond', in Peter Warr (ed.), *Thailand Beyond the Crisis*, Routledge, London.

——(2009a) 'Thailand's Crisis Overload', in Daljit Singh (ed.) *Southeast Asian Affairs 2009*, Institute of Southeast Asian Studies, Singapore, 334–54.

——(2009b) 'Poverty Reduction Through Long-term Growth: The Thai Experience', *Asian Economic Papers* 8(2): 51–76.

Warr, Peter and Bhanupong Nidhiprabha (1996) *Thailand's Macroeconomic Miracle: Stable Adjustment and Sustained Growth, 1966 to 1996*, World Bank and Oxford University Press, Washington, DC and Kuala Lumpur.

World Bank (various years) World Development Indicators, data.worldbank.org/indicator.

Young, Alwyn (1994) 'Lessons from the East Asian NICS: A Contrarian View', *European Economic Review* 38: 964–73.

23

Iran at a crossroads

Reza Ghorashi and Hamid Zangeneh

Introduction

The beginning

Iran's challenges could be summed up in one word: modernity.[1] Although the first encounter with modern Europe was under the Safavid dynasty in the 17th century,[2] it is the Russo–Iranian wars of the early 19th century that revealed the gap between Iran and the modern world. Despite its numerical advantage, the Iranian side was badly defeated by the superior arms and modern military tactics of the Russians. The quest for modernization thus began under the auspices of Crown Prince Abbas Mirza, the commander of the defeated Iranian army. The first meaningful steps, however, were taken by Premier Amir Kabir in the mid-19th century.[3] It was the consequences of his reforms and the 'enlightenment' movement of the second half of the 19th century that resulted in the Constitutional Revolution of 1905–07—Iran's first major encounter with modernity.

The 1905 revolution established a constitutional monarchy. It reflected the changes in attitude and expectations from the state. The country became a nation-state responsible for the welfare of its citizens and accountable to them. For a short while it was controlled by a democratically elected parliament (*Majlis*). This did not last long, however. With the coming to power of Prime Minister Reza Khan (later Reza Shah), it rapidly became an authoritarian regime. Nevertheless, it was a nation-state.

Reza Shah

Reza Shah's powerful central government provided nation-wide security and took steps towards modernizing Iranian society. Economic changes under Reza Shah were impressive. An infrastructure suitable for industrialization was built. Even though oil revenues were not substantial until 1936, they helped the process.

Most significant changes were social and cultural during the reign of Reza Shah. By introducing secular education and modern judiciary systems, the power and influence of the clergy (*Rowhanyyat*) was largely reduced. Before Reza Shah, *Akhunds* played a much more prominent role in the

440

everyday affairs of the people, and controlled the judiciary and education among other things. They were the only layer between the king's court and the ordinary people of the country. In a sense they functioned as a proxy for 'civil society' in pre-modern Iran. Their control of religious institutions and fiefs, in addition to religious taxes and charities, gave them financial independence from the state. Under Reza Shah most of these institutions were taken over by the state. Thus a numerically reduced and financially weakened clergy had to depend on the state for its survival. Additionally, despite the opposition of the clergy, attempts were made to improve the status of women and religious minorities. Advocacy of the national identity as a substitute for religious ones, emphasis on Iran rather than Islam, and other aspects of a secular state did not sit well with the clergy or their ardent followers.

The last shah

Iran was invaded during the Second World War by the USSR from the north and the UK and the USA from the south. Its facilities, particularly railroads, were used to send troops and materials to the 'Eastern Front' in the USSR against Nazi Germany. Reza Shah was forced into exile and his young son Muhammad Reza was put in his place. The vacuum of power at the top provided an excellent opportunity for the development of civil society in the next decade or so. Political parties were established and played a major political and social role. Genuine unions were formed and became active. Women's economic and social engagements increased. A free media kept the public informed. Although there was no orchestrated effort by the state to reduce the role of the clergy, the emergence and advancement of the aforementioned civil societies naturally limited the clergy's role and made their return to pre-modern-era dominance impossible.

The culmination of these developments was the premiership of Dr Muhammad Musaddeq in the early 1950s. He managed to nationalize the petroleum industry and cut off British Petroleum (BP) and its oversized influence in Iran's domestic affairs. He managed to equalize the balance of payments despite the oil boycott imposed by the 'seven sisters' (seven major oil companies at that time) to stop Iran's oil exports. The opportunity for domestic private sector investments increased. He also pushed the royal court and young king to their constitutional limits. Musaddeq was not opposed to constitutional monarchy and wanted the shah to 'reign, not rule'. His reforms turned out to be too much for the shah, his loyalists and, in particular, the British and US governments. In August 1954 the Central Intelligence Agency (CIA, in its TPAJAX Project) and MI6 (in Operation Boot) arranged the infamous *coup d'état* that overthrew Musaddeq and returned the shah to Iran from his short-lived self-exile. This was the end of an era during which in addition to resembling a modern nation-state, Iran actually experienced real political democracy.

The next 25 years were a period of major change. Political achievements such as free media and free elections were gradually lost. The creation of the infamous Sazamare Etelaat Va Amniate Kechvar (SAVAK—the shah's secret police) resulted in a politically oppressive environment in which no dissent was tolerated. Political parties and workers' unions were replaced by empty, impotent and fraudulent façades of political parties, and trades unions and were tightly controlled by the SAVAK. Student organizations and leftist groups, in particular, were brutally oppressed. The clergy, although limited and controlled by the state, were permitted to operate and retain some of their social networks. In later years, when fear of the spread of Marxist ideas among the youth completely overpowered and preoccupied the regime, the clergy were tacitly allowed a more active and prominent role.

Things were not as bleak in the sphere of the economy. Oil revenues provided the necessary 'primitive accumulation' of capital. Although wasteful and corrupt, the regime made significant

Reza Ghorashi and Hamid Zangeneh

improvements in infrastructure. Social actions such as land reform enhanced economic development. In the end, however, heavy involvement of polity (government) in economic affairs may have been a major cause of the 1979 Revolution.[4]

There were major social changes as well. Here the regime was more tolerant of openness and even encouraged social changes as long as they were not deemed threatening to its absolute power. More open male-female inter-relationships, modern arts and fashion, and similar 'Western-style' behaviours were tolerated and even encouraged. It is not an exaggeration to suggest that living in Tehran was not much different from major European cities in the early 1970s. These developments in social and economic modernization and openness, which symbolized the new state of affairs in urban areas of Iran, were most despised by the ever decreasing (in number and influence) clergy and their followers from more conservative segments of society.

The 1979 Revolution

The causes of the 1979 Revolution have been discussed by many and the ranges of explanations cover a wide variety of factors.[5] It is reasonable to argue that it was not due to poverty, be it absolute or relative (income gap). No doubt they both existed, but they were not at a level that should have resulted in such major nation-wide unrest. Social discontent, particularly among the more conservative, less educated 'shanty town' residents existed, but the majority of young, educated city dwellers were content with their status. Thus social discontent could not have been a major cause of the Revolution. The lack of democratic rights such as freedom of speech, free media, real and diverse political parties, and free and meaningful elections were major factors. Looking back today, these shortcomings do not seem to justify the 1979 Revolution either, but one must have in mind that events of the last 30-plus years have been so horrendous that they bend and bias our view of the past. Today, those shortcomings do not seem to matter, but then the expectations were much higher and the lack of the above-mentioned rights justified the discontent at the time. It is not far-fetched to suggest that people expected the 1979 Revolution to 'modernize' the polity and bring it up to the level of the economy and society. Had this happened, Iran's challenge with modernity would have been over. It would have been a 'modern' country with the typical challenges that other modern nation-states face. This, unfortunately, did not happen.

The events of the last three decades show that, unfortunately, the society and economy were forced to retreat backward rather than moving forward after the Revolution. That is, rather than modernizing the political system to make it compatible with modernized social and economic conditions, the country took a backward step. The Revolution forced social and economic backwardness, compatible with the political backwardness that had existed, on the citizenry of the country. This, in a nutshell, is the plight of Iran since 1905, and certainly since the 1979 Revolution. At no time did Iran experience social, economic and political modernity simultaneously.

The Islamic Republic of Iran (IRI)

The 1979 Revolution was not Islamic. It was not started by Islamists. It was hijacked by Islamists due to the political vacuum that exists in any dictatorial system that by its very nature does not allow development of competent political rivals, selfishness and short-sightedness of organized and unorganized players of the time, and, of course, foreign influences. The first sparks came from shanty town residents who were protesting the destruction of their huts by municipalities, and by intellectuals and students who came to these downtrodden people's support. The shah was not criticized for his 'un-Islamic' behaviour by anyone other than the clergy, who were

442

insignificant at the time. The major direct complaint, the old and oft-repeated thorn in the side of the intellectuals, was the shah's relations with ('taking orders' from) foreigners—US influence, in particular.[6] Although chants of '*Allah o akbar*' (God is great) were common, so were chants of '*Azaadi, braabary, braadary*' (Liberty, equality, fraternite). Slogans such as 'free all political prisoners', and other, though vague and general, political demands, are another indication that, if anything, the 1979 Revolution was about modern political demands, not the lack of an Islamic way of life. Demonstrators were united on one thing: *the shah must go.* Surprisingly missing were affirmative demands. For a population that was demonstrating in the millions for close to two years, one would have expected the articulation of freedom of speech, freedom of association, gender equality, recognition of ethnic and religious minorities, and basic human rights to be an integral part of their demands. This is even more surprising considering the recent history of Iran, particularly the Musaddeq era. One possible explanation is that none of these (modern) values were institutionalized and part of popular culture.[7]

The process of Islamization took a few very brutal years. We doubt that anyone, including leaders such as Ayatollah Ruhollah Khomeini, knew where exactly they were going. The fact that the mosques and other places of worship were the only non-governmental network of institutions surviving the oppressive state apparatus during the shah's tenure enabled the clergy and their allies to take over the everyday affairs of the Revolution. Mosques become the 'headquarters' of opposition. More important was a lack of 'vision' with specific demands and goals for 'after the shah was gone'. Only this vague notion of an Islamic Republic was being offered,[8] reflected in the slogan 'Neither East, nor West, Islam is best'.[9] This suggested that neither modern capitalist values of the 'West', nor 'socialist' ones of the Soviet bloc were acceptable. Supposedly, Islam offered a 'third way'. This has been the 'background noise' of the IRI's universe of problems and challenges.[10]

The political meaning of the IRI

As mentioned above, to the extent that the 1979 Revolution had affirmative demands, they were political. There were vague notions of demands for democracy and freedom of speech and the media. There was a strong negative sentiment towards the shah's dependence on his foreign benefactors, specifically the USA. Thus there was a demand for an independent foreign policy. The root causes of Iran's problems and shortcomings were perceived to be foreigners. This notion of holding foreigners (others) responsible for the plight of a country in not unique to Iran, nor the Third World, although it has much more currency there. In many cases, including Iran, there is ample evidence of interference in the past, such as the coup against Musaddeq, to support such claims. However, this 'blame game' sometimes goes too far. Blaming others (foreigners) becomes a convenient excuse for the ineptitude, mismanagement and corruption of these governments. In the case of the IRI it went beyond that: it became the IRI's identity.

For the first few months after the 1979 Revolution Iran was a free country. Speech and media were free. Most daily affairs were handled by citizens' volunteer committees. There was a strong sense of optimism that everything would be rosy from then on. Gradually, however, things began to change and the reality of the complexity of the challenges faced started to settle in. Unable to respond to these challenges, and some excesses, the leaders of the IRI started to look for excuses. They took a number of steps to restrict the freedom of speech and association.[11] Their big break came with the hostage crisis. A number of 'students' took the personnel of the US embassy hostage to protest at the US government permitting the shah to enter the USA. He travelled to New York for medical reasons. This tragic takeover was supposed to last a couple of days, but ended up lasting for 444 days. This was a heaven-sent 'gift' for Ayatollah

Khomeini and his supporters. They managed to divert all the frustrations of the people, who were disappointed (disillusioned) with the Revolution. It was the 'great Satan' whom they should blame for all their unfulfilled expectations. The recent past close relationship of the shah and the USA made for an easy diversion. All the IRI leaders needed was to tap into the already potent suspicion of foreigners, i.e. xenophobia. The populace's response was overwhelming. It seemed that everyone was looking for someone or something to blame for all the mistakes and shortcomings. The hostage crisis shaped the policies and approaches of what is now referred to as the Islamic Republic of Iran. The Islamists used the occasion to rid themselves of their partners in power.[12] This is really the moment when the Islamic Republic became Islamic. They pushed their agenda, specifically adopting a new constitution which in many ways was worse than the existing one. It gave the Supreme Religious Leader (*Valy-e Faghih*) ultimate power on every major aspect of government. The constitution restricted anything that was not perceived to be compatible with Islamic norms and practices, as interpreted by the Supreme Leader and the appointed 'Guardian Council'.

Forcing other allies out of power created a vacuum in the state apparatus. This was filled primarily by the clergy from seminaries or their close relatives and confidants. Initially, there were some reservations about the clergy having a direct role in running the affairs of state. Ayatollah Khomeini specifically banned the clergy from running for the office of the presidency. He wanted them to be more 'spiritual' leaders and jurisprudents. In practice they took control of the judiciary and were present in the parliament. Within a few years, however, the heads of all three branches were from the clergy. The increased influence of the clergy had been so dramatic that anybody with political ambition would then be advised to attend a seminary and don a turban and robe rather than attend a modern college or university. The legitimization of this took the form of the 'commitment' versus 'expertise' debate, with the eventual winners of this often bloody and murderous struggle, of course, being the advocates of commitment, who are in charge today.

Another major consequence of the hostage crisis was to make a habit of using, or even creating, pseudo-crises as a way of governing. Rather than resolving an issue through dialogue and compromise, an emergency situation is used to demonstrate why it is not resolvable and, quite often, why no one should complain or criticize the authorities on such occasions. The IRI leaders only let dropped the US hostage crisis when they had a new and better crisis on which to focus their attention—the war with Iraq. The eight-year war was, both in terms of human casualties and economic debasement and destruction, a very costly one by almost any standard. Yet, on numerous occasions, Khomeini referred to it as a 'blessing'. It was indeed a blessing for the Islamic regime because the war enabled it to consolidate its power and introduce more reactionary, backward Islamic measures, and crush any opposition to them under guise of being at war with the enemy. The same logic applies in the latest crisis: the nuclear issue. The existence of the crisis has been much more important than its eventual outcome. It is important to have a crisis of national importance to use for the suppression and subjugation of the citizenry and to whitewash the mismanagement of the socio-economic and political affairs of the country. This nuclear crisis has had the added advantage that the IRI has won the public relations war inside Iran and has convinced the majority that it is 'our right' that is being denied by the USA. It has convinced the citizenry that the harsh and crippling sanctions are a reasonable price to pay for their national yearning to achieve progress.

The social meaning of the IRI

The most challenging aspect of Islamization since the 1979 Revolution has been the socio-cultural one. This has caused the most friction between the people and the regime and, as far as modernity is concerned, has been the most damaging aspect of the Islamization of Iranian society. While there was some support among the more conservative segments of society for 'restoring Islamic values' at the beginning, little was agreed on what this meant. They had different understandings of what, for example, 'modestly dressed' meant. In general, the restoration was an attempt to bring back old (pre-modern) traditions. However, society had changed a great deal, particularly in urban areas and among the educated and middle and upper classes. Tolerance for 'otherness' (religious, ethnic) had gone up among a large majority of the population. The 'Western' (modern) ways of life regarding fashion, music, socialization and so forth were very different from the traditional Islamic ones.

The most drastic change had been in the social status of women, who during almost a century of progress had seen major achievements. The clash between the Islamists who are in control of the state apparatus and other, and the rest of society is a daily affair. People—women in particular—have resisted in any way possible every push by the Islamists.[13] Such clashes have defined everyday social life for the affected segments of society, such as women, religious minorities, many of the youth, etc., to a large extent. For most women, stepping out into the street is akin to stepping into a battle ground. This attempt to deny women's social space and segregate them has, due to the earlier advances and valiant resistance of women, changed Iranian society in a rather unique way. In some ways it has backfired on the regime. For example, there are many more female doctors, particularly gynaecologists, in Iran today than pre-Islamization.[14]

Another major consequence of the 'restoration of values' has been the dramatic increase in the dominance of the traditional clergy and seminaries (*Howzeh*) over the intellectual and cultural domains. In restoring Islamic values, sooner or later the question becomes 'What is Islamic?' The highest authority is of course the clergy. Their interpretation of Islamic/traditional values would trump any other.[15] Gradually, these interpretations have been more and more backward, conservative and impractical. The resulting tensions are among the most difficult challenges that the IRI faces.

The economic meaning of the IRI

The promise early on was an Islamic economy that was neither socialism nor capitalism. Soon it was realized that there is not much of a third way in the realm of economy.[16] As was mentioned earlier, Iran's economy prior to the revolution was suffering from heavy doses of government involvement. For a number of reasons, this problem was exacerbated after the revolution. The war with Iraq, which started in September 1980 and lasted close to a decade, forced Iran into a 'war economy' with consequent rationing and other government-imposed restrictions. For all practical purposes the government was solely in charge of the economy during the war period. Finally, the fact that the dominant attitude among Islamists at the time, reflected in the constitution,[17] was in favour of government control added to the problem. The emergence of quasi-governmental foundations (*bonyads*) and religious shrines and the increasing role of the Revolutionary Guard will be discussed below.

Today, the root cause of the IRI's economic problems is political. Usually states make political decisions (domestic as well as foreign) to improve their economies. In the IRI, it is the reverse. As a rentier state, the private sector produces precious little extra value. The IRI has used its huge oil revenues to hide this deficiency by subsidizing inefficient production and importation of a wide variety of necessities. It has also used oil revenues to further its political causes. The main domestic goal is its survival via the suppression of dissent. The denial of basic human rights such as freedom of speech, or respect for privacy and property on their own are deplorable. Additionally, they have a chilling effect on entrepreneurship and investment. Investment in productive activities such as industry and agriculture need clear and stable effective commercial and criminal laws for its survival. In a country where the whims of the Supreme Leader or even a powerful Friday prayers imam can ruin one's investment, capable investors and entrepreneurs will rarely commit themselves to a long-term project. In today's globalized economy investment and investors are very mobile. They will quickly leave an environment that is not conducive to profit and prosperity. A large number of Iranian professionals and entrepreneurs in the diaspora, who have been forced to leave Iran, are probably the most damaging to the IRI economy.

The main trait of the IRI's foreign policy is its antagonistic, anti-Western (more specifically anti-US) stance, which has become part of its identity. Thus, despite the high socio-economic and political price that has been paid, it is difficult for it to let go of this. Economic sanctions, inflation and the related currency crisis are three heavy tolls on the economy. They will now be discussed as well as the impact of quasi-governmental enterprises.

Semi-autonomous economic institutions

One of the phenomena that characterize the composition of the Iranian economy is the creation of a number of quasi-independent foundations (*bonyads*) that are currently among the largest conglomerates in the world. These foundations took control of most factories and businesses left behind by those who fled the country after the 1979 Revolution. The original intention was to redistribute the wealth among the masses, but they have increasingly forsaken their social welfare functions and have turned to straightforward commercial endeavours for their own benefits. They finance political campaigns of various ruling factions and in return receive exemption from taxes, import duties and most other government regulations. They have access to subsidized foreign currency and low-interest loans from state-owned banks. Furthermore, they are not accountable to the central bank, the Ministry of Finance, or any other government institution. Formally, they are directly under the jurisdiction of the Supreme Leader. It has been said that these *bonyads* count for 20%,[18] perhaps 50%, of gross domestic product (GDP). These numbers are vague and broad because the foundations are not accountable to the regular auditing and reporting of the rest of the economic institutions.

The Mostazafan Foundation, for example, is the second largest commercial enterprise in the country behind the state-owned National Iranian Oil Company (NIOC). Founded in 1979 with the assets of the last shah's family (the Pahlavi Foundation), it operates a wide variety of economic and charitable activities. It employs over 200,000 people and is worth tens of billions of dollars. It owns and operates approximately 350 subsidiary and affiliate companies in numerous industries including agriculture, manufacturing, transportation and tourism.[19] A decade after the revolution, the foundation's assets totalled more than US$20 billion, and included 'some 140 factories, 470 agribusinesses, 100 construction firms, 64 mines, and 250 commercial companies'.[20] It controls 40% of Iran's production of soft drinks, including Zam Zam Cola, which it owns and produces; and the newspapers *Ettela'at* and *Kayhan*.

According to the RAND study group,[21] the Mostazafan Foundation's largest subsidiary is the Agricultural and Food Industries Organization (AFIO), which owns more than 115 additional companies. Some of the foundation's contract work also includes large engineering projects, such as the construction of terminal one of the Imam Khomeini International Airport.

Another type of these autonomous institutions is the shrines and religious fiefdoms. There has been a huge increase in their number since the revolution. Shrines of sages and saints alone have increased from fewer than 1,500 in 1979 to about 11,000 today.[22] They own a large number of residential and commercial properties. Donations and other income, including financial assistance from government, are their other sources of income. They, too, are tax exempt and usually operate outside the control or supervision of government. Astan Quds Razavi (Imam Reza's shrine), is by far the largest of these fiefdoms. Only his sister's shrine in Qom comes close to it. *Forbes* magazine put its worth at $15 billion in 2003,[23] but to many observers this is a gross underestimation. The institution has been around supposedly since the death of the eighth Shi'a imam some 1,200 years ago. Even under the shah's regime it was a semi-autonomous foundation. Since the 1979 Revolution, its influence and endowments have increased manifold. Its custodian, in charge since 1979, is dubbed the Sultan of Khorasan. Mashhad, the burial site of Imam Reza is the capital of Khorasan province. For all practical purposes Astan Quds is an autonomous state within the state. It employs more than 20,000 people. The land occupied by the shrine has grown four-fold since 1979 according to the head of the foundation's international relations department. The foundation owns most of the real estate in Mashhad and rents out shop space to retailers and hoteliers.[24] The economic endeavours range from carpet weaving to insurance companies, to Razavi Brokerage House and Razavi Transportation Corporation. It includes farmland, dairy produce and orchards with flour mills, a bread-making factory, canning and cold-storage company. It is involved in construction and mining via the industrial and mineral development units of Astan Quds.

Astan Quds Razavi is a major provider of health care, with its own specialized hospital and pharmaceutical company called Samen. Its educational and cultural institutions include Imam Reza University, the Islamic Research Foundation, the Youth Counselling Service, the Social Research Institute, Razavi Cultural Foundation, the Artistic Creativity and Audio-Visual Media Institution, the Museums of the Astan Quds Razavi, Malek Library and National Museum. It owns Behnashr Publishing Company and publishes *Quds Daily*, *Za'ir Magazine*, and *Haram Magazine*. It runs Astan Quds Razavi sports complex.

The Revolutionary Guard—officially the Army of the Guardians of the Islamic Revolution, or Islamic Revolutionary Guard Corps (IRGC)—is another major economic power in Iran. As a military unit, the IRGC was originally banned from political and economic activities. Its retired leaders (generals), however, were not. They gradually infiltrated a large number of government agencies. Today, several cabinet ministers, a large number of MPs and many top-level managers of quasi-governmental enterprises come from the IRGC. It openly interferes in the political life of the country, but it is its economic role that is even more amazing. It controls most of the *bonyads*, including the aforementioned *bonyad* Mostazafan. According to the *Los Angeles Times*, the IRGC has ties to over 100 companies, with its annual revenue exceeding $12 billion in business and construction. The IRGC has been awarded billions of dollars in contracts in the oil, gas and petrochemical industries, as well as major infrastructure projects. The following commercial entities have been named by the USA as owned or controlled by the IRGC and its leaders: Khatam al-Anbia Construction Headquarters, the IRGC's major engineering arm, one of Iran's largest contractors employing about 25,000 engineers and staff on military (70%) and non-military (30%) projects[25] worth over $7 billion in 2006; Oriental Oil Kish (oil and gas industry); Ghorb Nooh; Sahel Consultant Engineering; Ghorb Karbala; Sepasad Engineering Co. (excavation and tunnel construction); Omran Sahel; Hara Company (excavation and tunnel construction); Gharargahe Sazandegi Ghaem; Kayson Construction Company (foreign branch, active in Venezuela).

In September 2009, the government of Iran sold 51% of the shares of the Telecommunication Company of Iran to Mobin Trust Consortium (Etemad-e-Mobin), a group affiliated with the Guards, for the sum of $7.8 billion. This was the largest transaction on the Tehran Stock Exchange in its history. The IRGC also owns 45% of shares in the automotive Bahman Group and has a majority stake in Iran's naval giant SADRA through Khatam al-Anbia.[26]

Economic sanctions

Political enmity between the Islamic Republic of Iran and the USA started right after the Iranian Revolution of 1979. The game of cat and mouse between the two countries has had its ebbs and flows, but has never disappeared long enough to give politicians a breather and time to sit at the negotiations table and resolve all their real and perceived bilateral and multilateral problems and misunderstandings. It seems that both sides believe that they can only negotiate if they have the upper hand or if the other side is submissive. As a result, sanctions have been ratcheted up again and again, with no end in sight.

Ostensibly, at the outset, US sanctions were enacted to put pressure on Iran to abandon its support of terrorism, subversion of the region's stability, efforts to produce weapons of mass destruction, and its opposition of the Arab–Israeli peace process. However, competition over the control of foreign policy between the US Congress and the president to satisfy the pro-Israeli and Zionist lobbies may have resulted in further US intransigence and adoption of harsher measures, while the seemingly perpetual power struggle among competing factions in Iran has made the resolution of US-Iran relations more intractable and a deeper strategic issue for both sides than it need be.

Sanctions started almost immediately after the revolution with the ill-conceived and opportunistic takeover of the US embassy. In response, President Jimmy Carter broke off diplomatic relations with Iran, froze Iranian assets in the USA, and banned the importation of Iranian oil to the USA. President Ronald Reagan basically followed suit and tightened the noose by putting Iran on the list of states 'sponsoring terrorism'. During the eight-year Iran–Iraq war the USA flagged ships traversing the Persian Gulf to protect them from the Iranian threat, and prohibited the exportation of what was designated 'dual-use technology'. During the 1990s, both the US Congress and President Bill Clinton were more active against Iran.

In 1987 the import of goods from Iran to the USA was prohibited. However, foreign affiliates of US companies continued to buy substantial amounts of Iranian oil. President Clinton's Executive Order of 1995 prohibited the export of US goods, services and technology to Iran. It banned investment by US companies in Iran, and prohibited Americans from approving, facilitating or financing US-owned companies to make transactions involving Iran, thus closing the loopholes of the Executive Order of 1987.

The D'Amato Law, authored by Senator D'Amato of New York, was fashioned around the 1995 Clinton Executive Order. It declared that 'it is the policy of the United States to deny Iran the ability to support acts of international terrorism and to fund the development and acquisition of weapons of mass destruction and the means to deliver them by limiting the resources of Iran'.[27] To this end Congress directed the president to impose a number of sanctions on companies that make an investment of $20 million or more or any combination of investments of at least $10 million each that in the aggregate equals or exceeds $20 million in any 12-month period, 'that directly and significantly contributed to the enhancement of Iran's ability to develop petroleum resources of Iran'.[28]

The D'Amato Law extended these prohibitions to companies and nationals of other countries involved with the Iranian oil and gas industry. In particular, the president might impose a number of sanctions on companies that invested in Iran's petroleum industries.[29] These sanctions included the denial of assistance from the Export-Import Bank, denial of permits to export goods and technology to the sanctioned persons, the prohibition of US financial institutions from making loans to the offending companies, and refusal of the US government to procure goods and services from violators. If the violators were financial firms, they may not be designated as primary dealers in US government debt instruments, or serve as its agents, or as repository for government funds.[30]

President George W. Bush was mostly distracted with Iraq and Afghanistan—so much so that no major new sanctions were added. The most notable step was including Iran among the 'axis of evil' countries. His Administration perused a policy of making the financial life of Iranians more difficult by going after secondary partners of Iran, as well as putting pressure on companies

Iran at a crossroads

directly trading with it. The Bush Administration froze the assets of companies that dealt with Iran, pushing the IRI to camouflage its foreign transactions.

For a long time sanctions were not universally applied. It was only the USA that severed most of its trade with Iran. Thus, while Iran had suffered economic costs, the damage to the country, unlike that to US businesses, was not initially substantial. It was true that Iran needed the US market, capital and technology, but both Western and Eastern European countries, as well as Japan and other Asian countries, had been happy to oblige and supplant the USA. Also, Iran learned to engage in inefficient and costly sanction mitigation schemes such as barters and bilateral exchanges with regional partners that allowed them to bypass these sanctions.

The cat and mouse game between Iran and the USA took a sharp turn with the presidency of Barack Obama. President Obama tightened the noose to the point that Iranian citizens have started to suffer in all aspects of life. His Administration managed to unite, more or less, the world against Iran. They took the issue to the United Nations Security Council and obtained sanction resolutions that makes every country a player against Iran and, like it or not, a participant in the game. This has forced many countries to cut off or significantly reduce their trade relation with Iran to the extent that the country today is selling almost half the volume of oil that sold in 2011, at bargain basement prices. However, the most important development has been the initiative by the European Union to sever Iran's financial lifeline by denying the country's participation in SWIFT (the Society for Worldwide Interbank Financial Telecommunication). This has forced Iran to sell off its oil in terms of currencies of the buying countries and unavoidably to spend the money on that country's goods and services. This has translated into cheap prices for its oil and having to accept whatever price a country wants to charge for its goods and services—a lose-lose situation for Iran.

However, these schemes have proved tremendously costly to Iran without yielding what the USA and its allies expected. Figure 23.1 depicts a set of actual and hypothetical trend lines for

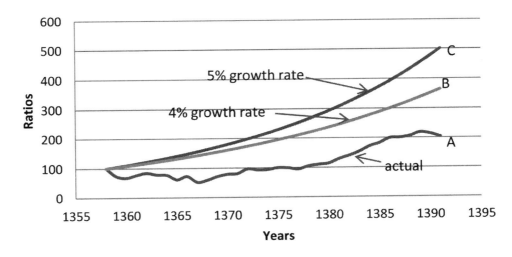

Figure 23.1 Actual and hypothetical trend lines

the Iranian economy. Trend line A represents an index of actual GDP over time. We took 1979 to be our base year (100). All of the data are actual statistics except for the last two years, for which data were not publicly available. We assumed that the economy kept growing at 1% in those two years, which is more than generous for this purpose, since we know that the economy has actually been in a recessionary mode within this time span. Trend lines B and C are based on the assumption that the economy grew at 4% (B) and 5% (C).

The graph shows that the Iranian economy is about 2.23 times bigger in absolute amount relative to 1979 (1357 Iranian calendar). That is, given the fact that the Iranian population is much larger in proportion to the country's GDP, per capita GDP is still less than what it was before the revolution. The graph also shows that had the economy grown at 4% per annum, it would have been 3.65 times larger and a 5% growth rate would made it 5.0 times larger.

The graph explainst a great deal about the performance of the Iranian economy since the revolution. Had it not been for the mismanagement, war and sanctions, the economy could have been potentially much larger and the standard of living much higher than what it is today. Given the fact that these data show a static progression, they do not show the mind-boggling cumulative and dynamic negative impact on the economy of the sanctions and mismanagement.

Given the ferocity of these sanctions, the question to ask is whether they are the optimum tools to achieve their stated goal of reshaping and redirecting Iran's political and strategic policies.[31] One could safely say not, because the government of Iran is founded on ideological principles that prohibit submission regardless of the cost—the martyrdom doctrine that has symbolized Shi'ism. This point was well demonstrated in the eight-year war that was the result of the Iraqi invasion of Iran. Iranians have paid a very high price so far and there is no wisdom to balk and announce to the country and to the world that they were wrong. It is not feasible or conceivable either politically and/or ideologically. One argument is that by creating deprivation, these sanctions will provoke citizens to rise up and overthrow the regime or force it into submission. Again, though, we do not see evidence of this in Iran or in any other instance anywhere in the world, yet. The sanctions against Iraq, a much smaller economy, could be used as an example. The draconian sanctions did not lead to the overthrow of Saddam Hussain—in other words regime change. The main consequence of the deprivation of the people of Iran may be a change in their so far positive attitude towards the USA.[32]

Inflation

Table 23.1 shows annual inflation rates grouped into different time periods. The first grouping covers the early years before the 1973 oil price rise. The second time period includes the years after the oil price increase and up to the revolution. The third period covers the post-revolutionary

Table 23.1 Inflation rates

Years	Explanation	Average
1968–79	Before the oil price increase	3.87
1973–79	Before the Revolution	13.81
1980–88	The Iran–Iraq War period	19.58
1989–97	Rafsanjani years	24.62
1998–2005	Khatami years	15.34
2006–12*	Ahmadinejad years	18.44

Note: * 2012 is an estimate.

years, most of which were taken up by the Iran–Iraq War. The fourth period reflects the post-war and post Khomeini era, Hashemi Rafsanjani's presidency. The next two groups belong to Sayed Muhammad Khatami's and Mahmoud Ahmadinejad's presidencies.

As Table 23.1 shows, prior to the 1970s and before the oil price rise, inflation in Iran was rather tame, with an average rate approximating 3.87% per year. However, this does not hold true for the subsequent time periods.

Budgetary constraints became almost irrelevant to Iran's economic planning, at least for a short while, when huge oil revenues were earned due to the spiralling oil prices triggered by the Arab oil embargo of 1973.[33] Prior to the oil revenue hike, the availability of foreign exchange dictated the government's project selection. Therefore imported inflation[34] was not a problem. The tremendous increase in the price of oil gave the government an opportunity to engage in grandiose nation-wide projects that were beyond the absorption capacity of the country. Iran's infrastructure was too limited to accommodate these new projects, and inflationary pressure started to mount.

The government's use of oil revenues to finance its rapid economic development increased the monetary base and money supply (discussed below), and therefore aggregate demand. On the other hand, due to the limited capacity, the higher aggregate demand could not be satisfied internally, hence goods had to be ordered from abroad. Due to the universal inflationary situation of the 1970s, all of the ordered materials carried with them an inflationary premium. However, due to inadequate capacity of ports and transport facilities, the open door policy was ineffective in fighting inflation because of the inability of importers to bring their merchandise into the country. There was a waiting period of over six months for ships to unload their cargo in the port cities of the Persian Gulf, and when they did unload, importers were unable to transfer the merchandise to their final destinations. Since there were no storage facilities, the imported goods could not be safely stored in these port cities. As a result, the imported items were stored in open facilities located around the outskirts of the port cities, a practice that resulted in their ruin. Therefore, the inflationary pressure could not be eased by a greater volume of imports.

Another factor contributing to the inflationary build-up prior to the revolution was higher per capita income. As purchasing power trickled down to the masses, demand for goods and services increased, which in turn increased the intensity of inflation. Pre-revolutionary Iran provided a classic example of a country in which there were too many dollars chasing too few goods.

The sudden rise in inflation immediately after the jump in oil prices jolted the economic system because people were not used to that magnitude of instability. However, the years following the revolution were no better. Although inflation rates reported by official sources are high, unofficial anecdotal estimates are at even higher levels. One must be cognizant of the fact that the official estimates include the prices controlled by the government directly or through its agencies, companies and bonyads. These goods and services, such as electricity, water, bread, tobacco and tobacco products, tea and sugar, are subject to government-mandated price controls and subsidies. Since the controlled prices of these commodities are combined with the prices of other free market goods, it results in much more moderate official inflation rates. This implies the existence of a serious hidden inflationary bias, which will show itself when these controls and subsidies are removed in the future.

Subsidies and inflation outlook

In the last two years of Ahmadinejad's first term, the central bank controlled the rate of money supply and therefore the economy experienced a rather sharp reduction in the rate of inflation. However, the inflation rate in his second term was no more encouraging because of the changes in the government's redistribution policies, as well as confused monetary policies.

Early in 2010 (in the last months of the Iranian year 1388), the parliament passed a law eliminating subsidies on 16 basic staples and instead allocated $20 billion for direct cash payments to the public. According to this law all subsidies on gas, diesel fuel, natural gas, electricity, water, wheat, flour, rice, milk, sugar, cooking oils, aviation, railroad transport and postal services were eliminated.

The intentions of the law, enunciated by the regime, were to reform consumption patterns and reduce excessive consumption/waste, especially of cheap energy, by raising prices to world levels; the redistribution of income in favour of the lower economic classes; the reduction of subsidies and allocation of saved resources to improve economic infrastructure; the removal of subsidy-generated distortions and allowance of the more efficient allocation of resources through the market mechanism.

One potential negative consequence of this law is the increased cost of exportables and therefore a reduction in non-oil exports. This was somewhat compensated for by the falling value of the Iranian rial, but that contributed to the higher inflation rate by causing import prices to rise further.

According to the current scheme, a family is expected to receive 50,000 toman (one toman equals 10 rials) as a cash subsidy. Assuming a 35% inflation rate, the cash subsidy would compensate a loss of purchasing power of those with an income of 142,857 toman. So, 50,000 is sufficient compensation for a family earning 142,857 toman to stay on an even keel. It means, other things being constant, a loss of purchasing power for any income higher than that. This favours the government and those who are not wage earners, i.e. producers and merchants. Given the fact that a 142,857 toman income is even lower than that of the lowest of the low-income workers, this implies that all wage earners will lose out.

As Table 23.2 shows, the higher the wages, other things remaining the same, the higher the losses of purchasing power of different income groups. Also, given the low elasticity of demand for most of these necessities,[35] total expenditures (revenues) on these products are going to increase. These losses of purchasing power are going to go to the producers, merchants and the government, which implies a redistribution of income of the worst kind: from have-nots to haves. That means greater inequality and eventually a lower standard of living for lower-income echelons of the population.

Another outcome of this law in the short run is a change in the composition of consumption baskets of lower-income classes. That is, people have cut or modified their expenditure on what they might consider 'marginal' goods, such as good-quality food, health care, education and leisure. However, in the medium and long run, this could add to and enlarge the size of the impoverished lower-income classes. That is, in the medium and long run, these cuts will deprive them of the opportunity to move into a higher class through better education. In other words, many more could fall into the vicious circle of poverty: low education–low-paying job–poverty.

Table 23.2 Inflation and purchasing power

Money income	Purchasing Power (PP)35% inflation	PP plus subsidy 50,000	Loss of PP
142,857	92,857	142,857	0
200,000	130,000	180,000	−20,000
300,000	195,000	245,000	−50,000
500,000	325,000	375,000	−125,000

The other side of the story of this law is a recessionary environment. It created stagflation. On the one hand, the removal of these subsidies increased the cost to producers and merchants, who would pass them along to consumers. For example, it would eventually increase the cost of energy from $9.8 to $49.00. On the other hand, the cash subsidies will increase aggregate demand. Depending on the strength of these changes, output could increase, decrease, or stay the same, but prices will definitely rise.[36]

The value of the Iranian rial (currency crisis)

Iran's policy with respect to the value of the rial could be analysed under either a short-run or a long-run scenario. Under a fixed exchange rate regime there is a de facto suppression of exchange rate volatility and incremental adjustments according to relative changes in other economic variables. So, when enough pressure is built up and the government, through the central bank, decides to relent and give in to the legitimate or speculative pressures on a currency, it would allow the currency to reach a different, perhaps more appropriate, level. In this environment we would see wild devaluations or revaluations of the currency in question.

Iran has never followed a truly free market approach to exchange rates. Rather, it has always followed variations of fixed and flexible exchange rate regimes—at times a single exchange rate, but mostly a more complicated and harmful multiple exchange rate system. Effectively, the government uses different rates for imports and exports and even different rates for each category of imports or exports. Therefore, Iran's exchange rate policy has gone through several metamorphoses in attempts to advance development policies while fighting inflation. Regardless of the intentions of the policy, legitimate or otherwise, oil revenues have been pivotal in determining the exchange rate regime and its par values. That is, the government's ability to provide more or less foreign exchange at lower or higher prices depends on the scarcity of oil revenues.

Until March 1993 there were three official exchange rates—the basic rate, used for oil export revenue, imports of basic necessities and official foreign debt repayment; the competitive rate, used for other imports not eligible for the basic rate; and the floating rate, for all other transactions. In that month, all these rates were replaced with a single rate, which effectively depreciated the rial to Rls 1,750/US$1, a rate similar to the parallel market rate. Six months later, the policy was abandoned and a new fixed rate of Rls 2,345/US$1 was established to discourage imports and promote exports.

In 1995 high inflation in Iran combined with US sanctions put a great deal of pressure on the central bank to change the parity rate of the rial to correspond to the parallel market rate again. These pressures led to the devaluation of the rial to Rls 3,000/US$1 in 1995. The cat and mouse game between the parallel free markets, effectively a black market, and the fixed government rate have been the story of Iran's exchange rate policy. The government allows the free market to function alongside the government-approved system until the discrepancy between the two reaches a boiling point. At that moment, the central bank develops a new scheme to close the gap.

Currently, due to uncertainties created by the elimination of subsidies for essential staples and the tightening of international sanctions, individuals and many corporations are trying to cover themselves by hoarding foreign currency and importing more than they would normally do at lower exchange rates. However, many factors favour the short-run ability of the government to deal with higher-than-usual demand for foreign currency in the market.

At this point in time, the government does have a reasonably large amount of foreign reserves, which combined with high global oil prices will shield the country from much hardship in the short term.

Iran has probably learned a lesson or two from the way the Organization of the Petroleum Exporting Countries (OPEC) members have dealt with oil speculators. They allow financial speculators to cause the price of oil to rise on paper and if these exceed a desirable level, they raid the market and push the price down by taking profits on the paper oil supplies. The Iranian government does the same in the market for currencies. It allows prices to rise and then intervenes in the market and sells its holdings of foreign currency at the new par values and earns an enormous profit, while at the same time creating a new 'parity' until another 'crisis'.

Even though the central bank is capable of inflicting short-term pain on speculators, or letting the market find a new equilibrium price before setting a new par value, it cannot control confidence in the fundamentals of the economy as well as other socio-political concerns of domestic and international players.

Observations and conclusions

Iran's unimpressive socio-politico-economic record during the last three decades has come about as a result of the Iran–Iraq War and the inevitable collapse of oil prices, both of which were beyond the government's control, in combination with economic sanctions and many self-inflicted and self-destructive policies. Many of the negative conditions could easily be reversed if Iran's ideological straightjacket were removed from the policymaking process.

Foremost among the self-inflicted and self-destructive wounds is the insecurity of individual citizens. Human rights violations are repeatedly acknowledged by officials of the United Nations and independent researchers, and are highlighted by the media with a troublesome frequency. Second is the ease and frequency with which laws and regulations are revoked and modified. It seems that when a law or regulation does produce instant results, it is changed. These laws may or may not stand the test of time. They may be dismissed for a variety of reasons. This contributes to the sense of uncertainty about laws and regulations that is felt by potential foreign and domestic investors.[37] A lack of uniformity in the application of the laws of the land, and uncertainty due to political instability, add to the sense of individual insecurity that these conditions instil. Court decisions as well as other official rulings depend on who you are, where you are, and with whom you are acquainted. Individual government officials could and would interpret the law to suit the person and not the situation. It is notoriously well known that nothing is impossible if you know the proper authorities and have the monetary ability to buy their favour.

Third, since the revolution, Iran has been paying for its political leanings in other less quantifiable ways. One punitive method, promoted by the USA, is the circuitous international prohibition of the transfer of technology that might be considered capable of serving dual purposes. This means that Iran cannot openly buy what it needs without a great deal of European and Japanese governmental red tape. These countries do not want to be accused of supporting or arming a 'rogue' nation, thus they have been making it increasingly difficult and costly to buy state-of-the-art machinery and equipment.

As of now, the Obama Administration has been tightening the sanctions noose and is making doing business as usual more difficult and costly. The USA has managed to get the UN Security Council to adopt a number of resolutions against Iran, including the prohibition of trade in oil with Iran and the transfer of technology to the country. However, probably the worst and costliest undertaking against Iran so far, has been the exclusion of Iran from SWIFT, which supplies secure messaging services and interface software to wholesale financial entities. This action has effectively cut Iran off from the international financial world and forced it into cash transactions and barter. This has meant that Iran needs to sell its oil at bargain basement prices to

Iran at a crossroads

countries that have 'exemption' (for which read permission) from the USA. Since they cannot use the normal financial means of paying for the oil they buy, the countries deposit the proceeds in their own banks, which Iran cannot withdraw. The only option is for Iran to spend the money and buy what is not prohibited by sanctions in that country at whatever price is set: a lose–lose bargain for Iran and a win–win bargain for the People's Republic of China, India, Japan, etc.

Finally, as one could expect, while they have fine-tuned the circumvention and bypassing of sanctions, it has not been without cost. In doing so, a large community of Iranian expatriates in the littoral sheikhdoms of the Persian Gulf have amassed large fortunes by importing and re-exporting commodities to Iran. By necessity, merchants who engage in circumvention of sanctions must fabricate false documents at high cost to Iran, which is helpless to confront them.

Notes

1   Well aware of the rich literature on 'modern', 'modernity' and 'modernism', we are neither able nor intend to add to it. Here, we are concerned with the impacts of this unique and monumental development in the history of mankind on Iran. Thus, we discuss its three major characteristics. The socio-cultural characteristic is prevalence of 'reason', most identifiable with scientific approach to all phenomena. 'Rationale' replaces 'God's will' in explaining natural and social phenomena. Socially, it is transformation of the source of law and power from heavens to earth. More important, however, is tolerance of 'otherness'. Be it other religion, ethnicity, or lifestyle. This is the most challenging aspect, partly because accepting change is difficult and partly because its advantages are not clear to the masses. What has been presented as a 'clash of civilizations', particularly in the Islamic world, could indeed be attributed to this aspect.
2   See, for example, Rudi Matthee, 'The Safavids under Western Eyes: Seventeenth-Century European Travelers to Iran', *Journal of Early Modern History* 13, 2009: 137–71.
3   See, for example, Abbas Amanat, *The Downfall of Mirza Taqi Khan Amir Kabir and the Problem of Ministerial Authority in Qajar Iran*, Cambridge University Press, Cambridge, 1991, 577–99, Vol. 23, No. 4, www.jstor.org/stable/163885.
4   Compatibility of economy and polity is nothing new. One way to look at it is that at early stages of capitalist development when markets are undeveloped and the private sector is weak, government is the producer of public goods such as roads and communication. It may additionally have to produce basic industries such as steel. At a later stage when the markets are expanded and the private sector is strong and able to provide the necessary investment, the government becomes more of a facilitator. By providing unified weights and currency and 'enforcing contracts', it enables markets to function. Timely switching of the role from producer to facilitator is crucial for a successful transformation. For a more detailed explanation, see Reza Ghorashi, 'Iran's Economy: Pre-modern vs. Modern', *Asian Affairs* 25, 2004: 48–59.
5   See, for example, Bina and Zangeneh (eds), *Modern Capitalism and Islamic Ideology in Iran*, St Martin's Press, New York, 1992; Hamid Zangeneh, *Islam, Iran, and World Stability*, St Martin's Press, New York, 1994.
6   He never succeeded in shedding the image of being a 'lackey' of the USA and UK since the 1954 *coup d'état*, despite the fact that documents released later by the US government agencies showed him to be 'stubborn' and 'hard to work with'.
7   This phenomenon is not unique to Iran. It is more a characteristic of pre-modern societies. Due to an undeveloped (non-existent) civil society, modern 'causes' such as gender equality will not become an integral part of culture, thus a persistent and automatic demand by social movements. This is because there is no institution to advocate the cause. Leadership is 'charismatic' (individual and their virtues) rather than institutional (political party with set demands, or organized advocacy group). Whatever the leader thinks and wants becomes the movement's demands. With the disappearance, usually the death, of the leader, the cause will be forgotten, unless there is another charismatic person to take up the cause. There are many who wonder what would have become of the 1979 Revolution had Musaddeq been alive. Would he and his ideas, rather than Khomeini's, prevail? What if Khomeini were not in exile abroad, therefore able to take a harder line and demand the overthrow of the monarchy? What if he had not been moved to Paris and the centre of media attention? Would leaders in Tehran shape the revolution's major demands?

8 Many claim that this was a plot. Khomeini and his disciples well knew what they wanted. They point to Khomeini's earlier writings about the characteristics of an Islamic government. Accordingly, he and his aides implemented this dictatorship of Velayat Faqih (Supreme Jurist) step by step. We are not so sure that they knew what they wanted. It seems that Khomeini himself was thinking that the if the shah were to go, all would be taken care of. He even announced that afterwards he would retire to a seminary in Qom. Indeed, he did go to Qom for few months but the everyday affairs of running a country were much more complicated and delicate that he and his disciples anticipated. There were constant demands on him from Tehran about how to resolve issues, mostly disputes among various decision-making individuals and authorities. The end result was that he returned to Tehran and took over the authoritarian role that he played till his death.

9 Literal translation from Farsi is 'neither eastern, nor western, Islamic Republic'.

10 First of all, there is not one version of Islam (or for that matter, any religion) despite claims by the followers of 'the true' version. Shi'a itself has been questioned by Sunni Muslims and is considered borderline heresy by some. Within Shi'a, Khomeini's views, particularly on the concept of Islamic government, have been criticized and rejected by many prominent clergy and scholars. Even among his disciples there is no unanimity. His second in line and heir apparent, Montazeri, was discredited by Khomeini himself. The same has happened to some of his close followers since his death. There is a never-ending debate about his heritage, and what he would have done. Second, contrary to the claims by IRI officials, Islam does not have solutions for everything. There are many (modern) challenges that are new and do not have precedent in history. Third, and most important, to the extent that there has been precedent, implementation has been a major problem. More modern social strata, women and minorities have resisted most of these traditional 'solutions'.

11 For example, in August 1979 Khomeini ordered the closure of nearly 100 newspapers and magazines. The ensuing protests were brutally crushed by pro-regime militias, which used various devices such as stones, knives and chains.

12 In terms of their outlook, forces opposed to Shah could be categorized in three broad groups: first, the left consisted of the Tudeh party and others sympathetic to the 'socialist camp' of the USSR, plus other smaller, independent leftist groups. They were never partners in power. Their crackdown started few months after the revolution. The 'Cultural Revolution' meant to force them out of college campuses and underground. Later, most of their leaders, even the rank and file, were arrested, tortured and mostly executed. Second, the liberal, pro-Musaddeq National Front, and Freedom Movement of which Prime Minister Bazargan and his cabinet ministers came. They were forced out of power after the 'hostage crisis', never to return. Most of them were forced to exile or put under house attest. Third, the Islamists, who consisted mostly of disciples of Khomeini, although some independent elements such as the first elected president were among them. Later, many from the seminaries joined them. The last 30 years have been dominated by clashes between various factions of the Islamists.

13 It is interesting to note, alongside the point raised in Note 7, that to the extent that a practice or way of life has been institutionalized and has had the support of the populace, the attempt to remove it or replace it with the 'traditional' way has failed. A good example is modern sports such as football (soccer). Although there is nothing Islamic or traditional about it, no major clergy or group has questioned its 'value' or compatibility with Islam because there is strong popular support for it. They have been successful, however, in preventing women from attending men's games.

14 There are many examples of these 'unintended consequences' that have made the Islamic Republic of Iran like nowhere else.

15 Of course, there has not been unanimity among the clergy on these concepts. Usually, the view of those in control of institutions such as Friday prayers and the Guardian Council who have enjoyed the support of the state apparatus and control over the media has prevailed.

16 Much has been said and written on Islamic banking. In Islam, like Judaism and Christianity, usury is prohibited. Money is barren and one cannot earn money on money. Profits, on the other hand, are permitted. So, while the lender cannot charge 'interest', it can 'share' the profit. Banks have come out with fancy names for interest rates, the dullest one being a dividend, and have 'solved' the problem. See Hamid Zangeneh, 'Islamic Banking: Theory and Practice in Iran', *Comparative Economic Studies* XXXI(3), Fall 1989: 67–84.

17 Although the constitution recognized a tripartite economy of government, private sector and co-operatives, it was the government that was in charge. For example, it was the sole agent in foreign trade—something that, due to its impracticality, was ignored and later changed.

18 Molavi Afshin, *Soul of Iran*, Norton, 2006, 176.
19 Ervand Abrahamian, *A History of Modern Iran*, Cambridge University Press, New York, 2008.
20 Ibid.
21 rand.org/pubs/monographs/2008/RAND_MG821.pdf.
22 Nikki Mahjoub, quoting Hassan Rabeie an IRI spokesperson, BBC Persian, 29 January 2013.
23 Paul Klebnikov, 'Mullahs Millions', *Forbes*, 21 July 2003.
24 Christopher de Bellaigue, 'The Struggle for Iran', *New York Review of Books*, 2007, 15, cited in Wikipedia.
25 Kim Murphy, 'Iran's $12-billion Enforcers', *Los Angeles Times*, 26 August 2007.
26 IMF, *IMF Staff Report for 2009 Article IV Consultation*, Washington, DC, 11 January 2010, 15.
27 Sec. 3(a) of Public Law 104–72 [H.R. 3107], 5 August 1996.
28 Ibid. Sec. 6. The law stipulated a limit of $40 million, but in August it was lowered to $20 million.
29 Ibid. Sec. 8(a).
30 Kamran Dadkhah and Hamid Zangeneh, 'International Economic Sanctions are Not Zero-Sum Games: There are Only Losers', *CIRA Bulletin* 14(1), March 1998: 24–29. A complete version of this is also published in the *Iranian Journal of Trade Studies Quarterly* 2(5), Winter 1998: 1–14. A Persian translation of this article is published in *Mehregan* 6(4), Winter 1998: 113–22.
31 The new sanctions, which came in the form of an amendment to the National Defence Authorization Act (NDAA), would impose sanctions against foreign companies or individuals engaged in trade with Iran in several sectors, including energy, ports, shipping and shipbuilding, which allegedly support Tehran's nuclear or arms programmes.
32 John Glaser, 'Iran Sanctions Passed the Point of Effectiveness, Says Expert', antiwar.com/blog/2013/01/24/iran-sanctions-passed-the-point-of-effectiveness-says-expert/. Among other provisions, they would also penalize foreign buyers of Iranian oil and natural gas if they paid for them with gold or other precious metals—a measure apparently aimed specifically at Turkey, a key US ally, which reportedly exported $6.4 billion in gold to Iran in exchange for natural gas during the first nine months of this year: original.antiwar.com/lobe/2012/12/01/us-senate-passes-new-sanctions-on-iran/.
33 This section is substantially from Hamid Zangeneh, *Iran's Fixed, Flexible and Harmful Economy*, www.worldpolicy.org/blog/2010/10/20/irans-fixed-flexible-and-harmful-economy.
34 Under a regime of fixed exchange rates, inflation could be imported through several channels, including higher imported goods prices, monetization of foreign reserves by the central banks, and higher demand for exportable goods.
35 The IMF estimates the short-term elasticity of demand for gasoline to be −0.124 and the long-term elasticity of demand for gasoline to be −0.494. Dominique Guillaume and Roman Zytek, *Islamic Republic of Iran: Selected Issues*, International Monetary Fund, 11 January 2010, www.imf.org/external/pubs/ft/scr/2010/cr1076.pdf, 11.
36 According to the IMF estimates, the new subsidy law would lead to a jump in consumer prices by about 33% in the first year (1389; 2010) and, if proper monetary and fiscal policies are undertaken, 'the inflation would gradually subside thereafter'. In the same report, the IMF predicts a slowdown of the economy to a sluggish growth of under 2% for the first year (2010) and, with a proper mix of fiscal and monetary policies, to 6.5%–7.5% growth in the medium term. Ibid.
37 H. Zangeneh, 'International Trade in Iran: An Appraisal', *Research in Middle East Economics* 2, 1997; H. Zangeneh and J.M. Moore, 'Economic Development and Growth in Iran', in H. Zangeneh (ed.), *Islam, Iran, and World Stability*, St Martin's Press, New York, 1994, 201–16; H. Zangeneh, The Iranian Economy and the Globalization Process', in A. Mohamadi (ed.), *Iran Encountering Globalization, Problems and Prospects*, RoutledgeCurzon, London 2003, 105–33; H. Zangeneh, 'An Estimate of Iran's Underground Economy: A Monetary Approach', in J. Assadipour (ed.), *Iran: Market & Democracy*, 2010; H. Zangeneh, 'Saving, Investment and Growth: A Causality Test', *The Iranian Economic Review* 11(16), 2006: 165–75.

24

Colombia

Seeking prosperity through peace

Nake M. Kamrany, Danielle N. Ramirez and Laura E. Armey

The recent global transition to a more diffuse distribution of economic power points to a shift in the balance of global growth from rich to low- and middle-income economies. Colombia may be a prime example as its recent rapid per capita income growth of 10.2% on average per annum since 1999 points to the potential for Colombia's convergence to the ranks of rich countries. However, Colombia's economic growth has been constrained by over 40 years of a costly and ineffective drug war policy that has failed. The illicit activity of drug production and trafficking grosses approximately US$10–$20 billion per year; it does not enter into the gross domestic product (GDP) accounting. In addition, the FARC (Revolutionary Armed Forces of Colombia) has stifled Colombia's drive towards economic prosperity. Barring this social and political impasse, the economy would flourish.

Inequality in the distribution of wealth, land and income in Colombia, which is among the highest in the world, is at the forefront of ongoing conflict. The result appears to be in part an abandonment of legitimate market activity, and an entrenchment of violence that threatens to undermine future growth.

Drug trafficking dominates the Colombian black market economy; cocaine is produced at $1,500/kilo and is sold on US streets for as much as $50,000/kilo. With so much profit to be made in drugs trafficking, many government officials fall victim to temptation. This is part of the reason why Plan Colombia has only provided the world with false hope. Colombians have rightfully lost faith in their government and crime goes largely unreported, which only provides more incentive and opportunity for criminals who have little fear of being caught.

Moreover, the aid from Plan Colombia ends up targeting poor Colombian farmers, thereby strengthening the leftist guerrilla groups and drug cartels that Plan Colombia is intended to uproot. The Colombian government has been at war with these organizations since 1966. Plan Colombia has instigated violence from the FARC because it focuses resources on aerial herbicide spraying to kill the coca plants from which cocaine is derived. The herbicides are also killing the legal crops of the small Colombian farmers. Moreover, farmers complain that the herbicides damage their health and water. These farmers suffer unremunerated losses and resentment grows. They, in turn, support the leftist groups who protect them from the injustice of the government, and rely on these groups to bring drug crops to market through an inhospitable environment at high profits to the guerrillas.

To combat this resentment, Colombia must address corruption and dramatic income and land inequality. Corruption has led to a loss of trust in the government among the Colombian population. Corruption must be rooted out of the government so that it can finally put an end to the drug problem and the violence and crimes that come with it through public trust. Taken together, addressing these problems, the Colombian government, with the help of international forces, must make it economically unappealing for the FARC's guerrilla fighters to continue fighting in support of the FARC's leaders and their ideology. Economic incentives and transition must be offered to these fighters that surpass the benefits they receive for fighting and to help them to become part of productive economic activity.

No doubt the FARC's mission will become superfluous when Colombia's per capita income rises and distribution becomes more equitable. Indeed, the end of the FARC–government conflict would also free many of Colombia's resources that would be put to better uses instead of being wasted on the exhausting civil war. Also, currently the FARC provides armed protection for the Colombian drug cartels that operate out of the land that the FARC controls. Without this strong demand for protection, the drug cartels would be automatically weakened. With the major drug cartels gone, peace could invade Colombia.

Colombia's economic prospects

Colombia, nestled in the northern part of South America, with a population of 46 million and a GDP of $333.4 billion, is the fourth largest economy on the continent. Although Colombia's

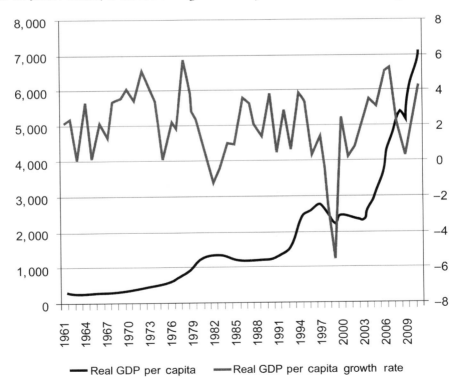

Figure 24.1 Colombia: patterns of GDP and per capita GDP growth, 1991–2011

per capita GDP is well below that of the USA, following a crisis in 1999, a rapid increase can be seen starting around 2000.

Despite economic shocks, Colombia has experienced solid growth since the 1980s, avoiding most of the implications of the debt crisis at that time which negatively impacted the rest of Latin America. Notably, however, that growth has been accompanied by an increase in volatility, and in the 1980s was reduced by falls in total factor productivity (TFP).[1]

Considering recent increases in Colombia's GDP per capita at 10% per annum, there is great potential for economic convergence, and in fact, estimates point to a possible convergence of GDP per capita between Colombia and the USA in roughly 29 years, i.e. by the year 2040. Modelling Colombia's future growth through various methods such as mean projection, ordinary least squares trends and evidence of unconditional income convergence one arrives at a similar time frame for economic convergence. Moreover, the presence of an S-shaped growth pattern explains the observed rapid progression of per capita income convergence. This reconciles the current observations with the well-documented stylized hypothesis of twin peak distribution of income.

During the past century the world has become increasingly globalized. With this, a trend of per capita GDP convergence can be observed between already developed and developing countries. Kamrany and Vassilev (2010) explain the drivers of economic conversion: 'This converging process is mainly achieved through the successful transfer and implementation of technologies by developed countries to less-developed countries. Using developed countries such as the United States of America as a benchmark; the focus is on the development of the respective growth rate of the GDP per capita income of less developed countries.' The phenomenon we observe in Colombia is consistent with this recent global transition from stagnant economic growth performance in the developing world to dynamic growth. It corresponds with a shift in the distribution of economic growth in favour of low- and middle-income

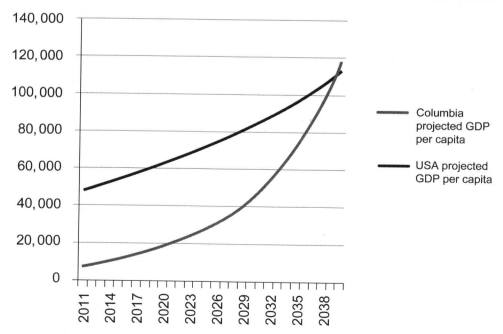

Figure 24.2 Colombia and U.S.: projected GDP per capita growth paths, 2011–2040

Figure 24.3 Real GDP per capita ratio

countries in the global economy such as the People's Republic of China, India, Brazil and Colombia, among others.

Looking at Colombia's economic indicators, there are several positive trends that make convergence possible. Colombia is experiencing enhanced productivity and a shift from relatively low value-added industries to higher value-added industries. Colombia's annual growth rate of per capita productivity (income) as well as its advances in technological growth, abundance of natural resources, control of fertility rate and educated labour force, place it among the middle-income countries that are poised to reach the ranks of the First World within the 21st century. The World Bank reports Colombia's capital formation (as a percentage of GDP) was 23% in 2011 compared to the USA's 15%. The valued added of the industrial sector, as a percentage of GDP, is relatively close for the two countries with Colombia at 38% and the USA at 20%. Problematically, the USA's value added of the services sector as a percentage of GDP is well over that of Colombia's, with 79% and 55% in 2010, respectively. Colombia is more agricultural, with 7% of its GDP coming from agriculture, compared to roughly 1% for the USA in 2011. Colombia's inflation was high but not overly problematic: 7% in 2011 compared to the USA's 2% in the same year. Colombia's external debt, while relevant to its economic prospects, is not overly pressing, as the 51st most indebted nation in the world.[2]

Social indicators show a generally positive environment for economic growth. Adult literacy in Colombia is at 93% compared with 99% in the USA. Life expectancy is 75 years in Colombia compared to 78.4 years in the USA. Infant mortality is still problematically just over double that of the USA, at 15.92 per 1,000 in 2012, and birth rates remain slightly higher in Colombia at 17.23 per 1,000, compared to the USA at 13.70 per 1,000.[3]

Early Colombian development was largely driven by industrial policies that began in the 1950s. These policies included trade protection and tax exemptions. Significant growth, industrialization and modernization have taken place, but only after the debt crisis of the 1980s that was a result of these measures.[4]

In recent years, however, Colombia has experienced a renaissance in the deployment of modern technologies and systematic industrial policies. Ostensibly, Colombian leadership has promoted industrial and services upgrading. Agriculture used to be the biggest sector in Colombia but has since been surpassed by the services and industrial sectors. Currently, the services sector makes up over half of GDP, while the industrial sector follows not too far behind with 37.6%. Other drivers of growth and prosperity include the rapid growth of trade and finance, a growing equity market, public finance, educational development and incentives to attract more trade and talent.[5]

International investment, as well as tourism, has greatly increased over recent years, largely due to Juan Manuel Santos's administration's favourable commercial relations and crackdown on corruption and the drug war. Moreover, in addition to signing a free trade agreement with the USA, Colombia continues to negotiates free trade agreements with a number of other countries.

However, Colombia seems caught in a web of violence, drug trade and corruption that may hamper its long-run growth potential. Political indicators could be harbingers of slow growth ahead.[6] Political indicators show widespread corruption and lawlessness, despite being Latin America's oldest republic. The World Bank's governance indicators for 2011 show some improvement since 2009, but the picture is not promising: political stability scored -1.25; rule of law was at -0.26; control of corruption at -0.31; and accountability at -0.15.[7] Colombian welfare is distributed unequally across Colombia, and in regions like Montes de Maria politicians use aid for development money for their own personal gain and eliminate companies that would bring actual development to the region.[8] Thus corruption is a real impediment to development, especially in the poorest regions of Colombia.

Ongoing violence in Colombia undermines stability and economic growth. Several authors have attempted to understand the impact of violence on growth in Colombia. Colombia has one of the world's highest homicide rates. Both Cárdenas[9] and Rubio[10] estimate that the high homicide rate in the 1980s and 1990s cost Colombia 2 percentage points per year in economic growth, plus an additional 0.7% of growth through reductions on aggregate investment. Cárdenas similarly finds that the slow down in total factor productivity that Colombia experienced between 1980 and 2000 was largely driven by its growing homicide rate and inequality. Using a 3SLS approach to test the impact directly of conflict on growth, Riascos and Vargas[11] estimate that the increase in the intensity of the Colombian conflict slowed GDP per capita growth by 0.3 percentage points per year on average in the 1990s. This impact is primarily through a reduction in total factor productivity growth and through a reduction in accumulation of capital. To deal with omitted variable bias, Borrero[12] addresses department-specific fixed effects. His results find similar reductions in growth from increases in homicides, kidnapping and actions of illegal armed groups.

Recent authors have attempted to understand the channels by which violence impacts economic growth. Camacho and Rodriguez (2010) show that firms are more likely to exit markets when violence increases. Rodríguez and Sánchez[13] also find that armed conflict exposure encourages children over the age of 11 to drop out of school early. Camacho[14] traces negative growth back to the negative impact on infant health from a mother's exposure to terrorism during pregnancy, while Vargas,[15] on the other hand, does not find consistent impacts of violent incidents on growth.

Dramatic inequality also threatens Colombian development. With an income Gini coefficient of 0.51 and land Gini of 0.86, Colombian inequality is among the highest in the world.[16] This is despite a trend in Latin America towards a growing middle class. A growing number of Latin Americans find their basic needs met, but feel they are lacking economic security: a growing lower-middle class. Cárdenas estimates that at least 43% of all Latin Americans have changed classes between the late 1990s and the 2000s. Intergenerational mobility, however, has remained stagnant, with educational attainment remaining largely determined on the basis of parental education levels.[17]

In his paper, *Fiscal Policy in Colombia: Tapping its Potential for a More Equitable Society*, Moller[18] claims that the poor, in Colombia and other Latin American countries, are largely left out of the benefits of development, feeding the cycle of violence and stalling growth. The middle class has been the primary beneficiary of social security transfers, and has been allowed to avoid paying taxes by opting out of government services. A 2010 LAPOP survey demonstrates that the majority of Colombians believe that the government should address inequality, and 42% are willing to pay higher taxes for this to be a reality. Moller[19] explains that the tax base is far too small—less than 2% of Colombians 'actually declare income and pay personal income taxes', owing to the extremely high threshold. Individuals have to earn three times the average household income per person before being liable for income taxes in Colombia, and then tax exemptions are available. He goes on to explain that 'Income tax exemptions raise the Gini coefficient by 0.7 percentage point and cost the treasury close to 1 percent of GDP in revenue forgone'. Furthermore, 'independent low-income workers are penalized as they are taxed presumptively at the source, without the right to reimbursements through the filing of annual income declarations'. The current administration has begun implementing policies in order to address inequality.

Despite the upward mobility trend, intergenerational mobility, a better proxy for inequality of opportunity, remains stagnant. Educational achievement and attainment remain strongly dependent upon parental education levels. Despite the recent growth in pro-poor programmes, the middle class has benefited disproportionately from social security transfers and is increasingly opting out from government services. Central to the region's prospects of continued progress will be its ability to harness the new middle class into a new, more inclusive social contract, where the better-off pay their fair share of taxes and demand improved public services.[20]

Colombia's economic convergence with the USA would in fact be possible if the country could resolve some of its major issues. Here, we have developed the cost of inequality, corruption and violence to Colombia's growth. In the following sections we look at the history of ongoing violence in Colombia, the drug trade, and possible ways out of a vicious cycle of illegal activity and violence that hampers Colombian prosperity.

A history of violence

Colombia's history has been riddled with political division, unstable central government and civil war. Colombia's struggles with common identity are rooted in some of these political divisions. Unfortunately, the vacuum they create is a perfect environment within which the drug business has taken hold.

Founded in 1848, Colombia was the first constitutional government in South America, and its Liberal and Conservative parties are two of the oldest surviving political parties in Latin America. A civil war ensued in 1863, leading to the creation of the 'United States of Colombia', lasting only 23 years until the country finally became the Republic of Colombia.[21] These 'United States of Colombia' developed as self-sufficient units because of the vast geographic differences and separations. In fact, 'geographical heterogeneity may account for the breaking of Ecuador and Venezuela from the Gran Colombia a few years after independence'.[22]

Unsurprisingly, internal divisions only continued to fester between the bipartisan political forces once Colombia transitioned into a republic, occasionally igniting very bloody civil wars. The most significant civil war, the Thousand Days War (1899–1902), ultimately led to the secession of Panama from Colombia in 1903 with help from the USA. Two decades later, in 1921, the USA constructed the Panama Canal and paid Colombia $25,000,000 for compensation and recognition of Panama under the terms of the Thomson-Urrutia Treaty.[23]

During the late 1940s and early 1950s Colombia was engulfed in the more famous bloody conflict known as *La Violencia* (The Violence). The civil war, centred around tensions between the two leading political parties, erupted after the assassination of the Liberal presidential candidate, Jorge Eliécer Gaitán, on 9 April 1948. The riots, known as El Bogotazo, began in the nation's capital, Bogotá, and quickly spread throughout the country, claiming the lives of almost 200,000 Colombians. The violence subsided during the decade of 1953–64, when Gustavo Rojas deposed the president in a *coup d'état* and negotiated with the guerrillas. During this time, the military junta of General Gabriel París Gordillo established law and order.[24]

Jostling for power subsided when Rojas himself was deposed and the Colombian Conservative Party and Colombian Liberal Party agreed to govern the country jointly through a coalition called the National Front. Under the deal, the presidency would alternate between Conservatives and Liberals every four years for the following 16 years. The National Front ended *La Violencia*, and subsequent administrations attempted to institute far-reaching social and economic reforms. However, the political and social discord and contradictions between each successive Liberal and Conservative administration made it impossible to come to any agreement.[25]

In addition, discord with the compromise led to the emergence of leftist guerrilla groups such as the FARC, ELN (National Liberation Army) and M-19 (19 April Movement), who continued to fight the government. The Revolutionary Armed Forces of Colombia (the People's Army), infamously known as the FARC, is the largest Marxist-Leninist guerrilla organization and has been at war with the Colombian government since 1966. These groups base their continued fight on the rampant inequality within Colombia. FARC funding comes primarily through ransom kidnappings and taxing the drug trade out of the south Colombian region where it operates.[26] Just like the FARC, the ELN also fights for equality, being an advocate for communist ideology and liberation theory. It is the lesser-known of the two communist fighting groups, but still has a sizable army of about 5,000 guerrillas.[27]

M-19, on the other hand, is a rebel group that resides primarily in Colombia's major cities. Some of M-19's founders were actually part of the FARC but broke off in order to expand beyond the rural areas and have a greater impact on their cause. However, their cause was identical to that of the FARC and ELN, to fight for the poor and overthrow the greed that plagued the government.[28]

During the late 1970s powerful and violent drug cartels emerged, most notoriously the Medellín Cartel under Pablo Escobar and the Cali Cartel. These drug cartels, in particular, have exerted extensive political, economic and social influence throughout Colombia. The '8000 case', the biggest political scandal of the 1990s, is infamous for revealing the extent of the cartels' political influence. During these proceedings Colombia ultimately investigated the role of drug money in electing Ernesto Samper as president in 1994.[29] These cartels have also financed and influenced different illegal armed groups across the political spectrum.[30]

The first group of Autodefensas Unidas de Colombia (far-right paramilitary group, AUC, or United Self-Defence Forces of Colombia) was formally promoted by the governor of the Department of Antioquia, Álvaro Uribe, who became president 16 years later. A coalition of drug dealers and landlords formed alliances to fight the leftist guerrillas through the creation of paramilitary groups. One such group is the AUC. 'This right-wing umbrella group was formed in 1997 by drug-traffickers and landowners to combat rebel kidnappings and extortion.'[31] The AUC funds itself through business investors and landowners who are negatively affected by the guerrilla groups, as well as through the drug trade. While initially a sanctioned counterpoint to the guerrillas, the militias began to look much like the guerrilla groups they were fighting. In an attempt to carry out justice and keep the peace, the Colombian government has extradited thousands of militia members to the USA to face drug charges; however, many of the most prominent and violent members have escaped any form of punishment entirely, leading to much criticism of both the government and the paramilitary groups alike.[32] In 2005 the Colombian government offered the paramilitaries a kind of truce. The Defence and Peace Law offered the paramilitary groups an opportunity to disarm and confess in exchange for sentences of a maximum of eight years for their crimes, and most paramilitary groups agreed (Acemoglu and Robinson 2012b).

The new Colombian Constitution of 1991 included key provisions on political, human and gender rights. As further testament to the influence of the drug cartels, the new constitution initially prohibited the extradition of Colombian nationals. Owing to ensuing controversy, the prohibition was repealed in 1996.[33] The cartels responded with terrorist attacks and mafia-style executions.

More practically, the 1991 Constitution increased checks and balances enhancing the role of Congress and the Constitutional Court, and reducing the power of the president.[34] Despite these reforms, the bloody internal conflict between guerrilla insurgent groups and paramilitary groups and effects of the drug trade continue to plague Colombia. President Andrés Pastrana and the FARC attempted to negotiate a solution to the conflict between 1999 and 2002. The government set up a 'demilitarized' zone, governed by the FARC, but repeated tensions led the Pastrana administration to conclude that the negotiations were ineffective.[35]

With the dual goal of ending the armed conflict and promoting a strong anti-narcotic strategy, Pastrana began to implement Plan Colombia. Signed in 1999, Plan Colombia is an agreement with the USA in which US military and monetary aid is given to Colombia to combat the drug cartels and the violence that comes with them.[36]

Supported by aid from the USA, President Uribe's administration applied more military pressure on the FARC and other outlawed groups, leading to an overall improvement of security indicators. However, this improvement has been undermined by the Colombian Army's continued violations of human rights and also questionable statistics.[37]

President Uribe's administration attempted to defeat the insurgent groups militarily. Security throughout Colombia improved under Uribe's watch, but at the potential cost of human rights violations and civilian casualties. Reported kidnappings showed a steep decrease as did intentional homicides. The rate of reported abductions declined steadily for almost a decade until 2010, when 220 cases were reported between January and October.[38] An overall reduction in violence has led to an increase of travel and tourism since 2002, but the US State Department and the British Foreign Office still warn travellers against wandering into rural areas where the FARC and cartels reside.[39]

Colombia has experienced modest progress in the fight against insurgents. The FARC's commander in chief, Alfonso Cano, was killed by security forces in November 2011. He was replaced by Timoleón Jiménez, who assumed the duty of first commander just days after Cano's death. Jiménez is thought to reside in the mountain corridor covering the Department Norte and the Bolívar Department.[40] Following the demobilization of the prominent right-wing paramilitary group AUC, the country has seen the rise of a number of neo-paramilitary groups that have been accused of widespread murder, drug trafficking and land grabbing.[41]

The drug trade supports this ongoing violence, and in turn many support the rebel factions owing to their dependence on the drug trade. The resulting chaos allows drug traffickers and corrupt local officials to maintain local political legitimacy.

The web of the drug business

The illicit economy has evolved over time to meet the fiscal needs of competing players, and to adapt to changing counter-narcotic and counter-insurgent policies. The ongoing civil war enables the narco-economy at the same time as it provides financial fuel for it. In Colombia, the production and sale of drugs is equal to nearly 4% of GDP.[42] The war on drugs has entrenched the role of insurgent groups in the drug business. As Thoumi (2010) explains, most repressive anti-drug policies increase risks to low-level producers and lower their returns, but have the unintended consequence that they increase the returns to the insurgents who are able to offer protection and facilitate the trade in drugs.

Prior to the 1990s the drug trade was largely limited to the Medellín and Cali Cartels. From the 1960s to the 1990s the focus was primarily on processing and trafficking cocaine. The death of Medellín kingpin Pablo Escobar in 1993, along with the capture of the majority of the Cali inner circle (Colombian President Samper, elected in 1994, having been revealed to have risen to power as a result of financial backing from the Cali, felt pressure to pursue the network to remove the black mark against himself and his country) begat the changes to the Colombian drug business in the mid-1990s.[43] The networks became more dispersed and their leadership decentralized. These short-term successes have led to the drug networks being much more difficult to track down, and make it challenging to target critical hubs and leadership.

Following the decentralization of the drug trade and the US strategy to interrupt the South American drug networks by disrupting the so-called 'airbridge' in the mid-1990s (policies included tearing up small landing strips and shooting down small planes, whether or not they were involved in drugs trafficking), which cut off the access of Colombian drugs traffickers to the producers in Peru and Bolivia, Colombia became a prominent grower of cocaine. Colombia also became the western hemisphere's leading heroin producer, producing a high-quality, lower-cost heroin.[44]

Colombia's cocaine growing continues to adapt to crop-destruction tactics. In 2004 police discovered a new strain of cocaine plant, which drugs traffickers reportedly spent over $100 million developing, that produces a much higher yield (the plant is nearly 10 feet tall instead of the normal five-foot tall plants) and a purer drug. It is also harder to kill and easier to grow in inhospitable regions.[45] Along with protecting plants with molasses to make them harder to kill, these hardier strains account for how, despite destroying nearly half the coca crop with aerial spraying, coca production has stayed constant (Mejia and Restrepo 2009).

The cost of the narco-economy can be measured across a variety of dimensions. In coca-producing regions,[46] homicide and other violence are notably higher. These regions also tend to attract clashes between the government, which targets drug production, and insurgent groups who protect it and gain funding from it. This leads, however, to these coca-growing regions becoming battle grounds with all of the civilian costs that that engenders in Colombia's ongoing civil war.[47]

Yet, despite these kinds of costs, coca still plays an important role in giving the insurgents a foothold within local populations. Angrist and Kugler[48] find that unemployment is reduced in coca-growing regions. Acemoglu and Robinson (2012b)' elaborate that the drug lords and insurgents have created law and order in the parts of the country where drugs are produced, and that most of the producers were displaced from other parts of the country by the ongoing political violence. A striking example of post-government order occurs in the town of La Danta, Antioquia. Here the local militia kingpin enforces laws, engages in taxation including that of the drug lords, and invests in local community development (Acemoglu and Robinson 2012b).

Insurgents further play a role in protecting the local populations from the abuses of drug traffickers, as well as in helping drugs traffickers to get their goods to market. Local populations are thus ingratiated with the insurgents. Attempts at crop eradication only strengthen the bond between insurgents and local populations.[49] Keefer and Loayza[50] reiterate that crop eradication has increased the productivity of remaining coca crops in the Andean region.

Political disparities and resentment towards the government help to create the environment in which coca thrives. Thoumi (2010) explains that in order to have a competitive advantage in drug production, a country needs to be both hospitable to growing drugs, but also to having a complex illegal system that exists within its borders. These kinds of countries must not only have a power vacuum, but also a place where social norms allow evading legal authority. He goes on to explain how the web of violence grows with drugs—the Medellín Cartel had close connections with law enforcement through helping to establish a right-wing militia to counter the left-wing guerrillas.

Most policy solutions to the drug-violence-poverty web depend on a more lenient US drug policy. Krebs et al.[51] use a theoretical model and simulations to argue that levels of interdiction would have to be too high to curb drug trafficking effectively or that drug use would have to be made legal to lower the benefits of smuggling. Becker et al.[52] similarly argue that taxation of legal drugs might be a more effective and less costly way to reduce consumption. Echeverry[53] finds that empirically the demand for drugs appears to be fairly price inelastic, and as a result the war on drugs has the primary impact of increasing prices, not reducing consumption. Using similar simulations to the above authors, Mejia and Restrepo[54] calculate that a three-fold increase in US counter-narcotics funding would only reduce consumption in developed countries by 15%. More troublingly, Keefer and Loayza[55] observe that prices for cocaine and heroin have been dropping because of increased supply, not decreased demand.

The irony of the illegality of drugs is that it further impoverishes the farmers who produce it, in addition to subjecting them to violence. Risk increases as a result of crop eradication that poor farmers, often not viewed as criminals within their own world view and community, are forced to endure. In addition, because the crops are illegal, the profits to the grower are much lower as the trafficking network requires greater compensation to get drugs to market.[56]

The narco-economy thus creates a kind of poverty trap whereby people become more dependent on it because of the policies that are meant to destroy it, and people become more tolerant of the traffickers and the insurgents because they depend on them for their livelihood. Violence perpetuates the drug trade, making people more dependent on durable crops such as coca, and it also provides the financial fuel for violence to continue. It flourishes because of weak institutions and in turn weakens them further.

The challenges to Colombia's peace that stem from drugs are manifold. Certainly if the narco-economy were tamed, insurgents would find themselves politically and financially disadvantaged, but the policies currently underway to try to deal with the narco-economy only entrench it further.

Unravelling the problem

> I think we have to stop pretending to ourselves that all the violence, misery and dissension that afflicts Latin America is the result of a plot hatched thousands of kilometers away, as if we couldn't imagine any other destiny, for ourselves than being at the mercy of the global powers.
> *(Gabriel García Márquez)*[57]

We could argue in this section that developed countries are to blame for Colombia's problems and that Plan Colombia, along with its failures, has entrenched the rebels and created greater divisions in Colombian society. We could argue that Colombia would be better off if the USA were to change its drug policy. We could argue that Colombia would be better off if the USA were simply to stop spending money on crop eradication. However, the USA cannot untangle Colombia's problems. So we encourage, rather, forward movement on the part of Colombia and its allies to find a peaceful solution to its problems. We think this stems from making the whole of Colombian society part of the solution, including giving the FARC a stake in the outcome of Colombia. We also believe it rests in tapping into a common Colombian identity, one that is intolerant of violations of law and violence against fellow Colombians.

Arguably, the drug trade continues in Colombia owing to a lack of common identity across the country, and feelings of distance from the authority and benefits of the central government. Francisco Thoumi (2010) argues that comparative advantages in drug production emerge in places where there are marginalized ethnic groups, a weak central state and internal conflict. Groups who have good reason to feel isolated from the state often perform the bulk of illegal activity. Additionally, social norms must allow for the evasion of the law. That is, a broader segment of society is tolerant of undermining law and order.[58] This means that the problem of drugs is grounded in a problem of identity, and Colombia must struggle to realign the identity of its marginalized groups with its population as a whole and its legal structure.

Colombia's cultural leaders have charted a way forward towards that kind of common identity. Gabriel García Márquez calls upon Colombians to identify with their pan-Latin heritage:

> to understand our current problems, we have to go back to the time before the Conquest. The borders that were drawn between the Latin American countries were only created to manipulate us, and still, whenever there's a need for it, the cry of nationalism goes up. Obviously, that only sets us against one another, stops us from seeing and feeling the problems that we have in common. Each country has its own special circumstances, but what really matters is our underlying common identity.[59]

Almost mournfully, Márquez, in the same interview, asks Colombians not to fight over issues of 'inequality, oppression, exploitation and neglect', but rather to answer such injustice with life. Germán Arciniegas, also a prolific Colombian writer and intellectual, was an undying proponent of the potential for the success of Latin American culture. He answered a series of pamphlets by Giovanni Papini, who argued in 1947 that Latin America was a failure. He wrote: 'America is a common project, of people, of European immigrants, united with blacks and Indians, in the formation of what [Mexican philosopher José] Vasconcelos called the "cosmic man".'[60] Sadly, this voice feels all too lost in the midst of the Colombian conflict. We cannot overstate the importance of finding this kind of common ground in recreating an identity to build an environment that fosters peace.

The peace process

The peace negotiations of the Andrés Pastrana government between 1998 and 2002 were a dismal failure. The government granted the guerrillas their own territory, which the guerrillas in turn used as a safe haven for securing their grasp on the drug business and mounting future attacks. The Uribe government did its best to undo the 'peace process', escalating the conflict and the policy of drug eradication in an effort to make continued violence appear pointless.[61]

On 4 November 2011 Alfonso Cano, the FARC's leader, was killed, opening up a new chapter in this conflict. His replacement Timoleón Jiménez is considered one of the 'least visible of the rebel commanders',[62] and it was difficult to predict what his reign would mean for the vicious war that has lasted half a century. However, despite continued armed conflict, the FARC, under Jiménez, agreed to participate in peace talks with the Colombian government, leading many to believe there might actually be hope for a brighter Colombian future.

There was much buzz and anticipation in the coming months for the peace talks that were scheduled to begin in October 2012 in Norway. Unfortunately, despite all of the excitement and perhaps overly inflated hopes, the Colombian government and the rebel army could not agree on anything, or even jointly participate in a temporary cease-fire.[63]

In order for the second round of peace talks that took place in Havana, Cuba, in 2013 to be successful, the two groups would undoubtedly need to make tough concessions. Promisingly, the government argued for the FARC to legitimize itself and use the political system to fight for its cause. However, the Colombian government had some hard choices as well. The FARC has had staying power because the Colombian government has failed to take the FARC and their voice seriously, and has not adequately addressed many of the legitimate complaints that strengthen the FARC's cause. Without honouring the FARC's legitimacy, the hope that they would behave legitimately is unrealistic. Treating the FARC as a legitimate entity, despite its distasteful past, could help to facilitate peace. Addressing the issues that enrage much of the population and give the FARC power is even more important.

The FARC has legitimate issues that they wish to address but it must also take its role in creating peace and prosperity seriously. The FARC's argument that 'land-ownership issues' are at 'the root of the problems' that Colombian peasants face is reasonable, and there are policy solutions to begin to ameliorate the inequality in land rights in Colombia. The FARC, for its part, however, has refused to be a legitimate voice for the rights of Colombia's poor, arguing instead that they 'want to denounce the crime of capitalism and neo-liberalism'.[64] This position, obviously, is not tenable, and keeps the FARC from being able to address the real issues it has aptly identified and fought a war over.

Effective drug policy

Clearly the counter-narcotics strategy of crop eradication has failed, but there are barriers to making a crop replacement strategy effective. Crop eradication policies play a role in entrenching insurgents. They potentially harm the environment more broadly along with the health of peasants, though evidence to this end is mostly circumstantial. More significantly, aerial spraying is not carried out from the prescribed distance above the ground, which leads to damage to water supplies and neighbouring legal crops, making development more rather than less difficult. This points to an overall lack of co-ordination to date between aerial spraying, alternative development and state-financed infrastructure development (Sherret 2005). While we argue that continuing aerial spraying is expensive and harmful, a first step might point towards co-ordination of efforts.

There is mixed evidence on the effectiveness of crop replacement programmes. Peru, through crop substitution and alternative employment programmes, successfully replaced nearly 50% of its coca production.[65] Promising stories abound of communities in Colombia that have replaced coca production with licit production (see Ferrer[66] for a community that replaced coca with coffee in Colombia). Unfortunately, efforts have stalled in Peru and in Colombia, because although one region or project may succeed in replacing coca, other producers and regions step in to fill the void in production.[67]

Many of the factors that make coca an attractive crop in certain regions create challenges in replacing it. Reuter[68] enumerates the challenges of successful crop replacement programmes: one must persuade farmers that the government will maintain its commitment in the long term. With political instability, it can be difficult to convince people that the government can provide protection and infrastructure to get more sensitive crops to market. In places where land is of poor quality, it can be hard to find substitute crops. The USA has reduced its funding for crop replacement, relative to crop eradication, citing a lack of security, the Colombian government's failure to follow through and the difficulty in finding crops to grow in poor soil.

Perhaps most persuasive is the idea that crop replacement works best where it is grounded in cultural norms and in a greater policy of development. In the story of the community that replaced coca with coffee, community leaders claimed that it was a way to help 'reinstate values'. Strikingly, projects to replace poppy crops in Afghanistan have been most successful when coupled with a push towards Islamic values.[69]

There appears to be a glimmer of hope that the new peace process may lead to a commitment by both the Colombian government and the FARC towards crop replacement. President Santos has said that agreeing to terms of a policy for crop replacement will be part of the peace process.[70]

Effective development could help to ameliorate the grievances that drive the FARC. Making the FARC a stakeholder in Colombia's future development could help them to cease being an impediment to the process. Moreover, if Colombia's government and warring factions are all involved, there is a chance it might be part of an adequately total makeover that could move the economy in a better direction.

However, if the peace process cannot work, if the two sides cannot be reasonable and come to an agreement, our argument, at the end of the day, is very simply one of crowding out. Eliminate the need for the FARC by addressing economic grievances and with a drug policy that decriminalizes growing coca. The Colombian government must exploit the methods it has available to it to make its people better off, and focus on development, not winning a futile war on drugs. Colombia has experienced incredible amounts of economic growth, and this growth ultimately gives Colombia the potential to address unemployment, poverty, and shortages of food, medical care and education. Colombia must work to combat the corruption and violence that diminish the impact of the benefits of this growth, and we hope that the Santos government will continue on its course to address massive inequality that also limits the benefits of growth. In so doing, we think that Colombia can unravel the underlying causes of violence, and push itself forwards.

Notes

1 Alvaro J. Riascos and Juan F. Vargas, 'Violence and Growth in Colombia: A Review of the Quantitative Literature', *Economics of Peace and Security Journal* 6(2), 2011: 15–20.
2 The World Bank, *World Development Indicators*, data.worldbank.org (accessed 3 December 2012).
3 'CIA World Factbook: Colombia', 10 December 2012, www.cia.gov/library/publications/the-world-factbook/geos/co.html.
4 Marcela Meléndez and Guillermo E. Perry, 'Industrial Policies in Colombia', IDB Working Paper No. 37, June 2010, ssrn.com/abstract=1817239, or dx.doi.org/10.2139/ssrn.1817239.
5 The World Bank, *World Development Indicators*.
6 Roberto Perotti, 'Growth, Income Distribution, and Democracy: What the Data Say', *Journal of Economic Growth*, 1996, ideas.repec.org/a/kap/jecgro/v1y1996i2p149-87.html.
7 World Bank, *Worldwide Governance Indicators*, info.worldbank.org/governance/wgi/sc_country.asp (accessed 3 December 2012).
8 Daron Acemoglu and James A. Robinson, *Who's Afraid of Development? The Colombian Version*, 26 March 2012, whynationsfail.com/blog/2012/3/26/whos-afraid-of-development-the-colombian-version.html.
9 Mauricio Cárdenas, 'Economic Growth in Colombia: A Reversal of "Fortune"?' *Ensayos Sobre Política Económica*, 2007, ideas.repec.org/a/col/000107/004635.html.
10 Mauricio Rubio, 'Crimen y Crecimiento en Colombia', *Coyuntura Económica* 25(1), 1995: 101–28.
11 Riascos and Vargas, 'Violence and Growth in Colombia'.
12 Pablo Querubín Borrero, *Crecimiento departamental y violencia criminal en Colombia*, CEDE, 2003.
13 Catherine Rodríguez and Fabio Sánchez, 'Armed Conflict Exposure, Human Capital Investments, and Child Labor: Evidence from Colombia', *Defence and Peace Economics* 23(2), 2012: 161–84, doi:10.1080/10242694.2011.597239.
14 Adriana Camacho, 'Stress and Birth Weight: Evidence from Terrorist Attacks', *American Economic Review* 98(2), April 2008: 511–15, doi:10.1257/aer.98.2.511.

15 Juan F. Vargas, 'The Persistent Colombian Conflict: Subnational Analysis of the Duration of Violence', *Defence and Peace Economics* 23(2), 2012: 203–23, doi:10.1080/10242694.2011.597234.

16 Cárdenas, 'Economic Growth in Colombia'.

17 Ibid.

18 Lars Christian Moller, *Fiscal Policy in Colombia: Tapping its Potential for a More Equitable Society*, The World Bank, 1 June 2012, documents.worldbank.org/curated/en/2012/06/16383116/fiscal-policy-colombia-tapping-potential-more-equitable-society.

19 Ibid.

20 Ibid.

21 Meléndez and Perry, 'Industrial Policies in Colombia'.

22 Francisco Thoumi, 'The Impact of Organized Crime on Democratic Governance in Latin America: Organized Crime and Democratic Governance in Colombia', 2010.

23 Rex A. Hudson and Library of Congress, Federal Research Division, *Colombia: A Country Study*, Federal Research Division, Library of Congress, Washington, DC, 2010.

24 Ibid.

25 Ibid.

26 'Profiles: Colombia's Armed Groups', BBC, 28 August 2012, sec. Latin America & Caribbean, www.bbc.co.uk/news/world-latin-america-11400950.

27 Ibid.

28 'Colombia: Information on the Former Guerrilla Group M-19', US Citizenship and Information Services, 25 March 2003, www.uscis.gov/portal/site/uscis/menuitem.5af9bb95919f35e66f614176543f6d1a/?vgne xtoid=f67c361cfb98d010VgnVCM10000048f3d6a1RCRD&vgnextchannel=d2d1e89390b5d010Vgn VCM10000048f3d6a1RCRD.

29 'Ernesto Samper Pizano', *Encyclopædia Britannica*, 2013, www.britannica.com/EBchecked/topic/520653/Ernesto-Samper-Pizano.

30 Hudson and Library of Congress. Federal Research Division, *Colombia*.

31 'Profiles: Colombia's Armed Groups'.

32 Ibid.

33 Hudson and Library of Congress. Federal Research Division, *Colombia*.

34 Meléndez and Perry, 'Industrial Policies in Colombia'.

35 Vargas, 'The Persistent Colombian Conflict'.

36 Juan Carlos Echeverry, *Colombia and the War on Drugs, How Short is the Short Run?* Documentos CEDE (Universidad de los Andes-CEDE, 2004, ideas.repec.org/p/col/000089/002133.html.

37 Hudson and Library of Congress. Federal Research Division, *Colombia*.

38 Human Rights Watch, *Human Rights Watch World Report 2011*, 2011, www.hrw.org/sites/default/files/reports/wr2011.pdf.

39 Hudson and Library of Congress. Federal Research Division, *Colombia*.

40 'Colombia: Timoleon Jimenez FARC Rebels New Chief', *Huffington Post*, 15 November 2011, www.huffingtonpost.com/2011/11/15/colombia-timoleon-jimenez-farc-n_1095654.html.

41 'Profiles: Colombia's Armed Groups'.

42 Echeverry, *Colombia and the War on Drugs, How Short is the Short Run?*

43 'Colombian Labyrinth', product page, 2001, www.rand.org/pubs/monograph_reports/MR1339.html.

44 Ibid.

45 Jeremy McDermott, 'Drug Lords Develop High-yield Coca Plant', *The Telegraph*, 27 August 2004, www.telegraph.co.uk/news/worldnews/southamerica/colombia/1470339/Drug-lords-develop-high-yield-coca-plant.html.

46 Joshua D. Angrist and Adriana D. Kugler, 'Rural Windfall or a New Resource Curse? Coca, Income, and Civil Conflict in Colombia', *The Review of Economics and Statistics* 90(2), 2008: 191–215.

47 Tomás González and Ron Smith, *Drugs and Violence in Colombia: A VECM Analysis*, Birkbeck Working Papers in Economics & Finance, 9 June 2009, www.ems.bbk.ac.uk/research/wp/PDF/BWPEF0906.pdf.

48 Angrist and Kugler, 'Rural Windfall or a New Resource Curse?'

49 Vanda Felbab-Brown, *Shooting Up: Counterinsurgency and the War on Drugs*, Brookings Institution Press, Washington, DC 2010.

50 Philip Keefer and Norman Loayza, 'Drug Prohibition and Developing Countries: Uncertain Benefits, Certain Costs', in Philip Keefer and Norman Loayza (eds), *Innocent Bystanders: Developing Countries and the War on Drugs*, World Bank Publications, Washington, DC 2010.

51 Christopher P. Krebs, Michael Costelloe and David Jenks, 'Drug Control Policy and Smuggling Innovation: A Game-Theoretic Analysis', *Journal of Drug Issues* 33(1), 1 January 2003: 133–60, doi:10.1177/002204260303300107.

52 Gary S. Becker, Kevin M. Murphy and Michael Grossman, 'The Market for Illegal Goods: The Case of Drugs', *Journal of Political Economy* 114(1), 1 February 2006: 38–60.

53 Echeverry, *Colombia and the War on Drugs, How Short is the Short Run?*

54 Daniel Mejia and Pascual Restrepo, 'The War on Illegal Drug Production and Trafficking: An Economic Evaluation of Plan Colombia', SCID Working Paper 387, 19 May 2009, scid.stanford.edu/publicationsprofile/1959.

55 Keefer and Loayza, 'Drug Prohibition and Developing Countries'.

56 Ibid.

57 Manuel Osorio, 'Interview with Gabriel Garcia Marquez', *The UNESCO Courier*, October 1991.

58 Francisco E. Thoumi, 'The Rise of Two Drug Tigers: The Development of the Illegal Drugs Industry and Drug Policy Failure in Afghanistan and Colombia', in Frank Bovenkerk and Michael Levi (eds), *The Organized Crime Community*, Studies in Organized Crime 6, Springer, New York, 2007, 125–48, link.springer.com/chapter/10.1007/978-0-387-39020-8_8.

59 Osorio, 'Interview with Gabriel Garcia Marquez'.

60 Steven Ambrus, 'German Arciniegas: Guardian of Our Distinct History', The Free Library, 1 May 1997, www.thefreelibrary.com/German%20Arciniegas:%20guardian%20of%20our%20distinct%20history.-a 019396827.

61 Echeverry, *Colombia and the War on Drugs, How Short is the Short Run?*

62 'Colombia: Timoleon Jimenez FARC Rebels New Chief'.

63 'Colombian Peace Talks Resume in Havana', *Huffington Post*, 14 January 2013.

64 'Colombia Peace Talks Launched', *Huffington Post*, 18 October 2012, www.huffingtonpost.com/2012/10/18/colombia-peace-talks_n_1980078.html.

65 Mejia and Restrepo, 'The War on Illegal Drug Production and Trafficking'.

66 Yadira Ferrer, 'Colombia: Farmers Replace Coca Crops with Coffee', 21 December 2004, www.ipsnews.net/2004/12/colombia-farmers-replace-coca-crops-with-organic-coffee/.

67 Daniel Mejia and Carlos Esteban Posada, 'Cocaine Production and Trafficking: What Do We Know?' in Philip Keefer and Norman Loayza (eds), *Innocent Bystanders: Developing Countries and the War on Drugs*, World Bank Publications, Washington, DC, 2010.

68 Peter Reuter, 'Can Production and Trafficking of Illicit Drugs Be Reduced or Only Shifted?' in Philip Keefer and Norman Loayza (eds), *Innocent Bystanders: Developing Countries and the War on Drugs*, World Bank Publications, Washington, DC, 2010.

69 William Byrd, 'Responding to the Challenge of Afghanistan's Opium Economy: Development Lessons and Policy Implications', in Philip Keefer and Norman Loayza (eds), *Innocent Bystanders: Developing Countries and the War on Drugs*, World Bank Publications, Washington, DC, 2010.

70 Jacob Stringer, 'Coca Crop Replacement Will Be Part of Peace Process: Santos', *Colombia Reports*, 14 December 2012, colombiareports.com/colombia-news/peace-talks/27437-coca-crop-replacement-will-be-part-of-peace-process-santos.html.

Bibliography

Acemoglu, Daron and James Robinson (2012a) *How Walter Ochoa Guisao Became 'El Gurre'*, 28 March, www.whynationsfail.com.

——(2012b) *Nice Schools Nice Roads*, 28 March, whynationsfail.com.

——(2012c) *Who's Afraid of Development? The Colombian Version*, 26 March, whynationsfail.com/blog/2012/3/26/whos-afraid-of-development-the-colombian-version.html.

Ambrus, Steven (1997) 'German Arciniegas: Guardian of Our Distinct History', The Free Library, 1 May, www.thefreelibrary.com/German%20Arciniegas:%20guardian%20of%20our%20distinct%20history.-a019 396827.

Angrist, Joshua D. and Adriana D. Kugler (2008) 'Rural Windfall or a New Resource Curse? Coca, Income, and Civil Conflict in Colombia', *The Review of Economics and Statistics* 90(2): 191–215.

Becker, Gary S., Kevin M. Murphy and Michael Grossman (2006) 'The Market for Illegal Goods: The Case of Drugs', *Journal of Political Economy* 114(1), 1 February: 38–60.

Borrero, Pablo Querubín (2003) *Crecimiento departamental y violencia criminal en Colombia*, CEDE.

Byrd, William (2010) 'Responding to the Challenge of Afghanistan's Opium Economy: Development Lessons and Policy Implications', in Philip Keefer and Norman Loayza (eds), *Innocent Bystanders: Developing Countries and the War on Drugs*, World Bank Publications, Washington, DC.

Camacho, Adriana (2008) 'Stress and Birth Weight: Evidence from Terrorist Attacks', *American Economic Review* 98(2), April: 511–15, doi:10.1257/aer.98.2.511.

Camacho, Adriana and Catherine Rodriguez (2010) *Firm Exit and Armed Conflict in Colombia*, Working Paper, World Institute for Development Economic Research (UNU-WIDER), ideas.repec.org/p/unu/wpaper/wp2010-94.html.

Cárdenas, Mauricio (2007) 'Economic Growth in Colombia: A Reversal of "Fortune"?' *Ensayos Sobre Política Económica*, ideas.repec.org/a/col/000107/004635.html.

Echeverry, Juan Carlos (2004) *Colombia and the War on Drugs, How Short is the Short Run?* Documentos CEDE. Universidad de los Andes-CEDE, ideas.repec.org/p/col/000089/002133.html.

Felbab-Brown, Vanda (2010) *Shooting Up: Counterinsurgency and the War on Drugs*, Brookings Institution Press, Washington, DC.

Ferrer, Yadira (2004) 'Colombia: Farmers Replace Coca Crops with Coffee', 21 December, www.ipsnews.net/2004/12/colombia-farmers-replace-coca-crops-with-organic-coffee/.

González, Tomás and Ron Smith (2009) *Drugs and Violence in Colombia: A VECM Analysis*, Birkbeck Working Papers in Economics & Finance; 9 June, www.ems.bbk.ac.uk/research/wp/PDF/BWPEF0906.pdf.

Hudson, Rex A. and Library of Congress. Federal Research Division (2010) *Colombia: A Country Study*, Federal Research Division, Library of Congress, Washington, DC.

Kamrany, Nake and George Vassilev (2010) *The World Economy's Convergence of Per Capita Income*, University Readers, San Diego, CA.

Keefer, Philip and Norman Loayza (2010) 'Drug Prohibition and Developing Countries: Uncertain Benefits, Certain Costs', in Philip Keefer and Norman Loayza (eds), *Innocent Bystanders: Developing Countries and the War on Drugs*, World Bank Publications, Washington, DC.

Krebs, Christopher P., Michael Costelloe and David Jenks (2003) 'Drug Control Policy and Smuggling Innovation: A Game-Theoretic Analysis', *Journal of Drug Issues* 33(1), 1 January: 133–60, doi:10.1177/002204260303300107.

McDermott, Jeremy (2004) 'Drug Lords Develop High-yield Coca Plant', *The Telegraph*, 27 August, www.telegraph.co.uk/news/worldnews/southamerica/colombia/1470339/Drug-lords-develop-high-yield-coca-plant.html.

Mejia, Daniel and Carlos Esteban Posada (2010) 'Cocaine Production and Trafficking: What Do We Know?' in Philip Keefer and Norman Loayza (eds), *Innocent Bystanders: Developing Countries and the War on Drugs*, World Bank Publications, Washington, DC.

Mejia, Daniel and Pascual Restrepo (2009) 'The War on Illegal Drug Production and Trafficking: An Economic Evaluation of Plan Colombia', SCID Working Paper 387, 19 May, scid.stanford.edu/publications profile/1959.

Meléndez, Marcela and Guillermo E. Perry (2010) 'Industrial Policies in Colombia', IDB Working Paper No. 37, June, ssrn.com/abstract=1817239, or dx.doi.org/10.2139/ssrn.1817239.

Moller, Lars Christian (2012) *Fiscal Policy in Colombia: Tapping its Potential for a More Equitable Society*, The World Bank, 1 June, documents.worldbank.org/curated/en/2012/06/16383116/fiscal-policy-colombia-tapping-potential-more-equitable-society.

Osorio, Manuel (1991) 'Interview with Gabriel Garcia Marquez', *The UNESCO Courier*, October.

Perotti, Roberto (1996) Growth, Income Distribution, and Democracy: What the Data Say, *Journal of Economic Growth*, ideas.repec.org/a/kap/jecgro/v1y1996i2p149-87.html.

Reuter, Peter (2010) 'Can Production and Trafficking of Illicit Drugs Be Reduced or Only Shifted?' in Philip Keefer and Norman Loayza (eds), *Innocent Bystanders: Developing Countries and the War on Drugs*, World Bank Publications, Washington, DC.

Riascos, Alvaro J. and Juan F. Vargas (2011) 'Violence and Growth in Colombia: A Review of the Quantitative Literature', *Economics of Peace and Security Journal* 6(2): 15–20.

Rodríguez, Catherine and Fabio Sánchez (2012) 'Armed Conflict Exposure, Human Capital Investments, and Child Labor: Evidence from Colombia', *Defence and Peace Economics* 23(2): 161–84, doi:10.1080/10242694.2011.597239.

Rubio, Mauricio (1995) 'Crimen y Crecimiento en Colombia', *Coyuntura Económica* 25(1): 101–28.

Sherret, Laurel (2005) 'Futility in Action: Coca Fumigation in Colombia', *Journal of Drug Issues* 35(1), www2.criminology.fsu.edu/~jdi/35n1.htm.

Stringer, Jacob (2012) 'Coca Crop Replacement Will Be Part of Peace Process: Santos', *Colombia Reports*, 14 December, colombiareports.com/colombia-news/peace-talks/27437-coca-crop-replacement-will-be-part-of-peace-process-santos.html.

Thoumi, Francisco (2007) 'The Rise of Two Drug Tigers: The Development of the Illegal Drugs Industry and Drug Policy Failure in Afghanistan and Colombia', in Frank Bovenkerk and Michael Levi (eds), *The Organized Crime Community*, Studies in Organized Crime 6, Springer, New York, 125–48, link.springer.com/chapter/10.1007/978-0-387-39020-8_8.

——(2010) 'Competitive Advantages in the Production and Trafficking of Coc-Cocaine and Opium-Heroin in Afghanistan and the Andean Countries', in Philip Keefer and Norman Loayza (eds), *Innocent Bystanders: Developing Countries and the War on Drugs*, World Bank Publications, Washington, DC.

——(2010) 'The Impact of Organized Crime on Democratic Governance in Latin America: Organized Crime and Democratic Governance in Colombia'.

Vargas, Juan F. (2001) 'Colombian Labyrinth', product page, www.rand.org/pubs/monograph_reports/MR1339.html.

——(2003) 'Colombia: Information on the Former Guerrilla Group M-19', US Citizenship and Information Services, 25 March, www.uscis.gov/portal/site/uscis/menuitem.5af9bb95919f35e66f614176543f6d1a/?vgnextoid=f67c361cfb98d010VgnVCM10000048f3d6a1RCRD&vgnextchannel=d2d1e89390b5d010VgnVCM10000048f3d6a1RCRD.

——(2011) 'Colombia: Timoleon Jimenez FARC Rebels New Chief', *Huffington Post*, 15 November, www.huffingtonpost.com/2011/11/15/colombia-timoleon-jimenez-farc-n_1095654.html.

——(2011) *Human Rights Watch World Report 2011*, Human Rights Watch, www.hrw.org/sites/default/files/reports/wr2011.pdf.

——(2012) 'Profiles: Colombia's Armed Groups', BBC, 28 August, Latin America & Caribbean, www.bbc.co.uk/news/world-latin-america-11400950.

——(2012) 'The Persistent Colombian Conflict: Subnational Analysis of the Duration of Violence', *Defence and Peace Economics* 23(2): 203–23, doi:10.1080/10242694.2011.597234.

——(2012) 'CIA World Factbook: Colombia', 10 December, www.cia.gov/library/publications/the-world-factbook/geos/co.html.

——(2012) 'Colombia Peace Talks Launched', *Huffington Post*, 18 October, www.huffingtonpost.com/2012/10/18/colombia-peace-talks_n_1980078.html.

——(2013) 'Colombian Peace Talks Resume in Havana', 14 January, www.huffingtonpost.com/huff-wires/20130114/lt-colombia-peace-talks/?utm_hp_ref=style& ir = style.

——(2013) 'Ernesto Samper Pizano', *Encyclopædia Britannica*, www.britannica.com/EBchecked/topic/520653/Ernesto-Samper-Pizano.

——(n.d.) 'World Development Indicators', The World Bank, data.worldbank.org (accessed 3 December 2012).

——(n.d.) 'Worldwide Governance Indicators', World Bank, info.worldbank.org/governance/wgi/sc_country.asp (accessed 3 December 2012).

25

The Saudi Arabian model

Robert E. Looney

Introduction

Saudi Arabia is in many ways a paradox, its austere Wahhabist Islam contrasting sharply with the highly advanced corporate efficiency of its gigantic state-owned oil company, Saudi Aramco. A country of enormous wealth, it none the less has a youth unemployment rate unofficially approaching 30%.[1] While its government has spent billions to upgrade the educational system and improve the country's human capital, private employers still complain that the lack of a qualified Saudi workforce keeps them almost entirely dependent on foreign labour.

Saudi Arabia is encircled by Syria, Bahrain and Yemen—countries in the throes of civil unrest or even outright civil war. Yet, to the surprise of many observers, the Kingdom has remained largely immune to the tumult of the Arab Spring, to the point where an organized 'day of rage' became a non-event.[2] Even so, a siege mentality seems to be developing and perhaps with good reason.

In 2011 the country ranked in the top 10 on *The Economist*'s Shoe-Thrower's Index,[3] a weighted average of factors designed to predict the propensity for rebellion and regime change in Middle Eastern states. The factors include the share of the population under the age of 25, the number of years the government has been in power, corruption and lack of democracy, gross domestic product (GDP) per person, censorship and the absolute number of people younger than 25 years. It omits dissent, as being too hard to measure, and unemployment, for which there is a lack of comparable data across the region.

Not surprisingly, Yemen topped the list, followed by Libya, Egypt, Syria and Iran. Saudi Arabia came in seventh, between Mauritania and Algeria, and would no doubt have fared even worse had unemployment been factored in. Given its lack of democracy, widespread corruption, massive income disparity and small monarchical elite linked to a fundamentalist religious establishment, the Saudi Arabian model appears primed for instability and revolution.

The Saudi monarchy has thus far been able to survive by virtue of its resilience and adaptability. Traditionally, it has shown itself to be skilled at balancing competing domestic forces, as well as adopting a hard line when its survival is at stake. The regime also has two unique strengths: the legitimacy it derives from its historic alliance with the Wahhabi religious establishment and its vast oil wealth. Will these attributes be enough, however, to allow the royal family to meet the challenges that lie ahead in an increasingly unstable part of the world?

475

Saudi Arabia: an emerging economy?

Perhaps for some of the factors implied above, Saudi Arabia is not included in many of the lists of emerging economies: BRICS (Brazil, Russia, India, People's Republic of China, South Africa), the Next 11, or N-11[4] (Turkey, Nigeria, Iran, Egypt, Mexico, Viet Nam, Republic of Korea (South Korea), Philippines, Pakistan, Indonesia and Bangladesh), MIST[5] (Mexico, Indonesia, South Korea and Turkey), and the CIVETS[6] (Colombia, Indonesia, Viet Nam, Egypt, Turkey and South Africa). The country is included in this volume for the simple reason that the Kingdom is the single largest economy in the Middle East and North Africa, and because it possesses an estimated 16.1% of the world's proven oil reserves. As long as regional and domestic stability prevail, Saudi Arabia will remain a key player in the region and around the world.

Whether the country should be included in the group of success stories is more open to debate. Looking at long-term trends in per capita income different pictures emerge, depending on how one measures GDP. Using the International Monetary Fund's (IMF) measure[7] of per capita GDP based on purchasing power parity (PPP) in current international dollars, the Kingdom's progress, with the notable exception of Singapore, has been more or less in line with that of other 'success stories', with per capita income increasing more or less in line with those of South Korea and Israel and more rapidly than Chile, especially after 2000 (see Figure 25.1). By

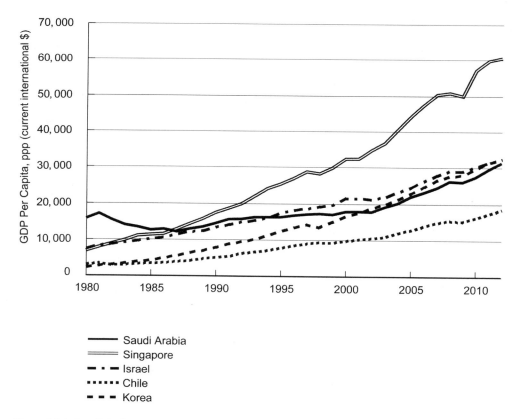

Figure 25.1 Saudi Arabia and the "Success Stories" current prices (ppp, current international $s)
Source: data IMF, WEO Database; May 2013

The Saudi Arabian model

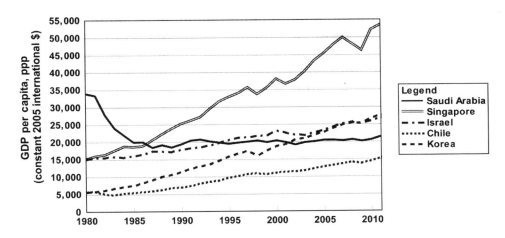

Figure 25.2 Saudi Arabia and the "Success Stories" constant prices (ppp constant 2005 international $s)
Source: data IMF, WEO Database; May 2013

this income measure, the Kingdom's per capita income nearly doubled between 1980 and 2011, increasing from US$15,659 to $29,400.

A very different picture emerges using the World Bank's measure[8] of GDP per capita PPP in constant 2005 international dollars. By this measure, Saudi Arabia had a wide lead over the other success stories in 1980. However, following the drop in oil prices in the early 1980s, combined with relatively high rates of population growth, the Kingdom's per capita income has stagnated at around $20,000 since the early 1990s (see Figure 25.2).

Because the World Bank's measure uses constant dollars it is probably more reflective of the extent of the Saudi economy's progress over the years. However, for anyone who visited the Kingdom in 1980 and again in 2013, the extent of progress would be readily apparent. Still, one can't help but wonder what would happen in the event of a prolonged slump in oil markets. Would its progress be easily reversed? Or has the country laid a solid enough foundation to sustain respectable rates of economic growth and rising standards of living in a manner similar to other emerging economies?

Patterns of growth

As a major oil-producing country, Saudi Arabia's growth mechanisms[9] differ somewhat from those found in the other emerging economies discussed in this volume. Further complicating the discussion is the fact that these mechanisms have changed over the years as the country develops more sophisticated institutions and a more viable non-oil sector.

Over the years, Saudi Arabian economic growth has been driven by developments in international oil markets. The rapid run-up in oil prices in 1973/74 resulted in growth rates reaching 10% per year in the late 1970s. However, the Kingdom's rate of expansion in GDP fell off rapidly and was negative for a few years with the fall in oil prices in the early 1980s.

As oil prices recovered and Saudi oil production levels increased in the second half of the 1980s GDP growth and stability were restored. Since then, oil production has been more stable. In turn, oil sector stability has been reflected in greater economic stability, with decade-average real GDP growth, despite year-to-year volatility with oil price fluctuations, averaging around 3.13% a year during the 1990s and 2000s. While the country is still vulnerable to external

Robert E. Looney

Table 25.1 Saudi Arabia: vulnerabilities

	Vulnerability to EZ slowdown	Vulnerability to China slowdown	Vulnerability to food shock	Ability to absorb capital	Stimulus ability
Saudi Arabia	8.1	4.7	7.4	7.6	8.0
UAE	9.7	5.3	8.6	8.2	8.9
Qatar	8.7	4.7	n/a	7.6	8.9
Bahrain	8.8	6.3	n/a	6.7	7.5
Kuwait	9.5	4.5	n/a	7.0	8.4
Oman	10.0	0.0	n/a	7.4	8.9
Algeria	2.2	4.4	5.0	4.8	6.6
Libya	0.0	2.9	5.1	6.5	6.0
Iraq	6.6	n/a	n/a	4.1	4.0
Iran	8.9	4.8	5.4	5.0	6.3
Egypt	6.8	7.1	5.2	5.1	3.8
Tunisia	0.0	9.4	6.0	6.9	4.4
Morocco	2.7	9.5	5.6	4.9	4.7
Lebanon	9.3	7.0	7.0	2.8	4.2
Jordan	9.4	10.0	6.8	4.7	3.9
MENA average	7.1	4.9	5.5	5.6	5.9

Source: Roubini Country Risk, RGE, December 2012 Scores
Note: Countries are scored on a scale of 0–10, with 10 being the strongest. Ability to absorb capital based on an average weighing of macroeconomic instiutional qualities and medium-term growth potential.

Table 25.2 Saudi Arabia: volatility and correlation of oil revenue, spending and non-oil growth, 1980–2010

	Oil revenue growth and volatility (std)	Spending growth volatility (std)	Correlation between oil revenue and spending	Non-oil growth volatility (std)
1980s	44.1	19.8	0.9	4.6
1990s	21.1	16.2	0.7	1.6
2000s	38.5	6.4	0.2	0.7

Source: International Monetary Fund, *IMF Country Report*, No. 12/271, Saudi Arabia 2012 Article IV Consultation, September 2010, 15

developments, its strategy of diversifying the export market and developing a wide spectrum of energy-based exports has created a higher degree of stability than found in other oil exporters (see Table 25.1).

The country's evolution to a more sophisticated economy is readily apparent in the weakening link between fiscal spending and oil revenues (see Table 25.2). As a result, fiscal spending volatility has fallen over the past decade, and the correlation between spending and oil revenue growth has declined.[10]

The Kingdom's emerging non-oil sector has been gradually ramping up its rate of growth from an average of 2.7% a year in the 1990s to 4.3% during 2000–11. As a result, the oil sector's share of total real GDP has declined from almost 40% in 1991 to less than 30% in 2011 (see Table 25.3). Despite high oil prices and production rates over the last several years, the contribution of the non-oil sector to the country's GDP has outpaced that of the oil sector (see Table 25.4).

However, these patterns should not be interpreted as a sign of a declining influence of the oil sector on the economy. It is open to debate just how much the non-oil sector would be able to

The Saudi Arabian model

Table 25.3 Saudi Arabia: output and employment by sector

	Oil sector	Non-oil manufacturing	Construction	Non-governmental services	Other non-oil	Total non-oil economy	Total economy
GDP (Saudi rial billion, constant 1999 prices)							
1989	131	24	32	129	124	308	439
1999	191	45	39	157	162	403	594
2009	219	83	58	257	210	608	827
Share in total GDP							
1989	29.8	5.5	7.3	29.4	28.2	70.2	100.0
1999	32.2	7.6	6.6	26.4	27.3	67.8	100.0
2009	26.5	10.0	7.0	31.1	25.4	73.5	100.0
Employent ('000s)							
1989	54	415	800	2,714	1,071	5,000	5,054
1999	97	484	653	3,503	1,433	6,073	6,170
2009	91	505	965	4,937	1,650	8,057	8,148
Share in total employment							
1989	1.1	8.2	15.8	53.7	21.2	98.9	100.0
1999	1.6	7.8	10.6	56.8	23.2	98.4	100.0
2009	1.1	6.2	11.8	60.6	20.3	98.9	100.0
GDP per employee (Saudi rial '000s, constant 1999 prices)							
1989	2,417	57	40	48.0	115.0	62.0	87.0
1999	1,962	92	60	45.0	113.0	66.0	96.0
2009	2,403	165	60	52.0	127.0	76.0	102.0
Average annual increase in labour productivity (%)							
1990s	−1.6	5.1	4.6	−0.5	−0.2	0.8	1.2
2000s	2.6	6.3	0.3	1.6	1.3	1.3	0.6

Source: International Monetary Fund, *Saudi Arabia: Selected Issues*, September 2012, 16

Table 25.4 Saudi Arabia: contributions to overall GDP growth, 2008–11

Year	Contributions to growth		
	Oil	Non-oil manufacturing, construction and retail	Other non-oil sectors
2008	1.2	1.3	1.7
2009	−2.3	0.5	1.9
2010	0.6	2.0	2.5
2011	1.2	3.0	2.9

Source: International Monetary Fund, *IMF Country Report*, No. 12/271, Saudi Arabia: 2012 Article IV Consultation, September 2012, 6

grow on its own without a steady infusion of oil-based government consumption expenditure. In this regard, the pattern of government consumption differs markedly from that found in non-oil economies (see Figure 25.3) in that it has averaged around 40% of total consumption since the mid-1970s. In contrast, comparable figures have been 23% for high-income countries and 15% for lower-middle-income economies, with upper-middle-income countries gradually increasing their share to rates found in the high-income economies. Through expanded public

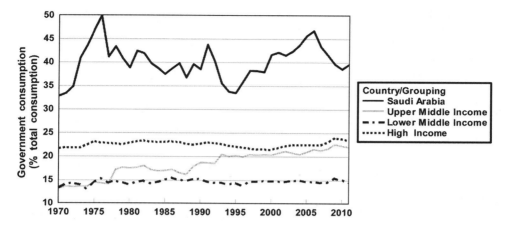

Figure 25.3 Government consumption (% total consumption)
Source: World Bank, World Development Indicators database

sector employment, and wage increases, the Kingdom uses government consumption to maintain a buoyant domestic market. Without this key source of demand, many local firms would not be viable.[11]

Sources of growth

In an effort to gain a deeper understanding of the factors driving Saudi Arabia's economic growth, several attempts have been undertaken to estimate the relative contribution of capital, labour and total factor productivity (TFP) to the Kingdom's observed rates of GDP growth. These efforts apply the neo-classical growth model originally developed by Robert Solow[12] in the late 1950s.

Solow's model applied to the advanced industrial countries often finds that capital contributes about 20% to the observed rate of growth, labour 30%, with the remaining 50% attributed to non-factor inputs such as technological change and increased efficiency. In contrast, many developing countries often find a much greater role for direct factor inputs, with TFP often zero or even negative. For example, Bruton[13] found TFP declining, and even turning negative, during much of Latin America's phase of import substitution.

In a similar fashion, Baier *et al.*[14] found TFP per worker in Saudi Arabia has been negative during the last several decades. Similar findings were obtained by Bisat *et al.*,[15] the IMF,[16] Keller and Nabli,[17] and Sala-i-Martin and Artadi.[18]

On the other hand, similar studies applied to the Kingdom's non-oil sector have produced a notably different pattern. For example, Bisat *et al.*'s estimates suggest that TFP growth was strongly positive during 1975–84, only to turn negative in the years 1986–95. Similarly al-Khatib[19] estimated TFP growth in the non-oil economy to have been positive for most of the 1970s, mainly negative in the 1980s and 1990s, and then positive again during 2000–07, with a near-zero average annual growth rate over the whole period.

Finally, the IMF's[20] estimates suggest that overall GDP for Saudi Arabia has in the past two decades been mainly the result of increased labour and capital inputs. Specifically, of the 3.2% average annual rate of real GDP growth during 1990–2009, 1.5 percentage points can be attributed to the accumulation of physical capital. Another 1.5 percentage points can be attributed to increasing human capital, most of it from growing employment and a smaller part from the change in composition towards higher education levels. As a result, the Fund found overall TFP growth to have been only marginally positive. On an annual basis, however, the results show considerable variation, with large positive TFP growth in some years. However, for most years since 1990, TFP growth was found to have been negative. The Fund also found that TFP in the non-oil sector has on average been somewhat higher (0.5% per year) than for the economy as a whole.

Summing up its findings, the IMF noted that:

> In both the economy as a whole and the non-oil sector, over the past two decades the pace of factor accumulation has generally been increasing and TFP growth falling. Reflecting the surge in investment, physical capital's contribution to both overall and non-oil GDP growth more than doubled from the 1990s to the 2000s. The contribution from human capital also increased, mainly as a result of raw employment numbers. For the economy as a whole, the increase in factor accumulation coincided with almost flat GDP growth, leading to a considerable reduction in TFP. For the non-oil economy, however, GDP growth also accelerated, leaving only a slight decline in TFP growth.[21]

The very low and often negative year-to-year values for TFP suggest that possibly a number of factors may be preventing the Kingdom's resources from fulfilling their potential. In effect, the country has relied on a fairly inefficient model of growth built around applying massive amounts of capital and labour to increase output rather than attempting to get more out of the existing resource base. A similar pattern developed in the old USSR and the former communist countries of Central and Eastern Europe. There the result in nearly all cases was zero TFP and a long-term secular decline in the rate of growth as demographics slowed and the investment rate reached maximum sustainable levels.[22]

In Saudi Arabia's case, it is very unlikely that surges in increased numbers of labourers (see Figure 25.4), due to internal demographics and increased restrictions on the use of expatriate labour, will occur in the future. In addition, as discussed in a final section below, it is also doubtful that the Saudi government will have as many resources at its disposal for capital formation as in the past. To sustain acceptable rates of growth the Kingdom will have to shift its growth model in a way that facilitates increased total factor productivity.

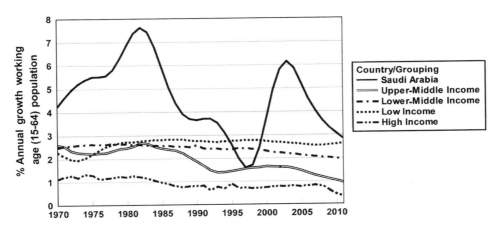

Figure 25.4 % Annual growth working age (15–64) population

Despite its current vast wealth, the Kingdom is likely to find that without unleashing TFP, its chances of joining the emerging economy club are problematic. There are a number of possible explanations for the Kingdom's low rates of productivity, each with implications for achieving a more effective use of resources. These are explored in the following sections.

Possible impediments to sustained growth

Saudi Arabia's oil wealth and production capabilities place it in a unique position. As many countries have discovered, however, the mere possession of natural resources does not guarantee economic prosperity and sustained rates of high economic growth. In fact, over the years there has been an ongoing debate over the possible presence (or absence) of an oil curse that impedes and/or distorts growth and development of oil-exporting countries. Stimulated by scholars such as Richard Auty[23] (who coined the term 'resource curse'), Terri Lind Karl,[24] Jeffrey Sachs and Andrew Warner,[25] and Michael Ross,[26] the debate has spawned a long list of studies, both empirical and descriptive, that purport to show the corrosive economic effects that stem from the production and export of oil.

The oil curse

At least four main channels have been identified through which the oil curse can harm an economy, and in doing so contribute either directly or indirectly to the reduction in TFP.

- pro-cyclical fiscal and monetary policies;
- crowding out of manufacturing;
- high volatility of commodity prices; and
- deterioration of governance and supporting institutions.

All or combinations of these factors can lead to a spectrum of undesirable outcomes:

- unsustainable growth—bubble economy;
- wasteful public investment programmes;
- an over-expansion of the public sector;
- destruction of the agricultural sector;
- lack of competitiveness outside the oil sector;
- underdevelopment of the private sector; and
- high levels of chronic unemployment.

These effects are far from uniform, with some countries experiencing few if any negative effects, while others have been plagued with all or most of the negative effects over long periods of time.

The literature on foreign aid provides a possible insight as to these differential impacts. The World Bank,[27] along with many researchers,[28] has found that countries with good levels of governance and sound institutions are able to obtain a number of positive benefits from economic aid such as increased economic growth and poverty reduction. On the other hand, countries that have made little or no progress on improved governance experience few aid-related benefits. Even worse, there are a number of documented[29] cases where aid produced negative outcomes similar to those often associated with the oil curse.

While the oil curse literature is instructive, there has been a tendency for many researchers to over-generalize the occurrence of the phenomenon. Clearly, since all oil-exporting countries are not alike, one would expect a variety of outcomes and effects associated with oil. As a starting point in our analysis of Saudi Arabia, the Legatum Prosperity Index[30] was used in an exploratory manner to identify clusters of countries that might possess environments similar enough for oil to produce roughly equivalent results, either positive or negative.

The Legatum Prosperity Index comprises measures that depict: (a) the economy; (b) entrepreneurship and opportunity; (c) governance; (d) education; (e) health; (f) safety and security; (g) personal freedom; and (h) social capital.

Two of these dimensions, the economy (five-year growth rate (2010), confidence in financial institutions (% yes), and satisfaction with living standards (% yes)), and governance (confidence in the government (% yes), confidence in the judiciary (% yes), and government effectiveness as measured by the World Bank), separate the oil countries into three separate environments (see Figure 25.5), dubbed here as: (a) classic oil curse countries, with both poor governance and economic underperformance; (b) partial oil curse countries, with poor governance but moderately good economic performance; and (c) oil blessing countries, with good levels of governance as well as strong economic performance.

The diagonal line in Figure 25.5 depicts a one-to-one relationship between governance and economic performance.[31] While the oil curse countries conform roughly to this pattern, both the partial oil curse countries and oil blessing countries lie above the line. This pattern suggests that the economies of both groups are over-performing. Specifically, given the levels of governance in

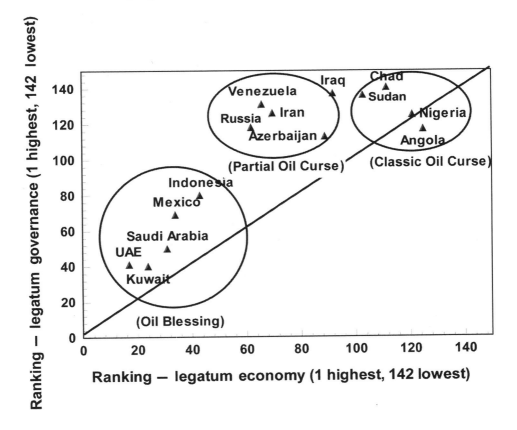

Figure 25.5 Oil curse mapping

both groups, one might expect economic performance to be somewhat less than the levels both groups are currently experiencing. As the oil curse and partial oil curse countries have roughly the same levels of governance, the somewhat better performance of the partial oil countries must be due in part to their progress in other areas and/or simply larger volumes of oil production and export. Similarly, the oil blessing group, which includes Saudi Arabia, can attribute its better economic performance to improved governance and possibly these other factors.

Since oil prices and revenues have been quite buoyant in recent years, one might expect, given their relative distance above the diagonal, the partial oil curse countries to experience a fairly sharp economic contraction during a prolonged slump in oil markets. Owing to their superior governance levels and relative closeness to the diagonal, Saudi Arabia and the other oil blessing countries appear better situated to withstand a negative oil shock (see also Figure 25.1). Still, the threat of a drop in oil revenues no doubt explains why Saudi Arabia and the other oil blessing countries maintain fairly high levels of foreign exchange reserves.

In sum, while not addressing the issue of productivity or TFP directly, Figure 25.5 suggests that the partial oil curse countries and the oil blessing group's economies are not sustainable—it is doubtful that their productive resources could not support their recent levels of economic performance in the absence of improved governance.

Limited progress in improved governance

Owing to the central role of governance in supporting longer-term growth in Saudi Arabia and the other oil-exporting countries,[32] a closer examination of its key components and their respective trends is warranted. What progress has been made to date? Has there been improvement with time? Are levels of governance approaching that commonly found in the more successful emerging economies?

The World Bank's Governance data set[33] provides estimates of the six key dimensions of governance: (a) voice and accountability; (b) political stability, absence of violence; (c) government effectiveness; (d) regulatory quality; (e) rule of law; and (f) control of corruption, for the years 1996–2011. The data present a mixed picture for Saudi Arabia: progress in some areas, with serious deficiencies in others.

Voice and accountability

In the case of voice and accountability (see Figure 25.6), the oil blessing countries averaged roughly in the 30th percentile. This is not a high figure by international standards, but is consistent with the observed pattern[34] of higher levels of authoritarianism in oil-producing countries.

After a period (1996–2001) of improvement in this critical governance dimension, the oil curse countries have remained in roughly the 15th percentile. Of interest, the partial oil curse countries while initially (1996) on par with the oil blessing countries, have experienced such a continuous drop in voice and accountability as to nearly converge with the oil curse countries.

In this area of governance, Saudi Arabia has not followed the typical pattern found in oil blessed countries. In fact, the Kingdom has scored consistently below the oil curse countries with the gap between the two widening over time.

These patterns are not necessarily reflective of increasing authoritarianism in Saudi Arabia. In reality, Saudi Arabia is a monarchy overseen by the Al Sa'ud family, and specifically the direct descendants of King Abd al-Aziz, the Kingdom's founder. The Basic Law, which was passed by King Fahd in 1992, served to codify the government's relationship with, and responsibilities towards, its citizens.[35] Still, the harsh reality remains that the Kingdom scores 163 out of 167

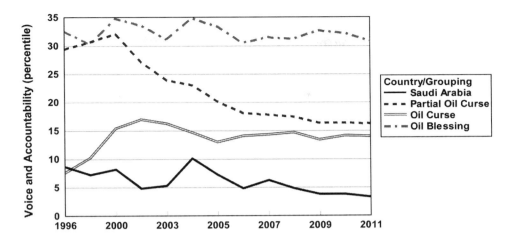

Figure 25.6 Voice and accountability (percentile)
Source: World Bank, Worldwide Governance Indicators, 1996–2011

countries on the Economist Intelligence Unit's 2012 Democracy Index,[36] receiving a score of zero for electoral process and pluralism.

Political stability, absence of violence

The three-country grouping again follows the pattern of declining governance as we proceed from the oil blessing countries to partial oil curse countries and finally the oil curse countries (see Figure 25.7). Each group of countries has experienced a slight improvement in governance starting around 2004. On the other hand, Saudi Arabia, after having slightly better attainment in this area than the oil blessing countries, has experienced a deterioration beginning around 2000.

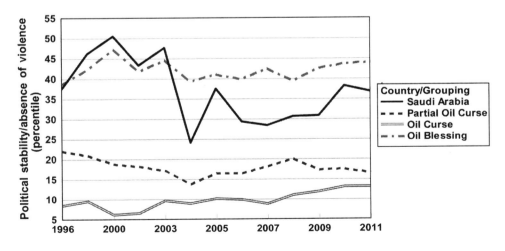

Figure 25.7 Political stability/absence of violence (percentile)
Source: World Bank, Worldwide Governance Indicators, 1996–2011

By 2011 the Kingdom had fallen from the 50th percentile in 2000 to the 37th percentile. At that time, the oil blessing countries were averaging around the 44th percentile.

Government effectiveness

This key dimension of governance reflects perceptions of the quality of public services and the degree of its independence from political pressures, the quality of policy formulation and implementation, and the credibility of the government's commitment to such policies. The country grouping pattern again has the predicted levels of relative governance attainment (see Figure 25.8). In contrast to the first two dimensions of governance, the oil blessing countries are in a relatively high percentile (60th).

There has been fairly good improvement in the partial oil curse countries, with these countries reaching the 30th percentile in around 2009. Unfortunately, the oil curse countries, after starting in the 19th percentile, experienced a fairly consistent drop in government effectiveness, winding up in the 10th percentile in 2011.

Again, Saudi Arabia's progress has been somewhat below that found in the oil blessing countries. While the Kingdom achieved a fairly sharp improvement up to the 50th percentile in 2005, a sharp decline set in, causing the country's ranking to fall to the 41st percentile by 2011.

Regulatory quality

This governance dimension, reflecting perceptions of the ability of the government to formulate and implement sound policies and regulations that permit and promote private sector development, is critical for assuring the Kingdom's sustained growth. In this area, Saudi Arabia has performed (see Figure 25.9) more or less in line with the other oil blessing countries. Initially (1996), the Kingdom (41st percentile) lagged the oil blessing countries (60th percentile) by 13 percentiles. However, by 2003 the gap had closed. Saudi Arabia, along with the other oil blessing countries, ended the period with a fairly respectable ranking in the 53rd percentile.

Still there is considerable room for improvement—a lot that needs to be done. Overall progress in easing constraints on business formation and operation often lags considerably behind

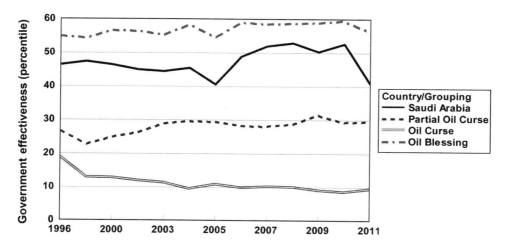

Figure 25.8 Government effectiveness (percentile)
Source: World Bank, *Worldwide Governance Indicators*, 1996–2011

The Saudi Arabian model

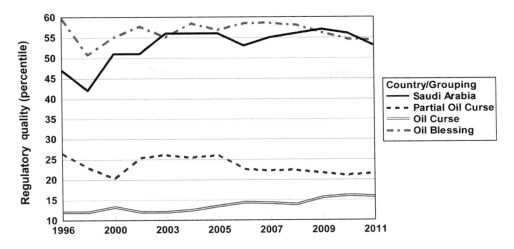

Figure 25.9 Regulatory quantity (percentile)
Source: World Bank, *Worldwide Governance Indicators*, 1996–2011

improvements in many of the other emerging economies. A new employment quota system that enforces 'Saudization'[37] has come into effect. There is no mandated minimum wage. The government influences prices extensively through subsidies and state-owned enterprises.[38]

Unfortunately, the large gap between the oil blessing countries and the oil curse/partial oil curse countries has not lessened with time. The oil curse countries ended the period in the 16th percentile, and the partial oil curse countries in the 22nd percentile.

Rule of law

Again, on this important governance dimension a fairly significant gap exists between the oil blessing and oil curse countries. The oil blessing countries have maintained (see Figure 25.10) a fairly steady position around the 50th percentile, while the oil curse countries have not been able to improve past the 10th percentile. Similarly, little progress has taken place in the partial oil curse countries, with their ranking falling from slightly over the 20th percentile in the late 1990s/early 2000s to the 18th percentile after 2007.

In contrast to the previous governance dimensions, Saudi Arabia has scored somewhat above the oil blessing countries. From 2000 the Kingdom's ranking improved from the 50th percentile to the 60th by 2011, only to fall off slightly in 2011.

Despite the country's efforts at improving the rule of law, organizations such as the Heritage Foundation caution[39] that the 'Saudi courts do not always enforce contracts efficiently. The judicial system is slow, non-transparent, and vulnerable to interference from the ruling elite. Laws protecting and facilitating the acquisition and disposition of private property are subject to Islamic practices. Enforcement of laws protecting intellectual property rights has been weak'. Government decision making lacks transparency and corruption remains a concern.

Control of corruption

Traditionally, the oil countries have been plagued with corruption. The opportunities for rent seeking, project kickbacks and patronage are all too numerous and tempting to government

Robert E. Looney

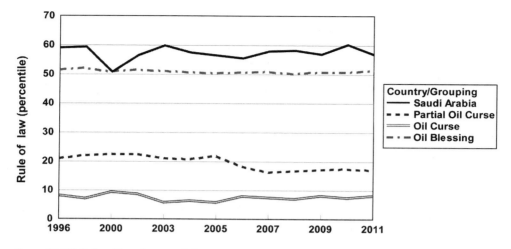

Figure 25.10 Rule of law (percentile)
Source: World Bank, *Worldwide Governance Indicators*, 1996–2011

officials. As with the other dimensions of governance, over-generalization in this area should be cautioned against. Again, the three clusters of oil-exporting countries exhibit somewhat different patterns and levels of governance attainment.

The oil blessing countries have achieved (see Figure 25.11) fairly decent levels of control over corruption, rising from the 43rd percentile in 1998 to nearly the 60th percentile in 2008, only to fall back to 53rd by 2011. Saudi Arabia follows a somewhat similar pattern, rising from the 46th percentile in 2004 to the 63rd by 2011. Still, corruption remains a concern, especially with regard to the Kingdom's attempts to increase foreign investment. In February 2007, in a serious effort to combat corruption, the country's Council of Ministers approved a National Strategy for Maintaining Integrity and Combating Corruption. Unfortunately, the country had fallen back to the 48th percentile in 2011. Clearly, it will take a concerted, ongoing effort to wring

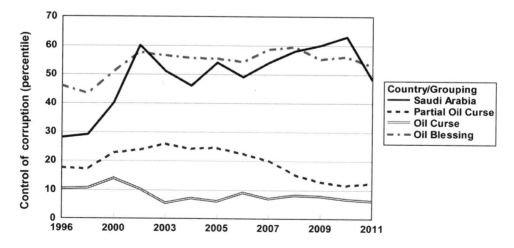

Figure 25.11 Control of corruption (percentile)
Source: World Bank, *Worldwide Governance Indicators*, 1996–2011

corruption out of Saudi society. As events have demonstrated, gains made in combating corruption can be lost quickly if the country is not constantly vigilant.

As with the other dimensions of governance, the oil curse and partial oil curse countries lag considerably behind the progress made by the oil blessing countries. In both cases these countries had lower percentile rankings in 2011 than at the start of the period (1996). Corruption levels in the partial oil curse countries appear to have stabilized at around the 12th percentile, while progress in the oil curse countries has not been able to rise above the 6th percentile in recent years.

Composite governance

Aggregating the six dimensions of governance provides a useful summary (see Figure 25.12) of progress made in each of the three clusters. The oil blessing countries appear to have stabilized at around the 50th percentile, with little progress made after 2002. During several periods (1996–2003 and 2004–10) Saudi Arabia appeared to be closing the gap with other oil blessing countries, but each time was unable to sustain the momentum.

The partial oil curse countries have had a gradual slippage in governance attainment over the years, with total governance declining from the 24th percentile in 1996 to the 19th in 2011. Finally, the oil curse countries have made little or no progress over time. Instead, these countries have stabilized at around the 11th percentile.

The observed patterns reported above raise some important questions for Saudi Arabia and the other oil-exporting countries. With the exception of government effectiveness, regulatory quality and control of corruption, Saudi Arabia has not made significant progress in the area of governance. In addition, the country lags behind other oil blessing countries in several key areas including voice and accountability, government effectiveness, and political stability and absence of violence.

Also instructive is a comparison of Saudi Arabia's pattern of governance with that of the other 'success stories' contained in the present volume—Chile, Israel, Singapore and South Korea. Looking at just the aggregate of the World Bank's six measures of governance, the contrast (see Figure 25.13) is stark. As noted earlier, Saudi Arabia's composite measure of

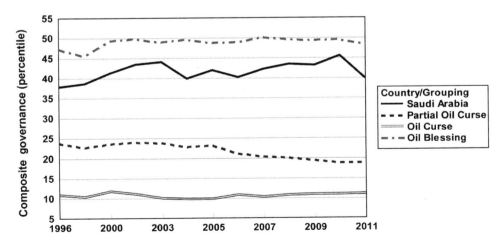

Figure 25.12 Composite governance (percentile)
Source: World Bank, *Worldwide Governance Indicators*, 1996–2011

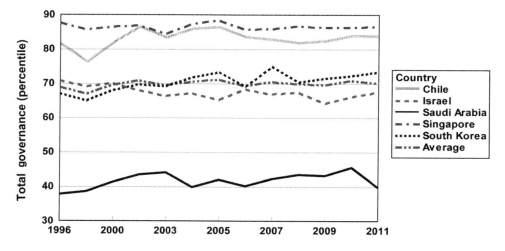

Figure 25.13 Total governance (percentile)
Source: World Bank, *Worldwide Governance Indicators*, 1996–2011

governance averages in the low 40th percentile. In contrast, Singapore and Chile average in the mid- to high 80th percentile, while Israel and South Korea have remained close to the 70th percentile. Clearly, it is problematic whether Saudi Arabia can truly join this group of countries without more effort put into the reform process—there is only so much that massive inflows of oil revenues and government expenditures can accomplish without being severely constrained by the country's current governance barrier.

To what extent will the country's governance deficiencies inhibit future growth and development? Or, as long as oil revenues are buoyant, can the government, by stepping up expenditure, sustain growth without establishing a firm governance/institutional framework? Put simply, can the country overachieve economically indefinitely?

Economic reforms

Part of the answer to these questions may lie in the Kingdom's efforts at economic reform and the government's effort to create an atmosphere of greater economic freedom. The Heritage House index of economic freedom suggests that the country has made relatively more progress in this area. The Kingdom's overall economic freedom score (see Figure 25.14) is roughly similar to the average of the oil blessing countries, and considerably above that of the oil curse and partial oil curse groupings.

In the critical economic freedom sub-component, trade freedom, the Kingdom has made steady progress (see Figure 25.15), especially starting around 2005. As a result, the country's trade freedom score surpassed that of the oil blessing countries for several years before converging to their average in 2012.

However, the picture is much less favourable when comparisons are made with the 'success story' countries (see Figure 25.16). While Saudi Arabia scores above the world average, its score converged towards that average (1996–2004) for a number of years. After improving with respect to the world average in 2007–11, the Kingdom's score has converged towards that average during the last several years. For a number of years the Kingdom's overall economic freedom score mirrored that of Israel. Starting in 2005, however, Israel has opened up a considerable gap over the

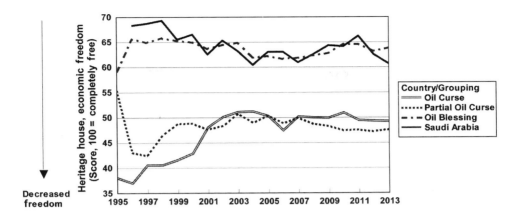

Figure 25.14 Heritage house, economic freedom score: oil countries

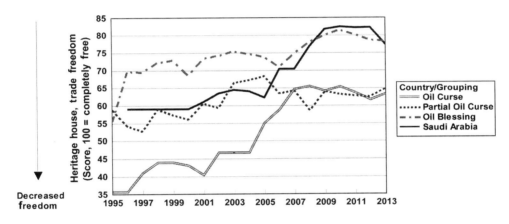

Figure 25.15 Heritage house trade freedom score: oil countries

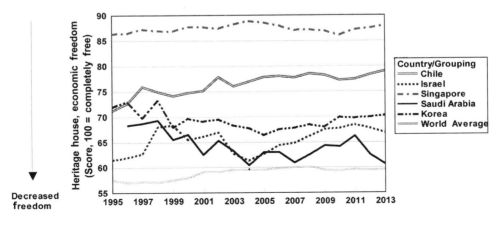

Figure 25.16 Heritage house, economic freedom score: "success countries"

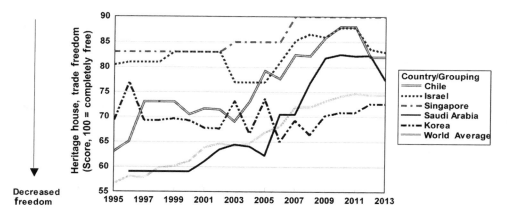

Figure 25.17 Heritage house, trade freedom score: "success stories"

Kingdom. A similar, but even less favourable pattern existed with South Korea. However, in recent years South Korea has managed to open up a considerable lead over the Kingdom.

As in the case of the oil country comparisons, Saudi's progress in trade freedom has been its strong suit (see Figure 25.17). The Kingdom's progress since 2005 has propelled it well past the world average and that of South Korea. Currently, the Kingdom has attained trade freedom scores comparable to those found in Chile and Israel, although considerably below Singapore.

In sum, the Kingdom has a considerable way to go before reaching levels of overall governance commensurate with that found in the oil blessing countries. Even greater gaps exist with respect to the group of success story countries. While many of the success story economies appear to have achieved sufficient reform momentum to sustain improvements over time, Saudi Arabia's reform efforts in both governance and economic freedom have been characterized more by starts, stops and frequent reversals.

A large body of oil curse literature[40] suggest that enthusiasm and commitment to reforms in oil exporters is counter-cyclical to that of oil revenues: a fall in oil revenues creates the imperative for increased efficiency and productivity associated with improved governance and economic freedom. On the other hand, oil booms provide the sense of illusion that reforms can be postponed or delayed without any adverse effects on the economy.[41] There is little doubt that in recent years the oil boom has been a factor in the reversal of several governance and economic freedom indicators.[42] This will create a major problem in the future for the government as vested interests have a larger and larger stake in the status quo.

Patterns of competitiveness

In a manner similar to reforms in governance and economic freedom, the Kingdom has a mixed record in improving the economy's competitiveness. On the positive side, the country has risen to 18th place (out of 144 countries) in the World Economic Forum's Global Competitiveness Rankings[43] (see Table 25.5). This is up from 21st place in 2010–11. The Kingdom also ranked highly in the three broad components of the WEF's Competitiveness Index: basic requirements (13th); efficiency enhancers (26th); and innovation and sophistication factors (29th).

While these aggregates paint a fairly rosy picture, many of the sub-components reveal a mixed picture of remarkable gains in some areas mixed with very below-par progress in others

The Saudi Arabian model

Table 25.5 Saudi Arabia: Global Competitiveness Index rankings, 2012–13

	Rank (out of 144)	Score (1–7)
GCI 2012–13	18	5.2
GCI 2011–12 (out of 142)	17	5.2
GCI 2010–11 (out of 139)	21	4.9
Basic requirements (43.4%)	13	5.7
Institutions	15	5.3
Infrastructure	26	5.2
Macroeconomic environment	6	6.5
Health and primary education	58	5.8
Efficiency enhancers (47.5%)	26	4.8
Higher education and training	40	4.8
Goods market efficiency	14	5.1
Labour market efficiency	59	4.5
Financial market development	22	4.9
Technological readiness	35	4.9
Market size	24	4.9
Innovation and sophistication factors (9.2%)	29	4.5
Business sophistication	25	4.9
Innovation	29	4.0

Source: World Economic Forum, *The Global Competitiveness Report 2012–13*, Geneva, 2012, 308
Note: % refers to the percentage contribution to the overall GCI of each sub-index. The weights reflect Saudi Arabia's transition from stage 1 to stage2.

(see Table 25.6). Some of the areas in which the Kingdom ranks extremely highly are: government services for improved business performance (5th); business costs of organized crime and violence (4th); number of procedures to start a business (8th); FDI and technology transfer (8th); and local supplier quality (6th).

This stellar performance contrasts sharply with some glaring weaknesses: primary education enrolment, net % (94th); tertiary education enrolment, gross % (69th); redundancy costs, weeks of salary (89th); women in the labour force, ratio to men (141th); legal rights index (89th).

The observed pattern of high attainment is some critical areas of competitiveness co-existing with very low level in other areas may account in part for the country's low rate of total factor productivity growth. Clearly, many of these factors complement each other, so great deficiencies in certain areas are likely to take a heavy toll in others.

Areas for policy focus

The country stage framework developed in Chapter 8 provides some rough guidelines for the Kingdom's future policy efforts, especially those undertaken with the intent to put the Kingdom on a path of sustained growth independent of developments in the oil markets. Clearly, in a dynamic context, the proper sequencing of reforms may be just as important as the selection of reforms themselves. Which areas are reforms likely to be most effective in stimulating the country's growth potential as well as the entrepreneurship needed to create sufficient jobs for the country's young population?

As indicated in Chapter 8, Saudi Arabia is presently in the WEF's transition stage from Stage 1 (factor driven) to Stage 2 (efficiency driven).

Robert E. Looney

Table 25.6 Saudi Arabia competitiveness: strengths and weaknesses

Strengths (ranked in top 10)		Weaknesses (ranked lower than 50th)	
Indicator	*Rank/ 144*	*Indicator*	*Rank/ 144*
1st pillar: institutions		1st pillar: institutions	
Public trust in politicians	5	2nd pillar: infrastructure	
Wastefulness of government spending	5	Fixed telephone lines/100 pop.	75
Government services for improved business performance	5	3rd pillar: macroeconomic environment	
Business costs of crime and violence	4	Inflation, annual % change	74
Organized crime	6	4th pillar: health and primary education	
Protection of minority shareholders' interests	9	Business impact of malaria	75
2nd pillar: infrastructure		Malaria cases/100,000 population	76
Mobile telephone subscribers/100 population	3	Infant mortality deaths/1,000 live births	69
3rd pillar: macroeconomic environment		Life expectancy, years	63
Government budget balance (% GDP)	4	Primary education enrolment, net %	94
General government debt (% GDP)	8	5th pillar: higher education and training	
4th pillar: health and primary education		Tertiary education enrolment, gross %	69
HIV prevalence, % adult population	1	6th pillar: goods market efficiency	
5th pillar: higher education and training		Trade tariffs, % duty	60
6th pillar: goods market efficiency		Prevalence of foreign ownership	76
Total tax rate, % profits	6	Imports as % of GDP	122
Number of procedures to start a business	8	7th pillar: labour market efficiency	
Agricultural policy costs	9	Redundancy costs, weeks of salary	89
7th pillar: labour market efficiency		Women in labour force, ratio to men	141
8th pillar: financial market development		8th pillar: financial market development	
9th pillar: technological readiness		Legal rights index	89
FDI and technology transfer	8	9th pillar: technological readiness	
10th pillar: market size		Individuals using internet, %	61
11th pillar: business sophistication		Mobile broadband subscriptions/100 pop.	71
Local supplier quality	6	10th pillar: market size	
Control of international distribution	7	11th pillar: business Sophistication	
12th pillar: innovation		12th pillar: innovation	
Government procurement of advanced tech products			

Source: World Economic Forum, *The Global Competitiveness Report 2012–13*, Geneva, 2012, 308

The first step in the analysis was to form a new country grouping by merging Stage 1 countries with the group (that includes) in transition from Stage 1 to Stage 2. A factor analysis of this combined group of countries was undertaken to determine the areas in need of immediate attention to assure continued growth. At this stage of development, those variables highly associated with growth potential were:[44] (a) health and primary education (WEF); (b) higher education and training (WEF); (c) infrastructure (WEF); (d) technological readiness (WEF), and trade freedom (HH). Those factors associated with entrepreneurship were: (a) labour freedom (HH); and (b) labour market efficiency (WEF).

494

As noted above, Saudi Arabia has some key deficiencies in several of these areas, especially with regard to health and education and labour markets (labour market efficiency and freedom). These are the policy areas that need immediate attention and reform. The country's progress in the trade area is paying high dividends, but there is still much more that could be accomplished in moving towards a freer trade environment. If the Saudi government makes satisfactory progress in these areas, the country will be well positioned to move on to the WEF's efficiency stage. While previous sections stressed the importance of improved governance, actions in this area, while desirable in and of themselves, do not appear to be critical in moving the country up the development ladder.

Assuming that Saudi Arabia is able to take effective action in the areas noted above, a similar analysis was undertaken by first merging Saudi Arabia's current group transition from Stage 1 to the group of countries already in Stage 3 (efficiency driven). A factor analysis of this new grouping found that a somewhat different set of variables were associated with growth potential, with governance reforms taking on greater importance than previously. At higher levels of income the growth process appears to become more complex. Specifically, the key variables associated with growth potential are now: (a) government effectiveness (WB); (b) property rights (HH); (c) institutions (WEF); (d) goods market efficiency (WEF); (e) business sophistication (WEF); (f) rule of law (WB); (g) financial market development (WEF); (h) freedom from corruption (HH); (i) infrastructure (WEF); (j) innovation (WEF); (k) control of corruption (WB); and (l) technological readiness (WEF).

For supporting increased levels of entrepreneurship the factor analysis also identified several key areas of governance as of prime importance: (a) voice and accountability (WB); (b) trade freedom (HH); and (c) political stability and absence of violence (WB).

Simply spending more money on some of the key areas noted above is obviously not enough. Furthermore, the Kingdom's effective, short-term policy options are limited by institutional constraints, shortages of human capital and religious restrictions. As a result, a more nuanced approach is needed if Saudi Arabia hopes to sustain satisfactory rates of economic growth combined with meaningful job creation.

Sources of instability

As it contemplates reforms, the Saudi royal family can expect to face a number of challenges.[45] The first set centres on the issues fuelling the Arab Spring uprisings in other parts of the region: unemployment, housing shortages and Shi'ite unrest. The second set, which will largely define the ability of the Saudi government to respond to these threats, involves the royal succession and uncertainty over the government's longer-term fiscal capacity. Other potential problems— for example, a looming water crisis as aquifers are depleted—will undoubtedly complicate matters for the monarchy, but will not in themselves pose a threat to its survival.

These new challenges may upset the delicate balance that has thus far allowed the Saudi royal family to maintain its close ties to the Wahhabi religious establishment while implementing reforms to stabilize and slowly modernize the country. Given the type of reforms necessary to weather the rapidly changing global economic, social and political environment, there is a distinct possibility that this balance may be evolving into a new trilemma of a type unique to the Kingdom (see Figure 25.1).

In the classic monetary system trilemma, the objectives of monetary autonomy, fixed exchange rates and capital mobility are not achievable simultaneously—countries have to choose two objectives at the expense of the other. In Saudi Arabia's case, mounting stresses stemming from the Arab Spring and internal frictions may require that the Wahhabis relax their doctrinaire hold on the country. In the worst-case scenario, ties between the current royal

Assessment

Many of Saudi Arabia's domestic problems stem from demographics. The country's population grew from 15 million in 1990 to over 28 million in 2011, an average annual increase of nearly 3%.[46] While not particularly high by international standards, these demographic changes create a major problem in an emerging economy whose comparative advantage is in capital-intensive petroleum and petrochemicals, and in which job creation does not progress in line with overall growth due. The limited potential of the country's agricultural sector, which would ordinarily absorb many of the new entrants to the labour force, is a further complication. On top of all this, Saudi Arabia's largely religious, tradition-bound educational system has been slow to respond to the needs of a modern, private sector economy, leaving most graduates sorely under-skilled.

The government has attempted to compensate for the skills deficit by subsidizing university education. An estimated 800,000 Saudis are enrolled in universities domestically and approximately 110,000 overseas.[47] Even among university graduates, expectations are soon dashed by the poor quality of most degrees.[48] Tellingly, 90% of Saudis currently in prison have university degrees.[49]

As noted previously, unofficial figures suggest that youth unemployment is as high as 30%. This fact has so far been obscured by the safety nets provided by strong family networks and the state—a situation that is unsustainable. In the short run, the government's attempts to address unemployment have centred on the Saudization[50] of the private sector, a carrot-and-stick approach that attempts to persuade employers to replace foreign labourers with Saudi nationals. In the longer run, the government is making massive investments in infrastructure and, more specifically, the creation of 'new economic cities'.

Saudization programmes have been around for years but have produced little in the way of meaningful job creation. The original Saudization plans called for replacing nearly 320,000 foreign workers with Saudis between 1995 and 2000. The number of immigrant labourers actually grew by 58,400 during this period. In the early 2000s Saudi Arabia's consultative legislature, the Shura Council, decreed that Saudi nationals must comprise 70% of the country's workforce by 2007.[51] As of 2012 Saudis accounted for only about 10% of private sector employees.

It's easy to see why attempts at Saudization have failed. The programme levies fines on employers who do not comply, essentially a tax on businesses that many firms resist. Some simply relocate outside the country, especially to the business-friendly United Arab Emirates (UAE), to avoid replacing skilled workers with more expensive and less qualified Saudis. Firms that attempt to comply by offering training programmes to their Saudi workforce find retention difficult, as their newly trained employees are bid away by other firms seeking to meet their Saudization quotas. Furthermore, since the rules, red tape and quotas of Saudization often change without warning, foreign firms opt for more predictable settings in which to invest.

Rather than learning from past mistakes, the government responded to the Arab Spring by rolling out a new, more bureaucratic version of the Saudization programme. Now dubbed the Nitaqat[52] programme, this latest Saudization effort is likely to meet the same fate as earlier attempts: scaring away private investors and doing little to decrease unemployment. The initiative is further hobbled by the welfare packages, expansion in government jobs and higher public minimum wage that were part of the government's myopic response to the Arab Spring. As a result, it is now even harder for the private sector to recruit Saudi workers.

The risk of this initiative is that private sector employers may choose simply to close down if the combination of low Saudi productivity and a government push for higher wages takes too heavy a toll on their profit margins. Larger businesses could easily relocate to the UAE, where work permits are freely issued. There are already more than 2,000 Saudi-owned businesses in Dubai, and as there are no restrictions on capital outflows, others are likely to follow. To avert such capital flight, the government is looking at a broad-based strategy for matching job seekers to employer needs, which includes scaling-up placement, training and education programmes to give Saudi graduates the skills actually needed in the workplace.

The longer-term 'new economic cities' programme of 2007 holds more promise. The programme takes its inspiration from the success of Jubail and Yanbu, industrial cities created from scratch in the 1970s. More than 30 years on, initial scepticism as to their economic viability have been firmly dispelled, thanks to the successful development of downstream industries, such as petrochemicals. To date, the two cities have created 107,000 jobs and 233 industries, many of which are major exporters.

The 2007 'new cities'[53] programme aims to replicate these earlier successes on a bigger and faster scale, this time with an emphasis on preparing Saudi Arabia for a post-oil future. The new cities are to serve as the basis for creating a modern knowledge economy—one significantly diversified away from the crude oil sector. Located in areas that trail the rest of the Kingdom economically, each will have a mix of industries designed to diversify the economy and generate jobs. In 2008 the government provided a fiscal outlay of $400 billion to fund the programme to 2013, after which it anticipates expanded local Saudi private sector and multinational investment to offset at least a portion of future costs.

The new cities programme is especially important given Saudi Arabia's future fiscal outlook. Riyadh-based Jadwa Investment estimates[54] that Saudi finances will remain viable under reasonable assumptions concerning oil prices for the next decade. Beyond that, the country will face a long-term fiscal deterioration. Even as government expenditures rise to accommodate a much larger population and honour past commitments, oil exports and revenues will decline due to increased domestic oil usage, domestic fuel subsidies and the rising costs of bringing new oil to market. Saudi Arabia's estimated break-even oil price will increase from a manageable $71 a barrel in 2012 (see Figure 25.18) to $90.7 a barrel in 2015, $175.1 in 2025 and $321.7 by 2030 (see Table 25.7). Given the unlikely chance that oil prices will reach these heights, the consequences are rapidly growing fiscal deficits.

The implications are clear. The Saudis face a rapidly closing window to transition to an economy that is less dependent on oil and more capable of self-sustained, job-creating growth. The good news is that the new cities programme could potentially kick in before the fiscal crisis. While the initial new cities of Jubail and Yanbu took 15 to 20 years to come into their own, the government now has considerably more expertise and resources at its disposal to undertake ventures of this size and scope. If priority is given to the programme, results could be significant as early as in the next several years.

The Saudi situation is a bit like global warming. Year-to-year developments don't produce enough change to elicit a dramatic shift in policies or actions, yet the situation remains a ticking time bomb. Saudi policymakers, under the illusion that the situation is manageable through short-term expediency measures can easily be lulled into a false sense of security. However, this approach will only hasten the arrival of the Kingdom's impending fiscal crisis by locking the country into a vicious circle, whereby short-term economic expediency leads to falling private investment, further increasing pressure on the state to increase social expenditures and public sector job creation. These expenditures will, in turn, divert resources from the oil sector, resulting in lower oil exports, cutbacks in the country's long-term economic cities programme, and ultimately the inability of the government to meet the growing demands of an increasingly

Robert E. Looney

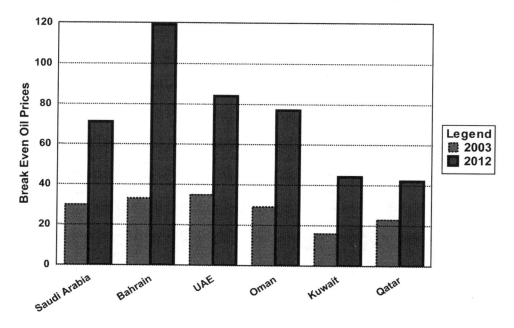

Figure 25.18 Break even oil prices

Table 25.7 Saudi Arabia key variables: forecast to 2030

	2005	2010	2015f	2020f	2015f	2030f
Oil indicators (million barrels per day)						
Oil production	9.4	8.2	9.3	10.0	10.7	11.5
Oil exports	7.5	5.8	6.3	6.0	5.6	4.9
Domestic consumption	1.9	2.4	3.1	3.9	5.1	6.5
Budgetary indicators (SR billion)						
Total revenue	564	735	843	961	1,108	1,120
Total expenditure	346	627	893	1,147	1,620	2,453
Balance	218	109	−50	−186	−512	−1,334
SAMA net foreign assets	564	1,652	1,958	1,331	375	375
Domestic debt	475	167	167	167	949	5,889
Break-even oil price ($ per barrel)						
Saudi export crude	30.3	71.6	90.7	118.5	175.1	321.7

Source: *Saudi Arabia's Coming Oil and Fiscal Challenge*, Jadwa Investment, Riyadh, July 2011, 24

restive populace. Saudi Arabia's best hope for escaping this bleak vision and averting its own Arab Spring is to break with its current myopia, focus on the longer-term necessities and undertake the reforms needed to sustain growth.

Notes

1 Ellen Knickmeyer, 'Saudis Push Young People, Including Women into Jobs', *Wall Street Journal*, 31 January 2012.

The Saudi Arabian model

2 Neela Banerjee, 'Saudi Arabia "Day of Rage" Fizzles', *Los Angeles Times*, 12 March 2011.

3 'Arab Unrest Index: The Shoe-Thrower's Index', *The Economist*, 9 February 2011.

4 Media Eghbal, 'The Next 11 Emerging Economies', Euromonitor International, 4 February 2008, blog.euromonitor.com/2008/02/the-next-11-emerging-economies.html.

5 Udayan Gupta, 'MIST: The Next Tier of Large Emerging Economies', *Institutional Investor*, 7 February 2011, www.institutionalinvestor.com/Article/2762464/Research/4120/Overview.html#.UbX2RZw qU_M.

6 Ruth Walker, 'BRICs, CIVETS, and PIGS: What's in a Name?' *The Christian Science Monitor*, 20 January 2012.

7 International Monetary Fund, World Economic Outlook Database, April 2013 Edition, www. institutionalinvestor.com/Article/2762464/Research/4120/Overview.html#.UbX2RZwqU_M.

8 World Bank, *World Development Indicators*, May 2013, data.worldbank.org/data-catalog/world-development-indicators.

9 See, for example, Robert Looney, 'The Saudi Arabian Quandry: The Economy's Inability to Sustain Growth', *METU Studies in Development* 31(1), June 2004: 171–86; and Robert Looney, 'Saudi Arabia: Measures of Transition from a Rentier State', in Joseph Kechichian (ed.), *Iran, Iraq, and the Arab Gulf States*, Palgrave, New York, 2001, 132–59; and Robert Looney, 'A Dual-Track Development Strategy for Saudi Arabia', *Journal of Energy and Development* 30(2), Spring 2005: 171–86.

10 International Monetary Fund, *Saudi Arabia: 2012 Article IV Consultation*, September 2012, 15.

11 Robert Looney, 'Real or Illusionary Growth in an Oil Based Economy: Government Expenditures and Private Sector Investment in Saudi Arabia', *World Development* 20(9), 1992: 1367–75.

12 Robert M. Solow, 'Technological Change and the Aggregate Production Function', *Review of Economics and Statistics*, 39(3), 1957: 312–20; see also Robert M. Solow, 'The Last 50 Years in Growth Theory and the Next 10', *Oxford Review of Economic Policy* 23(1), Spring 2007: 3–14.

13 Henry J. Bruton, 'Productivity Growth in Latin America', *American Economic Review* 57(5), December 1967: 1099–116.

14 S.L. Baier, G.P. Dwyer and R. Tamura, 'How Important are Capital and Total Factor Productivity for Economic Growth?' *Economic Inquiry* 44(1), 2006: 23–49.

15 A.M. Bisat, M.A. el-Erian and T. Helbing, 'Growth, Investment and Saving in the Arab Economies', IMF Working Paper No. 97/85, International Monetary Fund, Washington, DC, 1997.

16 International Monetary Fund, *Qatar: 2010 Article IV consultation: Staff Report*, IMF Staff Country Report 11/64, IMF, Washington, DC, 2011.

17 J. Keller and M.K. Nabli, 'The Macroeconomics of Labor Market Outcomes in MENA over the 1990s: How Growth has Failed to Keep Pace with a Burgeoning Labor Market', The Egyptian Center for Economic Studies Working Paper No. 71, The Egyptian Center for Economic Studies, Cairo, 2002.

18 X. Sala-i-Martin and E. Artadi, 'Economic Growth and Investment in the Arab World', in K. Scwab and P. Cornelius (eds), *The Arab World Competitiveness Report 2002–3*, Oxford University Press, New York, 2002.

19 M.A. al-Khatib, 'The Impact of Economic Diversification on the Saudi Non-Oil Economy', *Arab Journal of Administrative Sciences* 18(2), 2011.

20 International Monetary Fund, *Saudi Arabia: Selected Issues*, IMF, Washington, DC, 2012.

21 Ibid., 11.

22 William Easterly and Stanley Fischer, 'What We Can Learn from the Soviet Collapse', *Finance & Development*, December 1994.

23 Richard M. Auty, *Sustaining Development in Mineral Economies: The Resource Curse Thesis*, Routledge, London, 1993.

24 Terry Lind Karl, *The Paradox of Plenty: Oil Booms and Petro-States*, University of California Press, Berkeley, CA, 1997.

25 Jeffrey D. Sachs and Andrew M. Warner, *Natural Resource Abundance and Economic Growth*, Development Discussion Paper no. 517a, Harvard Institute for International Development, Cambridge, MA.

26 Michael L. Ross, 'The Political Economy of the Resource Curse', *World Politics* 51, January 1999: 297–322.

27 Cf. Carlos Santiso, 'Good Governance and Aid Effectiveness: The World Bank and Conditionality', *The Georgetown Public Policy Review* 7(1), Fall 2001: 1–22; and The World Bank, *Aid Effectiveness*, econ.worldbank.org/WBSITE/EXTERNAL/EXTDEC/EXTRESEARCH/EXTPROGRAMS/EXTPUBSE RV/0,contentMDK:21073824~menuPK:3084766~pagePK:64168182~piPK:64168060~theSite PK:4 77916,00.html.

28 Cf. William Easterly, *The White Man's Burden: Why the West's Efforts to Aid the Rest Have Done So Much Ill and So Little Good*, Penguin Press, New York, 2006.

29 Muhammad Abdul Wahab and Vaqar Ahmed, 'Foreign Assistance and Economic Growth: Evidence from Pakistan 1972–2010', *World Economics* 12(4), October–December 2011: 137–52.

30 The 2012 Legatum Prosperity Index, The Legatum Institute, London, 2012.

31 Roughly in a manner noted in Chapter 8, governance improves with increased levels of income.

32 Robert Looney, 'Governance-Constrained Growth in the MENA Region', in Abbas Kadhim (ed.), *Governance in the Middle East and North Africa: A Handbook*, Routledge, London, 2013, 3–32.

33 World Bank, *Worldwide Governance Indicators*, info.worldbank.org/governance/wgi/sc_country.asp.

34 Cf. Michael Ross, 'Does Oil Hinder Democracy?' *World Politics* 53, April 2001: 325–61.

35 Oxford Business Group, *The Report: Saudi Arabia*, 2013, 13.

36 Economist Intelligence Unit, 2012 Democracy Index.

37 Courtney Trenwith, 'Saudization to Cost Nearly $4bn in 2013-Study', Arabian.business.com, 1 May 2013, www.arabianbusiness.com/saudisation-cost-nearly-4bn-in-2013-study-500254.html.

38 Heritage House, Index of Economic Freedom, 2013, www.heritage.org/index/country/saudiarabia.

39 Index of Economic Freedom, 2013.

40 See, for example, Robert Looney, 'Russia's Economic Prospects', *Milken Institute Review*, Second Quarter, 2010: 38–45; and Robert Looney, 'The Emergence of Iranian Petro-populism', *Gulf Research Center Yearbook, 2006–7*, Gulf Research Center, Dubai, 2006, 417–27; and Robert Looney, 'The Iranian Economy: The Glass Half Empty London', Legatum Institute, 2012, www.li.com/docs/default-document-library/prosperity-in-depth-the-iranian-economy-the-glass-half-empty-Looney.pdf?sfvrsn=8.

41 Robert Looney, 'Middle East Reform Initiatives: A Stage Theory Perspective', with a commentary by Morton Kaplan, *International Journal of World Peace* 28(1), March 2005: 1–33.

42 Cf. Hossein Askari, *Collaborative Colonialism: The Political Economy of Oil in the Persian Gulf*, Palgrave Macmillan, New York, 2013.

43 *The Global Competitiveness Report 2012–13*, World Economic Forum, Geneva, 2012, 308.

44 The data source of the variable is given in parentheses—i.e. WEF is the World Economic Forum, WB is the World Bank and Heritage House is HH.

45 Cf. Fahad Nazer, 'Limits to Saudi Oil Power', *Yale Global Online*, 30 May 2012, yaleglobal.yale.edu/content/limits-saudi-oil-power.

46 World Bank, *World Development Indicators*.

47 David B. Ottaway, *Saudi Arabia's Race Against Time*, Wilson Center, Washington, DC, Summer 2012, 4.

48 Leigh Nolan, *Managing Reform? Saudi Arabia and the King's Dilemma*, Brookings Doha Center, May 2011, 4.

49 *The Political Outlook for Saudi Arabia*, Chatham House, London, May 2011, 4.

50 Robert Looney, 'Saudization: A Useful Tool in the Kingdom's Battle Against Unemployment?' *Journal of South Asian and Middle Eastern Studies* XXVII(3), Spring 2004: 13–33.

51 Kasim Randeree, *Workforce Nationalization in the Gulf Cooperation Council States*, Georgetown University School of Foreign Service in Qatar, Doha, 2012, 13.

52 Siraj Wahab, 'Saudi Arabia: Labor Ministry Outlines Details of Nitaqat Program', *Zawya*, 12 June 2011, www.zawya.com/story/Saudi_Labor_Ministry_Outlines_Details_Of_Nitaqat_Program-ZAWYA20110612032535/.

53 Crispin Thorold, 'New Cities Rise from Saudi Desert', BBC, 11 June 2008, news.bbc.co.uk/2/hi/middle_east/7446923.stm.

54 *Saudi Arabia's Coming Oil and Fiscal Challenge*, Jadwa Investment, Riyadh, July 2011.

Part VII

Assessing the future

26

The emerging powers and global governance

Why the BRICS matter

Leslie Elliott Armijo and Cynthia Roberts[1]

Governments spanning the globe, international organizations, the world's biggest banks, major think tanks, the European Union (EU), and the US national intelligence community all agree: economic power is shifting at a rapid pace and the next half-century will see major changes in the relative size and rankings of the world's economies.[2] The US National Intelligence Council (NIC) bluntly summarized the situation thus: 'In terms of size, speed, and directional flow, the transfer of global wealth and economic power now under way—roughly from West to East—is without precedent in modern history.'[3] By 2030 the diffusion of power is expected to have a significant impact, 'largely reversing the historic rise of the West since 1750 and restoring Asia's weight in the global economy and world politics'.[4] The financial and economic crisis since 2008 has exposed serious structural challenges and fiscal constraints facing the US economy and weighing even more heavily on the USA's key Western partners, but it is the rapid rise of other powers that ended the 'unipolar moment', according to the NIC, and is causing a 'fast winding down' of Pax Americana—the period of unrivalled US primacy since 1945.[5]

Likewise, countries that were once constrained by the structural imperatives of Cold War confrontation—from Germany to the People's Republic of China—now have greater freedom to manoeuvre, including to withhold co-operation from Washington's preferred agenda. In addition, the global shift in economic power is coinciding with widespread dissatisfaction with the management and governance capacity of the USA and its European partners, whose credibility has been challenged by fresh evidence of double standards and regulatory scandals surrounding such previously untouchable capitalist icons as the neutrality of the Libor (London Interbank Offered Rate) benchmark interest rate, to Moody's credit rating procedures. To the emerging powers, the international financial and economic crisis that began in US subprime mortgage markets in 2007 revealed that the much-vaunted West was not necessarily the font of all financial wisdom or the institutional gold standard it claimed to be, but instead suffered from its own variants of crony capitalism and irresponsible debt overhang.

This shift in relative interstate capabilities (power shift), coupled with the end of the Cold War, is providing exceptional opportunities for rising powers to assert themselves both geopolitically and in global governance arenas. This chapter focuses on understanding what changes

503

emerging powers may seek in contemporary global governance regimes—and why. Since late 2008 the G7 club of advanced economies has been partially supplanted as the dominant international economic steering group by the financial G20 group of developed and developing nations (see Table 26.1). New multilateral clubs have emerged and are demanding greater influence. In fact, the group of countries that arguably has had the most discernible impact in challenging the existing global governance architecture and creating expectations for real, if incremental, change is also the most improbable coalition: the BRICs, later BRICS (Brazil, Russia, India, China, and since late 2010, South Africa).[6] Back in 2001, Jim O'Neill, research director for investment bank Goldman Sachs, coined the BRICs acronym to signal a hot new investment class of large, emerging economies with high growth potential going forward. In the mid-2000s Russian leaders saw the opportunity to make the BRICs a political grouping, and by 2006 the Russian foreign minister was organizing informal caucuses of his counterparts on the sidelines of meetings of international governmental organizations (IGOs) such as the opening of the General Assembly of the United Nations (UN), and the semi-annual meetings of the World Bank and the International Monetary Fund (IMF). In April 2009 the BRICs held their first leaders' summit, in Yekaterinburg, Russia.

Since that time, the BRICS have been the clearest, although not the only, institutional manifestation of the efforts of rising powers to assert themselves in global governance, and one of the few that China has prioritized. By their fifth leaders' summit, in Durban, South Africa, the BRICS governments were not only demanding reforms of global governance institutions, but also discussing widening the scope of their co-operation through such headline endeavours

Table 26.1 Key global governance clubs, 2013

	G7/G8	*UN Security Council permanent five*	*Major economies (aka 'financial') G20*
Advanced industrial countries	Canada France Germany Italy Japan UK USA	France UK USA	Australia Canada France Germany Italy Japan UK USA EU
BRICS	Russia	China Russia	Brazil China India Russia South Africa
Other emerging economies			Argentina Indonesia Mexico Russia Saudi Arabia South Africa South Korea Turkey

as building a BRICS development bank (possibly with regional subsidiaries) to offer preferential funding for infrastructure development in developing countries, and creating a foreign exchange contingency reserve pool (with an initial US$100 billion in contributions) similar to the Chiang Mai Initiative and partly replicating the role of the IMF, to defend their economies against a possible balance of payments crisis while deterring potential currency speculators. The BRICS also are holding regular meetings of their permanent representatives of the UN in New York and Geneva, Switzerland, to co-ordinate policies, and are creating a virtual secretariat, a business council and a consortium of think tanks to collaborate on the development of a long-term vision for the BRICS and begin the process of developing an independent databank and new indicators to measure the socio-economic and -political progress of these emerging countries. By June 2013 India and Russia had already articulated their BRICS strategies, with Moscow being the first to publish a detailed official concept developed in an inter-ministerial process over 18 months and approved by President Vladimir Putin on 9 February 2013.[7]

This investigation follows several tracks. First, what is the objective evidence for the claim that an international power shift may be underway? The chapter's first section suggests that there is now a mismatch between the distribution of material resources among countries and influence within major global governance regimes. Second, what does international relations theory anticipate from power shifts and the formal and informal influence of powerful states on international institutions? This is the topic of the chapter's second section. Third, what can be deduced from recent statements and actions of major emerging powers vis-à-vis key global governance institutions? The chapter's third and fourth sections examine key interactions of the BRICS and the traditional advanced industrial powers in two important venues: the UN Security Council (UNSC) and the institutions of global financial governance, particularly the World Bank and the IMF. These empirical sections reveal several important findings about BRICS interaction and influence, including the importance of power asymmetries within the group as well as clues that China's interest in creating outside options may be spurring the BRICS' nascent development of parallel institutions, such as a BRICS bank. The conclusions return to our original questions.

Power is diffusing

Economic capabilities are diffusing. China will pass the USA in total gross domestic product (GDP) measured in purchasing power parity (PPP) terms in 2016, and within a decade thereafter in dollar terms at market rates.[8] The high point of the US share of global GDP was reached in 1960 at 38.5%.[9] It dropped to 22.7% in 2011 and is projected to decline to 17.8% by 2030. The USA's allies are experiencing even more dramatic declines relative to rising powers, with Japan's share of global output falling from 6.7% to 4.2% from 2011 to 2030, and the eurozone from 17.1% to 11.7% over the same period. By comparison, China's share is projected to rise from 17.0% to 27.9% and India's from 6.6% to 11.1%; together their share of global GDP in 2030 outdistances the USA, Japan and the eurozone combined.[10] The BRICs have accounted for more than half of global growth since the start of the financial crisis in 2007. In 2020 the four original BRIC countries will rank as four of the top seven economies (in PPP terms), displacing every European power except Germany, which will be surpassed by Russia by 2030.[11] BRIC countries also hold nearly 50% of total global hard currency reserves of $4.4 trillion, with the lion's share of $3.44 trillion held by the Chinese government.[12] The World Bank estimates that by 2030 half the total world capital stock of about $158 trillion (in 2010 dollars), embodied in investments in factories, equipment and infrastructure, will belong to developing countries, while their share in global aggregate investment activity is projected to triple to three-fifths, from one-fifth in 2000.[13] Of this amount, China will account for 30% of global investment, while estimates for Brazil, India and Russia combined amount to an additional 13%. For the present, the USA remains *primus inter pares*, but with a declining relative share of power, while Japan and particularly the major European countries are slipping ranks more rapidly. Among developing and transitional countries, those that now loom largest are the four original BRICs, but the greatest share of BRICS economic and financial weight is due to China alone.

Among the positive consequences of this shift in the distribution of global GDP are the reduction of poverty and emerging growth of a global middle class.[14] Although significant differences in living standards will persist, the global middle class will surge from about two billion in 2012 to 3.2 billion in 2020 and 4.9 billion (66% in Asia, of a total world population of about eight billion) by 2030. Not only will more people be in the middle class, but they will also have greater access to capital, education and digital technology.[15] Already they are starting to demand a larger voice in how their societies are run, on issues ranging from corruption, inequality and the environment, to state governance, as seen in recent protests in Brazil, China, Russia and Turkey.

Meanwhile, another pillar of the USA's global power and influence, strong military alliances, is experiencing significant change. Asian defence spending (excluding Australia and New Zealand) surpassed that of the North Atlantic Treaty Organization (NATO) Europe in 2012, reflecting in part the impact of Europe's high debt-to-GDP ratios and anaemic growth.[16] In fact, European defence budgets have been contracting at a faster rate than their economies have been declining, raising questions about demilitarization and the viability of the Atlantic Alliance.

None the less, in many dimensions of power, the USA remains overwhelmingly dominant: it is the world's sole contemporary superpower. Although it is experiencing relative economic decline vis-à-vis large, faster-growing states, the USA still possesses notable advantages in the global arena, including an open, innovative economy, favourable demographics, strong democratic institutions, a capable military with global reach, and the US dollar. With a 2012 defence budget of $645 billion, the USA spends more on its armed forces than the next 15 countries combined, at approximately 5% of GDP.[17] China's double-digit annual growth in defence spending, if sustained, will not approach US levels until around 2025. Moreover, US dominance of the major post-Second World War institutions of global governance has proven resilient for the first 13 years into the 21st century.

Insights from international relations theories about power shifts and international change

What are the implications of the tectonic diffusion of interstate influence and power identified in the previous section? Much contemporary international relations theory begins from the realist premise that the international system is defined by the power and interests of states, particularly the major powers. States operate in an anarchic system in which there is no supreme political authority or world government. The incentives in this structure incline states toward 'self-help', mistrust and competition. The structure also socializes states, encouraging emulation of winning strategies and technological innovations.[18] Given that there is no automatic enforcement of rules or bargains in anarchy, realists emphasize that states seek ample power to advance their goals, defend their sovereignty and prevent others from constraining their autonomy of action. A shift in relative material capabilities among major states in the international system consequently threatens the ability of the prevailing dominant actors to exert their will. In this competitive arena, states are positional players and fear relative losses, not only

The emerging powers and global governance

absolute ones. Realist scholars, moreover, conceptualize international institutions as largely epiphenomenal. IGOs and the rules they promulgate can overcome co-ordination issues but have little binding force, especially in the security realm. Powerful states strongly influence who plays the game, writes the rules and changes the pay-off matrix.[19] It follows that they employ their influence to construct the institutions in every order to pursue their own interests foremost, and ignore them when they prove too constraining. Dominant actors therefore do not necessarily seek Pareto-optimal solutions to collective action problems. Realists further hold that institutionalized co-operation is often derailed by distributional conflicts where dominant countries with favourable outside options often can exit if they fail to secure a superior distribution of benefits in international bargains. Likewise, IGOs that are prone to counter the interests of the dominant powers, such as the UN General Assembly, are sidelined.

Neo-liberal institutionalist scholars, while accepting a paramount role for systemic structure, none the less wish to explain the considerable, often well-institutionalized, international policy co-operation—or 'global governance'—that they observe. The genesis of interstate co-operation typically is a crisis, or a realization that a pressing policy problem will not go away on its own. Such acute policy challenges tend to be economic challenges (opening markets and maintaining free trade), or technical co-ordination issues (waterways management or the prevention of pandemics), but rarely involve universal security matters. Institutions can thus be useful by reducing transactions costs, increasing information and expertise, providing focal points for co-operation, stabilizing expectations and in some cases formalizing commitments through legalization of the rules.[20] To solve major 'collective action' problems it is often necessary for a hegemon and other dominant partners to create the institutions, and sometimes to supply the public goods themselves.[21] As the order becomes more institutionalized over time, a certain degree of legitimacy may emerge from voluntary participation by strong and weak states alike that will grow as the gains from co-operation increase. Even when the underlying distribution of capabilities shifts, the path dependence embodied in the existing rules of the institutional game tends to be continued—until the next crisis, when the institution itself fully or partially fails, and is replaced or subjected to renegotiation.[22] Moreover, neo-liberal institutionalists often assume that most global governance institutions provide valuable public goods. Although IGOs operate according to formal and informal rules that allocate special privileges and leverage to the dominant powers, they are more likely to endure when they provide benefits to weaker members as well.

With respect to power shifts, realists generally assume that rising power(s) will eventually be driven to challenge the status quo power(s).[23] However, emerging powers 'will attempt to change the system only if the expected benefits exceed the expected costs'.[24] If, as realists argue, rising power also leads to expanding ambition and determination to exert greater control over the rising state's autonomy and external environment, then conflict cannot be ruled out. Since the end of the Cold War, Washington has repeatedly used force to get its way. Similarly, some scholars believe that China's rapidly rising defence expenditure reflects its aim to maximize the power gap between itself and its neighbours in the Asia-Pacific region.[25] However, large-scale territorial expansion is improbable in the nuclear age.[26] Despite the possibility of regional disputes, it is important to distinguish the risks of conflict in power transitions from the likely global governance effects.

In principle, international change may range from territorial conquest to revising the prevailing rules, norms and institutions.[27] Although the BRICs and other emerging powers remain outside of the US-led system of alliances, they have been integrated to a large extent into Western economic institutions and are members of the UN. However, the extent to which rising powers have actually embraced Western global norms and international rules is widely debated, not only from one issue area to the next but also over time. Some Western scholars

507

dismiss rising powers as 'irresponsible stakeholders' unwilling 'to accept the rules under which they rose'.[28] Others perceive China, for example, as having adapted to global norms, variously attributing this outcome to the legitimacy of international regimes, domestic political incentives, or China's strategy of peaceful rise.[29] However, as China's power (and Russia's) has continued to grow, so do concerns about these countries' international ambitions and assertiveness.[30] Yet, so far none of the rising powers is in a rush to wrest leadership away from the USA and assume the responsibilities—and costs—of global leadership.

In any case, countries do not go to war over being denied a seat on the UNSC or to protect their greater voting shares in the IMF. So the question in this context becomes whether the liberal international institutions created after the Second World War can endure 'after hegemony'.[31] We can unpack this puzzle by considering why rising powers want to participate in existing global governance organizations. First, IGOs provide their members with a variety of goods: public or collective goods (from agreed technical standards to global economic monitoring; the World Trade Organization (WTO), given its near-universal membership is also a quasi-public good); club goods, which are excludable but non-rivalrous (such as private parks or membership in the EU); and private goods, which are both excludable and rivalrous.[32] In its first stage of institutional evolution, the BRICS organization has functioned like a club with some privileged members while excluding non-members, such as other large emerging economies like Indonesia, which has unsuccessfully petitioned to join. The BRICS club none the less provides benefits that may have positive externalities for other emerging economies, such as greater representation in the IMF. Additionally, to boost its legitimacy and influence, there is discussion of adding a new member to represent the Islamic civilization (for example, Indonesia or Turkey), and also inviting 'partners for dialogue', others with 'observer status', or 'associate members' in future 'BRICS plus' meetings.[33]

By comparison, the strongly institutionalized Western order is rooted not only in democracy and capitalism; its success also grows out of its accessible, expansive qualities and ability to generate remarkable economic growth while integrating a widening array of stakeholders. Liberal US specialists argue that it is 'easy to join' and 'hard to overturn', and thus functions as a quasi-public good.[34]

However, leaders of emerging powers are acutely aware that international institutions also have provided the dominant powers with two varieties of de facto private goods. First, and as noted, the design of such institutions inevitably reflects the preferences of those actors who created them. Consequently, dominant countries can secure a more favourable distribution of benefits in international bargaining and restrict the choice sets of others.[35] Thus the daily operations of institutions will tend to generate outcomes that replicate the status quo. As President Barack Obama explained, 'it was America that largely built a system of international institutions that carried us through the Cold War ... Instead of constraining our power, these institutions magnified it'.[36]

Second, current preponderant power(s) gain the de facto private good of an implicit right to demand exceptions from inconvenient rules and to exercise their influence in multilateral organizations behind closed doors where they can set the agenda and control the decisions that are most consequential to their interests. Unlike everyone else, the most powerful countries (currently only the USA in most areas) have attractive outside options that create a strong disincentive to commit to formal obligations when they run counter to important interests. If a dominant power cannot secure a favourable bargain, it can threaten to walk away. At the same time, in return for selectively overriding formal rules or agreeing to bargains on disproportionally uneven terms, the preponderant power is willing to compensate weaker states with a range of side payments, such as some privileges beyond the reach of their current capabilities, or economic carrots in other areas.[37] Examples include the Clinton Administration's invitation to

Russia to attend G7 meetings in the 1990s and join a reconstituted G8 in 1998, primarily in return for swallowing NATO enlargement and promoting liberal reforms, and possibly China's 2010 invitation to South Africa to join the BRICS, despite some discomfort among incumbents, perhaps in return for South Africa's help in opening markets.

Powerful countries continue to exercise disproportionate influence in IGOs, both formally and informally. Lesser powers may benefit from liberal global governance institutions because they are open, integrated and rule-based. Some scholars further maintain that such institutions also constrain the hegemon, which agrees to bind itself to the rules so that 'political authority within the order flows from its legal-constitutional foundation rather than from power capabilities'.[38] However, hegemons are never entirely constrained, benefiting from exceptions, escape clauses, veto rights and other mechanisms that allow the most powerful countries to use institutions as 'instruments of political control'.[39] It follows that emerging powers are likely to seek greater privileges within the existing global governance regime to shape the agenda and its application to issues they care about, both through adjustments in the formal rules and via enhanced informal influence. One means to achieve this end is to have an ability to exert pressure on an existing IGO by the threat of exiting to pursue unilateral options. The USA frequently uses such 'outside options' to bolster its bargaining power: if the UNSC is not in accord with US objectives, for example, then the USA may signal its willingness to forego a co-operative deal and go it alone or with its allies.[40] Similarly, a hegemon disgruntled with a wayward IGO or a rising power dissatisfied with the prevailing distribution of power and benefits could also seek to gain a bargaining advantage by threatening to leave and even by starting parallel institutions.

Over time, the BRICS could enable China's use of its rising power capabilities. Thus far BRICS countries have demonstrated only moderate interest in pushing to change the formal rules of the game. They would like to play by the same informal rulebook as the major advanced industrial powers, but tilted to their own advantage. China has already signalled that it also seeks its own outside options—for example, by constructing East and Central Asian regional organizations, building a robust military capability, enhancing the role of its currency and in other areas. Although less successful, Russia has also attempted to build and dominate regional organizations, while Brazil has worked to balance the USA by preferring to construct new South American institutions rather than work through existing hemispheric ones.[41]

Through the BRICS and other forums, China appears to be building a basis for co-operation and exerting its influence informally. Within the BRICS, China's immense power has created some concerns in Russia and particularly in India, where beyond long-standing security issues, discontent over perceived slights as well as China's institutional advantages and more active diplomacy and trade agenda has surfaced. The governance structure and eventual location of the new BRICS development bank, which China, Russia and India would like to house, will be indicators of whether China's disproportionate economic power will determine the outcome. The emergence of a potential hegemon within the BRICS bears monitoring because China, clearly the most influential of the BRICS and the single indispensable participant, is perfectly willing to employ support from its fellow BRICS for its own ends, but is unlikely to let itself be bound by intragroup obligations that infringe on its core interests.

BRICS and the UN Security Council: imbalances of power, representation and norms

In their summit declarations, the BRICS repeatedly call for the democratization of international governance and for greater equality in international politics. Although the UN is the most frequently mentioned international organization in BRICS documents,[42] the group's record with

Leslie Elliott Armijo and Cynthia Roberts

respect to reforming the UNSC has been unimpressive. By comparison, when, by chance, all five BRICS sat on the UNSC in 2011, and four remained in 2012, their votes were surprisingly aligned. The five found it valuable to interact and adopt joint positions that would not have been predicted from self-interest or differences in regime type and values. These actions appear to reflect not only a common interest in affirming the norm of state sovereignty but also an attempt to conciliate other BRICS partners, while setting aside their many bilateral differences. This section first explains the conundrum of Security Council reform and then turns to the surprising collaboration of all five BRICS while serving simultaneously on the UNSC.

Broadening representation on the UNSC

Through the years, multiple high-level panels, commissions and UN General Assembly resolutions have concluded that the UNSC should be made 'more representative, efficient and transparent'.[43] On the one hand, the fact that the members of the Security Council have never engaged in direct military conflict and managed to co-operate on several notable international security problems in the last two decades is a measure of the usefulness of the institution.[44] However, few global steering groups are more anachronistic than the UNSC, which is composed of 10 rotating members from UN regional groups and five permanent members (P-5—the USA, Russia, China, the UK and France). Only the permanent members, which earned their seats largely as the victors of the last world war, wield vetoes.

Since the UN's inception, India and Brazil have been the most active advocates for expanding the Council and securing their own inclusion as permanent members. They have long complained that developing countries make up the overwhelming majority of the UN's members and should play a role in shaping decisions instead of just being the objects of Security Council actions. The world's largest democracy, India, also contributes the third largest contingent of peace-keeping troops and ranks as the 10th largest economy (third by PPP). Brazil is currently the sixth largest economy, surpassing the UK, and also the 12th largest contributor of peace-keeping forces to the UN. Their respective contributions to the UN budget for 2012–13 were also scheduled to rise from 0.5% to 0.66% (India) and from 1.6% to 2.9% (Brazil). They are currently in a powerful coalition of the so-called 'G4' aspirants to permanent membership, which also includes Germany and Japan. These countries rank as the second and third largest contributors to the UN budget (accounting for 25%), behind the USA (22%) and just ahead of the UK and France (combined about 13%). China, Brazil, India and other emerging powers agreed to major increases in their UN payments as part of a new agreement for the revised UN budget for 2012–13 that will also reduce Japan's and European contributions. China will pay an extra 61%, increasing its share of the budget from 3.2% to 5.1%, overtaking Canada and Italy to become the sixth largest UN contributor. The G4 faces opposition, however, from a group of regional rivals which advocate for increasing the number of rotating, elected UNSC seats. The Africa bloc forms the third main coalition, and claims the right to at least two new permanent seats for Africa. Contention over competing claims has led to a deadlock over new seats and privileges that few observers believe will be surmounted in the near future. It is worth noting that any resolution to expand the UNSC needs the support of two-thirds of the 193 members of the UN General Assembly, or 129 votes, as well as endorsement by the P-5 to succeed.

A common BRICS position on Security Council reform and other security-related policies has evolved incrementally since the group was formed. By the 2011 BRICS leaders' summit, in Sanya, China, the official declaration reaffirmed the need for a comprehensive reform of the UN, explicitly including the Security Council. It further noted: 'China and Russia reiterate the importance they attach to the status of India, Brazil and South Africa in international affairs and

The emerging powers and global governance

understand and support their aspiration to play a greater role in the UN'. The 2012 New Delhi Declaration added that the BRICS governments 'recall our close coordination in the Security Council during the year 2011, and underscore our commitment to work together in the UN ... in the years to come'.[45] It is unlikely that Russia and China would have been willing to issue such supportive statements had the BRICS club not emerged, although the usual implicit caveat—*in the event that a future bargain on UNSC reform can be reached*—renders these still somewhat ambivalent statements not entirely satisfactory to their three BRICS partners. The Russians are willing to support the other BRICS as 'strong candidates' in the eventuality of actual reform, but insist that the future legitimacy of the UNSC demands overwhelming international support for such an outcome, not just the required two-thirds' majority necessitated by the UN.[46]

In fact, China and Russia are reluctant to expand the permanent membership of the UNSC, which would dilute the uniqueness of their own access to the veto. This situation reveals an important paradox inherent in BRICS demands to rebalance power in global governance institutions. Rising economic powers are not always dissatisfied, disenfranchised outsiders, pressing for a larger role. Typically, there are clubs within a global club, such as in the G7/G8 or the G7 and BRICS, respectively, within the G20. Club-within-the-club dynamics create tension between insiders and outsiders and strong incentives by existing institutional members to defend the status quo rather than to change it, even if change would promote progressive and more representative outcomes that benefit others.[47] In theory, a more representative and efficient UN security structure could be designed, involving a new bargain that adjusts the status quo without necessarily destabilizing current arrangements or a renegotiation that starts from scratch. However, in reality, it is difficult to get there from here. As noted above, in the real world, opportunities to create new institutional orders tend to occur after major shocks like war.

Regardless of their ideological and political differences, existing dominant powers, such as the P-5, are strongly motivated to protect their important institutionalized advantages and not dilute or undermine them. The veto, provided for in Article 27 of the UN Charter, is coveted because it allows a state to block resolutions condemning its uses of force and also resolutions to use force or employ other means of coercion by others of which it disapproves. However, permanent members of the UNSC with superior capabilities gain the most leverage from their veto power if they prefer to bargain from a position of strength instead of exercising the attractive outside options that their greater resources permit.[48] All of the current P-5 are committed to retaining their veto power and some, such as Russia, have vowed to veto any resolution to remove it.

Former US Ambassador to the UN Zalmay Khalilzad bluntly revealed the US position against enlargement in a 2007 cable which opposed extending the veto to new permanent members because it would 'dilute US influence' and 'increase the risk to US interests ... exponentially'. Tactically, Khalilzad proposed that the USA 'should quietly allow discontent with P-5 veto prerogatives to ensure the veto is not extended to new members while joining Russia and China in stoutly defending existing P-5 vetoes'.[49] Khalilzad went on to consider the different models for UNSC expansion that were then gathering momentum:

> To take just the G-4 countries plus the yet-unidentified African state(s) that would join them in permanent membership, we are confident we could reliably count on Japan's support, and to a lesser degree, on Germany's. However, on the most important issues of the day—sanctions, human rights, the Middle East, etc.—Brazil, India, and most African states are currently far less sympathetic to our views than our European allies.

This proved a prescient observation in view of the BRICS' voting record in 2011. Publicly, Washington had only supported Japan in the event of any enlargement, until President Obama

511

in late 2010 also endorsed India's bid. However, Obama refrained from extending the same endorsement to Brazil following Brasilia's abstention on the UNSC resolution authorizing the use of force against Libya in 2011 and its 2010 diplomatic intervention in the dispute over Iran's nuclear programme, which the US State Department decried as naive and irresponsible meddling.

Russia and China share US preferences despite their cheap talk about enlargement for developing countries. After President Obama signalled US support for India in a future bargain, Chinese officials tweaked the official position to underscore that China sincerely seeks a qualitative improvement in relations with India and that it is not opposing India's bid for a permanent seat in the UNSC. However, a 2009 State Department cable revealed that the Chinese then Vice-Foreign Minister He Yafei was also concerned about gathering momentum on UNSC reform and sought to prevail on the USA not to 'dilute' the P-5 'club' by making it a P-10. In that case, both China and the USA would 'be in trouble'.[50] Here is concrete evidence of how multiple memberships in exclusive clubs can create strains between insiders and outsiders that risk jeopardizing relationships with less privileged members of the out group.

Relatedly, despite the BRICS' statements calling for greater representation in IGOs, it is not self-evident that the UNSC is experiencing a legitimacy crisis simply because representation of permanent members is skewed and because the P-5 countries possess the veto. Compared to the Cold War, the UNSC has been more productively engaged with security issues. The UNSC adopted only two Chapter VII resolutions between 1977 and the start of the Gulf War. By comparison, 304 Chapter VII resolutions were approved between 1990 and 2004.[51] Likewise, the UN embarked on more numerous, ambitious and difficult peace-keeping operations (PKOs), illustrated by the more than 113,000 personnel from 114 countries currently deployed in 16 missions across four continents. Also notable is that China, which refused to participate in peace-keeping missions when it joined the UN in October 1971, had deployed 1,869 Chinese peace-keepers in nine UN operations around the world as of 31 December 2012 (making it the biggest contributor of troops to PKOs of the P-5), and is the seventh largest financial contributor to PKOs, after the USA, Japan, UK, Germany, France and Italy.[52]

Some scholars make a strong case that since 1991, the UNSC has become a more legitimate institution than was possible during the Cold War.[53] Reflecting a rise in internal conflicts, in 2005 191 member states endorsed the 'Responsibility to Protect' (R2P) doctrine, which holds that the UNSC may authorize measures, including force to protect civilians in the event of mass killing or other crimes. However, all of the BRICS, including the democracies, have voiced objections about the risk to state sovereignty from operationalized pretexts of R2P that fast-track punitive or coercive means, especially the use of force, and opposed such measures in Zimbabwe, Sudan, Myanmar (Burma) and elsewhere, despite their own occasional unilateral actions.[54]

The USA often has also sought the legitimizing imprimatur of the UNSC, even during the George W. Bush Administration, while still reserving the right to exercise its outside options. In Khalilzad's revealing description, the US mission 'starts most discussions about important Council statements or resolutions with at least six votes (the USA, the UK, France, and the three European delegations) and must secure three more to reach the required nine votes—barring a P-5 veto—for adoption'. It was not uncommon, then, for the USA to offer side payments and sweeteners to holdouts to get its way. Such prudent bargaining by both the predominant power and weaker members of the Security Council reflects the recognition that states with credible outside options will not commit to abide by rigid binding rules when their preferences are intense.[55] A larger UNSC membership, however, would likely complicate the conduct of serious negotiations without necessarily being fully representative of the UN membership.[56] A stronger China, by comparison, would perhaps enable a similar process but one resulting in different kinds of bargains, reflecting China's priorities.

Voting patterns in the UN Security Council

Whether the recent spurt of UNSC interventionist activity is likely to be sustained as global power shifts away from the West is an important question. The coincidence of all five BRICS simultaneously serving on the UNSC in 2011 (and 2012 minus Brazil), and the tendency of the three democratic BRICS to hew to Russian and Chinese positions, raise serious doubts about whether an enlarged UNSC would continue to back humanitarian action to the same degree.[57] The first UNSC resolution on Libya (UNSCR 1970), which imposed sanctions, an arms embargo, provided for humanitarian access and referred the matter to the International Criminal Court (ICC), passed unanimously in February. However, as the crisis escalated, with urging from the League of Arab States, the members authorized on 17 March UN Security Council Resolution 1973 approving a military operation to impose a 'no-fly zone' to protect civilians in Libya. All of the BRICS (minus South Africa, which voted 'yes') and Germany abstained and subsequently complained that the mandate was exceeded when it morphed into 'regime change'. Critical of the military operation, Brazil issued a paper arguing that the use of force in support of the new R2P norm needed to be subjected to higher standards and accountability, for 'Responsibility While Protecting'.[58] However, this proved a non-starter for those countries actually undertaking the military burden of intervention.

Meanwhile, Russia and China were probably disturbed by the rapid dislodging of Muammar al-Qaddafi and the costs to their interests. According to the Chinese government, 75 Chinese enterprises operating 50 joint projects were affected by the conflict in Libya. Nearly 36,000 workers were forced to leave, abandoning materials, machines and vehicles for projects valued at billions of dollars.[59] A well-connected Chinese academic official later remarked that it would not be surprising if in future incidents China decided to intervene on the side of the government, to protect its people, property and interests.[60]

When the UNSC subsequently turned to the escalating crisis in Syria in October 2011, the BRICS refused to support a draft resolution condemning the 'grave and systematic human rights violations' committed by Syrian forces against civilians. In early 2012 India and South Africa (after Brazil's term ended) did vote for resolutions that endorsed international efforts to facilitate a Syrian-led political transition to a democratic political system, but Russia and China vetoed these on grounds that the international community should not force Bashar al-Assad from office. Then the draft resolution in July 2012 threatening sanctions if the Syrian government failed to comply with the Annan Plan was vetoed by Russia and China, with South Africa abstaining, while India broke ranks and voted 'yes'.

The record shows that the BRICS countries co-ordinated their positions, and were often obstructive on sanctions or the use of force. Susan Rice, then the US Permanent Representative to the UN, questioned the voting of the three democratic BRICS as not always 'consistent with their own democratic institutions and stated values'. For the USA and other UNSC members, she added, this was 'a very interesting opportunity to see how they respond to the issues of the day … we've learned a lot and, frankly, not all of it encouraging'.[61] Such concerns parallel the EU's apprehensions that it is losing influence to China, Russia and their associates, and therefore is less able to win support at the UN for multilateral action on human rights and justice.[62]

As noteworthy as these revelations are, it is important not to draw overly firm conclusions about the degree of BRICS solidarity on the basis of a limited number of cases. The BRICS do share a common stake in defending the international norms of state sovereignty, independence and territorial integrity from what they see as excessive use of force and coercion by the USA and Europeans to achieve their strategic and humanitarian goals.[63] However, even the autocratic BRICS countries have supported or abstained on sanctions and other measures so long as their direct interests are assured—in instances ranging from sanctioning Libya and referring Qaddafi to the ICC, to supporting limited sanctions against the Democratic People's Republic of Korea (North Korea) and Iran.[64] Overall, major powers are reluctant to commit to precise thresholds that must be reached to justify interventions, as evident in Syria even after apparent use of chemical weapons in early 2013. Consequently, there has been more common ground and consistency in voting patterns than would seem likely among the diverse permanent members. Even in the 1980s the rates of affirmative votes shared by the autocratic powers with the Western UNSC members were above 91% (with only two vetoes by the USSR). During the 1990s China abstained twice as often as Russia but its voting affinity with the USA soared to 92.1%, while Russia's overall affirmative rate with the P-5 was 96.4%. Between 1990 and 2011 veto use on average declined to slightly over one per year for all P-5 members. Thus, it is premature to conclude that 2011 was a harbinger of change, marking the start of a more assertive BRICS bloc obstructing Western attempts to use coercion in support of humanitarian action. Moreover, any signal to this effect could undercut the standing of the BRICS democracies with the USA and Europeans, and leave them out in the cold.

Global economic governance: the BRICS in search of formal and informal influence

The international relations theories discussed above suggested that rising powers will desire a larger share in global governance, both in terms of formal power, as in access to leadership positions and votes, and in terms of informal influence within IGOs and in framing the international debates on key issues. The circumstances of the BRICS' rise to international prominence suggest that their increase in relative capabilities has been duly noted by the traditional powers. The BRICS group has been particularly noticeable as a club within the club of the financial G20. After the September 2008 crash of US investment bank Lehman Brothers induced financial ripples in all major global markets, the USA and other major powers realized that they would need more co-ordinated macroeconomic firepower than the G7 alone could muster, and thus convened the first financial G20 leaders' summit in Washington, DC. By the end of 2009 the financial G20—increasingly referred to as the 'major economies' G20—had explicitly declared itself the replacement for the G7/G8 as the senior co-ordinating body for global economic governance.[65]

Leadership of the Bretton Woods twins

Intellectuals from a number of developing countries—prominently including India, the only one of the original four BRICS whose head of government, Prime Minister Manmohan Singh, was a professional economist with long experience interacting with the IMF and World Bank— for years had been critical of the informal process of reserving the right for dominant countries to appoint the head of the so-called Bretton Woods twins, with the IMF managing director position going to a Western European, and the World Bank presidency to an American.[66] Having a national occupying either chairperson position has been presumed to confer considerable informal influence in setting the direction for the multilateral organization.

Therefore it was natural that in April of 2011 the BRICS, anticipating the end of the term of World Bank President Robert Zoellick in 2012, proclaimed their desire to end the de facto Western monopoly on appointing the heads of the two Bretton Woods institutions. The following month they unexpectedly got their first opportunity to exert collective influence, when IMF Managing Director Dominique Strauss-Kahn suddenly resigned over alleged improprieties.

The BRICS' IMF directors for their respective countries quickly issued a statement reiterating their desire for an open, competitive, merit-based process. Mexican Central Bank President Agustín Carstens became the first declared candidate, followed by French Minister of Finance Christine Lagarde, and former IMF Deputy Managing Director and then Israeli Central Bank President Stanley Fischer. Although Fischer, a dual US and Israeli citizen, had strong support in sub-Saharan Africa and elsewhere in the developing world, the race quickly devolved to a two-person contest between Carstens and Lagarde. Breaking with past tradition, both candidates embraced the opportunity to campaign openly and globally. Lagarde immediately focused on wooing the BRICS, as she travelled in rapid succession to Brazil, China, India and Russia, all of which refrained from early endorsement of either principal candidate. Russia briefly promoted the central bank governor of Kazakhstan and in the same week spoke out, together with its BRICS partners, against tradition prevailing over merit. Then at the G8 summit, Russia agreed that Christine Lagarde was a fine candidate. The IMF election, carried out within the executive board and with weighted voting reflecting country quotas, not unexpectedly went to Lagarde. None the less, the election was considerably more open and competitive than any previous process to choose the heads of the international financial institutions.

The next year's vote for the new World Bank president was much the same story. Early entrants to the race were former Colombian Minister of Finance and prominent left-leaning economist José Antonio Ocampo, and former World Bank neoclassical economist and current Nigerian Minister of Finance Ngozi Okonjo-Iweala, the latter nominated and strongly supported by South Africa. The USA nominated Korean-American university president and public health specialist Jim Yong Kim. Again, both developing country candidates complained that the selection process was insufficiently merit-based, particularly given that Kim was not an economist.[67] However, and in contrast to earlier nomination years, candidate Kim, like candidate Lagarde the previous year, visited various constituencies and discreetly campaigned on his own behalf. Once again, the BRICS demurred from declaring early for any candidate. Moreover, on the same day that Ocampo withdrew in favour of Okonjo-Iweala, hoping to force the hand of pro-diversity waverers, Russia abruptly endorsed Dr Kim, who was formally selected three days later, on 16 April 2012.

In both of these cases, opinions on the BRICS role were mixed, with some commentators concluding that the group was so weak and divided that it could not even agree to support a joint candidate. Others stressed that these elections for heads of the major international financial institutions had been the most open and competitive to date, speculating also that the individual BRICS might well have cleverly concluded some back-room *quid pro quo* deals from the traditional powers along the way. It also was noted that for the first time, neither global financial governance position had gone to a Caucasian male.

Formal votes in the Bretton Woods twins

The larger existential dilemma shared by both the World Bank and the IMF is that in a world of globalized capital, they are simply too small. If they wish to retain their influence in shaping global economic models, then they must locate additional funds. The obvious sources for increases in capital subscriptions are the large emerging economies in the financial G20, and particularly the BRICS. The large emerging powers also took a hit in 2008–09 from the international crisis, but most, including the BRICS, quickly bounced back.[68] Even prior to the crisis the emerging powers were becoming more important in global finance, and the lingering turmoil in advanced countries, especially Western Europe, has only underscored this. For example, in 2010, there were five Chinese, three Brazilian and one Russian bank among the top 25 banks globally ranked by profits, and the two top slots were held by Chinese institutions.[69] Since 2009 China has been the largest foreign sovereign owner of US Treasury securities, replacing Japan.

However, while the advanced industrial countries covet the financial resources of the BRICS, they resist yielding political control over the lending policies of the World Bank and the IMF. The root of the traditional powers' formal dominance of the Bretton Woods twins lies in the distribution of quotas—capital subscriptions and their associated voting rights—among countries. The basic patterns of quota allocations were determined at the 1944 conference in Bretton Woods, New Hampshire, as the soon to be victorious Allies sought to design viable and enduring post-war global governance institutions. Quotas were roughly proportional to the economic and other power resources that each founding member country controlled. As of 2008, and prior to the current recent rounds of quota renegotiations, the USA held a 15.00% quota in the World Bank and a 17.41% quota at the IMF. In both institutions, a super-majority (ranging from 70% to 85%, depending on the type of issue) has been required for significant decisions, implying that the USA plus one or two key allies has always had an effective veto.

Quota redistribution—popularly known as the debate over 'chairs and shares'—has been a long-standing demand of developing countries.[70] In the aftermath of the global financial crisis, both the BRICS club and the first Obama Administration in the USA sought to make 'reform' of the international financial institutions an issue that could work for them. New quota negotiation rounds began in late 2008 in both the Bank and the Fund, as well as in five other regional development banks to which the USA and other major powers contribute.[71] The BRICS found seemingly easy agreement on the broad topic of linking increased contributions (capital subscriptions) to quota reform: developing and transitional countries deserve a larger say in how the Bank and the Fund are run. Already by early 2009 the then IMF Managing Director Dominique Strauss-Kahn had requested that total IMF resources be doubled or tripled to $500 billion or even $750 billion, which he and others hoped would be pledged by the world leaders planning to attend the second financial G20 summit in London in late April 2009. In mid-March 2009, and even in advance of their first leaders' summit in June of that year, the BRICS issued a joint communiqué explicitly linking quota readjustment to an expansion of their financial contributions to the IMF and the World Bank, and they have repeated this demand on successive occasions. When the IMF announced its first ever bond issue in early 2009, the four BRICs quickly promised to invest up to $80 billion, with China contributing $50 billion, and the others $10 billion each.[72]

Through the years each new general capital increase round for both international financial institutions has been enormously slow and subject to much wrangling over allocation formulae, and the rounds whose negotiations began in 2008 have been no exception.[73] For example, the USA has favoured a calculation of economic size based on GDP calculated at market rates, which makes its economy appear relatively larger, while most developing countries would prefer to assess GDP at purchasing power parity—by which measure their economies are relatively larger. The current, and theoretically quite arbitrary, compromise is a 60%–40% blend of market and PPP calculations of relative economic size. In the IMF, whose quota formula always has incorporated a greater range of variables, groups of countries doggedly argue for allocation rules that favour themselves, panning or championing such variables as their national share in global foreign exchange reserves, the openness of their economies in trade and/or finance (measured variously), or even their comparative sensitivity to annual fluctuations in trade—an odd but historically included variable that allocates votes to the vulnerable rather than the powerful.[74]

In 2009 and early 2010 the Obama Administration, committed to finding additional capital for the international financial institutions, decided to twist the arms of Western European leaders, in order to get agreement on quota reallocation away from Western Europe and towards the emerging powers.[75] Prompted by continuous pressure from both the BRICS and the US Obama Administration, the executive directors at both major international financial institutions (IFIs) completed torturous negotiations resulting in 2010 multilateral capital increase and reallocation deals that included a 3.3% quota reallocation away from the advanced industrial (Part I) countries and towards developing (Part II) countries in the World Bank, and a 6% readjustment between roughly the same groups in the IMF. The major beneficiaries were the emerging powers, including China, Brazil, Mexico and India, leading some poorer countries and their advocates to cry foul. Unfortunately, by the time the provisional deals for the Bank and the Fund were announced in April 2010, US support for them already had unravelled. The US Senate Foreign Relations Committee's report, introduced by the senior Republican member Richard Lugar, recommended against any capital increase for any of the international financial institutions until they tackled the 'invidious corruption that has thwarted so many development projects', while also recommending that they 'should concentrate more clearly on "putting themselves out of business" by creating stable, self-sustaining economic growth in their client countries'.[76] Eventually, the Obama Administration gave up, declining in both 2012 and 2013 even to submit the package to Congress, and thus rendering the entire complex deal moot.[77] In October 2012 newly appointed World Bank President Kim announced that the time was not favourable for a capital increase.[78] IMF Managing Director Lagarde meanwhile threw herself into promoting a new capital-cum-quota renegotiating round, recognizing, however, that the emerging powers were unenthusiastic about allocating additional funds to an institution whose five largest borrowers as of 2012—Greece, Portugal, Ireland, Romania and Ukraine—had incomes per capita mostly higher than theirs.[79] At the G20 summit in Los Cabos, Mexico, in June 2012 the BRICS again pledged their willingness to increase their contributions to the IFIs by $75 billion, but reiterated that they expected the quota readjustments to also go forward.[80]

Through these varied negotiations, the BRICS were able to hang together reasonably well. They have not yet achieved their aims of greater voting power in the IFIs, but they have demonstrated that they are a force to be reckoned with. Moreover, and despite some objective intra-BRICS interest conflicts, club members have demonstrated some willingness to make tactical concessions for the sake of group cohesion. For example, in the World Bank, Russia, historically grouped with the wealthy countries and with a significantly smaller economy since the break-up of the USSR, would lose rather than gain under most possible adjustment schemes. Russia none the less has supported the principle of readjustment in favour of Part II (borrower) countries. Of course, when the 2010 deal on World Bank quota readjustment was about to be struck, Russia, along with Saudi Arabia, successfully threatened to scuttle the whole bargain unless a back-door fix was found to keep their shares from falling.[81] Moreover, in the World Bank negotiations leading up to the 2010 provisional deal, China chose to behave as a benevolent hegemon, not pushing in the World Bank negotiations for the maximum readjustment in its favour that it arguably could have claimed by virtue of economic size, but instead generously insisting that other countries receive additional increments.[82] One also could interpret the initial announcements, at their New Delhi (2012) and Durban (2013) summits, of the BRICS' intention to establish their own BRICS development bank as raising the spectre of an outside option.

The 'currency war'—of words

Perhaps the most interesting test case of intra-BRICS solidarity—and the skill of China in being able to profit from this—has been over the question of relative currency values, or 'global imbalances', as this source of tension is often referred to in the USA and Western Europe. On the one hand, the exchange rate and trade balance nexus lies at the heart of contemporary USA–China rivalries. Many US academics and a clear majority of US economic policymakers are convinced that Chinese capital controls and central bank market interventions have been designed not to protect China's domestic economy from unhealthy volatility, as Chinese officials claim, but instead to hold the value of China's currency artificially low, thus fuelling China's enormously successful exports of manufactures.[83] In 2007 China's current account surplus reached its zenith, at fully 10% of Chinese GDP. By the third quarter of 2012 global slow down had brought China's external surplus down to only 2.6% of GDP, yet the IMF still found this level worrisome.[84] Chinese authorities, of course, have consistently denied that their export surplus revealed evidence of exporting economic problems abroad, instead blaming lack of competitiveness and/or irresponsible macroeconomic policies in their trading partners.

On the other hand, and this is the interesting puzzle piece, China's BRICS partners also believe themselves to have suffered from China's export juggernaut, and have sometimes criticized Chinese currency policies. India, in particular, has a significant bilateral trade deficit with China ($39.4 billion in financial year 2011/12). Brazil has a reliable bilateral surplus ($10.5 billion in 2011), but worries because its imports from China are manufactures, while it mainly sells commodities to China. Moreover, Brazilian policymakers have become increasingly worried about Chinese trade competition in South America, the most important destination for Brazil's manufactured exports.[85] None the less, since Brazil's finance minister first publicly proclaimed his fears of an international 'currency war' in September 2010, the BRICS, notably including both Brazil and India, have tended to support the Chinese position that the major offenders to the implied norm of responsible currency policies have been the USA, Western Europe (the European Central Bank and the British), and in 2013 also Japan.

Vocal public support from the other BRICS on the currency levels issue, arguably in defiance of their own immediate best interests, has been an important resource for China to call upon in dealing with the USA. Thus far, US presidents, aware of the gamut of different spheres in which the two countries interact (for example, in attempting to restrain North Korean adventurism), successfully have dissuaded the US Congress from labelling China a 'currency manipulator', which would automatically trigger trade sanctions. Instead, US executive branch officials have tried repeatedly to get the financial G20 and/or the IMF to censure China, and the Chinese have employed their bureaucratic in-fighting skills to push back. In this ongoing *sub rosa* tussle, the USA tries to gain support from its major allies, the other G7 countries, while China attempts to keep the BRICS in its corner.

The USA has consistently tried to enlist the IMF in its battles to paint China as the guilty party in generating global trade and currency mismatches, while China has adamantly resisted being so labelled. Thus, for example, in August 2007 the IMF announced a plan to monitor global imbalances.[86] The Chinese correctly understood this as primarily aimed at themselves, which they found particularly unfair given the concurrent suspicion greeting their plans to invest some of their excess cash in the USA through sovereign wealth fund purchases of real assets such as infrastructure facilities (ports) and manufacturing plants.[87] In November 2010 the Korean hosts of the fifth G20 summit in Seoul tried to get agreement to implement a proposal, widely attributed to US Treasury Secretary Timothy Geithner, although he denied authorship, to discuss 'trade imbalances'. The Chinese (but also the Germans, another strongly trade surplus country) adamantly refused to engage in any such dialogue in the context of the G20. By late 2010 large economies G20 members Brazil, China, Germany and Russia all were publicly criticizing US monetary expansion, and India and South Africa later joined the rising chorus. In April 2011 the IMF once again announced a plan to provide data on trade imbalances, which the USA

The emerging powers and global governance

desired, but that same month also proposed a framework for how to deploy selective, temporary controls on inward capital flows (gratifying China, Brazil and India, among others).

Some observers see China's clear goal as promoting the renminbi as a global transactions and reserve currency, alongside the US dollar and the euro. None the less, the Chinese themselves remain ambivalent about how quickly they might want to move in this direction, as there would be a number of difficulties generated for their current development model.[88] Meanwhile, the BRICS have in their summits in 2011 (in Sanya, China), 2012 (New Delhi, India), and 2013 (Durban, South Africa) taken incremental steps to enhance their bilateral and multilateral financial co-operation, such as pledging to invoice more of their intra-BRICS trade and credits in local currency and taking initial steps to establish their own multilateral development bank.[89] These steps represent movement towards significant monetary co-operation, but they also mask potential conflicts. For example, local currency invoicing of trade saves on the service fees associated with converting transactions, even temporarily and electronically, into US dollars, but it is not at all clear that China's BRICS trading partners would not rather have dollars for their goods than renminbi. If the proposed BRICS bank made renminbi-denominated loans, this effectively would require borrowers to spend this currency on Chinese goods, and also to earn back renminbi to repay the loan, which would not necessarily be easy.

Meanwhile, the 'war' of words and phrases employed to discuss currency levels, capital controls and similar issues in the global economic governance institutions goes forward. These skirmishes will continue, and the BRICS club will likely remain a useful ally for China in its rivalry with the USA.

Conclusions and possible futures

This chapter set out the task of discerning how the rise of emerging powers might affect existing, Western-dominated, global governance regimes. We looked for evidence that the BRICS club is 'making a difference', first by reference to shifting patterns of material capabilities and then by reference to theory explaining what the BRICS, as rational actors, might seek to do in order to expand their influence in existing global governance regimes. The chapter then examined both the security and financial governance arenas through the lens of this analytical framework. Our analysis suggests these conclusions.

First, an underlying interstate shift in material capabilities is indeed underway, and at some point in the future there will be two dominant powers: the USA and China. In many dimensions of power, of course, especially those shaped by existing economic, political and military capabilities, the world today is still shaped by US primacy and Western institutions. Thus, it is not surprising that none of the emerging powers is directly provoking or balancing against the USA. None the less, the USA's pre-eminent position in both hard and soft dimensions of power will be challenged as rising states increase their own political, economic and military capabilities, and develop the concomitant bargaining power that propels international institutions in different directions and in pursuit of new agendas. For the foreseeable future, China will dwarf the other emerging powers combined, and thus should be expected to play a key role in shaping the BRICS' agenda and other coalitions it chooses to support.

Second, BRICS policymakers are eager to enhance their global influence by discovering common preferences that they can join forces to pursue. The BRICS' principal collective goal thus far has been the creation of greater ongoing global influence for themselves. Instead of dismissing the BRICS as trivial for their limited achievements thus far, it makes more sense to conceptualize them as in the process of building capacity, adjusting to China's looming presence within the club itself, and working through common positions. It remains to be seen whether

519

the BRICS in the future will co-ordinate to tackle important global issues, such as climate change and building effective domestic institutions that might be emulated in the developing world.

Third, it appears likely that the BRICS organization itself functions most readily as an 'outside option' for China to employ to exercise leverage within the major existing global governance institutions, particularly in the economic sphere, as with China's desire to sideline discussions of global imbalances and deflect criticisms of itself in the IMF or G20. Since there is intrinsically a lesser commonality of interests and policy preferences among the BRICS today than among the USA and its major allies (essentially the G7), we expect in the future either to see the conscious construction of a larger intra-BRICS set of shared views and preferences, or to observe cracks within the group as other members increasingly see their interests as competitive with the rise of China.

Fourth, the BRICS' preferences, singly and jointly, for global governance turn on reform and evolution, not revolution. It is striking that none of the emerging (or re-emerging in the case of China and Russia) powers has displayed revolutionary aims with respect to reordering the international system, at least so far. They have neither coalesced around the developing world's traditional agenda of redistribution, nor developed a radically new alternative model for international order. To varying degrees, all of the rising powers, including the principal challenger, China, benefit from engaging with the existing US-led order. None seeks to pay the costs of constructing a wholesale replacement, although nascent parallel institutions, including the BRICS themselves as a leadership club, and a possible BRICS development bank, are germinating.

Fifth and finally, the BRICS may make a growing difference, but not always and not necessarily in ways that improve global governance or serve the collective good, as perhaps is shown by their collective opposition to Western humanitarian action against the Assad government in Syria—although even in this case the efficacy of direct outside intervention is open to question. Similarly, the incremental development of the BRICS has given China a prominent new club to shield its rise. Given that rising power tends to correlate with rising geopolitical ambition, it follows that China's arrival as a great power is likely to create policy contradictions as it strains old loyalties and diplomatic commitments, for example, to solidarity among developing countries. None of this is entirely good news for a world that faces urgent global challenges that appear to be overwhelming the capacity of existing international institutions to produce meaningful co-operation, but it matters for understanding how the world works.

Notes

1 Author order according to alphabetical convention.
2 Å. Johansson, Y. Guillemette, F. Murtin, D. Turner, G. Nicoletti, C. de la Maisonneuve, P. Bagnoli, G. Bousquet and F. Spinelli, 'Looking to 2060: Long-Term Global Growth Prospects: A Going for Growth Report', OECD Economic Policy Papers No. 3, OECD Publishing, 2012; US National Intelligence Council (NIC), *Global Trends 2030: Alternative Worlds*, US Government Printing Office, Washington, DC, 2012; Álvaro de Vasconcelos (ed.), *Global Trends 2030—Citizens in an Interconnected and Polycentric World*, European Union Institute for Security Studies, Paris, 2012; D. Wilson, K. Trivedi, S. Carlson and J. Uri'ia, 'The BRICs 10 Years On: Halfway Through the Great Transformation', Global Economics Paper No. 208, Goldman Sachs, 2011.
3 National Intelligence Council (NIC), *Global Trends 2025: A Transformed World*, US Government Printing Office, Washington, DC, 2008, iv–vii.
4 NIC, *Global Trends 2030*, 15.
5 NIC, *Global Trends 2030*, 98.
6 Jim O'Neill, 'Building Better Global Economic BRICs', Global Economics Paper No. 66, Goldman Sachs, 2001; Cynthia Roberts (ed.), *Polity Forum: Challengers or Stakeholders? BRICs and the Liberal World Order* 42(1), January 2010.
7 'BRICS Development Bank a Done Deal', 'Background', and 'eThekwini Declaration', Fifth BRICS Summit, Durban, South Africa, 26–27 March 2013, www.brics5.co.za; 'Kontseptsiia uchastiia

Rossiiskoi Federatsii v ob'edinenii BRIKS' [Concept of the Participation of the Russian Federation in the BRICS], kremlin.ru/acts/17715; and author's interviews, Moscow, June 2013. The Russians were also among the first to produce a report (marked 'for official use') on their long-term vision, 'Russia in the BRICS: Strategic Objectives and Means for Their Realization', prepared by the Russian National Committee on BRICS Research for circulation in the second track diplomatic activity involving BRICS research centres.

8 Cynthia Roberts, 'Measuring the Chinese Economy', posted on 'H-Diplo: Lieber Roundtable: Is the US Declining?' 31 August 2013.

9 World Bank, World Development Indicators (WDI) database, data.worldbank.org/data-catalog/world-development-indicators (accessed May 2013).

10 Johansson *et al.* 'Looking to 2060'.

11 Author's calculation, using data available in OECD, *Economic Outlook No. 91*, 'Long-term Baseline Projections', June 2012 (database), stats.oecd.org (accessed January 2013).

12 Ilya Arkhipov, Mike Cohen and Arnaldo Galvao, 'BRICS Nations Need More Time for New Bank, Russia Says', 27 March 2013, www.bloomberg.com/news/2013-03-27/brics-nations-need-more-time-for-development-bank-russia-says.html (accessed 24 May 2013).

13 World Bank, *Capital for the Future: Saving and Investment in an Interdependent World*, Global Development Horizons, World Bank, Washington, DC, 2013, 3, 5, 17.

14 Vasconcelos, *Global Trends 2030*; Homi Kharas and Geoffrey Gertz, 'The New Global Middle Class: A Cross-over from West to East', *China's Emerging Middle Class: Beyond Economic Transformation*, Brookings Institution Press, Washington, DC, 2010; Dominic Wilson and Raluca Dragusanu, 'The Expanding Middle: The Exploding World Middle Class and Falling Global Inequality', Global Economics Paper 170, Goldman Sachs, 2008.

15 Vasconcelos, *Global Trends 2030*; Kharas and Gertz, 'The New Global Middle Class'; Glenita Amoranto, Natalie Chun and Anil B. Deolalikar, 'Who are the Middle Class and What Values do they Hold? Evidence from the World Values Survey', Asian Development Bank Economics Working Paper Series No. 229, 2010.

16 International Institute for Strategic Studies (IISS), *The Military Balance 2013*, Routledge, London, 2013.

17 IISS, *The Military Balance 2013*.

18 Kenneth N. Waltz, *Theory of International Politics*, Addison Wesley, Reading, MA, 1979.

19 Stephen D. Krasner, 'Global Communications and National Power', *World Politics* 43(3), April 1991.

20 Robert O. Keohane, *After Hegemony: Cooperation and Discord in the World Political Economy*, Princeton University Press, Princeton, NJ, 1984; Robert O. Keohane, 'The Theory of Hegemonic Stability and Changes in International Regimes, 1967–77', in Ole Holsti (ed.), *Change in the International System*, Westview Press, Boulder, CO, 1980; Robert O. Keohane and Lisa L. Martin, 'Institutional Theory as a Research Program', in Colin Elman (ed.), *Progress in International Relations Theory: Appraising the Field*, MIT Press, Cambridge, MA, 2003; and Judith Goldstein, Miles Kahler, Robert O. Keohane and Anne-Marie Slaughter, 'Legalization and World Politics', *International Organization* 54(3), Summer 2000.

21 Charles P. Kindleberger, *The World in Depression, 1929–1939*, University of California Press, Berkeley, CA, 1973; Keohane, 'Theory of Hegemonic Stability'; Robert G. Gilpin, *U.S. Power and the Multinational Corporation*, Basic Books, New York, 1975; Robert G. Gilpin, *The Political Economy of International Relations*, Princeton University Press, Princeton, NJ, 1987; Stephen D. Krasner, 'State Power and the Structure of International Trade', *World Politics* 28(3), April 1976.

22 Stephen D. Krasner, 'Approaches to the State: Alternative Conceptions and Historical Dynamics', *Comparative Politics* 16, 1984; James L. True, Bryan D. Jones and Frank R. Baumgartner, 'Punctuated-Equilibrium Theory: Explaining Stability and Change in Public Policymaking', in Paul Sabatier (ed.), *Theories of the Policy Process*, 2nd edn, Westview, Boulder, CO, 2007.

23 Robert G. Gilpin, *War and Change in World Politics*, Cambridge University Press, Cambridge, IL, 1981; A.F.K. Organski and Jacek Kugler, *The War Ledger*, University of Chicago Press, Chicago, IL, 1981; Ronald L. Tammen, Jacek Kugler, Douglas Lemke, Carole Alsharabati, Brian Efird and A.F.K. Organski, *Power Transitions: Strategies for the 21st Century*, Chatham House Publishers of Seven Bridges Press, New York, 2000.

24 Gilpin, *War and Change in World Politics*, 50.

25 Aaron L. Friedberg, *A Contest for Supremacy: China, America, and the Struggle for Mastery in Asia*, W.W. Norton & Company, New York, 2011; John J. Mearsheimer, 'The Gathering Storm: China's Challenge to US Power in Asia', *The Chinese Journal of International Politics* 3(4), Winter 2010.

26 Robert Jervis, *The Meaning of Nuclear Revolution: Statecraft and the Prospect of Armageddon*, Cornell University Press, Ithaca, NY, 1989; see also Robert Powell, 'Nuclear Deterrence Theory, Nuclear Proliferation, and National Missile Defense', *International Security* 27(4), Spring 2003.

27 G. John Ikenberry, Michael Mastanduno and William C. Wohlforth, 'Unipolarity, State Behavior, and Systemic Consequences', *World Politics* 61(1), January 2009; Jeffrey Legro, *Rethinking the World: Great Power Strategies and International Order*, Cornell University Press, Ithaca, NY, 2005.

28 Stewart Patrick, 'Irresponsible Stakeholders? The Difficulty of Integrating Rising Powers', *Foreign Affairs* 89(6), November/December 2010; Ian Bremmer and David Gordon, 'Rise of the Different', *The New York Times*, 18 June 2012.

29 Alastair Iain Johnston, 'Is China a Status Quo Power?' *International Security* 27(4), Spring 2003; Rosemary Foot and Andrew Walter, *China, the United States, and Global Order*, Cambridge University Press, Cambridge, 2010.

30 Friedberg, *A Contest for Supremacy*; Thomas J. Christensen, 'Advantages of an Assertive China: Responding to Beijing's Abrasive Diplomacy', *Foreign Affairs* 90(2), March/April 2011; Alastair Iain Johnston, 'How New and Assertive is China's New Assertiveness?' *International Security* 37(4), Spring 2013.

31 Robert O. Keohane, *After Hegemony: Cooperation and Discord in the World Political Economy*, Princeton University Press, Princeton, NJ, 1984.

32 Daniel W. Drezner, *All Politics is Global*, Princeton University Press, Princeton, NJ, 2007.

33 Cynthia Roberts, 'The Rising Power of the BRICS Club: Club Dynamics and Interests in Global Governance Institutions', Paper prepared for the International Studies Association Annual Convention, San Francisco, 3–6 April 2013; author's interviews, Moscow, June 2013 and June 2012.

34 G. John Ikenberry, 'The Future of the Liberal World Order', *Foreign Affairs* 90(3), May/June 2011; G. John Ikenberry, 'The Rise of China and the Future of the West', *Foreign Affairs* 87(1), January/February 2008; for contrary view see Cynthia Roberts, 'Russia's BRICs Diplomacy: Rising Outsider with Dreams of an Insider', *Polity* 42(1), January 2010.

35 Krasner, 'Global Communications and National Power'; Lloyd Gruber, *Ruling the World: Power Politics and the Rise of Supranational Institutions*, Princeton University Press, Princeton, NJ, 2000.

36 Stephen G. Brooks and William C. Wohlforth, 'Reshaping the World Order: How Washington Should Reform International Institutions', *Foreign Affairs* 88(2), March/April 2009: 50.

37 Randall W. Stone, *Controlling Institutions: International Organizations and the Global Economy*, Cambridge University Press, Cambridge 2011.

38 G. John Ikenberry, *Liberal Leviathan: The Origins, Crisis, and Transformation of the American World Order*, Princeton University Press, Princeton, NJ, 2012, 83; G. John Ikenberry, *After Victory: Institutions, Strategic Restraint, and the Rebuilding of Order after Major Wars*, Princeton University Press, Princeton, NJ, 2001.

39 Richard K. Betts, 'Institutional Imperialism', *The National Interest*, May/June 2011; Randall L. Schweller, 'The Problem of International Order Revisited: A Review Essay', *International Security* 26(1), Summer 2001.

40 Erik Voeten, 'The Political Origins of the UN Security Council's Ability to Legitimize the Use of Force', *International Organization* 59(3), July 2005.

41 Roberts, 'The Rising Power of the BRICS Club'; Leslie Elliott Armijo, 'Equality and Regional Finance in the Americas', *Latin American Politics and Society*, 55 (3) Winter 2013.

42 Marina Larionova, 'BRIKS v sisteme global'nogo upravleniia' [BRICS in the System of Global Governance], *Mezhdunarodnaia zhizn'* [International Affairs] 4, April 2012: 10.

43 Erik Voeten, 'Why No UN Security Council Reform?' in Dimitris Bourantonis and Kostas Ifantis (eds), *Multilateralism and Security Institutions in an Era of Globalization*, Routledge, New York, 2008, 289.

44 Keohane and Martin, 'Institutional Theory as a Research Program'; Jochen Prantl, 'Informal Groups of States and the UN Security Council', *International Organization* 59(3), July 2005.

45 BRICS Information Centre, University of Toronto, *BRICS Official Documents: Summits*, www.brics.utoronto.ca/docs/index.html, database, 2013.

46 Author's interviews, Moscow, June 2013.

47 Roberts, 'The Rising Power of the BRICS Club'; Cynthia Roberts, 'Introduction', *Polity Forum: Challengers or Stakeholders? BRICs and the Liberal World Order* 42(1), January 2010.

48 Erik Voeten, 'Outside Options and the Logic of Security Council Action', *American Political Science Review* 95(4), December 2001; Voeten, 'Political Origins of the UNSC's Ability to Legitimize'.

49 Roberts, 'The Rising Power of the BRICS Club'.

50 Ibid.

The emerging powers and global governance

51 Voeten, 'Why No UN Security Council Reform?' 292.
52 United Nations, 'Peacekeeping Factsheet 2013', 2013 www.un.org/en/peacekeeping/.
53 Voeten, 'Political Origins of the UNSC's Ability to Legitimize'.
54 Gareth Evans, Ramesh Thakur and Robert A. Pape, 'Correspondence: Humanitarian Intervention and the Responsibility to Protect', *International Security* 37(4), Spring 2013; Andrew Garwood-Gowers, 'The BRICS and the Responsibility to Protect: Lessons from the Libyan and Syrian Crises', in Vasilka Sancin and Masa Kovic Dine (eds), *Responsibility to Protect in Theory and Practice*, GV Založba, Ljubljana, Slovenia, 2013; Joel Wuthnow, *Chinese Diplomacy and the UN Security Council: Beyond the Veto*, Routledge, London, 2012, 29–30.
55 Voeten, 'Outside Options and the Logic of Security Council Action'; Voeten, 'Political Origins of the UNSC's Ability to Legitimize'; Stone, *Controlling Institutions*.
56 Thomas G. Weiss, 'The Illusion of UN Security Council Reform', *Washington Quarterly* 26(4), Autumn 2003.
57 This discussion draws on Roberts, 'The Rising Power of the BRICS Club'.
58 Government of Brazil, 'Responsibility While Protecting: Elements for the Development and Promotion of a Concept', A/66/551–S/2011/701, 11 November 2011, www.un.int/brazil/speech/Concept-Paper-%20RwP.pdf (accessed 4 January 2013).
59 Jingjing Huang, 'China Counting Financial Losses in Libya', *Global Times*, 4 March 2011, www.globaltimes.cn/china/diplomacy/2011-03/629817.html (accessed 6 January 2013); Ying Ding, 'Out of Libya', *Beijing Review*, 8 March 2011, www.china.org.cn/world/2011-03/08/content_22082446.htm (accessed 6 January 2013).
60 National Committee on American Foreign Policy, 'New Team in Beijing, New Term for Obama: How to Improve U.S.-China Relations', author's notes on panel discussion, Waldorf Astoria, New York, 6 May 2013.
61 Howard LaFranchi, 'Syria Vote May Prove Costly for Three Countries Seeking More UN Clout', *The Christian Science Monitor*, 5 October 2011, www.csmonitor.com/USA/Foreign-Policy/2011/1005/Syria-vote-may-prove-costly-for-three-countries-seeking-more-UN-clout (accessed 4 January 2013).
62 See for example, European Parliament, Committee on Foreign Affairs, 'Report on the EU Foreign Policy Towards the BRICS and Other Emerging Powers: Objectives and Strategies', 2011/2111 (INI), A7-0010/2012, 10 January 2012.
63 Roberts, 'Introduction', *Polity Forum*.
64 Wuthnow, *Chinese Diplomacy*.
65 On the financial G20 see Colin I. Bradford (ed.), *Global Leadership in Transition: Making the G20 More Effective and Responsive*, Brookings Institution, Washington, DC, 2011.
66 Devesh Kapur, 'The Changing Anatomy of Governance at the World Bank', in Jonathan R. Pincus and Jeffry A. Winters (eds), *Reinventing the World Bank*, Cornell University Press, Ithaca, NY, 2002; Arvind Subramanian and Devesh Kapur, 'Who Should Lead the World Bank?' *Project Syndicate*, 17 February 2012, www.project-syndicate.org (accessed May 2013).
67 James Fontanella-Khan, 'BRICS Nations Threaten IMF Funding', *Financial Times*, 29 March 2012.
68 Carol Wise, Leslie Elliott Armijo and Saori Katada (eds), *Unexpected Outcomes: How Emerging Markets Survived the Global Financial Crisis*, book manuscript, under review.
69 Philip Alexander, 'Top 1000 Banks 2011', *The Banker*, 30 June 2011.
70 Kapur, 'The Changing Anatomy of Governance'; Edwin M. Truman (ed.), *Reforming the IMF for the 21st Century*, Peterson Institute of International Economics, Washington, DC, April 2006.
71 Martin A. Weiss, 'Multilateral Development Banks: General Capital Increases', Congressional Research Service, Washington, DC, 27 January 2012; Robert H. Wade, 'Emerging World Order: From Multipolarity to Multilateralism in the World Bank, IMF, and G20', *Politics & Society* 39(3), 31 August 2011.
72 Bob Davis, 'Brazil, China, and Russia Consider IMF's First Bond Offering', *Wall Street Journal*, 25 April 2009; IMF, 'Bolstering the IMF's Lending Capacity', updated to 18 June 2012, www.imf.org/external/np/exr/faq/contribution.htm.
73 Truman, *Reforming the IMF*; Wade, 'Emerging World Order'.
74 New Rules for Global Finance (New Rules), online document collection on IMF quota reform, www.new-rules.org/what-we-do/imf-governance-reform/imf-quota-reform (accessed May 2013).
75 Douglas Rediker, 'Losing at the IMF', *Foreign Policy*, 10 October 2012; Johannes F. Linn, 'Charting a New Course for the World Bank: Three Options for its New President', Brookings Institution, Washington, DC, 17 April 2012.

76 US Government, Senate Committee on Foreign Relations, 'The International Financial Institutions: A Call for Change', Washington, DC, 111th Congress, 2nd session, 10 March 2010, 1.

77 Rediker, 'Losing at the IMF'; Linn, 'Charting a New Course'.

78 Sandrine Rastello, 'World Bank's Kim Sees "No Appetite" to Increase Capital', Bloomberg News, 4 October 2012, www.bloomberg.org.

79 International Monetary Fund (IMF), *Financial Statements, Quarter ended January 31, 2013*, IMF, Washington, DC, 2013, 9.

80 Krista Mahr, 'After the G20: Can the BRICS Save the Day?' *Time*, 22 June 2012; see also Oliver Stuenkel, 'The Case for IMF Quota Reform', Council on Foreign Relations Online, 10 October 2012, www.cfr.org. The commitments pledged in response to the crisis are not permanent quotas, but bilateral standby credit lines under the New Arrangements to Borrow (NAB) facility, to be activated as needed. The pledges are in the IMF's virtual basket of currencies known as Special Drawing Rights (SDRs). As of 1 July 2013 the IMF had total pledges worth US$556 billion (SDR 370 billion), including $104 billion from the USA, $99 billion from Japan, $47 billion from China, and about $13 billion each from Brazil, India and Russia. IMF, 'IMF Standing Borrowing Arrangements', IMF Factsheet, IMF, Washington, DC, April 2013.

81 Wade, 'Emerging World Order', 362.

82 Ibid., 362.

83 See, for example, Steven Dunaway, 'Global Imbalances and the Financial Crisis', Council on Foreign Relations, Washington, DC, March 2009.

84 Nick Edwards, 'Urbanisation Key to Curing China Imbalances—Report', *Financial Times*, 15 November 2012.

85 Russia has a small surplus with China, while South Africa hopes for substantial inward direct investment, so these two countries are less conflicted over the issue.

86 David Robinson, 'IMF-backed Plan to Cut Global Imbalances', *IMF Survey*, 7 August 2007.

87 Edwin M. Truman, 'The Rise of Sovereign Wealth Funds: Impacts on US Foreign Policy and Economic Interests', Testimony before the Committee on Foreign Affairs, U.S. House of Representatives, Washington, DC, 21 May 2008; Benjamin J. Cohen, 'Sovereign Wealth Funds and National Security: The Great Tradeoff', unpublished paper, 20 August 2008.

88 Ulrich Volz, 'All Politics is Local: Prospects of the Renminbi to become a Global Currency', in Leslie Elliott Armijo and Saori N. Kateda (eds), *The Financial Statecraft of Emerging Powers*, Palgrave, New York, forthcoming.

89 BRICS Information Centre, *BRICS Official Documents, Summits*; see also Cynthia Roberts, 'Building the New World Order BRIC by BRIC', *The European Financial Review*, February–March 2011.

27

Challenges of managing emerging economies

Domingo F. Cavallo

Advanced economies have well-functioning and long-established institutions that normally do not require significant changes to sustain growth and stability. By contrast, backward societies trapped in stagnation and international isolation, in trying to become emerging economies have to introduce deep institutional changes. For this reason, in managing emerging economies, policymakers face challenges quite different from those faced in advanced economies.

Policymakers in emerging economies need to design new rules and institutions that depart from those inherited in ways that may become very disruptive of the traditional social order. Furthermore, in the course of applying economic policies quite different from those of the past, policymakers have to dampen the risk that at time of crisis, the defenders of the old order push to reverse the institutional changes already implemented.

The rules and institutions created after the Second World War to help to organize a global economic order for reconstruction and development provide an institutional anchor for the national economies that want to change their traditional economic structures and become emerging economies.

All of today's emerging economies, at some stage, decided to become members of the World Trade Organization (WTO) and started to play by its rules and disciplines. The opening-up to foreign trade and investment promotes clearer definition and improved protection for property rights, at the same time as bringing increased competition in domestic markets. The access to more advanced technologies and the increased competition help to reach higher productivity levels, particularly in the sectors that produce internationally tradable goods and services.

Given the level of domestic savings, the availability of more advanced technologies and higher-quality capital goods means faster economic growth. Foreign savings in the form of foreign direct investment (FDI) usually help to finance higher levels of investment, reinforcing the process of growth.

Emerging economies, at the same time as opening up to foreign trade and investment, need to organize monetary and financial institutions so as to be able to control inflation, encourage domestic savings, develop local financial intermediaries and create favourable conditions for FDI. In the quarter of a century following the Second World War the international monetary system created in Bretton Woods provided an anchor for national monetary institutions and control of cross-border capital movements.

Since the mid-1970s most emerging economies have had to use the US dollar as the 'patron' currency in a more unstable global monetary environment. The wild fluctuations between the dollar and the currencies of other advanced economies, reflecting a very limited degree of international monetary co-ordination, have made it more difficult for the emerging economies to manage their monetary policies.

Those countries with high rates of local savings could somehow prevent crisis associated with sudden stops of financial flows by restricting inflows of capital to the FDI that was needed to access foreign technologies and management.

In order to finance a higher level of investment, countries with low rates of domestic savings rely on larger proportions of foreign savings. To the extent that foreign savings came as financial capital rather than FDI, in some emerging economies, the volatility of financial flows provoked financial crises that, at best, meant delays in the process of growth. In other cases, financial crises generated very damaging reversals in the pro-market institutional reforms.

Main challenges

Ten challenges identified from historical experience of emerging economies' reforms and policies deserve closer discussion.

First challenge: to generate enough domestic savings to finance the investment required to reach GDP per capita growth of at least 3% per year

For emerging economies to catch up with the level of growth of advanced economies at an acceptable pace they need to grow by at least 3% per year in per capita terms. Advanced economies have been growing between 1% and 2% in per capita terms for long periods of time. If the emerging economies do not grow by at least 3% per year, it will take hundreds of years to catch up with today's advanced economies' income levels.

Asian countries and countries rich in natural resources have no problem in generating domestic savings above 30% of national income, but for most Latin American, Eastern European and African economies, to generate domestic savings above 20% of national income is a real challenge, particularly in those countries with a long history of persistent inflation and very weak public finances.

To increase the rate of domestic savings it is necessary to implement fiscal consolidation reforms, to reduce inflationary expectations, to free interest rates so as to generate positive interest rates, and to remove taxes that discourage savings.

Second challenge: to invest in human capital and to enable the adoption of the most advanced available technologies in all areas of production

Some of today's emerging economies had well-organized primary and secondary education systems and incipient professional education in universities that provided fairly good training in sciences. These countries, mainly the Asian and Eastern European former communist societies, at the same time as they decided to open up their economies to foreign trade and investment, started to send students to universities in North America and Europe to be trained in business, economics and other disciplines necessary to facilitate the implementation of market reforms and the introduction of more advanced technologies.

Latin American and African economies, particular those with more traditional social structures and indigenous populations that had been marginalized for centuries, did not inherit educational systems as effective of those of Asian and Eastern European countries. Nor did they encourage professional training in North America and Europe with the same emphasis as the Asian and Eastern European emerging economies. This explains the greater difficulties these economies encountered to absorb advanced technologies and include migrants from low-productivity activities into the expanding modern urban economy.

Countries that inherited fiscal deficits due to poorly prioritized public spending and corruption and ineffective tax systems had a hard time in reconciling fiscal consolidation with increased fiscal resources devoted to education and health care.

Third challenge: to create the conditions that will enable foreign savings to complement domestic savings in providing financing for investment

The ability to attract FDI is crucial to achieve high rates of economic growth for two reasons: (a) FDI brings together advanced technologies and improved management, and (b) it complements domestic savings as a source of financing for investment. The first property of FDI is important in all emerging economies. The second property is crucial for economies that do not have high enough rates of domestic savings.

Generally, to create conditions favourable for FDI, emerging economies have to liberalize the capital account of their balance of payments which facilitates the movement not only of medium- and long-term financing but also of short-term capital. It is the instability of these cross-border, short-term capital movements that explains most of the currency and financial crises that plagued many emerging economies during the 1990s and the early 2000s.

For this reason, most emerging economies have started to introduce controls on financial capital flows under the umbrella of the so-called 'macro-prudential' monetary policies. Emerging economies that restrict the flow of purely financial flows have to be careful not to discourage FDI, which means essentially to avoid imposing restrictions on remittance of dividends and repatriation of capital.

Fourth challenge: to facilitate the external expansion of local firms in order to reassure the creation of global networks that will enrich the integration of the national economy into the global markets

The transformation of local firms into successful global companies is the best manifestation that an economy has finally emerged and became well integrated into the global markets. This development requires freedom for the local companies to invest abroad and respect for the rules and disciplines of the WTO so as to avoid retaliations from commercial partners.

Locally based global companies may enjoy strategic advantages for capturing and implementing the most advanced available technologies in the world for the production of their goods and services. They may also become strategically suited to reassure adequate supply of raw materials and to organize efficient distribution networks for the exportation of their products.

Fifth challenge: to find efficient ways to reach private-public partnerships in building the economic infrastructure required to improve competitiveness through increased productivity

Countries that have high rates of domestic savings and are able to absorb the available technology in transport, communications and energy may develop modern economic infrastructure through public investment as many of the Asian countries, particularly China, have done in the last decades.

However, countries that do not have high enough domestic savings, particularly those that historically had weak public finances, cannot develop modern infrastructure unless they find suitable ways to attract private capital. Adequate rules for the private provision of infrastructural services and efficient private-public partnerships are crucial to ensure financing for investment in infrastructure.

Emerging economies require high rates of investment in infrastructure in order to increase productivity throughout the economy and to improve competitiveness without resorting to extremely undervalued currencies and export subsidies.

Sixth challenge: to offer a safety net to the population marginalized by the process of modernization

The workers who lose employment in the process of modernization have to be compensated during the period required for the retraining that will allow them to be reinserted into the productive economy. Providing compensation and retraining programmes is crucial to assure social peace and remove resistance to the adoption of productivity-improving techniques in crucial sectors of the economy, particularly those that produce exportable goods or have to compete with imported goods.

People living in rural areas who are employed with relatively low levels of productivity and do not get sufficient income to pay for good education and health care, need to be assisted with public provision of those services. This assistance is necessary to improve their well-being and, at the same time, to prepare better those who will eventually migrate to cities to become employable in expanding productive activities.

Seventh challenge: to avoid damaging reversals in the process of opening up to foreign trade and investment

The forces that try to reverse the opening-up of the economy are normally present throughout the economic reform process but they may become very powerful at times of recession and high unemployment. The most common causes of recession and high unemployment are collapses of important foreign markets and sudden stops in inflows of foreign capital.

If the fiscal position of the economy is relatively strong and it does not have a large debt in foreign currency, currency devaluation can dampen the recessionary impact of the foreign shocks much better than restrictions on trade.

In economies with weak public finances and large debts denominated in foreign currency, a combination of an internal devaluation (through labour market and tax reforms) and an eventual orderly debt restructuring to eliminate the debt overhang may also be much more effective that restrictions on foreign trade.

The key for the resumption of sustainable growth in emerging economies is to avoid reversing the opening-up to foreign trade and investment. Otherwise there is the risk of recreating the vices of the old institutional framework, which instead of promoting growth kept the economy trapped in stagnation and international isolation.

Eighth challenge: to avoid the reintroduction of two-digit, persistent inflation

When emerging economies with weak public finances and large foreign currency debts suffer a long recession, if instead of relying on internal devaluation and orderly debt restructuring their policymakers decide to default on the debt and to produce a large devaluation, the most probable outcome will be the reintroduction of persistent inflation in the economy.

When that happens, the most likely reaction of those policymakers will be to introduce trade restrictions and exchange controls, in an attempt to limit the size of the devaluation without tightening monetary policy. This happened, for example, in Argentina and Venezuela after the crises of the late 1990s and early 2000s. The consequence is both a reintroduction of two-digit, persistent inflation and a closing of the economy to foreign trade and investment. The economies that do not avoid the reintroduction of those two diseases risk completely derailing from their emerging economy track and getting submerged again into stagnation and isolation.

Since the monetary policy of the mature market economies became very expansionary and nominal interest rates in those economies are close to zero, the risk of reintroducing double-digit, persistent inflation is also present in well-managed emerging economies that are receiving large inflows of foreign capital and try to prevent the appreciation of their national currencies. This is more a consequence of the expansionary monetary policies of the advanced economies than of the economic policies of the emerging economies and, therefore, there is not much that policymakers in emerging economies can do to prevent domestic inflation without suffering deflation in their tradable sectors of production. This is a problem that needs to be discussed as part of the negotiations to recreate an international monetary system and a global financial architecture capable of securing enough monetary policy co-ordination among the participating nations.

Ninth challenge: to develop the institutions that will secure respect for human rights and rule of law

Low inflation and rapid economic growth are necessary but not sufficient conditions to sustain convergence of emerging economies to the standard of living of advanced economies, because the economic changes create, simultaneously, social conflicts and demand for greater individual freedom and political participation. If these conflicts are not solved and these demands are not satisfied, they may derail the whole process of reform.

Whatever the previous political and social system, emerging economies will have to develop institutions that help to mediate and solve social conflicts and offer to the people higher degrees of freedom and political participation.

An increasing sense of respect for basic human rights and rule of law will help to consolidate the economic achievements and transform today's emerging economies into open societies, as happened with Western European nations and Japan after the Second World War.

Tenth challenge: to participate constructively in world affairs so as to contribute to global progress and preserve peace and security

Emerging economies, particularly those that for their size and importance may exercise influence in international forums, have to participate in discussions and negotiations to improve and extend the rules and institutions that may contribute to global progress and to preserve peace and security around the world.

The increasing interdependence of nations and the global character of many of the economic and social problems with which individual economies have to cope, make it necessary to organize effective ways to reassure the supply of global public goods, like financial stability, defence of the environment, the fight against global diseases, co-operation in scientific research and development, the fight against cross-border organized crime and terrorism, and preservation of peace.

Domingo F. Cavallo

The Great Recession of 2008 and its aftermath

Most emerging economies have enjoyed rapid growth during the last 10 years and were able to overcome fairly rapidly the negative effects of the Great Recession that started in the USA in 2008. The picture is different in the USA, Europe and Japan. Their economies either are still in recession or are growing at a very slow pace.

In spite of the pessimism that prevails in the advanced economies, emerging economies should emphasize in international forums the complementarities between those economies and the emerging world. If trade and currency wars are avoided, those complementarities could help to restart growth in the advanced world.

Two engines, operating from the supply side of the economies, are ready to restart growth in the advanced economies and sustain rapid growth in the emerging world: (1) investment in R&D research and development in the advanced economies, taking advantage of their scientific and research network, which will move the technological frontier; and (2) investment to implement available technologies across all sectors and regions in the emerging economies.

There are historical precedents that illustrate the point. The technological progress that started in the UK in the mid-19th century was rapidly implemented and reinforced by investment in the USA and the other Western offshoots. The countries that did not open up their economies and were kept isolated from this first wave of globalization predictably lagged behind those that joined it.

A similar process took place after the Second World War: the technological advances that had accelerated during the war, particularly in the USA, were rapidly implemented in Western Europe and Japan as they reconstructed their economies. Once again, those emerging economies that did not open up lagged behind those that did.

Similarly, and more recently, the technological progress originated in the R&D efforts of the USA, Western Europe and Japan has been introduced quite rapidly in many emerging economies since the early 1990s—most impressively in China and India. Again, the key to this rapid process of expansion was the opening-up of emerging economies to foreign trade and investment.

After the shock of 2008, most emerging economies could cushion the internal effect of the drastic drop in international trade by implementing counter-cyclical fiscal and monetary policies. Soon, they resumed rapid growth, which, in turn, benefited the advanced economies.

This emerging economy contribution to global dynamism was absent when the Great Depression of the 1930s interrupted the first wave of globalization. It was also absent in the aftermath of the first oil shock that interrupted post-Second World War growth. In those two cases, there were no economies with large enough domestic markets and savings to counteract the depressive effects in the leading economies.

Increased investment in R&D in the advanced economies and a larger role of the emerging world as absorptive markets for the technological advance will help both sets of economies. In particular, it will help the emerging nations to continue coping with the challenges of managing their economies with a view to achieving sustainable growth and prosperity.

28

Lessons of Korea for emerging economies

An unexpected journey from rags to riches, from crisis to recovery

Bernhard J. Seliger

In the 1960s the Republic of Korea's (South Korea) president Park Chung-Hee, among other things influenced by a visit to Germany in 1964, embarked on the building of the first national motorway, from Seoul to Busan, linking the two economic centres of the poor South Korea until now dependent on foreign aid and still devastated by the war. A major international institution (the World Bank) called this plan utopian, calling attention to some basic missing ingredients for such a large project: there was no major construction industry with experience in such large-scale projects, no steel industry, no car industry and, accordingly, even if the project succeeded, no traffic could be expected on the planned highway. Today, Korea is one of the major international contractors for construction projects, with a number of heavyweights in the industry, has a world-leading steel factory and indeed a whole steel city (Posco in Pohang), is one of the leading car manufacturers of the world and among the largest trading nations. A veritable journey from rags to riches.

However, this journey was not smooth and, indeed, in 1997, when the Asian Financial Crisis hit the country, it seemed to have come to an abrupt end. Again, South Korea underwent dramatic change in the last one and a half decades, from being considered a 'tiger in trouble' in the wake of the Asian crisis to a showcase of economic development. Today, South Korea is an active donor of development aid, receiving countless delegations from countries interested in the specific Korean way of development and also supporting its trade policy with sending out development officials and engineers. The judgement of 1998 was itself a complete reversal of previous enthusiastic reviews of world record high growth for several decades, from the 1960s to the 1990s. Korea, once considered a shrimp between two mighty whales, Japan and China, as neighbours, veritably made a jump to become a tiger. After the steep decline of 1998, this tiger again showed its claws, a transformation almost as astonishing as its original 'economic miracle', as the following comparison of Korea in 1998 and 2011 shows.

In 1998 South Korea suffered from a severe recession, triggered by the currency crisis it had experienced a year before. After two years of growing macroeconomic imbalance, in particular

531

growing current account deficits, as well as a contagion from the spreading currency crisis in South-East Asia since the summer of 1997, by the end of the year Korea had a record low of usable foreign reserves of barely more than US$7 billion. The South Korean won, previously managed in a narrow band to the US dollar, had to be floated and drastically depreciated, and South Korea's sovereign rating was lowered, which made repaying debt more costly and caused the stock market to crash.

In 2011 the South Korean economy marked for the first time a trade volume of more than $1 trillion. The nominal per capita gross domestic product (GDP) reached a record $24,000. South Korea's economy, though hurt by the subsequent financial crisis in 2008 and the lingering woes over the world economy, grew throughout this period. In July 2011 the free trade agreement between South Korea and the European Union (EU) took effect, and in late 2011 the free trade agreement with the USA (KORUS FTA) was approved in a tumultuous session of the Korean Parliament. From 2012, South Korea enjoyed free trade with an area representing two-thirds of the world's GDP. Also, South Korea's national success has become increasingly a benchmark for other countries as South Korea transforms into a leading world economy. From being a receiver of development aid it has become a major donor, hosting an Organisation for Economic Co-operation and Development (OECD) Development Assistance Committee (representing the most important donors of development aid) forum in November 2011 in Busan. It also took a leading role in the G20 during the financial crisis of 2008 and 2009, hosted a G20 summit in 2010, and is leading efforts to implement a new vision of green growth at the regional and international levels.

What triggered this remarkable resurgence of South Korea? While international aid under the umbrella of the International Monetary Fund (IMF), a steep depreciation of the Korean won and improving macroeconomic factors certainly helped to overcome the immediate crisis, it does not explain Korea's post-crisis development. Other countries working under the same external environment had much less success. To understand Korea's outperformance, one needs to look at institutional change after the crisis. While the popular explanation of the Korean crisis made it macroeconomic, and even an 'IMF crisis', blaming international forces for the downfall, nevertheless, the Korean government and companies understood that unresolved structural issues were at the heart of the crisis and started to embrace change, beginning with the unprecedented election of an opposition candidate and peaceful democratic power transfer in 1997 and 1998, and then implementing change in the public sector, the labour market, the private sector, monetary and financial policy, the foreign direct investment (FDI) regime, trade relations and other areas. In this sense, recent South Korean economic history is also a story from crisis to recovery.

Let us first look back at the origins of the 'miracle at the Han river', as South Koreans like to call their rapid economic development since the early 1960s. For centuries Korea had been a feudal agrarian society in which economic well-being was less a question of industriousness, and mostly dependent on the harvest, largely determined by the weather, and sometimes on political events, like wars, local turmoil, extortionist landlords, etc. Trade (for example, export of porcelain to Japan) was marginal, and traders belonged to the lowest class of society (*sang*) in the strict hierarchy formed according to a Confucian model of in the period of the Chosun kingdom (1392–1910). Accordingly, the monetization and commercialization of society were extremely low. The invasions by Japan in 1592 and the Manchu in 1637 lowered trade to a minimum. The decline of the Chinese Empire after the opium wars (1839–42 and 1856–60) was understood in Korea as a warning, with the lesson being to withdraw into almost complete isolation, which brought Korea the reputation of being a 'hermit kingdom'. After successfully fighting off various French and US trade and military missions and persecuting foreign missionaries, the newly rising Japan forced Korea to open up with the so-called Gangwha treaty of 1876. This was a prelude to 30 years of fighting between China, the old though mostly nominal tributary

Lessons of Korea for emerging economies

overlord Japan, and Russia over domination of Korea, which ended with Korea becoming a protectorate of Japan in 1905 and an outright colony in 1910. The opening of Korea brought foreign trade missions, more trade, and new ideas and innovations into the country. In 1900 the railway between Seoul and Incheon was opened. Treaties with a number of states were concluded. Nevertheless, trade remained marginal and is estimated to have been not more than 5% of GDP before colonization.

This changed dramatically with the modernization forced upon the Korean economy after Japanese colonization. The share of export goods in total production rose until the Second World War to more than 25% of GDP, the share of import goods to almost 35%. Foreign trade was clearly focused on Japan and dependent on Japan; for example, rice exports from the early colonial period to the beginning of the Pacific war in 1937 rose seven-fold. After the end of the colonial era, which brought many painful memories to Koreans, among them the attempt to erase the Korean cultural identity, many scholars focused on Korea's dependence on Japan and negated any positive impact of its colonization on the economy. However, from a purely economic point of view, modernization by Japan brought many advantages and laid some foundations for the later economic development: Japan paid prices for Korean rice and raw materials like iron that were higher than world market prices; in the northern part of Korea an industrial base developed and began to open up new markets abroad (obviously, mainly in the Japanese-dominated area); modern education in schools and universities, which barely began in the pre-colonial period, brought new educational opportunities to Korea's middle class; but most important of all, Korea for the first time was thoroughly integrated into an Asian production network. Some of the predecessors of the later large Korean conglomerates originated in this period, like Samsung in 1938.

The independence of Korea in 1945 and the subsequent division into South and North brought new problems for South Korea. The industrial base of Korea was mostly in the raw material-rich north of the country, and at the same time Japan as a destination for Korean rice exports ceased to exist. Anyway, the turmoil after independence brought a massive decline in production and in 1948 Korea, a traditional rice exporter, even had to import large quantities of its main staple food. The Korean War from 1950 to 1953 torpedoed the attempts to rebuild the economy and led to a new strong dependence, this time on its main ally, the USA. From 1952 to 1961 the South Korean government budget was almost half-financed by foreign aid. Exports, later the drivers of economic success, almost completely ceased, accounting for 1% of GDP in 1954 and 2% in 1962. Among the main export goods were women's hair (to make wigs), pig bristle, octopus and other seafood, and some raw materials.

South Korea's first post-independence president, Rhee Syngman tried, in accordance with the prevailing development theories of the time, to develop domestic industries like cement and steel by protecting them from foreign competition and substituting, thereby, foreign with domestic production. This policy of import substitution, unfortunately, did not work, since the lack of competition domestically as well as internationally worked as a disincentive for the growth of competitive industries. A fixed and overvalued exchange rate for the Korean currency, paired with high inflation rates, did not help economic development either. The reduction of military aid led to bottlenecks in urgently needed imports. In 1960, following mass protests due to election fraud and corruption, Rhee Syngman had to resign and leave the country. His successor, President Chang Myon, had no luck in governing the country, seeing a time of growing anarchy. Only when Park Chung-Hee, a relatively young officer educated in a Japanese military academy, led a *coup d'état* and afterwards reigned the country with an iron fist, did South Korea's rise as a trading nation, a developmental state and dictatorship, begin.

After the coup, Park Chung-Hee faced the following challenges: the economy, having grown after the end of the Korean War, already in 1956 was again in recession and in the crisis

533

year of 1960 barely grew by 1.2%. Widespread corruption had been the reason for the ousting of President Rhee, but it could not effectively be stopped by President Chang. Frequent strikes and demonstrations substituted for political debate and crippled the economy. Much more serious, in the competition of systems in the global Cold War, Korea was particularly exposed and South Korea compared unfavourably to the North. There, the introduction of a centrally planned economy and forced accumulation led initially to high growth rates, Also, politically, systemic competition was tough. Kim Il-sung, after successfully getting rid of rivalling factions, became an important representative of socialism in Asia, with good relations, too, with the USSR and the People's Republic of China. South Korea was dependent in political, military and economic matters on its main ally, the USA, but after the coup it drastically reduced aid, leading to severe current account problems.

In this situation the reform of economic policy had the highest priority. The introduction of an efficient and corruption-free economic administration was the precondition for the strategy of indicative planning chosen by the new president to develop the economy. Indicative planning, which in contrast to central planning does not force companies to comply with plans, but relies on developing broad government guidelines and targets for economic development, had been used with varying success in a number of countries, in particular developed countries, after the Second World War, including France and the Netherlands. In Korea it became an outright success. The Economic Planning Board from 1961 to 1996 designed a series of seven five-year plans, and guided companies with selective incentives to realize these plans. In particular, politically guided credit allocation was important, since due to uncertainty about market and political conditions for most companies, medium- or long-term financing of projects without state support was impossible. Successful economic development was achieved with the help of three new policies.

The most important element was the change from a strategy of import substitution to a strategy of export orientation in foreign trade. This was officially done in only the second document of the first five-year plan of 1966. Besides infrastructure development and a few other industries, where import substitution remained in place as a goal, the government focused all efforts on direct export promotion. This included advantages for exporting companies in the tax system, subsidies, priority in credit allocation and foreign currency availability, as well as administrative support for export-oriented companies. Selective liberalization of trade meant that imports of raw materials, intermediate products and investment goods were free, while imports of consumption goods and for production for the domestic market were restricted. The former positive list of imports was changed to a negative list (all not explicitly restricted imports were allowed). Administrative support meant, for example, faster administrative procedures, but most of all less corruption. From 1963 to 1971 mainly industrial exports were supported, e.g. in textiles and consumer electronics and appliances. In the 1970s a period of support for heavy industry and chemical industry followed. The focus of the 1980s was rather macroeconomic stability, after the second oil price shock and domestic political turmoil (Park Chung-Hee was killed in 1979 and after another unsuccessful democratic interlude a new dictator, Chun Doo-Hwan, governed until 1987). In 1987 political democratization was accompanied by economic liberalization and the decline of the importance of indicative planning.

The second important element of the new policy was collaboration with the emerging conglomerates. Export orientation for the Korean industry was towards compliance with the quality and prices of the world market, an important advantage compared to import substitution policies. At the same time it brought the problem that success on world markets could only be achieved through using economies of scale (i.e. lower average costs, when quantities of production are rising). The rise of competitive industries large enough to use economies of scale in

Lessons of Korea for emerging economies

the policy of import substitution theoretically should happen through protection of domestic markets. In the new policy of export orientation this was no longer possible. Therefore, the state began to promote the development of large conglomerates, some of which had already started in the Japanese period as small trading companies. These conglomerates, called *chaebol* and closely resembling their Japanese counterparts, the *keiretsu*, grew to become a trademark of South Korea's economic success, including such household names as Samsung, Hyundai or LG. Relations between government and *chaebol* were not free from tension; however, the government actively supported them, in particular in new overseas markets like the Middle East, when the building boom began in this region. At the same time, the government forced the *chaebol* in times of crisis (like during the oil price shocks) to soften the impact of economic shocks. If a company went bankrupt, healthy *chaebol* were forced to acquire and restructure it, thereby reducing social problems due to lay-offs in crisis times and having near-zero unemployment. This was an important element of social policy during the military dictatorship. At the same time, this policy led to a widespread attitude among *chaebol* owners that turnover growth is more important than profit growth, and to a form of unchecked, irrational acquisitions and diversification in often completely unrelated branches. Internal subsidies for unprofitable parts of conglomerates became widespread. Acquisitions were supported by politically allocated credit, and furthered by close collusion of banks and *chaebol*. Later, this was one of the structural reasons for the economic and financial crisis of 1997 and 1998.

The third new policy, besides the export orientation and collaboration and promotion of conglomerates, was the active development of new trade destinations and also the search for new donors. After the USA reduced military aid due to the coup by President Park, South Korea from 1963 sent more than 20,000 guest workers (miners and nurses) to West Germany, at that time in urgent need of workers, as a guarantee for German credits when normal credit sourcing on international capital markets was impossible. In 1965, even more important for the future development of Korea, relations with Japan were normalized. This was highly unpopular among the Korean population, but not only stabilized the government budget through cheap credit, but also allowed access to Japanese technology, which until today is a main ingredient in many of South Korea's most successful export goods.

The success of these new policies was extraordinary. The average growth rate of GDP from the 1960s to the 1990s was around 8% annually, the average per capita income in 1995 reached $10,000, starting in the 1950s with less than $200. Inflation and unemployment were low, and from 1977 there was even a lack of workers. Exports grew in the 1970s on average more than 45% annually. This also led to the growth of imports, fuelling a growing standard of living of the population and the rise of a large new middle class. The government budget was mostly in balance, which the World Bank in its famous 1993 report on the East Asian miracle sees as an important recipe for macroeconomic stability. Exports not only grew in quantity, but also changed from raw materials to industrial goods and, from the 1990s, high technology. In the mid-1990s South Korea was the world's fifth largest car manufacturer, the second largest shipbuilder, and a leading producer of semiconductors. These industries, using the low wages of largely uneducated workers, were substituted by capital-intensive production with highly specialized workers earning good wages, though the labour market remains divided between these export-oriented industries and a domestic industry relying mainly on low-paid workers. The success of the Korean export-oriented policies can be seen in its growth in US dollar value, from $0.04 billion in 1961 to $466.38 billion in 2010. By the mid-1980s South Korea was a world trading power. Intra-industrial trade played a growing role in its development, capital-intensive exports increased and Korean brands (e.g. in electronics or the automotive industry) gradually became more important, while comparative cost advantages due to low wages decreased. While export growth was high, imports even grew faster until 1986, when Korea for the first time had a trade surplus, which lasted until 1989, furthered by the Seoul Olympic Games of 1988. Then again, until the crisis year of 1997, imports grew faster, spurred by liberalization of formerly restricted imports for consumer goods. Additionally, easier access to capital markets, in particular short-term capital, at the time when the so-called East Asian economic miracle first gained international attention, was recklessly used by *chaebol* to finance further growth, leading to record debt levels of *chaebol*—another contributor to the crisis of 1997. For example, Kia Motors had a debt-to-equity level of 520% in 1997, and the 30 largest *chaebol* had an average level of 330%.

The cost of servicing these debts greatly reduced the profitability of many projects. According to estimates by the Hyundai Economic Research Institute in 1997, the 12 Korean companies ranking among the world's 500 largest had some of the lowest profitability indicators among the 500 companies. *Chaebol* had the biggest share in Korean economic growth, and the 30 largest ones produced approximately 80% of Korean GDP. In addition to low profitability, many *chaebol* diversified without following a coherent strategy. For example, the fur maker Jindo, which went bankrupt in 1998, had container, automotive parts, construction, waste management and retail subsidiaries. The five biggest *chaebol* in 1997 (Hyundai Group, Daewoo, Samsung Group, SK Corporation and LG Corporation) each had more than 100 subsidiaries, but only 10% to 20% of them were profitable. Internal cross-subsidization of a conglomerate's subsidiaries was the norm. This allowed also unprofitable business to stay in the market and reduced the allocative efficiency of the Korean economy. The lack of transparency in their business organization, caused by ties among families, financial institutions and areas of the media, led to allegations of 'crony capitalism'.

South Korea's admission to the OECD in 1996, after being a founding member of the World Trade Organization (WTO) a year earlier, was the visible expression of the success of the developmental model of Korea. Equally impressive was that economic success finally, after many decades of thinly disguised military dictatorship, brought peaceful democratization. However, the policy of high growth through the particular Korean model also was prone to crises. Neo-mercantilist policies focusing on exports and restricting imports led to the development of narrow oligopolies, collusive behaviour and inefficiency on domestic markets. When WTO and OECD membership brought pressure for the opening of markets, not least the capital markets, President Kim Young-Sam, the first civilian president elected by free elections since 1993, initiated a 'globalization' (*segewha*) programme to prepare to open up the markets, but failed to achieve this due to opposition from conglomerates, which had outgrown political pressure and at the same time had become 'too big to fail'.

When in 1997 the Korean economy was shaken by the downfall of the South-East Asian economies, the Kim Young-Sam government made some mistakes. The government tried to maintain the unrealistic exchange rate of the won against the dollar, thereby aggravating speculation in the currency, which led to its eventual fall. Eager to avoid bad press, the government did not correctly inform the public about the steady depletion of foreign exchange reserves. Consequently, the government's request for IMF assistance came as a shock and humiliation to many Koreans. A few months after he took over office, Kim Dae-Jung and his government developed a reform programme which was publicized by the Ministry of Finance and the Economy as 'DJnomics', named after the initials of President Kim Dae-Jung. Based on strict adherence to IMF conditions (which were relaxed several times due to Korea's worsening economic situation), the core of the reforms was the 'four plus one' policy. This policy involved the simultaneous reform of the labour market, the financial sector, the public sector and the private sector, together with the opening of Korea's markets to foreign competition.

Lessons of Korea for emerging economies

The first project of 'four plus one' was the reform of the labour market, which was formerly characterized by strong antagonism between activist trade unions and powerful employers. In the late 1980s and early 1990s, following their legalization, trade unions frequently resorted to long and sometimes violent strikes to gain wage raises far above productivity levels. Negotiations between employers and trade unions lacked a legal framework and institutional routine. Under the reform programme, tripartite (government-business-labour) negotiations were institutionalized, which allowed for more consensus-oriented negotiations. While strike threats are frequent and the tripartite negotiations often break down in some sectors, labour negotiations after the crisis improved dramatically.

The second part of the reforms concerned the financial sector, which showed its weaknesses in the crisis when numerous banks and financial institutions went bankrupt. Banks, insurance companies and investment trust funds were all riddled with bad loans. As part of the IMF conditions, stakes in Seoul Bank and Korea First Bank were sold to foreign investors to guarantee a freer market and increased competition. However, negotiations with foreign investors were slow and problematic, since the foreign buyers wanted government guarantees on bad debts, while the government wanted to prevent the Korean public from having the impression it was selling off Korean assets cheap, as well as employment guarantees. Ultimately, only massive state subsidies made the deals possible. Overall, results of financial reforms were mixed, with a considerable success of the Korean Asset Management Company (KAMCO) in buying and restructuring bad debt, but subsequent smaller crises in the investment trust and credit card business costing additional taxpayer money.

The third group of reforms was of the public sector, characterized by a strong bureaucracy in the Confucian tradition, which acted closely with the *chaebol*. While the meritocratic bureaucracy in Korea's history was held in high esteem, the problems of corruption and favouritism as a result of its dominant position were well known. The last two military rulers, Chun Doo-Hwan and Roh Tae-Woo, have been convicted of corruption involving several hundred million dollars. Also, after democratization corruption flourished, as shown by the 1997 bribes-for-loans scandal at Hanbo Iron & Steel Company, one of the events directly preceding the Korean financial crisis. The government has tried to resolve this problem from two angles. First, deregulation and privatization made corruption pay less: in private companies free from state involvement, only profits count. Second, an anticorruption commission was formed to erase corruption in office. This second part, however, has been inhibited by the frequent cases of corruption in the government itself, most visibly in the corruption cases surrounding practically every presidency, in particular the wider presidential families. Another aspect of public sector reform was increased transparency and the reduction of red tape. Here again, reforms have been successful, reducing the number of business regulations by half and thereby reducing the necessity and scope for corruption.

The last reform was the reform of the private sector, especially of the debt-ridden, secretive *chaebol* and their system of maintaining unprofitable businesses by cross-subsidization. Here again, results of the reform were mixed. While cross-subsidies almost disappeared and debt-equity ratios have fallen due to the improved economic situation after 1999, many *chaebol* have only superficially reformed. For example, even after formal reorganization, the firms' strong old family ties did not disappear. Together with the four major reform programmes, the process of opening the market to foreign competitors began. In some sectors, state regulations that acted as obstacles to trade were abolished. In the tourism industry, for instance, foreign firms previously were not allowed to invest in the Seoul area, and in the alcohol trade, discriminatory taxes against foreign brands were eliminated. In other sectors, such as the wholesale and retail systems, the de facto oligopolistic Korean market structure made market opening necessary. FDI is the field where the reform policy has brought major successful changes. For a long time, Korea had been hostile to foreign investment. While the Kim Young-Sam administration gradually lowered barriers to investment, the Kim Dae-Jung administration more boldly opened markets and aggressively wooed FDI. Not only did FDI mean an inflow of capital, it also involved injections of management expertise or technological capability. This was not only seen as instrumental in overcoming the currency and financial crisis, but also in furthering Korean efforts to restructure its ailing corporate and financial sectors. Already in 1999 Korea seemed to be back to the old path, with double-digit growth. However, subsequently growth became lower again and it became clear that the non-inflationary growth rate after the crisis was much lower than before. Given that decades of growth had considerably increased the economic basis, this does not seem surprising, and the ability of South Korea to steer through the latest world financial crisis without a recession has been very impressive.

Some 15 years after the onset of the Asian crisis, South Korea is a vibrant economy that has withstood the international financial crisis of 2008 to 2009 in a remarkable manner, exercising international leadership in the field of green growth and rising to the status of a large and respected middle power on an equal footing with Japan, for instance. Though economic debates and fears of the past still resound, as protests against the KORUS FTA in 2011 have shown, Korea underwent major change. It embraced institutional changes, it opened its markets further and overcame some of the old traumata haunting the former Japanese colony and divided nation, in particular the fear of losing its cultural identity by opening up. On the contrary, today Korean culture, in particular popular culture, has made great advances in South-East Asia, in China, in Japan and other parts of the world. South Korea has become a confident (and that does not always mean easier) middle power in world affairs, and a model for many countries searching for a recipe for development. Certainly, the South Korean developmental success cannot be emulated in a simplistic manner. The ingredients of its success were very specific and some of them may not work at all outside Korea. However, the Korean case certainly offers hope for all countries searching for a way to develop their economy, not least South Korea's own dismal brother in the North, that poverty can be overcome, though it is not an easy path and means sacrifices of hard-working generations, and that crises, perhaps unavoidable, can be used to get rid of institutional 'sclerosis' and free the economy to embark anew on a growth path.

29

China and India, 2025

A macroeconomic assessment

Charles Wolf, Jr and Alisher Akhmedjonov

Two centuries ago, Edmund Burke advised a British parliamentarian: 'Never plan the future by the past.'

A century later Winston Churchill cautioned: 'If we open a quarrel between the past and the present, we shall find that we have lost the future.'

These admonitions recall a more recent truism, often attributed to Yogi Berra: 'It's dangerous to make predictions, especially about the future!'

The assessments described in this chapter violate these precepts by using data from the past and the present to make forecasts about the future.[1] Consequently, I should emphasize not only the uncertainties that generally and inherently surround forecasts, but especially the uncertainties accompanying the forecasts described in this chapter because they pertain to two rapidly changing economies and polities that are affected by, as well as interacting with, a rapidly changing regional and global environment.

Forecasts of economic growth in the People's Republic of China and India

Economic growth in China and India has become the focus of increased attention in Asia, in the Asia-Pacific Economic Cooperation (APEC) forum, in the G20, and in the global economy. In recent decades, growth in both countries has exceeded expectations. China recorded an average annual growth in real gross domestic product (GDP) of 9%–10%, while India's growth during the same period was 7%–8%. Both countries face the challenge of sustaining such high rates of growth. This chapter summarizes a meta-analysis of growth estimates for China and India for the period to 2025, based on 27 separate studies, undertaken in three different institutional settings: universities, business and international organizations.[2] The meta-analysis also summarizes and evaluates several of the key assumptions underlying the estimates. Finally, the chapter compares five different scenarios of high, low and average growth estimates for the two countries, and concludes with several inferences based on this analysis.

539

The 27 studies included in the analysis were done between 2000 and 2008, and covered the two countries' recent and prospective levels and growth of GDP, capital, employment and total factor productivity (TFP). The studies were culled from a larger set of four dozen studies, with selections based on the sufficiency and comparability of their data for the comparative assessment that was our aim. Most of the studies contained explicit projections of these macro-economic indicators to 2025. Where estimates of the indicators were implicit, we derived the relevant values using either incremental capital-output ratios, or Cobb-Douglas production functions, or a combination of both methods. The detailed steps of this meta-analysis are described in the Appendix to this chapter.

The analytic methods used in the underlying studies vary widely. Some rely on simple extrapolation and trend analysis in forecasting growth of GDP and its components, while other studies used more sophisticated models. Some analyses concentrate on a single aspect of economic growth—for example, the role of capital accumulation and its determinants in explaining differences between the two economies—while other studies consider other factors such as demographics, labour markets and education, as well as trade and fiscal policies affecting growth. Some of the studies provide forecasts only to 2020, while others extend to 2050. A few of the studies focus more on either China or India, rather than giving equal attention to both countries. In these few cases, we supplemented some details that were implicit in a particular study to provide comparable results using similar methods and data for both countries.

Our review of forecasted GDP growth rates in the pooled studies of China and India to 2025 suggests that the recent rapid growth of these countries is only likely to be sustainable in the future at a slower pace. As shown in Table 29.1 and Figure 29.1, for the pooled studies, average annual GDP growth rates are projected to be 5.7% in China and 5.6% in India during the period from 2020 to 2025. During the same period, the average annual estimates of growth in the accumulated stock of capital are 6.1% for China and 6.9% for India; for growth in employment the average estimates are 0.4% for China and 1.6% for India; and for growth in TFP the average estimates are 3.4% for China and 2.1% for India.

These estimates of average rates are, unsurprisingly, accompanied by major uncertainties, as suggested by the wide range between the highest and lowest growth estimates, and their corresponding variances.[3] In the 27 studies we selected, the estimates for GDP growth rates for the 2020–25 period range from 3.8% to 9.0% for China and from 2.8% to 8.4% for India. For the growth rates in capital stock, estimates range from 4.2% to 9.4% for China and from 3.9% to 9.8% for India. For employment growth rates, the range is from −0.1% to 0.6% for China and

Table 29.1 China-India macro-economic meta-analysis: summary of salient estimates, 2020–25

	GDP		TFP		Employment		Capital	
	China	India	China	India	China	India	China	India
Mean	5.7	5.6	3.4	2.1	0.4	1.6	6.1	6.9
Max	9.0	8.4	5.6	3.6	0.6	1.9	9.4	9.8
Min	3.8	2.8	2.1	0.1	−0.1	0.7	4.2	3.9
Variance	2.2	2.3	1.0	1.0	0.0	0.1	2.1	2.5
n (obs)	28	26	28	26	28	26	28	26
n (studies)				27				

Notes: Growth rates are given in percentage per year. The number of observations does not match the total number of studies because some studies provide estimates for either China or India but not both. TFP = total factor productivity.

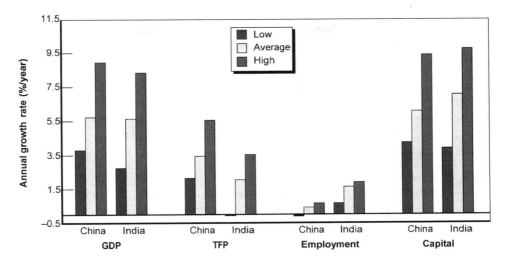

Figure 29.1 China–India macroeconomic comparisons: salient estimates, 2020–2025

from 0.7% to 1.9% for India. For TFP, the estimated growth rates range from 2.1% to 5.6% for China and from 0.1% to 3.6% for India.[4]

In the following section, we review these estimates by separating them into three clusters: (1) those by academic authors and institutions; (2) those by business organizations and authors (e.g. Goldman Sachs, PricewaterhouseCoopers, McKinsey); and (3) those by international organizations (e.g. the World Bank, the International Monetary Fund—IMF). We also evaluate the differing assumptions that may contribute to the wide range of the estimates, and highlight several other contrasting aspects of the three clusters.

Studies by academic authors and institutions

Of the studies in the meta-analysis, 11 are by university-based academic authors.[5] Interestingly, the academic cluster generates the widest range of growth estimates for both China and India, as summarized in Table 29.2. Within this cluster, the highest estimate for China's annual GDP growth for 2020–25 is 9%, and the lowest is 3.8%. For India, the estimates for annual GDP growth within this cluster range from 7.2% to 2.8%. Again, the variances of estimates in this group are higher than for the studies by business groups and international organizations. That the variance in the academic authors' estimates is by far the largest among the three clusters will be surprising

Table 29.2 China-India GDP growth estimates by 2020–25, by academic authors (%/year)

	China	India
Low	3.8	2.8
High	9.0	7.2
Average	5.5	4.3
Variance	2.6	2.4
n (observations)	15	9
n (studies)	11	7

Note: Differences between the numbers of observations and of studies arises because several studies included both high- and low-growth forecasts by their authors.

to some, but unsurprising to others. Later in this chapter we will suggest some hypotheses—more accurately, some conjectures—that may account for the variances.

In making these estimates, the academic authors tend to focus especially on one or two particular aspects of each country's growth. For example, some studies in this cluster focus especially on demographic changes in China and India (Golley and Tyers 2006; Tyers *et al.* 2006). Another forecast in this cluster focuses on the two countries' roles in global energy markets, their greenhouse gas emissions, and the presumed effects on growth (Paltsev and Reilly 2007a). Still another study in this cluster focuses particularly on China's regional economic structure, basing its estimates on sectoral and regional economic growth (Huang *et al.* 2003). Several studies base their long-term forecasts on a standard Cobb-Douglas production function (Holz 2005; Poncet 2006).

Holz (2005), from the Hong Kong University of Science and Technology, projects the highest annual GDP growth rate for China (9%) for the 2020–25 period, arguing that China can expect many years of rapid economic growth. Holz's forecast mainly rests on projecting recent growth rates into the future; he concludes that China's GDP will surpass that of the USA in purchasing power terms by the middle of the next decade.[6] He suggests this trajectory would follow the examples of Japan, Taiwan and the Republic of Korea (South Korea) in the early stages of their development. Holz contends that the structural changes taking place in China, along with factor price equalizations, will match the patterns of growth achieved by these other Asian countries.

In sharp contrast, another author in the academic cluster (Laurent 2006) suggests that China's average annual GDP growth rate in 2020–25 will decline to 3.8%, reasoning that declining numbers of prime working-age workers will inhibit China's growth. Laurent contends that India's growing labour force might enable India to grow more rapidly if its populace were more highly educated. However, unlike other economists who compare the two economies, Laurent is pessimistic about India's ability to educate its population. He expresses little confidence that this will happen, and forecasts that India's average annual GDP growth in 2020–25 will fall to 3.4%.

The effect of declining population on economic growth is also among the most significant issues raised in the study by Tyers *et al.* (2006) from the Australian National University (ANU). Their study suggests that relative labour abundance in India will bring higher capital returns and attract a rising share of global foreign direct investment to India.[7] Accordingly, the Tyers *et al.* forecast for India's annual growth rate in 2020–25 is 7.2%. The authors believe that India will displace China as the world's most rapidly expanding economy.

The ANU authors also examine the economic impact of a hypothetical increase in fertility in China that might occur if: (1) China were to abandon its one-child policy; and (2) a more-rapid-than-expected reduction of fertility were to occur in India. The ANU authors question the plausibility of this scenario by noting that even if China were to abandon its one-child policy, fertility might not rise substantially; the authors point to the reduction in fertility in China that occurred before the introduction of the one-child policy in 1979 (Carnell 2000) to show that forces other than policy have influenced China's fertility rate. For example, fertility is sensitive to cultural norms as well as economic incentives. Consequently, if a norm of low fertility has indeed taken root in China, it may be difficult to reverse. In India, too, fertility has been falling slowly.[8] An acceleration of fertility reduction in India might occur either as a consequence of economic development or because of exogenous societal reasons.

A contrasting study from scholars at the Massachusetts Institute of Technology (MIT) (Paltsev and Reilly 2007b) forecasts that India's average annual GDP growth rate in 2020–25 may be as low as 2.8%, due especially to high energy prices which would put a heavier burden on India's increasing oil imports. However, the MIT paper ignores the possible effects of new technologies that might partly reduce dependence on fossil fuel imports as well as lower their prices.

Similar to Holz (2005), researchers at CEPII, a French academic research centre on international economics (Poncet 2006), use a production function based on a neo-classical model in which GDP growth depends on growth of the labour force, of capital and of TFP. Poncet's GDP projections for both China and India are modest, placing them at average annual rates of 4.6% and 4.5%, respectively, during the period to 2025.

Unlike other studies in the three clusters of the meta-analysis, in which TFP enters the growth forecasts exogenously (Poddar and Yi 2007; Hofman and Kuijs 2007; Rodrik and Subramanian 2004), or is modelled as a process of 'catch-up' (Wilson and Purushothaman 2003), Poncet links the growth of factor productivity to investment in human capital. Growth in TFP becomes an endogenous function of average years of education and the income gap compared with income in the USA. The resulting differences in TFP and in the growth projections for India and China are thereby enlarged. Taking into account expected improvements in education, Poncet projects the average annual growth of TFP in 2020–25 as 2.5% in China, and 1.9% in India. In particular, Poncet projects that China's and India's GDP could grow at yearly average rates of 4.6% and 4.5%, respectively, during the period to 2025.

One paper in the academic cluster (Hofman and Kuijs 2007) estimates an average annual GDP growth rate for China of 6.7% during the 2020–25 period, while suggesting that China's recent 9% growth rate is unlikely to be sustainable. The authors believe that the greatest threat to China's future growth lies in the internal imbalance between aggregate domestic savings and domestic investment that has developed since 2005. They estimate that China's aggregate national savings have come to exceed aggregate domestic investment by 12% of GDP. Some researchers have paid less attention to this imbalance, focusing instead on the external imbalances reflected in China's large and continuing current account surpluses. In fact, the two sets of imbalances are exactly equal to one another because of the basic accounting identity that defines how the external and internal flow of funds is calculated.[9]

According to Hofman and Kuijs, China's aggregate surplus of savings is due largely to rapid increases in enterprise saving, whereas household and government savings have been stable or declining in recent years (Hofman and Kuijs 2007).[10] China's corporate sector has been enjoying high profits, while the wage share of GDP has been declining. The authors argue that this disparity is at the heart of China's growing income inequality, and they suggest that this is further exacerbated by the low returns earned by China's savers in financial markets (about 2.5%), despite the economy's rapid growth.

Studies by business organizations and authors

We included nine studies by business organizations and authors in the pool of 27 studies.[11] Table 29.3 summarizes the range of GDP growth estimates generated by this cluster. The

Table 29.3 China-India GDP growth estimates by business organizations and authors, 2020–25 (%/year)

	China	India
Low	4.5	5.4
High	5.2	8.4
Average	4.7	6.3
Variance	0.1	1.1
n (observations)	6	9
n (studies)	6	9

studies in the business cluster are typically based on the neo-classical growth model referred to above, and they generate a relatively narrow range of annual GDP growth estimates for China in the period from 2020 to 2025: between 4.5% and 5.2%. In contrast, the range of growth estimates for India is considerably wider: between 5.4% and 8.4%. The 8.4% estimate is from a Goldman Sachs paper (Wilson and Purushothaman 2003) that optimistically posits high productivity growth, generally favourable demographic conditions, and improvements in educational attainment.

In contrast to the average growth estimates of the academic cluster, the business cluster places India's expected GDP growth rates in the 2020–25 period *above China's*—specifically, an average estimate of annual GDP growth of 6.3% for India versus 4.7% for China. These figures compare with the academic cluster's average estimate of 5.4% for China and 4.3% for India, cited earlier. Furthermore, the variance estimates for the business cluster are substantially lower than for the academic cluster.

Not surprisingly, the papers in the business cluster, especially those sponsored by Goldman Sachs, accord particular importance to the prevailing regulatory environment and the protection of property rights in influencing their growth forecasts. This emphasis is missing in the papers by the academic institutions discussed earlier, and in the international organizations' studies to be discussed later.

The studies sponsored by the business organizations also tend to compare their estimates for China and India with those of other Asian economies, in particular South Korea—a characteristic that the business cluster shares with the cluster of studies by international financial institutions.

The study sponsored by Goldman Sachs (Wilson and Purushothaman 2003) suggests that if certain conditions prevail in China—namely, macroeconomic stability, high investment rates and a large labour force—the result will likely make China the world's largest economy by 2041, when China's per capita income is estimated to be US$30,000.[12] According to this study, India's growth rate is likely to remain above 5% for several decades, and its GDP will exceed Japan's by 2032, reaching a level of per capita income 35 times its current level, yet still significantly lower than China's in 2050.

Wilson and Purushothaman make several simplifying assumptions that indeed cast doubt on their final estimates. For example, they do not consider changing demographic conditions in China, instead making the erroneous assumption that the proportion of the working-age population in China will remain stable. In reality, the percentage of China's working age population is expected to peak in 2010–12 and to decline thereafter.[13] Furthermore, Wilson and Purushothaman make an unrealistic assumption that the investment rate of economies seeking to catch up with the developed countries will remain very high and constant. It is more realistic to assume that as India's and China's per capita income levels approach those of the developed countries, they will experience lower rates of return on investment, and therefore will reduce their rates of investment, leading to lower rates of growth in TFP. These reduced rates will tend to converge more closely with those prevailing in more advanced economies. For example, developing countries that previously maintained an investment rate of 25%–30% of GDP are likely to find these rates converging toward prevailing levels in the Organisation for Economic Co-operation and Development (OECD) countries (about 15%–20%),[14] due to the lower rates of return on new investment.

A sequel Goldman Sachs paper (Purushothaman 2004) places India's annual GDP growth at about 5.7% during the 2020–25 period, reasoning that the two crucial conditions of improved infrastructure and expanded education may be insufficient to keep India on a steady and higher growth path. Another Goldman Sachs paper (Poddar and Yi 2007) calls attention to certain constraints on doing business in India as potential threats to private enterprise.[15]

A paper sponsored by Deutsche Bank (Bergheim 2005) projects India to grow more rapidly than China in the period to 2020. The Bergheim paper forecasts India's average annual GDP growth at 5.5%, compared with projected Chinese GDP growth of 5.2% over the same period. The major contributor to this gap, according to Bergheim, is China's slower population growth rate (at 0.8% annually, about half that of India's growth rate), a presumed consequence of its one-child policy.

Analysts from the McKinsey Global Institute (2007) suggest that India's likely continuation of its recent rapid growth will result in the tripling of India's average household income over the next two decades. If this trend is sustained, India will become the world's fifth largest economy by 2025, compared with its current position of 12th. Unlike other studies in the business organization cluster, and while noting the progress that India has made to date, the McKinsey paper emphasizes the significant challenges it still faces. These include, for example, the large regional disparities in growth and in poverty levels: for example, India's southern and western states prosper while the northern and eastern states lag far behind. Furthermore, while India has been slowly urbanizing over the past two decades, the McKinsey study suggests that it remains the least urbanized of the emerging Asian economies. According to analysts from the McKinsey Global Institute, only 29% of the Indian population currently lives in cities, compared with 40% in China and 48% in Indonesia. The McKinsey analysts project that the level of urbanization will increase to only 37% by 2025 in India. Finally, they note that while more Indians are completing secondary and higher education, India's education system remains severely strained and that opportunities for schooling vary widely, as does the quality of schooling. Indeed, nearly all of the business group authors stress educational inequality in India as a significant impediment and a relative disadvantage in comparison with the educational conditions in China.[16]

Studies by international organizations

We included seven studies by international organizations in the pooled set.[17] Table 29.4 summarizes the international organizations' GDP growth estimates for China and India in the 2020–25 period. This cluster projects higher growth estimates than those made by the business cluster, but the international organizations' estimates are similar to those in the academic cluster. Whereas the business cluster's range of growth estimates is wider for India than for China, the

Table 29.4 Business conditions in China and India, 2007

	India	China	South Korea
Starting a business			
Time required (months)	1.1	1.2	0.6
Cost (% of GDP per capita)	74.6	8.4	16.9
Contract enforcement			
Procedures required	46	35	35
Time (months)	47.3	13.5	7.7
Property registration			
Procedures required	6	4	7
Time (months)	2.1	1	0.4
Closing a business			
Recovery rate (cents on the dollar)	11.6	35.8	81.2
Time (months)	120	20.4	18

Source: World Bank, undated 2010a

Charles Wolf, Jr and Alisher Akhmedjonov

international organization cluster shows a wider range in the estimates for China than for India, although the variance of the estimates for China is still lower than the variance in the academic cluster's estimates.

An anthology published by the World Bank (Winters and Yusuf 2007) provides several analytical models for assessing developments in the Chinese and Indian economies and their impact on global markets to 2020. In addition to providing forecasts of the two countries' economic growth, the World Bank study analyses what would occur if China were to grow at an annual average rate of 6.6%, and India at 5.5%, to 2020. Several essays explore other facets of China's and India's growth, including effects on the geographical location of global industry, changes in the international financial system, effects on the global environment, and the relationship between growth and governments.

A paper from the IMF (Rodrik and Subramanian 2004) estimating India's annual GDP growth during the 2020–25 period employs a growth-accounting model based on inputs of capital and labour and increases in factor productivity. Rodrik and Subramanian acknowledge that their estimates may be low if India succeeds in expanding and improving its educational system. They note that India's productivity growth has benefited from its stock of highly educated people, although the authors do not provide much supporting evidence. They also acknowledge that their growth forecasts rely on continuation of effective economic and social reforms in India. Rodrik and Subramanian also contend that, unlike China, India already has strong economic and political institutions, so that further reform need not be burdensome. Instead, they suggest that India 'has done the really hard work of building good economic and political institutions—a stable democratic polity, reasonable rule of law, and protection of property rights', concluding that 'countries with good institutions do not in general experience large declines in growth' (Rodrik and Subramanian 2004: 7–8).

As previously noted, not all of the authors and clusters of studies agree with this judgement. Instead some of the other studies contend that the effectiveness of India's institutions leaves much to be desired (e.g. Poddar and Yi 2007).

Similarities and differences among the clusters: observations and hypotheses

As indicated in Table 29.1 and the preceding sections, forecasts of the absolute and relative macroeconomic performance of India and China in the 2020–25 period reflect deep and pervasive uncertainty. Estimates of both China's and India's annual economic growth over this period vary by a factor greater than two (3.8%–9.0%) for China and by a factor of three (2.8%–8.4%) for India, across the 27 studies included in the analysis. The range in forecasts for the USA and most OECD countries would be much narrower.

Table 29.5 and Figure 29.2 summarize how the three clusters of our pooled studies differ from each other. For example, the widest variation in growth estimates for both China and India comes from the academic cluster. Table 29.5 also shows that the estimates of growth rates made by scholars at international organizations tend to be the highest among the three clusters, while the estimates from the business cluster show the widest difference in the growth estimates between India and China. Furthermore, the business cluster also projected distinctively higher growth estimates for India than for China.

The contrasting forecasts of the three clusters are also displayed in the box diagram of Figure 29.3, in which India's annual growth is indicated along the vertical axis, and China's on the horizontal axis. The three rectangles show the distribution of the summary statistics for, respectively, the business cluster, the academic cluster and the international cluster. The means for

546

Table 29.5 China-India GDP growth rate estimates by the three clusters, 2020–25 (%/year)

	Country	Minimum	Maximum	Average	Variance
Academic institutions	China	3.8	9.0	5.5	2.6
	India	2.8	7.2	4.3	2.4
Business organizations	China	4.5	5.2	4.7	0.1
	India	5.4	8.4	6.3	1.1
International organizations	China	5.9	9.0	6.8	1.1
	India	5.2	8.0	6.2	0.9

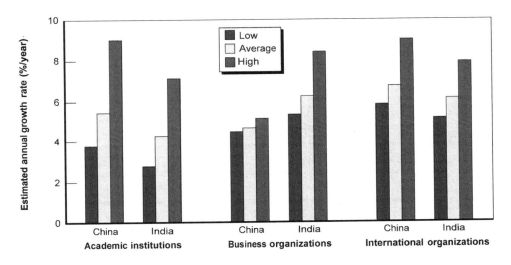

Figure 29.2 China-India GDP growth rate estimates by the three cluster, 2020–2025

each cluster are indicated by the correspondingly shaded dots in each rectangle. The lowest growth estimates for India and China for each cluster appear at the lower-left corner of each rectangle, and the highest growth estimates appear at the upper-right corner of each rectangle. The xs shown in Figure 29.3 represent, from top right to bottom left, the high, average and low China-India growth estimates for the pooled set of all 27 studies included in the meta-analysis.[18]

Interpreting, let alone explaining, the notable differences among the three clusters is bound to be conjectural. For example, the widest variances characterizing the academic cluster's estimates might plausibly be attributed to greater awareness by the scholarly community of the enormous sources of uncertainty affecting economic forecasts a decade and a half into the future. Another influence contributing to this spread may lie in differences in worldviews among members of the academic community: for example, some academic economists are inclined to favour central planning and an expanded role of government in economic development, while others are inclined to favour greater reliance on competitive markets, market-based pricing and decentralized innovation in determining resource allocation. Those who favour central planning may tend to see a rosier outlook for China, while those who adhere to the free market view may be inclined to view India's prospects with greater optimism. The result of these differing dispositions and behaviours may be the widened variance of their respective forecasts within the academic cluster compared with the two other clusters.

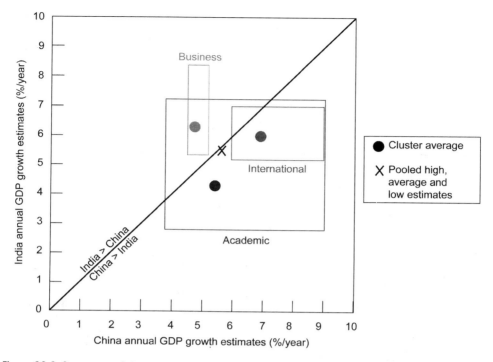

Figure 29.3 Summary of the average, high and low estimates, for all 27 studies and by cluster

By similar reasoning, it may be presumed that studies of economic growth sponsored by business organizations might tend to be led by economists inclined towards market-based development. Hence, such studies are probably more likely to view India's democracy, rule of law and legally protected property rights as constituting a more propitious environment for business innovation and long-term economic growth than that provided by China's one-party autocracy. Consequently, it is not surprising that the highest growth estimates for India relative to China come from the business-sponsored studies included in the meta-analysis.

Finally, that the forecasts made by the international organizations' studies show a marked advantage for China's expected growth relative to India's may plausibly be attributed to China's more prominent role in international trade and investment markets relative to India. As a consequence, one might expect international organizations to be particularly cognizant of this fact, and perhaps influenced by it in their estimates of the two economies' growth over the next 15 years, resulting in the relatively buoyant forecasts for China.

Underlying and contributing to the wide differences in forecasts are significant differences in the assumptions made by the forecasters. For example, some of the forecasts simply assume a continuation of recent growth trends in both countries, extrapolating linearly to forecast the 2020–25 period. Other forecasts focus especially on demographic trends and especially trends in labour supplies that inhere in the current circumstances of the two countries' population cohorts and fertility rates. Still other forecasts build their estimating models on assumptions relating to energy prices and the heavy dependence of the two countries on fossil fuel imports. Further, some of the forecasts make assumptions about the prevalence of macroeconomic stability, economic openness, the quality or the degree of inequality of educational opportunities, and the integrity of economic and social institutions. Embedded in most of the studies that use the neo-classical model described earlier are simplifying and arguable assumptions about constant returns to scale and competitive markets.

In turn, these assumptions and the selectivity of their focus affect the inputs to the analytic models that the authors use in generating their respective forecasts. In the process, the forecasts ignore cyclical fluctuations around long-term trend estimates. Furthermore, the studies generally ignore the possibility of major adverse political disturbances, natural disasters, or military conflict, or the possibility of a major technological jump that might trigger a new wave of innovation in either China or India, or that might cause a sharp change in the relative prices of the natural resources, fossil fuels, ferrous and non-ferrous metals of which China and India are major importers.

Always implicit, and sometimes explicit, in the forecasts is a recognition by the authors that China and India have taken quite different paths in pursuing economic development. China has emphasized the expansion of labour-intensive manufacturing, while India has charted a path from agriculture to high-end services with a limited increase in the manufacturing sector. In sum, the wide range of the estimates reflects both the assumptions and behavioural dispositions of the forecasters, the issues on which they focus as well as those they ignore, and the deep uncertainties that surround forecasts over the next decade and a half.

Five growth scenarios and concluding observations

The meta-analysis discussed in the preceding sections displays quantitatively the profound uncertainties that pervade attempts to forecast how two such dynamic and complex systems as the economies of India and China will fare over the next 15 years. This uncertainty pervades the 27 studies encompassed in our analysis, whether they are examined in the aggregate or within the three separate clusters of the academic, business and international organization studies.

In this section, we contrast five scenarios consisting of different pairings of the forecasts for the two countries: a scenario in which both countries grow at their respective average estimates, and scenarios that show the four combinations of the separate high and low growth estimates for China and India. On the implicit but not implausible premise that many of the factors affecting the economic performance of China and India (e.g. their respective fiscal and monetary policies, trade and investment policies, education policies, business regulatory policies, etc.) are uncorrelated with one another, these starkly contrasting high-low scenarios can serve two purposes: first, to highlight (and in some sense magnify) the uncertainties that emerge from the meta-analysis; and second, to provide a basis for contingency planning for policymakers. More specifically, the challenges that US policymakers, as well as policymakers in other countries, face will be very different depending on which of the contrasting scenarios ensues. That said, it should also be noted that the most appropriate policy responses to the contrasting scenarios are more likely to involve adjusting to the scenarios, rather than shaping them. However, it would be going too far to suggest that US policy is without some modest influence on which of the several scenarios occurs. However, realistically speaking, the extent of such influence, as well as of the resources that the USA is likely to be willing to deploy to affect scenario outcomes, will at most probably affect the scenarios only at their margins rather than their defining cores.

Figure 29.4 shows the five contrasting GDP growth pairings between China and India in 2020–25 under the five contrasting scenarios.

Figures 29.5 and 29.6 show the GDPs for India and China in 2025 in terms of market exchange rates (see Figure 29.5) and PPP conversion rates (Figure 29.6). As the two figures indicate, only in the scenario in which high growth in India is paired with low growth in China does India's GDP approach China's. In the four other scenarios, China's predominance is decisive. This outcome is the same whether conversions are calculated with market exchange rates or PPP rates.

Charles Wolf, Jr and Alisher Akhmedjonov

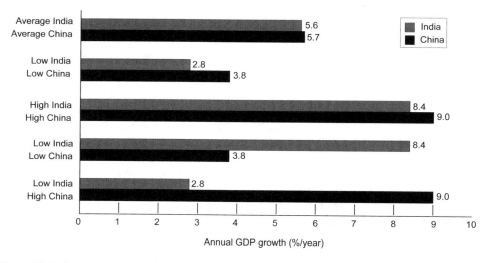

Figure 29.4 Fire GDP growth scenario, India and China, 2020–2025

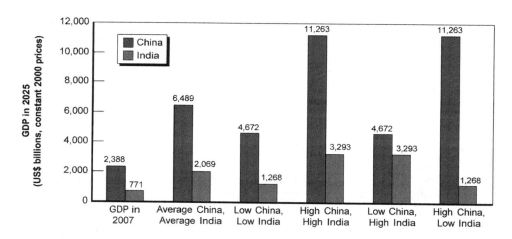

Figure 29.5 Five scenarios: GDP's of China and India in 2025, Harker Exchange Rates
Note: Conversion to market exchange rates based on The World Bank's World Development Indicators (World Bank, no date)

Turning to a more qualitative aspect of the China-India assessment, Table 29.6 distils from the meta-analysis our judgement about the advantages and disadvantages of China and India in their respective institutional and other circumstances. Whether and to what extent the factors listed in the table will enable India to move closer to, or ahead of, China after 2025 is worthy of separate consideration beyond that provided in this chapter.

Appendix: meta-analysis of economic growth in China and India

The first step in the meta-analysis involved collecting pertinent and accessible studies done between 2000 and 2008 addressing economic growth in China and India through the 2020–25

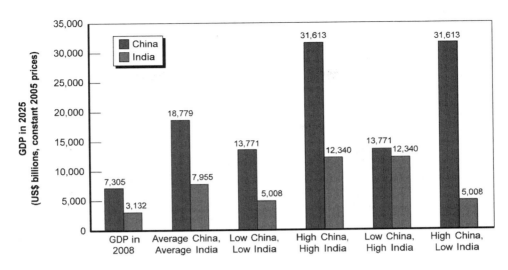

Figure 29.6 Five scenarios: GDP's of China and India in 2025, purchasing power party conversion rates

Table 29.6 Some qualitative factors affecting China and India's performance

Factor	Advantage of China or India
Democracy/rule of law	India
Information technology and service skills	India
Institutions	India
Property rights	India
Productivity growth	China
Foreign investment in and by each country	China
Infrastructure	China

period. The major sources consulted for the search included publication indexes, LexisNexis and internet search engines. This search yielded an initial pool of 47 studies.

The second step identified a subset of 27 studies that had the requisite data from India and China to permit their comparative assessment for the 2020–25 period. Twenty studies were excluded because of incomplete or otherwise insufficient data for the two-country comparison.

The third step required drawing data from each study to make calculations of the recent and out-year rates of growth of GDP, employment, capital and TFP, either directly from the study or indirectly using incremental capital/output ratios, or a Cobb-Douglas production function, or a growth-accounting methodology. Of the 32 studies, 27 met these criteria for inclusion in the meta-analysis.

In the fourth step, these 27 studies and the corresponding descriptive statistics on GDP and factor growth rates, means, minima, maxima and variances were arrayed into three separate groups or clusters of studies as follows:

- academic authors and institutions;
- business organizations (e.g. Goldman Sachs, PricewaterhouseCoopers, McKinsey); and
- international financial institutions (e.g. the World Bank, the IMF, Asian Development Bank).

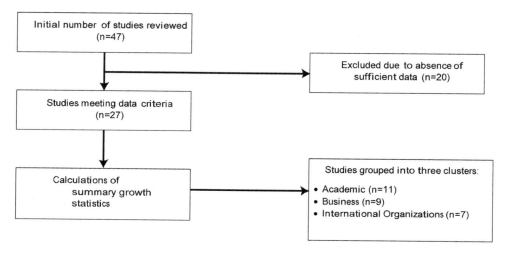

Figure 29.7 Meta analysis process

This step included comparisons of the descriptive statistics across the three clusters of studies, highlighting their similarities and differences.

In addition to the descriptive statistics, and the comparisons across the three clusters, the text discussion of the meta-analysis includes more detailed discussion of 17 of the 27 papers included in the meta-analysis.

Figure 29.7 summarizes the successive steps.

Notes

1 This chapter draws heavily from a prior RAND study, 'China and India, 2025: A Comparative Assessment', 2011, MG-1009, by Charles Wolf, Jr, Siddhartha Dalal, Julie DaVanzo, Eric Larson, Alisher Akhmedjonov, Harun Dogo, Meilinda Huang and Silvia Montoya. Chapter three of that book, 'A Macroeconomic Assessment', was jointly authored by Dr Akhmedjonov and myself. That chapter is, with some edits and elaboration, the source of the present chapter in this Handbook.
2 For the list of the 27 studies, see the bibliography at the end of this chapter. For their separation into the three institutional clusters, see below.
3 We deliberately focus on the extremes of the range, rather than on maximum likelihood estimates, in order to highlight the uncertainties involved in these forecasts. In turn, later in this chapter we use the maximum and minimum points of the range to formulate high- and low-growth scenarios to compare Indian and Chinese GDP forecasts for 2025.
4 The corresponding variances will be discussed below
5 The 11 in the academic cluster are: Brown 2005; Golley and Tyers 2006; Hofman and Kuijs 2007; Holz 2005; Huang et al. 2003; Laurent 2006; Linn 2006; Paltsev and Reilly 2007a, 2007b; Poncet 2006; and Tyers et al. 2006.
6 Holz assumes that the US average annual GDP growth rate during this period will be 3.0%.
7 The ANU paper by Tyers and colleagues assumes that with increasingly open capital accounts, both China and India stand to attract foreign investment the more rapidly their labour forces grow.
8 Cf. Wolf et al., 'China and India, 2025', Chapter two, 'Population Trends in China and India'.
9 The accounting identity specifies that the difference between an economy's aggregate savings and aggregate investment is equal to the difference between: (1) the sum of its exports and other current international earnings; and (2) its imports and other current international payments. Thus, the internal and external imbalances must be exactly equal.

10 One author of the current monograph (Wolf) considers this assertion to be wrong because data from the State Statistical Bureau indicate that household savings (and household holdings of liquid savings balances in the major state banks) have grown substantially in recent years.

11 The nine studies in the business cluster are Ablett *et al.* 2007; Bergheim 2005; Desai *et al.* 2007; Hawksworth and Cookson 2008; O'Neill *et al.* 2005; Poddar and Yi 2007; Purushothaman 2004; Wilson and Purushothaman 2003; and Wilson and Stupnytska 2007.

12 Wilson and Purushothaman assume that the US annual GDP growth rate during the same period is between 2.1% and 3.1%. Per capita income levels are in market exchange rates but closer to purchasing power parity (PPP) exchange rates. Wilson and Purushothaman assume that as countries develop, there will be a tendency for their currencies to converge towards PPP rates. PPP exchange rates are calculated as the ratio between a market basket of goods and services (e.g. consisting of consumer purchases or of the country's GDP as a whole), priced according to the country's own prices and weighted by their corresponding shares, divided by the same weighted market basket of goods and services but instead priced in prevailing US dollar prices. Hence, PPP rates omit the effects of capital transactions, which heavily influence market exchange rates, while market exchange rates omit the effects of non-tradable goods and services (e.g. residential property values and domestic household services). In developing countries, PPP exchange rates are predictably higher for domestic currencies (e.g. Indian rupees and Chinese renminbi) than are their market exchange rates.

13 See Wolf *et al.* 'China and India, 2025', Chapter two, 'Population Trends'.

14 World Bank and OECD statistical yearbooks, 2010, 2011.

15 See Figure 29.5.

16 Heng Quan, in his paper–titled 'Income Inequality in China and India: Structural Comparisons', observes Gini coefficients (reflecting socioeconomic inequality) for both China and India since 1980. He shows that China's regional differences were higher than those of India before 1990–91, reflected in India's lower Gini coefficient. However, India's coefficient has increased since 1991, evidently exceeding that of China.

17 The seven studies in the international organization cluster are: Cooper 2000; Das Gupta 2003; Rodrik and Subramanian 2004; Shiyang 2007; US Department of Energy, Energy Information Administration 2008; Winters and Yusuf 2007; and World Economic Forum 2006.

18 We are indebted to RAND colleague Michael Mattock for this graphic.

Bibliography

Ablett, Jonathan *et al.* (2007) *The 'Bird of Gold': The Rise of India's Consumer Market*, McKinsey Global Institute, Mumbai.

Bergheim, Stefan (2005) *Global Growth Centers 2020: 'Formel-G' for 34 Economies*, Deutsche Bank Research, Frankfurt am Main, 23 March.

Brown, Harold (2005) 'Managing Change: China and the United States in 2025', address at the 8th Annual RAND-China Reform Forum Conference, RAND Corporation, 28 June, www.rand.org/pubs/corporat e_pubs/CP505.html (accessed 21 July 2010).

Carnell, Brian (2000) 'China to Intensify One Child Effort; Immigration Case Throws Some Horror Stories in Doubt', 26 September, brian.carnell.com/articles/2000/china-to-intensify-one-child-effort-immigration-case-throws-some-horror-stories-in-doubt/.

Cooper, Richard N. (2000) 'Global Public Goods: A Role for China and India', *Public goods for economic development*, 2025, 315.

Das Gupta, Monica, Jiang Zhenghua, Li Bohua, Xie Zhenming, Woojin Ching and Bae Hwa-Ok (2003) 'Why Is Son Preference so Persistent in East and South Asia? A Cross-Country Study of China, India, and the Republic of Korea', *Journal of Development Studies* 40(2), December: 153–87.

Desai, Prashant, Richard Fairgrieve, Dippanker S. Haldar, A.P. Parigi and R. Subramanian (2007) *Tapping into the Indian Consumer Market*, McKinsey Global Institute, Mumbai.

Golley, Jane and Rod Tyers (2006) 'China's Growth to 2030: Demographic Change and the Labor Supply Constraint', Australian National University, Canberra.

Hawksworth, John and Gordon Cookson (2008) *The World in 2050: Beyond the BRICs: A Broader Look at Emerging Market Growth Prospects*, PricewaterhouseCoopers, London.

Heng Quan (2008) 'Income Inequality in China and India: Structural Comparisons', *The Asian Scholar* 4.

Hofman, Bert and Louis Kuijs (2007) *Rebalancing China's Growth*, Peterson Institute for International Economics.

Holz, Carsten A. (2005) *China's Economic Growth 1978–2025: What We Know Today About China's Economic Growth Tomorrow*, Hong Kong University of Science and Technology, Hong Kong.

Huang, Jikun, Linxiu Zhang, Qiang Li and Huanguang Qiu (2003) *National and Regional Economic Development Scenarios for China's Food Economy Projections in the Early 21st Century*, Chinese Academy of Sciences, December.

Laurent, Clint (2006) *India—Is it the Next China?* Asian Demographics Ltd, Hong Kong.

Linn, Johannes F. (2006) *Regional Cooperation and Integration in Central Asia*, Centennial Group, Washington, DC.

O'Neill, Jim, Dominic Wilson, Roopa Purushothaman and Anna Stupnytska (2005) 'How Solid are the BRICs?' Goldman Sachs Global Economics Paper No. 134.

Paltsev, Sergey and John Reilly (2007a) 'China and India in Energy Markets and its Implication for Global Greenhouse Gas Emissions', Massachussetts Institute of Technology, Cambridge, MA.

——(2007b) 'Energy Scenarios of East Asia: 2005–25', Massachussetts Institute of Technology, Cambridge, MA.

Poddar, Tushar and Eva Yi (2007) 'India's Rising Growth Potential', Goldman Sachs, London.

Poncet, Sandra (2006) 'The Long Term Growth Prospects of the World Economy: Horizon 2050', CEPII Working Paper No. 2006-16.

Purushothaman, Roopa (2004) 'India: Realizing BRICs Potential', Goldman Sachs Global Economics Paper No. 109, London.

Rodrik, Dani and Arvind Subramanian (2004) 'Why India Can Grow at 7 Percent a Year or More: Projections and Reflections', International Monetary Fund, WP/04/118, Washington, DC.

Shiyang, Cui (2007) *China: Opportunities, Challenges and Market Entry Strategies*, US Commercial Service and U.S. Consulate General, Chengdu, China.

Tyers, Rod, Jane Golley and Iain Bain (2006) 'Projected Economic Growth in China and India: The Role of Demographic Change', Australian National University, Canberra.

US Department of Energy, Energy Information Administration (2008) *International Energy Outlook 2008*, June, www.eia.doe.gov/oiaf/archive/ieo08/index.html (accessed 23 July 2008).

Wilson, Dominic and Roopa Purushothaman (2003) 'Dreaming with BRICs: The Path to 2050', Goldman Sachs Global Economics Paper No. 99, October, www2.goldmansachs.com/ideas/brics/brics-dream.html (accessed 23 July 2010).

Wilson, Dominic and Anna Stupnytska (2007) 'The N-11: More than an Acronym', Goldman Sachs Global Economics Paper No. 153, London.

Winters, Alan and Shahid Yusuf (eds) (2007) *Dancing with Giants: China, India, and the Global Economy*, World Bank Institute of Policy Studies, Washington, DC.

World Economic Forum (2006) *China and the World: Scenarios to 2025*, www3.weforum.org/docs/WEF_Scenario_ChinaWorld2025_Report_2010.pdf (accessed 21 July 2010).

Index

Abdel-Maguid, Sayed 413n39
Abdel-Razek, Sherine 412n26, 412n29, 413n45, 413n62, 414n76
Abeysinghe, T. and Jiaying, G. 222n37
Abeysinghe, T. and Meng, C.K. 221n34
Abeysinghe, Tilak 219n1, 223n56
Ablett, J. *et al.* 553n11
Abrahamian, Ervand 457n19
Abreu, M.de P. and Bevilaqua, A.S. 45n3
Abreu, M.de P. and Lago, L.A.C. do 34, 45n1
Abul-Magd, Zeinab 411n11
Accelerated and Shared Growth Initiative for South Africa (ASGISA) 129–30
accountability 236, 252, 277, 284–85n36, 462, 513; democratic accountability 360, 361; downward accountability 98; educational accountability 234; National Accountability Bureau (NAB) in Pakistan 383, 394; transparency and 316, 318, 324, 409; voice and 119, 142, 149, 153, 154, 156, 157, 159, 161, 162, 164–70, 407–8, 484, 485, 489, 495
Acemoğlu, D. 262n27, 283n5, 284n9
Acemoğlu, D. and Robinson, J.A. 62, 183, 184n14, 262n27, 381, 395n8, 465, 466, 470n8
Acharya, Shankar 70
Adelman, I. and Morris, C.T. 175n33, 175n36
Adly, Amr 408, 411n9, 414n90
Afghanistan 470, 472n58, 472n69; Iraq and, Bush administration and 448–49; Pakistan and 380, 383, 384, 385, 386–87, 389
Africa 15, 16, 22, 24, 25, 26, 42, 90, 91–92, 179, 510; North Africa 10, 188, 404, 476; sub-Saharan Africa 22, 23, 25, 27, 105, 114, 127, 515; world economy, key trends in 22, 23
Afshin, Molavi 457n18

Agenor, Pierre-Richard 174n8
agrarian reform: Chile 229; Viet Nam 350
Agrawal, M. and Bali, J. 80n1
Agrawal, Nisha 361n1
Agricultural and Food Industries Organization (AFIO) in Iran 446
agriculture 25, 36, 92, 330, 331, 333, 340, 373, 377, 390, 394, 397, 549; in Colombia 461, 462; de-collectivization in China 88–89; imbalances in Brazil 39; in India 61, 66, 68, 75, 76, 78, 80; in Indonesia 273, 279; in Iran 445, 446; in Israel 188, 190; land and agriculture in Viet Nam 346, 350–51, 360–61; productivity in Argentina 331; in South Africa 107, 108, 110; subsistence agriculture in Mexico 288; in Thailand 417, 425–27, 436–37
Ahluwalia, M.S. *et al.* 29n9
Ahmad, Meekal 378
Ahmadinejad, Mahmoud 451
Akhmedjonov, A. and Wolf, C.Jr. 552n1
Akhmedjonov, Alisher xviii, 539–54, 552n1
Akkari, Abdeljalil 413n51
Aldunate, Arturo Fontaine 241n9
Alessandri, Jorge 229
Alexander, Philip 523n69
Allende, Salvador 230, 232; statist revolution in Chile 229–30
Alliance Party (formation, 1957) in Malaysia 312
Aloui, R., Aïssa, M.S.B. and Nguyen, D.K. 284n16
Alsharabati, Carole 521n23
Amanat, Abbas 455n3
Ambrus, Steven 472n60
Amoranto, G., Chun, N. and Deolalikar, A.B. 521n15

555

Index

Anand, J. *et al.* 285n45
Anand, S. and Kanbur, R. 29n9
Anderson, James 361n1
Anderson, Jonathan 92, 104n21
Angrist, J.D. and Kugler, A.D. 466, 471n46, 471n48
Aon Hewitt 2012 People Risk Index 406
Aquino, Corazon 368
Arab community in Israel 197
Arab Spring in Saudi Arabia 496
Arbor, Ann 241n10
Arciniegas, Germán 468
Arellano, José Pablo 241n15, 241n21
Argentina 8, 329–38; agricultural productivity 331; Convertibility Law (1991) 335; countercyclical fiscal policy 329; debt problem 330; default 330; economic developments (since 2002) 329–31; economic frustrations, history of 331–38; expansionary fiscal policy 330; fiscal policies 329, 330, 366–69, 370; GDP per capita 332, 338; good economic management, prospects for return to 330–31; human resources 331; hyperinflation 330, 331, 335, 338; inter-war trauma (1913–45) 332–33; International Monetary Fund (IMF) 336; Marxist-Keynesian ideological glasses 331; monetary policy 329–30, 338; National Constitution enacted (1853) 331; natural resources 331; Perón presidencies (1945–75) 333–35; price stability 329–30; private investment 330; rational economic policymaking, potential for 331; stability and growth, deflation and counter-reform (1990–2012) 335–38; stagflation 335, 338
Arkhipov, I., Cohen, M. and Galvao, A. 521n12
Armey, L., Kamrany, N. and Ramirez, D. 9
Armey, Laura E. xviii–xix, 458–74
Armijo, L.E. and Kateda, S.N. 524n88
Armijo, L.E. and Roberts, C. 10
Armijo, Leslie Elliott xix, 503–24, 522n41
Armington, P. and Dadush, U. 28n6
Arriagada, Genaro 241n7
Arrow, Kenneth J. 201n7
Arroyo, Gloria Macapagal administration 368
Asaad, Ragui 413n66, 413n67, 414n89
Ashraf, Raja Pervaiz 382, 383
Asian Development Bank (ADB) 314–15, 325n3
Asian Financial Crisis (1997) 7, 26, 85, 88, 99, 276, 324, 392, 418, 436, 438; Malaysia 306; Philippines 365, 368–69; Republic of Korea (South Korea) 531, 536; Singapore 207–8; Thailand 416, 438
Asian Tigers 203, 204, 205, 206–7
Askari, Hossein 500n42
Assadipour, J. 457n37
Association of Southeast Asian Nations (ASEAN): Free Trade Area-Comprehensive Effective

Preferential Tariff (AFTA-CEPT) 374; Indonesia 272, 274, 281; Viet Nam 351
Astan Quds Razavi in Iran 446–47
Atiyas, İ and Bakiş, O. 261
Atkinson, Doreen 132n22
Australia 20, 29n15, 89, 90, 104n18, 143, 222n41, 223n58, 225n82, 331, 332, 333, 504; Australian National University (ANU) 542
authoritarianism 6, 38, 47, 161, 182–83, 403, 408, 434, 440, 456n8, 484; in Chile 227–28, 230–31, 233, 238, 240; in Mexico 288, 289; in Singapore 204, 205, 212, 215–16
Auty, Richard M. 482, 499n23
Auty, R.M. 285n51, 285n53
Avnimlech, G. and Teubal, M. 201n9
Ayala, E.A. and Villarreal, M. 304n18
Aylwin, Patricio 234, 238
Azcárraga, Emilio Jean 298, 299
al-Aziz, King Abd 484

Bachelet, Michelle 235
Bagnoli, P. 520n2
al-Baharna, Nazar 414n89
Baier, S.L. *et al.* 480, 499n14
Baker, Aryn 380, 395n5
balance of payments (BOP) 441, 505, 527; China 103n11; crisis in Brazil 37; crisis in Mexico 289–90; crisis in Philippines 369–70, 375; deficits 6, 391; Israel 189–91, 192, 195, 200; problems in Turkey 247, 250; South Africa 112; surpluses in Russia 51; surpluses in Singapore 219n10; Viet Nam 357
Balassa, B. 28n7
Balassa, B. and Samuelson, P.A. 69
Balassa-Samuelson effect 20
Bales, Sarah 361n1
Banco Nacional do Desenvolvimento Econômico e Social (BNDES) in Brazil 42, 43, 44
Banerjee, Neela 498n2
Banking Act (1985) in Turkey 247
Banyan column *(The Economist)* 226n104, 387, 396n18
Barisan Nasional (BN, or Coalition Front) in Malaysia 313
Barr, M.D. and Skrbis, Z. 224n77
Barro, R.J. and Sala-i-Martin, X. 62
Barros, Robert 241n13
Barsukov, Yurii 60n23
Bartelsman Stiftung 131n1, 131n3, 131n4, 132n32
Barth, James R. 147
Basher, S.A. *et al.* 285n48
Basher, S.A., Haug, A.A. and Sadorsky, P. 283n1
Basher, S.A *et al.* 284n15
Bassat, Avi Ben 202n22
Bauer, Peter T, Lord 65
Baulch, B. *et al.* 345
Baumol, W., Litan, R. and Schramm, C. 176n40

Bayrak, M.M. *et al.* 345
Bazargan, Prime Minister 456n12
Beaty, Thalia 414n93
Bebchuk, Lucian 201n19
Becker, G. 376n24, 376n26
Becker, G., Murphy, K. and Tamura, R. 376n23
Becker, G.S. *et al.* 467
Becker, G.S., Murphy, K.M. and Grossman, M. 472n52
Beijing Consensus 5, 129, 177–83; authoritarianism 182–83; foreign direct investment (FDI) 178, 179; gradualism *versus* shock treatment 178–79; innovation, encouragement of 179; macroeconomic stability 179; market liberalization 180–82; open economy 179–80; summary of provisions 178
Beinin, Joel 412n28
Beintema, N. 285n55
Bello, Andrés 240n2, 242n24
Ben Ali 412n19
Benassy-Quere, A. *et al.* 262n27
Benazir Income Support Fund in Pakistan 395
Benhabib, J. and Spiegel, M. 376n22
Benjamin, D. and Brandt, L. 351
Berg, Claudia 361n1
Berganza, Juan Carlos 304n6
Bergheim, Stefan 545, 553n11
Berra, Yogi 539
Bertelsmann Foundation 406
Bethell, L. 240n2
Betts, Richard K. 522n39
el-Bey, Doaa 412n20
Bhagwati, J. and Desai, P. 67
Bhalla, Surjit S. xix, 4–5, 61–82
Bhaskaran, Manu 219n1, 221n35, 223n52
Bhutto, Zulfikar Ali 382
Bi-national Industrial Research and Development (BIRD) 195
Bina, C. and Zangeneh, H. 455n5
biotechnology 25
Bisat, A.M. *et al.* 480, 499n15
Bisseker, Claire 133n57
Bitar, Sergio 241n8
Blanchard, O.J. and Fischer, S. 220n28
Blanke, J. 175n17
Boediono, Vice-President of Indonesia 278, 285n58
Boeninger, Edgardo 242n24
Bolsa Família in Brazil 33
boon-and-bust cycles 6, 227, 228, 229, 315, 366
Bordo, M.D., Meissner, C.M. and Stuckler, D. 284n29
Borrero, Pablo Querubín 462, 470n12
Borzutzky, Silvia 241n23, 242n29
Bosworth, B.P., Dornbusch, R. and Labán, R. 241n10

Bottelier, Pieter xix–xx, 5, 83–104
Bourantonis, D. and Ifantis, K. 522n43
Bousquet, G. 520n2
Bovenkerk, F. and Levi, M. 472n58
Brambilla, I. *et al.* 352
Brazil 4, 33–45; Banco Nacional do Desenvolvimento Econômico e Social (BNDES) 42, 43, 44; Bolsa Família 33; Brazilian miracle 38–40; coffee investments 35; coffee policy, role of 35; coffee prices 34, 35; coffee production 34, 35; coffee profits 37; coffee stockpiling 34; continuity from Lula da Silva, and promise of change 41–43; cotton exports 34; Cruzado Plan (1986) 40–41; debt-financed adjustment 39; external indebtedness 38–39; Fiscal Responsibility, Law of (2000) 41; foreign direct investment (FDI) 41–42; future prospects 43–45; Great Depression, saviour for 34–36; gross national product (GNP) 33; immigration from Italy 34; import substitution 36–38; income per capita 34; independence, emergence of 34; industrial structure 34–35, 36, 37, 38, 43–44; industrialization, evolution of 35, 36, 37, 38; International Monetary Fund (IMF) 37, 40, 41; Organization for Economic Co-operation and Development (OECD) 43; Partido Democrático Social (PDS) 40; Partido do Movimento Democrático Brasileiro (PMDB) 40; Partido dos Trabalhadores (PT-Worker's Party) 40, 41, 42, 43, 44; Plano Real (1994) 33; Portuguese colonialism in 33–34; Programa de Aceleração do Crescimento (PAC) 42; protective policies 34, 35, 37, 38, 39, 44; railways, expansion of 34; SELIC interest rate 41, 42, 43; starting over (1985–2010) 40–41; sugar exports 34; Triple Alliance with Paraguay (1860s) 34; US Civil War, effect on trade 34; world economy 34
Breakout Nations: In Pursuit of the Next Economic Miracles? (Sharma, R.) 364
Breisinger, C., Ecker, O., al-Riffai, P. and Yu, B. 413n55, 414n74
Bremer, J. and Kasarda, J. 139–40, 142, 174n11, 175n13
Bremer/Kasarda Stage Theory 139–41
Bremmer, I. and Gordon, D. 522n28
Bretton Woods twins: formal votes in 515–17; leadership of 514–15
BRICs (Brazil, Russia, India and the People's Republic of China) 3–5, 7, 9, 10, 503–20; entry points to BRICS level 269–76; global economic governance, BRICS and 514–19; global governance, emerging powers and 504–5, 505–6, 509; Indonesia and, comparison between 265, 267–69, 280, 283; informal influence and global governance 509;

Index

institutional evolution of 508; UN Security Council and, imbalances in relationship 509–14
Brinkley, Joe 379, 395n4
Brooks, David 388, 396n20
Brooks, S.G. and Wohlforth, W.C. 522n36
Brosnan, Greg 304n13
Browder, Bill 58, 60n30
Brown, Bukit 218
Brown, Harold 552n5
Brück, T., Binzel, C. and Handrich, L. 414n70
Brückner, M. 286n70
Brunner, José Joaquín 241n17
Bruton, Henry J. 480, 499n13
Buehn, A. and Schneider, F. 172
Buhlungu, Sakhela 132n22
Burke, Edmund 539
Burki, Shahid Javed xx, 8, 377–96
Bush, George Sr. 199
Bush, George W. 448, 449, 512
Byrd, William 472n69

Cabral, Pedro Álvarez 33
Calderón, Felipe 294, 303
Camacho, A.and Rodriguez, C. 462
Camacho, Adriana 470n10, 470n14
Cameron, David 387
Canlas, Dante 8, 372
Canlas, Dante B. xx, 364–76
Canlas, D.B. *et al.* 366, 370, 376n11, 376n13, 376n14, 376n17, 376n20
Cano, Alfonso 465, 468
Canuto, Otaviano 174n8
capital: accumulation in India 63; deficiencies in entrepreneurial access to 144–46; markets in Israel, liberalization of 190–91; markets in South Korea, access to 536; stocks of, world economy and 16–17; subsidies in Singapore 211
capitalism 445, 469, 508; Brazilian commitment to 38; *Capitalism and Freedom* (Friedman, M.) 65; competing capitalisms 218; creative destruction power of 231; crony capitalism 503, 536; Western order rooted in 508
Cárdenas, E., Ocampo, J.A. and Thorp, R. 45n3, 45n5
Cárdenas, Mauricio 462, 470n9, 471n16
Cardoso, Fernando Henrique 40, 41
Carlson, S. 520n2
Carnell, Brian 542
Carstens, Agustín 515
Carter, Jimmy 448
Cass, Frank 220n23
Cassing, J.H. 284n33
Castel, Paulette 356, 361n1
Castiglioni, Rossana 242n29
Castillo, Eduardo 305n29
Catão, Luis A.V. 45n4

Catholic Partido Acción Nacional (PAN) in Mexico 291
Cavallo, A., Salazar, M. and Sepúlveda, O. 241n9
Cavallo, Domingo F. xx–xxi, 8, 10, 11, 329–38, 525–30
Central Provident Fund (CPF) in Singapore 206
Centre d'Etudes Prospectives et d'Informations Internationales (CEPII) 543
Cham, Rowena 372
Chan, Fiona 221n35
Chan-Hoong, Leong 221n35
Chan R. and Low, A. 226n96
Chang, H.-J. 62
Chase, R. S., Hill, E. B. and Kennedy, P. 304n3
Chaudhry, Mohammad 382
Chee, Ho Seng 221n35
Chen, Sharon 225n94
Cheong, Terence 221n33
Chile 5, 6, 227–40; agrarian reform 229; Allende's statist revolution 229–30; capitalism, creative destruction power of 231; centres for technical formation (CFT) 233; Chilean miracle, origins of 227–32; CODELCO 232; competitiveness 228–29; Concertación government 238; counter-majoritarian provisions 238; democracy, restoration of 228, 238; direct fiscal funding (AFD) 233; educational reform, case study of 232–37; Foreign Direct Investment Statute (Decree Law 600 of 1974) 232; GDP per capita (1960–2010) 227–28; General Law of Education (LGE, 2009) 235; health reform (2005) 237–38; indirect fiscal funding (AFI) 233; inequality 231; inequality, reductions in 239; institutional reforms 238; Lagos' constitutional reforms (2003) 234–35; market-friendly educational reforms 234; market-friendly institutional constraints 237–40; military, economic plans of 231–32; military coup (1973) 230; National Accreditation Commission (CNA) 236; National Undergraduate Accreditation Commission (CNAP) 236; neo-liberal reforms 231, 232; Organic Constitutional Law on Education (LOCE, 2007) 235; pension system privatization (1982) 237; Pinochet dictatorship (1973–90) 227, 230–31; population growth 229; poverty rates 239; pro-cyclic economic pattern (1960s) 229; professional institutes (IP) 233; public school enrolment 233; social spending 238–39; state role, limitations on 232; student protests (2011) 240; study loans – *crédito con aval del estado* (CAE) 236–37; substitution industrialization (ISI) policies 228–29; tax structure 239–40; tertiary education, expansion of 233–34, 235–36
China, People's Republic of 5, 8, 11, 16, 18, 22, 27–28, 83–102, 539–52; Australian National

558

University (ANU) 542; business conditions (2007) 545; business organizations and authors, studies on economic growth by 543–45, 547; Centre d'Etudes Prospectives et d'Informations Internationales (CEPII) 543; China 2030 (World Bank, 2012) 97–98, 98–99; consumption 92–98; Deutsche Bank paper on economic growth in 545; economic developments (2007–12) 83–86; economic growth, forecasts of 539–41; economic rebalancing 92–98; financial sector reform 99–101; GDP growth 83, 84, 85, 87, 90, 92, 93, 97, 102, 104n24; GDP growth, estimates of future growth 539–40, 541, 542, 543, 544, 545, 546, 547, 548, 549–50, 551; Goldman Sachs paper on economic growth in 544–45; growth scenarios 549–50; Hong Kong University of Science and Technology 542; housing bubble 86–89; institutions and academic authors, studies on economic growth by 541–43, 547; International Monetary Fund (IMF) paper on economic growth in 546; international organizations, studies on economic growth by 545–46, 547; investment 92–98; McKinsey Global Institute paper on economic growth in 545; macroeconomic meta-analysis, salient estimates (2020–25) 540; Massachusetts Institute of Technology (MIT) 542; meta-analysis of economic growth 550–52; Mexico, Chinese challenge to 299–300; Organization for Economic Co-operation and Development (OECD) 544, 546; purchasing power parity (PPP) exchange rates 89, 90, 549, 553n12; qualitative factors affecting performance in 551; shadow banking 101–2; similarities and differences in forecasts 546–49; total factor productivity (TFP) 540, 541, 543, 544, 551; US–China trade 91–92; Viet Nam, China factor in 347–48; World Bank paper on economic growth in 546; world economy 89–91

Ching, Ho 224n77

Ching, Y.C. and Soon, L.G. 220n23

Chong, Terence 221n34

Choon, Chia Ngee 224n69

Christensen, Thomas J. 522n30

Chung-Hee, Park 531, 533, 534, 535

Churchill, Winston 539

CIVETS (Colombia, Indonesia, Viet Nam, Egypt, Turkey and South Africa) 3

Claessens, Stijn 219n6

climate change 4, 13, 25, 26, 27, 28, 99, 520

Cling, J.-P. et al. 343

Clinton, Bill (and administration of) 291, 448, 508

Clinton, Hillary 386

cocaine growing in Colombia 458, 466–67

CODELCO in Chile 232

coffee production in Brazil 34, 35, 37

Cohen, Benjamin J. 524n87

Collins, J. and Lear, J. 241n23

Collor, Fernando 40, 41

Colombia 9–10, 458–70; agriculture 461, 462; cocaine growing 466; Constitution (1991) 465; corruption, problem of 459, 462, 463, 470; Defence and Peace Law (2005) 465; drugs policy, effectiveness of 469–70; drugs trafficking 458, 465–67, 468; economic indicators, positive trends in 461; economic prospects 459–63; fiscal policy 463; GDP (gross domestic product) 458, 459, 460–61, 462, 463, 466; GDP per capita 460, 461, 462; inequalities in 458, 459, 462–63, 464, 468, 469, 470; insurgency in 466; intergenerational mobility 463; international investment 462; LAPOP survey (2010) 463; leftist guerrilla groups 464; M-19 (19 April Movement) 464; National Liberation Army (ELN) 464; peace process 468–69; Plan Colombia 458, 465, 467, 472n54; political disparities, resentment towards government and 466–67; political indicators 462; problems of, towards finding a peaceful solution 467–70; Revolutionary Armed Forces of Colombia (FARC) 10, 458, 459, 464–65, 467–68, 469, 470; social indicators 461; systematic industrial policies 462; technological innovation 461–62; Thomson-Urrutia Treaty (1921) 463; Thousand Days War (1899–1902) 463; total factor productivity (TFP) 460; United Self-Defence Forces of Colombia (AUC) 464–65; violence, history of 462, 463–65; World Bank report on capital formation 461

commodity prices, trends in 24–25, 113, 315, 482

comparative advantage 24, 62, 194, 299, 404, 468, 496; in Singapore 203–4, 204–5, 207, 211, 214

competitiveness: Chile 228–29; competition blocking in Russia 58–59; competitive advantage in South Korea 534–35; emerging economies and 139, 143, 144, 148–54, 156–60, 161–65, 171; Global Competitiveness Report (WEF) 124, 127, 141, 143, 144, 162, 164, 165, 173, 219n12, 301, 310, 492, 493, 494; global governance, emerging powers and 518; improvements in productivity and 527–28; Indonesia 266, 274, 276, 278, 280, 281; Malaysia 320, 323; patterns in Saudi Arabia of 482, 492–93, 494; potential constraints on 141–42; Russia 50; Singapore 204, 207, 210, 213, 216, 217, 218; South Africa 123, 125, 126–27; World Economic Forum Competitiveness Indicators (WEF) 148

composite governance in Saudi Arabia 489–90

concentration in Israel 198

Concertación government in Chile 238

Index

conditional cash transfer (CCT) programme in Mexico 293

confiscation of assets in Egypt 397

conglomerates *(chaebol)* in Asia 340, 348, 359, 534–35, 536, 537

Congress of South African Trade Unions (COSATU) 129

Constitution (1991) of Colombia 465

constitutional monarchy in Malaysia 313

Constitutional Revolution (1905–7) in Iran 440

consumer price inflation 51–52, 84

consumption 34–35, 38–39, 44, 50, 84, 89, 237, 269–70, 271, 272, 282; Chile, expenditure in 231; Chinese consumption 92–98; Colombia, reducing drug consumption in 467; consumption goods, imports of 534; consumption-led growth in Russia 49–50; defence consumption in Israel 191–92; domestic/household consumption 5, 38, 44–45, 49, 92, 93–95, 108, 118, 208, 213, 269–70, 390, 498; energy consumption in Singapore 210; government consumption in Saudi Arabia 479, 480; investment and, balance between 92–98; Malaysia, private consumption in 309; natural resources, over-consumption in Indonesia of 282–83; oil consumption in Iran 391–92; patterns in Iran 452; South African government consumption 108, 110–11, 112, 126; taxes in Turkey 258; Viet Nam, private consumption in 345, 360

continuum approach to stages 137

Contreras, Dante 242n24

Convertibility Law (1991) in Argentina 335

Cooper, Richard N. 553n17

Corbo, V., Kreuger, A.O. and Ossa, F. 219n2

corruption 7–8, 10, 55, 56, 58–59, 506, 517, 527, 533–34, 537; Chile 236–37; Colombia 459, 462, 463, 470; Corruption Perception Index (CPI, TI) for Malaysia 320; Egypt 400, 407–8, 412–13n38; emerging markets and 141, 142, 144–46, 149, 151, 152, 154, 156, 157, 159, 163, 164, 166–70; Indonesia 282, 284–85n36; Iran 443; Malaysia 306–7, 316, 317, 318, 320, 324; Mexico 295; Pakistan 382–83, 393, 394; Philippines 375; Saudi Arabia 475, 484, 488–89, 495; Singapore 206, 215, 216, 225n80; South Africa 118–19, 121, 123, 124–26, 127; Thailand 434, 438; Viet Nam 353–54, 360

cotton production and exports 34, 103n15, 402

Cristi, R. and Ruiz-Tagle, P. 241n12

Cristi, Renato 241n12

Cruzado Plan (1986) in Brazil 40–41

Cuba 8, 230, 339, 469

currency 21, 61, 100, 105, 184n9, 192, 210, 213, 252, 254–55, 276, 294; convertibility of 101; crisis in Iran 453–54; foreign currency 14, 249, 252, 269, 446, 453–54, 528, 534; manipulation

of 80n1, 205, 518; undervaluation in India, real interest rates and 78–79; valuation of 5, 62, 66, 67, 69–70, 71, 79, 80, 180, 189, 291, 336, 517–18; war (of words), global governance and 517–19

Cyprus bail-out, Russian losses from 56–57

Dadkhah, K. and Zangeneh, H. 457n30

Dadush, U. and Shaw, W. 11n3

Dadush, Uri xxi, 4, 11, 13–29

Dae-Jung, Kim 536, 538

Dalal, Siddhartha 552n1

D'Amato, Senator 448

Dang, H.B. et al. 356

Daniel, John 132n22

Dao, King Tran Hung 348

Das Gupta, Monica 553n17

DaVanzo, Julie 552n1

Davidsen, Soren 361n1

Davis, Bob 523n72

de Bellaigue, Christopher 457n24

de Janvry, A. and Sadoulet, E. 351

de Vasconcelos, Álvaro 520n2, 521n14, 521n15

Death, Carl 120, 132n24

debt 15, 19, 27, 34, 41–42, 50, 53, 57, 252, 290, 330, 359, 398, 411, 461, 503; Argentina, debt problem in 330; Brazil, debt-financed adjustment in 39; debt crises 14, 26, 177, 182, 183, 291, 298, 300, 367, 375, 460, 461; Debt Policy Statement (2012–13) in Pakistan 378; debt servicing in South Korea 536; external indebtedness of Brazil 38–39; Fiscal Responsibility and Debt Limitation Act (2005, FRDLA) in Pakistan 378; foreign debt 34, 38, 39, 190, 191, 192, 253, 254, 268, 269, 289, 290, 367, 370, 378, 453; foreign indebtedness in Mexico, acceleration of 290; government debt 57, 192, 248–49, 321, 448, 494; Highly Indebted Poor Countries (HIPC) 8, 339; public debt 27, 53, 193, 245, 247–48, 251, 252, 257, 269, 275, 336, 338, 352, 366–67, 374, 378; sovereign debt 14, 291, 400, 401, 407; Turkey, debt-to-GDP ratio in 248, 252, 257, 262n18

Debusmann, Bernd 304n8

Defence and Peace Law (2005) in Colombia 465

Delong, J. Bradford 68

DeLong, J.B.and Kohli, A. 70

Demiroglu, U., Ersel, H. and Yalçin, C. 261n1

democracy: democratic transition in Viet Nam, challenge of 360–61; restoration in Chile 228, 238; Western order rooted in 508

Democratic People's Republic of Korea (North Korea) 8, 22, 339–40, 514, 518

demographics: bonus for Mexico 302; change (post-2008) in Russia 54, 55, 56; patterns in South Africa 106; of Saudi Arabia, problems of 495–96

Index

Deng Xiaoping 92, 178, 347
Denison, Edward 371, 376n28
depression, risk of 27
der Eng, P.Van 268, 284n23
Dervis, Kemal 414n89
Desai, P. *et al.* 553n11
Desai, Raj M. 414n89
Deutsche Bank paper on economic growth in China and India 545
development growth in Indonesia 266–67
development levels in Russia 46–47, 47–48
development stages (2010–11) 143
developmental and political challenges in Singapore, responsiveness to 206–12, 217
Dhillon, Navtej S. 414n89
Diez, J. and Franceschet, S. 242n29
Dilma, Rousseff 33, 43, 44, 45n7

el-Din, Gamal Essam 411n15
Ding, Ying 523n59
Dinh, Viet Tuan 361n1
direct fiscal funding (AFD) in Chile 233
Discount Investment Corporation in Israel 198
discriminant analysis, constraints on group advancement 156–62
diversity in Pakistan 384–85
Doan, Quang Hong 361n1
Dogo, Harun 552n1
Dom Pedro I 34
domestic savings, generation of 526
Doner, R.F., Ritchie, B. and Slater, D. 220n17
Doner, Richard 219n1
Doo-Hwan, Chun 534, 537
Doucouliagos, H. and Ulubaşoğlu, M.A. 183, 184n13
Dow, Ngiam Tong 212
Drake, Paul 240n2
Drezner, Daniel W. 522n32
drugs trafficking: Colombia 458, 465–67, 468; policy effectiveness in Colombia against 469–70; Thailand 432, 435
Dufey, Gunter 219n1
Dunaway, Steven 524n83
Ease of Doing Business Index (World Bank) in Egypt 398
The East Asian Miracle (World Bank, 1993): Singapore 203
Easterlin, Richard A. 201n2
Easterly, W. and Fischer, S. 499n22
Easterly, William 499n28
Echeverría, Luis 289
Echeverry, Juan Carlos 467, 471n36, 471n42, 472n53, 472n61
Econometrica (Lucas, Jr., R.E.) 364
economic balance of power 13; shift to South and East 15–16
Economic Development Board (EDB) in Singapore 205, 207, 218, 225n85

economic freedom, limits on 142–44
economic growth: China, People's Republic of 92–98, 539–41; Colombia 459–63; India 61, 62–65, 80, 539–41; Indonesia 266–67; Iran 445–46; Saudi Arabia 490–92; South Korea 534, 538; Thailand 416–28, 431–32; Turkey 247–49. *See also* GDP growth; growth scenarios
economic order, 2050 projections 20
Economic Planning Board in South Korea 534
Economic Planning Unit (EPU) in Malaysia 314
Economic Review Committee in Singapore 208, 210
economic sanctions against Iran 447–50
Economic Stabilization Fund (ESF) in Mexico 291
Economic Strategies Committee in Singapore 210
economic triad (China, India and USA), emergence of 21
The Economist 11; on Egypt 406–7, 410; Shoe-Thrower's Index, Saudi Arabia and 475
Edmonds, E.V. and Turk, C. 351
education: attainment in Turkey, high-tech exports and 260; General Law of Education (LGE, 2009) in Chile 235; investment in Philippines 372–73; reform in Chile, case study of 232–37; system in Egypt, underperformance of 404–5; tertiary education enrolment in Mexico 301; tertiary education in Chile, expansion of 233–34, 235–36
Edwards, L. and Lawrence, R.Z. 12n3
Edwards, Nick 524n84
Edwards, Sebastian 434
Efird, Brian 521n23
Eghbal, Media 498n4
Egypt 9, 397–411; Aon Hewitt 2012 People Risk Index 406; Bertelsmann Foundation 406; confiscation of assets 397; Ease of Doing Business Index (World Bank) 398; economic and political crisis (2013) 410–11; Economic Freedom Index 407; economic freefall, Mubarak's experience of 398; *The Economist* on 406–7, 410; education system, underperformance of 404–5; foreign direct investment (FDI) 398, 401; Freedom and Justice Party (FJP) 402, 403, 405; future prospects 408–10; GDP growth 398, 399, 405; GDP per capita 399, 404; General Authority for Investments (GAFI) 407; governance, deficiencies of 406–7; gross national product (GNP) 401; Gulf Cooperation Council (GCC) 408–9; Heritage Foundation 406–7; human resources 404; hydrocarbon rents 397–99; infrastructure, Sadat's upgrading of 397; International Finance Corporation (IFC) 406–7; International Monetary Fund (IMF) 402, 403, 406, 409; labour force 405; macroeconomic imbalances and uncertainties 401–3; manufacturing exports 399; MENA region

561

Index

(Middle East and North Africa) and 404, 405, 406, 407; military economy 399–400, 409; Muslim Brotherhood 402, 408, 409, 410; Operation Desert Storm 398; physical infrastructure 406; prognoses and signs, hope in 400–401; reforms of Nazif cabinet 398; rent seeking, geostrategic location and 397, 398, 399–400; structural adjustment 398; structural constraints 403–8; Supreme Council of the Armed Forces (SCAF) 402, 412–13n38; total factor productivity (TFP) 406; Turkish-Egyptian bilateral relations 400; World Bank 405, 406, 407

Eichengreen, B. *et al.* 260

Elacqua, G. and Gonzalez, P. 242n26

Elecqua, G., Contreras, D., Salazar, F. and Santos, H. 241n20

Elman, Colin 521n20

emerging economies, challenge of management of 10–11, 525–30; competitiveness, improvements in productivity and 527–28; domestic savings, generation of 526; foreign savings, finance for investment with 527; foreign trade and investment, avoidance of damage in process of opening to 528; GDP per capita growth, minimum target for 526; global networks and integration of national economies into global markets 527; global progress, contributions to 529; Great Recession (2007–9) and aftermath 530; human capital, investment in 526–27; human rights institutions, development of 529; inflation, avoidance of two-digit and persistent manifestations of 528–29; law, institutions to secure respect for rule of, development of 529; local firms, facilitation of external expansion of 527; monetary and financial institutions, organization of 525; peace and security, preservation of 529; private-public partnerships, efficient building of economic infrastructure with 527–28; rules and institutions, need for innovation in 525; safety net for those marginalized by modernization, creation of 528; technological innovation, adoption of 526–27; US dollar as 'patron' currency 526; world affairs, constructive participation in 529; World Trade Organization (WTO) membership 525

emerging economies, modern stage theories and relevance for 137–74; assessment and summary of empirical findings 172–74; Bremer/Kasarda Stage Theory 139–41; capital, deficiencies in entrepreneurial access to 144–46; competitiveness 139, 143, 144, 148–54, 156–60, 161–65, 171; competitiveness, potential constraints on 141–42; continuum approach 137; development stages of countries (2010–11) 143; discriminant analysis, constraints on group

advancement 156–62; economic freedom, limits on 142–44; emerging economies, growth patterns 138; entrepreneurship, contributory factors to increases in 163; entrepreneurship, governance and 163–71; financial sector development 147; GDP per capita 142, 161; governance, institutional development and 142; governance, sequencing economic reform and 139–40; growth and entrepreneurship, constraints on 146–48; growth potential and entrepreneurship, dimensions of 148–56; Harvard Business School, work of Michael Porter at 137–38; Heritage Index 144, 145, 146, 148; middle-income trap 138–39; Milken Institute, Capital Access Index (CAI) 144–46; per capita income relative to US (1960) 139; productivity growth, factors affecting 139; regression analysis, linkages surrounding entrepreneurship 163; shadow economy, determinants of 173–74; *Wall Street Journal* Index of Economic Freedom 142; World Bank paper on middle-income trap 139; World Economic Forum Global Competitiveness Index (WEF GCI) 141–42, 143, 148

emerging markets, economic development of 18–22, 28

Emerging Markets Bond Index (EMBI) in Turkey 249, 254

Emir, O.Y. *et al* 257

Emperor Dom Pedro I 34

endogenous growth theory 18, 266, 267–68, 280, 366, 371, 376n22

Engel, E., Fischer, F. and Galetovic, A. 242n30

Ensor, L. and Maswanganyi, N. 133n59

entrepreneurship: capital, deficiencies in entrepreneurial access to 144–46; contributory factors to increases in 163; governance and 163–71; growth and entrepreneurship, constraints on 146–48; growth potential and entrepreneurship, dimensions of 148–56; regression analysis, linkages surrounding entrepreneurship 163

el-Erian, Mohamed. 413n65

Ersel, H. and Özatay, F. 261n3

Escobar, Pablo 464, 466

Estrada, Joseph 'Erap' administration 368

Ethiopia 22, 24, 143

European Union (EU) 16; South Korean FTA with (2011) 532

Evans, G., Thakur, R. and Pape, R.A. 523n54

Evenett, S. and Hoekman, B. 219n6

exchange rates: floating exchange rate regime in Turkey 249–50; Indonesia 275–76; Republic of Korea (South Korea) 533; Russia 49. *See also* currency

exports: cotton production and exports 34, 103n15, 402; Egypt, manufacturing exports

562

399; Indonesia 272–75; Republic of Korea (South Korea) 534, 535; Singapore 204, 213; sugar exports 34; Turkey, high-tech exports from 260

Eyraud, Luc 132n34

Ezzat, Dina 412n36, 412n37

factor accumulation in India 62–63, 78

Fahd, King 484

Fahim, Y. and Sami, N. 413n54, 413n56

Fahmy, Nabil 412n35

Faulkner, D. and Loewald, C. 132n14

Faundez, J. 240n6

Felbab-Brown, Vanda 471n49

Feng, Hua Guo 92

Ferrer, Yadira 469, 472n66

Feteha, Ahmed 412n19

Fforde, A. and Vlyder, S. de 354

Ffrench-Davis, Ricardo 240n2, 241n10

financial recession (2007–9) see Great Recession (2007–9)

financial sector developments: China, People's Republic of 99–101; emerging economies 147; Republic of Korea (South Korea) 537

financial shocks, world economy and 15

finanical crisis, risk of 27

Findlay, R. and Wellisz, S. 219n2

al-Fiqi, Mona 412n31

fiscal deficits in India, growth and 71–73

fiscal policies: Argentina 329, 330, 366–69, 370; Colombia 463; Fiscal Policy Statement (2013) in Pakistan 378; Great Recession (2007–9) in Turkey 258; Philippines 366–69; Turkey 247–49

Fiscal Responsibility, Law of (2000) in Brazil 41

fiscal system in Mexico 296–98

Fischer, Stanley 515

Fishlow, Albert xxi, 4, 33–45

Fiszbein, A. and Schady, N. et al. 304n7

Fitch Group 401

Fong, Pang Eng 219n1, 221n35

Fong, P.E. and Lim, L.Y.C. 219n2, 221n29

Fontanella-Khan, James 523n67

Food and Agriculture Organization (FAO) 25, 274, 279

Foot, R. and Walter, A. 522n29

foreign direct investment (FDI): Beijing Consensus 178, 179; Brazil 41–42; challenge for companies in Viet Nam 358–59; Egypt 398, 401; Foreign Direct Investment Statute (Decree Law 600 of 1974) in Chile 232; India 69; Indonesia 271–72; Mexico 300–301; Philippines 374, 375; Republic of Korea (South Korea) 532, 537–38; Russia 56; Singapore 204, 205, 214, 223n66; South Africa 105; Thailand 419, 421, 422; Viet Nam 339, 352, 353, 354; world economy, key trends in 14, 24

Fox, Julia and Edberg, Shanna 304n1

Fox, Vincente 292

Franco, Itamar 40

Frankel, J.A. 255

free trade 43, 91, 189, 190, 287, 290, 300, 374, 462, 507, 532; Singapore pursuit of 203–4, 205, 215

Freedom and Justice Party (FJP) in Egypt 402, 403, 405

Frei, Eduardo 229, 232, 234

Friedberg, Aaron L. 521n25, 522n30

Friedman, Milton 65, 376n16

Friedman, Thomas L. 380, 384, 395n7

Fuentes, Claudio 241n14

Fukuyama, Francis 381, 395n9

future prospects: Brazil 43–45; Egypt 408–10; global governance, emerging powers and 519–20; India 78–79; Indonesia 278–80; Pakistan 377, 380–81, 383–84, 390–94, 394–95; Russia 56; South Africa 131

Gaddy, C. and Ickes, B.W. 59n5

Gainsborough, Martin 349

Gaitán, Jorge Eliécer 464

Galal, Ahmed 414n89

Gandhi, Indira 77

Gangwha treaty in Korea (1876), effects of 532–33

Ganioğlu, A. and Yalçin, C. 262n28

Garwood-Gowers, A. 523n54

Gaulle, Charles de 189

GDP (gross domestic product): Colombia 458, 459, 460–61, 462, 463, 466; global governance, emerging powers and 505, 506, 516, 518; Iran 446, 450; projections to 2050 for major economies 15; Russia, performance (2008–9), deterioration of 52–53

GDP growth 5, 25; averages (1997–2012), world economy 14; China, People's Republic of 83, 84, 85, 87, 90, 92, 93, 97, 102, 104n24; estimates of future growth 539–40, 541, 542, 543, 544, 545, 546, 547, 548, 549–50, 551; determinants of (1978–2012) for India 67; Egypt 398, 399, 405; factors in India of 1951–2012) 79; growth potential for India and 69, 70, 71, 72, 73, 74, 75–76, 78, 79–80; India, estimates for future growth 539–40, 541, 542, 543, 544, 545, 546, 547, 548, 549–50, 551; India (1951–2012) 63–65; India (1980–90) acceleration in 68; Indonesia 267, 268, 280; Israel 187, 193, 200–201; Mexico 288, 290, 300–301; Pakistan 377–78, 385, 388, 391, 394; Philippines 364–65, 367, 372, 375; projection to 2017 for Russia 56; projections (2012–50), world economy 20; Putin's requirement in Russia for 57; Republic of Korea (South Korea) 535; Russia (2010 and 2011) 54; Saudi Arabia 477, 479, 480, 481; Singapore 204, 205, 207, 209, 210–11, 213, 217, 223n50, 308;

563

Index

sources and determinants for India of 61, 79–80; South Africa 117; Thailand 417, 427, 436; total factor productivity (TFP) in Russia and 50; Turkey 245, 249, 250, 252; Urals oil price (1998–2009) in Russia and 49; Viet Nam 357

GDP per capita: Argentina 332, 338; Chile 227–28; Colombia 460, 461, 462; Egypt 399, 404; emerging economies, modern stage theories and relevance for 142, 161; growth of, minimum target for 526; Indonesia 277, 280; Iran 450; Malaysia 306, 307, 308; Philippines 365; Republic of Korea (South Korea) 532; Russia 46, 47; Saudi Arabia 475, 476, 477; Singapore 213, 220n26, 223n50; South Africa 108, 114, 117, 121, 127; Thailand 417, 418; Turkey 245, 246, 250, 260, 261; Viet Nam 341

Geiger, T. 175n17

Geithner, Timothy 103, 518

General Agreement on Tariffs and Trade (GATT) 290, 300

General Authority for Investments (GAFI) in Egypt 407

General Law of Education (LGE, 2009) in Chile 235

geopolitics 19, 200, 397, 400, 503–4, 520; geopolitical breakdown, risk of 26–27; Mexico and 287–88

Ghana 22, 24, 143

Ghanem, Hafez 414n89

Ghesquiere, Henri 212, 224n74, 224n78

Ghorashi, G. Reza xxi, 440–57

Ghorashi, R. and Zangeneh, H. 9

Ghorashi, Reza 455n4

Giachetti, Mariano 338n1

Gilani, Yousaf Raza 382

Gilpin, Robert G. 521n21, 521n23, 521n24

Glaser, John 457n32

Glewwe, P. et al. 344

Global Competitiveness Report (WEF): Mexico 301; South Africa 124, 127

global governance, emerging powers and 503–20; Bretton Woods twins, formal votes in 515–17; Bretton Woods twins, leadership of 514–15; BRICS 504–5, 505–6, 509; BRICS, informal influence and 509; BRICS, institutional evolution of 508; BRICS and UN Security Council, imbalances in relationship 509–14; capitalism, Western order rooted in 508; competitiveness 518; currency war (of words) 517–19; democracy, Western order rooted in 508; economic power, shift in 503; future possibilities 519–20; GDP (gross domestic product) 505, 506, 516, 518; global economic governance, BRICS and 514–19; global governance clubs (2013) 504; global norms and international rules, embrace of 507–8; IGOs, powerful countries and disproportionate influence on 509; inconvenient rules, international institutions and demands for exemptions from 508; international institutions, design of 508; International Monetary Fund (IMF) 504, 505, 508; interstate capabilities, power shift in 503–4; liberal international institutions, 'after hegemony' endurance of 508; military alliances 506; North Atlantic Treaty Organization (NATO) 506, 509; Pax Americana, winding down of 503; power diffusion 505–6; power options of preponderant states 508–9; power shifts and international change, insights from international relations theories about 506–9; purchasing power parity (PPP) 505, 510, 516; realist perspective 506–7; rising power capabilities 509; states, power and interests of 506–7; UN Security Council (UNSC), broadening of representation on 510–12; United Nations (UN) 504, 505, 507; US National Intelligence Council (NIC) 503; voting patterns in UN Security Council (UNSC) 513–14; World Bank 504, 505; World Trade Organization (WTO) 508

global middle and rich class (GMR) 22, 23, 24, 28–29n8, 29n11

global norms and international rules 507–8

global progress, contributions to 529

Goldman Sachs 3, 11, 15, 29, 287, 304n4, 504, 520n2, 520n6, 521n14, 541, 551, 554; paper on economic growth in China and India 544–45

Goldsmith, Raymond W. 36, 45n2

Goldstein, Judith 521n20

Golley, J. and Tyers, R. 552n5

Gonzales-Rozada, M. and Levy-Yeyati, E. 262n13

González, Francisco E. xxi–xxii, 7, 287–305

González, T. and Smith, R. 471n47

Gorbachev, Mikhail 347

Gordillo, Elba Esther 301

Gordillo, Gabriel París 464

Goulart, João 38

governance: deficiencies in Egypt 406–7; effectiveness of government in South Africa 120–21; government-linked companies (GLCs) in Singapore 204, 206, 210, 214, 217, 219n10, 223n59, 226n102; government-linked corporations (GLCs) in Malaysia 309, 314; institutional development and 142; relations between *chaebol* in South Korea AND 535; role in South Africa of 118–26; in Saudi Arabia, limited progress towards effectiveness 484; sequencing economic reform and 139–40; in Singapore 212, 213, 218, 224n77, 225n80

gradualism *versus* shock treatment 178–79

Graham, Carol 414n89

Granholm, Jennifer 216

Great Recession (2007–9): emerging economies in aftermath 530; implications for world economy of 14–15; sluggish recovery in Thailand 428; world economy, key trends in 13, 14, 15

Green, Hong Lim 223n52

green growth in Indonesia 282–83

greenhouse gas (GHG) emissions 282–83

Gresh, Alain 414n92

Griliches, Z. 371

Groh, A.P. and Wich, M. 271, 285n39

Gronau, Reuben 202n22

gross national product (GNP): Brazil 33; Egypt 401; Thailand 417

gross national savings: South Africa 110–11, 112–13; Turkey 253

Grossman, G. and Helpman, E. 376n30, 376n32

Growth, Employment and Redistribution (GEAR) in South Africa 129

growth scenarios: China 549–50; drivers of growth, developing countries and 16–18; emerging economies 146–48, 148–56; India 549–50; India (1950–90) 65–68; India (1992–96) 73–74; India (1997–2002) 74–75; India (2003–10) 75, 80; India (2011–12) 75–76; Mexico 287–88; modelling growth in India 68–73; Pakistan 379–80; Philippines 364–65, 373, 374–75; Philippines' long-term growth, criteria for 371–74; Russia 48–52, 52–57; Saudi Arabia 477–80, 480–82; Singapore 210; South Africa 107–14, 116–27; Thailand 420–23

Gruber, Lloyd 522n35

Grynberg, R. and Newton, S. 29n12

G20 13, 14, 15, 18, 19, 20, 21, 22, 23, 24, 27–28, 29n10

Guillaume, D. and Zytek, R. 457n35

Guillemette, Y. 520n2

Gulf Cooperation Council (GCC) 408–9

Gumede, William 133n56

Gupta, Udayan 498n5

Gwartney, J. and Lawson, R. et al. 175n24

Gwartney, J., Hall, J. and Lawson, R. 175n22

Hadiwibowo, Y. and Komatsu, M. 285n50

Haiti 22

Halper, Stefan 178, 184n6

Hammerstad, Anne 131n6

Hanouz, M. Drzeniek 175n17

Hanson, P. and Teague, E. 60n34

Hanson, Philip xxii, 4, 46–60

Haredi community in Israel 197

Harvard Business School, work of Michael Porter at 137–38

Hasan, Riaz 396n29

Hausmann, R. 146

Hausmann, R. et al 259, 260

Hausmann, R., Rodrik, D. and Velasco, Andrés 175n27

Havrylyshyn, O. and Wolf, T. 164, 176n41

Hawksworth, J. and Tiwari, A. 280, 283n2, 285n60

Hawksworth, John 28n4

Hayek, F.A. 65

Hayton, Bill 346

Hazri, Herizal xxii, 306–26

Heiss, C. and Navia, P. 241n14

Hendy, R. and Zaki, C. 414n68, 414n85

Henry, C.M. and Springborg, R. 411n2, 411n8, 411n10, 413n41, 413n44, 413n46, 413n63, 414n73, 414n88

Heritage Foundation 406–7

Heritage Index 144, 145, 146, 148

Heroles, Jesús Reyes 304n11

Heston, A. et al 261n2

Hevia, C. and Loayza, N. 411n1, 414n71

Higgins, Benjamin 174n4

Highly Indebted Poor Countries (HIPC) 8, 339

Hirschman, Albert O. 395, 396n28

H1N1 flu pandemic 294

Ho Chi Minh 347, 349

Hock, Kang Soon 221n35

Hofman, B. and Kuijs, L. 543, 552n5

Hofmeister, W. 284n30

Holocaust, effects on Israel 188

Holsti, Ole 521n20

Holz, C.A. 542, 543, 552n5, 552n6

Hong, K. and Tang, H.C. 284n34

Hong Kong University of Science and Technology 542

Hooi, Joyce 222n48, 223n58

hostage crisis in Iran 444–45

Housing Development Board (HDB) in Singapore 205–6, 209, 217, 220n19

Hsiao, C. 370, 376n18

Huang, J. et al. 542

Huang, Jingjing 523n59

Huang, M. et al. 552n5

Huang, Meilinda 552n1

Hudood Ordinance (blasphemy laws) in Pakistan 384–85

Hudson, Rex A. 471n23, 471n37, 471n39

human capital 55, 62, 68, 189, 213, 246, 260–61, 266, 267, 283, 319, 366, 420, 426, 437, 495; Argentina 331; Egypt 404; emerging economies' investment in 526–27; Mexico 301–2; Philippines 371–72, 374; South Africa 114

human rights 9, 183, 227, 230, 303, 318, 409, 465, 511, 513; institutions, development of 529; in Iran, denial of 443, 445, 454

Huntington, Samuel P. 395, 396n28

Hussain, Saddam 450

hydrocarbon rents 397–99

hyperinflation 330, 331, 335, 338

Hyundai Economic Research Institute 536

Ikenberry, G. John 522n34, 522n38
Ikenberry, G.J., Mastanduno, M. and Wohlforth, W.C. 522n27
immigration: to Israel, waves of 188–89; from Italy to Brazil 34
import substitution: Brazil 36–38; Mexico 288–89; South Korea 533
income per capita: Brazil 34; Iran 451
India 4–5, 11, 16, 18, 22, 27–28, 61–80, 539–52; Australian National University (ANU) 542; business conditions (2007) 545; business organizations and authors, studies on economic growth by 543–45, 547; capital accumulation 63; Centre d'Etudes Prospectives et d'Informations Internationales (CEPII) 543; currency undervaluation, real interest rates and 78–79; currency valuation 69–70; Deutsche Bank paper on economic growth in 545; economic growth, determinants of 61, 62–65, 80; economic growth, forecasts of 539–41; factor accumulation 62–63, 78; fiscal deficits, growth and 71–73; foreign direct investment (FDI) 69; future prospects 78–79; GDP growth, determinants of (1978–2012) 67; GDP growth, estimates for future growth 539–40, 541, 542, 543, 544, 545, 546, 547, 548, 549–50, 551; GDP growth, factors of (1951–2012) 79; GDP growth, growth potential and 69, 70, 71, 72, 73, 74, 75–76, 78, 79–80; GDP growth, sources and determinants of 61, 79–80; GDP growth (1951–2012) 63–65; GDP growth (1980–90) acceleration in 68; Goldman Sachs paper on economic growth in 544–45; growth (2011–12) 75–76; growth acceleration (2003–10) 75, 80; growth beginnings (1992–96) 73–74; growth faltering (1997–2002) 74–75; growth planning (1950–90) 65–68; growth scenarios 549–50; Hong Kong University of Science and Technology 542; independence, economic environment at 65–67; *India: Planning for Industrialization-Industrialization and Trade Policies since 1951* (Bhagwati, J. and Desai, D.) 67; industrial growth, low level of 76–78; institutions, role in growth development 62; institutions and academic authors, studies on economic growth by 541–43, 547; interest rates 70–71, 78–79, 79–80; International Monetary Fund (IMF) 69, 73, 75; International Monetary Fund (IMF) paper on economic growth in 546; international organizations, studies on economic growth by 545–46, 547; labour, reallocation from agriculture to industry 68; McKinsey Global Institute paper on economic growth in 545; macroeconomic meta-analysis, salient estimates (2020–25) 540; Massachusetts Institute of Technology (MIT)

542; meta-analysis of economic growth 550–52; modelling growth 68–73; Organization for Economic Co-operation and Development (OECD) 544, 546; productivity growth 62–63; purchasing power parity (PPP) exchange rates 549, 553n12; qualitative factors affecting performance in 551; sectoral growth forecasts 78; sectoral growth rates (1951–2012) 66; similarities and differences in forecasts 546–49; total factor productivity (TFP) 540, 541, 543, 544, 551; World Bank paper on economic growth in 546
indirect fiscal funding (AFI) in Chile 233
Indonesia 6, 7, 18, 265–83; Association of Southeast Asian Nations (ASEAN) 272, 274, 281; BRICS, comparison with 265, 267–69, 280, 283; competitiveness 266, 274, 276, 278, 280, 281; development growth 266–67; economic growth 266–67; emerging economy, predictions for 265–66; energy subsidies 282; entry points to BRICS level 269–76; exchange rates, controllable factors 275–76; exports 272–75; foreign direct investment (FDI) 271–72; future prospects 278–80; GDP growth 267, 268, 280; GDP per capita 277, 280; green growth 282–83; greenhouse gas (GHG) emissions 282–83; imports 272–74; inflation, controllable factors 275–76; infrastructure 281; Innovation 1–747, concept of 280; investment 271–72; logistics 281; Master Plan (MP3EI) 280; Masterplan of Indonesia's Economic Growth Acceleration (MIEGA) 281; natural resources, over-consumption of 282–83; Organization for Economic Co-operation and Development (OECD) 282; 'Paradox of Plenty' 282; productivity, inclusiveness and 282–83; purchasing power parity (PPP) 276, 279, 280; research and development (R&D) 278; resource curse 282; sustainable development, factors ensuring 276–78; sustainable growth 266–67; sustainable growth, challenges for 281; sustainable growth, engines of 269–71; total factor productivity (TFP) 267, 268; trade patterns 272–75; United Nations Conference on Trade and Development (UNCTAD) 271, 272; World Bank and 265, 269; *World Investment Prospects Survey* (UNCTAD) 272
industrialization: Brazil 34–35, 36, 37, 38, 43–44; India 76–78; Republic of Korea (South Korea) 533; Russia 46–47, 51; Turkey 256
inequalities: Chile 231, 239; Colombia 458, 459, 462–63, 464, 468, 469, 470; income inequalities in South Africa 114–15; Thailand 429–30, 430–31
infant mortality in Thailand 432–34

inflation: avoidance of two-digit and persistent manifestations of 528–29; Indonesia 275–76; Iran 450–51, 452. *See also* hyperinflation

infrastructure: Egypt 397; Indonesia 281

Ingram, James C. 417

innovation: encouragement of 179; Innovation 1–747, concept of 280

insecurity: Iran 454; Mexico 294, 295, 303

Inskeep, Steve 396n21

institutions and academic authors, studies on economic growth by: China, People's Republic of 541–43, 547; India 541–43, 547

integration in trade and finance, world economy and 23–24

Inter-Agency Planning Group (IAPG) in Malaysia 314

Internal Security Act 1960 (ISA) in Malaysia 320

International Bank of Reconstruction and Development (IBRD) 8, 339

International Finance Corporation (IFC) in Egypt 406–7

international governmental organizations (IGOs) 504, 507, 508, 512, 514; powerful countries' disproportionate influence on 509

international institutions, design of 508

International Monetary Fund (IMF): Argentina 336; Brazil 37, 40, 41; Egypt 402, 403, 406, 409; global governance, emerging powers and 504, 505, 508; India 69, 73, 75; Malaysia 314–15; Mexico 290, 292, 295; Pakistan 377–78, 380; paper on economic growth in China and India 546; Philippines 364–65, 366, 367, 370; Republic of Korea (South Korea) 532; Russia 56–57; Saudi Arabia 476, 477, 478, 479, 480–81; South Africa 126; Thailand 418; Turkey 249–50, 258, 263n26; world economy, key trends in 15, 16

international organizations, studies on economic growth by: China, People's Republic of 545–46, 547; India 545–46, 547

interstate capabilities, power shift in 503–4

investment: China, People's Republic of 92–98; in commodities 25; convergence in mature economies 17; Indonesia 271–72; international investment by Colombia 462; Singapore 207

Iran 9, 440–55; Agricultural and Food Industries Organization (AFIO) 446; Astan Quds Razavi 446–47; Constitutional Revolution (1905–7) 440; currency crisis 453–54; economic meaning of IRI 445–46; economic sanctions 447–50; foreign policy 446; GDP (gross domestic product) 446, 450; GDP per capita 450; hostage crisis 444; human rights, denial of 445; human rights, violations of 454; income per capita 451; inflation 450–51, 452; insecurity for individual citizens 454; Islamic Republic of Iran (IRI) 442–54; Islamization, process of 443; laws

and regulations, uncertainties about 454; Mostazafan Foundation 446; Muhammad Reza Shah 441–42; oil revenues 441–42, 445, 451, 453; Organization of the Petroleum Exporting Countries (OPEC) 454; political meaning of IRI 443–44; quasi-independent foundations *(bonyads)* 446; rentier state 445–46; Revolution (1979) 442; Revolutionary Guard 445, 447; Reza Shah 440–41; Russo-Iranian wars 440; sanctions against 444, 446, 447–50, 453, 454–55, 457n30, 457n31, 457n32; Sazamare Etelaat Va Amniate Kechvar (SAVAK) 441; semi-autonomous economic institutions 446–47; social meaning of IRI 444–45; socio-politico-economic record 454; subsidies, inflation outlook and 451–53; technology transfer, prohibition of 454; traditional clergy, dominance of 445; United States D'Amato Law, effects of 448; women, social status of 445

Islamic extremism in Pakistan 384

Islamic Republic of Iran (IRI) *see* Iran

Islamization, process in Iran of 443

Israel 5–6, 187–201; Arab community 197; balance of payments 189–91, 192, 195, 200; Bi-national Industrial Research and Development (BIRD) 195; capital markets, liberalization of 190–91; concentration 198; defence 191–92; Discount Investment Corporation 198; economic concentration 197–98; economic development since independence 187–91, 200; employment patterns, changes in 188, 194; financial strength 192–93; foreign trade, liberalization of 190–91; foundation of state, aspirations on 187–88; gas 200; GDP growth rates 187, 193, 200–201; Haredi community 197; Holocaust, effects of 188; ideology of Labour movement, weakening of 188; immigration, waves of 188–89; Israel Defence Forces (IDF) Science Corps 194; labour market 195–96; Law for the Encouragement of Industrial Research and Development (1985) 195; local industry, development of 189; National Insurance Institute 197; Organization for Economic Co-operation and Development (OECD) 191, 196–97; poverty, income distribution and 196–97; research and development (R&D) 194–95; Six-Day War (1967) 189, 190, 191; stabilization and liberalization, relationship between 190; Technion 194; technology, success in 193–95; Tel-Aviv Stock Exchange (TASE) 198; Weizmann Institute of Science in Rehovot 194; West Bank settlements, cost of 198–200; Yom Kippur War (1973) 190, 191

Jacob, Rahul 396n31

Jadwa Investment in Saudi Arabia 497

Japan 16; Korea as Japanese protectorate 533
Jelenic, Michael 174n8
Jervis, Robert 522n26
Jiabao, Wen 85
Jiménez, Timoleón 465, 468, 471n40, 472n62
Johansson, Å. 520n2, 521n10
Johnson, R.W. 132n33
Johnston, Alastair Iain 522n29, 522n30
Jones, Barry 175n37
Jones, C.I. and Klenow, P.J. 220n26
Jones, I. and Klenow, P.J. 222n38
Jones, Randal 175n36
Jorgenson, D. 371
Jorgenson, D. and Griliches, Z. 376n29
Jorgenson, Dale W. 427
Jupestaa, J. 286n71

Kabir, Amir 440
Kadhim, Abbas 499n32
Kahler, Miles 521n20
Kamrany, N. and Vassilev, G. 460
Kamrany, Nake M. xxii–xxiii, 458–74
Kanapathy, V. and Hazri, H. 7
Kanapathy, Vijayakumari xxiii, 306–26
Kaplan, Morton 500n41
Kapur, Devesh 523n66, 523n70
Kara, H. et al. 255
Karl, Terri Lind 482, 499n24
Karzai, Hamid 386, 387
Katouzian, Homayoun 9, 12n4
Katz, Sherman 351
Kaufman, Daniel 414n89
Kaufman, Robert R. 240n3
Kearney, C. 284n26
Kechichian, Joseph 498n9
Keefer, P. and Loayza, N. 466, 467, 471n50,
    472n55, 472n67, 472n68, 472n69
Keller, J. and Nabli, M.K. 480, 499n17
Kenney, P. and Serrano, M. 305n34
Kenny, C. and Williams, D. 283n5
Kenya 22, 24, 143
Keohane, R.O. and Martin, L.L. 521n20, 522n44
Keohane, Robert O. 521n20, 521n21, 522n31
Keong, Yeoh Lam 221n35, 223n52
Kesriyeli, M. et al. 255
Khalilzad, Zalmay 511, 512
Khan, M.E. 372
Khan, Reza (later Reza Shah) 440, 441, 456n12
Khan, Tanvir Ahmad 386, 396n16
Kharas, H. and Gertz, G. 521n14, 521n15
Kharas, Mr 141
Khatami, Sayed Muhammad 451
al-Khatib, M.A. 480
Khomeini, Ayatollah Ruhollah 443–44, 455n7,
    456n8, 456n10, 456n11
Kiani, Khaleeq 377
Kiani, Khaliq 395n2, 395n3

Kim, A.M. 355
Kim, Jim Yong 515, 517
Kim Il-sung 534
Kimhi, Ayal 201n13
Kindleberger, Charles P. 521n21
Kings, Sipho 133n47
Kirchner, Néstor 338
Klebnikov, Paul 457n23
Kleiman, Ephraim 202n29
Knaul, F.M. et al. 305n33
Knickmeyer, Ellen 498n1
Kohli, Atul 68
Korean Asset Management Company (KAMCO)
    537
Korean War (1950–53) 533
Korhonen, I. and Solanko, L. 59n8
KORUS FTA (2011) 532, 538
Kosenko, Konstantin 201n18
Kosuke, M. and Phongpaichit, P. 434
Kotb, Ahmed 412n29, 412n32
Krasner, Stephen D. 521n19, 521n21, 521n22,
    522n35
Krebs, C.P., Costelloe, M. and Jenks, D. 472n51
Krebs, C.P. et al. 467
Krichevskii, Nikita 53, 60n13
Krugman, Paul 63, 220n28, 284n24, 383, 395n10,
    437, 438n2
Kuboniwa, Masaaki 50, 59n8, 60n17
Kudrin, Aleksei 57, 60n25
Kurtz, Marcus J. 241n23
Kuvshinova, Ol'ga 60n12
Kux, Denis 395n14
Kydland, F. and Prescott, E. 376n12

labour force: Egypt 405; India, reallocation from
    agriculture to industry 68; shortages in Russia
    56; world economy, key trends in 16
labour market: Israel 195–96; reforms in Republic
    of Korea (South Korea) 537
Laden, Osama bin 385
LaFranchi, Howard 523n61
Lagarde, Christine 515, 517
Lagos, Ricardo 234
Laos 8, 281, 339, 432, 434
LAPOP survey (2010) in Colombia 463
Lardy, Nicholas 184
Larionova, Marina 522n42
Larraín, F. and Vergara, R. 241n10, 242n25,
    242n30
Larson, Eric 552n1
Laurent, Clint 542, 552n5
Lavery, Jerry 120, 132n23, 132n25
Lavie, Ephraim 202n29
law, rule of 7, 9, 141, 142, 144, 149, 151, 152,
    154, 156, 157, 159, 161, 162, 164, 166–70,
    171, 174, 546, 548, 551; Colombia 462; Egypt
    407–8; Indonesia 275, 284–85n36; institutions

to secure respect for rule of, development of 529; Law for the Encouragement of Industrial Research and Development (1985) in Israel 195; legislative reforms in Malaysia 319; Malaysia 315, 324; Mexico 302–3, 302–4; regulations in Iran, uncertainties about 454; Russia 53, 56, 58–59; Saudi Arabia 484, 487–88, 495; Singapore 212; South Africa 118–19, 122, 123–24

Le, H.Q. and Pomfret, R. 352

LeBel, P. 284n28

Ledeneva, Alena 60n32

Lee, J.W. and Hong, K. 271, 285n38

Lee, Mr 215

Lee Kwan Yew 348

Legatum Prosperity Index (2012) for South Africa 124–26

Legro, Jeffrey 522n27

Lehman Brothers 42, 83, 84, 514

Leila, Reem 412n23, 413n43, 414n76, 415n94

Lemke, Douglas 521n23

Lenin, Vladimir 349

Levy-Yeyati, E. and Sturzenegger, F. 255

Lewis, Arthur 62, 68

Li, Tong 147

Li, Yue 361n1

liability dollarization 253–55

Lian, Goh Chin 221n35

Lieberman, S.S. and Wagstaff, A. 356

Lim, Linda 6

Lim, Linda Yuen-Ching xxiii, 203–26

Lim, L.Y.C. and Ann, L.S. 221n34, 225n87

Lim, L.Y.C. and Min, G. 222n39

Lim, L.Y.C., Fong, P.E. and Findlay, R. 219n2

Lin, Justin 62

Linn, Johannes F. 523n75, 524n77, 552n5

Loayza, N. et al. 260

logistics 207, 208, 210, 225n86, 281, 283

Looney, Robert E. xviii, 3–12, 5, 10, 105–33, 137–76, 411n5, 414n91, 475–500

Loong, Lee Hsien 216, 223n50, 224n68, 224n77, 226n97

Lopez, R.E., Anriquez, G. and Gulati, S. 284n11

Loveman, Brian 241n11

Low, Aaron 223n64

Low, Donald 219n1, 221n35, 223n52, 224n73, 225n80, 226n96

Low, Linda. 220n22

Lu, Wenling 147

Lucas, R.E. 283n7

Lucas, Robert E. Jr. 364

Lugar, Richard 517

Luhnow, D. and Davis, Bob 305n21

Luhnow, D. and Montes, J. 304n17

Lula da Silva, Luiz Inácio 41, 42, 43

Lundahl, M. and Petersson, L. 133n46

Lutchman, Jessica 132n22

Lynch, Merrill 60n23

M-19 (19 April Movement) in Colombia 464

McCaig, B. and Pavcnik, N. 352

McCaig, Brian 352

McDermott, Jeremy 471n45

McKinsey Global Institute paper on economic growth in China and India 545

macroeconomics: aggregates for South Africa 107–10, 111, 112; challenges for Malaysia 307–12; imbalances and uncertainties for Egypt 401–3; indicators (% of GDP) for Turkey 250–51; macroeconomic stability 179; meta-analysis for China, salient estimates (2020–25) 540; meta-analysis for India, salient estimates (2020–25) 540; policy reforms in Philippines 366–71; stability in Turkey, establishment of (1980–2012) 246, 247–56; stability in world economy 28; stop-and-go macroeconomics in Viet Nam, challenge of 356–58

de la Madrid, Miguel 290–91

Magaloni, Ana Laura 305n34

Magubane, Bernard Makhosezwe 132n38

Mahdi, A. and Rashed, A. 413n67

Mahjoub, Nikki 457n22

Mahr, Krista 524n80

Mahtani, Shibani 222n44

Mai, Chiang 505

de la Maisonneuve, C. 520n2

Malaysia 6, 7, 306–24; Alliance Party (formation, 1957) 312; Asian Development Bank (ADB) 314–15; Asian Financial Crisis (1997) 306; Barisan Nasional (BN, or Coalition Front) 313; competitiveness 320, 323; constitutional monarchy 313; corporate restructuring and liberalization 308; Corruption Perception Index (CPI, TI) 320; Economic Planning Unit (EPU) 314; executive power, concentration of 315–16; financial restructuring and liberalization 308; GDP per capita 306, 307, 308; general elections (2013) 320–21; government-linked corporations (GLCs) 309, 314; Inter-Agency Planning Group (IAPG) 314; Internal Security Act 1960 (ISA) 320; International Monetary Fund (IMF) 314–15; legislative reforms 319; macroeconomic challenges 307–12; Malaysia Plan (1996–2000) 312; *Malaysian Economic Monitor* (World Bank) 314–15; middle income trap (MIT) 306, 307, 308, 315, 319, 321–22, 323, 324; multi-ethnic society 312; National Development Planning Committee (NDPC) 314; National Development Policy (NDP) 314; National Key Results Areas (NKRA) programme 320; national transformation process 318; New Economic Model (NEM) 307, 318–19; New Economic Policy (NEP) 306–7, 313–14; Outline Perspective Plan (2001–10) 312; Performance, Management and Delivery Unit (PEMANDU) 319; Police

Index

(Amendment) Act (2012) 320; policymaking process 314–15; political economy 312–21; political economy landscape, changes in 317–18; political system, strengths and weaknesses in 315–16; purchasing power parity (PPP) per capita 306; reform process 318–20; resource-richness 312; Rukunegara (National Principles) 313; Security Offences (Special Measures) 2012 Act (SOSMA) 320; socio-political challenges 316–17; socio-political framework, towards revision in 321–24; total factor productivity (TFP) 310, 311; United Malay National Organization (UMNO) 313, 315, 316, 318, 320, 321; University and University Colleges Act (1971) 320; World Bank 314–15

Malesky, E.J. and Taussig, T 353

Malesky, E.J. *et al.* 348, 353

Malkin, Elisabeth 305n32

Mandela, Nelson 131

Manorungsan, Sompop 416, 436

Mao Zedong 92

Marco, L.E. di 45n1

Margolis, Mac 224n70

Maroushi, Nadine 411n16

Márquez, Gabriel García 467, 468, 472n59

Marshall, S. 411n11

Marshall, S. and Stacher, J. 411n11

Martin, Eric 304n4

Martinet, V. and Rotillon, G. 284n10

Martínez, J. and Díaz, A. 242n24

Massachusetts Institute of Technology (MIT) reports on China and India 542

Master Plan (MP3EI) for Indonesia 280

Masterplan of Indonesia's Economic Growth Acceleration (MIEGA) 281

Matshiqi, Aubrey 133n58

Matthee, Rudi 455n2

Mattock, Michael 553n18

Mbeki, Thabo 129

Means, Gordon P. 325n9, 325n12, 325n13

Mearsheimer, John J. 521n25

Meirelles, Henrique 41

Mejia, D. and Posada, C.E. 472n67

Mejia, D. and Restrepo, P. 466, 467, 472n54, 472n65

Meléndez, M. and Perry, G.E. 470n4, 471n21, 471n34

Meller, Patricio 240n2

MENA region (Middle East and North Africa) and Egypt 404, 405, 406, 407

Meng, Choy Keen 221n33, 226n99

Menon, J. and Thiam, H.N 325n3

Merry, Robert W. 384, 395n12, 395n13

meta-analysis of economic growth in China and India 550–52

Mexico 6, 7, 18, 287–304; Catholic Partido Acción Nacional (PAN) 291; Chinese challenge to 299–300; conditional cash transfer (CCT) programme 293; credit scarcity 296–98; demographic bonus 302; economic populism, boom and busts (1970–82) 289–90; Economic Stabilization Fund (ESF) 291; emerging economy, birth and growing pains of 288–95; energy and fiscal conundrum 295–96; fiscal system 296–98; foreign direct investment (FDI) 300–301; foreign indebtedness, acceleration of 290; GDP growth 288, 290, 300–301; General Agreement on Tariffs and Trade (GATT) 290, 300; *Global Competitiveness Report* (WEF) 301; goepolitics 287–88; growth and development, potential for 287–88; H1N1 flu pandemic 294; human capital 301–2; import-substitution industrialization (ISI) 288–89; insecurity 294, 295, 303; International Monetary Fund (IMF) 290, 292, 295; media sector 298–99; Mexican miracle (1940–70) 288–89; monopolies, 'mismatch' of 287–88; neoliberalism, adoption of (1982–2000) 290–92; North American Free Trade Agreement (NAFTA) 291, 300; Organization for Economic Co-operation and Development (OECD) 295, 296, 298, 301; PAN governments (2000–2012) 292–94; Partido de la Revolución Democrática (PRD) 291; Partido Revolucionario Institucional (PRI) 7, 288, 289, 291, 292; Partido Revolucionario Institucional (PRI), return of 294–95; Petróleos Mexicanos (PEMEX) 295–96; private banking sector, oligopolistic structure of 297; rule of law 302–4; Sindicato Nacional de Trabajadores de la Educación (SNTE) 301; state-owned development banks 298; telecommunications 298–99; tertiary education enrolment 301; trading powerhouse 300–301; violence 294, 295, 303; World Bank 290, 295; World Trade Organization (WTO) 295, 299

Mia, I. 175n17

Middle East 10, 42, 43, 380, 381, 384, 400, 404, 476, 511, 535. *See also* Israel

middle-income trap (MIT) 7, 125, 138–39, 141, 172, 179; China 98; Malaysia 306, 307, 308, 315, 319, 321–22, 323, 324; Thailand 416, 434–35, 436–38

military: alliances 506; Chile, economic plans of 231–32; coup in Chile (1973) 230; economy in Egypt 399–400, 409; intervention in Pakistan, potential for 379

Milken Institute, Capital Access Index (CAI) 144–46

Miller, Matt 216, 225n93

Min, Geh 222n39, 226n104

Mincer, Jacob 371, 376n25

MinEkon in Russia 57–58

Minhajul Quran International (MQI) in Pakistan 385

miniaturization 25

Mirza, Abbas 440
Mizala, A. 241n19
Mohamadi, A. 457n37
Mohamed, Mahathir 306, 315, 316, 326n42
Moller, Lars Christian 463, 471n18
monetary and financial institutions, organization of 525
monetary policies: aggregate targeting in Philippines 369–70; Argentina 329–30, 338; Philippines 369–71; Turkey 258–59
Montoya, Silvia 552n1
Moody's 401
Moore, Elaine 11n2
Moreira, Mauricio Mesquita 305n20
Morris, Stephen D. 305n35
Mostazafan Foundation in Iran 446
motorbikes, social transformation in Viet Nam and 345
motorway building, beginnings of modern development in Korea 531
Mubarak, Muhammad Hosni 398, 399, 400, 401, 402, 406, 408, 410
Muhammad Reza Shah 441–42
Murphy, Kim 457n25
Mursheda, S.M. and Serino, L.A. 285n44
Mursi, Muhammad 402, 403, 409, 410, 412n38
Murtin, F. 520n2
Musaddeq, Dr Muhammad 441, 443, 455n7
Musharraf, Pervez 378, 382, 387, 393
Muslim Brotherhood in Egypt 402, 408, 409, 410
Myanmar (formerly Burma) 22, 281, 432, 434, 512
Myon, Chang 533, 534

N-11 (Bangladesh, Egypt, Indonesia, Iran, Republic of Korea (South Korea), Mexico, Nigeria, Pakistan, Philippines, Turkey and Viet Nam) 3
Nabli, Mustapha 412n19
Namatallah, A. and Shahine, A. 412n20, 412n21
al-Nasir, Gamal Abd (Nasser) 397, 402
Nathan, Gilad 201n11
National Accreditation Commission (CNA) in Chile 236
National Constitution enacted (1853) in Argentina 331
National Development Planning Committee (NDPC) in Malaysia 314
National Development Policy (NDP) in Malaysia 314
National Economic and Development Authority (NEDA) in Philippines 366
National Economic and Social Development Board (NESDB) in Thailand 417, 429, 431
National Insurance Institute in Israel 197
National Internal Revenue Code (NIRC) in Philippines 368

National Key Results Areas (NKRA) programme in Malaysia 320
National Liberation Army (ELN) in Colombia 464
National Statistical Office's Socio-Economic Survey (SES) in Thailand 429, 430, 431
National Undergraduate Accreditation Commission (CNAP): Chile 236
Nattrass, N. and Seekings, Jeremy 133n43
natural resources: Argentina 331
natural resources, over-consumption of: Indonesia 282–83
Navia, Patricio xxiii–xxiv, 6, 227–42
Nazer, Fahad 500n45
Nehru, V. 67
neoliberalism: adoption in Mexico (1982–2000) 290–92; reforms in Chile 231, 232
Netto, Antônio Delfim 39
Neves, Tancredo 40
New Economic Model (NEM) in Malaysia 307, 318–19
New Economic Policy (NEP) in Malaysia 306–7, 313–14
New Growth Path (NGP, 2010) in South Africa 130–31
Ng, Irene Y.H. 219n1, 221n36, 222n47
Ngiam, Tong Dow 224n72
Nguyen, D.T.H. and Sun, S. 352
Nguyen, H.T.M. et al. 345
Nguyen, Minh Van 361n1
Nguyen, Nga Nguyet 361n1
Nguyen, N.N. and Rama, M. 356
Nguyen, T. and Turk, C. 348
Nguyen, Thang 361n1
Nicoletti, G. 520n2
Nieto, Enrique Peña 288, 295, 296, 299, 301
Nigeria 19, 22, 24, 143, 476
Ning, Teh Shi 223n68
Nitaqat programme in Saudi Arabia 496
Nolan, Leigh 500n48
Noland, M. and Pack, H. 413n57, 414n84
Nomura, K. and Amano, T. 221n28
North, Douglas 62
North American Free Trade Agreement (NAFTA) 291, 300
North Atlantic Treaty Organization (NATO) 506, 509
North Korea see Democratic People's Republic of Korea (North Korea)
Norton, W.W. 12n3

Obama, Barack 104, 223n50, 380, 383, 384, 385, 386, 449, 508, 511, 512, 516, 517
Ocampo, José Antonio 515
Odhiambo, Nicholas M. 118, 132n17
offshore finance 56–57, 205, 226n100
Ohmae, Kenichi 16

Index

oil curse: Russia 50; Saudi Arabia 482–84

oil prices: Russia 49–50; world economy, key trends in 25

oil revenues in Iran 441–42, 445, 451, 453

Okonjo-Iweala, Ngozi 515

Olson, Mancur 172, 176n45

O'Neill, J. *et al.* 553n11

O'Neill, Jim 3, 11n1, 11n3, 504, 520n6

Ong, Andrea 226n97

Ong, Cheryl 222n44

Oostendorp, R.H. and Doan, Q.H. 360

open economies 63, 73, 179–80, 204; Mexico 300; Philippines 367, 374; Viet Nam 358

Operation Desert Storm 398

opium wars (1839–42 and 1856–60) 532

Organic Constitutional Law on Education (LOCE, 2007) in Chile 235

Organization for Economic Co-operation and Development (OECD) 25; Brazil 43; China 544, 546; Development Assistance Committee forum, Busan (2011) 532; India 544, 546; Indonesia 282; Israel 191, 196–97; Mexico 295, 296, 298, 301; Republic of Korea (South Korea) 536; Russia 58; South Africa 121–23; Turkey 260

Organization of the Petroleum Exporting Countries (OPEC) 454

Organski, A.F.K. 521n23

Organski, A.F.K. and Kugler, J. 521n23

Osorio, Manuel. 472n57, 472n59

Ottaway, David B. 500n47

Outline Perspective Plan (2001–10) for Malaysia 312

overseas development assistance (ODA) 422

Özatay, F. 249

Özatay, F. and Sak, G. 249, 261n3, 262n8, 262n9

Özatay, F. *et al.* 262n13

Özatay, Fatih xxiv, 6, 245–64

Özmen, E. *et al.* 262n12

Page, John M. 132n29, 284n25

Pakistan 8–9, 377–95; Afghanistan and 384; Benazir Income Support Fund 395; change, inevitability of 387–90; Debt Policy Statement (2012–13) 378; diversity in 384–85; economic fundamentals, stability of 377–78; external assistance, dependence on 380; extremist actions in 380; fault lines in economy of 378; Fiscal Policy Statement (2013) 378; Fiscal Responsibility and Debt Limitation Act (2005, FRDLA) 378; future development 390–94; future prospects 377, 380–81, 383–84, 394–95; GDP growth 377–78, 385, 388, 391, 394; growth, declining trend in 379–80; Hudood Ordinance (blasphemy laws) 384–85; International Monetary Fund (IMF) 377–78, 380; Islamic extremism 384; military

intervention, potential for 379; Minhajul Quran International (MQI) 385; nation failure, possibility of 383–84; negative commentary in Western press about 378–79; Pakistan People's Party (PPP) 379, 382–83; pluralism, potential for 380–81, 385; political order, establishment of durability in 381–83; precarious situation in 379; religious conflicts in 184–85, 380–81; *The Signal and the Noise* (Silver, N.) 380; social and political development 380; United States, relations with 385–87; World Bank 387, 391, 392

Palocci, Antônio 41

Paltsev, S. and Reilly, J. 542, 552n5

PAN governments (2000–2012) in Mexico 292–94

Panagariya, Arvind 68, 70

Papa, M. and Gleason, N.W. 283n1, 284n17

Papini, Giovanni 468

'Paradox of Plenty' in Indonesia 282

Parry, M. *et al.* 29n12

Partido de la Revolución Democrática (PRD) in Mexico 291

Partido Democrático Social (PDS) in Brazil 40

Partido do Movimento Democrático Brasileiro (PMDB) in Brazil 40

Partido dos Trabalhadores (PT-Worker's Party) in Brazil 40, 41, 42, 43, 44

Partido Revolucionario Institucional (PRI) in Mexico 7, 288, 289, 291, 292, 294–95

Pastrana, Andrés 465, 468

Patrick, Stewart 522n28

Paua, F. 175n17

Paudel, Ramesh 438n1

Pax Americana, winding down of 503

People's Action Party (PAP) in Singapore 206, 209, 220n21, 225n80, 225n87

Performance, Management and Delivery Unit (PEMANDU) in Malaysia 319

Perón, Juan Domingo 333

Perón, María Estela (Isabelita) Martinez de 335

Perotti, E.C. and Oijen, P. 284n31

Perotti, Roberto 470n6

Petras, J. and Morley, M. 241n6

Petróleos Mexicanos (PEMEX) 295–96

Petroski, Henry 383, 395n11

Pham, Duc Minh 361n1

Philippines 8, 364–75; Asian Financial Crisis (1997) 365, 368–69; Association of Southeast Asian Nations (ASEAN) Free Trade Area-Comprehensive Effective Preferential Tariff (AFTA-CEPT) 374; balance of payments (BOP) crisis 369–70, 375; boon-and-bust cycles 366; *Breakout Nations: In Pursuit of the Next Economic Miracles?* (Sharma, R.) 364; development convergence, criteria for 365–66; *Econometrica* (Lucas, Jr., R.E.) 364;

572

education, investment in 372–73; fiscal policy 366–69; foreign direct investment (FDI) 374, 375; GDP growth 364–65, 367, 372, 375; GDP per capita 365; growth performance 364–65, 374–75; growth potential 373; human capital, investment in 371–72; International Monetary Fund (IMF) 364–65, 366, 367, 370; long-term growth, criteria for 371–74; macroeconomic policy reforms 366–71; monetary aggregate targeting 369–70; monetary policy 369–71; National Economic and Development Authority (NEDA) 366; National Internal Revenue Code (NIRC) 368; open economy 374; political and economic shocks 365; research and development (R&D) 373; technological progress 373; total factor productivity (TFP) 371–72; trade policy 373; trade policy reforms 374; *World Development Indicators* (World Bank) 364; World Trade Organization (WTO) 374

Phong, Dang 361n1

Phongpaichit, P. and Baker, C. 435

Pinctus, J. *et al.* 357

Pincus, J.R. and Winters, J.A. 523n66

Piñera, Sebastián 235, 237

Pinochet, Augusto 227, 228, 230, 231, 234, 238

Pizano, Ernesto Samper 464, 466, 471n29

Plan Colombia 458, 465, 467, 472n54

Plano Real (1994) in Brazil 33

platinum group metals (PGMs) 113–14

Pliego, Ricardo Salinas 298, 299

PMET (Professional Management Executive and Technical) jobs in Singapore 211

Poddar, T. and Yi, E. 543, 544, 546, 553n11

Police (Amendment) Act (2012) in Malaysia 320

politics: Colombia, political disparities in, resentment towards government and 466–67; Iran, political meaning of IRI 443–44; Malaysia, political economy in 312–21; Malaysia, strengths and weaknesses in 315–16; Pakistan, political order in, establishment of durability in 381–83; Philippines, political and economic shocks in 365; Saudi Arabia, political stability 484–85; Singapore, political democratization in 204; South Africa, political stability 119–20; Thailand, political developments in 434–38

Poncet, Sandra 542, 543, 552n5

population growth: Chile 229; Thailand 432; world economy 25

Population Policy, White Paper on (2013) in Singapore 209, 210–11, 218, 223n52, 223n54

Porter, Michael E. 137, 141, 174n5, 174n7, 175n16, 175n20, 219n3

Portillo, José López 289, 290, 291

Portuguese colonialism in Brazil 33–34

poverty: Chile 239; Israel 196–97; South Africa 114–15; Thailand 429–30, 430–31, 431–32; world economy 22–23

Powell, Robert 522n26

power capabilities 509

power diffusion 505–6

power options of preponderant states 508–9

power shifts and international change, insights from international relations theories about 506–9

Prantl, Jochen 522n44

Pravin, Jadhav 284n36, 285n41

Pricewaterhouse Coopers 15

private-public partnerships 527–28

productivity growth: emerging economies 139; India 62–63; Indonesia 282–83; Thailand 423–28

Programa de Aceleração do Crescimento (PAC) in Brazil 42

protectionism: protective policies in Brazil 34, 35, 37, 38, 39, 44; risk of 27

Prothro, J.W. and Chaparro, P.E. 241n7

Puche, Jaime Serra 305n26

purchasing power parity (PPP): China, People's Republic of 89, 90, 549, 553n12; global governance, emerging powers and 505, 510, 516; India 549, 553n12; Indonesia 276, 279, 280; Malaysia 306; Russia 46, 47, 48; Saudi Arabia 476, 477; Viet Nam 339, 344, 345, 358; world economy, key trends in 20, 21, 22, 28

Purushothaman, Roopa 553n11

Puryear, J. *et al.* 305n30

Puryear, J., Santibáñez, L. and Solano, A. 305n28

Putin, Vladimir 56, 505

al-Qaddafi, Muammar 514

Qadri, Dr Tahirul 385

Quadros, Jânio 38

qualitative factors affecting performance in China and India 551

Quan, Heng 553n16

quasi-independent foundations *(bonyads)* in Iran 446

Rabeie, Hassan 457n22

Rabin, Yitzhak 199

Rafsanjani, Hashemi 451

Rajan, Raghuram 176n40

Rama, Martin xxiv, 8, 339–63

Ramirez, Danielle N. xxiv–xxv, 458–74

Ramo, Joshua Cooper 178, 184n3

Ramos, Fidel 368

Randeree, Kasim 500n51

Rao, Narasimha 73

Rashid, Ahmed 396n17

Rashid, Muhammad Rashid 413n38

Rastello, S. 524n78

Rathbone, J. P. and Thomson, A. 304n16

Rathbone, John Paul 304n10

Ravallion, M. and van deWalle, D. 350, 351

Ravallion, Martin 29n9
Razak, Najib 307
Reagan, Ronald 448
Real Estate Investment Trusts (REITs) in Singapore 210
Reconstruction and Development Programme (RDP) in South Africa 128
Rediker, Douglas 523n75, 524n77
Reed, S. and Hamdan, S. 412n26
reform issues: Egypt 398; Malaysia 318–20; Russia 58–59
regression analysis, linkages surrounding entrepreneurship 163
regulatory quality: Saudi Arabia 485–87; South Africa 121–23
Reich, Robert 219n3
relative prices, prospects for 24–25
rent seeking: Egypt 397, 398, 399–400; Iran 445–46; Russia 50
Republic of Korea (South Korea) 11, 531–38; administrative procedures, speeding up of 534; Asian Financial Crisis (1997) 531, 536; capital markets, access to 536; collaboration with emerging conglomerates (chaebol) 534–35; competitive advantage 534–35; cross-subsidization of chaebol subsidiaries 536; debt servicing 536; development aid donor 531, 532; Economic Planning Board 534; economic policy, reform of 534; economic vibrancy 538; European Union (EU), FTA with (2011) 532; exchange rate, fixed with overvalued currency 533; export orientation 534, 535; financial sector reforms 537; foreign direct investment (FDI) 532, 537–38; Gangwha treaty (1876), effects of 532–33; GDP growth 535; GDP per capita 532; government and chaebol, relations between 535; historical perspective 532–33; Hyundai Economic Research Institute 536; import substitution, policy of 533; independence (1945) 533; industrial base, post-independence 533; International Monetary Fund (IMF) and 532; Japanese protectorate 533; Korean Asset Management Company (KAMCO) 537; Korean War (1950–53) 533; KORUS FTA (2011) 532, 538; labour market reforms 537; motorway building, beginnings of modern development 531; OECD admission (1996) 536; opium wars (1839–42 and 1856–60) 532; Organization for Economic Co-operation and Development (OECD) Development Assistance Committee forum, Busan (2011) 532; origins of the 'miracle at the Han river' 532–33; Park Chung-Hee, challenges for 533–34; private sector reforms 537–38; public sector reforms 537; recession (1998) 531–32; resurgence and national success 532; role in G20 during Great Recession (2007–9) 532;

selective liberalization of trade 534; Seoul Olympic Games (1988) 536; World Trade Organization (WTO) founder membership of 536; world trading power 535–36
research and development (R&D): Indonesia 278; Israel 194–95; Philippines 373
Reserve Bank of South Africa 105
resource curse: Indonesia 282; Malaysia 312
Reuter, Peter 469, 472n68
Revolutionary Armed Forces of Colombia (FARC) 10, 458, 459, 464–65, 467–68, 469, 470
Revolutionary Guard in Iran 445, 447
Reza Shah 440–41
Riascos, A.J. and Vargas, J.F. 462, 470n1, 470n11
Rice, Susan 513
Rivlin, Paul xxv, 6, 187–202, 411n7, 412n21
Roberts, Cynthia xxv, 503–24
Robinson, David 524n86
Robinson, Sherman 68
Rocha, K. and Moreira, A. 275, 284n14, 285n47
Rodríguez, C. and Sánchez, F. 462, 470n13
Rodrik, D. and Rosenzweig, M. 132n18, 175n21
Rodrik, D. and Subramanian, A. 68, 70, 543, 546, 553n17
Rodrik, Dani 146, 177, 182, 184n2, 184n11, 219n5, 225n83, 259, 260, 262n27
Rogers, Jim 222n43
Rojas, Gustavo 464
Rolando, R., Salamanca, J. and Aliaga, M. 241n22
Romer, Paul 212, 219n3, 223n61, 224n76, 283n7, 376n21
Rongji, Zhu 88
Ross, Michael 482, 499n26, 499n34
Rossiya, Delovaya 60n31
Rosstat (Russian Statiscal Service) 48, 49, 51, 53, 54, 55
Rostow, Walt W. 137, 140, 174n6, 175n12
Rowley, C, and Benson, J. 220n23
Roxborough, I., O'Brien, P. and Roddick, J. 240n5
Rua, Fernando de la 41
Rubin, Robert 291
Rubio, Mauricio 470n10
Rukunegara (National Principles) in Malaysia 313
rules: inconvenient rules, international institutions and demands for exemptions from 508; institutions and, need for innovation in 525. See also law, rule of
Rup, J. and Rodie, J.B. 354
Russia 4, 18, 46–59; competition blocking 58–59; competitiveness 50; consumer price inflation 51–52; consumption-led growth 49–50; Cyprus bail-out, Russian losses from 56–57; demographic change (post-2008) 54, 55, 56; depreciation of rouble 49; development levels 47–48; development today, circumstances

574

surrounding 46–47; employment growth 51; equipment, investment in 51; exchange rate 49; foreign direct investment (FDI) 56; future prospects 56; GDP growth, projection to 2017 56; GDP growth, Putin's requirement for 57; GDP growth, total factor productivity (TFP) and 50; GDP growth (2010 and 2011) 54; GDP growth and Urals oil price (1998–2009) 49; GDP per capita 46, 47; GDP performance (2008–9), deterioration of 52–53; growth patterns 48–52; growth patterns post-Great Recession (2007–9) 52–57; industrial innovation 51; industrialization, beginnings of 46–47; inter-crisis (1998–2008) economic progress 50–51; International Monetary Fund (IMF) 56–57; inventory reductions (2009) 53; labour shortages 56; market reform 48–49; medium term change (1998–2008) 54–55; MinEkon 57–58; 'oil curse,' notion of 50; oil prices 49–50; Organization for Economic Co-operation and Development's (OECD) 58; policy issues 57–58; private capital outflow 55; purchasing power parity (PPP) in 46, 47, 48; reform issues 58–59; rents 50; restructuring 47; Russian stock market (RTS) index 49–50; Russo-Iranian wars 440; superpower inheritance 47; total factor productivity (TFP) 50, 51, 55; United Nations (UN) Human Development Index 47; urbanization, beginnings of 46–47; World Bank Ease of Doing Business rankings 58; world economy 54, 56

Sabatier, Paul 521n22
Sachs, J.D. and Warner, A.M. 286n69, 499n25
Sachs, Jeffrey. 482
Sadat, Anwar 397, 398
Sala-i-Martin, X. and Artadi, E. 480
Sala-i-Martin, Xavier 143, 175n17
Saleh, H. and Kerr, S. 412n26
Saleh, Heba 412n34
Salim, Zamroni xxv, 7, 265–86
Salinas, Carlos 290, 291, 298
Salinas, D. and Fraser, P. 241n19
Samuelson, Paul 28n7
Samuelson, Robert J. 415n95
Sancin, V. and Dine, M.K. 523n54
sanctions against Iran 444, 446, 447–50, 453, 454–55, 457n30, 457n31, 457n32
Sandbu, M. 285n64
Sandford, Robinson R. 241n6
Sandhu, K.S. and Wheatley, P. 220n20
Sanger, David E. 383, 395n12
Santiago, Grijalbo 241n9
Santiago, Zig-Zag 241n9
Santiso, Carlos 499n27
Santos, Juan Manuel 462, 470

Sarney, José 40
Al Sa'ud family 484
Saudi Arabia 10, 475–98; Arab Spring, responses to 496; competitiveness 482; competitiveness, patterns of 492–93, 494; composite governance 489–90; corruption, control of 488–89; demographics, problems of 495–96; economic reforms 490–92; *The Economist* Shoe-Thrower's Index 475; emerging economy? 476–82; GDP growth 477, 479, 480, 481; GDP per capita 475, 476, 477; governance, limited progress in improvement of 484; government effectiveness 485; growth, patterns of 477–80; growth, sources of 480–82; instability, sources of 495; International Monetary Fund (IMF) 476, 477, 478, 479, 480–81; Jadwa Investment 497; law, rule of 487–88; monarchy in, survival of 475; 'new economic cities' programme 497; Nitaqat programme 496; oil curse 482–84; policy focus, areas of 493–95; political stability 484–85; purchasing power parity (PPP) 476, 477; regulatory quality 485–87; Saudization programmes 496; skills deficit 496; sustained growth, possible impediments to 482–95; total factor productivity (TFP) 480–82, 484; transition from oil-based economy, difficulties of 497–98; violence, absence of 484–85; voice, accountability and 484, 485; World Bank 482, 483; youth unemployment 496
Saverin, Eduardo 222n43
Sayigh, Yezid 399, 411n14
Sazamare Etelaat Va Amniate Kechvar (SAVAK) in Iran 441
Schmitz, H. *et al.* 353
Schneider, F. and Buehn, A. 175n30
Schneider, F. and Enste, D. 175n32
Schulz, Heiner 304n12
Schwab, Klaus 143, 175n16, 175n17, 175n18
Schweller, Randall L. 522n39
Scully, Timothy R. 240n3
sectoral growth: India 66, 78; Thailand 423–28
Security Offences (Special Measures) 2012 Act (SOSMA) in Malaysia 320
Sehnbruch, K. and Siavelis, P. 242n26
Selassie, Abebe Aemro 133n45
Seliger, Bernhard J. xxv–xxvi, 11, 531–38
Senor, D. and Singer, S. 201n6
Seoul Olympic Games (1988) 536
Ser, Tan Ern 222n48
shadow banking 101–2
shadow economy, determinants of 173–74
Sharma, Ruchir 12n3, 364, 415n95
Sharp, Jeremy 411n6
al-Shater, Khairat 403
Shaw, W. and Dadush, U. 28n1
Sheikh, Dr Hafeez 377, 392
Sherret, Laurel 469

575

Shinawatra, Thaksin 418, 434, 435, 436, 437, 438
Shinawatra, Yingluck 434
Shiyang, Cui 553n17
Siddiqa, Ayesha 411n13
Sigmund, P.E. 241n6
The Signal and the Noise (Silver, N.) 380
Siluanov, Anton 57
Silver, Nate 380, 395n6
Simkins, Charles 133n50
Simons, Warwick 104
Sindicato Nacional de Trabajadores de la Educación (SNTE) in Mexico 301
Singapore 5, 6, 203–19; Asian Financial Crisis (1997) 207–8; Asian Tigers 203, 204, 205, 206–7; birth rates, impact of industrial and labour policies on 210; capital subsidies 211; Central Provident Fund (CPF) 206; comparative advantage 203–4, 204–5, 211, 214; comparative advantage, shifts in 207, 211; competitiveness 204, 207, 210, 213, 216, 217, 218; developed countries, lessons for and from 215–16; developmental and political challenges, responsiveness to 217; developmental challenges of 21st century 206–12; *The East Asian Miracle* (World Bank, 1993) 203; Economic Development Board (EDB) 205, 207, 218, 225n85; Economic Review Committee 208, 210; Economic Strategies Committee 210; emerging economies, lessons for 212–15; environmental sustainability 210; export manufacturing 204; export volatility 213; external shocks to economy 207–8; foreign direct investment (FDI) 204, 205, 214, 223n66; foreign workers, expansion in numbers of 208; free trade 203–4, 205, 215; GDP growth 204, 205, 207, 209, 210–11, 213, 217, 223n50, 308; GDP per capita 213, 220n26, 223n50; globalization as development strategy, limitations of 213; governance 212, 213, 218, 224n77, 225n80; government-linked companies (GLCs) 204, 206, 210, 214, 217, 219n10, 223n59, 226n102; growth and investment promotion policies 210; Housing Development Board (HDB) 205–6, 209, 217, 220n19; institutional innovation 205–6; investment incentives 207; 'miracle' economy 203–5, 216–17; 'miracle' economy, underpinnings of 205–6; multinational corporations (MNCs), reliance on 213–14; offshore finance 205; 'one-party state' 206; organizational efficiency 206; People's Action Party (PAP) 206, 209, 220n21, 225n80, 225n87; PMET (Professional Management Executive and Technical) jobs 211; political democratization 204; Population Policy, White Paper on (2013) 209, 210–11, 218, 223n52, 223n54; privatization 214–15; production

networks, internationalization of 205; public policy shortcomings 213, 217; Real Estate Investment Trusts (REITs) 210; Singapore Stock Exchange (SSE) 206; social subsidies, aversion to 208–9; state-driven development model 204; strategic investment sectors 214; sustainability of growth model, problem of 207, 208–9, 211, 213, 217; sustainable competitiveness 218; talent pool, limits of 208; urban density 209–10; well-being, perception of decline in 208–9
Singh, Manmohan 73, 514
Sirilaksana, Khoman 421, 438
Six-Day War (1967) in Israel 191
Slaughter, Anne-Marie 521n20
Sohnen, Eleanor 305n36
Soin, Kanwaljiit 219n1
Sokolinski, Stanislav 202n21
Solow, Robert M. 174n1, 266, 283n6, 371, 376n19, 376n20, 376n27, 438n2, 480, 499n12
Song. Tan Kim 221n35, 223n52
Soros, George 48
South Africa 5, 105–31; Accelerated and Shared Growth Initiative for South Africa (ASGISA) 129–30; accountability and voice 119; competitiveness 123, 125, 126–27; Congress of South African Trade Unions (COSATU) 129; contrasting images of 105; corruption, control of 124–26; demographic patterns 106; effectiveness of government 120–21; equitable growth, policy approaches for 128–31; foreign direct investment (FDI) 105; future prospects 131; GDP growth 117; GDP per capita 108, 114, 117, 121, 127; *Global Competitiveness Report* (WEF, 2012–13) 124, 127; governance, role of 118–26; gross savings rate 110–11, 112–13; Growth, Employment and Redistribution (GEAR) 129; growth, sources of 116; growth dynamics 116–27; growth patterns 107–14; human development 114; income inequalities 114–15; International Monetary Fund (IMF) 126; Legatum Prosperity Index (2012) 124–26; macroeconomic aggregates 107–10, 111, 112; mining sector 113–14; New Growth Path (NGP, 2010) 130–31; Organization for Economic Co-operation and Development (OECD) 121–23; platinum group metals (PGMs) 113–14; policy approaches for self-sustained equitable growth 128–31; political stability 119–20; poverty 114–15; product market regulation (PMR) 121, 123; progress 106–16; Reconstruction and Development Programme (RDP) 128; regulatory quality 121–23; Reserve Bank 105; rule of law 123–24; unemployment 114–15; violence 119–20; voice, accountability and 119; well-being, conversion of growth into 117–18;

well-being, factors affecting 116–18; World Bank 105, 123–24
South Korea *see* Republic of Korea (South Korea)
Southall, Roger 132n22
Spence, Michael 12n3
Spinelli, F. 520n2
Springborg, Robert xxvi, 9, 397–415, 411n5, 411n12, 414n80, 414n87, 414n91
Stancil, B. 28n1
Standard and Poor's 401
state-owned enterprises (SOEs) in Viet Nam 340, 341, 342, 343, 352, 353–54, 355–56, 357, 358–59
Stein, Howard 219n7
Stepan, Alfred 45n5
Stieglitz, Joseph 392
Stiglitz, Joseph E. 215, 216, 219n3, 225n90, 225n91–92, 226n97, 284n22
stock exchange index of Thailand (SET) 423
Stone, Randall W. 522n37
Strauss-Kahn, Dominique 514, 516
Stringer, Jacob 472n70
Stuenkel, Oliver 524n80
Subramanian, A. and Kapur, D. 523n66
Subramanian, Arvind 174n2
sugar exports 34
Summers, R., Heston, A. and Bettina, A. 246
Suphannachart, W. and Warr, P. 436
Supreme Council of the Armed Forces (SCAF) in Egypt 402, 412–13n38
Suri, Vivek 361n1
Sussankarn, C. and Tinakorn, P. 436, 438n4
sustainability: of development in Indonesia 266–67, 269–71, 276–78, 281; of growth in Saudi Arabia, possible impediments to 482–95; of growth model in Singapore, problem of 207, 208–9, 211, 213, 217; sustainable competitiveness in Singapore 218
Sweezy, P. and Magdoff, H. 240n5
el-Sweidy, Ahmed 412n29
Swinkels, R. and Turk, C. 345, 361n1
Swirski, Shlomo 202n28

Tae-Woo, Roh 537
Tammen, Ronald L. 521n23
Tamura, Robert 376n23
Tan, Amelia 222n42
Tanuwidjaja, E. and Choy, K.M. 285n49
Tat, Hui Weng 221n35
Tat, H.W. and Hasmi, A.R. 221n29
Taymaz, E. 260
Technion in Israel 194
technologies: centres for technical formation (CFT) in Chile 233; change in, world economy and 15–16; foreign technologies, adoption of 18; innovation in Colombia 461–62; internet technologies 18; mobile phone technologies 18;

progress in Philippines 373; success in Israel 193–95; technological innovation, adoption of 526–27; transfer in Iran, prohibition of 454
Teck, Hoon Hian 221n34, 225n95
Tel-Aviv Stock Exchange (TASE) 198
telecommunications 97, 193, 225, 232, 298–99, 345, 354, 358, 375, 402, 436, 437, 447, 449
Teo, Youyenn 223n54
Thailand 9, 416–38; aggregate economic performance 416–20; Asian Financial Crisis (1997) 416, 438; drugs trafficking 432, 435; economic growth 416–28; economic growth, poverty reduction and 431–32; Financial Recession (2007–9), sluggish recovery 428; foreign direct investment (FDI) 419, 421, 422; GDP growth 417, 427, 436; GDP per capita 417, 418; gross national product (GNP) 417; growth, sources of 420–23; inequality 429–30; inequality, rise in 430–31; infant mortality 432–34; International Monetary Fund (IMF) 418; maternal mortality 432–34; middle-income trap 436–38; National Economic and Social Development Board (NESDB) 417, 429, 431; National Statistical Office's Socio-Economic Survey (SES) 429, 430, 431; non-economic social change 432; overseas development assistance (ODA) 422; political developments 434–38; population growth 432; populism 434; poverty 429–30; poverty, decline in 430–31, 431–32; productivity growth 423–28; sectoral economic performance 423–28; social progress 428–34; stock exchange index of Thailand (SET) 423; Thaksin's agenda 434–36; total factor productivity (TFP) 420, 421, 426, 427
Thayer, Carlyle A. 347
Thomson, Adam 304n15, 305n22, 305n31
Thomson-Urrutia Treaty (1921) 463
Thorold, Crispin 500n53
Thoumi, Francisco 466, 468, 471n22, 472n58
Thousand Days War (1899–1902) in Colombia 463
Thurow, Lester 219n3
Tomic, Radomiro 229
Toronto, Nathan W. 411n3
total factor productivity (TFP) 16, 18; China, People's Republic of 540, 541, 543, 544, 551; Colombia 460; Egypt 406; India 540, 541, 543, 544, 551; Indonesia 267, 268; Malaysia 310, 311; Philippines 371–72; Russia 50, 51, 55; Saudi Arabia 480–82, 484; Thailand 420, 421, 426, 427; world economy, key trends in 16, 18
Tran, Huong Thi Lan 361n1
Tran, T.B. *et al.* 353
Trenwith, Courtney 499n37
Trivedi, K. 520n2
True, J.L., Jones, B.D. and Baumgartner, F.R. 521n22

Index

Truman, Edwin M. 523n70, 523n73, 524n87
Tsang, Donald 223n50
Tsangarides, C.G. 285n42, 285n43
Turkey 6, 245–61; Banking Act (1985) 247; borrowing requirement (1990–2011) 248; convergence, challenge of 259–61; debt-to-GDP ratio 248, 252, 257, 262n18; economic imbalances and 'home-made' crisis (1990s) 247–49; educational attainment, high-tech exports and 260; Emerging Markets Bond Index (EMBI) 249, 254; financial crisis (2001) 245; financial crisis (2001), aftermath of 249–52; financial crisis (2001), fiscal policy during 257–58; fiscal policy during Great Recession (2007–9) 258; fiscal problems, accumulation of 247–49; floating exchange rate regime 249–50; GDP growth 245, 249, 250, 252; GDP per capita 245, 246, 250, 260, 261; GDP per capita, comparison with US, South Korea and BRICs 245–46; global shocks, economic policymaking and 256–59; gross national savings and total investment (% of GDP) 253; industrial production, current account balance and (1981–2012) 256; International Monetary Fund (IMF) 249–50, 258, 263n26; international reserve position 254; liability dollarization 253; liability dollarization, impact on economic activity 253–55; liberalization (1980s) 247; macroeconomic indicators (% of GDP) 250–51; macroeconomic stability, establishment of (1980–2012) 246, 247–56; monetary policy (2010–11), capital inflows and 258–59; net capital inflow (1998–2012), real GDP and 255; Organization for Economic Co-operation and Development (OECD) 260; savings rate 252–53; savings rate, impact of low rate on economic activity 253–55; Turkish-Egyptian bilateral relations 400; World Bank 249–50, 252–53
Tyers, R. *et al.* 542, 552n5, 552n7
Tzuk, Yuval 201n19

unemployment 5, 27, 44, 528, 535; China 83, 84, 103; Colombia 466, 470; Egypt 399, 405; Israel 197; Malaysia 308, 315; Mexico 303; Pakistan 377; Russia 51; Saudi Arabia 475, 482, 495, 496; Singapore 205, 207, 223n50; South Africa 106, 114–15, 116, 129, 130, 131; Thailand 418; Turkey 247, 249, 250, 252; Viet Nam 343, 344; youth unemployment 475, 496
United Kingdom (UK) 17, 19, 20, 143, 191, 223n58, 265, 441, 455n6, 504, 510, 512, 530
United Malay National Organization (UMNO) 313, 315, 316, 318, 320, 321
United Nations (UN): broadening of representation on UN Security Council (UNSC) 510–12; Conference on Trade and Development (UNCTAD) 271, 272; global

governance, emerging powers and 504, 505, 507; Human Development Index on Russia 47; voting patterns in UN Security Council (UNSC) 513–14
United Self-Defence Forces of Colombia (AUC) 464–65
United States 3, 4, 10, 13–16, 18, 19, 20, 25, 26, 28, 143, 180, 182, 184, 503–6, 508–16, 518–19, 520; Argentina and 331–32, 336; Bi-national Industrial Research and Development (BIRD) 195; bilateral trade agreement (BTA) with Viet Nam 351–52; Brazil and 42, 44; Chile and 230, 241n23, 242n29; China and 83, 85, 86, 87, 88–89, 90, 91–92, 103–4n17, 103n9, 104n18, 542, 543, 546, 549; Civil War, effect on trade with Brazil 34; Colombia and 460, 461, 462, 463, 464–65, 467, 469; D'Amato Law, effects in Iran 448; dollar as 'patron' currency 526; Egypt and 397, 399, 409; GDP per capita 21; Great Recession (2007–8) and aftermath 530; India and 65, 66, 69, 79, 80n2, 542, 543, 546, 549; Indonesia and 265, 267, 272–73; Iran and 441, 443–44, 447, 448–49, 450, 454–55; Israel and 189–90, 191, 192, 194, 195, 199, 200; Mexico and 287, 288, 290, 291, 293, 294, 295, 297, 299, 300, 302, 303; National Intelligence Council (NIC) 503; Pakistan and 377, 383, 385–86, 389; per capita income in emerging economies relative to (1960) 139; Philippines and 365, 369, 375; recovery in, world economy and 15; relations with Pakistan 385–87; Russia and 46, 51, 53; Singapore and 205, 215, 222n41, 222n43, 222n47, 223n50, 223n53, 223n58; South Korea and 532, 533, 534, 535; Thailand and 428; Turkey and 245; US-China trade 91–92; Viet Nam and 341, 347, 348, 351–52
University and University Colleges Act (1971) in Malaysia 320
urbanization: beginnings in Russia of 46–47; urban density in Singapore 209–10; Viet Nam 354–55
Uribe, Álvaro 464, 465, 468
Uri'ia, J. 520n2
Urzúa, Sergio 242n28

Vadaketh, Sudhir 221n35
Valdés, Juan Gabriel 241n9
Valenzuela, Arturo 240n5, 241n7
Vargas, Juan F. 462, 471n15, 471n35
Vasconcelos, José 468
Vejjajiva, Abhisit 434
Velasco, A. 146
Velloor, Ravi 224n71
Viet Nam 8, 339–61; Association of Southeast Asian Nations (ASEAN) 351; bilateral trade agreement (BTA) with US 351–52; cadres,

selection and promotion of 348–49; challenges ahead 356–61; China factor 347–48; communist heritage 339–40; conglomerrates *(chaebol)* 340; democratic transition, challenge of 360–61; employment 342–44; foreign direct investment (FDI) 339, 352, 353, 354; foreign direct investment (FDI), challenge for companies 358–59; GDP growth 357; GDP per capita 341; global integration 351–52; International Bank of Reconstruction and Development (IBRD) 339; land and agriculture 350–51; leadership, vision and 345–50; middle class, emergence of 344–45; motorbikes, social transformation and 345; prosperity, path to 340–45; public finance 352–53; purchasing power parity (PPP) 339, 344, 345, 358; renovation process *(Doi Moi)* 339; social progress 345; social protection 355–56; socialism and new ideas 349–50; state-owned enterprises (SOEs) 340, 341, 342, 343, 352, 353–54, 355–56, 357; state-owned enterprises (SOEs), challenge for 358–59; stop-and-go macroeconomics, challenge of 356–58; structural change 340–42; transformational keys 350–56; urbanization 354–55; war, reunification and *Doi Moi* 346–47; wealth, legitimacy of 359–60; World Trade Organization (WTO) 351–52

Vines, D. and Warr, P. 437, 438n3

violence: Colombia 462, 463–65; Mexico 294, 295, 303; Saudi Arabia 484–85; South Africa 119–20

Virmani, Arvind 68, 70

Vo, Dang Hung 361n1

Vo Van Kiet 349, 361n1

Voeten, Erik 522n40, 522n43, 522n48, 523n51, 523n53, 523n55

voice, accountability and: Saudi Arabia 484, 485; South Africa 119. *See also* accountability

Volz, Ulrich 524n88

Voronova, Tat'yana 60n21

Vu, T.H. *et al.* 351

Vylder, Stefan de 240n5, 241n8

Wade, Robert E. 219n7

Wade, Robert H. 523n71, 524n81

Wahab, M.A. and Ahmed, V. 499n29

Wahab, Siraj 500n52

Wahish, Niveen 412n25

Walker, Ruth 498n6

Wall Street Journal Index of Economic Freedom 142

Wallis, W. and England, A. 132n26

Waltz, Kenneth N. 521n18

Warner, Andrew 482

Warr, Peter xxvi–xxvii, 9, 416–39

Washington Consensus 5, 129, 177–83, 391–92, 393–94; authoritarianism 182–83; Beijing Consensus, comparison with 177–83; foreign direct investment (FDI) 178, 179; gradualism *versus* shock treatment 178–79; innovation, encouragement of 179; macroeconomic stability 179; market liberalization 180–82; open economy 179–80

Watts, Jonathan 224n76

Weiss, L. Meredith 325n25

Weiss, Martin A. 523n71

Weiss, Thomas G. 523n56

Weizmann Institute of Science in Rehovot 194

well-being: conversion of growth in South Africa into 117–18; perception of decline in Singapore 208–9; in South Africa factors affecting 116–18

West Bank settlements, cost to Israel of 198–200

Wild, F. and Cohen, M. 133n60

Williamson, John xxvii, 5, 133n48, 177–84

Wilson, Christopher E. 304n19

Wilson, D. 520n2

Wilson, D. and Dragusanu, R. 521n14

Wilson, D. and Purushothaman, R. 28n3, 543, 544, 553n11, 553n12

Wilson, D. and Stupnytska, A. 553n11

Wilson, Rodney 413n40, 414n82

Winn, Peter 241n23

Winters, A. and Yusuf, S. 546, 553n17

Wise, C., Armijo, L.E. and Kateda, S.N. 523n68

Wolf, C. *et al.* 552n8, 553n13

Wolf, C. Jr and Akhmedjonov, A. 11

Wolf, Charles Jr. 552n1, 553n10

Wolf, Jr., Charles xxvii–xxviii, 539–54

Womack, Brantly 347, 349, 361

Wong, Tessa 223n60

Woo, Jung-en 219n7

world affairs, constructive participation in 529

World Bank: Ease of Doing Business rankings on Russia 58; Egypt 405, 406, 407; global governance, emerging powers and 504, 505; Indonesia 265, 269; Malaysia 314–15; Mexico 290, 295; Pakistan 387, 391, 392; paper on economic growth in China and India 546; paper on middle-income trap 139; report on capital formation in Colombia 461; Saudi Arabia 482, 483; South Africa 105, 123–24; Turkey 249–50, 252–53; world economy, key trends in 16, 18, 22

World Development Indicators (World Bank) 19, 138, 228, 229, 231, 364, 365, 417, 423, 425, 426, 428, 480, 550; Philippines 364, 365; South Africa 107, 108, 109, 110, 111, 112, 113, 115

World Economic Forum (WEF) 123, 142, 144, 145, 146, 281, 405, 407; Global Competitiveness Index (WEF GCI) 141–42, 143, 148

World Economic Outlook (IMF) 19, 48, 51, 52, 115, 251

Index

world economy, key trends in 4, 13–28; Africa 22, 23; balanced world 21; biotechnology 25; Brazil 34; capital stocks 16–17; China, People's Republic of 89–91; climate change, risk of 26; commodity prices, trends in 24–25; depression, risk of 27; economic balance of power 13; economic balance of power, shift to South and East 15–16; economic order, 2050 projections 20; economic triad (China, India and USA), emergence of 21; emerging markets, economic development of 18–22, 28; endogenous growth theory 18; energy usage 25; financial crisis, risk of 27; financial shocks 15; foreign direct investment (FDI) 14, 24; foreign technologies, adoption of 18; GDP growth averages (1997–2012) 14; GDP growth projections (2012–50) 20; GDP projections to 2050 for major economies 15; geopolitical breakdown, risk of 26–27; global middle and rich class (GMR) 22, 23, 24, 28–29n8, 29n11; global middle class, rise in 22–2, 24; Great Recession (2007–9) 13, 14, 15; Great Recession (2007–9), implications of 14–15; growth drivers, developing countries and 16–18; G20 13, 14, 15, 18, 19, 20, 21, 22, 23, 24, 27–28, 29n10; integration in trade and finance 23–24; International Monetary Fund (IMF) 15, 16; internet technologies 18; investment convergence in mature economies 17; investment in commodities 25; labour force 16; macroeconomic stability 28; manufactured goods, trends in prices for 25; miniaturization 25; mobile phone technologies 18; oil prices 25; population growth 25; poverty, reduction in extremes of 22–23; protectionism, risk of 27; purchasing power parity (PPP) 20, 21, 22, 28; relative prices, prospects for 24–25; risks 26–28; Russia 54, 56; technological change 15–16; total factor productivity (TFP) 16, 18; trade shocks 15; United States, recovery in 15; World Bank 16, 18, 22; World Economic Outlook (IMF) 19; World Trade Organization (WTO) 15, 26, 27
World Investment Prospects Survey (UNCTAD) 272

World Trade Organization (WTO) 508, 525; Mexico 295, 299; Philippines 374; Republic of Korea (South Korea), founder member 536; Viet Nam 351–52; world economy, key trends in 15, 26, 27
Worthington, Ross 224n77
Wu, Harry X. 96
Wu, Y. 284n19
Wuthnow, Joel 523n64
Wydick, B. 266, 283n8

Yafei, He 512
Yago, Glen 147
Yahya, Yasmine 223n63
Yakovleva, Yulia 60n31
Yang, C.H. and Chen, Y.H. 285n56, 285n62
Yao, X. *et al.* 284n18, 284n20, 284n21, 284n27
Yao, X., Watanabe, C. and Li, Y. 284n12
Yaqub, Mohammad 378
Yenn, Teo You 225n91
Yew, Lee Kuan 224n77
Yodhoyono, Soesilo Bambang 278
Young, Alwyn 63, 220n28, 438n2
Young-Sam, Kim 536, 538
Yousafzai, Malala 380, 384
youth unemployment 475, 496
Yuan, Lee Tsao 220n28
Yusof, Z.A. and Bhattasali, D. 325n16, 325n18
Yusof, Zainal Aznam 325n11
Yusuf, S. and Nabeshima, K. 310, 325n4

Zaidi, S. Akbar 391, 396n25
Založba, G.V. 523n54
Zangeneh, H. and Moore, J.M. 457n37
Zangeneh, Hamid xxviii, 440–57, 455n5, 456n16, 457n33, 457n37
Zapata, Francisco S. 241n8
Zardari, Asif Ali 382, 383, 387
Zedillo, Ernesto 291, 292, 293
Zhibin, Zhang 224n72
Zhuang, Juzhong 372
Zoellick, Robert 514
Zuern, Elke 132n11

580